The Democratic Experience

AN AMERICAN HISTORY

FIFTH EDITION

Carl N. Degler Stanford University
Thomas C. Cochran Eleutherian Mills-Hagley Foundation
Vincent P. De Santis University of Notre Dame
Holman Hamilton
William H. Harbaugh University of Virginia
James M. McPherson Princeton University
Russel B. Nye Michigan State University
Clarence L. Ver Steeg Northwestern University

Scott, Foresman and Company   **Glenview, Illinois**

Dallas, Texas   Oakland, New Jersey   Palo Alto, California
Tucker, Georgia   London, England

Library of Congress Cataloging in Publication Data

Main entry under title

The Democratic experience.

   Also issued in 2 vols.
   Includes bibliographies and index.
   1. United States—History. I. Degler, Carl N.
E178.1.D36 1981   973   80-25809
ISBN 0-673-15450-5 (pbk.)

1 2 3 4 5 6 7 8 —VHJ— 85 84 83 82 81 80

Credit lines for illustrations appearing in this work are
placed in the ''Acknowledgments'' section at the end
of the book.

Credits and additional information about the flags on the
cover will be found on page 775.

Foreword

The opportunity to take a fresh look at the nation's history is always an exciting one, especially when one looks through the eyes of the eight distinguished historians who have written this text. In the fifth edition of *The Democratic Experience,* each author has taken a thoughtful look at his time period and the latest scholarship. The result is a text that retains its strengths as a solid interpretation of traditional economic and political history, while adding new insights into social and cultural changes that have influenced and been influenced by economic and political events.

Within each of the eight parts, the lead chapter has been focused upon the social changes, the cultural trends, and the ideas that dominated that time period. Special attention has also been paid to the role of technology. What emerges is a clearer picture of the interrelationship of a nation's culture and its political and economic life. Through these improved chapters, students will gain greater insights into the ideas and events that inspired this nation's founding and continue to influence its development.

To help the student keep this larger perspective in mind, each of the authors has also given thoughtful attention to the issues that continue to affect the nation's development: the individual's liberty and opportunities, the government's authority, and the evolution of our political system.

To better teach the student, the authors have also added or improved the pedagogical features of this edition:

- *Time lines.* New to this edition are time lines, which precede the introduction to each part. Their purpose is to help students visualize the chronology and relationship of events within each era.
- *Reading questions.* The introduction to each part concludes with five or six questions the student should keep in mind while reading. The provocative questions often call for interpretation, challenging the student to question commonly held attitudes.
- *Bibliographies.* As in previous editions, each of the eight parts is followed by an annotated bibliography of additional source materials. These bibliographies, ranked among the best in the marketplace, reflect the scholastic integrity of the text.
- *Illustration program.* The previous edition's outstanding program of maps and charts has been revised and supplemented by an equally outstanding program of captioned illustrations, interspersed throughout the text. Through authentic political cartoons, etchings, posters, paintings, and photographs, the student will be able to see history as it was seen by the people who lived in that period.
- *Biographies.* Of special importance are the biographies, which are new to this edition.

To personalize the sometimes abstract events of history, each author has written two biographies, one of a person prominent in the culture and one of a person whose life reflects developments in the political and economic sector. The fascinating people profiled range from Phillis Wheatley to W. E. B. DuBois, from Parson Weems to Belva Lockwood, from George Gershwin to J. Robert Oppenheimer.

The book that results is an engrossing story of a young nation engaged in what Thomas Paine described as a "bold and sublime experiment" in goverment. We hope you enjoy the story of the continuing effort to realize the high ideals of this nation's founding, for this is the Democratic Experience.

SPECIAL ACKNOWLEDGMENTS

We must first extend our appreciation to the many historians and scholars whose work is reflected in this text. Special gratitude goes to those teachers and historians who read the manuscript for this edition and gave us the benefit of their comments: Frank W. Abbott, University of Houston, Downtown College; Thomas J. Archdeacon, University of Wisconsin at Madison; Morris H. Holman, Eastfield College; Arthur McClure, Central Missouri State University; and Thomas R. Tefft, Citrus College.

We also want to acknowledge the authors who have contributed to previous editions. Our gratitude goes to David M. Potter, noted historian of the Civil War era and former coauthor of Part 4, "A House Divided." Special thanks also go to the respected scholar of the Progressive era, Arthur S. Link, former coauthor of Part 6, "The Emergence of a Modern Nation."

We are also proud to have been associated with the distinguished scholar, Holman Hamilton, who died shortly after completing his work on this edition. His contribution is a valuable one and he will be missed.

The Publisher

Contents

MAPS AND CHARTS

The Democratic Experience

AN AMERICAN HISTORY

FIFTH EDITION

Time Line

1

THE FOUNDING OF AMERICA

The founding of America brought into contact, and conflict, Indians (whose early ancestors had come from Asia), blacks from Africa, and whites from Europe. Indians had occupied both American continents, and in some areas—Peru, Central America, and Mexico—had developed remarkable civilizations. The major "nations" along the eastern shoreline of the present-day United States—the Algonquins, the Iroquois, Cherokees, and Creeks—never reached the cultural heights of the Incas, Mayas, and Aztecs, but they, too, created sophisticated social organizations, strong political alignments, and thriving economies.

Millions of Africans came to the Americas in bondage. Of this number, at least 400,000 reached the English colonies by 1770—the great majority after 1700. Even though most came as slaves, these blacks brought with them skills and talents equal or superior to those of the contemporary European peasant and the ordinary Indian. For centuries the effects of this extraordinary migration were overlooked by historians, but there can no longer be any question that the cultural backgrounds brought to the New World by the Africans survived.

But it was Europe that most clearly put its stamp on the colonies that would become the United States of America. At the end of the fifteenth century Europe was stirring with new interests and fresh vitality. A spirit of secularism focused attention upon the goodness of the world that humans had inherited. No longer could the priest insist that this vale of tears was but a brief abiding place where people seasoned their souls for bliss in the world to come. They wanted comforts and pleasures here below in a greater quantity and variety than they had known before. The Venetians and the Genoese, enterprising Italian traders that they were, had long brought luxury goods from the Near East and the Orient to please the wealthy of Europe. Now the demand was greater. More money was available. Silver mines in the Tyrol and elsewhere in eastern Europe were producing more precious metal, and the circulation of money was increasing. With more money in more hands, the demand for goods and commodities multiplied, especially for those goods that came from Asia.

Bartholomew Diaz in 1487–1488 rounded the Cape of Good Hope and came back to suggest the possibility of a passage to India. A few years later, a Genoese in the service of Spain, one Christopher Columbus, persuaded Queen Isabella of Castile to help finance a western voyage that he promised would lead to Asia and riches. When Columbus sailed from Palos on August 3, 1492, he believed that he could open a new trade route that would enable Spain to tap the wealth of Asia. When on October 12 he made a landfall in the Caribbean (perhaps Watling Island), he thought he had reached the outskirts of China. A bit later, when he landed on Cuba, he sent messengers in search of the Great Khan. Even after four voyages across the Atlantic, Columbus died still believing that he had discovered a sea route to Asia.

Within a generation after Columbus' discovery of America, Europe witnessed other events that would in time profoundly influence not only the Old World but the development of the New. On October 31, 1517, Martin Luther nailed to the door of the castle church in Wittenberg his famous ninety-five theses challenging debate on alleged corruptions in the Catholic Church, then the only recognized church in western and central Europe. No one in Wittenberg could have foreseen that this gesture would begin a cataclysmic movement known to history as the Protestant Reformation, which would give birth to the various Protestant sects and split Christendom into rival, often warring, Protestant and Catholic nations. Nor was it foreseen that this movement would determine the nature of many of the settlements in North America. In England a few years later King Henry VIII renounced the authority of the pope of Rome and in a "Protestant" move had himself declared supreme head of the Church of England. The causes of Henry's action were not religious, nor did religious belief lead his daughter, Elizabeth I, to maintain the Protestant position in England; but the effects of England's change to Protestantism on the history of Europe and of the New World were enor-

mous. Under Elizabeth, Englishmen began a long contest with Catholic Spain, the great colonial power in the New World. Out of that contest came the determination to establish English colonies in America. Under Elizabeth's Protestant successor, James I, Englishmen in 1607 finally gained a permanent foothold on the Atlantic seaboard in Virginia.

The patterns that today are identified with the social and political system of the United States developed in the colonial period. No reliable study has yet been made of the social class of the newcomers from Africa during this period, but impressionistic evidence suggests that they came from every strata and included princes and skilled artisans as well as farmers, herders, and hunters. Most of the European settlers, on the other hand came from the middle classes. The wealthy were satisfied to remain at their comfortable firesides, while the poor could not afford the journey.

English law and custom and the tradition of local self-government flourished in colonial America and constituted an enduring legacy. Non-English immigrants from the European continent also enriched the social and cultural diversity of the colonies—a preamble to a nation of immigrants. Included in this diversity was a variety of languages, religious views, farming techniques, and individual and family behavior. Native Americans, whose tribes were considered and treated as nations, were seldom assimilated into colonial social and cultural life although there was uninterrupted contact and exchange of goods between them and the newcomers.

At one time historians wrote of the English colonies in America as the creation of a special breed of humans guided by God and divorced from the worldly decadence of Europe. Today historians study the lasting ties between Europe, England, and the Americas, noting in particular when, where, and why divergences occurred. After the English colonies in North America broke with the mother country over the issue of whether or not the powers of self-government had been granted to them irrevocably—a dramatic confrontation broadly identified as the American Revolution—each generation of historians, influenced by the interests and attitudes of its own times, interpreted that epochal event differently. Thus in the Progressive Era—from around the turn of this century until 1917 (see Part 6)—students of the colonial period saw the Revolution not only as a rebellion against British rule but also as an internal rebellion against control by an upper-class minority. Themselves in revolt against the power of big business and political bosses, they looked on colonial America as an undemocratic society in which the few suppressed the many until the political and social upheaval of the Revolution.

Around mid-century, after surviving the Great Depression and World War II, Americans looked at their society, present and past, much less critically. They were struck by the differences between themselves and Europeans, and students of the colonial period found that these differences had developed very early. Research indicated that older historians had been wrong. Instead of being suppressed and disfranchised, a great many ordinary Americans in the eighteenth century had been qualified to vote. The Revolution, then, had not been an internal revolt so much as a unified effort of Americans to break away from an Old World that had become foreign to them.

More recently, with the turning away from nationalism and the questioning of our success in practicing democracy, some historians have called attention to the fact that the breadth of the franchise in the colonial period did not mean significant participation and that, broad as it was, it still denied participation to blacks, to women, and to seamen and other males at the bottom of the white social hierarchy. These scholars emphasize the stability of colonial society, rather than the fluidity that the somewhat older generation of historians underscores.

Some students of revolution, Hannah Arendt for one, regard the American Revolution as a tranquil episode, hardly worthy of its label. Others, Robert R. Palmer for one, ask historians to note that more colonials went into exile during the American Revolution than Frenchmen during the French Revolution. The majority of historians consider the American Revolution as a period of transformation in which many innovative colonial practices and political practices were codified, and opportunities were opened that made way for a democratization of political, social, and cultural life.

TO THINK ABOUT AS YOU READ . . .

1. How were the sweeping political, social, and economic changes in sixteenth-century England reflected in the development of the colonies? How might their development have been different if these changes had not been occurring in England?
2. The colonies were founded at a time when new ideas in both religion and philosophy were challenging long-accepted "truths." How did these new ideas affect the development of the colonies?
3. In what ways did the migration of peoples from Britain, Western Europe, and Africa contribute to the customs and traditions that became a continuing part of American life?
4. The history of the United States is often discussed in terms of a mosaic of localities,

regions, and/or sections. Where did these pockets of sectionalism start and why? Evaluate the proposition that the New England colonies had more characteristics in common than did any of the other groups of colonies and, therefore, represented the earliest emergence of sectionalism in United States history.

5. Consider the American Revolution as (a) a civil war, (b) a war for independence, (c) a revolution. In each case, think about whether the break with Britain represented a departure from colonial and/or British political, economic, social, and intellectual traditions or a natural outcome of these traditions.

Chapter 1

Patterns of Colonial Culture

COLONIAL SOCIAL STRUCTURE

Influences on Cultural Development. In intellectual and social life, as in political and economic life, the first English settlers in America shared the attitudes, ambitions, and habits of thought of their peers in the home country. During the colonial period, however, these characteristics were modified. In part this was because of the changing intellectual life in England, which affected the colonies in a variety of ways. In part it was because the men and women born and educated in America knew first-hand only the ways of their colonial neighbors. They experienced English culture and English intellectual currents second-hand.

Furthermore, the immigration of non-English peoples brought added diversity and dimension to the social and intellectual scene. An evaluation of the degree of distinctiveness of American culture depends on the relative weight placed upon these elements—English, American, and non-English. Because individual historians have placed different emphasis upon these factors, their judgments have differed. But all agree that conditions in the New World influenced social and intellectual development.

Influence of English Society. In Elizabethan England, the social rank of a family was determined strictly by the status of the male head of the household. The top level of this patriarchal and paternalistic society consisted of noble families, whose position depended upon extensive landholdings and the favors which accrued to a privileged segment of society. The nobility was not quite a closed circle. Younger sons who did not inherit a substantial estate or title generally sought their fortunes through the life of the gentry, through commercial connections, or through such professions as the army and the church. It was possible for a highly successful entrepreneur to penetrate the nobility, though full-fledged acceptance was often delayed for several generations.

Below the nobility ranked the gentry, the country gentlemen. The life of the gentry centered around the land. The country gentleman knew his tenants and their problems, and he experienced at first hand the uncertainties, as well as the blessings, of farming. The gentry served as the backbone of governing authority, in part because the sovereign encouraged their participation as a shield against ambitious nobles. The gentry formed the largest group in Parliament, and they held those local offices which were mainly responsible for enforcing the statutes of the state. Marriage alliances between gentry and families engaged in trade were fairly frequent, and gentry families often contributed younger sons to trade, to adventure, to the military, to the church, and sometimes to the universities.

Below the gentry ranked the yeomen, who could be leaseholders or owners of small estates. A yeoman was the dirt farmer of Elizabethan days, a man attached to the soil who lived a simple life and farmed with frugality. The laborers and servant classes of Elizabethan England ranked below the yeomen. A laborer might be an apprentice who in time would enter a trade and make a good living, or he might be a man who worked for daily wages and whose chances of rising to a better social and economic position were remote. In the same fashion, to be a servant could mean to serve with a gentry family in the expectation that by means of a good marriage or hard work an elevation of status could be secured, or it could involve the meanest kind of position, from which no escalation of status seemed possible.

The English social structure was not transplanted intact to America. Members of the English aristocracy did not come to America. They were relatively content and well off at home, so they had no incentive to migrate to a primitive New World wilderness. Occasionally, younger sons of noble families came to America to try their fortune, but even this element was rare.

For the other end of the social structure—day laborers and servants—migration to the New World was restricted because of the transportation costs. But servants were transported by the gentry class. Laborers, too, sometimes migrated by taking advantage of the system of *indentured servitude,* in which they bound themselves to a master for service in the colonies for a specified length of time, usually three to five years, in exchange for their passage. This system became widespread after the mid-seventeenth century.

The first settlers, then, were drawn principally from the yeomanry and the gentry, the latter bringing servants with them. At the outset, these class divisions, and their patriarchal framework, were scrupulously maintained. In early Massachusetts, to cite an illustration, a laborer's wife who appeared at church wearing a frock or hat of a quality that, in the eyes of the elders, exceeded the social station of laborer was severely admonished.

Influence of the American Environment.
Modifications in this structure during the colonial period gave rise to a social structure indigenous to English America. The gradual growth of a system of indentured servitude enabled people without money to emigrate to America, where they eventually became yeoman farmers or free laborers. Men who arrived as hired servants or as yeomen sometimes acquired substantial estates through industry or good fortune. Ships' captains who brought immigrants to certain colonies claimed headrights—an allotment of fifty acres of land for each person transported—and these grants formed the nucleus around which some landed estates were formed. Labor was so scarce that a skilled workman not only could make a good living but also could become an employer. Men of modest means who engaged in trade built up strong mercantile firms, and wealth brought an elevation of social status and often political power.

Among the most important determinants of social position in America was the possession of land, and its very abundance helped encourage a more mobile society. Nowhere was this more clearly demonstrated than in the Chesapeake colonies. In the first century of settlement the vast majority of the settlers in Virginia and Maryland were yeomen or indentured servants who were able to rise to the status of yeomen after completing their term of servitude. During various crises of the seventeenth century, especially during the Puritan ascendancy in England of the 1640s and 1650s and immediately after the restoration of the Stuart monarchy in 1660, members of gentry families or, more rarely, younger sons of noble families migrated to Virginia. But they acted as no more than leaven to the loaf. The Virginia gentry class that gradually emerged was made up primarily of those who had risen to this status in America. It was not a gentry group transplanted to America.

Women in Colonial America.   The practice of bringing families to the New World set the English colonies apart from those of other nations. Women were in great demand, not primarily to serve as companions or to satisfy sexual appetites, but as partners in the enterprise of settlement. John Winthrop of Massachusetts, who preceded his wife to New England, wrote her most lovingly of the life and excitement they would share in America. Some women became influential. The religious views of Anne Hutchinson of Massachusetts led to her being ousted from the colony but attracted a following that found refuge with her near Providence. Anne Bradstreet is now recognized as the most sensitive writer of verse in colonial America. Most women, like most men, worked day in and day out in the fields and the household, making a living, raising a family, and looking forward to better times.

Women in colonial America did not have the vote and could not, in most cases, hold property. Their opportunities were severely restricted. None became lawyers or ministers. Some practiced a trade, such as blacksmithing, but almost none made a name in business. Yet their influence was keenly felt, and without them there could have been no society to win its freedom and found a nation.

The Structure of Colonial Society.   The structure that evolved in colonial society differed from that of English society in three important respects. First, the top level of English society—the nobility—was shorn off by the process of transplantation. Second, the composition of American classes was not the result of direct transplants from England. Third, the parts of society were present in somewhat different proportions.

In America there were more slaves who were condemned to perpetual servitude and who had little if any mobility; but there were fewer servants, because the opportunities to acquire land and other forms of wealth were so abundant. American society ranged, therefore, from the colonial elite—the important merchants in Massachusetts and Rhode Island, the planters along the Chesapeake and in the Carolinas, and the large landholders in New York and Pennsylvania—to the small farmers and skilled workers, to the unskilled workers and servants, and finally, at the base, to the slaves.

The special contours of American society also reflected a modification of male professional opportunities. An upper-class Englishman could advance professionally through the church, the military, or the law. In America, the church in New England offered an avenue for advancement for a time. But by the eighteenth century a man looking for advancement generally sought out land and commerce, not the church. Moreover, American men, accustomed to their special militia forces, could not advance professionally through the naval or military service. In America, a man who had already achieved status as a merchant or landholder was placed in command of a colonial expedition.

Not until the 1730s and 1740s did the practice of law gain sufficient status to become an avenue for advancement. In earlier periods, merchants and landholders frequently served as their own lawyers. Only as colonial society became more sophisticated did the practice of law become a profession. A number of colonials, some of whom were already in a substantial social position—James Otis and John Adams in New England, John Dickinson in the Middle colonies, and Patrick Henry and Charles Pinckney in the Southern colonies—improved their status by becoming expert in the practice of law.

The seed of American society was English, but the American environment dramatically affected its growth. Its evolution, as a result, was distinctive, not a replica.

MINORITIES IN THE COLONIES

In the eighteenth century, the population of the colonies included large groups of non-English: Irish, Germans, Scots, and French. These minorities gave a flavor to American society that endures to the present time.

Two groups of Americans, however,—the native Indians and the immigrant Africans—were excluded from the colonial social structure. True, black Americans were very much a part of the economic structure, and trade with the Indians had great economic significance for the colonists. But in both cases the relationship between the races was marked by a cultural clash rather than cultural fusion, and in both cases white culture had enough power to establish its dominance.

European Minorities. The reasons for the inflow of non-English Europeans were numerous, but a change of policy in England was a critical factor. By the eighteenth century England was less enthusiastic about exporting its population to America. As its agriculture became increasingly commercial, as trade expanded a hundredfold, and as manufacturing began to take root, its people were needed at home. As the supply of labor from the mother country was reduced, the Middle and Southern colonies, especially, brought indentured servants from northern and western Europe.

Francis Daniel Pastorious, a man of exceptional intellect, led the first German settlers into Pennsylvania in 1683, founding Germantown north of Philadelphia. But the principal migration of Germans did not begin until after 1710. From that date to 1770, a wave of 225,000 German immigrants came to the New World—almost half of whom migrated to Pennsylvania. Statistically, about 80 percent settled in the Middle colonies of Pennsylvania, New York, and New Jersey, and about 20 percent settled in the Southern colonies from Maryland to Georgia. Less than 1 percent settled in New England.

The settlement of newcomers from France, Scotland, and Ireland tended to conform to the pattern of the German migration. In fact, the migration of Scotch-Irish from northern Ireland to Pennsylvania became so heavy that James Logan of Pennsylvania observed: "It looks as if Ireland is to send all its inhabitants hither. . . . The common fact is that if they thus continue to come they will make themselves proprietors of the Province."

The consequences of non-English migration were numerous. The population of provincial America grew; demographic patterns changed, and new cultural patterns and influences, such as German Pietism, were introduced. In those colonies where immigration was greatest—such as Pennsylvania, where Quakers constituted the elite and the Germans and the Scotch-Irish were regarded as the lower classes—the social structure was affected. New sources of labor became available at a time when colonial economic expansion demanded them. The colonies became more cosmopolitan, with a broader interaction of cultures.

The non-English influence was primarily cultural, not political. English political customs and institutions, modified by American colonial conditions, continued to be practiced

Many of the new immigrants settled in the country, where they cleared thick forests to build their farms.

without challenge because most of the newcomers had never before experienced self-government. But non-English cultural life in the broadest sense—the classical music of the Moravians, the new languages, Scottish Presbyterianism, the special methods of breeding high-grade cattle brought by the Scottish Highlanders—enriched provincial America.

The population growth provided by the new immigrants occurred mainly in the country rather than in the cities. In fact, this was one of the few periods in American history in which the urban proportion of the population declined rather than increased. Yet the five major colonial cities—Boston, Newport, New York, Philadelphia, and Charleston—tripled their populations be-

tween 1690 and 1742. And, more significantly, a great number of smaller urban communities developed—port towns in Massachusetts and inland towns such as Albany.

In each case the importance of the urban areas exceeded a strict population count because, as centers of distribution for goods and commodities, they became more influential economically, politically, socially, and culturally. By 1776 Philadelphia ranked second among the cities within the British empire, an astonishing development. Furthermore, Philadelphia had become an important cultural center with its scientific societies, its university, its public library, its newspaper, and its first citizen, Benjamin Franklin, amateur scientist, inventor, and noted publisher of *Poor Richard's Almanac*.

The Rise of Slavery. By far the largest group of immigrants to come to the English colonies in North America during the eighteenth century were blacks from Africa and the West Indies. It was a forced migration. The first blacks were brought to Virginia in 1619, and evidence indicates that until the middle of the seventeenth century they were both slaves and servants. The numbers involved were relatively insignificant. Less than 4 percent of the population of Virginia in 1670 was composed of slaves, with similar percentages in New York and Rhode Island.

But in the 1690s slavery suddenly boomed. The proportion of slaves in the population of Virginia rose to 25 percent in 1720 and to 41 percent in 1750. Slavery became the labor base upon which the large-scale plantation system in Virginia, Maryland, and North and South Carolina was founded.

Two considerations in particular account for the abrupt change. First, neither intellectual nor moral restraint existed. Blacks were considered property rather than people. Liberty as understood in the seventeenth and eighteenth centuries protected property and, as a consequence, protected slavery. No important social institution within Virginia or, indeed, in the Western World condemned slavery in 1700.

Second, Virginia, Maryland, and South Carolina were desperately in need of workers. In the seventeenth century, indentured servants had been the primary labor force in Virginia and Maryland, and indentures in modest numbers were introduced into New England, where family labor predominated. Beginning in the late seventeenth century, however, and accelerating in the eighteenth century, indentured servants were increasingly attracted to the Middle colonies. As a result, the Southern colonies were correspondingly desperate for labor as large landholdings became more numerous.

The chief reason for the increase of black slave importation in the Southern colonies,

then, was economic. Although twice as expensive as an indentured servant at the outset, a slave provided permanent service, and in every colony the laws made slaves in perpetuity of the offspring of female slaves. Soon slaves outstripped land as an investment. In a broadside written by Thomas Nairne of South Carolina in 1704 informing prospective colonists of the relative costs of establishing a plantation, the cost of two slaves, even for a modest plantation of 200 acres, constituted one half of all costs, including tools, land, a house, livestock, and a year's provisions. The land cost only £6 compared with £80 for the two slaves.

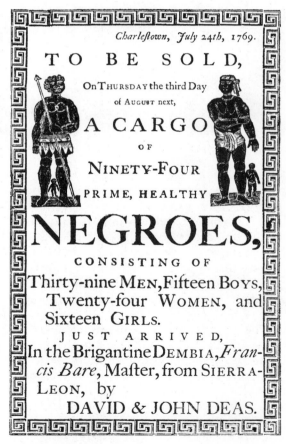

During the 1700s, blacks were viewed both as property and as an investment.

By 1775, 20 percent of the population of the English colonies in North America was composed of blacks, most of them slaves. More than 400,000 lived in the colonies of Maryland, Virginia, North Carolina, South Carolina, and Georgia—a number almost equal to the total population of New England.

Although it has often been asserted that the British Royal African Company brought most of the slaves to America, free traders were the principal conveyors of blacks. New Englanders, infrequently the Dutch, and later Southern merchants or planters imported slaves from the Caribbean as well as from Africa. Most of the colonies tried to end by law the increasing importation of slaves, but each act adopted by the individual colonial legislatures was rejected by the British Board of Trade. Because of the profitability of the slave trade, Britain considered it to be the basis for its entire trading structure. Indeed, a charge excised from the Declaration of Independence which condemned the crown for imposing slaves upon the colonies had a basis in fact.

That the slaves came to the English colonies with no skills and that the culture of Africa was vastly inferior to that of the Western World are myths that feed a racial bias. Most slaves came with skills equal to those of an ordinary laboring Englishman. For example, the original source of the rice that became a successful crop in South Carolina was Madagascar, where Africans had been cultivating it for centuries. When Eliza Pinckney of South Carolina was unsuccessful in making the commercial dye indigo with a white overseer, she imported a black slave whose knowledge, together with her own perseverance, culminated in an important marketable staple.

The agricultural tools of the African farmer and the English leaseholder did not vary greatly. In time, the transplanted African became the skilled worker in the Southern colonies—the cooper, cobbler, and blacksmith. It was not unusual for a planter to put in a request for a slave from a special region of Africa because of the particular skills of its inhabitants.

The devastating social consequences of slavery pervaded every aspect of colonial life. Conflict between blacks and whites led to the enactment of elaborate codes for the conduct of slaves. The Stono Rebellion of 1739 in South Carolina stunned the white population, and fear of future revolts prompted defensive measures. Laws were passed to restrict the importation of slaves and to encourage the importation of white indentured servants. White settlements were promoted on the frontier as protection for older slave-centered communities.

The most enduring effect of slavery was to set Africans outside the existing social strata and, with minor exceptions, to condemn them to perpetual bondage and lowest status in a caste system. The black was deprived of rights often described as peculiar virtues of the American system—the chance to improve one's position through hard work and the opportunity to provide a better life for one's children. Slavery alienated all but a few Africans from the American tradition. (See "Phillis Wheatley: Black Poet.")

The eighteenth century, therefore, witnessed a strange spectacle: a developing consciousness with respect to a definition of political liberty, consummated by the American Revolution, at the same time that slavery was being imposed on a vast number of human beings—the Africans who came to the colonies under compulsion.

The English and the Native Americans. The relationship between the English in North America and the native Americans was obvious yet subtle. A small number of Spanish conquistadors under Hernando Cortez were able to dominate Mexico by conquering the Aztecs, who held lesser tribes in subordination. But the English in North America faced a different situation that produced a decidedly different result. Powerful tribes blocked the westward expansion of the English settlers: (1) in the triangular area between Lakes Ontario, Erie, and Huron, the Hurons; (2) along the spine of the Appalachians, the Iroquois in New York and Pennsylvania, the Susquehannas in Pennsylvania and Virginia, and the Cherokees in the Carolinas; (3) in the Mississippi Valley below the Ohio River, the Chickasaws and, farther south, the Choctaws. And there were many other tribes interspersed throughout. However, no single nation had achieved ascendancy. Defeat for one tribe did not mean defeat for all.

Since the most powerful groups of native Americans in English America did not dwell along the Atlantic seacoast, the first white settlers from England frequently faced tribes that were friendly or, if warlike, easily defeated. If the Indians had joined forces to drive the English from North America at any time during the first half century of colonization, they could have succeeded. Lack of will—of unity of purpose—not an absence of power, explains their failure to do so.

From the beginning, the English treated native Americans as members of separate nations or separate tribes, never as subjects of the crown. Warfare and negotiation involved two nations: England and the particular tribe or nation in question. In contrast to the fusion of cultures that took place under the Spanish colonial system, the white and native American cultures remained separate in English America.

In need of labor, English settlers sometimes tried to make slaves of the native Americans

Phillis Wheatley: Black Poet

There are few enslaved Africans brought to the British colonies in North America whose lives are as well documented as that of Phillis Wheatley. Part of the explanation lies in the Wheatley family history. More important, Phillis Wheatley herself left a living, written record in her verses.

In both respects, her life was very different from those of the great majority of Africans brought to America. Yet her story represents the importance of the forced migration from Africa, not only because the numbers of people involved exceeded the migration of peoples from Western Europe in the colonial eighteenth century, but also because of the many talents brought to America by Africans. Unlike many other blacks, Phillis Wheatley was encouraged to develop her talents and was accepted into white society.

Phillis Wheatley was first seen in America as a delicate little girl, about eight years old, aboard a slave ship from Senegal that reached Boston in 1761. Susannah Wheatley, wife of tailor John Wheatley, wished to have a special personal servant. John purchased the young slave, brought her home, and named her Phillis.

At the time Phillis entered the Wheatley household, it included, in addition to the

captured in skirmishes. But it did not work. The captives could too easily slip off and return to their own people. In some colonies—South Carolina, for instance—captured native Americans were shipped off to the West Indies as slaves around 1700.

Efforts were also made to convert native Americans to English ways. Schools were established for them in several colonies, but once the native Americans returned to their own people, they took up their traditional ways and customs.

On occasion, the practice of treating a native American people as a foreign power had gratifying results for the English. When Iroquois and Cherokee leaders were brought to London to sign treaties of friendship, the crown made these occasions festive and special. Both Indian nations remained invaluable allies of England for a century.

In the colonial period powerful nations of native Americans blocked English access to the interior of the continent. These Indians controlled the interior trade by their defensive position along the Appalachian range and were strengthened by their ability to play off the European rivals, France and England, against each other. They held the balance of power in America for a century (1660—1760). Not until the French had been eliminated as a major participant in colonizing the continent were the English finally able to penetrate the Appalachian barrier in any great numbers.

Ironically, by forcing the American provincials to stay principally in the coastal areas, the native Americans contributed to their own

husband and wife, a son, Nathaniel, and a daughter, Mary. Three other children had died in their early years.

Susannah Wheatley and her daughter Mary, who was eighteen, observed that Phillis absorbed her lessons quickly. As a result, they began to instruct her, giving preference to Biblical teachings. Within about sixteen months Phillis could read difficult passages in the Bible with ease. Encouraged, Mary taught Phillis a smattering of astronomy, ancient and modern geography, ancient history, and even a few of the Latin classics. Homer became Phillis' favorite author, and soon she began to write verse. In the household, she was increasingly considered a daughter rather than a slave, and it became a familiar treat among the Wheatley friends to have Phillis recite the poetry of others or verses of her own. Her first poem, entitled "A Poem, by Phillis, a Negro Girl, in Boston, On the Death of the Reverend George Whitefield," appeared in print in 1770.

In 1771, Mary Wheatley married the pastor of the Second Church in Boston, the Reverend John Lathrop. In that same year, Phillis became a member of the congregation of the Old South Meeting House, a significant departure for that faith. Because Phillis' health appeared to fail, the Wheatley family physician recommended sea air. Nathaniel was about to leave for England on business, and so it was decided that Phillis would sail under protection of her foster brother. She was made a freed person before she left in May 1773.

Phillis was welcomed in England by the Countess of Huntingdon, for whom Whitefield had served as chaplain. She attracted wide attention, not only because of her writing talent but also because of her unusual gift of conversation. Brook Watson, the Lord Mayor of London, was sufficiently impressed to present Phillis with a 1720 Glasgow edition of *Paradise Lost*.

destruction. Prevented from moving westward, the colonists established a mature, vigorous, developed society from which to launch an assault to conquer the inland wilderness. If the English had been able to penetrate deeply into the interior of America soon after settlement, the strength provided by cohesive, highly developed colonies would not have been achieved.

Also, if deep penetration had been possible, the tie with England would unquestionably have been much less influential. The political experience of the settlements would have been less sophisticated, and therefore less valuable, for only relatively stable communities could provide such experience. In contributing to the creation of a vigorous, structured provincial society, the formidable Indian barrier thus contributed to the development of political, economic, and intellectual institutions. These institutions, in turn, became so deep-rooted that the sweeping westward movement of the nineteenth century failed to alter them in any fundamental way.

Trade represented one of the most important contacts between the settlers and the native Americans and accounted for the founding of many of the first modest provincial fortunes. In South Carolina, for example, the early road to riches was gained not by raising rice but by trading in deerskins, one of the most valuable exports from the Carolinas until well into the eighteenth century. In Pennsylvania James Logan's emergence as the first citizen of that colony was made possible

Phillis was urged to stay in London, but word reached her that Susannah Wheatley was seriously ill and longed for her return. Turning aside all entreaties to remain in London, Phillis left for Boston. However, before departing she arranged to have her collection of poems published under the title *Poems on Various Subjects, Religious and Moral.*

Little but despair greeted her on returning to Boston. Susannah Wheatley died in March 1774, and four years later Susannah's husband John died, followed soon after by Mary Wheatley Lathrop. Nathaniel, the only remaining member of the family, was living abroad.

In April 1778 Phillis became the wife of John Peters. In her letters she wrote of him as an agreeable man, but she quickly discovered that he lacked qualities to which she had become accustomed in the Wheatley household—among them diligence and industry. Pursued by poverty, deeply affected by the war which cut her off from friends in England, Phillis finally earned her living by doing daily chores in a lodging house. She died December 5, 1784, preceded in death by two of her three children.

Phillis Wheatley was a tragic figure, a victim of slavery who was rescued by a loving and talented family, a victim of a war which turned minds to politics rather than to poetry. Yet her verses live on. First editions of her poems appeared in 1793. Since then, her verses and her life have been the subject of continuous study.

Her piety and upbringing in the Wheatley family are revealed in these lines from "On the Death of the Reverend Mr. George Whitefield."

through what he called the "stinking" fur trade. In New York the trade brought a fortune and a title to Sir William Johnson.

During the eighteenth century the locus of the fur trade shifted. By 1730 New England's share was limited, if not negligible. The Middle colonies, the area of greatest expansion, had become the center of the trade, with New York and Pennsylvania well in the lead. In the South, Virginia had controlled the principal trade with the Cherokees and the Chickasaws in the late seventeenth century, but early in the eighteenth century South Carolina developed into a serious rival. Then Georgia moved into contention. By the mid-eighteenth century, New York and Georgia were perhaps the two colonies most deeply engaged in the trade with the natives.

Non-English Settlers in the Borderlands. While the English settlers were being held in check, Spanish and French colonists were settling in territory that would eventually become part of the United States. From the sixteenth to the early nineteenth century, the Spanish advanced into Florida, Texas, the American Southwest, and along the Pacific coastline of California. The French established their first settlement in Quebec, Canada, in 1608 and in the seventeenth and eighteenth centuries posted settlements of explorers and soldiers from New Orleans to the western Great Lakes and from the headwaters of the Ohio River, near present-day Pittsburgh, to its outlet into the Mississippi.

The Spanish and French coupled exploration and conquest with missionary stations.

> Thou, moon, hast seen, and all the stars of light,
> How he has wrestled with his God by night.
> He prayed that grace in ev'ry heart might dwell;
> He longed to see America excel;
> He charged its youth that ev'ry grace divine
> Should with full lustre in their conduct shine.

Somewhat surprisingly, Phillis' references to slavery are limited. When it surfaces, as in her dedicatory verses to the Earl of Dartmouth, she links it to a larger context of freedom, a commentary on her extraordinary perception, well in advance of her time and place, and a fitting epitaph.

> Should you, my lord, while you peruse my song,
> Wonder from whence my love of Freedom sprung,
> Whence flow these wishes for the common good,
> By feeling hearts alone best understood,
> I, young in life, by seeming cruel fate
> Was snatched from Afric's fancied happy seat:
> What pangs excruciating must molest,
> What sorrows labor in my parent's breast!
> Steeled was that soul, and by no misery moved,
> That from a father seized his babe beloved:
> Such, such my case. And can I then but pray
> Others may never feel tyrannic sway?

The English found their westward expansion blocked by a number of well-organized and well-established Indian tribes. This engraving by Theodore De Bry shows the village of Secoton in 1585, located in present-day North Carolina.

Many of the Spanish missions in the American Southwest and California, originally housing a garrison of soldiers, a parcel of priests, and a community of Indians, remain to be admired today. Those established by France proved to be somewhat less durable.

The objective of the Spanish defense of its borderlands was to extend the empire and, at the same time, "to Christianize, civilize, and purify" the native inhabitants—the Indians. To achieve these goals the Spanish established a chain of *presidios*, or army outposts, from Florida to California. These were linked to and often coupled with mission stations. A *presidio* consisted of some sixty or more soldiers, often living in a modest hut surrounded by a mud palisade. They were accompanied by their families, Indian servants, Indian warriors, and hangers-on of various types of frontier adventurers.

The missions, somewhat in contrast, tried to organize Indian society. On the whole the priests, largely Franciscans, did not find settled Indian communities and so set out to establish them. They gathered the Indians into mission stations typically made up of a *plaza*, or square, dominated by the church and surrounded by official buildings, granaries, blacksmith shops, tanneries, and stables, as well as living quarters for the Indians and the missionaries.

The object was to impose Spanish "civilization" upon this created Indian community. Indians learned to speak the Spanish language, to cultivate crops, to raise livestock, to raise and ride horses. They also learned carpentry, European style. They became winemakers and candlemakers. And, of course, they were held to daily sessions of work and prayer.

A traveler to the missions in California described how everyone, Indians and missionaries alike, awakened at first light. They attended prayers and mass, after which *atole*, a type of barley ground up and boiled, was served for breakfast. Then everyone was sent out to work. Men tilled the soil; women cared for the household and the children. A bell summoned the workers for the noonday meal of a stew made of wheat, corn, peas, and beans. The inhabitants of the mission station worked for several hours in the afternoon, after which everyone, once again, attended religious services.

Hunting and fishing were allowed, and the Indians raised livestock. At the same time, they retained some of their life-style. Their shelters, clothing, and games remained the same. Intermarriage between the Spanish and Indians was encouraged, and, in some mission stations, polygamy was permitted.

Out of this came the mixed Spanish-Indian customs: the rodeo and cattle roundup, the stylized concept of the cowboy with chaps, lasso, and lariat, riding a bronco. Out of it also came the fierce Apache warrior on horseback, defending the tribe against further colonial encroachment. Much more subtle as an outgrowth of the Spanish colonization of the borderlands was the hybridization of people and customs in the region, which has endured.

The French did not impose themselves in the same way on their mission-garrison stations. Trading played a larger role. The French did not attempt to keep whole Indian populations under their control, but they wooed and won the friendship of many tribes who stood against English encroachment. They also fortified the Mississippi and Ohio river basins, as well as the region surrounding the Great Lakes.

End of the Barrier to Expansion. In the wars that erupted during the eighteenth century between England and France, native Americans played a key role. Each side tried to win allies among them, and for almost a century there was a standoff. But in the Great War for Empire, 1754–1763, the English defeated the French and caused them to abandon North America. In the process the native Americans who had previously been able to take advantage of the rivalry between England and France to suit their own interests abruptly lost their strategic position. It was not by chance that the English settlements, which for 150 years had failed to penetrate more than 200 miles into the interior of North America, suddenly were able to surge thousands of miles in a few decades after 1800 to reach the Pacific Ocean.

THE SEVENTEENTH CENTURY: AGE OF FAITH

In America's intellectual and religious life, as in its social structure, English ideas and practices transplanted to the New World were modified by the American environment.

The late sixteenth and early seventeenth centuries in England were an Age of Faith, and the characteristics of this age were indelibly stamped upon the English colonies in America. The Protestant Reformation in Europe had unleashed a flood of ideas concerning the role of the church, qualifications for church membership, and the individual's relationship to God—particularly the degree of a person's freedom of will. Were individuals elected by God and thus saved from eternal damnation? Or could each person win salvation through individual faith and the exercise of free will? The English of the early seventeenth century were endlessly concerned with points of doctrine like these.

Puritanism in England. When Henry VIII broke with the Roman Catholic Church and established the Church of England, specific church practice and doctrine were little altered. But within the Anglican Church, opposition groups, who became known as Puritans, gradually emerged. All Puritans agreed that to become a member of God's elect, an individual must undergo a "conversion experience," in which a spiritual rebirth was sensed. Most agreed that certain rituals within the church service should be changed. Puritans disagreed, however, on the question of church government.

One group, the Presbyterian Puritans, followed the precepts of John Calvin. They believed in a close church-state relationship in which policies would be established by the ruling hierarchy and, once adopted, would be enforced among the individual congregations. In addition, the Presbyterian Puritans believed that the church should include the nonelect as well as the elect, since mortals were not capable of knowing with certainty whom God had elected for salvation.

Comprising a second group of Puritans were the Non-Conforming Congregationalists. They believed, first of all, that a church should be composed only of the elect and that such men and women could be identified. In their view the invisible church (God's elect) and the visible church (the church in daily operation) were one. The Non-Conforming Congregational Puritans held that individual congregations should rule themselves and that church doctrine and practice should be enforced by the individual congregation, not by a superior church hierarchy. Both these groups of Puritans—the Presbyterians and the Congregationalists—were willing to remain within the Church of England and to carry out their reforms, their "religious revolution," within the structure of the established church.

Closely related to the Puritans—though less influential—were the Non-Conforming Congregational Separatists. As their name indicates, these people held many of the same views as the Non-Conforming Congregational Puritans. But the Separatists believed that reforming the Church of England was an impossible task, so they wished to separate from it. In the eyes of the king their views were particularly dangerous, because by following their religious inclinations they were in effect repudiating the king as head of the church.

Puritanism in America. In New England, a small, uninfluential group of Non-Conforming Separatists founded Plymouth, while Non-Conforming Congregational Puritans founded Massachusetts Bay and spread throughout New England. Puritanism was to have a dramatic career in England, where the Presbyterian Puritans, at least for a time, gained control. But in America Puritan ideas were transformed into a distinct social organization only in New England.

The Puritans there conceived of themselves as a covenanted people. In essence, the "covenant theology" held that God had made a contract with humans setting down the terms of salvation. God had pledged Himself to abide by these terms. This covenant in no way changed the doctrine that God elected the saints, but it explained why certain people were elected and others were not. Individuals knew that they were numbered among the elect by experiencing God's grace and reflecting this *regeneration*—spiritual rebirth—before their peers.

Because the terms of the covenant were to be found in the Bible, the Bible was the source of the rules of conduct and was constantly searched for meaning and interpretation.

This detail of George H. Boughton's painting shows the Puritans walking to church with their guns and Bibles.

Because of the covenant, each law, each act, each policy demanded literal Biblical support. Believing in the vigorous use of reason, the Puritans supported the idea of a highly trained clergy and a literate laity. They firmly opposed all religious enthusiasms or any evidence of self-revelation (the doctrine that God revealed Himself directly to an individual). For this reason, both the Puritans and the Anglicans abhorred the Quakers. The notion of an "inner light" which, the Quakers claimed, involved a mystical force and a direct communication between God and the individual, was offensive to the New England Puritans. They demonstrated their abhorrence when they hanged several Quakers who refused to leave Massachusetts Bay.

The New England Puritans turned to congregationalism as a form of church government. But they attempted informally to establish close ties among the individual congregations by means of synods, or assemblies of delegates, for discussion and decision on ecclesiastical affairs. Theoretically, each congregation could select its own course of action, but in practice a consensus of the Puritan leaders usually determined the course.

It would be a mistake to think that the Puritan clergy were all-powerful; indeed, conformity to Puritan beliefs was enforced by civil authority. Lay leaders like John Winthrop, not the leading ministers, were primarily responsible for the banishment of colonials who protested against the Puritan doctrines.

The premises of New England Puritanism affected every sphere of life—political, economic, cultural, social, and intellectual. For example, land was distributed to church congregations so that a social-religious community could be created and sustained. Settlement by towns enabled the Puritans to center their lives and activities around the church, and designated practice could easily be enforced. With the Puritans in political control, and thus able to determine those groups who were to receive land grants, the objective of creating a Bible Commonwealth could be achieved.

Because the Puritans firmly believed in a rational religion, they soon began to think about establishing a center of higher learning to continue the tradition of a learned ministry untainted by divergent strains of theology. The upshot was the founding of Harvard College in 1636. Town settlements made schools practical. In 1642 an act was passed which required every town of fifty or more householders to establish an "elementary school" to teach the fundamentals of reading and writing. Both boys and girls attended. An enactment of 1647 required each community of one hundred householders or more to provide a "grammar school," a school to prepare students for college by means of vigorous instruction in the Greek and Latin classics.

New England Puritans expressed themselves in prose and poetry. Sometimes their tone was harsh, but it was always unmistakably clear. Sermons were cultivated as a literary form and were published by the press founded in Massachusetts Bay in 1639. This press became the voice of Puritanism in America. Its productivity was fabulous. Its output exceeded that of the presses of Cambridge and Oxford in England.

Changes in the New World. During the seventeenth century, Puritanism in America was gradually modified by New World conditions. Modifications were made in theology, in church practice, and in everyday life. The course of this change has been brilliantly analyzed by historian Perry Miller, but for purposes of this text a single example—the adoption of the Half-Way Covenant in 1662—will suffice.

The church, you will recall, was presumably made up exclusively of the elect, the covenanted people. Children of the elect, howev-

The Puritan's belief in a rational religion led them to found Harvard College, shown here in a 1726 engraving.

er, sometimes failed to evidence "conversion" and thereby to demonstrate the election which would qualify them for full membership within the church. As the body of church members became smaller in proportion to the total population, the clergy feared that the influence of the church in the community at large would be seriously undermined. By the terms of the Half-Way Covenant, therefore, the children of the elect who had not entered full membership in the church were nevertheless pemitted to have their children baptized. Baptism enabled the children to participate in some, though not all, of the sacraments of the church. This opening wedge made an association with the church possible without proof of "election." It was gradually widened until a number of prominent ministers advocated opening the church to those who tried to live according to the precepts of the church even though they could not demonstrate election.

The New World environment affected other areas of Puritan intellectual life as well. The intellectual vigor of Harvard College declined. Its intellectual direction became, at least to old-line Puritans, "radical," which meant that it diverged from early Puritan precepts and intellectual rigor. The enforcement of the school acts lagged, and few intellectuals of late seventeenth-century New England could match the intellectual creativity of the first-line Puritans.

Making the terms of church membership easier was important outside intellectual life as well. During most of the seventeenth century only church members could vote in the colony-wide elections of Massachusetts Bay. A substantial majority of the population, therefore, failed to qualify for the franchise. Thus, broadened church membership had direct political effects. When a new charter made property ownership the basis for franchise in 1691, the Puritans lost outright control of Massachusetts. Yet the Congregational Church as a social-religious institution was a powerful influence in New England well into the nineteenth century.

The Transplanted Anglicans.   In the Age of Faith the Anglican Church was transplanted to Virginia. From there it expanded into the Carolinas and Maryland, and, in the eighteenth century, to the Middle colonies and New England. In contrast to Puritanism in America, Anglicanism did not center around formal theological inquiries and dogmas. The theological structure of Anglicanism was exclusively the product and concern of the clerical hierarchy within England, and a highly learned Anglican ministry did not migrate to America.

As a result, the influence of the New World environment is measured in terms of its modifications of church practice and church ceremonials rather than modification of doctrine. For example, while the Anglican Church in England was highly centralized and carefully supervised by its hierarchy, in America it became a decentralized church ruled by lay members. The clergy who migrated to America were almost impotent before the lay leaders.

The Anglican parishes in seventeenth-century America were much too large, and this,

too, affected church practices. A minister could not readily serve a congregation when its membership was widely scattered. Lay leaders, therefore, began to read the services on the Sabbath, and they soon exercised a role in religious functions which violated the canons of the church.

Because people found it difficult to travel ten or twelve miles to church on horseback or by boat, attendance at services suffered. Moreover, because of the distances, weddings took place on a plantation rather than in church, and the dead were buried on the plantation in an unconsecrated family plot rather than in church ground—again a violation of church ordinances.

The absence of a guiding intellectual premise in the Chesapeake colonies dramatically affected education. The scattered nature of the settlements made community schools impractical: By the time the children arrived at the schoolhouse by horseback or boat, it would be time for them to return home. Consequently, responsibility for education was placed upon the family, not upon the community, and the finances and intellectual values of an individual family determined its response.

Obviously, in a plantation system which made public schools well-nigh impossible, the Virginia gentry had a decided advantage over lesser folk. Occasionally, when enough plantations were close to each other, Old Field Schools were founded in which the children were taught by a minister or by the wife of a planter. More often a family or a group of families hired an indentured servant to teach the children. With no way of obtaining an advanced education in the colony, those planters who wished their children to receive a college education sent them to England.

THE EIGHTEENTH-CENTURY MIND

The Enlightenment.   During the seventeenth century, English intellectual life underwent a transformation triggered by the momentous advance of science and the application of the theoretical framework of science to all phases of human experience. The writings of the father of scientific reasoning, Francis Bacon, marked the beginning of a movement called the Enlightenment. This movement was consummated by the great scientific discoveries of Sir Isaac Newton, whose *Mathematical Principles of Natural Philosophy* (1697) set forth, by precise demonstration, the laws of motion and gravitation. Newton was to the eighteenth century what Einstein has been to the twentieth.

The Enlightenment also affected religious thinking. Newton had used reasoning to discover laws in the physical universe. Many reasoned that laws must govern the relationship between the human race and the spiritual universe too. In this view, God was seen as the Prime Mover who had created the universe with a perfectly operating, harmonious system of unchangeable laws—the laws of nature. But once the universe had been created, so the reasoning went, God no longer took an active part in ruling it, and the natural laws set the requirements for human behavior.

Fortunately, these laws could be discovered, and once they were known, people had only to adjust their lives and their political and educational systems accordingly—in conformity with the requirements set by natural law. The closer to alignment between human activity and the laws of nature, the closer human institutions would be to perfection.

In this view, people were perfectible and progress was inevitable. These ideas about God and the universe were called *deism*. They contrasted sharply with many of the basic talents of Puritanism.

It should be emphasized that the ideas of the Enlightenment affected only a small minority of the English and far fewer colonials. Most people went about their daily lives unaware of intellectual trends. Enlightenment ideas did not gain strong advocates in America until the mid-eighteenth century, and even then their influence was sharply restricted. Whereas in England, Enlightenment ideas permeated literature as well as political thought, in America, they found expression chiefly in political thought. The Declaration of Independence appeals to the "laws of nature and nature's God."

The Enlightenment constituted only one current in the mainstream of intellectual life in eighteenth-century America. Whereas the English Age of Faith had dominated seventeenth-century colonial America, the widespread immigration of non-English groups brought a diversity of cultures. By the eighteenth century the colonies reflected what was to become a characteristic of the American mind—a wide diversity of intellectual streams.

The Growth of Toleration. The Toleration Act adopted by Parliament in 1689 gave sufferance to all Protestant sects in England. In America the background for toleration had been laid as early as 1636, when Roger Williams founded Rhode Island.

In a sense, Williams backed into the principle of religious toleration. He had found the Puritans of Massachusetts Bay imperfect in their religious fervor, and he consequently vowed to pray only with those he knew to be regenerate, spiritually reborn. Because he was unsure of other folk, he finally was forced to pray only with his wife. From this restricted, impractical position, Williams took the long step to religious toleration on the premise that since he could not determine precisely which persons were regenerate, he had no alternative but to extend toleration to everyone with religious convictions. Williams' ultimate attitude of toleration was well in advance of the mainstream both in England and in America.

The Maryland Toleration Act of 1649 lent impetus to the growth of toleration, though it arose not from broad humanitarian principles but from immediate circumstances. Maryland, established originally as a Catholic refuge, was being heavily populated by Protestants. Not only had the Catholics become a minority, but, because of the Puritan domination in England, they were seriously threatened by persecution. The Toleration Act, advocated by Lord Baltimore, was intended to protect the Catholic minority and to forestall action against Baltimore's proprietorship.

Toleration flourished in the eighteenth century, in part because of seventeenth-century precedents but, more important, because the realities of the eighteenth century made intolerance an anachronism. The migration of dissenter sects from Germany; the emergence of an intercolonial Presbyterian church increasingly fortified by newly arrived Scots and Scotch-Irish; the spread of Anglicanism throughout the colonies; the migrations from Pennsylvania south to Georgia; the settlements of Jews in Rhode Island, Georgia, and other colonies; the application of the English Toleration Act in America—these developments made toleration a necessity. The diversity of religious faiths made any other course impossible.

Toleration for provincial America did not mean disruption of church-state establishments. Householders of all faiths were taxed, for example, to maintain the Anglican church in Virginia and the Congregational church in Massachusetts, although in each colony people could practice other faiths without undue molestation. The separation of church and state did not become a question of principle until during and after the American Revolution, when it was apparent that no single church was sufficiently strong to be elevated to the status of a national church.

The Rise of Secularism. Greater toleration, in turn, provided a climate in which *secularism*— a concern with worldly rather than religious matters—could grow. The people who migrated to America in the eighteenth century were primarily seeking opportunity, not religious toleration. If toleration had been their principal desire, the German Pietists could easily have migrated to Rhode Island— and at an earlier date. But choice Pennsylvania land, in combination with religious toleration, proved to be a superior attraction. Moreover the new generations of Americans who were native-born turned with avidity to enrichment and advancement. They were less concerned than their seventeenth-century forebears with the saving of souls.

Perhaps the best index of the rise of secularism is the production of the provincial press. In the eighteenth century, newspapers flourished. The first was published in Boston in 1704, and by the 1750s almost every colony had one newspaper and a number had several. In contrast to Michael Wigglesworth's *Day of Doom* of the seventeenth century, almanacs became the best-sellers of the eighteenth century. *Poor Richard's Almanac*, which Benjamin Franklin edited in Philadelphia from 1732 to 1758, sold ten thousand copies a year and became the most popular reading matter in the colonies—except for the Bible.

The emergence of secularism can also be detected in the appearance of touring companies of English actors. Williamsburg had a theater in 1716. In the 1770s satirical patriotic plays by Mercy Otis Warren were published, as were the verses of Phillis Wheatley, who had been brought from Africa as a slave.

The Great Awakening. The growth of toleration and the emergence of secularism should not obscure a third significant and persistent theme of eighteenth-century intellectual and social life. It was the Great Awakening, an evangelical religious movement—a series of revivals preached by stirring evangelists— that swept through colonial America and caused great excitement.

The Great Awakening began in the Middle

colonies for three main reasons. German migration carried with it the Pietist movement from Europe. The rapid expansion characteristic of the Middle colonies tended to overtax traditional religious institutions and thus to encourage the creation of new organizations and new forms for religious expression. And a church-state relationship did not exist to thwart an evangelical movement.

In the 1730s the Great Awakening extended into New England, where its fire-and-brimstone preachers drew large revivalist crowds in cities and towns. In the 1740s and 1750s the movement reached into the Southern colonies, carried along in part by the migration of the Scotch-Irish and Germans southward along the eastern edge of the Appalachians.

Among the noted preachers associated with the Great Awakening was Jonathan Edwards of the Northampton Church in Massachusetts, often called the greatest theologian America has produced. He used Enlightenment reasoning to construct a theological contradiction to Enlightenment ideas. Beginning in the 1720s, many New England ministers were influenced by a theology basing salvation on human moral effort as well as divine grace. Edwards opposed this tendency and reasserted the absolute justice of God's power to elect or to condemn as He chose, defending with exceptional skill the basic Calvinistic position that God was omnipotent and that, before God, humans were impotent.

The Great Awakening caused divisions within existing church organizations. Church members attracted to the evangelical group were called "new lights", and they attempted to wrest control of the church from the conservative members who held power, the "old lights." The Awakening fervor also was responsible for the founding of four colleges by separate religious denominations: Dartmouth (Congregationalist), Princeton (Presbyterian), Brown (Baptist), and Rutgers (Dutch Reformed). The premise in each case

was that the existing institutions of higher learning—Yale, for instance, which had been founded in 1701—were unsuitable for training acceptable "new light" ministers.

The Awakening, because it was an intercolonial movement, strengthened intercolonial ties. Many historians have advanced the idea that, by emphasizing the individual and his or her relationship to God, it aroused a democratic spirit which influenced the revolutionary generation. This generalization cannot be proved or disproved, but it seems fair to suggest that in reviewing traditional institutions—which in this case happened to be ecclesiastical institutions—the Awakening encouraged a climate of freedom.

The Enlightenment in America. The greatest influence of the Enlightenment in America was the encouragement it gave to scientific inquiry. Cotton Mather, the most prominent New England clergyman in the late seventeenth and early eighteenth centuries, was attracted to scientific investigation. He was an advocate of smallpox inoculations when others greeted this medical advance with uncertainty or fear. William Byrd II of Virginia, along with other colonials, belonged to England's Royal Society and frequently sent observations of New World phenomena to his friends in England.

The contribution of most colonials was to that aspect of science called "natural history." Almost every botanical specimen collected in America constituted a contribution to knowledge because it added to the storehouse of scientific information. John Bartram, who collected specimens throughout the provinces and cultivated rare species in his garden at Philadelphia, was called the finest contemporary "natural botanist" by Carolus Linnaeus of Sweden, the foremost botanist in Europe. A celebrated work was Mark Catesby's extraordinary *Natural History of Carolina.*

Only Benjamin Franklin contributed to theoretical science, although many of his provincial contemporaries pursued allied investigations with vigor and persistence. Fortunately for Franklin, he entered a field of physics in which relatively little work had been done, and thus he was not handicapped by his lack of background, particularly his limited knowledge of mathematics. His identification of lightning as electricity and his observations concerning the flow of electricity and the equalization that took place between highly charged particles and those less highly charged were contributions that won him a reputation throughout Europe.

Although science became increasingly important in the colleges, it was pursued most fervently by those outside the institutions of learning. As proper eighteenth-century generalists, they were interested in politics, science, writing, and other broad-gauged, stimulating activities. As the impact of science

During the Enlightenment, many efforts were made to discover the natural laws of the universe. In this 1768 painting by Joseph Wright, a number of experimenters are shown exploring the effects of a vacuum upon a live chicken.

in colonial America makes clear, the Enlightenment, unlike Puritanism, was peculiarly the possession of the educated and social elite.

Yet in important ways Enlightenment ideas affected the whole people. For one thing, provincial America, because it represented a new, formative society, appeared in the eyes of some European and American observers to be the laboratory of the Enlightenment. American society, free from the incrustations of the centuries, could presumably adjust to the unchangeable laws of nature more readily than could that of Europe. Indeed, American intellectuals were confident that a perfect society was already being created.

In political thought and practice, too, provincial Americans regardless of status or location embraced many Enlightenment ideas. The right of citizens to challenge a governmental system when it stood athwart the laws of nature, and to replace such a government with one that conformed with nature's laws, were two assumptions of the Enlightenment which deeply penetrated the American mind.

Colonial Roots of American Culture.   Colonial America made no great progress in the arts, nor could such manifestations of cultural life be expected of a people whose principal energies were devoted to creating a new civilization. Yet Philadelphia stood as a cosmopolitan city, second in population only to London within the British empire. The American cities in the aggregate, as well as the American countryside, provided a stimulating atmosphere that nourished people of intelligence, indeed of genius, whose contributions would endure beyond those of most of their cultivated counterparts in England.

The standard criteria for evaluating the level of intellectual life, therefore, do not apply to provincial America. What were important were its zest for learning, its new modes of society, its mobility, its ability to prosper and to set examples that in time would be imitated. The promise of the American "minds" fashioned from the experience of the seventeenth and eighteenth centuries formed the foundation upon which American nationhood and an American culture were to be built.

How that promise would be realized is taken up in later parts of this book. In the remaining chapters of Part 1 we shall continue with our account of the founding of America. From the social and cultural aspects of colonial life we now turn to political and military aspects—to a record of epochal events preceding colonization and extending through the War for Independence.

Chapter 2

Evolution of the American Colonies

BACKGROUND TO COLONIZATION

The Beginnings of European Expansion.
America had been discovered as early as A.D. 1000, when the Vikings dominated northern Europe and the northern Atlantic. Yet their adventures did not stimulate European expansion into the New World. Obviously, a significant change had taken place in Western Europe by the time of Columbus' voyage in 1492, not only making overseas expansion possible but also instilling an adventurous spirit among Europeans so that they were eager to explore new lands and new opportunities.

Essentially, it was a change from medieval agrarianism and the feudal mind to economic developments characteristic of early modern Europe and the inquiring mind. In the Middle Ages, western Europe had been dominated by the feudal and manorial system in which each family's place in society—ranging from the peasantry to the nobility—was determined by the relationship of the male head of the household to the land. The commodities produced were consumed by the inhabitants of the manor. But the rise of early modern capitalism brought a revival of trade, the rise

of the city, the emergence of a merchant class, production for an outside market, and the growth of banking. As a result people were no longer dependent exclusively upon their relationship to the land. Business transactions brought an accumulation of money, and money could be employed to finance new enterprises.

The mind of Europe also was awakened. The Crusades, beginning in the eleventh century, introduced western Europe to the ways of the Near East and to such exotic commodities as spices and silks. Italian merchants—most notably, Marco Polo—journeyed all the way to China and Japan. The fear of the unknown and of new experiences which gripped many people in the Middle Ages gave way to the spirit of innovators, whose minds were stimulated by a curiosity about the unknown and a wish to exploit the riches of the East.

Portugal was the first nation bordering the Atlantic to engage in wide-scale exploration, especially along the western coast of Africa. This primacy was not accidental. Portugal was the first of the Atlantic nations to be unified, giving its leaders an opportunity to look outward rather than to be preoccupied with internal disorder. Among the most forward-looking was Prince Henry the Navigator (1394–1460), who established a center for the study of cartography and astronomy and for the improvement of ships and seamanship. Portugal was eventually rewarded when Bartholomew Diaz rounded Africa's southernmost Cape of Good Hope in 1488 and when Vasco da Gama reached India by way of the Cape of Good Hope in 1498.

The significance of national unity was underscored when Columbus' voyage in 1492 coincided with the expulsion of the Moors from Spain by the capture of Granada. Columbus' voyage, sailing west to reach the fabulous riches of the East, marked the great historical divide which eventually made the Atlantic rather than the Mediterranean the

Columbus' voyage, shown in this 1493 woodcut, marked the beginning of a new period of overseas exploration and expansion.

principal artery of trade and communication.

The efforts of Portugal and Spain to find new routes to the East were prompted in large part by their desire to challenge the commercial monopoly of the Italian cities. These cities, because of their geographical position, dominated trade with the East by way of the Mediterranean. By sailing around the world in 1519–1522 and showing a substantial profit despite the loss of all but one ship, the commander, and most of the men, the expedition of Ferdinand Magellan proved that the Mediterranean could be bypassed and the Italian monopoly broken.

Spain followed up the voyage of Columbus by establishing an American empire, thereby setting an example which the other nations of western Europe attempted to imitate. The Spaniards constructed a tightly knit, closely supervised colonial system whose object was to make its American colonies a source of wealth for the mother country and to prevent any encroachment by other nations.

In 1574, long before the English had established a successful colony in the New World, the Spanish population in Mexico City alone exceeded 15,000; throughout the New World it exceeded 160,000. More than 200 Spanish cities and towns had been founded, and Mexico City boasted a university. The principal agency used by Spain to transplant the culture of the Old World to the New was the Catholic Church, the only church in existence in the Western world at the time the Spanish colonial system was founded. The Spanish colonial policy, unlike that followed later by the English, considered native peoples as subjects of the sovereign. The result was a fusion of cultures, still characteristic of Latin America today.

The Spanish colonial system extended into territory that has since become part of the United States. As early as 1512 Ponce de Leon had launched an expedition from the West Indies to explore the coast of Florida, returning on a second voyage some seven years later. In 1728 Panfilo de Narvaez led a disastrous expedition of about 600 men, equipped with horses, livestock, and other supplies, which landed on the Gulf Coast of Florida. After exploring the region extending westward to Alabama and encountering illness, starvation, and hostile Indians, the survivors of the expedition were forced to build barges in an attempt to follow the coastline to Mexico. The barges foundered, and only four members of the group reached Mexico City some eight years later, after suffering almost unbelievable hardship, including enslavement by native tribes in Texas.

In 1565 Menendez de Aviles founded St. Augustine, the earliest continuous settlement within the present limits of the United States. The Spanish expansion into what is today Texas, the American southwest, and California was sufficiently powerful to leave an enduring imprint. Spanish soldiers and Franciscan priests established a chain of garrisons and mission stations throughout the territory. Santa Fe, New Mexico, was founded in 1610 and San Antonio, Texas, in 1718. In the eighteenth century more than twenty missions were organized in California, including San Diego, San Francisco, and Santa Barbara.

Factors in English Expansion. Although John Cabot, representing the English crown, explored the eastern coast of North America within a decade of Columbus' voyage, successful English settlement was delayed for a century. As a consequence, economic, religious, and political factors affecting the English colonies were entirely different from those that had influenced the Spanish colonies.

The two outstanding economic changes were in trade and agriculture. Whereas no trading companies flourished in 1500, over two hundred English trading companies operated aggressively by 1600, including the Muscovy Company (1553), the Levant Company (1592), and the famous East India Company (1600). In 1500 German and Italian merchants dominated English trade. By 1600 this domination had been eliminated and a strong group of English merchants had emerged. In 1500 most of the raw wool raised in England was shipped to Flanders to be made into cloth. By 1600 an English textile industry in England absorbed much of the wool produced in England.

These economic changes had a direct effect upon the development of the English colonies. The first three successful English colonies in America—Plymouth, Virginia, and Massachusetts Bay—were planted by cooperatively owned joint-stock companies, precursors of modern corporations, in which a number of investors pooled their capital. Many of those engaged in the American enterprises had gained their experience in trading companies elsewhere, and they continued to participate in trading enterprises throughout the world. As Charles M. Andrews, a prominent historian of the colonial period, has written: "English America would hardly have been settled at this time had not the period of occupation coincided with the era of capitalism in the first flush of its power."

The experience in trade influenced mercantilist thought in England. Mercantilism embodied a set of economic ideas held throughout western Europe from 1500 to 1800, though the precise measures taken differed from country to country. The mercantilist advocated that the economic affairs of the nation should be regulated to encourage the development of a strong state. A number of propositions were customarily included in this policy. A nation could become stronger by exporting more than it imported, resulting in a "favorable balance of trade." National self-sufficiency should be encouraged by subsidy of domestic manufactures. A nation's wealth was to be measured by the amount of precious metals it could obtain (thus the emphasis on the accumulation of bullion). Labor should be regulated for the well-being and benefit of the state. And colonies should be established to provide the nation with raw materials that it was unable to produce.

Although this does not exhaust the list of propositions supported by mercantilist thinkers, it does show that trade was considered one of the most important measures of a nation's wealth and that colonies were valued because they contributed to that wealth. In England the mercantile emphasis between 1500 and 1600 was upon internal regulation. After 1600 the emphasis was on external regulation, particularly the commercial relationship of England to its colonies. The phenomenal increase in English mercantile activity not only provided an agency—the joint-stock company—to create colonies but also provided a national purpose for doing so.

A second significant economic change took place in agriculture. Between 1500 and 1600 an enclosure movement gained strength in Britain. Essentially, "enclosure" meant that smaller landholdings in certain areas of England were incorporated into larger holdings, forcing some people off the land. The result was a dislocation of population which caused many political thinkers to conclude that England was overpopulated and that therefore almost anyone should be permitted to go to the New World to reduce "overpopulation." Spain, by contrast, had restricted immigration to selected individuals favored by the crown.

In the sixteenth century the Protestant Reformation swept through Europe and profoundly affected the religious and political development of England, which in turn placed an enduring stamp upon its colonies in America. In 1500 England (and the Continent) was within the fold of the Catholic Church. By 1600 not only had England broken away and established the national Anglican Church, but the religious rupture had also encouraged the rise of religious splinter groups.

The story of this religious rupture in

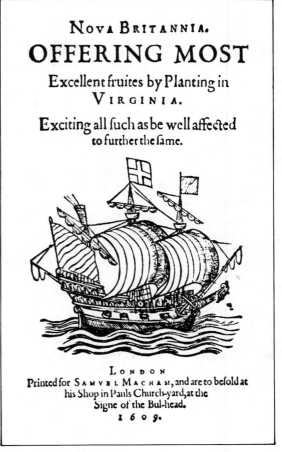

Overpopulation in England was thought to be so bad that tracts were printed, urging emigration to the New World.

England is too involved for extended treatment in this text. What is particularly important is that in the process of waging his contest with the Roman Catholic Church, King Henry VIII enlisted the aid of Parliament. Parliament passed a series of enactments creating a national church, culminating in the Act of Supremacy (1534), which made Henry, instead of the pope, the ecclesiastical sovereign of England. Eventually, by means of parliamentary acts, lands in England belonging to the Roman Catholic Church were taken over by the king, greatly enhancing his wealth.

The ramifications of these actions invaded almost every sphere of English life, but two had most effect on the colonies: (1) The king, by utilizing the support of Parliament, demonstrated that in practice the authority of the crown was limited—a concept carried to the English colonies in America and a concept in direct contrast to Spanish doctrine, which held the power of the sovereign to be without restriction; and (2) the break with the Catholic Church opened the way for a wide diversity of religious groups.

Some people, believing that separation from the Catholic Church should never have taken place, remained Roman Catholics. Others felt that Henry VIII and, later, Elizabeth I had not gone far enough. The Puritans, an impassioned and vocal minority, believed that the Reformation in England had stopped short of its goal, that ritual should be further simplified, and that the authority of crown-appointed bishops should be lessened. However, they resolved to stay within the Church of England and attempt to achieve their goals—that is, "purify" the church—without a division. The Separatists, a small minority, believed that each congregation should become its own judge of religious orthodoxy. They were no more willing to give allegiance to the crown than they had been to give it to the pope.

This religious factionalism was transferred to the American colonies. Of the first four settlements, Virginia was Anglican, Plymouth was Separatist, Massachusetts Bay was Puritan, and Maryland was Catholic.

Early in the seventeenth century, a number of English "dissenters"—men and women who were dissatisfied with political, economic, or religious conditions in England—were ready to migrate to the New World; English trading companies provided an agency for settlement.

THE ENGLISH SETTLEMENTS

One hundred fifteen years after Columbus' discovery of America, the English had not established a single permanent foothold in the Western Hemisphere. As late as 1600, although they had made several voyages and two attempts at settlement, they had not one colony to show for their efforts. But by 1700 some twenty colonies, with 350,000 inhabitants, stretched all the way from Newfoundland on the North Atlantic to the island of Barbados in the southern Caribbean. Heavy losses originally deterred growth, but promoters and settlers learned to adjust to the new environment. Thus by the end of the 1600s their settlements had taken root, attained prosperity, and entered upon a stage of steady growth. The English dream of expansion overseas had become a reality, and Britain looked with pride upon its American empire.

Founding Virginia. The first permanent English colony in America was Virginia. In the year 1606 King James I granted a group of London merchants the privilege of establishing colonies in "the part of America commonly called Virginia." Securing a charter, this Virginia Company of London raised sufficient funds by the sale of shares to outfit three ships and send them to Virginia, where on May 24, 1607, 120 men and boys established a settlement, Jamestown, on the banks of the James River.

The early Jamestown settlers had no experience in colonization. Many of them had come for adventure rather than from any desire to become permanent residents in the wilderness. They knew nothing of subsistence farming and displayed little ingenuity. Although the James River teemed with fish, they nearly perished for want of food. Of the first 5000 people who migrated to Virginia, fewer than 1000 survived.

Gradually, however, the Jamestown colonists devised ways of making a livelihood. Some traded with the Indians and began a traffic that would grow in importance with the years. Others planted foodstuffs and learned to raise Indian corn. John Rolfe, who married the Indian princess Pocahontas, developed the skill of growing tobacco profitably. Rolfe's contribution ensured Virginia's prosperity, for tobacco was a commodity much in demand in Europe.

In governing the colony, the Virginia Company at first adopted a policy of having severe laws administered by a strong-armed

Slaves are shown housing, airing, and vending tobacco, an important crop in Virginia.

governor. After this failed, it made the momentous decision to let the settlers share in their own government. When Governor George Yeardley arrived in Virginia in 1619, he carried instructions to call annually an assembly to consist of two members, or burgesses, from the various local units in the colony. These burgesses were to be elected by residents on a basis of almost complete male suffrage. This assembly, which met in the church at Jamestown in the summer of 1619, was the first representative law-making body in English America and as such was the forerunner of representative government in the United States. Even when the Virginia Company at last succumbed to bankruptcy in 1624 and lost its charter, with the result that Virginia became a royal colony, the company's greatest contribution was preserved intact: The Virginia House of Burgesses continued to meet. It was ironical that this transfer took place under King James I, for it meant that the very monarch who was the most severe enemy of Parliament in England was also, unwittingly, the one who permitted representative government in America to become a regular part of the system of colonial government under the crown.

The Coming of Africans. The first Africans came to Virginia in 1619. The records do not reveal whether they were brought as servants or slaves, but it is known that by 1650 Virginia had both black freemen and black slaves. African immigration grew slowly during the seventeenth century. In 1680 Africans, mostly slaves, comprised only 4 percent of the total population, widely scattered throughout the eastern seaboard.

Late in the seventeenth century the pace of importation of African slaves quickened. Most were brought to the Southern colonies of Maryland, Virginia, North Carolina, South Carolina, and eventually Georgia. By the beginning of the American Revolution blacks comprised 20 percent of the population, and the number of blacks — 400,000 —was equal to the total population of New England. Given the size of this single ethnic group, it is hardly surprising that the unwilling immigrants from Africa had an enduring impact on life in what was to become the United States of America.

The Pilgrims in Plymouth. The first permanent settlement in New England was made by colonists who arrived off Cape Cod in the *Mayflower* in December of 1620. They had been granted permission to settle farther south, but their ship had been blown off course. The core of the group of about a hundred settlers was a small, devoted band of Separatists, part of a larger number of religious dissenters who had left England for Holland in 1608. Unsuccessful there, thirty members of the congregation had decided to emigrate to the New World. The expedition, which put out from Plymouth, England, was financed by a joint-stock company in which the Separatists, their fellow passengers, and outside investors participated.

The story of these Separatists, who now called themselves Pilgrims, has become a part of the American legend: the hardships of the first winter, the friendship of the Indians Samoset and Squanto, who taught the settlers to plant corn, and the first harvest and thanksgiving festival.

The "Great Migration." Although the character and heroism of the Pilgrims bequeathed a poetic heritage to the American people, the larger colony of Massachusetts Bay contributed more to New England's civilization. The main body of settlers, under the leadership of John Winthrop, arrived in the summer of 1630 in the *Arbella*. This was one of four ships that carried the first wave of the "Great Migration" which between 1630 and 1640 brought some 20,000 people into Massachusetts.

The Winthrop group—most of them Puritans—had managed to obtain a royal charter for the Massachusetts Bay Company. Unlike other colonial enterprises, this company vested control not in a board of governors in England but in the members of the company who themselves were emigrating. They came bringing their charter with them and were self-governing, subject only to the English crown. Voting privileges were granted to those who were members of the Congregational Puritan Church of the colony, and during the early years of settlement a close relationship between church and state was the key to authority and life-style. But in all cases the civil magistrates, not the clergy, held preeminence.

During the ten years after the landing of the *Arbella*, Massachusetts Bay became the most populous English colony in the New World. From towns established at Boston, Cambridge, Dorchester, Salem, and elsewhere, groups from time to time broke away and moved into fresh territory. In the summer of 1636, for example, the Reverend Thomas Hooker, with about one hundred of his followers, set out on foot from Cambridge and settled a new township at Hartford, in what became Connecticut. Other towns proliferated in similar fashion.

The Spreading Colonies of New England. Occasionally colonists left Massachusetts Bay because they had offended the ruling authorities or because they were discontented with a thoroughgoing Puritan commonwealth that punished nonconformists severely and tried to impose its religious tenets upon all comers. Freedom of conscience or religion was not a virtue of Massachusetts Bay. Roger Williams, pastor of the church at Salem, was banished from the colony in 1635 because he had complained publicly that interference of the clergy in politics threatened the freedom of individual congregations, and because he questioned the right of the settlers to take land from the Indians. Williams fled in the dead of winter to the Narragansett Indians, and in

January 1636 he arranged to purchase land from the Indians for a little settlement which he called Providence. Before long, other fugitives from the persecution of the Puritan clergy in Massachusetts Bay found their way to Williams' colony, including a group led by the religious rebel, Anne Hutchinson.

The Providence settlers made a compact which guaranteed liberty of conscience to all, regardless of faith and which provided for the separation of church and state. Other groups came to the area and settled at Portsmouth, Newport, and Warwick, and in 1644 Parliament granted Williams a charter which united the various groups in what is now Rhode Island into one civil government. A royal charter in 1663 one more reiterated the liberties established earlier. This charter remained the basis of Rhode Island's laws until 1842. Rhode Island was far ahead of its time in its legal provisions. As early as 1647, for example, it outlawed trials for witchcraft and imprisonment for debt.

Massachusetts Bay emigrants settled a colony at New Haven under conservative Puritan leadership. As in Massachusetts, only church members were permitted to vote, a policy which in effect gave the church political control over the affairs of the colony. Since the Scriptures made no mention of jury trials, New Haven—in contrast to other New England colonies—forbade such trials and left the dispensation of justice in the hands of the magistrates.

In 1662 Connecticut received a royal charter which confirmed the rights of self-government and provided for the Fundamental Orders, a platform of government extending the franchise to nonchurch members. New Haven, to its distress, was absorbed into Connecticut, and its citizens thereby gained the guarantees of Connecticut's charter.

Other Massachusetts Bay residents moved into New Hampshire and Maine, where settlers had already established themselves in small fishing villages. Massachusetts laid claim to both regions, but after many disputes New Hampshire in 1679 gained a royal charter and freed itself from the domination of Massachusetts. Maine was not separated until 1820.

Catholic Maryland.   While Virginia was gradually gaining vitality, a neighboring colony developed on its northern flank. In 1632 Sir George Calvert, First Lord Baltimore, received from Charles I a charter for the tract of land extending from the fortieth degree of north latitude to the south bank of the Potomac River. Calvert, a Roman Catholic, intended to make Maryland a refuge for oppressed Catholics. He died before he could settle his grant, but his son Cecilius became lord proprietor and sent his brother Leonard to take possession of Maryland. The first group of Catholic settlers landed on March 25, 1634.

A "proprietary colony" such as the Calverts obtained was a return to a feudal and baronial system which in the seventeenth century was becoming outmoded. The manorial system of land tenure, which made the inhabitants of Maryland tenants of the Calverts instead of landowners, was the source of much unrest and would never have lasted at all had the Calverts not made tenancy similar to ownership.

In order to attract settlers and make the colony pay, the Calverts from the outset encouraged Protestants as well as Catholics to go to Maryland. Though most of the manorial families were Catholic, Catholics never constituted a majority of the population. Catholics and Anglicans held separate worship, and Lord Baltimore would not allow the Jesuits in the colony to place any restrictions upon Protestants. In 1649 he sponsored the famous Maryland Toleration Act, which guaranteed freedom of worship to all Christians. This was not yet full liberty of conscience, for there was a death penalty for non-Christians, but the act marked an advance in the direction of full religious freedom.

Proprietary Colonies.   Except for Maryland, the original colonies were established by joint-stock companies, but after 1660 almost all the newly founded colonies were proprietaries. Joint-stock companies as a whole did not make a profit, and business enterprisers became less interested in investing in colonial establishments. After 1660 King Charles II began to grant large segments of American land to those who had supported the Stuart claim to the throne during the period of Puritan control in England (1642–1660). Proprietors had been unsuccessful in the late sixteenth century because they could neither command sufficient capital nor sustain a colonizing effort over an extended period of time. But with the successful founding of Virginia, Maryland, Plymouth, and Massachusetts Bay, the risk of founding proprietary colonies was greatly reduced. As a result, the territory of the Carolinas was given to a number of proprietors in 1663, and Pennsylvania was founded as a proprietary colony in 1682. New Jersey began as a proprietorship but eventually was made a crown or royal colony, in which affairs were directed by crown officials. New York also began as a proprietary colony, under the Duke of York, after its capture from the Dutch. It became a crown colony when York ascended the throne as James II.

The Capture of New York.   In 1609 Henry Hudson, an Englishman in the employ of the Dutch East India Company, sailed the Hudson River as far as the present town of Albany. In 1623, after the monopoly of a private Dutch company in the area had run out, the Dutch West India Company was formed to develop trade in the region along the river that Hudson had discovered. Since the citizens of Holland were largely content, the new company had trouble finding colonists, so the early settlers included French Protestant refugees and non-Dutch emigrants from Holland. From the earliest times, New Netherland (later New York) was a polyglot region.

Despite incompetent governors, quarreling inhabitants, and frequent wars with the Indians, the colony made progress, and New Amsterdam (New York City) became an important shipping point for furs and farm products. By the 1660s, with a population of 2500, it was second only to Boston as a trading port. The colony as a whole had about 8000 settlers, some of them English.

The English had never admitted the right of the Dutch to the territory they had occupied. In 1664 Charles II named his brother James, Duke of York, proprietor over lands occupied by the Dutch in the New World. York sent out an expedition to take over New Netherland, the English claiming that this was not an act of war but merely an action to regain from the Dutch West India Company territory that was rightfully English. With an English fleet in the harbor of New Amsterdam, the Dutch governor, Peter Stuyvesant, surrendered on September 9, 1664. The town and territory were both rechristened New York in honor of the royal proprietor.

The Dutch occupation of the Hudson valley had benefited the English far more than the new overlords cared to admit. Had the Dutch not been in possession in the first half of the seventeenth century, when English settlements on the Atlantic seaboard were too sparse and weak to prevent the French from moving down the Hudson from Canada, the thin line of English colonies along the coast might have been divided by England's traditional enemy, France.

The Jerseys.   Soon after the Duke of York took over New Netherland in 1664, he granted the land between the Hudson and the Delaware to John Lord Berkeley and Sir George Carteret, royalists who had defended the island of Jersey against the Parliamentarians during the Puritan Revolution in England. Berkeley sold

The tradition of William Penn's "Great Treaty" has probably been kept alive by this painting by Benjamin West.

his proprietary right to two Quakers, and in 1676 the province was divided into East Jersey (belonging to Carteret) and West Jersey (which became a Quaker colony). The later division of the two portions of New Jersey among many heirs of the proprietors bequeathed a land problem so complex that it vexes holders of real estate in that state to the present day.

Penn's Experiment. In 1681 King Charles II granted to William Penn, a Quaker, a charter to the land between New Jersey and Maryland, naming him and his heirs forever owners of the soil of Pennsylvania, as the domain was called. Penn set about establishing a colony that would serve as a refuge for persecuted Christians from all lands. He drew up his celebrated first Frame of Government and made various concessions and laws to govern the colony, which already had a conglomerate group of English, Dutch, Swedish, and Finnish settlers scattered here and there. After his own arrival in Pennsylvania, he provided for the calling of a popular assembly on December 4, 1682, which passed the "Great Law," guaranteeing, among other things, the rights of all Christians to liberty of conscience.

Penn determined to keep peace with the Indians and was careful to purchase the land which his settlers occupied. The tradition of a single "Great Treaty" signed under an ancient elm at Kensington is probably a myth, but Penn held many powwows with the Indians and negotiated treaties of peace and amity after purchasing needed land. To the credit of Penn and the Quakers, these agreements with the Indians were, for the most part, conscientiously kept.

Pennsylvania's growth from the first was phenomenal. Penn's success was largely due to his own skill as a promoter, for he wrote enticing tracts and on preaching journeys described the opportunities offered by his colony. Mennonites from Switzerland and Germany—especially Pietists from the Rhineland, which had so often been overrun by invading armies—soon were coming to Pennsylvania in large numbers. Dutch sectarians, French Huguenots, Presbyterian Scots from Ulster, Baptists from Wales, and distressed English Quakers also came. Somewhat after the Mennonites, Lutheran emigrants from Germany swarmed into Pennsylvania's back country, where they cleared the forests and developed fertile farms. From the beginning Pennsylvania was properous.

Settlement of the Carolinas. Among the later colonies to be settled was Carolina, which also began as a proprietorship. Eight courtiers received from Charles II on March 23, 1663, a grant of territory between the southern border of Virginia and Spanish Florida. The proprietors drew up an instrument of government called the Fundamental Constitutions (probably the handiwork of the English political philosopher John Locke). This document provided for a hierarchy of colonial nobility and set up a platform of government with a curious mixture of feudal and liberal elements. Eventually it had to be abandoned in favor of a more workable plan of government.

The division of Carolina into two distinct colonies came about gradually. English settlers were already occupying land around Albermarle Sound when the proprietors received their charter, and Albermarle continued to attract a scattering of settlers. It was geographically remote from the other settlement on the Ashley and Cooper rivers to the south. As the two separate sections gained population, they set up separate legislative assemblies, approved by the proprietors. In 1710 the proprietors appointed a governor of North Carolina, "independent of the governor of Carolina," thus recognizing the separation of North from South Carolina. In 1721 South Carolina was declared a royal province, and eight years later North Carolina also became a crown colony.

Georgia. Georgia, founded in 1733, was administered for two decades by twenty trustees in England. Georgia was established to serve many purposes: as an extension of the southern provinical frontier; as a buffer or a first line of defense between the Spanish colony of Florida and the English settlements; as a planned Utopia where the trustees hoped to establish a model society; as a refuge for persecuted Protestants from Europe; as a new opportunity for men who had been released from debtor's prisons in England; and as a model "colony" that would produce commodities that England wanted, notably silk and citrus fruits. Because of these multiple objectives, no single one was carried out with success. In fact, by 1740 many of its colonists had left, and there were few new immigrants. Not until the crown took over the colony in the 1750s was Georgia rescued, and even then it did not flourish until after the American Revolution.

COLONIAL ADMINISTRATION AND POLITICS

English Administration of the Colonies. In London, administrative agencies to govern the colonies were slow in evolving. Originally, a committee of the King's Privy Council, the Lord Commissioners for Plantations, directly supervised the colonies. Variations of this committee operated until 1675, when the Lords of Trade was created—an agency whose vigorous actions set a new standard in colonial policy. It opposed the disposition on the part of the crown to issue proprietary grants and advocated revoking them, bringing such colonies under direct royal control.

The most important effort of the Lords of Trade was made in 1686, when it established the Dominion of New England. The charter of Massachusetts Bay had been annulled in 1684, and the Dominion represented an attempt to centralize the authority of the crown by creating a super-colony, including Massachusetts, New Hampshire, Connecticut, Rhode Island, New York, and New Jersey. It was expected that eventually Pennsylvania would also be incorporated within the framework of the Dominion. The crown, acting upon the recommendation of the Lords of Trade, appointed Edmond Andros as governor, to reside in Boston, with his deputy to reside in New York. No provision was made for an assembly, although there was to be a council of advisers. Andros, unfortunately, was of limited mind and petty spirit. He was scarcely the man to carry out such a dramatic, far-reaching colonial experiment. Resentment among the colonies included within the Dominion was intense, not only because their original charters had been arbitrarily set aside and the arbitrary Andros appointed, but because they lacked a representative assembly.

England's Glorious Revolution of 1688 deposed the despotic James II and firmly championed Parliament—and thus representative government, in England. This twist of fate provided an opportunity for the colonials to overthrow the Dominion. Acting on the premise that Governor Andros now represented a discarded royal regime, the colonials imprisoned him as a signal of their allegiance to the new government in England set up under William and Mary. Each colony that had been included within the Dominion hastily returned to its previous path of colonial self-government. Thus the Glorious Revolution marked the end of an experiment

to consolidate the colonies within a larger framework and administer them more directly by home authorities.

In many respects, the experiment of the Dominion of New England was a turning point in colonial political affairs. At this time the colonials were not yet strong enough to defeat the royal will. If the experiment had been a success, individual self-government within the colonies would have been eliminated and the entire course of American history might have been changed. With the fall of the Dominion, the individual colonies received a new lease on life, and they used it to gain strength politically and economically.

In 1696 the Lords of Trade were replaced by the Board of Trade, an administrative agency which survived into the period of the American Revolution. During the eighteenth century Parliament was overwhelmed with its own problems—namely, the internal political transition to parliamentary supremacy in England and the turmoil of foreign policy—and could not spare the time to formulate new policies for the empire. As a result, the general policies formulated very early in the century were followed throughout the period despite changing circumstances. An instruction issued to a governor in 1750 was little changed from instructions given in 1700. The American provinces were changing, England was changing, the world was changing, but British imperial policy remained, for the most part, unchanged.

Political Structures in the Colonies. English colonies in America experienced a vigorous political life, in contrast to the colonies of other western European countries. The concept of self-government was transferred to the English colonies almost from the outset in most settlements, but the political structure generally took more definitive shape early in the eighteenth century.

The political structures that evolved in royal, proprietary, and charter colonies were remarkably similar. Each colony had a governor who executed colonial laws, served as commander in chief of the militia, presided over the colony's highest court of appeals, and enforced relevant British enactments. In a proprietary colony like Pennsylvania the governor looked after the interests of the proprietor, most notably in the disposition of land, but he was also expected to enforce the imperial policies laid down by the home authorities. Usually the governor was appointed by the crown, although in proprietary colonies the proprietor held this prerogative and in Rhode Island and Connecticut the governor was elected by the legislature.

Most colonies had a council whose members served as advisers to the governor. This council comprised the upper house of the legislature and sat as the highest court of appeal in the colony. Generally council members were appointed by the crown upon the recommendation of the governor, but exceptions were made. Members of the council were customarily the more affluent colonials, many of whom had powerful friends in England. In a number of colonies the council, although acting in self-interest, was the spokesman for the people against the prerogative of the governor. The council wished to control office patronage, the distribution of lands, and the like.

A colonial assembly, which served as the lower house of the legislature, was elected by the freemen. By the eighteenth century every colony had instituted property requirements as a requisite for freemanship, but recent

Alexander Spotswood: Colonial Governor

When His Majesty's Ship *Deptford* dropped anchor off Hampton Roads, Virginia, on June 20, 1710, in preparation for its assignment to escort the tobacco fleet to England, it carried more than its usual complement of men and supplies. Aboard was Alexander Spotswood, with a commission as lieutenant governor of the colony of Virginia. Perhaps no royal governor better exemplified the political relationship that existed between the crown and the British colonies on the North American continent.

The Spotswoods had been royal and Anglican for five generations, and they had waged wars for the crown and church. Alexander's great-grandfather, Archbishop of St. Andrews and historian of Scotland, had assisted Archbishop Laud in introducing the Book of Common Prayer into Scotland, a defiant act in a Presbyterian stronghold. Alexander's grandfather, Secretary for Scotland, had been executed in 1646 for his opposition to the politics of the Presbyterian party and his loyalty to King Charles I.

Alexander was born in 1676 in Tangier, where his father was serving as physician to

research has demonstrated that these requirements did not seriously restrict the number of eligible voters. Property requirements for officeholding, however, were frequently much higher than the requirements for suffrage, so that a member of the assembly had to be a person of some means. "Professional politicians" who had no other means of livelihood were rare in the provinces.

During the eighteenth century the assemblies of every colony gained power. Among the specific powers obtained by most assemblies were the rights to initiate legislation, to judge the qualifications of their own members, and to elect their speakers. The assemblies were somewhat less successful in determining when elections should be held and in extending their membership.

Whereas the basic constitutional position of the home authorities was that the power of the assemblies and the grant of self-government itself were merely an extension of "the royal grace and favor," to be offered, modified, or even eliminated as the crown determined, the constitutional position held by the assemblies was that their power and authority derived from the consent of the governed. The assemblies conceived of themselves as replicas of the British House of Commons, and they attempted to imitate it in waging their contest for power against the prerogative of the governor, representing the crown or the proprietor.

Conflicts were inevitable between constitutional positions that differed so markedly. The principal expression of this conflict arose

the English garrison. Following his family's rugged tradition, he became an ensign in the regiment of the Earl of Bath at the age of seventeen, serving first in Flanders. Later, by then a lieutenant colonel, he was wounded at the Battle of Blenheim and captured by the enemy. No less a person than the Earl of Marlborough negotiated for his release.

Although his contemporaries and historians of early America refer to him as Governor, he was in fact the deputy of George Hamilton, the Earl of Orkney. The common practice of the time was to award a lucrative office in the colonies in return for a fee or favor to the crown. No work was required and the pay was excellent. The governor invariably appointed a lieutenant who actually conducted the official duties in the colony. The governor and lieutenant governor shared the salary and other perquisites of office.

Alexander Spotswood assumed his responsibilities at a difficult time. In the absence of a governor, Edmund Jennings, President of the Colonial Council, had governed Virginia by law during the previous four years. Although the council members had been appointed by the king, they had assumed executive power and used it to further their personal interests. Thus the Colonial Council had granted land, defended the colony, appointed subordinate officials, collected taxes, and, with the cooperation of the House of Burgesses, decided on the priority of expenditures.

Spotswood's early years can be read as a continuous attempt to regain and reinforce the authority of the royal governor. Measured against this standard, he failed. However, the contest for authority foreshadowed the growing tension between Britain and all of its colonies that would finally surface in the War for Independence.

between the assemblies and the governor. The assemblies attempted to restrict the scope of the governor's operations by controlling the disbursement of funds appropriated by the legislature, by failing to appropriate monies for projects asked for by the governor, and occasionally by refusing to pay the governor's salary until he accepted the legislation passed by the assembly.

Local Government. The structure of English local government at the time the colonies were founded was transplanted, for the most part, to the New World. Among the more important officials were the county sheriffs and the justices of the peace. Other positions that were important in England, such as lord lieutenant, did not flourish in the New World.

Local government in the United States today descends directly from the colonial period.

Local disputes over land titles and other matters were settled by the county courts. Colonial legislation was enforced by the justices of the peace in cooperation with the sheriff, and taxes were collected by the sheriff. In practice, therefore, local government served as a major link between the people and the colonial government.

Colonial Politics. In every colony, at some time or another, domestic disputes developed which were fought out in the political arena. The issues of land, currency, proportionate representation, defense, and the Indian trade were among those that arose most frequently. In a colony such as Virginia, where tobacco

Among Governor Spotswood's earliest concerns was the lucrative Indian trade. He believed that this trade should be strictly controlled for the British welfare, which (pleasantly enough) closely coincided with his own personal fortunes. To this end, he succeeded in persuading the Burgesses and the council to adopt an "Act for the Better Regulation of the Indian Trade." To participate in the Indian trade, a colonist or anyone else now needed to purchase a share in the Virginia Indian Company at a cost of 50 pounds—comparable to a year's salary for an experienced minister. To Spotswood's dismay, both the colonials and the London merchants raised strenuous objections, and the Indian Act was soon repealed.

Spotswood tackled another, even thornier, issue when he got a Tobacco Inspection Act passed. The idea had merit. Inferior tobacco was being shipped to England and passed off as tobacco of the highest grade. Because no standard existed, buyers had become wary, and the market for Virginia tobacco had sagged. How better to set things right, argued the governor, than to establish tobacco inspection points in Virginia and prohibit the export of all inferior grades?

But Spotswood had a hidden motive. He wished to appoint tobacco inspectors who supported his political objectives and thus, through patronage, to build a governor's party in Virginia.

To everyone's surprise, the small planters rebelled. The added expense of transporting their tobacco to places of inspection was burdensome. Moreover, they

was the principal staple, tobacco inspection acts aroused lively political disputes. (See "Alexander Spotswood: Colonial Governor.") Seldom did political parties develop. Generally, a coalition of forces, drawn in most cases from various parts of a province, united to support or defeat a particular measure. Once the issue was decided, the coalition disintegrated.

A political split between the eastern and western parts of a province was characteristic of Pennsylvania, which was growing at a swifter pace than most of its sister colonies. By contrast, the major political division in New York was between influential families whose wealth was based on land and influential families whose wealth was based on commerce. These political issues and the conflicts

they aroused were evidence not of internal disorder but of political maturity—of vigorous, healthy self-government in action.

COLONIAL ECONOMY

New England. The rise of capitalism throughout western Europe, which coincided with the founding of the English colonies, determined that the American provincial economy would be capitalistic in orientation, with an emphasis on trade, production for market, and eventual regional specialization. Each colony's economy at the outset was rather primitive—merely an appendage of the economy of the mother country—but shortly after the mid-eighteenth century an indigenous, well-developed capitalism emerged.

did not want to have the governor's favorites deciding whether their tobacco was fit for the London or Amsterdam market. In the next elections almost all of those who had accepted appointments as inspectors were turned out of office by the rebellious voters.

Angered and frustrated, Spotswood summoned the House of Burgesses and read a scathing attack on its members and their motives. Their laws were "Giddy Resolves," their quality as persons was "illiterate Vulgar," and their behavior was "drunken conventions."

The disputes over the Indian trade and tobacco inspection thereafter invaded all the political issues and affected basic social and economic policy in the colony, including the distribution of land. The strife ended only when Spotswood began to take on the self-interest of a Virginia planter and made peace with the Colonial Council and the House of Burgesses.

Spotswood was an able organizer and administrator. By 1722, when he was replaced as lieutenant governor, he had become a major landholder in the colony, an explorer of its western territories, and founder of the Spotswood Iron Works. After six years in England, he returned to Virginia where he spent his later leisurely years as a flourishing patrician planter. At his passing on June 7, 1740, he was mourned by Virginians who had pitted their political strength against him while he represented the authority of the crown.

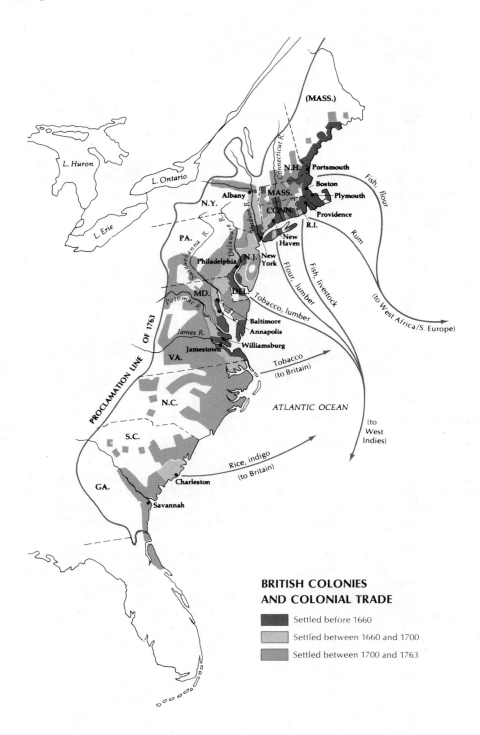

L. Huron

L. Ontario

L. Erie

(MASS.)

N.H.   Portsmouth

Albany   MASS.   Boston
                        Plymouth
N.Y.   CONN.
                        Providence
PA.   R.I.
                New
                Haven
Philadelphia   N.J.   New
                      York
MD.   DEL.

Baltimore
Annapolis
Williamsburg
Jamestown

VA.

N.C.

S.C.

Charleston

GA.

Savannah

Connecticut R.

Hudson R.

Delaware R.

Susquehanna R.

Potomac R.

James R.

PROCLAMATION LINE OF 1763

Tobacco, lumber

Flour, lumber

Fish, livestock

Fish, flour

Rum

(to West Africa/S. Europe)

Tobacco
(to Britain)

ATLANTIC OCEAN

(to
West
Indies)

Rice, indigo
(to Britain)

BRITISH COLONIES
AND COLONIAL TRADE

Settled before 1660

Settled between 1660 and 1700

Settled between 1700 and 1763

The economic development of New England was strongly influenced by the systems of land distribution and of trade. In the seventeenth century land was granted by the legislature to groups—usually church congregations—which in turn distributed the land among their members. The result was the encouragement of the famous New England township system, whose principal aim was to maintain an effective social-religious community. After provision for the church, sometimes a school, and a village green had been made, each family was customarily granted a town lot. Plots of land outside the town were then distributed among members of the group, with common land retained for grazing purposes and a specified number of acres reserved for latecomers.

Distributing the land in this fashion meant that all members of the group would be in close proximity to the church, the heart of the Puritan community. It also meant that sending youngsters to school would raise no serious problems and that towns would become the basis for representative government with town meetings providing the political structure to resolve local issues.

In the eighteenth century the New England land system changed. With a decline in importance of the central purpose of a concentrated social-religious community, settlement along western frontier lands seldom was made by church groups. Instead, people of influence and means began to buy large blocks of land for speculative purposes, selling off smaller parcels to individual farmers or prospective farmers.

Even in the older towns conditions changed. Original settlers or descendants of original settlers moved out, often selling their land to newcomers. Absentee ownership of town lots and township lands was common. Whereas in the seventeenth century town proprietors were nearly always residents of the town, this was less often the case in eighteenth-century communities.

Although farming was the predominant occupation in New England up to 1640, trade gained increasing importance thereafter. From 1640 to 1660 the English were preoccupied with civil war and political upheaval at home, and colonials began to replace the English merchants as the trading enterprisers. It was at this time that the developing resources of New England fisheries helped open up trade between the Puritans of New England and Puritans who had settled in the West Indies.

New England merchants gradually gained a position of economic and political primacy. By the end of the seventeenth century they had already begun to replace the Puritan magistrates as the source of economic and political power. By the 1760s they constituted the single strongest voice in New England.

It is important to remember that merchants were not alone in their dependence on trade for prosperity. The artisans who repaired canvas and built vessels and the farmers who exported meat products—in fact, the entire population in one way or another—were partly dependent upon prosperous commercial relations. Meat, fish, and lumber, the principal articles of export, found their major market in the West Indies. New England was also dependent on its role as a carrier of exports from other provinces and of imports from England.

For labor, New Englanders depended largely on members of their own families, though they sometimes hired local servants and imported indentured servants. New England, in contrast to some of the other regions, was attractive to skilled workers because they could find a ready market for their talent in an area dominated by a town system. Each town needed a carpenter and a blacksmith, for example.

The Southern Colonies.   Three significant factors affected the economic development of the Southern colonies: the distribution of land, the evolution of the plantation system, and the tremendous production of staples for market. In the seventeenth-century Chesapeake colonies (Virginia and Maryland) land was distributed directly to individuals, in contrast to the practice in early New England. Moreover, the colonials scattered up and down the rivers of the Chesapeake area instead of settling in groups. Each planter tried to have his own landing where an ocean-going vessel could readily load the tobacco he produced and unload the goods he had ordered from England. This method of settlement made the county the basis of local government, discouraged the establishment of a school system because of the distances involved, and markedly influenced the transplantation of the Anglican Church, as explained in Chapter 1.

In the seventeenth century the average landholding was relatively small, since labor to cultivate extensive landholdings was lacking. The headright system, whereby a planter could obtain fifty acres of land for each dependent or servant brought to the colonies, allowed the first accumulations of land to occur. But it was not until the eighteenth century, when American colonists obtained control of the machinery to distribute land, that large grants become fairly common.

Though slaves were imported into the Chesapeake colonies and into South Carolina in the seventeenth century, the principal labor force was composed of indentured servants, including convicts and paupers who were sentenced to labor in America. Over 1500 indentures were imported annually into Virginia alone in the 1670s and the 1680s.

While the Northern colonies were coming to rely upon trade, the Southern colonies were evolving the plantation system, with large tracts of land and a landing for ocean-going vessels.

But in the following years the plantation system became larger, the black slave became a relatively less expensive source of labor, and the Middle colonies—New York, the Jerseys, Pennsylvania, and Delaware—expanded to compete for indentured servants. At the same time the supply of English indentures decreased because the demand for labor in England increased. As a result, the institution of slavery became fastened upon the eighteenth-century Southern colonies. A society that had been made up largely of yeomen now became dominated by a planter elite, whose power was based on black slaves.

Tobacco continued to the main staple in the Chesapeake colonies, but rice became prominent in South Carolina, and the indigo introduced by Elizabeth Pinckney became an important crop. Naval stores became a major export of North Carolina. Deer skins were the important goods obtained through trade with the Indians.

In the seventeenth century no merchant group developed in the colonies because planters sold directly to English merchants. In the eighteenth century an important merchant group developed in strategically located Charleston, South Carolina, trade center for a vast hinterland. No major tensions developed between merchants and planters in the South, however, because the prosperity of one was directly related to the well-being of the other. In fact, the same individual might belong to both groups since many merchants bought land and planters sometimes became merchants.

The Middle Colonies. During the eighteenth century English migration decreased because demand for laborers and opportunities for advancement greatly increased at home as Britain expanded its trade and manufactures. However, a tremendous influx of non-English peoples—Germans, Scotch-Irish, Irish, Swiss, and French Huguenots—into the Middle colonies resulted in expansion of that region at a rate exceeding that of New England or the Southern colonies.

The reasons for the migration of non-English peoples were fundamentally economic, although religious intolerance and fear of destructive wars at home sometimes played a part. Opportunities for the Scotch-Irish in Ireland were limited, whereas opportunities in the New World appeared much more attractive. German Pietists came to Pennsylvania in large numbers because that colony offered an attractive land policy as well as religious toleration.

Land policies in Pennsylvania, the Jerseys, and New York varied greatly. In New York land was granted to royal favorites, who established extensive manors. An ordinary settler was often forced to accept a leasehold and become a renter instead of obtaining a clear title to the land. The distribution of lands in Pennsylvania was much more favorable. Small grants could be obtained by outright purchase. In fact, Scotch-Irish settlers on the frontier of Pennsylvania frequently assumed title to the land by right of settlement and refused to pay the proprietors.

New York and Philadelphia developed into major ports in the eighteenth century. Philadelphia, in fact, as already mentioned, became the second largest city within the British empire. Both cities developed a strong mercantile class and attracted skilled artisans—cabinetmakers, silversmiths, gunsmiths, and the like. Both exported grain. Grain was the principal commodity of the Middle colonies, which became the "breadbasket" of colonial America.

Pennsylvania's rapid growth and early economic maturity reflected the astonishing general growth of the colonies. The handful of English settlers had become 250,000 strong by 1700. By 1760 the colonies provided a good livelihood for a population of approximately 2,000,000 — almost half the population of England. No wonder, then, that trade quadrupled, that banking and currency became important issues, that tradesmen and merchants carried on sophisticated economic practices, that a stable society was formed, and finally, that the American economic system was sufficiently developed to sustain the shock of political separation from the mother country and to finance a war for independence. All the ingredients of a well-developed commercial capitalism were present.

English Regulatory Acts. As the economy of the American provinces matured, imperial regulations were enlarged to prevent foreign commercial competition and the competition of colonial manufactures with those of the mother country. Although restrictions were placed on the tobacco trade as early as the 1620s, a series of enactments passed from 1651 to 1700 laid the actual framework for the English imperial system.

The Navigation Act of 1651 was designed primarily to reduce competition from foreign shipping. It provided that non-European goods brought to England or its possessions could be transported only in English (including colonial) ships and that goods from the Continent could be brought into England or its possessions only in vessels belonging to the country that had produced the goods. A second Navigation Act (often called the Enumeration Act) passed in 1660 closed the loophole which had permitted colonials to import directly from Europe. It provided that all goods, regardless of origin, could be imported into or exported from any English colony only in English ships. "Enumerated" goods—including sugar, cotton, indigo, dye goods, and tobacco—of colonial origin were to be shipped only to England or its colonies; they could not be exported directly to other European countries.

The Enumeration Act was particularly hard on Virginia and Maryland, for it meant that colonial tobacco—which the English market could not absorb—had to be shipped to England and then reexported to Continental markets. Reexportation costs—including handling charges, storage charges, and the costs of frequent loss of tobacco stored in English warehouses—were extremely high. Historians have suggested that the enumeration of tobacco produced an economic depression in Virginia and Maryland in the late seventeenth century and was responsible for the later concentration of land ownership, since only the large-scale producer could meet the disadvantages of the market.

In 1663 a third Navigation Act—the Staple Act—required that most commodities (excluding salt, servants, and wine) imported into the colonies from Europe had to be shipped from England in English-built ships. But the colonists found a loophole. Often ships stopped at several colonial ports before returning to Europe. Colonial merchants would load enumerated goods at one port supposedly designated for a later colonial port; actually the goods would remain on the ship and go directly to Europe.

To close this loophole, a fourth Navigation Act was passed in 1673. It provided that whenever the vessel carried enumerated commodities, a plantation duty—that is, a bond—had to be paid before a ship could clear a colonial port. A final enactment in 1696 provided for the creation of vice-admiralty courts in America, to place the enforcement of the navigation laws in the hands of men appointed directly by the crown.

The research of historian Lawrence Harper indicates that the burden of the Navigation Acts was greater at the end of the seventeenth century than at any other time during the colonial period and that the acts were seldom evaded. Evasion was to come later with the Molasses Act of 1733.

Whereas in the seventeenth century the English regulations were directed principally at commerce, in the eighteenth century, with the maturing of the American economy, the regulations were directed principally at manufactures. The Woolen Act of 1699, which forbade colonial export of wool products, had little impact upon the American colonies because their exportation of textiles was limited anyway. But the Hat Act of 1732—which prohibited exportation of hats from one colony to another and severely restricted the colonial hat industry—adversely affected New York and New England, which had been usurping a vital European market. The act eliminated this colonial enterprise, greatly benefiting London hatters, who had exerted pressure in Parliament to pass the bill.

The Molasses Act of 1733 placed a heavy duty upon sugar, rum, molasses, and other commodities imported into the colonies from the non-British West Indies. This enactment seriously hampered the trade of the American colonies. They had been importing these commodities—molasses in particular—in quantity from Spanish and French colonies at a price cheaper than could be obtained in the British West Indies. Because the act seriously encroached upon this customary channel of trade, the Molasses Act was evaded by extensive smuggling.

The Iron Act of 1750 encouraged the colonial production of pig and bar iron for use by the English iron and steel industry but prohibited the building of slitting mills, forges, and other iron-finishing equipment in the colonies. Certain colonies, notably Pennsylvania, defied the prohibition, and when war broke out between France and England in 1752, the home authorities were unable to enforce the act with vigor. After 1763, of course, the continual crises between the mother country and the colonies prevented effective enforcement.

BRITAIN WINS SUPREMACY IN NORTH AMERICA

New France. France had originally laid claims to America because of the voyages of Giovanni da Verrazano in 1523 and of Jacques Cartier in 1534, but not until 1608 was the permanent settlement of Quebec established by Samuel de Champlain. New France, as the French settlements on the North American continent were called, was slow to grow. Trading in furs was the most lucrative enterprise, and it flourished in a wilderness setting. Settlers in farms and villages intruded upon the wilderness and its inhabitants.

In the 1660s the French became more determined in expanding their hold on North America. As a consequence, families were encouraged to settle in New France. They were provided with land, livestock, seed, and tools. Women were sent to become wives of unmarried men. Those who elected to remain unmarried were required to pay special taxes and were excluded from some of the subsidies provided to married settlers. In five years the population in New France doubled.

The French, much like the Spanish, encouraged exploration of the interior, sending Jesuit priests along with specially selected explorers. In 1673 Father Jacques Marquette, whose personal goal was to establish missions among the Illinois Indians, was ordered by his superior in Quebec to accompany Louis Jolliet, picked by the governor of New France, to explore the "Great River," the Mississippi. Accompanied by five trappers, Marquette and Jolliet followed the Wisconsin River down to the Mississippi River, which awed them with its grandeur. No less a surprise downstream was the roar of the Missouri River emptying into the Mississippi.

Marquette kept a lively journal describing the buffalo, the Indians along the route, the heat—it was mid-July—and their experiences and encounters along the route. After feasting on dog meat and other delicacies with the Indians on the Arkansas River, the explorers decided to return to Canada, in part because of their fear of capture by the Spanish should they proceed to the mouth of the Mississippi.

Robert de La Salle launched a less successful expedition in 1683, although he did reach the mouth of the Mississippi. Both explorations not only gave New France a strong claim to the interior of the territory of mid-America but also encouraged the French to fortify the Mississippi and Ohio rivers, laying the background for an inevitable clash of interests between the British and French colonies on the North American continent.

Early Border Conflicts.   The shifting balance of power in eighteenth-century Europe, brought about in part by the emergence of France and Britain as the major nations of the Western world, produced a ceaseless contest for position in both the Old World and the New. To the English colonials, the strength of New France was a particular danger. French fur traders in the wilderness were capable of stirring up the Indians to hostility against English traders and settlers who began to penetrate the transmontane region, and French control over the interior threatened to curb the westward expansion of the English colonies in America.

The War of the Spanish Succession (1702–1713), or Queen Anne's War, as it is known in America, saw a conflict of the colonists with both Spanish and French forces. In 1739 Great Britain attacked Spain in a conflict which soon merged into the War of the Austrian Succession, or King George's War (1740–1748). Believing that the time was ripe to neutralize French power in Canada, the governor of Massachusetts organized a force of militia. On June 17, 1745, the Americans, in one of the most audacious—and lucky—episodes in the colonial wars, captured Louisbourg, a fort on Cape Breton Island. In 1748, however, the British returned the fortress to the French in exchange for Madras in India.

Start of the Great War for Empire.   The French now showed a greater determination than ever to hold Canada and the Ohio and Mississippi valleys. In 1755 they erected blockhouses to fortify the Ohio and Allegheny river valleys against the British.

In the meantime, planters from Virginia and Maryland had organized the Ohio Company to exploit virgin lands as far west as the present site of Louisville, Kentucky. To prevent these western lands from falling into possession of the French, the governor of Virginia in 1753 sent George Washington, a young surveyor, into the Ohio valley to remonstrate with the French commander. The mission accomplished nothing, and when Washington was sent the next year with a force of men, his little army was surrounded, captured, and sent home. Thus began the conflict that was to develop into the French and Indian War and explode in Europe as the Seven Years' War (1756–1763), allying England and Prussia against France, Austria, and Spain.

With the danger of an Indian war threatening the whole frontier, the colonies were particularly concerned with counterbalancing the Indian allies of the French. To conciliate the powerful Iroquois, who had given invaluable support to the English in the past, the British government called a conference in Albany of commissioners from seven Northern and Middle colonies. This "Albany Congress" was more important for its political proposals than for its few accomplishments in dealing with the disaffected Iroquois. Because the delegates realized that a closer union of the colonies was needed to provide better collective defense and control of Indian affairs, they listened attentively to the "Plan of Union" put forward by one of Pennsylvania's leading citizens, Benjamin Franklin. Franklin's proposals would have brought all of the colonies under "one general government" with an executive and legislature, but with each colony retaining its separate existence and government. No colony gave the plan serious consideration, however, and the British government disregarded it altogether.

To protect the colonies, the British government sent two regiments of regulars and a British fleet. In an attempt to dislodge the French from Fort Duquesne, a strategic position that controlled the upper Ohio valley, a detachment of regulars and colonial militia under British General Edward Braddock marched toward the fort, but it was ambushed and routed by French and Indian forces. After Braddock's defeat, George Washington was given the responsibility of protecting more than three hundred miles of the Virginia frontier against incursions of Indians and French marauders.

The year 1755 was a period of almost unrelieved misfortune for the British, and for the next two or three years the war raged intermittently and disastrously along the whole frontier, with the French under the Marquis de Montcalm winning a succession of victories in the north.

The Capture of Quebec. William Pitt, who had become British Secretary of State for War in 1757, realized that part of the trouble in America lay in the incompetence of Britain's officers. To remedy this, he ordered to America fresh troops under a new command. He also won more wholehearted cooperation from the American provincials by promising

In the first American political cartoon, printed in 1754, Benjamin Franklin urged the colonies to join the Albany Congress—or die.

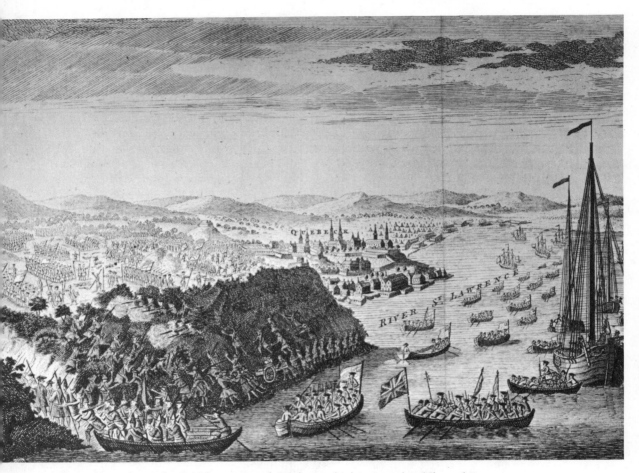

This etching shows the British capture of Quebec, which meant the defeat of France in North America.

that Britain would reimburse the individual colonies for their war expenditures.

The campaign against the French soon began to show favorable results. The victory that finally decided the issue in Canada came on September 13, 1759, when General Wolfe led a successful attack on Quebec, which had been under siege since late June. The capture of Quebec sealed the fate of France in North America. Elsewhere—in Europe and India—

British arms were also victorious, and France could do nothing but capitulate. In 1762 France ceded Louisiana to Spain in recompense for aid in the war and a year later, by the Treaty of Paris, ceded to Great Britain all of Canada except the tiny islands of St. Pierre and Miquelon. Paradoxically, the very magnitude of the British victory paved the way for the disintegration of the British Empire in America.

Chapter 3

Revolution and Independence 1763–1783

BACKGROUND OF THE REVOLUTION

The Character of the Revolution. The American Revolution was one of the greatest epochs in human history, not only because it brought a separation between Great Britain and its colonies in America but also because it was the first revolution of modern times founded on the principles of self-government and the protection of individual liberty. In this context, the American Revolution became a beacon to light the way for peoples the world over.

The American Revolution was, in fact, many-sided. It was a War for Independence in which the colonies fought to be separated from the strongest nation in the world, Great Britain. It was a civil war in which Englishmen fought Englishmen and occasionally colonials fought colonials. It was part of a world war. It involved a struggle for power within each colony. And it was a nationalist movement in which the colonies, after separating from Britain, formed a lasting union—an important decision that Americans today take for granted but that was not necessarily predestined.

Although the purpose of the Revolution was not to establish democracy any more than it was to establish a union, one of the results of the struggle within certain states was to give the average Amerian a greater voice in government.

Finally, it should be remembered that the first revolt by colonials against the homeland in modern times—the American colonies against Britain—occurred under the most enlightened and least burdensome imperial system of contemporary Europe. The whites who lived in the English colonies enjoyed far more privileges in every sphere of life than did their counterparts in the French and Spanish colonies.

Why were the least restricted colonials the first to revolt? The American colonials had enjoyed what they thought of as their liberties for a century or more, and they had no intention of seeing these liberties restricted, even if, comparatively, they were better off than colonials elsewhere. Although the Revolution was not inevitable, any action to limit existing privileges automatically produced friction. How deep the friction was to become depended upon the course of events and the response to these events by American colonials and by the authorities in Britain.

Early Provocations and Crises. The crises within the empire from 1763 to 1776 were provoked by a series of specific enactments, but to review the prelude to revolution in such narrow terms is to misconstrue the essential issues that were in dispute. An adjustment in the relationship between Britain and its colonies was made inevitable by several sweeping changes that had been occurring during the eighteenth century.

The colonial and commercial systems of Britain had been established in the seventeenth century, based on a theory already several centuries old. When the system was inaugurated, England possessed only a few colonies. After the Peace of 1763, Britain had more than thirty colonies scattered throughout the world, each with its individual characteristics. Did the policies initiated in the 1660s suit conditions in the colonies in the 1760s? Should the same system apply to India and Massachusetts?

Even before the specific crises that occurred between 1763 and 1776, the British-colonial relationships required adjustment to meet the new realities. Three major changes were

This 1777 cartoon shows "Poor old England endeavoring to reclaim [its] wicked American children." In actuality, the crisis between the "children" and the mother country had been developing for many years.

Poor old England endeavoring to reclaim his wicked American Children .
= One therefore to ENGLAND meaning & forced to go with a Staff!

clearly evident. The American colonies had matured. The political transition in England by which Parliament had steadily gained power at the expense of the crown required a redefinition of relationships within the empire. And the colonies in the New World had become a critical factor in the European balance of power.

By 1760 the British colonies in America were no longer infants dependent solely upon the protection of the mother country. From limited self-government to mature self-government, from inexperience to experience with authority, from a primitive to a complex, well-developed indigenous economy—this had been the course of the American colonies. Any imperial system that failed to recognize these realities was doomed. As it existed, the imperial system had become, in some of its parts, an anachronism. The American provinces had become an insatiable market for British goods, but the British system failed to adjust to this fact. The American colonies required a more enlightened money and banking policy, but the British tried to continue outworn theories. The American colonies produced statesmen, and even geniuses, but most American talent was unacknowledged.

The political transition in England required a rethinking of the constitutional structure of the empire. The colonies had been established under the auspices of royal charters. They had been administered through the king, the executive authority. As Parliament assumed greater authority, fundamental questions arose. Did Parliament have unlimited legislative supremacy over the colonies? Did Parliament gain the executive power previously exercised by the crown? The home authorities said yes; American colonials said no. Moreover, the Industrial Revolution of the eighteenth century in England introduced new problems with regard to mercantile theories—notably the importance of colonies as markets—which were never resolved.

During the eighteenth century the Spanish, French, and British colonies in the New World had become increasingly critical factors in the European balance of power. Beginning particularly with the Peace of Utrecht in 1713, the European powers attempted to establish an equilibrium in that balance. It was clearly tipped in England's favor by the Peace of Paris in 1763, when Britain acquired New France in North America as well as French possessions elsewhere in the world.

These British acquisitions created uneasiness and uncertainty throughout western Europe, and France began to explore avenues to redress the balance of power. Soon after 1763 the French recognized the possibility of doing so—not by recapturing its lost colonies or by capturing British colonies but by encouraging a separation between Britain and its colonies in America. This reasoning was responsible for French intervention in 1778 on behalf of the Americans.

Any one of these major changes in the eighteenth century—the maturation of the colonies, the political and economic transition in Britain, and the diplomatic evolution—was destined to produce problems in the relationship between England and the colonies. Together, they helped to produce a revolution.

The Constitutional Issue. As mentioned in the previous chapter, the British and the American colonials had differing concepts of the constitutional structure of the empire. The British asumed that the self-government practiced by the separate colonies was a favor granted by the mother country—a favor that could be enlarged, curtailed, or even eliminated. The ultimate authority rested in Britain. The colonies possessed no power except that granted by the home authorities. The colonials, on the other hand, held that self-government rested upon the consent of the governed (the colonial electorate), not upon royal grace and favor. The Americans believed they possessed rights (at first called the Rights of Englishmen, later called American Rights) which Britain could in no way curtail. Each colonial assembly viewed itself as struggling against a royal governor (and thus against the king), much like the House of Commons, in its struggle to gain power at the king's expense.

The rising power of Parliament posed an additional question: What were the limits to the legislative power of Parliament over the colonies? Conflict on this point was inevitable, and it became a critical issue in the revolutionary crisis that developed.

Constitutional Confrontations. During the French and Indian War several British policies annoyed the American provincials. In 1759 the Privy Council instructed the governor of Virginia to refuse to sign any bill which failed to include a "suspending clause"—that is, a clause preventing the act from becoming effective until it had been approved by the home authorities. In 1761 general writs of assistance empowered officers of the British customs service to break into and search homes and stores for smuggled goods. This provoked strong opposition from the provincials, who claimed that the writs were contrary to law and to the natural rights of men. In that same year the Privy Council prohibited the issuance in New York and New Jersey of judicial commissions with unlimited tenure, specifying that such commissions must always be subject to revocation by the king, even though in England judges no longer held their posts at the king's pleasure. In 1764 the Currency Act extended to all colonies the restrictions on the issuance of paper money that previously had applied only to Massachusetts.

Problems of Defense and Western Lands. The Peace of Paris of 1763 eliminated the French threat to English expansion on the North American continent and made available to English colonials opportunities in the West

that had been denied them for a quarter of a century. However, the Peace of Paris raised problems with regard to the administration and distribution of this land. It also raised the issue of revenue to pay the cost of administering the empire. Most important, the Peace of Paris, by eliminating the French threat, made the American provincials bolder in stating their views and, once they had adopted a position, more tenacious in clinging to it.

Among the principal problems faced by the British was the settlement of the territory west of the Alleghenies. The issue was complicated by the revolt in 1763 of the western Indians under the leadership of Pontiac, chief of the Ottawa tribe. Farms and villages along the whole of the colonial frontier from Canada to Virginia were laid waste. The uprising was put down largely by British troops, but the problem of future defense assumed great importance. This incident, together with a previous policy of appointing a commander in chief for America, produced a major decision on the part of the British: to quarter ten thousand British regulars on the American mainland and in the West Indies.

However well-intentioned, this action met with stern provincial opposition. Americans who had faced the French competition at close quarters for a century could not understand why British troops were needed now that the French menace had been eliminated. Ill will between the British redcoats and the colonials increased the tension, especially in New York (after 1765) and in Boston (after 1768), where the troops were stationed. Moreover, the colonials were not accustomed to the accepted British practice of expecting the people who were being "defended" to quarter the troops. The Quartering Act of 1765, which required New York colonials to house the soldiers and to make supplies available, was bitterly resented.

The solution to the problem of western lands beyond the Appalachians was equally irritating. If the colonies in immediate proximity to the western lands, like Pennsylvania, New York, Virginia, and the Carolinas, were permitted to extend their boundaries westward, colonies without a hinterland—Connecticut, Rhode Island, New Jersey, and Maryland, to name the most obvious—would be placed at a disadvantage. Should new colonies, therefore, be formed in the territory beyond the Appalachians?

The solution formulated by the British government was the Royal Proclamation Line of 1763, which established a line along the crest of the Alleghenies west of which colonials could not take up land. This policy of delay seemed sensible in London, but the colonials were impatient to take advantage of the new territory. Virginians had fought in the French and Indian War specifically to open this area to settlement. Not only were frontiersmen eager to exploit these opportunities, but land companies in Pennsylvania, Virginia, and New England, whose membership included affluent colonials and Englishmen, wished to act. For these men the Proclamation Line was a disappointment—an unexpected barrier to enterprise and opportunity.

The Proclamation Line, intended originally as a temporary measure to gain time for a permanent policy, was not revoked before the Revolution. Meanwhile, the Quebec Act of 1774 further annoyed the provincials by annexing the western lands north of the Ohio River to the Province of Quebec. The former French colony, viewed by the colonials as the enemy, was to be rewarded, while the faithful colonists who had fought to free that territory from French control were denied the fruits of their sacrifices.

The problems of western lands and defense did not bring on the Revolution, but they caused a lingering grievance. When added to the other irritations of British rule, they decreased the probability of compromise and increased the chances of hostility.

The Stamp Act.   George Grenville, who became Prime Minister in 1763, was neither an imaginative nor a clever man, but he was a determined one. Coming into office just at the close of the French and Indian War and feeling, as most of his countrymen did, that the American colonists would be the greatest beneficiaries of the vast territory bordering the Ohio and Mississippi rivers that had been won from the French, he was determined that the colonists should pay at least part of the costs of defending and pacifying this territory. Currently no revenue was coming from the colonists to aid in imperial defense. Duties imposed by the Molasses Act of 1733 were being evaded by smugglers. In fact, the American customs service was costing more to operate than it was collecting in fees.

Thus, in 1764 Grenville led Parliament to adopt the Sugar Act, an act intended to produce revenue—a purpose clearly stated in its preface—by enforcing the payment of customs duties on sugar, wine, coffee, silk, and other goods. Although it reduced the duty on molasses bought from non-British sources from 6 pence to 4 pence per gallon—on the surface, an attractive reduction—provincials actually had been smuggling in molasses for no more than a pence and a half per gallon as a bribe to customs officials. Now Grenville intended to enforce the trade laws by stricter administrative procedures. The crux of the issue, however, was the British intention to tax the colonists for purposes of revenue. Before this, duties had been imposed merely as a means of regulating the trade of the empire.

The issue of taxation, raised by the Sugar Act, was brought to a crisis in the Stamp Act of 1765, which provoked spontaneous opposition throughout the colonies. The Stamp Act placed a stamp fee on all legal documents, deeds and diplomas, custom papers, and newspapers, to name the most obvious articles. It directly affected every articulate element in the community, including lawyers,

Public outrage over the Stamp Act was so great that many used the skull and crossbones to mark the spot where the stamp was to be embossed on legal papers, while William Bradford ceased publication of his paper "in order to deliberate whether any Methods can be found to elude the Chains forged for us . . . "

merchants, preachers, and printers. Moreover, the act raised not only the question of who had the right to tax but also the more significant questions: Who had what power? Could Parliament legislate for the colonials in all matters? Was Parliament's authority without limit or were there bounds beyond which it could not reach—bounds based upon certain rights inherent in all Englishmen?

The conflict was contested on two levels, that of action and that of constitutional debate. In every colony the men appointed as Stamp Act collectors were forced to resign, sometimes under the threat of force. Sons of

Liberty were organized in key colonies to enforce the colonially imposed prohibition on the use of stamps. Occasionally mob spirit carried opposition to extremes, as it did in Massachusetts when a band of provincials ransacked the home of the lieutenant governor. The courts and the ports, which could not operate legally without using the stamps, continued after a momentary lull to carry out their regular functions in defiance of the act.

Each colonial legislature met to decide on a course of action, the most famous incident occurring in the Virginia House of Burgesses, where Patrick Henry introduced resolutions declaring that the "General Assembly of this Colony have the only and *sole exclusive* Right and Power to lay Taxes and Impositions upon the Inhabitants of This Colony." Any other course, said Henry, would tend "to destroy British as well as American Freedom." At the invitation of Massachusetts, nine colonies sent delegates to New York in October 1765 to form the Stamp Act Congress, in which a set of resolutions was adopted denying the authority of Parliament to tax the colonials. A boycott of British goods—the use of economic coercion to achieve political ends—was introduced on the theory that the colonial market was so necessary to Britain that it would abandon the act to regain the market.

On the second level, that of defining constitutional theory, the respective arguments of the colonials and the authorities in England developed differently. Colonials argued that they could not be free without being secure in their property and that they could not be secure in their property if, without their consent, others could take it away by taxes. This argument revealed the close tie between property and liberty in the minds of the eighteenth-century Anglo-Americans.

The British responded by saying that the Americans were not being taxed without their consent because they were "virtually," if not directly, represented in Parliament. They argued that many areas in Britain—notably Manchester and other substantial communities—were not directly represented in Parliament, but that no one denied that an act of Parliament had authority over those communities. The same concept of "virtual representation," asserted the British leaders, applied to the colonies.

The colonies vigorously opposed this interpretation of representation. Most of the colonial legislatures echoed Maryland's argument "that it cannot, with any Truth or Propriety, be said, That the Freemen of this Province of Maryland are Represented in the British Parliament." Daniel Dulany, a Maryland attorney, in his *Considerations on the Propriety of Imposing Taxes in the British Colonies*, argued that even those people in Britain who did not have the right to vote were allied in interest with their contemporaries. "But who," he asked, "are the Representatives of the Colonies?" Who could speak for them?

The Right of Exemption from all Taxes without their consent, the Colonies claim as *British* Subjects. They derive this Right from the Common Law, which their Charters have declared and confirmed . . . . A Right to impose an internal Tax on the Colonies, without their Consent *for the single Purpose of Revenue*, is denied; a Right to regulate their Trade without their Consent is admitted.

In brief, the colonists argued, Parliament had power, but not unlimited power. It could *legislate* and thus impose external duties to regulate trade, but it could not *levy a tax* for revenue. In time, as the revolutionary crisis deepened, the colonial position was modified to deny Parliament's authority to legislate for or tax the colonists for any purpose whatsoever.

A view much closer to the eventual stand taken by the colonists was expressed by George Mason of Virginia, who implicitly denied the indefinite subordination of the colonies. "We rarely see anything from your [the English] side of the water free from the authoritative style of a master to a school boy: 'We have with infinite difficulty and fatigue got you excused this one time; pray be a good boy for the future, do what your papa and mama bid you.' " He warned the British that "such another experiment as the stamp-act would produce a general revolt in America."

Parliament backed down—not on the principle at issue, but on the act itself. The Stamp Act was repealed in 1766. At the same time, however, the Declaratory Act was passed, stating that Parliament possessed the authority to make laws binding the American colonists. The Americans mistakenly believed not only that their arguments were persuasive but that the economic pressure brought on by the boycott of English goods had been effective. The boycott, in fact, only delayed British reaction, but the Americans, unaware of its failure, were to employ the boycott as a standard weapon against the British at each time of crisis.

The Townshend Duties.   The next major crisis arose in 1767. Misled by Benjamin Franklin, who in February 1766 had told the House of Commons that the provincials objected only to internal taxes, not to taxes on trade, the British Parliament in 1767 enacted the Townshend Duties on glass, lead, paper, paints, and tea. These import or "external" taxes were designed to exploit the distinction between internal taxes and external duties which Parliament mistakenly supposed the Americans were making.

At the same time, Parliament reorganized the customs service by appointing a Board of Customs Commissioners to be located at Boston. The following year, 1768, troops were sent to Boston, in part at least because of the urging of Customs Commissioners. The Townshend Duties failed to awaken the spontaneous reaction of the Stamp Act, but they tested once again the colonial versus British theory of the empire and posed anew

the question: What were the limits to the power of Parliament?

Again the American colonists resorted to a boycott, although no intercolonial congress was called. John Dickinson, in his *Letters from a Farmer in Pennsylvania,* reaffirmed the position of the colonials that duties, even "external" duties, could not be levied primarily to obtain revenue, though measures enacted to regulate trade were admitted as a proper prerogative of Parliament. Dickinson's essays were not revolutionary in tone or in spirit. Neither, however, did they back away from the fundamental position taken by the colonists—that they alone could levy a tax upon themselves.

As for the British, the Board of Customs Commissioners that came to enforce the Navigation Acts, the Sugar Act of 1764, and the Townshend Duties carried out its responsibility in such a perfidious way that the commissioners were properly accused of customs racketeering. But the real significance of the Board was the breadth of opposition it aroused. Not merely those colonists most vulnerable to its activity—particularly New England merchants—were disposed to stand against the British, but a consensus of opposition pervaded all the colonies, many of which experienced no serious problem with customs officials. This consensus was made possible because of the more profound issue: Where did the regulatory power of Parliament end and that of the colonials begin?

The Townshend Duties disappointed their advocates, for they did not produce the revenue expected. In 1770, therefore, the British repealed the Townshend Duties (except the duty on tea, which was retained as a symbol of Parliament's right to tax). The Americans relaxed their opposition and reopened their ports to British goods, though they condemned tea drinking as unpatriotic.

On March 5, 1770, by coincidence the same day the Townshend Duties were repealed, the

"Boston Massacre" took place. A small group of townspeople, described by the Boston lawyer John Adams as a "motley rabble of saucy boys, negroes, and mulattoes, Irish teagues and outlandish Jack Tars," shouted catcalls and insults and hurled snowballs and rocks at British troops on duty. A scuffle erupted, and the redcoats opened fire, killing three persons and wounding eight. Among the slain was Crispus Attucks, an escaped slave who, according to one witness, had led the charge against the redcoats.

'TIS TIME TO PART

The Boston Tea Party and the Coercive Acts. Beginning in 1772, provoked by a new British decision to pay the salary of the lieutenant governor out of customs revenues and thus free him from dependence on the colonial assembly, a Committee of Correspondence was established in Massachusetts at the urging of Sam Adams, John Adams' radical cousin. Many other colonies followed the Massachusetts pattern and formed such committees in order to keep one another informed of possible British action. In 1772 the *Gaspee*, a customs vessel that had gone aground while in pursuit of colonial shipping, was boarded and burned off Providence, Rhode Island, by a group that included prominent citizens.

These isolated incidents indicated that Americans had not abandoned their position but that, unless new provocations occurred, the situation probably would remain static. In 1773 and 1774, with the Boston Tea Party and the passage of the Coercive Acts, the conflict between Great Britain and its colonies entered a new and conclusive phase.

By the Tea Act of May 1773 the British government permitted the British East India Company, which had built up an excess stock of tea in England, to market—"dump" would perhaps be a more accurate term—it in

America. The company was also authorized to employ its own agents in this transaction, and thus, in effect, to seize monopolistic control of the American market. With this act the British reawakened the latent hostility of the American colonists. When the ships carrying the tea arrived, they were met with unbroken opposition. In some ports, the ships were forced to return to England without unloading; in other cases the tea was placed in a warehouse to prevent its distribution. In Boston a band of colonists, haphazardly disguised as Indians, dumped the tea into the harbor.

The reaction in England was prompt and decisive: Punitive legislation must be passed to teach those property-destroying Massachusetts provincials a lesson. This position was endorsed even by members of Parliament previously well disposed to the Americans. In quick succession, three Coercive or "Intolerable" Acts were passed: the Boston Port Act (March 31, 1774), which closed that port to commerce; the Massachusetts Government Act (May 30, 1774), which altered the manner of choosing the Governor's Council and, more significantly, indicated to the Americans that parliamentary power knew no limits; and finally, the Administration of Justice Act (May 30, 1774), which removed certain cases involving crown officials from the jurisdiction of Massachusetts courts.

The other colonies immediately rallied to the support of Massachusetts in opposing these "Intolerable Acts"—much to the surprise of the British authorities, who had expected the support rather than the condemnation of the colonies outside Massachusetts. After all, had not property been destroyed? No action on the part of the Americans revealed the basic issue so clearly. Essentially, the issue was not customs racketeering, or the presence of redcoats, or the problem of western lands, or even taxes. The issue was: Who had what power?

The Coercive Acts set in motion a series of

actions and counteractions which led directly to separation. If there was any one point at which the Revolution seemed to become inevitable it was in 1774, with the passage of the Coercive Acts and the colonial response to those acts. What would Parliament do next, the colonists asked themselves. Change the administration of justice in Virginia? Eliminate self-government in New York? Close the port of Philadelphia? Once the supremacy of Parliament in all areas was conceded, self-government would live merely on sufferance.

The colonials at this stage were not calling for independence. Such a step was too frightening. The Americans had lived within the British Empire for more than a century. It was the most enlightened government of its time, where liberty was a word that meant something. Separating from Britain in the 1770s was somewhat similar to abruptly changing today the form of government under which we have lived since 1789. It was not a step to be taken, as the revolutionary fathers later declared in the Declaration of Independence, for light and transient causes.

The Provincials Act. Events proceeded once again on two levels—that of action and that of theory. The First Continental Congress was called to meet in Philadelphia in September 1774. A number of important decisions made early in the deliberations set the tone of the meeting. Carpenters Hall, instead of the legislative chambers of Pennsylvania, was selected as the meeting hall—a victory for Sam Adams of Massachusetts and those who wished to take firm action against Britain. A more important show of strength came when resolutions proposing a union of colonies and regarded as conciliatory were offered. They were tabled by a close vote, and the Suffolk Resolves were adopted, asserting that the colonies should make no concessions until Britain first repealed the Coercive Acts. The burden of conciliation was thus upon the home authorities.

In addition, the First Continental Congress adopted a series of resolutions embodying its position and sent them off to the king. At the same time a Continental Association was established to cut off trade with the British. Although Congress avowed its "allegiance to his majesty" and its "affection for our fellow subjects" in Great Britain, the stand it took placed Britain on notice.

When the First Continental Congress adjourned, its members agreed to meet again in the spring of 1775 if no action was forthcoming from Britain. Conditions failed to improve; in fact, they became worse. In Massachusetts "minutemen" were training to guard against possible actions by British redcoats stationed in Boston. Guns, powder, and other military stores were being collected at Concord.

Many Londoners felt that the Port Act was too punitive, as shown by this cartoon of Bostonians forced to rely on other colonies even for the fish they ate, while British troops blockade the port.

When on April 18, 1775, the British military governor sent out from Boston about seven hundred British regulars to destroy the stores at Concord, they were met by minutemen companies in Lexington and Concord. At Lexington eight Americans were killed.

With minutemen swarming in from the countryside, the redcoats faced unexpected hazards on their return to Boston. Before the day was spent, they had suffered nearly three hundred casualties and escaped total destruction only because reinforcements came from Boston. Dogging the regulars all the way, the minutemen encamped on the land approaches to Boston and began a siege.

Meanwhile, on May 10, New England forces led by Benedict Arnold and Ethan Allen captured Fort Ticonderoga on Lake Champlain. Subsequently they moved northward to seize points along the Canadian border.

When the Second Continental Congress met in May 1775, the thin line between peace and war was in danger of vanishing. Congress appointed a Virginian, George Washington, commander in chief of the provincial forces surrounding Boston. His nomination by John Adams, a Massachusetts man, revealed the determined effort of the Americans to present a united front. Congress tried to win Canada to its cause but failed.

On July 6, 1776, Congress adopted the "Declaration of the Causes and Necessity of taking up Arms" in an attempt to assure fellow Britons that dissolution of the union was not intended but that neither would Americans back away from their convictions. "Our cause is just. Our union is perfect. Our internal resources are great, and, if necessary, foreign assistance is undoubtedly attainable."

In August 1775 the king declared that his subjects were in rebellion and began to recruit foreign mercenaries and prepare the British regulars. During the remainder of 1775 the Americans attempted the conquest of Canada, chiefly in order to deprive Britain of a base of attack. After capturing Montreal and being repulsed at Quebec, the Americans withdrew.

Beginning in January 1776 the movement for independence gained ground. Thomas Paine published his *Common Sense*, asserting "tis time to part." Appreciatively read by thousands upon thousands, *Common Sense* helped to crystallize opinion. By late spring a number of colonies instructed their delegates to the Continental Congress to advocate independence.

On June 7, 1776, Richard Henry Lee of Virginia, once again reflecting the unity of the colonials regardless of region, introduced a resolution calling for independence. It was adopted on July 2 by a close vote, the winning margin being provided by the deliberate absence of several Pennsylvania delegates who were not convinced that independence was the best policy.

The Declaration of Independence. Action and theory were moving together. In 1774 James Wilson, later a Supreme Court justice, had published *Considerations on the Authority of Parliament*, which posed a series of questions: "And have those, whom we have hitherto been accustomed to consider as our fellow-subjects, an absolute and unlimited power over us? Have they a natural right to make laws, by which we may be deprived of our properties, of our liberties, of our lives? By what title do they claim to be our masters? . . . Do those, who embark freemen in Great Britain, disembark slaves in America?" Wilson answered by affirming, without qualification, that Parliament had no authority over the colonies. Their dependence upon Britain was exclusively through the crown. The colonies were "different members of the British Empire . . ., independent of each other, but connected together under the same sovereign."

Wilson's assumption underlay the philosophy of the Declaration of Independence. The colonists directed the entire document against the king. Nowhere is Parliament mentioned.

Thomas Jefferson's rough draft of the Declaration of Independence shows the pains he took to explain why the law-abiding and substantial members of the Continental Congress felt they must separate from Britain.

The Continental Congress could have separated from Britain by means of a simple declarative resolution. An elaborate document to explain the reason for revolution was unnecessary. That such a document was written is in itself an insight into the nature of the Revolution, for it was not of tattered flags, of starved and desperate people, or of lawlessness. Its leadership included some of the most substantial and prominent individuals in America. Because of their influential position and their regard for law, they and their associates felt a deep need to explain to a "candid world" why they took such a drastic step.

Five delegates of the Continental Congress, among them John Adams and Benjamin Franklin, were assigned the task of writing the Declaration, but the draft was composed by Thomas Jefferson of Virginia. Modest changes were made by the members of the committee, and the document was then debated in Congress, where more changes were made.

The philosophy upon which the Declaration was based was that which underlay treatises written by John Locke on the occasion of the English Glorious Revolution of 1688. The similarity in ideas and even in phraseology is striking. The Declaration appealed to the highest authority within the intellectual structure of the eighteenth century, "the Laws of Nature and Nature's God." It asserted that all men are created equal, that each person is endowed with certain rights that cannot be set aside, that included among these rights are "life, liberty, and the pursuit of happiness."

What this felicitous phrase meant was to be defined more carefully later in state and national constitutions. But the Declaration reaffirmed what Americans in their experience had long practiced: that governments, based upon the consent of the governed, are established to secure these rights. The king, the symbol of the British government, had failed to honor his obligation.

The Declaration included a list of specific charges that add up to a devastating indictment, too often treated by historians as an excuse or a rationalization for an act already taken. With the acceptance of the Declaration by the Continental Congress, the British view that the rights of the colonies depended on the sufferance of the royal grace and favor was forever demolished.

With the Declaration, the character of the conflict changed too. Whereas the colonials had been secretly soliciting aid from France since 1775, the Continental Congress, representing an independent people, now established ministries throughout Europe to obtain recognition and help for the independent colonies, soon to become the United States. Washington, who had been leading a militia force to obtain recognition of the rights of colonials, now headed an army fighting for American independence. Thirteen colonies became thirteen states with the problem of working out appropriate constitutions.

Facing the experience of union, the Americans also had to work out an acceptable constitutional structure for the national government. With the Declaration, the Continental Congress was no longer an extralegal body of rebels but the symbol of a sovereign nation.

The Internal Revolution. Emphasis has been placed on the principal issue—what were the limits of the power of Parliament? But historians have investigated a second ques-

tion: Within each colony, who was to possess authority? Their point of view has ranged widely on this question. Some have insisted that the issue of who was going to rule at home was preeminent, that the break with Britain was brought about by radical dissenters within each colony who were so anxious to overthrow the power structure in their colony that they worked for revolution to accomplish this purpose. Other historians contend that those who held power in the late colonial period were willing to fight to maintain it.

The present consensus among historians is perhaps best expressed as follows: Conflicts within individual colonies contributed to the coming of the Revolution because some people hoped to correct grievances under a new regime. However, this internal struggle for control was not the decisive or preeminent force. The principal issue was the conflict over the constitutional framework of the empire. Even without an internal struggle, the Revolution would have occurred. The internal grievances were related, however, to later developments in the revolutionary and postrevolutionary periods as Americans set about to resolve their own problems.

The Loyalists. The Declaration of Independence was a divisive rather than a unifying document, and it had an impact upon every colony, county, and town and almost every family. With its adoption, people had a decision to make: Would they remain loyal to Britain and its government? Or would they join those who advocated independence and be called rebels?

Regardless of their political views or associations, the present generation of Americans claim the American Revolution as their rightful heritage, and, consequently, regard this decision as a foregone conclusion. But the literal "patriots" of 1776 were those who upheld the existing British government: The word *patriotism* derives from *patrios*, meaning "established by forefathers."

In discussing the division between those who supported separation from Britain and those who opposed it, historians have customarily used rather gross figures, holding that one third of the revolutionary generation remained loyal to Britain, one third remained uncommitted, and one third supported independence. Closer examination reveals that the percentage varied substantially among colonies as well as among localities within colonies.

The best recent figures indicate that 20 percent, about 500,000, of the white population became Loyalists. As many as 100,000 persons altogether left the colonies for Canada, England, the West Indies, and other places of exile. Historian Robert R. Palmer has calculated that twenty-four persons per thousand of the population left the colonies compared with five persons per thousand of the population of France during the French Revolution, a startling fact that raises the issue of Loyalists to a new level of importance.

These divisions were reflected among families and friends. Gouverneur Morris of New York took up the cause of independence. His mother and many other members of his family remained loyal to Britain. Benjamin Franklin's son William, who was governor of New Jersey, became a Loyalist, causing Franklin to write that his son caused him more personal grief by this act than he had experienced in a lifetime. Close friends and trading associates Thomas Willing and Robert Morris of Philadelphia took opposite sides: Willing remained a supporter of the crown, while Morris became a principal leader of the Revolution.

Some of the most distinguished and honored leaders in these and other provinces left. Daniel Dulaney of Maryland, who wrote so convincingly about the evils of the Stamp Act, could not bring himself to accept independence. Neither could Joseph Galloway, Speaker of the House in Pennsylvania. Chief Justice William Smith of New York finally decided to migrate to Canada after refusing to take a loyalty oath to the revolutionary government in New York.

To list these names tends to imply that only the upper social strata became Loyalists, but the total of 500,000—full 20 percent of the population—demonstrates that people from every social class became Loyalists. Slaves left plantations to follow the British in the hope of gaining freedom, but servants and artisans also sought the protection of the British government and army.

During the course of the War for Independence, it is estimated that as many as 30,000 Loyalists served in the British army. In 1780 alone as many as 8,000 Loyalists served in the British forces. Washington's forces at that time numbered no more than 9,000.

What is more difficult to ascertain is the number of Loyalists who remained in the colonies, trying not to offend the supporters of the Revolution but assisting the British troops when they came. The colonies of Georgia, New York, and South Carolina were the strongest Loyalist strongholds, followed by New Jersey and Massachusetts. Indeed, the British planned military campaigns in these provinces in the expectation that Loyalists would flock to their standard. The decision to concentrate on New York in 1776 and again in 1777 was based, at least in part, on this assumption. The decision in 1779–1780 to redirect the military effort to Georgia and South Carolina was also prompted by the expectation of winning support throughout the countryside.

Loyalists who did not wish to speak out had good reason to retain a low profile. To leave was to abandon their homes and land, for few Loyalists were able to convert their possessions into cash. Revolutionary governments confiscated Loyalists' property to be resold to the highest bidders. For this and many other reasons, few Loyalists, with the critical exception of those who migrated to Canada, left an imprint upon their adopted homelands.

Those who left for England were probably the ones who became most disenchanted. The nation and the government they had held in such high esteem seemed unrecognizable at close range. The rampant corruption, the flagrant bidding for position and favor, even the life-style of eighteenth-century England seemed alien to provincial leaders. Persons accustomed to leadership in the colonies became, for the most part, inconsequential in England. A dedicated Loyalist, Henry Van Schaack, longed to return to America and eventually did so.

On the whole, the Loyalists, because they chose the losing side, became lost among their contemporaries and, in many respects, to history.

PROSECUTING THE WAR

The Continental Congress. To make independence a reality, the war had to be won. Though the Continental Congress had neither a specific grant of authority nor a fixed constitutional basis until 1781, it resolved financial, military, diplomatic, and constitutional questions during this critical period. Occasionally, action lagged and arguments centered upon trivialities, but the Continental Congress should be remembered for its major achievements rather than for its minor failures. It unified the American war effort and fashioned an instrument of national government without violating individual liberty and without producing dissension so divisive as to splinter the Revolution. Most of America's greatest leaders served at one time or another in the Congress, gaining their first political experience at the national rather than at the colony-state level.

Revolutionary Finance. One of the early problems facing Congress was how to finance the war. Four major methods were used: Loan Office Certificates, the equivalent of present-day government bonds; requisitions, that is, requests for money and later supplies from individual states; foreign loans, which were insignificant until 1781; and paper currency.

The first issues of paper money were made by Congress before the Declaration of Independence. This avenue of revenue was one that had been used by many colonies during the colonial period. At first the paper money circulated at its face value, but as more money was issued, its value declined (although intermittently the value of the currency increased when successful military operations revived hopes for a quick victory). By the spring of 1781 the value had declined so precipitously that paper currency cost more to print than it was worth once it was printed. Up to that point, however, paper money paid for no less than 75 percent of the cost of the war.

After 1781 foreign loans became especially important, because these loans provided capital for the establishment of a national bank, the Bank of North America. From it the government borrowed money in excess of the bank's capitalization. After 1781, Morris Notes—a form of paper currency backed by the word of Robert Morris, the Superintendent of Finance—helped to restore the public credit. At the conclusion of the war the national government as well as the various states had incurred a substantial debt that was to figure in the movement to write the federal Constitution of 1787.

Military Strategy. The British did not take advantage of their most promising military strategy until 1782, when, too late, they managed to blockade all the American ports. An intensive blockade, if it had been coordinated with swift, devastating land campaigns to lay waste the resources of the Americans, might have brought success, for the British, in order to win, had to demand unconditional surrender. The Americans, to be successful, needed an army in the field as a symbol of resistance. Any negotiations automatically recognized the United States as an independent nation because a sovereign power does not negotiate with rebels.

The first military operations of the British were concentrated in the Middle states, with an eye to dividing the United States physically, crippling its unity, and exploiting the possibility of support from American Loyalists. When this failed, the emphasis shifted to the Southern theater of operations beginning in 1780.

Slavery and the Revolution. The policy on enlisting blacks in the Continental forces changed throughout the course of the war. At the beginning of the fighting the Continental army and most state militias accepted black enlistments, both slaves and freemen. Prince Estabrook, a black, fought at Lexington, for example, and Peter Salem fought at Lexington, Concord, and Bunker Hill. One Rhode Island regiment included 125 blacks, of whom 30 were freemen.

Early attitudes changed. A Council of War convened by General Washington in Massachusetts in October 1775 decided not to accept further enlistment of blacks because other troops, especially those from the South, refused to accept them as equals. Free blacks protested to Washington, and in December 1775 he ordered the reopening of enlistments to free blacks. Meanwhile, he requested the Continental Congress to review the issue. In January 1776 Congress ruled that free blacks who had already served could reenlist, but other blacks, whether slave or free, were excluded. The pattern set by the Continental army was followed by state militias.

The British attitude fluctuated as much as that of the American provincials. The British recognized that recruiting slaves would cripple the planter colonies, so they promised freedom in exchange for service. They offered indentured servants the same promise. When planters found their slaves leaving to answer the British call, they became alarmed and angry. In Virginia slave patrols were doubled to catch runaways. Each planter in the Southern colonies tended to keep a sharper eye on the men and women in bondage.

Toward the end of 1776 and early in 1777, Continental policy changed once again. Blacks were recruited for the Continental and state navies. The state of Maryland enlisted blacks in its militia, and even the Virginia militia was willing to accept blacks. By 1779 the Continental Congress recommended that South Carolina and Georgia raise a military force of five thousand black soldiers. Owners of slaves who enlisted were to be compensated, and the slaves in return would receive freedom and $50 in cash. The two states rejected the recommendation, but enlistment of blacks did grow in the North. In 1781 Baron Von Closen found that one fourth of the encampment of soldiers at White Plains was composed of blacks.

A few faltering steps were taken toward emancipation during the war years. In 1780 Pennsylvania provided for the gradual abolition of slavery. In 1784 Connecticut and Rhode Island followed Pennsylvania's lead, and soon thereafter New York and New Jersey followed suit. In 1783 the Supreme Court of Massachusetts ruled that the phrase "men are created free and equal" meant what it said, thereby freeing slaves in that state. In contrast, a proposal in the Maryland legislature to free slaves lost by a vote of 32 to 22. Significantly, no grand plan of emancipation was adopted anywhere in the new nation.

The reason was largely the attitude of the whites toward the blacks. Jefferson, in a public statement called *The Summary View*, acknowledged that slaves should be freed, but he also declared that blacks were inferior human beings. He could never bring himself to free his own slaves, even though Washington eventually did. The fear of living with blacks as equals, the loss of property, and the

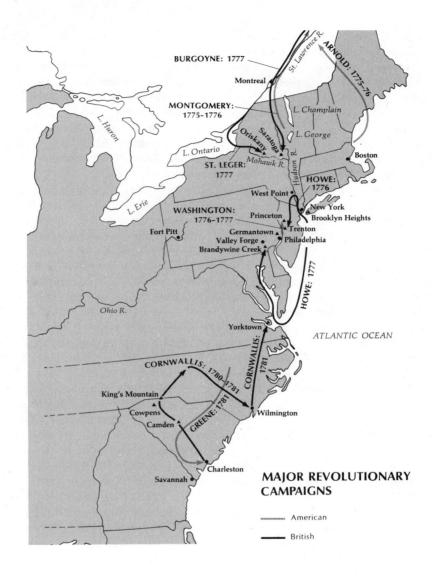

BURGOYNE: 1777

MONTGOMERY:
1775–1776

ST. LEGER:
1777

WASHINGTON:
1776–1777

ARNOLD: 1775–76

St. Lawrence R.

Montreal

L. Champlain

L. George

Oriskany

Saratoga

L. Huron

L. Ontario

Mohawk R.

Boston

L. Erie

Hudson R.

HOWE:
1776

West Point

New York

Brooklyn Heights

Princeton

Trenton

Fort Pitt

Germantown

Valley Forge

Brandywine Creek

Philadelphia

Ohio R.

HOWE: 1777

Yorktown

ATLANTIC OCEAN

CORNWALLIS: 1780–1781

CORNWALLIS: 1781

King's Mountain

Cowpens

Camden

GREENE: 1781

Wilmington

Charleston

Savannah

**MAJOR REVOLUTIONARY
CAMPAIGNS**

————— American

————— British

social consequences paralyzed the movement to free the slaves. So the possibility faded, to be taken up again by a later generation that resolved the issue on the battlefield.

The War in the North. Washington forced the British under General Sir William Howe to abandon Boston by capturing Dorchester Heights in March 1776. Howe loaded his troops on transports and sailed to Nova Scotia

to prepare for an attack on New York. He took with him more than a thousand Loyalists who preferred residence in Canada to independence from Great Britain.

In an effort to prevent Howe's taking New York, Washington moved south and occupied Brooklyn Heights on Long Island. There on August 27, 1776, Howe with an army of thirty-three thousand attacked and defeated Washington, who withdrew to Manhattan

Island. After the British had occupied New York, Washington retreated to New Jersey. British troops continued to occupy the city for the duration of the Revolution.

With an army that seemed destined to disappear entirely at times—it once dwindled to three thousand men—Washington could not hope to recapture New York or prevent the British from making further advances. Only the stupidity or laziness of General Howe prevented the annihilation of the American forces. But Washington managed to keep the semblance of an army together and on two occasions won startling victories over British units. On Christmas night, 1776, he crossed the Delaware, fell on a garrison of Hessian troops at Trenton, and captured or killed most of them. Again, on January 3, he won a small battle at Princeton and marched with his army to Morristown, where he established winter quarters.

In 1777 Howe bestirred himself sufficiently to send an army by sea against Philadelphia. Washington proceeded overland south of Philadelphia and met units of Howe's army at Brandywine Creek on September 11, 1777, suffering defeat after being badly outmaneuvered. Howe entered Philadelphia with ease, but British units were severely tested when Washington launched an unexpected counterattack at Germantown on October 4. Though the American army was defeated, its offensive spirit aided the cause of independence at home and in France.

In the meantime the British had planned a three-pronged attack to capture the Hudson Valley and thus isolate New England from the colonies to the south. From Canada, General Sir John Burgoyne was to push southward down Lake Champlain and the upper Hudson with the expectation of joining Howe moving up the Hudson from New York City. Burgoyne would then join Howe in an attack on Philadelphia and the occupation of other rebel territory to the south. But Howe had received conflicting orders and decided that the immediate capture of Philadelphia was more urgent than cooperating with Burgoyne.

Burgoyne had also expected to converge with a third British force (mostly Loyalists and Indians) moving eastward from Lake Ontario along the Mohawk Valley, but this force was beaten back by American troops at the Battle of Oriskany. Nevertheless, throughout the summer of 1777 Burgoyne pressed southward toward Albany. At last, failing to receive aid from either Howe or the force from Lake Ontario, he suffered complete defeat in two battles fought near Saratoga. On October 17, 1777, he surrendered his entire army of 5800 men to American General Horatio Gates. Thus ended the British hope of isolating New England by occupying the Hudson Valley.

European Aid to the Americans. The victory over Burgoyne and the Battle of Germantown had significant political results. They indicated to European politicians that the Americans could win independence and that British power could be crippled by the loss. France, of course, was anxious for revenge upon its ancient enemy, and the efforts of American diplomats in Paris now began to bear fruit. Benjamin Franklin proved a most effective ambassador to France. Wearing a fur cap as the symbol of republican and frontier simplicity, he soon became the toast of Paris and made friends with those politicians best able to help the American cause.

On February 6, 1778, he consummated an alliance with France. France immediately supplied limited funds to aid the American cause and in 1780 dispatched troops and ships. French ports were now opened to such war vessels as the Americans had, and privateers could attack British vessels and stand a better chance of getting away to a safe haven. The French navy provided sea power that the colonies had previously lacked.

Eager to gain the access to American

markets that Great Britain had long prevented, Holland also provided aid, largely in the form of loans underwritten by the French. Thus European aid, prompted by self-interest, contributed to the American victory. Since Spain was at the time closely allied to France, America expected aid from Spain also, but these hopes were never fulfilled.

New Campaigns in the North.   The winter of 1778 was a bitter one for Washington. His army went into winter quarters at Valley Forge, not far from Philadelphia, where Howe and the British were quartered. Because the British could pay in gold, farmers kept them supplied with everything they could want, while Washington's troops nearly starved and went barefoot in the snow, not because supplies were unavailable but because their distribution was badly administered.

Howe, notorious for his dilatoriness, was relieved in 1778 by Sir Henry Clinton, who evacuated Philadelphia and returned to New York for a new campaign in the North. Washington, without the power to inflict defeat, could only hang on the flanks of the British army. He established a base at White Plains, New York, and saw to it that West Point on the Hudson was fortified. The arrival off New York of a French naval force under Count d'Estaing did little to help the American cause, for D'Estaing showed little audacity and soon sailed away to the West Indies. Only from the western frontier was the news encouraging. George Rogers Clark, leading a group of frontiersmen, helped to hold the West against the British.

The War in the South.   In the southern theater of operations the British captured Savannah (1778) and Charleston (1780) and hoped to collaborate with the Loyalists in the interior, thus gaining control of Georgia and the Carolinas. Despite the efforts of American guerrilla bands the fate of the South remained in doubt. In August 1780 the British under Cornwallis inflicted a disastrous defeat upon American forces at Camden, South Carolina, but this defeat was redeemed in October by the destruction of a Loyalist force at the Battle of King's Mountain near the North Carolina border and the brilliant victory of Daniel Morgan and his farmer-cavalrymen at the Battle of Cowpens, South Carolina, in January 1781.

These successes turned the tide in the Carolinas. Through the winter, spring, and summer of 1781, General Nathanael Greene, commander of the American army in the South, skillfully threw militia, cavalry, and guerrilla forces against the British armies. By autumn those British who had not moved north to Virginia with Cornwallis were pocketed in a small area about Charleston, South Carolina.

Battle of Yorktown.   Meanwhile, in 1780 the French dispatched an army of 5500 men under an able soldier, the Count de Rochambeau, to aid Washington. These troops encamped at Newport, while Rochambeau and Washington waited to see what success collaborative effort would bring. The Count de Grasse, a brilliant French naval commander with a well-equipped squadron, had arrived in the West Indies.

After an exchange of correspondence, de Grasse decided that his squadron could attack more successfully in the Chesapeake than in the harbor of New York, so a decision was made for a coordinated land and sea attack in Virginia, where Cornwallis' army, supplemented by troops under the turncoat Benedict Arnold, was being engaged by forces led by French general Lafayette. Washington and Rochambeau began to move their armies southward, a maneuver which the British believed was a feint to catch them off guard in New York, where they expected the main attack to take place.

With de Grasse controlling the Chesapeake Bay area and with a French and American force of 15,000 men surrounding Cornwallis' camp on the York peninsula, Cornwallis was doomed. He surrendered on October 19, 1781. As his men marched out to lay down their arms, a band played "The World Turned Upside Down." When the news of Yorktown reached Britain, the king's ministers agreed that peace must be made with the rebellious colonies.

The War in Retrospect.   The war had been a strange and at times hopeless one for the Americans. But Washington had emerged as a persistent, determined leader. He may have lacked brilliance as a military tactician, but he had the courage, integrity, and character essential to successful command. Despite the demoralization of his forces by lack of supplies, by desertions, and occasionally by mutinies, he held on until the Americans, with French help, achieved victory.

British incompetence played a part in the eventual outcome of the war. Without the assistance that British commanders—Howe and Clinton, particularly—unwittingly gave the patriots, the end might have been different. It was the good fortune of America that Great Britain had been engaged in a world war, and that some of its best troops and more competent commanders were in India, Africa, the West Indies, and elsewhere.

Although a few young Frenchmen like Lafayette came to America to fight for the patriots out of sheer idealism, the alliance of the Bourbon powers, France and Spain, against Great Britain was not motivated by love of liberty or of the republican principles so nobly stated in the Declaration of Independence. By a trick of fate, these very principles of liberty would exercise an enormous influence in France within a few years and would overturn the French monarchy. But in the conflict between the colonies and Great Britain, France was merely playing the game

of power politics. It hoped to wreak revenge on an ancient enemy and perhaps to regain some of the American territory it had lost.

Spain also had an interest in territory west of the British possessions in North America. To weaken Great Britain's strength in the New World would provide possible opportunities for later aggrandizement there for both France and Spain. A weak and struggling republic without money and friends would be easy to dominate and perhaps to devour.

France had promised its satellite, Spain, that it would help wrest Gibraltar from the British, but had attacked Gibraltar in vain. Now France proposed to appease Spain with territory west of the Appalachians. In the peace negotiations, which had begun even before Yorktown, the disposition of western territories was a critical consideration.

The Peace of Paris, 1783.   To negotiate a peace with England, Congress appointed five commissioners: Benjamin Franklin, envoy in France; John Jay, American agent in Spain; John Adams, envoy in Holland; Henry Laurens; and Thomas Jefferson. Only the first three, assembled at Paris, took an active part in the discussions. At the outset, Jay was suspicious of the motives of the Count de Vergennes, the French foreign minister, and of the British agent, Richard Oswald. Oswald had come with instructions to treat with the commissioners as if they represented rebellious colonies. Jay insisted that Oswald go back and obtain new instructions to treat with the representatives of the "Thirteen United States," which would be tantamount to recognizing at the outset the independence of the new republic. This Oswald did.

Although the commissioners had received from Congress full power to negotiate the best treaty possible, Congress had specifically instructed them to take no steps that France would not approve. Since Jay was convinced that France was determined to sacrifice American interests to satisfy Spain, he persuaded Adams and Franklin to deal secretly with England and to make a preliminary treaty that promised favorable terms.

The news leaked out and Vergennes was incensed, but Franklin, a great favorite of the French, managed to placate him by admitting that their action was merely an "indiscretion." Nevertheless, the preliminary treaty had established the pattern for the final treaty, which was signed on September 3, 1783.

Great Britain, partly to sow dissension between the Bourbon allies and partly to win the friendship of the late colonies and keep them from becoming satellites of France, offered such favorable terms that Vergennes in anger declared that the English were ready to "buy peace rather than make it." Instead of letting Spain have the trans-Appalachian region, Great Britain agreed that the Mississippi should be the western boundary of the United States. Although Franklin had tried to obtain all of Canada "to insure peace," it was agreed that the Great Lakes should determine the northern border. In the end, Great Britain gave the Floridas back to Spain, and the treaty set the southern border of the United States at 31° north latitude. The provisions of the treaty seemed clear, but in some areas the boundary lines were not stated precisely. In Maine (at that time still part of Massachusetts) the border remained in dispute for years.

The treaty also provided that American citizens were to enjoy the same fishing rights in Canadian waters as British subjects. The two countries agreed that the Mississippi River would be forever open to navigation by both American and British shipping. The British demanded restitution of Loyalist property confiscated during the war, but all Congress could do was to recommend that this be done. Since Congress had no authority over the states, it was agreed that suits might be brought by British subjects in the state courts for the recovery of debts. The Treaty of Paris was ratified by Congress on January 14 of the next year, 1784.

EFFECTS OF THE WAR

Unrestricted Trade.   Wars traditionally result in social and financial upheavals, and the American Revolution was no exception. Within the twenty years of controversy and war, old and settled traditions were altered, and the patterns of a new society emerged.

No longer were the American colonies the source of raw materials supplied exclusively to Great Britain. Dutch, French, Spanish, and Portuguese ships could slip into American ports and load tobacco, wheat, corn, meat, rice, and other products needed in Europe. Despite the war—even as a result of it—some American merchants made more money than ever before, and some European commodities, received in exchange for produce, were more abundant during the war than previously.

A few fortunes were made by war profiteers, but, more important, a network of colonial merchants experienced the challenges and problems of unrestricted trade on an international scale. Patriotism did not keep some dealers from making 200 or 300 percent profit on clothing and supplies needed by the Continental soldiers. New industries, particularly war industries, developed. Iron foundries multiplied. Gunsmiths flourished, and factories for the manufacture of muskets, gunpowder, and cannon were built, particularly in New England and in Pennsylvania. Since the usual trade in English woolens and other fabrics was cut off, cloth making was encouraged.

The Westward Movement.   With the elimination of the prohibition against movement into the trans-Appalachian region that the British had tried to enforce after 1763, fresh migrations began. Frontiersmen were soon filtering into valleys and clearings beyond the mountains. In 1776 Virginia had organized into a county a portion of what later became the state of Kentucky. Before the Revolution, frontiersmen from Virginia had settled on the Watauga River in what became Tennessee. After the Revolution, uprooted citizens and restless souls all along the frontier began a trek west that would continue until one day the American continent as far west as the Pacific would be occupied. Land companies were organized, and within a few years speculation in western lands became an obsession.

Modifications of American Society. Socially, the Revolution brought changes too. The most immediate result was the elimination of royal governors, other British officials, and the cliques of socially elite that gathered about them. Even in colonies that had had no royal officials, those who were subservient to the mother country were swept out and new leaders took their places.

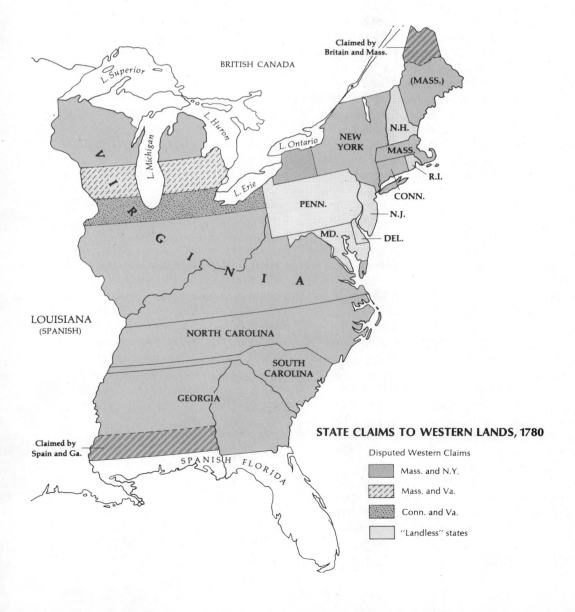

STATE CLAIMS TO WESTERN LANDS, 1780

Disputed Western Claims

Mass. and N.Y.

Mass. and Va.

Conn. and Va.

"Landless" states

Yet as important as these changes were, the United States nowhere experienced the kind of social revolution that swept France a few years later. The structure of American society was modified rather than radically altered. In Virginia, for example, the influence of the tidewater aristocrats diminished somewhat, and back-country politicians of the type represented by Patrick Henry gained power. But the families that had produced leaders before the Revolution still continued to supply many of the leaders·in the new nation.

One reason the new republic moved with relative ease from the status of a colony to that of a self-governing nation was the tradition of local responsibility established in all of the colonies early in the development of the British settlements. This inheritance from the British tradition of local self-government ensured a reservoir of leadership from which individuals could be drawn for any level of responsibility required.

The Articles of Confederation. Soon after the Declaration of Independence, a committee was appointed to draw up Articles of Confederation to bind the thirteen states together into a union. It took more than a year to draft the Articles, and they then had to be submitted to the states for ratification. This took until the spring of 1781.

In the meantime—during almost the entire war—the rebel colonies operated under the authority of the extralegal Continental Congress.

Among the most important contributions of the Articles were their preservation of the union and their definition of powers to be granted to the central government as opposed to the state governments. The operation of the Articles, together with the formation and operation of state governments, is more properly the subject of Chapter 5 on the postwar period.

The delay in ratifying the Articles of Confederation was due chiefly to a conflict of economic interests. Massachusetts, Connecticut, New York, Virginia, Georgia, and the Carolinas—under the terms of colonial charters, royal grants, Indian treaties, or proprietary claims—asserted ownership of tremendous grants of lands in the West. To be able to retain these western lands would be a great economic boon since the sale of the back regions would provide the state governments with a steady income and make it unnecessary for them to tax their citizens at all.

Naturally the advantage that would come to states with western land claims was resented by the states with fixed boundaries. They protested that the War for Independence was being fought for the benefit of all and that every state should share in the rewards to be found in western territory. Thus these landless states were reluctant to sign the Articles of Confederation until the westward limits of the existing states were set and until Congress, the central government, was given authority to grant lands and to create new states beyond these limits.

The debate was not motivated entirely by the question of the equality of the states. Land speculators had formed companies in Maryland and Pennsylvania, for example, and had made purchases from the Indians in the Ohio valley. Now they wished governmental validation of their titles. How could they secure clear title to land claimed by Virginia and New York when such states were inclined not to recognize the Indian purchases made by out-of-state residents?

Eventually, after considerable political maneuvering and propagandizing, both sides gave in. Between 1777 and 1781 the land companies vacated their claims to western territory purchased from the Indians, and upon recommendation of a congressional committee in 1780, the landed states, led by Virginia, New York, and Connecticut, gave up claim to most of the trans-Appalachian country, thus making the western lands the territory of the nation. In February 1781 the last of the landless states, Maryland, ratified the Articles, and on March 1 the Confederation was formally proclaimed. The problem of western lands was now placed squarely before the new central government (see Chapter 5).

When the war was over, many thoughtful citizens throughout the country feared that the loose provisions of the Articles of Confederation would not permit the evolution of a nation strong enough to survive. For example, in foreign policy much would depend upon the power of a centralized authority. Furthermore, a central authority was required to establish the financial stability of the nation and to deal with problems of credit, the issuance of money, and the maintenance of national defense. These problems and their solution would form an important chapter in constitution making.

A final word should be said about the American Revolution not only as a symbol in the history of the United States but as a guiding light for generations of people the world over. As the first anti-imperialist, anti-monarchial revolution of modern times, the American Revolution inspired imitators in Europe and Latin America in the nineteenth century and in Africa and Asia in the twentieth. The principles of revolution—government by consent of the governed, and inviolate rights that no government can invade—spoke to the hearts and minds of people in other nations. The fact was and is that the American Revolution is not exportable: Other people and other nations are the products of their own particular circumstances and experience. But the language, idealism, and ideas—these have taken on a life of their own.

BIBLIOGRAPHY

The most comprehensive studies of the settlement of the English colonies in America are Charles M. Andrews, *The Colonial Period of American History,* 4 vols. (New Haven: Yale University Press, 1934–38), Herbert Levi Osgood, *The American Colonies in the Seventeenth Century,* 3 vols., and Osgood, *The American Colonies in the Eighteenth Century,* 4 vols. (Gloucester, Mass.: Smith, 1957). Lawrence H. Gipson, *The British Empire Before the American Revolution,* 15 vols., rev ed. (New York: Knopf, 1958–65), views the colonies within the framework of the whole empire. For the discoveries, see David P. Quinn, *England and the Discovery of America, 1481–1620* (New York: Harper and Row, 1974).

Useful single-volume treatments of the colonial development are Curtis P. Nettels, *The Roots of American Civilization,* 2nd ed. (New York: Appleton-Century-Crofts, 1963), Louis B. Wright, *The Atlantic Frontier* (Ithaca, N.Y.: Cornell University Press, 1963), Clarence L. Ver Steeg, *The Formative Years* (New York: Hill & Wang, 1964), and David Hawke, *The Colonial Experience* (Indianapolis: Bobbs-Merrill, 1966). For the Spanish colonies, see Charles Gipson, *Spain in America* (New York: Harper and Row, 1966).

Excellent biographical material is to be found in Samuel E. Morison, *Builders of the Bay Colony* (Boston: Houghton Mifflin, 1963). Important studies of New England communities include Richard Bushman, *From Puritan to Yankee* (Cambridge: Harvard University Press, 1967), Sumner C.

Powell, *Puritan Village* (Middletown, Conn.: Wesleyan University Press, 1970), and Kenneth A. Lockridge, *A New England Town* (New York: Norton, 1970). Perry Miller, *Orthodoxy in Massachusetts 1630–1650* (New York: Harper & Row, 1970), is a valuable introduction to the religious history of the Puritans. Miller's *The New England Mind: From Colony to Province* and *The New England Mind: The Seventeenth Century* (Cambridge: Harvard University Press, 1953, 1954), are accounts of Puritan theology. A revised account is Robert Middlekauff, *The Mathers* (New York: Oxford University Press, 1971). For education, see Lawrence Cremin, *American Experience: The Colonial Experience* (New York: Harper and Row, 1970).

For information about family structure and demography see John Demos, *A Little Commonwealth* (New York: Oxford University Press, 1971), and Philip Greven, *Four Generations* (Ithaca, N.Y.: Cornell University Press, 1969). Winthrop D. Jordan, *White over Black* (Baltimore: Penguin Books, 1969), describes attitudes of white colonists toward blacks, as does Peter Wood, *Black Majority* (New York: Knopf, 1974), while studies of Indian-white relations include Verner W. Crane, *The Southern Frontier* (Ann Arbor: University of Michigan Press, 1956), George T. Hunt, *The Wars of the Iroquois* (Madison: University of Wisconsin Press, 1960), and Alden Vaughan, *New England Frontier: Indians and Puritans 1620–1675* (Boston: Little, Brown,

1965). See also Wilcomb E. Washburn, *The Indians in America* (New York: Harper and Row, 1975).

Establishment of all the Southern colonies except Georgia is treated in Wesley F. Craven, *The Southern Colonies in the Seventeenth Century* (Baton Rouge: Louisiana State University Press, 1949). Richard L. Morton, *Colonial Virginia*, 2 vols., (Charlottesville: The University Press of Virginia, 1960), is a recent and detailed treatment. A study of the transit of English social ideas to Virginia is Louis B. Wright, *The First Gentlemen of Virginia* (Charlottesville: The University Press of Virginia, 1964), and of slavery in Virginia, Edmund S. Morgan, *American Slavery, American Freedom: The Ordeal of Colonial Virginia* (New York: Norton, 1975). Edward McCrady, *The History of South Carolina Under the Proprietary Government 1670–1720* (New York: Russell & Russell reprint of 1899 ed.), is a detailed account, and Samuel A. Ashe, *History of North Carolina*, 2 vols. (Greensboro, N.C.: Van Noppen reprint of 1925 ed.), gives considerable space to the colonial period. More recent are Hugh T. Lefter and Albert R. Newsome, *North Carolina*, rev. ed. (Chapel Hill: University of North Carolina Press, 1963), and E. Merton Coulter, *Georgia*, 2nd ed. (Chapel Hill: University of North Carolina Press, 1960). Alexander C. Flick, ed., *History of the State of New York*, 10 vols. in 5 (Albany: State University of New York Press, 1933–37), is a synthesis of material on the subject. For material on Pennsylvania see Gary B. Nash, *Quakers and Politics* (Princeton: Princeton University Press, 1968).

For the structure of eighteenth-century colonial politics see Patricia Bonomi, *A Factious People: Politics and Society in Colonial New York* (New York: Columbia University Press, 1971), Charles S. Sydnor, *American Revolutionaries in the Making* (New York: Free Press, 1965), and Bernard Bailyn, *The Origins of American Politics* (New York: Random House, 1970). Carl L. Becker, *The Declaration of Independence* (New York: Knopf, 1942), and Bernard Bailyn, *The Ideological Origins of the American Revolution* (Cambridge:

Harvard University Press, 1967), discuss ideas leading up to independence, as does Michael Kammen in *People of Paradox* (New York: Random House, 1972), while political aspects of those years are covered in Lawrence H. Gipson, *The Coming of the American Revolution 1763–1775* (New York: Harper & Row, 1954), Edmund S. Morgan and Helen M. Morgan, *The Stamp Act Crisis* (New York: Macmillan, 1963), Edmund S. Morgan, *The Birth of the Republic 1763–1789* (Chicago: University of Chicago Press, 1956), and Allan Nevins, *The American States During and After the Revolution 1775–1798* (Clifton, N.J.: Kelley reprint of 1924 ed.).

Among the informative books on Loyalists are the following: Mary Beth Norton, *The British-Americans: The Loyalist Exiles in England, 1774–1789* (Boston: Little, Brown, 1972); William Nelson, *The American Tory* (New York: Oxford University Press, 1961); and Robert Calhoon, *The Loyalists in Revolutionary America* (New York: Harcourt, 1973). See as well Pauline Meiers, *From Resistance to Revolution* (New York: Random House, 1972). The British-Colonial contest for authority is ably developed in Jack P. Greene, *The Quest for Power* (Chapel Hill, N.C.: U. of North Carolina Press, 1963). A useful survey is Evarts B. Greene, *The Revolutionary Generation 1763–1790*, ed. Arthur M. Schlesinger and Dixon R. Fox (New York: Watts, 1971). Piers Mackesy, *The War for America* (Cambridge: Harvard University Press, 1964), surveys the campaigns of the Revolution. See as well Howard Peckham, *The War for Independence* (Chicago: University of Chicago Press, 1958) and John Shy, *Toward Lexington* (Princeton: Princeton University Press, 1965). Jackson T. Main describes the social contests and conflict of the Revolution in *The Social Structure of the American Revolution* (Princeton: Princeton University Press, 1965). A more recent version of Revolutionary politics is Jack N. Rakov, *The Beginnings of National Politics* (New York: Knopf, 1979). For an overall synthesis, see Gordon Wood, *The Creation of the American Republic* (Chapel Hill, N.C.: University of North Carolina Press, 1969).

Time Line

2

THE YOUNG REPUBLIC

The first four decades of American life after the Revolution were important decades—years in which the work of independence was completed, the Republic shaped, the national character determined, the federal system established, and a foreign policy developed. This was a period of important events and crucial decisions, yet we have no good name for it. It was dominated by no single great figure, but by several. This era exhibits no internal consistency, for during these years everything that was done was being done for the first time. If it could be characterized at all, it might be called a period of precedents.

The problems faced by the postrevolutionary generation were considerable and urgent. Solutions had to be found or compromises made swiftly if the Republic was to survive. The new nation was, of course, not yet a nation at all, but thirteen separate societies, settled at different times by people with different aims, backgrounds, even dialects. During the Revolution these "thirteen clocks" (as John Adams called them) had indeed "struck as one." But the question now was whether *E Pluribus Unum*—"One Out of Many," the motto placed on the Great Seal in 1776 — could be made to come true.

Although the colonists had called themselves the "Thirteen United States of Ameri-

ca" in their Declaration of Independence and although the new nation now had symbols, legends, heroes, monuments, flags, and celebrations, it was not yet a "people," as the era used the word. Its sense of identity would derive from none of these but rather from the belief that, as James Madison wrote, "the *people*, not the government, possess the absolute sovereignty." On this fragile premise the postwar leaders had first of all to construct a new, viable political system, based on a somewhat dubious trust in the ability and integrity of the average citizen.

Visitors to the new nation in the years after the war found this trust difficult to understand. The United States was defiantly *not* like England or the Continent (which made it puzzling enough), and its principles and aims, in terms of the old order, simply did not seem to make sense. In the light of contemporary judgments, there was not much reason to believe that the United States would succeed.

The majority of American leaders, however, faced the future with vigor and confidence. They began with certain advantages, as the astute French traveler Alexis de Tocqueville observed, in "that the American arrived at a state of democracy without having to endure a democratic revolution, and that he is free without having to become so." Americans did not have to destroy a feudal society in order to evolve a new one. The country began its existence without hereditary royalty, a standing army, or an entrenched aristocracy. Americans had committed themselves to a certain kind of nation, based on a belief in progress, natural rights, and rationality. The full intellectual strength of two generations of Americans was focused on the problem of achieving a society whose goal, in Jefferson's words, was to be nothing less than "the happiness of associated man."

Postwar leaders joined forces, then, as William Miller phrased it at the time, "to make liberty a *practical* principle, and to *prove* it." (Miller was using *prove* in the sense of *test*—to see if it worked.) However much these leaders may have argued about the *means* of realizing the principles of the Revolution, none wished to undo it. Successful self-government by a sovereign people, they believed, rested on the maintenance of the essential freedoms embodied in the new Constitution and its Bill of Rights: freedom of speech and assembly (including a free press); limitation of the government's power to control the lives of its citizens; equal privilege and protection under the laws.

But these were ideals, not reality. The present necessity, all agreed, was to strike the proper balance between the two extremes which the Constitution came to represent. How well they, and the generations that followed them, have succeeded is the central thread of American history.

America's "bold and sublime experiment," as Thomas Paine called it in *Common Sense,* could not be conducted in a vacuum. There were urgent issues of foreign policy to be debated and settled as the United States took its place in the company of nations. The War of 1812 tested for the first time the question of the country's position vis-à-vis foreign wars. Should America be neutral? Could it be, when the outcome might irrevocably affect its future? The Monroe Doctrine represented the beginnings of the nation's long search for security, independence, and equality in its international relations.

In domestic policy there were other turning points. During the 1790s the Supreme Court considered itself a quasi-governmental economic force, whose aim, Justice Samuel Chase said, was to protect the rights of property, "for the protection whereof the government was established." But John Marshall made the Court literally supreme, in its check on the executive and legislative branches of government, and its assumption of the right to interpret the Constitution.

Given the precarious state of the Republic, its self-confidence was remarkable. The postrevolutionary generation felt that its example might provide the spark to activate an age of revolutions, toppling all other existing forms of government in the Western world. Jefferson found it "impossible not to be sensible that we are acting for all mankind."

No period in American history, perhaps, exhibited more ebullience—yet these Americans were realistic, too. They hoped to create a free, just, and equal society, but they knew the frailties of human nature (their own included) and were well aware of the limitations of human will and knowledge. Those who sought to make a society that guaranteed the rights of life, liberty, and property also followed a policy of conquest against the Indian, protected (in common with other nations) a system of slavery that refused those rights to a sizable segment of the population, and maintained (also in common with other nations) a system that limited those rights for their mothers, wives, and daughters.

Not surprisingly, historians have made, and continue to make, differing assessments of the people and events of these years. The nationalist historians of the early nineteenth century, to whom the concept of class conflict was unknown, drew the Founding Fathers in primary colors as statesmen of more than mortal wisdom. Some nineteenth-century historians saw the Constitution as a temporary victory of nationalism over sectionalism; others as the climax of the Revolution. Still others saw it as the attempt of a counterrevolutionary minority to curb the powers of the majority. In the twentieth century some have seen it as motivated primarily by economic self-interest, others as the product of consensus among men whose differences were not so great as they had formerly seemed.

In the same way, views of the War of 1812 have shifted over the years. Nineteenth-century interpreters tended to accept Madison's claim that it was fought to preserve the national honor and guarantee America's maritime rights. Later historians saw it, in part at least, as an imperialist push toward acquisition of Canada and Spanish America or as a means for the new Western states to protect and extend their frontiers—by defeating both the Indians and England.

From the vantage point of two hundred years of subsequent experience, one can easily find flaws in what the postrevolutionary generation planned and failures in what it did. But it is only just to recognize that these men did not have the tools and concepts of modern anthropology and psychology to deal with their social problems and that the techniques of modern political and social research were not available to them. That is to say, in effect, that the Founding Fathers were products of their times—possessed of the same biases and virtues, the same blindness and perceptions that human nature is heir to in any time and place.

Yet the goal they set for their new nation still remains one of dazzling promise. If their reach exceeded their grasp, what they accomplished should not be disparaged just as it should not be overpraised. They *did* make a nation, against great odds and out of great principles, which they hoped would be, as Jefferson called it, "the last best hope of mankind."

TO THINK ABOUT AS YOU READ . . .

1. Historians have long called the 1780s the "critical period" of American history. How would the nation have developed if the Philadelphia convention had *revised* the Articles of Confederation instead of writing a new document? What if the states had failed to ratify the Constitution?
2. Congress forbade slavery in the Northwest Territory in 1787, stopped the importation of slaves into the United States in 1808, and banned slavery in much of the Louisiana Purchase in 1819. Why did Congress find such legislation possible in these years but not in 1850 or 1860?
3. British historians have pointed out that Americans in 1812 might better have fought against Napoleon, who —in their opinion—was a much greater threat to the peace and liberty of the contemporary world than England. Why do you think that the Americans did *not* fight France? Were the grievances against the British sufficient to justify war? Were other alternatives open to the American government?
4. In the light of our contemporary racial theory and the tremendous surge of population westward during that period, can you suggest practical alternative policies toward the Indian problem that Congress and the states might have developed?
5. Europeans have long considered Americans the most nationalistic people in the Western world, most thoroughly convinced of their historical importance and ultimate destiny. Can you trace the development of this trait (if such it be) in the latter years of the eighteenth and the earlier decades of the nineteenth century? Is it characteristic of us today? If so, why? If not, why not?

Chapter 4

The Emergence of a National Culture

THE DEVELOPMENT OF AN AMERICAN CREDO

A Time of Optimism and Pride. The period between 1783 and 1824 was a time of extraordinary political, economic, and social revolution. This was the age which saw the close of the American Revolution, the ratification of the Constitution, and the development of the two-party system of government. It was the age of George Washington and Thomas Jefferson, of the Louisiana Purchase and the Lewis and Clark expedition, of the War of 1812 and the growth of textile and iron industries, of Henry Clay and John C. Calhoun, of the Missouri Compromise and the Monroe Doctrine. In Europe it was the age of the French Revolution and the rise and fall of Napoleon, of the Romantic Movement, and of the Industrial Revolution.

In launching a new system of government, Americans looked ahead with a strong sense of hope and experiment. They were optimistic about the future, for they had no significant record of failure to disillusion them. They were impatient of "established" institutions or traditions, for they had just established

some of their own and disestablished a good many British ones. Though the society did not grant the Declaration's "unalienable rights" to free blacks, slaves, and Indians, or full political and social equality to women or to all classes, nonetheless—thoughtful Americans believed—it afforded more freedom to its citizens than any other society.

This pride in what they had accomplished, joined to their anti-British feelings, made Americans aggressively self-confident. Triumphant in their newly won independence, they became less aware of their social, cultural, and religious indebtedness to Great Britain. Having rejected all the prejudices, superstitions, and errors of the Old World, so Americans felt, they were ready to outdistance it in every sector.

American Nationalism. Several events favored the growth of American nationalism. For one thing, many democratic and humanitarian tendencies were accentuated or set in motion. During the Revolution and the early national period large Loyalist estates were confiscated and divided. Small businesses and manufacturing were stimulated. Church establishments were attacked. Slavery, imprisonment for debt, and humiliating punishments were regarded with growing disfavor. The idea of universal education at state expense was voiced. Americans were far from being of one mind about these matters, but they did believe that they could, by honest effort and the fortunate circumstances of their society, forge ahead in ways that the nations of the Old World could not. The Americans were a "new" people, as Crèvecoeur put it. They were ready to teach the rest of the world and were no longer content to be taught.

Indeed, Americans considered the United States to be superior to England and Europe in every way. It was, they hoped, the model of a new kind of New World. "Americans are fanatically proud of their own wild country," remarked an English traveler during the period, "and love to disparage the rest of the world." It was America's mission to lead other nations to revolution against the forces of ignorance and oppression or, as Joel Barlow wrote, "to excite emulation throughout the kingdoms of the earth, and meliorate the conditions of the human race." It was America's responsibility to extend the concepts of liberty, equality, and justice over all the earth. This responsibility, said James Wilson at the Constitutional Convention, was "the great design of Providence in regard to this globe."

In order to accomplish this mission, Americans felt compelled to cultivate their Americanness, emphasize their differences with Europe, and develop their own culture in terms of their own national purpose. "Every engine should be employed to render the people of the country national," wrote Noah Webster, "to call their attachment home to their own country." If the United States was to succeed as an experiment in self-government, the people who governed themselves must have deep faith in it. The patriotic impulse was considered essential to the creation of a national character.

THE FRAMEWORK OF THE AMERICAN MIND

The structure of ideas within which Americans achieved their independence was provided by the two great intellectual movements embodied in the Age of Reason and the Age of Romanticism. The United States itself, almost purely a creation of the eighteenth century, emerged at a time when the Western world was shifting from one system of thought to another, the two involving quite different views of human nature, the world, and the deity.

Adapting the Enlightenment. The American colonies were children of the Age of Reason, or the "Enlightenment." (See Chapter 1 for an earlier discussion.) John Locke, an English philosopher, probably wrote a charter for the Carolinas. Rousseau and Montesquieu were friends of Franklin. Sir Isaac Newton and Cotton Mather were contemporaries. Voltaire was still living when the Continental Congress signed the Declaration of Independence. It was the Enlightenment, not the Puritanism of New England, that provided the first *national* pattern of American thought.

The Age of Reason rested upon three principles: the possibility of human *perfectibility*, the inevitability of *progress*, and the effectiveness of *reason*. It emphasized the scientific method over the theological, reason over faith, skepticism over tradition and authoritarianism. The thinkers of the Enlightenment believed that humans could subject themselves, their society, the past, and the universe itself to rational analysis. In this way they could discover general laws that would supply them with precise, definitive explanations of human and natural activity. With this knowledge, they could so direct their energies and construct their institutions that their progress would be swift and sure. The Americans who chose the path of revolution, and who, after its successful conclusion, accepted the challenge of making a new nation on new principles, reflected these attitudes.

There was an American Enlightenment, but it was late, eclectic, and singularly American. Eighteenth-century America was not merely an extension or a reflection of contemporary Britain or Europe. First of all, there was a culture lag in the transmission of patterns of thinking from one side of the Atlantic to the other. The Founding Fathers worked with ideas fifty to one hundred years old by European standards, developed on another continent for different purposes—and mixed them with latter borrowings and adaptations. The Romanticists—Goethe, Wordsworth, Coleridge, Schiller, and Kant—were writing at nearly the same time that Americans were still quoting the leaders of the Age of Reason—Newton, Locke, and Montesquieu.

Second, Americans chose from British and European thought only those ideas they needed, or those in which they had special interest. They adopted Locke's justification of a century-old English revolution as vindication of their own, for example, and used French "radicalism," aimed at Gallic kings, to overthrow a tyranny that really did not exist. The Americans thus bent the Enlightenment to American uses.

The Professionalization of Science. The intellectual impact of the Enlightenment manifested itself most clearly in the advancement of American science in the late eighteenth century. The colonies had been settled in the scientific age of Galileo and Newton. American intellectuals were never far from the center of the great scientific revolution that marked the European Enlightenment, and, like other educated people of their times, lived by contemporary scientific attitudes. They believed that all problems would respond to scientific investigation. Deriving their view from Newtonian science, they saw the universe as mechanistic, governed by constant natural laws which were discoverable by human reason. They believed that all knowledge was fundamentally scientific and that the inductive method of thinking was quite possibly the only trustworthy method of arriving at truth. From science, the leaders of American thought believed they might find solutions to the problems of human society.

The Revolution suspended practically all scientific activity. But immediately after it, as Dr. Amos Eaton, himself a scientist, wrote, "A thirst for natural science seemed to pervade the United States like the progress of an epidemic." The nation was especially fortunate in receiving a number of brilliant immigrants and refugees during and after the war. Thomas Cooper, geologist and economist, came from England, as did Joseph Priestley, one of the world's greatest chemists; Pierre du Pont de Nemours, a noted chemist, arrived from France. Meanwhile, the United States possessed a number of highly competent scientists among its native-born. President Jefferson was a scientist of repute himself, and the Lewis and Clark expedition which he sent westward in 1804 was one of the most significant scientific projects in American history.

Though long neglected by the colleges and universities, the study of science began to appear in the curriculum, usually as astronomy, chemistry, or physics. Indeed, science itself was becoming a profession rather than a hobby for interested amateurs. The tremendous growth in the amount of scientific knowledge, and the equally great impact of that knowledge on contemporary life, meant that there was no longer a place for the "natural philosopher" who took all scientific knowledge as his province. The day of the academic jack-of-all-trades like Dr. Samuel Latham Mitchill of Columbia, who ranged through chemistry, medicine, mathematics, botany, zoology, and poetry, was nearly over.

American scientists readily admitted that they had made no major contributions to

On their expedition, Lewis and Clark took copious notes and observations of the flora and fauna of the new land. This page from their notebooks shows their notes on the Sage Grouse and a black-and-white pheasant they found in the Rocky Mountains.

scientific theory and that Europe and England still dominated the various fields. Yet their achievements were not negligible, especially in identifying and classifying the flora and fauna of their continent and in exploring the extent of its resources. And Americans were confident that their own great scientific contributions would inevitably come.

"The Best Mechanics in the World." While America had produced few scientists of

worldwide repute (always excepting Franklin), Americans were quick to apply scientific knowledge to practical ends. Born in the midst of the Industrial Revolution, the United States knew no other than a technological environment. The steam engine, the iron industry, the chemical revolution, and the discovery of electricity, for example, all preceded Yorktown. Americans embraced technology with great enthusiasm. Machinery, wrote Salmon P. Chase, "is an almost infinite power. It is in modern times by far the most efficient cause of human improvement, producing almost unmingled benefit, to an amount and extent of which we have as yet but a very faint conception."

Technology was particularly important to a new nation that needed to catch up with the rest of the industrialized world. One of Congress' first acts in 1790 was to pass a patent law, and the first patent went to a process for making potassium carbonate, essential to the glassmaking industry. By 1830 the United States Patent Office was issuing annually four times as many patents as were being issued in England. Foreign visitors often commented on "Yankee ingenuity." Americans, a French observer wrote, "are the best mechanics in the world . . . , engineers from birth." The country had ample power, unparalleled natural resources, and a chronic shortage of labor. A stream of new processes and new machines supplied the missing element needed for an efficient, productive society.

When the country needed something done, somebody quickly invented or adapted a machine, tool, or technique to do it. Examples are too numerous to list, but the iron I-beam, the copying lathe, the breechloading rifle, the iron plow, the electromagnet, the milling machine, the miner's lamp, the compound steam engine, Portland cement, the screw propeller, the stone-crusher, the high-speed steam printing press, insulated wire, wire nails, the spinning mule, the ice refrigerator,

The steam engine was just one of the many technologies that helped the new nation cope with a chronic labor shortage. Besides powering boats, such as Robert Fulton's Paragon, *shown in this watercolor, steam engines were used to power many newly invented factory machines.*

canned food, the railroad T-rail—to name a few—were all in use before 1830. These, and many other technologies like them, had immediate economic value and powerful influence on the way Americans lived and worked.

The New England textile industry is a case in point. The area had plenty of water power, good transportation, and a labor shortage. Before 1800 cloth was made almost wholly by hand. After 1820 it was made almost wholly by machinery. Cheap factory-made cloth of good quality had effects in the home, in

society, in the domestic market, and in world trade. This example could be duplicated in a hundred other cases.

The Arrival of Romanticism. The rise of Romanticism disturbed the orderly patterns of the Age of Reason. During the latter years of the eighteenth century, philosophers and critics in America and Europe became increasingly uncomfortable within the framework of thought erected earlier by Newton, Locke, and Pope. They were no longer content with a rationalism and classicism which, it seemed to them, had hardened into traditionalism. Thinkers on both sides of the Atlantic began to question seriously some of the attitudes of the Enlightenment and to alter their conceptions of nature, human nature, and society.

Many of these "Romantic" ideas were not new, nor were they ever assimilated into a unified system. But the climate of opinion that characterized the intellectual activity in both America and Europe from the closing decades of the eighteenth century to the middle of the nineteenth was coherent and consistent enough to warrant calling the period the Age of Romanticism.

The Romantic view of society rested on three general concepts. First, it rested on the idea of *organism*— of wholes, or units, with their own internal laws of governance and development. A society had a life of its own, a "national spirit," a "national destiny." Second, it rested on the idea of *dynamism*, of motion and growth. Institutions and beliefs were assumed to be fluid, changing, capable of improvement and adaptation. The age had a dislike of finality. Third, it rested on the idea of *diversity*—the value of differences in opinions, cultures, tastes, societies, and characters—as opposed to the value of uniformity of the Enlightenment.

To the Age of Reason, conformity meant rationalism. Diversity meant irrationality, and therefore error. To the Age of Romanticism, consensus seemed less important than individual judgments. It was "natural" and "right" for things and people and ideas and societies *not* to be all alike.

Those who fought the Revolution, wrote the Constitution, and set the Republic on its way were largely products of the Age of Reason and derived their intellectual inspiration from it. The next generation of leaders were shaped less by the Enlightenment than by Romanticism. What Americans thought about their country, their arts, and the organization of their political and social relationships, as well as about themselves and the natural world around them, was powerfully influenced in the early 1800s by this new set of ideas.

The Secularization of Theology. At the time of the Revolution there were approximately three thousand churches in the United States. The majority of these were Calvinist and belonged to the Presbyterians and Congregationalists, whose differences lay less in creed than in matters of church government. The Anglican Church was seriously divided by the Revolution, supplying, on the one hand, the largest number of Loyalists of any church and, on the other hand, the majority of the signers of the Declaration of Independence.

The Methodists, whose first missionaries had arrived only in 1769, were growing rapidly, as were the Baptists, though both groups were still relatively small and dispersed. Lutheran and Reformed church membership lay chiefly in German- and Dutch-settled areas. The small Catholic population was concentrated primarily in Maryland. In 1782 there were still fewer than twenty-five priests in America. The first American bishop, Father John Carroll, was appointed in 1789.

During the Revolution the states immediately set about to establish proper relationships with the various churches. Each former colony had its own religious history, but it was plain that no single church could satisfy a diverse, expanding population that already worshipped under seventeen different creeds. The legislatures wisely chose to allow, as New York's did, "free enjoyment of the rights of conscience." The Continental Congress, and later the Constitutional Convention, reaffirmed the prevailing belief that religion, as Jefferson phrased it, was "a matter which lies solely between man and his God." Most of the state constitutions contained clauses or bills of rights guaranteeing freedom of worship on much the same terms as the federal Constitution.

This painting shows Samuel Slater's mill on the far side of the bridge crossing the Blackstone River in Pawtucket, Rhode Island. It was here that the first spinning frame was used, leading to the mass-production of cloth.

Also during the war years each legislature, in one way or another, with the exception of New Hampshire, Connecticut, and Massachusetts, provided for a clear separation of the churches from state authority. The Congregationalists in these states successfully resisted disestablishment for another thirty to fifty years. In Virginia, Jefferson saw the passage of the Statute for Religious Freedom in 1786, which he counted among his proudest accomplishments.

Nevertheless, there was still widespread doubt whether religious freedom and toleration could be fully extended to everyone. For full civil and political rights a number of states required religious tests or qualifications which discriminated against Catholics, Jews, and nonconformist Protestant sects. Most of these, however, had disappeared by 1830.

Ministers of the postwar years generally believed American Protestantism to be in a "low and declining state." The Presbyterian Assembly of 1798 noted "a general dereliction of religious principles and practice among our citizens." Congregations were often restive with authority and impatient of the old doctrines. In 1800 even the powerful Congregational and Presbyterian churches could count less than ten percent of the people of New England and the Middle Atlantic states as church members. All the major Protestant sects were split by argument and dissension. None of the older Calvinist groups, in fact, had been able to make the necessary adjustments to the great new surge of scientific information, and none had kept direct touch with the secular, optimistic, republican spirit of the time.

Nor was this all. The churches faced a threat in the form of a religious philosophical movement transported from England and Europe in the latter decades of the eighteenth century under the name of *deism*. (See Chapter 1 for an earlier discussion.) Rooted in the Enlightenment's faith in reason and science and closely in tune with the secular, rationalistic temper of the period, deism had a strong appeal to intellectual and political leaders such as Franklin, Jefferson, Paine, Joel Barlow, and Philip Freneau. Cutting away the twisted intricacies of Calvinistic doctrine, the deists proclaimed God's benevolence but His detachment from the running of the Universe. They also believed in human rationality, goodness, and free will, and in nature's order, harmony, and understandability. If people would but live by these beliefs, said Ethan Allen of Vermont, "they would . . . rid themselves of blindness and superstition, gain more exalted ideas of God, and make better members of society."

Against the deists the orthodox theologians put up a sturdy defense, but against the inroads of another "heresy," *unitarianism*, they had less success. Partly imported from England and partly the legacy of the Great Awakening of the early eighteenth century, unitarianism was so named because it rejected the idea of the Trinity and emphasized the human personality, rather than the divinity, of Jesus. "Liberal" unitarian doctrines, which assumed that most persons possessed the ability to discern religious truth, interested more and more orthodox Calvinist parishioners and ministers after 1790.

Harvard College, the traditional fortress of New England Calvinism, surrendered to the "liberals" in 1805. The "Conference of Liberal Ministers," called in 1820 to furnish leadership for those dissatisfied with Calvinistic orthodoxy, six years later became the American Unitarian Association. This association was a separate group of 125 churches, among them twenty of the oldest Calvinist churches in New England.

Frontier Evangelism. At the same time, there were indications, as early as the 1790s, that the religious evangelism of the Great Awakening might once again provide a revitalizing force within the orthodox Calvinist churches. The Methodists and Baptists especially produced a number of evangelist preachers, but revivalism was never really popular in Presbyterian and Congregational circles. On the frontier, however, the evangelists' simple, direct, and emotionally satisfying version of Christian faith was well suited to the needs of the pioneer community. There the camp meeting took on great importance, and by 1800 traveling preachers had spread revivalism through western Pennsylvania, Kentucky, Ohio, and Tennessee. Famous exhorters such as James McGready and Barton Stone, preaching a vivid religion of hellfire, rigid morality, and salvation, attracted huge crowds.

At the great Cane Ridge camp meeting of 1801 in Kentucky, between ten thousand and twenty thousand people heard forty evangelists preach over a six-day period. Such meetings spread across the country—Methodist Bishop Francis Asbury counted four hundred of them in 1811, chiefly in the South and West—and continued through the 1850s.

While frontier evangelism sometimes encouraged emotional excess, it helped bring stability and order to new communities, increased church membership, and gave churches great influence in social and political affairs. Calvinism itself was powerfully affected by the impact of this "second Great Awakening," which, in addition to exerting a strong democratizing force on religion, emphasized individual responsibility, morality, and social action. The new Romanticism, by reason of its insistence on the individual, the validity of human emotions, and the ability of the individual to make things better, also contributed significantly to the impetus of revivalism. From the religious enthusiasm generated by this "Awakening," churches became involved in reform causes such as temperance, social welfare, prison reform, and eventually the abolition of slavery.

Freedom and Equality: The Ideal. Thomas Jefferson put into the Declaration the phrase "all men are created equal," using the word *men* in the eighteenth-century sense of "any human being." Those who signed the Declaration apparently agreed that this was part of that body of "self-evident" truth enumerated in the document and supported by natural law. Equality and liberty, the Declaration implied, were coexistent. *Liberty* was the more easily defined; *equality* was more difficult, yet the need for defining its meaning was imperative.

Neither Puritans nor Virginians came to the colonies looking for equality. The company settlers were in search of more wealth, while the Puritans brought with them the elements of an aristocratic theology. Both carried to the new country many of the distinctions of the British social system.

But Calvinism also pointed in another direction: It rejected much of the church hierarchy, believed in the priesthood of all believers, and introduced elective methods into portions of church policy. Later, philosophers of the Enlightenment included the principle of equality within their listings of "natural rights," and John Locke and Jean Jacques Rousseau added wider dimensions to the term's meaning.

More important, however, the idea of equality had a strong practical basis in the American colonial experience. The wilderness stripped away the distinctions of civilization and put everyone on an equal footing. Indians, disease, starvation, and other hazards of frontier life killed an earl's or a tinker's child with equal disregard. The lack of fixed organization in a new society made it possible for Americans to be both free and equal in an actual, visible sense. Social mobility allowed them to change their status, within limits, rather rapidly. The rough equality forced on American society by the frontier was the most compelling fact about it.

Colonial and republican society, like England's, was built on stratifications which no one questioned. Everyone recognized, a Virginian wrote in 1760, that there were "differences of capacity, disposition, and virtue" among people, which divided them into classes. Yet these strata were broader and more vague than England's. Colonial society possessed the whole range of criteria for class distinctions, including wealth and property, dress, manners, speech, and education, but these carried less weight than they did abroad. There was not so much doffing of caps, bowing or curtseying, and pulling of forelocks; British General Carleton complained that it was hard to uphold "the dignity of the throne and peerage" in American society. Few foreign travelers failed to remark on the fluidity of American classes, much of it the result of broad economic opportunities offered by an expanding society.

The Social Problem. After 1783, when Americans faced the necessity of implementing the terms of the Declaration, almost every leader gave attention to the problem of equality and of how to make it an integral part of the new nation's life. Jefferson's "glittering generality," as John Adams called it, had provided an inspirational rallying cry for revolution but had not provided a practical definition for constructing a government in a disjointed postwar society. Some, like Fisher Ames, believed the doctrine "a pernicious tool of demagogues"; others, like Thomas Paine, thought it "one of the greatest of all truths" in political theory.

Franklin, while remarking that "Time, Chance, and Industry" created social and economic distinctions, believed that everyone was equal in "the personal securities of life and liberty." Jefferson and John Adams discussed the matter in their old age, concluding, in Jefferson's phrase, that there was a "natural aristocracy" of "virtue and talents," but that there was also an equality of rights belonging to all. (Or, as Nathaniel Ames said succinctly in his popular *Almanac*, "Men are by nature equal, but differ greatly in the sequel.")

Generally, the leaders of the postwar generation agreed that the new nation needed a government in which the better and more able governed, and also one in which the rights of all were equally protected and maintained. On this basis the nation began to build its society, with the implications of the term *equality* still to be explored more fully by future generations.

Thoughtful Americans were well aware that it was inconsistent to have slavery in a society based on "natural rights" and to wage a revolution to free people who held others in bondage. There was no dearth of opposition to slavery. Between 1776 and 1804 seven states passed legislation for emancipating slaves. Jefferson included an antislavery clause in his instructions to the Virginia delegates to the Continental Congress and tried unsuccessfully to place an antislavery provision in the Virginia constitution of 1776. Revolutionary leaders Charles Carroll and William Pinkney also unsuccessfully sponsored an antislavery bill in the Maryland legislature in 1789. But while slavery was a matter of legal condition, it was also a matter of race, which made a great difference when emancipation legislation and the black slave's future status in an overwhelmingly white society were discussed.

Theories of race were not well developed until the eighteenth century, when continuing contact with Indians and blacks forced Europeans to speculate about the different kinds of human beings, their origins, and their qualities. Eighteenth-century scientists, who arranged all life forms in systems, considered the different races as varieties of one human *species*. That species, created by God to occupy a particular place in the design of nature, existed within fixed, unchangeable limits. The varieties of races were the result of geography, climate, and other factors, which produced differences within the species but did not alter its boundaries. Beginning with the Biblical account of the creation of Adam, scientists postulated that at one time all humans had been alike but that different environments had changed them into members of related races, differing in color, size, hair, and other characteristics. Though color was not a wholly satisfactory criterion for identifying these varieties of human beings, it provided the most visible and logical basis for classifying them.

There were also those who believed—with Biblical support—that the different races were the result not of environmental influence but of a second creation. And later there were still others who believed that each race had originated in one of a series of separate creations. Whatever the theory, it was generally agreed that there were five biologically identifiable groups of humans: Caucasian or white; Mongolian or yellow; Malayan or brown; "American" or red; and Ethiopian or black. Whether or not these races were equal in abilities—or, if not, possessed the potential to be made so—became a question of major importance to the Enlightenment.

Some philosophers believed that since all people, whatever their color, were created as members of the same species, they had the same potentialities and, through education, favorable environment, and other means, could reach equality. Among the American writers who belonged to this school, one of the most influential was Professor (later President) Samuel Stanhope Smith of Princeton. Others disagreed, arguing that the races were separate and not necessarily equal. Thomas Jefferson, in *Notes on Virginia* (1786), took the view that certain races, particularly the red and the black, probably did not possess the proper potential for progressive change and that while their status might be improved, it was doubtful they could attain actual equality. He later modified his ideas, expressing the hope that blacks would someday be "on an equal footing with the other colors of the human family."

As the debate over race continued into the nineteenth century, Jefferson's hope seemed increasingly less likely of realization. Philosphers and scientists on both sides of the Atlantic tended to assume that each race had inherent and quite separate traits. They were not equal, nor could they be made so. Most authorities ranked them in descending order as white, yellow, brown, red, and black, on the basis of pseudoscientific evidence subject to much debate. This theory of racial abilities dominated American thinking about race over the next half century. It both shaped and was used to justify the national policy toward Indians and blacks.

SHAPING AMERICAN SOCIETY

Feeding and Clothing the Republic. From the earliest settlement, soil and sea provided Americans with God's plenty. Nowhere else in the world did people have food in such quantity and variety as in the United States. A visitor to New York City in 1796 counted sixty-three kinds of fish, fourteen kinds of shellfish, fifty-two kinds of meat and fowl, and twenty-seven kinds of vegetables for sale. Contemporary accounts show that American appetites were impressively large: Count Volney, who was almost hospitalized during a tour of the United States by a breakfast of fish, steak, ham, sausage, salt beef, hot breads, and cider, wrote that Americans seemed to pass "the whole day . . . in heaping indigestions upon one another."

Such abundance was unavailable, however, to the less affluent. Habit and ignorance of nutrition made the average American meal ill-balanced and monotonous. Frontier diet leaned heavily on game, mush, molasses, beans, peas, and "hawg and hominy." The city laborer's diet was not much different, except that it had less game and fewer vegetables. Its staples were bread and meat— usually salt pork, pickled beef, salt fish, and sausage.

Meat was salted or smoked because preservation was a problem. A freshly killed chicken lasted only about eighteen hours in a city market. Neither country nor city people, unless they could afford it, consumed much fresh milk, vegetables, or fruit. Scurvy and rickets were common in the lower walks of life.

A great change in diet came after 1820, when new methods of refrigeration and canning partially solved the ancient problem of food preservation. Commercial canning began in 1819, and the substitution of tin containers for glass in the 1830s made the process better and cheaper. Icehouses for storage had been common since the seventeenth century, and efficient home iceboxes came on the market as early as 1803. By 1840, according to the New York *Mirror*, an icebox was as much a necessity as a kitchen table.

American men in the post-Revolutionary years dressed much the same as Britishers of similar social and economic situation. Though a few older men still wore wigs in 1800, most men wore long hair tied in a queue. Madison was the last President to wear a queue, and by the 1820s the style was gone—James Monroe wore his hair shorter, parted in the middle, and combed in shaggy waves in the reigning style. Beards did not appear until the 1830s and then mostly on radical-bohemian types. They did not gain respectability until the Civil War (Lincoln was the first bearded President) and then flourished in luxuriance until the 1890s.

A well-to-do city man's attire in the 1790s might include a beaver hat, blue cutaway coat with high collar and broad lapels, striped waistcoat, white linen scarf, light-colored doeskin breeches buttoning below the knee, and high soft boots with turned-down tops. Gone were the gaudy colors, gold embroidery, and decorative ruffles of the 1770s. Colors were muted, the emphasis on quality cloth, skilled tailoring, and understated elegance.

By 1810 the full-length pantaloon had replaced knee breeches, and by the 1820s men wore tight-waisted, high-collared, wide-shouldered coats with rolled lapels, contrasting vests, shirts with wide collars, and colored cravats. The city laborer and artisan wore buckskin or ticking (heavy cotton) breeches, a thick shirt of linen (or deerskin or "linsey woolsey," a linen-wool mixture), a coat of "duroy" or coarse woolen cloth, and heavy boots. He probably also had a suit of broadcloth or dark corduroy for church, weddings, christenings, and burials. Fustian, a cotton-flax combination, was widely used in the South for both men's and women's ordinary clothes. Jeans, a wool-cotton mixture, was common in the North.

Improved spinning and looming machinery and the rise of the textile industry changed male clothing habits. A plentiful supply of cheap cloth and the appearance of factory-made, ready-to-wear clothing made class distinctions in style, cut, and fabric less obvious. Without close inspection, foreign travelers observed, it was often difficult on a Sunday to distinguish a mechanic from a clerk or even a banker.

As men's fashions followed London, so women's followed Paris. In the postwar period the tremendous hair arrangements dictated for women during the preceding years (some had to be mounted on wire forms) gave way to shoulder-length curled hair, secured by ribbons and combs and sometimes lightly powdered. Rouge and "pearl powder" were common cosmetics. By 1800 hair was shorter, pomaded into tight curls. By 1812 it was longer again, curled into loose tendrils

and decorated with leaves, flowers, jewels, and the like.

The trend in fashion at that time was toward sheer, clinging materials, the basic dress a straight narrow tube (almost always white) with drawn-in high waist, puffed sleeves, and a single petticoat or pink tights underneath. Over the next decade there evolved the "Empire" style, patterned after that of Napoleonic Paris, with long narrow sleeves, plunging necklines, and sweepingly draped skirts, done in rich damasks, brocades, silks, and fine light wools or cottons. Fashions shifted dramatically in the 1820s toward bright colors, low waistlines, ankle-length skirts, wide sleeves, large collars, and ballet slippers or low shoes. In the 1830s came stays, stomach boards, French pantelettes, leg-of-mutton sleeves, and full skirts that were soon to give way to hoopskirts.

All this, of course, was high style. A visitor to the White House reported that, like most American women, Dolley Madison at home wore "a plain stuff dress protected by a large apron with a linen kerchief pinned about the neck." The usual costume for housework was a no-nonsense, long-sleeved wool or cotton dress buttoned up to the neck, with light-weight knee-length linen or flannel under-drawers for protection against the chill of unheated houses.

Marriage, Morals, and Family Life. "Marriages in America," wrote Franklin in 1782, "are more general, and more generally early, than in Europe." With agriculture pushing westward and industry expanding in the cities, young couples did not need to wait for capital to marry—as in Europe they often had to do. And in the newer settlements young women, considerably outnumbered by the men, were in much demand as wives and had much greater freedom of choice.

American marriages tended to be not only early but unusually productive. Families of six to eight surviving children were common, while South Carolina authorities recorded one woman with thirty-four living children. In America, in contrast to Europe, the delicate business of marriage agreements was either neglected or left to the principals. The "arranged" marriage never found wide acceptance in the United States, and much of Europe's nuptial apparatus—the dowry or *dot*, the contract, banns, and the like—had disappeared by the turn of the century. Young men and women could, of course, recognize the advantages of a good match, but observers agreed that American partners paid less attention to economic benefits.

Attitudes toward divorce differed from those current in Britain and Europe. Divorce seemed more frequent (except in Catholic and strict Anglican circles) and somewhat easier to obtain, especially for men. Laws varied from state to state, but cruelty and desertion, as well as adultery (and nearly twenty other reasons), were recognized as grounds for divorce earlier in America than in Europe. In sparsely settled areas, where courts met infrequently, couples sometimes simply separated without legal formalities. Similarly, couples might live together for months or longer until a circuit-riding parson arrived.

The frontier also accepted so-called left-handed marriages, in which the ceremony

Unlike their European counterparts, American couples could afford to marry early and have many children.

was performed by militia captains, unlicensed ministers, or even the bride's father. As churches and organized government caught up with settlement, of course, there was less casualness.

Foreign travelers often noted that the American family lacked the unity and patriarchal structure of the European. Although it formed a strong social unit, with clear educative, religious, economic, and protective responsibilities, it was noticeably less tightly knit than its British and Continental counterpart. In the cities, as factories sprang up, young people soon became a vital component of the labor market, and on the farms of the West the same was true. Though shamefully exploited, mill girls could earn enough to be independent, while boys could find work at eleven or twelve. Family wealth, social caste, and parental influence—matters of importance in European society— counted for less in a fluid society where sons and daughters, by hard work and a bit of luck, could outdo their parents. In America a young man might easily own more land than his father. A young woman might as easily marry, leave home, and set up her own household, better than her mother's. Meanwhile, the spread of public school meant that the family need no longer serve as the sole medium of education and culture.

Travelers were also amazed at the lack of strict parental control in the United States and at the responsibilities parents placed on children. One British visitor wrote that even at thirteen "female children rejoice in the appellation of 'Misses' and begin to enjoy all the privileges of self-management." Boys, it seemed to Europeans, were on their own much earlier than abroad. Some thought this the result of lax discipline in an unformed society, while others attributed it to the American feeling of equality. More probably, the fact was that in the new society where population was scattered and opportunities great, children necessarily took on greater responsibilities. In a frontier setting, boys and girls had to make their own way as soon as they could and grew up quickly because they had to.

American moral attitudes were much the same as those of contemporary England, but the powerful Calvinistic tradition (and more rigid Anglicanism) in the United States probably produced a stricter code of morals in small town and rural areas. French emigré Moreau St. Mèry found Philadelphia's morals no looser than Europe's, though he was continually surprised at American frankness about sex. The European custom of keeping mistresses, though uncommon in the United States, was not unknown in sophisticated circles. One traveler noted "young and pretty street walkers" in Philadelphia, saw a bevy of attractive "sailors' girls" in Baltimore, and found an entire section of New York, called "Holy Ground," set aside for prostitution.

Travelers rarely failed to comment on the freedom granted to American youth. A study of Massachusetts church records later indicated that of two hundred couples married over a fourteen-year span, sixty-six admitted to premarital relations. The practice of "bundling," or sharing the same bed, was a result of frontier housing conditions. Its innocence no doubt varied with the participants. But travelers also agreed that there was probably less extramarital activity in America than in Europe. St. Mèry believed that although American girls enjoyed "unlimited liberty before marriage," an American wife "lived only for her husband, to devote herself without surcease to the care of her household and her home."

Women's Legal Status. The legal status of women during the later eighteenth century remained much as it had been in colonial days. Many of the earlier laws were carried into the lawbooks of the new states without substantial change. Unmarried women were considered the wards of relatives, married

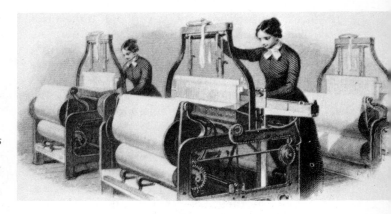

Due to the chronic labor shortage, farm girls were often employed to operate the looms in the growing textile industry. "Lowell girls," such as those shown above, lived in the Lowell Company's free dormitories in the company town of Lowell and were chaperoned and treated as proper young ladies. Although they worked long hours for low wages, they earned enough to be independent.

women their husband's chattels. Although they varied from state to state, a wife's rights to property were closely limited. She could not make a will, sign a contract, or witness a deed without her husband's permission. For a woman to get a divorce, no matter what the provocation, was so difficult in most states as to be next to impossible.

Almost all professions and trades were closed to women, and of course they could neither vote nor hold office—a handicap they shared with some males. In the eyes of the law, as Blackstone tersely put it, "The husband and wife are one, and that one is the husband."

Not only the law but the church supported this view. According to both Catholic and Protestant clergy, woman's subordinate place in society was established by those intellectual and physical limitations placed upon her at her creation, as the Bible said, and forever fixed by her weaknesses as a daughter of Eve.

Nonetheless, the American woman held a higher status in this new and flexible society than it might appear. In the city or country, woman's work—spinning; weaving; sewing; making shoes, soap, candles, clothing; and much else—was absolutely necessary to the maintenance of the home and the functioning of society. Nor were such mundane tasks the extent of her obligations. The development of the child-centered family, which had begun in

the Renaissance, powerfully influenced the position of the woman within the home during the eighteenth century. With it came the idea that the family—not society at large—had the crucial task of preparing the young—socially, intellectually, and spiritually—to enter society. This belief placed major responsibility on woman as supervisor of home and teacher of children. By the early nineteenth century men were ready to agree that, from this point of view, women's function in society was equal to—possibly superior to—their own. Herein lay the beginnings of a reevaluation of women's place in the world.

Women were not restricted to purely domestic duties. The system of household manufacturing provided opportunities for them to learn a craft and become part of the home labor market. They also helped their husbands in their work, ran the farm or shop when the men served in the militia or went to sea or hunted game, and often took over management of farm or shop when husbands died. Thus Franklin's sister-in-law Ann ran her husband's print shop after his death, and John Singleton Copley's widowed mother kept her late husband's tobacco store.

Chronic labor shortages made female labor much more acceptable in America than in Europe. The growth of the textile industry was particularly influential in opening the way to the employment of women outside the home. Extending them the privilege of working fourteen hours a day at a loom naturally raised some doubts about their presumed inferiority. Other trades began to accept women workers until, by the early 1830s, Harriet Martineau could list seven kinds of employment dominated by females—teaching, sewing, typesetting, bookbinding, domestic service, textile mill work, and running a boardinghouse.

New Thinking About Women's Rights. The Revolution itself encouraged new ways of thinking about women's status. The Daughters of Liberty, though not so well publicized as the Sons, aided in the boycott of British goods and the harassment of Loyalists. Not only did the departure of men to serve in the army and the government create vacancies that women had to fill, but the whole drift of the revolutionary argument worked to their benefit. If all human beings were endowed with natural and unalienable rights, why were women not granted them in full? Strongminded women like Mercy Warren, Margaret Winthrop, and Abigail Adams (not to mention the legendary Molly Pitcher, who joined her husband's artillery crew at the Battle of Monmouth) were likely to ask such questions. Thus Judith Sargent Murray demanded that an American woman be treated as "an intelligent being" with interests beyond "the mechanics of a pudding or the sewing of the seams in a garment." Enlightened men like Franklin, Paine, and Benjamin Rush joined her in asking for a reconsideration of women's rights.

Meanwhile, the winds of feminist thought abroad blew westward across the water. Americans read Godwin and Condorcet and especially Mary Wollstonecraft's *Vindication of the Rights of Woman* (1792). Women's rights became a topic of discussion in magazines and drawing rooms everywhere. Charles Brockden Brown's tract *Alcuin* (1798) was intended to serve as the American version of *Vindication,* and several of his novels, notably *Ormond,* explored issues raised by the feminist debate. Judith Sargent Murray could thus confidently predict in 1798 the advent of "a new era in female history."

This was not soon forthcoming however. Both in England and in the United States, distrust of "radical theories" after the French Revolution led once-enthusiastic reformers to revise their concepts of female rights and return to earlier, more conservative views of woman's place in society. Part of the reaction derived from a revised concept of "motherhood" and of woman's "place in the home." In contrast to the Puritan and neo-Puritan emphasis on the father as chief agent in childrearing, the eighteenth century gradually shifted responsibility for family life to the mother. By 1800 the mother was considered uniquely qualified, by biological and spiritual design, for raising and educating the next generation. This idea of woman's role in American life, with its stress on domesticity, was in a sense an elevation of woman's status. But it also served to rationalize a change in attitude toward her rights. If mothers played such a crucial social and moral role in determining the nation's future, their political and legal emancipation seemed really of secondary importance. Their right to rule the home seemed of greater importance than their right to vote or hold property.

Since it was assumed that most would become wives and mothers, the position of the unmarried woman was not of great social concern. Those who did not marry often served as caretakers in a relative's household (as "maiden aunts") or followed careers in teaching or in one of the semi-skilled professions open to them.

The key to legal (and social) equality, most postwar feminists believed, lay in the right of self-development through education. The struggle for equal education was hard, for women faced the old tradition of female inferiority, summarized in Rousseau's dictum that woman's "whole education ought to be relative to man." Although men like Jefferson and Burr believed in educating their daughters in something more than the polite and domestic arts, most Americans considered women's minds to be incapable of contending with subjects like law, philosophy, science, or theology.

Here the argument from domesticity proved useful, however. A mother must be well-educated herself in order to educate her children. If she was to be responsible for maintaining house, family, and husband, she obviously must be educated in such a way as to enable her do so effectively.

The thrust for female education gained momentum swiftly during the early decades of the century. Emma Hart Willard, herself an accomplished mathematician, first cracked the wall (with the help of Governor DeWitt Clinton and others) by establishing in 1821 at Troy, New York, the first endowed school for women that was equal to those for men—Troy Female Seminary. A few others appeared during the twenties and thirties—notably Mt. Holyoke Seminary, opened at South Hadley, Massachusetts, in 1837 by Mary Lyon. But it was left to the next generation to give the women's rights movement measurable momentum.

THE QUEST FOR AMERICAN ARTS

A Native Literature Having gained political independence, Americans sought their own culture as a way to express—in literature, drama, and the other arts—the fundamentals of their civilization. Critics, editors, and authors agreed on the need for native, original art. As Noah Webster wrote, "America must be as independent in *literature* as she is in politics." But it was easier to demand art than to produce it.

The first step toward artistic independence was to declare America's freedom from English and European domination. The second was to define the circumstances and standards by which the new nation could produce a distinguished literature of its own. The author must have something American to write about and a defined, recognizable, native manner of writing it. True, Timothy Dwight admitted, the United States lacked "ancient castles, ruined abbeys, and fine pictures." But on the other hand, the American artist possessed a number of things that neither British nor other European artists possessed.

The American artist had the Indian, the frontier, and a brief but eminently usable past. After 1790 every author of note made at least one attempt to use the American frontier or American history in a major work. In addition, American artists possessed ample material for studies of manners—what dramatist James Nelson Baker called "the events, customs, opinions, and characters of American life."

Patterns in American Prose. The distinguishing development in literature during the period from 1783 to 1830 was the growing popularity of the novel, the poem, the essay, and the drama. This growth was accompanied by a decline of such once-popular forms of writing as the sermon, the journal, and the travel narrative. It reflected in part the higher level of appreciation and sophistication of American society and in part a greater effort by American writers to enter into the mainstream of contemporary literary fashions.

The essay, modeled chiefly after the work of the great British essayists, attracted a number of talented Americans, among them Washington Irving, who became famous with the appearance of *The Sketch Book* (1819–1820). Although most critics did not consider the novel an art form worthy of serious effort, the popular demand for fiction increased rapidly.

Magazines printed novels by the score, and libraries stocked greater numbers of them each year.

The most popular ones, such as William Hill Brown's *Power of Sympathy* (1789) and Susannah Rowson's *Charlotte Temple* (1791), copied the novels of the English author Samuel Richardson. The Gothic novel of suspense and terror found a gifted American practitioner in Philadelphia's Charles Brockden Brown, whose *Wieland* (1798) and *Ormond* (1799) were uneven in quality but indicative of genuine talent.

Most popular of all, however, was the historical romance, patterned on the works of Sir Walter Scott, whose novels enjoyed a tremendous vogue in early nineteenth-century America. Dozens of American novelists imitated him, but none successfully fitted the Scott formula to the American scene until James Fenimore Cooper wrote *The Spy* (1821), *The Pioneers* (1823), *The Last of the Mohicans* (1826), and thirty other novels. When Cooper's buckskin-clad hero Natty Bumppo walked into American fiction and leaned on his long rifle, the American novel came of age.

Meanwhile, another American, Washington Irving, had included several pieces of short fiction in his *Sketch Book*. Two of these, "Rip Van Winkle" and "The Legend of Sleepy Hollow," provided a pattern for a new literary form, the short story, and their central characters quickly became a part of the American cultural heritage. Irving's popularity, combined with Cooper's, furnished a decisive answer to English critic Sydney Smith's sneer in 1820, "Who reads an American book?"

Reading for the People. With a near doubling of population between 1790 and 1830, there was a large new mass audience for books. People were unusually literate because of the spread of popular education, and they had a taste for books of every kind. At the close of the Revolution, Boston counted fifty bookstores, New York and Philadelphia thirty or more each. Peddlers and "book agents" hawked books, along with pots, ribbons, and liniments, up to the edge of the frontier. Subscription and rental libraries, developed in the mid-eighteenth century, swiftly multiplied. In 1825 the libraries of the five largest American cities had twenty times more books to *lend* than the entire country *owned* in Washington's day.

With this growing audience in mind, publishers, booksellers, and writers soon worked out better marketing and publication methods. New machinery for papermaking, typesetting, and printing increased production a hundredfold. The steam-powered cylinder press, perfected by the 1830s, turned out thousands of impressions an hour. Improved mail services and the expanding network of roads meant cheap, quick distribution of reading matter.

This great new market naturally demanded a supply. Fiction was a particularly lucrative field for writers and publishers. "Sentimental" novels, in which characters had to distinguish between "false" and "true" love and surmount heartrending domestic disaster, flooded the market. Written by and for women—some quite skillfully—these novels were the "true confessions" of the day. They reinforced the role of woman as household manager and mother and at the same time carried implicit messages of female pride and independence.

Women produced the bulk of American fiction written in the postwar decades and provided by far the largest market for it. Of the approximately two hundred American novels published between 1790 and 1820, two-thirds were by female authors. While they tended to feature highly emotional and melodramatic plots, with names such as *The Coquette*, *The Beggar Girl*, or *Virtue Rewarded*, they nevertheless showed that women's concerns and values were legitimate literary subjects and emphasized the importance of women in the society of the new Republic.

Equally popular were tales of mystery, terror, and crime, such as *Adventures in a Castle* and *The Asylum*, patterned on the British Gothic novel. So, too, were stories of Indians, war, and adventure, like *The Prisoners of Niagara*, *The Champions of Freedom*, and *The Mysterious Chief*. Nearly as much fiction as fact, Parson Mason Weems' biographies of Francis Marion, Benjamin Franklin, and George Washington (including the hatchet-and-cherry-tree story) left indelible impressions on the American mind. (See "Parson Weems: The Hero Maker.")

Poetry in the New Republic. Poetry found hard going in the period after the Revolutionary War. There were plenty of young people interested in writing verse but the way of the poet was difficult in a world torn by two wars with England, a near-war with France, bitter political rivalries at home, and a whole new political system a-building. Some talented writers, like Joel Barlow, tried their hands at "epics" and retreated to politics; John Trumbull, one of the cleverest, went into law. Timothy Dwight, whose poetic aims were high but whose gifts were of doubtful quality, turned to theology and education.

This was not the case with Philip Freneau, the first authentic poetic voice to be heard in the United States. His poems, dealing with nature, beauty, the past, and personal experience, show genuine poetic gifts. The delicacy and skill of his lyric verse were unmatched by any American poet of his day—and by few British poets.

These early poets, however, belonged to the formal English tradition. Colonial Americans had imported the British broadside, a sheet of paper with ballad verses written on one side, sold for a penny by street hawkers. These remained popular after the turn of the century. Really a form of versified journalism, they dealt with crimes, battles, deaths of the famous, holidays, natural disasters, and anything else of public interest.

The Revolution and the War of 1812 elicited hundreds of such poems, many anonymous, printed either as broadsides or in magazines, with titles like "A Patriot's Prayer," "A Song for the Redcoats," and "Hale in the Bush." Similarly, funeral poetry, written to commemorate the passing of famous and ordinary alike, constantly appeared in newspapers.

The Theater and Other Entertainments. Immediately after the Revolution, people flocked back to the theaters, which had been closed by the Continental Congress in 1774, along with "horse racing, gambling, cockfighting . . . , and other expensive diversions." Companies catering to elite and relatively affluent audiences presented British, Continental, and some American plays.

American dramatists tended to follow foreign models, using American materials. Royall Tyler's *The Contrast* (1787), patterned on Sheridan's comedy of manners, contrasted true-blue American Colonel Manly with Billy Dimple, an Anglicized fop, much to the latter's disadvantage. James Nelson Barker's *The Indian Princess*, or *La Belle Sauvage* (1808), focused on the Indian-white conflict, a persistent theme. John Howard Payne's *Clari* (1823), introduced the song, "Home, Sweet Home."

The growth of audiences stimulated a wave of theater building in the cities between 1790 and 1840—big theaters, seating as many as four thousand. Where theaters did not exist, companies played in tents, taverns, ballrooms, barns, and anywhere else that an audience could find seats. As audiences increased, prices decreased. Whereas a New York theater box cost $2 in 1800, most city theaters by 1820 had a 75¢ top price, with tickets for the gallery as low as 12½¢. Shakespeare, Goldsmith, and Sheridan, well acted and presented, were successful at the box office. But theatrical emphasis clearly began to shift to mass entertainment. Farces like *The Double-Bedded Room*, melodramas like *Metamora: The Last of the Wampanoags*, and roaring comedies like *The Lion of the West* gave the popular theater audience what it wanted.

"Spectacles" or "pageants," presented either as separate exhibitions or as portions of plays, were as popular as plays. *The Battle of Bunker Hill*, staged at Boston in 1793, reproduced the entire engagement, with troops, cannon, gunfire, burning houses, fireworks, and parade. *The Young Carolinian* (1818) included a full-scale battle between the United States Navy and the Barbary pirates. *The Last Days of Pompeii*, presented in Philadelphia in 1830, had twenty-two spectacular scenes, the last one the eruption of Vesuvius. An evening at the theater in 1820 might also include between-the-acts skits, afterpieces, comic routines, and parodies with names like *Hamlet and Egglet* and *Much Ado About Pocahontas*.

Another popular theatrical form featured the panorama or diorama. A panorama was a painting on the inner walls of a rotunda. To view it, the spectator stood in the middle and slowly turned full circle. A diorama was a continuous strip of painted canvas about twelve feet wide, cranked from one roller to another across a stage to make a moving picture. Both were often accompanied by music, a lecture, and program notes. Panoramic views of cities—Paris, Rome, London, Jerusalem—were particularly popular. One could take *A Trip to Niagara*, or view *The Battle of Trenton*, or have *A Tour of the Pyramids* for a dollar or less. Probably the largest panorama displayed was the one shown in 1831 of the Battle of Waterloo, Napoleon at St. Helena, and Napoleon's funeral procession, all covering a total of twenty thousand square feet.

Animal shows, equestrian shows, jugglers, acrobats, puppeteers, and other itinerant entertainers traveled the countryside in America as they did in England. In 1815 Hachaliah Bailey of Somers, New York, took to the road with a few animals and an elephant named Old Bet. Within a few years more and larger shows followed, some with clowns.

Quite logically, these shows teamed up with traveling acrobatic groups and horse shows to become "circuses," as we use the word. Where roads did not go, circuses went by boat, down the Ohio and the Mississippi in the 1820s, as far west as Detroit by 1830. The more prosperous shows began to use canvas walls, and later tents, to accommodate larger audiences.

The first circus to travel under "the big top" was probably the Turner show in 1826. A few years later tents were standard for all but the smallest shows. Copying the stage "spectaculars," circuses introduced costumed parades and pageants. Well aware of the popularity of the city "dime museums," they also added "side shows."

Architecture. The Enlightenment, as befitting an Age of Reason, preferred spare, clean, harmonious designs derived from Greek and Roman building over the intricate and ornamental baroque and medival styles inherited from the seventeenth century. There were very few professional architects in the United States at the time of independence, and most existing public buildings were copied from designs imported from Britain. The typical colonial style was, therefore, a modification of Georgian, made popular in England by Inigo Jones and the Adam brothers.

After the Revolution there was an immediate demand for buildings to serve the new state and federal governments, and a corresponding need for professional architects. The current vogue for things Greek and Roman, as well as the prevailing English style, created two distinct architectural traditions— a modified Georgian style, exemplified in Philadelphia's State House, or Independence

Hall, and a Romanized style characteristic of the Middle and Southern colonies, best illustrated by Jefferson's Virginia State Capitol at Richmond.

The two greatest practitioners of these architectural styles were Charles Bulfinch of Boston and Thomas Jefferson of Virginia. Deeply impressed by the British style, Bulfinch developed an American version of it, called the Boston or "Federal" style. It emphasized simplicity and balance, with cleanly symmetrical brickwork, graceful doorways separating equal numbers of sash windows, white trim, and classical cupolas. He rebuilt Faneuil Hall in Boston, designed capitols for Boston, Hartford, and Augusta, built a number of churches, and served for a time as architect in charge of the national Capitol in Washington. His influence may still be seen in the small towns of Ohio, Michigan, and Illinois, or wherever the next generation of New Englanders migrated.

Jefferson believed that the United States needed to develop an architectural tradition of its own, free of British influence and worthy of a young, great nation. Perceiving an analogy between the grandeur of the classic past and the future of the Republic, he drew on his study of Roman remains in Europe, and of French and Italian adaptations of the Classical style, to create an American tradition well illustrated by his plans for the University of Virginia. His home at Monticello, on which he worked for forty years, was his crowning achievement and is one of the gems of American architecture.

Parson Weems: The Hero Maker

Parson Mason Locke Weems occupies a unique place in American history. He gained immortality with one book and one anecdote. The book was *The Life of George Washington, with Curious Anecdotes Equally Honourable to Himself and Exemplary to His Young Countrymen*, published in 1800. The story was, of course, about young George, his hatchet, and his father's cherry tree. These seem scant reason to warrant fame, but with them Weems created the first authentic, enduring American hero.

Mason Weems was born in Maryland in 1759. Little is known of his childhood and youth. He may have served in the Royal Navy and he may have studied medicine in Scotland. He appeared in England, however, after the Revolution and with the help of John Adams was ordained a minister in the Church of England in 1784. He returned to take up a church in Maryland and, as was not uncommon for preachers in poor parishes, took another job. He signed up as a book agent and travelled on horseback through the country settlements peddling broadsides, recipes, pamphlets, books, and prints. He did well, married Frances Ewell, a local girl, in 1795, and moved to Virginia.

Here his growing family required more income than his pulpit provided, so he hired on as agent for Matthew Carey of Philadelphia, one of the most aggressive publishers in the East. Weems proved as good at selling as he was at preaching and

After Jefferson, the Classical tradition was further modified by Benjamin Latrobe, whose source was Greek, not Roman, and who with his followers helped initiate what soon became the Greek Revival era in American architecture. The Federal, Classical, and Greek Revival styles, though they added grace, beauty, and charm to the American scene, still could not yet be called wholly American architecture.

The laborer, farmer, and frontier settler, of course, could not afford a Monticello or a Boston townhouse. The early colonists quickly replaced the medieval gables, thatched roofs, and exposed timbers of the English cottage with shingles and clapboards, better suited to American weather. The result was the graceful, functional (and usually unpaint-ed) Cape Cod cottage, translated into brick in the Middle colonies and built with variations throughout the country. In the South the "shotgun" cabins, introduced by Scandinavian settlers, were still built on the frontier, but in the growing settlements people preferred the plank-built, four-square cottage or two-story house.

Musicians and Painters.   The eighteenth-century colonists loved music as ardently as their English contemporaries. French and German immigrants, too, brought their musical tastes to America, and after 1800 such cities as New York, Philadelphia, Boston, and Charleston supported good orchestras, musical societies, studios, and academies. However, American composers and musicians, such as William

combined the two until he found he was spending more time taking orders than saving souls. Since he was also an accomplished fiddler, he was much in demand at weddings, dances, and holiday celebrations, and he was well known and well liked in the back-country settlements from Georgia to Pennsylvania.

Weems was a superb salesman, and wherever he found a crowd he stopped to tout Carey's list of seventy-six titles and fifty-six maps and prints. In fact, Weems set a kind of record by selling over three thousand copies of Carey's *Family Bible* at the then-astronomical price of $30.00 each. He sensed, though, that the market was ready for something different from anything on Carey's lists. His countrymen were religious and patriotic and liked a good story; they needed a history, and they needed heroes. So Weems suggested to Carey that a series of books about famous Americans "of Courage and Ability" would provide exactly what the public warranted. Washington was the obvious first choice, and when the ex-President died suddenly in late 1799 Weems put out a short biography (dedicated to Martha Washington) within a few months. Three editions, each expanded over the previous one, were sold out within the year.

Weems was, after all, a "parson," whose purpose in life was to "uplift his fellowman" and put his country on the path to righteousness. He believed that Washington's "unparreleled [sic] rise and elevation was due to his virtues," and that he was therefore the best possible model for Americans to emulate. Washington's virtues, he wrote Carey, were "his Veneration of the Diety [sic], his Patriotism, his Industry, his Temperance and Sobriety, his Justice, etc.," all of which (and more) he illustrated by "anecdotes apropos Interesting and Entertaining."

Since Weems conceived of his book as a kind of sermon, he could see no harm in embellishing his anecdotes a bit, or for that matter making up ones he needed. Any legend or rumor, if it would add to the story, was therefore fair game. As a

Billings or James Hewitt, could hardly hope to match their powerful European contemporaries or to compete with the talented, trained immigrants who came to America from the finest European orchestras and schools.

As for popular music, eighteenth-century colonists imported large numbers of songbooks from England. "Singing meetings" were common diversions, and "singing schools" trained not only church choirs but secular choruses, some of professional skill. After the Revolution publishers put together "songsters" or "musical miscellanies" by the hundreds, including such songs as "The Blue Bell of Scotland," "Drink to Me Only with Thine Eyes," "Yankee Doodle," "Auld Lang Syne," and many others that became enduring favorites. These collections (such as the 1808 *Missouri Songster*, which Lincoln remembered using as a boy) proliferated after the 1790s and served as the main source of American popular music over the next century.

Samuel Miller, in his *Retrospect of the Eighteenth Century* (1803), admitted apologetically that American art had as yet produced no great painters, though he could point with pride to Benjamin West, John Singleton Copley, Charles Willson Peale, Gilbert Stuart, and John Trumbull. These painters, all born into the prerevolutionary generation and rooted in an English and European tradition, looked to Paris, Rome, and especially London for instruction and inspiration.

West became court painter to England's King George III and successor to Sir Joshua

dedicated Jeffersonian, Weems was also anxious to show Washington not as a lofty, aristocratic Federalist, but rather as "a pure Republican," a heroic, statesmanlike man of the people. The book sold hugely, entranced his readers, and created a legendary Washington who still endures.

Parson Weems, of course, wrote not history but fiction, and he wrote it well. *Washington* was a skillful mixture of adventure, patriotism, morality, and hero worship that struck the public exactly right. The cherry-tree incident did not appear until the fifth edition in 1806, and other unverifiable anecdotes appeared from time to time—the Indian who fired at Washington seventeen times at the Battle of the Monongahela and mysteriously missed every time; the Quaker observer who saw him praying alone in the woods at Valley Forge; his mother's dream of how little George put out the fire that threatened their home, just as he later saved the nation from the consuming blaze of war and dissension.

There were other stories of Washington's youthful wisdom and strength of character—of how as a boy he refused to allow his classmates to fight and instead adjudicated their quarrels with even justice; of how he showed his precocious military talent by organizing his school friends in mock battles. The man who emerged from the book was precisely the larger-than-life figure the public wanted—strong, pious, just, virtuous, and everything else an American hero should be—a "patriot Hero, a Christian statesman, great in goodness and good in greatness."

Weems, unfortunately, sold the rights to his book to Carey for $1000 in 1808, but the book had a life of its own. It went on and on, through at least ninety editions, and was still on sale for a dime in an abridged edition as late as 1930. William McGuffey picked up the cherry tree story and others for his famous series of school *Readers* (1836–1857), thus introducing Weems to uncounted millions of youthful readers.

Reynolds as President of the British Royal Academy. A painter in the so-called grand style, he specialized in huge canvases of such famous events as *The Death of General Wolfe*. Copley, one of West's students, was probably the best portrait painter in London. Peale not only painted well but founded the first museum in the United States (1786), organized the first public art exhibition in the country (1794), and in 1805 helped establish the Pennsylvania Academy of Fine Arts.

Gilbert Stuart, another pupil of West's, dominated American portrait art for nearly thirty years, producing the amazing total of 1150 portraits. His realistic, luminous style and his feeling for the person behind the painting made him the best portrait painter of the period. His *Washington*, which appears on a well-known postage stamp, is an example of Stuart at his best. Trumbull, strongly affected by West's manner, became head of the American Academy of Arts in 1817 and exerted considerable influence on American taste and critical standards for many years.

Since the Romantic Age was intensely interested in the individual, the most popular form of painting was the portrait. The market for official portraits of businessmen, judges, legislators, militia officers, and the like was excellent, and the market for family portraits of ordinary folk was even better. From polished professionals to self-taught "limners," painters traveled the land taking commissions, while the better-known maintained thriving studios in the cities. There were so many that Gilbert Stuart grumbled in

Nobody really knows, to this day, how many copies of the Parson's *Washington* have been sold.

Loss of the *Washington* did not discourage Weems. He went on to write similar exemplary—and touched-up—lives of *Francis Marion* (1809), *Benjamin Franklin* (1815), and *William Penn* (1822), all successful. He still wanted to make the United States the world's most moral, Christian nation, and he believed that the right kind of reading would help his countrymen accomplish it. Therefore he began a series of books under the general title of *God's Revenges*, directed against duelling, adultery, gambling, murder, and drunkenness. They warned effectively against those and other sins and were also whacking good melodramas, the soap operas of their times. Who would not be interested, for example, in how handsome, elegant James O'Neale seduced pretty, trusting Matilda L'Estrange, whose brother then pursued the miscreant and shot him twice in the head—all illustrated with seven lurid engravings?

All in all, before he died in South Carolina on May 23, 1825 (leaving ten children) Parson Weems had authored twenty-five pamphlets and books in addition to the *Washington*. As one of Weems' friends remarked of his writings, they were "most admirable in their effect except that you know not what to believe." His readers obviously did not care. His books appeared in a total of 218 different editions and probably sold over a million copies, which made him clearly one of the best-selling authors of his day.

Later biographers de-fictionalized *Washington* and made him gradually into the Virginia planter-aristocrat, professional soldier, and indispensable statesman that he no doubt really was. Yet he remains to Americans, in an equally real sense, the boy who could not tell a lie and who grew up to be Father of His Country—as Parson Weems said he was.

Thomas Jefferson, one of the greatest architects of this period, adapted classical styles to American needs, as shown in his design of the University of Virginia.

his old age that "you kick your feet against a dog kennel, and out will start a portrait painter." For those who could not afford the best, some would "paint in" customers' faces on prepainted figures. For even less, a silhouette cutter provided cheaper immortality.

There were limited opportunities for women to receive art training until after 1800, when female seminaries and art academies introduced studio instruction and a few male painters took female pupils. Nevertheless, there were a few notable women painters in this field traditionally dominated by men— Ellen and Rolinda Sharples, who came from England to do portraits; Jane Stuart, Gilbert's daughter; Sara Goodrich, the miniaturist. There were also Angelica Kaufmann Peale and her cousins Sarah Miriam and Anna Claypoole of the "painting Peale" family.

Sarah Peale and her sister, in fact, were both elected to the prestigious Pennsylvania Academy. Sarah, who had her own studio in Boston for twenty years and in St. Louis for thirty, was recognized as one of the more successful portrait painters of her time. She was the first professional woman painter in the United States, supporting herself entirely on her commissions.

In areas free of male competition, however, there developed a strong female aesthetic sense and a tradition of craftsmanship displayed in quilting rugs, lace, furniture decoration, homemade water colors, folk painting, and the like. Female academies and private teachers taught needlework, the best of which required great skill and years of training in technique and design. Though the sampler was the most common form of self-expression, the highest technical and artistic performance was the needlework picture of silk embroidery, based on paintings or original sketches, which could take a year or so to complete. Only in recent years have art historians begun to take such early women's art seriously, and much work remains to be done.

Winning Artistic Independence.   During the period from 1787 to 1830 all the arts in the United States were in large part derivative and imitative—dependent upon Britain and Europe for standards and inspirations. Literature showed much more of an American disposition than painting, architecture more than music. Artistic production on the whole was becoming increasingly nationalistic in spirit, though artists and writers still lacked confidence in their own tastes and ideas. They were fearful about not conforming to traditional, time-tested artistic norms.

What the United States wanted was a Golden Age of its own, built out of American materials and ideas but couched in artistic terms and derived from traditional esthetic theories. Real artistic independence was yet to come. At the popular level, however, there was already a sturdy, quite American tradition that would flourish and grow more independent in the half century ahead.

The story of American culture will be resumed in Chapter 7. In the following two chapters we shall be concerned with the political, diplomatic, and military events of

Charles Wilson Peale painted his own portrait to show himself drawing the veil on his museum, the first in the United States.

the period under consideration—the period which witnessed the establishment of the Republic and the developments of the Jeffersonian Era. It was, as we mentioned earlier, a period of precedents, a time in which the new government was seeking to establish its identity and to begin functioning as a viable political system.

Chapter 5

Establishing the Republic 1781–1800

THE KING'S FRIENDS

The Treaty of Paris of 1783 contained two clauses concerning the American Loyalists. One recommended that they be restored their "estates, rights, and properties"; the other, that refugees be allowed to return for a year, without persecution or prosecution, to settle their affairs. But the States did not always follow these recommendations. The bitter war that "set Nabor against Nabor " had left fierce antagonisms. Loyalists who had served with the British—there were twenty-one Loyalist regiments in the British army—faced beatings, tar and feathers, and possibly hanging. Most Loyalists who fled did not return.

There were two waves of Loyalist migration, one in the early years of the war, the other near and after its close. Refugees in the first wave went chiefly north to Canada. Of those in the second wave of "late Loyalists" in 1781–1784, some were probably motivated as much by the promise of cheap land as by loyalty to the King. In 1789 the Governor of Canada designated those who arrived before 1783 and their descendants as "United Empire Loyalists." These individuals would be enti-

tled to attach U.E. to their surnames; about 3½ million Canadians today may do so.

Estimates are hard to substantiate, but about 60,000 Loyalists in all left the United States. Of these, 40,000 went to Canada, 10,000 to England, and most of the rest (including over 1000 free blacks and slaves) to the West Indies and Africa.

"Our Old Home." The Loyalists who went to England, chiefly to London and Bristol, were first lionized and then neglected. Governor Hutchinson of Massachusetts, who on arrival was offered a baronetcy (which he could not afford) and an honorary Oxford degree, wrote two years later, "We Americans are plenty here, and cheap. Few if any of us are much consulted or inquired after."

Some liked London, of course, but others found that they did not like the British and that the British, with their prejudice against colonials, did not particularly like them. Britain's tightly woven, hierarchical society had few openings for them in the usual vocations—church, military, law, politics— and not many had the capital or connections needed for business.

Then too, the Loyalists were not British, but British-American, and England was not home. "I would rather die in a little country farmhouse in New England," said Hutchinson, "than in the best nobleman's seat in Old England." Nevertheless, a parliamentary commission, appointed in 1783 to deal with Loyalist war claims, eventually paid out three million pounds to about two thirds of the claimants.

"Go to Hell or Halifax." Loyalists who went to Canada did much better. The British promised half-pay to ex-officers as well as land, lumber, seeds, stock, tools, and clothing, and kept most of their promises. The larger number went to Nova Scotia—to the great port city of Halifax or to the fertile St. John valley. Others went to the St. Lawrence area. Since the Maritime provinces of Canada were a geographical and economic extension of New England, and central Upper Canada, north of the St. Lawrence River, was a similar extension of New York State, the Loyalists easily fitted into Canadian society. In fact, the British in 1784 created the Province of New Brunswick to separate them from the more conservative society of Nova Scotia.

The arrival of the Loyalists had significant impact on subsequent Canadian history. It placed thriving English-speaking settlements where none had been before, thus reinforcing Canada's Britishness at a crucial point in its development. Without them Upper Canada might have gravitated toward New York State, the Maritimes toward New England, and present-day Canada might not exist. Refugees from one North American nation, in a sense, became the founders of another. "By Heaven," wrote Loyalist Edward Winslow from New Brunswick, "we will be the envy of the American States. I am in the midst of as cheerful a society as any in the world." But one Loyalist wife wrote, as she saw the last ships depart for Massachusetts, "Such a feeling of loneliness came over me that though I had not shed a tear through the entire war, I took my baby in my lap and sat down on the moss and wept."

THE SEARCH FOR STABILITY

Balancing Federal with Local Authority. Of prime importance in the political life of the United States throughout it history has been the problem of federalism—the division of power between the states and the federal government—or, more simply, the issue of local control or "states' rights" versus central authority. The origins of this problem are to be found in the British imperial system of the mid-eighteenth century. At the center of this system had stood Great Britain, whose government had directed foreign affairs and intercolonial relations with the view of keeping the machinery and policies of the empire working in harmony. At the extremities of this sytem had been the colonies themselves, each of which had attained the right to govern its internal affairs.

In practice, however, the dividing line between imperial and local affairs was variously interpreted, and out of the conflict of interpretations arose the American Revolution. With the Declaration of Independence, the American colonies rejected the government in London altogether and, under the pressures of war, united sufficiently to set up a central authority of their own making—the Confederation.

When Richard Henry Lee on June 7, 1776, offered a resolution to the Continental Congress declaring American independence, he also proposed that "a plan of confederation be prepared and transmitted to the respective colonies for their consideration and approbation." A little over a month later, on July 12, a committee headed by John Dickinson of Pennsylvania presented such a plan to the Continental Congress. On November 15,

Many of the Loyalists fled north to Canada, where some settled along the St. Lawrence River. Through settlements like this one at Johnston, the Loyalists helped to found a new country.

1777, after more than a year of debate, the Articles of Confederation were approved and sent to the states for ratification, a process that took four years. During almost the entire war, therefore, as we have seen, the country operated under the authority of the Continental Congress without a formal central government.

Because the loyalty of individual Americans was strongly attached to their states, it was readily agreed that the states should hold the sovereign powers of government. The Articles were designed to create an assembly of equal states, each of which retained its "sovereignty, freedom, and independence, and every Power, Jurisdiction, and right." The Articles of Confederation therefore created a quasi-federal system with a New Congress almost exactly like the wartime Continental Congress then in existence, in which each state—regardless of size, population, or wealth—had an equal vote. The Articles delegated to Congress the power to declare war, make peace, conclude treaties, raise and maintain armies, maintain a navy, establish a postal system, regulate Indian affairs, borrow money, issue bills of credit, and regulate the value of the coinage of the United States and the several states. However, nine of the thirteen states had to give their consent before any legislation of importance could be enacted, and enforcement of the decisions of Congress depended upon the cooperation of all the states. For example, Congress could make treaties but could not force the states to live up to their stipulations. It could authorize an army but could not fill its ranks without the cooperation of each state. It could borrow money but had to depend on requisitions from the states to repay its debts.

Nor did the Articles provide standing agencies of enforcement. Congress could pass laws, but there was no formal executive or judicial branch to execute and adjudicate them. The day-to-day operations of government were handled rather precariously by officials or committees appointed by Congress.

Because of their recent quarrels with Parliament over questions of taxation and commercial regulation, the states also withheld two key powers from their new central government: the power to levy taxes (Congress could merely request contributions from the state legislatures) and the power to regulate commerce. Without these powers the Confederation government could not depend upon a regular and adequate supply of revenue to sustain its own functions, nor could it attempt to foster a national economy, a factor essential to the political unity of America.

The central government, therefore, was what the Articles called it—nothing more than "a firm league of friendship." Sharing a common cause of facing common danger, its members could work together with some measure of effectiveness. Any suspicion that Congress would infringe upon their own right of independent action, however, would throw the states on their guard.

The State Governments. The Declaration of Independence in 1776 had made necessary the creation of two kinds of government: central and local. While only tentative motions were made toward centralization, the people were quick to make the transition from colonial government to state government. Actually the process was one of revision and adaptation, since each of the former colonies already possessed a government with its own methods of operation. Indeed, two states (Connecticut and Rhode Island) continued to operate under their colonial charters by simply deleting all references to the British crown. Ten other states completed new constitutions within a year after the Declaration of Independence, and the last (Massachusetts) by 1780. The state constitutions, though varying in detail, reflected both the colonial experience and the current revolutionary controversy.

The framers of the constitution placed the center of political authority in the legislative branch, where it would be especially responsive to popular and local control. As a Massachusetts town meeting bluntly resolved in 1778, "The oftener power Returns to the hands of the people, the Better . . . Where can the power be lodged so Safe as in the Hands of the people?" Members of the legislature, if they wished to be reelected, had to keep in mind the feelings of their people "back home." Legislators were held constantly accountable by being restricted to brief terms: in ten states the lower house, which originated tax legislation, was newly elected every year; in Connecticut and Rhode Island it was every six months; in South Carolina, every two years.

Framers of the constitutions, remembering their recent troubles with royal governors and magistrates, restricted the powers of governors and justices almost to the vanishing point. The average governor, contemporary jokesters claimed, had just about enough authority to collect his salary.

The imbalance of power among the branches of government often severely hampered the states' abilities to meet and solve the political and economic problems which faced them during and after the war. Yet whatever their shortcomings, these constitutions were the first attempts to translate the generalities of the Declaration into usable instruments of government. They were constructed on the premise, novel to the eighteenth century, that a government should be formed under a *written* document, thus recognizing the first time in modern political life the difference between fundamental and statute law. The introduction of such precisely formed instruments of governmental law, on such a grand scale, was a major contribution to the science of government.

The state constitutions reaffirmed the powerful colonial tradition of individual freedom in their bills of rights, which guaranteed each citizen freedom of religion, speech, and assembly, trial by jury, the right of habeas corpus, and other natural and civil rights. In general, they extended the voting franchise to the majority of white male citizens. In all states, a man had to own some property to vote. In many, he had to own a more substantial amount to hold office. Since property formed the basis for voting qualifications, and since the states quickly enlarged opportunities to own land, most white males could probably meet the requirements. New Jersey even gave the vote to women, only to withdraw it later. Over the years, gradual abolition of property qualifications further widened the suffrage.

The popular fear of governmental power tended to render the state governments politically and financially impotent. Afraid to antagonize the voters, who could quickly run them out of office, legislators had difficulty, for example, in passing effective measures of taxation. Even when they did so, revenue men were hard put in forcing collections from the people.

THE CONFEDERATION PERIOD

Such was the political framework within which the new nation entered the "critical period," 1783–1789, from the close of the Revolutionary War to the inauguration of the federal government under the Constitution. Long after the label of "critical period" was first introduced by historian John Fiske in 1889, historians came to acknowledge that the years of the Confederation were more creative and constructive than once was supposed.

During these years a peace was won on terms highly favorable to the United States. An orderly policy for western territorial expansion was established. A postwar recession was overcome and replaced by economic prosperity. The population increased. The Constitution was born. Nevertheless, except in regard to western lands, the achievements of the period were due largely to the efforts of particular individuals and groups and to some of the more foresighted state governments. The central government was much too dependent on the conflicting whims of the several states to be consistently effective.

Establishing a Western Policy. The solution to the western land problem (see Chapter 3), which had kept the last state, Maryland, from ratifying the Articles until 1781, was of paramount importance to the new government. It represented a first step toward nationalization and made certain that the nation, as it moved west, would gradually evolve as a unit rather than as thirteen colonies with a set of permanent dependent territories. It also meant that since Congress now controlled all the western lands, it could determine a central policy for the development of this vast unpopulated territory.

During and after the Revolution a stream poured west, creating an urgent need for a systematic plan of land sale and territorial government. A Land Ordinance passed by Congress in 1785 provided for a government survey to divide the land of the Northwest Territory (north of the Ohio River, west of Pennsylvania, and east of the Mississippi River) into townships of thirty-six square miles. Each township was to be split into thirty-six sections of one square mile (640 acres) each and each section into quarter sections. Four sections in every township were reserved as bounties for soldiers of the Continental army, and another section was set aside for the use of public schools. The remainder of the land was to be sold at public

NORTHWEST TERRITORY

SEVEN
RANGES
First area surveyed
under Ordinance of 1785

auction for at least one dollar an acre, in minimum lots of 640 acres.

The Ordinance of 1785 proved advantageous to wealthy land speculators, who bought up whole townships and resold them at handsome profits. Sensing even greater returns, a group of speculators (including some congressmen and government officials) pressed for further legislation to provide a form of government for the Northwest. The result was the Northwest Ordinance of 1787, based largely on a similar ordinance drafted by Jefferson in 1784 but never put into effect.

Though it favored the wealthy land speculator over the indigent farmer, the Northwest Ordinance did provide a model for translating the unsettled Northwest, by orderly political procedures, from frontier to statehood. It provided that Congress should appoint from among the landholders of the region a governor, a secretary, and three judges. When the territory reached a population of 5,000 free adult males, a bicameral legislature was to be established. When there were 60,000 free inhabitants (the population of the smallest state at the time), the voters might adopt a constitution, elect their own officers, and enter the Union on equal terms with the original thirteen states. From three to five states were to be formed from the territory. Slavery was forbidden in the area, and freedom of worship and trial by jury were guaranteed.

So successfully did the Northwest Ordinance accomplish its political aims that it set the pattern for the absorption of the entire West (as well as Alaska and Hawaii) into the Union. Settlers flooded into the Northwest Territory as soon as the ordinance went into effect. The great drive westward had begun, not to cease for another hundred years.

Relations with Europe. Perhaps the most serious problems facing Congress under the Articles arose from its lack of a unified, coherent foreign policy and its lack of authority to evolve one. The core of diplomatic power lay equally among the states, each of which possessed the right to arrange its own foreign affairs, with the national government virtually helpless to operate independently.

The United States was in a most delicate position in regard to England, France, and Spain. There was no reason to suppose that Britain intended to allow America to remain independent without interference if Britain's interests dictated otherwise. The United States, for its part, desperately needed trade agreements with Europe and especially with England, its largest market.

It was also involved in a border dispute with Spain over Florida, and when the Spanish, who controlled the lower Mississippi and New Orleans, closed them to American trade in 1784, the nation was in trouble. If Congress could not open the Mississippi to trade, a number of Western leaders favored either taking New Orleans by force or joining a British protectorate which might help them to do so. Washington felt that the West in 1784 was so near to secession that "the touch of a feather" might divide it from the country.

The Spanish, who needed American trade, seemed willing to negotiate, and in 1785 the Spanish minister Diego de Gardoqui discussed terms with Secretary of Foreign Affairs John Jay. Both diplomats were bound by specific instructions which led to a stalemate, but eventually Jay in 1786 agreed to a commercial treaty. This treaty would have allowed the United States to trade with Spain but not with its colonies—if the Americans would "forbear" navigation of the Mississippi River though not the *right* to use it.

Such a roar of protest went up from the West that Jay let the negotiations lapse. The Spanish helped matters in 1788 by opening the river under restrictions with which the West could live, though not happily, until the issue was settled by the Pinckney Treaty of 1795. These negotiations with Spain not only pointed up the impotence of the Articles in foreign affairs but left behind in the West a lingering suspicion of the East.

The Difficulties of Trade. When the colonies left the imperial system, thus giving up their favored economic position, American merchants and shippers found themselves in cutthroat competition with the British, Dutch, and French for world markets. John Adams tried unsuccessfully for three years to make some kind of trade agreement with England, but as Lord Sheffield commented, putting his finger squarely on the commercial weaknesses of the Articles of Confederation, "America cannot retaliate. It will not be an easy matter to bring the Americans to act as a nation. They are not to be feared by such as us."

Sheffield proved to be correct, for when Congress asked the states in 1784 for exclusive authority to regulate foreign trade over a fifteen-year period, the states immediately refused. Under the Articles of Confederation, Congress was powerless to do more than protest.

Domestic commerce as well as foreign trade suffered from interstate rivalries. The states used their power to levy tariffs against each other, creating barriers that seriously hampered domestic commerce and caused further dissatisfaction with the central government. At the same time, American industry was struggling to survive. The war and blockade had stimulated American manufacturing by cutting off imports from Britain and the Continent. Some of the states, in fact, had offered premiums and subsidies for the production of manufactured goods. But with the return of peace much of the artificial stimulation which had encouraged American industry was withdrawn, and the inevitable postwar slump set in. Capital was short, the currency disordered, transportation deficient, and investments risky.

Frenzied Finances. The Articles of Confederation gave the national government no power to tax. If the states refused to pay their levies in full or on time, Congress simply was forced to accumulate ever larger foreign and domestic debts. The states responded erratically to Congress' requests for revenue, so that while Congress occasionally had money, it never had enough at the right time. Although Congress repudiated most of its war debts by simply canceling out millions of dollars in the currency issued under the Continental Congress, the country in 1785 still owed about $35 million in domestic debts and had a growing foreign debt. The states, meanwhile, had war debts of their own, which they increased after the war by taking on the amounts of the congressional debt that were owed to their citizens.

In addition to the problem of these debts, both national and state governments lacked a uniform, stable, sound currency. There was no trustworthy federal currency, and the states were loaded with badly inflated wartime paper money. The postwar slump which hit the country in 1783, sinking to its lowest point in mid-1786, affected the farmer and the small debtor most of all. In states where they controlled the legislatures, the solution seemed easy: Seven state legislatures simply approved the issue of paper money in larger quantities. In addition, to help distressed farmers, these states passed "stay laws" to prevent creditors from foreclosing mortgages.

Crisis and Rebellion. At the depth of the depression in 1786 there was a severe hard-money shortage. Farmers, especially, were in difficulty. Protest meetings in several states won some concessions from the legislatures, but in Massachusetts, when mobs of unruly men closed the courts at Northhampton, Worcester, and Springfield, thus preventing farm foreclosures and prosecutions for debt,

Governor James Bowdoin sent militia to scatter them.

In reply to Bowdoin, Daniel Shays, a veteran of the Revolution, organized a band of farmers in 1786 for an attack on the Springfield Arsenal, from which he hoped to get arms. The governor sent a force of militia (paid for by contributions from Boston businessmen) to protect the arsenal, and Shays' poorly mounted attack in February 1787 failed miserably. In a few weeks the leaders of the rebellion had been captured and convicted, and a few sentenced to death. The legislature pardoned them all, however—even Shays, who was released in 1788.

Shays' Rebellion had swift effects in Massachusetts. Governor Bowdoin was defeated in the next election by John Hancock, and the legislature prudently decided to grant the farmers some measure of relief. The effect on the country at large was equally swift, and

Shays' attempt to storm the Springfield arsenal was seen as a threat not only to the authority of Massachusetts but to the entire nation.

much greater. As Abigail Adams wrote Thomas Jefferson, when "ignorant, restless desperadoes, without conscience or principles" could persuade "a deluded multitude to follow their standards . . ." who could be safe, anywhere in the land? "There are combustibles," wrote Washington, "in every state which a spark might set fire to."

FRAMING A NEW CONSTITUTION

The Drift Toward a New Government. Even the most earnest states' rights advocates were willing to admit the existence of imperfections in the Articles of Confederation, and proposals for conventions to discuss amending them had already appeared in the New York legislature in 1782 and in Massachusetts in 1785. In 1786, under the cloud of Shays' Rebellion, Congress agreed that the Articles needed revision, though as James Monroe told Jefferson, "Some gentlemen have inveterate prejudices against all attempts to increase the powers of Congress, others see the necessity but fear the consequences."

It remained for Alexander Hamilton of New York to seize the initiative. When Virginia invited representatives from the states to meet at Annapolis in 1786 for a discussion of problems of interstate commerce, Hamilton called upon the states to appoint delegates to a meeting to be held in May 1787 at Philadelphia, to discuss ways "to render the Constitution of the Federal Government adequate to the exigencies of the Union." Since at almost the same time Daniel Shays' men, pursued by Boston militia, were providing an example of the kind of "exigency" Hamilton referred to, his call found receptive audiences in the states. Congress adopted his suggestion and authorized a convention "for the sole and express purpose of revising the Articles of Confederation and reporting to Congress and the several legislatures such alterations and provisions therein."

While there were those who believed that the Articles could be amended and reworked into an effective and efficient government, a number of determined political leaders— among them Alexander Hamilton, James Madison, John Jay, and Henry Knox—were convinced that the country's interests demanded a much stronger central government: They believed in executive and judicial control rather than legislative and did not fully trust the decentralized, mass-dominated state governments. There was a general belief among the mercantile and financial classes that, as Madison wrote, the United States needed the kind of government which would "support a due supremacy of the national authority, and leave in force the local authorities so far as they can be subordinately useful."

The Question of Federalism. The meetings at Philadelphia began on May 25, 1787. Conspicuously absent were many of the popular leaders of the prerevolutionary era. These "antifederalists," men like Samuel Adams and Patrick Henry, had involved themselves in the Revolution when it still comprised a scattering of colonial protests and then state revolts, rather loosely guided by the Continental Congress. Deeply devoted to winning independence for their own states, most of them continued to believe that the states should be governed without the interference of a strong central government. Some antifederalists, like George Clinton of New York, had a vital stake in local state politics, which the enlargement of the powers of a continental government might endanger. Others saw the need to strengthen the Confederation but insisted that the supremacy of the states should not be basically altered. All of the antifederalists were passionately convinced that a republican system could survive only on the local level, under their watchful eyes. A republic on a continental scale was beyond their imagination.

The fifty-five delegates who made their appearance in the Philadelphia State House held generally broader views. George Washington (chosen presiding officer of the convention) and Benjamin Franklin were distinguished representatives of an older generation, long experienced in guiding the military and diplomatic affairs of the colonies as a whole. Most of the delegates, however, were in their thirties or forties. Their careers had only begun when the Revolution broke out and their public reputations had been achieved as a result of their identification with the continental war effort. With the coming of peace, these "nationalists" had been disquieted by the ease with which the states slid back into their old provincial ways. In vainly advocating revenue and commercial powers for the Confederation Congress, Robert Morris, James Wilson, Gouverneur Morris, James Madison, Alexander Hamilton, Charles Pinckney, and others began to see the futility of trying to govern a large country with thirteen states following diverse policies.

These federalists distrusted unchecked power in government as much as their opponents did. However, they believed that under the current system power *was* being exercised in one quarter without effective restraints. Jefferson branded it the "legislative tyranny" of the states. There was no way to appeal the decisions of the state legislators. The state executive and judicial branches, and even the central Confederation, were powerless to overrule the legislative branch. In addition, nations abroad were beginning to look with contempt upon the disunited states, and there were even dangerous signs of territorial encroachments—by Britain in the Northwest and by Spain in the South and Southwest. National survival and prestige, the federalists insisted, demanded that a stronger central government be created.

The Philosophy of the Constitution.   The feeling of urgency which permeated the minds of the delegates goes far toward explaining their eagerness to reach compromises on matters in dispute. Whenever the debates became deadlocked, speakers would arise and warn of the consequences should the Convention fail. Said Elbridge Gerry at mid-session: "Something must be done or we shall disappoint not only America, but the whole world. . . . We must make concessions on both sides." And Caleb Strong warned, "It is agreed, on all hands, that Congress is nearly at an end. If no accommodation takes place, the Union itself must soon be dissolved."

Such warnings climaxed a series of heated arguments during the meetings. While differences of opinion continued to arise, they were mostly over matters of detail and method. The Founding Fathers were in essential agreement in regard to the broad outlines of the new government and in regard to political principles, learned through years of experience in dealing with a "tyrannous" Parliament and serving in state legislatures and in Congress.

First, they believed that the central government must be empowered to act without the mediation of the states and to exercise its will directly upon individual citizens. It must have its own administrative agencies, with the ability to enforce its own laws and treaties, to collect its own revenues, and to regulate commerce and other matters of welfare affecting the states generally.

Second, they believed that power in government, though imperative, must somehow be held in check. Like most enlightened people of the eighteenth century, they recognized that human nature was not perfect. "Men are ambitious, vindictive, and rapacious," said Alexander Hamilton, and while his language was strong, his appraisal of human nature was generally shared by his colleagues. They agreed with the French political philosopher Montesquieu that "men entrusted with power tend to abuse it." The system advocated by Montesquieu to prevent this evil was to distribute the functions of government among three coequal branches of government, each of which would hold a veto or check on the power of the others. This doctrine of "separation of powers" had earlier been outlined by John Adams:

A legislative, an executive, and a judicial power comprehend the whole of what is meant and understood by government. It is by balancing each of these powers against the other two, that the efforts in human nature toward tyranny can alone be checked and restrained, and any degree of freedom preserved in the constitution.

That a three-branch system had failed in the state governments did not shake the delegates' faith in the *principle* of separation of powers. The states had only gone through the motions of creating three branches. In actuality they had not given the executive and judicial branches sufficient checks on the legislatures, which in some states were running riot in control of government.

Finally, most of the delegates were committed to some form of federalism, the political system which would unite the states under an independently operating central government while permitting them to retain some portion of their former power and identity. Few agreed with George Read of Delaware that the states "must be done away." Even Alexander Hamilton, who formally introduced such a scheme, acknowledged that the Convention might "shock the public opinion by proposing such a measure." It was generally agreed that the states must remain. The argument arose over how, in operating terms, power could be properly distributed between the states and the national government.

The Convention at Work. Four days after the Convention opened, Edmund Randolph of Virginia proposed fifteen resolutions, drafted by his colleague James Madison. The general intent was clear at once: to proceed beyond mere revision of the Articles of Confederation in favor of forming a new national government. This "Virginia Plan" proposed a na-

tional executive, a national judiciary, and a national legislature consisting of two houses, both representing the states proportionally according to either population or tax contributions, with the lower house popularly elected and the upper house chosen by members of the lower one. Although William Paterson proposed a rival "New Jersey Plan," which in substance would merely have enlarged the taxation and commerce powers of the Confederation Congress, it was never seriously considered. The Virginia Plan, after four months of debate, amendment, and considerable enlargement, became the United States Constitution.

Although the delegates agreed upon the main features of the new government, discord over the details almost broke up the Convention. That a breakup was avoided is attributable in part to the delegates' recognition of the undeniable need for compromise and concession. They were pressed to balance special interest against special interest, the large states against the small, section against section, in order to work out a constitution that the majority could accept. No state could be perfectly satisfied with the result, but each could feel that the half loaf it garnered for its interest was far better than none.

Major opposition to the original Virginia Plan came from the small states. In the existing Congress each of their votes was equal to that of any large state, but under the proposed system of proportional representation in the national legislature they would be consistently outvoted by the larger, more populous states. Delegates from the large states retorted that government should represent people, not geography. "Is [a government] for *men*," asked James Wilson, "or for the imaginary beings called *States?*" The issue came down to the question of how federal the federal government should be. In acknowledging the permanence of the states, were the delegates obligated to go further and introduce the concept of the states into the very structure and representation of the new central government?

The final answer to this question was yes. In the end, the large states gave in. After the New Jersey Plan was rejected and the principle of a bicameral (two-house) legislature established, the small states, while hesitating to object to proportional representation in the lower house, persisted in claiming the right of equal representation for states in the Senate, or upper house. And by threatening to walk out of the Convention, they won. In essence, this "Great Compromise," as it came to be called, was hardly a compromise at all. The major issue concerned representation in the Senate, and when the large states conceded on this point, they received no concession in return. However, the major crisis of the Convention had been resolved.

In the process of accepting this two-house legislature, the delegates acknowledged not only a balance between large and small states but also a balance between the common people and propertied, supposedly conservative interests. Many delegates had argued against giving the people a direct voice in government; "The people," said Roger Sherman, "should have as little to do as may be about the government. They want information, and are constantly liable to be misled." Elbridge Gerry pointed to the "evils" that "flow from the excess of democracy." Other delegates agreed, however, with James Madison, who stated "that the great fabric to be raised would be more stable and durable, if it should rest on the solid foundation of the people themselves." Thus the basis of representation in the lower house was set at one representative for every forty thousand persons—each representative to be elected by voters eligible to elect "the most numerous branch of [their] State legislature." On the other hand, the senators of the upper house—two from each state—were to be chosen by the state legislatures, putting them at a second remove from popular control. As a result, the Senate was expected to represent the more conservative interests, "to consist," as John Dickinson noted, "of the most distinguished characters, distinguished for their rank in life and their weight of property." In sum, the two houses of Congress were to balance the rights of the lower and higher ranks of society, but with the edge given to the higher.

Another issue arose over the manner of choosing the President, the head of the executive branch of the new government. To have the national legislature appoint him, as the original Virginia Plan proposed, might mean, it was argued, that a candidate to that high office would be "a mere creature of the legislature." A second plan, championed by James Wilson, called for popular election of the President, but the delegates had too great a distrust of unchecked democracy to find this plan fully acceptable. Other proposals sought to bring the states into the elective process by having either the state legislatures or the governors combine to elect the nation's chief executive.

The final compromise embodied elements from all these plans. Each state legislature was to appoint a number of presidential "electors" equal to the total number of senators and representatives to which the state was entitled in Congress. The electors would meet in their own states and vote for two presidential candidates, and the candidate receiving the majority of votes from all the states would become President. It should be noted that the method of choosing the electors was left to the decision of the state legislatures. Thus, the legislatures might decide to keep the power of appointment in their own hands, as most of them did, or they could submit the appointment to popular vote, a method which became widespread only much later. In either case, the electoral system was intended to minimize popular influence in the choice of the President.

Few of the delegates, however, believed

that the election would end in the electoral college. It was believed that each state would try to advance a native son, and thus no candidate would receive a majority vote. In that event, the election would be referred to the House of Representatives, where votes would be taken by state delegations, each state having one vote. In effect, this presidential compromise echoed the earlier issue over proportional representation. In the first phase of the election, votes would be drawn on the basis of population. In the second phase, voting would be on the basis of statehood.

The conflict between North and South was not so serious in the Convention as it was later to become, but the differing sectional economies did arouse specific issues of governmental structure and powers. Because the South was an agricultural region dependent on a world market for its staple exports like tobacco and rice, it wanted commercial regulation—tariffs and export duties—eliminated or minimized. Southerners were also committed to slavery, not necessarily through moral conviction of its justice but because of their inescapably large investment in slave labor. Finally, the Southern states, six in number and comparatively less populous than the Northern states, were aware that in Congress they would be outnumbered by the North. They thus felt compelled to secure constitutional guarantees for their sectional interests before launching a new government in which they could be consistently outvoted.

In the North, on the other hand, agricultural products like grain and livestock had for the most part a ready domestic market. Many Northerners were more interested in having the government promote shipping and foster manufacturing by means of protective tariffs. Many also roundly condemned slavery and demanded an end to the "nefarious" slave trade. Their attitude, however, was not entirely without self-interest. The Convention had already agreed that direct taxes were to be assessed on the basis of population. The North was quite willing to have slaves counted as part of the population in apportioning such taxes, thus upping the South's assessments. But Northerners objected to counting slaves in apportioning representation in the House of Representatives, a plan which would enlarge the Southern delegations.

The Convention resolved these differences by negotiating compromises. In regard to commerce, the South won a ban on export taxes and a provision requiring a two-thirds vote in the Senate for ratification of treaties. In return, the North secured a provision that a simple congressional majority was sufficient to pass all other acts of commercial regulation. The slave trade was not be prohibited before the year 1808, but a tax of ten dollars might be imposed on each slave imported. The so-called three-fifths compromise specified that five slaves would equal three free men for purposes of both taxation and representation.

The influence of the states in the framework of the new constitution was greater than some nationalists would have liked. But one of the most important factors shaping the delegates' decisions was their practical recognition that they had to offer a constitution which the people would approve, and popular loyalty to the respective states was too strong to be ignored.

Referral to the States. By the close of the summer the Constitution was slowly taking shape, and on September 17, 1787, twelve state delegations voted approval of the final draft. Edmund Randolph and George Mason of Virginia, along with Elbridge Gerry of Massachusetts, refused to sign it, feeling that it went too far toward consolidation and lacked a bill of rights. (Randolph, however, later decided to support it.) The remaining thirty-nine delegates affixed their signatures and sent the document to Congress with two recommendations: that it be submitted to state ratifying conventions especially called for the purpose, rather than directly to the voters; and that it be declared officially operative when nine (not thirteen) states accepted it, since there was real doubt that any document so evolved could ever get unanimous approval. Some of the delegates feared that they had far exceeded their instructions to *revise* the Articles, for the document they sent to Congress certainly represented much more than revision.

Federalists and Antifederalists. The new Constitution met with great favor and equally great opposition in the states. Its strongest supporters, who adopted the name "Federalists," were drawn from the ranks of bankers, lawyers, businessmen, merchants, planters, and men of property in the urban areas. Hamilton and Jay favored it in New York. Madison, Randolph, and John Marshall argued for it in Virginia. And the fact that Washington and Franklin, the two most honored Americans, supported it was much in its favor. Opposition to its ratification came from the small farmers, laborers, and the debtor, agrarian classes. However, it is misleading to arrange the argument over ratification on lines of economic interest alone, however convenient. Obviously there were businessmen and merchants who voted for the document because they felt it would mean expanded markets, better regulation of commerce, greater credit stability, and less control of trade by the states. Just as obviously there were farmers and debtors who voted against it for equally self-interested economic reasons.

But the lines of demarcation between rich and poor, or mercantile and agrarian interests, were by no means so clear in the voting as one might expect. Claiming that the nation could obtain progress and prosperity under the Articles if they were revised, the Antifederalists accused the Convention of creating a government that eventually, as George Mason of Virginia thought, might "produce either a monarchy or a corrupt aristocracy."

There was "apprehension," Rufus King of New York told Madison, "that the liberties of the people are in danger."

On the other hand, the Federalists, who might more accurately have been called "nationalists," possessed a group of leaders of great drive and organizing skill. It was not easy to outargue or outmaneuver men such as Hamilton, Jay, Madison, James Wilson, or Henry Knox. Furthermore, they had the initiative and kept it, giving their opposition little time to temporize or organize. The Federalists immediately began an energetic campaign for ratification in their own states. In New York, where opposition was strong, the Constitution was brilliantly defended in a series of eighty-five newspaper articles written by Hamilton, Madison, and Jay. The essays later were collected in a single volume called *The Federalist*.

The Antifederalists had only a few such talented leaders. George Clinton, Patrick Henry, Elbridge Gerry, Luther Martin, and James Warren were able men, but none, for example, was capable of producing the brilliant *Federalist* papers or of handling the New York campaign as Hamilton did. The Antifederalists tried to fight the battle piecemeal, without a positive program, and showed a curious reluctance to match the aggressive, shrewd campaigning of the Federalists.

It has long been fashionable among historians, particularly in the earlier twentieth century, to consider the struggle over ratification as a contest between "conservatives" and "liberals." If the Declaration of Independence represented "radical" or revolutionary thought, the Constitution, it was assumed, therefore represented a conservative counterrevolution which undid some of the Revolution's work. On reexamination, however, it becomes less clear which side deserves which label. It was the Federalists, after all, who proposed the bold, decisive change to carry out to completion the powerful nationalism engendered by the revolutionary effort. This was a daring step—to create from a bundle of disparate states a single, unified nation bound together by common consent and national pride. The Antifederalists, fearful of any power not under their direct restraint, preferred the status quo. To them, apparently, the great experiment in federalism suggested by the Constitution seemed too new, too dangerous. They could not conceive of a nationalized government which did not threaten republican principles.

Ratification of the Constitution. The ratification of the document proceeded smoothly in most of the smaller states, which were generally satisfied with the compromises set up to protect them. By January 1788 five states (Delaware, New Jersey, Georgia, Connecticut, and Pennsylvania) had accepted it, with strong opposition recorded only in Pennsylvania. The Massachusetts state convention ratified the Constitution by a vote of 187 to 168 after a long dispute, and then only after attaching a strong recommendation for a bill of rights. Maryland and South Carolina ratified, while New Hampshire, the ninth state, took two conventions (the second by a margin of nine votes) to accept it in June 1788. Legally the Constitution could now go into effect, yet most people understood that without New York and Virginia it could not function successfully.

In Virginia, the Federalists won a narrow victory, 89 to 79, on June 25. Like Massachusetts, Virginia attached proposals for twenty changes and a recommendation for a specific bill of rights. In New York, Hamilton and the Federalists pulled the document through on July 26 by the breathtakingly small margin of 30 to 27. North Carolina refused to ratify the Constitution until a bill of rights was actually attached to it and finally approved it in late 1789. Rhode Island held out until 1790.

The debates over the ratification indicated that the chief issue was the Constitution's lack of a bill of rights, so in 1789 the First Congress proposed ten amendments (ratified in 1791) to guarantee popular government and individual freedom. Of the ten, the First prohibited Congress from interfering with freedom of speech, press, religion, and assembly. The Fifth placed the citizen under "due process" of law, and the Sixth and Seventh guaranteed trial by jury. The Tenth reserved to the people and to the states all powers not delegated to the federal government, thereby providing a guarantee of decentralized political power. Thus this "bill of rights" wrote into law those "self-evident truths" and "natural rights" on which the Declaration had based its case for independence.

The ideas expressed in the Constitution were themselves implicit in the Articles of Confederation, the Declaration of Independence, and the revolutionary argument. The Constitution merely gave those ideas explicit, final form. The idea that government should protect life, liberty, and property was already accepted. The idea that government should be powerful enough to perform its functions was already recognized, even in the Articles—though there were sharp differences of opinion over how powerful that need be.

No one at the Convention, and very few people in the states, argued for retention of the Articles without change. The question was, did the Constitution change the direction of government too much? The difference between the Articles and the Constitution lay almost wholly in the amount and quality of the authority granted to that "more perfect union."

LAUNCHING THE GOVERNMENT

Washington and Federalist Rule. After the balloting for President in January 1789, and for Congress under the terms of the new Constitution, the presidential electors met in February to choose George Washington as the first President of the United States. John Adams,

REDEUNT SATURNIA REGNA.

On the erection of the Eleventh PILLAR of the great National DOME, we beg leave most sincerely to felicitate " OUR DEAR COUNTRY."

Rise it will.

The foundation good—it may yet be SAVED.

The *FEDERAL EDIFICE.*

ELEVEN STARS, in quick succession rise—
ELEVEN COLUMNS strike our wond'ring eyes,
Soon o'er the *whole*, shall swell the beauteous DOME,
COLUMBIA's boast—and FREEDOM's hallow'd home.
   Here shall the ARTS in glorious splendour shine !
And AGRICULTURE give her stores divine !
COMMERCE refin'd, dispense us more than gold,
And this new world, teach WISDOM to the old—
RELIGION here shall fix her blest abode,
Array'd in *mildness*, like its parent GOD !
JUSTICE and LAW, shall endless PEACE maintain,
And *the* " SATURNIAN AGE," *return again.*

According to this 1788 caricature, the nation's foundation was sound once powerful Virginia and New York ratified the Constitution, but the refusal of North Carolina and Rhode Island seemed like crumbling pillars in the nation's temple.

who had received the smaller number of electoral ballots, was installed as Vice-President in mid-April, and on April 30 Washington, standing on the balcony of the Federal Building at Broad and Wall Streets in New York, was inaugurated as President.

For the first few months of the new administration, Congress and the President moved carefully. Congress quickly created the three executive departments of State, Treasury, and War, and Washington chose Thomas Jefferson, Alexander Hamilton, and Henry Knox to serve as their Secretaries. Congress then passed a tariff on imports and a tonnage duty on foreign vessels, both intended to raise revenue and to protect American trade. The Judiciary Act of 1789 created the office of Attorney General, a Supreme Court, three circuit courts, and thirteen district courts, filling in the outlines of the federal legal system.

Federalist Finance.   Washington left the most critical problem of his first term to Alexander Hamilton, his confident young Secretary of the Treasury. Hamilton believed, as most Federalists did, that the government should play an active, even decisive role in economic affairs, so that the nation might achieve a self-sufficient, expanding economy, balanced among agriculture, manufacturing, and trade. To this end he proposed, in his *Report on the Public Credit* (1790), *Second Report on the Public Credit* (1791), and *Report on Manufactures* (1791), a firm, unified policy enforced by a strong federal authority.

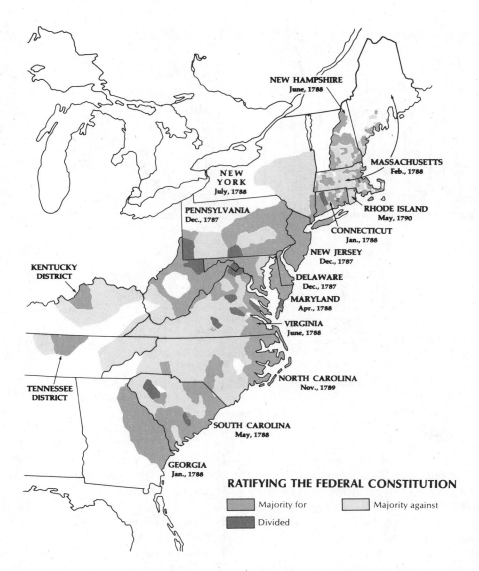

NEW HAMPSHIRE
June, 1788

MASSACHUSETTS
Feb., 1788

NEW YORK
July, 1788

RHODE ISLAND
May, 1790

PENNSYLVANIA
Dec., 1787

CONNECTICUT
Jan., 1788

NEW JERSEY
Dec., 1787

KENTUCKY
DISTRICT

DELAWARE
Dec., 1787

MARYLAND
Apr., 1788

VIRGINIA
June, 1788

TENNESSEE
DISTRICT

NORTH CAROLINA
Nov., 1789

SOUTH CAROLINA
May, 1788

GEORGIA
Jan., 1788

RATIFYING THE FEDERAL CONSTITUTION

Majority for   Majority against

Divided

Hamilton's economic program also had clear political aims. He was convinced that the new government could not last unless the Constitution were strengthened by interpretation and made responsive to changing needs, and unless the forces of wealth and property supported it. Thus he hoped to win business and financial groups to the support of the federal government, and to bind these groups to the national interest. Hamilton fashioned his program from three basic components.

The first laid the foundation for the Hamiltonian system. Under the previous regimes—that is, the Continental and Confederation congresses—the general government had accumulated a foreign debt of about $12 million, owed chiefly to France and Holland, and a domestic debt of about $40 million, owed to American nationals. The separate states owed a total of about $22 million more. Hamilton proposed that the federal government promise full payment of all these debts at par value, thus taking over, or *assuming,* the unpaid debts of the states. Since the federal government did not possess the money to pay this debt, totaling about $74 million, Hamilton recommended *funding* the entire debt. That is, in exchange for their old Continental and Confederation bonds, creditors would be issued new interest-bearing bonds which would be the direct obligation of the new federal government.

No opposition was voiced against payment of the foreign debt in full, but full payment of the domestic debt at face value was another matter. On the open market these old domestic bonds had been selling at far below their original face value. Because the previous central governments had failed to meet interest payments or provide for retirement of the debt, the original owners of the bonds had lost faith in them and had sold them for whatever they could get. The purchasers were usually men of means who were willing to buy cheap on the chance that the government would make good.

Hamilton did succeed in getting Congress to make the old bonds good at face value (many congressmen were themselves bond holders), but in so doing he aroused charges from his opponents that the new government was being operated in the interest of the wealthy. Hamilton's intentions, however, were actually both honorable and farsighted. In his plan, he believed, the middle and upper classes would find a strong motive for sustaining the national government, and their confidence in the solvency and good faith of the government would stimulate business activity. In addition, the funded debt, in the form of negotiable bonds, could be used by creditors as capital to finance new enterprises.

Vehement opposition to the assumption of the state debts by the federal government was also evoked in the Southern states, which had already paid off most of their debts. Southerners protested the use of national funds to help pay off the obligations of states with large outstanding debts, such as the New England states. Hamilton's assumption program was defeated on its first vote in the House, but he finally won in a bargain with Jefferson. In exchange for an agreement to locate the new national capital on the Potomac across from Virginia, Jefferson's congressional forces agreed to assume the debts of the states.

The second part of Hamilton's program called for the creation of a central bank, somewhat like the Bank of England, which would serve as a depository for federal funds, issue paper money (which the Treasury by law could not do), provide commercial interests with a steady and dependable credit institution, and serve the government with short-term loans. Some leaders in and out of Congress objected to this proposal on two grounds: Four fifths of the bank's funds were to come from private sources, which might then control the bank's (and the nation's) fiscal policies. More important, the scheme was probably unconstitutional. Jefferson and Madison, among others, argued that since the federal government was not specifically authorized by the Constitution to create a national bank, it would be unconstitutional for Congress to do so.

Hamilton, aware that the bank bill might set an important precedent, argued that Congress was authorized by the Constitution to do what was "necessary and proper" for the national good. If the proposed bank fell within this definition, as he believed it did, the Constitution gave Congress "implied powers" to act in ways not precisely defined in the document. He took the position "that every power vested in a government is in its nature *sovereign* and includes, by *force* of the *term,* a right to employ all the *means* requisite and fairly applicable to the attainment of the *ends* of such power. . . ."

Jefferson, to the contrary, argued that the

federal government possessed only those powers explicitly granted to it in the Constitution, and that all others, as the Tenth Amendment said, were reserved to the states. The language of the Constitution must be strictly construed. "To take a single step beyond the boundaries thus especially drawn around the powers of Congress," he wrote, "is to take possession of a boundless field of power, no longer susceptible of any definition." Neither the "general welfare" nor the "necessary and proper" clause of the Constitution, he maintained, could be so broadly interpreted. Washington and Congress, however, accepted Hamilton's argument and in 1791 created the Bank of the United States with a charter for twenty years.

The Whiskey Rebellion. Third, Hamilton proposed to levy an excise tax on a number of commodities to supply money to the federal Treasury for, he wrote, ". . . the creation of debt should always be accompanied by the means of its extinguishment." Among the items included in the bill, passed in 1791, was whiskey. In western Pennsylvania and North Carolina, where conversion into whiskey was a cheap and efficient way of getting grain to market, Hamilton's excise tax was therefore a tax on the farmer's most valuable cash crop.

Collections fell off in this area in 1792, and a few tax collectors were manhandled by irritated Pennsylvania farmers in 1793. In 1794 a sizable force of angry whiskey makers vowed to march on Pittsburgh to challenge federal authority at its nearest point.

Memories of Daniel Shays were still fresh in Congress, and President Washington acted quickly. He issued a proclamation ordering the Pennsylvanians to return to their homes,

Opposition to the nation's first tax, Hamilton's excise tax on whiskey, was so high that United States officers were treated much the same as British tax collectors before the Revolution—tarred and feathered and ridden out of town on a rail.

declared western Pennsylvania in a state of rebellion, and sent Hamilton and Henry Lee with a force of 15,000 militiamen to Pennsylvania. The farmers promptly scattered, but Hamilton, determined to teach the unruly frontiersmen a lesson in federal authority, saw to it that a score of the ringleaders were arrested, tried, and sentenced to death. Washington wisely pardoned them, but neither Hamilton nor Federalism was ever popular in that region again.

DEVELOPING AN INDIAN POLICY

At the close of the Revolution the issue between Indians and white Americans remained as insoluble as ever. It seemed impossible to divert or delay the American drive westward, where the tribes possessed undeveloped lands of great value.

Of the losers in the Revolution, the Indians—most of whom had fought with the British—lost most. The Peace Treaty simply left them out. Britain ceded the lands west to the Mississippi to the Americans without mentioning the Indians who lived there, while the Americans considered them a conquered people whose lands were subject to confiscation.

"With respect to the Indians," wrote one of the negotiators, "we claim the right of pre-emption; with respect to all other nations, we claim the sovereignty over the territory." Though tribal leaders protested to the British negotiators that they had no right to give away Indian lands, and to the Americans that they had no right to abrogate previous treaties, neither side listened.

"Noble Red Man" or "Barbaric Savage?" Federal and state policy toward the Indians was greatly influenced by the white Americans' perception of them. Whites found Indians difficult to negotiate with, for few Americans understood much of Indian psy-chology, politics, or culture. Both Indians and whites were heirs of two hundred years of constant and vicious warfare. White explorers and settlers, almost from their first contacts with the Indians, had developed contrasting images of the "noble red man" on the one hand, and the "barbaric savage" on the other. These images persisted in the minds of later Americans.

Some Americans, particularly the educated minority, viewed the various Indian cultures with respect and sympathized with the Indians' plight. These Americans hoped the tribes could be assimilated into American society. Both President Washington and his secretary of war, Henry Knox, who had charge of Indian affairs, believed in assimilation. Knox reaffirmed Indian land claims in a series of reports in early 1789. "Instead of exterminating part of the human race," he wrote, Americans should instead take pride in having "imparted knowledge of cultivation and the arts to the aboriginals of the country. . . ."

Others tended to see the Indian as irredeemably—though tragically—savage, incapable ever of learning the ways of civilization. Frontiersmen, too, had vivid recollections of Indian attacks during the French and Indian wars and bitter, still-fresh memories of Loyalist-Indian raids in New York and Pennsylvania during the Revolution. (See "Simon Girty: The White Savage.") Meanwhile, the possibility of an alliance between the western tribes and the British army, still in Canada, posed a threat to the Ohio-Indiana frontier.

In fact, although the British had promised at the Peace of Paris to give up their posts in the Northwest, they apparently intended to hold them as long as possible. Orders from the Colonial office to the governor-general of Canada, one day before the proclamation of the Treaty in 1784, instructed British commanders to do exactly that. So many Americans were convinced that the only sound policy toward the Indians was removal.

Assimilation or Removal. Relations with the Indians developed over two phases in the years before 1812. From the end of the war until the election of Washington in 1789, Congress assumed that all Indian lands belonged to the United States and that all tribes were under government control. Congress appointed commissioners to handle Indian affairs, but most direct dealings with the tribes were carried out by the states.

Land was the issue. Both federal and state policy was to move Indians off lands that settlers wanted, but this required more military power and money than either federal or state governments possessed. The removal policy also raised questions among those who saw this as a moral problem as well as a military and political one.

By 1786, both state and federal governments realized that establishing an effective, acceptable Indian policy involved a large set of complex issues. The central problem was how to establish white settlements in Indian country and still treat the Indian with humanity and justice. The lure of open, fertile land, a growing nationalism, and the need for strategic defenses against France, Spain, and British Canada all had to be balanced against the new nation's desire to act in accordance with the principles of its revolution and a Christian conscience.

American leaders therefore reactivated the British colonial policy of recognizing Indian

Simon Girty: The "White Savage"

The North American Indian wars of the eighteenth century were really not Indian wars at all. They were, rather, wars between white groups—British and French, British and American—in which the Indian served as an instrument by which the whites settled the fate of the Indian's homelands. Savage, pitiless wars, they exposed the seamier side of the frontier, where the environment was sometimes too strong for the person. Life in the wilderness could blur distinctions. It was easy, very easy, in the frontier country, to cross the cultural line that separated red and white.

More than a few white men and women crossed it. Within a few years after Virginia's settlement, more than forty English men had taken Indian wives and several English women had married Indian husbands. Some crossed over simply to escape the rules and responsibilities of their own culture. Others found it the best way to survive on the frontier. Still others found security and status in tribal life. Children who were captured and brought up by Indians were particularly susceptible.

Simon Girty was one of these, and two hundred years ago almost every American knew his name. His reputation stretched from New England to the Gulf and far into the West. To his era he was the ultimate traitor, the "White Savage of Ohio" who turned against his heritage and his race.

land rights and acquiring the necessary acres by treaties and purchases, meanwhile establishing strict boundaries to control the advance of white settlers. The Northwest Ordinance of 1787, which had officially opened the West to settlement, stated that Indians should be dealt with in "utmost good faith," their "property, rights and liberty" protected, their lands "never to be taken from them without their consent."

This new policy did not fully satisfy the national conscience, however. At best, it was a temporary solution. If land and game disappeared and the tribes were pushed ever farther west by treaty and expansion, the whole race might soon disappear.

Plenty of Americans, particularly on the frontier, did not care. But many others did not want their country, which they believed to be a new and better experiment in enlightened government, held responsible for the destruction of an entire people.

In the view of the Enlightenment, Indians were as much part of the human race as were white men. Such differences as existed between them were seen as the results of education and environment. The solution, then, was to "civilize" Indians by giving them education, religious training, and the means of making a living, thus bringing them into the mainstream of American society. "In leading them to agriculture, to manufacture, and civilization," said Jefferson, "I trust and believe we are acting for their greatest good."

Westward expansion was thus given a moral basis by being seen as an extension of

---

Simon Girty was born in 1741 in Pennsylvania, the son of an Irish immigrant who was killed in 1751 in a fight with an Indian named The Fish. His father's friend John Turner then killed The Fish, married the Widow Girty, and took over her sons, Thomas (the oldest), Simon, James, and George. The entire family, however, was captured in an Indian raid in 1756. After burning Turner at the stake, the Indians divided the rest of the family with the exception of Thomas, who escaped. The mother and George went with the Delawares, James with the Shawnees, and Simon with the Senecas, who renamed the boy Katepacoma, taught him their language, and turned him into a skilled woodsman and hunter.

Two years later the Girtys were released and reunited at Fort Pitt. All except Thomas (who entered business) seem to have been rough, violent young men—three among many such hangers-on around the post who earned a precarious living as scouts and translators. When American independence seemed near, Simon threw in his lot with the British, then changed his mind and found work as an American agent to the Senecas, his old captors. He was soon disciplined for "ill behavior" (probably brawling) and in 1778 changed sides again. This time he went with James and George to Detroit, where they offered their services to British General Henry Hamilton, known as "Hairbuyer" Hamilton because of his reputation for paying bounties on American scalps.

Hamilton sent Simon to Ohio to organize Indian raids against frontier settlements, which he did quite successfully. Ritual torture of captives was a traditional element of the culture of some Eastern Woodland tribes and characteristic of the Shawnee and Mingos that Girty led. (On the other hand, some tribes regarded the white custom of death by hanging as exceptionally cruel and barbaric.) Torture was not restricted to white captives, nor was it considered demeaning to captive or captor. In fact, it was sometimes regarded as an opportunity for a prisoner to demonstrate his

the advantages of a "higher" social order to a "lower" group. The concept was neither new nor American. It was a common principle in European thought and would continue to be, whether the subjected people were Gauls, or Aztecs, or Maoris.

Clashes on the Frontier. Treaties negotiated with the tribes of the Northwest brought only temporary peace, while in the South the Spanish encouraged the Creeks' harassment of frontier settlements. In response, the Americans took military action.

In 1790 General Josiah Harmar's expedition against the Indians in the Ohio country was ambushed and scattered. In 1791 General Arthur St. Clair's larger force did no better. In 1793—1794 Tennessee militia temporarily sta-bilized the Southwestern frontier in a series of small, sharp engagements.

Washington then gave command to General "Mad Anthony" Wayne, who took 4000 men into northwestern Ohio, where the British had authorized the construction of a fort inside American boundaries. Wayne defeated the Indian forces at the Battle of Fallen Timbers in the late summer of 1794. The next year the twelve strongest tribes ceded most of the Ohio country to the United States by the Treaty of Greenville.

THE PERILS OF NEUTRALITY

The French Revolution. The outbreak of the French Revolution forced the Washington administration into the first real test of its

personal courage. To the frontier settler and militiaman, however, it understandably represented a barbaric violation of all the codes of war.

Girty, of course, leading Indians in battle, did as they did. Soon the Girty legend began to form—stories were told of his cruelty, his pleasure at torture, and his implacable hatred of the Americans. The commandant at Fort Pitt offered $800 in gold for him, to which Simon sent back word that he "expected no quarter and would give none."

In 1782 Girty was part of a British-Indian force that defeated an American militia command near Upper Sandusky, Ohio, under Colonel William Crawford. Girty's Indians captured eight prisoners and killed six, saving Crawford and the company doctor for death by torture. Surgeon Knight, who escaped the next night to tell the tale, witnessed Crawford's long and painful death, and the story sped swiftly through the settlements. In August that year, Daniel Boone's militia drove off Girty and 600 Indians at Bryant's Station, Kentucky, the last major Indian battle on that bloody ground. Girty's reputation was by that time secure.

After the end of the war in 1783, Simon married a white girl twenty years his junior who had spent four years as a Wyandot captive, and then took up farming (and according to local stories, heavy drinking) near Amherstburg in Canada. The British, however, soon found they could use him to stir up trouble in Indian country and sent him out once more with war parties into Ohio. But the era of border warfare was drawing to a close. General "Mad Anthony" Wayne's tough frontier army broke the Indian alliance at Fallen Timbers, near Maumee, Ohio, in August 1794, though Girty and his Wyandots escaped.

Girty's life after 1796, when the British finally left the Northwest, was a long anticlimax. In Amherstburg he became a local celebrity, known as a hard-drinking,

foreign policy. A good many Americans in 1789 welcomed the news of the French uprisings as the logical outcome of their own revolution; "in no part of the world," wrote John Marshall later, "was the Revolution hailed with more joy than in America." The execution of Louis XVI and the Reign of Terror which followed, however, led many to sober second thoughts, while the French declaration of war against England, Holland, and Spain in February 1793 introduced the difficult question of neutrality directly into American foreign policy.

One segment of opinion, holding that Britain was still the United States' major enemy, favored the French cause. Others felt that British trade was so essential to American prosperity that the United States, whatever its sympathies with revolution, could not afford to offend the world's greatest naval and economic power. Still others, observing the chaos of Jacobin Paris, saw France as a threat to the security and order of society everywhere—even to Christianity itself.

In April 1793, when he received news of the outbreak of war between France and Britain, Washington immediately issued a proclamation. Although avoiding the word "neutrality," it guaranteed the belligerents the "friendly and impartial conduct" of the United States. America, he believed, needed peace—the opportunity to build up its strength—more than anything else. "If this country is preserved in tranquility twenty years longer," he wrote, "it may bid defiance in a just cause to any power whatever. . . ."

boastful man given to periodic frightening rages. His wife, tired of beatings, left him in 1798, taking their four children. Girty took no part in the War of 1812, and legend has it that when the British began to evacuate Detroit in 1813 Girty stayed until the last British soldier had left, then jumped his horse from the river bank and swam to Canada (a highly unlikely feat) as a gesture of defiance.

When General Harrison's American army crossed into Canada to occupy Amherstburg, Girty prudently disappeared among the Mohawk villages. He came back to his farm in 1816, old and half-blind but no less vicious and violent than before. He died on February 8, 1818, after a drunken spree, and was buried in the iron cold of Canadian winter. When spring came, no one remembered to mark his grave.

There were other renegade white men who played more important roles than he in the Indian wars, but Simon Girty became the frontier's symbol of fear. Tales of tortures clustered about his name. Balladeers chronicled his misdeeds. Soldiers and settlers alike vowed horrible vengeance upon him. Yet in contrast to his reputation, Simon Girty was rather small fry. The British never gave him a responsible military post, nor did they entrust him with any mission that required intelligence or trustworthiness—they used him simply as a guerilla leader who knew Indians and was skilled in forest warfare.

But Americans needed heroes and villains for the Indian wars. For heroes there were Anthony Wayne, Simon Kenton, Daniel Boone, and others. For villains they had such men as Hamilton, Tecumseh, and Girty, the White Savage—the one who most typically personified all that war in the wilderness meant on the frontier. His life, as one chronicler put it, "presents nothing to be imitated. It would be well if the name of this monster could be erased from the annals of history."

His proclamation, which was to influence American foreign policy for the next half-century, derived from his firm conviction that the United States should avoid, at all reasonable costs, the "brawlings of Europe." The following year Congress passed a Neutrality Act which made Washington's position the official American policy.

Strained Relations with Britain. The British navy was large, the French navy small, and the British blockade of France very effective. When the French, desperate for trade, opened up their West Indian ports to American ships, the British immediately declared that any trade with France was a military act and that ships caught at it were subject to seizure. Not only did British men-of-war confiscate American cargoes, but, claiming that some American sailors were really deserters from the British navy (as, indeed, a few were), they forcibly "impressed" a number of American seamen into naval service. Still, though American ships were in danger wherever they went in Atlantic waters, wartime trade was so lucrative that many American merchants felt that the profit was worth the risk, and incidents multiplied.

Jay's Treaty. Hoping to reduce tensions, Congress passed an embargo act in 1794 which forbade British ships to call at American ports and American ships to sail in areas where they might be subject to British seizure. Since this hurt American trade more than it hindered the British navy, the embargo lasted less than two months. However, American protests induced the British to relax some of their rules, and in 1794 Washington requested Chief Justice John Jay to sail for London to discuss a treaty to settle outstanding differences.

Jay's arguments were no doubt good ones, but perhaps more important, French military successes persuaded the British that it was unwise to antagonize the United States

unduly. Under the terms of Jay's Treaty (the Treaty of London, signed in 1794) the British agreed to evacuate the frontier posts by 1796; to open the British West Indies to American trade under certain conditions; to admit American ships to East Indian ports on a nondiscriminatory basis; and to refer to a joint commission the payment of pre-Revolutionary War debts and settlement of the northwest boundary dispute.

However, they simply refused to discuss other important points at issue, including impressment and the Indian question, and they made far fewer concessions than Jay had been instructed to get. Washington reluctantly submitted the treaty to the Senate, which ratified it by only one vote. Not only was the Washington administration severely criticized for the settlement, but Jay himself was burned in effigy in various cities.

Not all the news was bad, however. Spain, badly mauled by France in the land war, had signed a separate peace in 1795 and, fearing British retaliation for its defection, needed American friendship. In the Pinckney Treaty (the Treaty of San Lorenzo), signed on October 27, 1795, Spain recognized the line of 31° latitude as the United States' southern boundary and granted the United States free navigation of the Mississippi with a three-year right of deposit at New Orleans.

EARLY POLITICAL PARTIES

The Emergence of Party Politics. The dispute over Jay's Treaty revealed a deep division in Washington's administration, as well as growing public opposition to a number of Federalist policies. The French Revolution, the Franco-British War, and subsequent problems in foreign relations created further political differences in Congress. By 1792 opposing factions had begun to coalesce around the two strong men of Washington's cabinet, Hamilton and Jefferson.

Hamilton and Jefferson represented contrasting views of what the American government should be. Both views were implicit in the Declaration and the Constitution, and both still lie beneath the stream of partisan politics. These contrasting views have come to be known as Hamiltonian and Jeffersonian democracy.

Hamilton had no confidence in "the people in the mass." "I have long since learned," he wrote Washington, "to hold public opinion of little value." Most people, he believed, were unreliable, easily swayed by passions, self-interest, and false rhetoric. Since political, social, and economic systems were intertwined, an effective government should be an active force ("a strong government, ably administered," John Jay of New York put it) in promoting the good of the total society. Its control should be vested in those few who had skill and talent—"the rich and wellborn," Hamilton once called them—who would use it best to ensure the forward thrust of the nation.

Jefferson believed deeply in the ability of the majority of people to govern themselves, if properly prepared and allowed to do so. In his view, the individual—in whom he found "substantial and genuine virtue"—was much more important than the state, and the individual's right to pursue liberty and happiness was paramount. People were capable of ruling themselves; thus they needed no strong central government to do it for them. "That government is best," he said, "which governs least." A central government was needed, of course, for foreign policy, defense, commerce, and like matters, but too much control of the individual "begets subservience and venality" and corrupts him. It was ironic that it was Jefferson, the Virginia planter-aristocrat, who did not trust the "rich and wellborn" few and Hamilton, the illegitimate child of a Scottish merchant, who did not trust the "unstable rabble."

Though John Adams had written, "There is nothing I dread as much as the division of the Republic into two great parties, each under its leader," such a split seemed inevitable. This political division, first observable in the arguments over Hamilton's fiscal program, widened noticeably throughout Washington's first administration. The pro-Hamilton, pro-Washington group, using the name adopted by the forces favoring the Constitution during the ratification campaign, called themselves Federalists. The opposition at first called themselves Antifederalists, a somewhat unsatisfactory label but the best that could be devised at the moment.

The Antifederalists opposed the administration's program chiefly because of what they felt was its tendency to concentrate wealth and influence in a relatively small class. Certainly neither Jefferson nor his followers objected to sound currency and credit or to economic stability and prosperity. Rather, they opposed the Hamiltonian methods of obtaining them—the Bank, tariffs, excise taxes (but not the assumption of state debts)—because these measures might serve to create a permanently privileged class whose interests could well become inimical to the opportunities and welfare of the greater number of people.

Through Washington's first term the rivalry between the two factions increased. Despite these internal tensions, however, the Federalists easily reelected Washington for a second term in 1792 against token opposition, with John Adams as his Vice-President.

The Election of 1796. James Madison gave the anti-administration forces a better name when, in 1792, he spoke of "the Republican party." This designation (sometimes "Democratic-Republican") shortly displaced "Antifederalist." Into this loosely organized opposition group, formed about the commanding figure of Thomas Jefferson, came such men as Monroe and Madison of Virginia, George Clinton and Aaron Burr of New York, Albert Gallatin and Alexander Dallas from Pennsylvania, Willie Jones, the North Carolina back-country leader, and others from the Middle and Southern states. Among the Federalists were Hamilton, Schuyler, and John Jay of New York, Timothy Pickering and John Adams of Massachusetts, Thomas Pinckney of South Carolina, and John Marshall of Virginia, with Washington, of course, at the head of the party.

When Jefferson, convinced that he could no longer work with Hamilton and the administration party, resigned as Secretary of State in 1793, Republican partisan politics began in earnest. Hamilton resigned from the Treasury in 1795, partly because he could not afford to neglect his law and business interests, but he still remained the most powerful Federalist leader, since Washington decided not to run again in 1796.

Washington's achievements as President have been overshadowed by his image as "The Father of His Country" and by the dramatic contest during his second term between Hamilton and Jefferson. More recently, historians have pointed out Washington's real skill as an administrator and the importance of his contributions to the efficiency of the fledgling government. Since almost every act of his first term set a precedent, Washington did more than anyone else to establish the tone of the presidential office and to establish the whole set of delicate relationships among the executive, the cabinet, the Congress, and the judiciary.

When Washington decided in September 1796 not to seek a third term as President, he submitted to the press a "Farewell Address" which he had written with the aid of Madison and Hamilton. In his valedictory, published in newspapers throughout the nation, Washington explained his reasons for declining to seek a third term. He stressed the necessity of preserving the Union, the "main prop" of individual liberty, and pointed out the obligation of all Americans to obey the Constitution and the established government, " 'till

changed by an explicit and authentic act of the whole People." He warned of the dangers of a party system, particularly one based on a division along geographical lines; urged that the public credit be cherished; and admonished Americans to observe "good faith and justice towards all Nations."

The most enduring passages of the Farewell Address, however, are those in which Washington counseled Americans to steer clear of permanent alliances with the foreign world. Washington's admonitions for a foreign policy of neutrality have been quoted consistently by isolationists in the past century and a half

Washington, far right, is shown with the key members of his Cabinet: from left to right, Franklin, Jefferson, and Hamilton. The opposing views of Jefferson and Hamilton helped create our system of party politics.

Courtesy Chicago Historical Society

to justify the dominant American policy of avoiding involvement in international politics:

. . . The great rule of conduct for us, in regard to foreign Nations, is, in extending our commercial relations, to have with them as little *Political* connection as possible. . . . Europe has a set of primary interests, which to us have none, or a very remote relation.—Hence she must be engaged in frequent controversies, the causes of which are essentially foreign to our concerns.—Hence therefore it must be unwise in us to implicate ourselves, by artificial ties in the ordinary vicissitudes of her politics. . . . Taking care always to keep ourselves . . . on a respectably defensive posture, we may safely trust to temporary alliances for extraordinary emergencies.

After eight years in office, Washington left behind a government that possessed a reasonably good civil service, a workable committee system, an economic program, a foreign policy, and the seeds of a body of constitutional theory. He also left behind a party beginning to divide. The election of 1796 gave clear indication of the mounting strength of the Republican opposition. Thomas Jefferson and Aaron Burr campaigned for the Republicans, John Adams and Thomas Pinckney for the Federalists. The margin of Federalist victory was slim: Adams had 71 electoral votes, Jefferson 68. Since Jefferson had more votes than Pinckney, he became Vice-President.

Federalists and Republicans. It is too broad a generalization to say that the Federalists represented the conservative, commercial, nationalistic interests of the Northeast and Middle Atlantic states, and the Republicans the more radical, agrarian, debtor, states' rights interests of the South and West. The fact is that the two parties drew support from all kinds of people in different parts of the country.

The differences in the parties reflected many factors—personalities, religious and educational backgrounds, ideologies, economic interests, political necessities, and the like. It would be more accurate to say that these parties were loose combinations of certain economic, social, and intellectual groupings, held together by a set of common attitudes and interests.

Fundamentally, they reflected two different opinions about the qualities of human nature. Hamiltonians were acutely aware of the "imperfections, weaknesses, and evils of human nature." They believed that if people were fit to govern themselves at all, it must only be under rigid controls imposed upon them by society and government. Jeffersonians, on the other hand, believed that people were by inclination rational and good. If freed from the bonds of ignorance, error, and repression, they might achieve real progress toward an ideal society. Others, of course, took positions between these two extremes.

These contrasting concepts of human fallibility were reflected in contemporary political opinions about the structure and aim of government. The Federalists emphasized the need for political machinery to restrain the majority. They believed in a strong central government and a strong executive, with the active participation of that government in manufacturing, commerce, and finance. They believed that leadership in society belonged to a trained, responsible, and (very likely) wealthy class which could be trusted to protect property as well as human rights.

The Jeffersonian Republicans distrusted centralized authority and a powerful executive, preferring instead a less autonomous, more decentralized government modeled more on confederation than on federalism. They believed in the leadership of what Jefferson called "a natural aristocracy," founded on talent and intelligence rather than on birth, wealth, or station. Most Republicans believed that human nature in the aggregate was naturally trustworthy and that it could be

improved through freedom and education—
and therefore that wise self-government,
under proper conditions, would be possible.

THE TRIALS OF JOHN ADAMS

The XYZ Affair.   John Adams took office at a
difficult time, for the Federalist party that had
elected him was showing strain at the seams.
Hamilton still dictated a large share of party
policy from private life. He did not like Adams
and had maneuvered before the election in an
attempt to defeat him. Adams himself was a
stubbornly honest man, a keen student of
government and law, but blunt, a trifle
haughty, sometimes tactless.

Adams' administration promptly found
itself in trouble. Within his party there was a
violently anti-French group who virtually
demanded a declaration of war against
France. The French, angry at Jay's Treaty and
at an American neutrality that appeared to
favor Britain, seemed willing to cooperate.
Adams, who did not want war, sent John
Marshall, C. C. Pinckney, and Elbridge Gerry
to Paris in 1797 to try to find some way out.

The French foreign minister Talleyrand,
dealing with the American commission
through three mediaries called (for purposes
of anonymity) X, Y, and Z, demanded not
only a loan to the French government but also
a bribe, which the Americans indignantly
refused. When the news of the "XYZ Affair"
leaked out, the ringing slogan "Millions for
defense, but not one cent for tribute!"
(presumably Pinckney's reply) became a
rallying point for the anti-French faction in
Congress.

The Treaty of 1800.   Capitalizing on the war
fever, Congress created a Department of the
Navy, built a number of new ships, armed
American merchantmen, and authorized an
army of 10,000 men. Though his own party
leaders (Hamilton among them) argued that
war with France was inevitable, Adams

refused to listen, and as it turned out, the
French did not want war either. After nearly a
year of undeclared naval war, the French
government suggested that if an American
mission were to be sent to Paris it would be
respectfully received.

By the time the American commissioners
arrived in France in March 1800, the country
was in the hands of Napoleon Bonaparte, who
quietly agreed to a settlement of differences.
The Treaty of 1800 was not popular with the
Federalists or Congress, but it was ratified. It
avoided a war and also dissolved the French-
American alliance forged during the Revolution. "The end of war is peace," said Adams,
"and peace was offered me." John Adams got
his peace, but probably at the expense of
victory in the coming elections for himself and
his party.

The Alien and Sedition Acts.   The popular
outcry against France, and the near-war that
carried through 1797–1799, gave the Federalists a good chance, they believed, to cripple
their Republican political opponents under
cover of protecting internal security. The
country was honeycombed, so the Federalist
press claimed, with French agents and propagandists who were secretly at work undermining the national will and subverting public
opinion. Since most immigrants were inclined
to vote Republican, the Federalist Congress
capitalized on antiforeign feeling in 1798 by
passing a series of Alien Acts which lengthened the naturalization period from five to
fourteen years, empowered the President to
deport undesirable aliens, and authorized
him to imprison such aliens as he chose in
time of war. Though he signed the bill, Adams
did not like the acts and never seriously tried
to enforce them.

As the second step in its anti-Republican
campaign, Congress passed the Sedition Act,
also in 1798. Under this act, a citizen could be
fined or imprisoned or both for "writing,
printing, uttering, or publishing" false state-

The American frigate Constellation's *capture of the French frigate* L'Insurgente *on February 9, 1799 was just one of the many battles in the undeclared naval war with France.*

ments or any statements which might bring the President or Congress "into contempt or disrepute." Since this last clause covered almost anything Republicans might say about Federalists, its purpose was quite plainly to muzzle the opposition. Under the Sedition Act twenty-five editors and printers were prosecuted and convicted—though they were later pardoned and their fines returned by the Jeffersonians.

With the Alien and Sedition laws the Federalists went too far. Public opinion sided with the Republicans. The legislatures of Kentucky and Virginia passed resolutions in 1798 and 1799 (Jefferson drafted Kentucky's; Madison, Virginia's) condemning the laws and asking the states to join in nullifying them

as violations of civil rights. Actually none did, but the Kentucky and Virginia resolutions furnished the Jeffersonians with excellent ammunition for the approaching presidential campaign. And although the United States had no strong tradition of civil liberties, the Alien and Sedition laws helped to create one by pointing out how easily those rights of free speech and free press, guaranteed by the Bill of Rights, could be violated.

The Election of 1800. Washington's death in December 1799 symbolized the passing of the Federalist dynasty. The party that he had led was in dire distress, divided into wrangling factions. The Republicans were in an excellent position to capitalize on a long string of political moves which had alienated large blocs of voters—the handling of the Whiskey Rebellion, Hamilton's tax policies, the Jay Treaty and Jay's negotiations with Spain in 1786, the Alien and Sedition Acts—as well as conflict and resentment within the Federalist party.

As a matter of fact, the Federalists had been unable to maintain a balance between the nationalist business interests which formed the core of their support, and the rapidly growing influence of the middle and lower urban and agrarian classes of the South, the West, and the Middle Atlantic states. After Washington, who had held the party together by the force of his example, no Federalist leader found a way to absorb and control the elements of society which, after 1796, began to look to Jefferson for leadership. The clash of personalities within the Federalist camp, of course, damaged the party further.

John Adams, who through his entire term had to face the internal opposition of the Hamiltonians as well as the Republicans from without, deserves more credit than he is often given. Except for Adams' stubborn desire to keep the peace, the United States might well have entered into a disastrous war with France, and without him the Federalist party under Hamilton's control would probably have killed itself ten years sooner than it did. Adams' decision to stay out of war, made

against the bitter opposition of his own party, was not only an act of courage but very likely his greatest service to the nation.

Although Hamilton circulated a pamphlet violently attacking the President, the party had no other satisfactory candidate for the election of 1800 and decided to nominate Adams again, choosing C. C. Pinckney to run with him. The Republicans picked Jefferson and Burr once more, hoping thus to unite the powerful Virginia and New York wings of the party. The campaign was one of the bitterest in American history. In the end, the Republicans, who won the Middle Atlantic states and the South, emerged with a small edge in total electoral votes.

Under the Constitution, the candidate with the most votes was President and the next Vice-President, but when the Republican electors all voted for Jefferson and Burr, they created a tie. This threw the election into the House of Representatives, still controlled by lame-duck Federalists. The Federalists' hatred of Jefferson was so intense that many of them preferred Burr. At the same time, Burr's own party wanted Jefferson, but Burr refused to step aside. Hamilton, much as he disagreed with Jefferson's principles, considered Burr a political adventurer and deeply distrusted him. He therefore threw his influence behind Jefferson, who was declared President on February 17, 1801.

Chapter 6

The Jeffersonian Era 1800–1824

JEFFERSON IN POWER

"The Revolution of 1800."   Thomas Jefferson usually referred to his presidential election victory as "the revolution of 1800," though it was hardly a "revolution" in the usual sense. It was, nonetheless, an important election, for it shifted national political authority toward the South and West and introduced a new emphasis on decentralized power and state sovereignty. It marked the first successful alliance of agrarian and urban forces later consolidated by Jackson. And since it was also the first really violent American political campaign, it set "faction" and partisanship firmly into the political process. In actual practice, however, Jefferson did surprisingly little to erase what his predecessors had done, and there was much greater continuity from the Federalist decade into his own than appeared at first glance.

Settling the Barbary Corsairs.   Jefferson's administration had hardly caught its breath before it was plunged into a vortex of swift-moving foreign affairs. The President's first problem involved the depredations of pirates from the Barbary states of North Africa (Tunis, Algiers, Morocco, and Tripoli), who had preyed on Mediterranean commerce for a quarter century, enslaving seamen and levying tribute on shipping. During their administrations, Washington and Adams paid out more than $2 million in ransom and bribes to the Barbary potentates, and Jefferson determined to end the affair. Beginning in 1803 the United States sent to the Mediterranean four naval squadrons, which in a series of brilliant actions finally forced some of the pirate states to sue for peace. A final treaty was not established until 1815, but after 1805 American rights were generally respected in the Mediterranean and the shameful practice of extracting ransom and tribute was on its way to extinction.

The Purchase of Louisiana.   In 1801 Napoleon Bonaparte recovered the territory of Louisiana, lost by France to Spain in 1763. Jefferson recognized the potential danger to the United States of this sudden shift in ownership of half the American continent from impotent Spain to imperial France. The United States could not afford to have New Orleans, he wrote,

LOUISIANA PURCHASE

possessed by "our natural and habitual enemy," Napoleon. "The day that France takes possession of New Orleans, we must marry ourselves to the British Navy." And of course the United States needed the West if its empire was ever, as Jefferson hoped, to stretch from sea to sea.

The President therefore sent James Monroe to Paris to discuss the possible purchase of Louisiana. It was either buy now, Jefferson said, or fight for it later. Napoleon, for his part, did not want to face a British-American alliance in case of war and knew that, since New Orleans was almost indefensible against American attack, he would probably lose Louisiana anyway.

Napoleon therefore decided to sell, and after some haggling the United States purchased the Louisiana territory and West Florida in April 1803 for $15 million. Jefferson, though overjoyed at the bargain, was also embarrassed by the fact that nowhere in the Constitution could he find presidential authority to make it. He finally accepted Madison's view that the purchase could be made under a somewhat elastic interpretation of the treaty-making power. The brilliance of the maneuver obscured the constitutional question involved, but the "strict constructionist" doctrine was never the same again.

Whatever its constitutionality, the Louisi-ana Purchase was one of the most important presidential decisions in American history. At one stroke the United States became a continental power, master of the continent's navigation system, and owner of vast new resources that promised greater (and perhaps final) economic independence from Europe. It also put an end to the likelihood that the West could ever be split from the East and set a precedent for future territorial expansion.

The Problems of Political Patronage. In addition to the need for keeping a watchful eye on Europe and the Mediterranean, Jefferson had political problems at home. His cabinet, a particularly able group, included James Madison of Virginia as Secretary of State and the brilliant Swiss from Pennsylvania, Albert Gallatin, as Secretary of the Treasury. Quite aware of the utility of patronage, Jefferson quietly replaced Federalist appointments with his own, so that before the close of his first term he had responsible Republicans in positions where it counted.

One of his thorniest problems, however, was that of the so-called "midnight judges" appointed by John Adams under the Judiciary Act of 1801. The act reduced the number of Supreme Court justices to five, created sixteen new circuit courts, and added a number of federal marshals and other officials. About a month before Jefferson's inauguration Adams had nominated Secretary of State John Marshall as Chief Justice of the Supreme Court. Then on the eve of the inauguration, Adams filled many of the new judicial posts with solid Federalist party men.

John Marshall was a stalwart Federalist, but beyond that he was a convinced nationalist who believed that the Constitution was the most sacred of all documents, "framed for ages to come . . . , designed to approach immortality as nearly as human institutions can approach it." He did not trust the Jeffersonians, and he entered the Court determined that none should play fast and loose with the Constitution so long as he could prevent it.

Jefferson versus Marshall.   Jefferson was sure that Marshall, that "crafty chief judge," would set as many obstacles as he could in the administration's path and that the "midnight judges" would undoubtedly follow his lead. In 1802, when Jefferson persuaded Congress to repeal the Judiciary Act of 1801, all of Adams' judges were left without salaries or duties. This, the Federalists claimed, was unconstitutional.

To test the constitutionality of Congress' repeal, William Marbury (one of the "midnight" appointments) asked Secretary of State Madison to give him his commission as justice of the peace of the District of Columbia. This Madison refused to do. Marbury then applied to the Supreme Court for a writ ordering Madison to do so. Marshall used the case to promote what Jefferson did not want established—the Supreme Court's right of judicial review of legislation. The Constitution, wrote Marshall, is "the *supreme* law of the land, superior to any ordinary act of the legislative." "A legislative act contrary to the Constitution is not law," Marshall went on, and "it is the province and duty of the judicial department to say what the law is."

The Jefferson administration then launched an attack directly on the Federalist-dominated judiciary itself, using as its tool the constitutional power of impeachment for "high crimes and misdemeanors." The first target was John Pickering of the New Hampshire district court, who was apparently both alcoholic and insane. Pickering was impeached by the House, judged guilty by the Senate, and removed from office. Next, in 1804, the Republicans picked Associate Justice Samuel Chase of the Supreme Court, a violently partisan Federalist who had presided over several trials of Jeffersonian editors under the Sedition Act of 1798. In 1805, when the Senate decided it could not convict Chase, Jefferson conceded that impeachment was ineffective as a political weapon. Congress then gradually created a series of new judgeships and filled them with Republicans, a slower process but one that worked.

Marshall and Constitutional Law.   Jefferson's differences with Marshall were temporarily settled, but Marshall's long tenure as Chief Justice was a most important influence on the rapid growth of the power of the federal

As seen by the Federalists, "Mad Tom" Jefferson was in league with the devil in trying to pull down the federal government. Ironically, Jefferson actually broadened the interpretation of the Constitution's provision for federal authority.

MAD TOM in A RAGE

government over the next three decades. Marshall served on the Court from 1801 to 1835, participated in more than a thousand opinions and decisions, and wrote some five hundred of them. Whenever opportunity presented itself, as it often did, Marshall never failed to affirm two principles: that the Supreme Court possessed the power to nullify state laws that were in conflict with the Constitution; and that the Court alone had the right to interpret the Constitution, especially in regard to such broad grants of authority as might be contained in terms such as "commerce," "general welfare," "necessary and proper," and so on. His opinion did not always become the final version of constitutional issues, but the consistency of his attitudes, carried over a whole generation of legal interpretations, had much to do with the shaping of American constitutional law.

Opening the West.   After the Louisiana Purchase there was great anxiety to find out about what the nation had bought, more or less sight unseen. Jefferson, who had already made plans for the exploration of these newly acquired lands, persuaded Congress to finance an expedition up the Missouri River, across the Rocky Mountains, and if possible on to the Pacific. To lead it Jefferson chose his private secretary, a young Virginian named Meriwether Lewis, and William Clark, brother of George Rogers Clark, the frontier soldier.

In the spring of 1804 Lewis and Clark's party of forty-eight, including several scientists, left St. Louis for the West, mapping, gathering specimens of plants and animals, collecting data on soil and weather, and observing every pertinent detail of the new country. They wintered in the Dakotas and with the help of a Shoshone Indian woman, Sacajawea, crossed the Rockies and followed the Columbia River to the Pacific, catching their first glimpse of the sea in November 1805. By autumn of 1806 the expedition was back in St. Louis.

At almost the same time a party under Lieutenant Zebulon Pike was exploring the

Charles M. Russell's mural, Lewis and Clark Meeting the Flatheads, *shows the sweep and grandeur of the unexplored territory.*

upper Mississippi and the mid-Rockies. Other explorations followed, and the Louisiana Territory was soon organized on the pattern of the Northwest Ordinance of 1787 (its first state, Louisiana, entered in 1812). The West was no longer a dream but a reality.

The "Essex Junto." The prospect of more states being carved out of the wide new West greatly disturbed the Federalist party leaders. Ohio entered the Union in 1803, a soundly Republican state, and the probability that all the new states from the Northwest Territory, plus all those to be developed from the Louisiana Purchase, might lean politically to the Jeffersonians was profoundly worrisome. United only in their common hostility to the President, the Federalists had neither issue nor leader to counter his popularity and had little chance of finding either.

The gloom was especially thick in New England, so much so that a small number of Federalists (nicknamed the "Essex Junto") explored the possibilities of persuading the five New England states, plus New York and New Jersey, to secede from the Union to form a separate Federalist republic—a "Northern Confederacy," said Senator Timothy Pickering of Massachusetts, "exempt from the corrupt and corrupting influence and oppression of the aristocratic democrats of the South."

Alexander Hamilton of New York showed no inclination to join them, so the New Englanders approached Aaron Burr. Since Burr felt it unlikely that he would be nominated for Vice-President again, he consented to run for the governorship of New York, an office from which he might lead a secession movement.

Hamilton disliked Jeffersonians too, but he considered Burr a dangerous man and campaigned against him. After Burr lost, he challenged Hamilton to a duel on the basis of certain slurs on Burr's character reported in the press and killed him in July 1804.

Alexander Hamilton died as he had lived, a controversial man who aroused strong feelings. His blunt distrust of "King Mob" and his frank preference for British-style constitutionalism had never endeared him to the public, but the leadership he provided for the country during the crucial postwar years had much to do with its successful transition from a provincial to a federal philosophy. Woodrow Wilson once characterized Hamilton, quite unfairly, as a great man but not a great American. It is more accurate to say that he may not have been a great man, but he was an indispensable one.

The duel ruined Burr's reputation and helped to complete the eclipse of the Federalist party. Yet Burr himself was not quite finished. After the Republicans passed him over as their vice-presidential candidate in 1804 in favor of George Clinton of New York, he apparently entered into a scheme to carve a great empire of his own out of the American West, a conspiracy which ended with his trial for treason in 1807. Although he was acquitted, everyone drawn into his plan was ruined, and Burr was forced to flee to England to escape further prosecution for Hamilton's death and additional charges of treason. Meanwhile, the Federalist party approached the election of 1804 with its brilliant leader dead, its reputation tarnished, and neither candidates nor issues of any public value.

The Election of 1804. The election of 1804 was very nearly no contest. The Republican caucus nominated Jefferson for a second time, with George Clinton of New York as his running mate. The Federalists ran the reliable C. C. Pinckney and Rufus King of New York. Jefferson carried every state except Connecticut and Delaware, garnering 162 of the total 176 electoral votes and sweeping in an overwhelmingly Republican Congress with him.

Jefferson's first administration ended on a high note of success—as John Randolph said later, the United States was "in the 'full tide of successful experiment.' Taxes repealed; the public debt amply provided for, both principal and interest; sinecures abolished; Louisiana acquired; public confidence unbounded." Unfortunately, it could not last.

AMERICA AND THE WOES OF EUROPE

Neutrality in a World at War. Napoleon Bonaparte loomed large in the future of both America and Europe. Jefferson did not like him, but to Jefferson and many other Americans France was still the country of Lafayette, Rochambeau, De Grasse, and the great French philosophers of the Enlightenment. Against Napoleon stood England, whose aim Jefferson believed was "the permanent domination of the ocean and the monopoly of the trade of the world." He wanted war with neither, nor did he wish to give aid to either in the war that flamed up between them in 1803.

It would be an oversimplification, of course, to assume that American foreign policy of the period was governed primarily by a like or dislike of France or England. The objectives of Jefferson's foreign policy, like Washington's and Adams', were first, to protect American independence and second, to maintain as much diplomatic flexibility as possible without irrevocable commitment to any nation.

In the European power struggle between England and France that developed after 1790, Jefferson saw great advantages to the United States in playing one against the other without being drawn into the orbit of either. An American friendship with France would form a useful counterbalance against the influence of Britain and Spain, the chief colonial powers in North and South America. A British and Spanish defeat might well mean the end of their American empires.

At the same time Jefferson did not want to tie America's future to the fortunes of Napoleon, who might be an even greater threat to American freedom if he won. The wisest policy therefore lay in neutrality toward all and trade with anyone—or, as the British wryly put it, America's best hope was "to gain fortune from Europe's misfortune."

Maintaining neutrality was as difficult for Jefferson as it had been for Washington and Adams before him. The British navy ruled the seas, and Napoleon, after the Battle of Austerlitz in 1805, ruled Europe. The war remained a stalemate while the two countries engaged in a battle of proclamations over wartime naval commerce. Each side set up a blockade of the other's ports, but since neither had sufficient ships to enforce the quarantine, American vessels filtered through these "paper blockades" with comparative ease when the risk was warranted.

The British at Sea. From 1804 to 1807 the British and French issued a confusing series of orders and decrees aimed at controlling ocean trade, with the result that American vessels were liable to confiscation by either one if they obeyed the rules of the other. In addition, British men-of-war insolently patrolled the American coast to intercept and inspect American ships for contraband almost as soon as they left port. And as if this were insufficient provocation, the British claimed the right to search American ships for British deserters.

Conditions in the British navy encouraged desertion, and doubtless a number of British sailors turned up in the American merchant marine. It was also evident that British captains were notoriously careless about citizenship and in many cases simply kidnapped American sailors. Protests from the United States government about these "impressments" were loftily disregarded.

Finally, in the summer of 1807 the British *Leopard* stopped the United States navy's *Chesapeake* (a warship, not a merchant vessel), killed or wounded twenty-one men, and took four sailors. This was by any standard an act of war, and America burst out in a great roar of rage. Had Congress been in session, it almost certainly would have declared war on the spot. But Jefferson held his temper, demanded apologies and reparations, and ordered British ships out of American waters to prevent further incidents. Though the British apologized, they also reaffirmed their right to search American ships and seize deserters. The *Leopard-Chesapeake* affair rankled in American minds for years and had much to do with the drift toward war with Britain in 1812.

The "Obnoxious Embargo." Jefferson and Secretary of State Madison bent every effort to avoid provocation that might lead to war. There were only two choices—war or some kind of economic substitute. The easier choice would have been war, for which Jefferson could have obtained public and congressional support. Instead he chose peace, pinning his hopes on "peaceful coercion," as he called it, by means of a boycott of British goods and a set of nonimportation acts which Congress passed in 1806 and 1807.

Neither was sufficiently effective to do much good, however. As the situation between the two nations steadily deteriorated, Jefferson asked Congress for a full-scale embargo, a logical move since Britain needed American trade, especially foodstuffs, in increasing quantities as the war progressed. In late 1807 Congress therefore passed the Embargo Act, which forbade American ships to leave the United States for any foreign port or even to engage in the American coastal trade without posting a heavy bond. Jefferson hoped that the Embargo Act of 1807 would do two things: first, that it would discourage the British from seizing American ships and sailors and force them to greater regard for American rights; and, second, that it would encourage the growth of American industry by cutting off British imports.

England suffered shortages, but not enough to matter; France approved of the embargo since it helped at second hand to enforce Napoleon's own blockade of England. American ships rotted at anchor along the Eastern seaboard. Merchants went bankrupt, and farm surpluses piled up. In New York, one traveler wrote, "The streets near the waterside were almost deserted. The grass had begun to grow upon the wharves."

While the shipping interests suffered, however, New England and the Middle Atlantic port states did begin a transition to manufacturing that was soon to change their economic complexion. With foreign competition removed, capital previously invested in overseas trade was available for new factories and mills, which sprang up in profusion along the seaboard. But the future economic advantages were difficult to see in the midst of the paralyzing effects of the embargo. Jefferson was violently attacked in the taverns and counting houses, and finally Congress repealed the Embargo Act. On March 1, 1809, three days before his successor Madison took office, Jefferson reluctantly signed the bill.

The end of Jefferson's second term came during the bitterest disputes over the embargo, and the President, who had wished for some time to retire to his beloved Monticello, was relieved to accept Washington's two-term precedent and announce his retirement. His eight years in the presidency, begun in such high confidence, ended on a much more equivocal note. Ironically, Jefferson, the believer in decentralized government, found himself under the Embargo wielding more power over American life than any Federalist would have dreamed of. Though a "strict constructionist," Jefferson had discovered authority in the Constitution to buy Louisiana. And though a believer in states' rights, he had coerced the New England states into an economic boycott which hurt their commerce badly.

The Election of 1808. Jefferson trusted and admired James Madison and easily secured the Republican nomination for him. The

Federalists nominated the tireless C. C. Pinckney again, but in spite of the embargo and divided Republican sentiment Madison won by 122 to 47 electoral votes.

James Madison, far from being a mere graceful shadow of Jefferson, was very much his own man. His role in the formation of the Republican party was a decisive one, and the political philosophy of the Jeffersonian group owed much to his thinking.

The Drift to War. Madison was an astute practitioner of politics as well as a profound student of it, but when he succeeded Jefferson, he inherited a large bundle of thorny problems. The Non-Intercourse Act, with which Madison replaced the Embargo Act in 1809, allowed American ships to trade with any nations except France and England. When this failed to work, Congress replaced it with Macon's Bill No. 2 (named after the chairman of the House Foreign Affairs Committee), which relieved American shipping from all restrictions while ordering British and French naval vessels out of American waters.

This failed to influence British policy, but "peaceable coercion" was beginning to hurt England more than the British admitted and more than Madison realized. Parliament was preparing to relax some of its restrictions even as Congress moved toward a declaration of war. It simply did not happen soon enough to change the course of events.

The War Hawks. Jefferson's "peaceful coercion" policy was probably the best that could have been pursued under the circumstances, and except for some exceedingly clumsy diplomacy abroad and mounting pressures for war at home, it might have worked. Much of the pressure came from a group of aggressive young congressmen, the first of the postrevolutionary generation of Western politicians—Henry Clay of Kentucky, John C. Calhoun and Langdon Cheves of western South Carolina, Peter B. Porter of western New York, Felix Grundy of Tennessee, and other so-called "buckskin boys." Intensely nationalist and violently anti-British, this group of "War Hawks," as John Randolph of Roanoke called them, clamored loudly for an attack on Britain via Canada and on the seas.

The regions from which these "War Hawks" came believed they had special reasons to dislike England. The West had fallen on hard times in the years from 1805 to 1809, and it blamed the British navy rather than the Embargo Act. More serious, however, was the charge that the British, from their Canadian posts, were stirring up the Indians and arming them for marauding raids across the American frontier.

"Mr. Madison's War." The origins of war are never simple, and the War of 1812, especially, seems to have developed from a bewildering complexity of causes. Historians have advanced a number of explanations as to why the United States, after seven months of somewhat disordered debate in Congress, decided on June 18, 1812, to declare war on Great Britain. The vote was close in the Senate—19 to 13—and not overwhelming in the House—79 to 49.

Nineteenth-century historians tended to agree that the causes of the war were first, to "vindicate the national character" (as the House Foreign Affairs Committee said); and second, to retaliate against British violations of America's maritime rights. Yet the largest vote for war came from the South and West, where sea trade was less important. New England, the center of American sea trade, opposed the war. At the news, flags flew at half-mast in New England and there were minor riots in some port cities.

The Eastern Federalist press dubbed it "Mr. Madison's War," and so it remained. Some, too, regarded it as a stab in Britain's back when that nation stood alone against Napoleon, who in 1812 was on his way to Moscow for what seemed likely to be his last great conquest.

Later historians, noting the rhetoric of the Congressional debates and the distribution of the vote, concluded that the South and West hoped by the war to annex Canada and Florida as room for expansion, an expression of what later became known as America's "manifest destiny" to occupy the continent. Some still favor this expansionist interpretation, but other historians have suggested that fear of Britain's economic dominance—a reassertion of England's old imperial power over her former colony—also played an important role. Whatever the motivations, it was a brief, confused, and, except for a few instances, not very heroic war which nonetheless had a crucial role in the national development.

THE WAR OF 1812

War on the Land: First Phase.   Many Americans believed that Canada not only ought rightfully to join the United States, but wanted to. The Articles of Confederation had provided for Canada's admission to the Union, while the first Congress called itself "Continental" by design. Secretary of War William Eustis wrote in 1812 that "We have only to send officers into the Provinces and the people, already disaffected toward their own government, will rally to our standard."

There was, in fact, a good deal of pro-American sympathy in the Western St. Lawrence region—then called Upper Canada, later Ontario. But American Loyalists controlled both the Assembly and the Governor's Executive Council, and as the Anglican Bishop of Upper Canada wrote, they and the British Canadians wanted no part of that "degenerate government . . . equally destitute of national honor and virtue," that lay to the south. French Quebec, with vivid memo-

ries of Revolutionary anti-Catholic propaganda, feared the loss of its language and its religion under American rule, while neither British nor French merchants in Montreal could see any advantage in a change.

The United States was totally unprepared for war, its defenses outmoded, its army, reduced to about 7000 men, badly equipped and poorly led. The British situation was no better. Canada had a thousand miles of border, with 6000 scattered British regulars and a militia pool of perhaps 60,000 to defend it. John C. Calhoun figured that a complete conquest of Canada might take a month. Henry Clay thought one company of Kentucky militia could do it.

American strategy was threefold: first, take Montreal and seal off the St. Lawrence route to the interior; second, invade the Niagara region and secure control of the central St. Lawrence Valley; third, invade western Canada from Detroit, securing the Great Lakes and the Northwest.

None of it worked. The expedition into Quebec failed at Crysler's Farm and at Châteauguay, due chiefly to the stubborn defense of the French-Canadian militia. General William Hull, the American commander at Detroit, crossed into Canada in July of 1812, lost his courage, and quickly returned. British General Isaac Brock, with a smaller force, bluffed Hull (who was later courtmartialed) into surrendering Detroit on August 14, and when Fort Michimilimackinac in upper Michigan and Fort Dearborn in Illinois fell soon after, the British controlled the Northwest. Brock then rushed his army toward Niagara, where he defeated an American invasion at Queenston Heights in mid-October. Brock was killed in the battle, but he had saved western Canada.

In the middle of these military failures, Madison was nominated for another term. An Eastern antiwar wing of the Republicans, however, nominated De Witt Clinton of New

York against him, and the Federalists added their support for Clinton. Madison won, 128 to 89 electoral votes, but, significantly, Clinton carried all of New England and the Middle Atlantic states except Vermont and Pennsylvania. At the same time the Federalists doubled their delegation in Congress.

War on the Land: Second Phase.   Despite its early disasters, the army kept trying for Canada. In the winter of 1812–1813 American sailors commanded by Captain Oliver Hazard Perry hammered and sawed out a small fleet and in September 1813 met and smashed the British lake squadron at the Battle of Lake Erie, near Sandusky, Ohio. Lake Erie was one of the most savage naval actions of the era (Perry's flagship suffered 80 percent casualties), but after three hours of fighting, Perry dispatched his message to General William Henry Harrison commanding the forces near Detroit, "We have met the enemy and they are ours." Without control of Lake Erie, the British evacuated Detroit and fell back toward Niagara, but Harrison's swiftly advancing force caught and defeated them at the Battle of the Thames on October 5, 1813.

By reason of Perry's and Harrison's victories, the United States now commanded the Northwestern frontier. London, however, was sending more British regulars and the Canadian militia was gaining experience. Two American invasions were turned back at Stoney Creek and Beaver Dam, and on July 25, 1814, a bitter battle at Lundy's Lane near Niagara Falls stopped a third attempt. The British then struck back at Buffalo and captured and burned it. Later that year they took Fort Niagara.

War at Sea.   The American navy entered the War of 1812 with sixteen ships. The British had ninety-seven in American waters alone. The out-numbered Americans therefore limited themselves to single-ship actions, in which they did surprisingly well. The *Constitution* ("Old Ironsides"), a forty-four gun frigate commanded by Yankee Isaac Hull, defeated the British *Guerriere* on August 19, 1812, in one of the most famous sea fights in history. The big frigate *United States*, commanded by Captain Stephen Decatur, captured the British *Macedonian* a few weeks later, but the American *Chesapeake* lost a bitter fight to the British *Shannon* in 1813.

American privateers contributed most to the success of the war at sea. These swift ships sailed circles around the British, captured or destroyed 1300 British merchantmen, and even had the impudence to sack British shipping in the English Channel in full sight of the shore. They gave the American public something to crow about now and then, though the overall effect on the outcome of the conflict was negligible. The British naval blockade was quite effective, and by 1813 the majority of American ports were tightly bottled up.

War on the Land: Final Phase.   Napoleon abdicated in April 1814 and was exiled to the isle of Elba in the Mediterranean. With Bonaparte gone and the French war finished, England turned its huge army of veterans toward American shores. The strategy of the British general staff was to make three coordinated attacks: one from the north, from Canada down Lake Champlain into New York state; a second on the coast, through Chesapeake Bay, aimed at Baltimore, Washington, and Philadelphia; a third up from the south, at New Orleans. The end was in sight, wrote the London *Times*, for this "ill-organized association" of states. Indeed, it looked that way.

The northern campaign began in July 1814. Since Lake Champlain in upstate New York was the vital link in the invasion route, British General Sir George Prevost wanted it cleared of American ships. But in September 1814 the American lake squadron under Captain

Thomas Macdonough decisively defeated the British. Without control of the lake the British drive stalled and eventually dissolved.

The British were more successful at Chesapeake Bay, where in August 1814 General Robert Ross landed a strong force that marched on Washington. The American government fled into Virginia and the British, in retaliation for the American burning of York (Toronto) in 1813, set fire to the White House and the Capitol before moving toward Baltimore. Here they were stopped at Fort McHenry, where a spirited defense inspired Francis Scott Key to write "The Star-Spangled Banner." Unable to crack the Baltimore defenses, the British set sail for the West Indies.

The third British offensive, aimed at New Orleans and commanded by General Edward Pakenham, sailed from Jamaica in November 1814 with 7500 seasoned veterans. To oppose Pakenham, Andrew Jackson took his frontier army on a forced march in December. Though neither Jackson nor Pakenham knew it, American and British representatives were already at work in Belgium on a treaty of peace. Two weeks after the Treaty of Ghent was signed on December 24, 1814, Jackson's Western riflemen almost annihilated Pakenham's army. The British lost 2000 men (including Pakenham), while Jackson's loss totaled 8 dead and 13 wounded in a battle that did not really affect the war or the peace.

The Hartford Convention. In 1814, when American prospects seemed darkest, the Federalist Massachusetts legislature called a convention at Hartford, Connecticut, to discuss "public grievances and concerns"—that is, the Republican conduct of the war. The delegates, who came primarily from the Massachusetts, Connecticut, and Rhode Island legislatures, had a great deal to discuss. Some advised amending the Constitution to clip Congress' war-making powers. Others

suggested negotiating a separate peace with England.

Curiously enough, the delegates, all Federalists, appealed to the doctrine of states' rights, the same doctrine that the Jeffersonians had used against Federalist centralization during Adams' administration. They argued that since the Republican Congress had violated the Constitution by declaring an unwanted war, those states which did not approve had the right to override congressional action. At the conclusion of the meeting Massachusetts and Connecticut sent commissioners to Washington to place their protests before Congress. But when the commissioners arrived, the war was over, and whatever they had to say was forgotten.

A Welcome Peace. Early in 1813 Czar Alexander I of Russia had offered to mediate between the United States and England, since he wanted the British free to concentrate their full military force on Napoleon. Madison sent commissioners to Russia, but Lord Castlereagh, the British foreign minister, refused to accept the czar's suggestion. Late that same year, however, Castlereagh notified Secretary of State James Monroe that he was willing to discuss differences between the two nations, and in August 1814 American and British representatives met in Ghent, Belgium.

As the meetings dragged on, it became plain that the British could not successfully invade the United States—or the United States, Canada. Weary of war, both British and Americans wanted to finish it, and on December 24, 1814, the commissioners signed a peace treaty. Interestingly, it did not mention impressment, blockades, seizures at sea, or any of the major disputes which seemed to have precipitated the war.

The Results of the War. The reaction of war-weary Americans to the news of the Treaty of Ghent, which arrived in the United

Although "Mr. Madison's War" accomplished little, many citizens felt proud that the country had weathered the threat symbolized by the British capture of Washington.

States in February 1815, was swift and spontaneous. Bells rang, parades formed, newspapers broke out in headlines to proclaim the "passage from gloom to glory." Yet "Mr. Madison's War" had accomplished very little in a military or political sense. The treaty realized few if any of the aims for which the war had presumably been fought.

The most that can be said is that the treaty opened the way for future settlements to be worked out over the next decade with Britain, Spain, and France. The war dislocated business and foreign trade, deranged currency values, and exposed glaring cracks in the national political organization.

But to the American people the outcome, ambiguous as it was, marked a turning point in patriotic self-esteem. True, the war might

have been avoided by better statesmanship, and it might even have been fought with France on equally reasonable grounds. Yet from the American point of view, the War of 1812 gave notice to the rest of the world that the United States had arrived as a nation. "Who would not be an American?" crowed *Niles' Register*. "Long live the Republic! All Hail!"

The War and Canada. The War of 1812 marked the first step in the creation of Canada, which was to emerge a half-century later as a sovereign nation. In the conflict between England and the United States, British and French Canadians were caught in the middle, as they had been in the American Revolution. For England to strike at the

United States, the route lay through Canada. For the United States to strike at England, the only vulnerable point was Canada.

But to the average Canadians, British or French, the war's causes meant little and they had small stake in it. Canada's problem was simply survival, and it survived. Whatever their differences, French, British, and Loyalists joined in common cause to outlast a long, hard war and preserve their part of the British Empire.

America's attempted invasions intensified already strong anti-American feelings, while Canada's repulse of them was understandably a source of growing national pride. Opposition to the United States and wariness of its motives thus became continuing factors in subsequent Canadian-American relations. The war strengthened Canada's Britishness, and at the same time gave it the beginnings of its own sense of identity.

AMERICA MAKES A NEW START

A Confident Nation.   The War of 1812 marked the end of America's lingering sense of colonial inferiority. It was hardly a "second war of independence," as some called it, but from it there did come a new spirit of national consciousness. Albert Gallatin wrote, "It has renewed and reinstated the national feeling and character which the Revolution had given, and which were daily lessening. The people now have more general objects of attachment. . . . They are more Americans, they feel and act more as a nation."

After the Treaty of Ghent the United States turned toward the great hazy West, where half a continent lay virtually empty. America could now concentrate on its domestic problems with less concern for European standards, ideals, and entanglements. Indifference to foreign affairs after 1814 was so great that even Napoleon's escape from Elba, his return to France, and his final defeat at Waterloo in June 1815 excited little attention in the American press. The interest of the United States centered on perfecting and expanding the nation it had constructed out of two wars and a generation of experiment. In other words, its chief task lay in developing modern America.

The Aftermath of War.   The most persistent postwar problems were economic. Finances during the war had been handled almost as ineptly as military affairs. Banks had multiplied profusely and without proper control. The country was flooded with depreciating paper money. Prices were at the most inflated level in America's brief history. The shipping industry had been badly hurt by war and blockade. On the other hand, the value of manufacturing had increased tremendously—the total capital investment in American industry in 1816, it was estimated, was somewhat more than $100 million. The West, now producing foodstuffs and raw materials in abundance, balanced on the verge of a tremendous boom. As soon as peace was established, the Republican Congress began to consider a three-point program for economic expansion: a tariff to protect infant American industry; a second Bank of the United States, since the charter of Hamilton's original Bank had expired in 1811; and a system of roads, waterways, and canals to provide internal routes of communication and trade.

A Protective Tariff.   The protection of America's infant industries was a matter of first priority. New factories, encouraged by the war, had grown in great numbers, especially in the textile industry. As soon as the wartime blockade ended, British-made products streamed toward the United States, and young industries that had flourished under conditions of embargo and war found it quite another matter to compete in an open peacetime market. Whereas the total value of United States imports in 1813 had been $13 million, by 1816 it had leaped to $147 million, while American manufacturers begged for protection.

Congress in 1816 passed a tariff to protect the new factories—the first United States tariff passed not to raise revenue but to encourage and support home industry. The argument over this protective tariff exposed some potentially serious sectional economic conflicts and marked the first appearance of a perennial political issue. Southern producers and New England shippers opposed the tariff, but the growing factory towns of New England supported it, as did some of the younger Southern cotton politicians, who hoped to encourage industrial development in the South. The Middle Atlantic states and the West favored it, and the Southwest divided on the issue.

Renewing the Bank of the United States.   In 1816 Congress turned its attention to the national Bank. The charter of the first Bank of the United States had been allowed to expire because the Republicans believed that, as Jefferson originally claimed, banking powers properly belonged to the states and Hamilton's centralized bank was therefore unconstitutional. But the new contingent of Western congressmen were much less interested in the Bank's constitutionality than in its usefulness. Henry Clay, who had opposed the first Bank in 1811 on constitutional grounds, now supported the second Bank, he explained, because it was necessary for the national (especially Western) interest to have a stable, uniform currency and sound national credit. Therefore, Congress in 1816 gave the second Bank a twenty-year charter, on much the same terms as before but with about three and a half times more capital than the first and substantially greater control over state banks.

Building Better Connecting Links.   The British wartime blockade and the westward movement had exposed a critical need for roads,

improved waterways, and canals. When coastal shipping was reduced to a trickle by British offshore naval patrols, forcing American goods to move over inland routes, the roads and rivers were soon choked with traffic. The Republican program of improved internal communications was especially popular in the West, but more conservative Easterners, including President Madison, doubted the constitutionality of federal assistance for roads and canals unless an amendment to the Constitution was adopted for the purpose.

Calhoun introduced a "bonus bill" into Congress in 1816, empowering the use of federal funds for internal improvements. It cited the "general welfare" clause of the Constitution as providing authority for such action. The bill was passed, but Madison vetoed it on his last day of office in 1817. Many of the states began digging canals and building roads themselves. President Monroe later agreed that the federal government did have the authority to fund such internal improvements, inaugurating the great canal and turnpike era of the 1820s.

AMERICA MOVES WEST

The Treaty of Ghent released a pent-up flood of migration toward the West. In 1790 a little more than 2 percent of the population lived west of the Appalachian mountain chain. In 1810 it was 14 percent; in 1820, 23 percent, with the proportion still rising. The stream of migration moved west in two branches following the east-west roads and rivers—one from the South into the Southwest, the other from the northeastern states into the Northwest Territory.

There were a number of reasons for this great westerly movement. One was America's soaring population, which almost doubled in the first two decades of the nineteenth century, from 5.3 million in 1800 to over 9.6

million in 1820. Another was the discharge of war veterans, accompanied by a rush of immigrants from Europe, who moved west to look for new opportunities. Still another was improved transportation. Whereas there had been few good routes to the West, the number of roads and turnpikes now grew, while the Great Lakes-Ohio River waterway provided an excellent route for settlers to move into the Northwest.

But the most compelling force behind the westward migration was land—the rich black bottom lands of the Southwest, and the fertile forest and prairie lands of the Northwest.

Governor William Henry Harrison of Indiana Territory persuaded Congress in 1800 to reduce the minimum requirement for the sale of land to a half section at two dollars an acre, with four years to pay. In 1804 Congress reduced the minimum to a quarter section, and in 1820 to eighty acres at a base price of $1.25 an acre. This was the great magnet that drew settlers west. Unfortunately, the land was sometimes already occupied by Indians.

Land Hunger versus Indian Rights. While it was clear from the first that the new American government wanted swift access to the In-

Thomas Ruckle's Fairview Inn *shows the eagerness with which settlers set off to claim their own portion of the rich, black land in the West, where they would clash with the Indians already living there.*

dians' tribal lands, Congress in 1789 had assured the Indians that their "land and property shall never be taken from them without their consent." And in appropriating funds to pay certain tribes for land claims, Congress had tacitly recognized, as Secretary of War Henry Knox said, the Indians' right to ownership as "prior occupants." At the time, however, Washington had remarked that despite the government's good intentions, he doubted that "anything short of a Chinese wall" would ever keep land-hungry settlers out of the Indians' lands.

Washington was right. The Indians, reported Thomas Forsyth from frontier country in 1818, "complain about the sale of their lands more than anything else." The settler, he wrote, "tells the Indian that that land, with all that is on it, is his," and, treaty or not, "to go away or he will kill him etc."

Such constant clashes between Indian and settler had forced the Indians to surrender much of their land. Congress' Indian policy was neither sufficiently definite nor sufficiently aggressive to satisfy impatient settlers, traders, land speculators, or Indians.

Resistance to Federal Policy. The hope that the two races might live together in "perpetual peace and affectionate attachment," as Jefferson had hoped, quickly faded. Particularly in the South, state governments resisted federal Indian policy. On the frontier few paid attention to boundaries or treaties.

Nor were Indians willing to give up more and more land, treaties or not. Each advancing encroachment brought resentment and retaliation. Turning hunters and warriors into farmers was not easy, and American frontiersmen were much more interested in getting the Indians' land than in teaching them to farm it.

Indians, of course, were expected to relinquish their lands at once. Conflicts between settlers and Indians became increasingly violent and frequent, and the emergence of a remarkable leader, the Shawnee Tecumseh, crystallized Indian resistance. Rejecting all American claims to Indian lands, Tecumseh and his medicineman brother, the Prophet, after 1800 began to organize the tribes of the Northwest into a loose and effective alliance.

This alliance was finally broken by General William Henry Harrison, governor of Indiana Territory, at the Battle of Tippecanoe in November 1811, while Tecumseh was absent. Tecumseh then joined the British army in Canada and reappeared with his Indians in the War of 1812. He was killed at the Battle of the Thames in 1813, and with him died the Indians' efforts to organize and resist.

At the close of the war, with the British threat removed from the Northwest and the French from the Southwest, the federal government could at last proceed with its policy of assimilation or removal. After 1815 the political power of those who, like Andrew Jackson, wanted to clear the Indian lands immediately, was too strong to resist. In 1817 the Senate Committee of Public Lands recommended exchanging public lands in the trans-Mississippi region for the Indian lands east of the Mississippi, but only with the consent of the tribes.

Very soon it became clear that the Indian tribes were not willing to consent. The only remedy, John C. Calhoun wrote in 1820, was to place them "gradually under our authority and laws." "Our opinions, and not theirs," he continued, "ought to prevail, in measures intended for their civilization and happiness." In 1825 Calhoun, then Secretary of War, and President Monroe presented Congress with a plan to remove the eastern tribes into the region beyond Missouri and Arkansas—a plan opposed by those who felt such an act a betrayal of the national honor. But the opposition was inadequate, and by the 1830s the tribes were removed—many to present-day Oklahoma and Kansas. By 1848 twelve

**INDIAN CESSIONS AND ORIGINAL
LOCATIONS OF THE TRIBES**

Prior to 1784   1784 to 1810   1810 to 1850

new states had been created from what had once been Indian country.

That the postwar policy of peaceful expansion and assimilation did not succeed did not necessarily mean that other solutions to the problem would have been possible. For example, the creation of an Indian state, closed to white settlement, in the rich lands of the Mississippi-Ohio basin—as some proposed—would never have succeeded. Considering the alternatives and the limitations imposed by them, what *should* have been done about the Indian and what *could* have been done were not necessarily the same.

GROWING PAINS

The Election of 1816. Madison selected James Monroe of Virginia for his successor in the presidential election of 1816, and although some Republicans favored William H. Crawford of Georgia, the party caucus agreed to choose the third Virginian in succession for the presidency. The Federalists, disheartened by the Hartford Convention, failed to nominate an official candidate, though in some states they supported Rufus King of New York. King received only the votes of Massachusetts, Connecticut, and Delaware, and Monroe won easily by 183 to 34 electoral votes.

A tall, distinguished, quiet man, James Monroe had studied law with Jefferson and was the older statesman's close friend and disciple. He drew his advisers impartially from different sections of the country, choosing John Quincy Adams of Massachusetts as Secretary of State, William H. Crawford of Georgia as Secretary of the Treasury, John C. Calhoun of South Carolina as Secretary of War, and William Wirt of Maryland as Attorney General. Henry Clay of Kentucky, the Speaker of the House, and others of the Western group dominated Congress, with Daniel Webster of New Hampshire and other New Englanders furnishing the opposition.

The "Era of Good Feelings." Because of the virtually unchallenged Republican control of political life until 1824, these years are labeled "The Era of Good Feelings." The Federalist party was dead, and it seemed for a time that the two-party system itself was ending. There were no European wars of consequence during the period to involve the United States, nor any crucial issues in foreign affairs. But, like all labels, this one was true only in part: Feelings were "good," but subterranean conflicts were soon to destroy the political peace.

Sectional interests and aspirations were growing and changing. The new Northwest, as it gained stature and stability, demanded greater influence in national policy. The South, tied more and more to cotton, and New England, changing from an agricultural to a manufacturing economy, were both undergoing inner stresses that took outward political form. Specifically, these sectionalized rivalries were shortly to appear in two issues—tariffs and slavery—which terminated the good feelings and produced new bad ones.

Prosperity and Panic. After 1815 the national economy flourished mightily. The wartime boom continued, industry grew strong behind its tariff wall, and American ships carried goods and raw materials over all the world. Yet much of this prosperity had a hollow ring. Too many small Southern and Western banks had issued far too much paper money in excess of their capital reserves, and in 1818 the second Bank of the United States (which suffered from mismanagement itself) began to close out some of these "wildcat" banks by collecting their notes and demanding payment.

The purpose was fiscally sound—to force stricter control of banking practices. But the effect was disastrous. By early 1819 a number of shaky banks had already collapsed and others were about to follow. In fact, the entire national banking system, which had not been sound for several years, was nearly ready to topple.

In 1819 more and more banks crashed, businesses failed, and a wave of losses and foreclosures swept over the nation, especially through the West. The consequences of the 1819 crisis continued to be felt until 1823. For the part they had played in precipitating the crisis, the second Bank of the United States and the financial interests of the East earned the undying resentment of the West.

"FIRE BELL IN THE NIGHT"

Sectionalism and Slavery. As the tariff issue of 1816 had exposed some of the sectional economic tensions beneath the surface of "good feelings," so the panic of 1819 revealed more. The second great issue, the question of the existence and extension of the institution of slavery, was projected into Congress by Missouri's impending statehood in 1819.

Slavery had been a submerged issue in national politics since Washington's time. In 1793, during his administration, Congress had passed a fugitive slave law and later forbade the further importation of slaves, beginning in 1808, without unduly arousing sentiment in North or South. In fact, there were many in both sections who hoped that the 1808 act might lead to the eventual extinction of the entire system. In the North, where slavery was unprofitable and unnecessary, all the states had legally abolished it by 1804 (as the Ordinance of 1787 already had abolished it from the Northwest Territory). In the South antislavery societies actively campaigned against it. Still, after 1816 there was growing harshness in Northern and Southern discussions of the slavery question.

The most important area of disagreement over slavery concerned its economic relationship to Southern cotton culture. Eli Whitney's invention of the cotton gin (1793), the introduction of new strains of cotton, the expanding postwar textile market at home and abroad, and the opening to production of the rich "Black Belt" lands of the Southwest, all combined to make cotton an extremely profitable cash crop. Cotton was on the way to becoming "King" in the South.

Cotton required a large, steady supply of cheap, unskilled labor. Many believed that black slaves filled this need. At the same time, it was found that the delta lands of Louisiana and Mississippi were ideal for sugar cane, while tobacco culture moved from the coastal South into Kentucky and Tennessee. These too needed cheap labor.

In 1800 there were about 894,000 blacks in the United States, almost wholly concentrated in the eastern South. In 1808, when the importation of slaves ceased, the figure stood at over one million, and by 1820 the South's investment in slaves was estimated to be nearly $500 million. It was perfectly clear that slavery and cotton provided the foundation of Southern society and would continue to do so.

The Missouri Compromise. Missouri, early in 1819, counted 60,000 persons and applied for entry to the Union as a slave state. No doubt the bill for its admission would have passed without appreciable comment, had not James Tallmadge, Jr., of New York introduced in the House an amendment requiring the gradual abolition of slavery in the new state as a condition of its admission. This amendment immediately exposed the heart of the issue.

As the nation moved west, the tendency had been to maintain a rough balance of power between slave- and free-state blocs in Washington. The North and Northwest, however, had gained a million more persons than the South and Southwest since the 1790 census, thereby proportionately increasing their congressional representation. The slave states were already outvoted in the House; only in the Senate were the sections equally represented, a situation which might not continue for long.

Of the original thirteen colonies, seven became free states and six slave. Between 1791 and 1819 four more free states were admitted and five slave. So when Missouri applied for entrance to the Union in 1819, the balance was even, and Tallmadge's amendment involved far more than Missouri's admission alone.

Slavery was already barred from the Northwest Territory but not from those lands acquired through the Louisiana Purchase. Should Missouri and all other states subse-

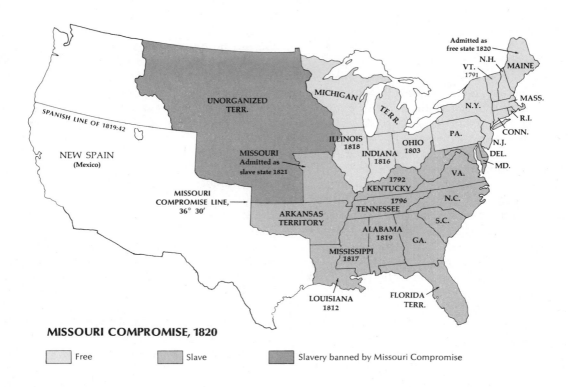

MISSOURI COMPROMISE, 1820

☐ Free   ◩ Slave   ■ Slavery banned by Missouri Compromise

quently admitted from the Louisiana Purchase lands be admitted as slave states, the balance of federal political power would be tipped toward the South and slavery. If they were to be free states, their entry favored the North and emancipation.

At stake lay political control, present and future, of the Union. "It is political power that the northern folk are in pursuit of," Judge Charles Tait of Alabama wrote to a friend concerning the Missouri question, "and if they succeed, the management of the Gen'l Gov't will pass into their hands with all its power and patronage."

Tallmadge's bill finally passed the House in February, after hot and protracted debate. Congress adjourned, however, until December, and during the interval Maine, long attached to Massachusetts, applied for statehood. Sensing compromise, the Senate originated a bill accepting Maine as a free state and Missouri as slave, thereby preserving the balance. The House accepted it, but added a proviso that slavery be banned forever from the Louisiana Purchase lands above the line of 36°30'.

The bill was passed and signed in March 1820, but this so-called Missouri Compromise merely delayed the ultimate confrontation of the problem of slavery, and everyone knew it. The "momentous question," wrote Jefferson from Monticello, "like a fire-bell in the night, awakened me and filled me with terror."

EVOLVING A FOREIGN POLICY

Catching Up on Old Problems. Following the Treaty of Ghent the United States and Britain gradually worked out their differences one by one. The Rush-Bagot Agreement of 1817 demilitarized the Great Lakes. The Convention of 1818 gave U.S. nationals fishing rights off the coasts of Labrador and Newfoundland, established the northern boundary of the

Louisiana Purchase at the 49th parallel, and left the Oregon country, which both claimed, under joint occupation for ten years.

America and Spain, too, settled some old disputes. The United States took one section of Florida in 1810 and another in 1813. Secretary of State John Quincy Adams continued negotiations for the rest of the territory, but his diplomacy was disturbed by Florida's Seminole Indians, who kept up raids (with Spanish and British assistance) on the Georgia border. In 1818 General Jackson marched into Florida, captured two Spanish forts, and executed two suspected British agents in what is known as the First Seminole War. The posts were quickly returned to Spain, but Jackson's action helped precipitate a treaty, signed by Adams and Spanish minister Luis de Onís in February 1819, by which Spain renounced its claims to West Florida and ceded East Florida to the United States. In the Adams-Onís Treaty the Spanish also agreed to a boundary line stretching across the continent to the Pacific, redefining the Louisiana Purchase line, and dividing the old Southwest from Spanish Mexico. In addition, the Spanish gave up their somewhat vague claims to Oregon in return for a clear title to Texas.

The Monroe Doctrine.   Reduced to a third-rate power and racked by internal dissension, Spain was losing its empire in Central and South America. Beginning in 1807, its colonies revolted one after another until, by 1821, nearly all had declared themselves independent republics. By 1830, all of Latin America except Cuba and Puerto Rico had gained independence. Sympathetic to such revolutions and alert to opportunities for new markets, the United States waited until its treaty with Spain was accepted and then recognized these republics early in 1822.

Spain, of course, continued to consider the new Latin American nations simply as Spanish colonies in rebellion. In Europe, mean-while, Austria, Prussia, Russia, and France had formed an alliance and "congress system" for the purpose of crushing popular revolutions wherever they occurred. The United States feared that the alliance would decide to send an army to restore Spain's lost colonies, making royal Catholic Spain once more a power in the New World. Nor was the alliance the only threat to the Americas. Russia had already established trading posts in California, and in 1821 Czar Alexander's edict claimed part of the Oregon country for Alaska and barred foreign ships from a large area of the northwest Pacific.

The British, who had no desire to see Spain regain its empire or Russia expand its colonial holdings, offered to join with the United States in a declaration against any interference in the Americas on the part of the alliance, but Secretary of State John Quincy Adams convinced President Monroe and the cabinet that the United States should handle the problem alone. For one thing, Adams did not want his country, he said, to "come in as a cockboat in the wake of the British man-of-war." Furthermore, Adams and others recognized the potential value of the new Latin American republics as markets. And lastly, no one wanted to write off the possibility of American expansion southward if one or more of the new republics asked to be annexed to the United States.

President Monroe in his annual message to Congress on December 2, 1823, therefore stated the official attitude of the United States on the issue. The Monroe Doctrine, as it came to be called, rested on two main principles—noncolonization and nonintervention.

Concerning the first, Monroe stated that any portions of the Americas were "henceforth not to be considered as subjects for future colonization by any European power." In regard to the second, he drew a sharp line of political demarcation between Europe and America. "The political system of the allied powers is essentially different . . . from that of

America," he said. "We should consider any attempt to extend their system to any portion of this hemisphere as dangerous to our peace and safety." At the same time, Monroe promised that the United States would not attempt to interfere with the internal affairs of European nations or with any of their existing colonies in the New World, such as Cuba.

These ideas had been implicit in all American foreign policy since Washington's Farewell Address, but Monroe's message restated in precise terms the classic American principles of hemispheric separation and avoidance of foreign entanglements that had motivated the diplomacy of his predecessors. His enunciation of American domination over half the globe seemed "arrogant" and "haughty" to European statesmen, nor were the Latin American republics particularly pleased with such doubtful protection. Both knew, whether Monroe or the American public cared to admit it, that it was the British navy and not the Monroe Doctrine that barred European expansion into the Americas.

The Triumph of Isolation.   The Monroe Doctrine simply articulated what Americans

By the 1820s, many nations envied the British for having the world's richest, most extensive, and most powerful empire, while others feared that the British hunger for colonies knew no limits. American cartoonist Thomas Nast took his own jab by portraying "John Bull" (Britain) grossly swollen from swallowing so much of the world.

A LITTLE MONROE DOCTORING MIGHT BE GOOD FOR HIM.

had believed since the beginnings of their foreign policy—that there were two worlds, old and new, contrasted and separate. The Old World of England and Europe seemed to Americans regressive, corrupted, plagued by wars and ancient hatreds. The New World was thought to be democratic, free, progressive, hopeful. The objective of the United States, reflecting these attitudes, was to keep these worlds apart, lest the "taint" of the old besmirch the "fresh future" of the new.

The first generation of American statesmen, from Washington to Monroe, unanimously insisted that the United States should, whenever possible, avoid entanglements in Old World politics or problems. At the same time it was perfectly clear to them that the United States could not exist without European trade and that, since the major European powers still held territorial possessions in the New World, it would be extremely difficult to avoid some sort of implication in their almost continuous wars. The foreign policy of every President from Washington to John Quincy Adams was shaped by this constant tension between the dream of isolation and the reality of involvement.

Still, there were certain accepted positions on foreign affairs that the United States throughout the period believed it must maintain—freedom of the seas, freedom of trade, neutrality in European disputes, national integrity, and, above all others, the promotion of the cause of liberty throughout the world. In practice, American diplomats found it hard to work out solutions within this somewhat rigid framework. Did maintenance of freedom of the seas, for example, justify involvement in a European war? Would American assistance to other nations' revolutions justify entanglement in European affairs, even for the best of motives? Should American policy, when it coincided with that of a European power, be pursued jointly? Ought the United States to assume responsibility for internal affairs of democracy in other American republics?

In attempting to answer these and similar questions, the makers of American foreign policy during the early years of the Republic followed rather closely the principles laid down by Washington and the first generation. Fortunately for them, Europe was so preoccupied with its own power conflicts that American diplomacy had time to temporize and room to make a few mistakes. Still, every statement about foreign affairs in the early decades of the nineteenth century derived from the American assumption that the United States was detached from Europe and must remain so, always free to pursue its special ends.

BIBLIOGRAPHY

General studies of the early national period include Edmund S. Morgan, *The Birth of the Republic 1763–1775* (Chicago: University of Chicago Press, 1956), Marcus Cunliffe, *The Nation Takes Shape 1789–1837* (Chicago: University of Chicago Press, 1959), and Charles M. Wiltse, *The New Nation 1800–1845* (New York: Hill & Wang, 1961). R. R. Palmer, *The Age of Democratic Revolution*, 2 vol. (Princeton: Princeton University Press, 1969–1970), places American events within the larger European context. Thomas D. Clark, *Frontier America* (New York: Scribner's, 1969), and Richard A. Bartlett, *The New Country: A Social History of the American Frontier 1776–1890* (Ithaca, N.Y.: Cornell University Press, 1972), provide insight into frontier life in the late eighteenth and early nineteenth centuries. John A. Krout and Dixon R. Fox, *The Completion of Independence* (New York: Quadrangle, 1971), and Russel B. Nye, *The Cultural Life of the New Nation* (New York: Harper & Row, 1963), treat social and cultural developments. See also the latter chapters of Howard Mumford Jones, *O Brave New World!* (New York: Viking Press, 1972), Russel B. Nye, *American Literary History 1607–1830* (New York: Knopf, 1970), John C. Burnham, ed., *Science in America* (New York: Holt, Rinehart and Winston, 1971). Daniel Boorstin, *The Americans: The National Experience* (New York: Random House, 1965), and Richard B. Davis, *Intellectual Life in Jefferson's Virginia* (Chapel Hill: University of North

Carolina Press, 1964), for additional studies in cultural history. The best source on Parson Weems is Marcus Cunliffe, ed., *The Life of Washington, by Mason L. Weems* (Cambridge, Mass.: Harvard University Press, 1962).

Carl L. Becker, *The Declaration of Independence* (New York: Knopf, 1942), remains the classic treatment of the ideological backgrounds of revolutionary philosophy. Merrill Jensen's *The Articles of Confederation*, 2nd ed. (Madison: University of Wisconsin Press, 1959), and *The New Nation* (New York: Random House, 1965), have had great influence in shaping interpretations of the Confederation period. The standard account of the Constitutional Convention is Max Farrand, *The Framing of the Constitution* (New Haven: Yale University Press, 1913), while A. T. Prescott, *Drafting the Federal Constitution* (Baton Rouge: Louisiana State University Press, 1941), reorganizes Madison's notes for convenient study and discussion. Clinton Rossiter, *1787: The Grand Convention* (New York: Macmillan, 1966), is thorough, while Merrill Jensen, *The Making of the American Constitution* (New York: Van Nostrand Reinhold, 1964), is an excellent brief treatment. Gordon S. Wood, *The Creation of the American Republic 1776–1787* (Chapel Hill: University of North Carolina Press, 1969) is a first-rate study.

An important study that has influenced historical thinking for a half century is Charles A. Beard, *An Economic Interpretation of the Constitution*, rev. ed. (New York: Macmillan, 1935). The Beardian economic thesis, however, has been challenged by Robert E. Brown, *Charles Beard and the Constitution* (New York: Norton, 1965), and Forest MacDonald, *We the People: The Economic Origins of the Constitution* (Chicago: University of Chicago Press, 1958). Jackson Turner Main, *The Antifederalists* (Chapel Hill: University of North Carolina Press, 1961), and Celia Kenyon, ed., *The Antifederalists* (Indianapolis: Bobbs-Merrill, 1966), are studies of the opponents of the Constitution. Louis M. Sears, *George Washington and the French Revolution* (Detroit: Wayne State University Press, 1960), and Paul A. Varg, *Foreign Policies of the Founding Fathers* (Baltimore: Penguin Books, 1970), are valuable. Richard B. Morris, *Seven Who Shaped Our Destinies: The Founding Fathers As Revolutionaries* (New York: Harper & Row, 1973), is a thoughtful study of leadership. Staughton Lynd, *Class Conflict, Slavery, and the United States Constitution* (Indianapolis: Bobbs-Merrill, 1968) provides a differently angled interpretation.

John C. Miller *The Federalist Era* (New York: Harper & Row, 1963) is an excellent general survey of the period. Leonard White, *The Federalists: A Study in Administrative History* (New York: Macmillan, 1965), and *The Jeffersonians* (New York: Macmillan, 1965), analyze the respective administrations as political operating units. Recent general studies of political developments are John R. Howe, *From the Revolution Through the Age of Jackson: Innocence and Empire in the Young Republic* (Englewood Cliffs, N. J.: Prentice-Hall, 1973), and Richard Buel, Jr., *Securing the Republic: Ideology in American Politics 1789–1815* (Ithaca, N.Y.: Cornell University Press, 1972). Shaw Livermore, Jr., *The Twilight of Federalism* (Princeton: Princeton University Press, 1962), covers that party's rise and fall. Stephen Kurtz, *The Presidency of John Adams* (Cranbury, N.J.: Barnes, 1961), and Alexander de Conde, *The Quasi-War* (New York: Scribner's 1966), deal with the Adams administration. Charles M. Wiltse, *The Jeffersonian Tradition in American Democracy* (New York: Hill & Wang, 1960), is a thoughtful consideration of Jeffersonian ideas, while Merrill D. Peterson, *(The Jeffersonian Image in the American Mind* (New York: Oxford University Press, 1963), is a provocative study of Jefferson's impact on the American self-concept. Adrienne Koch, *Jefferson and Madison: The Great Collaboration* (New York: Oxford University Press, 1964), traces the development of political theory and practice through both men's administrations. Marshall Smelser, *The Democratic Republic 1801–1815* (New York: Harper & Row, 1968), and Noble E. Cunningham, Jr., *The Jeffersonian Republicans in Power* (Chapel Hill: University of North Carolina Press, 1958), and Richard Ellis, *The Jeffersonian Crisis* (New York: Oxford University Press, 1971) concern the Republican administrations. Two special studies throw light on the Alien and Sedition Acts: James M. Smith, *Freedom's Fetters* (Ithaca, N.Y.: Cornell University Press, 1956), and John C. Miller, *Crisis in Freedom* (Boston: Little, Brown, 1964).

George Dangerfield, *The Era of Good Feelings* (New York: Harcourt Brace Jovanovich, 1952), is the best general history of the pre-Jacksonian decades, while Herbert J. Clancy, *The Democratic Party: Jefferson to Jackson* (New York: Fordham University Press, 1962), is concisely considered political history. Also important for an understanding of the period is Dangerfield's *Awakening of American Nationalism 1815–1828* (New York: Harper & Row, 1965) and Bradford Perkins, *Castlereagh and Adams: England and America 1812–1823* (Berkeley: University of California Press, 1964). Bradford Perkins, *Prologue to War: England and the United States 1805–1812* (Berkeley: University of California Press, 1961), and *The Causes of the War of 1812* (New York: Holt, Rinehart, Winston, 1962), Harry L. Coles, *The War of 1812* (Chicago: University of Chicago Press, 1965), and Roger Brown, *The Republic in Peril* (New York: Columbia University Press, 1964), all treat the War of 1812.

A general source of popular arts and entertainment is Russel B. Nye, *The Unembarrassed Muse: The Popular Arts in America* (New York: Dial Press, 1970). Frank L. Mott, *Golden Multitudes* (New York: Macmillan, 1947), and James D. Hart, *The Popular Book* (Berkeley: University of California Press, 1961), are the best sources for popular fiction. There is no single study of American popular theater, but Richard Moody, ed., *Dramas from the American Theater* (Boston: Houghton Mifflin, 1969), Richard Moody, *America*

Takes the Stage (Bloomington: Indiana University Press, 1955), and Daniel Grimsted, *Melodrama Unveiled: The American Theater and Culture 1800–1850* (Chicago: University of Chicago Press, 1968), are good sources. John Durant, *The Pictorial History of the American Circus* (Cranbury, N.J.: Barnes, 1957), is pleasant and informative.

Richard O. Cummings, *The American and His Food* (Chicago: University of Chicago Press, 1940), is the best single-volume history of American culinary habits. Two older but still useful sources for dress are Alice M. Earle, *Two Centuries of Costume in America*, 2 vols. (New York: Blom reprint of 1903 ed.), and Elisabeth McClellan, *Historic Dress in America 1800–1870* (Philadelphia: Jones, 1910). A standard study of family life is Arthur W. Calhoun, *A Social History of the American Family*, 2 vols. (New York: Arno Press, 1973).

The materials of the period are rich in biography. Dumas Malone's life of Jefferson has reached five volumes, **Jefferson and His Time* (Boston: Little, Brown, 1948–1974). The definitive biography of Washington is Douglas Southall Freeman's multi-volumed *George Washington* (New York: Scribner's, 1948–1957), while James T. Flexner, *Washington, the Indispensable Man* (Boston: Little, Brown, 1975) is the best one-volume study. John C. Miller, **Alexander Hamilton* (New York: Harper & Row, 1959), is the most readable single-volume biography of Washington's Secretary of the Treasury. Irving Brant's *James Madison*, 6 vols. (Indianapolis: Bobbs-Merrill, 1948–1961), and William P. Cresson's *James Monroe* (Chapel Hill: University of North Carolina Press, 1946), cover the lives of Jefferson's successors; Gilbert Chinard, **Honest John Adams* (Gloucester, Mass.: Smith, 1933), remains the best biography. Samuel F. Bemis, *John Quincy Adams and the Foundations of Foreign Policy* (New York: Knopf, 1949), is the classic treatment of foreign relations during Adams' times, and Bemis' *John Quincy Adams and the Union* (New York: Knopf, 1956), is an excellent one-volume biography. Dexter Perkins, **A History of the Monroe Doctrine* (Boston: Little, Brown, 1955), is a definitive study. A good modern biography of John Marshall is Leonard Baker, *John Marshall, A Life in Law* (New York: MacMillan, 1974).

A general history of the women's rights movement is Eleanor Flexner, **Century of Struggle: The Woman's Rights Movement in the United States* (Cambridge: Harvard University Press, 1959); see also Robert E. Riegel, *American Woman: A Story of Social Change* (Rutherford, N.J.: Fairleigh Dickinson Press, 1970), Barbara Welter, *Dimity Convictions: the American Woman in the 19th Century* (Athens, Ohio: Ohio University Press, 1976), and the documents edited by William L. O'Neill, **The Woman Movement* (New York: Watts, 1971). Recent studies of American Indians include Alvin M. Josephy, *The Indian Heritage of America* (New York: Knopf, 1968), and Wilcomb E. Washburn's outstanding volume, *The Indian in America* (Harper & Row, 1975). The development of postwar Indian policy is treated in Bernard Sheehan, *Seeds of Extinction: Jeffersonian Philanthropy and the American Indian* (Chapel Hill: University of North Carolina Press, 1973), and Robert Berkhofer, *Salvation and the Savage* (Lexington, Ky.: University of Kentucky Press, 1965). Edward Spicer, **A Short History of the Indians of the United States* (New York: Van Nostrand Reinhold, 1969), and William T. Hagan, **American Indians* (Chicago: University of Chicago Press, 1961), take somewhat different views of the Indian in American history. American attitudes toward Indians are treated historically by Roy H. Pearce, *The Savages of America* (Baltimore: Johns Hopkins University Press, 1965). For more information about Simon Girty, consult W. Butterfield, *The History of the Girtys* (Cincinnati: R. Clarke Co., 1890), and Thomas Boyd, *Simon Girty: The White Savage* (New York: Minton Balch, 1928). For racial theory in America, see Winthrop D. Jordan, **The White Man's Burden: Historical Origins of Racism in the United States* (New York: Oxford University Press, 1974), Thomas F. Gossett, **Race: The History of an Idea in America* (New York: Schocken Books, 1965), Gary B. Nash, *Red, White, and Black* (Englewood Cliffs, N.J.: Prentice-Hall, 1974), and the documents edited by Louis Ruchames, *Racial Thought in America* (Amherst, Mass.: University of Massachusetts Press, 1969). David B. Davis, *The Problem of Slavery in an Age of Revolution 1770–1823* (Ithaca, N.Y.: Cornell University Press, 1975), is an essential background study.

*Denotes availability in paperback.

Time Line

3
DEMOCRACY AND MANIFEST DESTINY

Eighteenth-century British statesman Edmund Burke once defined a political party as "a body of men . . . united upon some particular principle in which they all agree." This definition, however, could not be applied to the Jacksonian Era of American history. Although almost all citizens called themselves Republicans, there was little agreement on particular principles.

The years 1824–1848, the Jacksonian Era, years of vitality and diversity, were marked by the spectacular growth of the second American party system. This growth was especially obvious after 1828, when Andrew Jackson won the presidency. Among the issues that divided American politicians were free trade, protective tariffs, and bank and land policies.

Agreement on these issues was the exception, rather than the rule. Increasingly, opinions were influenced by a growing sectionalism. Some of this sectionalism may be seen as mainly geographic—East versus West, South versus North. But the determining factors were economic conflicts, with agriculture ranged against industry, for example, and manufacturing interests opposing foreign trade. These economic conflicts, in turn, recalled long-standing debates about the federal government's proper role in the economy. Should federal policies protect one section or one group's interests at the expense of other sections? These became the main questions behind all sectional conflicts.

A counterpoint to these sectional interests was sounded by the growing number of reform movements. Directed at specific social ills, these reform movements sought to bring the country closer to the ideals that had inspired its founding. The full effect of some reform movements, like the movements for women's rights, would not be felt until the twentieth century. Others, such as the powerful antislavery movement, strongly influenced sectional and national politics from the 1840s on.

Overall, these were exciting, exuberant years, which also witnessed a wondrous literary surge and new developments in religion and philosophy. They too invited conflicting views.

The governmental format of the Jacksonian Era bore a striking resemblance to the plans and expectations of the preceding period. Structurally, there was no change remotely resembling the change of the 1780s which had replaced the Articles of Confederation with the Constitution. Not a single constitutional amendment was adopted between 1824 and 1848. Nor were any new executive departments added.

The number of new free states entering the Union continued to be equaled by new slave states. Thus free-state and slave-state strengths maintained their balance in the United States Senate. While the percentage of Northerners in the House of Representatives steadily increased, this reflected the population trend and adherence to a rigid constitutional provision rather than a departure from law or precedent.

On other counts, however, 1828–1848 differed dramatically from the days of the Virginia Dynasty. "Jacksonian democracy," a favorite expression of modern scholars, is used to denote a far greater participation in government by ordinary people than had been the case in Jefferson's time. This spread of political interest and political effort resulted, in part, from the "westernizing" of so many American people. On and near the western frontier, away from long-established cities and towns, life naturally proved less sophisticated and rougher—and more socially democratic than in communities "back east."

These attitudes were not limited to the West, however. Across the country, growing numbers of "average" people—the less well educated, the poorer, and the less aristocratic—became more individualistic, more aggressive, and less deferential. Unlike their parents, they were confident of their own ability to run things.

Jacksonian democracy also involved increased power for state and local political bosses, more emotional appeals to the mass electorate, and more intense partisanship. With the much larger number of voters, it was equally logical for party newspapers to multiply, for national nominating conventions to come into being, and for the hiphurrah and ballyhoo of torchlight campaigning to establish themselves as part of the American scene.

Two developments of the Jacksonian Era would have been particularly startling to the founders of the Republic. Dreams of American imperialism had been largely lacking in 1787, when the Constitution was being shaped in Philadelphia. Yet the 1840s witnessed the annexation of Texas, the Mexican War, and the acquisition of California and New Mexico by the United States. There was even serious talk in high governmental circles of adding all of Mexico plus Canada, Cuba, Hawaii, and other areas to the national domain. Should such action and sentiment be considered imperialistic, with the conflict in Mexico the least defensible aspect? Numerous Americans, especially in the Northeast, said yes.

The second development concerned the basic controversy over states' rights. Should the country be a "consolidated nation" or the "consolidated states"? Jefferson and Madison had both stressed states' rights. But during Jackson's time, the trend was toward a stronger national government. This disturbed Southerners in particular. Not a few pointedly expressed allegiance to "the Union as our fathers knew it"—meaning the preconsolidated Union.

What alarmed Southerners most was that an increasingly powerful central government would be controlled by, or mainly answerable to, the Northern majority in the House and the surging Northern population. Northern interests were bound to be favored in this context, critics thought, and Southern interests would suffer.

Both Southern concern over centralization and Northern charges of imperialism were obviously related to the slavery issue. This issue could not be called new. Many eighteenth-century Americans, including Constitution-makers, had debated it. But prior to the 1860s, even Northern objectors to the "peculiar institution" rarely subscribed to abolitionists' demands that slavery be ended everywhere at once. As slavery was legal in half the states, Northern respecters of the Constitution—like their Southern counterparts—believed that the slave states had a constitutional right to retain slavery.

Extending slavery, however, was a different matter. From 1845 on, larger and larger numbers of Northerners opposed slavery's expansion, associating it with imperialism and a malevolent "slave power." Meanwhile, what seemed to be magnified Northern power in an ever more centralized Union compounded Southerners' resentment of the Yankees. On each side of the Mason-Dixon line,[1] ignorance of the other side bred suspicion, and calm discussion succumbed to passion.

TO THINK ABOUT AS YOU READ . . .

1. The period from 1824 to 1848 saw the growth of reform movements concerned with many issues, from antislavery to prohibition. What were the forces that contributed to people's concern over these conditions within society?
2. What were the movements and trends of thought, feeling, and conviction that influenced the transcendentalists on the one hand and such authors as Hawthorne and Melville on the other? How were these intellectual trends reflected in their books?
3. How were the themes of (a) federal authority over the states and (b) federal authority over the economy illustrated in events that occurred while Andrew Jackson occupied the White House?
4. Why did American political parties and the party system evolve and change as they did between 1824 and 1848? What new factors, methods, and emphases became influential in choosing presidents?
5. Much attention has rightly been given to American expansion in the Far West in 1824–1848. How do you account for the various kinds of expansion and economic changes that were occurring *east* of the Mississippi River during this same period? How did these changes contribute to sectionalism?
6. What factors contributed to the belief in the "Manifest Destiny" of America? What arguments were used to justify it? How well do those arguments stand up today?

---

1. Mason and Dixon's line was a boundary line between Pennsylvania and Maryland, named for the original surveyors. The "Mason-Dixon line" has come to symbolize the demarcation line between the North and South.

Chapter 7

The Culture of the Jacksonian Era

NATIONAL PRIDE

The Excitement of Progress. In the half-century preceding 1830, the United States had made astounding progress. The victory at Yorktown, the Constitution, the Bill of Rights, the Louisiana Purchase, the Battle of New Orleans, the Missouri Compromise, and the Monroe Doctrine were landmarks passed within the memory of many citizens living in 1830. The increase in the population, the growth of the national domain, and the development of cities and industries were only a few of the reasons for Americans' sense of gratification.

The wonder was that one could see such substantial cultural growth in so short a time. At the close of the Jacksonian Era, in 1848, only six decades had elapsed since the eventful months of ratification of the Constitution. Yet distinctive intellectual, artistic, and scientific progress had been made, especially during the most recent twenty years. Authors, artists, and scientists already were giving eloquent and sustained proof of the richness and variety of American life and thought. Ordinary Americans were participating. They and their descendants reaped the benefits.

The Triumph of Technology. Such heady developments should not obscure the fact that the majority of Americans lived simple lives. In 1824–1848, most of them still were farmers and most farms still were small. But, subtly or abruptly, what happened to them from dawn to dusk was changing. With the coming of the cast-iron plow, the steel plow, and the mechanical reaper, more food and fiber could be produced by the same amount of land. This led many farmers to acquire and cultivate more soil. It also meant that increasing numbers of them, no longer agriculturally essential, would be free to move to cities where—mainly in the Northeast—mills and factories were springing up.

No invention wrought more changes in everyday living than the steam engine. Machines found their way into what had been gardens, factories into towns and cities, and once-rural people into urbanized communities where steam, iron, and their byproducts promised year-around income for workers. Steam-propelled riverboats, with their cheap and smooth transportation, speeded the expansion of river cities like Cincinnati and St. Louis. Railways, from the 1830s and 1840s on, were to have a similar impact on inland communities. One of the most amazing changes, barely beginning in this period, was the coming together of ship and rail traffic, notably at a spot where a small village, Chicago, was incorporated in 1837.

Concurrently, the ever increased use of the cotton gin (invented in 1793 for separating the cotton lint from the seed) combined with the stepped-up demands for cotton to influence Southerners' way of life. Because of the gin, the southern climate, the nature of the land, and the presence of cheap slave labor, the South was in an economic position to supply what expanding American and international markets needed. If there had been no cotton gin, slavery might have been far less profitable. Thus it is clear that the gin was a potent factor, affecting both the status

of slavery and the proslavery thinking of many Southerners.

Other scientific thought and technological action had similar economic and social impacts. Samuel F.B. Morse, an admirable portrait painter, invented the telegraph and sent his first message in 1844. Charles Goodyear discovered the process known as the vulcanization of rubber. From the mind and skill of Samuel Colt came the first practical firearm with a revolving chamber, and Elias Howe is given credit for the first sewing machine.

During this period, too, medical and dental pioneers in Georgia and New England helped ease the suffering of future millions by applying anesthesia to surgery. William

Cyrus McCormick's mechanical reaper, enabling farmers to harvest their grain much faster and more efficiently than before, paved the way for the development of the large farms that became characteristic of American agriculture.

Beaumont, an American army doctor on the Michigan frontier, was the first student of gastric digestion in a living patient. And Oliver Wendell Holmes, the Massachusetts poet-physician, saved the lives of countless mothers and babies by showing that antiseptics could prevent puerperal ("child-bed") fever.

THE ROLE OF REFORMERS

American Women. By twentieth-century standards white women received very unfair treatment. Most of them spent their lives at hard, repetitious labor in frontier cabins, isolated farm houses, or urban dwellings, though some left farms and villages to tend machines in such new "mill towns" as Lowell and Lawrence, Massachusetts. Recently arrived immigrant girls took menial jobs—often as domestic servants—in Atlantic Seaboard cities and interior communities.

To place the pre–1825 status of women in clearer perspective, however, it should be recalled that women were usually freer and more esteemed in America than in Europe. We should realize, too, that as daughters and wives and mothers and grandmothers and valued members of their communities, many women were deeply loved and respected by relatives and neighbors. Still fame and even prominence were deemed unladylike, despite the fact that such first ladies as Abigail Adams and Dolley Madison had been recognized as persons of ability when their husbands reached the presidency, and a minority of other women became arbiters of fashion or local doers of good works.

Certain legal restrictions on women carried over from earlier periods into the Jacksonian Era and down toward modern times. Women still could not vote. Wives' property rights were circumscribed at best. Often wives were prevented by law from controlling their own inheritances. And with rare exceptions, women, no matter how talented or ambitious,

found themselves excluded from most professions.

The 1820s, 1830s, and 1840s marked the start of major reforms, many of them spearheaded by women. Emma Willard and Mary Lyon were two notable pioneers in the effort to improve educational opportunities for girls. Sarah and Angelina Grimké, of a prominent South Carolina family, were among the many who crusaded in the North for the abolition of slavery. Dorothea Dix was another earnest friend of the unfortunates. (See Dorothea Lynde Dix: Humanitarian.) Many women were widely known as writers and editors. It was an augury of the future when Elizabeth Blackwell entered medical school in the 1840s, receiving her M.D. degree in 1849.

Meanwhile, Lucretia Mott and Elizabeth Cady Stanton labored for women's rights. In 1848 at Seneca Falls, New York, they sponsored a women's rights convention; its *Declaration of Sentiments* listed discriminations against women and declared that "all men and women are created equal."

Fighting Ills, Woes, and Evils. The zeal of reformers, both men and women, found many targets in the very nation where so many opportunities for improvement and advancement beckoned. The number of people arriving from Europe, particularly from the 1840s on, was larger than America could neatly accommodate. Many immigrants, poor and uneducated, crowded into port cities where they received low wages for long hours and lived in squalor in what came to be known as slums.

Attempts to cope with such problems in 1842–1848 proved rudimentary and, on the whole, unsuccessful. Most of the effort to improve the lot of urban workers came from the relatively weak labor unions, which will be analyzed in greater detail in Chapter 9. But the unions consisted mainly of skilled artisans. They were interested principally in bettering their own lot, not that of the unskilled newcomers. In general, the chief gain for both groups stemmed from workers' demands for free public schools, which were established in New York in 1832 and Philadelphia two years later.

Both urban and rural Americans ate too much fat meat, too many fried foods, and too few fruits and vegetables. Reformers like Sylvester Graham, for whom Graham bread and Graham crackers were named, did their best to promote dietary change. Yet victims of surplus poundage, dyspepsia, and dysentery were less inclined to heed sensible advice than to rely on patent medicines.

The heavy drinking in America, by children and teenagers as well as adults, had been appalling (by modern standards) ever since colonial times. The evil of what we now call *alcoholism* and the reformers' determination to reduce or exterminate it are set forth in Chapter 10. Many men, women, and children "took the pledge" that they would drink no more alcoholic beverages. Then as now, of course, there was cynicism as to how well such pledges would be kept. But vast improvement in drinking habits did occur in the Jacksonian period—far more than with respect to eating.

Reformers similarly progressed substantially in the struggle to eliminate imprisonment for debt. Headway was made in the movement to end the traditional flogging of wayward sailors. The horrors of war anywhere and everywhere led Elihu Burritt, the learned blacksmith of Connecticut, to champion the cause of pacifism. Thomas H. Gallaudet labored ably on behalf of the deaf. Samuel G. Howe, with equal dedication, educated the deaf and the blind. And Dorothea Dix was horrified by the neglect of the insane and strove as a lobbyist to provide institutionalized residence and humane treatment for them.

One may logically ask why there was all this concern for the handicapped portion of the populace. Unquestionably, religion was a factor. The Golden Rule of Christianity inspired people to care sincerely, doing unto others what they would want others to do unto them. The theory and practice of democracy, when carried to their logical conclusions, likewise led humanitarians to devote days, years, and even lifetimes to helping unfortunates. Numerous reformers were motivated also by the desire to impose order on the fast-changing society of which they were a part. Finally, it was a highly optimistic age, with a decidedly individualistic bent.

Just as not everyone was politically active, the number of steadfast participants in some of these reforms was small. But enough Americans believed in human perfectibility to make reform a key characteristic of this period.

Communitarianism. For some idealists, devotion to reforms *within* established society could not suffice. A small minority of American men and women looked upon the current social order, in which the majority toiled and suffered so many privations and indignities, as so utterly harsh and materialistic that it should be forsaken in favor of communitarianism. The communitarians' idea was for a limited number of people to live together in a little community, wholly or mainly self-sufficient and more or less apart from the general society surrounding it.

These communities could be either religious or secular. Among the Christian communitarians were the Shakers, who founded settlements in New England, New York, Kentucky, and elsewhere, and who believed in separation from the cruel and wicked world, in simplicity of language, and in celibacy. Religious communities were sponsored also by the Mormons and by several Adventist sects.

Secular communities resembled the Christian communities in that the purpose was to join people together so as to face collectively the challenge of the frontier or to confront collectively the trends toward industrialization. Among the secular experiments were New Harmony in Indiana, the North American Phalanx in New Jersey, and Fruitlands in Massachusetts. A number of transcendentalists (see p. 179) inaugurated a Massachusetts community named Brook Farm, widely known because of its gifted residents.

Religious and secular communitarianism usually shared such features as vegetarianism, prohibition of alcoholic beverages, equitable division of labor, and community ownership and control of property. Many secular communities had their philosophical bases in the social contract theories of the eighteenth century.

Most secular experiments did not last long, perhaps owing to an absence of explicitly Christian zeal which, in the case of the Mormons and the Shakers, proved a reliable source of community strength. In all, only a few thousand people committed themselves to communitarianism. The vast majority of Americans concentrated on making ends meet, trying to save something for a rainy day, and giving what spare time they had to efforts to improve the society they had inherited.

Progress in Education. Among the most striking reforms of the Jacksonian period were those in the field of education. If some citizens objected to paying for the instruction of other people's children, most of them—at least in the Northeast— endorsed the drive for public

Dorothea Lynde Dix: Humanitarian

by James M. McPherson

The remarkable career of Dorothea Lynde Dix illustrates several important themes in early and mid-nineteenth century America: the upswelling of humanitarian reform; the changing role of women; the development of modern institutions for deviant members of society; the growth of more humane and scientific concepts of "insanity." She is known primarily as a pioneer in the field of mental health. Although her achievements were built on the foundation of earlier reforms, her single-minded dedication to improving conditions for people suffering from mental illness or retardation was the most important agency of progress in this field.

Dorothea Dix was born on April 4, 1802, in the frontier village of Hampden, Maine (then part of Massachusetts). From her Puritan forebears she gained an intense commitment to education, duty, hard work, and self-discipline. But these Protestant Ethic values seem to have skipped her improvident, ne'er-do-well father, from whose chaotic household Dorothea escaped at the age of twelve to live in Boston with her stern but supportive grandmother, the widow of a successful physician and businessman.

schools below the college level. The impetus came from sources as contrasting as Harvard graduates and New York union members. Parents wanted sons and daughters to have the educational exposure they themselves had lacked. More and more children grew familiar with Noah Webster's excellent grammar and speller. As young Americans read and memorized the offerings of William Holmes McGuffey, whose first reader appeared in 1836, some of the finest literature of the ages became part of their consciousness.

What we now take for granted as public grade and high schools did not spread evenly across the face of the land. Primary and secondary education in rural regions was handicapped by the long distances separating farm families, with the resultant problem of assembling students under one roof. As there were more situations of this sort in the South and West than in the Northeast, it was Southern and Western girls and boys living outside towns and cities who were most frequently deprived of the advantages of public education. Wealthy parents tried to compensate by sending their children to private academies or by hiring tutors for them. But this practice was of no help to any but the well-to-do.

In higher education, prestige continued to be identified with Harvard, Yale, and Princeton. The University of Virginia admitted its first students in 1825. Generally, however, small denominational colleges were more typical, making Latin, Greek, and mathematics available in out-of-the-way places. Such

---

At the age of nineteen, Dorothea opened a grammar school for girls in Boston, the type of school then known as a "dame school." For the next twenty years she alternated between teaching and periods of recovery from incipient tuberculosis. Much influenced by the great Unitarian clergyman, William Ellery Channing, she became a Unitarian and published several undistinguished books of a devotional and poetic nature.

Approaching her fortieth year, Dix seemed headed for a typically genteel but sterile existence as a New England spinster. But an incident in March 1841 changed her life and launched her career as a reformer. Visiting an East Cambridge jail to teach a Sunday School class for women inmates, she found female "lunatics" freezing in filthy, unheated cells. Shocked by such cruelty, she publicized the conditions and won public support for improving them.

From this experience, Dix went on to make an eighteen-month study of jails, almshouses, and other public institutions in Massachusetts. In 1843 she presented to the legislature a hair-raising report of "helpless, forgotten, insane and idiotic men and women" confined "in *cages, closets, cellars, stalls, pens: Chained, naked, beaten with rods,* and lashed into obedience!" Five years later, after traveling 30,000 miles to make similar investigations in more than a dozen states, she presented a petition to Congress: "I have myself seen *more than nine thousand idiots, epileptics, and insane in these United States, destitute of appropriate care and protection* . . . bound with galling chains, bowed beneath fetters and heavy iron balls attached to drag chains, lacerated with ropes, scourged with rods, and terrified beneath storms of profane execrations and cruel blows."

In truth, the treatment of the mentally ill was not everywhere this bad. There had been much progress beyond the medieval practice of treating insanity as a form of

institutions received marginal support from their respective churches.

There were few medical schools, and fewer still in engineering. Most young lawyers got their training in older attorneys' offices. Nevertheless, sons of farm and village families had access to opportunities denied their fathers—even though few state universities thrived. The era also provided a beginning for the higher education of women when coeducation was inaugurated at Ohio's Oberlin College.

FAITH AND INTELLECT

Religion and the People. Religion played an important part in the lives of average Americans. The Baptist and Methodist churches had more members than any others, but the Presbyterian, Congregational, Episcopal, and other denominations appealed to substantial numbers. Sunday schools constituted a standard medium for indoctrinating the young. And Methodists and Baptists were successful in developing black congregations.

Religious diversity should likewise be stressed. With the influx of Irish and German immigrants by the hundreds of thousands during the 1840s and 1850s, more Americans adhered to the Roman Catholic and Lutheran faiths. And supplementing churches with European origins were indigenous ones like the Disciples, Mormons, and various Adventist groups.

Widespread evangelistic endeavors also characterized the era. Especially in the South

possession by demons, to be cured or punished by exorcism or scourging. The Quakers, in particular, had in the eighteenth century influenced the establishment of "lunatic asylums" where the mentally ill received humane treatment. About a dozen such asylums existed in the United States at the time Dix began her crusade.

But these hospitals reached only a small percentage of the mentally ill. Most persons believed to be insane were either locked up at home by embarrassed relatives or incarcerated as lunatic paupers in jails and poorhouses, where conditions were often as bad as Dix portrayed them.

Dix's tireless, selfless work in state after state, all the more heroic because of personal shyness and chronic ill health, paid off with extraordinary victories. Her first success was the enlargement of the state insane asylum at Worcester, Massachusetts, in 1843. From there she went on to persuade the New Jersey legislature in 1845 to establish the state's first mental hospital, which Dix called "my firstborn child."

During the next thirty years she was directly responsible for the founding of 32 mental hospitals at home and abroad, and indirectly responsible for the establishment of many more. From 1854 to 1856 she visited several European countries and inspired the same kinds of reforms in the care and treatment of the insane there as she had done in the United States. Wherever Dix went, a network of voluntary associations was created to aid her cause and sustain her initiatives after she moved on. By 1880, when she retired from active work, the dozen American mental hospitals of 1840 had increased tenfold to 123.

and West, the example of Bishop Francis Asbury inspired his Methodist successors to "ride the circuit" and present in graphic language the punishments for sin and the rewards of salvation. In the East and then in Ohio and Indiana, Lyman Beecher and his sons preached powerful Calvinistic sermons and attacked such social ills as dueling and alcoholic indulgence.

More popular than any other evangelist in the West and North, Charles Grandison Finney in countless revival meetings emphasized the individual's ability to repent. Salvation, Finney believed, represented only the start of a useful life: The person saved should then save others. Finney's theology, lacking orthodox Calvinistic tenets, won converts by the tens of thousands.

No longer were clergymen as apt as in the past to bewail a "low state" of American Protestantism. No longer did religion—as in the 1790s—appear to be removed from the masses in Middle Atlantic and other communities, with church memberships declining and the dissensions and arguments of ministers severely damaging their sects. If—as the French traveler Alexis de Tocqueville thought in the 1830s—religion was the foremost American institution, there were solid reasons for its number one rank. The "Second Great Awakening," which had begun with the turn of the century, continued into the time of de Tocqueville's visit and its spiritual force was felt long after that.

The evangelists of the Second Great Awakening did much of their preaching and

Dix's observations of jails and penitentiaries led her into the cause of prison reform, a subject on which she produced influential writings. She also sympathized with other reform movements, especially the movements for temperance, women's rights, and education. But she focused her active efforts on the plight of the mentally ill, except during the Civil War when she served as Superintendent of Female Nurses for the Union army.

Single-minded in her ideas of how things should be done and no longer shy about expressing herself, Dix sometimes clashed with army surgeons and intimidated inefficient nurses, who called her "Dragon Dix." But she also won the commendation of the secretary of war for her services. Dix's wartime activities were part of a broader development in which nursing was evolving from a menial occupation into a genuine profession. This in turn opened up new career opportunities for women.

After the war Dix resumed her work for better institutional treatment of the insane. Although she favored therapeutic rather than merely custodial care, she contributed little directly to the development of psychiatry or to the psychology of mental illness. But her institutional achievements did create a framework for future advances in psychiatry. In 1881, old and infirm, she retired to live with her "firstborn child," the Trenton state mental hospital, where she died on July 18, 1887.

An architect's projection of a community of 2,000 persons at New Harmony shows public buildings, offices, shops, botanical and food gardens, and exercise grounds, all set in 2,000 acres in southern Indiana. This structure was never built.

exhorting outside the doors of churches, reaching the people at huge camp meetings in the countryside or at medium-sized revivals. But a significant part of their ultimate effect was to lead zealous converts into Baptist and other church folds, where continuing inspiration, strength, and comfort could be found.

There was also a close relationship between the assailing and reforming of social sins and the Protestant Ethic concept of hard work as a glorification of God. The excitement of economic progress and the challenge of technology had an undeniable identification with thrift, industry, and self-discipline. So it was not accidental that Christianity was far from being a Sunday-only affair in the Jacksonian period. Both rural and urban faithful attended prayer meetings on week nights. Grace was said before meals in innumerable homes, and devotional services were held in family circles with parents and children devoutly kneeling.

The Unitarian Influence. For the Christians whose ardor and faith have just been depict-

ed, God the Son and God the Holy Ghost were as integral in the Deity as God the Father. But concurrently spreading in New England was the influence of Unitarians, who rejected the doctrine of the Trinity, believing that God exists in only one person.

Unitarians accepted Christian revelation, but only so far as it accorded with what they conceived to be human reason. The Calvinistic belief in the doctrine of election was not for them because it implied an arbitrary God. Instead, Unitarians underscored the Deity's benevolence. They declared that Jesus was divine in the sense that all people are divine. To a degree, they were reacting against both the creed and the formalism of Congregationalists and the fire-and-brimstone evangelism of the Great Awakenings, although one also finds links between the latter and Unitarian individualism. To Unitarians, the life of Jesus represented an example to be emulated by persons who already were innately good and spiritually free.

A spokesman for Unitarian thought and

action was the Boston clergyman, William Ellery Channing. Implicit in his ideas was the prominence of the individual—independent, yet spiritually obliged to "transcend" individualistic self by intimate identification with the Deity. Though Channing had been reared in the creed of Calvinism, he came to deny the doctrine of original sin and to believe firmly in the freedom of the will.

Romanticism Revisited. It is not difficult to understand why Channing and other Unitarian thinkers appealed to young scholars and writers who had been impressed by the ideas of Romanticism. Romanticism had had an important influence on the thinking of the young republic. Now, in 1824–1848, Romanticism's influence was, if anything, even more pervasive.

Romantic writers and artists had as their goal the "liberation" of the individual—the full realization of the human potential. To accomplish this, they felt that individuals should give free rein to imagination and emotion, experimenting with new ways and new ideas. The emphasis was on informality, the picturesque, the exotic, and the sensuous as ways of appreciating external nature and capturing the transient aspects of life. They shunned tradition, feeling that human intuition and poetic sensibility were best qualified to lead people to truth.

The growth of democratic government during the Jacksonian period reflected this new emphasis on the value of the individual and faith in the ability of the common person. This individualism was not necessarily "nonconformist": Most Americans still took their cue for behavior from the majority. But in the main, those who invaded the wilderness and established settlements in the West saw themselves as economically self-reliant and capable of almost any achievement. They developed versatility, robustness, and resilience, along with the physical courage that was expected of them.

The Romanticists felt that society was a growing organism that could be changed and improved. Thus Romanticism as well as Christianity nourished the reform movements of the period. Most American Romanticists, however, thought their country already had the political foundations it needed and so concered themselves largely with social and humanitarian reforms.

THE GOLDEN AGE OF LITERATURE

Emerson and Transcendentalism. The period from the triumph of Jacksonian democracy to the Civil War was one of the greatest eras in American literary history. It has been called "The Golden Day," "The New England Renaissance," and "The Flowering of New England." Two memorable figures, Ralph Waldo Emerson and Henry David Thoreau, share credit for much of the flowering. Each a Harvard graduate and each a resident of Concord, Massachusetts, Emerson and Thoreau were the leading proponents of transcendentalism—into which the two intellectual streams we have just observed, Unitarianism and Romanticism, flowed.

Transcendentalism has been defined philosophically as "recognition in man of the capacity of knowing truth intuitively, or attaining knowledge transcending the reach of the senses." In his first little book *Nature*, published in 1836, Emerson asked penetrating questions:

Foregoing generations beheld God and nature face to face; we, through their eyes. Why should not we also enjoy an original relation to the universe? Why should not we have a poetry and philosophy of insight and not of tradition, and a religion by revelation to us, and not the history of theirs?

Emerson pointed out that Jesus "spoke of miracles," for Jesus felt "man's life was a miracle" and man's "daily miracle shines, as the character ascends." But the churches' interpretation of the word miracle, Emerson

Evangelist preachers of the Second Great Awakening inspired fervent avowals of religious faith and drew many people into the church fold. The camp meeting depicted here took place about 1835.

added, gave a false impression and was "not one with the blowing clover and the falling rain."

The allusion to clover and rain as miracles symbolized the transcendentalists' search for revelations of divinity in external nature as well as in the individual's own nature. Emerson viewed the different aspects of the universe as diverse manifestations of a central spirit, which he called the Over-Soul. Man and woman, according to Emerson, could be channels for the higher truths of the Over-Soul by developing their intuitive powers to the fullest. Emerson's doctrine of the Over-Soul also implied a belief in self-reliance, as

expounded in his famous essay of that name. When he wrote about self-reliance, Emerson's meaning was that the human being could reach a direct, exalted relationship with the universal spirit.

Emerson's philosophy was essentially a variety of philosophical idealism, as distinct from materialism. Broadly speaking, an idealist is one who sees basic reality as spiritual; the materialist is one who sees it as physical or material. But Emerson's idealism was concerned ultimately with the conduct of life. For this he felt that men and women have the capacity to draw upon a power greater than their own.

Thoreau. Although Emerson published many volumes of poetry and essays, he was more widely known in his lifetime as the most popular lecturer of his day. By contrast, Thoreau's contacts with his contemporary Americans were minimal. Very few bought or read his *A Week on the Concord and Merrimack Rivers* (1849) or even his now-celebrated *Walden* (1854), both of which related his experience and thinking in the 1840s.

Today Thoreau is considered one of the major American writers of all time. Emerson comprehended the younger man's greatness as a stylist, testifying that "Thoreau illustrates with excellent images that which I convey in a sleepy generality." An erstwhile schoolteacher and local handyman, Thoreau spent the years 1845–1847 in a shack on the edge of Walden Pond near Concord. Here he dwelt among the birds and beasts, reading and writing with few distractions. "I went to the woods because I wished to live deliberately." he explained, "to front only the essential facts of life."

Any Romanticist, any fellow-transcendentalist, would have no trouble grasping the logic of what Thoreau said. " . . . I had not lived there a week before my feet wore a path from my door to the pondside. . . . How worn and dusty, then, must be the highways of the world, how deep the ruts of tradition and conformity."

Independence and self-reliance dominated Thoreau's life. He actively helped the "underground railroad" to convey runaway slaves to the freedom of Canada. He spent a night in jail rather than pay a tiny tax to support a government then prosecuting what he considered an unjust war against Mexico.

Out of the latter experience came *Civil Disobedience,* a highly influential political essay which the modern author and critic Henry S. Canby was to call "Gandhi's textbook in his campaign of passive resistance" against the British in twentieth-century India. (Together Thoreau and Mahatma Gandhi greatly influenced the nonviolent resistance of Martin Luther King, Jr.) Thoreau declared it the duty of citizens to deny allegiance to a government they feel is wrong.

Such an attitude is essential to the health of a democracy. It is the opposite of that apathy which prevents citizens from taking a stand, allowing important contests to go by default. Thoreau was not antisocial. He merely took his duties as a citizen more seriously than most Americans.

The Boston Brahmins. In his own day, Thoreau was not nearly so well-known as Henry Wadsworth Longfellow, James Russell Lowell, or Oliver Wendell Holmes. Each of these was an admired poet (and Holmes, somewhat later, the author of well-regarded prose). Although Lowell and Longfellow attacked slavery in verse, all three were primarily literary aristocrats. Holmes applied

A sketch by Thoreau's sister, Sophia, shows the cabin where her brother retreated "to live deliberately."

the label "Brahmin caste of New England" to the cultivated, exclusive class he typified.

These "Brahmins" were inclined to view literature as something lofty and ennobling. Much of the time in their writing, they erected barriers against unpleasant or perplexing social and philosophic questions. The dreamy utopias of Emerson and the back-to-nature living of Thoreau were not for them in the 1830s and 1840s—nor were the portrayals of evil that characterized the books of Nathaniel Hawthorne and Herman Melville. Benevolent toward others, the "Brahmins" were usually satisfied to savor the pleasant intellectual life of Boston and Harvard—where all three were professors. Although (or perhaps because) he had a sense of humor, Holmes considered Boston "the thinking center of the continent, and therefore of the planet."

Hawthorne. The writer who most brilliantly opposed transcendentalist tendencies was Nathaniel Hawthorne of Salem, Massachusetts. He was the chief inheritor, in literature, of the old Puritan tradition and his works—particularly his novel *The Scarlet Letter* (1850)—embodied Puritan ideas. His ancestors had been Puritan magistrates charged with persecuting Quakers and condemning "witches" at Salem court. While disapproving of their bigotry and cruelty, he recognized the ancestral tie: "Strong traits of their nature," he said, "have intertwined themselves with mine."

Hawthorne rejected both the optimism inherent in transcendentalism and the reform movements abetted by it. He held the Puritan belief that people are innately sinful, that evil is an ever present reality (not an illusion to be brushed aside), and that self-reliant individualism alone cannot save a person from destruction. In Hawthorne, we see the persistence of the Puritan point of view into the Jacksonian Era.

Unlike Emerson, who denied that evil existed in an ultimate form, Hawthorne made evil central in his stories and novels. *The Scarlet Letter* deals with secret guilt, the effects of crime on man and woman, and the need for expiation through confession or love. In *The House of the Seven Gables* (1851), evil appears as a hereditary taint visiting the sins of the fathers on the children in a study of degeneration and decay. *The Blithedale Romance* (1852) is, in part, a satire on the secular community Brook Farm—the villain showing how a reformer's zealotry can mesh with unconscionable ambition and thus serve evil rather than good.

Melville. A writer close to Hawthorne both in his concern with the "deep mystery of sin" and in his revulsion against Emersonian currents of optimism was Herman Melville. Born in New York, reared there and in the Berkshires of Massachusetts, Melville as a youth shipped as a sailor on a merchantman plying the Atlantic and later on a whaler bound for the South Seas. On these voyages he saw at first hand a world of violence, crime, and misery.

Such early Melville books as *Typee* and *Omoo* were popular, but his increased pessimism caused the novelist to be neglected after the 1840s. He was "rediscovered" in the 1920s by post-World War I readers, to whose mood of disillusionment *Moby Dick* (1851) had a powerful appeal.

Although Melville, like Hawthorne, was a philosophical pessimist, he arrived at his pessimism along intellectual avenues differing from Hawthorne's in three ways. First, Hawthorne still cherished Calvinist values though critical of them and all others, whereas Melville rebelled against the religious conservatism he had known as a boy. Second, in Liverpool and in the South Seas Melville was shocked by the roughness and cruelty of "civilized" men—brutalities that neither Hawthorne nor Emerson experienced. Finally, just as he lacked Emerson's optimism, he lacked Hawthorne's resignation.

Said Hawthorne in reference to an 1856 meeting with Melville in England:

Melville, as he always does, began to reason of providence and futurity, and of everything that lies beyond human ken, and informed me that he had "pretty much made up his mind to be annihilated"; but still he does not seem to rest in that anticipation; and, I think, will never rest until he gets hold of a definite belief. It is strange how he persists—and has persisted ever since I knew him, and probably long before—in wandering to-and-fro over these deserts, as dismal and monotonous as the sand hills amid which we were sitting. He can neither believe, nor be comfortable in his unbelief; and he is too honest and courageous not to try to do one or the other.

Modern literary critics give Melville high ratings and are fascinated by his imagery. Sometimes they remind us that we should not forget his love of the exotic, the sensually attractive, and the humorous, for Melville was a many-sided man. While the dilemma of the author of *Moby Dick* has been variously analyzed, it is probable that Hawthorne's interpretation was not wide of the mark.

James Fenimore Cooper. The disparity between the dream of a peaceful, democratic society in the virgin wilderness and the reality of frontier life was frequently reflected in the thought and literature of this period. The real Western frontier posed many problems of adjustment for its settlers. Land speculation, political corruption, and immorality were common in the poorly organized towns. In short, the real frontier bore little resemblance to the literary legend or to the popular tall tale.

The first major writer of fiction to exploit the literary potential of the frontier was James Fenimore Cooper, whose series of "Leatherstocking Tales" both romanticized the wilderness and conveyed the loss many Americans felt when they became aware of the crude fashion in which the frontier was being settled. For instance, Cooper convincingly expressed the tragedy of the American Indian, pushed out of ancestral lands by the advancing white settler.

Although it is easy to lampoon his didacticism, stock characters, and strained and starchy dialogue, at his best Cooper was a captivating storyteller with a talent for both description and perceptive social criticism. "The Leatherstocking Tales" represent a Romantic view of the West, just as Sir Walter Scott's novels and ballads romanticized with charm and skill the people and places of a lost Europe. Cooper's West, however, was confined mainly to upper New York State before 1800. He himself never saw the prairie, never neared the Rocky Mountains—in fact never even crossed the Mississippi River.

Southern Romanticism.   The South produced numerous authors before the Civil War, yet there were few direct literary connections with New England. Sectional interests influenced literature, just as they influenced politics. With many Southerners convinced that slavery must be maintained and allowed to spread, Southerners liked to idealize their plantations as happy feudal domains where blacks benefited from the most humane treatment. Southern writers praised Greek democracy, where *inequality*, rather than *equality*, had prevailed. There and in the American South, they held, competent individuals directed and cared for the less competent—acting in the interest of all.

Because of the feudal emphasis, the dominant influence on Romantic Southern literature in 1824–1848 was the British author Sir Walter Scott. Scott's fictional recreation of the Middle Ages, his knights in shining armor, his defenders of glamorous ladies in distress, and his heroes' exemplary characters fitted in with notions of Southern chivalry—as opposed to Northern commercialism and reformism.

A number of American writers attempted to romanticize the "feudal" South. One of the best of those novels was John P. Kennedy's

Swallow Barn (1832), which depicted rural Virginia in the 1820s. A resident of Baltimore, Kennedy strung together sketches of idealized plantation aristocracy with a minimal plot. In it the master of the estate of Swallow Barn is genial and generous, his relatives and friends are virtuous, their hospitality is bountiful, and the blacks are cheerful.

Edgar Allan Poe. Reared as a foster child in Virginia, Edgar Allan Poe nevertheless can be treated only partly as a Southerner. Although in his personal life he was—or wanted to be—a conservative Southerner, and although he supported the works of other Southern authors and praised the Southern defense of slavery, Poe's writings rarely reveal a Southern tone or setting. In his tales he was more influenced by the "Gothic" tradition in English fiction—the kind of fiction that used certain stock properties like old castles, decayed houses, dungeons, secret passages, ancient wrongs, and supernatural phenomena.

Poe was not concerned with portraying contemporary scenes or providing moral reflections on life. He believed that poetry, for example, should exist for its own sake, never as an instrument of instruction. It may be that no other American has maintained more consistently that literature exists primarily and perhaps solely to entertain. But Poe did not take this function lightly. In his own poetry and prose, he applied the theories of literary technique that he expounded in his critical writings. There was a great deal of orginality in Poe's writing, particularly in his short stories and detective stories. Both his poetry and his prose were enormously admired abroad, especially in France.

JOURNALISM AND POPULAR CULTURE

Writing for the People. Americans of the time read newspapers more avidly than even the most exciting fiction. New York City pro-

duced some of the best journalism in Horace Greeley's *Tribune* and poet-editor William Cullen Bryant's *Post*. James Gordon Bennett's New York *Herald*, a pioneer in the "penny press" field, presented national and world news alongside lurid accounts of murders and sex scandals. Nowhere else had there ever been so many newspapers as there were then in America. While quality varied from town to town, Americans knew more about what was going on than any other general population anywhere.

After stereotyping began in 1811 and electrotyping in 1841, the influence of technology on popular culture was evident. Printers used steam presses to mass-produce books which, cheaply bound and extensively distributed, sold for as little as twenty-five cents. Intellectuals read such magazines as the *North American Review* and the *Southern Literary Messenger*. Tillers of the soil preferred the *American Farmer*, the *American Agriculturist*, and the *Southern Cultivator*. In addition to agricultural articles, these offered fiction and verse to farm families.

Religious periodicals abounded—notably the *Biblical Repertory* (Presbyterian), the *Biblical Repository* (Congregationalist), the *Christian Review* (Baptist), the *Christian Examiner* (Unitarian), the *Methodist Magazine*, and the *United States Catholic Magazine*. Carrying theological arguments and sectarian messages, many of them also disseminated miscellaneous culture. "Of all the reading of the people," a commentator observed in 1840, "three fourths is purely religious." In 1848, fifty-two religious journals were published in New York City alone.

Magazines and Books for Women. Discerning innovators discovered that women could compose one of the most dependable magazine markets. From 1830 on, a Philadelphia periodical called *Godey's Lady's Book* enjoyed an enviable circulation. By the 1850s, its subscription list reached 150,000. Eventually, its publisher amassed a million-dollar fortune.

Graham's Magazine, which made its bow in 1841, instantly appealed to both women and men. Soon it had 40,000 subscribers and a $50,000 annual profit. Its contents? Short stories, essays, poetry, colored fashion plates, book reviews, and a department on fine arts. Bryant, Cooper, Lowell, and Longfellow contributed to *Graham's.* For a time Poe was literary editor, and some of his best work graced its pages. Combining the insipid and sentimental with better things, *Graham's* and *Godey's* provided exactly what their readers wanted.

Women writers were widely published during the Jacksonian period. Authorship lent opportunity to women when most other vocational doors were shut. Mrs. Ann Stephens, co-editor of the *Ladies' National Magazine,* sent florid but thrilling tales to the *Lady's Wreath* and similar media. Poems (often lachrymose) and articles by Mrs. Lydia Sigourney won acceptance in countless journals. Among women authors with large followings were Catharine M. Sedgwick and Mrs. Anna Mowatt. Mrs. Caroline Lee Hentz and Mrs. E.D.E.N. Southworth, popular novelists of the 1850s, got their start in the previous decade. Margaret Fuller edited the *Dial* in Boston and later, in New York on Greeley's *Tribune,* gained more admirers of her astute criticism. Her volume, *Women in the Nineteenth Century,* projected advanced views on women's rights.

Sports, Humor, and Realism. One of the liveliest periodicals was New York's *Spirit of the Times.* Its editor featured sports and pastimes like horse racing, boxing, hunting, shooting, and fishing. He also had an eye for realism and amusing exaggeration in fiction. In the *Spirit* and in books, small farmers and reckless frontiersmen of the Old Southwest— from Georgia to Arkansas—became subjects of wildly humorous yarns by such frontier writers as Thomas B. Thorpe, William T.

Thompson, Augustus B. Longstreet, J.J. Hooper, and George W. Harris. Authentically depicting the speech, customs, and scenery of their region, they produced comedy combined with realism.

Harris, who wrote for the *Spirit* in the 1840s, created his fictional character Sut Livingood a bit later. There is no better example of the breed of men inhabiting these humorists' stories. A lanky mountaineer and self-confessed "nat-ral-born durn'd fool," Sut loves liquor and women but hates Yankees and circuit-riding preachers, whom he describes as "durn'd, infurnel, hiperkritical, potbellied, scaley-hided, whiskey-wastin'." These storytellers delighted in the boast and brag of the "tall tale":

I'm that same David Crockett, fresh from the backwoods, half-horse, half-alligator, a little touched with the snapping-turtle; can wade the Mississippi, leap the Ohio, ride upon a streak of lightning, and slip without a scratch down a honey locust; can whip my weight in wild-cats—and if any gentleman pleases, for a ten-dollar bill, he may throw in a panther. . . .[1]

Chauvinism, boastfulness, and exaggeration here all reflected the influence of the West and Southwest on thinking and reading tastes. There are historians who believe that the "starting point of a truly American literature" can be located on the frontier, in just such tales, more logically than in the East.

ARTS, SCIENCES, AND POPULAR TASTE

The "Higher Culture." As in literature, so in other arts: Americans valued both the light and the serious. Classical music had numerous appreciators, particularly in urban centers with their orchestras and choral societies. No actor won more plaudits than Edwin Forrest,

---

1. Vernon Louis Parrington, *Main Currents in American Thought,* II (New York: Harcourt Brace Jovanovich, Inc, 1927), p. 176.

who played major Shakespearean parts like Brutus and King Lear. No lecturer was more respected than Emerson, who discoursed on intellectual topics annually from New England westward. Margaret Fuller's "conversations," in Boston, attracted audiences of women—eager participants—hungry for mental stimulation. And in 1826 in Millbury, Massachusetts, Josiah Holbrook organized a series of public lectures that were to form the basis of the National American Lyceum movement. This movement, which was dedicated to the spread of information about the arts, sciences, history, and public affairs, spread to other states and became an important force in adult education and social reform.

Despite the fact that serious research was beyond the reach of most teachers, the period witnessed advances along scientific lines. There was keen public interest in science, and young and older people crowded scientific exhibitions and marveled at scientific experiments. Benjamin Silliman, professor at Yale, published *Elements of Chemistry* in 1830 and wrote learnedly on subjects ranging from gold deposits to sugar planting. Other scientific pioneers were Elisha Mitchell, geologist and botanist at the University of North Carolina; Edmund Ruffin, Virginia soil chemist; and Matthew F. Maury of the U.S. Navy, his generation's expert in navigation and oceanography. George Ticknor at Harvard was the American trailblazer in the study and teaching of modern foreign languages. In the historical field, William H. Prescott was publishing his monumental works on Mexico and Peru, and another first-rate historian, Francis Parkman, was writing *The Oregon Trail* and *The Conspiracy of Pontiac*.

In some of the arts and sciences, America still leaned on Europe for much of its leadership. Thus John James Audubon, the ornithologist and painter whose *Birds of America* is a classic, was born in the West Indies and reared in France. Duncan Phyfe, famous for the furniture he produced in New York, came to America from Scotland. Louis Agazziz of Switzerland, who joined the Harvard faculty, did as much as anyone to

Although this speaker seems to be getting a mixed reaction to his discourse on the weather, the public lectures of the Lyceum Movement were an important source of information and intellectual stimulation in the Jacksonian Era.

arouse American interest in zoology and geology. Young Americans of promise went to Germany and France for graduate study.

In philanthropy, too, the Old World pointed the way: Washington's Smithsonian Institution was endowed by an Englishman. Among highly regarded performing artists appearing in the United States were an Austrian ballet dancer, a Norwegian violinist, a Swedish soprano, and British actors and actresses.

Popular Music and Drama.   But Americans by no means depended exclusively on Europe for all their culture. Much folk art and folk craft—the beautiful furniture of the Shakers, for example—was far from being purely derivative, although many songs Americans hummed—"Home, Sweet Home" is an illustration—were at least partly of European origin. Well-loved ballads, fiddle tunes, and folk songs fused the native and imported. The same was true of hymns, work songs, political chants, and comic airs. Some were totally native. All were intimately integrated into the lives, worship, and fun of average people.

On the stage, light plays and musicals competed with the classical. With low admission prices, the urban theater boomed. Rowdy comedies and farces played to rowdy audiences. The versatile James H. Hackett helped make Rip Van Winkle famous and ridiculed "high society" in *The Moderns, or A Trip to the Springs*. The lighter side of cultural life developed with zest in rural areas as well. Heroes were applauded and villains hissed and booed in smaller cities and towns—even in barns and log houses and on boats on Western waters.

Among indigenous American entertainments was the minstrel show with its interlocutor and end men, banjos, bones, and tambourines. Both American and European audiences cheered minstrels like Ohio's Daniel Emmett, the singer and composer who subsequently gave "Dixie" to the South. Enchanting were the tunes of Stephen Collins Foster, the Pennsylvanian who immortalized Florida's "Swanee" River and evoked tears with the strains of "My Old Kentucky Home." Love of the spectacular as well as good music led multitudes to line the pockets of Phineas T. Barnum, who amazed gaping compatriots with his museum of curios—from the woolly horse and bearded lady to the midget "General Tom Thumb"—and in 1850 sponsored the first American tour of Jenny Lind, "the Swedish Nightingale."

Sculpture, Architecture, Painting.   American sculptors had a remarkable vogue. Among the most celebrated were Hiram Powers, whose "Greek Slave" Londoners greeted with admiration, and Thomas Crawford, whose "Armed Freedom" surmounts the Capitol in Washington, D.C. Pseudoclassical portrait busts were produced by the thousands. Average Americans took pride in this art form, although the nude "Greek Slave" did not please the prudish and Horatio Greenough's "George Washington"—partly

Audubon's classic studies of American birds included this painting of the passenger pigeon, a once-abundant species that became extinct in 1914.

draped in a Roman toga—drew its share of outraged criticism.

The Jefferson-Latrobe influence remained strong in Greek Revival architecture. But in the 1830s and 1840s young architects considered classical columns and porticos too formal and artificial. Devotees of Romantic theories, they stressed the organic in plan and construction. A multiplicity of styles, especially the Gothic, characterized the work of Alexander J. Davis and of Richard Upjohn, who designed Trinity Church in New York City. While most Americans did not employ architects, thousands of houses showed the influence of architectural handbooks.

Although, like Upjohn, the most successful portrait painter, Thomas Sully, had come to the United States from England, the canvases of the American-born artists John Neagle and Henry Inman also were popular. "Storytelling" or anecdotal painting—in which common human situations were depicted nostalgically or humorously—likewise was growing in public favor. Scenes of life on the farm or of raftsmen poling their flatboats upstream or of prairie schooners and Indians appeared in the work of George Caleb Bingham, William Sidney Mount, and Alfred Jacob Miller. Romanticism and American pride in the land combined to inspire a group of painters known as the Hudson River School, who romantically portrayed the wilderness of forests, mountains, and streams.

SLAVERY AND DEMOCRACY

Garrison and Abolition. For all the progress and all the pride in the American of 1824–1848—for all the artistry of the gifted, the technology of the inventive, and the fun and frolic and misery and strivings and achievements of the masses of people—the dark cloud of slavery deeply troubled first the few and then the many.

In the 1820s ordinary citizens like the Philadelphia Quaker, Benjamin Lundy, led the fight to abolish slavery. Then in Boston in 1831 a journeyman printer named William Lloyd Garrison founded *The Liberator*, a violently abolitionist paper. Garrison could see no good in the legal sanctions protecting slavery in half the country. Constitutionalism meant far less to him than securing freedom for his fellow human beings. It was no happenstance that Garrison's insistence on this reform occurred at the very time when other movers and shakers were spurring other reforms—both religious and secular.

According to Garrison's concept of Christianity, slavery was sinful. As *The Liberator's* editor, he was motivated primarily by this sinfulness. Fanatical in his conviction, he attacked the Constitution as "a covenant with death and an agreement with hell" and called for an immediate end to slavery. It was hardly surprising that neither Emerson nor Hawthorne nor Holmes would subscribe to such extremism in a day when John Quincy Adams, himself against slavery but no Garrisonian, described the abolitionist faction as small and shallow.

But Garrison was persistent. In 1843, he began the first of twenty-two terms as president of the American Anti-Slavery Society. The seed nourished by Garrison and fellow abolitionists eventually flowered in the emancipation of blacks from bondage. In that sense, Garrison may be regarded as one of the era's most influential reformers. Yet, as we have seen, it was the possibility of slavery's westward extension—rather than the existence of slavery in states where it was legal—to which millions of Northerners strenuously objected from the outbreak of the Mexican War forward. The approach to the slavery issue of Abraham Lincoln and other political leaders was anything but that of Garrison.

No discussion of antislavery efforts should neglect the work of blacks who, with Garrison and like-minded whites, carried the abolition banner. Outstanding in this regard was Frederick Douglass, who escaped from slavery and became an agent of the Massachusetts Anti-Slavery Society. Of commanding appearance and an orator, Douglass established an antislavery paper—the *North Star*—and was well-received by both American and British audiences. The eloquent Charles L. Remond, born free, for a time rivaled Douglass on abolitionist platforms. Black clergymen also had significant parts in the antislavery cause. Two, the Presbyterian Henry H. Garnet and the Congregationalist Samuel R. Ward, held pastorates in upstate New York but were known chiefly as abolition spokesmen.

The Literary Civil War. From 1833 on, the New England Quaker, John Greenleaf Whittier, contributed poems and prose to the abolitionists' campaign. Longfellow in 1842 published a few antislavery poems but never became a Garrison adherent. James Russell Lowell wrote for the *National Anti-Slavery Standard*. Other younger authors—Thoreau, Melville, and Walt Whitman—were repelled by slavery and said so. Then, while Holmes and Hawthorne continued to abstain from the agitation, Emerson swung around in the 1850s to laud the abolitionist crusader John Brown and to compare Brown's gallows to the cross of Jesus.

It is not astonishing to find William Ellery Channing and other Unitarians among outspoken antislavery recruits. Nor does it seem strange that Harriet Beecher Stowe—daughter, wife, and sister of Calvinist ministers and a woman abundantly aware of her own powerful New England conscience—would write *Uncle Tom's Cabin* (1852). Mrs. Stowe contended that the book, which depicted the separation of families, maternal loss, and other evils inherent in slavery, was inspired by God. Inspired or not, it turned out to be the greatest work of propaganda ever written by an American. Southern fiction produced by way of reply had no comparable punch.

The ablest Southern arguments were in essay form and came mostly from politicians and educators. Many slaveholders agreed with John C. Calhoun and William Harper of South Carolina and Thomas R. Dew of Virginia that far from being harmful, slavery was a positive good. Other Southerners merely saw—or thought they saw—a practical necessity for retaining the slave labor system.

When *The Impending Crisis of the South*, a book attacking slavery on economic grounds, was published in 1857, its author, Hinton R.

George Caleb Bingham was one of many painters who showed everyday situations, such as these frontiersmen relaxing at an informal shooting competition.

Helper of North Carolina, was bitterly assailed by Southerners. On the other hand, the writings of a Virginian, George Fitzhugh, were warmly praised in the 1850s by those who denounced Helper. In *Sociology for the South,* Fitzhugh said slavery was a social, political, and economic blessing—and avowed that people trying to eliminate it were blind to Southern realities.

Alexis de Tocqueville's America. Alexis de Tocqueville, the young French magistrate who spent nine months in the United States in 1831 and 1832, has been mentioned previously for his views on life in America. His noteworthy contribution to political science,

sociology, and history was *Democracy in America* (1835). He concluded that American democracy was functioning successfully; that its success depended chiefly on separation of church and state and on the absence of centralization; that American political morality was important; and that American democracy was not for export to Europe until such time as Europeans elevated their standards of governmental morality.

The Frenchman was particularly struck by what he saw as an American tendency toward the practical, an avoidance of traditions, and an optimistic hope that in the new social system people would be able to progress rapidly toward perfection. One of his principal theses was that the American system of government derived from a dominant principle—the will of the people—which had been felt all during the nation's history.

The French magistrate, who stayed long enough to look around thoroughly and to reflect on what he saw and heard, was by no means oblivious to problems involved in the questions of slavery and race. "The most formidable of all the ills which threaten the future existence of the Union," he wrote, "arises from the presence of a black population upon its territory; and in contemplating the cause of the present embarrassments or of the future dangers of the United States, the observer is invariably led to consider this as a primary fact."

Social mobility was a feature of American life that intrigued de Tocqueville. He believed that, with one exception, such mobility would prevent both class stratification and extreme social conflict resulting from it. This exception he found in black-white relationships. If and when Southern blacks "are raised to the level of freemen," he predicted, "they will soon revolt at being deprived of almost all their civil rights; and as they cannot become the equals of the whites, they will speedily show themselves as enemies." Northern whites, he observed, "avoided the Negroes with increasing care in proportion as the legal barriers of separation are removed."

The French observer was not without other doubts concerning the American experiment. He saw a potential danger to freedom of the individual in the possibility that majorities would crush minorities or nibble away at minority rights. He also thought he discerned a trend toward mediocrity in popular leaders and in American culture—this in a country where Emerson, Thoreau, Hawthorne, Melville, Whitman, and Lincoln all were living when de Tocqueville's book went to press. Still, while the French visitor guessed wrong at times, he was remarkably correct in the aggregate.

Harriet Beecher Stowe's best seller, Uncle Tom's Cabin, was a powerful weapon in the literary civil war.

Chapter 8

The Growth of Democratic Government 1824–1848

THE ELECTION OF 1824

Four Political Factions. The sands of political allegiance never shifted more swiftly than in the last year and a half of James Monroe's administration. The partisanship of the days of Jefferson was fast giving way to factional feuds. Although the Federalist party continued to exist for a while in enclaves like Delaware, most citizens called themselves Republicans, including the four leading candidates for the presidency in 1824.

Before 1824, the congressional caucus of the Republican majority had chosen the party's presidential candidates. But during Monroe's second administration the caucus met with increasing opposition. The public looked on the caucus as undemocratic and sought a reform in much the same spirit as the other efforts toward reforms discussed in Chapter 7.

There was growing conviction, too, that it was not in the country's best interest for a newly elected President to feel that he owed his office to Congress. Here we find an excellent example of the evolution of our party system, for criticism of the caucus eventually led to establishment of national party conventions in the 1830s.

Politicians, impressed by the strenuous objections against the caucus, moved to dissociate themselves from it. In a number of states either the legislature or state conventions nominated their own favorite sons. Three quarters of the states elected candidates by popular vote. The result was that when the Republican caucus was held in February 1824 only 66 of the 216 Republican congressmen even attended.

The caucus chose Secretary of the Treasury William H. Crawford, a Georgian, for their candidate. Most of Crawford's strength was in the Southeast, and his selection was scorned by his rivals and their many followers. New England supported John Quincy Adams of Massachusetts, son of John Adams and Secretary of State in Monroe's cabinent. Kentucky, Missouri, and Ohio looked to Speaker of the House Henry Clay of Kentucky. Meanwhile, Pennsylvania, most of the West, and some of the Southeast rallied behind "Old Hickory," General Andrew Jackson of Tennessee, the famous hero of New Orleans. Secretary of War John C. Calhoun of South Carolina had early dropped out of the race, seeking the vice-presidency instead.

Adams Defeats Jackson.   The real contest in the presidential election of 1824 was between Jackson and Adams. Jackson received approximately 153,000 popular votes to Adams' 108,000 and 99 electoral votes to Adams' 84. But Crawford and Clay, with 41 and 37 electoral votes respectively, split the total sufficiently that neither Jackson nor Adams received a majority.

Constitutional procedure now called for the decision to be referred to the House of Representatives. Here each state had one vote, and the three candidates with the most electoral votes—Jackson, Adams, and Crawford—remained in the running.

House Speaker Clay, no longer a presidential candidate, held the balance of power in the House decision. Although he earlier had instigated an anti-Adams campaign in the West, Clay personally disliked Jackson more than Adams and feared him as a future Western rival. He therefore decided to support Adams.

As a result Adams was elected on the first ballot on February 9, 1825. The new President promptly appointed Clay his Secretary of State. Just as promptly, Jacksonians angrily charged that a "corrupt bargain" accounted for both Adams' election and Clay's appointment. There probably was an implicit—if not explicit—understanding between Adams and Clay, but no evidence exists to demonstrate corruption.

One of the often unseen pivots of history is discernible in the election of 1824. Adams was almost exclusively a New England candidate until the New York General Assembly gave him twenty-six of New York's thirty-six electors. This resulted from tricky maneuvering by Adams' Albany managers, who were able to divert from Clay several of the electoral votes he had counted on. If Clay instead of Crawford had been the third candidate, it is possible that the popular Speaker of the House of Representatives would have appealed to his fellow representatives more than either Adams or Jackson.

THE J.Q. ADAMS INTERLUDE

Adams in the White House.   President Adams projected a bold domestic program. In his first annual message he called for laws creating a national university (first proposed by Washington), a naval academy, and a national astronomical observatory. Adams likewise advocated a uniform national militia law, a uniform bankruptcy law, and an orderly, federally financed system of internal improvements. Most of these ideas were highly imaginative, and had his program gone into effect, the second Adams today would be

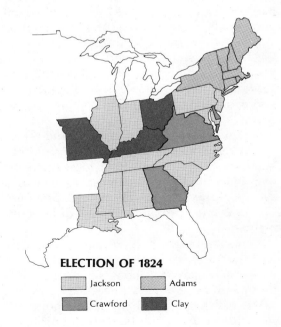

ELECTION OF 1824

	Jackson		Adams
	Crawford		Clay

identified with legislation of those kinds.

But such accomplishments simply were not forthcoming. From the outset Adams made little effort to push his policies once he had enunciated them. A principal cause of this failure was his view that the executive should abstain from what he considered undue interference in the legislative branch. As a consequence, numerous White House proposals, made year after year, were never introduced in Congress as legislative bills or resolutions.

In addition, Adams had personal defects that prevented his being a natural leader. Aloof and unpleasant toward many associates, he disliked public contact and was incapable of appearing to good advantage when little knots of admirers gathered to greet him on his limited travels. Though a man with his diplomatic background should have overcome such traits, he was ungracious and petty in the most minor human relations.

Compounding such personal handicaps were continuing complexities as to what was constitutional and what was not. Politicians had conflicting ideas on (1) what the federal government's role in the economy should be and (2) how much authority the federal government should have over the states. While these problems were not peculiar in 1825–1829, the White House provided no strong directing force toward helping to solve them.

Disagreements among senators and representatives over the construction of the Constitution, coupled with their local interests, contributed to Congress' refusal to develop a systematic national public works program. This was one of Adams' greatest disappointments.

Congressional appropriations followed no logical pattern, and legislative logrolling—the exchange of favors among lawmakers—left undone some of the most necessary projects.

Despite this slapdash approach, however, internal improvements were significant.

Rivers were dredged and harbors made more serviceable, with more federal appropriations voted for those purposes than in the previous thirty years. Lack of funds had halted work on the National Road in 1818. Federal money permitted construction to resume in 1825. By mid-century this important highway stretched from Cumberland, Maryland, to Vandalia, Illinois.

Democratic Republicans, National Republicans. Off to an inauspicious start in the first half of his term, Adams was hopelessly beset after 1826 by a congressional coalition fighting him at every turn. The old Republican party was no more. Increasingly, Jackson people were known as Democratic Republicans, and Adams-Clay people as National Republicans. Jacksonians would not forget that a "deal" had made Adams President despite the electorate's clear preference for Jackson. Sectional hostilities were increasing, and states' rights adherents opposed Adams' bold plans to expand federal authority. Political idealists might praise Adams for being one of the least dominating of all our chief executives, but his effectiveness suffered for this very reason. His opponents played politics to the hilt, especially after they came to control Congress.

Sectionalism and partisanship were most flagrant in the area of tariff debates and tariff votes. One reason for the passage of the tariff of 1824, enacted while President Monroe was still in office, had been its inclusion of duties on raw wool and other farm products. These schedules were attractive to the West, but Eastern manufacturers of woolen textiles complained that their profits diminished because raw materials were so expensive. Yet in 1827 a bill containing a compromise that was supposedly acceptable to both Northeast and Northwest was defeated in the Senate by Vice-President Calhoun's tie-breaking vote.

The next year a tariff crisis occurred that would lead to others. In drafting the tariff bill of that year, Jacksonians in Congress gave top priorities to the protectionist features desired by Middle Atlantic states, where Jackson hoped for potent backing in the next presidential election. His congressional friends virtually ignored New England interests, assuming that Adams' fellow New Englanders could not avoid voting for a high tariff in any case. But the measure was offensive to a wide variety of individuals and sections, especially the Southeast.

Painted into a corner by the shrewd strategy, Adams signed the bill with loathing. Then, because of his signature, he—not the Jacksonians—bore most of the blame for it. Thereafter his name was associated with what critics appropriately labeled the "Tariff of Abominations."

Foreign Relations. Adams' background in diplomacy had led his supporters to believe he would leave a memorable record in foreign affairs. Yet he achieved nothing as President on a par with his earlier success as Secretary of State in getting Russia to agree to Alaska's southern boundary. During his presidency the United States failed to obtain from England the right of free navigation of the St. Lawrence River. And American shippers had to resort to a roundabout trade when the ports of the British West Indies remained closed to Yankee merchantmen as tightly as they had ever been. Old claims against France for damages arising out of the wars of the French Revolution were no nearer settlement in 1829 than in 1825. And though delegates were sent to the Congress of Panama in 1826—called for the purpose of establishing cooperation among the republics of the Western Hemisphere—one died en route to Panama, and the other arrived too late, so the mission accomplished nothing.

In the entire field of foreign relations, Adams could point with pride only to an unprecedented number of minor treaties and to the renewal in 1827 of the Anglo-American agreement covering joint occupation of Ore-gon. With these exceptions, his administration was a negative interlude in diplomatic history.

JACKSON TRIUMPHANT

The Election of 1828. Even if Adams' personality had been more attractive, his attitude more gracious, and his leadership more compelling, he would have had trouble in any contest with the forces arrayed against him. As early as 1825, the general assembly of Tennessee placed Andrew Jackson on the track for the 1828 presidential race. Moreover, except for New England, enthusiasm for Jackson appeared everywhere. From New York to Illinois and from Pennsylvania to Louisiana, acclaim for Jackson reverberated.

Jackson had impressive allies. Vice-President Calhoun, an outstanding South Carolinian who had been Monroe's Secretary of War, did little to conceal his antipathy toward Adams. An important addition to the Jackson high command was Senator Martin Van Buren of New York. Formerly a Crawford lieutenant, the ingratiating Van Buren worked dextrously with Calhoun and others to weld a powerful combination of Southerners and Northerners opposing Adams and favoring Jackson.

In the 1828 election, backers of both Adams and Jackson indulged in discreditable tactics. Pro-Adams journalists made much of Jackson's reputation for military highhandedness. They dragged the name of Mrs. Jackson through the gutters of partisan filth by reminding voters that her divorce from another man had not been final in the 1790s when she became Jackson's wife. This infuriated Jackson and may have had something to do with Mrs. Jackson's death soon after the election. Pro-Jackson editors, however, were no innocent bystanders when the mud was slung, and Adams was pilloried as an aristocrat out of touch with the plain people.

Substantive issues were not entirely ignored. Since the country had not reached the

ELECTION OF 1828

Jackson   Adams

Vote divided

period of national conventions and platforms, there was no formal enunciation of principles, but Jackson in some minds was linked with proposals for tariff reform, and Adams—fairly or unfairly—with the Tariff of Abominations. Critics of the Second Bank of the United States hoped that Jackson, as President, would oppose it. Some advocates of the federally funded construction of roads and canals and the dredging of rivers and harbors preferred Adams because he had spoken out in favor of federal appropriations for these purposes. Yet there was no unanimity here; others believed that Jackson would support federal funding for internal improvements more heartily than Adams.

If serious opinions were held by serious citizens, a simple "Hurrah for Jackson!" was the rallying cry that appealed to most Americans. About three times as many people voted in 1828 as four years before, and the results were recorded with more care. Jackson, the Democratic-Republican candidate, scored a clear triumph with approximately 647,000 popular votes to 508,000 for Adams. In the

electoral college the margin was two to one, with 178 votes for Jackson and 83 for Adams.

"King Mob." Jackson's inauguration in March 1829 was accompanied by a demonstration unparalleled in American history. The thousands of people assembled in Washington behaved well outside the Capitol while Jackson read his inaugural address. But when the time came for the White House reception, "King Mob" took over. Men, women, and children crashed, trampled, and crushed their way in muddy boots and shoes into and through the mansion. Only when someone thought of placing refreshments on the White House lawn did the crowd move outdoors.

Jackson's political enemies were shocked by this public demonstration. They talked darkly of a reenactment of French Revolution excesses on American soil. Actually, the scene had been more a matter of bad manners and an explosion of pent-up energy than anything else. The base of governmental support had broadened appreciably in the past few years, but no excesses other than social ones upset the evolutionary development of an increasingly democratic state. Nevertheless, when the multitude faded away shortly after inauguration day, the symbol of "King Mob" remained as a counterweight to "King Caucus" of old.

Reorganization of the Cabinet. The Democratic-Republican party of 62-year-old President Jackson charted its administrative course in an atmosphere of confusion. Though Van Buren became Secretary of State, several cabinet members were more closely identified with Vice-President Calhoun than with either Jackson or Van Buren.

Almost at once there erupted one of those odd controversies that occasionally have influenced American political history. Secretary of War John H. Eaton, a Jackson appointee who had long been on intimate terms with the new President, had recently married a young widow whose comeliness was said to have attracted him before her first husband's death. The story goes that Mrs. Calhoun and the wives of Calhoun's cabinet friends took the lead in snubbing Mrs. Eaton. Jackson resented the social chill, associating it with the shameful treatment of his own late wife during the campaign.

Van Buren, who endeared himself to Jackson by siding with the Eatons, offered to resign from his cabinet post, knowing that a cabinet reorganization would enable Jackson to be rid of the problem. Eaton followed Van Buren's example, and in the spring of 1831 Jackson requested resignations from all the remaining cabinet members except one. Calhoun's supporters were excluded from the succeeding cabinet, while Van Buren retained the confidence of Jackson, who promptly named him minister to Britain.

Changing Problems, Changing Arguments. Meanwhile, a more fundamental division between Jackson and Vice-President Calhoun developed over two other issues. First, the

English artist Robert Cruickshank portrayed the rowdy scene that occurred when "King Mob" came to call on President Jackson at the White House.

President was greatly disturbed by the discovery that, years before, Calhoun had recommended that Jackson be court-martialed for his conduct during the Seminole War of 1818. Second and more significant, Jackson hotly disapproved of Calhoun's contention that a state had the right to nullify a federal statute. It was concerning this "nullification" question that the smoldering antipathies of the two ranking officials of the country flared into the open.

The nullification stand of the Vice-President and his fellow South Carolinian, Senator Robert Y. Hayne, resulted from their state's opposition to the tariff tendencies of the United States—especially the Tariff of Abominations. They believed that while the industrial Northeast benefited, the agricultural South was damaged by the rising customs duties.

Economic conditions in the Southeast were steadily worsening. The extension of cotton planting to the rich bottom lands of Alabama, Mississippi, and Louisiana had expanded production of the staple, and cotton prices consequently dropped. Many planters in the Southeast, threatened with ruin by their inability to compete on relatively poor soil, pulled stakes and took their slaves to the Southwest for a fresh start. The consequent loss of population compounded the Southeast's financial difficulties. There were also political reverberations, since fewer people would mean smaller representation in Congress for South Carolina and similarly affected states.

Calhoun had lately joined Hayne and other South Carolina politicians in the conviction that most of their state's troubles could be traced to the tariff. In 1828, while running for reelection to the vice-presidency as a Jackson adherent, Calhoun had secretly written the "South Carolina Exposition." This document, published without his name, declared protective tariffs unconstitutional. It went on to assert the right of any state to "nullify" or prevent the enforcement within its boundaries of an unconstitutional act of Congress. Calhoun's authorship of the "Exposition" was not generally known in 1830, but his new position was becoming clear in some minds, including Jackson's.

In 1830, the Vice-President carefully coached the less brilliant Hayne when the latter eloquently defended the extreme states' rights position in a dramatic Senate debate with Senator Daniel Webster of Massachusetts. As Massachusetts had become more industrialized and accordingly adopted a high tariff policy, Webster had abandoned his low-tariff convictions (he opposed the Tariff of 1824), and by 1830 he was a high-tariff advocate. Moreover, Webster identified Massachusetts' changed economic attitude with a political nationalism that contrasted with the growing sectionalism of South Carolina. In so doing, he sought to equate the North's economic interest with patriotic virtue.

The famous Senate debate of 1830 arose as the result of a resolution by Connecticut Senator Samuel A. Foot, which had as one aim a restriction of the sale of public land. The land question was a vital matter to congressmen from the West. Current land laws, in effect since the early 1820s, provided for (1) a minimum purchase of eighty acres, (2) a minimum price of $1.25 an acre, (3) no credit system, and (4) exceptions which recognized but did not wholly satisfy Western insistence on lower land prices and on the preemption principle by which genuine settlers would have the first chance to buy at the minimum price. Already in the air were proposals for liberalizing land policies. Eastern laborers joined Western farmers in favoring such liberalization, and Southerners saw an advantage in linking Western land desires to Southern low-tariff hopes. Thus the opposition to Foot's restrictive resolution was not limited to any single section.

Senator Thomas H. Benton of Missouri resoundingly assailed the Foot Resolution. Benton saw it as a scheme of New England

manufacturers, fearful of losing factory opera-
tives to the lure of the West, to make cheap
land inaccessible and so keep their workers in
the East. Hayne went to Benton's support but
took a different tack. If Foot's proposition
were put into effect, he said, future prices of
Western land would be high. The income
would then constitute "a fund for corruption," adding to the power of the federal
government and endangering the independence of the states. Thereupon Webster
launched his first reply to Hayne. Denying
that the East was illiberal toward the West, the
erstwhile sectionalist from Boston proclaimed
his nationalism.

Hayne again spoke, reminding his hearers
of New England's anti-Union attitude during
the War of 1812. Where, he asked, were New
England nationalists then? Had not residents
of Webster's section, plotters of the Hartford
Convention, favored the same constitutional
arguments contained in the "South Carolina
Exposition"? The Northeastern sectionalists
of old, Hayne insisted, currently championed
theories which they formerly had decried.
Their sincerity, he implied, was open to grave
doubts. And their past words and tactics
hovered as reminders of appalling inconsistencies.

Webster's "Second Reply to Hayne."   After
Hayne spiritedly elaborated on the extreme
states' rights point of view, Webster answered
him in what is widely regarded as the greatest
speech ever delivered in Congress. In New
England, he said, what Hayne had discussed
was consigned to a bygone time. New
Englanders were thinking not of the past but
of the present and the future. Vital now was
the well-being of America as a whole. Nothing
could be more preposterous than the idea that
twenty-four states could interpret the Constitution as each of them saw fit. The Union
should not be "dissevered, discordant, belligerent." The country should not be "rent with
civil feuds, or drenched . . . in fraternal

blood." It was delusion and folly to think of
"Liberty first, and Union afterwards." Instead, "dear to every true American heart"
was that blazing sentiment—"Liberty *and*
Union, now and forever, one and insepara-
ble!"

Although generations of young Americans
memorized the peroration of Webster's "Second Reply to Hayne," there was at least as
much logic—of the sort premised on the
recorded performances of the various sections—on Hayne's side. Hayne was both
consistent and persistent over a perod of six
years, while Calhoun (who soon overshadowed Hayne as the personification of antina-
tionalist sentiment) was as inconsistent as
Webster and as illogical on the basis of his
long-established position. Both in the "Exposition" and in subsequent documents, Calhoun contributed to his state's cause the
thoughts and theories of a resourceful mind.
Still, modern scholarship cannot ignore the
circumstances under which Calhoun and
Webster made their shifts. Under the pressure
of politico-economic necessity, each now
occupied the other's previous position.

Calhoun and Jackson succeeded Hayne and
Webster in the public spotlight during the
spring of the same year, 1830, when
a Jefferson birthday banquet was held in
Washington's Indian Queen Hotel. Jackson
offered fellow Democratic-Republicans a
toast: "The Federal Union, it must be preserved!" Calhoun countered with a toast of his
own: "The Union, next to our liberty, most
dear!" The disparate sentiments were not lost
upon the diners. The President had hurled
down the gauntlet. The Vice-President had
picked it up. After that, their relations became
ever more strained, and before Jackson's first
term ended, Calhoun had resigned the vice-
presidency.

Two Controversial Vetoes.   Jackson sternly
opposed the Bank of the United States and
objected to most proposals to use federal

funds for internal improvements. The improvements question bulked large in 1830, when Congress passed a bill authorizing subscription of stock in a private company constructing a road between Maysville and Lexington, Kentucky. Jackson vetoed the proposition on the ground that the Maysville Road lay wholly in one state and therefore was not entitled to financial support from Washington.

Jackson's controversial veto seemed tyrannical and enemies dubbed him "King Andrew." Henry Clay and many other transportation-minded Americans charged the President with being an impediment in the march of progress. But the veto was well received by Southern strict constructionists and by others resentful of what they deemed undue interference by the federal government in purely state affairs. Moreover, Jackson's selection of a Western road as a target of his disapproval pleased those in New York and Pennsylvania who had financed their own projects locally and saw no reason why people in other regions should get the kind of Washington help they themselves had failed to obtain.

Jackson was hostile to the Bank of the United States for at least four reasons. First, he held the Jeffersonian strict-construction view, maintaining that Congress was not empowered by the Constitution to incorporate a bank outside the District of Columbia. Jackson also doubted that the Bank would serve the nation's welfare and accused it of not having established a sound and uniform currency. His third objection was that the Bank played politics in election campaigns and influenced congressmen by lending them money or placing them on its payroll. Finally, Old Hickory had an ingrained suspicion of the note issues of all banks—with the Bank of the United States the most notorious offender because it was far and away the most powerful.

Actually, under Nicholas Biddle's leadership the Bank of the United States had made important contributions to American economic stability. Regardless of what Jackson said, it did provide a sound currency, and its monetary standards and the financial power it wielded often exerted a salutary effect on the fluctuating currencies of state banks—many of which were dangerously weak. But the charge of political activity and legislative influence was, for the most part, warranted. Jackson came to consider the Bank a monopoly, but though government deposits were exclusively entrusted to it, the Bank was not a monopolistic enterprise in the customary sense of the term.

The Bank's charter had four years to run in 1832, but Clay, now a United States senator, was in full accord with Bank President Biddle's desire to see the institution rechartered long in advance of the legal deadline. Clay pushed a Bank Bill through both houses of Congress. Then, chosen by the National Republicans as their standard bearer in opposition to Jackson, he strove to make the Bank the main issue in the campaign of 1832. Jackson lost no time in vetoing the rechartering act in July 1832. Thus he and Clay set the stage for a showdown on the issue.

The Election of 1832. It can be argued that Clay was handicapped in his presidential race by the existence of an Anti-Masonic third party which considered the Masonic fraternity an aristocratic threat to democratic institutions and objected to both Jackson and Clay because they were Masons.

The Anti-Masons nominated William Wirt of Maryland, himself ironically also a Mason and for twelve years Attorney General under Monroe and Adams. They chose their candidate by a party convention, foreshadowing the method soon to be adopted by all the parties. The National Republicans' choice was Clay, while the Democratic-Republicans (now beginning to be called Democrats) of course were for Jackson, with Van Buren as his running mate. In most states the anti-Jackson

BORN TO COMMAND.

OF VETO MEMORY.

HAD I BEEN CONSULTED.

KING ANDREW THE FIRST.

This political cartoon depicts Jackson as "King Andrew," an autocratic dictator trampling on the U.S. Constitution and the Bank of the United States.

following was concentrated behind either Clay or Wirt, with the other man staying out of the contest. But even with this tactical advantage, neither Clay nor Wirt had a very good chance to oust the well-liked Jackson. Futhermore, the Bank issue did not aid Clay any more than criticism of Masonry helped Wirt.

Not all historians agree on the exact size of the popular vote. It is clear, however, that Jackson won easily; his popular vote was approximately 687,500 against 530,000 for Clay and Wirt combined. Jackson was victorious in nearly the entire South and West, plus the "big" states of New York and Pennsylvania. In the electoral college, Jackson scored 219

to Clay's 49 and Wirt's 7. South Carolina, still voting through its legislature, refused to back any of the regular candidates and cast eleven protest ballots for John Floyd of Virginia.

"KING ANDREW"

Crisis Over Nullification.   No sooner was the 1832 election decided than South Carolina brought the nullification controversy to a head. The issue immediately in question was the Tariff of 1832, which lowered customs duties but not enough to satisfy critics in Charleston and Columbia. The newly elected state legislature, composed predominantly of "nullifiers," ordered a special state convention to deal with the problem. The convention met in Columbia in November and took three major steps: It declared the tariffs of 1828 and 1832 null and void within South Carolina. It called on the state legislature to prohibit collection of duties in the state after February 1, 1833. And it warned that South Carolina would secede if the federal government used force to collect duties.

Jackson responded to South Carolina's saber-rattling by dispatching naval and military units to that state and issuing a stirring Nullification Proclamation, which declared in part:

I consider, then, the power to annul a law of the United States, assumed by one State, incompatible with the existence of the Union, contradicted expressly by the letter of the Constitution, unauthorized by its spirit, inconsistent with every principle on which it was founded, and destructive of the great object for which it was formed.

Possible bloodshed was averted when Senator Clay of Kentucky sponsored a compromise tariff bill providing for a gradual reduction of duties year by year until 1842. Though the protectionist New England and Middle Atlantic states bitterly opposed such a tariff reduction, Congress passed the compromise bill and Jackson signed it on March 2, 1833. On the same day, a Force Bill—giving Jackson congressional authority to use arms to enforce collection of customs—became law.

The Compromise Tariff of 1833 was much more reasonable by South Carolina's standards than preceding tariffs had been. The Columbia convention met once again and withdrew its nullification ordinance, but as a face-saving gesture the convention nullified Jackson's Force Bill. The President regarded this last defiant act as of little practical significance. Both sides now considered the issue closed, and both claimed victory.

The United States Bank.   Jackson, interpreting his success in the 1832 election as a mandate from the voters to continue action against the Bank of the United States, decided to remove federal deposits from the Bank gradually and deposit them in selected state banks. An order to this effect was issued on September 26, 1833, and when Secretary of the Treasury Duane refused to carry it out, Jackson replaced him with Roger B. Taney, until then Attorney General. By the end of the year twenty-three state banks—dubbed "pet banks" by anti-Jacksonians—had been selected as depositories.

Jackson's move against the Bank met with considerable political opposition, and his policy was attacked in Congress. In December 1833 Henry Clay introduced Senate resolutions to censure both the Treasury action and the President for having "assumed upon himself authority and power not conferred by the constitution and laws, but in derogation of both."

When those resolutions were adopted, Jackson formally protested that the Senate had charged him with an impeachable offense but denied him an opportunity to defend himself. The Senate, however, rejected Jackson's protest and, as a further measure of defiance, would not approve Taney's nomination as Secretary of the Treasury. Only after a three-year Senate battle did Jackson's supporters succeed in having the resolution of censure expunged from the Senate record.

Hard Money and Land.   Jackson's Bank policy contributed to a series of severe nationwide economic reverses. Even though the administration withdrew federal funds from the United States Bank only gradually, using them to meet current expenses while depositing new revenue in "pet banks," the Bank's decline was sharp enough to touch off an economic recession in 1833–1834. Nicholas Biddle's actions aggravated the situation: To make up for the lost federal deposits and to force congressional reconsideration of the Bank's charter, Biddle took the unneccessarily harsh step of calling in outstanding loans, thus creating demands for credit from state banks which they could not meet. Only under strong pressure from businessmen and from the governor of Pennsylvania did Biddle at last reverse his policy.

The country pulled out of the economic doldrums and almost immediately headed into a dangerous inflationary spiral. State banks used their newly acquired federal funds for speculative purposes. At the same time, the federal government greatly increased its sale of public land, inadvertently encouraging the most reckless speculators.

Although political leaders were divided in their reaction to the inflationary trend, Jackson agreed with Senator Benton's prediction that "the present bloat in the paper system" could foreshadow another depression. On July 11, 1836, Jackson chose to issue a Specie Circular, which provided that after August 15 all public lands purchased from the federal government were to be paid for in gold or silver, with one exception: Until December 15 people actually settling on the land were permitted to use state bank notes to purchase parcels of land up to 320 acres.

Jackson's sudden policy reversal sharply curtailed western land sales and weakened

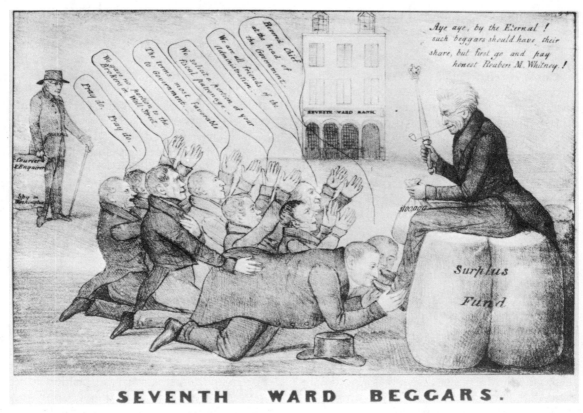

SEVENTH WARD BEGGARS.

Jackson's opponents accused him of depositing federal funds in "pet banks." The cartoon shows a group of bankers groveling before him, begging for money.

public confidence in the state banks. It encouraged the hoarding of specie (hard money) and was a factor in bringing on the Panic of 1837.

The western land problem figured repeatedly in congressional debates from Jackson's day to Lincoln's and beyond. Benton and other Westerners favored the policy of "graduation," by which prices for the less desirable portions of the public domain would be reduced from $1.25 an acre to $1.00, 50 cents, or less, depending on the length of time they had been on sale. Westerners also wanted the policy of preemption, which favored squatters rather than speculators.

Although Congress passed no graduation

bill until 1854, a temporary Preemption Act in 1830 authorized settlers to buy up to 160 acres of public land at a minimum price of $1.25 an acre. The act was renewed regularly and remained in force until 1842.

Not to be confused with preemption was Henry Clay's advocacy of "distribution." In 1833, the Kentuckian drove through both the House and Senate a bill stipulating that most of the revenue derived from public-land sales be distributed among all the states, with a smaller fraction earmarked for states where the sales took place. That was a typical example of Clay's desire to appeal politically to two sections at once. Jackson, however, pocket-vetoed the bill, thwarting his adversary and identifying himself further with the actual settlers of the Northwest and Southwest.

Jackson's Foreign Policy Jackson's handling of foreign affairs was at times as forthright and unconventional as one might expect of an old border captain. The only real diplomatic crisis of his two terms concerned claims against France for seizures of American ships during the Napoleonic wars. Adams and preceding Presidents had failed to collect, but at Jackson's urging France agreed to pay $5 million in a series of indemnity installments. The first $1 million was due in 1833. When the French made no payment then or the following year, Jackson urged Congress to authorize reprisals on French property unless the money were speedily sent. For a few months there appeared to be danger of war, but French officials finally saw that the President meant business. Payment of the debt began in 1836.

Jackson also faced the problem of whether to recognize the independence of Texas, established in 1836. Because it was a potential slave state, Jackson trod carefully in order not to inflame the American people over the slavery issue and possibly jeopardize Van Buren's presidential hopes in the election of 1836. Jackson was fearful also of angering Mexico, which insisted that the United States enforce its neutrality statutes. Though there was no question about Jackson's personal sentiment—his sympathy for the Texan revolutionists was strong—he withheld recognition from the Texas republic until the very day he left office in 1837.

The Supreme Court. Andrew Jackson's most enduring influence on the Supreme Court came indirectly through the justices whom he elevated to the bench. When he retired, five of the sitting judges were his appointees. The number included Roger B. Taney, who had succeeded John Marshall as Chief Justice on the latter's death in 1835.

Among the principal early decisions under Taney was *Briscoe* v. *The Bank of Kentucky* (1837), which reduced the application of constitutional limitations on state banking and currency matters. This decision held that it was not unconstitutional for a state that owned stock to issue bank notes. More famous is *Charles River Bridge* v. *Warren Bridge* (1837), which stressed community responsibilities of private property and modfied the contract doctrines of Marshall. In *Bank of Augusta* v. *Earle* (1839), the Chief Justice denied that corporations had all legal rights of natural persons. He also held that while corporations could take part in interstate commerce, any state had the right to exclude another state's corporations.

In later cases there sometimes was a lack of agreement or consistency regarding federal commerce power on the one hand and the states' internal police power on the other. This is traceable in part to the Court's changing personnel after Jackson's presidency, and in part to the alterations in Taney's own ideas.

For many years, it was the fashion to be hypercritical of Taney's Supreme Court record. Continuing on the tribunal until he died during the Civil War, he became very unpopular in the North because of his position in favor of states' rights and because of the Dred Scott decision in 1857 (see Chapter 11). Actually, the judicial philosophies and influences of Marshall and Taney had many similarities. Taney and most of his associates believed that the growing power of corporations needed supervision by states in the public interest. But they were not unsympathetic toward property rights as such, and modern authorities on judicial history see no sharp break between most constitutional interpretations of the two able jurists.

JACKSONIAN DEMOCRACY—A LOOK BACK

The Influence of Economic Factors. In Jackson's time, as now, political changes were often tied to economic changes and alliances formed and reformed over economic issues. What had been the Republican party had, by 1836, split into two parties known as Democrats and Whigs, with opposing views on government and its proper role in the economy.

To find consistency in the political actions of Democrats and Whigs is difficult, chiefly because of shifts brought about by economic factors. Daniel Webster, for example, had begun his career as a champion of New England shipping interests and free trade. But after the War of 1812, domestic manufacturing was growing and Webster caught the spirit of industrial progress. He and other Whigs felt that the fledgling industries needed all the government protection they could get.

Thus by the late 1820s Webster had become an aggressive advocate of protective tariffs that would foster American industry. Besides a protected market, he and his fellow Whigs felt that industry also needed a sound banking system, which would provide a stable currency and ample credit.

Henry Clay, too, had changed his political convictions with changing times. Reared in the Virginia of Jeffersonian agrarianism, he migrated to Kentucky and was awakened to new Western economic ambitions. A spokesman for Western Whigs, Clay believed in a nationalistic program—his so-called American System. Through federally funded internal improvements, a liberal policy of public-land sales, a central bank, and tariffs, the aim of this system was to reduce American dependence on foreign trade and provide a home market for the exchange of the North's manufactured goods and the West's agricultural products.

The Whigs felt that government aid to business would promote the economic progress and well-being of all Americans. However, the Whig party also contained prominent Southern planters, though their reliance on cotton exports and low-cost imports caused them to oppose the protective tariffs advocated by the Northern Whigs. Like the leaders in other sections, those in the South took anguished turns in their search for adjustment. John C. Calhoun of South Carolina began as a "War Hawk" nationalist during the days of Jefferson and Madison. Later, he became a defender of states' rights in defiance of federal "authoritarianism." Politically, he shifted from the Democrats to the Whigs and back to the Democrats.

Jackson was able to cope with these shifting factions. With a military reputation that aided him in politics, he was looked upon as a champion of the plain people and an enemy of "privilege" to any one class or section. Often arbitrary in method, Jackson was basically pragmatic in most of his policies. He favored a "judicious" tariff. He approved or opposed federal funding for internal improvements on the merits of each individual case. And he and his Democratic followers were more aware than the Whigs of the potential dangers of "monopolies" like the Bank of the United States.

Characteristics of Jacksonian Democracy. The policies identified with Jacksonian democracy have been associated with five major trends. First, Jacksonian democracy represented a trend toward equality, with more people participating more fully in the political process. While Jackson drew support from persons in many walks of life, poorer people were most inclined to identify themselves with Jackson and his policies. Second, Jacksonian democracy marked a departure from the domination of bankers and merchants, even though some bankers and merchants were steadfast Jacksonians. Third, Jacksonians were expansionists, committed to making room for white settlers on what had been Indian lands. Fourth, as seen in the South Carolina controversy, Jacksonian democrats resolutely opposed weakening the Federal union. Fifth, Jackson's followers approved

Jackson's exercise of federal authority over the American economy.

To understand Jackson's influence, it is essential to understand why Jackson was so popular and what caused him to retain his popularity. The War of 1812, as we have seen, involved no other military victory on a par with Jackson's brilliant one. Fervidly admired because of his achievement, he intrigued fellow-Americans who found in him no mere child of luck but a man of iron will and ingenious battlefield prowess. Also (and this was nearly as important), he seemed to symbolize the "outs" or nonestablishment people in contrast with the "ins" of Washington. He had come up in the world on his own and was a leader of forcefulness and determination—the very sort of dynamic figure who makes enemies and yet attracts hosts of followers and friends. No understanding of Jacksonian democracy can be complete without awareness of the charismatic Jackson image.

Evaluation of Jackson's Administration. As President, the active and dominant Jackson continued both to arouse strong adverse criticism and to inspire praise bordering on idolatry. The Tennessean's enemies did not hesitate to call him every unpleasant name in the book. They depicted him as "King Andrew," a would-be tyrant with slight regard for the ways of free people and with a ruthless intent to impose his will on the country. On the other hand, Jackson's friends (and they were a majority) loved him personally and held his political talents in the highest esteem.

In the perspective of the years, Jackson's record shows marked differences from issue to issue. Although moderation is not traditionally considered a trait of Jackson's, he was essentially a moderate on the tariff, and his attitude toward land policy was generally temperate. Though he did not block all internal improvements financed with federal funds, he was apt to be conservative or reactionary (depending on one's point of view) on projects in that category.

Many scholars are agreed that Jackson's greatest mistake was his hostility to the Bank, and that his Specie Circular reflected a miscalculation in timing if not in principle. On the other hand, Jackson's foreign policy was successful, and his nationalism was tellingly asserted in opposition to the nullifiers.

A slaveholder with the manners and tastes of a Southern planter, Jackson was limited by his lack of formal education and was especially handicapped in economics. But he had an acute awareness of public preferences and the public interest. He also had an instinct for reaching the "common" people and for identifying their desires with his own. A simple man with a fighting heart, Jackson was no democratic doctrinaire. He was wedded neither to indigenous abstractions nor to imported systems of dialectics. Jackson judged each issue on its merits—as he understood them—and contributed vigorous leadership to every cause he championed.

Historians' opinions of Jackson, like their judgments of Jefferson and other Presidents, have changed from generation to generation. The principal recent charges against Jackson are that his Indian policy was too harsh. Yet, for the last thirty years, scholarly consensus has been that as President he was great or near-great.

DEMOCRATS AND WHIGS

The Election of 1836. As Jackson's second term neared its end, Vice-President Martin Van Buren was the Democratic presidential nominee. The opposition, now called the Whig party, tried to throw the contest into the House of Representatives by sponsoring several candidates on a regional basis. Van Buren faced Daniel Webster in the Northeast,

Ohio's William Henry Harrison in the Northwest, and Tennessee's Hugh L. White in the South. These three Whigs won 14, 73, and 26 electoral votes respectively. South Carolina gave its 11 votes to the anti-Jacksonian Willie P. Mangum of North Carolina. Their combined total of 124 was well under Van Buren's figure of 170, and the Whig popular vote of 739,000 failed to match Van Buren's 765,000. So while the Whigs made gains, the 1836 regional scheme fell apart, and again the Democrats were victors.

The Panic of 1837. The "Little Magician" or "Red Fox of Kinderhook," as Van Buren was nicknamed, proved to be an unlucky President. A New York lawyer of ability and a politician who up to now had proved himself adroit in difficult situations, Van Buren found himself confronted by an economic disaster beyond his control. In May 1837, only two months after his inauguration, a New York bank panic signaled the start of one of America's deep depressions. In part, the trouble stemmed from an English financial crisis during which many British creditors canceled their American investments. Yet Jackson and Van Buren drew much of the blame. Some of Jackson's "pet banks" were among those that failed. And while the Specie Circular checked speculation in western lands, it curtailed the activities of financiers who had been supplying funds to speculators.

The depression affected the lives and fortunes of people in every part of the country. Widespread unemployment developed in seaboard cities of the Northeast, spreading into interior communities and fanning out to the South and West. Bread lines and soup kitchens relieved the hunger of poor families, including thousands of recent immigrants. Farmers received low prices for their crops. Factories closed. Laborers walked the streets. Canal and railroad projects were halted. In 1839 the worst of the depression

seemed to be over, but another decline occurred later that same year, and good times did not return to America as a whole until 1843.

In the meantime, Van Buren's fine display of statesmanship belied his reputation as a crafty politician. Beginning in 1837, he induced Congress to agree to a temporary issue of short-term Treasury notes. These amounted to $47 million in the next six years and enabled the government to meet its obligations. He also advocated an independent treasury, where federal funds could be safely retained without either running pet-bank risks or resorting to another Bank of the United States.

Most Whigs and some Democrats opposed the banking bill on the grounds that removal of federal funds from the state banks where they were deposited would restrict credit at a time when credit was sorely needed. The Independent Treasury Act finally was passed in 1840, but Van Buren's victory was short-lived. The next year, under the Tyler administration, the act was repealed, and for the next five years the Whig majority in Congress defeated Democratic efforts to reestablish this "subtreasury system."

The *Caroline* Affair. Another problem of the Van Buren regime concerned a spat along the Canadian border. In 1837 Canadian insurgents, dissatisfied with London's rule, fled to an island in the Niagara River, where American Anglophobes reinforced them with recruits and arms. The American steamer *Caroline* was employed in the supply service.

Canadian soldiers, crossing to the American side of the Niagara, set the *Caroline* afire and turned her adrift. Because of the high state of excitement, there was danger of mob invasions in either direction, and the slaying of an American citizen on the night the vessel burned seriously complicated the situation. Three years later a Canadian deputy sheriff

The election campaign of 1840, pictured in this lively scene, served as a model for over a century of future presidential contests.

named Alexander McLeod was arrested in Lockport, New York, and indicted for murder and arson in connection with the *Caroline* affair.

There was loose talk of war, and on both sides of the border additional sums were appropriated for the strengthening of boundary defenses. Even after McLeod was acquitted by a New York court in 1841, the case seemed an unpromising preliminary to the Webster-Ashburton negotiations on border disputes that were to take place the next year.

Tippecanoe and Tyler Too. During Van Buren's presidency, Webster and Clay continued to be prominent in the senatorial spotlight. Webster's oratorical ability was as outstanding as ever, and Clay distinguished himself as a parliamentary leader.

Northern Whigs favored the creation of a new national bank and advocated a high tariff and federally financed internal improvements. If their anti-Jackson and anti-Van Buren confreres of the South did not agree about the tariff and the bank, the common bond linking all Whigs was the issue of "executive tyranny." Less domination by the President and more authority vested in Congress were aims that Southern and Northern Whigs shared. They also capitalized on the country's economic distress and were as one in their criticism of Van Buren as the 1840 election approached.

The Whigs played their cards cannily in the 1840 test of skill. In the first place, their standard-bearer was neither Clay nor Webster—able men who had many friends, but also many enemies—but William Henry Harrison of Ohio. Harrison had run well as a regional Whig candidate in 1836 and had won a measure of military glory in the dim past at the Indian Battle of Tippecanoe. Second, the Whigs turned to their own advantage a journalist's taunt that Harrison was unfit for

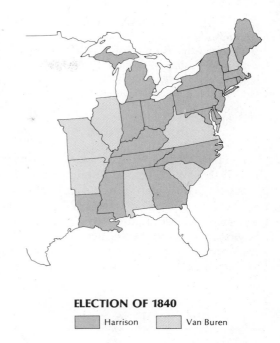

ELECTION OF 1840

Harrison   Van Buren

the presidency. "Give him a barrel of hard cider, and settle a pension of two thousand a year on him," the newsman sneered," and [take] my word for it, he will sit the remainder of his days in his log cabin by the side of a 'sea coal' fire, and study moral philosophy."

Yes, the Whigs replied, their nominee was a man of the people who preferred a log cabin and hard cider to the frippery of red-whiskered Van Buren. In reality, Harrison dwelt in a mansion near Cincinnati and was an aristocratic Virginian by birth and rearing. But log cabins, barrels of cider, coonskin caps, and even live coons became Harrison symbols in the campaign.

For the vice-presidency the Whigs had chosen John Tyler of Virginia, a former states' rights Democrat who now was a spokesman for the minority Southern element within the Whig party. The Whigs' most typical campaign verse contained the best known of all jingles associated with elections:

What has caused the great commotion,
  motion, motion,
Our country through?
It is the ball a rolling on
For Tippecanoe and Tyler too—
  Tippecanoe and Tyler too,
And with them we'll beat
  little Van, Van, Van.
Van is a used up man.

As expected, the Whigs were victorious in 1840. Harrison's electoral showing was impressive (234 to Van Buren's 60), and his popular vote was 1,274,000 to 1,127,000 for the Democrat. Although the Whig margin was not vast in a number of critical states, it was large enough. North of the Mason-Dixon line Van Buren carried only New Hamsphire and Illinois.

The 1840 election was not a "critical" or "realigning" one like those of 1800 and 1828. No permanent party changes stemmed from it. But the Tippecanoe campaign did have importance as it (1) showed how adroitly Whigs could play the Democrats' game and (2) served as a model for presidential contests for more than a century.

President Without a Party.   The sweet taste of triumph soon turned bitter in Whig mouths. Inaugurated in March 1841, the 68-year-old Harrison died after a single month in office. Tyler, the first man to reach the presidency through the death of his predecessor, shared few of the ideas of the dominant Whig group in Congress. Twice he vetoed attempts to revive the Bank of the United States. Twice he

Sam Houston:
Texas Hero and Jacksonian Democrat

Few Americans of 1828–1848 rival Sam Houston in epitomizing so many prominent characteristics of the Jacksonian period. First in war and then in politics, he was intimately identified with Andrew Jackson. Not even Jackson himself so vividly personified the dynamic thrust for Western expansion. Few fellow-Americans became so involved, in and out of Congress, in the issue of federal-state authority. Significantly, Houston looms today as a consistent and colorful human link between the Unionism of President Jackson and the Unionism of Abraham Lincoln.

In a curious way, Houston also symbolized two major reform trends—temperance and religious conversion. He was a romantic personage who lived as close to nature as Thoreau, yet repeatedly combined his romanticism with an on-again-off-again practicality.

Born in Virginia in 1793, young Sam grew up in Tennessee and by choice spent three of his adolescent years living with the nearby Cherokee Indians. The Cherokees liked the teenager so much that they adopted him into their tribe. Returning to his white kinsmen, he volunteered at nineteen for combat in the War of 1812. In 1814 his bravery at Horseshoe Bend, where General Jackson defeated the Creek Indians, won Houston great commendation. Severely

vetoed Clay-sponsored tariffs. Thrice he defeated distribution to the states of proceeds from public-land sales. All members of Harrison's cabinet, which Tyler inherited, resigned after six months, with the exception of Secretary of State Webster, who stayed on only long enough to complete ongoing negotiations over the border with Canada.

John Tyler found himself in the unenviable position of a President without a party. He did agree with Northern Whigs that the Independent Treasury law should be repealed, and this was done in 1841. But his vetoes of Clay's tariff measures made him a deserter in their eyes. The Tariff of 1842, which Congress reluctantly passed and Tyler signed, was but mildly protective. Tyler also approved a General Preemption Act and cooperated more and more with Democrats, whose nomination he hoped to obtain in 1844. Northern Whigs and border-staters like Clay rued the day when "Tyler too" had been tapped to run with "Tippecanoe."

The Webster-Ashburton Treaty. Before Webster entered the State Department, the *Caroline* affair was not the only border incident fanning the flames of international misunderstanding. There was also the undeclared Aroostook War, caused by conflicting claims to the Aroostook River region on the undefined Maine-New Brunswick boundary. Ten thousand Maine troops were committed in 1839 to the defense of a large area subject to dispute. At length, representatives from both sides negotiated a truce.

wounded in this encounter, he managed to survive, although the battlefield injury he had received never healed.

Following the war, Houston studied law and served as district attorney in Nashville. A political protégé of Jackson, he won two elections to Congress and then the governorship of Tennessee. In 1829 Eliza Allen, an attractive girl half his age, became Houston's wife but abruptly left him after only two months of marriage. (Rumors spread as to the reason, which may have been related to his unhealed wound, but he and Eliza forever maintained absolute silence on the subject. Ultimately he divorced her on the ground of abandonment.) Immediately, in "moments of awful agony" [his words], he resigned as governor. He felt "overwhelmed by sudden calamities" and thought it "more respectful to the world" to retire. Boarding a riverboat and leaving all the familiar scenes of past political triumphs, he steamed away from white society.

Houston's destination? That part of what is now Oklahoma where his old Cherokee friends had gone, and where he was welcomed as one of them. Taking an Indian wife, Houston operated as a merchant and gave legal advice on the side. He also served his adopted Indian father and other Indian chiefs by twice representing Cherokee interests in Washington. There his old mentor, President Jackson, greeted him warmly. Sam was a rarity among whites—a Westerner who not only sympathized with Indians but, owing to the Jackson-Houston friendship, negotiated successfully on their behalf.

Houston drank heavily in the Cherokee country, as he had done previously and would also do later. He even acquired the nickname "Big Drunk." Still it would be wrong to think of this as a "lost" period of his life. From the Cherokees' point of view, his achievements were impressive.

As the crisis eased, the British government at long last saw the need for determining what portions of the disputed area should be acknowledged as belonging respectively to New Brunswick and to the United States. Secretary Webster met in a series of conferences with England's envoy, Lord Ashburton. In their treaty of 1842, New Brunswick received 5000 square miles out of 12,000. The treaty was resented and Webster's popularity forever damaged in Maine, which felt itself shortchanged. Nevertheless, the Webster-Ashburton Treaty did help to achieve order and peace.

Return of the Democrats. Fresh issues exerted a vital impact on the election of 1844. Some had to do with the West, others with chattel slavery. Texans had won independence from Mexico in 1836, and now there was considerable sentiment for the annexation of the Republic of Texas by the United States. (See "Sam Houston: Texas Hero and Jacksonian Democrat.") Southerners particularly favored such a step, while expansion-minded Northerners hoped that Oregon would be wholly occupied by Americans instead of being divided between the United States and Britain.

Henry Clay's 1844 presidential nomination by the Whigs came as no surprise. But Van Buren was shunted aside by the Democrats because he was thought to be anti-Texas, and little attention was paid to Tyler as a candidate since he was not a reliable party man. Instead, delegates to the Democratic national conven-

---

By 1833 Sam Houston was in Texas. Here he identified himself with the independence cause. In 1836, when war broke out between Texas and Mexico, he was chosen to lead troops assembled to oppose the Mexican army under Santa Anna. Houston's victory at San Jacinto that spring exemplified brilliant strategy and tactics. His trouncing of Santa Anna took only a few minutes but made the victor a hero in Texans' eyes and a natural choice for the new republic's presidency. Serving two nonconsecutive terms as president, Houston did much to strengthen and lend prestige to the Texas government.

Houston's Indian wife, who had not come to Texas, died a few years later, and in 1840 the hard-fighting, hard-drinking frontiersman wed Margaret Lea, a woman of deep religious conviction who set out to reform him and succeeded. This marriage was a happy one, blessed with eight children.

When the United States annexed Texas in 1845, Houston took his seat in the U.S. Senate and remained in that body thirteen years. Here devotion to the Union distinguished him. He was one of only four senators who supported every provision of the Compromise of 1850. Though hailing from a slave state, he attacked the weaker 1854 Kansas-Nebraska Bill because it undid the Missouri Compromise of 1819, which had established a line dividing future free and slave states.

Later, as governor of Texas in 1859–1861, he opposed Texas' secession from the Union—a stand totally unpopular with most of his constituents. Houston could have resorted to arms once more, leading Unionists against the Texas majority. Instead he relinquished the governorship at the age of sixty-eight and retired to his Texas farm, where he died two years later. The year was 1863.

A mere résumé of his career fails to provide anything like an adequate impression of the impact of Houston's personality. Six feet two, with brown hair and penetrating

tion nominated James K. Polk, the first "dark horse" presidential nominee.

A former governor of Tennessee and Speaker of the House of Representatives, Polk seemed thoroughly at home on the Democratic platform, which euphoniously but none too accurately described the desired Western policy as "the reannexation of Texas" and "the reoccupation of Oregon." Whigs made light of Polk's qualifications. "Who *is* James K. Polk?" they asked. But Polk's campaign strategy proved more effective than that of Clay, who tried to straddle the Texas dilemma and was impaled on the horns of equivocation.

Into the close contest came James G. Birney, heading the antislavery Liberty party, who siphoned off Clay votes in New York and

caused its electors to go to Polk. This made the difference. Polk received 170 electoral votes, Clay 105. The popular outcome favored the Tennesseean much more narrowly. Polk's 1,338,000 supporters outnumbered Clay's by only 38,000.

Features of American Democratic Growth.
The years 1824–1828 were characterized by an increase in the number of elected officeholders, by a relative decrease in appointed officials at the state and local levels, and by some reflection of the popular will by the Supreme Court. There was far greater participation in government than had been the case in prior eras. By the time the period was well launched, all states except one chose presidential electors by popular vote. And the

gray eyes, he created the illusion of being bigger than he was. Extraordinarily popular when a young politician, and time and again as a Texas officeseeker, he had military qualities like Jackson's and a gift for what really counted in battle. Possessing a natural dignity, he also could be charmingly informal. Spectators enjoyed spotting him in the Senate—wearing a leopardskin vest and other quaint clothes—relaxed and whittling in the back row while colleagues strutted in the limelight. This casualness, together with his unswerving Unionism and his reputation for courage, made him a legend in his life.

Occasionally, Houston hurt his prospects with faulty decisions, like his identification with the anti-immigrant Know-Nothing movement of the 1850s. Another fault was his love of liquor. Converted to the Baptist faith and taking the anti-liquor pledge, Houston in his fifties and sixties not only reformed personally but spoke eloquently for the temperance cause far and wide on the lecture platform.

Houston's strong stand for the Union, in 1850 and thereafter, was signally reminiscent of Jackson's position earlier in the nullification crisis. While more attuned to Indians' needs than "Old Hickory" ever was, Houston fully shared Jackson's forthright expansionism and was the Southwest's outstanding statesman in the years after Jackson's death.

Governor of two states, congressman from two, and twice president of Texas, Houston might have made it to the White House if he had not been from the remote frontier and if, when young, he had flaunted fewer free-and-easy personal habits.

No other leader, active from the 1820s to the 1860s, was a more confirmed nationalist than the vibrant, exotic Sam Houston.

popular vote itself steadily increased from campaign to campaign, not only because the population was greater but because such barriers as religious and property qualifications were gradually lowered on a state-by-state basis. Jacksonians regarded changes of these kinds as desirable reforms, whose democratizing purposes and spirit bore resemblances to the era's social reforms.

The development of democratic government was not without its growing pains. One of the most criticized aspects of the political scene was the "spoils system," by which governmental posts were allotted as "spoils" of victory to members of the party triumphant at the polls. Under Monroe and Adams a small coterie of federal clerks and minor administrators had held offices on what amounted to a lifetime good-conduct basis. Jackson removed a number of these perennials because they had played the partisan game against him, because they were corrupt and inefficient, or because he wanted to make room for partisans of his own. In 1832 Senator William L. Marcy, a Jackson adherent, had remarked, "To the victor belong the spoils of the enemy"; and Jackson's enemies applied the phrase "spoils system" to Jackson's program of rewarding his political supporters with public office.

During his entire presidency Jackson removed only a fifth of those holding office in 1829, but he did take a decisive step toward perpetuating an undesirable system. Jacksonians defended the policy as the quickest and surest path to reform, but for every Adams man like embezzler Tobias Watkins who was removed, Jackson's party contributed a scamp of its own—such as collector Samuel Swartwout of the port of New York, who embezzled more than a million dollars.

National party conventions, which came into being with the Anti-Masonic assembly held in 1831, were thoroughly established in the political structure by the end of Jackson's second term. Sometimes they have resulted in the choice of second-rate candidates for first-rate posts, but in the main the decisions of conventions have been sound, and they were and are more directly representative and democratic than "King Caucus" ever was. After momentarily striking a pose of aloofness from Jacksonian electioneering tactics, Whigs imitated their rivals by adopting slogans and symbols similar to Democratic ones. And for over a century styles of campaigning were patterned, to an appreciable degree, on the 1840 ballyhoo techniques that promoted "Tippecanoe and Tyler Too!"

During Jackson's administration the personal advisers on whom the President relied came to be known as the "kitchen cabinet"—because they ostensibly conferred with Jackson more intimately than did members of his official cabinet. Later chief executives have followed Jackson's example by surrounding themselves with capable but unofficial counselors whose advice supplemented—or supplanted—that of department heads. It is doubtful that the "kitchen cabinet" would have originated as and when it did if Jackson had not owed his election in part to Calhounite Deep South support, which at least two cabinet members personified but on which he chose not to rely once his administration was underway.

It would be a mistake to minimize the role of the West in the period 1824–1848. Public lands, the tariff, internal improvements, the United States Bank, and almost all other issues were of interest to Westerners. The West had its own viewpoint or viewpoints of a predominantly sectional variety, yet it also exerted a nationalizing influence. The Southwest had much in common with the Northwest, and Jackson the Southwesterner proved himself a foremost nationalist who was supported as consistently in the Northwest as in any other portion of the country.

Chapter 9

Westward Expansion and Economic Growth 1824–1848

THE BACKGROUND OF EXPANSION

Manifest Destiny. New York magazine editor John L. O'Sullivan proclaimed in 1845 that it was "the fulfilment of our manifest destiny to overspread the continent allotted by Providence for the free development of our yearly multiplying millions." O'Sullivan's exuberant words reflected the optimism of fervid nationalists that the American banner soon would wave over all of North America and beyond. For the exponents of Manifest Destiny, even the addition of Texas, New Mexico, California, and the Oregon country to the nation would not be enough: God had destined the United States to extend its sovereignty over Canada, Alaska, Mexico, Cuba, other West Indian islands, and Hawaii.

The dream of Manifest Destiny was less fantastic than it may now appear: it was no less realistic to contemplate the annexation of Canada or Cuba than to dream of extending American sovereignty to Alaska or Hawaii. Furthermore, in the light of America's im-

pressive achievements since 1776, nearly anything seemed possible in the next half century. In 1803 the Louisiana Purchase had doubled the area of the American republic. By 1830 commerce with Europe was flourishing, and trade with Asia was burgeoning, with adventurers extracting fortunes from China. Wealthy speculators were willing to invest in almost any feasible enterprise.

Dreams of Manifest Destiny were both an augury of future hemispheric expansion and a concomitant of the westward expansion actually taking place between 1824 and 1848. During this period the Indian barrier was surmounted and the immense areas of the new Southwest and the Far West were added to the United States. It was a period which saw a rapid influx of European immigrants into the United States. Between 1830 and 1850 more than two million Europeans—most of them impoverished farmers or manual workers—crossed the Atlantic. Many were of the new German and Irish wave of immigrants. Between 1830 and 1850 the population of the

United States as a whole almost doubled, from about 12.9 million to over 23 million.

Although much of the emphasis on the theme of expansion was frankly materialistic, and some would be called racist today, idealistic motives were present, too. Protestant and Catholic missionaries, active in Oregon and elsewhere, hoped for numerous Indian converts. Many Americans took pride in the contrast between freedoms flourishing in their own country and oppressions evident in foreign lands. There was widespread concern that the intrigues of European imperialists would endanger the opportunities and liberties of ordinary Americans. Rumors spread that Britain and other powers were scheming to influence the internal and diplomatic policies of the Republic of Texas, to acquire Hawaii, and to control the Bays of San Francisco and San Diego as well as Puget Sound. (Some of the rumors had more substance than skeptics realized.) Would not encroachments of inimical courts and kings imperil the future of American democracy? Might they not also limit areas otherwise available for millions of oppressed Europeans, still hoping to come to American shores? Surely, it was God's and America's way to counter and remove the threat through a constructive program of rapid expansion. This was the sincere conviction of idealistic believers in Manifest Destiny.

The Indian Barrier. In 1830 the nation's land and water area covered more than 1,780,000 square miles. In addition, more than 12,000 square miles in the far Northeast and approximately half a million square miles in the far Northwest were claimed by both Washington and London. Substantial numbers of Americans were living in Texas, which then was still part of Mexico, on land which the Mexican government had granted to Moses Austin and his son, Stephen F. Austin.

Most pioneers, however, were less concerned with Mexican Texas or with Anglo-American boundary differences than with the nearer Indian barrier. From Indians' points of view, it was utterly wrong for them to be forced out of their ancestral lands in order to make places for white settlers. Most whites had a very different attitude, considering Indians inferior and looking on them as in the way.

During this period, the pressure of frontiersmen and their families pushed tens of thousands of Indians west of the Mississippi River. In ninety treaties signed during Jackson's presidency—some less honorable than others—the Indians reluctantly accepted new western lands in lieu of their old homes.

North of the Ohio River there was relatively little trouble for the white Americans when what was left of the Shawnees, Wyandots, Delawares, and Miamis were moved to western reservations. Although the move was a difficult one, the Northern tribes were to suffer less than the tribes of the South.

The most dramatic example of resistance by Northern Indians in the 1830s was an exception to the rule. This involved a resolute Sauk, Black Hawk by name, who believed that a treaty ceding the Rock River region of southern Wisconsin and northwestern Illinois to the hated whites had been signed under conditions of trickery. Black Hawk reluctantly moved his people to the west bank of the Mississippi, but in 1832 he led them back to southern Wisconsin in search of fertile farm land. The ensuing Black Hawk War, won by the whites that summer, marked the end of organized Indian resistance in the Old Northwest. Westward migration of Sauk, Fox, Winnebago, and other tribes increased. Within six years both Wisconsin and Iowa became territories; within sixteen years they became states, as settlers from the East populated the country of red men again dispossessed.

In the judgment of many white men, Southern Indians generally were making more progress toward "civilization" than those being prodded westward north of the

Americans surged westward, inspired by the dream of Manifest Destiny. Note the development of "progress" as the symbolic spirit of America moves across the land.

Ohio. Sequoya, inventor of a set of characters for Cherokee syllables, enabled thousands of Cherokee adults and children to read and write. Because by white standards they were more advanced than other Indians, the Cherokees, Chickasaws, Choctaws, Creeks, and Seminoles are known in American history as the Five Civilized Tribes. Some of them, notably the Seminoles and the Creeks, did not always prove civilized if placidity is a criterion. But there is small wonder that enlightened and virile leaders could not invariably remain placid in light of the whites' tricks and treachery.

The Indian Springs Treaty of 1825, involving Creek land in southern Georgia, was so unfair to the Indians that the U. S. Senate rejected it. Often treaties were said to be the result of corrupt deals in which Indian "leaders" sold out to the whites in return for handsome rewards. In any case, the treaties secured the land for the whites. The Treaty of Dancing Rabbit (1830) relinquished nearly eight million Choctaw acres in Alabama and Mississippi, and in the next decade other substantial cessions were made. Many Cherokees and other Indians were forced to move west. Not a few died along the way on what has been called the "Trail of Tears," suffering not only indignities but agonies on the long trek from their homes.

Not all Southern tribes submitted passively to the whites' intrusions. Osceola, a Florida Seminole subchief, so resented the Treaty of Payne's Landing, which authorized removal of the Seminoles to west of the Mississippi, that he is said to have plunged his knife into the document when he was expected to sign it with his "X."

Resistance on the part of Micanopy, Alligator, Osceola, and other Indians—supported by some runaway slaves—culminated in the Second Seminole War. In 1835 the Seminoles ambushed and massacred 107 of the 110 officers and men of Major Francis L. Dade. Taking full advantage of Florida's maze of inland rivers and swamps to hide their women and children, they harassed United States troops, then rushed back to cover. Osceola was seized and imprisoned when, under a flag of truce, he came for an interview with an American general. He died in a military prison, but the war—the bloodiest and most expensive of all our conflicts with Indians—continued until 1842. Although there are Seminoles in Florida in our own time, most of the original tribesmen were forced to surrender or were tricked into capture by the whites. Usually they settled in the Indian Territory of present-day Oklahoma.

The Pathfinders. By the 1830s, with the removal of the Indians, the trans-Appalachian West was a great complex of newly admitted states, and already people were moving beyond the Mississippi River. Missouri had been admitted as a state as early as 1821, and Arkansas followed in 1836. The wilderness beyond the Mississippi provided attractive commercial opportunities for aggressive American frontiersmen. The lucrative fur trade in the Northwest, for example, had early drawn rugged trappers and traders to that area.

The most successful of the early fur traders was German-born John Jacob Astor, who organized the American Fur Company in 1808 with the intention of establishing a monopoly of the fur trade throughout the West. Astor's acquisitiveness, ruthlessness, enormous capital, and efficient administration helped him take over Great Lakes and Mississippi valley trading posts which originally had belonged to other companies. In the 1820s he pushed west and northwest, absorbing the Columbia Fur Company in the Oregon country and ruthlessly crushing rival trappers and traders.

Astor's business methods met with severe criticism on the frontier. An army officer had this to say: "Take the American Fur Company in the aggregate, and they are the greatest scoundrels the world ever knew." But Astor, undaunted by criticism, continued to prosper. In 1834 he withdrew from the fur business to concentrate on New York City real estate.

William Henry Ashley of St. Louis was another who made a fortune from furs in the Northwest. Ashley's Rocky Mountain Fur Company originated the revolutionary "rendezvous" method of fur trading, by which company agents, instead of trading with the Indians, bought furs directly from white trappers at an annual "rendezvous" in the mountains. From 1822 to 1826, Ashley and the rugged trappers on his payroll pushed north and west, penetrating the country of hostile tribes and trapping beaver there.

When Ashley retired, he sold his Rocky Mountain Fur Company to Jedediah S. Smith, the "Knight in Buckskin" whose explorations greatly fostered American interest in the Far West. In the autumn of 1826 Smith led the first American overland expedition from Missouri to California. He carved an amazing career as "mountain man" and plainsman. Another fabulous character was Jim Bridger, who may have been the first white man to see Salt Lake.

Astoria

Columbia R.

LEWIS JAND CLARK

Yellowstone R.

Missouri R.

ASTOR'S TRADERS

ASHLEY'S TRADERS

ZEBULON PIKE

JEDEDIAH S. SMITH

Snake R.

JOHN C. FRÉMONT

GREAT
SALT LAKE

JEDEDIAH S. SMITH

San
Francisco

Monterey

Platte R.

St. Louis

PIKE'S PEAK

Colorado R.

Los Angeles

San Diego

Santa Fe

STEPHEN LONG

Arkansas R.

Red R.

Mississippi R.

Rio Grande

ZEBULON
PIKE

**WESTERN
EXPLORATIONS**

Still another was Thomas Fitzpatrick, the noted guide and genuine friend of grateful Indians.

Smith, Ashley, Bridger, Fitzpatrick, and the employees of the Astor interests all were experts with the knife, the rifle, and the trap. But more important, they contributed significantly to frontier expansion and marked the paths for others. They had much to do with the development of communities like St. Louis and of states and future states in what is now the western part of the Middle West. Accounts of their exploits also turned Eas-

terners' eyes and imaginations out to the Rockies and beyond.

Perhaps the most famous explorer among his contemporaries—so famous that he was known as the "Pathfinder" and won the Republican nomination for President in 1856—was John C. Frémont. Son of a French émigré schoolteacher, Frémont early in life formed a strong taste for meeting and mastering wilderness challenges. It was in 1838–1839, when employed on a survey of the broad plateau between the upper Mississippi and upper Missouri Rivers, that this

A huge caravan, led by Smith, Jackson, and Sublette, leaves for the Northwest in 1830.

army officer got his real start as a geological observer, mapmaker, and scientific reporter. In the 1840s he led several expeditions to the West, exploring the Oregon Trail, the Sierra Nevada, California, the Colorado River, and the Rio Grande. His well-written reports, avidly read in the East, stimulated further emigration to the West.

The Santa Fe Trail.   Santa Fe, in the Mexican territory of New Mexico, also provided attractive commercial opportunities for enterprising Americans. Though the volume of American trade in Santa Fe never was large, it was economically significant because American merchants were able to dispose of goods at handsome profit and because they brought away silver in an era when silver was at a premium.

William Becknell of Arrow Rock, Missouri, initiated the Santa Fe trade in 1821, when he sold his goods for ten to twenty times what they would have brought on the banks of the Mississippi. Venturesome American merchants and farmers followed Becknell's example, carrying goods along the 800-mile Santa Fe Trail from Independence, Missouri, to the great bend of the Arkansas and into New Mexico. Though the trip was arduous, confronting caravans with the dangers of rattlesnakes, heat, and storm, only eleven whites are reported to have been slain by Indians on the trail before 1843—a figure which illustrates that the Santa Fe Trail was less dangerous than it sometimes has been depicted.

The Oregon Trail.   Mention of the Oregon Trail also conjures up visions of caravans moving west, but in this case the wagon trains carried not merely merchants but farmers and other permanent settlers. Back in Jefferson's time, Lewis and Clark had traversed part of what was to become the celebrated route to the Pacific Northwest. Other hardy spirits followed, adding discoveries of their own.

The Oregon idea was not difficult to sell to land-hungry Americans. Oregon at that time was jointly occupied by the United States and Britain. The Hudson's Bay Company, an English concern, had long been established on the Columbia River. Church interest heightened when such American Protestant missionaries as Jason Lee, Samuel Parker, and Dr. Marcus Whitman went out to Oregon to convert Indians. Thus national pride, missionary zeal, the lure of cheap land, and the favorable reputation of the region all played a part in enticing thousands to Oregon.

As in the case of the Santa Fe Trail, Missouri towns like Independence and St. Joseph were takeoff spots for the Oregon-bound. For a couple of days of travel, the two routes even coincided. Then, as one went south, the other bent north. Out across various rivers including the Platte, and beyond to Fort Laramie, the covered wagons and pack trains of those seeking homes in the Northwest wound their way in the 1840s. On to Fort Bridger and along the Snake they proceeded to Whitman's mission. At last they saw the storied Columbia and reached Astoria, or wherever they were going. The Oregon Trail stretched two thousand miles—two and a half times the length of the Santa Fe journey.

Western Army Posts. The exploits of the mountain trappers, the Santa Fe traders, and the Oregon pioneers should not tempt us to overlook the tremendous contributions of the professional soldiers. From the 1820s well into the 1840s, the United States army never was large, but its role in aiding the settlement of the West can hardly be exaggerated. Specula-

tors and homesteaders were more likely to bring their families to areas when the military was nearby. Army posts in time became villages, towns, and cities. It was not unusual for a retired officer to become a respected civilian in a new community. Soldiers brought steamboats to Western rivers, constructed sawmills, and built their own forts. They farmed adjacent fields, introduced cattle, and disproved the widely credited legend that a "Great American Desert" existed between the Mississippi and the Rockies.

When it came to exploration, the army also played its part. Although these military expeditions were not so colorful as the exploits of a Jim Bridger or of the famous trapper, Indian fighter, and scout Kit Carson, they were nevertheless essential in opening up the previously unknown West.

WINNING THE WEST

A National Question. As long as the westward movement was confined to a few explorers and commercial adventurers, Washington could act indecisively and put off any attempt to reach terms with London and Mexico City in connection with territorial disputes in the West. But as American settlers poured into the Far West and the Southwest, setting up communities and then local governments, the United States government could no longer hesitate. The dispute with Britain over the boundaries of the Oregon country had to be settled. And the aspirations of fellow Americans living in Texas had to be heeded. What had been social and economic developments in the West had by the 1840s risen to the level of national political questions.

The Oregon Dispute. The "Oregon country" was a great deal larger than the present state of Oregon. It was bounded roughly by the "Great Stony" Mountains on the east, the

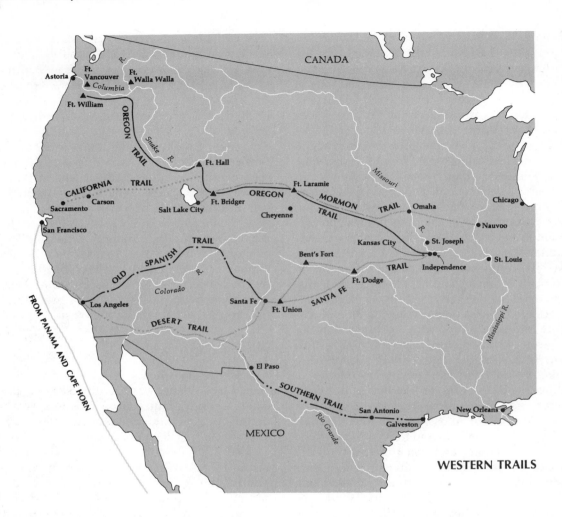

WESTERN TRAILS

Pacific on the west, California on the south, and Alaska (then Russian) on the north. When informed men chatted about Oregon in the era after the War of 1812, they referred to a wondrously varied land with towering mountains and fertile valleys, swift-coursing rivers and magnificent forests. Details, however, eluded even the best-informed of commentators; lack of surveys made it impossible to define its area precisely.

Early in the nineteenth century both Russia and Spain laid claim to sections of Oregon. But Spain bowed out of the picture in 1819, and Russia in the next decade acknowledged 54°

40' as Alaska's southern line. Britain and the United States were left in contention over the Oregon country.

The principal area in dispute was the territory between the Columbia River and the line of 49° latitude to the Pacific—the northwestern two thirds of the present state of Washington. Britain based its claims on the exploration, discovery, and occupation of the region by British subjects. American claims also were based on exploration and occupation, including Captain Gray's original discovery of the Columbia River in 1792, the Lewis and Clark expedition of 1804–1806, and the presence of American missionaries and settlers in the area in the 1830s and 1840s.

During Anglo-American negotiations in 1818 the United States proposed the boundary line of 49° to the Pacific Ocean. Britain agreed except for the part north and west of the Columbia River; it was unwilling to relinquish its claims to the Columbia River, the "St. Lawrence of the West." Unable to reach a satisfactory agreement, the two nations settled upon a treaty of ten-year joint occupation of the area "on the northwest coast of America, westward of the Stony Mountains." In 1827 the treaty was renewed for an indefinite period, with the provision that either party could terminate it on a year's notice.

Neither in 1818 nor at any other time until 1845 did the United States or Britain provide for civil government in Oregon. No marshal, no sheriff, no jury, no judge was empowered to carry out legal procedures. No laws could be executed because none had been enacted, there being no enacting authority. Often men took justice, or what they deemed was justice, into their own hands. A missionary, without the shadow of authority, might name a constable or a magistrate. There were times when American traders and trappers tried alleged culprits for murder and other crimes. But maintenance of order, while frequently successful, was unofficial at best. Indians did not become subject to the slightest American official authority until 1843, when President Tyler appointed Oregon's first Indian agent.

That was the year when the first large body of American immigrants arduously entered the Willamette valley in Western Oregon. It was also then that a committee, composed of American pioneers and their French-Canadian neighbors, met in Champoeg and formed a provisional government. Once the government came into being, it was almost immediately effective. People of stamina and initiative determined to do in Oregon what Washington agencies had not done.

Soon the "Oregon fever" had hit the eastern United States, and British settlers in Oregon began to find themselves vastly outnumbered. This rapid influx of Americans prompted both Britain and the United States to try once again for a peaceful boundary settlement.

Soon after the Democratic victory in the election of 1844, the newly elected President Polk, faced with the possibility of war with Mexico, once again proposed to Great Britain the boundary line of 49°. When the British minister in Washington peremptorily rejected the American offer, the United States on April 26, 1846, gave the required one year's notice to terminate the joint-occupation treaty of 1818. Later that year the British government decided to settle for the 49° line. Britain submitted a draft treaty to this effect to the United States and Polk submitted the treaty to the Senate, which approved it on June 12 and formally ratified it a week later.

OREGON BOUNDARY DISPUTE

Claimed by U.S.

Claimed by both U.S. and England

The Anglo-American settlement did not meet with unanimous approval in the United States: Northwestern exponents of Manifest Destiny and antislavery men charged that they had been betrayed by a South which, smugly complacent over the annexation of all of Texas, had been satisfied with less than all of Oregon. But the Oregon Treaty did have the important effect of preventing a possible third war between the United States and Great Britain at a time when the United States was involved in a war with Mexico over the question of Texas.

Settlement of Texas. In the 1820s and 1830s a number of Americans—mostly South-erners—took Mexico's liberal colonization law at face value and migrated to Texas. With the help of slaves and cotton gins they farmed the fertile soil and conducted business under the aegis of Stephen Austin and other *empresarios* who had contracted with the Mexican govern-ment to settle a certain number of families in Texas in return for grants of land.

In three centuries the Spanish government had brought only 4000 subjects to Texas. Now the population of the Austin communities alone expanded from 2000 in 1828 to more than 5500 three years later. By 1836 more than 25,000 white men, women, and children were scattered between the Sabine River and San Antonio de Bexar. Colonists from the United States far outnumbered those of Spanish ancestry.

Friction between Mexicans and Americans in Texas was probably inevitable. Mexicans, long accustomed to Spanish procedures, naturally were unprepared for the kinds of administrative and legislative responsibilities so readily assumed by the immigrants. Blunt and self-assertive Americans in Texas were certain that their way of life was freer, healthier, happier, and in all ways superior to that of the Mexicans. They looked upon themselves individually and collectively as proper agents to impose reform and progress on what they deemed to be a benighted society, handicapped for generations by su-perstition and sloth. The average newcomer failed to recognize the spirituality and gentili-ty of Spanish culture and criticized the Mexican peasants for being illiterate and ignorant. Americans also overlooked the equally pertinent truth that both Mexican peasants and their grandee overlords were sensitive and proud.

Americans in Texas were distressed by gyrations in Mexican policy and the uncertain-ty of their own status. The Mexican govern-ment appeared indifferent to educational needs and law enforcement, and it did nothing to meet the Americans' request for the separation of Texas from the state of Coahuila, to which it had long been joined. This neglect, as well as the government's pressure to force the Roman Catholic religion on the settlers and to abolish slavery, contrib-uted to a drift that widened the gulf between the native Mexicans and the immigrants from the north.

War for Independence. In Mexico City, meanwhile, a growing trend toward dictatori-al rule reduced the likelihood of conciliation. The master spirit of despotism was Antonio Lopez de Santa Anna, who became president of Mexico in 1833. Santa Anna, "the Napoleon of the West," was ambitious, adept at intrigue, and an able field commander as long as fate favored him. As president he ruthlessly crushed every semblance of liberalism in Mexico's central government and then turned his attention to Texas, where Americans were vehemently protesting his abandonment of the eleven-year-old "enlightened" Mexican constitution. The Texans' protests culminated in a proclamation of independence from Mexico on March 2, 1836.

Four days later Santa Anna and his Mexican troops swept into Texas and massacred every one of the 188 Americans at the Alamo mission in San Antonio. Davy Crockett, Jim

Bowie, and William B. Travis were among the American heroes who died defending the Alamo. That same month, at Goliad on the south bank of the San Antonio River, the severely wounded James Walker Fannin surrendered his tiny command to Mexican General José Urrea, with the understanding that the Texans would be accorded the humane treatment normally extended to prisoners of war. Instead, acting under Santa Anna's orders, Urrea mercilessly executed most of the prisoners in cold blood, with Colonel Fannin the last to go. If the shots that killed them were not heard 'round the world in the tradition of Concord bridge, "Remember the Alamo!" and "Remember Goliad!" long served as rallying cries in Texas.

During the war for Texan independence, as we have seen, the young republic's forces were in the capable hands of General Sam Houston, who had fought under Andrew Jackson in the War of 1812 and had later settled in Texas. Not quite two months after the Texans' stunning defeats at the Alamo and Goliad his troops surprised and defeated Santa Anna's forces at San Jacinto on April 21, 1836 and captured the Mexican dictator himself. Houston forced Santa Anna to sign the Treaty of Velasco, by which Mexico agreed to withdraw its forces from Texas and to recognize the Rio Grande as the southwestern boundary of the new Republic of Texas.

The Republic of Texas.   The Texans' proposal for annexation was initially rejected by the United States because of fear that a serious sectional controversy might develop over extending slavery into the area. Thus the young republic, under the leadership of

The fall of the Alamo mission was a stunning defeat for the Texans, but it provided a rallying cry that is remembered today.

Presidents Sam Houston (who served two nonconsecutive terms) and Mirabeau B. Lamar, proceeded to develop its own foreign and domestic policies. One of its first problems was Mexico's refusal to recognize its independent status. Because Santa Anna had signed the Treaty of Velasco under duress, while a prisoner of war, the Mexicans denied its validity. Thus, though both Europe and the United States officially recognized Texas independence, Mexico withheld recognition.

Though the sizable volunteer army of the San Jacinto campaign was disbanded in 1837, Texas maintained armed troops against the danger of another military campaign by Mexico. The Texas Rangers, loosely organized until then, were developed into a tight-knit corps. And the Texas navy made itself felt in the Gulf of Mexico. As late as 1843, Texan sailors fought against Mexican steam warships.

Maintenance of the navy and defenses against marauding Indians demanded more money than Texas had. The republic's civil government also desperately needed financial support. Though bond issues were floated with varying degrees of success, the fiscal structure was never very solid in the period of the republic.

Nevertheless, Texas prospered. Its population grew rapidly, most of the immigrants continuing to be Americans. Large in territory and rich in untapped resources, Texas was regarded with covetous eyes by those American politicians who viewed it as a promising field for expansion, exploitation, and the extension of slavery.

Annexation of Texas.   Presidents Jackson and Van Buren had been concerned about the North's opposition to the annexation of Texas. Jackson favored annexation and was more outspoken about it after he retired from the presidency. Van Buren marked time, but neither Tyler nor Polk had qualms about working toward annexation. Although both were slaveholders, neither seems to have been thinking primarily about considerations of slavery. (Polk's diary gives abundant evidence to this effect.) Both couched their motives in terms of expansion: Would it be to the country's advantage to limit expansion of the federal domain? This was substantially the same question Jefferson had asked himself in 1803 with reference to the Louisiana Purchase. Like Jefferson, Tyler and Polk answered with a ringing "No!"

But antislavery elements in the North viewed the situation differently. Most Northerners—excluding the tiny minority of abolitionists—agreed with their Southern brothers that the Constitution protected slavery where slavery then existed. Extension of slavery into the West, however, they strongly disapproved. Thus the addition of Texas as a slave state was opposed by many citizens north of the Mason-Dixon line.

Early in 1844 President Tyler, anticipating the presidential campaign of that year, sent a treaty for the annexation of Texas to the Senate. When the Senate rejected it by a vote of 35 to 16, Tyler recommended that Texas be annexed by joint resolution of both houses of Congress, since a joint resolution could be passed by a simple majority in both houses plus the President's signature, in contrast to the two-thirds Senate majority needed for treaty ratification. Congress adjourned before the measure could be brought to a vote, but when the second session convened on December 2, 1844, Tyler again urged a joint resolution to annex Texas.

This time the resolution passed both House and Senate, and Tyler signed it on March 1, 1845. Under the terms of the resolution, Texas was offered statehood with the understanding that its territory might be subdivided into not more than four additional states. The Missouri Compromise line of 36° 30' was extended westward to permit slavery in Texas.

Before the annexation resolution was

passed, there had been hints and fears of British involvement in the fate of the Texas Republic. It was to England's, as well as to Mexico's, interest to see that Texas stayed out of the United States. A pending arrangement whereby Texas would ship cotton directly to Liverpool, for example, would mean the tightening of mutually advantageous Anglo-Texas economic ties.

The London government tried to induce Mexico to recognize Texas independence on the condition that the Lone Star republic would not become part of the United States. Mexico did assent to this proposal in May 1845, and Texans had a choice of being annexed to the United States or negotiating such a treaty with Mexico. The Mexican offer had come too late, however. Now that annexation to the United States was theirs for the taking, Texans found this alternative the more desirable.

War with Mexico.   Already irate over Texas' independence, the Mexican government became exceedingly resentful when, in 1845, its erstwhile possession was formally annexed by the United States. Mexico had threatened to declare war on the United States if Texas was annexed. Now it withdrew its minister to the United States and severed official relations with the American government.

In June 1845 President Polk ordered General Zachary Taylor and his troops into Texas to defend the territory. Taylor set up camp on the south bank of the Nueces River, about 150 miles from the Rio Grande. In November Polk dispatched John Slidell to Mexico on a special mission to discuss the outstanding issues between Mexico and the United States. Slidell was to propose that the United States assume the $2 million in claims of American citizens against the government of Mexico, in return for Mexico's recognition of the Rio Grande as the southwestern boundary of Texas (Mexico claimed the Nueces River as the southwestern line). Polk also authorized Slidell to offer $5 million for New Mexico or $25 million for both New Mexico and California.

When the new Mexican government under President José J. Herrera refused to receive Slidell, Polk ordered Taylor to proceed to the Rio Grande. There, on April 25, 1846, Taylor's troops were attacked without warning by Mexican troops, and Congress declared war on the Republic of Mexico.

The battles of Palo Alto and Resaca de la Palma followed; the first was an inconclusive artillery duel, the second a smashing American victory. These opening engagements of May 1846 were followed by the major encounters of Monterrey the next September and Buena Vista in February 1847. General Zachary Taylor, bearing battlefield and theater responsibility in the Monterrey area, displayed great gallantry and was popular with his men. However, he did not make much progress in the direction of Mexico City, partly because Polk transferred most of the seasoned soldiers from Taylor's command to that of Major General Winfield Scott.

It was Scott, who, landing at Vera Cruz in March 1847, made that Gulf port his supply base and advanced inland to the mountain pass of Cerro Gordo, where he routed Mexican General Santa Anna. Other battles took place in 1847, and all were American victories. Scott entered Mexico City in September, but it was bloodsoaked Buena Vista, more than half a year before, that would make Taylor the next President.

Although the United States declared war on Mexico in May 1846, the news did not reach California for a number of weeks. Meanwhile, a group of California settlers, aided by explorer John C. Frémont and by American naval officers, had revolted against Mexican rule and proclaimed California an independent republic. They raised a flag on which a grizzly bear, a red star, and the legend "Republic of California" were juxtaposed. When news that the United States had declared war against Mexico was received,

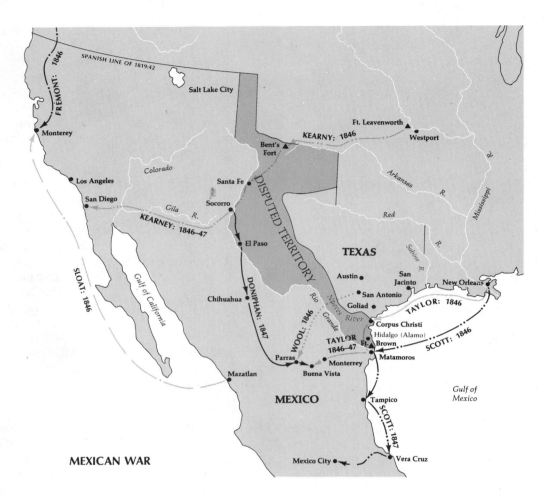

MEXICAN WAR

however, the significance of the Bear Flag Revolt was greatly diminished.

In the summer of 1846 Colonel Stephen W. Kearny and a detachment of about 1700 troops took possession of Santa Fe in the name of the United States. Polk subsequently ordered Kearny to take charge of American operations in California. The American elements previously led by Commodore R. F. Stockton were brought together under Kearny, and by autumn of 1846 the conquest of California was complete.

The Treaty of Guadalupe Hidalgo. In April 1847 President Polk, eager to end the fighting

as quickly as possible, delegated Nicholas P. Trist, chief clerk of the State Department, as peace commissioner to Mexico. Trist's instructions were to negotiate a treaty recognizing the Rio Grande as the southwest boundary of Texas and ceding to the United States for $15 million the Mexican states of upper California and New Mexico. The United States also would assume the claims of United States citizens against Mexico up to $3.25 million.

Once in Mexico, Trist badly bungled the negotiations and was peremptorily recalled by Polk. Trist, however, refused to return to Washington and, with no official authority, signed on February 2, 1848, a treaty which incorporated all the provisions of his annulled instructions. Polk was furious at Trist's disobedience, but he immediately sent the treaty to the Senate for ratification. Though the Treaty of Guadalupe Hidalgo was denounced by two vocal minorities—those who had demanded the cession of all of Mexico and those who wanted none of the southwestern territory—it was ratified by the Senate on March 10, 1848. The United States now found itself in possession of the mammoth region which includes the present states of California, Nevada, and Utah, most of Arizona and New Mexico, and parts of Colorado and Wyoming. It also found itself with a considerable number of Spanish-speaking residents, many of whom had lived there for generations.

Eruption of the Slavery Issue.　Northern reactions to the War with Mexico were even more intense than Northern reactions to Texas' annexation. No matter how moderate they had previously been, antiextension Northerners began to heed the abolitionists' propaganda that the South's vicious "slave power" must be checked. According to this version of affairs, the South, having dominated the federal government since its establishment, now was afraid that population growth in the North and the proliferation of free states in the Northwest would destroy its political advantage. Therefore, it was argued, this nefarious Southern "power"—arrogant, determined, and utterly unscrupulous—sought to strengthen itself by spreading an evil which enlightened folk righteously deplored. The threat would affect the Southwest (as a result of the Mexican War), the West as a whole, and Northern states as well. The "slave power," the argument continued, would try to annex every Mexican mile and Central America and the West Indies in the bargain.

At the same time, many Southerners blamed the North as the aggressor. The pamphlets of abolitionists stirred up blacks, they asserted. Slave insurrections had resulted and would continue to result from the "senseless" agitation. Antislavery virulence had long been limited to a few Northern hotheads, but now they saw the zealotry as epidemic. Northerners had petitioned to do away with slavery in the District of Columbia and on federal property in the South, and the same "intolerance" had been manifested in opposition to annexing Texas. And did not Northern states abysmally fail to live up to their constitutional commitments when they repeatedly refused to enforce the Fugitive Slave Law of 1793? So ran the Southern arguments.

As the world has often seen in situations where emotion interferes with reason, there were exaggerations on both sides rather than complete departures from truth. On the one hand, there simply was no "slave power" in the abolitionist sense of the term. There was no unanimity of Southern opinion as to policies. From Jefferson's day through Jackson's to Polk's, not all Southern officeholders in high places had been of one political mind. Chief Justice Taney, for example, did not invariably hand down Supreme Court opinions resembling those of Chief Justice Marshall. Taney was a Marylander and Marshall a Virginian, yet their legal tenets and those of other Southerners were poles apart. Contrary to what was charged, there was no widespread Southern *or* Northern conspiracy.

In the 1840s, the issues of slavery and antislavery, expansion and containment became intermeshed. If the Civil War had never taken place, we might not now be inclined to stress North-South antipathies respecting the West. But since the war did occur, it is evident that the relationship of the slavery question to the West involved problems loaded with political dynamite.

Filling Out the West.　While settlement of Texas and the Oregon country was proceeding, other areas were luring pioneers westward in search of land or mineral wealth. Some who had started out on the Oregon Trail bound for the Northwest changed their destination to California. The path to California followed the Oregon Trail to the Continental Divide where, turning southwestward, it became the California Trail and led through the Sierra Nevada into California.

Before 1840, only fur traders penetrated to California, and whaling ships stopped there for supplies occasionally. In the early 1840s some farmers began to move into the Pacific Coast valleys, but when war with Mexico broke out in 1846, there were only about 700 Americans in California. The discovery of gold at Sutter's Mill near Sacramento in 1848 started the "gold rush," which brought the total population of the area to 90,000 by 1850, when California became a state. The gold seekers came by sea around Cape Horn, or by sea after an overland crossing of Mexico or Central America, or by various overland routes across the North American continent. The transcontinental journey was chosen by most immigrants, an estimated 40,000 using it in 1849 alone.

By the 1850s there were two frontiers in America, one moving westward beyond the Mississippi and the other moving eastward from California and Oregon into the Rocky Mountain area. The first settlement to fill the gap between them was made by the Mormons, who moved to Utah in 1847. This religious group had been organized by Joseph Smith in New York state in 1830. They had moved to Ohio in 1831 and to Illinois in 1839 to escape persecution. Then, for the same reason and under the leadership of Brigham Young, they decided to move to a desert valley around the Great Salt Lake, where they hoped to find peace. They had some misfortunes and near disasters in the first few years but eventually became prosperous.

With the close of the Mexican War the Mormons lost the nominal Mexican jurisdiction under which they had been free to do as they pleased. Congress organized the Mormon lands into Utah Territory in 1850, naming Brigham Young as territorial governor. By 1860 there were 40,000 persons in Utah, but it was not admitted as a state until 1896 because the Mormon church did not renounce the practice of polygamy until 1890. For a few years after 1849 the Mormons profited substantially from the sale of supplies to gold seekers on the way to California.

The treaty ending the war with Mexico filled out the present continental limits of the United States with the exception of a strip of land in what later became southern New Mexico and Arizona. It was purchased from Mexico in 1853 because it was thought to provide the best route for a railroad to California. With the Gadsden Purchase, the American "empire" was complete from Atlantic to Pacific.

THE ECONOMICS OF EXPANSION

The West and the Transportation Revolution. From the beginning of human life on earth, people have lived in close association with rivers and streams. Waterways were the natural routes over which travelers moved both themselves and their goods, for rivers cut through wildernesses they could not penetrate in other ways. Therefore, when the settlers moving into the American frontier were forced to return to the most primitive conditions of living, rivers naturally became their first important means of inland transportation.

One of the great drawbacks to river transportation is that the river does not always go where the traffic needs to go. That became true in the United States as soon as the territory west of the Appalachian Mountains was opened for settlement. Rivers descended eastward from the Appalachian watersheds to the Atlantic or westward to meet the Ohio and Mississippi, but no waterway connected East and West. Thus the great enthusiasm for

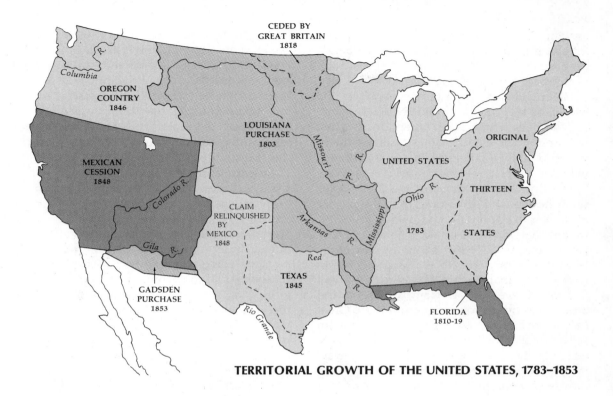

TERRITORIAL GROWTH OF THE UNITED STATES, 1783–1853

building national roads during the "Turnpike Era" from 1800 to 1830 was occasioned partly by the fact that roads were needed to connect the Ohio River system with the Atlantic coastal rivers.

However, transportion of goods between West and East over these road and river routes was prohibitively expensive except for light and very valuable merchandise. The best outlet for the bulky Western produce was not eastward but southward on flatboats down the Ohio and Mississippi Rivers to New Orleans. But to try to propel flatboats back up the river against the current was still impractical. Manufactured products needed by Western settlers—such as guns, ammunition, traps, axes, plows, tools, and even shoes and cloth—still had to come in overland from the East.

Because America's immediate economic problem was the need to move goods over great distances inexpensively, the new steam power developed in England in the eighteenth century was applied in America to water transportation even earlier than to industry. Beginning with John Fitch in 1786, a series of American inventors worked on the problem of driving a boat with steam, culminating with Robert Fulton's commercial success in powering his *Clermont* up the Hudson River in 1807. In the following decade steamboats were successfully tried on the Ohio and Mississippi Rivers. By 1829 there were 200 steamboats in operation on the Western rivers, and by 1842 the number had reached 450. A decade later there were considerably over 1000. Partly because of the special needs of the West and partly because early steamboats were too fragile for ocean use (trans-Atlantic steamer service was not frequent until mid-century), more steamboats were in service on the Mississippi River system than anywhere else in the world. Pittsburgh, Cincinnati, and Louisville began as river towns, and New Orleans became one of America's greatest ports.

Meanwhile, in an attempt to avoid the roundabout route through New Orleans, Northerners turned their attention to canal building, which had been so successful in England in the 1760s and 1770s. The first such waterway of great importance was New York's Erie Canal, connecting the Great Lakes with the Hudson River (and thus the port of New York). Upon its completion in 1825, freight charges from Buffalo to New York City were cut from $100 to $10 a ton, the time of the trip from twenty days to six. Migrants began to use the canal to gain access to the West. Buffalo, Cleveland, Detroit, Chicago, and other cities began to sprout around the Great Lakes, and the area began to fill up with settlers just as the Ohio valley had earlier. As a result of the canal trade, New York City grew rapidly in wealth and population, becoming the greatest port on the Atlantic seaboard. The nation was propelled into the "Canal Era" (1825–1840), with other sections from Illinois to Massachusetts trying to imitate the success of New York.

Yet rivers and canals had their shortcomings. During winter, frozen waterways could not be used in the North. Rivers followed inconvenient courses, and canals could not be built in rough or hilly country. The railroads would overcome all these limitations.

Steam-powered rail locomotives had already won success in England when the Baltimore and Ohio Railroad started the first few miles of American rail service in 1830. Soon other short lines were built elsewhere, and by 1840, 2808 miles of track had been laid. Ten years later the mileage had more than tripled, to 9029 miles, and by 1860 it had tripled again, to 30,626 miles (as compared to industrial Britain's 10,410 miles). The railroads, which connected the Atlantic coast with Chicago and St. Louis by the 1850s, for

the first time provided the West with exactly the kind of transportation it needed. Western products, no matter what their bulk, could now be moved regardless of weather or terrain directly to Eastern markets for overseas shipment. Manufactures from the East and abroad could come in freely. Traffic on the rivers and canals declined. With the coming of the rails, the commercial and industrial Northeast and the agricultural Northwest were tied more closely together by common economic bonds.

The Northeast and the Industrial Revolution. Under the impact of continually expanding trade, each section of the country underwent a characteristic economic evolution of its own. New England, for example, the section which had achieved the lead in population in the colonial era, was the first to pass from agriculture to commerce and industry. The absence of good soil for agriculture and the abundance of good harbors adjacent to ample supplies of pine and hardwood had turned its people to shipbuilding, fishing, and overseas commerce in colonial days. It was no accident, too, that industrialism should have entered America through New England, for towns well located for commerce were also attractive for manufacturers. Mills and factories need to be near shipping points.

Other circumstances contributed to the growth of industrialism in the Northeast. In the early stages, streams were still a must for turning the water wheels that drove the machinery of mills and factories, and the Northeast was favorably endowed with water power. In Chapter 6 we saw how the Embargo and the War of 1812, in restricting overseas trade, had driven idle commercial capital into investment in domestic industry. The tremendous potentialities of trade with the West, facilitated first by the Erie Canal and then by the railroads, provided further incentive for the manufacture of industrial products. Final-

The Erie Canal, shown here at Rochester in 1853, provided a vital connection between the Great Lakes and New York.

ly, even after steam had replaced water power in industry, manufacturing continued for a time to be located where capital and labor were already concentrated—in the Northeast.

The rise of industrialism in the northern United States had economic and social consequences of such a revolutionary character that it has been called—as in England—the Industrial Revolution. It revolutionized the nature of business organization, of labor, of population distribution, and of the life and welfare of all Americans.

The Corporate Revolution. The arrival of industrialism meant the beginning of the growth of large factories and large railroad networks. And as the size of businesses increased, the old methods of organizing and financing business enterprises by means of individual ownership or partnership became inadequate. The costs of maintaining trading ships or small mills did not exceed the personal fortune of individuals, but with the coming of railroads and large-scale manufactures, the enormous costs of buildings, equipment, and stock began to run into millions of dollars. This was far beyond the financial resources of even the wealthiest person, and the risks were too great to be undertaken singly. As a consequence, entrepreneurs turned increasingly to the corporate form of enterprise.

The chief disadvantage of the partnership was its "unlimited liability" for business debts: If the firm failed, creditors could force the sale of the owners' personal property, as well as their business property, to satisfy claims. The partnership, therefore, usually comprised a very few individuals who knew and trusted one another and who were willing to take the risks together. Moreover, the partnership had no permanence. It dissolved and the company collapsed when any single member withdrew. The corporation, on the other hand, is a separate legal entity or "person," distinct from its owners. An owner may sell his stock in the corporation without the assent of the other owners, and the corporation continues.

Most important is the feature of "limited liability." If the corporation fails, the owners are liable to lose only what they paid for stock in the corporation. The creditors have no claim on their personal resources. Finally, by the issuance of stock, the corporation can draw on the contributions of literally thousands of investors and accumulate the large amounts of capital needed for big industry.

In spite of its advantages, the corporate form was not without its opponents in the Jacksonian period. Jackson, Jefferson before him, and even the father of free enterprise or laissez faire, the English economist Adam Smith, had attacked corporations as according "exclusive privilege"and limiting "free competition." But what they were attacking was the kind of incorporation that was known before the 1830s. Before then corporation charters had been granted only through special legislation and only for some specific

enterprise that had to be run as a monopoly in order to be profitable. Thus turnpikes, canals, bridges, and banks—enterprises of a semi-public character—were often conducted under charters granting exclusive privileges. Part of Jackson's hostility toward the Bank of the United States can be traced to its monopolistic charter. And even less clearly beneficial to all the public was the construction of industrial establishments.

Many thought that the government should have no authority over the economy. But the wider markets in the West and the new technical processes made increased capital so necessary to industry that corporation charters were sought more and more in spite of possible public opposition. To make incorporation democratic and consonant with Jacksonian equal-rights principles, Whigs and like-minded Democrats urged "general incorporation laws" (as distinct from special legislative grants) which would make corporation charters available to all who could meet certain legal requirements. Beginning in the 1830s and continuing into the 1840s and 1850s, corporations began to proliferate under the new system of general laws.

The Whig party, which generally favored business interests (as would later its successor, the Republican party), had advocated free incorporation as a method of inaugurating a kind of "democratic" capitalism. That is, business would no longer be dependent upon rich men but could gather the combined resources of countless small investors. However, this multiplication of ownership eventually resulted in a revolutionary change in the nature of business organization. As the number of stockholders or owners in a corporation rose into the thousands and as they were dispersed about the country, actual management or "control" of the company fell into the hands of individuals who were not dominant owners or perhaps not even stockholders at all.

Under the system of individual proprietorship or partnership, ownership and control had been in the hands of the same person. The corporate system began the process of divorcing ownership from control and of creating a vast class of investors dependent, insofar as their profits were concerned, on the actions of others—the corporate managers. The inherent danger was that the managers might not act in the interests of the owners. In former days when the owners managed their own businesses, owners who defrauded the company defrauded themselves. With the separation of ownership and control, the "insiders" or managers could systematically loot a company for their own profit. Said a contemporary observer concerning the stock market scandals of 1854:

The spring trade of '54 opened gloomily. . . . In June it was discovered that the Parker Vein Company had flooded the market with an immense and unauthorized issue of stock. The first of the next month New York was startled by the intelligence that Robert Schuyler, President of the New York and New Haven Railroad, had been selling some 20,000 illegal shares at par,—and was now a defaulter for two millions. Almost simultaneously it was ascertained that Alexander Kyle, Secretary of the Harlem Railroad Company, had made an issue of forged stock to the amount of $300,000. Other developments of breaches of trust came flocking from the inland cities.[1]

Scandals, very fortunately, represented only one phase of America's part in the Industrial Revolution. Another phase, at least equally significant, was the entirely new evaluation of the forces that affected the location of industry.

The Rise of Industrial Populations. Before the steam engine was developed, the almost

complete reliance on water power resulted in scattering manufacturing among a large number of small or medium-sized towns, for the capacity of any given dam site was limited. The triumph of steam made it feasible for manufacturing to concentrate in large cities.

Industrial employment brought new problems not imaginable in the previous handicraft period of individual workshops. In America, as in England, people did not know how to cope with the problems of health and safety in the new factories because never before had such problems existed. (Even in England factory laws were not introduced until the 1840s.) Moreover, congested living quarters in the growing industrial cities of New England and the Middle Atlantic states often resulted in a deplorable lack not only of sanitation but also of the minimum requirements for decent human existence. Hours of work were usually long, wages low, and schools for the children of workers inadequate. Workers could afford little for housing. The idea of public transportation had not been developed, so employees had to live within walking distance of their place of employment. All these conditions worked together to produce a type of housing for industrial workers which would become slums of the worst sort.

Unlike the earlier hand industries, the new steam-driven machines did not require workers with great skill or physical strength. Increasingly, women and even children were hired to perform the simple but arduous and monotonous tasks of factory work. On the other hand, conditions were perhaps not so disagreeable as in England, and there were bright spots on the American industrial landscape. The novelist Hawthorne in one of his rambles about the New England countryside remarked on the bright, cheerful faces looking out through the factory windows. The factory girls of Lowell, Massachusetts, were known for their neat dress and published a

---

1. James K. Medbury, *Men and Mysteries of Wall Street* (Boston: Fields, Osgood, 1870), p. 309.

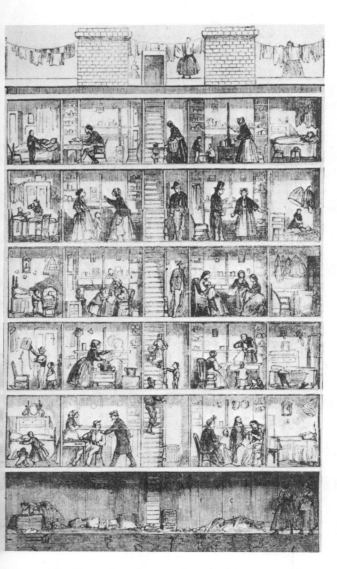

The illustration above and on the facing page shows two sections of a larger tenement of two-room apartments, which were joined under a common roof.

literary weekly. But these pleasant scenes were fast fading into the past.

Urban industrialism resulted not only from new production techniques and new Western markets but also from increased efficiency in agriculture: Improved farm methods and farm machinery permitted more people to be siphoned off into industrial production. In addition, a good many immigrants settled immediately in the cities. As a result, between 1820 and 1850 the cities grew much faster than the population as a whole. In 1820 only one person in fourteen lived in a city of 2500 or more. In 1850 nearly one person in six lived in such a city. This meant an increase of more than fivefold in the population of cities, while the whole population had increased just over twofold during those years.

The great majority of Americans were still rural, still untouched by conditions developing in the Northeast. But those who watched the cities fill with immigrants and develop slums, vice, and crime were deeply disturbed. Many associated crowded cities and the factory grind with a Europe of decadence and oppression. The traditional Jeffersonian vision of America—the land of democratic simplicity—seemed to be threatened by new problems of industrial complexity.

The Rise of Labor. Among the first to react to these unsatisfactory conditions were the workers themselves. Although workers were influential in contributing to trends toward better education, their moves in the direction of unionization were in the main separate and distinct from most other reforms of the period.

The oldest labor organizations in America date back to the late eighteenth century, when various skilled craftsmen banded together to obtain higher wages, shorter hours, and other benefits from their merchant-artisan employers. But it was not until the late 1820s and the 1830s that aggressive union activity began with the establishment of strong craft unions in Philadelphia, Boston, New York, Providence, and other cities. An attempt was even made in 1834 to form a National Trades Union, but though the group held conventions for several years, the effort failed to achieve an enduring result.

The most successful of the early unions were local groups which were primarily political in their objectives, working especially hard for various social reforms like free public schools. Aided by favorable public opinion, they were able to make substantial gains by legislative action. By the middle of the nineteenth century the idea of free public education, at least through the primary grades, was pretty generally accepted.

Beginning in the late 1840s, a number of important states began to establish the ten-hour day as the legal maximum work day. But it was usually possible for workers to make a special contract with their employers to work longer, and economic necessity frequently drove them to do so, nullifying the effect of the statutory provision. Nevertheless, such laws represented a gain for labor, since they helped to establish the idea of a ten-hour limit.

Finally, in the 1850s, unions less interested in political activity than in "bread-and-butter" issues (wages, hours, and working conditions) gathered momentum. During this period, the first permanent national unions of separate trades were set up, beginning with the National Typographical Union in 1852.

The appearance of solid and enduring national unions was a sign of the end of America's industrial adolescence. Many more decades were to pass before economic conditions would convince even a substantial minority of American workers or employers that unions were a good and permanent element in industrial relations. The individualistic tradition and conditioning of both workers and employers, and an excess of labor, prevented that result sooner. But national unions were here to stay, and their

Increasing industrial employment forced people to live in congested tenements, under deplorable sanitary conditions. Workers could afford little for housing and had to live near their place of employment.

very existence testified to the arrival of a new period in American economic history.

Growing Sectionalism. While the economic bonds were tightening between Northeast and Northwest, the South depended increasingly on selling cotton and other plantation products on the European market. Although there were notable exceptions, basically Southerners were pulling away from their earlier common interests with other parts of the country. The South's growing identification with an international market economy was natural for the specialized producer of seven eighths of the world's cotton fiber.

However, certain financial obstacles prevented the South from completely freeing itself from dependence on the North. A growing demand for slaves meant continually rising prices for them. To buy land and slaves for the expansion of cultivation required new increments of capital, which the planter class—a leisure-loving economic aristocracy—simply could not provide for itself. The new capital, therefore, had to be acquired in the financial markets of the North and Europe in competition with an expanding and increasingly productive mechanized industry.

Likewise the shipping and sale of cotton tended to be handled by mercantile agencies

Trade unions organized to improve wages and working conditions. A contemporary illustration shows the Shoemakers' Strike of 1860, in Lynn, Massachusetts, in which 800 women workers paraded, demanding higher pay.

in the principal Northeastern seaports, because the highly specialized shipping requirements of the Southern economy could not be met efficiently except in conjunction with the more general trade of the major ports. Southern ports did not offer such possibilities of pooling cargo and warehouse space. Southerners complained that their own business was taken away from them by Northern merchants who obtained the profits of the cotton trade and kept the Southern planters dependent upon them for mercantile credit.

Nevertheless, the South continued to follow its policy of determined divergence from the economies of the other sections of the nation and continued to seek a free world market. Not all whites living in the South were in agreement on means and methods, but the most extreme elements felt that there was only one way in which their section could escape economic submission to the North and West. Only through secession from the Union, they were convinced, could the Southern states avoid being damaged by future economic policies which would destroy slavery and the plantation system. Ultimately the South would indeed choose the path of secession, a path that would lead not only to the end of the institutions they had sought to save but also to the most destructive event in our national history—the Civil War.

BIBLIOGRAPHY

Vols. IV and V of Edward Channing's *History of the United States* (New York: Macmillan, 1905–1925), chronicle the growth of democratic government from 1824 to 1848. For a briefer assessment of the period by an expert in political theory, see Charles M. Wiltse, *The New Nation 1800–1845* (New York: Hill & Wang, 1961). Chilton Williamson, *American Suffrage from Property to Democracy 1760–1860* (Princeton: Princeton University Press, 1960), contains specific data on voting which had never before been compiled.

Many students will find Russel B. Nye, *Society and Culture in America 1830–1860* (New York: Harper & Row, 1974), the most useful one-volume account of topics discussed in Chapter 7. Social, cultural, economic, and political aspects of the Jacksonian period are treated in Edward Pessen, *Jacksonian America: Society, Personality, and Politics* (Homewood, Ill.: Dorsey Press, 1978), and in two Daniel J. Boorstin volumes, *The Americans: The Democratic Experience* (New York: Random House, 1973) and *The Americans: The National Experience* (New York: Random House, 1965). Paul W. Gates, *The Farmer's Age: Agriculture 1815–1860* (New York: Harper & Row, 1968), is excellent. A valuable assessment of transportation, manufacturing, and the wage earner is contained in George R. Taylor, *The Transportation Revolution 1815–1860* (New York: Harper & Row, 1951). Edwin S. Gaustad, *A Religious History of America* (New York: Harper & Row, 1966), provides basic factual data and sound interpretation. Also recommended are Bernard A. Weisberger, *They Gathered at the River* (New York: Quadrangle, 1966), Timothy L. Smith, *Revivalism and Social Reform* (New York: Harper & Row, 1975), E. Brooks

Holifield, *The Gentlemen Theologians* (Durham: Duke University Press, 1978), and Herbert Hovenkamp, *Science and Religion in America 1800–1860* (Philadelphia: University of Pennsylvania Press, 1978).

Reform trends and specifics are provocatively presented in Alice F. Tyler, *Freedom's Ferment* (New York: Harper & Row, 1962), David J. Rothman, *The Discovery of the Asylum* (Boston: Little, Brown, 1971), Ronald G. Walters, *American Reformers 1815–1860* (New York: Hill & Wang, 1978), and David B. Davis, ed., *Ante-Bellum Reform* (New York: Harper & Row, 1967). The standard biography of Dorothea Dix is Helen E. Marshall, *Dorothea Dix: Forgotten Samaritan* (Chapel Hill: University of North Carolina Press, 1937). Books that place Dix's career in its historical context include Albert Deutsch, *The Mentally Ill in America* (Garden City: Doubleday, 1937), Norman Dain, *Concepts of Insanity in the United States, 1789–1865* (New Brunswick, N.J.: Rutgers University Press, 1964), and Gerald N. Grob, *The State and the Mentally Ill: A History of the Worcester State Hospital in Massachusetts, 1830–1920* (Chapel Hill: University of North Carolina Press, 1966). Gerald Carson, *Cornflakes Crusade* (New York: Holt, Rinehart and Winston, 1957), is a readable history of dietary reform. Authoritative on a frightening scourge of the times is Charles E. Rosenberg, *The Cholera Years: 1832, 1849, and 1866* (Chicago: University of Chicago Press, 1962). Eleanor Flexner, *Century of Struggle: The Woman's Rights Movement in the United States* (Cambridge: Harvard University Press, 1959), can open vistas, as can Robert F. Gleckner and Gerald E. Enscoe, eds., *Romanticism: Points of View* (Englewood Cliffs, N.J.: Prentice-Hall, 1970). Octavius B. Frothingham, *Transcen-*

dentalism in New England (Philadelphia: University of Pennsylvania Press, 1972), is old but still standard. For literature, see several works by Van Wyck Brooks including *The Flowering of New England* (New York: Dutton, 1936), Chapter 11–16 in Vol. I of Harvey Wish, *Society and Thought in America* (New York: McKay, 1950–1962), and especially Chapters 18–46 in Robert E. Spiller et al., eds., *Literary History of the United States*, 2 vols. (New York: Macmillan, 1974).

Frank L. Mott's *American Journalism: A History of Newspapers* (New York: Macmillan, 1962) and Vol. I of his *A History of American Magazines* (Cambridge: Harvard University Press, 1938–1968) are storehouses of information. Nye's *Society and Culture*, previously cited, is especially good on popular writing and entertainment; it may be supplemented by his *The Unembarrassed Muse: The Popular Arts in America* (New York: Dial Press, 1970). See also Richard Moody, *America Takes the Stage* (Bloomington: Indiana University Press, 1955), Gilbert Chase, *America's Music* (New York: McGraw-Hill, 1966), Wayne Andrews, *Architecture, Ambition, and Americans* (Glencoe, Ill.: Free Press, 1964), and particularly Oliver Larkin's handsome *Art and Life in America*, rev. ed. (New York: Holt, Rinehart and Winston, 1960).

Among the most discerning commentaries on educational developments is Frederick Rudolph, *The American College and University* (New York: Knopf, 1962). For science see George H. Daniels, *American Science in the Age of Jackson* (New York: Columbia University Press, 1968), and Dirk J. Struik, *Yankee Science in the Making* (New York: Macmillan, 1962). Abolitionists are accorded detailed treatment in Louis Filler, *The Crusade Against Slavery 1830–1860* (New York: Harper & Row, 1960), Merton L. Dillon, *The Abolitionists: The Growth of a Dissenting Minority* (DeKalb: Northern Illinois University Press, 1974), and Ronald G. Walters, *The Antislavery Appeal: American Abolitionism after 1830* (Baltimore: Johns Hopkins University Press, 1976). For Northern blacks, consult Leon F. Litwack, *North of Slavery: The Negro in the Free States* (Chicago: University of Chicago Press, 1961); for free Southern blacks, Ira Berlin, *Slaves Without Masters: The Free Negro in the Antebellum South* (New York: Pantheon Books, 1974); for urban slavery, Richard C. Wade, *Slavery in the Cities* (New York: Oxford University Press, 1964); for political antislavery, Richard H. Sewell, *Ballots for Freedom* (New York: Oxford, 1976); and for slavery as a whole, Kenneth M. Stampp, *The Peculiar Institution* (New York: Knopf, 1956). Many additional books on slavery are listed in the bibliography at the end of Chapter 12.

The most famous discussion of democracy in the Jacksonian period is contained in the French observer Alexis de Tocqueville's *Democracy in America*, 2 vols., published in several editions since 1835–1840. Arthur M. Schlesinger, Jr., won a Pulitzer Prize for *The Age of Jackson* (Boston: Little,

Brown, 1945). Claude Bowers vividly describes *The Party Battles of the Jackson Period* (New York: Octagon Books, 1965). For other interpretations of the age of Jackson see Glyndon G. Van Deusen, *The Jacksonian Era 1828–1848* (New York: Harper & Row, 1959), Leonard D. White, *The Jacksonians* (New York: Free Press, 1965), Marvin Meyers, *The Jacksonian Persuasion* (Stanford: Stanford University Press, 1957), Richard P. McCormick, *The Second American Party System* (Chapel Hill: University of North Carolina Press, 1966), James C. Curtis, *Andrew Jackson and the Search for Vindication* (Boston: Little, Brown, 1976), Michael P. Rogin, *Fathers and Children: Andrew Jackson and the Subjugation of the American Indian* (New York: Knopf, 1975), Peter Temin, *The Jacksonian Economy* (New York: Norton, 1969), and Lee Benson, *The Concept of Jacksonian Democracy* (Princeton: Princeton University Press, 1961).

John W. Ward, *Andrew Jackson: Symbol for an Age* (New York: Oxford University Press, 1962), places emphasis on nonpolitical aspects of the Jackson period. Marquis James, *Portrait of a President*, Vol. II of *Andrew Jackson* (New York: Grosset & Dunlap, 1956), is a sympathetic account of "Old Hickory" and his political career. James Parton, *The Presidency of Andrew Jackson*, Vol. III of *The Life of Andrew Jackson*, ed. Robert V. Remini (New York: Harper & Row, 1967), has an illuminating introduction by Remini. Remini's own writings include *Martin Van Buren and the Making of the Democratic Party* (New York: Norton, 1970), *The Election of Andrew Jackson* (Philadelphia: Lippincott, 1963), *Andrew Jackson* (New York: Harper & Row, 1969), and *Andrew Jackson and the Bank War* (New York: Norton, 1968). Although Remini's *Andrew Jackson and the Course of American Empire 1767–1821* (New York: Harper & Row, 1977) does not reach the period covered in this part of our text, it will appeal to many students interested in Jackson the man and the leader.

Charles S. Sydnor, *The Development of Southern Sectionalism 1819-1848* (Baton Rouge: Louisiana State University Press, 1968), is a scholarly treatment of this important Southern trend. A detailed discussion of the important nullification controversy will be found in Chauncey S. Boucher, *The Nullification Controversy in South Carolina* (Westport, Conn.: Greenwood Press, 1969). A more recent interpretation is found in William W. Freehling, *Prelude to Civil War: The Nullification Controversy in South Carolina 1816–1836* (New York: Harper & Row, 1966). Jackson's anti-Bank policies are discussed in Ralph C. H. Catterall, *The Second Bank of the United States* (Chicago: University of Chicago Press, 1903; reprint, 1960), and in Thomas P. Govan, *Nicholas Biddle: Nationalist and Public Banker 1786–1844* (Chicago: University of Chicago Press, 1959).

Robert G. Gunderson has written a delightful account of events surrounding the election of 1840 in *The Log-Cabin Campaign* (Lexington: University of Kentucky Press, 1957).

Robert J. Morgan deals with Tyler's presidency from the viewpoint of a political scientist in *A Whig Embattled* (Lincoln: University of Nebraska Press, 1954). John Tyler's White House bride, the vivacious and very young Julia Gardiner, lives again in Robert Seager, *And Tyler Too* (New York: McGraw-Hill, 1963). Bray Hammond, *Banks and Politics in America from the Revolution to the Civil War* (Princeton: Princeton University Press, 1957), is valuable for political-entrepreneurial interpretations of the period. Douglass C. North, *The Economic Growth of the United States 1790–1860* (New York: Norton, 1966), is recommended. And few basic books are fresher or more provocative than Henry Cohen, *Business and Politics in America from the Age of Jackson to the Civil War: The Career Biography of W. W. Corcoran* (Westport, Conn.: Greenwood Press, 1971).

Bernard De Voto, *Year of Decision: 1846* (Boston: Houghton Mifflin, 1961), is a dramatic treatment of Western developments. Nicholas P. Hardeman, *Wilderness Calling* (Knoxville: University of Tennessee Press, 1977) is perhaps the best-written account of one family's western pioneering experiences. Commercial interests and westward expansion are discussed in Norman A. Graebner, *Empire on the Pacific* (New York: Ronald Press, 1955). Frederick Merk, *Manifest Destiny and Mission in American History* (New York: Knopf, 1963), and *The Monroe Doctrine and American Expansionism 1843–1849* (New York: Knopf, 1966), are products of a major authority's mature scholarship. Albert K. Weinberg, *Manifest Destiny* (Gloucester, Mass.: Peter Smith, 1958) is a reprint of an older book of continuing value. Frederick J. Turner, *Frontier and Section* (Englewood Cliffs, N.J.: Prentice-Hall, 1961), is an important collection of essays by an oft-cited master.

For a discerning reevaluation of the West in history and literature, see Henry N. Smith, *Virgin Land* (New York: Vintage Books, 1957). Walter P. Webb, *The Great Plains* (New York: Grosset & Dunlap, 1957), is a regional study by an authority. A classic of the frontier, Josiah Gregg's *Commerce of the Prairies,* abr. ed. by Milo M. Quaife (Lincoln: University of Nebraska Press, 1967), presents the retouched account of a Sante Fe trader. Scholarly and readable books about Indians, dealing in whole or in part with the period, are Grant Foreman, *Five Civilized Tribes* (Norman: University of Oklahoma Press, 1971), and his

Indian Removal (Norman: University of Oklahoma Press, 1969), William T. Hagan, *American Indians* (Chicago: University of Chicago Press, 1961), and Ronald N. Satz, *American Indian Policy in the Jacksonian Era* (Lincoln: University of Nebraska Press, 1975).

Students who enjoy the biographical approach to history may wish to read all or parts of Samuel F. Bemis, *John Quincy Adams,* 2 vols. (New York: Knopf, 1949 and 1956), Charles M. Wiltse, *John C. Calhoun,* 3 vols. (New York: Russell & Russell, 1970), Glyndon G. Van Deusen, *The Life of Henry Clay* (Boston: Little, Brown, 1937), R. L. Rusk, *The Life of Ralph Waldo Emerson* (New York: Columbia University Press, 1957), Charles Sellers, *James K. Polk,* 2 vols. to date (Princeton: Princeton University Press, 1957 and 1966), Charles H. Foster, *The Rungless Ladder: Harriet Beecher Stowe and New England Puritanism* (New York: Cooper Square reprint of 1954 ed.), Holman Hamilton, *Zachary Taylor,* 2 vols. (Hamden, Conn.: Shoe String Press reprint of 1951 ed.), Claude M. Fuess, *Daniel Webster,* 2 vols. (New York: Plenum, 1968), Walter M. Merrill, *Against Wind and Tide: A Biography of William Lloyd Garrison* (Cambridge: Harvard University Press, 1963), and Kathryn K. Sklar, *Catharine Beecher: A Study in American Domesticity* (New Haven: Yale University Press, 1973. For the colorful details of political campaigns from 1824 through 1848, see Vols. I and II of Arthur M. Schlesinger, Jr., and F. L. Israel, *History of American Presidential Elections,* 4 vols. (New York: McGraw-Hill, 1971).

Otis A. Singletary, *The Mexican War* (Chicago: University of Chicago Press, 1960), Robert S. Henry, *The Story of the Mexican War* (New York: Ungar, 1960), William R. Hogan, *The Texas Republic* (Austin: University of Texas Press, 1969), Frederick Merk, *Slavery and the Annexation of Texas* (New York: Knopf, 1972), David M. Pletcher, *The Diplomacy of Annexation: Texas, Oregon, and the Mexican War* (Columbia: University of Missouri Press, 1973), and Gene M. Brack, *Mexico Views Manifest Destiny 1821–1846* (Albuquerque: University of New Mexico Press, 1975) are recommended. For an Englishwoman's view of Jacksonian America see Frances Trollope, *Domestic Manners of the Americans,* ed. Donald Smalley (New York: Random House, 1970). *Fluctuations in American Business 1790–1860* (New York: Russell & Russell, 1969), by Walter B. Smith and Arthur H. Cole, is an invaluable reference work.

---

*Denotes availability in paperback.

Time Line

4

A HOUSE DIVIDED

By 1850 the United States had attained the size and physical resources of a powerful nation, but it was not yet a nation in the full sense. In fact, there was some doubt whether it was a nation at all, or whether it could become one. Nation or not, the United States had grown with remarkable speed. In forty-seven years this country had moved its western border from the Mississippi River to the Pacific Ocean and had almost trebled its area. What had begun as a string of states along the Atlantic coast had now become a transcontinental two-ocean republic. During the same half century the population had increased more than fourfold and the economic output at least sixfold. No other country in the world matched these growth rates.

In some respects the United States had also made great progress toward resolving the tensions between individual liberty and central authority that had been the main preoccupation of the Founding Fathers. In previous history the governments of nation-states had gained strength at the expense of the individual freedom and local self-government. But under America's federal system, many domestic decisions were left for local action, while the collective weight of all the states

could be thrown behind the central government in matters that concerned them as a group. Thus, strength was not gained at the sacrifice of democratic self-rule.

The United States had also succeeded in maintaining a remarkable cohesion, considering the dimensions of continental expansion. In the first decade of the nineteenth century, after the acquisition of the Louisiana Territory, the problem of communication and transportation over vast distances had created a danger of national disintegration. But the rapid development of turnpikes, steamboats, canals, and railroads—not to mention the telegraph—had reduced these distances to manageable proportions, knitting the country together physically even as it grew larger.

Nevertheless, at mid-century there was still uncertainty whether centralizing forces would complete the forging of a nation or whether they might drive out of the Union those who felt threatened by them. The slavery issue—more precisely, the question of whether slavery should be allowed to expand into the new territories—was rapidly polarizing the American people into two sectional factions. And by 1860 the polarization of the political parties, which until then had bridged sectional antagonisms, was identical with sectional polarization.

The Republican party had become spokesman for the dynamic, expansive, freelabor ideology of Northern commercial/industrial capitalism as well as for the moral idealism of the antislavery movement. Its leaders viewed slavery as incompatible not only with the future of a democratic, competitive, capitalist society but also with the ringing phrases of the Declaration of Independence and the Preamble to the Constitution, which proclaimed all men to be created equal, possessing the unalienable rights of liberty and justice. Southern whites, who considered slavery essential to their domestic tranquility and general welfare, feared that Abraham Lincoln spoke for the Northern majority in expressing the hope that a Republican triumph would place slavery on the road to ultimate extinction. When Lincoln was elected President, the South invoked its version of the Jeffersonian heritage—that ultimate power lay in the states and not in the Union, that the Union was a voluntary association of separate and autonomous states, and that the states could go out of the Union by their separate acts just as they had come into it.

The effort of the Southern states to put this theory into practice led to a four-year civil war (1861–1865) which constituted the greatest internal crisis in American history. Each side appealed to the revolutionary tradition of the Founding Fathers to justify its cause. For the South it was a war to gain independence from what Southern whites perceived as the oppressive domination of an alien government. The revolutionary nature of Northern war aims by 1863 were best expressed by Lincoln in the Gettysburg Address. The Founders of the Republic, said Lincoln, had brought forth a new nation conceived in liberty and dedicated to the proposition that all men are created equal. But although conceived in liberty, this new nation had become the largest slaveholding country in the world. Now the North was engaged in a great civil war to determine whether the nation would have a *new birth of freedom* and whether, freed from the evil of slavery, it could survive.

Northern victory settled the question of the nature of the American system. The Union became a single nation consisting of member states whose powers were subordinated to those of the central government, thereby fulfilling the dreams of some Founding Fathers while destroying the hopes of others. After the Civil War the Thirteenth, Fourteenth, and Fifteenth Amendments wrote into the Constitution the ultimate ascendancy of national authority. These Amendments emancipated four million slaves and granted them civil and political equality. By doing so, they broadened the application of democracy and reaffirmed—at least in principle—the worth and right to freedom of each human being. But except during the few years of Reconstruction this affirmation existed only in principle, for in the decades after 1877 the whole nation acquiesced in the segregation and disfranchisement of black Americans.

The Civil War was the most important turning point in American history. During that era, Americans made choices and took actions that decisively affected the future, not always in ways they intended. The preservation of the Union meant also the triumph of industrial America, and this triumph meant that Americans were moving into a different era in which the values of individualism, competition, democracy, and the general welfare would have to be reinterpreted and reaffirmed in a social and economic environment much more complex than that envisioned by the Founding Fathers.

The histories written of the Civil War and Reconstruction offer a vivid example of how interpretations of the past reflect preoccupations and attitudes of the present. By 1890 most white people in both North and South agreed that while slavery had been wrong and Northern victory in the war probably a good thing, Reconstruction was a disastrously ill-advised attempt to elevate freed slaves to positions of equality and power for which they were not qualified. This national consensus in favor of white supremacy formed the basis for most historical treatments of Reconstruction until the 1950s. According to these treatments, vengeful Republicans forced black suffrage upon a prostrate South that for more than a decade reeled helplessly under the corrupt and ignorant rule of carpetbaggers, scalawags, and freedmen. Goaded to a just fury, white Southerners turned on their tormentors and finally overthrew the "Black Republicans" in 1877 to redeem the South from plunder and ruin.

In the 1930s and 1940s some historians extended this interpretation backward in time to include the causes of the Civil War. They portrayed the South as the victim of vicious abolitionist propaganda and of demagogic antislavery politicians who stirred up sectional hatred. Slavery, in this view, was a benign institution that would have gradually and peacefully evolved into freedom if Northern agitators had not provoked a war that, while abolishing slavery, so embittered race relations in the South that reconciliation was postponed for generations.

A fundamental revision of these interpretations accompanied and followed the civil rights movement of the 1950s and 1960s. This revision had been anticipated, of course, by some earlier scholars, especially by black historians such as W.E.B. Du Bois and Carter G. Woodson. The new interpretations drew parallels between the abolitionists and Radical Republicans of the Civil War generation and the civil rights workers of the 1960s, between Southern slaveholders or the Reconstruction Ku Klux Klan and the Citizens Councils or the Klan of the 1960s. Instead of an avoidable and tragic conflict, the Civil War became an inevitable clash between irreconcilable ideologies that accomplished a desirable social revolution—emancipation. Instead of a vengeful effort to humiliate a beaten foe, Reconstruction became an admirable attempt to create an interracial democracy in the South, an attempt that nevertheless failed because it did not go far enough in the direction of redistributing wealth and power.

These conflicting interpretations illustrate that history is not what *happened*, but rather what historians say about what happened. The past, like the present, is complex and ambiguous. We can never know all of it and must be content with flashes of insight that illuminate small corners of reality. Historians must ask questions of the past, but their answers (and indeed the questions themselves) will inevitably be colored by their own biases and limitations as fallible human beings.

TO THINK ABOUT AS YOU READ . . .

1. If you were writing a history of the Civil War, why would you say it happened? Could it have been avoided?
2. Could the problem of slavery have been solved by peaceful means? If so, how? If not, why not?
3. A noted historian once wrote that the poor whites of the South, of all Southerners, suffered most from slavery. Do you agree? If so, why? If not, why not?
4. What were the war aims of the opposing sides in the Civil War? How did these aims evolve or change during the four years of conflict?

5. How was it possible for Southerners to think realistically that they could win the war against the North? What factors in the end accounted for Northern victory?

6. Was Reconstruction a nightmare of suppression, corruption, and plunder or a fulfillment of the American dream of equality? Did Southern whites, Northerners, or freed slaves bear most of the responsibility for the collapse of Reconstruction governments? What Reconsruction policy would have made most sense?

Chapter 10

The Changing Nation

THE MODERNIZATION OF AMERICA

Characteristics of Modernization. The best word to describe the rapid changes experienced by Americans in the middle decades of the nineteenth century is "modernization." The consequences of modernization were as profound for the United States a century ago as they are for non-Western societies today.

In economic development, modernization, such as was occurring in the North, is characterized by four factors. The first is a heavy investment in "social overhead capital," or improved transportation and communication. This produces a transition from a localized subsistence economy to a regionally or nationally integrated market economy. The second factor is a rapid increase in the output per man-hour that results from technological innovation and the substitution of machines for human labor. The third factor is the evolution from decentralized handcraft manufacturing to centralized industry producing standardized, interchangeable parts. Last is the accelerated growth of the industrial sector as compared with other sectors of the economy.

Socially, modernization is marked by a growth in education, literacy, and mass communication and by a transition from a static, predominantly rural populace to an urbanizing population in which farms and villages become cultural as well as economic satellites of the urban/industrial market. Politically, modernization is accompanied by the rise of nationalism and centralized authority and by increased popular participation in government. Ideologically, modernization is characterized by an outlook that emphasizes change rather than tradition. In sum, modernization is the transition from a rural, village-oriented system of traditional personal and family ties to a dynamic, urban, market-oriented system of impersonal relationships.

Modernization was both cause and effect of the rapid advances in technology that had been taking place since the Revolution. It was also both cause and effect of the growing differences between North and South. As a labor-intensive economy, tying up large amounts of capital in the ownership of human beings, slavery inhibited technological innovation. The South feared change, while the North welcomed it and came increasingly to

247

see slavery and the South's conservatism as obstacles to the progress and greatness of America.

American Modernization. In nearly every index of modernization, this period marked the transition of America—with the partial and significant exception of the South—from a pre-modern to a modern society. In the 1850s middle-aged Americans could look back upon unprecedented changes in their own lifetimes. Since 1815 the development of steamboats, canals, macadamized roads, and railroads had radically increased the speed and reduced the cost of inland transportation. In 1815 the average cost of shipping freight had been 40¢ per ton-mile by wagon and 6¢ by water; in 1855 it was less than 3¢ by rail and 1¢ by water. Goods sent from Cincinnati to New York in 1817 took more than fifty days to reach their destination; by the early 1850s they required only six days. The same trip for passengers was reduced from three weeks to less than two days.

A few simple statistics will illustrate the pace of change in other indices of modernization also. While all sectors of the economy grew rapidly from 1840 to 1880, the rate of growth in the manufacturing sector was more than twice that of agriculture. The percentage of the labor force engaged in manufacturing nearly doubled during the same period, and the proportion of the population living in urban areas increased more than two and one half times. As a measure of the increased efficiency and higher standard of living produced by a modernizing economy, the *per capita* commodity output increased 72 percent and per capita income doubled during the same years.

This growth was a mixed blessing. The industrial working class did not share equally in the rising prosperity, for the real wages of blue-collar workers rose less than the income of other groups. And who can measure the human consequences of the transition from a craft-oriented system of manufacturing, in which skilled journeymen and apprentices worked alongside master craftsmen in small shops, to a factory system in which unskilled or semiskilled workers performed repetitious tasks at a machine? The loss of skills and of pride in craftsmanship, the growing separation of a working "class" from its employers, and the sense of relative deprivation caused by unequal distribution of increasing national wealth lay behind much of the labor unrest of this period.

In contrast with Europe, however, wages in America were high because of a relative shortage of labor. Despite rapid population growth, the supply of workers was never sufficient to meet the demand. This labor shortage in turn continued to stimulate technological innovation. New machines and new methods of production had to compensate for labor scarcity. Eli Whitney's attempt in 1798 to manufacture interchangeable rifle parts was sparked by the lack of skilled labor to make rifles in the traditional way. Although making interchangeable parts by machine was not exclusively an American development, it became known as the "American System" of manufacturing. By the 1850s, according to a team of visiting British industrialists, the American System was used for the production of a wide variety of goods including "doors, furniture, and other woodwork; boots and shoes; ploughs and mowing machines; wood screws, files, and nails; biscuits; locks, clocks, small arms, nuts and bolts."

Education and Innovation. A high level of literacy, an openness to change, and that intangible quality known as "Yankee ingenuity" also contributed to American technological progress. Economists consider education an investment in "human capital" that is vital to economic growth. The United States (with the exception of the South) had a higher percentage of its population in school than any other country in 1850. Literacy in the

North and especially in New England was nearly universal. It was no accident that most technological advances came out of New England, the most industrialized and modernized section of the country. As one observer wrote in 1829: "From the habits of early life and the diffusion of knowledge by free schools there exists generally among the mechanics of New England a vivacity in inquiring into the first principles of the science to which they are practically devoted. They thus frequently acquire a theoretical knowledge of the processes of the useful arts, which the English laborers may commonly be found to possess only after a long apprenticeship."

Although Prussia and France were far ahead of the United States in basic science and Britain had a clear lead in engineering and machine-tool capacity, American entrepreneurs and engineers, much like those of Japan today, had a knack for adapting foreign technology to their own needs and improving it through dozens of incremental changes. Thus, while the basic inventions of textile machinery were British, most of the important improvements in such machinery in the 1820s and 1830s were American. "Everything new is quickly introduced here," wrote a German visitor. "There is no clinging to old ways, the moment an American hears the word 'invention' he pricks up his ears."

Technology and Agriculture. Although industrial and urban growth outpaced that of

Education was an important factor in the economic growth of the United States. A contemporary painting shows young women attending evening school.

farm and village during this period, farming remained the principal occupation of Americans and the backbone of the economy. It provided most of the exports that earned foreign exchange, and helped provide the capital to launch America's industrial growth. Yet in most elements of husbandry, American farmers were incomparably careless and wasteful. Crop rotation was only occasionally practiced, fallow lands were not plowed to preserve fertility, and millions of tons of manure were allowed to wash away unused each year. Not until after the Civil War did most American farmers begin to approach the careful scientific farming of Europe.

The reason for such wastefulness, of course, was the existence of seemingly limitless fertile virgin land. It was cheaper to exhaust the soil in one area and move westward than to nourish the fertility of Eastern land. The constant extension of the frontier was the main reason for the abundance of American agriculture. But after 1830 the mechanization of farming and especially of the harvesting process became an increasingly important cause of rising productivity. Insofar as the substitution of machines for human muscles is an index of modernization, Northern agriculture (there was little mechanization in the South) was at the forefront of this process before the war.

For centuries there had been little improvement in farm implements. Plows were hardly better than those used by pre-Christian Egyptians: "In culture, harvesting and threshing of grains," writes one historian, "the colonists were not much advanced beyond Biblical times." Suspicion of "newfangled" ideas was stronger among farmers than among other groups. But the same problem that stimulated innovation in manufacturing—a shortage of labor—overcame this conservatism on the expanding frontier. The first improvements came with the development of an iron plow by Jethro Wood of New York in the 1810s and of a steel plow by John

Deere of Illinois in the 1830s (further improved by John Oliver of Indiana in the 1850s). Drills for faster planting of seed also came into use during the early nineteenth century. But these implements, which increased the acreage a farmer could plow and plant, actually made worse the chief bottleneck of farming—the harvest. A farmer could grow more grain than he and his family could reap.

The reaping process was vastly improved with the invention of horse-drawn reapers by Cyrus McCormick of Virginia and Obed Hussey of Maine in the 1830s—the most revolutionary development in nineteenth-century agriculture. Two workers and a horse could now harvest as much grain in a day as twenty workers with sickles. Of course, even this quantum leap in productivity would have meant little had not similar improvements in threshing come along at the same time. Here the principal invention was a combined threshing and fanning machine patented by John and Hiram Pitts of Maine in 1834. These inventions and the continued expansion of grain farming onto the prairies enabled wheat farmers to double their productivity per man-hour between 1835 and 1880 and to multiply the total wheat harvest sixfold. McCormick's reaper even made it possible for Northern farms to increase the production and export of wheat during the Civil War, despite the military enlistment of nearly a million farmers.

THE SOCIAL IMPACT OF MODERNIZATION

Ready-Made Clothing. Although crude sewing machines had been developed in France and America during the 1830s, the first patented machine with the crucial capacity to sew interlocking stitches was perfected by Elias Howe of Massachusetts in 1846. Howe exhibited his machine at the Quincy Hall Clothing Manufactory in Boston, where amazed visitors watched him sew 250 stitches in a minute, seven times the speed of a fast seamstress. In the next few years several other technicians made improvements in Howe's original machine. One of them, Issac M. Singer of upstate New York, began to sell sewing machines, without paying Howe a royalty. Howe finally won the resulting patent suit in 1854. To avoid more patent battles several manufacturers merged in 1856 to form the "Great Sewing Machine Combination," the first monopoly in American industrial history. By the 1870s nearly a million sewing machines were manufactured each year, three quarters of them by I. M. Singer Company, heir of the 1856 merger.

The Civil War was the catalyst for the ready-made clothing industry. The demand for millions of uniforms was a powerful spur to standarized production. When the Union government supplied manufacturers with a series of graduated measurements for soldiers, producers developed the concept of "sizing" and soon began to make clothes in regular sizes. By the end of the century, nine tenths of the men's clothing in the United States was ready-made. Although a smaller percentage of women's clothes was commercially manufactured, the development of standardized dress patterns helped democratize female fashions as well.

Technological changes and the Civil War also profoundly affected the shoemaking industry. In the 1850s adaptation of the sewing machine to leather hastened the trend to standardized production. But the sewing of uppers to soles remained handwork until 1862, when Gordon McKay, a Massachusetts entrepreneur, patented an improved sewing machine that mechanized this process. This invention and later ones not only enabled manufacturers to fill government contracts for army boots but laid the groundwork for a mechanized, mass-production shoe industry after the war. By the century's end factory shoes, like ready-made clothing, dominated the market.

These developments illustrated both the positive and negative impacts of mechanization. On the one hand, they lowered the cost of clothes and shoes, improved their quality and fit for the lower and middle classes, and democratized a consumer product that in Europe continued to function as a symbol of class differences. The sewing machine also lightened the drudgery of housewives while providing new employment opportunities for women and children outside the home. On the other hand, sweatshops (shops or lofts where women and children worked long hours at sewing machines for piecework wages) became a byword for labor exploitation. Not until unionization in the twentieth century did garment workers begin to win decent wages and working conditions. The mechanization of boot and shoe production destroyed an ancient craft and caused strikes and strife as skilled workers were replaced by machines or demoted to the status of machine tenders.

The "Balloon-Frame" House. Americans lived in a greater variety of houses a century ago than they do today. Ranging from the rickety wooden cabin of the slave or sharecropper and the log cabin or sod hut of the pioneer farmer to the substantial stone house of the Pennsylvania Dutch farmer and the Georgian or Neo-classical mansion of the rich, these structures had the virtues of variety and individuality. But in an era of rapid growth they also had disadvantages. Stone or brick construction was slow and required many skilled workmen. The same was true of substantial wooden houses, which for centuries had been built with thick timbers joined by mortise and tenon and fastened by wooden pegs. The skilled carpenters necessary for this kind of construction were in short supply in the mushrooming Midwestern cities of the period.

The lack of skilled workers inspired a new technique of inexpensive, speedy, standardized home construction—the "balloon-frame'' house. This was the now-familiar combination of machine-sawed boards (two-by-fours, two-by-sixes, etc.) nailed together as wall plates, studs, floor joists, and roof rafters to form the skeleton of a frame house. The technique was probably invented by a Connecticut Yankee, Augustine Taylor, who in 1833 moved to Chicago, the boom town of that decade. A severe housing shortage was solved by these balloon-frame structures, so-called by skeptics who sneered that the first strong wind would blow them away. In fact they were remarkably strong, for the boards were nailed together in such a way that every strain went against the grain of the wood. Such houses could be built in a fraction of the time and at a fraction of the cost of a traditional house. So successful was the "Chicago construction" that it spread to all parts of the country. By the end of the nineteenth century

at least half of all American homes were built in this fashion. The proportion today is three quarters.

The balloon-frame house would not have been possible without a related revolution in the manufacture of nails. New England factories pioneered in the mechanization of the handcraft methods of nail making in the 1820s, cutting the price of nails by two thirds and creating another mass-production industry.

Plumbing, Lighting, and Heating. Changes inside homes also had a large impact on the way middle-class urban Americans lived. Bathing was a once-a-week occurrence at best when water had to be pumped by hand, heated in an open fireplace, carried to a tin tub, and drained by bailing after the bath. Before mid-century, wealthier homeowners

A severe housing shortage and a revolution in manufacturing nails led to the success of the "ballon-frame" house, shown here under construction. This method of building is still in use.

and better hotels had installed tubs with running water heated by pipes passing through a boiler, but such contrivances were rare in modest urban homes and virtually nonexistent for the majority who lived in rural areas. The same was true of toilets, which first appeared in the 1830s but made little headway at a time when relatively few cities had municipal water systems (about one hundred places had them by 1860) and even fewer had sewer systems. By the 1880s many middle-class urban homes had hot and cold running water and "modern" bathroom equipment, but the outdoor privy and the Saturday night hand-filled bathtub remained standard for rural Americans. Even as late as 1900 Baltimore had 90,000 outdoor privies.

Improvements in lighting, cooking, and heating spread more widely than improvements in plumbing. For light, most houses before 1860 used candles or lamps that burned one of several kinds of animal or vegetable oil. Whale oil was the cleanest and safest fuel, but it was expensive. Coal, oil, lard, and camphene (turpentine and alcohol) were cheaper, but the first two were dirty and the last dangerous. Gas derived from coal had been used for lighting as early as 1806. While most cities had piped-in gas supplies by the time of the Civil War, this form of lighting was confined mainly to streets, public places, and a few wealthy homes. After the discovery of petroleum at Titusville, Pennsylvania, in 1859, kerosene lamps became the ubiquitous source of home lighting, persisting long after Thomas A. Edison perfected the incandescent electric light bulb in 1879.

As late as 1840 in most homes, food was still cooked in an open fireplace. In 1834 Philo P. Stewart, a Connecticut-born abolitionist, missionary to the Indians, founder of Oberlin College, and inveterate tinkerer, patented a stove that with subsequent improvements became the standard wood- or coal-burning kitchen appliance for the second half of the nineteenth century.

Another Connecticut Yankee, Eliphalet Nott, president of Union College, patented several improvements of the basic Franklin heating stove and invented the first stove to burn anthracite coal. By the 1840s many homes were heated by such stoves, and European visitors were already complaining that Americans kept their houses too warm. Central heating with hot air first made its appearance in the 1830s. The "radiator" heated by steam or hot water piped from a basement boiler became common in the last three decades of the century.

The Icebox. The use of ice to preserve food was mainly a nineteenth-century development. The icebox was entirely so. Nothing better illustrated Yankee ingenuity and enterprise than the career of Frederic Tudor of Boston, the "Ice King." A passing remark at a party in 1805 gave him the idea of exploiting one of New England's few natural resources—the ice on its ponds. By 1825 Tudor and his Cambridge partner Nathaniel Wyeth had perfected an ice-cutting machine that mechanized the "harvesting" process, and through trial and error had worked out the best methods for building and insulating ships to transport the ice as well as icehouses to store it. The old underground icehouses had suffered a seasonal loss from melting of at least 60 percent. Inside Tudor's heavy-timbered double walls with sawdust insulation, the loss was only 8 percent.

In 1833, Tudor sent one of his ships with 180 tons of ice from Boston to Calcutta, crossing the equator twice in a voyage of four months and arriving with the cargo intact. Although the main export markets for ice were the American South and the West Indies, Tudor shipped his product all over the world. In the 1850s Boston exported up to 150,000 tons of ice per year.

Tudor's achievements helped make possible the "icebox" (an American word), which by 1860 was a common feature of American households. These large wooden boxes on legs, lined with tin and zinc and interlined with charcoal, improved the American diet and extended the season for fresh fruits and vegetables. Meat could be preserved longer without salting. Ice cream became a widely enjoyed pleasure instead of a rare luxury. Americans began to put ice in their drinks, to the consternation of European visitors. Even that abomination in British eyes, iced tea, made its appearance before the Civil War. After the war the development of refrigerated railroad cars further improved the quality and variety of fresh fruits and vegetables available in all parts of the country. It also permitted the meat-packing industry to become centralized in Chicago and to serve a national market with its products.

MODERNIZATION AND REFORM

The Protestant Ethic and Reform. Economic growth and a rising standard of living depend not only on material factors but also on intangibles such as social values. The openness to change and the emphasis on education in Northern states have already been mentioned as important contributors to economic development. Equally important were attitudes toward work. There is universal agreement that nineteenth-century Americans (at least those in the North, and especially those

Refrigeration permitted the centralization of the meat-packing industry. This view is of the Union Stockyards in Chicago in 1866.

in New England) were infused with the work ethic. "The national motto," wrote a British observer of the United States, "should be 'All work and no play.' " This produced some unlovely habits, such as the tendency of Americans to bolt their food in order to lose little time from labor. But it also reinforced a value system that was well adapted to modernization.

This value system was more or less synonymous with what is generally called the Protestant Ethic—or sometimes the Puritan Ethic, since its roots lay in Puritan attitudes toward work as a glorification of God and idleness as an instrument of Satan. Emphasizing hard work, thrift, sobriety, reliability, self-discipline, self-reliance, and the postponement of immediate gratification for the sake of long-range goals, the Protestant Ethic reinforced precisely those values best suited to modernization and capitalist development. There was also a close relationship between the Protestant Ethic and many of the reform movements. These movements grew out of the evangelical enthusiasm of the Second Great Awakening (1800–1830) and the radical idealism of transcendentalism. In addition to urging Christians to stop committing such social sins as fornication, drunkenness, violation of the Sabbath, and enslavement of other human beings, reformers sought to instill in the poor, the idle, the depraved, and the intemperate "the virtues of true Protestantism—industry, sobriety, thrift and piety"—to enable them to reform themselves.

Another link between reform and modernization was provided by the voluntary associations that carried on reform activities. The social network of pre-modern societies is confined mainly to kin and village. An essential element of modernization is the transcendence of these localized and prescriptive ties by supralocal voluntary organizations formed for a specific purpose—trade unions, missionary societies, reform associations, pressure groups, and the like. This was

precisely what happened in the United States. There were only a few such associations in the eighteenth century, but by 1832 their number and variety astonished the French visitor, de Tocqueville. "Americans of all ages, all conditions, and all dispositions constantly form associations," he wrote in *Democracy in America*," associations to give entertainments, to found seminaries, to build inns, to construct churches, to diffuse books, to send missionaries to the antipodes . . . to found hospitals, prisons, and schools. . . . Wherever at the head of some new undertaking you see the government in France, or a man of rank in England, in the United States you will be sure to find an association."

Four of the reform movements that were related to modernization and had a crucial impact on American society after 1848 were the movments for temperance, education, women's rights, and abolition.

Temperance.   In the early nineteenth century Americans consumed an extraordinary amount of liquor. The average annual intake of spirituous and fermented alcohol per person of drinking age in the 1820s, for example, was seven to ten gallons—at least five times today's average. The most common distilled liquor in New England and seaport cities was rum. In the rest of the country it was usually whiskey. Beer and wine were drunk everywhere, but the most popular fermented drink in those days was hard cider (about 20 proof). No social occasion, whether a corn-husking bee or the installation of a clergyman, was complete without heavy drinking. Whiskey was a form of money on the frontier, and even church subscriptions were payable in liquid coin. Wretched transportation facilities before the 1820s meant that grain could be marketed over distances only in distilled form. Liquor was cheap, untaxed in most areas, and constituted a considerable portion of people's daily calorie intake. Many men greeted each day with a gill (four fluid ounces) of grog. John Adams regularly drank a pint of hard cider before breakfast. European visitors were astonished by the "universal practice of sipping a little at a time . . . [every] half an hour to a couple of hours."

The temperance movement arose partly as a reaction to excessive consumption. Beginning as a local religious and moral reform led by ministers, doctors, and women, the movement had expanded by the 1830s into a well-organized national crusade. At the height of its power in 1836, the American Temperance Union, a federation of 8000 local and regional societies, claimed a membership of 1.5 million. But this Union fragmented as members divided over the question of temper-

Militant prohibitionists demanded total abstinence from alcohol. After four hours in a bar room, this man has decided to "take the pledge."

THE TEMPERANCE CRUSADE.
FOUR HOURS IN A BAR ROOM.

1ST HOUR
NICAL INDIFFERENCE.

2ND HOUR
MOCKERY AND DEFIANCE.

3RD HOUR
AGE AND DESPAIR.

4TH HOUR
UNCONDITIONAL SURRENDER.

ance *vs.* prohibition. At first the movement had been for *moderation* in drinking, urging the elimination only of distilled spirits while endorsing temperate consumption of beer, wine, or cider. But by the 1830s temperance advocates became more militant, taking on the character of Christian perfectionism and moral regeneration that characterized other reform crusades of the decade. Like the abolitionists, who demanded universal emancipation, prohibitionists began to call for the total abolition of *all* alcoholic beverages. The requirement that members pledge total abstinence caused a dramatic drop in the membership of the American Temperance Union by 1840.

Up to this time temperance had been primarily a middle-class Protestant movement. Its goal was to impose the values of the Protestant Ethic, especially sobriety, upon the whole society. It was here that temperance intersected with modernization. Work patterns in pre-modern society were task-oriented rather than time-oriented. Artisans typically worked in bursts of effort until a particular job was completed, then took several days off, perhaps to spend their wages in heavy drinking. This irregularity was unsuitable to mechanized factories in which successful operation of complex and dangerous machinery required punctuality, reliability, and sobriety. Work became time-oriented rather than task-oriented.

It was no coincidence that the temperance movement in both Britain and America coincided with the Industrial Revolution in those countries. As part of the effort to instill the values of reliability and self-discipline in the working classes, employers supported the temperance movement and often forbade their workers to drink on *or* off the job.

Many workers, especially Irish and German immigrants, did not take kindly to such discipline. But in 1840 Protestant workingmen began to organize the Washington Temperance Societies. The first such society was founded in Baltimore by six heavy-drinking workmen who had been converted by a temperance lecture. Proudly declaring themselves "reformed drunkards," they moved with missionary zeal to organize societies all over the Northern and Western states. Native-born workers pointed to their endorsement of temperance as evidence of their superior dependability as compared to immigrant laborers.

The Washingtonian movement rejuvenated the temperance crusade. It was this period that produced an outpouring of sentimental songs with such titles as "Father, Dear Father, Come Home with Me Now" and the play *Ten Nights in a Bar Room*, which did for temperance what *Uncle Tom's Cabin* did for the antislavery movement.

The alliance of middle-class prohibitionists and Washingtonians helped push prohibition laws through fifteen state legislatures in the decade after Maine passed the first in 1846. But these laws had little impact on drinking habits. In a dress rehearsal for the national prohibition of the 1920s, they were widely evaded and most were eventually repealed. Whatever success the temperance cause enjoyed was the result of other factors, especially the evangelical revivals of the Second Great Awakening. In any case, the per capita consumption of alcohol appears to have declined sharply, perhaps as much as fivefold in the two decades before 1850. It never again approached the earlier level and rum and hard cider almost disappeared as American drinks.

Public Education. Traditional histories of education emphasize the great reforms inspired by Horace Mann, Secretary of the Massachusetts State Board of Education from 1837 to 1849. Before then, so the story goes, the New England common schools had fallen into decay, the few public schools elsewhere were "pauper" schools to which self-respecting parents would not send their children, teachers were semiliterate, and most children outside New England grew up with scarcely any formal schooling. Although this picture contains some truth, historians have recently uncovered evidence of a vigorous and growing educational system in the generation before 1837. It now appears that in New England and New York at least three quarters of the school-age children were in school and that in 1830 the average adult in those states had completed eight or nine years of schooling (though the typical school term was only three or four months each year).

Elsewhere the picture was less bright, although a mixture of public, private, and church schools provided some education for well over half the white population except on the frontier and in parts of the South. If this had not been true, one would have difficulty explaining the 95-percent literacy rate for the Americans in the North.

In some respects, however, things were as bad as the reformers of the 1840s painted them. Formal teacher training was almost nonexistent. Educational standards varied widely. Schools were generally ungraded. With rare exceptions, no public school system worthy of the name existed in the Deep South. The white illiteracy rate in the slave states was above 20 percent. Black illiteracy was close to 90 percent. Pennsylvania, New Jersey, and the Western states had little in the way of public school systems before 1835.

What Horace Mann and his fellow New England reformers did was to rationalize and centralize the existing patchwork pattern of public schools, to professionalize the calling of teacher, and by force of example and crusading zeal to spread this system through most of the North by 1860. Mann founded the first "normal" school for training teachers at Lexington, Massachusetts, in 1839. During the next two decades such institutions were established in several states. A half century later they evolved into teachers' colleges.

Massachusetts also pioneered in other reforms: a standardized graded curriculum, extension of public education to the secondary level, and the first compulsory attendance law (1852). Indeed, Mann did his work so well that some revisionist historians have criticized him for inaugurating a bureaucratic educational establishment that they regard as rigid and reactionary.

Revisionists have also condemned the school reformers for creating a system designed to impose Protestant middle-class values on all children in order to perpetuate the class structure through repression of ethnic minorities and the poor. It is true that the schools tried to teach the values of the Protestant Ethic. An essential task of education, wrote the Massachusetts Superintendent of Schools in 1857, was "by moral and religious instruction daily given" to "inculcate habits of regularity, punctuality, constancy and industry." *McGuffey's Readers* and the various readers and spellers of Noah Webster, which taught hundreds of millions of nineteenth-century children to read, reiterated these lessons. But the reformers of the time considered this progressive, not reactionary. The purpose of reform, after all, was not to keep the poor content in their humble station but to lift them out of povery by equipping them with the skills and values they needed to function and hold their own in a modernizing, fluid, competitive, capitalist economy. "Nothing but Universal education can counterwork this tendency to the domination of capital and the servility of labor," wrote Horace Mann in 1848. Education "does better than to disarm the poor of their hostility toward the rich; it prevents being poor." If this was unrealistic, it nevertheless bespoke the faith that all classes of Americans have placed in education.

Higher Education.

Ever since the founding of Harvard College in 1636, higher education had been associated primarily with the churches. In 1860, of the 207 colleges existing, 180 had been founded by churches—most of them during the previous generation as population flowed westward and the Protestant denominations struggled to educate a ministry and a lay leadership that would preserve and expand the faith on the frontier.

Many of the 6000 "academies" (with only 12,000 teachers) that provided nearly all the country's secondary education were also church-supported. In 1860 there were only 321 public high schools, nearly a third of them in Massachusetts.

After the Civil War, higher education became more secular and more broadly available. By 1890 twenty-five states outside the South had followed the lead of Massachusetts and passed compulsory school-attendance laws. By 1900 there were 6000 public high schools. The need for technical and scientific training to keep pace with rapid advances in these fields led to the founding of several schools modeled on the earlier examples of Rensselaer Polytechnic Institute (1824) and Massachusetts Institute of Technology (1865). In 1862 the Morrill Act created the land-grant colleges.

In the postwar decades the modern university outgrew the confines of the old Christian college. In 1869 Charles W. Eliot became the first nonclergyman president of Harvard and proceeded to liberalize the curriculum. In 1868 Andrew D. White launched another real university at Cornell, and in 1876 Daniel Coit Gilman started America's first true research university at Johns Hopkins.

The "Media."

Not all education took place in schools, of course. In addition to such institutions as the family, church, and voluntary associations, many channels existed for the dissemination of information and ideas. One of the most important was the public lecture. Abolitionists, temperance workers, and other reformers found lecturing to be the most effective means of spreading their message. Debating societies, literary associations, and the like grew up in almost every crossroads village. In 1826 Josiah Holbrook, a Massachusetts educator and friend of Horace Mann, founded the American Lyceum of Science and the Arts. The Lyceum was the first national agency for adult education, bringing lecturers on almost every conceivable subject to cities and hamlets throughout the nation.

Overshadowing all other means of communication, however, was the popular press. America was a newspaper culture. Technological advances in printing brought explosive growth in newspaper circulation after 1830. The expansion of the railroad network enabled urban dailies to print weekly editions for rural areas. By 1860 the weekly edition of Horace Greeley's New York *Tribune* had the unprecedented circulation of 200,000 copies. Samuel F.B. Morse's invention of the telegraph in 1844 made possible the instantaneous transmission of news over long distances and led to the formation of the Associated Press in 1848. The number of newspapers, which had doubled between 1825 and 1840, doubled again by 1860, reaching a total of 3300. Widespread literacy, the highly partisan nature of American journalism, and universal white manhood suffrage help explain the remarkable politicization of the population, an important factor in the emotion-charged controversies that led to civil war.

Popular magazines such as *Godey's Lady's Book* (started 1830), *Harper's Monthly* (1850), and the New York *Ledger* (1851) also enjoyed an expanding readership. These magazines fostered the spread of what might be called middle-brow culture. Prominent features in newspapers as well as magazines were sentimental poetry and moralistic fiction. Most novels were serialized in weeklies before appearing between hard covers. Harriet Beecher Stowe's *Uncle Tom's Cabin* was an outstanding example of this genre, unusual only in that it dealt with a controversial issue. Most popular novels focused on conventional domestic situations revolving around such themes as marriage, home, family, religion, and death. All of them championed God, motherhood and virtue. Most of the authors were women, who poured forth serialized novels year after year, reaching a huge audience—also mostly women—through the mass-circulation magazines and inexpensive books. Susan Warner's *Wide, Wide World* (1850) and Maria Susanna Cummins' *The Lamplighter* (1854) set the tone for literary soap opera. Marion Harland's first novel, *Alone* (1854), sold half a million copies. She wrote dozens more, the last one in 1919. Mary Jane Holmes produced a book a year from 1854 to 1907.

By all odds the leader of this school was Mrs. E. D. E. N. Southworth, who wrote her first novel, *Retribution* (200,000 copies), in 1849 after her husband had deserted her. She followed with sixty-one more in the next four decades. Serialization of her books lifted the *Ledger's* circulation to 400,000 by 1860.

Women's Rights. The preeminence of women in popular literature was only one sign of the growing opportunities and achievements of women at mid-century. But there was ambivalence in these achievements. Literary themes and popular culture reinforced the cult of domesticity and the sexual double standard that tied women to home, marriage, and family while men managed affairs in the outside world. At the same time, however, economic modernization was taking many women out of the home and putting them into the wage-earning labor force. The textile and garment industries were large-scale employers of women (and children). The inventions of the telegraph (1844), typewriter (1874), and telephone (1876) created new white-collar jobs for women.

The expansion of public education and the professionalization of teaching opened a major career opportunity for women, though women were paid less than male teachers. By the 1850s the "schoolmarm" was a familiar figure, especially in the Northeast. In the decades after Oberlin opened its doors to women in 1837, several other colleges followed suit. Beginning with Vassar (1865) and Wellesley and Smith (1875), numerous women's colleges were founded after the Civil War. (Mount Holyoke, founded in 1837, did not become a full-fledged college until 1888.)

The spirit generated by antebellum reform movements spurred demands for an end to women's inferior legal and political status. Female abolitionists began to speak out against sexual as well as racial slavery. The first women's rights convention was organized by Elizabeth Cady Stanton and Lucretia Mott and held at Seneca Falls, New York, in 1848. The movement's first priority was abolition of laws that treated unmarried women as minors and forced married women to turn over all property to their husbands. By 1861, more than half the states had taken steps toward ending such legal inequalities.

After the war, feminist leaders decided to concentrate on winning the right to vote, believing that the ballot was the key to open other doors to sexual equality. (See "Julia Ward Howe: Hymnist of Freedom.") By 1890 women had won the right to vote in school-board elections in seventeen states and territories. Wyoming territory granted women general suffrage in 1869 and, with its admission to statehood in 1890, became the first state to do so. Colorado followed in 1893, Utah and Idaho in 1896. Although no more states enfranchised women until 1910, the nineteenth century movement laid the

Julia Ward Howe: Hymnist of Freedom

by Holman Hamilton

It would be very easy—but utterly misleading—to depict Julia Ward Howe (1819–1910) solely in terms of literary success. She was successful in that very way, for she wrote "The Battle Hymn of the Republic," containing the most celebrated lyrics connected with the Civil War. In her long, fruitful life, she became the most famous American woman in the eyes of her contemporaries.

But there is a far greater significance in the Howe story—significance not alone in terms of her own times but also as people see her today. To grasp the importance of what she did, and all she represents, it is essential to understand the status of women in the first half of the nineteenth century. Most daughters of upper-class families, sheltered from infancy on, had no active part in improving the lot of the masses of humanity and were not supposed to. They took it for granted that they were not to plunge into causes, particularly those deemed unpopular or unfashionable. It was a rare wife and mother, with courageous conviction, who chose to dedicate herself to helping black

groundwork for passage of the Nineteenth Amendment in 1920.

The Broadening Antislavery Movement. Beginning as a moral-religious movement, abolitionism entered politics in 1840 with the founding of the Liberty party. Although some Liberty men insisted that the Constitution empowered the federal government to abolish slavery, officially the party stood only for the exclusion of slavery from new territories and states, for its abolition in the District of Columbia, and for prohibition of the interstate slave trade. In 1848 the Liberty party was absorbed by the more broad-gauged Free Soil party, which adopted a similar platform (omitting reference to the slave trade) but attracted many members who were more opposed to Southern political power than to slavery as such.

Genuine abolitionists watched these and subsequent developments leading to the founding of the Republican party in 1854 (treated in Chapter 11) with mixed feelings. While they welcomed the growth of antislavery sentiment in the North, they were well aware that it was often based on dislike of both slavery *and* blacks. Abolitionists kept their societies alive and continued to work for the equal rights and education of Northern blacks.

The emancipation of four million slaves by the Civil War enabled them to extend this work into the South as well. Northern freedmen's aid societies and abolitionist-led missionary associations founded hundreds of

people or to leading the fight to obtain the right to vote for the female half of the population. Such a wife and mother was Mrs. Howe.

Born in New York City, Julia Ward moved to Boston upon marrying Dr. Samuel Gridley Howe. Her choice of a husband indicated the qualities she valued, for Dr. Howe, a Massachusetts physician, devoted his career not to conventional practice but to aiding seriously handicapped children, adolescents, and adults. He gave "light" to the blind, "sound" to the deaf, and meaning to the retarded. Samuel's was a pioneering venture in medicine, psychology, and mercy. Encouraging him every inch of the way, and meanwhile bearing their four daughters and two sons, was his wife Julia.

Yet Julia was not a mere cheerleader. She was sincerely religious, and she worked with zeal to help fellow human beings of all kinds—through better public schools, through the training of qualified teachers, and through improving conditions in prisons and jails.

In an era when most whites looked down on blacks and did little or nothing on their behalf, she gave her best efforts to opposing slavery with her sharpest weapon—her pen. Together, Samuel and Julia Howe edited *The Commonwealth,* an antislavery paper. Julia had a major role in the enterprise, possessing both talent as a writer and persistence as a reformer.

Nor were writing and editing the only means the Howes used in their antislavery activities. Abolitionist men and women needed a headquarters where they could gather and exchange ideas and plan the next moves in their campaigns. Julia Ward Howe provided that headquarters in her own house, not simply as hostess but as a

elementary schools for freed blacks in the 1860s. These schools laid the foundation for the public school system established by Reconstruction governments in the Southern states. Abolitionist missionary societies also founded more than a hundred secondary schools and colleges, which provided nearly all of the higher education for Southern blacks until the twentieth century.

Most of the teachers in freedmen's schools were from New England. They conceived their mission to be the founding of "a real New England civilization" in the South. They modeled their curriculum on that of New England academies and colleges and they taught the same values—sobriety, thrift, work, austerity, and self-discipline.

The missionary schools trained most of the men and women who became leaders of the black community in the three generations after emancipation, but they failed to create a New England civilization in the South. Also doomed to failure for at least a century was the abolitionist hope for racial equality. Although most of the wartime and Reconstruction programs advocated by abolitionists were adopted—universal emancipation, enlistment of black soldiers, creation of a Freedmen's Bureau, equal civil and political rights incorporated into the Constitution, and a civil rights law barring segregation in public facilities (1875)—these measures were backed by too little moral conviction in the white population apart from the abolitionists. The war changed white racial attitudes enough to abolish slavery, but it did not change them

catalytic agent for freedom's cause. As she later said, she had "the honor of pleading for the slave when he was a slave."

Most authors become famous only when they address themselves to topics in which they have deep interest. Julia Ward Howe's literary growth perfectly illustrates this fact. In 1854, at thirty-five, she published a first volume of poems. Three years later, a second book of poetry followed, as well as a play. But the latter was no stunning triumph and the verses received little attention. The limelight, where she would soon shine, was reserved for a period of national upheaval. Author, subject, mind, and emotion found their inspiration in the Civil War. The accomplishment was entirely logical because now religious conviction and aggressive opposition to slavery blended with the cause of the Union, in which she also devoutly believed. Visiting the city of Washington, D.C., and Union soldiers stationed nearby, she was inspired to write a series of stanzas to the familiar tune of "John Brown's Body."

Lyrics came to Julia one night when she could not sleep. She was scarcely able to read what she scrawled in the dim light, and then—at last drowsy—was asleep.

When she wakened, she reviewed the words of the "Battle Hymn":

> Mine eyes have seen the glory of the
> coming of the Lord:
> He is trampling out the vintage where
> the grapes of wrath are stored;
> He hath loosed the fateful lightning of
> His terrible swift sword;
> His truth is marching on.

enough to abolish prejudice, discrimination, and segregation.

PREJUDICES, POLITICS, AND POLARIZATION

Immigration and Modernization. In the first forty years of the Republic immigrants did not come in large numbers. As late as the 1820s the number of immigrants averaged less than 13,000 per year. But rapid population growth, land shortages, and labor surpluses in Northern Europe, combined with cheap land, labor shortages, and higher wages in America, brought a quadrupling of this average in the 1830s. And during the decade from 1845 through 1854, the number of immigrants averaged nearly 300,000 annually.

Although these newcomers provided much of the labor force necessary for rapid economic growth, many of them received a cold welcome in the United States. Actually, anti-immigrant sentiment (or nativism) was not directed primarily against immigrants as such, but against *Catholic* immigrants. Nearly 40 percent of the immigrants to America during these years were Irish Catholics, driven to emigrate by the potato famine after 1845. Another 12 or 13 percent were German Catholics.

Settling mainly in cities, the Irish were the most concentrated and visible of the immigrant groups. They were poor, clannish, fiercely loyal to their church, hostile toward abolitionists and toward free blacks (with whom they competed for jobs), and therefore

Although it brought her only four dollars in cash, the poem had a sensational impact. So stirring were her lines that almost immediately they echoed and re-echoed throughout the North. Eventually they became integral in the nationwide musical and poetic tradition.

Julia did not rest on "Battle Hymn" laurels. With blacks freed and the Union saved, the vote for women was her next theme. This was another unpopular cause from many people's points of view, yet she adhered to it and led it, with all the enthusiasm she had earlier devoted to freeing the slaves. The Nineteenth Amendment, granting women suffrage, would not be adopted until 1919, nine years after Julia Ward Howe's death at the age of ninety-one. But younger women with whom she had been working carried to spectacular completion this second major reform.

The intellectual, philanthropic, and literary roots of Julia Ward Howe were planted in soil originally nurtured by the Emersons and Thoreaus. Thus she linked pre-Civil War Americans with citizens of our own times. And in a period characterized by social and political reforms of many kinds, she sustained and symbolized the ceaseless struggle to improve the lot of all who are disadvantaged, neglected, and underrated.

favorable toward slavery and the Democratic party. This aroused a nativist anti-Irish movement that strongly influenced the politics of several states in the 1840s and 1850s. The movement was fueled by traditional Protestant anti-Catholicism and by temperance reformers, abolitionists, proponents of public schools, and Protestant workingmen, who saw the Irish influx as a threat to their reforms, values, or status. In the 1840s there were numerous anti-Catholic riots and some pitched battles between Protestant and Catholic workingmen.

Nativism reached its height in the Know-Nothing movement, whose main goal was to exclude "foreigners" from political power by lengthening the naturalization period from five to as much as twenty-one years. In 1849 a secret nativist society called the Supreme Order of the Star-Spangled Banner was organized in New York City. When questioned about the Order, members would reply, "I know nothing." The Know-Nothings began to endorse political candidates, and by 1854 their strength had mushroomed to formidable proportions in several states,

where under the name of the American party they elected legislators, governors, and congressmen.

Then, within two or three years, the Know-Nothing movement subsided as quickly as it had risen. This was partly because of a falling off in immigration after 1854. More important, however, was the blazing intensity of the slavery issue. Northern nativists were absorbed into the new Republican party, while those in the South (remnants of the Whig party) retained the name American party and nominated Millard Fillmore for President in 1856.

The Know-Nothing legacy persisted in Northern politics, however, and during the next forty years most Catholics voted Democratic, while evangelical Protestants usually voted Republican. Local and state elections often turned on such "ethnocultural" issues as temperance, parochial schools, and the like. The animosities expressed by the Know-Nothings flared up again in the American Protective Association (APA) of the 1880s and 1890s and in continuing patterns of prejudice against Catholics and immigrants.

The Know-Nothings charged that Irish and German immigrants were stealing American elections and running the big city political machines.

Stereotypes, Sectionalism, and Modernization. The role of the new Republican party as the vehicle for both antislavery *and* anti-Catholic sentiment can be explained by the concept of modernization. The Republican ideology spoke for the dynamic, innovative forces of modernizing capitalism. Republicans considered slavery incompatible with modernization, for it was labor-intensive, tied up huge amounts of capital, inhibited technological innovation, kept labor at a low level of education and motivation, froze the social order, and denied masses of people the right of political participation. At the same time, Irish immigrants in the North were proslavery, antiblack, antitemperance, and a perceived threat to the values of Protestantism and the goals of reform. Many reformers considered Catholicism itself a sort of slavery, hostile to the modernizing values of an open, competitive, mobile society. Nativism and antislavery came out of the same social milieu.

The priest, the "papist" immigrant, and the swaggering, whip-wielding slaveholder thus became the principal negative reference symbols for the antislavery vanguard of Northern Protestantism. In turn, "Black Republicans" and "Puritan Republicans" were interchangeable negative reference symbols for Southern whites and Northern Catholics, who together were the backbone of the Democratic party. Indeed, a small civil war within the North paralleled the larger one between North and South. In 1862–1863 there were several Irish working-class riots against blacks and "Black Republicans," culminating in the terrible New York draft riot of July 1863.

Several historians have seen the Civil War as a revolution of modernization. According to this view, the North won mainly because its modernizing economy could mobilize the resources for modern war better than could the Southern economy. The war crippled the Southern ruling class, thereby removing the chief obstacle to the triumph of competitive, democratic, commercial-industrial capitalism. It freed the Southern labor force and opened to blacks new opportunities for education, social mobility, and political participation. It brought at least a partial remolding of Southern institutions in the New England image. But the effect of the Southern "counterrevolution" of the 1870s—and Northern acquiescence—in overturning many of the achievements of Reconstruction can be measured in the extent to which America's most serious social problems remain unsolved yet today.

Chapter 11

The Sectional Crisis 1848–1861

THE ORIGINS OF SECTIONALISM

The Transcontinental Republic. Between 1846 and 1848, with the settlement of the Oregon question and the Treaty of Guadalupe Hidalgo, the United States became in the full sense a two-ocean transcontinental republic. Except for Alaska, Hawaii, and a small segment of Arizona and New Mexico which would be acquired by the Gadsden Purchase in 1853, the country had reached its present territorial limits.

In one sense, the acquisition of the Southwest marked a fulfillment of American nationalism. No other nation on earth had grown so rapidly, and no people were prouder of their nation than the Americans, who boasted incessantly of the superiority of republican institutions. Yet, ironically, the climax of national growth also brought with it a crisis of national unity, for it precipitated a bitter rivalry between two dissimilar sections of the country—areas divided by the Mason-Dixon line and the Ohio River.

The problem of geographical rivalries was not a new one in the United States. In a country larger than all of western Europe, with immense diversity of soil, terrain, and climate, conflicts had arisen more than once between the economic interests of one area and those of another. In fact, American history has been full of such conflicts, and they have often been marked by a division between East and West. This was true, for instance, in the contest over the Bank of the United States at the time of Jackson, and later in the battle between the advocates of the coinage of silver and the defenders of the gold standard in 1896. The theme of sectional rivalry has been so persistent that historians sometimes dispute whether the deepest antagonisms in American history have been between conflicting social classes or ethnic groups or religious denominations or between conflicting sections.

Thus, the sectional crisis between North and South, which approached its climax between 1848 and 1860, was in no sense unique. But it did reach a unique pitch of intensity. Usually, competing sectional forces have sought only to gain advantage over one another within a Union which both accept, but on this occasion the South became so alienated that it made a titanic effort to withdraw from the Union.

The Southern Way of Life.

Historians have never been able to agree on any one factor as the primary cause of this division, but they do agree in recognizing a cluster of contributing factors. As far back as the seventeenth century, North and South had developed along dissimilar lines. Virginia, Maryland, and the colonies to the South had based their economy on crops which were limited to latitudes of warm climate and a long growing season. Tobacco, the first of these to be introduced in the colonies, was followed by rice and indigo in Carolina and sugar in Louisiana, and, most important, by cotton throughout the lower South after the invention of the cotton gin in 1793. For the cultivation of these crops the plantation had evolved as the economic unit of production. Within the plantation system the labor supply had grown to consist of black slaves.

Actually, slave labor did not become dominant until the eighteenth century, but by the time of the American Revolution, slaves had come to outnumber free persons in many plantation districts. In 1850, 32 percent of the South's total population was held in slavery. In South Carolina and Mississippi a majority of the population consisted of slaves.

Slavery.

Slavery presented a supreme paradox, for while slaves were human beings, they were also mere property. The complex relationships between masters and slaves reflected this paradox. On the one hand, most white Christians recognized the slaves' humanity and believed that they had immortal souls to be saved. (Of course the idea of a better life after death could also be useful in diverting slave unrest into religious zeal.) The law viewed slaves as human beings to the extent of making them liable to punishment for serious crimes. Some masters permitted a wedding service for slave couples even though they could not legally be married. On plantations where blacks and whites mingled closely in everyday life, relations of intimacy and affection often developed. Even the proslavery stereotype of the "happy and carefree" slave, a reflection more of the whites' wishful thinking than of reality, was a backhanded way of admitting the slave's right to human happiness.

The Southern way of life was supported by the labor of slaves. These workers are removing the seeds from cotton bolls in a cotton gin.

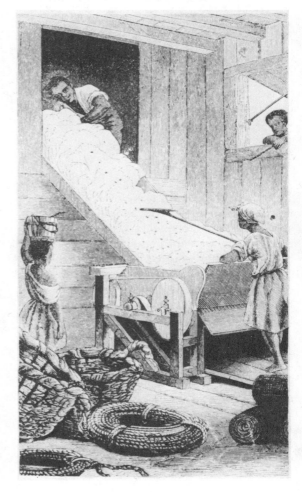

Slaves were property to be bought, sold, or raffled off at the will of their owners, as the poster shows.

On the other hand, slaves were chattels—pieces of property. They could be bought, sold, mortgaged, bequeathed by will, or taken in payment for debt if their owners became bankrupt. They could not legally marry, or own property, or in most states, be taught to read or write. Owners might let them have a family, earn money, and even buy their freedom, but until they were free, money, spouse, and children could be taken away at any moment.

The evils of slavery can be looked at in several ways. Many abolitionists condemned slavery primarily for its physical harshness—the flogging and branding of slaves, the separation of mothers from children at the auction block, the brutal labor conditions, especially for slaves who had been "sold down the river" to work in the sugarcane fields, and the low standard of diet, clothing, and housing. Slaves experienced much cruelty and hardship no doubt, but many slaves were kindly treated.

The worst feature of slavery may well have been its social and cultural impact on both slave and master. The slave's powerlessness tended to create a sense of dependency and to discourage self-reliance. Stable family life was difficult in a situation where parents and children might be sold away from each other, female slaves could be sexually exploited by white men, and a slave father was legally helpless to protect his wife and children. The master's power over fellow human beings tended to create feelings of superiority and domination. The racial theories that bolstered slavery bred in most white people a belief in black inferiority. Some blacks themselves subscribed to this notion.

Of course this does not mean that all or even most slaves carried the psychological scars of dependence and inferiority. On many plantations the black driver, rather than the overseer, exercised authority in day-to-day operations. As a sort of labor leader as well as "boss," the driver could do much to win better working conditions for the slaves. Drivers, slave artisans, and other blacks with critical skills played important roles in Southern life and provided other slaves with role models of self-respect and limited power *within* a system from which few could hope to escape.

Moreover, despite repression the slaves sustained a vigorous black culture largely independent of surrounding white institutions. Natural leaders in the slave quarters often became eloquent preachers in the "invisible institution" of the black church, whose congregations worshipped apart from whites (sometimes secretly) in spite of laws against separate worship. Some of these preachers, especially Gabriel Prosser in 1800 and Nat Turner in 1831, plotted armed insurrections to strike for freedom. The slaves created the most original and moving music in antebellum America—the spirituals—which expressed their longing for freedom as well as their resignation to sorrow, and evolved after the Civil War into the blues and eventually jazz.

Recent research suggests that while slavery made stable family life difficult, a majority of slaves nevertheless formed strong ties of kinship and family. Thus although slavery's impact on black people could be repressive, the countervailing force of a positive black culture provides an impressive example of survival in the face of adversity.

Slavery also put Southern whites on the defensive, ever fearful of slave insurrection and ever conscious that slavery was condemned throughout most of the Western world. As a result they isolated themselves more and more, imposing an "intellectual blockade" to keep out not only abolitionist ideas but any social ideas implying freedom or change. To defend their system, they idealized the society as romantic and chivalric. At best, they realized their ideal in the attainment of a real aristocracy. But the tradition was maintained at a high cost.

By 1850 the Southern system, its rural life and its slave labor, had led to the development of a somewhat conservative temper, a marked stratification of social orders, and a paternalistic type of society. The power of all landowners to rule their own workers on their own plantations had prevented the growth of a strong public authority. As a result, violence was frequent, and qualities of personal courage and physical prowess were especially valued. For instance, the practice of dueling, which had died out in the North, still prevailed. The taboo against women working outside the home was far stronger than in the North. Even women schoolteachers in the South were often Northerners.

The Northern Way of Life. It would be a mistake to think of the North as presenting a total contrast, for the majority of people in the free states also engaged in agriculture and lived a rural life. But the Northern economy and Northern life were more diversified. In the absence of a valuable export crop such as tobacco or cotton, many New England Yankees had turned early to commerce as a means of securing money to buy the imports they needed. During the Napoleonic wars, when their commerce was disrupted and the supply of imported manufactures was cut off, they had begun a manufacturing industry. As manufacturing grew, cities grew with it.

Prosperity and rapid economic growth in the North fostered a belief in progress and innovation quite different from the more traditional (or static) attitudes of the South. Although the factory system brought with it a certain amount of exploitation of labor through low wages, the fact that all men were free made for greater mobility, greater equality, more democracy, and less sharply defined social stratification than in the South. The modernizing North grew to value the commercial virtues of thrift, enterprise, and hard work, in contrast to the more military virtues which held a priority in the South.

Such differences as these can easily be exaggerated, for a great deal of frontier Americanism prevailed in both the North and the South. Evangelical Protestantism was the dominant religion of both sections. The materialistic pursuit of wealth motivated cotton planters as well as Yankee industrialists. To a European, all Americans seemed bumptiously democratic, and in the South the Whig party, favored by most planter aristocrats, could not have competed against the Democratic party at all unless it had adopted the democratic symbols of the log cabin, the coonskin hat, and the cider barrel.

THE BASES OF SECTIONAL ANTAGONISM

Regional dissimilarity, however, need not lead to conflict. In the United States today, states of the farm belt differ greatly from those of the Atlantic seaboard, but we tend to think of these differences as making the areas complementary, rather than antagonistic to each other. The antagonism which drove North and South to war in the mid-nineteenth century, therefore, needs to be explained.

Economic Causes.   In one sense the antagonism was economic, for the dissimilar economic interests of the North and the South caused them to favor opposite economic policies and therefore to clash politically. Essentially, the South, with its cotton economy, produced raw materials for a textile industry centered in Britain. Accordingly, the South sold on the world market, and in return it needed to buy its manufactured goods where they were cheapest, which was also in the world market, and to keep down taxes and governmental costs as much as possible.

For the more diversified Northern economy, the needs were different. Northern manufacturers and workers wanted tariffs to protect them from the competition of low-priced goods produced by cheaper labor abroad. Manufacturers and farmers alike needed improved transportation facilities ("internal improvements") in the form of roads, canals, and railroads to foster inter-regional exchanges of goods. Northern economic groups and their congressional representatives therefore supported state and federal appropriations to build better roads and to assist canal and railroad construction.

Some of the upper South states like Kentucky and Maryland, with urban and manufacturing centers of their own, supported appropriations for these purposes. But the cotton-growing South did not fit into this scheme. Most of the cotton and tobacco crop was shipped by river or by short, locally built railroads to river or coastal port cities for export abroad. Internal improvements meant only that the South would be paying part of the governmental costs of a program from which it did not benefit. Indeed, the new

transportation routes diverted trade away from the South's own Mississippi River system, which drew trade southward toward New Orleans. In addition, the tariff meant that the South would be prevented from buying its manufactures from those who bought its raw materials and would be forced by law to pay a higher, tariff-supported price for its manufactures. As the Virginian, John Randolph of Roanoke, had angrily declared, "we shall only pay more for worse goods."

Because of these economic factors, North and South tended to vote against each other on questions of tariff, internal improvements, and other extensions of the power of the central government. Their rivalry had reached a crisis at the time of the Nullification Controversy in 1833, when South Carolina was ready to defy federal law (see p. 201). The crisis had been averted when other Southern states had not supported South Carolina. The South as a whole had resented federal economic policies but had never opposed them to the point of breaking up the Union, to which most Southerners felt strong patriotic loyalty.

The Growth of the Slavery Issue.   A deeper cause of division, however, was the institution of slavery. Until the 1770s slavery had scarcely been regarded as a moral question at all, except by the Quakers. In one form or another the institution had existed in other lands for thousands of years. The slave trade had been essential to the colonization of the Western Hemisphere. As late as 1780 there was no division into slave states and free states; slaves were held in every state of the Union. They were less numerous in the North only because they were less profitable there. But in the late eighteenth century (during the Age of Reason, or the Enlightenment), slavery came under attack from believers in natural law, human equality, and human rights. At the same time, emphasis in the churches shifted from a limited concern with the personal salvation of the individual to a fuller application of Christian teaching in relation to human society. Thus, the savage penal code of earlier times was modified, various social reforms were adopted, and slavery came under attack.

The states from Pennsylvania northward shared in this movement against slavery. By 1804 all of them had adopted laws for the gradual or immediate emancipation of their slaves, and Congress had prohibited the importation of any more slaves from Africa after 1808. For a time it appeared that the South might also participate in this movement. Southern Enlightenment leaders like Jefferson condemned slavery in the abstract, and antislavery societies were active in the South. Furthermore, slavery was restricted to the rice and tobacco economy, which was static and no longer very profitable. This meant that the Southern economy as a whole did not depend on slave labor.

But Jefferson never freed more than a handful of his own slaves. The Southern antislavery societies devoted their efforts mainly to encouraging the emigration of free blacks. And the tenor of antislavery sentiment among Southerners, apart from the Quakers and the early Methodists, was one of anguished handwringing over an inherited evil rather than vigorous action for its abolition.

The introduction of cotton injected greater vitality into the slave system. In one generation, the cultivation of short-staple cotton spread across the lower South from middle Georgia to the banks of the Brazos in Texas. Every decade from 1800 to 1860 the value and the volume of the crop doubled. In this dynamic and expanding economy, the price of slaves rose and fell with the price of cotton. Slavery went with cotton into the new areas. By 1820 it was completely interwoven into the whole Southern system.

While this was happening, the humanitarian crusade against slavery in Great Britain (which abolished slavery in the West Indies in 1833), in France (which abolished it in 1848), and in the Northern states (where the abolitionists became increasingly militant in their denunciations) led the South to a defensive reaction. By 1830 Southern leaders were no longer saying, as some had said earlier, that slavery was an evil but too deeply rooted to be abolished at once. Instead, they were beginning to assert that slavery was a positive good. They defended it with claims that it had been sanctioned in the Bible and that the Negro was biologically inferior to the white. They argued that the exploitation of Negro workers by the slavery system was not so harsh as the exploitation of white workers by a wage system in which the worker received only a bare subsistence when he was working and no subsistence at all when he was not. They held that, since social divisions were inevitable, assigning leadership to one class and subordination to another was better than having an endless struggle between classes.

These clashing arguments polarized the two sections more and more with each decade after 1830. As the abolitionists became more militant in their crusade against the "sin" of slavery, the South became so defensive about criticism that it would not tolerate any expression of antislavery opinion.

In spite of this disagreement on the ethics of slavery, several factors prevented a legal or physical clash over the question. To begin with, slavery was widely regarded as a matter for the states locally rather than for the federal government nationally. (South Carolina's attempt at nullification was actually a challenge to the government's authority in this area as well as in setting tariffs.) At that time, people regarded the federal system more as a loose association of states and less as a consolidated nation, and they were willing to leave many important questions to state action. Further, it was generally understood that the Constitution, in its "three-fifths" and fugitive slave clauses (see p. 122), protected the South's right to practice slavery. It was on the basis of such provisions that the Southern states had agreed to join the Union.

Apart from the question of legal or constitutional obligation, many Americans took the position that the harmony of the Union was simply more important than the ethics of slavery—that the slave question must not be permitted to weaken the Union and that the abolitionists were wrong to keep up constant agitation on an issue which caused sectional antagonism. The abolitionists, who were in the minority, felt that the Union was not worth saving unless it was based upon freedom.

The Question of Extending Slavery. All this meant that as long as the institution of slavery was confined to the existing slave states, few Northerners were willing to act against it, and it was not an explosive question politically. But when the question of extending slavery to new areas arose, the opposition was far more determined. As early as the Ordinance of 1787, the old Congress under the Articles of Confederation had agreed to exclude slavery from the region north of the Ohio. Some people, motivated by sincere antislavery sentiments, were determined to "contain" slavery. Others cared nothing about the evils of slavery but wanted to reserve unsettled areas for white residents only. And many people wanted to bring these new areas to the support of the North in the economic struggle between North and South. The South, conversely, was equally convinced that the growth of the country should not be all on the side of the North, reducing the South to a defenseless minority. This feeling made the South unwilling to concede even the areas where there was little prospect of extending slavery.

Because of these attitudes, the acquisition of any new area, the organization of any new territory, and the admission of any new state had always involved a possible flare-up over the slavery question. There had been such a crisis in 1819, when Missouri applied for admission to statehood as the first state (except Louisiana) to be formed out of the Louisiana Purchase. In the same way, the prospect of acquisition of territory from Mexico as a result of the Mexican War brought on a more protracted and more serious crisis beginning in 1846.

A few months after the beginning of the Mexican War, President Polk asked Congress to appropriate $2 million to be used in negotiating for land to be acquired from Mexico at the termination of the war. Many Northern Democrats were at this time angry with Polk, partly because he had vetoed a rivers and harbors bill important to midwestern economic development and partly because they felt he had violated the expansionist promises on which he was elected. His platform had called for the "reoccupation" of Oregon and the "reannexation" of Texas, and for "all of Oregon or none." This had put the question of expansion on a bisectional basis by promising Oregon, sure to be free territory, for the North, and Texas, which already had slavery, for the South. But after becoming President, he had compromised on Oregon, accepting the boundary at the 49th parallel instead of at 54° 40', while pushing expansion toward the southwest to the fullest extent by waging war with Mexico.

The Wilmot Proviso. This was the state of affairs when David Wilmot, a Democrat from Pennsylvania, introduced a resolution in the House of Representatives that slavery should be prohibited in any territory acquired from Mexico with the $2 million Polk requested. This free-soil resolution passed the House, where the North was stronger, but failed to pass in the Senate, where the South had equal strength. The disagreement of Senate and House marked a deadlock in Congress which lasted for four years, blocking the organization of governments for the new areas. The result was a steady increase in sectional tension.

In 1848, at the end of the Mexican War, the victorious United States acquired territory embracing the present states of Nevada, California, and Utah, most of Arizona and New Mexico, and parts of Colorado and Wyoming. Mexico also relinquished all claims to Texas above the Rio Grande. In the same year gold was discovered in California, and by 1849 the Gold Rush was in full swing.

The need for organizing the new land was urgent, and the territorial question became the foremost issue in public life. At one extreme on this question stood Wilmot and the "free-soilers," both Whig and Democrat, who demanded the exclusion of slavery from the new areas by act of Congress. At the other extreme, most Southern Whigs and Democrats adopted the position of John C. Calhoun. Calhoun argued that the territories were owned in common by all the states (rather than by the federal government, which was only a joint agent for the states) and that all citizens had an equal right to take their property (including slaves) to the common territory. Therefore, Congress had no power under the Constitution to exclude slavery from any territory.

The Doctrine of Popular Sovereignty. Political leaders who wanted some kind of adjustment or middle ground were not satisfied with either Wilmot's or Calhoun's alternative, one of which conceded nothing to the South, the other nothing to the North. They sought a more "moderate" position, and some of them advocated an extension of the Missouri Compromise line of 36° 30' to the Pacific. But most of them were more attracted by a proposal sponsored by Lewis Cass, senator from Michigan, for what was called "popular sovereignty" or "squatter sovereignty." Cass contended that the fairest and most democratic solution would be to let the people in the territories decide for themselves whether they would have slavery, just as the people in the states had already decided. Cass' proposal offered an attractive means for keeping the slavery question out of federal politics, but it contained one ambiguity which he adroitly refused to clarify. It did not specify *when* the people in the territories should make the decision. If they could make the decision as soon as the territory was organized, free soil could be attained by popular vote as easily as by congressional vote. According to Calhoun, popular exclusion at this stage would be just as wrong as congressional exclusion, for it would mean that Congress was giving to the territory a power which Congress did not have and therefore could not give. But if the voters in a territory could decide on slavery only when they applied for statehood, this would mean that the territories would have been left open to slavery quite as much as by Calhoun's position.

Far from reducing the amount of support for popular sovereignty, however, this ambiguity actually added to the attractiveness of the doctrine. Antislavery people argued that popular sovereignty would result in free territories, while proslavery advocates contended that it guaranteed slavery a fair chance to establish itself during the period before statehood.

THE COMPROMISE OF 1850

While these various positions on the territorial extension of slavery were being developed, the impasse in Congress continued. For three entire sessions, covering most of the Polk administration, nothing could be voted for California or the Southwest. It was only after long delay that an act to organize Oregon Territory without slavery was adopted.

In 1848, when the two national parties faced this question in a presidential election, both of them evaded it. The Democrats nominated Cass, on a platform that still did not say *when* the people of a territory could vote on slavery.

The Whigs nominated a military hero, Zachary Taylor, who had never been in politics, without any platform whatever. In the election campaign, which was a kind of contest between frank evasion and concealed evasion, Taylor was triumphant. He became President in 1849.

Early Secessionist Sentiment. Meanwhile, the House of Representatives had repeatedly voted in favor of Wilmot's principle of free soil by congressional action. The seeming imminence of a free-soil victory had, in turn, aroused bitter resentment in the South. For the first time many Southerners began to think of withdrawing from the Union if Congress voted to prevent them from taking their slaves into areas they had helped to win and to pay for. By 1848, Southerners in Congress were beginning to speak rather freely of disunion. After Taylor was elected, Southerners realized that, although he was a Louisiana slaveholder, he was not going to block free-soil legislation, and they began to organize Southern resistance. In October 1849 a state convention in Mississippi called for a convention of Southern state delegates to meet at Nashville, Tennessee, the following June to work out a united Southern position. Five Southern states officially elected delegates to such a convention, and representatives were unofficially chosen from four others.

Thus, when Taylor's first Congress met in December 1849, the need for organizing the area acquired from Mexico was urgent, and the relations between North and South were at a crisis. This crisis became more acute when Taylor announced his support for admitting California directly to statehood, without going through a territorial stage, and his intention to support the same plan for New Mexico in due course. Technically, this plan bypassed the question of congressional exclusion from the decision on slavery, but in substance it would represent a free-soil

victory, for the proposed states seemed fairly certain to be free states. At this prospect Southern protests were intensified. Though historians today disagree as to whether the country was close to disunion, certainly many prominent leaders at the time feared that it was.

The Clay Compromise Proposals. Among those leaders fearing disunion was Senator Henry Clay of Kentucky. As a spokesman of the border states, which were always anxious to promote sectional harmony, and as one who had played a leading part in arranging the compromises of 1820 and 1833, Clay was a natural leader of compromise. Although a Whig, he was at odds with President Taylor. Accordingly, Clay came forward, early in the congressional session of 1850, with an elaborate compromise designed to cover the slavery question in all its national aspects. Clay's plan called for: (1) admitting California as a free state; (2) organizing the rest of the Mexican cession into two territories, Utah and New Mexico, which were to decide for themselves whether slavery should be permitted or abolished; (3) awarding New Mexico part of the area on the upper Rio Grande claimed by Texas, but compensating Texas through federal payment of the Texas debt contracted before annexation; (4) abolishing the sale of slaves in the District of Columbia but guaranteeing slavery itself in the District; (5) enacting an effective law to compel the return of fugitive slaves who had escaped into the free states.

Clay's proposal brought on a long, brilliant, and famous series of debates in Congress. Clay himself made an immensely eloquent appeal for his plan as a means of saving the Union. Calhoun, who did not support the compromise directly, helped it indirectly by coming into the Senate almost in a dying condition to warn solemnly of the danger to the Union and the determination of the South to maintain its rights. The most important

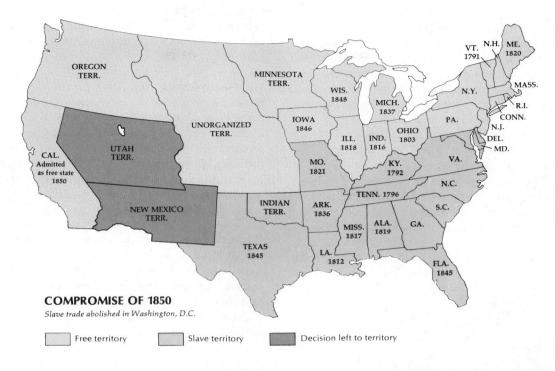

COMPROMISE OF 1850

Slave trade abolished in Washington, D.C.

| | Free territory | | Slave territory | | Decision left to territory |

speech of the session was made by Daniel Webster, who was Clay's only peer as an orator and who was generally regarded as an antislavery man. On the seventh of March, Webster announced his support of the compromise and made a powerful argument that slavery was naturally excluded from the west by climatic, physical, and agricultural conditions and that there was no need to bring on a crisis by adopting an antislavery law, such as the Wilmot Proviso, to accomplish what had already been settled by physical environment. "I would not re-enact a law of God," said Webster, impressively, "I would not reaffirm an ordinance of nature."

Despite great oratorical support, Clay's "omnibus bill," incorporating all his proposals in one measure, faced heavy opposition. President Taylor was waiting to veto it, and in July it was cut to pieces on the floor by a process of amendment in which Northern and Southern extremists voted together to prevent its passage. Clay—old, worn out, and badly discouraged—went off to Newport for a rest.

The Douglas Strategy.   Even before this vote was taken, however, the tide had turned. President Taylor died. His successor, Millard Fillmore, favored the compromise and immediately began to exert presidential influence to support it.

Meanwhile, Stephen A. Douglas, a young and vigorous senator from Illinois, took over the management of the compromise forces in Congress. Douglas was not a great orator, but he was a supremely effective rough-and-tumble debater, a man of immense energy ("a steam engine in breeches" was the phrase), and a most sagacious political tactician. He perceived that there was not a clear majority in favor of the compromise and that it could not be passed in the form in which Clay had presented it. But he realized that if Clay's proposals were taken up one by one, they could be passed by a combination of those who favored the compromise as a whole and those who favored each particular measure. (For instance, California would be admitted by a majority composed of compromise men and antislavery men, while the Fugitive Slave Act would be adopted by a combination of compromise men and proslavery men.) Douglas applied this strategy so effectively that within a few weeks Clay's entire program was enacted into law.

The adoption of the "Compromise of 1850" ended the crisis. It also broke the long deadlock and gave badly needed political organization to California and the Southwest. Because it brought a great sense of relief to those who had feared for the safety of the

The runaway slave could be hunted down like a wild animal, pursued by dogs and armed men.

Union, it was hailed as a great and final settlement which defused the slavery issue once and for all as a source of discord in the Union.

The Fugitive Slave Act. In fact, the Compromise of 1850 settled far less than it appeared to settle. For Utah and New Mexico it still left open the explosive question Lewis Cass had so carefully avoided: Could the citizens of the territory outlaw slavery in the territory? More important, while laying to rest the explosive issue of the Wilmot Proviso, it brought to life the even more explosive issue of the fugitive slave. The question of the slave in the territories was a legal and abstract question—a question of what was later called "an imaginary Negro in an impossible place"—but the question of the runaway slave was dramatic and real, involving a human creature in quest of freedom who was being hunted down by his fellow humans.

Finally, the compromise had never commanded a real majority and had been enacted only by finesse. The Southern states accepted it somewhat reluctantly, but Georgia spoke for the rest of them when its legislature voted resolutions that if the compromise were not fully enforced, Georgia would withdraw from the Union. In fact, while the Southern disunionists were agreeing not to demand secession at this time, the Southern unionists were almost forced to agree to the *principle* of secession in order to get the secessionists to agree not to exercise it at that time. Meanwhile, in the North the antislavery forces were pouring their denunciations upon the Fugitive Slave Act and upon Daniel Webster for supporting it. Perhaps never before in American politics had political invective been so bitter.

For a time, the fugitive slave question raised a terrific furor. To appreciate the uproar, one must understand that the law contained a number of very extreme features. It denied trial by jury in the case of alleged fugitives and provided for their cases to be decided by a special federal commissioner. Further, it paid the commissioner a fee that was higher in cases where the alleged fugitive was returned to slavery than in cases where the fugitive was set free. Though this arrangement was defended on the ground that there was much more paper work in one case than the other, it led to severe criticism. Still further, the law stipulated that any citizen could be called upon to participate in the enforcement process, which meant that those who opposed slavery must not only permit the capture of fugitives but might possibly be made to help in their capture.

Apart from these features of the law itself, the act aroused criticism because in operation it applied not only to slaves who were then running way but also to any slaves who had ever run away. There were many fugitives who had lived quietly in the North for many years and who had been quite safe from arrest under the relatively ineffectual Fugitive Slave Law of 1793. But now, under the act of 1850, they found themselves in real danger. In 1851 a black who had lived in Indiana for nineteen years was torn from his family and sent into slavery. Throughout the North, blacks were terrorized by the law, for those who were not fugitives had reason to fear being kidnapped quite as much as actual runaways had reason to fear being arrested. Consequently, a wave of migration to Canada set in, and several thousand blacks moved to Ontario.

Resistance Against the Fugitive Slave Law. A series of fugitive slave episodes followed which kept the country at a high pitch of excitement. In Boston, leading citizens openly asserted their intention to violate the law. In October a "vigilance committee" headed by one of the foremost citizens of Boston, the Reverend Theodore Parker, smuggled two undoubted slaves out of the country. Four months later a crowd, mostly black, seized a prisoner, Shadrach, from the courtroom and

spirited him away to Canada. Finally, in April 1851 the government succeeded in returning a slave from Boston, from which city it was boasted that no slave had ever been returned. This was accomplished only after mobs had surrounded the courthouse for several days. Only once again was a slave, Anthony Burns, returned from Boston. In his case a mob stormed the courthouse in an effort to rescue him, and a large military force was required in order to prevent his rescue.

It other cities, also, rescues and attempted rescues kept the pot boiling, and the fugitive slave question became for a time the foremost issue of the day. Yet the excitement and emotion which the issue generated have made

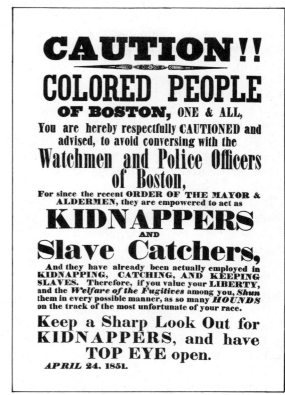

The Reverend Thomas Parker, who actively opposed the Fugitive Slave Act, circulated a cautionary broadside in 1851.

it hard to get at the facts about whether the escape of slaves from the South was numerically significant. On the one hand, Northern antislavery advocates boasted of their resistance to the law and claimed that they were operating a vast "underground railroad" which had helped 80,000 slaves to escape their pursuers. On the other, spokesmen of the South, indignant at the open violation of the law, complained bitterly that 100,000 slaves had been abducted over a forty-year period. These were probably inflated figures. The underground railroad was more extensive in legend than in reality and more important as a weapon of psychological warfare than as an escape route for slaves. It also appears that in many parts of the North the Fugitive Slave Act had public support and was well enforced.

There is no doubt, however, that the fugitive question dramatized the issue of slavery to a spectacular degree. The human being in quest of freedom, trying to escape from bloodthirsty pursuers, was an immensely moving figure. By changing the focus of the slavery question from the legal status of an imaginary chattel in a remote territory to the human plight of an individual human being in a nearby street, the Compromise of 1850 had, perhaps, created more tension than it relieved.

It is by no means an accident that *Uncle Tom's Cabin* (1851-1852), the classic literary protest against slavery, was published less than a year after the enactment of the fugitive law. The book's most dramatic scene was that of the fugitive slave girl, Eliza, crossing the icebound Ohio River as she was being pursued by a slave trader. This book, one of America's all-time best sellers, wrung sympathy and tears from countless people who had never previously been moved by the abolitionists.

The Election of 1852. If the Fugitive Slave law dramatized the issue of slavery, the crisis preceding the Compromise had dramatized

the issue of Union. Many Northerners who thoroughly disapproved of slavery felt that the question of Union was more important and must have priority. Consequently, despite fugitive slave episodes, the Compromise received strong support throughout the country, and though there had not been a clear majority in favor of adopting it, there was certainly a clear majority in favor of maintaining it.

The firmness of public support for the Compromise showed up clearly in the election of 1852. As it approached, Millard Fillmore, who had signed the compromise acts while serving out the term of Zachary Taylor, aspired to a term of his own. But in the party convention Northern Whigs blocked the effort of Southern Whigs to nominate Fillmore and forced the nomination instead of General Winfield Scott, who had captured Mexico City in the Mexican War. Scott was the Whigs' third military hero, and they hoped that, like Harrison and Taylor he would get to the White House on his military record.

The adoption of a platform revealed a deep division among the Whigs. The majority secured the adoption of a plank accepting the Compomise of 1850, including the Fugitive Slave Act, as a final settlement. But there was strong opposition, consisting mostly of delegates who supported Scott. Scott, who was pompous and politically clumsy, tried to get out of this dilemma by saying merely, "I accept the nomination with the resolutions attached." But it was clear that he was not a thoroughgoing supporter of the Compromise.

The Democrats settled their differences between rival candidates by agreeing on a dark horse, Franklin Pierce of New Hampshire, who had served with gallantry in the Mexican War. Pierce later proved a weak man, but he was an attractive candidate—handsome and pleasing in his manner—and the Democrats gave him united support on a platform that proclaimed the finality of the Compromise.

The position of the two parties gave the voters a fairly clear choice on the question of compromise—Pierce and his party were united on it, The Whigs were not. The voters exercised their option in a decisive way. Pierce carried all but four states—two in the North, two in the South.

The defeat smashed the Whig party, which was already badly divided between the "Cotton Whigs" of the South and the "Conscience Whigs" of the North. Though many important figures—including Abraham Lincoln—remained in the Whig organization somewhat longer, it was never a national party after 1852. This meant that only one national party—the Democratic—was left, which in turn meant that there was now only one remaining political organization in which Northern and Southern leaders were still seeking to smooth out sectional disagreements for the sake of party victory.

KANSAS AND NEBRASKA

The Douglas Bill. Pierce's campaign had promised harmony for the Union and finality for the Compromise, but his administration brought just the opposite. His first Congress had barely met in December 1853, when the territorial question arose again in a new form. Stephen A. Douglas wanted to organize territorial government for the region west of Iowa and Missouri. This area lay within the Louisiana Purchase, and since it was north of 36° 30′, it had been closed to slavery by the Missouri Compromise of 1820. Douglas, therefore, at first introduced a bill to organize free territories.

But Southern senators voted against his legislation and thus blocked it. They did this in part because they knew that Douglas wanted to promote a transcontinental railroad west from Chicago or some other Northern teminus to the Pacific. They were equally eager to run such a road west from New Orleans. There was simply no reason for them to give their votes to organize another free-soil territory for the purpose of facilitating a Northern railroad.

Douglas felt that he had to have their votes. Thus in January 1854 he was led to take the fatal step of agreeing to change his bill so that it would repeal the Missouri Compromise line and would leave the status of slavery in the Kansas-Nebraska region to be settled by popular sovereignty. Douglas made the plausible argument that what he advocated was nothing new and that the legislation of 1850 had already replaced the principle of geographical division with the principle of popular sovereignty.

"Appeal of the Independent Democrats." In a widely disseminated tract entitled "Appeal of the Independent Democrats," antislavery

KANSAS-NEBRASKA ACT, 1854

<table>
<tr><td>Free territory</td></tr>
<tr><td>Slave territory</td></tr>
<tr><td>Slavery question to be decided by people</td></tr>
</table>

advocates rejected Douglas' argument with furious indignation. They insisted that the act of 1850 applied only to the Mexican cession and was thus merely supplementary to the Missouri Compromise. The South, they asserted, was violating a sacred pledge; in 1820 it had promised to recognize freedom north of 36° 30′ in return for the admission of Missouri, and now it was defaulting on the agreement.

This argument was not entirely accurate. To mention but one point, a majority of Southern congressmen had voted against the act of 1820 to begin with. But the act had stood for thirty-four years, and Douglas was at least reckless, if not wrong, to tamper with it.

The furious blast of indignation that greeted his amended Kansas-Nebraska bill must have told him that he had made a major blunder. But Douglas was bold, aggressive, and tenacious. After committing President Pierce to his bill, he staged an all-out parliamentary battle for enactment. His own resourcefulness in debate enabled him repeatedly to throw his attackers on the defensive, and he conducted a brilliant campaign by which he succeeded in forcing the bill through both houses of Congress.

The Election of 1854. Douglas' success came at a terrible price. He himself had correctly foreseen that the repeal of the Missouri Compromise would "raise the Hell of a storm," but he had not foreseen, as he later said, that he would be able to travel to Chicago by the light of his own burning effigies. Six months after the act was adopted, the congressional elections of 1854 took place. All over the North "anti-Nebraska" parties sprang up to capitalize on free-soil anger at the Kansas-Nebraska Act. In Wisconsin and Michigan these parties took the name "Republican." This name soon spread to other states. In the Northeast, however, the main beneficiary of the voter uprising in 1854 was not the newborn Republican party but rather the anti-Catholic Know-Nothings, who shared the Republicans' hostility to the extension of slavery but were even more concerned about the apparent threat of Catholic immigrants.

Whatever the name of their opponents, the Democrats suffered a stunning setback in the Northern congressional elections. The number of Northern Democrats in the House fell from 91 to 25, and the Northern congressional Democrats functioned thereafter as the tail to the Southern Democratic dog.

In the long run, however, the Republicans rather than the Know-Nothings proved to be the main beneficiaries of the 1854 electoral revolution. Northern opposition to the expansion of slavery was deeper and more intense than Protestant dislike of Catholic immigrants. By the end of 1855 the Republican party had emerged as the successor to the Whigs as the country's second major party. Unlike the Whigs, however, the Republicans were entirely a sectional party with no strength at all in the slave states.

"Bleeding Kansas." The worst thing about the new Kansas-Nebraska Act was that, even at the price of causing the bitterest kind of sectional hostility, it did not create a real basis for stability in the new territory. It merely changed the terms of the contest, for Douglas and many Northern Democrats believed that popular sovereignty could make Kansas and Nebraska free territories just as well as congressional action could, while proslavery leaders took the repeal of the Missouri Compromise to mean that slavery should prevail in at least one of the two new territories.

Both antislavery and proslavery groups prepared to rush supporters into Kansas to defend their respective positions there. From Missouri, proslavery advocates, known as Border Ruffians, had a way of riding over into Kansas on election day to vote and to intimidate the free-soilers and then riding back to Missouri. In New England, antislavery advocates organized an Emigrant Aid Society to send free-soil settlers to Kansas. Though the society never officially purchased weapons for these settlers, the leaders of the society bought rifles with separate funds to arm the emigrants against the proslavery groups.

It would have taken a strong President to keep order in Kansas, and Pierce was not strong. He appointed a succession of able governors for the territory, but he would not vigorously support them when they needed his backing. Affairs therefore went from bad to worse. After the proslavery faction had stolen an election and Pierce had given recognition to the government thus elected, the free-soil advocates formed another government of their own. Kansas then had two governments—a proslavery one at Pawnee,

legal but not honest and an antislavery one at Topeka, honest but not legal.

It is a great mistake to think of frontier Kansas as inhabited entirely by people who went there as missionaries for slavery or for freedom. Many settlers were simply land-hungry pioneers like those who swarmed into all new territories. Such settlers were always quick to violence, and not all the shooting that took place in Kansas was because of slavery. But the slavery issue did accentuate the violence and give a pattern to the lawlessness of the frontier.

With President Pierce denouncing the free-soil government for its illegality, the proslavery forces secured an indictment of the free-soilers by a grand jury which was, of course, of the proslavery men's own choosing. With this indictment an armed mob, or "posse," as it called itself, marched on the

Hostility erupted frequently in Kansas following passage of the Kansas-Nebraska Act. The painting depicts antislavery Kansans firing on a proslavery settlement.

The Cavalry engagement.

free-soil headquarters at Lawrence, where they destroyed the printing press and burned or looted a good deal of property.

Four days later John Brown, a free-soiler who carried his views to fanatical lengths, avenged the sacking of Lawrence and the killing of several free-soil settlers by leading a body of men to Pottawatomie Creek, where they took five unarmed proslavery settlers from their homes in the dead of night and murdered them. These events were part of an escalation of terror and violence in "Bleeding Kansas." Probably two hundred people met violent deaths before a new territorial government used federal troops to restore order four months later.

"The Crime Against Kansas." Meanwhile, the intensity of sectional ill will was both illustrated and heightened by an occurrence in Washington. Charles Sumner, an antislavery senator from Massachusetts, delivered an oration entitled "The Crime Against Kansas" in which, in addition to castigating the slave power as bitterly as he could, he spoke in extremely personal terms about elderly Senator Andrew P. Butler of South Carolina. He alluded, for instance, to "the loose expectoration" of Butler's speech. A nephew of Butler's in the House of Representatives, Preston Brooks, went to the Senate chamber when the Senate was not in session, found Sumner seated at his desk, and beat him severely with a cane.

For several years after the assault Sumner was incapacitated, either by the blows which he received or, according to the best modern medical opinion, by his psychological reaction to the assault. The public significance of this affair, however, lay less in the attack itself than in the fact that a large part of the Northern press made a martyr of Sumner and pictured all Southerners as barbarians, while the South made a hero of Brooks and typed all Yankees as rabid fanatics.

The Character of Franklin Pierce. By this time the Pierce administration was ending as a disaster because of the weakness of the President and the extent to which he let himself be dominated by Southern influence. After failing to prevent repeal of the Missouri Compromise, Pierce might still have saved the peace of the country if he had stood firm for real popular sovereignty in Kansas. But he had instead backed a proslavery regime which was palpably fraudulent, had allowed violence to go unrestrained, and had finally given his support to the idea of statehood with a proslavery government. At this point Stephen A. Douglas had broken with the administration and was fighting hard in Congress to defeat this proslavery government. Thus the political division now was less between free-soil and proslavery forces than between the honest application of popular sovereignty and the perversion of it.

Indeed, Pierce had backed the south at almost every point. He had negotiated the Gadsden Purchase (1853) with Mexico for what is now the southernmost part of Arizona and New Mexico because the land in question was strategic for the construction of a transcontinental railroad by the southern route from New Orleans. He had permitted three of his diplomatic emissaries in Europe to meet at Ostend, Belgium, in October 1854 to propose American annexation of Cuba by purchase or, if that failed, by "wresting it from Spain." Cuba had almost 400,000 slaves and would strengthen the power of slavery. (This "Ostend Manifesto," however, aroused such worldwide indignation that the administration was forced to repudiate it.)

Moreover, the administration did nothing effective to prevent expeditions by adventurers, called *filibusterers*, who invaded Latin countries from American shores. One such expedition from New Orleans against Cuba failed. Another, against Nicaragua, was temporarily successful. These efforts to acquire

Ill feeling between antislavery and proslavery forces was heightened by an assault upon Senator Sumner in the Senate chamber.

new slave territory for the United States sparked Northern anger and brought new recruits into the Republican party.

ON THE EVE OF WAR

The Election of 1856. At the end of Pierce's term even the Southern Democrats knew that he could not be reelected. The Democrats nominated James Buchanan of Pennsylvania, who, as minister to England, had been out of the country at the time of the Kansas-Nebraska Act (although as one of three authors of the Ostend Manifesto, he was particularly ac-

ceptable to the South). Buchanan had been Secretary of State under Polk and was a veteran of American politics—an old Public Functionary, as he called himself.

To run against him, a remnant of the Know-Nothings and Southern Whigs calling themselves the American party nominated Millard Fillmore. But the principal opposition came from the new Republican party. They passed over their most prominent leaders to nominate the dashing but politically inexperienced young explorer of the Rocky Mountains and the Far West, John C. Frémont.

In the election that followed, Buchanan carried all the slave states (except Maryland, which voted for Fillmore) and four free states, thus winning the election. But the majority of the North was now backing the Republican party, which denounced slavery as a "relic of barbarism" and which had no organization whatever throughout half the Union.

It is questionable whether, by this time, anyone could have brought the disruptive forces of sectional antagonism under control. Certainly Buchanan could not do it. His cabinet, like Pierce's, was dominated by Southern Democrats. In February 1858 he forfeited his claim to impartial leadership by recommending admission of Kansas to statehood under a proslavery constitution fraudulently adopted by a rump convention that met at Lecompton. Douglas and other Northern Democrats resisted the Lecompton constitution. Thus Douglas lost the Southern support which he had won in 1854, and the Democratic party became deeply divided.

The Dred Scott Decision.   Meanwhile, in 1857 the Supreme Court had handed down a decision that may have been intended to restore sectional peace but had exactly the opposite effect. This ruling concerned a Missouri slave, Dred Scott, who had been carried by his master first to the free state of Illinois and then into Wisconsin Territory, which was within the Louisiana Purchase north of 36° 30′ and was therefore, under the Missouri Compromise, free territory. After he had been taken back to Missouri, Scott sued for his freedom, and the case was eventually carried up on appeal to the Supreme Court. The justices divided in various ways on several questions that were involved, but essentially the five justices from slave states held that Scott was still a slave, while the four from the free states divided two and two.

The principal opinion was rendered by Chief Justice Roger B. Taney, who stated that, during colonial times, blacks had "been regarded as beings so far inferior that they had no rights which the white man was bound to respect." Following Taney, the majority of the court held that a person born a slave or the descendant of slaves was not a citizen and therefore could not bring suit in federal courts. In strict logic, therefore, the court need not have ruled on the other questions Scott raised, but it went on to state that even if he could have sued, he still would not have been free, for the Missouri Compromise was unconstitutional because Congress had no power to exclude slavery from the territories.

In a literal sense the Dred Scott decision added nothing new, for it merely declared void a law which had already been repealed by the Kansas-Nebraska Act three years earlier. But in another sense, it had a shattering effect. It strengthened a conviction in the North that an evil "slave power," bent on spreading slavery throughout the land, was in control of the government and must be checked. It justified Southerners, on the other hand, in believing that the free-soilers were trying to rob them of their legal rights.

It even struck a deadly blow at the one moderate position—that of popular sovereignty—which lay between the extremes of free-soil and proslavery contentions. If, as the Court ruled, Congress had no power to exclude slavery from a territory by its own act, certainly it could not give a power which it did not possess to the territorial legislatures, and without such power there could be no effective popular sovereignty. It made compromise by act of Congress almost impossible.

The decision also convinced many free blacks that they had no future in a country that denied them citizenship. It intensified the growing mood of black nationalism and spurred movements for emigration to Haiti or Africa.

The Lincoln-Douglas Debates.   The effect of the Dred Scott decision in polarizing sectional extremism showed up clearly in 1858, when

Stephen A. Douglas ran for reelection to the Senate from Illinois and was challenged to a series of debates by his Republican opponent, Abraham Lincoln. Lincoln, a former Whig, was deeply opposed to slavery. He regarded it as morally wrong—"if slavery is not wrong then nothing is wrong"—and he insisted that the Dred Scott decision be reversed. Slavery must be kept out of the territories and placed "in the course of ultimate extinction."

But Lincoln was by no means an abolitionist. He did not advocate racial equality. He recognized both the complexity of the slavery question and the fact that slavery was protected by constitutional guarantees which he proposed to respect—even to the enforcement of the fugitive slave law. Lincoln defined the dilemma the Dred Scott decision had created for Douglas and for all moderates. If slavery could not be legally excluded from the territories, how could the people of the territory, under popular sovereignty, exclude it?

Douglas replied at Freeport, Illinois (the "Freeport doctrine"), that unless a territory adopted positive laws to protect slavery by local police regulations, slavery could not establish itself. Thus by merely refraining from legislation, lawmakers could keep a territory free. This answer was enough to gain reelection for Douglas, but it cost him what was left of his reputation as a national leader with strong bisectional support. At one time, Southerners had applauded him for repealing the slavery exclusion of the Missouri Compromise. Now they saw him as a man who was supporting the free-soilers in Kansas and who was advocating a theory that would deprive the South of rights guaranteed by a decision of the Supreme Court.

John Brown's Raid. If the Dred Scott decision brought to a climax the Northern feeling that freedom was being dangerously threatened by a sinister conspiracy of the "slave power," John Brown's raid on Harpers Ferry created an even more intense feeling below the Mason-Dixon line that abolitionist fanaticism posed an immediate danger to the social order and even to human life in the South. After the "Pottawatomie massacre" in Kansas, Brown had dropped out of sight, but during the night of October 16, 1859, he suddenly descended, with a band of eighteen men (including five blacks), on the town of Harpers Ferry, Virginia, seized the federal arsenal there, and called upon the slaves to rise and claim their freedom.

Within thirty-six hours Brown was captured. Later he was tried and hanged. But his act had touched the South at its most sensitive nerve—its fear of the kind of slave insurrection that had caused immense slaughter at Santo Domingo at the beginning of the century and had periodically threatened to erupt in the South itself. Southern alarm and resentment would perhaps have been less great if the North had denounced Brown's act—as many Northerners, including Lincoln, did. But the fact soon came out that Brown had received financial backing from some of the most respected figures in Boston, and the day of his execution became one of public mourning in New England. Brown was called Saint John the Just, and Ralph Waldo Emerson declared that Brown would "make the gallows glorious like the cross."

The Election of 1860. By this time, developments were rapidly moving toward a showdown. For more than a decade, sectional dissension had been destroying the institutions which held the American people together in national unity. In 1844 it had split the Methodist church. In 1845 the Baptist church had divided into separate Northern and Southern bodies. Between 1852 and 1856, sectionalism had split the Whig party, and as matters now stood, the Democratic party was the only remaining major national institution, outside of the government itself. In 1860, with another presidential election at hand, the

ELECTION OF 1860

■ Lincoln	■ Douglas
■ Breckinridge	□ Bell
▨ Vote divided (Lincoln and Douglas)	

Democratic organization, already strained by the tension between the Buchanan and the Douglas wings, also broke apart.

The Democrats.   Meeting at Charleston, the Democratic convention divided on the question of the platform. Douglas Democrats wanted a plank which promised in general terms to abide by the decisions of the Supreme Court but which avoided explicit expression of support for slavery in the territories. Southern Democrats, led by William L. Yancey, a famous orator from Alabama, wanted a categorical affirmation that slavery would be protected in the territories. When the Douglas forces secured the adoption of their plank, Yancey and most of the delegates from the cotton states walked out of the convention.

The accusation was later made that they did this as part of a deliberate plan or conspiracy to break up the Union by splitting the Democratic party, letting the Republicans win, and thus creating a situation which would cause the South to secede. But, in fact, many of those who bolted were hoping to force Northern Democrats to come to terms or to throw the election to Congress, where there was a chance that the South might have won.

For weeks, desperate efforts were made to reunite the Democrats, but in the end the Northern wing of the party nominated Douglas and the Southern wing nominated John C. Breckinridge of Kentucky, Vice-President under Buchanan.

Some of the conservative successors of the Whigs, now calling themselves Constitutional Unionists, nominated John Bell of Tennessee for President and Edward Everett for Vice-President on a platform that said nothing about the territorial question, and called only for "the Constitution, the Union, and the enforcement of the laws."

The Republican Victory.   The principal opposition to Douglas, it was understood, would come from the Republicans, whose convention was meeting at a new building called the Wigwam in Chicago. The leading candidate before the convention was William H. Seward, U. S. senator from New York, who had been the foremost Republican for some years. But his talent for coining memorable phrases—"a higher law than the Constitution" and "the irrepressible conflict between freedom and slavery"—had won him a reputation for extremism. The Republicans, seeing a good chance of victory after the Democratic split, decided to move in a conservative direction in order not to jeopardize their prospects. Accordingly, they nominated Abraham Lincoln, who had made his reputation in the debates with Douglas but who had never been militant on the slavery question. To balance this nomination they made Hannibal Hamlin, a former Democrat from Maine, their vice-presidential candidate.

To win, the Republicans needed only to hold what they had won in 1856 and to capture Pennsylvania and either Illinois or Indiana, which Buchanan had carried. As the election turned out, they won every free state except New Jersey (part of which went to Douglas), while Breckinridge won all the slave states except Virginia, Kentucky, and Tennessee (which went to Bell) and Missouri (which went to Douglas). Douglas ran a strong second in popular votes but a poor fourth in electoral votes, while Lincoln was in the curious position of winning with only 40 percent of the popular vote. His victory resulted not from the division of his opponents, however, but from the fact that his strength was strategically distributed. His victories in many of the free states were narrow, and he received no votes at all in ten Southern states. Thus the distribution of his popular votes had maximum effectiveness in winning electoral votes.

Secession. Lincoln's victory at last precipitated the sectional split which had been brewing for so long. As we can now see in the light of later events, Lincoln was moderate-minded and would have respected the legal rights of the South even though he deplored slavery. But to the South, fearful of Northern aggression, his victory was a signal of imminent danger. Here was a man who had said that a house divided against itself could not stand and that the Union could not continue permanently half slave and half free. To the South he denied rights in the territories which the Supreme Court had said that the South possessed. He was supported by swarms of militant antislavery men. And his victory clearly represented the imposition of a President by one section upon the other, for 99 percent of his vote had come in the free states.

Southerners had controlled the United States government most of the time since its

THE UNITED STATES ON THE EVE OF CIVIL WAR *(Dates of secession are given under state names)*

- Free states
- Border slave states that did not secede
- Slave states seceding before firing on Ft. Sumter, Apr. 12, 1861
- Slave states seceding after firing on Ft. Sumter, Apr. 12, 1861

(slavery abolished in territories: 1862)

founding. Although, as we have already seen, there was some diversity in their political opinion, especially before 1845, their prominence had been a matter of pride in the South and—increasingly—a matter of concern in the North. From 1789 to 1861, twenty-five of the thirty-six Presidents Pro Tem of the Senate and twenty-four of the thirty-six Speakers of the House were Southerners. Twenty of the thirty-five Supreme Court justices were from the South. A Southerner was Chief Justice during all but twelve of these years. At all times the South had a majority on the Court. During forty-nine of these seventy-two years the President of the United States was a Southerner—and a slaveholder. And during twelve additional years, including most of the crucial 1850s, the Presidents were Northern Democratic "doughfaces" who were sometimes more pro-Southern than Southerners themselves might have dared to be.

Thus when the news of Lincoln's election came in 1860, Charles Francis Adams, the son and grandson of the only truly Northern Presidents the United States had ever had and himself a founder of the Republican party, wrote jubilantly: "The great revolution has taken place. . . . The country has once and for all thrown off the domination of the slaveholders."

The slaveholders, too, regarded the 1860 election as a political revolution which foreshadowed a future dominated by the ideology and institutions of the North. To the Old South this would be disaster. A counterrevolution of independence seemed the only answer.

Proponents of secession invoked the doctrine that each state had retained its sovereignty when it joined the federal Union. Thus, in the exercise of this sovereignty, each state, acting through a special convention like the conventions that had ratified the Constitution, might secede from the Union. As soon as it learned of Lincoln's election, the South Carolina legislature called a convention to take the state out of the Union. Within six weeks the six other states of the lower South—Mississippi, Florida, Alabama, Georgia, Louisiana, and Texas—also called conventions. Delegates were elected by popular vote after short but intensive campaigns. Each convention voted by a substantial and in most cases an overwhelming majority to secede. By February 9, 1861, three months after Lincoln's election but almost a month before his inauguration, delegates from the seven seceded states had met in Montgomery, Alabama, to adopt a provisional Constitution for the Confederate States of America and to elect Jefferson Davis and Alexander Stephens as provisional President and Vice-President of the new republic.

The Failure of Compromise.   The actual arrival of disunion, which had been dreaded for so long, evoked strenuous efforts at compromise—especially by leaders in the border slave states, where loyalty to the Union was combined with sympathy for the South. From Kentucky, Senator John J. Crittenden, heir to the compromise tradition of Henry Clay, introduced proposals in Congress to revise and extend the Missouri Compromise line by constitutional amendment. Virginia took the lead in convening a Peace Convention, with delegates from twenty-one states, which met in Washington in February. Congress actually adopted a proposed amendment which would have guaranteed slavery in the states that wanted to keep it. This amendment was submitted to the states for ratification before the war came and made it obsolete.

But Lincoln was unwilling to make any concessions that would compromise the basic Republican principle of excluding slavery from the territories. The Crittenden Compromise would have permitted slavery in all territories south of 36° 30′ "now held, *or hereafter acquired.*" In view of the South's appetite for the acquisition of new slave territory in the Caribbean and Central Ameri-

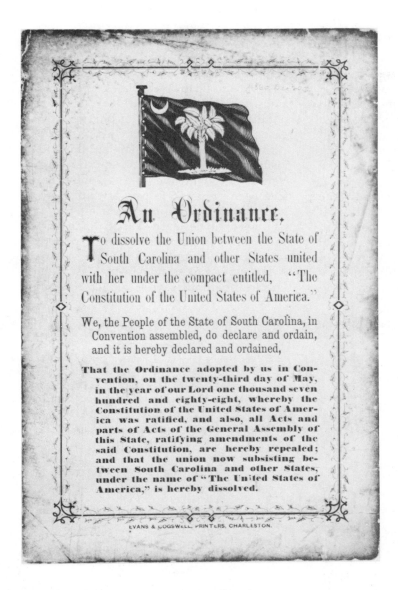

An Ordinance,

To dissolve the Union between the State of South Carolina and other States united with her under the compact entitled, "The Constitution of the United States of America."

We, the People of the State of South Carolina, in Convention assembled, do declare and ordain, and it is hereby declared and ordained,

That the Ordinance adopted by us in Convention, on the twenty-third day of May, in the year of our Lord one thousand seven hundred and eighty-eight, whereby the Constitution of the United States of America was ratified, and also, all Acts and parts of Acts of the General Assembly of this State, ratifying amendments of the said Constitution, are hereby repealed; and that the union now subsisting between South Carolina and other States, under the name of "The United States of America," is hereby dissolved.

EVANS & COGSWELL, PRINTERS, CHARLESTON.

The secession of South Carolina from the Union was soon followed by that of six other southern states. The nation was on the brink of civil war.

ca, Republicans feared that adoption of such a compromise "would amount to a perpetual covenant of war against every people, tribe, and State owning a foot of land between here and Terra del Fuego" and turn the United States into "a great slavebreeding and slave-extending empire." Therefore they defeated the Crittenden Compromise. In any case, it is unlikely that adoption of this or any other compromise would have stemmed the tide of secession in the lower South, where by February 1861 the Confederacy was a *fait accompli.*

Fort Sumter. Thus, when Lincoln was inaugurated on March 4, 1861, he was faced by a new Southern republic where seven states of the Union had been. This new Confederacy had seized federal post offices, customs houses, arsenals, and even federal forts, with the exception of Fort Sumter in Charleston harbor and Fort Pickens in Pensacola harbor. From North Carolina to the Rio Grande, these were the only two places where the Stars and Stripes still flew. There was great speculation at the time as to what position Lincoln would take, and there has been great dispute among historians since then as to what position he actually *did* take.

Certainly he made it absolutely clear that he denied the right of any state to secede and that he intended to preserve the Union. But whether he intended to wage war in order to preserve it is not so clear. There were eight slave states (Virginia, North Carolina, Kentucky, Tennessee, Missouri, Arkansas, Maryland, and Delaware) still in the Union. Lincoln was extremely eager to keep them loyal. And so long as they remained in the Union, they might help to bring the other slave states back. This split among the slave states represented a failure on the part of the secessionists to create a united South. Thus Lincoln had every reason to refrain from hasty action.

If he had been able to maintain the federal position at Fort Pickens and Fort Sumter, or even at one of them, he apparently would have been prepared to play a waiting game. But less than twenty-four hours after becoming President he learned that Major Robert Anderson, commander at Fort Sumter, was running out of supplies and would soon have to surrender unless food were sent to him. Lincoln apparently gave serious consideration

Hinton Rowan Helper: Antislavery Southerner

Hinton Rowan Helper was the self-proclaimed spokesman for the non-slaveholding whites who constituted three fourths of Southern white families. His book *The Impending Crisis of the South,* published in 1857, attacked slavery as an evil institution that retarded Southern progress and destroyed the prosperity of non-slaveholders. *The Impending Crisis* ranks with *Uncle Tom's Cabin* as one of the most important documents of the growing sectional conflict. It provoked a crisis in Congress and helped bring on the Civil War. In the end, however, Helper achieved little that he had hoped for and died of self-inflicted violence.

Hinton Rowan Helper was born December 27, 1829, in a section of North Carolina populated mainly by small farmers. After working as a youth on his father's farm and gaining a respectable education at a local academy, Helper went West in 1850 to seek his fortune in the newly opened goldfields of California. His unhappy failures there caused him to return East and publish in 1855 a derogatory book about California, *The Land of Gold*. The book's failure further disappointed him, and he poured some of the bitterness from this disappointment into the writing of his second and far more significant book, *The Impending Crisis,* published two years later.

to the possibility of surrendering Sumter, and he might have done so if he had been able to reinforce Fort Pickens and make it the symbol of an unbroken Union. But attempts to reinforce Pickens were delayed, and on April 6 Lincoln sent a message to the governor of South Carolina that supplies would be sent to Sumter. If they were allowed in, no military reinforcement would be attempted.

Historians have disputed whether this was a promise not to start shooting if supplies were allowed or a threat to start shooting if they were not allowed. In any event, the Confederate government decided that the supplies could not be allowed. On April 12, 1861, after Major Anderson had rejected a formal demand for surrender, Confederate batteries opened a bombardment before dawn that forced Fort Sumter to surrender after twenty-six hours of furious shelling.

On April 15 Lincoln issued a call for the loyal states to furnish 75,000 militia to suppress the Southern "insurrection." All the free states responded with alacrity and enthusiasm. The four slave states of Virginia, North Carolina, Tennessee, and Arkansas responded by joining the Confederacy. The other four slave states—Maryland, Delaware, Kentucky, and Missouri—remained uneasily in the Union, though many of their men went South to fight for the Confederacy. The bombardment of Fort Sumter marked the beginning of a war which lasted four years and which, with the exception of the Napoleonic wars, was the greatest military conflict the world had seen up to that time.

Using selected statistics from the 1850 census, Helper portrayed a South stagnating in economic backwardness, while the free-labor North strode forward in seven-league boots. He contrasted the nearly universal literacy and comfortable living standard of Northern farmers and workers with the apparent ignorance and poverty of Southern "poor whites." The cause? "Slavery lies at the root of all the shame, poverty, ignorance, tyranny, and imbecility of the South," wrote Helper. Slavery monopolized the best land, degraded all labor to the level of bond labor, denied schools to workers, and impoverished all but the "lords of the lash" who "are not only absolute masters of the blacks [but] of all non-slaveholding whites, whose freedom is merely nominal, and whose unparalleled illiteracy and degradation is purposely and fiendishly perpetuated."

Although he demanded the total abolition of slavery, Helper wasted no sympathy on the slaves, whom he wanted shipped back to Africa. His book was aimed at the non-slaveholders who, like himself, disliked slavery because they disliked black people and resented their competition as laborers. Helper therefore assumed that the non-slaveholding whites would rally to the antislavery standard. He urged them to form state Republican parties in the South, use their votes to overthrow the slaveholders' rule, and free themselves from the curse of bondage.

But few non-slaveholding Southern whites read his message. No Southern printer had dared to publish the book, so Helper had had to move from his native North Carolina to the North to get it published in New York. *The Impending Crisis* was virtually banned in the South. Some states made it a criminal offense to possess or circulate copies of it.

Even if Southern whites had been able to read the book, however, it is unlikely that many of them would have accepted its arguments. Helper underestimated the

"CAUSES" OF THE CIVIL WAR

Ever since 1861, writers have disputed what caused the Civil War and whether it was an "irrepressible conflict" in the sense of being inevitable. Southerners have argued that the war was fought not over slavery but over the question of states' rights. Several of the Confederate states, they point out, seceded only when the others had been attacked. Economic determinists have contended that the Northern public never would support the abolitionists on any direct question (which is certainly true), that Lincoln did not even venture to issue the Emancipation Proclamation until the war had been in progress for a year and five months (which is also true), and that the conflict was really between an industrial interest which wanted one kind of future for America and an agrarian interest which wanted another. Other historians, going a step beyond this, have pictured the North and the South as two "diverse civilizations," so dissimilar in their culture and their values that union between them was artificial and unnatural.

In the 1940s another group of writers, known as revisionists, emphasized the idea that Northerners and Southerners had formed distorted and false concepts of each other and that they went to war against these images rather than against the people they were really fighting. The war, they argued, grew out of emotions, not out of realities.

Every one of these points of view has something to be said for it. The causes of the

strength of the ties that bound most whites, slaveholder and non-slaveholder alike, in a common culture. Although many residents of the South's upland and mountain regions were hostile to the plantation regime, most non-slaveholders elsewhere were loyal to the "Southern way of life," including slavery. Many were relatives of slaveholders. Others aspired to become slaveowners themselves. Even most whites who had no connection with slavery or the planters supported the "peculiar institution" as the best means of controlling the black population and maintaining white supremacy.

The principal effect of *The Impending Crisis* in the South was to create a defensive-aggressive reaction to its popularity in the North. Republicans praised the book's economic indictment of slavery as a forceful expression of their own free-labor views. Leading Republicans raised money to print an inexpensive abridged edition and distributed it as a campaign document in the Congressional elections of 1858. This angered Southerners and contributed to one of the most serious sectional deadlocks in the history of Congress.

Republicans had a plurality but not a majority in the House of Representatives that convened in December 1859. Because their candidate for Speaker had endorsed Helper's book, the Democrats and ex-Whig conservatives refused to vote for him. The House remained deadlocked over the election of a Speaker for eight weeks until a compromise candidate finally won on the forty-fourth ballot. Tempers grew short, Northern and Southern congressmen hurled insults at each other, and nearly every member came to the House armed. Many observers actually expected a shootout on the floor of Congress. When war came, a little more than a year later, the clash over Helper's book was remembered as one of the many sectional irritants that had burst the bonds of Union.

Civil War were certainly not simple. But though each of the explanations points to something other than slavery, it is significant that the factor of slavery was involved in all of them. It is true that the South believed in the right of the states to secede whereas the North did not, but this belief would have remained an abstraction and never been acted upon if the Republican crusade against slavery had not impelled the South to use the secession weapon. Slavery was important not only as a moral issue, but also as an economic institution that divided two different and in many ways antagonistic societies. Both of these societies—the modernizing, free-labor, capitalist North and the conservative, agrarian, slave-labor South—were expansionist. Each believed that its social system must expand into the new territories in order to survive. Each saw the expansion of the other as a threat to its own future.

It is hard to imagine that without slavery the general dissimilarities between North and South, even their social and cultural separateness, would have been brought into such sharp focus as to precipitate a war. It is true that in the 1850s extremist leaders came to the fore and each section formed an emotional stereotype rather than a realistic picture of the other. (See "Hinton Rowan Helper: Antislavery Southerner.") But this is a process that always occurs as antagonism deepens.

The point is that slavery furnished the emotional voltage that led to deep distrust and dislike in each section for the people of the other. In his second inaugural, Abraham

During these years Helper lived in the North and tried with indifferent success to make a living as a lecturer. Described by a contemporary as a "tall, slim, peculiar-looking person, with short black hair, whiskers and mustache, a very bronzed complexion, and a fierce military expression," Helper had become one of the most-hated men in the country as far as slaveholders were concerned. A North Carolina senator denounced him in a scathing congressional speech. Outraged and insulted, Helper rushed to the floor of the Senate and engaged the senator in a rough-and-tumble fistfight. Sympathetic Republicans paid his fine.

In 1861 President Lincoln appointed Helper U.S. Consul in Buenos Aires, where he served until 1866. While there he married an Argentine woman. After his return home his dislike for blacks turned into a pathological hatred. Sensitive of his heritage as a "poor white" and plagued by a sense of failure, he made blacks the scapegoats for the frustration and disappointments of his careeer. His 1867 book, *Nojoque: A Question for a Continent*, reaffirmed his earlier goal to "write the negro out of America" and expressed a desire "to write him out of existence." Another book of similar tenor, *Negroes in Negroland*, followed in 1868. Helper denounced the Republican Reconstruction program of equal rights for freed slaves. This time he received a much more sympathetic hearing in the South.

Much of the remainder of Helper's life was consumed in futile attempts to promote a trunk railroad from Canada to Argentina. During these years he made a scanty living as a lobbyist in Washington for claims against South American countries. In 1899 his wife left him. On March 8, 1909, living alone and in poverty in Washington, he took his own life.

Lincoln said, "All know that slavery was somehow the cause of the war." The operative word in his statement was "somehow," for the war was not in any simple sense a fight between crusaders for freedom all on one side and believers in slavery all on the other. Robert E. Lee, to name but one Southerner, did not believe in slavery at all, and many a Northern soldier who was willing to die, if need be, for the Union was deeply opposed to making slavery an issue of the war. But both antislavery Southerners and proslavery Northerners were caught in the web woven by the issue of slavery.

Could this issue have been settled without war? Was the crisis artificial? Was the territorial question a contest over "an imaginary Negro in an impossible place"? Was war really necessary in a situation where it seems doubtful that a majority of Southerners wanted to secede (only seven out of fifteen slave states seceded before the firing on Fort Sumter) or that a majority of Northerners wanted to make an issue of slavery? (Lincoln had only 40 percent of the popular vote, and he promised security for slavery where it was already established.) Were the American people, both North and South, so much alike in their religion (overwhelmingly evangelical Protestant), their speech (American variants of English), their ethnic descent (mostly from British, Irish, and German stock), their democratic beliefs, their pioneer ways, their emphasis upon the values of self-reliance and hard work, their veneration for the Constitution, and even their bumptious Americanism—were they so much alike that a war between them could and should have been avoided? This in turn raises the question whether disagreements are any less bitter among parties who have much in common.

What was happening in America was that the center of gravity was gradually shifting from a loosely organized agricultural society to a modern industrial society with much greater concentration of power. As this happened, the United States was being transformed from a loose association of separately powerful states to a consolidated nation in which the states would be little more than political subdivisions. In America's startling growth the North had outstripped the South and the equilibrium that previously existed between them had been destroyed. The proposal of the victorious Republicans to confine slavery—and in this sense to exclude the South from further participation in the nation's growth—dramatized this shift in equilibrium. It seems most unlikely that the South would ever have accepted the political consequences of this basic change without a crisis, especially since Southern whites greatly feared the possibility that a preponderant North in control of the federal government might ultimately use its power to abolish slavery.

The brooding presence of race permeated this issue. Slavery was more than an institution to exploit cheap labor. It was a means of controlling a large and potentially threatening black population and of maintaining white supremacy. Any hint of a threat to the "Southern way of life," which was based on the subordination of a race both scorned and feared, was bound to arouse deep and irrational phobias and to create a crisis. Whether this crisis had to take the form of armed conflict and whether this phase of armed force had to occur precisely when it did, or might have come a month, a year, or a decade sooner or later, would seem to be a matter for endless speculation.

Chapter 12

Civil War and Reconstruction 1861-1877

THE BLUE AND THE GRAY

The "American" War. The American Civil War lasted four years, from April 1861 to April 1865. It was fought over more than half of the United States, for battles took place in every slave state except Delaware, and Confederate forces made incursions into Pennsylvania, Ohio, West Virginia, Kansas, and (raiding from Canada) Vermont.

From a total of 14 million white males, 2.9 million were in uniform—2.1 million for the Union and 800,000 for the Confederacy. This was over 20 percent—a higher proportion than in any other American war. The Union total included 180,000 black soldiers and perhaps 20,000 black sailors, nearly one tenth of the men in the Northern armed forces. Either as battle casualties or as victims of camp maladies, 618,000 men died in service (360,000 Union troops and 258,000 Confederates). More than one soldier in five lost his life—a far heavier ratio of losses than in any other war in our history. For the Confederate soldiers it was one in three.

Partly because the cost was proportionately so heavy, and partly because the Civil War was distinctly an American war, this conflict has occupied a place in the American memory and the American imagination that other wars—more recent, more destructive, and fought on a global scale—have never held. On both sides, men were fighting for what they deeply believed to be American values.

Southerners were convinced that their right to form a Confederacy was based on a principle of the Declaration of Independence—that governments derive their just powers from the consent of the governed. They were also fighting to defend their states from invasion. "All we ask is to be let alone," said Jefferson Davis in his first war message to the Confederate Congress. Early in the war some Union soldiers captured a Southern soldier, who from his tattered homespun butternut uniform was obviously not a member of the planter class. They asked him why he, a nonslaveholder, was fighting to uphold slavery. "I'm fighting because y'all are down here," was his reply.

The North was fighting to defend the flag and to prove that a democracy was not too weak to hold together. Secession was the "essence of anarchy," said Lincoln. "The central idea pervading this struggle is the necessity of proving that popular government is not an absurdity. We must settle this question now, whether in a free government the minority have the right to break up the government whenever they choose."

The Resources of North and South. In later years, after the Confederacy had gone down to defeat, men said that the Lost Cause, as Southerners called it, had been lost from the beginning and that the South had been fighting against the census returns. In many respects this seems true, for the South was completely outnumbered in almost all the factors of manpower and economic strength that make up the sinews of modern war. The eleven Confederate states had a white population of 5,450,000, while the nineteen free states had 18,950,000. These figures leave out both the population of the four border slave states of Missouri, Kentucky, Maryland, and Delaware and the slave population of the Confederate states.

The four border states were divided, but most of their people and resources supported the Union side. Slaves strengthened the Confederate war effort in an important way, however, for they constituted a majority of the South's labor force and thereby enabled most white men to leave home to fight in the army.

The Union was far ahead of the Confederacy in financial and economic strength. It had a bank capital more than four times as great as that of the South. It led the South in the number of manufacturing enterprises by six and a half to one; in the number of industrial workers by twelve to one; and in the value of its manufactures by eleven to one. In railroad mileage, it led by more than two to one.

But against these ratios of strength must be placed the fact that the Union was undertaking a vastly more difficult military objective. It was seeking to occupy and subdue an area larger than all of western Europe. This meant that armies had to be sent hundreds of miles into hostile territory and be maintained in these distant operations. This necessity involved the gigantic tasks of transporting the immense volume of supplies required by an

COMPARATIVE RESOURCES OF NORTH AND SOUTH, 1861

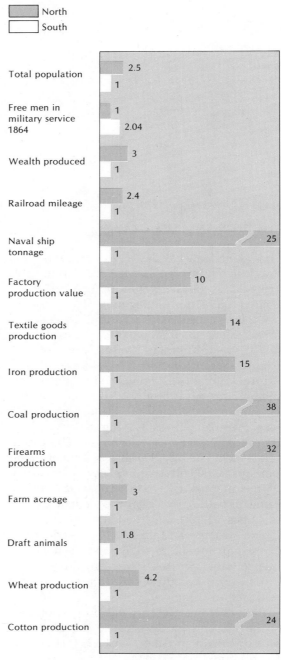

North
South

Total population	2.5 / 1
Free men in military service 1864	1 / 2.04
Wealth produced	3 / 1
Railroad mileage	2.4 / 1
Naval ship tonnage	25 / 1
Factory production value	10 / 1
Textile goods production	14 / 1
Iron production	15 / 1
Coal production	38 / 1
Firearms production	32 / 1
Farm acreage	3 / 1
Draft animals	1.8 / 1
Wheat production	4.2 / 1
Cotton production	24 / 1

Based on U.S. Census, 1860

army in the field and defending long lines of communication, which would be worthless if they were cut even at a single point. In wars prior to the Civil War, armies had depended upon the use of great wagon trains to bring supplies. As the supply lines lengthened, the horses ate up in fodder a steadily increasing proportion of the amount they could haul, until there was scarcely any margin left between what the supply lines carried and what they consumed in carrying it.

During the Civil War, for the first time in the history of warfare, railroads played a major part in the supply services. If these more efficient carriers of goods had not changed the whole nature of war, it is questionable whether invading armies could ever have marched from the Ohio to the Gulf of Mexico. Ten years earlier the United States had not possessed the railroad network which supplied the Union armies between 1861 and 1865. At an earlier time the defensive position of the South would have been far stronger.

But even with railroads, superior muni-

tions, and superior industrial facilities, the military tasks of the Union were most formidable. America was a profoundly civilian country. The peacetime army numbered only 16,000, and few people on either side had any conception of the vast problems involved in recruiting, mobilizing, equipping, training, and maintaining large armies. It was an amateur's war on both sides, and many of its features seem inconceivable today.

Most of the troops were recruited as volunteers rather than drafted. The Confederacy enacted conscription in April 1862 and the Union in March 1863. But the real purpose of these laws was to stimulate volunteering rather than to institute a genuine draft. Both the North and the South allowed drafted men to hire substitutes, until the Confederacy abolished this privilege in December 1863. The Union government also exempted a drafted man upon payment of a $300 commutation fee, until this privilege was abolished in July 1864.

Union conscription was applied only in

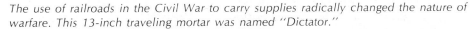

The use of railroads in the Civil War to carry supplies radically changed the nature of warfare. This 13-inch traveling mortar was named "Dictator."

localities which failed to meet their quotas. Thus communities were impelled to pay "bounties" to encourage men to volunteer. This resulted in the practice of "bounty-jumping." A man would enlist, collect his bounty, desert, enlist again in some other locality, collect another bounty, and desert again.

Volunteers enlisted for specified periods, normally three years. The Confederacy's draft laws compelled them to reenlist even when their enlistment terms were up. On the Union side, by contrast, volunteers could not be compelled to reenlist, and in 1864 the North had to rely on bounties and patriotic persuasion to induce more than half of its three-year volunteers to reenlist.

Volunteer regiments at first elected their own officers, up to the rank of captain, and they frequently preferred officers who were not strict in matters of discipline. This was to handicap them in battle, however. Men without prior training as officers were placed in positions of command, and recruits were often thrown into combat with little basic training as soldiers. Even physical examinations for recruits were often a farce. It was, to a considerable extent, a do-it-yourself war.

THE WAR IN THE FIELD

The Virginia Front. From the very outset of the war, attention was focused on the Virginia front. After fighting had begun at Fort Sumter and the states of the upper South had joined the Confederacy, the Confederate government moved its capital to Richmond, Virginia, about one hundred miles south of Washington. With the two seats of government so close together, the war in the East became a struggle on the part of the Union to capture Richmond and on the part of the South to defend it.

Between Washington and Richmond a number of broad rivers—the Potomac, the Rappahannock, the York, the Chickahominy, and other tributaries—flow more or less parallel with one another from the Allegheny Mountains in the west to Chesapeake Bay in the east. This grid of rivers afforded a natural system of defense to the South and presented an obstacle course to the North. Southern armies on the defensive could lie in wait for their attackers on the south banks of these streams, as they did at Bull Run, Fredericksburg, Chancellorsville, and the Wilderness. When the Southern army was driven back after going on the offensive, it could recross to safety, reorganize, and recoup, as it did after Antietam (Sharpsburg) and Gettysburg.

For four years the principal army of the North, the Army of the Potomac, struggled against the principal army of the South, the Army of Northern Virginia, over this terrain. Each side placed its foremost commander here. Robert E. Lee headed the Army of Northern Virginia after Joseph E. Johnston was wounded in 1862, while Ulysses S. Grant was brought east to take overall command of Union armies in 1864 after his great successes in the West. Public attention centered primarily upon these campaigns, and they have continued to receive more than their share of attention in history.

During the first half of the war, the Union met with a long succession of disappointments and defeats on the Virginia front. In July 1861, when both armies were still raw and unseasoned, the Union sent General Irvin McDowell south with the slogan "Forward to Richmond" and with expectations of an easy victory. But when he encountered the Confederate armies of Generals Pierre G. T. Beauregard and Joseph E. Johnston at Manassas Junction (the first battle of Bull Run), he was defeated. His army, which was too green to absorb a defeat, lost all organization and retreated in panic to Washington. McDowell was replaced by George Brinton McClellan, who had campaigned successfully in West Virginia—a little man of supremely self-confident manner who was inevitably compared with Napoleon. McClellan possessed real

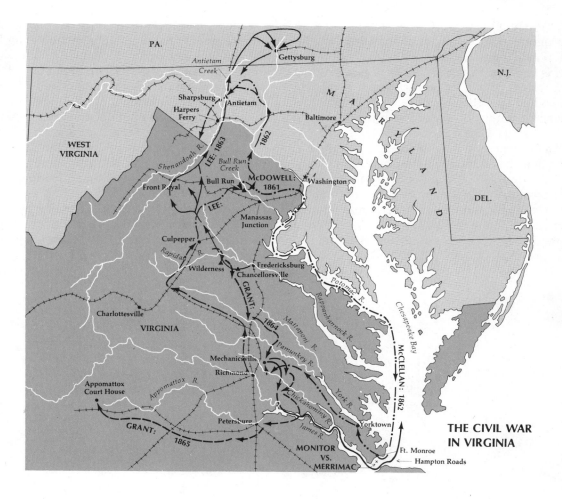

THE CIVIL WAR IN VIRGINIA

ability as an organizer, and he had the good sense to realize that he must make his troops into an army before he took them campaigning. Consequently, there was no more major fighting on the Virginia front for almost a year. When McClellan did at last move in April 1862, he persuaded President Lincoln to let him transport his troops by ship to Fort Monroe, a point on the Virginia coast within striking distance of Richmond. From this point he proposed to move up the peninsula between the York and the James Rivers (hence called the Peninsula Campaign) to capture the Confederate capital.

McClellan's plan was a brilliant solution to the difficult problem of supply, for he could now bring provisions for his army by ship without fear of Confederate raiders getting to his rear and cutting his lines. But the plan had one important drawback. It left, or appeared to leave, Washington exposed to the Confederates. Therefore, for the defense of the capital, President Lincoln insisted on withholding part of the troops that McClellan wanted. So although McClellan launched his invasion from Fort Monroe toward Richmond, he failed to push his offensive with the vigor the North expected.

While these developments were in progress, the Confederate commander, Joseph E. Johnston, was badly wounded and was replaced by Robert E. Lee. Lee, a Virginia aristocrat, mild of speech and gentle of manner but gifted with a daring that was terrible to his adversaries, quickly perceived that he could play upon the Union's fear that Washington was too exposed. Accordingly, he sent his brilliant subordinate, Thomas J. ("Stonewall") Jackson, on a raid up the Shenandoah Valley, appearing to threaten Washington and causing the administration to hold there defensive troops that had previously been promised to McClellan.

When Jackson returned from his raid with phenomenal speed, Lee's reunited forces took the offensive against McClellan's original forces south and east of Richmond in a series of engagements known as the Seven Days' Battles (June 25–July 1, 1862). McClellan fought hard and was not decisively defeated, but he lost his nerve, moved back to a base on the James River, and sent Washington a series of frantic messages that the government had deserted him. Lincoln, who had never fully accepted the basic idea of operating by sea, withdrew McClellan's troops from the peninsula to northern Virginia and placed most of them under the command of General John

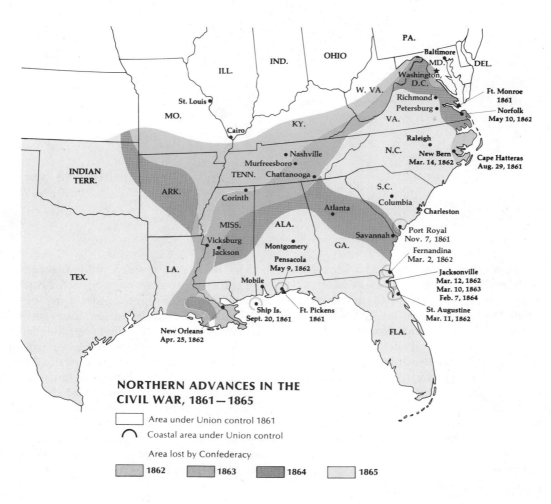

NORTHERN ADVANCES IN THE CIVIL WAR, 1861—1865

☐ Area under Union control 1861

⌒ Coastal area under Union control

Area lost by Confederacy

▨ 1862   ▨ 1863   ▨ 1864   ☐ 1865

Pope, who had gained a reputation in the West.

Pope promptly ran afoul of the Lee-Jackson combination at the Second Battle of Manassas (the second battle of Bull Run) in August 1862, and McClellan was restored to command and given a second chance. When Lee marched north, crossed the Potomac, and advanced into Maryland, McClellan shadowed him. Again Lee divided his forces, sending part of his army to capture Harpers Ferry. But even when a copy of Lee's secret orders fell into McClellan's hands and he knew exactly what to expect, he still did not move quickly or decisively. After a supremely hard-fought engagement at Antietam (Sharpsburg), Lee withdrew, bloodied, but not crushed, to the south bank of the Potomac. Lincoln again replaced McClellan, this time with Ambrose E. Burnside.

In December 1862 Burnside made an unimaginative frontal attack across the Rappahannock at Fredericksburg, Virginia, against prepared Confederate defenses. Fighting the Confederates on ground of their own choosing, he sustained terrible losses and was replaced by Joseph Hooker. Hooker seemed a man of boldness and decision, but in May 1863, after executing an excellent flanking march to maneuver Lee into battle on unfavorable terms, Hooker lost his poise and allowed Jackson's corps to roll up the Union right flank in a surprise attack that rocked the Federals and eventually drove them back across the Rappahannock. Although a great victory, the South paid a fearful price for Chancellorsville. Jackson was accidentally wounded by his own troops and died a few days later.

Hooker remained in command until Lee launched a second offensive against the North, this time into Pennsylvania. When Lee escaped from Hooker on the northward march, Lincoln again changed commanders, turning this time to George Gordon Meade. Meade's army and Lee's army met at Gettys-

burg, though neither had planned it that way. On the first three days of July 1863 the South made its supreme effort. The little town in Pennsylvania became the scene of the greatest battle ever fought in North America. Lee, facing Meade across a valley, threw his troops against the Union positions in a series of bold attacks, the most famous of which was Pickett's Charge. But Meade was too strong to be dislodged. Lee's forces, which had been fearfully punished, waited for more than a day to receive a counterattack that never came and then marched south. Meade did not pursue until too late, and ten days after the battle Lee recrossed the Potomac unmolested. The Army of Northern Virginia had still never been driven from a battlefield, but its great offensive power was forever broken.

The War in the West.   On July 4, 1863, the day on which Lee began his uncontested withdrawal, another Confederate general, John C. Pemberton, at Vicksburg, Mississippi, surrendered an army of about thirty thousand men—the largest that has ever been captured in North America. The man to whom he surrendered was Ulysses S. Grant, and the event marked the culmination of a series of campaigns in the West which had been much more decisive in their results than the eastern campaigns.

The whole region beyond the Alleghenies was far vaster and more broken up geographically than the Virginia theater, and the campaigns in the West never had a single focus as they did in Virginia. Operations along the Mississippi were scarcely coordinated with operations in the central and eastern parts of Tennessee and Kentucky, and neither of these was synchronized with activities "west of the River" in Missouri, Arkansas, most of Louisiana, and Texas. Essentially, however, it was the objective of the Union to gain control of the Mississippi and thus to cut off the western wing of the Confederacy. In this way Confederate armies would be deprived of reinforcements and supplies—especially of Texas cattle—which they vitally needed. A further division of the Confederacy would be undertaken by driving southeast through Kentucky and Tennessee, cutting vital Confederate rail connections at Chattanooga in eastern Tennessee, and continuing thence into the heart of the Confederacy, across Georgia to the sea. Such an operation would cut off the Gulf Coast region from the Atlantic seaboard and leave only Virginia, the Carolinas, and part of Georgia to support a hopeless cause.

It took three years and eight months for the Union to carry out these plans, although they had begun sooner than the great campaigns in Virginia. In February 1862, Grant, a man who had resigned from the army in 1854 as a failure and later been reinstated, captured two Confederate forts, Henry and Donelson, in western Tennessee, which controlled the Tennessee and Cumberland Rivers. Unlike the streams of Virginia, which cut across the paths of advancing armies, each of these rivers flowed in a "U"-shaped course from the southern Appalachians southward into northern Alabama (in the case of the Tennessee) or central Tennessee (in the case of the Cumberland) and then, reversing their course, almost due north to the Ohio River. Control of these river highways gave Grant easy entry deep into the South.

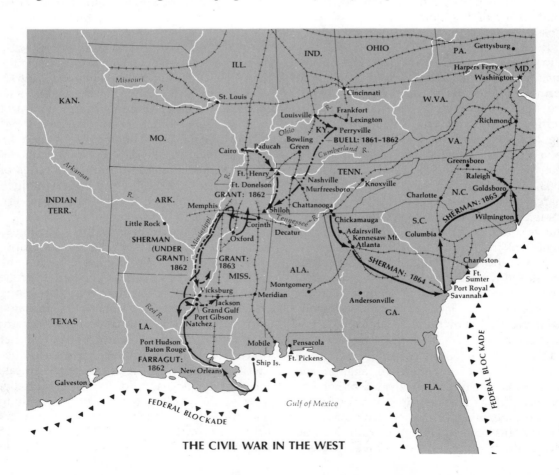

THE CIVIL WAR IN THE WEST

On the Cumberland, Nashville, the capital of Tennessee, fell to the Union as soon as Fort Donelson was captured, and by April Grant had advanced up the Tennessee almost to the border of Mississippi. In that same month, when all was still very "quiet along the Potomac," the Union army and navy, by skillful combined operations, captured New Orleans, the largest city of the Confederacy.

After these early successes, the Union forces found themselves blocked for some time. A Confederate army under Albert Sidney Johnston struck Grant unexpectedly at Shiloh, Tennessee, on April 6, 1862. In two days of fierce fighting that cost Johnston's life, the Union forces blunted the Southern attack and with reinforcements on the second day Grant counterattacked and drove the Confederates back to Mississippi. The next six months saw inconclusive thrusts and counterthrusts by both sides in the Western theater.

During the winter of 1862–1863 Grant began a campaign against the Confederate stronghold at Vicksburg, where towering bluffs command the Mississippi. Deep in enemy country, Vicksburg was rendered almost impregnable by vast swamps, by a succession of steep hills, and by the river itself. After making a series of unsuccessful moves against this natural fortress, Grant at last hit on the bold and unorthodox plan of moving down the west side of the river, crossing below Vicksburg, abandoning his lines of communication, and living off the country during a final drive against the Confederate defenses. It was by this plan that he finally captured Pemberton's entire army at Vicksburg on July 4, 1863, and gained complete control of the Mississippi artery.

Among the many unsuccessful attempts to take the Confederate stronghold at Vicksburg was a canal, dug in hopes of cutting the city off from the Mississippi River.

Grant Takes Command. Grant confirmed his reputation as the North's best general by taking command of the Union forces at Chattanooga after their bloody defeat in the Battle of Chickamauga (September 19–20, 1863) and launching a coordinated attack that drove General Braxton Bragg's Confederate army all the way to Dalton, Georgia, in battles on November 23–25. In March 1864, Lincoln brought Grant east to serve as general-in-chief and to take personal charge of the Army of the Potomac (Meade was not removed but was under Grant's command).

By this time the Confederacy, outnumbered from the beginning, was fearfully handicapped by losses of men which could not be replaced as Union losses could. Grant, recognizing this handicap, settled upon a plan of operations that was far less brilliant than his operations in the West, but no less decisive. By steadily extending his flanks, he forced the Confederacy to extend also and to make its lines very thin. And by continuing pressure, he gave his adversaries no rest. Lee resisted with immense skill, while Grant sacrificed men so freely between May 5 and June 3 in the Virginia campaign that his losses almost equaled the total number of men in Lee's army.

In June 1864, after being terribly punished at the Battle of Cold Harbor, Grant decided to move his base to the James River (as McClellan had done two years earlier), to attack from the south. He succeeded in this maneuver and thus pinned Lee's forces at Petersburg, which is actually south of Richmond. With Petersburg under siege and Lee no longer mobile, it was only a question of time, but Lee held on for nine long months while Richmond remained the Confederate capital.

Sherman's March. While Grant and Lee faced each other across the trenches at Petersburg, the Confederacy was being cut to pieces from the rear. Grant had first cut it at Vicksburg on the Mississippi, and the next cut was to take place from eastern Tennessee into Georgia. When Grant left for Virginia, William T. Sherman, a trusted subordinate, remained to face the Confederate forces under Joseph E. Johnston in the mountains of north Georgia.

Johnston, a "retreating general" but a resourceful obstructionist, blocked and delayed Sherman at every step, all the way to Atlanta. There he was removed because of his unwillingness to take the offensive, and John B. Hood was put in his place. Hood made the mistake of challenging Sherman in a series of direct attacks and was so badly defeated that Sherman, after taking Atlanta on September 2, 1864, was able to march unopposed across Georgia to the sea. Sherman reached the port of Savannah on Christmas, 1864, while Grant was still outside Petersburg.

Of all the Civil War generals, Grant and especially Sherman had the most "modern" conception of warfare. They were pioneers in the practice of total war. Sherman had become convinced that "we are not only fighting hostile armies, but a hostile people." Defeat of the Southern armies would not be enough to win this war. The railroads, farms, and factories that fed and supplied the armies must also be destroyed and the will of the civilian population that sustained the armies must be crushed. "We cannot change the hearts of those people of the South," said Sherman in 1864, "but we can make war so terrible. . .and make them so sick of war that generations would pass away before they would again appeal to it." The march of his army from Atlanta to the sea not only destroyed Confederate resources but also functioned as a form of psychological warfare. "It is a demonstration to the world," wrote Sherman, "that we have a power which Jefferson Davis cannot resist. This may not be war but rather statesmanship."

Appomattox. From this time, the South was completely fragmented and the Confederacy's cause was hopeless. But Johnston, having

Sherman's policy of total war called for the bombardment of Southern cities as a form of psychological warfare. This photo shows part of Charleston, South Carolina, in ruins.

returned to his command in the Southeast, held together a force that retreated across the Carolinas, with Sherman pursuing and wreaking havoc in South Carolina as he pursued. Lee, meanwhile, held against steadily increasing odds at Petersburg. By April 1865, however, the inevitable defeat could be put off no longer. Petersburg fell and Richmond was evacuated. Lee met Grant on April 9 at a farmhouse near Appomattox Court House, and in a moving scene surrendered the Army of Northern Virginia to Grant, who accorded generous terms and told his troops not to cheer because, he said, "the rebels are our countrymen again." Johnston also surrendered at Greensboro, North Carolina, before the end of the month, and the Confederate government, which had fled south after the fall of Petersburg, simply evaporated.

THE WAR BEHIND THE LINES

The Problems of the Confederacy.   Writers on the Civil War have piled up a vast literature— one of the largest bodies of literature on any historical subject—detailing the military aspects of the war: the battles and leaders, the campaigns and maneuvers, the strategy and tactics. This military record, however, does not fully explain the outcome of the war. For, in terms of strategy and tactics, the Confederate performance equaled that of the Union and, on the Virginia front, surpassed it until the last year of the war. The final result was registered on the battlefield, but the basic factors which caused Confederate defeat lay behind the lines. Essentially, the Confederacy failed to solve the problems of organizing its society and its economy for war. It faced these problems in a particularly difficult form, and when it proved unable to solve them, it went down to defeat.

One basic handicap of the Confederacy lay in the fact that while the North had a balanced agricultural and industrial economy that was invigorated by war, the Southern economy was based primarily on cotton production, which was dislocated and almost paralyzed by the war. In the North, war stimulated employment, and while wages failed to keep pace with inflation, civilian morale was generally high except among the underpaid urban poor. In the South, economic conditions deteriorated so badly that what may be called economic morale declined even while fighting morale remained good. During the spring of 1863 "bread riots" occurred in Richmond and several other Southern cities.

Essentially, the Confederacy, with its rural and agricultural society, needed two things. First, it needed access to the products of European—especially British—industry. Second, it needed to stimulate production of food, of horses, and of strategic supplies within the South. Ultimately, it was unable to meet most of those needs.

In order to be able to draw on British industry, the Confederacy needed to have buying power in the European market and to be able to ship goods freely to and fro across the Atlantic. But once war broke out, Lincoln proclaimed a blockade, which meant that federal naval vessels would try to seize the merchant vessels of any neutral country bringing goods to Confederate ports.

Southerners thought that the blockade would not work, partly because there were not enough Union ships to enforce it and even more because they believed in what has been called the "King Cotton delusion." They were firmly convinced that cotton was an absolute economic necessity to Britain, because textiles were the heart of British industry. Without cotton this industry would be prostrated. Britain's factories would stand idle, and its workers would be unemployed and would literally starve. When this started happening, the British government would decide to intervene to get cotton. The British navy, which still dominated the seas, would break the blockade.

Southerners were so confident of this idea that they were quite willing to see the British supply of cotton cut off for a while. In the first months of the blockade, while it was still largely ineffective, they deliberately kept their cotton at home instead of sending a part of it abroad to be held in British warehouses for later sale to give them funds for the purchase of supplies. But the bumper crops of the previous two years had produced such a surplus that British manufacturers were able to operate without interruption for nearly a year after the war broke out.

The Importance of Sea Power. For this and other reasons, the faith in cotton ultimately proved to be a fallacy. Britain got increased supplies of cotton from Egypt and India. Also, British antislavery sentiment generated a strong resistance to taking steps that would help the Confederacy. And Britain was pleased to see America adopting a doctrine of international law concerning the right of blockade which she had always advocated and which was bound to be favorable to a nation with large naval power. But most of all, British industry was not paralyzed because Northern wartime purchase stimulated it. Britain, as a neutral, enjoyed an economic boom from supplying war materials to the Union—a boom very similar to the booms the United States later enjoyed in 1914–1917 and 1939–1941 as a neutral supplying war materials to Britain.

Consequently, Britain and France, which was following Britain's lead, never did give diplomatic recognition to the Confederate government, although they did recognize the existence of a state of war in which they would be neutral. This meant that they would treat Confederate naval vessels as warships and not as pirates.

The British recognition of belligerency was much resented in the United States, but in fact the real danger for the Union cause lay in the possibility of diplomatic recognition of the Confederacy, which would probably have resulted in efforts by the British to break the blockade. Such efforts would, in turn, have led to war with Britain. But this recognition, for which the Confederacy waited so anxiously, never came.

In November 1861 Confederate hopes were high when an eager Union naval officer, Charles Wilkes, stopped the British ship *Trent* on the high seas and took off two Confederate envoys to Britain, James Mason and John Slidell. Britain, at this point, actually prepared to fight, but President Lincoln wisely admitted the error and set the envoys free. Meanwhile, the blockade steadily grew tighter. One Confederate port after another was sealed off. Small Confederate vessels, built for speed and based in the Bahama Islands, continued to delight the South by running the blockade and bringing in cargoes of goods with high value in proportion to their bulk. But their volume was small, and they did not in any sense provide the flow of goods that the Confederacy so vitally needed.

In addition to depending on British naval might, the Confederacy made two important efforts to establish sea power of its own. To begin with, it fitted out the first large ironclad vessel ever to put to sea. A powerful steam frigate, the U.S.S. *Merrimac,* which the federals had scuttled in the Norfolk Navy Yard, was raised, renamed the *Virginia*, covered with armor plate, and sent out in March 1862—an iron giant against the wooden vessels of the Union navy. In its first day at sea it destroyed two large Union vessels with ease.

The entire Union navy appeared to be in acute danger, and there was panic in Northern coastal cities. But the Union had been preparing a metal-clad vessel of its own—a small craft that lay low in the water, with a revolving gun turret. This *Monitor*, as it was called, challenged the *Virginia* on March 9, 1862. The battle ended in a draw, but with Monitor-type vessels the Union navy was again safe.

The Confederacy's second major endeavor at sea was to buy vessels and equipment in England. Under the technicalities of British law, these could be combined on the high seas to produce fighting ships without violating Britain's neutrality. Such vessels could then raid merchant vessels flying the Union flag.

There were several of these raiders, most famous of which was the *Alabama*. This great marauder, commanded by Admiral Raphael Semmes, roamed the seas for two years, from Newfoundland to Singapore, capturing sixty-two merchant ships (most of which were burned, after careful attention to the safety of their crews and passengers). It also sank the U.S.S. *Hatteras* in a major naval battle. It was at last cornered and sunk off Cherbourg, France, by the U.S.S. *Kearsarge*, but its career had made the American flag so unsafe on the high seas that prohibitive insurance costs caused more than 700 American vessels to transfer to British registry. The American merchant marine never again attained the place in the world's carrying trade that it had held before the *Alabama* put to sea.

The Confederacy sought to have additional raiders built in British shipyards, and two immensely formidable vessels—the Laird rams—were actually constructed. But there were vigorous protests from Charles Francis Adams, the American minister to England, and the British were aware that in spite of technicalities this was really a violation of neutrality. So the British government stopped their delivery in September 1863. After this the Confederate cause was lost at sea as well as on land, and the federal blockade tightened like a noose to strangle the Confederacy economically.

Economic Failures of the South. Meanwhile, on the home front, the Confederacy failed economically because it was caught between the need to stimulate production and the need to keep down prices and control inflation. The Southern government began with few financial assets other than land and slaves, neither of which could be readily transformed into negotiable currency. It faced a dilemma. It could either encourage production by buying goods in the open market at an uncontrolled price, in which case inflation would mushroom. Or it could control inflation by a system of requisitioning goods for its armies at arbitrarily fixed prices, in which case production would be discouraged rather than stimulated. Help in reducing this problem would have required a program of heavy taxation, by which the government would take back the inflationary dollars that had been spent. But the Confederacy was afraid to use its taxing power. It raised less than 5 percent of its revenue from taxes—a smaller proportion than any other nation in a modern war. Its bond drives to raise funds by borrowing also fell short of hopes.

The South's main source of money was the printing press—the most inflationary method of all. Prices rose by 9,000 percent in the four years of war. Goods grew scarcer while money grew more plentiful. It was grimly said that at the beginning of the war people took their money to market in a purse and brought their goods home in a basket, but that by the end they took the money in a basket and brought their purchases home in a purse.

In short, the Confederacy died of economic starvation—an insufficiency of goods. Its government was too weak to cope with the nearly insoluble economic problems the war had caused. President Jefferson Davis was a bureaucrat who thought in legalistic rather than in dynamic terms. He was not an innovator but a conservative miscast as a revolutionist. The state governments also competed against the Confederate government for the control of manpower and supplies. They insisted upon their sovereign status so strenuously that it has been said that the Confederacy was born of states' rights and died of states' rights.

The only chance the Confederacy ever had—and it was perhaps a fairly good one—was to win a short war before the results of economic malnutrition set in. Once that failed, the cause was hopeless. A few Confederates, like Josiah Gorgas in the Ordnance Department, improvised brilliantly, and others did so desperately. But in a country where a vitally necessary rail line could be laid only by tearing up the rails somewhere else and re-laying them, a long war against a dynamic adversary could have but one end.

Northern Industrialism and Republican Ascendancy. The problems and limitations of the Confederacy—problems of localism and decentralization, of an agricultural economy and of small-scale economic activities—were characteristic features of the kind of folk society the Confederacy was defending. But while the South was making a last stand against the forces of the modern mechanized world, the war was rushing the North along the path toward industrial domination. Before the Southern states withdrew from the Union, they had blocked some of the governmental measures most conducive to the new industrial economy. Southern secession, however, left the new Republican party in control. The Republicans combined a free-soil, antislavery ideology with the traditional Whig policy of using the government to stimulate economic growth. While this program was designed to promote the mutual interests of capital and free labor, Republican economic legislation in practice usually helped the former more than the latter.

Thus secession and the war enabled the Republicans to enact what one historian has called their "blueprint for modern America." In February 1861, while the empty seats of the departing Southern congressmen were still warm, and even before President Lincoln took office, Congress adopted the Morrill Tariff, which, though not very high, was higher than the existing tariff of 1857. This was the first of many tariff increases. There was not another perceptible reduction until 1913. Meanwhile Congress repeatedly strengthened the measures by which it gave American industrial producers more exclusive control in the American market, even if this forced American consumers to pay higher prices than they would have had to pay on the world market.

The Transcontinental Railroad. In 1862 Congress broke the long deadlock the sectional conflict had created over the building of a railroad to the Pacific. For a decade, advocates of a southern route and supporters of a northern route had blocked each other. Now, with the Southerners absent, Congress created the Union Pacific Railroad Company, incorporated with a federal charter, to build westward from Omaha and to meet another road, the Central Pacific, a California corporation, building eastward from Sacramento. To encourage this enterprise, Congress placed very large resources at the disposal of the railroads. For each mile of track built it gave to the roads ten square miles of land, running back in alternate blocks from the tracks. And it granted loans (not gifts) of between $16,000 and $48,000 a mile—according to the difficulty of the terrain where construction took place.

The value of the lands at that time was not great, and the munificence of this largesse has often been exaggerated. But the point is that

When the final spike was driven, the Union Pacific and the Central Pacific railroads were united, allowing rail travel from coast to coast. The event was a cause for great celebration.

the government was paying most of the costs of construction, whereas it might well have controlled or even owned the railroad. Instead, it placed these resources in the hands of private operators, who, if they succeeded, would become owners of the world's greatest railroad. And if they lost, they would be losing the government's money rather than their own. It was "venture capitalism," as it is now called, but the government was doing most of the venturing and the private interests which constructed the road were getting most of the capital.

In 1869, four years after the war ended, the Union Pacific and the Central Pacific met at Promontory Point in Utah, and a golden spike was driven to mark the event. Travelers to California no longer were obliged to go by wagon train or sail around Cape Horn. The United States was a long step closer to being a transcontinental, two-ocean republic in an operative sense as well as in a purely geographical one.

The National Banking System. One other major economic measure resulting from Republican ascendancy was the creation of a new and far more centralized system of banking and money. Ever since Andrew Jackson's overthrow of the Bank of the United States in 1832, the country had had a decentralized, loose-jointed financial system—one which today it is difficult even to imagine. The United States, of course, issued coins and also bills. For each bill in circulation, a corresponding value of precious metal was held in the Treasury and could be claimed by the holder of the bill. The government handled all its own transactions in such currency and was thus on a "hard money" basis.

Actually, however, this kind of money was not nearly sufficient to meet the economic needs of the country for a circulating medium. The principal circulating medium, therefore, had been provided by notes issued by banks operating under charters from the various states. State laws governing the incorporation of banks naturally varied, which meant that the financial soundness of the various banks also varied. This in turn meant that some of the notes circulated at face value, while others circulated at various degrees of discount from face value. So although the government was on a hard money basis, the economy of the country was not, and the federal government exercised no control whatever over the principal component in the monetary system of the country.

The Legal Tender Act of 1862 and the National Banking Act of 1863 changed all this. They grew out of the government's need to raise the immense sums required to fight the war. The Legal Tender Act authorized the issuance of Treasury notes—the famous greenbacks—which circulated as authorized money without a backing in metal held in the Treasury.

But primarily the Treasury relied upon borrowing—that is, upon selling bonds. To borrow it had to make the bonds attractive as holdings for the banks. Accordingly, the National Banking Act provided that a bank which purchased government bonds to the amount of one third of its paid-in capital might issue federally guaranteed notes, known as national bank notes, in an amount equal to 90 percent of its bond holdings.

In 1865 a tax was laid on the notes issued under state authority by state-chartered banks. The tax had the effect of making these notes unprofitable and thus driving them out of circulation. As a result of government borrowing policy, therefore, the United States acquired a new, uniform, federally sanctioned circulating medium of national bank notes.

These notes became the principal form of money for the next fifty years, but they had a great defect—they made the amount of money dependent upon the volume of federal debt rather than upon the economic needs of the country. They were inflexible, and in 1913 they were largely replaced by Federal Reserve notes as a result of the establishment of the Federal Reserve System. But the principles that the United States should have a uniform currency in use throughout the nation, and that the federal government should be responsible for this currency, had come to stay.

Women and the War. Although the Civil War brought suffering and loss to hundreds of thousands of American women, the war meant progress toward independence and equality for women as a group. It meant new opportunities for employment, broadened social and political interests, and demonstrations of competence in activities previously reserved for men. Some women went to war—as nurses, spies, even as soldiers. But the vast majority who served at home—including those who stayed in the home—did most damage to the myth of the helpless female.

As in earlier wars, but in much greater numbers, women had to take their husbands' places as heads of households, running shops, managing farms and plantations, finding jobs to earn food for their families. In the South, many had to do housework—and field work—for the first time. Some had to face armed, hostile blacks as well as enemy soldiers. In Minnesota and elsewhere on the frontier, women had to survive Indian uprisings.

Job opportunities for women multiplied as men went off to fight or quit old occupations for better-paying ones. The war quickened the movement of women into school teaching, a profession once dominated by men. Many Northern women also went South to teach in schools for freed slaves. In both the Union and the Confederacy women also went to work for the government. By the end of the war thousands held government office jobs. Here, too, the change was permanent: Washington, D.C., would never again be without its corps of women workers. Many were employed, and some were killed, in government arsenals.

When the war began, women dominated the work force in the mills and factories of New England, while in the South women industrial workers were a small minority— another situation that favored the Union war effort. As men joined the service, women took their places in industry and helped produce military equipment and supplies. The demand for what was considered women's work also expanded: Sewing women were hired by the thousands, and brutally exploited. In self-protection, the women organized, protested, and went out on strikes.

In addition to work for pay, there was a tremendous amount of unpaid activity by women in both South and North. Women volunteered to nurse and to teach. They joined aid societies. They organized activities to raise funds. They wrote and spoke for the causes they believed in. Many of them demonstrated talents of efficiency and leadership. They were also passionately partisan, pushing men and boys into enlisting and preaching hatred of the enemy to their children. In the South some turned food riots into excuses for looting; in the North some helped turn draft riots into murderous assaults on blacks.

The Civil War gave American women a chance to enter many new areas and prove themselves quite as capable as men. They proved their smartness and their toughness. When the war ended, many lost their jobs to returning veterans. Some returned gratefully to domesticity. But there was no turning back the clock.

EMANCIPATION AND RECONSTRUCTION

The Road to Reunion. Wars always bring results not intended by those who fight them. The Civil War accelerated the growth of mass production and economic centralization in the North while it destroyed much of the economic plant in the South and convinced the rising generation of Southern leaders that future regional prosperity would depend upon industrialization. The war also caused an increase in federal power at the expense of the states, for no government could spend the funds, organize the forces, and wield the strength the federal government did, without increasing its power. But the main purpose of the war was to reunite a broken union of states, and there was a question whether the abolition of slavery was necessary to the objective of reunion. Some Republicans wanted to make emancipation one of the objects of the war, simply because they deplored slavery and did not believe that a Union which had slavery in it was worth saving. Others, who were relatively indifferent to the welfare of the blacks, believed that the slaveholding class, which they called the "slave power," was guilty of causing disunion, that to make the Union safe this power must be destroyed, and that the way to destroy it was to abolish slavery. Still others, including many of the "War Democrats" and the Unionists in the border states, regarded the war as one against secession, having nothing to do with slavery.

Emancipation. For his part, Abraham Lincoln had stated his belief, long before he became President, that the Union could not endure permanently half-slave and half-free. He knew, however, that he could not free any slaves unless he won the war and that he could not win the war if he antagonized all the Unionists in the slave states of Delaware, Maryland, Kentucky (his own birthplace), and Missouri. As a result, he moved very slowly on the slavery question, and when two of his generals tried to move more quickly by emancipating slaves in the areas they had occupied, he countermanded their orders.

Few people realize it today, but the war had raged for seventeen months and was more than a third over before Lincoln moved to free the slaves in the Confederacy. In July 1862 he made up his mind to proclaim the freedom of slaves in the insurrectionary states, but he decided to wait for a victory before doing so. The Battle of Antietam (Sharpsburg) in September was not a great victory, but it sufficed. In that month Lincoln issued a proclamation that after January 1, 1863, all slaves in areas which were at that time in rebellion should be "forever free." This still did nothing about slaves in places like New Orleans, which was occupied by federal forces or in the border slave states. It also gave all the states of the Confederacy one hundred days during which they could save slavery by coming back into the Union.

Strongly believing in persuasion rather than force, Lincoln in December 1862 proposed a constitutional amendment for the gradual emancipation of slaves in the border states by the year 1900, with compensation to the owners. But this proposal was overtaken by events as the escalating impact of the war accelerated the destruction of slavery. On January 1, 1863, Lincoln issued the Emancipation Proclamation, to apply in all areas under Confederate control. Although it would require Northern victory to become a reality, this Proclamation announced a new Union war aim—freedom for the slaves as well as restoration of the Union.

The caution with which Lincoln had proceeded with emancipation reflects his own scruples about the Constitution and the prudence of his own temperament, but it also reflects the fierceness of the divisions within the North and the dangers that these divisions held for the administration. On one flank, Lincoln was assailed by the Democrats. A minority of War Democrats gave him vigorous support, but a majority of the Democrats, known as "Copperheads," constantly called for a negotiated peace, and especially assailed any move against slavery. Democratic propagandists helped convince white workingmen that they were being used in a war to free blacks who would take their jobs away. It was this conviction that turned the "draft riots" in New York in July 1863 into mob assaults on blacks. More than a hundred people were killed in these assaults, most of them white rioters shot down by police and troops.

On the other flank, the more militant antislavery men in the Republican party denounced Lincoln because he did not instantly take drastic action to end slavery. These "radical Republicans" hoped to dominate the administration by forcing all moderates on the slavery question out of the cabinet, and in 1864 some of them sought to prevent Lincoln's nomination for a second term. But by unrivaled political dexterity and skill Lincoln frustrated these attacks from both directions and maintained a broad base of support for the war.

As late as 1864 the House of Representatives defeated a constitutional amendment for the abolition of slavery. The Thirteenth Amendment, abolishing slavery, was not finally voted by Congress for submission to the states until January 31, 1865. Maryland, Tennessee, and Missouri abolished slavery by state action at about this same time, but slavery was still legal in Kentucky and Delaware when the Civil War ended, and the amendment was not ratified until eight months after Lincoln's death.

Lincoln as a War Leader. Long after these events, people who had grown up with an oversimplified image of Lincoln as a Great Emancipator became disillusioned by this record, and in the twentieth century some critics have sought to tear down his reputation. But he remains a figure of immense stature.

Born in 1809 in a log cabin in Kentucky, Lincoln grew up on the frontier in Indiana and

Abraham Lincoln is portrayed with members of his Cabinet at the first reading of the Emancipation Proclamation in 1863.

Illinois, doing rough work as a rail splitter and a plowboy and receiving only a meager education. Later he became a self-taught lawyer with a successful practice in Springfield, served in the state legislature as a Whig, and rode the circuit on horseback to follow the sessions of the court. Except for one term in Congress, 1847–1849, he rarely went East and was relatively unknown until the debates with Douglas gained him a reputation in 1858. In 1861, at a moment of crisis, this tall, gangling, plain-looking man, whose qualities of greatness were still unsuspected, became President.

Lincoln's relaxed and unpretentious manner masked remarkable powers of decision and qualities of leadership. Completely lacking in self-importance, he seemed humble to some observers. But he acted with the patience and forbearance of a man who was sure of what he was doing. He refused to let the abolitionists push him into an antislavery war which would antagonize Union men who did not care about slavery, and refused to let the Union men separate him from the antislavery contingent by restricting war aims too narrowly. He saw that the causes of Union and emancipation must support each other instead of opposing each other, or both would be defeated.

Patiently he worked to fuse the idea of union with that of freedom and equality ("a new nation conceived in liberty and dedicated to the proposition that all men are created equal"). Thus he reaffirmed for American nationalism the idealism of freedom and gave to the ideal of freedom the strength of an undivided union. Knowing that in a democracy a man must win political success in order to gain a chance for statesmanship, he moved patiently and indirectly to his goals. His opportunism offended many abolitionists, but in the end he struck slavery the fatal blow.

Black Americans and the War. For black Americans, the Civil War years were a time of elation and rejoicing, frustration and despair. Black men and women alike worked hard for the Union cause. Black intellectuals wrote and lectured, at home and abroad. Blacks organized their own aid and relief societies for the great numbers of freed slaves and went to them as teachers. Black women volunteered their services as nurses and hospital aids. Black men by the hundreds of thousands went to war for the Union as sailors in the navy and as servants, cooks, and laborers with the army. When they were finally allowed to, they also went as soldiers.

But for a long time blacks were not allowed to serve in the army. Not until the autumn of 1862 were blacks officially permitted to enlist, and it was another year before the bravery of black regiments in battle began to change the scornful attitude of whites, in and out of the service. Overall, black servicemen established an admirable record, and twenty-one received the Congressional Medal of Honor. But the officers in black regiments were mostly white men. Only a handful of black soldiers were promoted to the rank of lieutenant or captain. Not until June 1864 was the pay of black and white soldiers equalized.

Throughout the war, then, blacks continued to face injustice and discrimination, despite their major contribution to the Union cause. From the beginning, their most influential spokesman, Frederick Douglass, looked on Lincoln as much too conservative, and when the President delayed taking decisive steps toward freeing the slaves, Douglass was outspoken in his criticism.

Although Lincoln had his black supporters, including the beloved Harriet Tubman, he also gave offense by his continuing interest in some programs to move blacks out of the country to a colony in the tropics. In fact, there were some blacks who were so embittered that they welcomed the possibility of such separation. Martin R. Delany, who later joined with Douglass in working for black recruitment, favored the migration of Ameri-

A regiment of black soldiers from Massachusetts stormed Fort Wagner in a heroic battle in 1863. As this engraving shows, their officers were white men.

can blacks to Haiti, a project that was tried unsuccessfullly early in the war. After the rejection of black volunteers by the army, the subsequent mistreatment of black soldiers, and attacks on both black soldiers and black civilians in several Northern cities, there were blacks who agreed with white racists that the Civil War was indeed a white man's war in a white man's country, to which blacks owed no allegiance.

Nevertheless, there was progress. The Emancipation Proclamation was finally issued. The Thirteenth Amendment was adopted. The great slave population (which, as Douglass had repeatedly pointed out, enabled the Confederacy to put so large a proportion of its whites into uniform) was finally freed. Many blacks, Union soldiers as well as former slaves, were also freed from the bonds of illiteracy by dedicated teachers—both black and white—and through their own efforts.

After the war blacks were recognized as full citizens by the federal government and campaigns against discrimination in the law courts, the polling places, the schools, and public conveyances won victories in several states. In 1864 black representatives from eighteen states formed the National Equal Rights League. The long, agonizingly slow march toward equality had begun.

Lincoln's Plan of Reconstruction. Although he had always opposed slavery on moral as well as political grounds, Lincoln was skeptical about the prospects for racial equality in the United States. The legacy of slavery and race prejudice, he believed, would prevent blacks from rising to the level of whites or prevent whites from allowing blacks to rise to their level. This was why Lincoln had supported the colonization abroad of freed slaves as a possible solution of the race problem.

By 1864, however, the President was convinced of the impracticality if not the injustice of this policy. The contribution of blacks to the Union war effort and the growing strength of Northern antislavery convictions also made him more hopeful about the chances for eventual black advancement and racial adjustment. On this question, though, Lincoln remained a moderate and a gradualist to the end of his life.

Lincoln and the Northern moderates also believed that victory in war could not really restore the Union. It could only prevent secession. After that, the Union would be really restored only if the Southern people again accepted the Union and gave their loyalty to it. To bring them back, Lincoln wanted a conciliatory policy. So when in 1864 Congress adopted a measure known as the Wade-Davis Bill, imposing stringent terms for the restoration of the former Confederates, Lincoln vetoed it. When people raised technical questions about the legal status of the Confederate states (Were they still states, or conquered territories? Had they committed "state suicide"?), he was impatient about such "pernicious abstractions." All that mattered was whether the the states could be brought back into their proper relationship with the Union.

By 1864 the Union had regained enough control in Louisiana, Tennessee, and Arkansas to start a process of restoring these states to the Union, and Lincoln laid down generous terms on which this could be done. He would grant amnesty to former Confederates who took an oath of allegiance, and when as many

as one tenth of the number who had been citizens in 1860 did so, he would permit them to form a new state government. When this government accepted the abolition of slavery and repudiated the principle of secession, Lincoln would receive it back into the Union. It did not have to recognize the rights of blacks or give a single one the vote.

Louisiana was the first state reorganized on this basis, and despite its denial of black suffrage, Lincoln accepted it, though he did ask the governor "whether some of the colored people may not be let in, as for instance the very intelligent, and especially those who have fought gallantly in our ranks." In Virginia, Tennessee, and Arkansas, also, Lincoln recognized state governments which did not enfranchise the black Americans.

But it was clear that Republicans in Congress were suspicious of these states—more because of their leniency toward the former Confederates than because of their treatment of the blacks. It was also clear that Congress might deny them recognition by refusing to seat their newly elected senators and representatives.

In 1864, when the time came for a new presidential election, the Democrats nominated General McClellan to run against Lincoln. Some of the so-called Radical Republicans, who were dissatisfied with Lincoln's leniency, tried to block his renomination and put up the Secretary of the Treasury, Salmon P. Chase, in his stead. But this effort failed, and Lincoln was renominated. In an effort to put the ticket on a broad, bipartisan basis, the party dropped the name Republican, called itself the Union party, and nominated for the vice-presidency a Southern Democrat who had stood firmly for the Union, Andrew Johnson of Tennessee.

In November 1864 Lincoln and Johnson were elected, carrying all but three Union states (New Jersey, Delaware, and Kentucky). In the following March, the new term began, and Lincoln delivered his Second Inaugural Address, calling for "malice toward none and charity for all," in order "to bind up the nation's wounds." On April 9, Lee surrendered the Army of Northern Virginia. It was clear that the work of Reconstruction must now begin in earnest. On April 14, Lincoln attended a performance at Ford's Theater, where he was shot by an assassin, John Wilkes Booth. He died the next morning, without ever recovering consciousness, and Andrew Johnson became President of the United States.

Johnson's Policy of Reconstruction. Although a Southerner, Johnson was expected to be more severe in his Reconstruction policy than Lincoln. Johnson was a former tailor who had been illiterate until his wife taught him to write. He was a man of strong emotions and he hated both aristocrats and secessionists. But when his policy developed, it turned out that he disliked abolitionists and radicals even more. In the end, Johnson proved more lenient toward former Confederates than Lincoln had been.

On May 29, 1865, he issued a broad amnesty to all who would take an oath of allegiance, though men with property valued at more than $20,000 (in other words, planters) were required to ask special pardon, which was freely given. In the six weeks after May 29 he appointed provisional governors in each of the remaining Southern states to reorganize governments for these states. Only men who had been voters in 1860 and who had taken the oath of allegiance could participate in these reorganizations. This meant, of course, that blacks were excluded. When the new governments disavowed secession, accepted the abolition of slavery, and repudiated the Confederate debt, Johnson would accept them. As to what policy should be followed toward the freedmen, that was to be determined by the states themselves.

The Southern states moved swiftly under this easy formula. Before the end of the year, every state except Texas, which followed soon after, had set up a new government that met the President's terms. But two conspicuous features of these governments were deeply disturbing to many Republicans.

First, these Southern states had adopted a series of laws known as "Black Codes," which denied to blacks many of the rights of citizenship—including the right to vote and to serve on juries—and which also excluded them from certain types of property ownership and certain occupations. Unemployed Negroes might be arrested as vagrants and bound out to labor in a new form of involuntary servitude.

Second, the former Confederates were in complete control. Between them, the newly organized states elected to Congress no fewer than nine Confederate congressmen, seven

Through the use of force as well as law, the Southern states denied many citizenship rights to blacks—including the right to vote.

Confederate state officials, four generals, four colonels, and Confederate Vice-President Alexander Stephens.

Congressional Radicals. When Congress met at the end of 1865, it was confronted by presidential Reconstruction as a *fait accompli.* At this point, the Republicans were far from ready for the kind of all-out fight against Johnson that later developed, but they were not willing to accept the reorganized states. They were especially resentful because these states could now claim a larger representation in Congress with the free black population (only three fifths of the blacks had been counted when they were slaves), without actually allowing the blacks any voice in the government. It would be ironical indeed if the overthrow of slavery should increase the representation of the South in Congress and if the Rebels should come back into the Union stronger than when they went out.

For some months, the Republicans in Congress moved slowly, unwilling to face a break with a President of their own party, and far from ready to make a vigorous stand for the rights of blacks. But they would not seat the Southern congressmen-elect, and they set up a Joint Committee of the Senate and the House to assert their claim to a voice in the formulation of Reconstruction policy. They also passed a bill to extend the life and increase the activities of the Freedmen's Bureau—an agency created to aid blacks in their transition from slavery to freedom.

When Johnson vetoed this measure and also vetoed a Civil Rights bill, tensions increased, and in June 1866, Congess voted a proposed Fourteenth Amendment. This amendment clearly asserted the citizenship of blacks. It also asserted that they were entitled to the "privileges and immunities of citizens," to the "equal protection of the laws," and to protection against being deprived of "life, liberty, and proprty without due process of law."

Lawyers have been kept busy for more than a century determining exactly what these terms meant, but one thing was clear. The amendment did not specify a right of black suffrage. It did, however, provide that states which disfranchised a part of their adult male population would have their representation in Congress proportionately reduced. It almost seemed that Congress was offering the Southerners a choice. They might disfranchise the blacks if they were willing to pay the price of reduced representation, or they might have increased representation if they were willing to pay the price of black suffrage. This might not help the blacks, but it was certain to help the Republicans. It would either reduce the strength of Southern white Democrats or give the Republicans black political allies in the South.

The Fourteenth Amendment also provisionally excluded from federal office any person who had held any important public office before the Civil War and had then gone over to the Confederacy. This sweeping move to disqualify almost the entire leadership of the South led the Southern states to make the serious mistake of following President Johnson's advice to reject the amendment. During the latter half of 1866 and the first months of 1867, ten Southern states voted not to ratify.

Radical Reconstruction. Southern rejection of the Fourteenth Amendment precipitated the bitter fight that had been brewing for almost two years. Congress now moved to replace the Johnson governments in the South with new governments of its own creation. Between March and July 1867, it adopted a series of Reconstruction Acts which divided ten Southern states into five military districts under five military governors. These governors were to hold elections for conventions to frame new state constitutions.

In these elections adult males, including blacks, were to vote, but many whites, disqualified by their support of the Confederacy, were not to vote. The constitutions these conventions adopted must establish black suffrage, and the governments they established must ratify the Fourteenth Amendment. Then and only then might they be readmitted to the Union. Thus, two years after the war was over, when the South supposed that the postwar adjustment had been completed, the process of Reconstruction actually began.

The period that followed has been the subject of more bitter feeling and more controversy than perhaps any other period in American history, and the intensity of the bitterness has made it hard to get at the realities. During 1867 the military governors conducted elections. In late 1867 and early 1868 the new constitutional conventions met in the Southern states. They complied with the terms Congress had laid down, including enfranchisement of the blacks, and within a year after the third Reconstruction Act (of July 1867), seven states had adopted new constitutions, organized new governments, ratified the Fourteenth Amendment, and been readmitted to the Union. In Virginia, Mississippi, and Texas the process was for one reason or another not completed until 1870.

All of these new governments, except the one in Virginia, began under Republican control, with more or less black representation in the legislatures. In one state after another, however, the Democrats, supporting a policy of white supremacy, soon gained the ascendancy. Military and "Radical" rule lasted for three years in North Carolina; four years in Tennessee (never under military government) and Georgia; six years in Texas; seven years in Alabama and Arkansas; eight years in Mississippi; and ten years in Florida, Louisiana, and South Carolina.

The experience of this so-called "carpetbag" rule has been interpreted in completely different terms by historians of the past and those of the present. The earlier interpretation reflected the feelings of the Southern whites, who resented this regime bitterly, seeing it as one of "military despotism" and "Negro rule." According to this version, later elaborated by a pro-Southern school of historians, the South was at the outset the victim of military occupation in which a brutal soldiery maintained bayonet rule. Then came the "carpetbaggers"—unscrupulous Northern adventurers whose only purpose was to enrich themselves by plundering the prostrate South.

To maintain their ascendancy, the carpetbaggers incited the blacks, who were essentially well disposed, to assert themselves in swaggering insolence. Thereupon, majorities made up of illiterate blacks swarmed into the legislatures, where they were manipulated by the carpetbaggers. A carnival of riotous corruption and looting followed, until at last the outraged whites, excluded from all voice in public affairs, could endure these conditions no longer and arose to drive the vandals away and to redeem their dishonored states.

This picture of Reconstruction has a very real importance, for it has undoubtedly influenced Southern attitudes in the twentieth century, but it is an extreme distortion of the realities. Historical treatments since 1950 have presented quite a different version, stressing the brief nature of the military rule and constructive measures of the "carpetbag" governments. As for bayonet rule, the number of troops in the "Army of Occupation" was absurdly small. In November 1869 there were 1000 federal soldiers scattered over the state of Virginia and 716 over Mississippi, with hardly more than a corporal's guard in any one place.

As for the carpetbaggers, there were indeed looters among the newcomers who moved into the South, but there were also idealists. Many Northern women came to teach the freed slaves. Many men came to develop needed industry. Many others worked with integrity and self-sacrifice to find a constructive solution for the problems of a society devastated by war and left with a huge population of former slaves to absorb and provide for. Many native Southerners, who joined with the "carpetbaggers" in their programs and who were therefore denounced as "scalawags," were equally public-spirited and high-minded.

As for "Negro rule," the fact is that the blacks were in a majority only in the convention and the first three legislatures of South Carolina. Elsewhere they were a minority, even in Mississippi and Louisiana, where they constituted a majority of the population. In view of their illiteracy and their political inexperience, the blacks handled their new responsibilities well. They tended to choose educated men for public office.

Thus many of the black legislators, congressmen, and state officials they chose were well qualified. They were, on the whole, moderate and self-restrained in their demands, and they gave major support to certain policies of long-range value, including notably the establishment of public school systems, which the South had not had in any broad sense before the Civil War.

As for the "carnival of corruption," the post-Civil War era was marked by corruption throughout the country. All the Southern states combined did not manage to steal as much money from the public treasury as did the Tweed Ring in New York City. It was true, however, that the impoverished South could ill afford dishonesty in government. Nevertheless, much that was charged to "corruption" really stemmed from increased costs necessary to provide new social services such as public schools and to rebuild the Southern economy laid waste by war.

Finally, it should be noted that the Southern whites were never reduced to abject helplessness, as is sometimes imagined. From the outset they were present in all of the Reconstruction conventions and legislatures—always vocal, frequently aggressive, and sometimes dominating the proceedings.

The Fall of Radical Reconstruction. For an average of six years, then, the regimes of Radical Republican Reconstruction continued. After that they gave way to the Democratic Redeemers—those who wanted to "redeem" the South to white rule—delaying until the twentieth century further progress toward equal rights for blacks.

When one considers that the South had just been badly defeated in war, that Radical Reconstruction was the policy of the dominant party in Washington, and that black and white Republicans constituted a majority of the voters in a half-dozen Southern states, it is difficult to understand why the Radical regimes were so promptly—almost easily—overthrown. Several contributing factors must be recognized.

First, the former slaves lacked experience in political participation and leadership. Largely illiterate and conditioned for many decades to defer to white people, they grasped the new opportunities with uncertain hands. Very often they seemed to wish, quite realistically, for security of land tenure and for education more than for political rights. At the same time, however, a number of articulate and able blacks, some of them former slaves, came to the fore and might have provided effective leadership for their race if Reconstruction had not been abandoned so soon.

Second, and more important, one must recognize the importance of the grim resistance offered by the Southern whites. With their deep belief in the superiority of their own race, these Southerners were convinced that civilization itself was at stake. They fought with proportionate desperation, not hesitating to resort to violence and terror. In 1866 a half-whimsical secret society was formed in Tennessee. Known as the Ku Klux Klan, it began to take on a more purposeful character and to spread across the South. Soon every Southern state had its organization of masked and robed riders, either as part of the Klan or under some other name. By use of threat,

Concealed by hoods and robes, two Ku Klux Klan members posed for the camera in 1868.

horsewhip, and even rope, gun, and fire, they spread fear not only among blacks but perhaps even more among the Republican leaders. The states and even Congress passed laws to break up this activity, but after 1873 the laws proved almost impossible to enforce. The Klan-like organizations ceased to operate only when their purposes had been accomplished.

The dramatic quality of the Klan has given it a prominent place in the public's mental picture of Reconstruction. But though violence played a prominent role, the white South had other, less spectacular weapons which were no less powerful. Southern whites owned almost all of the land. They controlled virtually all employment. They

dominated the small supply of money and credit that was to be found in the South. And in unspectacular ways they could make life very hard for individuals who did not comply with the system. These factors, perhaps more than the acts of night riders and violent men, made the pressure against Radical rule almost irresistible.

Another important reason for the downfall of "Radical" Reconstruction was that it was not really very radical. It did not confiscate the land of plantation owners and distribute that land among the freed slaves, as radicals and abolitionists such as Thaddeus Stevens and Wendell Phillips had urged. It did not reduce the former Confederate states to the status of territories for a probationary period, as many Radicals also advocated. It did not permanently disfranchise the South's former ruling class, nor did it permanently disqualify more than a handful of ex-Confederate leaders from holding office. It did not enact Charles Sumner's bill to require universal public education in the South and to provide federal aid for schools there. These would have been genuinely radical measures, but they went beyond what a majority of Northern voters were willing to support.

Indeed, even the limited radicalism of the Fourteenth Amendment and the Reconstruction Acts strained the convictions of most Northerners to the utmost. The North was not a racially equalitarian society. Black men did not have the right to vote in most Northern states at the time the Reconstruction Acts of 1867 enfranchised them in the South. The enactment of Negro suffrage in the South was accomplished not because of a widespread conviction that it was right in principle but because it seemed to be the only alternative to Confederate rule.

Later, Republicans found that many Northern voters cared little about black suffrage in the South. They also found that the white South would not consent to a real reunion on this basis and that the restoration of former

Confederates to political power did not threaten Northern or national interests. As a result, the Republicans let the existing forces in the South find their own resolution, which was one of white supremacy.

Yet Reconstruction was far from a total failure. It established public schools in the South that gradually brought literacy to the children of freed slaves. It brought abolitionists and missionaries from the North to found such colleges as Howard, Fisk, Morehouse, Talladega, and many others. These colleges trained future generations of black leaders who in turn led the black protest movements of the twentieth century.

And although Reconstruction did not confiscate and redistribute land, many freed slaves became landowners through their own hard work and savings. In 1865 scarcely any black farmers owned their farms. By 1880, one fifth of them did. Finally, reconstruction also left as a permanent legacy the Fourteenth and Fifteenth Amendments, which formed the constitutional basis for the civil-rights movements of the post-World War II generation.

Johnson Versus the Radicals. The Republicans did not abandon their program all at once. Rather, it faded out gradually although the Radicals remained militant while Johnson remained President.

Johnson had used his administrative powers to evade or modify the enforcement of some Republican Reconstruction measures. This convinced most Republicans that his removal was necessary if their policy was to be carried out in the South, and in 1868 they tried to remove him by impeachment. The immediate pretext for impeachment was Johnson's dismissal of Secretary of War Stanton in February 1868.

A year earlier Congress had passed a law, the Tenure of Office Act, which forbade such removals without senatorial consent and which has since been held by the courts to be unconstitutional. But when Johnson removed Stanton, who was reporting to the Radicals what went on in administration councils, there had been no judicial ruling, and the House of Representatives voted to impeach Johnson, which meant that he must be tried by the Senate on the articles of impeachment.

The trial was conducted in a tense atmosphere and scarcely in a judicial way. Immense pressure was put on all Republican senators to vote for conviction. When a vote was finally taken on May 16, 1868, conviction failed by one vote of the two thirds required. Seven Republicans had stood out against the party. Johnson was permitted to serve out his term, and the balance between executive and legislative power in the American political system, which had almost been destroyed, was preserved.

The determination of Republicans to achieve congressional domination of the Reconstruction process also manifested itself in restrictions on the judiciary. When a Mississippi editor named McCardle appealed to the Supreme Court to rule on the constitutionality of one of the Reconstruction Acts, under which he had been arrested by the military, Congress in March 1868 passed an act changing the appellate jurisdiction of the Court so that it could not pass judgment on McCardle's case.

The Grant Administration. In 1868 the country faced another election, and the Republicans turned to General Grant as their nominee. He was elected over the Democratic candidate, Governor Horatio Seymour of New York, by a popular majority of only 310,000—a surprisingly close vote. Without the votes of the newly enfranchised blacks in the seven reconstructed Southern states, Grant might have had no edge in popular votes at all.

To implant Negro suffrage permanently in the Constitution—for the North as well as the

South—Congress in 1869 passed the Fifteenth Amendment, forbidding the states to deny any citizen his right to vote "on account of race, color, or previous condition of servitude." The Amendment was ratified in 1870.

President Grant supported the measures of the Radicals and in some ways gave his backing to their policies. Like the good military man he was, he believed that where violence broke out, it should be put down uncompromisingly. Accordingly, he favored the adoption of Enforcement Acts for the use of federal troops to break up the activities of the Ku Klux Klan. When these laws were passed, he did not hesitate to invoke them, and troops were sent in on a number of occasions.

Fundamentally, however, Grant was not a Radical. He wanted to see tranquillity restored, and this meant reuniting North and South on any basis both would be willing to accept. Accordingly, he urged a broader extension of amnesty to all former Confederates, and he grew to resent the frequent appeals of Republican governments in the South for troops to uphold their authority. Though he realized that the tactics of the Redeemers were very bad—"bloodthirsty butchery," "scarcely a credit to savages"—he became convinced that constant federal military intervention was worse in the long run.

During the eight years of Grant's presidency, Republican governments were overthrown in eight of the Southern states. As Grant's second term neared its end, only three states—Louisiana, Florida, and South Carolina—remained in the Republican ranks. The program of Radical Reconstruction still remained official policy in the Republican party, but it had lost its steam. The country was concerned about other things.

In foreign affairs, Secretary of State Hamilton Fish was busy putting through an important settlement by which Great Britain and the United States adopted the principle of international arbitration as a means of settling American claims that had grown out of the raiding activities of the *Alabama* and other ships which British shipyards had built for the Confederacy.

In financial circles there was a controversy over what to do about the greenback dollars issued during the war. Since greenbacks were not backed by gold, people had saved the more valuable gold dollars and spent the less valuable greenback dollars, thus driving gold out of circulation. The government was willing to give gold for greenbacks even though such a policy would tend to increase the value of the dollar. Debtor interests (such as farmers), who wanted a cheap dollar, fought hard against the policy of redemption, but the policy was adopted in 1875.

In politics, public confidence in the government was shaken by a series of disclosures concerning government corruption. In 1872 it was revealed that several congressmen had accepted gifts of stock in a construction company, the Crédit Mobilier, which was found to be diverting the funds of the Union Pacific Railroad—including the funds the government had granted to it—with the knowledge of the officers of the road. In 1875 Grant's private secretary was implicated in the operations of the "Whiskey Ring," which, by evading taxes, had systematically defrauded the government of millions of dollars. The following year, the Secretary of War was caught selling appointments to Indian posts. Meanwhile, in the New York City government, the Tweed Ring, headed by Tammany boss William Marcy Tweed, was exposed as guilty of graft and thefts that have seldom been equaled in size and have never been surpassed in effrontery.

The epidemic of corruption inspired a revolt by reform Republicans, who bolted the party in 1872, organized the Liberal Republican party, and nominated Horace Greeley, editor of the New York *Tribune*, for President.

Although the Democrats also nominated Greeley and formed a coalition with the Liberal Republicans, Grant easily won reelection because most Northern voters were not yet prepared to trust the Democrats.

In the economic orbit, the country was trying to weather the financial depression that began with the panic of 1873. All in all, the problems posed by the South and the blacks seemed more and more distant, less and less important, to the people of the North.

The Hayes-Tilden Election of 1876.

The election of 1876 brought to an end the program of Reconstruction, which probably would have ended soon in any case. In this election the Republicans, who were badly divided, turned to a Civil War veteran and governor of Ohio, Rutherford B. Hayes, as their nominee. Hayes was a conspicuously honest man, and so was his Democratic opponent, Samuel J. Tilden of New York, who owed his reputation to his part in breaking up the Tweed Ring.

When the votes were counted, Tilden had a popular majority (obtained partly by the suppression of black votes in some Southern states) and was within one vote of an electoral majority. But there were three states—Florida, Louisiana, and South Carolina—in which the result was contested, and two sets of returns were filed by rival officials. To count the votes in such a case, the Constitution calls for a joint session of the Congress. But the House of Representatives, with a Democratic majority, was in a position to prevent an election by refusing to go into joint session with the Senate. Congress agreed to appoint an Electoral Commission to provide an impartial judgment, but the commission divided along party lines, voting eight to seven for Hayes. As late as two days before the inauguration it was doubtful whether the Democrats in the House would accept the decision.

Many Northern Democrats were prepared to fight to a finish against what they regarded

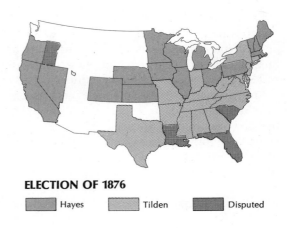

ELECTION OF 1876

| | Hayes | | Tilden | | Disputed |

as a stolen election, but the Southern Democrats had found that one civil war was enough. Moreover, various negotiations had been in progress behind the scenes. Important groups of Southern Democrats who had been left out when the government largesse of the Union Pacific-Central Pacific was distributed now hoped for a Texas and Pacific Railroad which would provide bountiful federal grants for Southern interests. They received assurances from friends of Governor Hayes that he would look with favor upon such programs of internal improvement. Moreover, they were assured that he would withdraw the last remaining federal troops from Louisiana and South Carolina, which meant that their Republican governments would collapse and the score of states would be: redeemed, eleven; reconstructed, none.

With these understandings, Southern congressmen voted to let the count proceed so that Hayes would be elected. Later, when they were explaining their conduct to their constituents, they thought it best to say quite a great deal about how they had ransomed South Carolina and Louisiana and very little about their hopes for the Texas and Pacific Railroad and other such enterprises. Thus a legend grew up that there had been a "compromise" by which Reconstruction was ended.

What had really happened was that Southern Democrats and Northern Republicans had discovered that there were many features of economic policy on which they were in close harmony. The slaves were emancipated, the Union was restored, and bygones were bygones. The harmony of their views made reconciliation natural and Reconstruction unnecessary. There was still the question of the blacks, but only a few whites had ever supported black suffrage or racial equality for its own sake. It had been an expedient, and now that the expedient was no longer needed, it could be laid aside. Such was the spirit of reconciliation.

Thus, the country ended a period of intense friction and entered upon a long era of sectional harmony and rapid economic growth. But this was done at the expense of leaving the question of racial relations still unattended to, even though slavery itself had, at immense cost, been removed.

BIBLIOGRAPHY

Older but still useful accounts emphasizing the social history of this period are Arthur C. Cole, *The Irrepressible Conflict 1850–1865 (New York: Macmillan, 1934), and Allan Nevins, *The Emergence of Modern America 1865–1878 (New York: Macmillan, 1927). Richard D. Brown, *Modernization: The Transformation of American Life 1600–1865 (New York: Hill and Wang, 1976), is a useful introduction to the modernization theme. Relevant parts of the following books illuminate the impact of modernization on everyday life: Daniel J. Boorstin, *The Americans: The National Experience (New York: Random House, 1965), Boorstin, *The Americans: The Democratic Experience (New York: Random House, 1973), Joseph C. Furnas, *The Americans: A Social History of the United States 1587–1914 (New York: Putnam's, 1969), Russell Lynes, The Domesticated Americans (New York: Harper & Row, 1963), Roger Burlingame, *March of the Iron Men: A Social History of Union Through Invention (New York: Scribner's, 1938), and H. J. Habakkuk, *American and British Technology in the Nineteenth Century (Cambridge, Eng.: Cambridge University Press, 1962).

For the growth and modernization of the American economy, see especially George R. Taylor, *The Transportation Revolution 1815–1860 (New York: Harper & Row, 1951), Douglass C. North, *The Economic Growth of the United States 1790–1860 (New York: Norton, 1966), North, *Growth and Welfare in the American Past, 2nd ed. (Englewood Cliffs, N.J.: Prentice-Hall, 1974), Stuart Bruchey, *The Roots of American Economic Growth 1607–1861 (New York: Harper & Row, 1968), and Gruchey, *Growth of the Modern American Economy (New York: Dodd, Mead, 1975).

The best study of agriculture is Paul W. Gates, The Farmer's Age: Agriculture 1815–1860 (New York: Harper & Row, 1968). Popular culture and the press are treated in Russel B. Nye, Society and Culture in America 1830–1860 (New York: Harper & Row, 1974), Nye, *The Unembarrassed Muse: The Popular Arts in America (New York: Dial Press, 1970), and

Carl Bode, The Anatomy of American Popular Culture 1840–1861 (Berkeley: University of California Press, 1959).

The best general history of antebellum reform is Ronald G. Walters, American Reformers 1815–1860 (New York: Hill and Wang, 1978). Enlightening surveys of drinking and the temperance movement can be found in W. J. Rorabaugh, The Alcoholic Republic (New York: Oxford University Press, 1979), and Ian R. Tyrell, Sobering Up: From Temperance to Prohibition in Antebellum America 1800–1860 (Westport, Conn.: Greenwood Press, 1979). Two recent studies of education are David B. Tyack, *The One Best System (Cambridge: Harvard University Press, 1974), and Frederick M. Binder, *The Age of the Common School 1830–1865 (New York: Wiley, 1974). Still the standard history of higher education is Frederick Rudolph, *The American College and University (New York: Knopf, 1962). The large body of scholarship on the abolitionists is concisely embodied in James B. Stewart, *Holy Warriors: The Abolitionists and American Slavery (New York: Hill and Wang, 1976).

For the role of abolitionists and the development of racial attitudes and black education during and after the war, see two books by James M. McPherson: *The Struggle for Equality (Princeton: Princeton University Press, 1964), and *The Abolitionist Legacy: From Reconstruction to the NAACP (Princeton: Princeton University Press, 1975). Still the most thorough accounts of antebellum immigration and nativism are Marcus Lee Hansen, *The Atlantic Migration 1607–1860 (Cambridge: Harvard University Press, 1940), and Ray Allen Billington, *The Protestant Crusade 1800–1860: A Study of the Origins of American Nativism (New York: Macmillan, 1938).

For the political and military history of the entire 1850–1877 period, still the most comprehensive one-volume work is James G. Randall and David Donald, The Civil War and Reconstruction, 2nd ed. rev. (Boston: Heath, 1969), though some of its scholarship is now quite dated. A superb modern study which focuses mainly on the war but includes long chapters on the antebellum and postbellum decades is Peter J. Parish, *The American Civil War (New York: Holmes and Meier, 1975). For the 1848–1865 period, the most detailed and authoritative treatment is Allan Nevins, Ordeal of the Union, 2 vols. (New York: Scribner's, 1947), The Emergence of Lincoln, 2 vols. (New York: Scribner's, 1950), and The War for the Union, 4 vols. (New York: Scribner's, 1959–1971).

The best study of the crucial years between the Mexican War and the Civil War is David M. Potter, *The Impending Crisis 1848–1861 (New York: Harper & Row, 1976). For the background and causes of the Civil War, the view that unrealistic emotionalism and blundering leadership played a large part is expressed in Avery O. Craven, *The Coming of the Civil War, 2nd ed. rev. (Chicago: University of Chicago Press, 1957), and in various writings of James G. Randall, including Lincoln the President, 4 vols. (New York: Dodd, Mead, 1945–1955). Important essays disputing this viewpoint and developing alternative causal interpretations are reprinted in Edwin C. Rozwenc, ed., *The Causes of the American Civil War, 2nd ed. (Boston: Heath, 1972). This controversy is admirably reviewed in Thomas J. Pressly, *Americans Interpret Their Civil War (Princeton: Princeton University Press, 1954). On the compromise of 1850 and the impact of the Fugitive Slave Law, see Holman Hamilton, *Prologue to Conflict: The Crisis and Compromise of 1850 (Lexington: University of Kentucky Press, 1964), and Stanley W. Campbell, The Slave Catchers: Enforcement of the Fugitive Slave Law 1850–1860 (Chapel Hill: University of North Carolina Press, 1970). An excellent account of the origins and ideology of the Republican party is Eric Foner, *Free Soil, Free Labor, Free Men: The Ideology of the Republican Party Before the Civil War (New York: Oxford University Press, 1970). A major account of the last four years preceding the war is Roy F. Nichols, *The Disruption of American Democracy (New York: Free Press, 1967). Don E. Fehrenbacher, The Dred Scott Case: Its Significance in American Law and Politics (New York: Oxford University Press, 1978) is a superb study not only of that crucial case but also of the political context in which it occurred. The most thorough study of Hinton Helper is Hugh C. Bailey, Hinton Rowan Helper, Abolitionist-Racist (University, AL: University of Alabama Press, 1965). Good brief biographies and appraisals of Helper's career can be found in the introductions to two modern reprintings of his most important book: George Frederickson, ed., The Impending Crisis of the South (Cambridge, MA: The Belknap Press of Harvard University, 1968), and Harvey Wish, ed., Ante-Bellum: Writings of George Fitzhugh and Hinton Rowan Helper on Slavery (New York: Capricorn Books, 1960).

For interesting interpretations of the South's course toward secession, see William L. Barney, *The Road to Secession (New York: Praeger, 1972), Barney, The Secessionist Impulse: Alabama and Mississippi in 1860 (Princeton:

Princeton University Press, 1974), Steven A. Channing, *Crisis of Fear: Secession in South Carolina (New York: Norton, 1970), and Michael P. Johnson, Toward a Patriarchal Republic: The Secession of Georgia (Baton Rouge: Louisiana State University Press, 1977). On the Northern response to secession and the Fort Sumter crisis, see David M. Potter, *Lincoln and His Party in the Secession Crisis (New Haven: Yale University Press, 1942), Kenneth M. Stampp, *And the War Came: The North and the Secession Crisis (Baton Rouge: Louisiana State University Press, 1950), and Richard N. Current, *Lincoln and the First Shot (Philadelphia: Lippincott, 1964).

On slavery there is a huge literature, one of the richest and most controversial in American historiography. The classic pro-Southern interpretation of slavery as a benign institution is Ulrich B. Phillips, *American Negro Slavery (New York: Appleton, 1918). The classic Northern interpretation of slavery as a harsh institution is Kenneth M. Stampp, *The Peculiar Institution (New York: Knopf, 1956). The controversial interpretation of slavery's destructive impact on black personality is Stanley M. Elkins, *Slavery: A Problem in American Institutional and Intellectual Life, 2nd ed. (Chicago: University of Chicago Press, 1968). For scholarship inspired by Elkins' book, see Ann Lane, ed., *The Debate over Slavery: Stanley Elkins and His Critics (Urbana: University of Illinois Press, 1971). Three important books by Eugene D. Genovese develop a complex portrait of interrelationships between the economic environment of the Southern plantation, the ideology of the master class, and the culture of the slaves: *The Political Economy of Slavery (New York: Pantheon Books, 1965), *The World the Slaveholders Made (New York: Pantheon Books. 1969), and *Roll, Jordan, Roll: The World the Slaves Made (New York: Pantheon Books, 1974). Two self-proclaimed "cliometricians"—Robert W. Fogel and Stanley L. Engerman—used econometric theory and methodology in a controversial reinterpretation of slavery, *Time on the Cross; The Economics of American Negro Slavery, 2 vols. (Boston: Little, Brown, 1974). For a sampling of the devastating critical reaction that has discredited large parts of Time on the Cross see Herbert G. Gutman, *Slavery and the Numbers Game (Urbana: University of Illinois Press, 1975), and *Reckoning with Slavery: Critical Essays in the Quantitative History of American Negro Slavery (New York: Oxford University Press, 1976). Three important studies that focus on the culture of the slaves are Herbert G. Gutman, The Black Family in Slavery and Freedom 1750–1925 (New York: Pantheon Books, 1976), Leslie Howard Owens, *This Species of Property: Slave Life and Culture in the Old South (New York: Oxford University Press, 1976), and John W. Blassingame, *The Slave Community: Plantation Life in the Ante-Bellum South (New York: Oxford University Press, 1972). On slave revolts, Herbert Aptheker, *American Negro Slave Revolts (New York: Columbia University Press, 1943), chronicles every actual and rumored uprising. For fugitive slaves and the underground railroad, Larry Gara, *The Liberty Line: The Legend of the Underground Railroad (Lexington: University of Kentucky Press, 1961), is important. Two good studies chronicle the history and ideology of black abolitionists: Benjamin Quarles, *Black Abolitionists (New York: Oxford University Press, 1969), and Jane H. Pease and William H. Pease, *They Who Would Be Free: Blacks' Search for Freedom 1830–1861 (New York: Atheneum, 1974).

The military history of the war has been treated with distinction by four writers; Douglas S. Freeman, whose R. E. Lee, 4 vols. (New York: Scribner's, 1935), is a classic, and who also has written Lee's Lieutenants, 3 vols. (New York: Scribner's, 1942–1944); Kenneth P. Williams, who died before completing his account of the Union Armies, Lincoln Finds a General, 5 vols. (New York: Macmillan, 1949); Bruce Catton, who is known for many works, especially A Stillness at Appomattox (Garden City, N.Y.: Doubleday, 1953), This Hallowed Ground (Garden City, N.Y.: Doubleday, 1956), and the Centennial History of the Civil War, 3 vols. (Garden City, N.Y.: Doubleday, 1961–65); and, finally, Shelby Foote, who wrote The Civil War: A Narrative, 3 vols. (New York: Random House, 1958–1974).

Noted Civil War historians have written five short essays in David Donald, ed., *Why the North Won the Civil War (Baton Rouge: Louisiana State University Press, 1960). Good studies of political, social, and constitutional dimensions of the conflict include William L. Barney, *Flawed Victory: A New Perspective on the Civil War (New York: Praeger, 1975), David Donald, *Lincoln Reconsidered (New York: Knopf, 1956), James G. Randall, *Constitutional Problems Under Lincoln, 2nd ed. rev. (Urbana: University of Illinois Press, 1964), and Harold M. Hyman, A More Perfect Union: The Impact of the Civil War and Reconstruction on the Constitution (New York: Knopf, 1973). Two good general histories of the Confederacy are Clement Eaton, *A History of the Southern Confederacy (New York: Macmillan, 1954), and Emory M. Thomas, *The Confederate Nation 1861–1865 (New York: Harper & Row, 1979). The role of blacks in the war is treated in Bell I. Wiley, *Southern Negroes 1861–1865 (New Haven: Yale University Press, 1938), Benjamin Quarles, *The Negro in the Civil War (Boston: Little, Brown, 1953), and James M. McPherson, ed., *The Negro's Civil War (New York: Pantheon Books, 1965). For the role of women see Mary Elizabeth Massey, Bonnet Brigades: American Women and the Civil War (New York: Knopf, 1966).

On Reconstruction the traditional, anti-Radical interpretation by William A. Dunning, *Reconstruction: Political and Economic, 1865–1877 (New York: Harper & Row, 1907),

has been subjected to extensive revision. The two best general revisionist treatments—both brief—are John Hope Franklin, *Reconstruction After the Civil War (Chicago: University of Chicago Press, 1961), and Kenneth M. Stampp, *The Era of Reconstruction 1865–1877 (New York: Knopf, 1965). Among more intensive studies, the following are especially important: Eric L. McKitrick, *Andrew Johnson and Reconstruction (Chicago: University of Chicago Press, 1970), La Wanda Cox and John H. Cox, *Politics, Principle, and Prejudice 1865–1866 (New York: Free Press, 1963), William R. Brock, *An American Crisis: Congress and Reconstruction 1865–1867 (New York: St. Martin's Press, 1963), Michel Les Benedict, A Compromise of Principle: Congressional Republicans and Reconstruction 1863–1869 (New York: Norton, 1974), Willie Lee Rose, *Rehearsal for Reconstruction: The Port Royal Experiment (Indianapolis: Bobbs-Merrill, 1964), Joel Williamson, *After Slavery: The Negro in South Carolina During Reconstruction 1861–1877 (Chapel Hill: University of North Carolina Press, 1965), Allen W. Trelease, White Terror: The Ku Klux Klan Conspiracy and Southern Reconstruction (New York: Harper & Row, 1971), W.E.B. DuBois, *Black Reconstruction in America (New York: Russell & Russell, 1935), and C. Vann Woodward, *Reunion and Reaction: The Compromise of 1877 and the End of Reconstruction, 2nd ed. (Boston: Little, Brown, 1956). An important study of the economic impact of emancipation and Reconstruction is Roger L. Ransom and Richard Sutch, *One Kind of Freedom: The Economic Consequences of Emancipation (Cambridge, Cambridge University Press, 1977).

Of the many important biographies for this period, only a few can be mentioned here. Robert W. Johannsen, Stephen A. Douglas (New York: Oxford University Press, 1973), is an exhaustive study of this key Democratic figure. On Lincoln, the best one-volume biographies are Benjamin P. Thomas, Abraham Lincoln (New York: Knopf, 1952), and Stephen B. Oates, *With Malice Toward None: The Life of Abraham Lincoln (New York: New American Library, 1977), but for the period before the presidency, see the brief but cogent *Prelude to Greatness by Don E. Fehrenbacher (Stanford: Stanford University Press, 1962). Three important Republican leaders are treated in David Donald, Charles Sumner, 2 vols. (New York: Knopf, 1960–1970), Fawn M. Brodie, *Thaddeus Stevens: Scourge of the South (New York: Norton, 1959), and Glyndon G. Van Deusen, *William Henry Seward (New York: Oxford University Press, 1967). For a detailed study of a key figure in the Northern victory, see Benjamin P. Thomas and Harold M. Hyman, Stanton: The Life and Times of Lincoln's Secretary of War (New York: Knopf, 1962). The most concise biography of Frederick Douglass is Benjamin Quarles, *Frederick Douglass (Washington: Associated Publishers, 1948).

*Denotes availability in paperback.

Time Line

5

THE AGE OF INDUSTRIALISM

Americans in the years following the Civil War—a time which has become known as the Gilded Age—lived in a nation quite different from that of their parents. It had become a nation where traditional ideas of democracy were modified by the values of a new industrial and urban society. The most important single change was the rise of industrial capitalism and the burgeoning of corporations that controlled nationwide industries. But American life was fundamentally altered by other far-reaching developments: settlement of the last American West, construction of the transcontinental railroads, revolutionary changes in agriculture, urban growth with all its attendant problems, the rise of the labor movement, a huge influx of immigrants, and the emergence of the United States as a world power. These developments gave the period its dramatic character and its importance in our history. They also established the foundations of modern America.

The triumph of industrialism in the post–Civil War generation launched the United States on the road to becoming the richest and most powerful nation in the world. But at the same time it transformed the country from one of economic democracy with opportunity for all to one of economic plutocracy with great opportunities for only the few. Industrial growth led to extreme economic inequities and sharpened class differences.

Although the old agrarian ideals of freedom, personal dignity, and individual worth gave ground under the impact of industrial expansion, they remained essential to the American view of life. President Abraham Lincoln had restated these ideals in his first annual message to Congress in December 1861, when he described the United States as a nation where "a large majority" of the people "neither work for others or have others working for them" and where a "free man" was not "fixed for life in the conditions of a hired laborer. . . ."

Most Americans wanted a society based on these Jeffersonian ideals, and probably most of them continued to believe—despite evidence to the contrary—that big business was compatible with such a society. But if they did, they were either misled or confused about what was going on, because the growth of big industry could not help but create inequities. A small class of businessmen, whose economic interests were protected and advanced by the government, organized American industry and employed in its factories and mills a large class of workers who had virtually no economic rights. In the process a fundamental change in American life took place. The ordinary American became the hired employee of a large corporation and, as a consequence, lost much economic freedom along with a sense of responsibility and initiative. Economic equality largely gave way to economic progress.

One of the most important effects of enormous economic growth of the post–Civil War years was the concentration of wealth and power in the hands of a few individuals and corporations. Strong and ambitious men, like John D. Rockefeller in oil, Andrew Carnegie in steel, Cornelius Vanderbilt in railroads, and Jay Cooke and J. P. Morgan in finance, controlled the economic life of the nation.

The rise of this economic plutocracy can be considered a victory for some of the economic ideas of Alexander Hamilton, one of the Founding Fathers. A commanding leader of the Federalists, Hamilton had devised an economic program for the early Republic that had an enduring influence on American development. Wanting a government by and for the upper classes, he had advocated an alliance between the federal government and business. Hamilton believed that American business should be encouraged and supported by the government—a belief that became a fixed part of business thought in this country. Thus he favored government intervention in the economy, as in the imposition of a protective tariff, in behalf of the moneyed class. In the decades that were to follow, as we have seen, the government's proper relationship to the national economy became a source of continuing controversy.

Following the Civil War, Hamiltonian ideas were very much in evidence in the attitudes and activities of business. The leaders and defenders of American business believed that big businessmen should run the economy and that the government should assist big business to encourage economic growth. They also maintained that they should be allowed to develop the nation's resources without interference, since this, too, would benefit all Americans. And most Americans in the era following the Civil War agreed with these propositions.

The term "Gilded Age," coined by Mark Twain and Charles Dudley Warner in their novel of that name, was used by contemporaries, and has been used by historians ever since, to describe these years. It seemed a fitting epithet for a period marked by the "all-pervading speculativeness" and the "shameful corruption" which, Twain observed, had "lately crept into our politics."

History is often not what actually happened but rather what historians say happened, and at the hands of historians the Gilded Age has fared badly. When twentieth-century historians began to study the era closely, most of them adopted the interpretations of social reformers who had lived during the period. Vernon Louis Parrington in the widely read and profoundly influential third volume of his *Main Currents in American Thought* (1930) set the modern tone when he wrote of these years: "Exploitation was the business of the times."

Two other very influential historians who dealt with the period, Charles A. Beard and Matthew Josephson, writing the 1930s, strengthened and expanded this view. Like Parrington, Beard deplored the accumulation of power by business leaders, and he condemned "the cash nexus pure and simple" that produced the era's vulgarities and inequities. Josephson saw the period in terms of economic, political, and social exploitation of the many by the few, for whom he popularized the damning phrase "Robber Barons."

The impulse to spring to the aid of the underdog brought forth champions of the cultural, literary, and technological achievements of the Gilded Age, but the stereotype of its business leadership, industrial development, and political activity has not changed substantially despite the extensive study given to the period since the 1940s. This is because few scholars have made serious attempts to investigate the Gilded Age in its own context and in accordance with the standards and ideas that then prevailed. Instead, historians have continued to accept the harsh indictments that contemporary reformers and intellectuals like E. L. Godkin and Henry Adams made of the era, preferring their judgments to those of the politicos and industrialists of the Gilded Age. In addition, it has been pointed out, the historians—usually liberal Democrats—have not been much impressed by a presumably conservative and Republican period.

Nevertheless, these later historians have sought to present a fuller, more balanced picture by emphasizing the important contributions the business leaders of the Gilded Age made to the economic development of the nation, the technology they introduced into industry, and the social good they sometimes did with their money. While the moguls were shown to be destructive, they were also depicted as creative, pioneering entrepreneurs. Allan Nevins, Thomas C. Cochran, Edward C. Kirkland, and others launched this reevaluation of American business leadership in the Gilded Age in the 1940s and 1950s, and

the trend has continued without interruption and with only occasional dissent. Recent historians have also stressed the impersonal forces at work in an industrial society, leading to the standardization of life, the growing dependence of people upon one another, the increasing feeling of insecurity, and the decline of interest in nonmaterial things that still characterize and affect our lives today.

In an effort to counterbalance the traditional censure of the political life of the Gilded Age for its barren monotony, modern historians have tried to show the importance of politics to Americans of the period and the vitality of the democratic spirit. They point out that public interest in government was very much alive and that political issues were deeply significant, attesting to the emergence of the United States as a great industrial nation and an international power. They dismiss the charge that no basic issues divided the major parties and argue that politics, in the words of historian H. Wayne Morgan, was "an ever-present, vivid, and meaningful reality to that whole generation." In the last few years Morgan and others, making extensive use of primary sources and without blinking away the corruption and blandness in many areas of politics, have led the way in reassessing the influence of the politics and politicians of the Gilded Age.

Whatever its flaws and shortcomings, the America of the Gilded Age believed in itself. The era was a time of relative prosperity and of rapid growth and change. And, unlike the America of today, the nation was largely free of involvement in international affairs and devoted itself to its own self-interest.

TO THINK ABOUT AS YOU READ . . .

1. Do you think the American Industrial Revolution during the last part of the nineteenth century was a good thing or a

bad thing for America and Americans? Some of Rockefeller's contemporaries, for example, maintained he had done more for the world than Shakespeare, and others contended that material progress is the source of all other progress. Did many Americans agree with these views? What do you think of them?

2. The Gilded Age was a period in which a few acquired vast wealth, while many lived in abject poverty. What lines of reasoning were used to justify these wide differences? Was this logic applied equally to both "haves" and "have nots"? Did people believe that the government could or should adjust the unequal distribution of wealth?

3. Some critics of the American political system of politics argue that it does not produce the ablest persons for the presidency. Would the record of the Gilded Age support or refute this view? The same critics blame poor city government on city bosses. Would the record of the post–Civil War years support or refute this belief?

4. As you know from earlier units, Americans have viewed their country as a grand experiment in forming "a more perfect union" and have sponsored reform movements aimed at correcting specific social ills. During the Gilded Age, however, some reformers blamed social ills on the social order itself. Considering the various proposals of the Mugwumps, the socialists, the anarchists, the Social Darwinists, and the reform Darwinists, how do you evaluate the efforts of these groups and their place in the continuing story of reform?

5. How did the loss or gain of rights for blacks, women, and Indians affect them and the course of American history during this period? What is your view on the actions taken to promote these rights during the Gilded Age? Do present-day Americans have a different view of the struggles for rights?

Chapter 13

Industrialism and American Life

LIFE IN THE GILDED AGE

The Growth of Industry.   The years following the Civil War were a period of rapid and vast economic expansion known as the American Industrial Revolution. Between 1860 and 1900 the total railroad mileage increased from 30 thousand to 193 thousand, while the capital invested in manufacturing jumped from $1 billion to almost $10 billion, the number of workers from 1.3 million to 5.3 million, and the value of the annual product from under $2 million to over $13 billion. Industry had come of age, and the United States had become the greatest industrial nation in the world.

This enormous economic growth not only made the United States potentially the most powerful country in the world but transformed it from a rural and agrarian nation into an urban and industrial one. By 1890 the value of this country's manufactured goods exceeded that of its agricultural products. Ten years later manufactured products were worth twice as much.

Big business came to dominate economic life. Antebellum factories and plants—where the relationship between owners and employees was close, where the workshop was small and the market was local, where the owner-

ship comprised an individual or a partnership—gave way to large, impersonal corporations. The hitherto scattered banking institutions now became concentrated in four or five financial centers. And east of the Mississippi River factory and foundry workers and their families helped build towns into cities and create sprawling industrial centers. Into these centers swarmed millions of immigrants, who were to alter the racial and ethnic composition of the nation.

Although the Civil War is generally regarded as marking the beginning of the triumph of industrial capitalism, it did not produce the Industrial Revolution. The forces responsible for the rapid postwar expansion of American industry had been developing for more than half a century. In the 1850s railroads had revolutionized transportation, and many inventions had transformed both industry and agriculture.

Then, in the post–Civil War years, major advances in every field of science, especially in chemistry and physics, provided the principles for new technology. Inventions that spurred industrial growth were made in transportation, communications, electrical power, the production of steel, and the use of oil.

As we shall see in Chapter 14, railroad development played a key role in the expansion of industry, the economy, and the nation. By 1900 the American railroad system extended into every section of the country. Through the use of standard-gauge track, the rolling stock of railroads could travel over each other's lines all over the country, greatly facilitating the shipment of goods. Equipment improved when steel replaced heavier and more brittle iron in the construction of tracks, locomotives, and freight and passenger cars. Service also improved. The Westinghouse airbrake, the automatic coupler, and the block and signal system increased safety, while the Pullman sleeping car, the dining car, and improved lighting offered both comfort and safety.

The telegraph had been widely used before the Civil War, and in the following decades came the submarine cable, the telephone, the stock ticker, the typewriter, and wireless telegraphy. Cyrus W. Field succeeded first in laying a cable across the Atlantic Ocean in 1866, and Alexander Graham Bell and his assistant Thomas A. Watson invented the telephone in 1876. Even more significant was the development of wireless telegraphy by Italian electrical engineer Guglielmo Marconi in 1901, from which came the radio, television, and radar.

Also vital to industrial growth was the typewriter, the first practicable one invented by Charles L. Scholes in 1867. By the mid-eighties the typewriter was used by most large business concerns. It assisted business by making communication more legible, preserving records, and providing carbon copies of correspondence and other papers. These advances were as essential as those in transportation to the development of business.

The use of electricity also contributed to industrial growth. In 1879, after much trial and error, Thomas Edison invented a practical incandescent light bulb that enabled entire towns and even large cities to be illuminated. Another major accomplishment was his development of a system of central power stations for generating the electric current necessary for any extensive lighting system. The opening of the Pearl Street Central Station in New York in 1882 was considered to be the beginning of the electrical age. Early customers were *The New York Times* and the banking firm of J. P. Morgan and Company. Out of these developments came in the 1880s a workable electric railway, a practical dynamo, and electric motor. The use of electric light and

This view of New York City in 1890 shows the maze of electrical and telephone wires that contributed to the rapid industrial growth of the nation.

power brought a revolution in the home, in transportation, and in the factory, where electric motors would replace the steam engine.

Of major importance too was the development of ways to mass-produce steel. In the 1850s William Kelly of Kentucky and Henry Bessemer, an Englishman, independently invented the open-hearth process of making steel, which came to be known as the Bessemer process. The air burned most of the carbon and other impurities in the iron, and when certain amounts of carbon, silicon, and manganese were added, the product was steel. What had previously been a rare metal could now be mass-produced, and the country's vast supplies of iron ore and coal could be more fully utilized.

In 1870 only 77,000 tons of steel were manufactured. But by 1880 1.39 million tons were produced yearly and by 1900 nearly 11.4 million tons. Historians regard this rapid expansion of the steel industry as one of the most important reasons for the Industrial Revolution of the late nineteenth century. At the same time the petroleum industry expanded from a state of nonexistence before the Civil War to that of about 50 million barrels annually by the early 1890s.

All these inventions increased productivity. They also offered opportunities for vast wealth to entrepreneurs with drive, initiative, and the courage to compete in a free-enterprise system that accepted graft, corruption, and the worship of material goods. Many took the chance, and many acquired immense fortunes.

Popular Culture.   Since they shared neither the cultivated tastes of the intellectuals nor the bankrolls of the industrialists and financiers, most Americans sought their own cultural pleasures. In time, catering to this mass audience would create whole new industries.

Most Americans knew no more about the lives of the very rich than what they read in their newspapers and magazines. And these media were developing as never before. The Gilded Age was the age of the warring newspaper barons, Joseph Pulitzer and William Randolph Hearst, of the first major newspaper chains and press services. Magazines were being aimed at particular segments of the public—lowbrow, middlebrow, and highbrow. As circulations mounted, advertising began to surge.

Since readers of the time did not know that Mark Twain was a major figure in American literature, they simply enjoyed his books. They also enjoyed the hacks who turned out dime novels and books for boys—the writers of historical romances, sentimental stories, exposés, inspirational works, love stories. A few are remembered: Horatio Alger, Jr., and his successful young heroes; Lew Wallace and his sensational success, *Ben Hur*; George Barr McCutcheon and his Graustark novels. And there were the popular poets, James Whitcomb Riley, Eugene Field, Mrs. Ella Wheeler Wilcox. In at least one way the writers for mass audiences had a kinship with the captains of industry. They believed in production: poets turned out a daily poem, novelists a hundred novels. But with few exceptions what they wrote ignored the real world and offered escape.

Family fun was largely do-it-yourself. The middle-class family would leave its home—often a wooden "Gothic" structure surrounded by a lawn and shade trees—to have a picnic. After consuming quantities of food, the men and boys might pitch horseshoes. Later on, the women and girls might join them for a game of croquet. In the 1890s every American seemed to want a bicycle, and as the turn of the century approached, so did the phonograph, the automobile, and the movies.

There were no movies in the Gilded Age, but many towns had theaters where plays, vaudeville, and minstrel shows were performed. One of the great thrills of the late nineteenth century was the circus. When the circuses of Barnum and Bailey or the Ringling Brothers or "Buffalo Bill's Wild West Show" came to town, hundreds of patrons bought tickets to get into the big tents. Another big attraction was the county fair with its horse racing, sideshows, fireworks, livestock exhibitions, and possibly even a baseball game. Here families had picnics and reunions with relatives and friends from other towns.

There was growing interest in outdoor sports in the Gilded Age, but it was not until the end of the century that athletic contests began to draw large crowds. In 1869, a professional baseball club, the Cincinnati Red Stockings, was organized. In 1871, the National Association of Professional Baseball Players was created in an effort to deal with abuses then afflicting the game, such as foul language by the players, gambling, and bribing the players. Then in 1876, the National Association of Professional Baseball Clubs came into being. But though professional baseball became more respectable, not everyone thought it was proper to attend games, especially those played on Sunday. And in some cities—Philadelphia, Cleveland, and Boston—Sunday baseball was prohibited. Baseball in the Gilded Age was a simpler, far less expensive game than it is today. There were no huge salaries for players or imposing grandstands and playing fields. Nor did the games receive much space in the newspapers.

Football was played almost entirely at universities and colleges, with Harvard, Yale, and Princeton leading the way. Virtually all the players who made Walter Camp's All American team were from Eastern schools. Little money was budgeted for football, and

Bicycling was enormously popular at the turn of the century. These well-dressed riders are cycling on Riverside Drive in New York City.

there were no large, high-salaried coaching staffs, huge stadiums, or intersectional games.

The New Rich. At the top of the social and economic structure in the United States in the Gilded Age were the Captains of Industry, as they were called by many contemporaries and as they considered themselves to be. They were the new rich—Rockefeller leading the way with his nearly $900 million. By 1900, it was estimated, one tenth of the population owned nine tenths of the wealth in the country, and the few millionaires at the time of the Civil War had increased to 3,800.

One of the symbols of the great capitalists' position in society was their style of living, which included palatial mansions and gold-trimmed carriages. Their big houses had libraries, billiard rooms, art galleries, several dining rooms, even small theaters and chapels. They lived in brownstone houses in the large cities and in manor houses in the suburbs or in the country. Built in virtually every known style and copied from those of the Europeans and Persians, these residences often showed bad and even vulgar taste. It was a time when the jig-saw, the cupola, the mansard roof with its dormer windows, and an orgy of decoration were in vogue. Historian and socioliterary critic Vernon L. Parrington described it as "flamboyant lines and meaningless detail" with "tawdry decorations" and "a stuffy and fussy riot of fancy."

"The Gilded Age" was a fitting label for the tawdriness characteristic of this period. This term captured the cynical spirit and crudeness of the new age. The United States, wrote E. L. Godkin in *The Nation* in 1866, is a "gaudy stream of bespangled, belaced, and beruffled barbarians. . . . Who knows how to be rich in America? Plenty of people know how to get money; but . . . to be rich properly is, indeed, a fine art." The new rich were unsure of themselves and used gaudy display to impress others. The conspicuous waste of money was the measure of social status. This

prompted the craze of wealthy Americans for European antiques and art collections and launched perhaps the greatest plunder of the continent since the sacking of Rome.

Though perceptive social critics assailed the new rich for their coarse taste and lack of business ethics, the typical American saw the rich as respected members of society, pillars of the churches, and philanthropists who occupied positions of prestige and power both at home and abroad. And Parrington, though sharply critical of the period, was also fascinated. He interpreted the Gilded Age as one in which the energies damned up by the limitations of frontier life and the inhibitions of backwoods religion had been suddenly released.

Economist Thorstein Veblen considered this extravagant and ostentatious living intentionally conspicuous waste and a clear sign of the increasing inequality of wealth. He maintained that ornamentation, too, was a form of conspicuous waste and that buildings, household interiors, and even spoons should be designed simply for use. The young Gifford Pinchot, later to be a leading progressive in the country and a governor of Pennsylvania, working as a forester on Vanderbilt's Biltmore estate, observed about the chateau: "As a feudal castle, it would have been beyond criticism, and perhaps beyond praise. But in the United States of the nineteenth century and among the one-room cabins of the Appalachian mountaineers it did not belong. The contrast was a devastating commentary on the injustice of concentrated wealth."

The Middle Class. Probably too much has been made of this conspicuous display of wealth. More representative of the American life-style of these years was that of the middle class—the clerks, professional people, shopkeepers, and lower-level executives. For these people, home was a simple house or an apartment (something rather new then) with heavy furniture and draperies, marble-topped tables, and considerable bric-a-brac. Their standard of living was usually better than that of their parents. They could educate their children, and they could hope and work for a better status. They enjoyed the increased comforts resulting from the inventions of the day: the telephone in the seventies, the electric light in the eighties, and the gas burner after 1890. If they lived in a city, they might enjoy the benefits of electric trolley cars, elevated railways, better sewage disposal, improved water distribution plants and street paving, and more efficient fire departments. But they would also suffer the dreadful noise of the "el," the congested traffic of wagons and hacks, and the constant danger of great fires, such as the great Chicago fire of 1871, laying waste to large sections of cities.

Walking city streets was dangerous, especially at night, and wise citizens stayed at home after darkness came. In the *Centennial Guide to New York City and Its Environs,* published in 1876, travelers were advised to "reach the city in the day-time," to "avoid being too free with strangers," to "avoid all crowds, particularly at night," and, if they were obliged to make inquiries on the street, to "apply to a policeman or go into a respectable place of business." Present-day Americans may find small comfort in the knowledge that the dangers of urban living are nothing new.

In the country, travel was still by horseback, wagons, or buggies over muddy trails and roads filled with bumps and holes. A trip to the village or to the county seat, accomplished now in a matter of minutes or, at most, an hour or so, was then generally an all-day event. Mail reached post offices only several times a week, and rural free delivery did not come to some areas until the nineties. With no radios and only weekly newspapers in rural areas, the general store was the center for news and gossip.

The Worker. In contrast with the visible wealth and comfort of the new entrepreneurs were the wretched living conditions of the workers, brought in great numbers to the cities by the lure of jobs. Many of them lived in tenements that were cheerless, cold, frequently without running water, and cut off from the sun and air. Tenements were built to crowd as many people as possible into the smallest possible space. For block upon block in the slum areas, these ugly structures were to be found covering every inch of building space. Jacob Riis, the reformer, estimated in 1890 that about 330,000 persons were living in one square mile on the lower East Side of New York City. Even the stables of the rich cost more and were more comfortable than the tenements of the poor.

Despite these miserable living conditions, the industrial growth of the Gilded Age did bring material benefits for American workers. The technological advances expanded production and thus made higher wages possible. Between 1870 and 1890 both money and real wages increased, the former by more than 10 percent, the latter from 10 to 25 percent. In the same decades the cost of living fell, with the price index (taking 1860 as 100) going down from 141 to 98.

But whether the worker received a fair share of the great economic growth of the last quarter of the nineteenth century is a debatable matter. With half of the period in a depression or recession it is uncertain how many workers shared the benefits. And the benefits were unequal even among those receiving them. Skilled and white-collar workers received the highest wages. Adult males received about 75 percent more for similar work than women, and two to three times as much as children.

As for the length of the working day and week, there were many variations. By 1890, the typical worker labored ten hours a day, six days a week. But bakers averaged more than

65 hours a week, steelworkers over 66, and canners about 77. In the construction industry the average work week was slightly more than 55 hours.

Although it was commonly believed that workers had unlimited opportunities to advance and thus had much upward economic mobility, studies do not support this assumption. The evidence shows that few unskilled workers went beyond the ranks of the semiskilled and virtually none achieved middle-class status. But the myth, popularized by the stories of Horatio Alger and others, persisted, and a number of Americans continued to believe that anyone who worked hard and was thrifty and virtuous could, with some luck, become a millionaire.

The New Immigration. Europeans came to the United States in unprecedented numbers

Cities teemed with poor working people drawn by the lure of jobs. Thousands were housed in these rows of tenements on the Lower East Side of New York City.

during this period. By the 1890s New York City has as many Italians as Naples, as many Germans as Hamburg, and twice as many Irish as Dublin. By 1900, three fourths of the people of Chicago were foreign born.

The most important thing about this huge movement of peoples was not its size but the immigrants' origins. Previously, nearly all immigrants had come from northern and western Europe—Germany, Ireland, England, and Scandinavia. Now the tide flowed from southern and eastern Europe—particularly from Italy, Austria-Hungary, Poland, and Russia. In the 1860s these groups had constituted only 1.4 percent of all immigrants. Their percentage rose to 7.2 in the seventies, to 18.3 in the eighties, to 51 percent in the nineties, and to 70 percent in the first decade or so of the twentieth century. This heavy influx, the "new immigration," brought a variety of ethnic groups who had never been here before in appreciable numbers.

Most of the "old" immigrants had been able to read and write, most were Protestants, and most settled on farms. In contrast, the newer immigrants came from "backward" countries, and most were illiterate. Most were Roman Catholic, Greek Orthodox, or Jewish, and most of them turned to industry and settled in the cities.

Promoters of American industry recruiting cheap labor and agents of steamship companies seeking passengers spread the news that America was the land of opportunity and the haven of the oppressed. Their claims were amply substantiated in letters from immigrants already here and in stories told by those who returned to their native lands. Transportation was cheap and wages, by European standards, were high. And there was religious freedom, no compulsory military service, and best of all, the overpowering lure of freedom.

Strangers in a new world and ignorant of its language and customs, immigrants of the same nationality flocked together in the same areas, spoke the same languages, and clung to their own customs and beliefs. Crowding into the large cities, they formed their own communities with newspapers and even theatrical productions in their own languages.

Because the newcomers were so different and so clannish, older Americans wondered whether these immigrants could ever be assimilated into the mainstream of American life. They also feared that the waves of "racially inferior" immigrants would annihilate the native American stock and resented the fact that so many immigrants were Catholics and Jews. Columnist Finley Peter Dunne's "Mr. Dooley" expressed a popular position when he said,

As a pilgrim father that missed th' first boats, I must raise me claryon voice again' th' invasion in this fair land by th' paupers an' anychists in effete Europe. Ye bet I must—because I'm here first.

"Old" immigrants did not understand or welcome the various ethnic groups of the "new" immigration. These descendants of northern European stock are against the immigration of Chinese laborers.

THE NEW DECLARATION OF "INDEPENDENCE."

"...FOR TWENTY YEARS NO MORE CHINESE LABORERS SHALL COME TO THE UNITED STATES; ...AND NO COURT SHALL ADMIT CHINESE TO CITIZENSHIP.

Labor leaders contended that the new workers from abroad were degrading American labor standards by accepting lower wages, working longer hours, and allowing themselves to be used as strike breakers. Labor leaders also found it hard to unionize people who spoke so many strange and different languages.

These hostilities and fears led to anti-immigrant movements that bore various names— the United Order of Deputies, the American League, the Red, White, and Blue, and so on. The most powerful group, the American Protective Association, was organized in 1887 to rally Americans for a fight against Catholicism. It grew with startling rapidity after the onset of the Panic of 1893 and stirred hostilities that would affect American society for decades to come.

The influx created acute problems in the cities. Too many people moved in too rapidly, and wretchedness resulted. There were too many to be housed, too many for water or sewage or transportation facilities to accommodate, too many for the police and fire departments to look after. For employers seeking cheap labor, the situation was splendid. And so it was for the middle-class family looking for servants. An amazing number of ordinary American households had live-in maids and cooks. But for others, urban living was a horror. In 1890 the immigrant journalist Jacob Riis published his shocking report on New York's slums, *How the Other Half Lives*. It was in part upon this "other half " that the vast fortunes of the Gilded Age were built.

"SURVIVAL OF THE FITTEST"

The Shock of Darwinism. A very strong influence on Americans in the Gilded Age was the theory of evolution set forth by Charles Darwin in his *Origin of Species,* published in 1859 and soon applied to social and economic life by English philosopher Herbert Spencer. According to Darwin's theory, all complex

forms of plant and animal life, including human beings, had evolved over a long period of time from lower organisms. In the process there had been a natural selection of those individual organisms best adapted to survive in their environment. Thus there was "survival of the fittest," with the strong and hardy surviving and the weak falling by the wayside.

Darwin's theory of evolution directly challenged the Biblical story of creation and, according to Sigmund Freud, severely wounded the self-love of human beings when they learned that the presumed gulf between themselves and lower forms of life did not really exist. The new biology of the nineteenth century, wrote Jacques Barzun, a leading cultural historian, "seemingly made final the separation between man and his soul." Naturally such a theory and such a trauma provoked considerable debate among Gilded Age Americans, especially scientists, theologians, and clergymen.

Social Darwinism. Spencer's theory, applying Darwin's biological theory to economic and social life, was invaluable to the new industrial order because it seemed to justify the acquisition of wealth and power and gave an explanation of why some became wealthy while others stayed poor. Spencer maintained that evolution was leading inevitably to a society in which people would enjoy "the greatest perfection and the most complete happiness," and that competitive struggle was the natural means whereby this would come about. The weak would fall by the wayside, while the strong and able would push forward.

The new doctrine thus opposed poor relief, housing regulations, and public education and justified poverty and slums. Any governmental attempt to alter the situation would be interfering with natural law and impeding progress.

Spencer's ideas were especially attractive to

American businessmen, who could thus feel that they themselves were the finest flower of evolution. Of his first reading of Spencer, Andrew Carnegie exclaimed, "I remembered that light came in as a flood and all was clear. Not only had I got rid of theology and the supernatural, but I had found the truth of evolution."

Spencer enjoyed a great vogue in the United States from 1870 to 1890. Numbered among his many devoted American followers were Edward Livingston Youmans and John Fiske, who spread the gospel of Social Darwinism all over the country through magazine articles, popular books, and lectures. Such leading universities as Harvard, John Hopkins, and Yale included the Spencerian philosophy in courses on religion, biology, and social science.

Spencer's most influential American disciple was William Graham Sumner, who taught sociology and political economy at Yale from 1872 until his death in 1910. Sumner vigorously supported economic individualism and hailed the millionaires as products of natural selection. He scornfully derided reformers and their programs to protect the weak. He ridiculed democracy as the "pet superstition of the age" and repudiated the idea of human equality.

Laissez-faire. Much of the reasoning of Social Darwinism was found in the other dominant theory of the times—laissez-faire, which included ideas of the classical economists going back as far as Adam Smith's *Wealth of Nations* (1776). Beyond what was necessary to maintain law and order and to protect life and property, the government was not to interfere in the conduct of business or in personal matters. According to this view, those pursuing their business interests free of government meddling would achieve the best possible use of resources, would promote steady economic progress, and would be rewarded, all according to their deserts.

Acquisition of wealth was considered evidence of merit, for did not wealth come as a result of frugality, industriousness, and sagacity? Poverty carried the stigma of worthlessness, for did it not result from idleness and wastefulness? During most of the late nineteenth century these attitudes prevailed in America and were upheld by prominent educators, editors, clergymen, and economists.

Somewhat paradoxically, philanthropy also was expected to play a part in the behavior of those who were successful in business. They were expected to be humanitarian and to relieve distress but were forbidden by the dictates of Social Darwinism from offering any aid that might undermine self-reliance, initiative, and ambition. The solution to this dilemma was offered by Andrew Carnegie in *The Gospel of Wealth* (1889). While asserting that wealth must necessarily be concentrated in the hands of the few, Carnegie also set forth the maxim that the man who dies rich dies disgraced. The duty of the man of wealth, he maintained, was to administer his surplus funds as a trust to yield the greatest value to the community. Funds should be given, for example, to help found public libraries, improve education, and promote world peace. To support a needy individual, on the other hand, was wrong. Carnegie argued that every person maintained by charity was a source of moral infection to the community. He asserted that of every thousand dollars spent for poor relief nine hundred fifty would better be thrown into the sea.

INDUSTRIALISM AND RELIGION

Protestantism and Darwinism. The churches had to adapt themselves to industrialism and the challenge of Darwinism. This proved to be difficult for the Protestant churches. Most Protestants considered the Bible to be the supreme authority and had closely identified their ethics with the economic individualism

A prevalent belief in late nineteenth-century America was that the fruits of success would reward industrious and prudent behavior.

of the middle class. But the Darwinian theory of evolution undermined confidence in the authority of the Bible, and the concentration of power and wealth by a few weakened belief in the virtues of economic individualism.

In the eighties and nineties, however, an increasing number of Protestant clergymen accepted the theory of evolution and reconciled it with their religious beliefs. Henry Ward Beecher, one of the most celebrated preachers of the time, declared in his *Evolution and Religion* (1885) that evolution was merely "the deciphering of God's thought as revealed in the structure of the world." A few clergymen went beyond this to deny some of the supernatural events in Christianity. This alarmed the "fundamentalists," who reasserted their literal belief in the supreme authority of the Bible as the only solid foundation for religious faith. A struggle ensued between the fundamentalists and the liberals.

Throughout the Gilded Age most Protestant clergymen believed that the existing economic order was just. For instance, Beecher condemned the eight-hour day, insisted that poverty was a sign of sin, and advocated the use of force, if necessary, to put down strikes. Commenting in 1877 on the sharp wage cuts suffered by railway workers, Beecher concluded:

It is said that a dollar a day is not enough for a wife and five or six children. NO, not if the man smokes or drinks beer. . . . But is not a dollar a day enough to buy bread with? Water costs nothing; and a man who cannot live on bread is not fit to live.

Perhaps Beecher and other clergymen like him were conservative because wealthy businessmen in their congregations made heavy contributions to church funds. In any case, the conservative sentiments of many of the clergy and their lack of sympathy for the workers' demands caused a drop in working-class attendance in the churches.

The Social Gospel. In the 1880s a few socially conscious Protestant clergymen took issue with Beecher's teachings on current economic questions and began to preach the Social Gospel. They insisted that the problems created by industrialism could be solved only by a universal application of the teachings of Christ. Among the chief exponents of the Social Gospel were Josiah Strong, Washington Gladden, and Walter Rauschenbusch. In his writings and sermons Gladden upheld the right of labor to organize and recommended that industrial disputes be eliminated by an "industrial partnership" that would allow workers to recieve "a fixed share" of industry's profits. Gladden espoused the idea of government ownership of public utilities although he rejected socialism as a system. Rauschenbusch severely censured industrial capitalism as a "mammonistic organization with which Christianity can never be content."

The Catholic View. The position of the Catholic Church on evolution was that the hypothesis had to stop short of human beings. The attitude of the Church toward social reform was more negative than positive, more tolerating than approving. Only in part was the hierarchy moved by considerations of justice and charity. James Cardinal Gibbons, Archbishop of Baltimore, insisted that Catholics cultivate a patriotic citizenship in keeping with the nation's civil institutions and customs. Gibbons asserted, "The accusation of being un-American—that is to say, alien to our national spirit—is the most powerful weapon which the enemies of the Church can employ against her." Only in this sense—as an aspect of Americanization—did the Catholic Church display any marked interest in social reform before the second decade of the twentieth century.

Archbishop John Ireland of St. Paul minimized the economic problems of the time and advocated only temperance and conservative trade unionism. In 1903 he said publicly, "I have no fear of greater fortunes in the hands of individuals, nor of vast aggregations of capital in the hands of corporations." Ireland's friendship with President McKinley and with James J. Hill, the railroad builder, brought him under the criticism of reformers. Yet he often expressed strong sympathy for organized labor, saying on one occasion, "Until their material condition is improved it is futile to speak to them of spiritual life and duties."

Through its indifference to social reform, the Church jeopardized its hold on the loyalty of its communicants. Catholics in large numbers lost interest in a church which seemed indifferent, if not hostile, to movements promoting their economic welfare. As the Church began to lose members to Protestantism and socialism, it developed a greater interest in social problems. Also helping to change the Church's attitude was Pope Leo XIII's famous encyclical *De Rerum Novarum* (1891), which condemned the exploitation of labor and asserted that it was the duty of the state to bring social justice.

Idealism. From the 1870s on probably the most important new influence on philosophy was German idealism, particularly as expressed by Georg Wilhelm Friedrich Hegel (1770–1831). Hegel viewed the whole course of history as the working out of divine purpose by certain general laws of nature, culminating in the achievement of perfect freedom. But Hegelianism rationalized existing conditions, and what Hegel meant by freedom was very different from the traditional American conception. Hegel's philosophy glorified the state and taught that individuals could be free only by subordinating themselves to their national government and to their social institutions.

The idealist movement was strongest in New England, where its leaders were Josiah Royce of Harvard and C. E. Garman of Amherst, but the idealist awakening was evident also at such universities as California, Columbia, Cornell, Johns Hopkins, Michigan, and Princeton. The idealists believed in the priority of the mind over matter and in the fundamental unity of the universe, but they modified these concepts to support American individualism.

American Pragmatism. Meanwhile a school of philosophy more distinctively American and opposed to idealism was growing in popularity. Pragmatism, unlike most earlier philosophies, did not offer theories about God and the universe. It presented instead a way of evaluating acts and ideas in terms of their consequences in concrete experience. Pragmatism says that we cannot reject any hypothesis if consequences useful to life flow from it. The pragmatist's decision regarding the truth or falsity of an idea, then, is based on experiential test: One decides whether an idea is true or false by seeing whether it works. This concept was closely associated with two ideas that had gained wide currency in American thought—the idea of progress through evolution, and the idea of truth obtained through scientific investigation. The forerunners of pragmatism were Chauncey Wright and Charles S. Peirce, but two other men, William James and, later, John Dewey, developed it.

William James, philosopher and psychologist at Harvard, rejected Spencerian determinism, which afforded no place for chance or human will. He upheld the independence of the mind and "the right to believe at our own risk any hypothesis that is live enough to tempt our will." At times he was inclined to suggest that if someone felt happier or behaved better as a result of believing some idea, that idea should be regarded as true. But while James repudiated absolutes, he also spoke out against a skepticism that would inhibit impulsively generous commitment. He distrusted all general laws and abstractions that denied the human capacity for free action. James contended that a person's decisions would influence the course of events and that, in spite of the existence of God, good or evil would result from human device and intelligence.

In his *Principles of Psychology* (1890), James made the first important American contribution to the scientific study of the mind. In later books he expounded his views on pragmatism. Theories to him were "instruments, not answers to enigmas." Pragmatism "has no dogmas, and no doctrines save its method," which was a method for reaching the truth. "The true is the name of whatever proves to be good in the way of belief," James said, "and good, too, for definite, assignable reasons." Such views were a sharp departure from nearly all the philosophies and religions of the past, and they captivated many Americans. Yet they also laid James open to the charge that pragmatism was simply another name for expedience: Anything is good that works.

The New Legal Theory. There was also a revolt against formalism in law. The preceding generation had regarded the law as fixed and unchanging and as a standard measure which the judge simply applied to the question at hand like a yardstick. But a new school of legal theorists arose following the reasoning of Oliver Wendell Holmes, son of the poet of the same name and friend of William James, that law should be based on changing social needs or political policies rather than simply upon logic or precedent. "It is revolting," said Holmes, "to have no better reason for a rule of law than that it was laid down in the time of Henry IV. It is still more revolting if the grounds upon which it was laid down have vanished long since, and the rule simply persists from blind imitation of the past." The new school of theorists went on

to contend that the meaning of any general legal principle must always be judged by its practical effects.

CHALLENGES TO DARWINISM AND LAISSEZ-FAIRE

Reform Darwinism. In the 1880s a number of sociologists and economists revolted against the fatalism and lack of social responsibility of Social Darwinism. These "reform Darwinists" maintained that societies could command their own destinies and that human intelligence applied to social problems could improve the existing system.

A leader among the dissenters was Lester Ward, a largely self-educated sociologist. He came from a poor family in Illinois, endured privations in his early life, worked in factories, fought in the Civil War, and for many years was a government official. When he was sixty-five, Ward became Professor of Sociology at Brown University, where he taught "A Survey of All Knowledge." His ideas were first presented in his *Dynamic Sociology* (1883) but were more readable in *The Psychic Factors of Civilization* (1893). Ward believed that a laissez-faire economic system did not necessarily advance human progress, and he advocated state management and social planning.

Younger professors of sociology, such as Albion Small of Illinois, Charles Horton Cooley of Michigan, and Edward Allsworth of Wisconsin, seconded Ward's assault on Social Darwinism. Contrary to Spencer's notion that society was composed of separate individuals operating independently of one another, they asserted that each individual personality was shaped by social institutions which were themselves amenable to social control. In *Sin and Society* (1907) Ross argued that in the new industrial society morality required the impersonal corporation to accept full responsibility for its antisocial acts. Followers of

Spencer and Sumner declined in numbers and influence in the universities. In 1906 the American Sociological Society was founded and Ward was its first president. His ideas on government social planning eventually came to dominate American social thinking.

The New Economists. Similarly the viewpoint of economists changed. In the mid-1880s, a new group of scholars, many of whom had been trained in German universities, began to challenge laissez-faire sentiments. In 1885 they founded the American Economic Association, which boldly declared that the state was "an agency whose positive assistance is one of the indispensable conditions of human progress" and that "the doctrine of laissez-faire is unsafe in politics and unsound in morals." Among the leaders of this revolt were Richard T. Ely of Johns Hopkins University and the University of Wisconsin, Simon Nelsen Patten of the University of Pennsylvania, John R. Commons of the University of Wisconsin, and Wesley C. Mitchell of Columbia University. Although they differed in their economic and political programs, they all dissented from the classical belief in absolute economic laws valid for all societies. They insisted that society, constantly changing, had to be examined in terms of process and growth. Using the historical approach to study economic realities, they discovered that there were great differences between what actually had happened and what, according to classical economics, was supposed to have happened.

Thorstein Veblen. The leading academic rebel was Thorstein Veblen. Born in Wisconsin of Norwegian immigrants and educated at Yale and Johns Hopkins, he taught at Chicago, Stanford, and Missouri. Veblen bitterly assailed what he called the "kept classes" and their "pecuniary" society. He derided the idea that the wealthy leisure class was the most

biologically fit and that millionaires were a product of natural selection. Veblen argued that the millionaire was not responsible for the creation of the industrial technology but rather had taken possesion of the wealth produced by the skill and labor of other people. In his most widely read book, *The Theory of the Leisure Class* (1899), and a number of other volumes Veblen analyzed the role of the upper class in American society. Although he had little popular appeal, he wielded a great deal of influence among intellectuals of the twentieth century, particularly after the Great Depression of 1929.

Reformers. Outside of academic circles, increasing numbers of radical reformers began to attack the existing social and economic system and to propose new plans for economic organization. They, too, rejected Spencer's fatalism and the idea that progress resulted from the struggle for existence and the consequent removal of the unfit.

The most important of these reformers was Henry George. Born in Philadelphia, he moved to San Francisco as a young man and for twenty years watched a frontier society become transformed into a wealthy and class-stratified society. What was the cause of the imbalance that deepened the poverty of the masses and increased the wealth of a few? George believed the explanation lay in the inequities of private land ownership that allowed landowners to enrich themselves solely through the rise of real-estate values. Land took on value not because of anything the owner did but because people lived on it. George maintained that the unearned increment, instead of going to private individuals, ought to be taken by the government in the form of a "single tax" on land values. This would make other taxes and other forms of government intervention unnecessary, leave individual enterprise otherwise free, and promote "the Golden Age of which poets have sung and high-raised seers have told us in metaphor!''

George set forth his theories in *Progress and Poverty* (1879) and found a wide audience both in the United States and abroad. He spent the rest of his life working for the single tax program and continued to develop his theme in subsequent books. In addition, he edited a newspaper, gave many speeches, and came close to being elected mayor of New York City in 1886. George's ideas influenced virtually every reformer for years to come, and they still have appeal as a practical way to change the social system.

Somewhat more radical than George's program was that of his contemporary Edward Bellamy. Rejecting both classical eco-nomics and the fatalism of the Social Darwin-ists, Bellamy concentrated his attack on the free-enterprise system itself. He attacked excessive individualism, private monopoly, and competition, characterizing the latter as ''sheer madness, a scene from bedlam'' and the price system as ''an education in self-seeking at the expense of others.'' He assailed the ''imbecility of the system of private enterprise'' and the callousness of industrial-ists, who ''maim and slaughter [their] workers by thousands.''

In his utopian novel *Looking Backward* (1888), Bellamy portrayed an ideal community in the year 2000 whose beauty and tranquility contrasted sharply with the ugly industrial towns of his day. In this utopia the govern-

By the late 1800s some thinkers argued that the rich were not biologically superior but were ''kept'' by the labor of people like the men shown in this Pittsburgh steel mill.

ment owned all the means of production, and material rewards wee shared equally by everyone. At least 500,000 copies of the book were sold. Bellamy called his system "Nationalism," and "Nationalist" clubs sprang up to spread the new faith. "Nationalist" magazines advocated public ownership of railroads and utilities, civil service reform, and government aid to education. This served to renew interest in socialism and caused Americans to consider socialist ideas and programs. But both George and Bellamy rejected Marxian socialism. George regarded Karl Marx as "the prince of muddleheads," and Bellamy maintained that American Marxists were really in the pay of the "great monopolists," employed by them "to wave the red flag and talk about burning, sacking, and blowing people up, in order, by alarming the timid, to head off any real reforms."

Young social reformers seeking a way to refute Social Darwinism were influenced by the ideas of the reform Darwinists and of reformers like George and Bellamy. They were also influenced by the social-justice movement, which had its roots in European, especially English, reform movements. Nearly every leading English reformer had visited the country, and many young American progressives and reformers came under their influence. Implicit in all these new ideas and ferment was that of the life of service. Out of this emerged the idea of social work as a way young reformers could serve society. Jane Addams of Chicago's Hull House became a leading symbol in this country of these social reformers and their work. She had been a social worker at Toynbee Hall in the Limehouse area of London, and when she returned to the United States in 1889, she established Hull House, a slum-relief center in Chicago. Her experiences at Hull House showed her that people could become stronger and learn to deal with adversity. Thus she began to reject Social Darwinism.

Also involved in the social justice move-

ment was the Salvation Army, which had come from England at the end of the nineteenth century. It offered assistance as well as religion. So did the clergy of various faiths now working in the slums. Joining in the movement too were middle-class and upper-class women, who had begun to join literary circles and clubs and were pushing not only for the ballot and legal equality for themselves but also for a number of reforms on behalf of children, working women, and Indians. (See "Helen Hunt Jackson: Crusader for the Indian.")

Socialism. Bellamy and other reformers avoided the word *socialism* not only because they found it distasteful but also because they realized that in the United States it was often identified with *anarchism* and *communism*, labels that frightened most Americans. The first socialist political parties in this country appeared in New York, Philadelphia, Chicago, St. Louis, Milwaukee, and other large cities in the years immediately following the Civil War. In the beginning most American socialists, like their European counterparts, were followers of Karl Marx. Seeking to develop a revolutionary spirit among American workers, these socialists urged workers to "offer an armed resistance to the invasions by the capitalist class and capitalist legislatures" and exhorted them to overthrow American capitalism by "energetic, relentless, revolutionary and international action."

A National Labor Reform party was organized in 1868 with a platform declaring that "our government is wholly perverted from its true design. . . . [The] mass of the people have no supply beyond their daily wants and are compelled . . . to become paupers and vagrants." These appeals were too radical for the masses of wage earners and found only a small receptive audience among them. The National Labor Reform party's presidential candidate in 1868 polled fewer than 30,000 votes.

In 1877, a Socialist Labor party was formed. Marxian doctrines were the basis of its program, and recent European immigrants provided most of its members. The party's purpose was not to reform but to revolutionize the industrial order. It blamed the plight of the masses on the concentration of economic power in private hands, and it advocated having all the basic means of production run by the government in democratic association with the workers. For some years the Socialist Labor party avoided regular political activities and instead attempted to bore its way into control of the labor federations. But the leaders of post–Civil War unionism successfully opposed the efforts of socialists to control labor and rejected their radical solutions to economic and social problems.

Eventually, in the 1890s, the splintered factions of the Socialist Labor party united under the leadership of Daniel De Leon, who became known as "the socialist pope." Born on the island of Curaçao and educated in Germany, De Leon had come to the United States, where he studied law and taught for a short time at Columbia College. A brilliant orator and pamphleteer, he became a champion of Marxism and took a militant stand against traditional trade unionism. He derided the American Federation of Labor as "a cross between a windbag and a rope of sand" and called its founder, Samuel Gompers, "a labor faker" and "a greasy tool of Wall Street."

De Leon urged all workers to join an independent political movement that would win control of the government and establish

Helen Hunt Jackson: Crusader for the Indian

One of the most influential champions of the Indian during the late nineteenth century was the writer Helen Hunt Jackson. Her biting criticisms of federal Indian policy in *A Century of Dishonor* (1881) and her sentimental novel *Ramona* (1884) presented the classic statement of American injustice toward the Indian and aroused the national conscience. Described by some of her contemporaries as "the most brilliant, impetuous, and thoroughly individual woman of her time," she is, ironically, almost forgotten today.

She was born Helen Maria Fiske October 15, 1830, in Amherst, Massachusetts, the daughter of Nathan Welby and Deborah (Vinal) Fiske. A professor of Latin, Greek, and Philosophy at Amherst College, her father was also a Congregational minister and author. Her mother, a Bostonian, also wrote. Helen had two brothers, who died in infancy, and a sister, Anne. Her mother died when she was fourteen and her father three years later, leaving Helen in the care of an aunt. But her father had given her a good education at the well-known Ipswich (Massachusetts) Female Seminary and the private school of Reverend J. S. C. Abbott in New York City. She was a neighbor and schoolmate of Emily Dickinson, who would become one of America's great poets, and they remained lifelong friends.

"a socialist or co-operative commonwealth, whereby the instruments of production shall be made the property of the whole people." But in 1892 the Socialist Labor presidential ticket polled only 22,000 votes and in the next election only 34,000. The party was too foreign in its makeup and too radical in its program to attract wide support. To offset some of this deficiency, a rival organization, the Social Democratic party, was organized in 1896 by Eugene V. Debs, president of the American Railway Union. In 1901 the anti-De Leon group in the Socialist Labor party joined Debs to form the Socialist Party of America.

ACHIEVEMENTS OF THE GILDED AGE

Despite the obvious cultural excesses and the long list of social problems, intellectual and artistic developments of the Gilded Age were impressive. The original and creative thinkers of the eighties and the nineties made these two decades one of the most intellectually fertile periods in the whole of American history. In scholarship, the age saw the birth of two new social sciences: Lewis Henry Morgan founded anthropology and Lester Ward fathered American sociology. The period also witnessed a revolution in higher education. Until this time colleges and universities had concentrated on training ministers and lawyers, but now learning began to shake off its fetters and to range freely in the physical, natural, and social sciences, the arts, and the humanities.

The most famous of the daring new

In 1852, Helen married Army Captain Edward Bissell Hunt, brother of a former governor of New York. Helen's husband was an accomplished engineer officer and thus held high army rank. For the next eleven years she and her husband led the usual wandering life of a military family.

Then there were tragedies in store for her. Her first child, Murray, died in 1854 of a brain disease when he was eleven months old. In 1863 her husband suffocated while experimenting with an underwater naval vessel he had designed. Two years later her other son, "Rennie," died of diphtheria. With her parents, husband, and sons dead, she was now alone.

Up to this time, Helen Hunt had shown no signs of literary ability. In 1866, she returned to Newport, Rhode Island, where she and her husband had once been stationed. For a while, she was interested in spiritualism and clairvoyance. But after spending some time with Emily Dickinson and coming to know Thomas Wentworth Higginson, well-known author, soldier, and reformer, she decided to turn to a writing career.

She began to write travel sketches, children's stories, novels, poems, and essays under the pseudonyms "H. H." and "Saxe Holm," eventually writing over thirty books and hundreds of articles. The pseudonyms kept her from becoming more prominent, but it was still the convention for women writers to conceal their authorship. Only after she began to write her books about Indians did she use her full name. By that time she was perhaps the most productive woman writer in the country. In 1874 Ralph Waldo Emerson rated her "the greatest American woman poet" and placed her poetry above that of almost all American men.

In May 1872, Helen Hunt took a trip to California, and then, for bronchial trouble, spent the winter of 1873–1874 at Colorado Springs, Colorado. There she met

university presidents were Charles W. Eliot of Harvard and Daniel Coit Gilman of Johns Hopkins. At Harvard, Eliot greatly expanded the curriculum and sponsored the elective system, which had originated at the University of Virginia at the time of its founding. He also drastically reformed Harvard's medical and law schools and gave them true professional status. At Johns Hopkins, Gilman built the first great graduate school in America. The graduate school and the seminar method were introduced from Germany in the 1870s, and some graduate work was done at Harvard and Yale in that decade. But Johns Hopkins, designed primarily as a center for graduate work at its founding in 1876, took the lead in this field and held it for the next quarter of a century. At that time also, professional

schools got under way—the Columbia School of Mines (1864), the Massachusetts Institute of Technology (1865), Stevens Institute (1871), and the Johns Hopkins Medical School (1893).

Arts and Letters. During the two or three decades following the Civil War, there developed a new realism in American literature, stimulated by Darwinism, the influence of European writers, and a reaction against the sentimental gush that had come to dominate fiction. An early manifestation of the trend was the regional short story. Bret Harte in the West, Hamlin Garland in the Midwest, George Washington Cable and Joel Chandler Harris in the South, and Sarah Orne Jewett in New England gave readers a fresh and exciting view of regional America and contrib-

Pennsylvania Quaker William Sharpless Jackson, a wealthy banker and railroad manager, whom she married on October 22, 1875. Relieved of her financial concerns, she moved to Colorado. From that time on, the West and its Indians took up more and more of her attention.

During an 1879 visit to Boston, Helen Hunt Jackson heard a lecture by the Ponca chief, Standing Bear, about the sufferings of the dispossessed Plains Indians. This was a turning point in her life, and she began to champion the cause of Indians almost at once. Not only did she expose the government's mistreatment of Indians in her writings, but she sent out petitions, wrote letters to newspapers, and endeavored to awaken public opinion on behalf of the Indians. Soon she was a reformer at war with government officials over their Indian policy.

Her book, *A Century of Dishonor*, published in 1881, is a powerful story of dispossession, broken treaties, crooked dealings, unfulfilled promises, and the federal government's inhumane treatment of the Indian tribes who were its powerless wards. The book caused a national sensation. An emotional and partisan book, it is not a balanced history but an impassioned plea on behalf of the Indian. At her own expense, she sent a copy to every member of Congress with the following words printed in red on the cover: "Look upon your hands! They are stained with the blood of your relations."

The impact of this book was so great that it has been called the *Uncle Tom's Cabin* of the Indian cause. And Helen Hunt Jackson regarded herself an an "Indian Harriet Beecher Stowe," saying "If I can do one-hundredth for the Indians as Mrs. Stowe

uted to the reunification of the country.

In his own day Mark Twain (Samuel L. Clemens) was considered a regional author, but his novels, essays, and sketches have made a lasting reputation for him as a major figure in American literature. The materials for Twain's best narratives—*The Adventures of Tom Sawyer* (1876), *Life on the Mississippi* (1883), and *The Adventures of Huckleberry Finn* (1884)—were his boyhood home, Hannibal, Missouri, and the great Mississippi River which rolled before it. Along with many other writers of the period, he deplored the evils of crass materialism and ridiculed the get-rich-quick schemes of his money-mad countrymen. In *The Gilded Age*, for example, Twain and Charles Dudley Warner pointed out that sober industry and contentment with a modest income honestly earned are infinitely preferable to frantic money-making schemes. Yet Twain himself tirelessly sought ways to increase his wealth.

The growing social ills of the Gilded Age called forth specific indictments which became increasingly prominent in the realistic literature of the late nineteenth and early twentieth centuries. William Dean Howells, who by 1900 was considered by many young writers to be the dean of American letters, exhibited the grime and squalor of New York City in *A Hazard of New Fortunes* (1890). Stephen Crane's *Maggie: A Girl of the Streets* (1893) exposed the ugly life of New York's Bowery. Hamlin Garland in *Main-Travelled Roads* (1891) described the hardships and injustices suffered by farmers in Iowa and

did for the Negro, I will be thankful." Within a year of her book's publication, the strong Indian Rights Association was created. In 1883 President Chester Arthur appointed Mrs. Jackson a Commissioner of Indian Affairs, and in 1887 the first comprehensive reform legislation for Indians was enacted in the Dawes Act.

Helen Hunt Jackson continued her fight for the Indian and also continued to be a prolific writer of poetry, novels, and essays until her death. Probably her best known fictional work is *Ramona* (1884), an idyllic account of the Indian past. In 1886, the *North American Review* called this book "unquestionably the best novel yet produced by an American woman," ranking it with *Uncle Tom's Cabin* as one of the two famous ethical novels of the century. Since then it has gone through hundreds of printings and countless stage and screen showings.

She also continued to have personal tragedy in her life. In June 1884, she suffered a severe fracture of her leg. Then she was tranferred to a place in California that proved to be malarious. While confined there, a cancer developed. During all this period, "her sunny elasticity never failed," wrote one of her closest friends, "and within a fortnight of her death she wrote long letters, in a clear and vigorous hand, expressing only cheerful hopes for the future." On August 12, 1885, she died and was interred temporarily in San Francisco. Later she was buried near the summit of Mount Jackson, Colorado, one of the Cheyenne peaks named in her honor, about four miles from Colorado Springs. Still later, to escape commercialism and the possible vandalism of the spot, her body was taken to Evergreen Cemetery at Colorado Springs, where it remains.

Wisconsin. While they emphasized the abuses of the new industrial order, however, writers were comparatively gentle in their treatment of the captains of industry. In Howells' *The Rise of Silas Lapham* (1884), for example, the author implied that the great majority of American financiers were honest—that "robber barons" were the exception, not the rule.

Even the much more subtle and sensitive novelist and literary critic Henry James (brother of psychologist William James), who lived abroad most of his life, presented American financiers as men of integrity and charm in several of his books. James' particular interest was the interaction of men and women—American and European—in sophisticated international society. *The American* (1877), *The Portrait of a Lady* (1881), and *The Ambassadors* (1903) present Americans who are morally superior to their more cultured European counterparts.

Because many poets—Bryant, Longfellow, Holmes, Lowell, Emerson, and Whittier—whose careers had begun in an earlier period continued to satisfy tastes after the war, much of American poetry showed remarkably few effects of the changing intellectual climate. But by the end of the century American poets and prose writers were feeling its impact. For example, much of Stephen Crane's poetry inferred from the biological struggle for survival and the astronomical immensity of the universe that the individual is unimportant:

> A man said to the universe
> "Sir, I exist!"
> "However," replied the universe,
> "The fact has not created in me
> A sense of obligation."

The Gilded Age knew nothing of Emily Dickinson because only seven of her poems were published during her lifetime (1830–1886), but she is today considered one the leading poets of the post–Civil War period.

She began to write poetry in the mid-fifties and continued until her death, but she spent the last half of her life as a recluse in Amherst, Massachusetts.

In striking contrast was Walt Whitman, whose revolutionary volume of poetry, *Leaves of Grass,* had been published in three editions before the Civil War and who continued to be an important figure in American poetry of the postwar period. Although many critics objected to his departures from the conventions of versification and to his frankness about sex, he became for many others the very voice of America—enthusiastic, optimistic, energetic, and free. His Quaker inheritance contributed to the independence, love and peace, and sense of brotherhood celebrated in so many of his works—among them *Drum Taps* (1866), a volume of poems recounting the experiences and suffering shared by both North and South, and the richest account of the Civil War to be found in our poetry.

Increasing wealth and leisure after the Civil War contributed to a new awareness of art among Americans, and the work of the artists George Inness, Thomas Eakins, Winslow Homer, and Albert Pinkham Ryder was of such high caliber that the Gilded Age could be called the most important in American painting. Inness pioneered a new landscape school. Homer and Eakins were the leading American representatives of the naturalistic movement in painting. Homer grounded his art in direct observation of nature, while Eakins depicted ordinary middle-class city life of the United States in the late nineteenth century. Ryder, haunted througout his life by the sea, was the most original Romantic of his time. Two American expatriates, James McNeill Whistler and John Singer Sargent, both of whom lived most of their lives in London, enjoyed international reputations—Whistler for his muted, poetic compositions, Sargent as the most sought-after portraitist of the Anglo-Saxon world. A third expatriate artist, Mary Cassatt, the sister of a railroad executive, settled in Paris and exhibited with the great French Impressionists.

Although in architecture the Gilded Age has been said to mark the low point in taste, fine and outstanding architects did exist. Henry Hobson Richardson and Louis H. Sullivan were the first major architects to meet the demands of industrialism upon their art. To these men, buildings had a sociological function as well as an artistic one. In his *Autobiography of an Idea*, Sullivan wrote that "masonry construction was a thing of the past . . . [and] the old ideas of superimposition must give way before a sense of vertical continuity." For a number of architects it was a golden age. The rich commissioned them to design giant urban residences, baronial country homes, and great stone "cottages" on the shore. The imitation French châteaus and Italian palaces were sometimes ugly and often absurd. But gifted and imaginative architects like Richard Morris Hunt put the limitless funds of their patrons to good use.

The Chautauqua Movement.   There was a mass desire for knowledge in the Gilded Age, and various efforts were made to meet the demand. Most successful of these ventures

The great American thirst for knowledge that sparked the earlier Lyceum Movement continued in the open-air meetings held at Lake Chautauqua.

was the Chautauqua movement, founded in 1874 by Lewis Miller, an Ohio businessman, and John H. Vincent, a Methodist minister. The two-week summer course they organized for a few Sunday-school teachers at Lake Chautauqua in New York proved to be such an enjoyable experience for those who attended that the word spread and within a few years thousands from all parts of the country were coming to Lake Chautauqua. And the Chautauqua movement, like the earlier Lyceum Movement, expanded its activities. The founders broadened their range of instruction to include such subjects as economics, government, science, and literature. During the years of Chautauqua's greatest popularity, eminent authorities, including some of the Presidents of the period, gave talks to open-air audiences on every subject conceivable. In addition, the Chautauqua Literary and Scientific Reading Circle was organized and became a national society. This organization provided correspondence courses leading to a diploma. Textbooks were written for the program, and a monthly magazine, the *Chautauquan,* was published. According to the Reverend Vincent, the program was formulated to give "the college outlook" to those who did not have a higher education.

Because the Chautauqua movement was so successful, various imitators appeared. By 1900 there were about two hundred Chautauqua-type organizations. Most were of a more commercial character but were designed to satisfy the same craving for self-culture. They furnished a varied fare of music, humor, and inspirational lectures and probably provided more entertainment than enlightenment for those who attended.

The Chautauqua movement and its imitators helped popularize information that earlier had been the property of experts only. Too, thousands of Americans who sought cultural and intellectual improvement probably felt rewarded by many of the programs, and perhaps their interests were broadened by them.

From all contemporary accounts, Americans of the Gilded Age pursued diverse cultural interests. They listened to lectures, went to museums, plays, and circuses, sought more education at Chautauqua institutes, sat through religious revival meetings, and began to watch new phenomena such as baseball and football. In all this they had a sense of assurance and optimism that would begin to decline as the Gilded Age neared its close. In the rest of the unit, we will discuss some of the events that were to dampen the early optimism.

Chapter 14

The Age
of Big Business
1865–1900

THE AMERICAN INDUSTRIAL REVOLUTION

The Effect of the Civil War. It has been customary to credit the Civil War with a major role in bringing about the Industrial Revolution through the great impetus that it supposedly gave to the growth of manufacturing in the North. In fact, however, the Civil War may have retarded American industrial development, for growth rates slowed during the conflict. Between 1839 and 1899 total output for commodities, including agricultural products, increased elevenfold, or at an average rate per decade of slightly less than 50 percent. But growth rates varied widely from decade to decade. The 1840s and 1880s were periods of considerably more rapid advance than the 1850s, 1860s, and 1870s, and the lowest level of industrial growth occurred during the decade of the Civil War.

Nevertheless, the government gave strong encouragement to entrepreneurs during the Civil War. The Republican party, seeking the votes of businessmen in the 1860 campaign, promised them favorable legislation. In power, the Republicans carried out their pledges and through tariff, railway, banking,

and immigration legislation created conditions suitable for industrial capitalism.

The Post–Civil War Boom. A number of factors were responsible for the post–Civil War industrial boom. The United States possessed bountiful raw materials, and the government was willing to turn them over to industry for little or no money. Coupled with the abundance of natural resources and continuing technological progress was a home market steadily expanding through immigration and a high birth rate. Both capital and labor were plentiful. The increase in trade and manufacturing in the Northeast in the years before the war produced an accumulation of savings, while additional millions of dollars came from European investors. And from 1860 to 1900, unbroken waves of millions of European immigrants provided American industry with workers as well as with customers.

The Role of Government in Business. An essential factor in the growth of industrialism was the continuation of the government's friendly attitude toward business. The protective tariff—beginning with the Morrill Tariff of 1861 and expanded by the McKinley bill of 1890, the Wilson-Gorman law of 1894, and the Dingley Tariff of 1897—allowed American manufacturers to charge high prices without fear of foreign competition. The national banking system and the financial policies pursued by the Treasury Department resulted in a currency deflation benefiting creditors over debtors. Businesses also received grants of land and of natural resources. While these measures can be considered a sign of governmental favoritism, they can also be seen as a way to encourage economic growth, a traditional policy of American government since the days of the Federalists.

Equally helpful to the development of business was the lax public control of it. There were few investigations of business practices, no legislation to protect consumers, and few effective regulatory commissions or laws. Businessmen knew that almost any action could be justified by the doctrines of Social Darwinism and laissez-faire. Most Americans in the Gilded Age considered governmental regulation of business to be unnecessary, unjust, and even immoral. Even reformers felt that governmental regulation of business should be confined to those cases where it was clearly necessary and where a careful study had been made. With cheerful inconsistency, the business leaders who championed laissez-faire welcomed governmental intervention in the economy in the form of tariffs, grants, and subsidies—measures that clearly violated laissez-faire doctrine.

The Role of the Courts. Also beneficial to the growth of business was the protection given by the Supreme Court in its interpretation of the Fourteenth Amendment. This amendment, added to the Constitution in 1868, was presumably designed to safeguard the newly emancipated blacks. But the original intent of the amendment disappeared, and it became instead a refuge for private enterprise.

In its first section the Fourteenth Amendment declares: "No state shall make or enforce any law which shall abridge the privileges or immunities of citizens of the United States; nor shall any state deprive any person of life, liberty, or property, without due process of law." In the first postwar cases involving the question of governmental regulation of business, the Court interpreted this "due process" clause in favor of the state governments. In the Slaughterhouse Cases of 1873, involving a Louisiana law that granted a monopoly of the slaughterhouse business in New Orleans to one corporation, the Court declared the law to be a legitimate exercise of the police powers of a state to protect its citizens. In *Munn* v. *Illinois* (1877) the Court approved an Illinois law that fixed maximum storage rates for grain elevators on the grounds that a state could regulate "a business that is public in nature though privately owned and managed."

These decisions so alarmed American businessmen that some predicted the end of private property. Others believed that the only remedy lay in a constitutional amendment to protect business against state regulation. Then a change occurred in the make-up of the Court with the appointment of more conservative justices. The end of the depression years of the mid-eighties quieted radical demands, and a series of decisions beginning in the Santa Clara case of 1886 and culminating in *Smyth* v. *Ames* in 1898 made the Fourteenth Amendment into something quite new. In these cases the Court greatly broadened the interpretation of the amendment by holding that the word *person* in its first section meant corporations as well as individuals. It widened the application of the "due process" clause (which had originally been intended only to prohibit confiscation of property or other arbitrary violations of individual rights) to invalidate any regulation that would prohibit a corporation from making a "reasonable" profit on its investment. And, finally, the Court held that the courts and not the states should decide how much profit was reasonable. Thus it became corporations whose rights were protected by the amendment.

With these last cases the Fourteenth Amendment had practically been rewritten. Businessmen who denounced the rule laid down in *Munn* v. *Illinois* found protection in the later decisions. Lower courts handed down injunctions that tied the hands of regulatory commissions, and the Supreme Court became the stronghold of laissez-faire.

THE RAILROAD AGE

The new industrialism could never have been possible without the tremendous expansion of the railroad systems in America. In fact, they played such a dominant role that the period could well be called the railroad age. Between 1831 and 1861, 30,000 miles of railroad created a network connecting the Atlantic seaboard and the Mississippi valley. The war slowed down construction, but between 1867 and 1873 about 30,000 miles of railroad were added, and during the 1880s a record-breaking 73,000 miles were constructed. In 1900 the American railroad system, extending into every section of the country, measured 193,000 miles. This represented 40 percent of the world's railroad mileage and was more than the mileage of all European countries combined. Railroad building increased more rapidly than the population. In 1865 there was one mile of track in operation for every 1150 Americans. Twenty years later there was one mile for every 450. Capital invested in railroads jumped in this period from $2 billion to nearly $10 billion.

After the war most of the short lines were consolidated into a few large systems. Cornelius Vanderbilt, who had already made a fortune in steamboats, led the way. Before his death in 1877 he had extended the New York Central System to Chicago, offering improved service at reduced rates.

The New York Central's chief competitor for the traffic between the East and the Middle West was the Pennsylvania Railroad, which became the most important railroad and one of the foremost business enterprises in the country. At the end of the nineteenth century the Pennsylvania had lines tapping the most important Middle Atlantic and North Central industrial centers.

The Erie Railroad was a competitor for much of this traffic, but in the 1860s and 1870s it suffered from being in the hands of three of the most disreputable railroad manipulators of the era: Daniel Drew, Jay Gould, and Jim Fisk. Through bribery, chicanery, and fraud they made the Erie synonymous with all the vices of the Industrial Revolution. Consolidation enabled the Baltimore and Ohio to push into the Middle West, and the New York, New Haven, and Hartford to fan out into New England. By 1900 railroad consolidation had reached such vast proportions that more than two thirds of the railroad mileage of the country was controlled by groups led by Cornelius Vanderbilt, James J. Hill, E. H. Harriman, Jay Gould, John D. Rockefeller, and John Pierpont Morgan.

The Transcontinentals.   More spectacular and more important than railroad building in the older sections of the country was the construction of the transcontinentals. In 1862 Congress had chartered the Union Pacific and the Central Pacific railroads. Upon their completion of the transcontinental line in 1869, the two railroads had received 54 million acres of government land and government loans amounting to about $60 million. In addition the Union Pacific had issued one million shares of stock at $100 a share.

Much of the profiteering that accompanied the building of both roads can be ascribed to the separation of ownership and control in modern corporate enterprise. Managers systematically bled their companies for their own profit. The public first became aware of the

SELECTED TRAVEL TIMES AND COSTS 1870

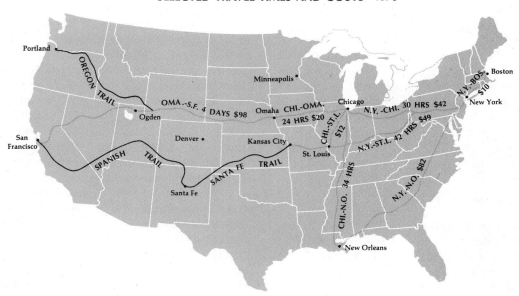

SELECTED TRAVEL TIMES AND COSTS 1900

Railroad

Wagon Trails

large scale of this practice in the Crédit Mobilier scandal of 1872. Officers of the Union Pacific Railroad had used a dummy construction company (the Crédit Mobilier), which they owned, to build the road and had turned over most of the assests of the road, including loans from the government and investments by shareholders, to themselves as constructors, paying themselves, by a conservative estimate, $73 million for a $50 million job. Their bribery of congressmen in connection with this deal was only incidental. More fundamental to an understanding of this evil is the fact that executives were placed in a position which gave them constant opportunity to enrich themselves at the expense of the investors and of the enterprise itself.

The Crocker Company, which built the Central Pacific, amassed a profit of about $63 million on an investment of $121 million. Most of this went to the four leading officials of the Central Pacific—Leland Stanford, Collis P. Huntington, Charles Crocker, and Mark Hopkins—each of whom left a fortune of $40 million or more at his death.

Governmental Aid to Railroads. While individual initiative and enterprise played a large part in the building of America's great railroad empire, it is doubtful if American railroads would have become so highly developed had it not been for the generosity of the federal, state, and local governments. Between 1850 and 1871 the railroads received from the federal government alone more than 130 million acres of land—an area as large as the New England states, Pennsylvania, and New York combined—and from the states about 49 million acres of land. It is nearly impossible to assess the value of this land, but a conservative estimate (based on $2.00 an acre) would place the value at $360 million. Some estimates have been as high as $2.5 billion.

Because they failed to meet all the conditions under which this land was granted, the railroads were able to retain only about 116 million acres. Even so, at the end of the land-grant era it was discovered that railroads had been granted one fourth of the entire area of Minnesota and Washington; one fifth of Wisconsin, Iowa, Kansas, North Dakota, and Montana; one seventh of Nebraska; one eighth of California; and one ninth of Louisiana. And at one point (1882) Texas discovered that its donations of land to railroads exceeded by 8 million acres the amount remaining in the public domain.

To such grants of land were added loans and subsidies. Towns, cities, and counties gave the railroads about $300 million, and the states, at a conservative estimate, furnished an additional $228 million. The federal government made loans of approximately $65 million, most of which went to the Union and Central Pacific. A town was at the mercy of a railroad, which could bypass it and thereby cause it to dry up. By this threat the railroads were able to secure cash grants, loans, exemption from taxation, and subscription to their stocks.

Yet many loans were made voluntarily and enthusiastically to get local railroad advantages. For, as the governor of Maine asked in 1867, "Why should private individuals be called upon to make a useless sacrifice of their means when railroads can be constructed by the unity of public with private interests, and made profitable to all?" By 1870, according to one estimate, public subsidies plus land grants contributed 60 percent of the costs of all railroad construction.

Public Benefits. The national railroad system no doubt brought great benefits to the economy. In addition to facilitating the movement of goods, the railroads used enormous amounts of iron and steel, coal, lumber, and other products and provided employment for hundreds of thousands of workers. In the decade of the 1880s the railroad companies

Federal land grants enabled the building of a railroad empire. To help accomplish this enormous task, Western railroads imported thousands of Chinese laborers like those shown here working for the Southern Pacific in 1851.

bought nearly 15 million tons of rails, purchasing in some years over 90 percent of the rolled steel manufactured in the United States.

The railroads were also one of the most active colonizers of the last West. They possessed vast tracts of land grants to sell, and they stood to gain in increased passenger and freight business as settlement expanded. They offered prospective settlers and buyers of land rail tickets at reduced prices and sometimes even provided free transportation

for a settler's furniture. The railroads kept agents at eastern seaports to welcome immigrants and to arrange for their transportation to the West. They even had immigration agencies in Europe to persuade Europeans to come to America.

THE INDUSTRIALISTS

"Robber Barons" or "Captains of Industry"? It is important to recognize that the foregoing factors were not wholly responsible for the American Industrial Revolution. It required the superb talent found among those Americans who mobilized the nation's productive energies to build the railroads and factories. The new industrialists were ambitious, resourceful, and extremely able. At times they were ruthless and dishonest but probably no more so than many other Americans of their day. They displayed the vigor, cleverness, and strength of will that have characterized the great entrepreneurs of all epochs of capitalistic expansion. They lived at a time when the highest goal was to acquire wealth and when one's position in society was determined by the amount amassed. In their day they were known as Captains of Industry and praised for the economic growth of modern America. But in time they came to be described in many quarters as Robber Barons, who exploited the working class and exacted tribute from the public.

Few of the industrialists were guided by the morality and ethics that had prevailed in business before the Civil War. To eliminate competitors and get around legal and political obstacles, they did not hesitate to use trickery, bribery, and corruption. Their attitude toward complaints about their methods was summed up in William Vanderbilt's famous reply to a reporter's questions about the motives for his management of the railroads: "The public be damned."

If we indict or criticize these industrialists for what they did to attain economic and industrial power, we must remember that they were the products of their time. Probably even the worst and coarsest of their activities reflected the dominant mores of American society in the Gilded Age. While they used wasteful and ruthless methods to promote economic development, they also faced such risks as overexpansion and unfair competition. Many now regard these businessmen more as creative agents in economic change whose long-run material contributions to society outweighed their short-run self-serv-

ing activities. They were launching the beginnings of a great economic expansion and economical mass production.

As already noted, there was great faith in the rags-to-riches story. Andrew Carnegie's success in climbing from the lowly position of bobbin-boy in a cotton textile mill at the wage of $1.20 a week to that of multimillionaire of the American steel industry is the classic American story of the poor boy making good. Carnegie's *Autobiography* and the work of historians helped to keep alive for many years the "rags-to-riches" dream and the belief that the Captains of Industry came from poor, immigrant, rural, uneducated families, without social advantages—that, in fact, they became rich and powerful by pulling themselves up not only by their own bootstraps but also by a strict adherence to the Calvinist ethic of hard work, thrift, chastity, and abstinence. New research, however, has shown that the bulk of the business leaders came from white Anglo-Saxon Protestant, urban, northeastern, educated professional and business families. It seems that the doors of business success were not generally opened to immigrants, farm boys, or youths of poor education and background.

While these tycoons accumulated large fortunes, they insisted they were not materialistic. "I know of nothing more despicable and pathetic than a man who devotes all the waking hours of the day to making money for money's sake," wrote John D. Rockefeller in his *Reminiscences*. He maintained it was "the association with interesting and quick-minded men," not money alone, that prompted him to follow his course to success. Andrew Carnegie expressed a similar view when he said that many of his "clever partners" in the steel business had been his friends from boyhood. He emphasized the joy he found in "manufacturing something and giving employment to many men."

A number of the new industrialists were of military age during the Civil War, but most of them took advantage of a law that allowed them to hire a substitute or to pay a certain amount of money in lieu of military service. Writing from Pittsburgh in 1863, Thomas Mellon, the founder of an aluminum fortune, declared that "such opportunities for making money had never existed before in all my former experience." When his son James asked permission to enlist, the elder Mellon wrote, "Don't do it. It is only greenhorns who enlist. Those who are able to pay for substitutes do so, and no discredit attaches." Then he added, "It is not so much the danger as disease and idleness and vicious habits. . . . I had hoped my boy was going to make a smart, intelligent businessman and was not such a goose as to be seduced from his duty by the declamations of buncombed speeches."

Simon Cameron, as Secretary of War, handed out war contracts left and right and asked only for production in return. Gigantic frauds and great fortunes resulted from shoddy contracts and shady deals. Vanderbilt supplied the government leaky ships. J. P. Morgan, twenty-four years old in 1861, purchased 5000 discarded carbines and sold them back to the army for $112,000. Both Morgan's and Vanderbilt's deals were exposed, but neither was punished. Jim Fisk went south to smuggle out cotton and sell it in the North for large profits. Gould's inside information enabled him to cash in on railroad deals and speculaton in gold. And so it went.

The Trust. Before the Civil War, American business was highly competitive and consisted of small units—mostly individual enterprises or partnerships. After the war, businessmen sought ways to check increasing competition, which they had come to regard as inefficient, wasteful, and threatening to their profits. They established trade agreements, associations, and pools to limit competition. But because these devices depended upon voluntary cooperation and were not enforceable in the courts, none proved suffi-

ciently reliable. The answer seemed to lie in the formation of industrial trusts, which provided businessmen with more efficient control over the policies of all members within a single industry.

Under the trust system the stock of several competing companies was placed under the control of a group of trustees in exchange for trustee certificates. Ownership remained with the original companies, but management was consolidated in a single board of directors. John D. Rockefeller was by far the most important figure in the trust movement, and the formation of his Standard Oil Company in 1879 established the trust pattern in the United States.

John D. Rockefeller and the Standard Oil Trust. Rockefeller was a young merchant in Cleveland, Ohio, when he decided to enter the oil industry during the Civil War. Here he found violence, lawlessness, and waste, and, being no exponent of such free enterprise, he took steps to end this competitive strife. Rockefeller adopted the most efficient methods of production, regularly saved a part of his profits, and surrounded himself with some of the ablest men in the industry. By 1867 he was the largest refiner of oil in Cleveland, and in 1870 he organized the Standard Oil Company of Ohio with a capitalization of $1 million. This was the original *trust* and the term came to be applied to any large combination with monopolistic powers.

With his trust, Rockefeller soon eliminated his Ohio competitors. He now proceeded to take on refiners in New York, Pittsburgh, and Philadelphia. Those who accepted Rockefeller's terms shared in the large profits. Those who continued to resist him were attacked with every weapon in cutthroat competitive warfare. He usually crushed his competitors with ruthless price cutting, but he also had an immense competitive advantage in the rebates[1] and drawbacks[2] he received from the railroads. By 1879 Rockefeller controlled about

90 percent of America's refining industry.

Of all the trusts that appeared in the eighties and nineties, none aroused more alarms or pointed up more moral issues than the Standard Oil Trust. Even the means Rockefeller used to gain a monopoly in the oil industry produced conflicting opinions. "I ascribe the success of the Standard Oil Company to its consistent policy of making the volume of its business large through the merit and cheapness of its products," declared Rockefeller. But Senator James K. Jones of Arkansas offered another explanation on the floor of the United States Senate in 1889: "The iniquities of the Standard Oil Company have been enumerated and recounted until some of them are familiar to everyone," said Jones, "and the colossal fortunes which have grown from it, which in all their vastness do not represent one dollar of honest toil or one trace of benefit to mankind, nor any addition to the product of human labor, are known everywhere."

And the controversy has continued. Some writers see in the rise of Standard Oil a dark record of unfair trade practices, railroad favors, bribery and blackmail, and an alliance between the corporation and politics by which legislators, officials, and judges closed their eyes to practices that violated the law. Others have argued that Standard Oil straightened out a disorderly industry and, by introducing efficiency and competency, lowered prices and created a great industry. Both sides, however, agree that Standard's methods

frequently were ruthless and that they would not be tolerated today.

Rockefeller had a way of being ahead of the law most of the time. William Vanderbilt, testifying about the leaders of Standard Oil before a congressional committee in 1879, expressed an opinion prevalent in those years: "Yes, they are very shrewd men. I don't believe that by any legislative enactment or anything else, through any of the States or all of the States, you can keep such men down. You can't do it! They will be on top all the time. You see if they are not." Be that as it may, in 1892 the Supreme Court of Ohio ordered the dissolution of the Standard Trust on the grounds that it was designed to "establish a virtual monopoly" and was "contrary to the policy of our state." But this decision did not produce the desired results, for the Standard trustees, although they returned the stock to the stockholders, continued to manage the member concerns as "liquidating trustees" until 1897, when the court forced them to abandon this stratagem.

Prior to this, in 1889, New Jersey had changed its corporation laws in such a way as to make legal the formation of a holding company—a company which owned a majority of the stock in a number of subsidiary corporations and was established to unify their control. In 1899 the various subsidiaries of Standard were legally combined through the creation of a giant holding company, the Standard Oil Company of New Jersey, capitalized at $110 million. Standard's control over the refining business continued as complete as ever. In 1911 the United States Supreme Court held that Standard had violated the 1890 Sherman Antitrust Act, but this decision, like earlier ones in the state courts, had little effect upon the management of Standard's affairs.

Carnegie and Steel. Just as Rockefeller captured the refining market from his competitors, so Andrew Carnegie captured much of

---

[1]Powerful industrial shippers, in a strong bargaining position with railroads, often demanded—and received—secret "rebates," or discounts from publicly posted shipping rates. Rebates sometimes were given in return for a specified volume of business or in return for the shipper's distributing his traffic in accordance with a pooling agreement made among competing lines.

[2]In exchange for the privilege of transporting the freight of a large shipper (e.g., Standard Oil), railroads agreed to pay the shipper "drawbacks," or subsidies drawn from a percentage of all receipts of its competitors.

A view of the Frick Coke Company, later bought out by Andrew Carnegie, shows the ovens producing coke to be used in the production of steel.

the steel market, although he never achieved a monopoly. He had made money in various ways in the fifties and sixties and was already a millionaire when he turned to steel production in the early seventies. Like Rockefeller, Carnegie secured rebates from the railroads. He also was materially aided by the depression of the seventies, for as he said about it afterward, "so many of my friends needed money, that they begged me to repay them [for their investments in early Carnegie enterprises]. I did so and bought out five or six of them. That was what gave me my leading interest in this steel business."

From this time on, Carnegie led the field in the steel industry. He bought out and took into his business Henry Clay Frick, who in the seventies had gained control of most of the coke ovens around Pittsburgh. Together they created a great vertical combine of coal fields, coke ovens, limestone deposits, iron mines, ore ships, and railroads. In 1892 the Carnegie Steel Company was formed at a capitalization of $25 million. It controlled all its sources of supply and was soon making one fourth of all unfinished steel in the United States. At the turn of the century it became a New Jersey corporation with a capitalization of $160 million.

Carnegie was essentially an *industrial capitalist* in that his money came from industry and not from bankers. He put a large part of his profits back into his business, and he did not allow his corporation's stock to be sold to persons outside his organization. He was successful because of his efficient business methods and driving energy and because he skillfully chose partners of almost equal ability, such as Frick and Charles Schwab. His labor policy, like that of most of the corporation leaders of this era, was one of long hours, low wages, and hostility to trade unions. Carnegie was willing to make innovations in methods and machinery, ready to discard equipment whenever better came along. He made improvements in times of depression, and when prosperity returned, he was ready to produce.

The Growth of Trusts.   Soon after Standard Oil Company had set the trust pattern, other business enterprises of this type appeared. The McCormick Harvester Company of Chicago secured almost a monopoly of mechanical farm equipment. James B. Duke's American Tobacco Company, established in 1890, and Henry O. Havemeyer's American Sugar Refining Company, founded in 1891, gained almost complete monopolies, while Philip D. Armour and Gustavus Swift won domination of the meat packing business. Other consumer goods controlled by trusts were salt, whisky, matches, crackers, wire, and nails.

Eventually, prosecution by states or state legislation declaring trusts illegal ended these organizations. But though the original form of trust disappeared, the term *trust* continued in use, applied to any type of monopoly. Many of the former trusts reorganized themselves into holding companies under the friendly corporate laws of New Jersey. Others became corporate combines created by mergers of separate firms. Fewer combinations occurred during the depression of 1893–1897, but after this they increased at an extraordinary rate.

Opposition to the Trusts.   As the American people watched the proliferation of trusts and millionaires, they became convinced that something must be done to restore competition. There arose a popular outcry against monopolies, and by the eighties public speakers and writers began to condemn them. In 1881 Henry D. Lloyd attacked the Standard Oil Trust in "The Story of a Great Monopoly" in the *Atlantic Monthly*. Similar articles against other examples of big business followed. Edward Bellamy in his *Looking Backward* (1887)

Trusts gave businessmen more control over their profits, but the destruction of competition aroused a popular outcry against monopolies. The base of the statue in this cartoon is the Standard Oil Trust.

assailed economic conditions of the time and pictured a future socialist utopian state where life's necessities and luxuries would be produced by a cooperative society for the benefit of all. Henry George in his *Progress and Poverty* (1879) maintained that the problems of the times were largely the result of a monopoly of land. "All who do not possess land," he argued, "are toiling for those who do, and this is the reason why progress and poverty go hand in hand." George proposed that the unearned increments in land values be confiscated by the government in the form of a single tax on land. This would benefit the whole of society and adjust those economic disparities from which American society was suffering. (The ideas of Bellamy and George were discussed more fully in Chapter 13.)

During the eighties a number of states passed laws prohibiting trusts, but these failed to check the increasing concentration of industry. Some trusts appeared more powerful than the states that attempted to regulate them, and when one device for creating monopoly ran afoul of the law, another was substituted. State legislation also proved ineffective so long as such states as New Jersey, Delaware, and West Virginia placed few restrictions on the chartering corporations and permitted the creation of holding companies.

The Interstate Commerce Act. These frustrations aroused the opponents of monopoly to demand federal action. Between 1873 and 1885 more than thirty measures were introduced in the House of Representatives providing for the regulation of interstate railroads. Some of them were passed, only to fail in the Senate. But under the pressures of Easterners as well as Westerners, the Senate yielded at last and appointed the Cullom Committee to investigate. In 1886 the committee made its report, concluding: "It is the deliberate judgment of the Committee that upon no public question are the people so nearly unanimous as upon the proposition that Congress should undertake in some way the regulation of interstate commerce." This recommendation together with the Supreme Court's Wabash decision in 1886, forbidding the states to continue their regulation of *interstate* railroad traffic, led to the Interstate Commerce Act of 1887.

This law provided that all railway rates "shall be reasonable and just." It prohibited such discriminatory practices as rebates and drawbacks and made illegal some of the long and short haul abuses.[3] It forbade pooling agreements[4] and required that all rates and fares be printed and publicly posted. The act established a five-man Interstate Commerce Commission, with power to investigate the railroads and to require reports from them. The Commission could hear complaints of violations of the law, but it had to depend upon the courts to enforce its rulings. Thus the Commission did not receive the powers necessary to regulate the transportation system. Also, the commissioners were virtually required by the act to be inexperienced in railroad practices, so they had difficulties fully understanding and acting on the complaints of the shippers.

The chief weakness of the law, however, was its vagueness in not defining "reasonable and just" rates. Such grave defects in the act were recognized even by such a staunch opponent of federal regulation as Senator

---

[3]The "long and short haul" abuse pointed up the fact that railroads charged rates based not on operating costs but on what the public could be forced to pay. Over "long hauls"—e.g., from Chicago to New York—competition between railroads was keen and freight charges were low (sometimes lower than operating costs); but over "short hauls"—i.e., between local points serviced by only one line—a railroad, in a noncompetitive situation, could charge rates as high as the public could bear, thereby recouping whatever losses it might have suffered on long hauls.

[4]By means of "pooling agreements" competing railroads sometimes agreed to maintain uniformly high rates in a particular locality by apportioning traffic among themselves or dividing accumulated earnings. Pooling was intended to avoid competitive rate wars.

Nelson Aldrich of Rhode Island, who described the new law as a "delusion and a sham, an empty menace to great interests, made to answer the clamor of the ignorant and unreasoning."

The Commission soon discovered that it could not compel witnesses to testify and that appeals to the courts produced endless delays. Even in those cases that reached the Supreme Court, the decisions generally favored the railroads over the Commission. Between 1887 and 1905 the Court heard sixteen cases appealed by the I.C.C. In fifteen it upheld the railroads.

The Sherman Antitrust Act.

Senator John Sherman of Ohio outlined the need for stronger federal control when he said in 1890:

Congress alone can deal with the trusts, and if we are unwilling or unable there will soon be a trust for every production and a master to fix the price for every necessity of life.

In 1890 Congress passed the Sherman Antitrust Act, another departure from laissez-faire policies, by an almost unanimous vote. Although Sherman introduced it, it was written mainly by Senators George F. Edmunds of Vermont and George F. Hoar of Massachusetts. The act declared that "every contract, combination in the form of trust or otherwise, or conspiracy in restraint of trade or commerce" was illegal. But Congress left it to the courts to determine the meaning of the terms and phrases in the law, and it could not be enforced without the cooperation of the Attorney General. Senator Orville Platt of Connecticut in commenting on the act stated, "The conduct of the Senate . . . has not been in the line of honest preparation of a bill to prohibit and punish trusts. It has been in the line of getting some bill with that title that we might go to the country with." Senator Shelby Cullom of Illinois thought that if the act "were strictly and literally enforced the business of the country would come to a standstill."

But it was not enforced. From 1890 to 1901 the Justice Department instituted only eighteen antitrust suits. And the Supreme Court—in *U.S.* v. *E. C. Knight Co.* (1895)—undermined the law by holding that manufacturing, being wholly intrastate in character even though ultimately affecting interstate commerce, was not subject to federal regulation. This limited definition of the "commerce clause" in the Constitution put trusts beyond federal control.

The Growth of Finance Capitalism.

During the 1890s industrial capitalism began to give way to *finance capitalism* as investment bankers became more influential in the development of American industry. The industrial capitalists like Rockefeller and Carnegie were producers who had grown rich with their own industries. Finance capitalists like J. P. Morgan and August Belmont, in contrast, came to power not because they were skilled industrial organizers but because they had enormous sums of money with which they could invest in and purchase control of an industry. A corporation in need of capital could ask a banking house to sell the corporation's securities. In return the investment banker demanded a share in the management of the corporations in which his customers had invested. Hard-pressed industrialists could not refuse, and gradually the bankers assumed supervision of corporate policies. By the turn of the century control of a number of corporations had passed from industrialists to bankers.

The leading American finance capitalist was J. P. Morgan, who was also a dominant figure in the national economy. The New York banking houses of August Belmont and Company and Kuhn, Loeb and Company and the Boston banking houses of Lee, Higginson and Company and Kidder Peabody and Company were also important. Morgan worked to bring about order and stability in one industry after another, for he wanted to make sure that dividends would be paid regularly to stockholders. He disliked competition because he felt it would lead to cutthroat price cutting, which would be bad for business. Instead, he wanted corporations to make prices and markets. Morgan's policies meant more protection to stockholders but higher prices to consumers.

Probably the biggest of Morgan's ventures was his launching of the United States Steel Corporation in 1901. He bought out the Carnegie Steel Corporation and combined it with ten other steel companies into one vast corporation capitalized at the unprecedented figure of slightly over $1 billion plus a bonded debt of over $303 million. The Bureau of Corporations later estimated that the total value of the combined assets of all the merged companies was actually only $676 million.

With Carnegie's sale to Morgan the era of industrial capitalism came to a close. Finance capitalism brought even greater economic consolidation. In 1893 there were twelve great companies with an aggregate capital of about $1 billion. By 1904 there were 318 industrial combinations—one of them Morgan's United States Steel Corporation—with a combined capital in excess of $7.25 billion. Together these 318 companies controlled more than 5000 separate plants.

LABOR

Labor had a difficult time in the industrial age. While businessmen solicited governmental assistance in the form of tariff protection and did not regard this as governmental intervention, they bitterly opposed any attempt to improve the conditions of labor by legislation on the ground that this would be unwarranted interference with the economic system. Most businessmen regarded as absurd the notion that employees had the same right to government protection and aid as had already been afforded business. Businessmen believed that they alone had the right to determine the terms and conditions of employment. They dismissed the idea of collective bargaining.

But as business formed combinations, so did labor. The National Labor Union, organized in 1866, was mainly a reform organization that summed up various grievance labor had had since the 1840s. It demanded an eight-hour day, the abolition of slums, and the establishment of cooperatives. It favored arbitration over strikes in labor disputes, and it frowned, at first, upon independent political action by labor groups. Its most important leader was William Sylvis, who died in 1869 after heading the organization for only a year. Had he lived longer, the union might have played a greater role in the history of labor. After his death, however, it turned more and more to political activity, and in 1873 its trade-union aspect disappeared when it became the National Labor Reform party. Even so, the National Labor Union prepared the way for more effective labor organizations, such as the Knights of Labor.

The Knights of Labor. The Knights of Labor were organized in 1869 under the leadership of Uriah Stephens. Believing in the solidarity of labor, the Knights admitted almost everyone to membership, excluding only lawyers, bankers, stockbrokers, liquor dealers, and professional gamblers. Their announced primary purpose was "to secure to toilers a proper share of the wealth they create." They hoped to achieve their goals through secrecy, the organization of cooperatives, and education and propaganda.

Secrecy was of prime importance to the members, for their jobs were at stake: Industries locked out workers who belonged to unions. Even the name of the organization was not made public until 1881. But their secrecy caused the Knights trouble with the churches, especially the Catholic church,

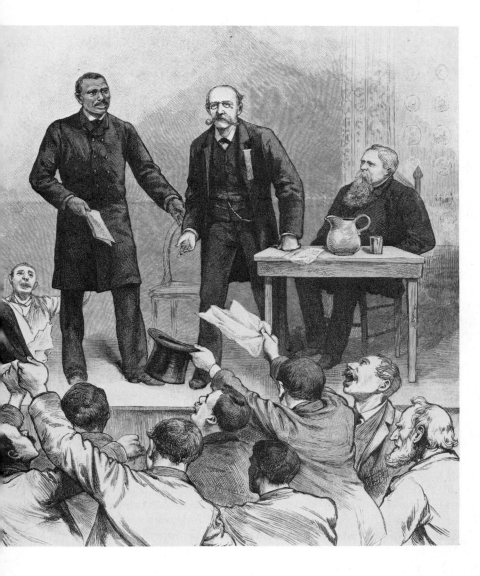

A black delegate is depicted introducing Terence Powderly to the 1886 convention of the Knights of Labor.

which feared the members might be taking a secret oath that was in conflict with their religion. Only the intercession of Cardinal Gibbons of Baltimore kept the Pope from excommunicating the Catholics in the federation.

The Knights were of national importance from 1879 to 1893, while Terence V. Powderly was their Grand Master Workman. Powderly was denounced by some as a revolutionary and by others as a faker who sold out labor. He seldom gave full attention to the union, considering it only a part-time position, and engaged himself in other activities such as being Mayor of Scranton, Pennsylvania, from 1878 to 1884 and a leader of the Irish Land League. His great strength with the workers was his oratorical power. Powderly supported land reform, temperance, and public education.

The Knights hoped to organize all workers, skilled and unskilled, black and white, into one big union for mutual protection against "the aggression of employers." They worked for the eight-hour day, abolition of child labor, settlement of labor disputes by arbitration rather than by strikes, and encouragement of cooperative stores and factories.

The Knights' official opposition to the use of strikes—like that of unions generally in the seventies—was because most strikes then had been unsuccessful. The depression of the seventies had dealt unions some severe blows. They lost strength and saw wages drop as much as 40 percent in textiles and on the railroads. They faced increasing unemployment, prosecution of strikers, and use of police and private detective agencies as strike breakers. In addition to lockouts (restricting employment to nonunion labor) employers resorted to blacklisting (circulating names of union leaders and members) and to "yellow dog" contracts (pacts whereby employees agreed not to join unions). So the seventies and the depression of that decade were a very difficult time for unions. Only a handful of the national ones pulled through these years.

Although Powderly himself was opposed to use of the strike as a weapon and was willing to come to terms with employers at almost any price, the hard times of the mid-eighties led to boycotts and strikes, notably on the Union Pacific in 1884 and Jay Gould's Wabash in 1885. Spontaneous strikes by shopmen and trainmen caught the companies off guard and compelled Powderly's support of his followers. These were labor's first major victories, and they forced Gould to negotiate with the Knights. An illusion of easy success arose, and suddenly the Knights were flooded with members. In 1886, their peak year, membership shot up to 700,000.

But fast on the heels of these successes came the Great Southwestern Strike of 1886 and

failure. Powderly had agreed in the Wabash settlement to have no more strikes without notifying the railroads in advance. It was an agreement he could not enforce. The strikes that had occurred were not of his making but were strikes of local origin that had drawn him in only after they had begun. In the Southwestern strike Gould refused to negotiate with the union because the Knights had given no advance notice to the railroad. The workers were unable to hold out.

Of all the labor upheavals of the period, none was more frightening to men of property and order or did more damage to the prestige of labor than the bombing at Haymarket Square in Chicago in 1886. On May 1 a number of independent trade unions struck for recognition of the eight-hour day, and two days later the police shot and clubbed some of the strikers who were beating up strike breakers. The violence of the police prompted growls of resentment and threats of retaliation in the labor press. The next day, May 4, a group of anarchists called a protest meeting in Haymarket Square. As the speeches were coming to a close, almost two hundred policemen arrived on the scene and ordered the crowd to go home. Before anyone could move, however, a bomb exploded, killing one policeman outright and fatally wounding several others. Almost immediately the police opened fire on the workers, and soon a riot was in full swing. Many civilians were killed, dozens wounded, and in the confusion and excitement several of the policemen shot each other.

The reaction in Chicago and throughout the nation was one of horror. In the resulting hysteria, eight men were arrested, tried, and convicted on what later has come to be seen as flimsy, inconclusive evidence. Four were executed and the others imprisoned.

Although the Knights of Labor had nothing to do with the Haymarket Riot, they were identified in the public mind with the anarchists, and skilled workers began to desert the Knights in large numbers. From this time on, the Knights declined in influence, and by 1890 the membership had fallen to 100,000. The failure of their cooperatives also contributed to their downfall.

In addition they were weakened by the same conflict that had earlier rent the National Labor Union. It was the division between a national leadership dedicated to general economic and political reform and the trade unions that preferred to concentrate on the immediate economic betterment of workers. This controversy came to a head, ironically, during 1886, when the Knights had their most spectacular growth, largely as a result of the success of strikes, and when Powderly and other union leaders refused to support new strikes. These and other dissensions over immediate strategy and long-range goals led to a loss in the numbers and influence of the Knights.

The Rise of the AFL.   While the power and influence of the Knights waned, a new labor organization, the American Federation of Labor (AFL), was created in 1886 under the leadership of Samuel Gompers. Gompers abandoned the Knights' idea of labor solidarity. Trade unionism was his aim, and his plan was to group workers according to crafts. The AFL pursued three practical objectives: higher wages, shorter hours, and better working conditions. Gompers opposed direct affiliation of labor unions with political parties and favored cooperation with employers and mediation of labor disputes. The Knights and the AFL competed for supremacy in American labor unions. By the end of the nineteenth century the AFL had won.

Violence and the Unions.   Most labor organizations rejected violence as a weapon in their struggle to improve the conditions of labor, but there were some exceptions. One was the Molly Maguires, an organization active among Pennsylvania coal miners from the mid-sixties to the late seventies who resorted to violence and to the destruction of property. Another exception was the Anarchists, a small group that supported acts of terror directed at ending capitalism.

There was, however, violence in some of the strikes. One bloody episode occurred in a strike of steelworkers against Carnegie's Homestead plant near Pittsburgh in 1892. Pinkerton detectives, hired by the Carnegie Company, fought with the strikers, and a number of men were killed or wounded. The strike was finally broken when the governor of Pennsylvania called out the National Guard to give protection to the company and to local law officials.

With the onset of depression in the summer of 1893, however, unrest and dissatisfaction among the working class deepened. Among the most violent of the labor upheavals, which aroused national apprehension, was the Pullman strike called by the American Railway Union in sympathy for the distress of Pullman workers. By the end of June 1894 some 20,000 railroadmen were on strike in and around Chicago, tying up every Midwestern railroad. In retaliation the railroad companies appealed to a federal court for an injunction against the strikers on the basis of the Sherman Antitrust Act, arguing that the strike was a restraint on trade such as the act forbade. The court issued the injunction.

At the same time, violence broke out in Chicago, and President Cleveland (over the protest of Governor Altgeld of Illinois) sent in 2000 federal soldiers to "protect the mails." Before order was restored, some twenty people were reported killed and 2000 railway cars destroyed. Eugene V. Debs, president of the American Railway Union, and other labor leaders were arrested, convicted of contempt of court—for violating the injunction—and sentenced to six months to a year in jail. The conviction of the A.R.U. leaders was upheld by the Supreme Court of the United States, which declared the injunction issued against the union to be a legitimate device for the

*A violent strike against Carnegie's Homestead plant was broken by the National
Guard. The wounded men in the lower right of the picture are Pinkerton detectives.*

protection of interstate commerce and the mails.

For thirty years after the Debs case, a federal court injunction was a potent weapon in the hands of employers threatened with a strike. Although the Clayton Act of 1914 appeared to limit the court's authority to interfere in labor disputes, many antilabor injunctions continued to be granted by the federal courts, and it was not until the Norris-La Guardia Anti-Injunction Act was passed in 1932 that labor gained the protection it had long sought against injunctions.

It is noteworthy that in the Homestead and Pullman strikes the companies were run by two of the leading industrialists in the country who themselves believed that they were among the most enlightened and concerned of American employers—and were so regarded in many quarters. Carnegie had written magazine articles supporting the rights of labor, and George Pullman had built what he considered a "model town" where his employees could live.

Most American workers in these years accepted existing working conditions as inevitable and made the best of it. Although they might be discontented, they did not protest. Industrial workers were a minority group and were much influenced by rural values. Many were unskilled, poorly educated, and socially underprivileged. They were also awed by the enormous achievements of the new industry and were proud of being a part of it. And those who were upwardly mobile generally identified with their employers and accepted the values of American capitalism. Thus as a class, American workers were silent.

Unions and the Black Worker. Unlike the politicians of the day, the national labor organizations of the post–Civil War decades had to deal with the race issue. Should they organize black workers? And if they did, should they allow them to join the same unions with white workers, or should they put them in segregated unions? This was a difficult problem for labor leaders, because they recognized that black workers were potential competitors. The National Labor Union, owing to the wide diversity of opinion among its members, never took any specific action on this matter. But the Knights of Labor, whose goal was to organize all workers, skilled and unskilled, sought to bring blacks into the labor movement. Thus it organized black as well as mixed locals, not only in the North, but in the South, where Knights organizers were attacked by vigilantes and lynch mobs. It is not possible to tell from the available records how many blacks became members of the Knights. At the 1886 convention of the union the general secretary reported that "the colored people of the South are flocking to us, being eager for organization and education . . . ," and that same year, the peak year for the Knights, it has been estimated that there were no fewer than 60,000 blacks in the Knights of Labor.

Since the American Federation of Labor was comprised of national craft unions, it had few black members, for few black workers had been admitted to craft unions. Gompers' position on the black worker was made clear in his annual report of 1890 when he emphasized the "necessity of avoiding as far as possible all controversial questions." It was not until the First World War, according to Spero and Harris in their history, *The Black Worker*, that blacks became "a regular element in the labor force of every basic industry."

THE LAST FRONTIER

The West. While industrial expansion was transforming post–Civil War America, there took place another movement of momentous consequence—the settlement of the western half of the country. It was a migration probably unparalleled in the history of the world. In one generation Americans established more than a million farms in this last

West and occupied more new land than earlier Americans had settled in two and a half centuries. From 1607 to 1870 Americans had occupied 407 million acres and had placed 189 million of them under cultivation. In the last three decades of the nineteenth century they took up 430 million acres and brought 225 million of them under cultivation.

The Mining Frontier. Miners were the first to reveal to the nation the resources and potentialities of the territory between the Missouri River and the Pacific. The discovery of gold in 1848 had lured many miners to California, and later, throughout the 1860s, miners hurried to "strikes" in Colorado, Arizona, Idaho, Montana, and Wyoming. In each case gold attracted the first settlers, the miners. When the pay dirt was exhausted, ranchers and farmers, aided by the government and the railroads, laid the foundations of the territory.

The discovery of gold in the foothills of the Rocky Mountains close to Pike's Peak, near Lake Tahoe on the eastern slopes of the Sierra Nevada, on the reservation of the Nez Percé Indians in the eastern part of Washington territory, in Last Chance Gulch in Montana, and in the Black Hills region of South Dakota on the reservation of the Sioux Indians brought thousands upon thousands of persons to these areas. Into them crowded all the elements of a rough and active civilization. A large number of the miners, such as those in Idaho, "were like quicksilver," said H. H. Bancroft, the historian: "A mass of them dropped in any locality, broke up into individual globules, and ran off after any atom of gold in their vicinity. They stayed nowhere longer than the gold attracted them." Others, as in Colorado, stayed on, once the mining boom had spent itself, to farm and to help their area become a territory.

The story of the mining towns is a familiar one in fiction and motion pictures. Their lawlessness has attracted much attention. To be sure, it existed. But it would be a mistake to represent the mining communities as mere nests of lawlessness, or to argue, as most Easterners did, that mining camps had abandoned the institutions of civilized society. Mining camps did have few churches, schools, newspapers, theaters, and so forth, but they quickly established them. For example, in the town of Deadwood, South Dakota,

This miner is washing gold—"pay dirt"—in Montana.

known as the most lawless place in the country and consisting mainly of two long rows of saloons, a stage company played Gilbert and Sullivan's *Mikado* for a record run of 130 nights. Each mining camp was a separate administrative and judicial district having its own governing officials who passed and enforced its own laws. The legal codes and practices of these mining camps were eventually recognized in American courts, and a number of them were incorporated into constitutions and laws of the Western states.

The miners' frontier came to an end in the 1880s. No more important discoveries were made, and the individual prospector was gradually replaced by big corporations, usually run by Eastern financiers. Between 1860 and 1890, $1,242,000,000 in gold and $901,000,000 in silver were taken out of the mines in the West. These amounts enabled the federal government to resume specie payment and helped precipitate the money question, a major political issue during the last quarter of the nineteenth century (see the next chapter).

The Settlers. The opportunities for obtaining cheap or free land induced many settlers to go West. They could buy a farm outright from the national government under the terms of the Preemption Act of 1841, which allowed them to obtain a quarter section (160 acres) at the price of $1.25 an acre. Or they could purchase their quarter section from one of the land-grant railroads or from one of the states, whose holdings of public domain were greatly increased by the passage of the Morrill Act of 1862. (This Act had given every state establishing a public agricultural college 30,000 acres for each senator and representative then in Congress.) Finally, western settlers could secure their quarter section free of charge under the Homestead Act of 1862. This law made it possible for any American citizen, or any alien who had declared the intention of becoming a citizen, to acquire 160 acres of unoccupied government land by living on it or by cultivating it for five years. A homesteader who wished to gain ownership sooner could, after six months of residence, buy the quarter section at the prevailing minimum price, usually $1.25 an acre. The residence requirement went up to fourteen months in 1891.

The Homestead Act has been called "the greatest democratic measure of all history," but it had a number of faults. The best farming lands east of the 100th meridian (the line approximately bisecting the Dakotas and Nebraska east and west) were largely taken by 1862, and in the region from the Great Plains to the Pacific, to which the law chiefly applied, small homesteads were inadequate. Moreover, the Homestead Act did not end land speculation. Larger purchases than ever were made by individuals. For example, William S. Chapman bought a million acres in California and Nevada, and Francis Palms and Frederick E. Driggs together procured 486,000 acres of timberland in Michigan and Wisconsin. There was also fraudulent administration of the law. False claims were made, and claims were turned over to speculators and to land, mining, and timber companies. Perjury and bribery of land officials were common. In practice the act was a perversion of the land reformers' ideas.

During this period a generous Congress passed other measures to dispose of the public domain. The Timber Culture Act of 1873 provided free grants of 160 acres in certain regions on condition that the settler plant forty acres (later reduced to ten acres) in trees and keep them growing for ten years. Under the terms of the Desert Act of 1877 the government offered semiarid lands in 640-acre tracts to those who would irrigate them. But since irrigation projects usually required more capital than most settlers had, the law benefited primarily the large-scale grazing companies. The Timber and Stone Act of 1878 permitted the sale of quarter sections of land not suited for agriculture but valuable for timber. Large corporations and speculators managed to get possession of more than 13 million acres of such government lands.

The Ranching Frontier. Flourishing on the Great Plains for about two decades after the Civil War was an open-range cattle industry, originating with the Long Drive of cattle from Texas northward to railroads on the Great Plains for shipment eastward to the large cities. One of the most accessible meeting places for ranchers and packers was at Abilene, Kansas, on the Kansas Pacific railroad line. Here Joseph G. McCoy, an enterprising meat dealer from Illinois, built a hotel and erected barns, stables, pens, and loading chutes. In 1868 Abilene received 75,000 head of cattle and in 1871, a record year, 700,000 head. Over the next dozen years a total of 4 million cattle were driven over the Chisholm Trail to Abilene and other Kansas cow towns. The cattle were moved slowly in herds of two or three thousand head. This procedure required the services of sixteen or eighteen cowboys, a cook with a chuck wagon, and a wrangler with extra cow ponies.

It was on the Long Drive that the cowboy came into his own as a unique character of the frontier. He was a picturesque figure, usually clothed in a flannel shirt, with a brightly colored handkerchief loosely knotted around his neck, high-heeled boots into which his trousers were tucked, a pair of leather chaps—or heavy riding overalls—and a broad-brimmed felt hat. Heavy spurs and a revolver completed his costume. The cowboy's work was hazardous. With only a cow pony, a lasso, and a six-shooter, he and his companions tried to keep under safe control several thousand head of steers during two months of continuous travel.

There were many risks along the trail—the danger of stampedes, which could be set off by a sudden noise or lightning flash, of thefts by rustlers, and of raids by Indians. One of the veterans of the Long Drive wrote, "It was

tiresome grimy business for the attendant punchers who travelled ever in a cloud of dust and heard little but the constant chorus from the crackling of hoofs and of ankle joints, from the bellows, lows, and bleats of the trudging animals."[5] The cowboy's life was also a lonely one. He sang sentimental words to soothe the restless cattle and to cheer himself as he whiled away the lonely hours on the Chisholm Trail. Although fans of Western stories and movies might never suspect the fact, blacks were numerous among the cowboys who drove the herds to market.

The cattle business reached its peak in the early 1880s, when profits of 40 to 50 percent were common. But such returns quickly attracted so many prospective ranchers that they overstocked the range. The unfenced plains of the public domain were bountiful and free, and the ranchers made use of this public land. Between 1882 and 1884 they sent as many young steers north to the ranges as they shipped east to the markets. But the two disastrous winters of 1885–1886 and 1886–1887 and the blistering summer of 1886 destroyed most of the feed and the cattle. What steers eventually reached market were so inferior in quality that the bottom fell out of beef prices despite the great shortage.

At this time, too, large numbers of sheepherders began to cross the plains. The sheep stripped the range of grass, so when the sheepmen came to stay, the cattlemen had to fight or leave. Farmers were also homesteading the plains and fencing the open range, and many of them turned to cattle raising. Soon they were able to produce beef of higher quality than that found on the open range. With the increase of railroad facilities, the Long Drive became unnecessary. Gradually this stage of the colorful cattle industry was ending, and with it came an end to the last frontier.

---

[5]Philip Ashton Rollins, *The Cowboy* (New York: Charles Scribner's Sons, 1922), p. 253.

A lone cowboy in fur chaps and high felt hat watches over a long line of cattle plodding through the snow.

The Indian. An essential step in the conquest of the last West was a solution of the Indian problem. The Indians of the Great Plains and the Rocky Mountains, about 250,000 in number, actively opposed white settlement in their areas. The land had been theirs for centuries, and they were determined to fight, if necessary, to keep it. The strongest and most warlike were the Sioux, Blackfoot, Crow, Cheyenne, Comanche, and Apache tribes. They clung tenaciously to their land and fought valiantly for it. Mounted on swift horses and armed with bows and arrows, the Indians of the Great Plains were more than a match for the whites until the repeater rifle was perfected.

Until the time of the Civil War, the Plains Indians had been relatively peaceful. Then the miners invaded the mountains, cattlemen moved into the grasslands, and white settlers followed the railroads across the prairies. Wanton destruction of the buffalo by the intruding whites threatened the Indians' very existence, because they depended on the animal for food, fuel, clothing, robes, bowstrings, tools, and other essentials. Faced with all these pressures, the tribes became dissat-

isfied with their treaties with the federal government.

During the war, whites clashed with the Apache and Navaho in the Southwest and with the Arapaho and Cheyenne on the Great Plains, and for the next twenty-five years Indian warfare constantly recurred. In the mountain areas most of the tribes were eventually persuaded to give up their lands and move to reservations, but the tribes on the plains were not willing to abandon their hunting grounds to the encroaching whites.

In 1867, Congress enacted legislation providing for the removal of all Indians to reservations, thereby breaking the promises given to the Plains Indians in the 1820s and 1830s that they could keep their lands forever. The federal government decided to create two reservations for the Plains Indians—one in the Black Hills of Dakota, the other in present-day Oklahoma. But then there were difficulties. While the tribal chieftains signed the treaties, individual Indians often refused to be bound by them. General W.T. Sherman wrote, "We have . . . provided reservations for all, off the great roads. All who cling to their old hunting grounds are hostile and will remain so till

Wholesale destruction of the buffalo threatened the existence of the Plains Indians. This photo shows a pile of 40,000 buffalo hides in Dodge City, Kansas, in 1874.

killed off. We will have a sort of a predatory war for years—every now and then be shocked by the indiscriminate murder of travelers and settlers, but the country is so large, and the advantage of the Indians so great, that we cannot make a single war to end it."

Sherman's prediction was accurate. Between 1869 and 1875 more than 200 battles between the United States army and the Indians took place. What went on in these conflicts can be derived from a statement of General Francis A. Walker, Commissioner of Indian Affairs, in 1871: "When dealing with savage men, as with savage beasts, no question of national honor can arise. Whether to fight, to run away, or to employ a ruse, is solely a question of expediency." A few years earlier General S. R. Curtis, United States Army commander in the West, had told his subordinate officers: "I want no peace till the Indians suffer more."

And the Indians did suffer. A white trader reported that Cheyenne "were scalped, their brains knocked out; the men used their knives, ripped open women, clubbed little children, knocked them in the head with their guns, beat their brains out, mutilated their bodies in every sense of the word." This barbarity surely raised the question: Who were the savages, the Indians or the whites?

The Indian wars after 1865 cost the federal

government millions of dollars and hundreds of lives, yet a solution to the problem seemed to be nowhere in sight. Much of the failure rested with the national government, whose officials regarded each tribe as a separate nation. Indians frequently misunderstood the terms of the tribal treaties, and many individual Indians did not feel obligated by them. Moreover, authority over Indian affairs was divided between the Department of the Interior and the War Department, which pursued different policies and objectives. Finally, frontiersmen in general believed that the only good Indian was a dead one, and most soldiers agreed.

Easterners, far removed from the scene of strife, had a different attitude. Here churchmen and reformers united to urge a policy of humanitarianism toward the Indians. And as the War Department followed its policy of fighting the Indians, new ideas about the problem began to have influence at Washington. A new civilian Board of Indian Commissioners, created in 1869, attempted to convert the nomadic Plains Indians to agriculture on the reservations and sought to persuade the government to break down tribal autonomy.

In 1871 Congress abolished the policy of dealing with tribes as though they were separate nations. In the seventies, too, the government began to establish Indian boarding schools removed from the reservations. To give Indians greater incentive, the Indian Commissioners recommended individual land holdings and the gradual elimination of the system of reservations. Books on behalf of the Indian began to appear, among them Helen Hunt Jackson's *Century of Dishonor*

(1881), which had the greatest influence in stirring up public opinion behind efforts to improve the Indians' lot.

Finally, in 1887, the Dawes Act initiated a new Indian policy that reversed the old military policy of extermination. The Act provided for the dissolution of tribal autonomy and the division of tribal lands, with each family head receiving 160 acres. To protect the Indian in his property, the right of disposal was withheld for twenty-five years. At the end of this probationary period the Indian received full rights of ownership and full United States citizenship.

The new policy did not work well either, however. In dividing up the reservations, the best tracts were usually sold to white settlers and the worst given to the Indians. Often the Indian owners were disheartened and failed to cultivate adequately the land they kept. And when individual Indians, without experience as property owners, acquired good land, they were too easily persuaded to sell it. (The Burke Act of 1906 gave the Secretary of the Interior discretionary authority to reduce the probationary period preceding legal sale.) Nor was the policy universally applied. Some tribes, especially in Arizona and New Mexico, retained their tribal organizations and continued to hold their land in tribal fashion.

Gradually the feeling developed that it had been a mistake to have the Indians abandon their traditional way of life. An effort was made to reverse the policy laid down by the Dawes Act and to allow the tribes to hold their land as communal property. This was to be realized in the Indian Reorganization Act of 1934.

Chapter 15

The Politics of Conservatism and Dissent 1877–1900

POLITICAL DOLDRUMS

Critics of the Gilded Age. In contrast to its dramatic industrial and economic progress in the post-Reconstruction years the political activity of the United States in this period seemed to lack the vitality and productivity of earlier periods. The Presidents had executive ability and high principles, but they, like most of the important men in Congress, proved to be mediocre and uninspiring leaders. "No period so thoroughly ordinary has been known in American politics since Christopher Columbus first disturbed the balance of power in American society," wrote Henry Adams, that biting commentator of the Gilded Age. "One might search the whole list of Congress, Judiciary, and Executive during the twenty-five years 1870 to 1895 and find little but damaged reputation. The period was poor in purpose and barren in results."

This era in American politics has been kicked and scuffed by historians until little remains of its reputation. Most critics believe that at no other time in American history was the moral and intellectual tone of political life so uniformly low and political contests so preoccupied with patronage. "Even among the most powerful men of that generation," said Henry Adams, speaking of the politicians, there were "none who had a good word for it." It has become a historical convention to censure the politicians of these years for degenerating into a group of spoilsmen who served the business community as they were themselves served by it.

The most serious charge leveled against the major parties was that they failed to meet the problems generated by the Industrial Revolution. Far-reaching economic changes necessitated extensive social readjustments, and problems arising from recurrent industrial crises and depressions demanded vigorous governmental action. However, a variety of factors dissipated the political energies that might have been directed at these social problems.

Two Empty Bottles. The common explanation for this failure is that there were no important differences on major issues between Democrats and Republicans. "Neither party has any principles, any distinctive tenets," wrote James Bryce, a contemporary English observer of the American party system. "The two major parties in this period," concluded Bryce, "were like two bottles. Each bore a label denoting the kind of liquor it contained, but each was empty." Historians have called the period the "age of negation" and its politics "the politics of dead center."

The Republican party was a loose combination of Northeastern business groups and upper Midwestern farming groups—an alliance that had been formed in 1860 and had fought and won the Civil War. In much of the North and West, Republicans were the party of wealth and respectability.

Two other large groups attached to the Republican party were blacks and Union army veterans. The blacks, loyal to the party of emancipation, had been able to elect a few congressmen from the South. But after the Republicans abandoned them in 1877, they become more openly critical of the party and rapidly lost what little political power they had previously enjoyed. War veterans, on the other hand, increased their political importance by organizing the Grand Army of the Republic in 1866 and pressuring Congress into voting for generous pension laws.

Sharply divergent views between Northeastern businessmen and Western farmers occasionally threatened party unity, but Republican orators tried to sidestep their differences by "waving the bloody shirt"—equating party loyalty with national patriotism and charging the Democrats with having fought under the Confederate flag.

The Democratic party, in contrast, was a more regional coalition than the Republican. Its support came chiefly from the "solid South" and the city machines of the Northeast, but it also had some support from the industrial workers of the big cities and from those Northeastern bankers and merchants—

"sound money" men—who opposed protective tariffs and government subsidies to special interests and who favored contraction of the currency.

In the South the Democrats were the party of white supremacy. Southern party leaders, often of Whig background, called themselves "Conservatives" and frequently were labeled "Bourbons" by their opponents. They had much in common with Democratic leaders in the Midwest, who shared their conservative economic views and were also known as "Bourbons." In large Northern cities the Democratic party had the allegiance of most immigrants, who were attracted by the name of the party and whose leaders had sometimes risen to places of influence in it. The rank-and-file Democrats—farmers, industrial workers, and small businessmen—were often restive under the conservative leaders, but those leaders prevailed until the mid-1890s.

Today the big cities of the country will usually vote Democratic, but in the Gilded Age most of the large urban centers outside the South were more likely to be Republican than Democratic. New York and Boston ordinarily went Democratic, but in the three presidential elections of the 1880s, for example, a majority of the cities of over 50,000 outside the South went Republican. The Republican party in these years was able to appeal successfully to urban voters and many immigrants as the party of prosperity and economic growth. In contrast the Democrats appeared as the more conservative and economy-minded party and did not have the same appeal.

To account for the seeming impotence of political parties during the era, it must be remembered that a generally held opinion in America, in line with laissez-faire, was that government should "let well enough alone." Consequently, government rarely concerned itself with economic and social problems.

However, there were other deterrents to

In line with laissez-faire, President Hayes is shown as pursuing a policy of "let'em alone."

LET'EM ALONE POLICY

BLOODY Shirt

BAYONET RULE

THE "WEAK" GOVERNMENT 1877—1881.

governmental action. Probably most important was the sharp contest between the parties and the failure of either to control the national government for any appreciable length of time. Contrary to popular belief, these were not years of Republican supremacy. Rather, they were a period of party stalemate and equilibrium.

In the six presidential elections from 1876 to 1896, the Republicans, while winning four, gained a majority of the popular vote in only one (1896) and a plurality in only one (1880)—and even that plurality was less than one tenth of 1 percent. In three of these elections the difference between the popular vote for the two major party candidates was less than 1 percent, although electoral vote majorities ranged from 1 in 1876 to 132 in 1892. The Democrats, while electing a President twice (1884, 1892), won a majority of the popular vote in 1876 and a plurality in 1884, 1888, and 1892. Each party managed to control the presidency and Congress at the same time for only two years—Republicans from 1889 to 1891 and the Democrats from 1893 to 1895.

In recent years, the two major parties in the Gilded Age have received much attention from historians. One might have expected the parties to show increasing centralization and bureaucracy, paralleling the centralization then going on in American business, with the national committees rising to a position of power over the state organizations. Instead there were decentralizaton, a lack of continuity between campaigns, weak national administrations, and even weaker national committees. Instead of a developing hierarchy of power in the parties, there remained a fundamental contradiction between state power and success in nominating a President.

In place of increasing professionalism, political adventurers—businessmen without firm state party bases—almost invariably beat the pros in presidential politics. Political coalitions were formed to serve during approaching elections and then fell apart soon afterwards, to be rebuilt, many times, in different forms. In general, the increased bureaucratization and centralization of American life were largely thwarted in political life.

The two major parties had few if any national leaders. Of course, there were Democratic and Republican officeholders, and some of these people were well known to voters beyond their immediate constituencies. But public office and a degree of popularity seldom transferred themselves into effective power. Leaders of both parties worked to keep abreast of the changes in the public mood but did not often try to change that mood. The greatest strength of the party system was its ability to reflect the diversity and diffuseness of the American electorate. Finding an issue to appeal to a broad cross-section of the party's voters or office-

holders in a country so large and diverse was a formidable task in the late nineteenth century and one rarely undertaken successfully. Politicians acted less to address the national problems arising from industrialism and more to satisfy newly created sectional interests.

The Pull of Sectionalism. Sectional interests resulting from the growth of industry and the expansion of the West served to dissipate and disrupt legislative activity during the seventies and eighties. The leading issues of the country, as indicated by party platforms and congressional action, were currency and banking, tariffs, public lands, internal improvements, railroad and trust regulation, and immigration. While all of these produced strong sectional feeling, they generally had one common feature—opposition of the agricultural regions to the industrial centers of the nation. One result was that political personalities seemed to play a subordinate role in determining the outcome of votes on national policies, while efforts to find adjustments between sectional interests and party allegiances took priority.

Because the Industrial Revolution had made them the new ruling class in the country, businessmen could obtain political favors, supplanting the Southern planters and Northeastern merchants in the seats of power. The usual explanation for this alliance between business and politics is that the politicians were the hirelings of the business community. "Business ran politics, and politics was a branch of business," writes one leading historian.

But despite its favored position, business did not control American politics. Businessmen had to pay heavily for political favors, and often they were blackmailed by threats of regulation or of withdrawal of government assistance. Businessmen complained that politicians treated them simply as customers, compelling them to pay for protection, selling political benefits to the highest bidders, and refusing to do the proper thing without pay. As we shall see, farmers and workers, too, were able to win political favors once they became organized and began to put pressure on politicians.

Voters did more sectional voting during depressions and showed more party loyalty in times of prosperity. Those sections hardest hit in a depression broke party ranks and combined with other distressed areas to attempt to do something about their grievances. The vagueness of party platforms until 1888 also stimulated sectional divisions, since it allowed representatives from discontented sections to interpret the planks to suit their own interests. In Congress sectional voting was more pronounced when the control of the houses was divided between the two parties than in those instances when one party was in control. This was equally true for depression and prosperity years in the seventies and eighties. Thus Presidents had to deal not only with divided Congresses, but with Congresses in which their own party members did more sectional than party voting.

The Disabled Presidency. The President might have been expected to mediate sectional interests, but the office of the presidency was at a low ebb in power and prestige during this period. National political power was vested chiefly in Congress. Congressional leaders had almost overthrown Andrew Johnson, had gained nearly complete control of Grant, and tried to put subsequent Presidents in the Gilded Age at their mercy. Senator John Sherman, Republican leader of Ohio and a perpetual aspirant to the office, wrote: "The executive department of a republic like ours should be subordinate to the legislative department. The President should [merely] obey and enforce the laws."

Congressional leaders acted accordingly. "The most eminent Senators," observed George F. Hoar, Republican of Massachusetts, about his colleagues in the Senate,

" would have received as a personal affront a private message from the White House expressing a desire that they should adopt any course in the discharge of their legislative duties that they did not approve. If they visited the White House, it was to give, not to receive advice."

The Party Bosses. The political rulers of the day were not the titular leaders but the party bosses, many of them United States senators, who headed powerful state machines and rewarded their followers with public offices. Among the important bosses were Senators James G. Blaine of Maine, Roscoe Conkling of New York, Zachariah Chandler of Michigan, and John A. Logan of Illinois, all Republicans; and Arthur P. Gorman of Maryland, a Democrat. Before 1883 these party bosses had at their disposal an enormous amount of spoils in the form of federal, state, and local offices. They controlled a hierarchy of workers down to the ward heelers, to whom they gave offices in return for faithful service. The assessment of officeholders and the sale of nominations and offices tightened the bosses' grip on local machines.

When the Civil Service Reform Act of 1883 (to be discussed later in this chapter) began to remove these powers by eliminating the federal spoils that produced them, politicians turned increasingly to businessmen for money and support. A new type of political boss appeared—a business type who resembled and worked closely with corporation executives, made few speeches, and conducted his activities in anterooms, caucuses, and committees. Matthew S. Quay of Pennsylvania, Leland Stanford of California, Philetus Sawyer of Wisconsin, Thomas Platt of New York, and Nelson W. Aldrich of Rhode Island were bosses of the new type. Some had been prosperous bankers and businessmen and had entered the Senate to protect their interests. In 1889 William Allen White could say: "a United States Senator . . . represented

A political cartoonist of the 1880s depicted the "real" bosses of the Senate.

something more than a state, more even than a region. He represented principalities and powers in business." According to White, one senator "represented the Union Pacific Railway System, another the New York Central. . . . Coal and iron owned a coterie from the Middle and Eastern seaport states. Cotton had half a dozen senators. And so it went." Many labeled this imposing body the "Millionaires' Club." Senator George Hearst of California, one of the group, echoed Darwinian theory when he said: "I do not know much about books; . . . but I have traveled a good deal and have observed men and things and I have made up my mind after my experiences that the members of the Senate are the survivors of the fittest."

Besides these prominent Establishment bosses, there were the backroom bosses, who often ruled without ever holding elective office. The principal effect of the spoils system was to transfer party control from publicly elected leaders to "inside" rulers. The most flagrant examples of "invisible government" occurred in the cities, many of which were run by corrupt political machines. Whether Democratic, like Tammany Hall in New York, or Republican, like the Gas Ring in Philadelphia, their methods were the same. Bryce expressed the opinion that municipal government was "the one conspicuous failure of the United States." And Andrew D. White in an article in *Forum* in 1890 stated that "with very few exceptions, the city governments of the United States are the worst in Christendom—the most expensive, the most inefficient, and the most corrupt."

New York City furnished the country its most notorious example of a municipal machine. There Tammany Hall, an organization dating back to the eighteenth century, controlled the Democratic party and the local government. William Marcy Tweed and his followers—A. Oakey Hall, the mayor, Peter B. Sweeney, county and city treasurer, and Richard B. Connally, the city controller—ran Tammany Hall and plundered the city. By every type of embezzlement this repulsive crew robbed the city treasury year after year until, at the height of their power, they were splitting among themselves 85 percent of the total expenditures made by the city and county.

Their technique was simple. Everyone who had a bill against the city was instructed to pad it—at first by 10 percent, later 66 percent, finally 85 percent. Tweed's gang received the padding. For example, the courthouse, originally estimated at $3,000,000, cost the taxpayers $11,000,000. The plastering bill alone amounted to $2,870,000 and the carpeting to $350,000, "enough to cover the whole City Park three times." The loot taken by the Tweed Ring has been variously estimated at from $45,000,000 to $100,000,000.

Although respectable citizens protested, they were powerless for several years to move against Tweed because he controlled every arm of the government. Finally, courageous editorials in *The New York Times* and the cartoons of Thomas Nast in *Harper's Weekly* exposed the corruption of the Tweed Ring and aroused the general public. His own followers, Tweed said, could not read, but they could "look at the damn pictures." Tweed

offered George Jones, owner of *The Times*, $1 million to quiet his paper and Nast $500,000 to study art in Europe, but they refused. A citizens' committee headed by Samuel J. Tilden and Charles O'Conor launched an investigation that was able by the end of 1872 to drive every member of the Tweed Ring out of office. Tweed himself died in jail.

Yet the traditional view of the boss as nothing but a corrupting force in American politics needs to be modified. Some recent studies of Boss Tweed and of the Cox machine in Cincinnati show that these political organizations furnished some element of order and stability in a rapidly expanding and disordered society. They point out that the boss provided a valuable service in giving services to many people who had no other institutional or social order to which to appeal.

Moreover not all bosses used politics to advance their material interest. Common as the various forms of graft and corruption were in the Gilded Age, not all bosses sought material profit. Boies Penrose, Republican boss of Pennsylvania, apparently never made a dollar out of politics. And according to Theodore Roosevelt, "Senator Platt [Republican boss of New York state] did not use his political position to advance his private fortunes—therein differing from many other political bosses. He lived in hotels and had few extravagant tastes."

The Reformers. In this age of corruption, voices such as those of the "single-tax" advocate Henry George and the socialist Edward Bellamy were calling for reform. Probably the most respectable of all the reformers were the "Mugwumps," as they were called by their opponents. The term was first used politically in 1884 to describe the independent Republicans who refused to support presidential candidate James G. Blaine. Mugwumps generally were newspapermen, scholars, and intellectuals, earnest men of high ideals and prominent social position, of conservative economic views, and usually of Republican background. Foremost among them were George William Curtis, editor of *Harper's Weekly*; E. L. Godkin, editor of *The Nation*; Carl Schurz; William Cullen Bryant; Whitelaw Reid; and Samuel Bowles. They lashed out against the spoils system and worked to purify politics through civil service reform. Since they believed in laissez-faire, however, they restricted their economic program to tariff reform and sound money.

The Mugwumps spoke in moralistic terms rather than in economic ones. They appealed primarily to the educated upper classes and seldom identified themselves with the interests of the masses, whom they viewed with an aristocratic disdain. They regarded the reform movements of labor and farmers as radical and dangerous and had little use for other reform movements of the period. But this was characteristic of most contemporary reform movements. They had little in common and had great difficulty in understanding one another. Divided and mutually suspicious, the reformers thus exerted little influence.

The Mugwumps have long been praised by historians, who accepted their censure of the Gilded Age. But recent studies of these reformers challenge both the indictment of that period and Mugwump beliefs. It will be difficult for future writers to extol these "independents," who condemned corruption, without recognizing that they too were elitists who opposed the democratizing direction of their time. The Mugwumps "seemed to dislike thinking about the working man as such," writes Geoffrey Blodgett. "They had no solution for the poor," doubting in fact that there *was* a solution because poverty "resulted from the poor people spending too much money." And unlike the Progressives of the succeeding generation, they "made no real effort to break the control of the elective process enjoyed by party professionals."

These liberal reformers of the Gilded Age believed that political independence helped to purify politics. But they also had a price for their reforms. They wanted a small, efficient government run by themselves or by men like themselves, reducing property taxes, encouraging individual effort, and cutting back public services. "Unable to come to terms with his age, the liberal reformer exaggerated its defects and overrated the past," observes John G. Sproat. "Everything considered, his campaign to reform postwar society was a pathetic failure." Liberal reformers of the Gilded Age are now found wanting almost as much as the Gilded Age was found wanting by them.

The Voters. There were limits to what could be done about relieving social and economic discontent, and these limits were imposed mainly by the voters themselves. For one thing, those interested in reform did not give consistent support to either party. Victory in national elections depended on heavily populated "doubtful" states, which had enough shifting voters to swing the results either way. These were Connecticut, New York, and New Jersey in the East and Ohio, Indiana, and Illinois in the Midwest. These states, especially New York and the three Midwestern ones, enjoyed strong bargaining power with which they secured favorable posts for their politicians and obtained most of the funds from the campaign treasuries at election time. The doubtful states were wedded to neither party but courted by both. The parties chose presidential and vice-presidential candidates from these areas and awarded their congressmen important committee assignments.

"Not the Republican politician but the voting public failed reform in the early years of the Gilded Age," writes La Wanda Cox about New York. "Civic improvement did not win the anticipated votes from New York City's Democratic faithful, and Republican support for equal suffrage brought political disaster. The hopeful union of idealism and practical politics within the state Republican party could not be consummated in the face of public repudiation at the polls."

In the Northeast, and in Massachusetts in particular, according to Blodgett, the political leaders were all acting in an essentially conservative manner because of these restraints. They realized that the country was changing, and they were willing to make adjustments. But their constituents—native Americans and immigrants alike—opposed basic change, because to them perpetuating their community was more important than improving it. As a result, the Democratic party in Massachusetts did not rise to the occasion and by the end of the nineteenth century could no longer be considered an effective instrument of social and economic change.

It is important to remember that some pieces of major legislation were passed during this period, despite the limitations imposed by voters and the politicians' reluctance to address the issues. The abiding belief that this was a period in which issues were steadfastly ignored is testimony to the lasting quality of the progressive-liberal historians' interpretation of the Gilded Age, which is echoed even by modern historians. The assumptions of the early historians also overlooked the fact that there was proportionately a heavier turnout of voters in the Gilded Age than in the twentieth century, evidence of their concern with politics and partisanship.

The new political history by Paul Kleppner, Richard Jensen, and Samuel McSeveney (see Bibliography) has altered the old assumptions about voter behavior and party alignment in the late nineteenth century, at least in the Middle West and in the Northeast. These new studies show that voters, unlike politicians, were more sharply divided on issues than historians later gave them credit for and were more interested in local questions such as

prohibition and the public school than in national questions such as the currency, the tariff, governmental corruption, and civil service reform. Politicians evidently tended to avoid these local issues, regarding them as being too explosive.

Both voter behavior and party alignment revolved primarily around ethno-cultural issues and responses, mostly religious and sectarian in nature. The expansion in the Catholic population in the country in the last third of the nineteenth century by the flood of immigrants from Europe greatly strengthened the Democratic party, which has traditionally been identified with Catholic voters. Then in the 1880s there was a revival of anti-immigrant nativism supported by many Republican Protestants. The very moralistic Protestants sharply assailed the drinking habits and the easy Sunday recreational activities of the immigrants, especially the Germans and the Irish. These Republicans wanted prohibition and Sunday laws, demands that angered many Americans who believed their personal liberties were in danger. German Lutherans and Irish and Polish Catholics were alarmed that the Republicans would also attempt to eliminate their parochial schools, which they considered essential for maintaining their religion and their culture. Thus they gave their support to the Democratic party.

The new political studies also confirm that economic or class antagonisms played an important role during the depression of the 1890s. They indicate, however, that in general these matters were of lesser importance than party loyalty and the issues of the day. The studies also show a shift in campaigning during the early 1890s from an "army style," featuring colorful rallies and other forms of hoopla usually associated with election campaigns in those years, toward a more intellectual appeal to the needs of the voters or a new approach to elections based on advertising—the "merchandising style."

THE FIGHT FOR RIGHTS

The Abandonment of the Blacks. The failure of Americans in the Gilded Age to deal adquately with the problems of industrialism can be clearly seen in the way they handled their greatest and most tragic problem—the plight of American blacks, who comprised one tenth of the population. Though the Civil War had settled the question of human slavery, it did not settle the problem of securing for all Americans the inalienable rights set forth in the Declaration of Independence. Nor did it alter the fact that white supremacy was generally taken for granted. During Reconstruction significant constitutional and legislative steps such as the Thirteenth, Fourteenth, and Fifteenth Amendments and the Civil Rights Acts of 1866 and 1875 were taken to insure the freedman's political and civil rights, but developments during the last quarter of the nineteenth century virtually destroyed these political gains.

When President Hayes removed the last of the federal troops and federal control from the South in April 1877, he left Southern blacks in the custody of Southern whites. Governor Wade Hampton of South Carolina had promised, "We . . . will secure to every citizen, the lowest as well as the highest, black as well as white, full and equal protection in the enjoyment of all his rights under the Constitution." Because of such promises Hayes believed that a new "era of good feeling" was developing in the South between the two races. Even before 1877 was over, he learned differently. "By state legislation, by frauds, by intimidation, and by violence of the most atrocious character, colored citizens have been deprived of the right of suffrage," he wrote in his diary. But he did practically nothing to correct the situation as he had earlier said he would.

The Republican party had emerged from the Civil War as the champion and protector of the Southern blacks. It had emancipated and enfranchised them and had provided them with the same political and civil rights as whites. In their platforms from 1876 to 1896 the Republicans solemnly pledged themselves to enforce the Fourteenth and Fifteenth Amendments, to secure to "every American citizen of whatever race and color complete liberty and exact equality in the exercise of all civil, political, and public rights," protect "honest voters" against terrorism, violence and fraud, and never to relax their efforts "until the integrity of the ballot and purity of elections . . . be fully guaranteed in every state." In Congress they sponsored investigations of fraud and violence in elections in the South, accused Southern Democrats of holding their seats illegally and of exercising a disproportionate voting influence, and focused attention upon indiscreet statements by Southern leaders and the press. But while Republicans talked much, they took few steps to remedy the situation or to meet their obligations to the freedmen.

Actually, throughout most of the last quarter of the nineteenth century, the Republicans were in no position in Congress to enforce the Fourteenth and Fifteenth Amendments. But their abandonment of blacks was also part of a well-planned policy. Their new plans called for a shift in Republican appeals in the South from blacks to whites. They wanted to maintain and even increase their black support, but their main aim was to swell their ranks with southern whites.

Thus Hayes abandoned the Southern blacks when he removed the troops in the hope of reconciling North and South, conciliating Southern whites, and ingratiating the Republican party with them. Arthur deserted the blacks when he chose to work with Independents in the South in the belief that it was necessary to subordinate the freedmen to exploit the Democratic cleavages in the South,

Currier and Ives viewed with alarm the willingness of the Federal government to let political considerations take precedence over the civil rights of the former slaves.

which he had concluded was the only path to Republican success there. And in 1890, when Republicans had control of the presidency and the Congress at the same time for the only period in these years, they again forsook blacks when they failed to pass the Federal Elections or "Force" Bill, providing for national supervision of federal elections as a way of protecting the rights of Southern blacks to vote. They did so because they had a greater interest in the tariff and silver measures, but also because there was considerable opposition to the elections legislation in party ranks.

The Republican abandonment of the blacks was also a part of a general abandonment by all Northerners. By the end of Reconstruction most Northerners probably agreed with Southern whites that the blacks were not prepared for equality and that the South should be allowed to deal with them in its own way. Northerners had also come to believe that the elimination of the issue of blacks from

politics was necessary for a return to national solidarity and a development of trade relations between the North and South.

The blacks were also abandoned by the courts. After 1877 practically every Supreme Court decision affecting blacks nullified their rights or curtailed them somehow. The Court drastically limited the powers of the federal government to intervene in the states to protect the rights of blacks. To all intents and purposes, it invalidated the Fourteenth and Fifteenth Amendments as effective safeguards for black people. When in 1883 the Court set aside the Civil Rights Act of 1875 on the ground that the Fourteenth Amendment was binding on states but not individuals, it ended federal attempts to protect blacks against discrimination by private persons. There would be no federal civil rights legislation thereafter until 1957. And in the 1870s, when the Court held that the Fifteenth Amendment did not confer the right to vote upon anyone and that Congress did not have the authority to protect the right to vote generally, sections of the Enforcement Act of 1870 were declared unconstitutional because they provided penalties for hindering a person in voting. In 1894 Congress repealed the entire law. Again, there was no further legislation on the subject until 1957.

Finally, in two decisions in the 1890s, the Court paved the way for additional curtailment of the rights of blacks. In *Plessy* v. *Ferguson* (1896) the Court laid down the "separate but equal" rule in defense of segregation. This became the law of the land until 1954. Then in *William* v. *Mississippi* (1898) the Court opened the road to legal disfranchisement by approving Southern plans for depriving blacks of the vote.

Blacks had continued to vote after the return of white supremacy in the South, though in reduced numbers. In some parts of the South they were prevented from voting by threats or intimidation, and in other parts their vote was nullified by artful means such as the use of tissue ballots and a complicated system of ballot boxes. In the 1890s, however, the Southern states proceeded to disfranchise them with laws. Within two decades practically all black voters had been disfranchised by means of poll taxes, white primaries, and literacy or property qualifications that were enforced against blacks but not against whites. In the same years the Southern states also passed numerous "Jim Crow" laws, segregating blacks in virtually every aspect of public life.

Most Northerners shared the Court's attitude toward blacks. They deplored agitation on behalf of blacks and were willing to accept the South's racial policies. Even educated, intelligent Northerners believed that black people were racially inferior, because most scientists at the time believed this. Most of the Northern press supported the decisions in the civil rights cases. And as Rayford W. Logan, a leading black historian, has shown, Northern newspapers usually described blacks in a derogatory manner, regardless of the actual circumstances, strengthening a stereotype of the "criminal Negro." The leading literary magazines of the North such as *Harper's, Scribner's* and the *Atlantic Monthly,* mirroring the refined tastes of the upper classes, regularly used derisive terms when they referred to blacks.

Most Americans did not especially wish blacks ill, writes John A. Garraty, a leading historian on the Gilded Age. ". . . They simply refused to consider them quite human and consigned them complacently to oblivion, along with the Indians."

The position of black leader Booker T. Washington among his race may have also contributed to the assault upon the rights of blacks. Washington, founder and principal of Tuskeegee Institute in Alabama was, according to Louis R. Harlan, a recent biographer, a "white man's black man" and a "safe, sane Negro" to Southern whites. In the Northern white world, Washington was "deferential but dignified," drawing philanthropy from such men as Carnegie. Among Southern whites, says Harlan, Washington made a point of not crossing the color line and sought to reduce social friction. He believed that for the time being blacks should forgo agitation for the vote and social equality and devote their efforts to achieving economic security and independence. "In all things that are purely social," he said in 1895, "we can be as separate as the fingers, yet one as the hand in all things for mutual progress."

"Washington unmistakably accepted a subordinate position for Southern Negroes," writes Rayford Logan. "This position was far different from the unequivocal standard for equal citizenship advanced by [Frederick] Douglass in 1889. He definitely renounced social equality. . . . In return he asked for a chance to gain a decent livelihood. Washington was convinced, and rightly so," continues Logan, "that it would have been folly to ask in

1895 for equal rights for Negroes." Washington's position won the enthusiastic support of the white community and had much to do with fixing the pattern of race relations in the country for most of the remainder of his lifetime. Most blacks of that time probably accepted Washington's view.

New Achievements for Women. While blacks were slowly losing their rights, women in the Gilded Age were struggling for more rights, opportunities, and privileges and for a more equal place with men in the participation in and conduct of American affairs. Much of this activity centered on the effort to win the vote.

There was considerable opposition to women's claim of equal political rights with men. Gilded Age politicians insisted that the political arena was a male preserve, that politics itself was masculine, and that any effort to change that situation was contrary to human nature. But politicians were not alone in holding this view. Francis Parkman, one of the era's most prominent historians, thought women's suffrage would leap over "Nature's limitations," disrupt the home and give women excitement and cares "too much for their strength." Publicly he wrote that especially in the "crowded cities" women's suffrage would be "madness" and would certainly make bad governments worse.

But a number of supporters of women's rights, including Wendell Phillips, a leading social reformer of the day, vigorously disagreed. "One of two things is true," declared Phillips, "either woman is like man—and if she is, then a ballot based on brains belongs to her as well as to him; or she is different, and then man does not know how to vote for her as well as she herself does."

The major political parties, however, either ignored or opposed the demand for women's suffrage, and many women—although probably not a majority—decided to take action themselves. They did several things. Under the leadership of Susan B. Anthony and Elizabeth Cady Stanton there was agitation for women's suffrage from the 1870s on. Then some women's groups, such as the Equal Rights party, took direct political action by nominating women for President of the United States—Victoria Claflin Woodhull in 1872 and Belva Ann Bennett Lockwood in 1884 and 1888.

Other women worked to unite the various women's suffrage groups. By 1890, the two principal competing groups had merged into the National American Women's Suffrage Association, which sought to win support for the cause from Congress and the state legislatures.

In the last third of the nineteenth century there was a great battle for women's suffrage in the nation's magazines, public meetings, legislative assemblies, and state constitutional conventions. As Thomas Wentworth Higginson, a Civil War commander of a black regiment and a well-known reformer and feminist of these years pointed out, "Mrs. [Harriet Beecher] Stowe helps to free Uncle Tom in his cabin, and then strikes for the freedom of women in her own 'Hearth and Home.' Mrs. [Julia Ward] Howe writes the 'Battle Hymn of the Republic,' and keeps on writing more battle hymns in behalf of her own sex. Miss [Louisa May] Alcott not only delineates 'Little Women,' but wishes to emancipate them." Other prominent persons such as George William Curtis, civil service reformer, and John Greenleaf Whittier, poet and abolitionist, as well as the two most important labor organizations of the day, the Knights of Labor and the American Federation of Labor, supported the movement for women's suffrage.

Women tried unsuccessfully to win the vote through the Fifteenth Amendment. And at first they failed in efforts in the states as seven states turned down women's suffrage proposals between 1867 and 1877. They also suffered

Women continued to struggle for more rights during the Gilded Age, but many people thought women's suffrage was highly undesirable.

a serious legal setback when the Supreme Court in *Minor* v. *Happersett* (1875) refused to accept the argument that women could vote because they were citizens and unanimously ruled that the Fourteenth Amendment had not conferred the vote upon women. And when some state laws barred women from the legal profession, the Supreme Court upheld such laws, with one justice saying, "The natural and proper timidity and delicacy which belongs to the female sex, unfits it for many . . . occupations." Women, he said, should stay with "the noble and benign offices of wife and mother."

In 1878, Senator Aaron Augustus Sargent of California introduced into Congress an equal suffrage amendment. During the remaining years of the century, Senate committees reported five times and House committees twice in favor of the amendment, but Congress never took action on it. Despite considerable effort by the suffragettes, the increasing militancy of the women's suffrage movement, and a growing sympathy and backing for it generally, only four states at the close of the nineteenth century had given the vote to women—Wyoming (1869), Colorado (1893), Utah (1896), and Idaho (1896).

Women seemed to make more progress in some other aspects of American life than they did politically. More women appeared to be working outside their homes and going to college than had been the case in earlier periods of American history. The old prejudice against self-support for women was beginning to weaken, and at the same time colleges and universities were preparing increasing numbers of women for positions previously held mainly by men. "We have reached a new era," asserted *Harper's Bazaar*, a leading woman's magazine, in 1883. "Slowly as woman has come to her inheritance, it stretches before her now into illimitable distance, and the question of the hour is rather whether she is ready for her trust than whether that trust is hampered by conditions."

As Arthur M. Schlesinger, Sr., one of America's most distinguished historians, pointed out more than a generation ago, "Women who would have shrunk from factory work and domestic service or even from teaching trooped forth with a sense of adventure to become typists, telephone girls, typesetters, bookkeepers, nurses, librarians, journalists, lecturers, social workers, doctors, lawyers, artists. Even in the realm of mechanical invention, a time-honored monopoly of men," added Schlesinger, "they were displaying surprising capacity in a variety of fields." According to Emily Faithfull, an English social worker and observer of American life in the late nineteenth century, there were in 1882, in Massachusetts alone, almost 300 branches of industry and business where women could earn from $100 to $3000 a year.

Though there had long been a large number of women who worked for a living outside the home, the great economic expansion of the late nineteenth century brought increasing numbers into the work force. From 1880 to 1890, the number of women workers went up from 2.5 million to more than 4 million, about one sixth of the total work force, and by 1900, to 5.3 million. Unfortunately, this was counterbalanced by the fact that women usually filled the lowest-paid jobs and received unequal pay in virtually every position they held for work equal to that done by men.

Since unions did not pay much attention to working conditions for women, not much was done to correct the injustice of the unequal wage scale. One gain was made when Congress in 1872 enacted the Arnell Bill giving women government employees equal pay with men for equal work. Belva Ann Bennett Lockwood had much to do with the passage of this act. She drafted the measure, and its passage was hastened by a petition she circulated at the meetings of the National and American Women's Suffrage Associations in New York in 1870. (See "Belva Ann Bennett Lockwood: A Campaigning Woman.") Another gain was that legislatures in the industrial states began in the 1880s to consider legislation regulating working conditions of women in factories.

Women also made progress in education in these years despite the fact that they were up against a generally held view, expressed by a minister in 1880, that women's emotional nature "painfully disqualifies" them from the effort to be educated. By this time women had been accepted in colleges for about twenty years. In fact, by 1870 one third of American colleges were coeducational.

Probably the greatest educational opportunities for women occurred in the Middle West and in the South where the new state universities began to admit women as well as men. President James B. Angell of the University of Michigan told a visitor to the campus in 1883 that while coeducation was still an experiment in the East it was definitely settled in the West, adding that "none of the ladies had found the curriculum too heavy for their physical endurance."

Angell's concern about women's physical

stamina for the rigors of study was shared by a number of Americans, both women and men. M. Carey Thomas, a graduate of Cornell in 1877 and the first president of Bryn Mawr, expressed this concern when she said, "The passionate desire of the women of my generation for higher education was accompanied . . . by the awful doubt, felt by women themselves as well as by men, as to whether women as a sex were physically and mentally fit for it."

Women clearly demonstrated their fitness for college, and coeducation grew rapidly in these years. Between 1880 and 1898 the proportion of coeducational colleges increased from 51 percent to 70 percent and the number of women students from 2750 to more

than 25,000. At the same time some women's colleges on a level with the top ones for men were established—Vassar (1861), Wellesley (1870), Smith (1871), and Bryn Mawr (1885). Mount Holyoke, a girl's seminary begun in 1836, became a college in 1893. Also, two of the country's leading universities, Harvard and Columbia, added women's colleges— Radcliffe in 1879 and Barnard in 1889. By the end of the nineteenth century four out of every five colleges, universities, and professional schools in the country admitted women.

Women, especially of the upper middle class, also turned their attention to club activities and joined in large numbers the women's organizations springing up all over

More women worked away from home than had earlier. The women shown here are operating a long-distance switchboard in 1888.

the country. "We have art clubs, book clubs, dramatic clubs, pottery clubs," wrote one woman in 1880 in the *Atlantic Monthy.* "We have sewing circles, philanthropic associations, scientific, literary, religious, athletic, musical, and decorative art societies." These various associations provided a good way for women to find out about the world in which they were now playing a larger role. And they also furnished good training for many women who became active civic and humanitarian leaders in their communities. In one decade, 1888–1897, three important groups were formed that placed more women in public affairs—the National Council of Women, the General Federation of Women's Clubs, and the National Congress of Parents and Teachers. By the close of the nineteenth century, the General Federation of Women's clubs claimed a membership of 150,000 and was supporting such reforms as child welfare, education, and sanitation.

Of course, as we have seen, the participation of women in reforms was not new to the Gilded Age. Women had taken an active role in reform movements before the Civil War, and this momentum continued. Probably the strongest women's reform group of this era was the Woman's Christian Temperance Union (W.C.T.U.) formed in Cleveland in 1874 to fight the saloon and to promote prohibition. The movement for prohibition had begun in the first half of the nineteenth century. By the time of the Gilded Age four states—Maine, New Hampshire, Vermont, and Kansas—had prohibition laws. The Unit-

Belva Ann Bennett Lockwood: A Campaigning Woman

Few Americans have achieved as much prominence and subsequently been forgotten as completely as Belva Ann Bennett Lockwood, who was twice nominated for President. Until she died at the age of 87, she spent more than fifty years of tireless work expanding the opportunities, privileges, and human rights of her sex. And she never doubted that women would eventually have an equal place with men in the conduct of American affairs.

Belva Ann Bennett was born October 24, 1830, on her parents' farm in Royalton, New York. She attended country schools and in later years recalled the hard benches of the one-room schools and the white line painted on the floor where she had to "toe the mark" when reciting. "I always wanted an education, even when a girl," she said, "and when I was fourteen I had enough money to attend the Royalton Academy a year." Belva gave great credit to her mother for both moral and financial support. However, at fifteen, a lack of funds and her father's opposition compelled her to give up her education and teach in various area country schools. Her pay was ten shillings a week and "boarding around." Even in these early years, Belva was vexed that men teachers were paid more for the same work.

ed States Supreme Court upheld such laws in 1847 but reversed itself in 1888 on the grounds that the interstate control of liquor belonged to Congress.

Frances E. Willard became the head of the W.C.T.U. in 1879 and began to campaign for legislation for the outright banning of strong drink. She also worked through schools and churches to arouse public opinion against liquor. Under her vigorous leadership the W.C.T.U. became the leading force in the prohibition movement. In 1893, the Anti-Saloon League, comprised of both women and men, joined the anti-liquor crusade. With pressure from the W.C.T.U. all states but two added the requirement of "scientific temperance instruction" to the school curriculum between 1882 and 1898.

Many women who saw the saloon as an implacable foe were also aware of a number of other social problems—such as child labor, unsanitary housing, lack of public-health measures, penal conditions that needed their support for reform. Not all women, however, agreed that the increased activities of women meant progress. "What is this curious product of today, the American girl or woman?" asked one woman writer in 1880 in the *Atlantic Monthly*. " . . . Is it possible for any novel, within the next fifty years, truly to depict her as a finality, when she is still emerging from new conditions . . . , when she does not yet understand herself . . . ?" She added, "The face of today is stamped with restlessness, wandering purpose, and self-consciousness."

Thus, by the end of the nineteenth century

Belva was first married on November 8, 1848, shortly after she became eighteen, to a young neighbor farmer, Uriah H. McNall. They had a daughter Lura in 1849, before her husband died of a foot injury in 1853. The young widow sold the farm, sent Lura to her grandparents, and went back to school: first a year at the nearby Gasport (N.Y.) Academy and then to Genesee Wesleyan Seminary and Genesee College (later Syracuse University). In her last year at school, Belva heard and met Susan B. Anthony, who also resented the inferior position of women in American life. This meeting increased Belva's determination to work for women's rights.

After graduating from Genesee in 1857 with honors and a B.S., Belva was elected preceptress (principal) of the Lockport (N.Y.) Union School. For the next four years she supervised the small staff, taught, and, despite some disapproval, promoted gymnastics, public speaking, nature walks, and skating. The school code allowed her assistant men teachers to receive nearly twice the salary she was paid. When she protested this injustice, she was told by a minister's wife, "You can't help yourself; it is the way of the world." So she resigned. As she reported later, "Those words opened my eyes and raised my dander."

In 1866 Belva moved to Washington, D.C., opened a successful private school, and in 1868 married Dr. Ezekiel Lockwood, a former Baptist minister and dentist twenty-seven years her senior. He ran the school until it was closed because of his ill health. He died in 1877, again leaving Belva a widow. Their only child, Jesse, had died in infancy.

With her husband's encouragement, Belva had begun reading law. Her application to the law school of Columbia College was turned down on the traditional ground that her presence would distract the young men. After being rejected at Georgetown and Howard Universities as well, Belva, along with fourteen other women, gained

increasing economic independence and more educational opportunities for women had enlarged their social freedom and widened their range of activity. They had gone far, but they had much farther to go.

FROM HAYES TO HARRISON

Hayes and the Presidency. Rutherford B. Hayes was chosen for President by an Electoral Commission, and historians have portrayed him as a respectable mediocrity with an average capacity and an impeccable public and private life. True, there was no dramatic flair in his personality, and he lacked brilliance, but he was a man of integrity and honest intentions, and his determination and steadfastness of purpose eventually frustrated even his bitterest foes. Hayes' presidency is an excellent illustration of how party stalemate and equilibrium can hamper effective executive leadership. Hayes worked under severe handicaps that have not been fully appreciated.

His right to the office had been disputed, and Republicans and Democrats alike referred to him as "the *de facto* President" and "His Fraudulency." His programs for the South and for civil service reform, plus his show of independence, caused such a deep split within his own Republican party that he was nearly read out of it. At one time Hayes had but three supporters in the Senate, one of them a lifelong friend and relative. Moreover, the Democrats controlled the House of Representatives throughout his administration and

admission to the newly established National University Law School in 1871. Only she and one other woman finished the course.

Even then, because of prejudice against women in the professions, the Law School finally refused to grant them diplomas. But after Belva wrote a spirited letter to President Grant, who was *ex-officio* President of the Law School, she received her diploma, signed by Grant himself. In September 1873 she was admitted to the District of Columbia bar, after overcoming the objection that she was a woman—and, in addition, a married woman.

In her law training, Lockwood had specialized in claims cases against the government. But because she was a woman, both the Court of Claims (1874) and the United States Supreme Court (1876) refused her admission. Undaunted, Lockwood pushed for the passage of legislation that would remove this restriction. In 1879, after her persistent lobbying, Congress enacted the "Lockwood Act" allowing women lawyers to practice before both the Supreme Court and the Court of Claims.

Some of the highlights of Lockwood's legal career include her successful efforts to obtain equal pay for women government workers (1872) and to secure equal property rights and equal guardianship of children for women in Washington, D.C. (1896). She also worked unsuccessfully (1903) to include women's suffrage clauses in the statehood bills for Oklahoma, Arizona, and New Mexico. And in 1906, she represented the Eastern Cherokee Indians, who were awarded $5 million in land claims against the government.

By the 1880s Lockwood was widely known for her work in the women's rights movement. She decided it was time for women to take political action and be nominated for public office. She contended that, while women could not vote, they could legally receive votes and, if elected, hold office. In 1884 the National Equal

the Senate the last two years of his term. Under these circumstances it is amazing that he could accomplish anything.

Hayes endeavored to reestablish presidential power and prestige and to redress the balance between the executive and legislative branches. He first challenged congressional dominance in the make-up of his cabinet when he picked men who were most unwelcome to the bosses, particularly the liberal Republican Carl Schurz for Secretary of the Interior and the Southern Democrat and former Confederate David M. Key for the important patronage-dispensing position of Postmaster General. At first the Senate balked and refused to confirm the entire cabinet list, but under much public pressure it finally gave in to the President.

Hayes gained another victory over congressional encroachment by refusing to yield the right given him by the Force Acts of 1870-1871 to intervene in federal elections in the states. Democratic majorities in Congress sought to nullify these Reconstruction laws by attaching to army appropriation bills riders aimed at removing federal supervision of elections. Hayes fought these attempts because they would have placed him under the "coercive dictation" of a "bare" majority in Congress and because he wanted to make the executive "an equal and independent branch of the government." He vetoed eight such bills, and Congress lacked enough votes to override him.

Hayes also struck a daring and spectacular blow for reform against the spoils system and

Rights Party nominated Belva Lockwood for President and Mrs. Marietta L. B. Stow for Vice-President.

Lockwood's nomination was a daring act, designed to receive long overdue recognition of women's rights. Her platform embraced all her interests—equal rights for all, including blacks, Indians, and immigrants; uniform marriage and divorce laws; reduction of the liquor traffic; and universal peace. Her campaign, ridiculed by many, was opposed by the two most important leaders of women's suffrage, Susan B. Anthony and Elizabeth Cady Stanton, who supported James G. Blaine, the Republican nominee. Nevertheless, Lockwood ran a strong campaign, received 4149 votes in six states, and claimed she was defrauded of more. She ran again in 1888 with less impressive results.

Disappointed with politics and estranged from the major women's suffrage groups, Lockwood worked for international peace, attending nearly every major peace conference from 1890 to 1914 and serving on the nominating committee for the Nobel Peace Prize. She also lectured and was prominent both nationally and internationally in promoting women's rights, temperance, peace, and arbitration.

Lockwood lived her last years in severe financial difficulty. Her lucrative law practice faded, and irregularity in the Cherokee claims case forced her to return half of her legal fee. Most of her remaining money was lost when she entrusted it to an unscrupulous male admirer. Evicted from her large Washington home at the age of 84, she lived on a pension provided by Andrew Carnegie. After a period of declining health, she died in Washington on May 19, 1917, and was buried in the Congressional Cemetery. Belva Lockwood had several lives and careers—teacher, lawyer, public speaker, wife, and mother—and her contribution to the cause of women's rights did not end with her death. She deserves to be remembered.

Hayes is shown as a sentinel protecting the Civil Service from the spoilsmen.

its greatest champion, Senator Conkling. Hayes had already vexed the bosses with his inaugural statement: "He serves his party best who serves his country best," and he really angered them with his comment, "Party leaders should have no more influence in appointments than other equally respectable citizens." He appointed a commission headed by John Jay of New York, grandson of the first Chief Justice, to investigate the largest patronage office in the federal service, the New York Custom House—long an example of the spoils system at its worst. The commission found that most of the employees had been appointed in the interest of the Conkling machine, that 20 percent of them were superfluous, and that the place was ridden with "ignorance, inefficiency, and corruption." When Conkling's lieutenants, Collector of the Port Chester A. Arthur and Naval Officer Alonzo B. Cornell, refused to clean up the corruption or to resign, Hayes boldly removed them and named two others to the posts. On Conkling's insistence the Senate refused to confirm the nominations, but Hayes persisted and within a year his choices were approved. He had won a battle, but he had not routed the spoilsmen.

The End of Resconstruction. Hayes removed the last of the federal troops from the South and ended military Reconstruction. He acted to restore harmony between North and South and between whites and blacks. He responded to a general demand for a change in policy in the South. He considered that Reconstruction governments had lost so much support that they had become completely unable to sustain themselves even with the use of force. And he dreamed of building in the South a strong Republican party that would no longer depend upon the blacks for its main strength and that could command the esteem and support of Southern whites.

Hayes became the first Republican President to experiment with the plan of appointing regular Democrats to important posts in the South in the hope of gaining Republican success there. He seldom was credited with any honest motives, however, for the public in 1877—and many years later—believed this was part of the bargain that had made him President. His experiment was a sharp departure from the strategy of the Radicals during Reconstruction. Had it worked, the "solid South" as a Democratic stronghold might not have come into being.

Depression and the Silver Question. When Hayes entered the presidency, the country was experiencing the worst years of a depression that had begun in 1873. Almost immediately he was confronted with the first great industrial conflict in our history—a railroad strike that began on the Baltimore and Ohio and spread through fourteen states, affecting two thirds of the railroad mileage in the country outside New England and the South. At the request of four state governors, Hayes sent federal troops to intervene in the strike and restore order.

Hayes ran further afoul of labor, especially on the West Coast, when he vetoed a bill passed in 1879 to restrict Chinese immigration. He felt the bill violated the Burlingame Treaty of 1868, which had given the Chinese the right of unlimited immigration to the United States. (However, Hayes sent a mission to China to negotiate a new treaty, and the resultant Treaty of 1880 gave the United

States the right to regulate or suspend Chinese immigration. The Exclusion Act, passed by Congress in 1882, suspended such immigration for ten years.)

The President also took an unpopular stand on the currency question. Discontented agrarians wanted "cheap money" and the repeal or modification of the Resumption Act of 1875, which obligated the Treasury to redeem greenbacks in specie at full face value on January 1, 1879. Many predicted that such redemption would wreck the monetary system, for everyone would want gold rather than paper notes. But Hayes resisted the pressure and aided Secretary of the Treasury John Sherman in accumulating a gold reserve to redeem the currency. Greenback dollars, which were worth only sixty-seven cents in 1865, rose to one hundred cents before the deadline of resumption, and people realizing this preferred the notes, which were easier to handle. Thus no run on the gold reserve developed.

Inflationists now pushed demands for free coinage of silver, and once again Hayes took the unpopular side. The old ratio between gold and silver had been 16 to 1: there was sixteen times as much silver in a silver dollar as there was gold in a gold dollar. But when the Gold Rush of 1849 lowered the price of gold, an ounce of silver became worth more than one sixteenth of an ounce of gold, and Americans sold their silver on the open market rather than have it coined at a loss. Silver dollars nearly disappeared from circulation, and in 1873 Congress abolished their coinage. Then silver mines in Nevada, Arizona, and Colorado produced such large quantities of silver that the price of silver fell, and miners and agrarians called for a return to the coinage of silver at the old ratio.

Congress responded by passing over Hayes' veto in 1878 the Bland-Allison Act, authorizing the Treasury to purchase not less than $2 million and not more than $4 million worth of silver each month and coin it into dollars at the former ratio of 16 to 1. The act, however, did not fully meet the demands of the silverites, who wanted the "free and unlimited coinage of silver." Moreover, the Treasury consistently purchased only the minimum amount of silver required by the act.

The Election of 1880.   Hayes did not seek reelection, and the Republican convention of 1880 was divided in its support. The "Stalwart" faction, led by party boss Roscoe Conkling, sought a third term for Ulysses S. Grant. But James G. Blaine of Maine and John Sherman of Ohio also had Republican supporters. When it became clear that none of the three could secure a majority, the delegates nominated Congressman James A. Garfield of Ohio on the thirty-sixth ballot. To appease the Stalwarts, second place on the ticket went to one of Conkling's closest associates, Chester A. Arthur, whom Hayes in 1878 had dismissed as head of the New York Custom House. When Samuel J. Tilden declined to run, the Democrats picked General Winfield Scott Hancock, a Pennsylvanian and a Union hero in the Battle of Gettysburg. His running mate was William H. English of Indiana.

The platforms of the two parties revealed few basic differences on policy and no real understanding of the country's problems. The campaign, which turned largely on personalities and irrelevant issues, produced a great deal of sound and fury but nothing of importance. Five sixths of the voters turned out, and Garfield won by fewer than 40,000 popular votes, although his electoral vote was 214 as compared to 155 for Hancock. Despite the failure of the major parties to discuss the vital issues of the day, less than 4 percent of the electorate voted for a protest party candidate—General James B. Weaver of Iowa of the Greenback Labor party, which advocated inflationary policies and stricter federal regulation of interstate commerce.

Garfield and Arthur.   Garfield had been an effective speaker and an able party leader in the House, but many of his contemporaries found him timid and vacillating. Overwhelmed with the demands of office seekers, he exclaimed, "My God! What is there in this place that a man should ever want to get into it?" After accepting the aid of the Stalwarts during the campaign and apparently reaching some understanding with them on patronage matters, Garfield antagonized Conkling by making Conkling's great rival, Blaine, Secretary of State and by appointing a Conkling opponent in New York Collector of the Port.

In the ensuing fight between the President and the Stalwarts, Conkling and his colleague from New York, Thomas "Me Too" Platt, resigned their seats in the Senate and were not reelected by the New York legislature. At the height of the conflict, on July 2, 1881, Charles J. Guiteau, a disappointed office seeker who was mentally unbalanced, shot Garfield and shouted, "I am a Stalwart and Arthur is President now." Garfield died of the wound on September 19, and Arthur became President.

To many Americans the succession of Arthur was a calamity, for he had the reputation of a New York machine politician. Reformers shuddered at the thought of a spoilsman in the presidency, and there was a widespread feeling that the Stalwarts would take over. But in spite of his unsavory past, Arthur was personally honest and did have ability. The responsibilities and dignity of the high office caused him to rise to the occasion and to give the country a good administration. He did not turn over the patronage to Conkling, as many thought he would. He supported civil service reform, prosecuted frauds in the Post Office, cleared the way for the construction of a modern navy, and had the Chinese immigration question settled. He also tried to bring about a reduction in the tariff and to check federal spending on unnecessary public works by vetoing an $18 million rivers-and-harbors bill, but both efforts were defeated by Congress.

The Civil Service Act.

The most important legislation during Arthur's presidency was the Pendleton Civil Service Act of 1883. Since the end of the Civil War, reformers had been denouncing the spoils system and advocating the establishment of a permanent civil service based on merit. Garfield's murder dramatically advanced their cause. The Pendleton Act authorized the President to appoint a Civil Service Commission of three members to provide "open competitive examinations for testing the fitness of applicants for the public service now classified or to be classified." In addition, the act forbade the levying of political campaign assessments on federal officeholders and protected them against ouster for failure to make such contributions.

At first the act affected only the lowest offices—about 14,000, or 12 percent of the total number of federal employees, leaving the remainder under the spoils system. But the President was given authority to extend the classified list at his discretion. Arthur demonstrated good faith by making excellent appointments to the Commission. Every subsequent President extended the classified list, and at the end of the century it included 40 percent of all federal positions.

The Election of 1884.

In 1884 the Republicans turned their backs on Arthur and nominated James G. Blaine of Maine for President. The Democrats named Grover Cleveland of New York. Viewing Blaine as an old guard politician inimical to good government, William Curtis, Carl Schurz, and other reformist Mugwumps bolted the Republican party and supported Cleveland. As in 1880 few real issues were discussed, and the campaign degenerated into one of personal abuse and vilification. "The public is angry and abusive," observed Henry Adams. "Everyone takes part. We are all doing our best, and swearing like demons. But the amusing thing is that no one talks about real issues." The Democrats publicized the "Mulligan letters" to prove that Blaine, as Speaker of the House, had been guilty of unethical conduct in connection with land-grant railroads, and the Republicans retaliated with the charge that Cleveland was the father of an illegitimate child, the responsibility for whom he had accepted. Since Blaine seemed to have led an impeccable private life but a culpable public one and Cleveland just the reverse, one Mugwump suggested that "we should elect Mr. Cleveland to the public office he is so admirably qualified to fill and remand Mr. Blaine to the private life which he is so eminently fitted to adorn."

Overall, the decision in 1884 was even closer than in 1880. Cleveland's plurality in popular votes was only 29,000 and his electoral vote was 219 to Blaine's 182. So narrow was the margin of victory for Cleveland that he carried the pivotal state of New York by a mere 1149 votes.

Cleveland and the Presidency.

Cleveland, a strapping figure of well over two hundred pounds, came to the White House in 1885 with a reputation as a reformer and a man of courage, integrity, and prodigious work habits. Actually he was unimaginative, stolid, obdurate, and brutally candid, and he lacked a sense of timing. He was also a thoroughgoing conservative, a believer in sound money, and a defender of property rights. In his inaugural he promised to adhere to "business principles," and his cabinet included conservatives and business-minded Democrats of the East and South. His administration signified no break with his Republican predecessors on fundamental issues.

Cleveland faced the task of pleasing both the Mugwumps and the hungry spoilsmen of his own party, who had been cut off from federal patronage for twenty-four years. At first he refused to yield to the bosses on appointments and thereby won the acclaim of reformers. But faced with a revolt within his own party, Cleveland gave in to the spoilsmen and replaced Republicans with "honest Democrats." Carl Schurz wrote, "Your attempt to please both reformers and spoilsmen has failed," and Cleveland broke with the Mugwumps. At the end of his presidency he had removed about two thirds of the 120,000 federal officeholders. On the credit side he increased the civil service classified list to 27,380 positions, almost double the number when he took office.

Cleveland had more success as a watchdog of the Treasury. He halted the scandalous pension racket by vetoing hundreds of private military pension bills that congressmen pushed through for constituents whose claims had been rejected by the Pension Office. Cleveland signed more of these bills than had all his predecessors since Johnson put together, but he was the first President to veto any. The Grand Army of the Republic screamed at the vetoes, and in January 1887 Congress responded by passing a Dependent Pension Bill, which provided a pension for all honorably discharged disabled veterans who had served as little as three months in the Union army, irrespective of how they had become disabled. Cleveland vetoed it and angered the G.A.R.

Aside from the Interstate Commerce Act, for which Cleveland deserves no credit and which he signed with reluctance and "with reservations," little significant legislation was enacted during his term. He did not compel railroad, lumber, and cattle companies to give up 81 million acres of public land that they had fraudulently occupied. In 1886 Congress passed a Presidential Succession Law, which provided that after the Vice-President, the succession should pass to the members of the cabinet, beginning with the Secretary of State,

in the order of the creation of their departments. In 1887 the Dawes Act was passed, initiating a new Indian policy.

The Tariff Issue. Cleveland devoted his entire annual message of December 1887 to the tariff question, advocating a drastic reduction in duties. The Democratic-controlled House responded with a low tariff measure, but the Republican-dominated Senate turned it down and passed a highly protective bill that the House would not accept. This led to a deadlock and the injection of the tariff question into the 1888 election. For the first time in this era both major parties were forced to take a position on the tariff issue.

The Election of 1888. The Democrats renominated Cleveland and chose the elderly ex-Senator Allen G. Thurman of Ohio as his running mate. The Republicans nominated Senator Benjamin Harrison of Indiana for President, and Levi P. Morton, a wealthy New York banker, for Vice-President. Two labor parties, voicing the industrial unrest of the period, entered the campaign. Union Labor and United Labor condemned the major parties for being under the control of monopolies and for being indifferent to the welfare of workers.

The campaign was waged largely on the tariff issue, with Republicans defending protection and Democrats advocating a reduction of duties. The Republicans appealed to the manufacturing interests, who would profit from a high tariff, and to veterans, who were promised generous pension legislation. Both parties used money freely; throughout the country voters were bribed in probably the most corrupt presidential election in our history. Although Cleveland had a plurality of more than 90,000 popular votes, Harrison carried the crucial states of Indiana, New York, and Ohio and gained 233 electoral votes to Cleveland's 168. The decisive factors were probably the efficiency of the Republican organization and the purchase of the floating vote in the doubtful states.

Harrison and the Republicans. Harrison possessed intellectual and oratorical gifts, but he was very cold in his personal relationships. "Harrison sweats ice water" became a popular phrase, and one of his close associates remarked, "Harrison can make a speech to ten thousand men and every man of them will go away his friend. Let him meet the same ten thousand in private, and every one will go away his enemy." Although Harrison had ability, he lacked forcefulness, and the leadership passed largely to the Republican leaders in Congress, especially to Senator Nelson W. Aldrich of Rhode Island and Speaker of the House Thomas B. Reed of Maine. Reed pushed through the House a revision of the rules that gave him almost dictatorial powers over proceedings and earned him the title of "czar."

For the first time since 1875 the Republicans had the presidency and a majority in both houses of Congress, and they began to pay off their political debts. The McKinley Tariff of 1890 raised rates to a higher level and protected more products than any previous tariff in American history. In the same year the Dependent Pension Act, substantially the same measure vetoed by Cleveland, granted pensions to all G.A.R. veterans suffering from any disability, acquired in war service or not, and to their widows and children. In the same year, to meet the demands of the silverites, the Sherman Silver Purchase Act increased the amount of silver to be purchased by the Treasury to 4.5 million ounces a month. To appease the popular clamor against monopolies, the Sherman Antitrust Act was also passed in 1890.

This same Congress earned itself the label "the Billion Dollar Congress." By distributing subsidies to steamship lines, passing extravagant rivers-and-harbors bills, offering large premiums to government bondholders, and returning federal taxes paid by Northern states during the Civil War, it handed out so much money that by 1894 the Treasury surplus was gone. The United States has never had a surplus since.

Instead of the widespread support that such policies were expected to bring, the public reaction was one of hostility, and in the congressional elections of 1890 the Republicans were severely rebuked. They retained only 88 of the 332 seats in the House and had their majority in the Senate reduced from 14 to 6. The appearance of nine new congressmen representing farm interests and not associated with either of the major parties indicated that a third-party revolt was shaping up and that a new phase in American politics was under way.

THE AGRARIAN REVOLT

The Plight of the Farmer. The third-party revolt took the form of agrarian insurgency in the West and South, which had been coming on since the Civil War and which reached its culmination in the 1890s. There were a number of causes for agrarian discontent. The conversion of American agriculture to a commercial basis made the farmer a specialist whose role was to produce a surplus by which the United States could adjust an unfavorable balance of trade. But unlike the manufacturer, the farmer had no control over his market or his prices. He worked alone and competed with other farmers, American and foreign. Instead of benefiting from the new order of things, he was one of its victims.

Prices for agricultural products had declined. Between 1870 and 1897 wheat prices dropped from $1.06 to 63.6 cents a bushel, corn from 43.1 to 29.7 cents a bushel, and cotton from 15.1 to 5.8 cents a pound. These were market prices, after warehouse and transportation charges were added. The net prices paid to the farmer were even lower. Farmers of the Old Northwest received only

42 cents a bushel for wheat which government economists estimated cost 45.1 cents a bushel to produce. In Kansas in 1889 corn sold for 10 cents a bushel and was commonly used for fuel, and in 1890 a farmer in Nebraska shot his hogs because he could neither sell nor give them away.

Farmers increasingly were shackled with debts and loss of proprietorship over their land. In 1900 nearly one third of the country's farms were mortgaged. In the Middle West the percentages were highest—45 percent in Wisconsin, 48 percent in Michigan, and 53 percent in Iowa. Mortgages were few in the South because of the crop-lien system, by which local merchants advanced seed, equipment, and personal necessities to planters in return for a first lien on the planter's future cotton crop. Throughout the country the number of tenant farmers increased from 25.9 percent of all the farms in 1880 to 29.4 percent in 1890 and to 35.3 percent in 1900.

The basic cause of the farmer's misfortune was an overexpansion in agricultural production. In addition to the continuing increase in agricultural production, the number of farmers also kept going up. Between 1860 and 1890 the number of farms increased from 2 million to 4.5 million, the wheat crop from 173 million bushels to 449 million, and the cotton from 5.3 million bales to 8.5 million. Supply was outrunning demand, and the farmers were falling behind in the economic race.

The farmers blamed others, in particular the railroads, the middlemen, and the banks. They resented railroad rate differentials and discriminations against them. On through routes and long hauls rates were low, because the railroads competed with one another, but on local or short hauls, where there was little or no competition, rates were high. Sometimes the Western local rate was four times that charged for the same distance and commodity in the East, where rail lines were more numerous. Farmers paid more to ship their grain from Minnesota towns to St. Paul

or Minneapolis than a shipper in Minneapolis had to pay for a haul to New York. In addition, farmers resented the way railroads favored shippers and dominated state politics.

The farmers also believed themselves to be at the mercy of the middlemen—local merchants, grain dealers, brokers, and speculators. The national banks' rules precluded loans on real estate and farm property and the banks did not respond to the farmers' seasonal needs for money.

The farmers complained that they bore the brunt of the tax burden. The merchants could underestimate the value of their stock, householders might exclude some of their property, the owners of securities could conceal them, but the farmers could not hide their land. Finally, the protective tariff hurt the farmers because they purchased manufactured goods in a highly protected market and sold their crops in an unprotected one. They shared none of the benefits of protection. Instead, they contributed heavily to the subsidization of business. This injustice was all the more difficult to bear in view of their belief that the tariff was "the mother of trusts."

The Granger Movement. Feeling they were being left behind and believing that politicians were indifferent and even hostile to their interests, farmers decided to organize and protest against their condition. In 1867 Oliver Hudson Kelley, a government clerk, founded the Patrons of Husbandry, which became better known as the Grange. The farmers saw in the Grange a weapon with which to fight their foes. By 1874, its peak year, it had an estimated membership of 1.5 million. The Grangers established a number of cooperatives in an effort to eliminate the profits of the middleman, but mismanagement and business opposition doomed most of them.

Although the Grange officially declared itself "nonpolitical," individual members joined various agrarian third parties organized in the Midwest. In coalition with either

SENATOR TILLMAN'S ALLEGORICAL COW.

The farmers complained that they contributed heavily to the subsidization of business. An allegorical cow feeds on the produce of Western and Southern farmers while her milk goes to big money interests in the East.

the Democrats or the Republicans, these third parties gained control of several state legislatures and enacted Granger laws to regulate the rates charged by grain elevators and railroads. They were challenged in the courts, but in *Munn* v. *Illinois* in 1877, the most important of these cases, the Supreme Court upheld the "police power" of the state regulation.

After 1875 Grange membership decreased rapidly. Out of the 20,000 local granges extant in 1874 only 4,000 remained in 1880. Many farmers had been attracted by the novelty and vogue of the Grange, and others had believed it would provide a panacea for all their ills. They left when they found there was not immediate and universal success.

The Greenback Movement. Farmers next were attracted to the Greenback movement. From 1867 to 1872, Eastern labor dominated the movement, and its primary objectives then were to lower the interest rate on money and to reduce taxation. After 1873 farmers

favored an expansion of the currency in the hope that it would bring higher prices for their products. When the panic of 1873 intensified the agricultural depression and the Granger movement failed to relieve the situation, farmers took over the Greenback movement. Its high-water mark was the election of fifteen congressmen in 1878. But with the resumption of specie payment in 1879 and with the rise of the price of corn in 1880, farmers lost interest in Greenbackism and its support rapidly declined. In the presidential election of 1880 the Greenback candidate, James B. Weaver of Iowa, received only 300,000 votes, about 3 percent of the total. By 1888 the party was dead.

The Farmers' Alliance. With the decline of the Grange and the disappearance of Greenbackism, a new set of farm groups appeared. Most important were the Farmers' Alliances, two distinct organizations of different origins. The Northwestern Alliance was organized by Milton George in Chicago in 1880. The

Southern Alliance was formed in 1875 in a frontier county of Texas for protection against horse thieves and land sharks. It remained small until 1886, when it expanded throughout the South under the vigorous leadership of C. W. Macune and absorbed rival farmers' organizations. For blacks there was a Farmers' National Alliance and Cooperative Union.

The Alliances experimented with cooperatives more than the Grange had but with no greater success. A merger of the Northwestern and the Southern Alliance was unsuccessfully attempted in a meeting at St. Louis in 1889. The Southern Alliance insisted upon the retention of its secret rituals and the exclusion of blacks, at least from the national body. The Northwestern Alliance wanted a federation in which each organization would keep its identity.

Then the Southern Alliance changed its name to the National Farmers' Alliance and Industrial Union and induced the three strongest state alliances of the Northwestern Alliance, those of Kansas and North and South Dakota, to join. It then gained the endorsement of the Knights of Labor.

The Emergence of Populism. Though the Alliances proclaimed themselves nonpolitical organizations, they issued demands each year which could be realized only by political means. For example, the Ocala, Florida, platform of 1890 called for the abolition of national banks, establishment of subtreasuries, a graduated income tax, direct election of United States senators, and government control of communication and transportation facilities.

By 1890 the Northwestern Alliance concluded that nonpartisan activities were a failure and decided to enter politics. Kansas led the way by organizing a People's (Populist) party in June 1890, and Alliancemen in other Western states set up independent parties under other names. The West was in the throes of a mighty upheaval. A later commentator called it "a pentecost of politics in which a tongue of flame sat upon every man and each spoke as the spirit gave him utterance."

"Sockless" Jerry Simpson, Ignatius Donnelly, Mary Elizabeth Lease, Anna L. Diggs, and General James B. Weaver were among the leaders of Western Populism. The party, though hastily constructed, was successful in three states. In Kansas it elected five congressmen and one senator in the 1890 elections. In Nebraska it gained control of both houses of the legislature and elected two congressmen. In South Dakota it elected a senator.

In the South the Alliance feared that the establishment of a third party might split the white vote and bring the Republicans and their black supporters into power again. So at first the Alliance tried to gain control of the Democratic party machinery. It attacked the industrial and urban leadership of the Democrats and endorsed candidates who pledged themselves to the Ocala platform. The Alliance appeared to have captured the Democratic party in the elections of 1890 when four governors, eight state legislatures, forty-four congressmen, and three senators promised to support Alliance demands, but after the election nearly all these elected officials reverted to Democratic orthodoxy once in office. This disillusioning experience, plus the prospects of Cleveland's renomination by the Democratic party, stimulated Southern Alliancemen to become Populists. In July 1892 the national People's party was formally organized in Omaha.

The Election of 1892. The Populist platform of 1892 restated earlier Alliance demands, including the free and unlimited coinage of silver at the ratio of 16 to 1; government ownership and operation of railroads and the telephone, telegraph, and postal systems; prohibition of alien ownership of land; restriction of immigration; and a graduated income tax. The death of L. L. Polk of North Carolina just before the convention met in Omaha on July 4 probably deprived the Populists of their strongest candidate. They nominated General James B. Weaver of Iowa for President and General James G. Field of Virginia for Vice-President. Both Cleveland and Harrison were renominated by the major parties. Their running mates were Adlai E. Stevenson of Illinois and Whitelaw Reid, editor of the New York *Tribune*.

The free silver plank was the only exciting issue in the campaign, and Weaver polled 1,040,000 popular votes and 22 electoral votes. Populists became the first third party since the Civil War to break into the Electoral College. They also elected ten representatives, five senators, three governors, and 1500 members of state legislatures. Cleveland defeated Harrison with 277 to 145 electoral votes and 5,555,426 to 5,182,690 popular votes.

Cleveland and the Depression of 1893.

Shortly after Cleveland assumed the presidency in 1893, the country began to experience the worst financial panic in years. Following the failure of a number of prominent firms, the stock market suddenly collapsed. Banks called in their loans, and credit just about dried up. Businesses failed daily. Before the year was out, 500 banks and nearly 16,000 businesses had gone into bankruptcy. According to the *Commercial and Financial Chronicle,* never before had there been such a sudden and striking cessation of industrial activity. And no part of the nation escaped it. Everywhere mills, factories, furnaces, and mines closed down in large numbers, and hundreds of thousands of workers lost their jobs. By the fall of 1893, the *Banker's Magazine* of London reported the American people to be "in the throes of a fiasco unprecedented even in their broad experience" and declared that "ruin and disaster run riot over the land."

The Panic of 1893 sent tremors through the New York Stock Exchange and bidding often became frenzied. A severe depression followed.

The panic developed into a major depression. There was no agreement as to its causes. Conservative business leaders attributed it to the Sherman Silver Purchase Act and to radical attacks on property. Labor leaders and agrarians blamed it on the capitalists. The Democrats blamed the Republicans, and the Republicans accused the Democrats.

There had been periodic panics followed by depressions ever since the end of the Civil War. In each instance reckless speculation overinflated values. Then confidence collapsed, with attendant business failures and unemployment. The primary cause for the debacle of 1893 was the overexpansion of transportation facilities and industrial production, accompanied by stock manipulation and reckless speculation. And as usual it had been preceded by a similar depression abroad.

Like his predecessors in office, Cleveland believed it was not the duty of the federal government to alleviate suffering in a depression. As he complacently stated in his second inaugural, ". . . while the people should patriotically and cheerfully support their Government, its functions do not include the support of the people." In his view the Sherman Silver Purchase Act had caused the depression, and his proposed remedy was to repeal the act and maintain the gold standard. The silverites disagreed. They contended that the cure lay in the free and unlimited coinage of silver at a ratio of 16 to 1 of gold and that the Sherman Act had provided inadequate relief. Many debtor agrarians agreed.

But Cleveland was convinced that the silver certificates issued under the Sherman Act and redeemed in gold were responsible for the drain on the gold reserve that was being lowered to the established minimum of $100 million. This was an oversimplification, for there were several causes for the drain on gold. But Cleveland summoned Congress into special session in 1893 and, through a combination of Gold Democrats and Republi-

cans, had the Sherman Act repealed. Most Western and Southern Democrats voted against the Democratic administration, widening the split within the party on the currency issue.

Repeal failed to restore prosperity, and the Treasury's gold reserve continued to fall. To keep the country on the gold standard, Cleveland had the Treasury sell government bonds for gold. A group of bankers headed by J. P. Morgan absorbed three bond issues in 1894 and 1895, but it was not until 1897, when the depression had finally run its course, that the Treasury crisis ended. Although the gold purchases enabled the Treasury to meet its obligations, the bond sales intensified the silverites' hatred of the President. Many Americans became alarmed over the government's dependence upon a syndicate of New York bankers.

Cleveland failed to bring about any substantial reduction of the tariff. In the House, the Democrats, fulfilling their campaign promises, had passed a tariff bill drawn up by William L. Wilson of West Virginia, which provided for a modest reduction in rates. In the Senate, though, a group of protectionists from both parties, led by Senator Arthur Gorman, influential Democrat from Maryland, attacked the bill with more than six hundred amendments, restoring some old rates and raising others. The resultant Wilson-Gorman Tariff of 1894, which Cleveland denounced as "party perfidy and party dishonor" and which became law without his signature, was a far cry from reform. It did provide for a small income tax of 2 percent on incomes over $4000, but the Supreme Court, as unpopular as Cleveland, held the tax to be unconstitutional.

For the remainder of his presidency, Cleveland confined his role to that of protector of the status quo. He vetoed the Seigniorage bill, which would have increased the supply of the currency. Through subordinates he rudely rejected the petitions of "armies" of unemployed workers who, under the nominal leadership of men like Populist Jacob S. Coxey, marched on Washington in 1894 to plead for public works relief programs. In the same year, Cleveland sent federal troops to crush the Pullman strike.

Three Supreme Court decisions in 1895 added to the general discontent in the country. The Court in a 5-4 decision in *Pollock* v. *Farmers' Loan and Trust Company* invalidated the income tax clause of the Wilson-Gorman Tariff, on the ground that it was a direct tax. Therefore, according to the Constitution, it had to be apportioned among the states on the basis of population. Moreover, Justice Stephen J. Field had earlier called the income tax "an assault upon capital" and a "stepping stone to others, larger and more sweeping, till our political contests . . . become a war of the poor against the rich."

Shortly after this the Court, in the case of *in re Debs*, unanimously upheld the injunction sending Debs to prison at the time of the Pullman strike. At the same time the Court in an 8-1 decision in *United States* v. *E. C. Knight Company*, in the first U. S. Supreme Court case involving the Sherman Antitrust Act of 1890, distinguished manufacturing from commerce and held that the Sherman Act did not apply to manufacturing combinations within states. This decision seriously weakened the enforcement of the antitrust laws and for some time

placed most monopolies beyond the reach of federal regulation.

Thus there was a widespread feeling in the country in the mid-nineties that there was a war on between the rich and the poor, and that the President, the Supreme Court, and Congress were on the side of the rich.

The Election of 1896.   The Republicans met in St. Louis in June and nominated William McKinley of Ohio for President and Garret A. Hobart, a corporation lawyer of New Jersey, for Vice-President. Marcus Alonzo Hanna, a wealthy Ohio industrialist, was largely responsible for McKinley's nomination. Hanna was a good example of the new kind of political boss then emerging—the businessman holding office and actually running the party instead of remaining in the background and paying out political favors. As a leader of the Republican party in Ohio, soon to become Republican national chairman, Hanna gathered the necessary delegate votes for McKinley's nomination and financed and managed his preconvention campaign.

On the monetary question McKinley's record was not consistent. He had voted for both the Bland-Allison Act and the Sherman Silver Purchase Act. Yet in 1891, in running for governor, he had condemned the free coinage of silver and advocated international bimetallism. Hanna had already decided upon a gold standard plank, but at the

ELECTION OF 1896: ELECTORAL VOTE

McKinley: 271   Bryan: 176

convention he gave the impression he had to be "persuaded" by the Eastern delegates that "the existing gold standard must be maintained." After a gold plank was adopted, a small group of silver advocates led by Senator Henry M. Teller of Colorado left the hall and organized the Silver Republican party.

The Democrats were torn by bitter strife when they met in Chicago in July. The agrarians looked upon Cleveland as an enemy. He personified the Northeastern conservatism against which they were in revolt. Within the Democratic party insurgency was rampant. In the elections of 1894 the Democrats had barely retained control of the Senate and had lost the House.

Insurgent Democrats prepared to outdo the silverites in denouncing Cleveland and advocating free silver. They hoped to win back the Populists and take over the Democratic party. Their work was so effective that by the summer of 1896 they had gained control of every state Democratic organization south of the Potomac and west of the Alleghenies except South Dakota, Minnesota, and Wisconsin.

The silverites dominated the convention, and Cleveland was denounced in resolutions and speeches. The platform repudiated the Cleveland program and attacked the protective tariff, national banks, trusts, and the Supreme Court. It called for an income tax and the free coinage of silver at the ratio of 16 to 1. The leading contender for the nomination was Congressman Richard P. ("Silver Dick") Bland of Missouri, who had fought for free silver since the seventies. But the convention passed him by and on the fifth ballot nominated William Jennings Bryan of Nebraska, who had captivated the silver delegates with a speech that rose to a stirring peroration: "You shall not press down upon the brow of labor this crown of thorns, you shall not crucify mankind upon a cross of gold."

Bryan, ony thirty-six at the time, seemed to have been nominated by the accident of a spontaneous speech. But he had been rounding up support for several years and had presented his ideas many times to other audiences. His convention speech was simply the last step. Bryan's running mate was Arthur Sewall of Maine, a wealthy shipbuilder, banker, and protectionist but an advocate of free silver.

The Populists faced a dilemma when their convention met in St. Louis in July. If they nominated their own candidate, they feared they would split the reform vote and permit McKinley to win. If they endorsed Bryan, they would surrender their identity to the Democrats and sacrifice their broad program of reform for one that placed a disproportionate emphasis on the silver question. Western Populists were eager to nominate Bryan, but Southern Populists wanted a separate party ticket.

The Populists finally were induced to nominate Bryan through trickery. Senator William V. Allen of Nebraska, chairman of the convention, told the Southerners that the Democrats had promised to withdraw Sewall and accept Thomas E. Watson, Populist leader of Georgia, as their vice presidential candidate if the Populists would nominate Bryan. Watson's decision to accept this compromise persuaded Southern opponents of fusion to vote for Bryan's nomination. This would have created a true Democratic-Populist partnership, but the Democrats refused to withdraw Sewall. Henry Demarest Lloyd watched the convention with great disgust and finally concluded, "The People's party has been betrayed, . . . but after all it is its own fault."

The campaign was a highly emotional and dramatic one. Bryan spoke in 21 states, traveled 18,000 miles and addressed some 5 million people in more than 600 speeches. McKinley remained at his home in Canton and read well-prepared speeches from his front porch to carefully coached delegations that visited him. But Hanna did the real work. The powerful response to Bryan's appeal frightened Eastern conservatives, and Hanna took advantage of their panic to collect campaign funds. From trusts, banks, railroads, and tycoons he raised a sum estimated at between $3.5 million and $15 million as against a bare $300,000 for Bryan.

Hanna used the money lavishly but wisely, and he received great assistance from the press, which heaped all kinds of abuse upon Bryan. The *Louisville Courier Journal* called him "a dishonest dodger . . . a daring adventurer . . . a political faker," and the New York *Tribune* referred to him as a "wretched, rattle-pated boy." The Philadelphia *Press* described the "Jacobins" of the Democratic convention as "hideous and repulsive vipers," and Theodore Roosevelt was reported as saying that the silver men might well "be stood up against the wall and shot." John Hay, writing to Henry Adams in London, said of Bryan, "The Boy Orator makes only one speech—but he makes it twice a day. There is no fun it it. He simply reiterates the unquestionable truths that every man who has a clean shirt is a thief and should be hanged, and there is no goodness or wisdom except among the illiterates and criminal classes." In addition there were dire warnings that Bryan's victory would bring disaster. Farmers were told that mortgages would not be renewed. Workers were informed that factories would be closed or wages cut.

Out of almost 14 million popular votes cast, McKinley won with a margin of over a half million and with 271 electoral votes to 176 for Bryan. Bryan failed to carry a single industrial and urban state and did not win a single state north of the Potomac and east of the Mississippi. Despite the widespread unrest among labor, he failed to elicit its support, and this failure was one of the principal reasons for his defeat. But also he had nowhere near the

material resources backing McKinley, and he represented the party blamed for the depression. The Republicans gained a majority in both houses of Congress.

McKinley lost all the mining states and the wheat-growing states of South Dakota, Nebraska, and Kansas, where Republicans had always been strong. But he held onto the corn-producing states of the Middle West, where the farmers were better off than those on the Plains. And he gained an ascendancy in the Northeast such as no previous Republican President had had. From Maine south to Virginia and from the Great Lakes to Tennessee he carried every state. While the margin by which he carried some was narrow, McKinley had a majority of the popular vote in the nation. The Republicans continued to hold the bulk of the Northern farmers and had gained new strength among the commercial and industrial interests of the North and the Upper South. For the first time since 1872, New England and the Middle Atlantic, Central, and North Central states were solidly Republican, and these sections were strong enough, if united, to control the electoral college and thereby the presidency itself.

Historians are generally agreed that the election of 1896 was the most important one since 1860, and they have regarded it as a turning point in American history. For one thing it gave the Republicans a clear majority of the popular vote in the country as a whole for the first time since Reconstruction. For another it ushered in a series of Republican triumphs and a period of Republican supremacy in the national government that was to last, except for Wilson's two terms, until 1932. McKinley's victory also marked a triumph for conservatism and industrialism. The backbone of agrarian resurgence was broken in 1896.

In the mourning for Bryan the fate of Populism was largely forgotten. Its passing seemed to be the concern of few, yet it was one of the most significant results of the election of 1896. Fusion with the Democrats and the abandonment of a broad program of reform for the sake of silver had all but destroyed the Populist party on the national level. It was Populism, not Bryanism, that furnished the backbone of agrarian resurgence, and when that backbone was broken in 1896, it meant that agrarian radicalism had made its last aggressive political stand.

The Populists in Perspective. Despite their defeat in 1896 and their disappearance from the political scene, the Populists have an important, albeit a controversial, place in American history. For quite a number of years historians portrayed the Populists as the champions of the common man and as the makers of modern reform in the country. The favorable and traditional point of view about the Populists was put forth by John D. Hicks in *The Populist Revolt* in 1931, and this remained the standard general account until recent years. According to Hicks, Populism represented "the last phase of a long and perhaps a losing struggle—the struggle to save agricultural America from the devouring jaws of industrial America." Hicks wrote in the tradition of the Progressive historians who were very critical of American industrial society and who regarded the older agrarian America as having many virtues.

This favorable view of the Populists came under attack in the 1950s when critics like Richard Hofstadter and Victor C. Ferkiss charged them with all kinds of mischief, including racism, anti-Semitism, jingoism, nativism, anti-intellectualism, xenophobia, and even being the forerunners of American fascism. Though the critics agreed that Populism was the first modern political movement of practical importance in the United States to insist that the federal government had some responsibility for the common weal, they also believed that the Populist leaders were haunted by nonexistent conspiracies and frequently were given to scapegoating rather than to rational analysis.

The 1960s witnessed another turnabout. A more favorable view of Populism reappeared. C. Vann Woodward and William P. Tucker, while conceding some of the points scored by the critics of Populism, found that the negative and unlovely characteristics of the Populists were not peculiar to them and that the irrational and illiberal side of Populism was no reason to repudiate its heritage.

Thereafter, some of the new writers saw the Populists as hoping to transform the American social system by putting forth a logical and reasonable analysis of industrial America, including the rejection of laissez-faire capitalism, Social Darwinism, and the success ethic. Others showed that Populism, at least in Kansas, the most Populist of the western states, was not hostile "to things non-American" but instead was a rational, legitimate political response to economic distress. Still others reported that the Populists in Alabama, at least, were neither revolutionaries nor reformers but repeatedly even voted against reforms to which they were pledged.

Then in 1976 Lawrence Goodwyn published the first scholarly, general study of the Populist movement on a national scale since that of Hicks. In *Democratic Promise: The Populist Movement in America,* Goodwyn contended that Hicks had missed the essential dynamics of Populism, thereby opening the way for the later distortions and misinterpretations. He accused Hicks of mistaking "the shadow movement" accompanying Populism for the real thing. The real thing, argued Goodwyn, was the political revolt growing out of the cooperative movement of the Alliance and the elaborate program of structural economic and political reforms developed in that struggle getting under way in the 1880s. The shadow movement was the effort to substitute for that entire program and the reform spirit behind it the single demand for the free coinage of silver.

And so it goes. Despite the extensive literature on Populism, it remains difficult to assess its place in American history.

The Crisis of the 1890s.   The work of the new political historians has thrown new light on the "crisis of the nineties" that culminated in the 1896 election. It appears that the ethnocultural issues and responses continued to be important well after the depression began in 1893, as evidenced by shifts away from the Democratic party in areas little affected by the economic downturn. The success of the Republicans in the 1894 elections resulted in part from their advocacy of what appeared to be plausible solutions to the depression and in part from the divisions and weaknesses within the Democratic party. The Republican party professionals also refused to commit their party to a single issue. Instead, McKinley in 1896 led a new coalition of business-backed pragmatists who favored a pluralistic approach to interest groups and national issues.

Bryan, on the other hand, turned his 1896 campaign into a moral crusade aimed at rural, pietistic, old-stock voters in the Midwest. This shift in appeals, along with the continuing depression, confirmed the voter realignment that had begun in 1894, insuring Republican dominance in the Midwest for nearly a third of a century. In the urban Northeast, Bryan failed not so much because he did not address himself to ethnic and religious differences among the voters as because workers there, regardless of background, rejected the economic arguments he advanced, instead favoring Republican arguments on the tariff, currency, and the return of prosperity.

In establishing its position as the majority party after 1894, the Republican party obviously benefited from the depression and Democratic mistakes. But the Republicans prevailed because they also more clearly met the needs and desires of the mass of American voters than any other party and because they seemed to provide plausible solutions to the depression. Meanwhile, the Democrats, awarded national power in 1892, failed to meet this challenge satisfactorily or to strengthen their party organization enough to insure continued Democratic election victories. If the voters turned after 1894 to the Republicans, they also turned against the Democrats.

McKinley and the End of an Era.   The McKinley administration was ushered in under highly favorable circumstances. Businessmen knew that their interests would be safeguarded for four years. There was a return to prosperity which was to continue for several years. Farmers largely dropped politics and were busy raising crops. Politicians were happy and looked forward to a long period of abundance. McKinley, well aware of the economic distress that had affected Americans, promised in his first inaugural that this would be his chief concern. To maintain recovery he advocated two principal measures—a higher tariff and a gold standard act. Congress responded with the Dingley Tariff of 1897, which raised duties to an average of 52 percent, the highest in our history, and the Gold Standard Act of 1900, which declared the gold dollar from that time on would be the sole standard of currency.

With these two laws the McKinley administration made good its campaign promises. Beyond this neither the President nor Congress intended to interfere with the economy. They planned to let it alone and to allow business to create prosperity. McKinley's inauguration marked the beginning of the greatest consolidation movement in American industry (1897–1904). This, coupled with the Spanish–American War, produced golden years of prosperity under McKinley and Hanna.

McKinley's presidency marked the beginning of a new era not only in national politics but in the running of the national government. As Professor Wilfred Binkley, a leading authority on the presidency and Congress, writes: "Not since the presidency of Thomas Jefferson, had there been achieved such an integration of the political branches of the federal government and such consequent

coherence and sense of direction in its functioning." The equilibrium and stalemate of the preceding two decades had given way to new political and economic changes under Republican supremacy.

BIBLIOGRAPHY

General studies of the intellectual history of the post–Civil War generation include Merle E. Curti, *The Growth of American Thought*, 3rd ed. (New York: Harper & Row, 1964), R. H. Gabriel, *The Course of American Democratic Thought*, rev. ed. (New York: Ronald Press, 1956), Henry S. Commager, *The American Mind* (New Haven: Yale University Press, 1950), Vernon L. Parrington, *Main Currents in American Thought*, Vol. III (New York: Harcourt Brace Jovanovich, 1930), and Clinton Rossiter, *Conservatism in America: The Thankless Persuasion* (Toronto: Random House, 1962).

Giving a more specialized treatment of ideas in this generation are Richard Hofstadter, *Social Darwinism in American Thought*, rev. ed. (New York: Braziller, 1959), Morton G. White, *Social Thought in America* (Boston: Beacon Press, 1957), and Charles Page, *Class and American Sociology: From Ward to Ross* (New York: Schocken Books, 1969). Perrry Miller, ed., *American Thought: Civil War to World War I* (New York: Holt, Rinehart and Winston, 1954), is a first-class anthology. Some informative essays on this subject can be found in H. Wayne Morgan, ed., *The Gilded Age: A Reappraisal* (Syracuse: Syracuse University Press, 1970). And see also Bruce Kuklick, *The Rise of American Philosophy* (New Haven: Yale University Press, 1977).

Biographies and special studies of some of the leading thinkers of the period include A. G. Keller, *Reminiscences (Mainly Personal) of William Graham Sumner* (New Haven: Yale University Press, 1933), Samuel Chugerman, *Lester F. Ward: The American Aristotle* (New York: Octagon Books, 1965), C. A. Barker, *Henry George* (New York: Oxford University Press, 1955), Lewis Mumford, *The Story of Utopias* (New York: Viking Press, 1962), Joseph Dorfman, *Thorstein Veblen and His America* (Clifton, N.J.: Kelley reprint of 1934 ed.), R.B. Perry, *The Thought and Character of William James*, 2 vols. (Cambridge: Harvard University Press, 1948), Arthur Ernest Morgan, *Edward Bellamy* (Philadelphia: Porcupine Press reprint of 1944 ed.), and Max Lerner, ed., *The Mind and Faith of Justice Holmes* (New York: Modern Library, 1943).

On religion in the Age of Industrialism the story is well told in Aaron I. Abell, *The Urban Impact upon American Protestantism 1865–1900* (Hamden, Conn.: Shoe String Press reprint of

1943 ed.), Aaron I. Abell, ed., *American Catholic Thought on Social Questions* (Indianapolis: Bobbs-Merrill, 1968), and Henry F. May, *Protestant Churches and Industrial America* (New York: Harper & Row, 1963). Charles Howard Hopkins, *The Rise of the Social Gospel in American Protestantism 1865–1915* (New Haven: Yale University Press, 1940), discusses the Social Gospel movement, and Paul A. Carter, *The Spiritual Crisis of the Gilded Age* (DeKalb: Northern Illinois University Press, 1971), analyzes the spiritual crisis of these years.

On American literature in the post–Civil War generation the following works are especially useful: Van Wyck Brooks, *New England: Indian Summer* (New York: Dutton, 1950), and *The Confident Years 1885–1915* (New York: Dutton, 1960); Jay Martin, *Harvests of Change: American Literature 1865–1914* (Englewood Cliffs, N.J.: Prentice-Hall, 1969); and Warner Berthoff, *The Ferment of Realism 1884–1919* (New York: Free Press, 1965). Alfred Kazin, *On Native Grounds* (New York: Harcourt Brace Jovanovich, 1972), treats American writing since 1890; so also does M.D. Geisman, *Rebels and Ancestors* (New York: Hill & Wang, 1953). The Chautauqua story is told in Victoria Case and Robert Ormond Case, *We Called It Culture: The Story of Chautauqua* (New York: Books for Libraries, 1948), and Joseph E. Gould, *The Chautauqua Movement: An Episode in the Continuing American Revolution* (Albany: State University of New York Press, 1961). And a prize-winning general history of American art is Oliver W. Larkin, *Art and Life in America*, rev. ed. (New York: Holt, Rinehart and Winston, 1960). For popular culture see Russel Nye, *The Unembarrassed Muse: The Popular Arts in America* (New York: Dial Press, 1970). See also Bernard De Voto, *Mark Twain's America* (Boston: Little, Brown & Co., 1932), Justin Kaplan, *Mr. Clemens and Mark Twain* (New York: Simon & Schuster, Inc., 1966), and Leon Edel, *Henry James* (New York: J.B. Lippincott Co. 1953–1962.)

An excellent survey of industrial growth can be found in Edward C. Kirkland, *Industry Comes of Age: Business, Labor and Public Policy 1860–1897* (New York: Quadrangle, 1967). Thomas C. Cochran and William Miller, *The Age of Enterprise* (New York: Harper & Row, 1968), covers industrial and business expansion since 1800. Roger Burlingame, *Engines of Democracy* (New York: Scribner's,

1940), emphasizes inventions and technology. Stewart H. Holbrook, *The Age of the Moguls (Garden City, N.Y.: Doubleday, 1953), contains entertaining anecdotes and dramatic incidents of the lives of business leaders. William Miller, ed., *Men In Business: Essays in the History of Entrepreneurship (Cambridge: Harvard University Press, 1952), has scholarly studies of the business community. Joseph Dorfman, The Economic Mind in American Civilization 1865–1918, Vol. III (New York: Viking Press, 1949), and Edward C. Kirkland, Dream and Thought in the Business Community 1860–1900 (Ithaca, N.Y.: Cornell University Press, 1956), analyze the dominant ideals in the business world. The trust problem is analyzed in H. R. Seager and C. Gulick, Trust and Corporation Problems (New York: Harper & Row, 1929).

Rendigs Fels, American Business Cycles 1865–1897 (Chapel Hill: University of North Carolina Press, 1959), is an excellent study of the cyclical course of American economic development in post–Civil War America. Samuel P. Hays, *The Response to Industrialism 1895–1914 (Chicago: University of Chicago Press, 1957), studies the impact of industrialism upon American life. Sigmund Diamond, ed., *The Nation Transformed: The Creation of Industrial Society (New York: Braziller, 1963), is an excellent anthology.

Thomas C. Cochran, Railroad Leaders 1845–1890 (New York: Russell & Russell, 1965), studies the attitudes of leading railroad executives on a number of business matters. R. E. Riegel, *The Story of the Western Railroads (Lincoln: University of Nebraska Press, 1964), is the most useful general account of the transcontinentals. Gabriel Kolko, *Railroads and Regulation 1877–1916 (New York: Norton, 1970), has new material on both management and reform. For a recent and significant study of the way businesses were organized and managed see Alfred D. Chandler, The Visible Hand (Cambridge: Harvard University Press, 1977). See also Lewis Mumford, *Technics and Civilization (New York: Harcourt Brace Jovanovich, 1938)

On the businessman see Allan Nevins, Study in Power: John D. Rockefeller, Industrialist and Philanthropist, 2 vols. (New York: Scribner's, 1953), Joseph F. Wall, Andrew Carnegie (New York: Oxford University Press, 1970), Frederick Lewis Allen, The Great Pierpont Morgan (New York: Harper & Row, 1949), and Wheaton J. Lane, Commodore Vanderbilt: An Epic of the Steam Age (New York: Johnson reprint of 1942 ed.), Matthew Josephson, The Robber Barons (New York: Harcourt Brace Jovanovich, 1934), Julius Grodinsky, Jay Gould (Philadelphia: University of Pennsylvania Press, 1957), Andrew Carnegie, Autobiography (Westport: Greenwood Press, Inc. 1920), and John D. Rockefeller, Random Reminiscences of Men and Events (New York: Arno Press, 1909).

The standard work on labor is John R. Commons, et al., History of Labor in the United States, 4 vols. (New York:

Macmillan, 1918–1935). Joseph G. Rayback, A History of American Labor (New York: Free Press, 1959), is an excellent short survey, and Norman J. Ware, The Labor Movement in the United States 1860-1895 (Gloucester, Mass.: Smith, 1959), deals with the Knights of Labor. Terence V. Powderly has left two autobiographical accounts: Thirty Years of Life and Labor 1859–1889 (Clifton, N. J.: Kelley reprint of 1890 rev. ed.), and The Path I Trod (New York: AMS Press, 1940). On the AFL see Samuel Gompers, Seventy Years of Life and Labour, 2 vols. (Clifton, N.J.: Kelley reprint of 1925 ed.), and Phillip Taft, The AFL in the Time of Gompers (New York: Harper & Row, 1957). For industrial workers see David Montgomery, *Beyond Equality (New York: Random House, Inc., 1967). John A. Garraty, *The New Commonwealth (New York: Harper & Row, 1968) has excellent chapters on labor in the Gilded Age and other aspects of life in these years, and Garraty, ed., *Labor and Capital in the Gilded Age (Boston: Little, Brown & Co., 1968) has some of the testimony from the 1883 Senate investigation of that matter. David Brody, *Steelworkers in America (New York: Russell & Russell, 1960) and Stephan Thernstrom, *Poverty and Progress: Social Mobility in a Nineteenth-Century City (New York: Atheneum Publishers, 1968), tell us much about the lives of workingmen.

Ray A. Billington, Westward Expansion: A History of the American Frontier, 4th ed. rev. (New York: Macmillan, 1974), is an excellent survey of the westward movement. See also Thomas D. Clark, Frontier America: The Story of the Westward Movement, 2nd ed. (New York: Scribner's, 1969), Walter P. Webb, *The Great Plains (New York: Grosset & Dunlap, 1957), Clark C. Spence, ed., *The American West: A Source Book (New York: Crowell, 1966), Allan G. Bogue, Thomas D. Phillips, and James E. Wright, eds., *The West of the American People (Itasca, Ill.: Peacock, 1970), and Robert G. Athearn, *High Country Empire: The High Plains and Rockies (Lincoln: University of Nebraska Press, 1956).

Thomas A. Rickard, A History of American Mining (New York: Johnson reprint of 1932 ed.), is a standard account of the miners' frontier. First-class modern studies of the mining frontier are Rodman W. Paul, Mining Frontiers of the Far West 1848–1880 (New York: Holt, Rinehart and Winston, 1963), and William S. Greever, The Bonanza West: The Story of Western Mining Rushes 1848–1900 (Norman: University of Oklahoma Press, 1963). Roy M. Robbins, *Our Landed Heritage: The Public Domain 1776–1936 (Lincoln: University of Nebraska Press, 1962), is excellent on the disposition of public lands. For a classic contemporary account of the mining frontier see Mark Twain, *Roughing It (New York: Harper & Row, 1872), and see also W. T. Jackson, *Treasure Hill: Portrait of a Silver Mining Camp (Tucson: University of Arizona Press, 1963).

On cattle ranching on the Plains see Everett Edward Dale,

The Range Cattle Industry: Ranching on the Great Plains from 1865 to 1925 (Norman: University of Oklahoma Press reprint of 1930 ed.), Lewis Atherton, The Cattle Kings (Bloomington: University of Indiana Press, 1961), E. S. Osgood, *The Day of the Cattleman (Chicago: University of Chicago Press, 1929), and Robert R. Dykstra, The Cattle Towns (New York: Knopf, 1968).

On the cowboy see Philip Ashton Rollins, The Cowboy: An Unconventional History of Civilization on the Old Time Cattle Range (Clifton, N.J.: Kelley reprint of 1936 3rd ed.), Andy Adams, Log of a Cowboy: A Narrative of the Old Trail Days (Lincoln: University of Nebraska Press, 1964), Joe B. Frantz and Julian E. Choate, The American Cowboy: The Myth and the Reality (Norman: University of Oklahoma Press, 1955), and Phillip Durham and Everett L. Jones, The Negro Cowboys (New York: Dodd, Mead, 1965).

William T. Hagan, *American Indians (Chicago: University of Chicago Press, 1961), is a good short survey, and John C. Collier, The Indians of the Americas (New York: Norton, 1947), is an impressive account. Helen Hunt Jackson, A Century of Dishonor (Williamstown, Mass.: Corner House reprint of 1881 ed.), is a powerful contemporary indictment of Indian policy. Two scholarly studies, Loring B. Priest, *Uncle Sam's Stepchildren: The Reformation of United States Indian Policy 1865–1887 (Lincoln: University of Nebraska Press, 1975), and Henry L. Fritz, The Movement for Indian Assimilation 1860–1890 (Philadelphia: University of Pennsylvania Press, 1963), deal with important subjects concerning Indians; and Ralph K. Andrist, *The Long Death: The Last Days of the Plains Indians (New York: Macmillan, 1969), is a vivid account of the Indian wars on the Plains. William Brandon, The Last Americans: The Indians in American Culture (New York: McGraw-Hill, 1974), is a revision with bibliographical annotations of *The American Heritage Book of the Indians (New York: Dell, 1964); it is a portrayal of American Indians in the entire Western Hemisphere from prehistory to modern times. Wilcomb E. Washburn, The Indian in America (New York: Harper & Row, 1975), is a recent general account of the American Indian. For an understanding of Indian reformers see Francis Paul Prucha, ed., Americanizing the American Indians: Writings by the "Friends of the Indians" 1880–1900 (Cambridge: Harvard University Press, 1973), and for a recent comprehensive treatment of Indian wars of the post–Civil War decades see Robert M. Utley, Frontier Regulars: The United States Army and the Indian, 1866–1891 (New York: Macmillan, 1973).

Matthew Josephson, *The Politicos (New York: Harcourt Brace Jovanovich, 1963), is the liveliest and the most comprehensive, but not the most detached, account of the political history of this period. H. Wayne Morgan, From Hayes to McKinley: National Party Politics 1877–1896 (Syracuse, N.Y.: Syracuse University Press, 1969), is a first-rate modern appraisal. A short, worthy account can be found in John A. Garraty, The New Commonwealth 1877–1890 (New York: Harper & Row, 1969), while H. U. Faulkner, *Politics, Reform and Expansion 1890–1900 (New York: Harper & Row, 1959), is a recent synthesis of the nineties. Two excellent sectional studies of politics are C. Vann Woodward, *Origins of the New South 1877–1913 (Baton Rouge: Louisiana State University Press, 1951), and H.S. Merrill, *Bourbon Democracy of the Middle West 1865–1898 (Baton Rouge: Louisiana State University Press, 1953). A brilliant but caustic commentary on the period may be found in the appropriate chapters in Henry Adams, *The Education of Henry Adams, ed. Ernest Samuels (Boston: Houghton Mifflin, 1973). James Bryce, *The American Commonwealth, 2 vols. (New York: Macmillan, 1895), is a classic contemporary account of American government and American politics by a brilliant Englishman. Leonard D. White, *The Republican Era 1869–1901 (New York: Free Press, 1965), traces the federal administrative history of these years.

Vincent P. De Santis, Republicans Face the Southern Question (Baltimore: Johns Hopkins University Press, 1959), traces Republican efforts in these years to break up the Democratic South, and Stanley P. Hirshon, *Farewell to the Bloody Shirt: Northern Republicans and the Southern Negro 1877–1893 (Bloomington: Indiana University Press, 1962), analyzes Republican strategy in the South. Robert D. Marcus, Grand Old Party: Political Structure in the Gilded Age 1880–1896 (New York: Oxford University Press, 1971), is an excellent study of the Republican party and its organizational structure. Keith Ian Polakoff, The Politics of Inertia: The Election of 1876 and the End of Reconstruction (Baton Rouge: Louisiana State University Press, 1973), is an excellent description and analysis of the two major parties in the 1870s and the presidential election of 1876.

Eric F. Goldman, *Rendezvous with Destiny: A History of Modern American Reform, abr. rev. ed. (New York: Knopf, 1956), and Richard Hofstadter, *The Age of Reform: From Bryan to FDR (New York: Knopf, 1955), deal with the mentality of reform. Ari Hoogenboom, *Outlawing the Spoils (Urbana: University of Illinois Press, 1968), surveys the course of the civil service reform movement in this period. John G. Sproat, *The Best Men: Liberal Reformers in the Gilded Age (New York: Oxford University Press, 1971), and Geoffrey Blodgett, The Gentle Reformers: Massachusetts Democrats in the Cleveland Era (Cambridge: Harvard University Press, 1966), are first-class studies of the Mugwumps.

Ray Ginger, *Age of Excess, 2nd ed. (New York: Macmillan, 1975), H. Wayne Morgan, ed., *The Gilded Age, rev. ed. (Syracuse, N.Y.: Syracuse University Press, 1970), and John A. Dobson, *Politics in the Gilded Age: A New Perspective on Reform (New York: Praeger, 1972), are able recent appraisals of the Gilded Age.

The new political history of the late nineteenth century, exploring the ethnocultural forces, is to be found in Richard J. Jensen, *The Winning of the Midwest: Social and Political Conflict 1888–1896* (Chicago: University of Chicago Press, 1971), Paul Kleppner, *The Cross of Culture: A Social Analysis of Midwestern Politics 1850–1900* (New York: Free Press, 1970), and Samuel McSeveney, *The Politics of Depression: Political Behavior in the Northeast 1893–1896* (New York: Oxford University Press, 1972).

Fred A. Shannon, **The Farmer's Last Frontier 1860–1897* (New York: Harper & Row, 1968), examines agricultural conditions and movements after the Civil War. A more recent study is by Gilbert C. Fite, *The Farmers' Frontier* (New York: Holt, Rinehart and Winston, 1966). Allan G. Bogue, **Money at Interest: The Farm Mortgage on the Middle Border* (Lincoln: University of Nebraska Press, 1969), and *From Prairie to Corn Belt: Farming on the Illinois and Iowa Prairies in the Nineteenth Century* (Chicago: University of Chicago Press, 1963), are revisionist views of the credit and farm situation.

The political repercussions of the depression of the nineties are dealt with by the new political history of this decade already mentioned and by George H. Knoles, *The Presidential Campaign and Election of 1892* (New York: AMS Press reprint of 1942 ed.,), and Stanley L. Jones, *The Presidential Election of 1896* (Madison: University of Wisconsin Press, 1964).

John D. Hicks, **The Populist Revolt* (Lincoln: University of Nebraska Press, 1961), is a standard work on populism. It should be contrasted with the revisionist account in Richard Hofstadter, *The Age of Reform*, mentioned earlier; and Hofstadter's revisionist account in turn should be contrasted with those found in Norman Pollock, **The Populist Response to Industrial America* (New York: Norton, 1966), and Walter T. K. Nugent, *The Tolerant Populists: Kansas Populism and Nativism* (Chicago: University of Chicago Press, 1963).

The plight of the black population after Reconstruction has received important attention in a number of studies. Some of the significant ones include Rayford W. Logan, **Betrayal of the Negro: From Rutherford B. Hayes to Woodrow Wilson* (New York: Macmillan, 1965), C. Vann Woodward, **The Strange Career of Jim Crow*, 3rd ed. rev. (New York: Oxford University Press, 1974), and Louis R. Harlan, **Booker T. Washington* (New York: Oxford University Press, 1972).

Some contemporary accounts of the increasing participation of women in American life in the Gilded Age are: Annie N. Meyer, ed., *Woman's Work in America* (New York: Henry Holt & Co., 1891), Thérèse Blanc, *The Condition of Women in the United States* (Abby L. Alger, tr., Boston: Roberts Bros., 1895), Carroll D. Wright, *Working Women in Large Cities* (Washington, D.C.: U. S. Government Printing Office, 1889), and Elizabeth Cady Stanton, Susan B. Anthony and others, eds., *History of Woman Suffrage* (6 Vols., New York and Rochester: C. Mann, 1881–1922).

Modern and more recent accounts of women include Aileen Kraditor, *The Ideas of the Woman Suffrage Movement, 1890–1920* (New York: Columbia University Press, 1965), William L. O'Neill, *Everyone Was Brave: The Rise and Fall of Feminism in America* (Chicago: Quadrangle, 1969), Page Smith, *Daughters of the Promised Land: Women in American History* (Boston: Little, Brown and Co., 1970), Sheila Rothman, *Woman's Proper Place: A History of Changing Ideals and Practices, 1870 to Present* (New York: Basic Books, 1978), and Carl N. Degler, *At Odds: Women and the Family in America from the Revolution to the Present* (New York: Oxford University Press, 1980).

* Denotes availability in paperback.

Time Line

6

THE EMERGENCE OF A MODERN NATION

By the turn of the twentieth century American society embodied a great paradox. The nation's material prosperity was the envy of all Europe, yet most of its social, cultural, and political institutions lagged far behind those of the advanced western countries. Its cultural life was barren or derivative, its educational system a mere shell, and its large pockets of rural and urban poverty a national disgrace. On no level of government—municipal, state, or federal—did public power compare to private economic power. In almost every sphere except the technological the nation's institutions cried for modernization.

The failure of limited government and free market forces to produce either a just or an orderly society sparked two decades of social, intellectual, and political ferment. Out of this ferment emerged a movement—really a set of attitudes—called *progressivism*. It encompassed all aspects of American life, from popular culture through art, philosophy, and political thought, and it began before and lasted long after its arbitrarily assigned dates of 1900 through 1917.

Culturally, progressivism inspired or embraced new modes of expression in music, painting, literature, and architecture. Philosophically, it supplanted the old absolutes with behaviorist and relativist values and goals. Politically, it constructed complex forms of government based on an application of the empirical findings of the maturing social sciences. From the art galleries of New York to the school districts of the rural South, progressivism had succeeded by the end of World War I in modernizing most American institutions and including subtle changes in the thought and outlook of much of the reading public.

In so far as progressivism possessed a unifying force, that force was political. But political progressivism itself was so divided in purpose, support, and leadership that it defies easy generalization. Some progressives were obsessed by the need to improve the order and efficiency of social, economic, and political institutions. Others were driven by compassion to soften the harsh conditions of people's life and labor. Probably most were animated by private concerns that happened to coincide with society's evident needs.

From one perspective, progressives sought to wrest control of politics from both the urban ethnic bosses and the representatives of corporate wealth. From another, they strove to create an informal partnership between the great corporations and the regulatory agencies charged to police them. From a third, they aimed simply to modernize American society. But from a fourth and much more inclusive perspective, progressives aspired to marshal the country's disparate elements—business, labor, agriculture, and professionals—behind a philosophy based on a renewed sense of the commonweal, with a commitment to the well-being of all factions of society. This meant the withering of laissez-faire. It also meant restraints upon the right of both business and private citizens to act without regard to the public interest. Theodore Roosevelt stated the essence of this public interest philosophy at the height of the Progressive Era: "We are for the liberty of the individual up to, and not beyond, the point where it becomes inconsistent with the welfare of the community."

Progressivism was most dramatically expressed in the struggle of Presidents Theodore Roosevelt, William Howard Taft, and Woodrow Wilson to restrict the excesses of big business by attacking monopolies, regulating the food and drug industries, settling industry-wide strikes, and conserving natural resources. These efforts produced a considerable expansion of federal power at the expense of states' rights. They also marked the beginning of the rise of the modern presidency. But on balance, progressivism's most singular accomplishment was the modernization of local, county, and state governments by the creation or expansion of thousands of agencies. Staffed by trained experts and subject only to nominal legislative supervision, these agencies were empowered to make administrative decisions on matters ranging from utilities' rates to inoculation against disease. Without their activities, chaos would have prevailed.

The emergence of the United States as a world power during the Progressive Era added to the tensions induced by the processes of modernization. A minority of progressives believed that the acquisition of far-flung colonies after the Spanish-American War violated the democratic ethos and that meddling in the internal affairs of Latin America distorted the Monroe Doctrine. Geographically isolated farmers and small townspeople could not understand that the nation's burgeoning industrial might make the United States a world force, for better or for worse. The belief of many progressives from 1914 to 1917 that both the Allies and the Central Powers were fighting for economic and territorial advantage made them reluctant to prepare the United States to enter World War I. Cultural sympathies and national rivalries brought over from Europe by millions of new and old immigrants made it difficult to frame a policy consistent with the national interest. Rejection of Wilsonian idealism after the war fostered a partial return to isolation and a reluctance to face the inescapable realities of international power politics.

In general, historical interpretations of the Progressive Era and World War I have reflected the values and perceptions of the times in which they were written. During the 1930s, the Great Depression sparked a revival of economic determinism—the idea that economic factors, rather than political movements, shape and determine the course of history. This Marxist view, together with the relative failure of progressivism in the 1920s and disillusionment about the war, spawned a negative historical judgment of progressivism. By the 1940s judgments had become mixed. Some historians perceived a causal link between the expansion of federal power during the Progressive Era and the much greater expansion of that power under the

New Deal. Others pointed out that progressivism had failed to develop the kind of broad-based political support by labor and agriculture that characterized the New Deal. Meanwhile, the war against Hitler stimulated a favorable reappraisal of American involvement in the First World War.

More recently, the society's failure to resolve the urban, racial, and ecological crises has induced a more cynical reappraisal. By attacking only surface inequities, so New Left historians argue, progressives created an illusion of reform, which actually strengthened the basic economic system instead of altering it.

Much of this same cynicism characterizes a quasi-Marxist interpretation of the progressives' foreign policy. This cynicism stems from more recent disillusionment over the Cold War, the prolonged conflict in Vietnam, and the rise of what President Eisenhower defined as the "military-industrial complex"—a loose alliance of military, industrial, and labor leaders committed to an all-powerful defense establishment. Thus New Left historians regard the United States' Caribbean and Far Eastern policies during the Progressive Era as *prima facie* evidence of the aggressive nature of capitalism. They further contend that economic interests drove the United States into World War I.

The virtual usurpation of the war-making power by a succession of presidential administrations, along with the deception of Congress by several Presidents, has also raised misgivings among traditional liberal historians about the sharp growth of presidential power in the twentieth century. These doubts have been accentuated by the exposure of gross violations of privacy, including the abuse of wiretapping, by the Kennedy, Johnson, and Nixon White Houses, as well as by the FBI and the CIA. The near-success of the Watergate coverup has further renewed historians' respect for the checks against executive power that the Founding Fathers wrote into the Constitution. Finally, the failure of state and federal regulatory agencies to fulfill their promise has prompted a reappraisal of the progressive movement's uncritical championing of "government by commission." By serving business rather than the public, many historians argue, Progressive Era commissions contributed to the rise of what the Marxist historian Gabriel Kolko has termed the "Corporate State."

Nevertheless, many historians continue to defend what they regard as the legitimate growth of state and federal power. They note that the enormous growth of nationwide corporations created an urgent need for an offsetting power responsive to the public interest. They argue that technology mandated the modernization and growth of government as much as it did that of business. They observe that the Great Depression proved the incapacity of small government—especially state and local government—to relieve unemployment. And they point out that a strong federal judiciary was utterly crucial to the long and tortured evolution of both civil rights and civil liberties.

TO THINK ABOUT AS YOU READ . . .

1. Before the Civil War, reform movements had been directed largely at specific social problems in the private sector. Now, between the 1890s and World War I, reform groups supported and won passage of an enormous amount of reform legislation by municipalities, state governments, and the federal government. How do you explain this shift from private to political action?

2. During the Progressive Era, the various

minority groups—such as "new" immigrants from different European countries, blacks, women, and dirt-poor farmers in the South—advanced themselves at different rates. How do you explain this? Why, in particular, did blacks fail to advance at the same rate as others?

3. What ideas most strongly influenced political progressivism? What forces in society produced them, and who pushed them most vigorously? On what issues, if any, did workers, ethnic groups, and industrialists agree? On what issues, if any, did they disagree? What differences were there among progressives themselves?

4. To what degree were the war against Spain and the decision to acquire the Philippines a function of economic considerations? Of other factors? Why do many historians regard the U.S. decision to take the Philippines and to pursue the Open Door policy a tragedy? Do you agree or disagree with them?

5. What was the stake of the United States in World War 1? Why was it virtually impossible to frame a peace treaty responsive to the interests of all the nations concerned? Did this doom the League of Nations to failure regardless of American participation in it? How did different ethnic groups in the United States react to the terms of the Peace?

Chapter 16

Society and Culture in the Progressive Era

THE GROWTH OF THE CITIES

The Flight from the Farm. The population of the cities increased sevenfold between 1860 and 1910. About 30 percent of this increase reflected a movement of native whites, and to a much lesser extent blacks, out of rural areas. Although farm prices rose so high during the Progressive Era that the years 1909–1914 are known as "The Golden Age of Agriculture," the exodus continued through World War I. By 1920 well under a third of all Americans still lived on farms and less than half in rural areas.

Three interrelated factors caused this migration to the cities. Rural births exceeded deaths, output per farmer increased, and the quality of rural life suffered a relative decline.

Just before the Civil War, it took 39 man-hours to produce 40 bushels of corn. By 1894 improved farm machinery had reduced that number to 15. The increase in the efficiency of wheat production was even more dramatic. In 1896 with full mechanization a wheat farmer could harvest 18 times more crop than in 1830. This increase in output per farmer, together with a high rural birthrate and a shortage of good new land, created a surplus of agricultural workers. The rise in output and increase in farm prices also drove up land values disproportionately. These same factors further contributed to a growth in tenancy from 25 percent of all farmers in 1880 to 37 percent in 1910. Partly because of the extraordinarily high incidence of black tenants, South Carolina, Georgia, Alabama, and Mississippi led the nation at between 60 and 70 percent. But even in Illinois the rate stood at 44 percent.

For the more substantial farmers, rural life remained moderately rewarding. But for those on the margins of existence, it became more depressing. Tens of thousands of farm families lived without church, school, or society. Thousands of mothers died in childbirth, and more thousands of children died from privations and inadequate medical care.

Southern farmers fared the worst. Both blacks and whites accepted the recurring fevers and chills of malaria as facts of life, and at least a half million whites were infected, through ignorance of elementary sanitation, with the debilitating hookworm disease. As a distraught southern physician wrote to Theodore Roosevelt, "I would prefer to see my own daughter, 9 years old, at work in a cotton mill than have her live as a tenant on the average southern tenant one-horse farm."

In 1909 the privately financed Rockefeller

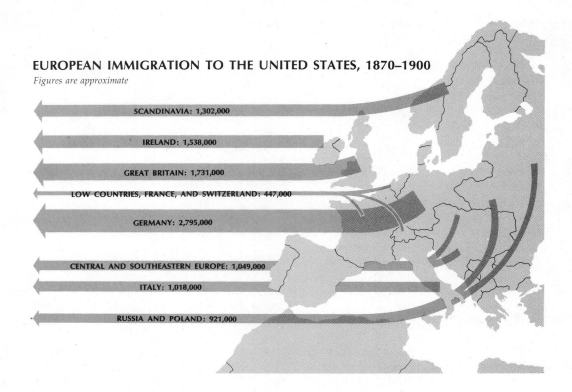

EUROPEAN IMMIGRATION TO THE UNITED STATES, 1870–1900

Figures are approximate

SCANDINAVIA: 1,302,000

IRELAND: 1,538,000

GREAT BRITAIN: 1,731,000

LOW COUNTRIES, FRANCE, AND SWITZERLAND: 447,000

GERMANY: 2,795,000

CENTRAL AND SOUTHEASTERN EUROPE: 1,049,000

ITALY: 1,018,000

RUSSIA AND POLAND: 921,000

Sanitary Commission opened a campaign that eventually wiped out the hookworm disease, and in 1912 the United States Public Health Service began a prolonged assault on malaria. But by then a generation or more of dirt-poor Southerners had lost all opportunity for normal development.

The New Immigrants: Problems and Achievements. The wave of "new immigrants," discussed in the previous unit, continued to rise until the outbreak of World War I. Between 1901 and 1914 some 3 million Italians, 1.5 million Jews, and 4 million Slavs poured into the United States. The relatively high literacy rate of male Jews and the skills they had learned in eastern European villages enabled them to adapt quite readily to urban economic and social life. But most new immigrants came from peasant backgrounds

and were ill-prepared for city life. A small number of Poles, Bohemians, and Italians settled on run-down farms, which their superior diligence and use of women and children in the fields made into productive units. But the lack of transferable skills forced most to take menial jobs in overcrowded cities or grime-ridden industrial and mining towns.

No society could have absorbed so many disparate people without social tension. Nor could any society have adequately housed such vast numbers upon arrival. One result—and the one most often emphasized—was a pronounced increase in social and economic discrimination. Next to Jews, Orientals suffered most. But all immigrants, including the Germans, Scandinavians, and Irish, who still came in large though sharply reduced numbers, suffered in degree.

Much of the social tension was rooted in

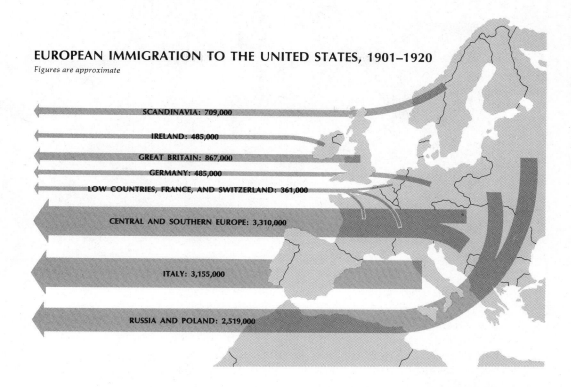

EUROPEAN IMMIGRATION TO THE UNITED STATES, 1901–1920

Figures are approximate

SCANDINAVIA: 709,000

IRELAND: 485,000

GREAT BRITAIN: 867,000

GERMANY: 485,000

LOW COUNTRIES, FRANCE, AND SWITZERLAND: 361,000

CENTRAL AND SOUTHERN EUROPE: 3,310,000

ITALY: 3,155,000

RUSSIA AND POLAND: 2,519,000

class and economic rivalries. Old-stock employers, for example, often used the most recent immigrants as strike breakers. They also kept certain ethnic groups from management positions in many industries. Conversely, members of a particular ethnic group would establish themselves in a certain occupation and close out other ethnic strains. In fact, virtually all ethnic groups discriminated to some degree against each other: German Jews against east European Jews; Germans against Slavs; Norwegians against Swedes; Irish against Italians, Slavs, Jews, and even French-Canadians.

Much of the tension was also religious. As such, it long antedated the American experience. Conflict between Catholics and Protestants went back to the Reformation; that between Christians and Jews, to the Roman Empire. Thus most of the Jews who came to the United States during this period were fleeing systematic discrimination and even outright persecution—both official and unofficial—by Rumanians, Russians, Ukrainians, and Poles, just as many Irish had earlier fled Ireland because of their long economic repression by the English. It is a tribute to the openness of American society and its institutions, including the absence of a state church, that discrimination proved mild on balance, at least by European and Oriental standards.

Meanwhile the rise of racist theory in Europe, much of it popularized in the United States, gave a pseudo-intellectual cast to the notion that the old immigrants from northwestern Europe were inherently superior and that the new immigrants should be refused entry. Even John R. Commons, progressive economist, Christian layman, and zealous friend of labor, favored immigration restric-

Public education was an important route of upward mobility for many ethnic groups. These adult immigrants are studying to become naturalized American citizens.

tion on genetic grounds. Markedly higher scores by northern Europeans on the crude intelligence tests then coming into use gave a further veneer of scientific truth to these views. Not until after the new immigration had ended did more sophisticated research indicate that cultural and environmental factors such as urban or rural origin, family occupational and educational background, and quality of schooling figured crucially in intelligence test scores.

Actually, the heavy environmental emphasis of reform Darwinism led many progressives to remain skeptical of the more sweeping racist theories. Unlike conservatives, they equated race more with culture than genetics, though they also believed that excessive immigration enabled employers to hold down wages and feared that immigrants from nondemocratic countries would not readily be assimilated, partly because many constituted a kind of migrant work force. In 1908, more Italians and Hungarians returned to their homelands than entered the United States.

Progressives strove, nevertheless, to "Americanize" those who were here and to give them a measure of political representation. "I grow extremely indignant at the attitude of coarse hostility to the immigrant," Theodore Roosevelt wrote privately in 1906:

I have one Catholic in my Cabinet . . . and I now have a Jew . . . and part of my object in each appointment was to implant in the minds of our fellow Americans of Catholic or Jewish faith, or of foreign ancestry or birth, the knowledge that they have in this country just the same rights and opportunities as every one else.

Yet probably a majority of progressives joined conservatives and the American Federation of Labor in supporting a literacy test designed to curtail the new immigration drastically. Passed four times and vetoed four times—by Cleveland in 1896, Taft in 1913, and Wilson in 1915 and 1917—it was finally enacted over Wilson's second veto in 1917.

Most new immigrants tended to enter lower-class occupations, obscuring another development of great importance. They, or at least their children, moved from unskilled to skilled jobs with the same or higher frequency as old-stock whites of the same economic class. Many also became homeowners with somewhat greater frequency, though Jews invested much more heavily in education than housing. But whether as owners or renters, most immigrants gravitated toward the familiar. Virtually every American city developed neighborhood pieces of Europe—"Little Italy," "Little Polonia," and so forth. Through foods, music, customs, and ways of looking at life, these distinctive settlements enriched American culture as a whole and helped transform the United States into a partially pluralistic society.

Education and Social Mobility.   Public education served as the broadest avenue of upward mobility in American society. For cultural and economic reasons, not all ethnic groups took that route in the same proportions. For the same reasons, most old-stock whites in the South and many in rural areas elsewhere did not take it either. But for those who did, including numerous sons and daughters of substantial Midwestern farmers and rural and small-town clergymen, it opened new social and economic opportunities.

The most notable advances were made by urban Jews. Despite the impoverishment of many of their immigrant parents, Jewish youngsters—especially males—graduated from high school in much higher proportions than the offspring of most other ethnic groups. One result was a lower delinquency rate; another, adequate preparation for college. In 1908, at a time when Jews made up about 2 percent of the population, male Jews of the first and second generations comprised 8.5 percent of the male student bodies at seventy-seven major colleges and universities. By the next generation they constituted a disproportionately high percentage of physicians and lawyers in the larger cities. This led to the institution of quotas at many private colleges—though not public ones—and a drive by the American Bar Association to eliminate night law schools.

The teaching profession itself became an agency of upward mobility for rural whites and blacks, for small-town Americans of older stock, and for urban Jews and Irish, especially in New York and New England. Teaching in grammar and secondary schools was one of the few careers open to women, and the proportion of female teachers rose from 70 percent in 1900 to 85 percent in 1920—though males maintained a firm hold on higher-paying administrative positions. In the colleges and universities, moreover, women were probably subjected to even greater discrimination than were Jews.

The Modern City.   If one word were to characterize the new urban society, it would be *mass*—mass transit, mass entertainment, mass circulation of written matter, mass education, mass production, and mass distribution.

In transit, the electric streetcar and the commuter train hastened the breakup of mixed residential sections in or near the city's core. The upper classes moved out first, but in time even clerks and factory workers bought or rented bungalows and flats in three-story frame houses far removed from offices and plants. Most new neighborhoods and suburbs had discrete ethnic and religious identities, but they tended to be more socially stratified than the old ones. No longer, for example, did workers, managers, and professionals reside on the same block, though all might live, say, in the new Irish or Jewish neighborhood. Meanwhile the vacated residences were replaced by new stores and plants or occupied by the latest immigrants and newly arrived rural families, both white and black.

Not until after World War I would the outlines of the modern city's central problem—loss of industry, tax base, and gainfully employed residents—become perceptible. During the Progressive Era many cities retained administrative cohesiveness by annexing suburbs, while the growth of small businesses, great department stores, and white collar industries like insurance and banking actually increased city tax bases. New civic leaders emerged among the offspring of the immigrants and the rural old stock and, especially, from the ranks of professional men, usually lawyers. Through much of the period America enjoyed an urban renaissance, characterized by beautifying movements, administrative reforms, improved schools, and new or expanded parks, playgrounds, libraries, museums, and zoos.

THE RISE OF MASS CULTURE

The Growth of Spectator Sports. The city further stimulated interest in mass spectator sports—football, boxing, and baseball. By the turn of the century the Yale-Princeton football game was drawing between thirty and forty thousand fans, the Army-Navy game had become a national event, and Walter Camp's "All-America" selections were an annual feature of the sports pages. The winning of the heavyweight boxing championship in 1909 by a black, Jack Johnson, induced race riots. His defeat in 1915 by a white, Jess Willard, brought a kind of national celebration. Six years later a new champion, Jack Dempsey, drew 80,000 fans and the first million-dollar gate in a bout in Jersey City. But it was baseball that came closest to being the national pastime.

Major league attendance climbed from 4.75 million in 1903 to 9 million in 1920. Through most of the period it was in fact the game of both the classes and the masses. Participation in the major leagues, though hardly the minor ones, also enabled many old-stock, small-town boys and Irish and German urban youths to escape dreary lives in the mills or factories. Significantly, throughout these years blacks were barred from organized baseball, as the white leagues were known.

The greatest "stars" of the era included Ty Cobb, a fiery Georgian whose .367 career batting average is still unequaled; Honus Wagner, probably the finest all-round player ever; Walter Johnson, whose 413 pitching victories, 110 shutouts, and 3499 strike-outs remain modern records; and gentlemanly Christy Mathewson, who won more than thirty games in three separate seasons and pitched three shutouts in the World Series of 1905. So attached to the game was the American male that the revelation that the Chicago White Sox had "thrown" the 1919 World Series drove the Red Scare (see Chapter 20) off the front pages. A year later, "Babe" Ruth, formerly a superb pitcher for the Boston Red Sox, transformed the game by hitting 54 home runs for the New York Yankees.

Motion Pictures. Movies were one of the rare popular amusements to come up from the masses rather than down from the classes. They began in the 1890s as extra attractions in cheap variety houses, and in 1905 found their own home in nickelodeons. Here the working class—both native-born and immigrant—embraced the new medium. When subtitles flashed on the screen, those in the audience who could read English often read them aloud to their neighbors. For many of the foreign-born, the movies offered a course in Americanization.

By 1910 motion pictures were playing to a weekly audience of 10 million in 10,000 theaters across the nation. With few exceptions American movie-makers fixed their sights firmly on the mass market, turning out films that delivered a good laugh or a good cry, some hair-raising excitement, or steamy passion (an un-American phenomenon portrayed by exotics like Theda Bara and Rudolph Valentino). American directors displayed an early awareness of the medium's technical potential, and beginning with D. W. Griffith's *The Birth of a Nation* in 1915, they created some great spectacles.

America's silent movies celebrated traditional moral values in sentimental and melodramatic clichés, but they also revealed a good-humored, street-smart cynicism. Besides seeing virtue triumph, movie fans could see the police portrayed as bumbling idiots (the Keystone Kops) and the high and mighty brought low by the plucky urchin (Mary Pickford) or the cheeky rogue (Douglas Fairbanks). Master of this subversive theme was the comic genius, Charlie Chaplin, one of the few silent stars who appealed to both sophisticated and unsophisticated tastes.

Popular Reading. Taste in reading matter was much like that in movies, though popular literature lacked the movies' cynical strain. Russel Nye writes of the pulp magazines, which replaced the dime novel by 1910: "Pulp stories were frankly mass-produced items, written to a rather rigid formula, never realistic, never disturbing, never disappointing. War could never be grim, a hero must never show fear, airplanes could never have accidents . . . courtship must end in marriage." By 1915 pulp magazines, led by *Argosy*, were enjoying monthly sales in the millions.

On a somewhat higher plane stood the better Western novels. Foremost among their authors was the Zanesville, Ohio, dentist Zane Grey. He published his first success, *Riders of the Purple Sage,* in 1912, then went on to write seventy more. Among mystery writers, Mary Roberts Rinehart was queen. Influenced by the domestic novel and the Gothic tale, as well as by both the stories of Edgar Allen Poe and Sir Arthur Conan Doyle's Sherlock Holmes, she added a parallel love story (always with a happy ending) to the crime story. The most successful popular novelists of the time were Gene Stratton-Porter, whose sentimental stories sold millions of copies, and Harold Bell Wright, who offered action and inspiration as well as sentiment. The most widely read poet of the era, the unassuming Detroit newspaperman Edgar A. Guest, was really a versifier whose talent lay in the expression of commonplace emotions and experiences in colloquial rhymes.

Today even more than the movie fare of that period, the most popular reading matter seems singularly innocent and unsophisticated. Ordinary Americans were beginning to have some leisure time, and their quest for diversion in reading led them to romance, moral uplift, and happy endings. But their tastes were not unremittingly mediocre. They also read with enthusiasm the books of Jack London and other authors whom the critics approved.

Music. Technology, mass distribution, and increases in per capita income also affected America's musical patterns. As early as the 1890s mass-production techniques made pianos available to people of moderate means, and the sale of sheet music consequently soared. In 1909, 5 million copies of "Meet Me Tonight in Dreamland" were sold and the following year 8 million of "Let Me Call You Sweetheart." Yet even as more and more Americans gathered around the piano in the parlor, Thomas Edison's recently developed phonograph was sounding the comparative decline of this homemade music-making. When given the choice, most people chose to listen rather than play or sing, and by the outbreak of World War I sales of phonograph records had skyrocketed while those of pianos and sheet music had plummeted. But the decline in participation in music-making was partly, perhaps largely, offset by the dance craze sparked by the glamorous husband-and-wife team, Vernon and Irene Castle, who came to New York in 1912. Soon almost every good restaurant had an orchestra and a dance floor and every middle-class party a phonograph and dance records.

Some of the new music was indigenous, and much of it was worth listening to. The first important development was highly syncopated ragtime, which crossed the color line late in the 1890s. Shelton Brooks write ragtime's most famous song, "The Darktown Strutter's Ball," and Scott Joplin, a Texas-born black, emerged as its finest composer. Hardly had ragtime captured the popular imagination than it was challenged by the blues, which evolved from black Southern folk music and became popular in white circles following the issuance of W. C. Handy's "Memphis Blues" in 1913. A black minister's son from Alabama, Handy composed several other classics, including "Beale Street Blues" and that perennial favorite, "St. Louis Blues."

Journalism. Another aspect of the new urban culture was Yellow, or "People's," Journalism. It began with the purchase of the *New York World* in 1883 by Joseph Pulitzer. Sports coverage was greatly expanded, comic pages were introduced, murders and sex crimes were reported in gruesome detail, and scandals of all sorts were given featured treatment. In fifteen years the *World's* circulation increased from 15,000 to 1.5 million. During the Progressive Era, Pulitzer and the *World* turned responsible, though the paper continued to be lively and popularly written. Meanwhile, Pulitzer's arch-rival, young William Randolph Hearst, perfected the new sensationalism in a nationwide chain of newspapers and magazines. The most demagogic of the mass-circulation publishers, Hearst forced his editors to promote his political ambitions and to propagandize his shifting political views. He was especially adept at catering to the passions and prejudices—religious, political, and even ethnic—of his largely lower-middle-class urban readers.

Concurrently, Adolph Ochs, scion of a Southern German-Jewish family, was transforming *The New York Times* from a partisan editorial sheet to "a newspaper of record." Under Ochs' aegis, *The Times* focused on nonsensational news in commerce, education, the arts, government, and foreign events. Its circulation remained small, for its stodgy make-up appealed only to the better educated. Nonetheless, editors and publishers the nation over subscribed to the *Times*, and its broad coverage and high reportorial standards had a pronounced effect upon the more highly principled of them.

Muckraking. Of more direct relevance to the emerging progressive movement was the rise of investigative reporting. In 1902 a group of journalists, later dubbed "muckrakers" by Theodore Roosevelt, began to publish articles about social, economic, and political problems in such middle-class magazines as *McClure's, Collier's, Everybody's,* and *Cosmopolitan.* Their subject matter ranged from the traffic in prostitutes to the perversion of democracy in city halls, statehouses, and the United States Senate. Their output varied greatly in quality. Some writers, like Ida M. Tarbell, who carefully documented the impersonal ruthlessness of John D. Rockefeller and his associates in the *History of the Standard Oil Company* (1904), established standards of research and reporting that few journalists have ever surpassed. Others resembled David Graham Phillips, author of *The Treason of the Senate* (1906), whose innuendo and misrepresentation obscured much of the real truth that underlay his work.

One muckraker, Lincoln Steffens, brought to his work extraordinary insight into contemporary practices of American politicians, businessmen, and ordinary citizens. His two chief contributions were *The Shame of the Cities* (1904) and *The Struggle for Self-Government* (1906). Steffens was neither unaware of the defects of character that made public officials accept bribes nor indifferent to the moral lassitude that made average citizens indulgent of bad government, but he was much more interested in the bribe givers than in the bribe takers. Refusing to cater to anti-immigrant biases, he showed that the old-stock Republican machine in Philadelphia was more corrupt than Irish-dominated Tammany Hall. He revealed that in Rhode Island rural Yankee legislators, not urban Italians, had sold out to the streetcar and other interests. He described how the Pennsylvania Railroad in New Jersey and the Public Service Corporation of that state had contrived to have the New Jersey legislature perpetuate low taxes and other special privileges for railroads and public service corporations.

The muckrakers' analysis of political corruption confirmed progressive leaders' belief that the American republic must be reformed or become a businessman's oligarchy, and the widespread circulation of their articles helped to create the support necessary for successful political action.

ARCHITECTURE, PAINTING, AND LITERATURE

Architecture.   The two most innovative architects of this period, Louis Sullivan and Frank Lloyd Wright, were too sophisticated for popular taste. Although Sullivan continued to do distinguished work until after World War I, his commissions became more and more infrequent. Meanwhile, a number of talented designer-engineers built functional and often esthetically inspiring bridges and factories of steel and reinforced concrete. But most architects and their businessmen-clients emphasized form rather than function. The overwhelming majority of the buildings of the era were more banal than creative, more pretentious than graceful. The same held for private houses. Sullivan, Wright, and a few others did imaginative work but most new construction was eclectic. When historical styles such as Cape Cod, Georgian, or Greek Revival were used, the end product almost invariably violated the lines and proportions that had given the originals their distinction.

Sullivan attributed this failure of taste to the appeal of the Roman façades, false monumentalism, and harmonious lagoons of the Great White City fashioned for Chicago's Columbian Exposition of 1893. "The damage

. . . has penetrated deep into the . . . American mind," he wrote, "effecting there lesions of dementia." More likely, however, the Exposition's imperial style touched the same impulses for grandeur that ordained the acquisition of an empire after the war with Spain in 1898.

Sullivan's student, Frank Lloyd Wright, also failed to exercise much immediate influence on the American skyline. "Early in life," Wright once wrote, "I had to choose between honest arrogance and hypocritical humility. I chose honest arrogance." Wright further developed Sullivan's concept of "organic" architecture. Professing a regional style (he was in fact influenced by the Japanese), he designed from the inside out, always emphasizing the unique texture of his materials. He used native woods, horizontal planes, and deep overhangs and often succeeded brilliantly in harmonizing his buildings with their natural surroundings. As early as 1900 the *Architectural Review* recognized Wright's genius, and by 1905 his work had deeply affected the modern movement in Germany, Holland, and France. But only as his ideas were brought back to the United States by Europeans like Walter Gropius did Wright make a vigorous imprint on American architecture. Meanwhile, the skilled traditionalists Stanford White, Ralph Adams Cram, and their disciples continued both to form and to reflect the widespread preference for Roman and Gothic.

Ironically, the maligned Columbian Exposition had a much greater impact on progressive public policy than did the works of Sullivan and Wright, the true intellectual progressives. Its classic spaciousness sparked a nationwide movement to beautify American cities. Uncounted urban open spaces were converted into parks, and sums commensurate with the nation's wealth were poured into public buildings. Unfortunately, little attention was given to the flow of traffic, and even less to the needs, interests, and habits of pedestrians. Almost always, moreover, the buildings erected were more derivative than original in design.

Painting. "There is a state of unrest all over the world in art as in all other things," the director of the Metropolitan Museum complained in 1908. "It is the same in literature, as in music, in painting, and in sculpture." This was the year that eight young painters, spearheaded by the realists Robert Henri, George B. Luks, and John Sloan, protested against the National Academy's near blackout of their work and staged a private show in New York. They rebelled not against the old painting techniques—they never mastered the new ones—but against the class bias that failed to see reality in all human activity, including the seamy. Their work of social protest grew more out of the political ferment of the era than the revolution in art forms that had already swept Europe. Inevitably, Victorian-minded critics dismissed them as "apostles of ugliness," "the revolutionary gang," "the black gang," and, most often, "the ashcan school."

Meanwhile, more creative European currents were beginning to affect American artists. By 1912 the work of the Postimpressionists was familiar to sophisticated habitués of the New York gallery of the revolutionary camera artist Alfred Stieglitz. The next year 1600 paintings, drawings, prints, and pieces of sculpture representing almost every mode in modern art appeared in a spectacular show at the New York Armory. Picasso, Matisse, Brancusi, Duchamp, Kandinsky, Cézanne, Van Gogh, Gauguin, and others had their work displayed, to the extreme discomfort of conservative critics. *The New York Times* labeled the show "pathological." *Art and Progress* compared many of its artists to "anarchists, bomb-throwers, lunatics, depravers." And an official of the Chicago Law and Order League demanded that the exhibition be banned from his city because the "idea that people can gaze at this sort of thing without it hurting them is all bosh."

The vehemence of the conservatives' criticism and the desperation of their counterattack served only to underscore their artistic bankruptcy. As the art historian Sam Hunter writes, "They were soon unable to pose with real conviction or enthusiasm a possible alternative, since even the art they defended was becoming a retarded and diluted academic derivative of some form of modernism." Nevertheless, the public proved as slow to accept the highly individualized abstractionism of the new painters (including the Americans Max Weber and John Marin) as it did the architecture of Sullivan and Wright.

The Novel. The trend toward realism in literature, begun in part by Henry James, continued in his own late works and in the novels of Willa Cather, author of *O Pioneers!* (1913) and *My Antonia* (1918), and Edith Wharton, whose novels of manners include *Ethan Frome* (1911) and *The Age of Innocence* (1920), a story of New York high society.

Meanwhile, Jack London and Frank Norris were writing the survival-of-the-fittest doctrine into a host of brutal novels ranging in subject from the individual's struggle against the elements to the battle with the trusts. But it was in the writings of Theodore Dreiser, the era's only literary giant, that naturalism, as literary determinism was called, proved most profound. The son of German Catholic immigrants who settled in Indiana, Dreiser early disavowed belief in religion and conventional morality. "Man was a mechanism," he wrote, "undevised and uncreated, and a badly and carelessly driven one at that." Yet Dreiser, no less than his predecessors, was a moralist at heart. All his work was charged by a tension between determinism and its antithesis. In the very act of denying free will and the importance of man, he affirmed them. "To have accepted America as he has accepted it, to immerse oneself in something one can neither escape nor relinquish, to yield to what has been true and to yearn over what has seemed inexorable," this, concludes Alfred Kazin, "has been Dreiser's fate and the secret of his victory."

Dreiser's first novel, *Sister Carrie* (1900), was withdrawn by his publisher because of its harsh reception. Critics, many of whom objected to the novel's sympathetic treatment of a "fallen woman," failed to see that its account of the purposelessness of life was counterbalanced by its emphasis on life's sheer vitality. His second book, *Jennie Gerhardt* (1911), like *Sister Carrie* the story of an otherwise virtuous "kept woman," struck at the failure of the conventional moral code to correspond to reality. Similar themes pervaded *The Financier* (1912) and *The Titan* (1914), though they were widely regarded as progressive indictments of the "robber barons."

Poetry. The years before World War I also witnessed a remarkable renaissance in poetry. Perhaps the most powerful voice was that of Edwin Arlington Robinson, a traditionalist who dealt with the abiding theme of the individual's search for God and truth amidst darkness and suffering. Robinson failed in his quest. Life and human destiny remained mysterious. Yet in the "black and awful chaos of the night" he felt "the coming glory of the Light." Rescued from obscurity by Theodore Roosevelt, who gave him a government sinecure after reading his *Children of the Night* (1897), Robinson failed nevertheless to receive full recognition until after the war.

By 1912, the year Harriet Monroe established the magazine *Poetry* in Chicago, a renaissance was at hand. Vachel Lindsay, now remembered more for his jazz-like odes than his sensitive lyrics, published his "General William Booth Enters into Heaven" in the first issue of *Poetry*, then went on to exalt the common people in numerous other works. Edgar Lee Masters, Clarence Darrow's law partner, startled traditionalists with his masterpiece, *Spoon River Anthology*, in 1915. There he laid bare the sham and moral shabbiness of small-town America in a brilliant compound of irony, sadness, and humor which closed paradoxically, on an affirmative note. A year later Carl Sandburg's first important volume appeared. A Whitmanesque romantic who employed free verse, Sandburg glorified Chicago as the roaring, brawling butcher and steel-maker to the world. During these same years Robert Frost was writing deceptively simple verse against a rural New England backdrop that masked his passionate, almost terrifying, life-force.

At the same time another revolt against the genteel tradition was brewing among a group of American and English poets in London, the so-called imagists. Led by Ezra Pound and Amy Lowell, they asserted that the poet should re-create impressions caught in the fleeting image. Holding that meter and rhyme made the creation of a pure image difficult, if not impossible, they reject these confining conventions. They also dismissed Romanticism as being the literary expression of a decadent humanistic culture. They were soon joined by T. S. Eliot, whose now classic "The Love Song of J. Alfred Prufrock" met a hostile reception when first published in *Poetry* in 1915.

TWO MILESTONES

Women and Woman Suffrage. The modest changes in the status of women that had brought coeducational education to two thirds of the nation's colleges and universities by the 1890s continued through the Progressive Era. The revolution in morals commonly ascribed to the 1920s had actually become a subject of social commentary well before World War I. Divorce became common, and though divorcees remained "tainted," by 1916 one marriage in nine was ending in divorce, as compared to one in twenty-one in 1880.

Meanwhile, working-class men, especially Irish, were deserting their families in appalling numbers. By 1920, despite religious scruples and high legal costs, the working-class divorce rate equaled that of the middle class.

Concurrently, the percentage of married women employed outside the home rose to 10.7 by 1910, as the number of working women passed 6 million. And the concept of "equal pay for equal work" even received a brief trial during the war, though the hostility of unions and the widespread belief that women's employment should be regarded as temporary or supplementary soon restored the old order.

Intellectually, Charlotte Perkins Gilman of the famous Beecher family levelled the era's most penetrating attack on prevailing sexual and familial arrangements. Woman's survival, wrote Gilman, depended on her ability to seduce and hold a husband; "men worked to live . . . /while/ women mated to live." Among many other solutions, Gilman proposed complete emancipation of women from domestic duties through the establishment of day nurseries.

Conceivably, as William R. Leach has recently argued, most early feminists privately believed that release from male sexual and economic domination of the family was the central issue of the women's movement and that the demand for suffrage was part of that. But probably Eileen Kraditor is also correct in holding that many feminists had no interest "in lowering women's moral standards to the

Florence Kelley: Social Feminist

The divisions within the women's movement are nowhere more sharply shown than in the life of Florence Kelley. A handsome, large-headed woman who dressed in black and refused to wear stays, she stood for protective legislation for working women against those who demanded full equal rights at the cost of such protection. Born in Philadelphia in 1859, she was a descendant of Quaker botanist John Bartram. Her father, Congressman William D. Kelley, was a former Jacksonian Democrat who left the party over slavery in 1854 and later earned the sobriquet "Pig Iron" for his vigorous defense of the protective tariff. An early advocate of woman suffrage, he encouraged Florence, the only one of his six daughters to survive infancy, to attend Cornell.

Although Florence's senior thesis on the legal status of children was published in the *International Review* the summer of her graduation in 1882, she was refused admission to the University of Pennsylvania graduate school because of her sex. She then enrolled at the University of Zurich, the first European university to admit women. There she became a socialist in the belief that Marxism explained both the cruel treatment of children, which she had earlier

level of men's," and the majority of Americans certainly continued to believe "that the family, not the individual, constituted the basic unit of society." Each home existed as a " 'state in miniature.' It had only one head—the husband—and he alone represented it in the world outside."

Most working women labored out of economic necessity, and their particular concerns were addressed by the most celebrated feminists of the era—Jane Addams, Lillian Wald, Florence Kelley—and by thousands of less well-known figures. (See "Florence Kelley: Social Feminist.") Whatever their private views on male domination, the social feminists, as this group is termed by historians, acted in the tradition of *noblesse oblige.* Working out of Chicago's Hull House and

New York's Henry Street Settlement, they strove to help immigrant women adjust to American life while maintaining their personal dignity by preserving the best of their own cultures.

More important—for the settlement movement reached only a comparative few—the social feminists both inspired and did much of the tedious research behind hundreds of state and federal laws prescribing working conditions for women, children, and even men. Time and again their testimony before state and congressional legislative committees tipped the balance. "If I wanted to put a measure through—no matter how silly or outrageous—," grumbled an arch conservative West Virginia assemblyman, "I would simply get a handsome woman—with a sort of

observed in England, and American slavery, as her Quaker relatives had described it to her. She also entered into correspondence with Marx's collaborator, Friedrich Engles, and later translated his *The Condition of the Working Class in England in 1844.*

While at Zurich, Florence married a Russian socialist medical student, Lazare Wischnewetsky, and bore the first of three children. In 1886 the couple went to New York and Wischnewetsky tried, with mediocre results, to establish a medical practice. They joined the Socialist Labor Party, but the Europeans who dominated the local group mistrusted her and soon expelled both of them, presumably because Florence was as explosive and hot-tempered as she was dedicated and nondoctrinaire. Meanwhile she bore two more children. Then, following several years of estrangement from her husband, induced partly by financial problems, she moved to Illinois to obtain a divorce under the state's more permissive laws. At first she lived in Jane Addams' Hull House while the children lived at the home of the reformer Henry Demarest Lloyd in Winnetka. After the divorce Florence resumed her maiden name and reunited the family in an apartment near Hull House.

Kelley's energy, incisiveness, and wit won her quick entry into Hull House's inner circle. As Addams wrote, she "galvanized us all into more intelligent interest in the industrial conditions about us." In 1893, largely in consequence of Kelley's lobbying, the state legislature enacted a statute to limit hours of work for women, prohibit child labor, and control tenement sweatshops. Appointed Chief Factory Inspector by Governor John Peter Altgeld, Kelley braved a smallpox epidemic to inspect sweatshops and once received a warning shot outside a factory.

Although her annual reports kept conditions before the public, prosecution of violators proved so difficult that she took a law degree in the evening division of the Northwestern University Law School in 1894. Three years later Altgeld's conservative

cheerful ring in her voice—to come down here & lobby for it."

Meanwhile the long struggle for woman suffrage was drawing to a successful conclusion under the leadership of Carrie Chapman Catt. A superb organizer and skilled politician of broad social concerns, Catt had served from 1900 to 1904 as Susan B. Anthony's successor in the presidency of the National American Woman Suffrage Association. She then put her unflagging energies into mobilizing suffrage sentiment in the states and, in 1915, to helping Jane Addams organize the Woman's Peace Party. Catt returned to the presidency of the N.A.W.S.A. the following year to combat the divisive tactics of Alice Paul's militant splinter group, the Woman's Party, and to confront the mounting opposition of conventional women to the movement for suffrage.

Publicly, at least, the suffragists justified the vote for women in terms of broad social and political policy. Their arguments frequently overlapped, and their emphases shifted with time and place. But, in general, several distinct approaches emerged. The social feminists contended that suffrage would produce a more just and compassionate society and even eliminate war. As Addams said, a woman cannot care properly for her family if she has no voice in making the laws and electing the officials who determine whether her home has pure water, fresh food, proper sanitation, and adequate police protection. Others, more politically conservative and probably more representative of suffragists as

successor dismissed her. Kelley continued to work out of Hull House two more years, supporting her family by working evenings at the John Crerar Library. Then, in 1899, she and the children moved to Lillian Wald's Henry Street Settlement in New York, and Kelley became executive secretary of the newly formed National Consumer's League.

The League strove to persuade consumers to press for improved working conditions, and under Kelley's forceful leadership it became one of the most effective reform agencies of the Progressive Era. At its height it had sixty leagues in twenty states. "No gentle saint," in the words of one of her intimates, Kelley gave her opponents no quarter. She favored "direct assault" but was not averse to "guerilla" tactics. Legislators shrank under the fury of her scorn and the power of her magnificent presence. "She had the voice and presence of a great actress," noted Frances Perkins, "though she was far from theatrical in her intentions."

By 1913, mainly because of Kelley's efforts, nine states had adopted minimum wage legislation for women. Meanwhile she had assembled much of the medical and sociological data on the differences between men and women which Louis D. Brandeis incorporated in his defense of Oregon's ten-hour-day law for women in *Muller* v. *Oregon* (1908).

The death of Kelley's only daughter from heart disease in 1905 seemed to give a special urgency to her abiding interest in the welfare of children. She played an important role in marshalling support for a federal children's bureau in 1912, the child labor bill of 1916, and the Sheppard-Towner maternity-aid measure of 1921. Irritated by Samuel Gompers' lack of interest in social legislation, she wrote him off as an "aged Dodo." Nor could she contain herself when the Supreme Court struck down state minimum wage legislation and the second child labor act early in the

a whole, argued that suffrage would reestablish Anglo-Saxon domination of urban politics and clean out corruption. Professional women tended to put the case almost solely in terms of career discrimination. Protestant church women, and most social feminists as well, argued that the women's vote would assure national prohibition legislation. Only a small minority of fervent radicals boldly declared that suffrage would enable women to free themselves of male domination within marriage.

By 1917, Catt's tactics had already won substantial support in the states, and the suffragists were urgently pressing most of the above considerations on Congress. Many congressmen—probably most—were privately unsympathetic. But by mounting pressure on them from within their home districts, shrewdly aligning themselves with the prohibitionists, and capitalizing on the Wilson administration's desire for wartime unity, Catt's forces persuaded the House to approve a federal suffrage amendment in January 1918. Eighteen months later a lobby-wearied Senate also submitted, and within fifteen months three fourths of the states had ratified the Nineteenth Amendment. In simple declarative language it stated that the right to vote should not be abridged "on account of sex."

Margaret Sanger and Birth Control. The swirling cross-currents of the turbulent women's movement engulfed the movement for birth control. Until well into the Progres-

---

1920s. Why, she asked, are "seals, bears, reindeer, fish, wild game in the national parks, buffalo, migratory birds, all found suitable for federal protection; but not the children of our race and their mothers?"

Kelley long served as vice-president of the National Woman Suffrage Association, partly in the conviction that municipal government and services would not be cleaned up until women got the vote. She had felt since 1885, however, that the N.W.S.A was preoccupied with problems of middle-class women, and she feared that the proposed Equal Rights Amendment of the twenties would wipe out the hard-won protective legislation for lower-class working women by eliminating laws based on the physical differences between men and women. "How cruel . . . ," she wrote, "is the pretension of certain organizations of professional and business women to decide for the wage-earners . . . what statutory safeguards they are henceforth to do without."

Kelley was equally scornful of the new Woman's Party's refusal to fight against the disfranchisement of blacks in the South. "An inglorious ideal of equality this!" she expostulated. "Acquiescence in the disfranchisement of millions of women, provided only that the men of their race also are deprived of their constitutional rights."

Kelley continued her leadership of the National Consumers' League and her campaign for social justice until her death. She maintained a nominal social affiliation over the years, prompting one conservative United States senator to declare in the 1920s that her proposed child labor amendment "derived straight from the communist manifesto of 1848." Yet, partly because of her Quaker heritage, she lacked the requisite temperament to be doctrinaire on anything but pacifism. More an activist than a theoretician, she believed that the moral sensibilities of the middle classes—especially women—would eventually bring the reforms she sought. She died from anemia in 1932, too early to see the partial harvest that came with the New Deal.

Mrs. Carrie Chapman Catt and another prominent suffragist, Dr. Anna Shaw, head a parade of 22,000 suffragists who marched in New York to win ratification of the Nineteenth Amendment.

sive Era Protestants and Catholics alike had regarded artificial contraception as a violation of the law of God, and by 1914 twenty-two states had anti-birth control statutes on their books. By then the shift to an industrial society had made large families an economic liability, especially in towns and cities. This latter reality had already induced a decline in the birth rate, notably among old-stock urban whites in the middle and upper classes. For the most part, this decline reflected natural controls.

So strong was the consensus against contraceptives at this time that Congress banned the dissemination of birth control information in interstate commerce in 1914. This ban provoked a bitter reaction, in particular among younger radical feminists and extreme political leftists—for different reasons. The

feminists saw contraception as a form of emancipation or as a means to reduce men's sexual exploitation of women. Those on the political left believed that capitalists wanted more births in order to create a surplus of labor and thus keep down wages. The views of these two groups fused in the early career of Margaret Sanger, who for forty years served as the knife's edge of the movement for birth control.

"A passionate romantic," according to her biographer, David M. Kennedy, Sanger was the daughter of an Irish-born workingman, an all-round iconoclast who had renounced his Catholicism. In 1912, following the death of a working girl from a self-induced abortion, Margaret stripped off her nurse's uniform and emerged as *l'enfant terrible* of the birth-control campaign. Inspired at first by the anarchist

Emma Goldman, she was also encouraged by William D. "Big Bill" Haywood of the radical Industrial Workers of the World, Eugene V. Debs of the Socialist party, and women's liberation groups.

Early concluding that the marriage bed was "the most degenerating influence in the social order" because it made sex-chattels of wives, Sanger declared that women "are determined to decide for themselves whether they shall become mothers, under what conditions, and when." Soon she was urging women to stop producing children "who will become slaves to feed, fight and toil for the enemy—Capitalism." Then, in 1916, she defied the law by opening a birth-control clinic in New York. Tried and found guilty, she won a partial victory on appeal in 1918 when the court's opinion gave physicians somewhat greater latitude to prescribe contraception.

Sanger's agitation broadened the movement's base. Partly in the conviction that smaller families would raise the standard of living of the poor, middle-class reformers organized the National Birth Control League in 1915. Two years later the philosopher John Dewey drafted a measure to make contraceptives freely available—to which the New York State legislature refused to give serious consideration.

Meanwhile eugenicists took up the cause in the persuasion that mental defectiveness was transmitted through the genes and could be greatly reduced through birth control. The ranks of these eugenicists included some of the most blatant racists and conservative elitists in the country. But as Kennedy writes, their greatest strength came from "people who saw daily the tragic consequences of hereditary disease—social workers, public health officers, charity workers, and supervisors of institutions for the defective."

Buoyed by the support of these and other respectable figures, Sanger began to abandon her socialist rationale for birth control. "More children from the fit, less from the unfit—that is the chief issue," she announced in 1919. Marxism, she contemptuously asserted in 1922, is "purely masculine reasoning."

Nevertheless, religious opposition to contraception remained vigorous—and among the lower classes, effective—through the 1920s. The Catholic Church became increasingly militant in its defense of the Papacy's standing disapproval of contraception, and it was not until 1931 that a major Protestant body—the Federal Council of Churches of Christ—formally endorsed birth control. Long before then, however, large numbers of Protestant clergymen had become silent converts to the movement.

By the mid-twenties the use of contraceptives was commonplace among middle-class Protestants, Jews, and non-church people. Old-line radical feminists like Charlotte Perkins Gilman were continuing to hold that only procreation justified intercourse, but there was wide acceptance among non-Catholics of the newer generation's contention that it should also be indulged in for reasons of pleasure. In time, even Margaret Sanger was counseling women to develop their distinctively feminine qualities to the utmost.

The Triumph of National Prohibition. The informal alliance of the suffragists and prohibitionists arose out of considerably more than convenience. As Norman H. Clark observes in his perceptive revisionist synthesis, *Deliver Us from Evil,* the prohibition movement aimed to "protect the values sheltered by the American nuclear family" at a time when it seemed that its security was more urgent to society's well-being than were the rights of individuals. Alcoholism had been a "WASP" (White Anglo-Saxon Protestant) problem since the founding of Jamestown, and Southern Baptist and Northern Methodist women had long been in the vanguard of the movement to restrict the indiscriminate use of liquor. By 1900 thirty-seven mainly rural Protestant states had enacted local option laws. In 1907

Oklahoma, an old-stock territory with a minuscule foreign population, came into the union with a completely dry constitution. And by 1919 ten of the twelve states in which women could vote had outlawed the saloon.

These facts suggest that prohibition's much remarked anti-ethnic and anti-Catholic thrust was more incidental than causal. Only because many Germans happened to be heavy beer drinkers and many Irish heavy whisky drinkers did the movement become identified as a "nativist" crusade. Pietist immigrants from Sweden supported prohibition vigorously, as did many Reformed and other non-Lutheran Germans. A group of priests organized the Catholic Clergy Prohibition League, and Father J. J. Curran served twenty-five years as a national vice-president of the Anti-Saloon League. The bishop of Montana, a state where hard drinking was notorious among Irish miners, even observed that prohibition would contribute to the "spiritual progress of the Catholic Church" in America.

Neither was prohibition an essentially rural phenomenon, despite its successes in rural states. Most sponsors of local option laws were town or city people, and most members of the W.C.T.U. and the Anti-Saloon League were urban. As Clark writes, "behind them in solid support were the deep ranks of urban business leaders, labor leaders, attorneys, physicians, teachers—both Catholic and Protestant." They stood behind them because, like their counterparts in Finland, Scandinavia, Germany, Britain, France, and the province of Quebec, all of which had serious temperance movements, they perceived alcoholism to be a grave social problem.

They realized, of course, that saloons served as workingmen's clubs. But they also saw that many embodied the worst features of urban industrial culture: "blatantly and aggressively masculine to the mood of a sneering *machismo*, linked sordidly to organized crime, organized prostitution, and the organized herding of mercenary voters." Hardly a social feminist with first-hand knowledge of the saloon's impact on family life and urban politics failed to support prohibition, probably with the silent support of hundreds of thousands of workingmen's wives.

New scientific evidence on the linkage between alcoholism and brain damage further strengthened the prohibition movement in business and professional circles. Physicians prescribed alcohol less frequently, and in 1914 a national meeting of psychiatrists and neurologists actually pronounced it a poison. At the same time, numerous investigations by social scientists revealed relationships between alcohol and crime, prostitution, and poverty. By

The prohibition movement gained momentum through the informal alliance of suffragists and prohibitionists. This poster urges the closing of saloons, which many thought were a serious menace to family life.

1916, as Clark concludes, science, no less than organized religion, had prepared the way for total abstinence.

Nevertheless, the moderate prohibitionists would probably have settled for a ban on hard liquor. But the so-called wets, who were liberally financed by the hard liquor industry as well as by German-American beer interests, stiffened dry lines by refusing to compromise. Soon after the United States entered the war, the War Department gave the prohibitionists an important victory by banning the sale of alcoholic beverages near army camps. When the Eighteenth Amendment, banning the manufacture, sale, and transportation of intoxicating liquor, still left it to Congress to define what was "intoxicating," prohibitionists won inclusion of beer and wines by playing up the need to conserve grain. The amendment, adopted by Congress in December 1917, went into effect in January 1920.

THE INSTITUTIONS OF CHANGE

Technology and Business. Chief among the many forces that made the Progressive Era a period of extraordinarily rapid change were technology and scientific management. In manufacturing, mechanization and time-and-motion-saving techniques pioneered by Frederick Winslow Taylor helped production to increase 76 percent between 1899 and 1909, while the labor force expanded only 40 percent. In organization and distribution, managerial innovations created nationwide markets.

In the automobile industry, assembly-line production enabled Henry Ford to cut the price of his Model T from $950 to $290. By 1917 almost 5 million vehicles were clogging a partially macademized highway system. By then, too, a 7-million telephone network had wrought a revolution in communication, and some fifty corporate research laboratories were forging another revolution in product development. Meanwhile the use of electricity

grew so fast that by the end of World War I it powered more than half of American industry and had spawned a booming appliance industry.

Not all the effects proved salutary. Skilled workers were downgraded in older industries like steel and textiles, and the dehumanizing efficiencies of the assembly lines made virtual automatons of everyone but supervisors in many of the newer industries. On the other hand, real wages in manufacturing rose 37 percent from 1897 to 1914 and rose again during the war. Outside the factories, moreover, the number of skilled workers—electricians, plumbers, carpenters, tool makers, automobile mechanics, and heavy equipment operators—grew greatly. An increase in the clerical and sales work force from 3 percent in 1880 to 8 percent by 1910 also raised the number of reasonably challenging jobs. Nor was that all. Increased wages, together with the spread of truck gardening, the rise of the citrus industry, and increased use of refrigerated railroad cars, induced a marked improvement in diet. By the early 1900s the average American worker and his family were consuming twice as much meat, to say nothing of citrus fruits, as their British counterparts.

Modernizing the Government. Years before the Progressive Era began, thoughtful observers of the American scene agreed that the art of government had not kept pace with the science of industry. Progressives proposed, consequently, to apply the techniques of business management to the bewildering complexities of the new urban and industrial society. With remarkable unanimity, they turned to experts—scientists, engineers, economists, physicians, political scientists, and social workers—for information, political support, and personnel to staff new or enlarged departments and regulatory commissions.

By the end of the era much of American

government had become thoroughly modernized and professionalized. Graduate engineers were planning and operating municipal sewer and water systems. Trained medical personnel were combating disease by enforcing public health measures. Experts with Ph.D.s in agronomy, chemistry, and other sciences were engaged in research sponsored by the Department of Agriculture at land-grant universities and experimental stations. Even police and fire department recruits, traditionally trained on the job, were attending newly founded academies.

Politically, the modernization of government increased the distance between the average citizen and the decision-makers. This doubtless contributed to a decline in voter turnout, one of the most pronounced trends of modern times. But the social benefits were almost incalculable. In the twenty years before the United States entered the war, advances in medical science and sanitation combined with improvements in diet to reduce the death rate from 17 to 12.2 per thousand and to increase life expectancy from 49 to 56 years.

THE SOCIAL SCIENCES

Psychology and Economics. By undermining classical economics, the psychology of this period powerfully influenced progressive thought and attitudes. Freed from its old metaphysical and theological commitment by the Darwinian revolution, psychology had begun to explore the whole range of human activity. By World War I two definite schools—the instinct and the behaviorist—had emerged. Both were European in origin, and both found a receptive audience in the United States.

The founder of the instinct school in America, William McDougall, felt strongly that psychology should concern itself with social behavior. He contended that humans were ruled by deep-seated instincts rather than by rational or moral considerations. And his charge that classical economic theory was "a tissue of false conclusions drawn from false psychological assumptions" reinforced the insights Thorstein Veblen had already written into his *Theory of the Leisure Class* (1899). In *The Instinct of Workmanship and the State of the Industrial Arts* (1914) Veblen echoed McDougall's strictures against the inadequate psychological base of classical economics. He especially charged that modern industrial institutions had failed to play upon people's constructive instincts. F. W. Taussig argued in *Inventors and Money-Makers* (1915) that the instinct of contrivance, or workmanship, did not depend necessarily on prospective gain, as the defenders of the profit-making system contended, but rather on the satisfaction of making something. But however much instinct psychology undermined classical economic thought, it produced no systematic theory of its own as a substitute.

The behaviorist psychology of the Russian Ivan Pavlov and the Americans E. L. Thorndike and John B. Watson proved both more receptive to, and more reflective of, progressive thought because it supported an environmentalist interpretation of society. Passing over everything that could not be verified by direct observation, the behaviorists sought to measure all human behavior in terms of stimulus and response. "It is the business of behavioristic psychology," wrote Watson, "to be able to predict and control human activity." Since consciousness was not observable, it should not be studied; thought was to be treated as latent speech.

Behaviorism offered too restricted and shocking a view of human nature to win universal acceptance. Humanists rejected it angrily. Nevertheless, it sired a school of psychology still powerful today and markedly influenced all subsequent social science. It also contributed enormously to both the hard and soft sides of progressivism—to the production efficiencies of Taylorism, and to the reformers' belief that the poor were the

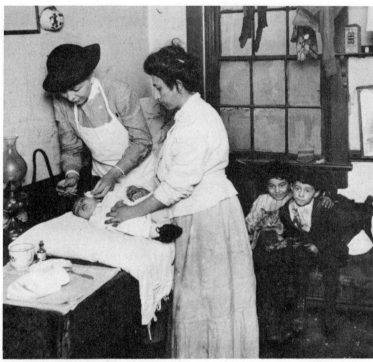

Courtesy Chicago Historical Society

Public health measures greatly reduced infant mortality. Here an Infant Welfare nurse examines the baby of an immigrant mother in her tenement home about 1913.

victims of their environment. Behaviorism further contributed to the rise of the consumer society by giving an intellectual base to the manipulative skills of advertisers.

The New History. The writing of history proved no more immune to progressive currents than did other disciplines. Nor did it escape their paradoxes. The influence of German methodology, first felt at Johns Hopkins, continued as historians now severed their ties with literature almost completely. Seeking scientific truth by the use of rigorously exact techniques, they destroyed hallowed beliefs, stripped history of its individual drama and romance, and lost their popular audience. Yet they added immeasurably to the general body of knowledge and contributed important new insights about the forces that had molded America.

The foremost characteristic of the new history was present-mindedness. As James Harvey Robinson and Charles A. Beard confessed in their pathfinding *The Development of Modern Europe* (1907), they had "consistently subordinated the past to the present" in the "ever-conscious aim to enable the reader to catch up with his own times." Implicit in this approach was a belief in laws of behavior as formulated by social scientists. The insights of philosophers, poets, and observers no longer sufficed. Implicit, also, was a desire to use history to create a better future. This last was not new: From Thucydides historians had concerned themselves with the usable past. By Robinson and Beard's time, however, probably a majority of America's professional historians had conceived their task as being merely descriptive. It was against them and their failure to search for causal explanations that might indirectly bear on the present—to be, in the new view, truly scientific—that Robinson and Beard revolted.

"The Constitution," Beard wrote in *An Economic Interpretation of the Constitution* (1913), "was essentially an economic document based upon the concept that the fundamental private rights of property are anterior to government and morally beyond the reach of popular majorities." He then set forth data to prove that through their interest in public securities, money, manufacturing, trade, and shipping, the framers of the Constitution had stood to gain directly from the establishment of the new government.

Beard insisted that his work was American-inspired. James Madison, he repeatedly pointed out, had offered "one of the earliest, and certainly one of the clearest" statements of economic determinism. But as Morton G. White observes, Beard's *An Economic Interpretation of the Constitution* actually reflected the worst, or at least the simplest, aspects of both Marx's and Madison's thought. Thus Marx neither denied man's capacity for high-minded action or accepted the idea that every political action derived directly from an economic interest. Conversely, Madison believed with Aristotle that factions and interests were rooted in human nature—not, as Marx contended, in economic systems. In Beard's analysis the framers had been moved by a narrow Marxist view of the deterministic force of economic systems and a similarly narrow Madisonian view of a direct relationship between self-interest and action. Recent scholarship has demolished, or at least seriously challenged, the evidence on which Beard based his economic thesis.

Beard always denied that he had written a tract for the times. "I simply sought to bring back into the mental picture of the Constitution," he said, "those realistic features of economic conflict, stress and strain, which my masters had, for some reason, left out of it, or thrust far into the background as incidental rather than fundamental."

Whatever his intentions, the work drove deeper the wedge between progressives and conservatives. In the span of a decade many people's attitudes toward the Constitution and the judiciary that upheld it had moved from reverence to begrudged respect to unbridled contempt. Perhaps the fairest judgment of Beard's work is the one that Roosevelt passed on the Armory Exhibition of Modern Art: "The necessary penalty of creativity is a liability to extravagance."

PROGRESSIVE EDUCATION

Public Education. The higher educational level required for entry into business and government inevitably transformed the public school system. Every strand of progressivism from the quest for order through the cult of efficiency to the belief in equal opportunity entered into the transformation. By the end of the era the foundations and much of the superstructure of modern education had been firmly established.

In 1900 the upper classes sent their children to private schools or had them tutored, and except for a few middle-class sections of large cities the public school system was in deplorable condition. Politics, corruption, and incompetence were rife. Rote instruction, over-sized classes, and an out-of-date curriculum were the rule. Teachers were poorly prepared and even more poorly paid, averaging $42.15 a month—less than the wages of a day laborer. In the South, three years schooling was the norm; in the North, seven years. Southern states spent $9.72 per pupil each year, Northern states $20.85.

The most pronounced changes occurred in the South, which experienced an educational revival comparable to the one that had swept the North before the Civil War. By 1910 school budgets had doubled, the enrollment of white children had risen almost a third, and the school term had lengthened from five to six months. White illiteracy had also declined from 11.8 to 7.7 percent.

Southern public schools generally were poor; those for black children the worst. In this Kentucky school over half the students are absent doing farm work.

Nowhere, however, did the increase in expenditures affect all social and economic classes equally. Even in the richest states of the North, dependence on local taxation produced wide disparities between rural, small-town, suburban, and metropolitan appropriations. Old-stock whites in the remote areas of upper New England and western New York frequently fared worse than immigrants in the large cities. Within the urban systems, the middle-class composition of school boards also produced inequities. Almost invariably, facilities tended to be poorer and student-teacher ratios higher in lower-class and ethnic neighborhoods.

Discrimination fell heaviest, of course, on blacks. Although they managed to decrease their illiteracy rate from 44.5 to 30.1 percent during the first decade of the century, no Southern state (and no Northern one either) made a conscientious effort to give black

people equal facilities. By 1910 only 8251 black youths were attending high school in the entire Southeast. As late as 1915 South Carolina was spending $13.98 annually for each white child and only $1.13 for each black one.

Meanwhile, an exceptionally high drop-out rate, especially among immigrants' children, prompted a wave of compulsory attendance laws and curriculum changes. Some progressives believed that early employment deprived children of their birthright. Others feared that lack of schooling would create a permanent urban proletariat.

Virtually all recognized that the technological society required greater education for everyone. Vocational and commercial high schools were established in the larger cities with strong business support and, after 1917, federal subsidization. In single-high-school towns, manual training and commercial courses were offered. For numerous reasons, including the failure of equipment and instruction to keep abreast of developments in industry, the vocational schools never flowered. But for years thereafter, the commercial courses produced a steady flow of male bookkeepers and female typists and stenographers.

In keeping with the spirit of the times, basic changes in the aims and methods of teaching accompanied the upgrading of physical facilities in the public schools. The most distinguished educational theorist of this period was philosopher John Dewey, a disciple of William James (see Chapter 13). Born in 1859 in Vermont, Dewey taught at the Universities of Michigan, Chicago, and Columbia and remained an influential and active force in American thought until his death in 1952.

To Dewey, valid thinking and understanding had to be based on one's own experience. Thus he abandoned authoritarian teaching methods and the use of rote practice. Subject matter, he felt, should be adapted to the needs and capabilities of children, and learning processes should be centered on their own experience and discovery. They should "learn by doing," inquiring and drawing their own generalizations instead of memorizing someone else's.

To foster such learning, he wrote in *School and Society* (1899), "means to make each one of our schools an embryonic community life, active with types of occupations that reflect the life of the larger society, and permeated throughout with the spirit of art, history, and science." Such schooling, he believed, would advance democracy and develop intelligence as a tool for social reform. The development of vocational education was in keeping with Dewey's interest in practical education.

Against the sustained and often irrational opposition of traditionalists, Dewey and his followers accomplished one of the major cultural revolutions of the century. By the end of World War I, Teachers College of Columbia University was well on the way to inculcating a new generation of teachers with a potentially creative approach to teaching. Dewey's most influential work, *Democracy and Education,* appeared in 1916. Three years later the Progressive Education Association was organized to advance the dynamic new program.

As in most creative changes, the costs proved high. Traditionalists within the universities failed at first to grasp the intellectual foundation of the reconstruction of primary and secondary education, thus forcing departments and colleges of education to organize without the help of the liberal arts faculties, who might have exercised a leavening influence on the new education curricula. At the same time, state teachers' colleges began to supplant the two-year normal schools. Directed by professional educators, they offered so many overlapping education courses as to make a mockery of the word *education*. On no level—B.S., M.S., or Ph.D. —did the quality of an education degree compare favorably with that of a degree in one of the traditional disciplines.

Higher Education. Colleges and universities were favorably influenced by the deepening of knowledge, the specialization induced by the new technology, and their own growing commitment to excellence. The quality of graduate and professional study rose notably. States greatly expanded their aid to higher education. Municipal colleges and universities multiplied. Major strides occurred in adult education. And between 1900, when the Association of American Universities was founded, and 1914, the total enrollment in colleges and universities nearly doubled, increasing from 109,929 to 216,493.

Concurrently, the status and salaries of college professors rose and the percentage of Ph.D.s increased. The principle of academic freedom was also receiving wider and wider acceptance, except for some notorious violations during the war. The improvements reflected in part the influence of the American Association of University Professors, organized in 1915. But in the main they marked the coming of age of American higher education.

Increased specialization, expanded research opportunities, and freedom to create led to great contributions to almost all areas of knowledge. By the end of the Progressive Era American scholarship had surpassed European scholarship in some fields and equaled it in many others. But once again the cost proved high. The social sciences developed their own vocabularies, often unnecessarily. And scientists, physicians, and engineers lost contact with the humanities and social sciences because of their need to specialize early in their undergraduate careers.

Legal education was beset by the same paradoxes. Pre-law training was steadily upgraded; by World War I two years of undergraduate work was a common requirement for admission to reputable law schools. But except in a handful of schools attached to the great universities, the nature and theory of law were largely neglected. Even though a law degree became a virtual prerequisite for election to public office, most law schools turned out little more than competently trained technicians.

Medical education, which had become a national scandal, underwent a dramatic upgrading following publication of Abraham Flexner's searching report for the Carnegie Endowment in 1910. For a few years progressive elements of the medical profession showed interest in institutionalizing medical service to the poor. By 1919, however, entrepreneurial attitudes had become dominant within the already powerful American Medical Association. Proposals for the mildest forms of socialized medicine (medicare) were fiercely repelled, and the United States' record of treatment of the poor, both black and white, became one of the worst in the Western world. Conversely, advances in medical science,

education, and technology, including an enormous hospital-construction program, put American care of the middle and upper-middle classes among the world's best.

In agriculture, federal grants-in-aid to land-grant colleges underwrote invaluable research in crops, soil properties, and conservation practices. County agents and farmer's institutes sponsored by university extension services also brought scientific knowledge to farmers themselves, though the more poorly educated and less prosperous farmers generally resisted it. In the long term, these developments sharply increased the quality and quantity of agricultural production. But they also spurred the growth of commercial farming and the increase in tenancy earlier noted.

CHURCH AND SOCIETY

Protestantism. The social and intellectual ferment of the Progressive Era affected religion and its institutions in profound and sometimes paradoxical ways. Organizations like the Young Men's Christian Association, the International Sunday School Association, and the American Bible Society blurred denominational lines, while fundamentalism, modernism (the attempt to reconcile contemporary scientific thought and traditional religion), and the Social Gospel cut across them. After 1908, the formation of the Federal Council of Churches of Christ in America by thirty-three evangelical bodies created a loose unity among their 17 million members.

Yet the Northern Presbyterian church preserved the purity of its doctrines only by expelling several of its most distinguished ministers and losing control of its leading seminary, Union, in New York to the modernists. Modernist clergymen also captured many Northern Baptist, Congregational, and Methodist congregations, while perhaps a majority of intellectuals left the church in spirit.

Rural migrants to the city decisively rejected

modernism. Uncomfortable in sophisticated urban congregations and uninterested in theological subtleties, they throve on the thundering fundamentalism of the Reverend Billy Sunday and a wave of revivalism that swept the established evangelical churches. Many became enthusiastic converts to Pentacostalism, to Holiness churches, and to the Jehovah's Witnesses. Many also responded to exhortations by spellbinders like the Baptist Russell Conwell to accept the prevailing social and economic order. In a thousand sermons the country over, Conwell affirmed the virtue of getting rich—"to make money honestly is to preach the gospel."

Conversely, a small but growing minority of urban ministers and laymen transformed the Social Gospel into a powerful progressive force during the prewar years. They agreed with the Congregational clergyman George Herron that the dualism of contemporary life was intolerable:

A corporation, greedy, godless, vicious in many of its operations, consists of men famous for their piety and benevolence. A nation governed by men of eminent Christian character goes mad with the spoils of unrighteousness. . . . A church containing many sincere, teachable, self-sacrificing Christians is as powerless a moral institution in the community as the town pump.

In 1908, one year after the publication of Walter Rauschenbusch's most important work, *Christianity and the Social Crisis*, the Methodist Episcopal Church came out for abolition of child labor and for a host of other reforms. Though they rejected his Christian Socialism, they accepted his graphic analysis of the brutalizing impact of the new industrial order. In that same year the newly organized Federal Council of Churches of Christ called for the end of exploitative capitalism by a program of social-welfare legislation.

The Social Gospel movement quickened many lay consciences and raised profound questions about business ethics and the morality of the laws of the marketplace. It thus broadened and strengthened the moral foundations of the progressive movement. Nevertheless, the countertruth remains: Evangelical Protestants spent more energy campaigning for prohibition and against parochial schools than they did in fighting exploitation of their fellow men and women.

Catholicism. Partly because of the Roman Catholic Church's authoritarian structure and partly because of the still low educational level of most of its members, the Catholic Church in America remained clear of the conflict over modernism that rocked Protestantism. For millions of immigrants, it was the one familiar institution in an alien culture. Despite the drop in membership during the Gilded Age, Poles and other workers supported the Catholic Church with much greater zeal than was being shown in Europe.

Assuredly, Catholicism was beset by other problems. A group of dissident Poles founded the National Polish Catholic Church in 1907. Italian males gave the Church only nominal support and broadly refused to send their children to parochial schools. There developed an acute shortage of priests of the same ethnic background as their parishioners. Then, after that problem began to be resolved, conflict ensued over whether instruction in the parochial schools should be in English or in the language of ethnic origin.

New immigrants also resented bitterly the reluctance of the Irish to share their domination of the Church hierarchy. Finally, public support of parochial education was resisted by non-Catholics and not sanctioned by American legal institutions, subjecting many Catholics to a heavy financial burden. But in spite of these difficulties, Church membership and parochial education grew rapidly throughout the entire period.

Although Catholic working people gave greater support than Protestants to the welfare aspects of progressivism, the Social

Gospel movement had slight impact on the Church as an organization. The Paulist priest, economist, and political scientist, John A. Ryan, emerged as one of the era's more influential reformers following publication of his *A Living Wage: Its Ethical and Economic Aspects* in 1906. Pope Leo XIII's charge in *De Rerum Novarum* (1891) that "a small number of very rich men have been able to lay upon the masses of the poor a yoke little better than slavery itself," also spurred uncounted parish priests to compassionate works. But the hierarchy's militant philosophic and theological conservatism, and especially its sharp perception of the Church's need for acceptance by the conservative Protestant business establishment, caused most bishops to continue to ignore the encyclical.

Judaism. Some developments within the Jewish community paralleled those within Protestantism and Catholicism. By 1900 the mainly German-Jewish immigrants of earlier years had risen in extraordinary numbers into the middle, upper-middle, and professional classes. Fearful that the great influx of Jews from eastern Europe would compromise their own hard-won social position, they were repelled by the political radicalism of many of the newcomers combined with what they regarded as the newcomers' "crude" religious Orthodoxy. They turned first to immigration restriction, then to paternalistic programs of uplift. Although tension persisted into the next generation and beyond, it was eased by modifications in Orthodox practices as the east Europeans became Americanized and educated. Late in the period, moreover, many of the more successful Orthodox Jews moved to the suburbs and joined Conservative congregations in a blend of Orthodoxy and German Reform Judaism. And large proportions of highly educated Jews—even more than Protestants—abandoned religion in all but name.

No comparable Social Gospel movement emerged within Judaism in America, partly because Jews came to the United States with a more refined sense of community than most old-stock Americans. Proudly, the German-Jewish social agency, the United Hebrew Charities, reported in 1900 that it had taken care of almost every poverty-stricken Jew it had found. Just as Jews made a disproportionately large contribution to the nation's cultural and intellectual life, they also supported the humanitarian aspects of progressivism with an intensity and strength out of all proportion to their numbers.

LEGAL AND POLITICAL MAIN CURRENTS

Sociological Jurisprudence. The vast changes in American thought and institutions wrought by progressivism were mirrored in the law. Admittedly, the old absolutes died hard. Not until the new industrial problems became acute did the liberating force of Oliver Wendell Holmes' *The Common Law* begin to be felt. Not until judges came abreast of the new pychological and sociological currents did a progressive synthesis begin to be formed.

In crudest form the new accommodation reflected the judiciary's realization that since it lacked the power of the purse or sword, it could not indefinitely hold back a nation bent on reform. As the humorous newspaper commentator "Mr. Dooley" phrased it, "Th' Supreme Court follows th' ilection returns." But in its broadest and highest form it reflected the same impulses that had inspired the progressive movement in general—the quest for social justice, the belief in progress, the urge to create, and the faith in science. Thus Harvard's Dean Roscoe Pound, who synthesized the historical insights of Holmes, the methodology of the social scientists, and the pragmatism of James and Dewey, conceived of the law as an agency for social reconstruction:

The sociological movement in jurisprudence is a movement for pragmatism as a philosophy of law;

for the adjustment of principles and doctrines to the human conditions they are to govern rather than to assume first principles; for putting the human factor in the central place and relegating logic to its true position as an instrument.

In spite of lingering opposition, the force of these and similar ideas was immediate and widespread, though hardly pervasive. Judges began to probe beyond the crime into its social or psychological origins and to view juvenile delinquency as environmental rather than hereditary in origin. Children's courts, modeled on one that Judge Ben Lindsey established in Denver, spread throughout the nation and even in Japan.

The law also began to adjust creatively, though again slowly, and inadequately, to labor problems. The common law concepts of "fellow-servant rule," and "contributory negligence" had made workers, not employers, liable for most industrial accidents. But these withered away as the courts upheld liability and workmen's compensation laws grounded on sociological realities. No one put the case more graphically than Roosevelt in a remarkable message to Congress on January 31, 1908:

It is hypocritical baseness to speak of a girl who works in a factory where the dangerous machinery is unprotected as having the "right" freely to contract to expose herself to dangers to life and limb. She has no alternative but to suffer want or else to expose herself to such dangers. . . . It is a moral wrong that the whole burden of the risk incidental to the business would be placed with crushing weight upon her weak shoulders.

Nevertheless, the Court struck down the Child Labor Act of 1916, and it ruled numerous state statutes unconstitutional. Yet, as a recent student of the Supreme Court concludes, many constitutional historians exaggerate in calling the period one of unrestrained judicial conservatism. The Court did uphold most of the basic progressive legislation of the period even though much of

About 1900 the concept developed that perhaps not all delinquency originated in heredity. Children's courts were established to protect youngsters like these homeless boys photographed by Jacob Riis in New York.

this legislation struck at the core of the free enterprise system—for example, at an employer's right to fix prices and wages.

Political Thought. While Dewey, Pound, and Beard were reconstructing education, law, and history, Herbert Croly, later one of the founders of the progressive weekly, *The New Republic*, was calling for a reconstitution of politics. He charged that the existing system was geared to the interests of the wealthy minority. The remedy, he concluded, was to infuse the political order with the new social and psychological concepts.

In *The Promise of American Life* (1909), Croly accepted the charges of Veblen and the instinct psychologists that industrialism had repressed the finer human instincts. He directed his fire, accordingly, at laissez-faire capitalism's basic precept—the belief that freedom to pursue individual gain leads inevitably to social progress. In words that came close to paraphrasing Theodore Roosevelt's presidential messages of 1907 and 1908, Croly called for the replacement of individualism by social togetherness. By the exercise of self-discipline, said Croly, people must create a community loyal to an ideal—a nation-state that would fulfill humanity's great promise.

Believing in big business' potential for good and despairing of the Democrats' devotion to states' rights, Croly at first fastened on the Republican party as the vehicle to achieve his purposes. He considered Roosevelt almost the ideal statesman: "The whole tendency of his programme is to give a democratic meaning and purpose to Hamiltonian tradition and method. He proposes to use the power and resources of the Federal government for the purpose of making his country a more complete democracy in organization and practice."

Like Roosevelt, however, Croly finally concluded that Republican nationalism served big business interests almost exclusively. In 1912 his *The Promise of American Life* became Theodore Roosevelt's "Bull Moose" party's bible and Croly its prophet.

By the end of the Progressive Era, most of these social, intellectual, and economic currents were influencing Washington in greater or lesser degree. Moving upward from the unions in some cases, downward from business in others, and in from the universities in almost all, they usually affected local and state politics first. Often, as in education and birth control, local and state influences remained strongest. On other matters, notably regulation of national corporations, Congress became preeminent. But in most instances, local, state, and federal governments divided responsibilities.

Chapter 17

The Forging of Modern Government 1900–1917

PROLOGUE TO CHANGE

Enter Theodore Roosevelt. On a September afternoon in 1901, at the Pan-American Exposition in Buffalo, New York, a young anarchist shot President William McKinley at close range. Eight days later the President died. Vice-President Theodore Roosevelt took the President's oath and the old order began to give way to what was to become known as the Progressive Era. It was symbolized at first by Roosevelt, at forty-one the youngest man to occupy the White House, then by Senator Robert M. La Follette of Wisconsin and President Woodrow Wilson.

Two and a half months after being sworn in, President Roosevelt sounded the dominant note of twentieth-century American politics. The old system, he said in his first annual message to Congress, must be changed to meet new social and economic problems: "When the Constitution was adopted, at the end of the eighteenth century, no human wisdom could foretell the sweeping changes . . . which were to take place by the beginning

of the twentieth century. At that time it was accepted as a matter of course that the several States were the proper authorities to regulate, so far as was then necessary, the comparatively insignificant and strictly localized corporate bodies of the day. The conditions are now wholly different and wholly different action is called for."

Presidential Initiative. Action soon followed words. On February 14, 1902, Roosevelt invoked the Sherman Antitrust Act against the Northern Securities Company, a mammoth railroad holding corporation controlled by the bankers J. P. Morgan and Company and Kuhn, Loeb and Company and the railroad operators James J. Hill and Edward H. Harriman.

Morgan was stunned. He exclaimed that Roosevelt had not acted like a "gentleman" and later tried to treat the President like a rival operator. Hill was even more embittered. "It really seems hard," he complained, "that we should be compelled to fight for our lives against the political adventurers who have

R is the Railroad Trust, always on time
To Run over the People, and get their
last dime.

THERE'S NOTHING LIMITED ABOUT ME

PLEASE LEAVE ME ENOUGH TO PAY MY FUNERAL EXPENSES

COPYRIGHT, 1902, BY W. R. HEARST.

In 1902 Roosevelt moved against a mammoth railroad trust, depicted here as a brutal giant extracting the "last dime" from the common people.

never done anything but pose and draw a salary." But the proceedings continued. Two years later the Supreme Court, in a five to four decision, ordered the Northern Securities Company to dissolve.

By the time the Northern Securities case was settled, Roosevelt had added another dimension to presidential leadership. In May 1902, John Mitchell, the moderate leader of the United Mine Workers, had called anthracite miners of northeastern Pennsylvania out on strike. The strikers demanded an eight-hour day, wage increases, and recognition of their union. The eight railroad companies which dominated the industry would neither recognize the United Mine Workers nor

mitigate the workers' near subhuman conditions of life. "[The miners] don't suffer," the operators' chief spokesman expostulated at one point; "why, they can't even speak English." And so the strike continued through the summer and into the fall.

Fearful of a coal shortage and infuriated by the operators' arrogance, Roosevelt considered filing an antitrust suit against the coal combine. But when the Attorney General advised that it would fail for lack of evidence, he decided to invite the contesting parties to the White House. The operators deeply resented this implied recognition of the U.M.W. and vehemently refused to make any concessions at the ensuing conference in October.

Roosevelt was so determined to end the strike that he issued secret orders to the army to prepare to seize the mines. He then warned prominent business leaders on Wall Street of his intent. These measures sufficed. The operators agreed to accept the recommendations of an independent arbitration committee appointed by the President. Their plan to crush the U.M.W. had failed. "This is the great distinguishing fact," the Springfield *Republican* proclaimed at the time, "for while the operators still nominally refuse to recognize the mine workers' union, that union nevertheless is a party to the President's plan of arbitration and is so recognized by him."

The political importance of both the Northern Securities Company suit and the President's intervention in the coal strike far transcended their immediate economic significance. By striking out boldly on his own, Roosevelt had asserted his independence of big business, revitalized the executive office, and helped prepare the way for the progressive movement to reach the national level. He had also given meaning to the Sherman Antitrust Act and had created the impression that the Republican party could become a viable instrument of reform.

THE REVOLT OF THE MIDDLE CLASSES

The New Consensus. The program that Theodore Roosevelt and Woodrow Wilson pressed on Congress and the nation from 1905 to 1916 was neither revolutionary nor original. Many reforms of the Progressive Era had been spelled out in the Populist party platform of 1892. Almost every major measure that Roosevelt and his successors would sign into law had been suggested earlier by William Jennings Bryan. Even the attack on the Northern Securities Company was based on a law enacted twelve years before. Why, then, did progressivism succeed when Populism and Bryanism had failed?

The middle-class character of progressivism's constituency and leadership made the crucial difference. Populism, despite its attempt to win labor support, had been essentially a movement of rural protest. Bryan's Populism had been more broadly based, but Bryan's identification with prohibition and evangelical Protestantism had alienated many normally Democratic Catholic and Jewish workers. In 1896 Bryan had failed to win middle-class support, even among well-to-do farmers.

Middle-class voters had been frightened mainly by Bryan's allegedly wild financial ideas. "How intellectually snobbish I was about 'sound economics,' " the editor William Allen White wrote later. ". . . It seemed to me that rude hands were trying to tear down the tabernacle of our national life."

Progressivism triumphed because tens of thousands of civic-minded Americans who shared White's virtues and prejudices were drawn into the movement. "Populism shaved its whiskers, put on a derby and moved into the middle of the class—the upper middle class," White wrote. That, of course, was poetic license. Progressivism did appeal more to educated, prosperous farmers than to uneducated, unsuccessful ones, but it also exerted a powerful pull on skilled laborers.

Urban blue-collar workers of old stock or of northern European origins gave it disproportionate support, especially on economic issues. Even in the Middle West, progressivism's voter strength lay more in cities and medium-size towns than in the countryside.

Assuredly, most first-echelon progressive leaders came from the old-stock middle or upper-middle classes. The secondary leadership was of similar background, though it contained some minor union officials, some old-line politicians, and a number of Jewish professionals. It was augmented, moreover, by the social feminists, voteless until 1920 but extraordinarily influential nonetheless.

On the average, the men who would "march to Armageddon" with Theodore Roosevelt in 1912 and form the Progressive ("Bull Moose") party were ten years younger than the conservatives who remained with the G.O.P. They had been college students or impressionable young men of affairs when the intellectual revolution of the Gilded Age challenged the economic and social values of their fathers. Although they might not have heard of Lester Ward and his *Dynamic Sociology*, they were thoroughly familiar with Henry George's indictment of poverty and Edward Bellamy's utopian vision of the potentialities of the new technology. They accepted the postulates of reform Darwinism, and they believed with varying intensity that the environment could and should be shaped to bring out the best in humankind and its institutions.

Despite their broad identity of background, few progressives thought alike on all issues. As we have already seen, the progressive movement was at once positive and negative, liberal and conservative, democratic and elitist. It possessed both a soft side and a hard side, both a social justice wing and a business wing. Thus many of the urban businessmen who joined early citizen's movements for local control, city manager government, and efficient administration had scant sympathy for much of the social justice progressive's economic program. They had no desire to reform the tax structure or create a welfare polity through minimum wage laws, workmen's compensation, and health insurance systems. Neither did rural and small town progressives evince much concern for social justice. In Connecticut, for example, small town state legislators voted down workmen's compensation in the same session in which they enacted a strong measure to regulate public utilities. In Congress, too, rural progressives gave considerably more support to measures regulating business than to those affecting workers.

Even the urban, middle-class professionals who comprised the heart of the progressive movement had divided allegiances. The narrower moralists among them wanted mainly to clean up politics by destroying "bossism" and its attendant evils. They believed that the Australian (secret) Ballot, the direct primary, and numerous other procedural reforms would shift power from the boss-manipulated masses to themselves and people like themselves. It can even be argued that a majority of those who supported progressivism were driven more by fear, resentment, and self-interest than by a creative desire to fashion a new society. They fumed over soaring tax rates and gas, electric, and streetcar monopolies. They attributed the increasingly high cost of government to corruption rather than to the root cause—expanding services. They blamed rising prices on the "trusts."

And they feared the aggrandizement of power by organized labor, though they sympathized with individual working men and women. Many felt that they were being squeezed between the upper and nether elements of society. A few of the aristocrats among them may even have been moved by desire to regain a status and prestige lost to the new business leaders, those *nouveaux riches* whom one critic described as being "without restraints of culture, experience, the pride, or even the inherited caution of class or rank."

Yet to view progressivism through one or another of its constituent parts is to miss the thrust of the movement as a whole. All but the most opportunistic progressives shared a vision of society that impelled them, within limits, to put what they saw as the public good above their private interest. Whatever their personal ambitions—even the purest idealists among them possessed normal drives for prestige and power—their breadth of outlook enabled them to transcend short-range economic and social considerations in pursuit of long-range civic goals.

As political activists, they forged a series of shifting political coalitions based on the mainly material concerns of labor, farmers, white-collar workers, and businessmen. As educated and highly well informed citizens, they based their program on the ostensibly objective findings of social scientists. As pragmatic idealists, they gave their designs unity and purpose by evoking the moral impulses roused by the Social Gospel and by the muckrakers' exposures of corruption and exploitation. In short, despite their differences and inconsistencies, they mobilized the new public interest philosophy in three areas of American life: social, economic, and governmental.

Social Problems. Everywhere that progressives looked they saw poverty, injustice, and political corruption in the midst of growing abundance and seemingly limitless opportunity. One percent of the nation's families owned seven eighths of its wealth, and 10 million Americans lived in abject circumstances. Many workers still toiled sixty hours a week. Almost 2 million children worked in the fields or in factories, frequently on night shifts. Thousands of workers were killed annually on the railroads alone—by one estimate over 7000. As late as 1913 industrial accidents caused 25,000 deaths a year.

Nor did there seem to be much hope that

Courtesy International Museum of Photography
at George Eastman House.

*Until child labor laws were enacted, many
children worked long, poorly paid hours with
dangerous machinery. Two boys working in a
Georgia cotton mill about 1910 are so small they
must stand on the machine frame to reach a shelf.*

employers would or could cope with these
problems. Wages were fixed by supply and
demand. In the absence of a strong labor
movement or minimum wage laws, even
those manufacturers who wished to be humane were forced to keep wages at the
subsistence level in order to survive competition. Thus Massachusetts, which had pioneered in strong child labor laws, steadily lost
textile mills to the South, where child labor
helped keep production costs low.

Labor's attempts to organize and strike for
higher wages and shorter hours had been
systematically weakened by injunctions and,
more important, by management's use of
immigrants as strike breakers. There was no
pension system, no automatic compensation

for injuries or death sustained on the job. The
widow who received $250 from her late
husband's employer could consider herself
blessed. Relief, when available, came largely
from private sources.

The Power of Business. The consolidation of
several firms into large industrial combines, a
movement described in Chapter 14, threatened to make conditions worse rather than
better. By 1904 combinations of one form or
another controlled two fifths of all manufacturing in the United States. Six great financial
groups dominated about 95 percent of the
railroads. Some 1320 utilities companies were
organized under a handful of giant holding
companies. As early as 1902 the United States
Industrial Commission reported, "In most
cases the combination has exerted an appreciable power over prices, and in practically all
cases it has increased the margin between raw
materials and finished products." The Commission added that the cost of production had
probably decreased and that profits had
doubtless increased. A subsequent report
revealed that the cost of living actually
increased 35 percent between 1897 and 1913.

As we have seen, efficiency was the
economic justification for these developments. But the consolidation movement, like
the protective tariff movement, was based
primarily on fear of competition and its
attendant instability. No one, not even J.
Pierpont Morgan, whose very gaze "forced
the complex of inferiority . . . upon all around
him," was immune. Fear of competition had
driven him and his associates to buy out
Andrew Carnegie and organize the United
States Steel Corporation in 1901. The desire
for stability and assured profits had also
prompted him and James J. Hill to organize
the Northern Securities Company in 1901.

The consolidation movement both tended
to destroy competition and, more important,
made it difficult for the nation to solve its
festering social and political problems. Great

corporations had the power to prevent labor from organizing basic industries and used this power ruthlessly. They also transformed economic power into political influence in various ways. If railroad, sugar, oil, and steel interests could not "buy" state legislatures as openly as they had twenty-five years earlier and if they could no longer send as many hand-picked men to Congress as they once had done, they nevertheless exerted great influence over both elections and legislative decisions. They made huge contributions to the Republican party, controlled countless newspaper editors and publishers, and kept lobbies in Washington and in state capitals.

Small industrialists, organized in 1895 as the National Association of Manufacturers (NAM), also fought social and economic change. They and other comparatively small businessmen and real estate promoters shared responsibility with big business for the already widespread pollution of America's cities and desecration of the countryside. Small industry fought minimum wage, child labor, and factory safety bills. Small businessmen lobbied most vigorously for low local and state taxes and thus for inadequate schools and social services.

Stranglehold on Government. The obstructionist role of small business should not obscure the major issue that Roosevelt and progressives faced on the national level. The inescapable fact was that big business in 1901 constituted the most potent threat to American democracy. The post–Civil War shift of power from Washington to Wall Street had accelerated under President McKinley. By Roosevelt's ascension, the presidency had become a kind of branch brokerage office, with the President himself little more than the Washington director of a nationwide financial operation. There was nothing particularly sinister or even secret about the system. Republican politicians such as McKinley and his friend Mark Hanna believed that national welfare depended upon cooperation between business and government.

But no national progressive movement could gain political power until the reign of big business was effectively challenged. This was why Roosevelt's action against the Northern Securities Company had such great symbolic importance. Progressives continued to emphasize direct democracy—the primary, initiative, referendum, recall of judicial decisions, and, above all, direct election of senators. These devices, they believed, would enable them to introduce bills in boss-dominated legislatures, undo the work of conservative legislatures and judges, and replace business-oriented senators with people more representative of the general citizenry.

THUNDER IN THE CITIES AND STATES

Origins of Urban Reform. The catalyst behind the shifting coalitions that formed the progressive movement was the prolonged depression of the 1890s. A business editor wrote at the time:

It is probably safe to say that in no civilized country in this century, not actually in the throes of war or open insurrection, has society been so disorganized as it was in the United States during the first half of 1894; never was human life held so cheap, never did the constituted authorities appear so incompetent to endorse respect for the law.

Appalled by the people's hardships and fearful of their social implications, the middle and upper-middle classes had begun to become politically active in large numbers for the first time. As we have seen, clergymen were trying earnestly to apply the Social Gospel. Women's literary societies developed an interest in social and economic problems. Men's civic clubs turned their sights on public utility monopolies. Untried reform politicians challenged conservative business leaders. And most important of all, farmers' organizations, labor unions, church clubs, and other

With virtually no government controls, many business operators exploited labor ruthlessly. At the bottom of the wage scale were the immigrants, like the woman shown here working in a factory in Lynn, Massachusetts.

civic groups formed common fronts. In so doing, they regularly crossed—though they rarely severed—the class, ethnic, and religious lines that had heretofore separated social units.

Between 1894 and 1897, municipal reform movements erupted across the nation. In city after city during the next decade, reform candidates—both Republican and Democratic—campaigned successfully for commission or city manager government, for local control, and for honest elections. Invariably, they found that the trail of privilege and corruption led from the city hall to the statehouse and

thence to powerful business interests. Government, they gradually—and often reluctantly—concluded, had to be transformed from a negative to a positive force. Only then could insurance and utility companies be brought under control, exploitation of men, women, and children stopped, and the power of the bosses destroyed.

State Reforms. As governor of New York in 1899, Theodore Roosevelt pushed through a corporation tax, strengthened factory and tenement inspection laws, and flouted business interests on so many other counts that the G.O.P machine eased him out of the state and into the vice-presidential nomination in 1900. In the same year, Robert M. La Follette abandoned Republican orthodoxy and won the governorship of Wisconsin. Much of his program had developed piecemeal in the East, especially in Massachusetts and New York, but La Follette, drawing on a general shift of progressive support from the countryside to urban centers, implemented his program so imaginatively that it became a model and gained renown as the "Wisconsin Idea." There and elsewhere, progressives won the direct primary, the short ballot, the initiative and referendum, and the recall of elected officials.

Progressives in state legislatures strengthened child labor laws, created commissions to regulate utilities and railroad rates, and began to impose inheritance, corporation, and graduated income taxes. They also made increasingly large appropriations for schools, state universities, mental and penal institutions, and welfare programs in general. Maryland enacted the first workmen's compensation law in 1902. Oregon limited women workers to a ten-hour day in the next year. Illinois established a public assistance program for mothers with dependent children in 1911. And Massachusetts created a commission to fix wages for women and children in 1912. By the end of the Progressive Era the number of students in high schools had almost doubled, most of the great industrial states had workmen's compensation laws, and the number of industrial accidents had been dramatically reduced by the forced or voluntary adoption of safety procedures. The epilog that Senator La Follette wrote in his *Autobiography* in 1913 was in reality a prolog:

It has been a fight supremely worth making, and I want it to be judged . . . by results actually attained. If it can be shown that Wisconsin is a happier and better state to live in, that its institutions are more democratic, that the oppor-

tunities of all its people are more equal, that social justice more nearly prevails, that human life is safer and sweeter—then I shall rest content in the feeling that the Progressive movement has been successful.

PROGRESSIVISM MOVES TO WASHINGTON

By 1904 President Roosevelt was girding for a mighty struggle with conservatives in his own party. He had come into office well aware that his party was a hostage to business and its spokesmen in Congress and that this situation placed limits on his ability to act. As he explained to intimates, he could do something about either the tariff or the trusts, but not both. He had opted for trust reform as the more popular issue, the issue less offensive to Congress, and the issue more vulnerable to executive leverage.

On the legislative side, the record of his first administration had been modest. A Democratic-sponsored reclamation measure, the Newlands Act, had been passed in 1902 with the President's support. The Elkins Act to prohibit railroad rebates had gone through in 1903 because the railroads favored it. And a Department of Commerce and Labor, including a Bureau of Corporations with investigatory powers, had been created the same year. But a handful of conservatives, called Old Guardsmen—Nelson W. Aldrich of Rhode Island, William B. Allison of Iowa, Marcus A. Hanna of Ohio, Orville H. Platt of Connecticut, and John C. Spooner of New York—had otherwise kept the legislative hatches closed.

Wealthy, able, and intelligent, these senators were also arrogant and dogmatic. Only Mark Hanna had sought to make peace with labor in 1900 by joining Samuel Gompers in forming the National Civic Federation to promote settlement of labor disputes. Other senators were insensitive to social and economic injustice. They supported governmental subsidies and other favors to business, even while invoking the principle of laissez-faire to prevent even the mildest reforms.

They did not want Roosevelt to run for a full term in 1904. But after he captured the party machinery, they and the financial and business interests helped him win a rousing victory over the conservative Democratic candidate, Judge Alton B. Parker of New York, who actually believed that the trust problem should be left to the states. As the New York *Sun* put it, better to have "the impulsive candidate of the party of conservatism than the conservative candidate of the party which the business interests regard as permanently and dangerously impulsive."

Significantly, not even Roosevelt's extraordinary popularity reversed the downward trend in voter turnout which had started in 1900 and would continue until 1928. This decline was strong in the North as well as in the South, especially among workers and marginal farmers. Most likely it reflected an alienation induced by the growing impersonality of society and politics, the ethnic and cultural conflicts within both major parties, and the supplanting of political campaigns by other forms of popular entertainment.

The Party Structure. The key to the conservative domination of the Republican delegation in Congress was malapportionment in the states and the election of United States senators by their legislatures. In every state east of the Mississippi the small towns and rural areas had become grossly overrepresented as the cities grew. In almost every state a handful of entrenched leaders with close ties to an intricate network of business lobbyists dictated the selection of senatorial candidates. By gerrymandering congressional districts, they assured the election of conservative Republicans to the House. Only in the northwest central states and on the Pacific Coast did progressive Republicans control the selection of senators and representatives with any consistency.

At no time, therefore—not even during the height of progressive Republican insurgency between 1910 and 1912—was as much as a fourth of the Republican delegation in Congress progressive. Yet neither was this dominant conservatism truly representative of rank and file Republicanism. "If I thought the Republican organization under the dome of the Capitol represented the Republican party of the country," a Wisconsin progressive protested in 1909, "I would be ashamed of being a Republican."

Roosevelt could find little support for his legislative program by turning to the Democrats, however. Most Southern state legislatures were gerrymandered in favor of rural

President Roosevelt's great popularity aided him in his battle with the conservatives in his own party. He is shown here campaigning in 1904.

"Tories," so progressive thought was far weaker in Congress than outside it. And though Southern Democrats willingly abandoned states' rights on issues that redounded to the South's advantage, they remained basically unsympathetic to Roosevelt's centralizing tendencies. Furthermore, the Democrats' strength in the Senate was too slight for Roosevelt to have forged a viable coalition with them and the small minority of progressive Republicans. He had no choice, therefore, but to work through those who controlled the party—the conservative Republican leaders.

Still, there were offsetting factors. The President controlled the patronage. He could enforce acts of Congress vigorously or indifferently. He could appoint fact-finding commissions. And he could use the vast moral force of his office to influence public opinion and thus, indirectly, the Congress. Reinforced by his understanding of these powers and emboldened by his popular mandate and the angry excitement whipped up by the muckrakers, Roosevelt prepared in December 1904 to present a full program of reform to Congress.

Railroad Regulation. His first major achievement was the Hepburn Act to strengthen the rate-making power of the Interstate Commerce Commission. Following publication in *McClure's* of a devastating account of railroad malpractices, a concerted demand for action arose in the Middle West and the South. It came not only from farmers but also from merchants, manufacturers, and civic leaders, whose national organizations protested less against high rates than against the discrepancies between charges for long and short hauls, the curtailment of services induced by the consolidation of lines, and similar abuses.

These powerful pressures drove a number of conservative Republican senators part way to Roosevelt's side. Spurred by brilliant presidential maneuvering, a coalition then passed a compromise measure in 1906. Although La Follette cried "betrayal" because the bill failed to authorize evaluation of a railroad's worth in determining rates, the Hepburn Act had many progressive features, including extension of the Interstate Commerce Commission's jurisdiction to oil pipeline, sleeping-car, and express companies.

Public Health Controls. Shortly after adoption of the Hepburn Act, the President signed two other significant measures—the Pure Food and Drug Act and the Meat Inspection Amendment to the Agricultural Appropriations Act. Each was necessitated by the callous disregard for the public's health by the industries concerned. Each reflected a growing conviction that only federal regulation could safeguard the people's health against avaricious business.

The Pure Food and Drug Act was a testament both to the new scientism and to the single-minded dedication of the Department of Agriculture's chief chemist, Dr. Harvey W. Wiley, "a very mountain among men, a lion among fighters." Wiley had long been pressing for a law to prevent the manufacture and sale of adulterated, misbranded, or poisonous foods and drugs. With powerful help from President Roosevelt, the American Medical Association, and muckraker Samuel Hopkins Adams, his bill finally came to the floor of the Senate in the spring of 1906. Sneering openly at chemists in the Department of Agriculture, Senator Nelson W. Aldrich said that "the liberty of all the people" was at stake. But Senator Porter J. McCumber of North Dakota rejoined that the real issue was the public's right to receive what it asked for and "not some poisonous substance in lieu thereof." An imperfect but pioneering pure-food-and-drug measure became law on June 30, 1906.

The fight for the Meat Inspection Amendment offered an even more penetrating insight into the business mind. Upton Sinclair's muckraking novel, *The Jungle* (1906), graphically exposed conditions in the meat-packing industry:

There was never the least attention paid to what was cut up for sausage, there would come all the way back from Europe old sausage that had been rejected, and that was mouldy and white—it would be doused with borax and glycerine, and dumped into the hoppers, and made over again for home consumption. There would be meat that had tumbled out on the floor, in the dirt and sawdust, where the workers had tramped and spit uncounted millions of germs. . . . [A] man could run his hand over these piles of meat and sweep off handfuls of the dried dung of rats.

After reading *The Jungle*, according to Finley Peter Dunne's humorous character "Mr. Dooley," Roosevelt rose from his breakfast table crying "I'm pizened" and threw his sausages out the window. Actually, the President ordered an immediate investigation. Meanwhile, lobbyists for the meat-packing industry charged that an inspection measure drawn by Senator Albert J. Beveridge of Indiana was "unconstitutional" and "socialistic." When European sales dropped precipitously, however, the meat packers abruptly reversed themselves. They demanded, in the words of Mark Sullivan, "an inspection law . . . strong enough to still public clamor, while not so drastic as to inconvenience them too greatly." The result was compromise in the Rooseveltian pattern.

For Generations Yet Unborn. By then the President was also deep in a bitter struggle for rational control and development of the nation's natural resources. On his side stood a great host of governmental scientists and experts headed by Gifford Pinchot, uncounted public-spirited citizens from all over the nation (but especially from the East), numerous homesteaders, and the great lumber corporations. Arrayed against him were small lumber companies, grazing, mining, and power interests of all types, most Western

state governments, and, in the end, a decisive majority in Congress.

The issues were simple in some instances and complex in others. Should homesteaders be sacrificed to big cattle and sheep men for reasons of efficiency? Should giant lumber corporations, which had the means to pursue scientific forestry, be favored over small companies, which did not? Should the moralistic and scientific assumptions of Roosevelt and his supporters prevail? These assumptions were that the country's natural resources belong to the people as a whole; that "the fundamental idea of forestry is the perpetuation of forests by use"; that the federal government should reclaim arid lands; that "every stream is a unit from its source to its mouth, and all its uses are interdependent"; and that the electric monopoly is "the most threatening which has ever appeared."

Early in his administration Roosevelt saved what would become the heart of the Tennessee Valley Authority in the 1930s by vetoing a bill that would have opened Muscle Shoals on the Tennessee River to haphazard development by private interests. He then set aside governmental reserves in Nebraska for a tree-planting experiment that would serve as a model for a more comprehensive program under the New Deal. In 1905 he rehabilitated the Bureau of Forestry, renamed it the Forest Service, and appointed Gifford Pinchot as its chief.

A small revolution followed. Trained and dedicated foresters staffed the new agency. Enlightened controls directed the development of water-power sites by corporations. The President vetoed numerous bills injurious to the public interest. More than 2500 potential dam sites were temporarily withdrawn from entry in order to assure orderly and constructive development. In addition, 150 million acres were added to the national forests. Half as many acres with coal and mineral deposits were transferred to the public domain. And most large lumber corporations (though not the small ones) were persuaded to adopt selective-cutting techniques which alone assured the perpetuation of timber resources.

Western congressmen beholden to private interests responded with near-hysterical charges of "executive usurpation" and destruction of states' rights. But Roosevelt was undaunted. He skirmished for the preservation of the country's natural monuments even as Congress passed laws depriving him of authority to create new national forests. Before he left office in March 1909 the number of national parks had doubled. Sixteen National Monuments like California's Muir Woods and Washington's Mount Olympus had been created and fifty-one wildlife refuges established. "Is there any law that will prevent me from declaring Pelican Island a Federal Bird Reservation?" Roosevelt asked. "Very well, then I so declare it."

The President also appointed a commission to investigate and make recommendations for multipurpose river valley developments such as the Tennessee Valley Authority later became. Then in May 1908 he urged the first conference of governors to implement the conservation movement in their states. No governor espoused the movement with Roosevelt's zeal and understanding, but spadework for moderate state programs had nevertheless begun. "When the historian . . . shall speak of Theodore Roosevelt," Senator La Follette later wrote, "he is likely to say . . . that his greatest work was inspiring and actually beginning a world movement for . . . saving for the human race the things on which alone a peaceful, progressive, and happy life can be founded."

Variations in Antitrust Policy. Neither La Follette nor most other progressives were altogether enthusiastic about Roosevelt's later attitude toward big business. The President had followed up action against the Northern Securities Company with a spate of suits. By

the end of his second term twenty-five indictments had been obtained and eighteen proceedings in equity had been instituted. His successor, William Howard Taft, intensified the pace, bringing forty-three indictments in four years. In 1911 the Supreme Court implicitly reversed the Knight decision of 1895 in two verdicts, decreeing dissolution of the Standard Oil Company and the American Tobacco Company. These decisions made it clear that manufacturing combinations were not exempt from the Sherman Antitrust Act, even though the Court qualified its position somewhat with the so-called rule of reason, which acknowledged that bigness *per se* was no crime.

"The example of these basic decisions served as a powerful negative factor in business affairs," concludes one recent scholar. "Certain lines of development were denied to ambitious men." Yet they wrought few

The cartoon applauds the apparent force and effect of Roosevelt's antitrust policies. The President looks on approvingly in the background.

basic changes in the American economy. Price leadership continued, as the producers in an industry followed the lead of a few dominant corporations. Moreover, control over credit remained highly concentrated in Wall Street.

As his administration progressed, Roosevelt himself experienced a metamorphosis in his attitude toward the "trusts." Because he appreciated the advantages of large-scale production and distribution, he sought to distinguish between "good" and "bad" trusts. Putting his faith primarily in regulation, he repeatedly called on Congress to strengthen and expand the regulatory Bureau of Corporations. Then, after he left office, he came out openly for government price-fixing in basic industries.

Otherwise, from this time on Roosevelt maintained cordial relations with the Morgan–U.S. Steel axis. In order to prevent the spread of a severe financial panic that struck New York in 1907, he went to the aid of the banks and acquiesced in U.S. Steel's absorption of a Southern competitor, the Tennessee Coal and Iron Company. In the next year he accepted without protest the inadequate Aldrich-Vreeland banking bill, which progressives and agrarians bitterly opposed as inadequate and banker-oriented.

Trouble on the Labor Front. Labor continued to make modest advances during the Roosevelt and Taft administrations, mainly because of the progressives' work in the states. The American Federation of Labor grew by fits and starts, and the standard of living of its highly skilled members rose appreciably. In manufacturing, as we have seen, real wages increased, while the average work week declined from sixty to fifty hours.

The AFL failed, however, to organize basic industry, mainly because of the massive counteroffensive by employers, spearheaded by the National Association of Manufacturers. To prevent labor from organizing, the NAM resorted to weapons ranging from propagan-

da to violence. Its most effective tactic was maintenance of the open shop (a shop in which union membership is not a precondition of employment), and its most important ally was the middle class. The employers understood that in practice an open shop meant a nonunion shop, but middle-class progressives often did not. Even when they saw the point, a lingering devotion to natural law and individual rights made it difficult for them to accept the idea of the closed shop. Roosevelt was unsure on the issue. And men like Woodrow Wilson, then president of Princeton, Charles W. Eliot, president of Harvard, were adamant in their opposition to the closed shop. Eliot actually acclaimed the strike breaker as "a very good type of modern hero." In consequence, labor received virtually no support during the Progressive Era for the one measure that would have assured it success—active governmental support of the organizing process.

To compound labor's difficulties, the basic right to strike was often grossly impaired by management's private police forces, the actions of corporation-dominated state governments, and the indiscriminate issuance of injunctions by judges who cared more for property than for human rights. In speech after speech from 1905 to 1912, Roosevelt inveighed mightily against the abuse of the injunction (six special messages to Congress between 1905 and 1908). But the NAM was so influential in Republican councils that he failed even to get an anti-injunction plank in the party platform in 1908.

Campaigns to organize the steel industry meanwhile suffered a series of setbacks and finally collapsed altogether. The United Mine Workers were successful in the East, but they failed in two bloody efforts in Colorado. The first, in 1903–1904, ended in a rout climaxed by the deportation of strikers to the desert. The second, in 1913–1914, ended in tragedy when National Guardsmen burned a striker's tent colony at Ludlow on April 20, 1914, accidentally killing eleven women and two children.

Against this background the formation in 1905 of the freewheeling and often violent Industrial Workers of the World ("Wobblies") was almost predictable. Concentrated in the West, the I.W.W. fought the battles of frontier miners, lumberjacks, and migrant workers.

Forecasts of the Welfare State. By 1907 the Republican majority in Congress had had their fill of Theodore Roosevelt. They approved no major domestic legislation during his last two years in office and repudiated him openly on several occasions. Nevertheless, the executive power continued to expand. The President appointed numerous investigatory commissions. He made further advances in conservation. He repeatedly lectured Congress and the people on the need to mitigate the harsh inequities of capitalism by welfare measures. He was outraged by the Supreme Court's ruling in *Lochner* v. *New York* (1905), which held a maximum-hours law for bakers to be unconstitutional on the grounds that it was an unreasonable interference with the right of free contract and an unreasonable use of the state's police power. And after a New York tenement law was invalidated and a workmen's compensation law declared unconstitutional, Roosevelt wrote Justice William R. Day that, unless the judiciary's spirit changed, "we should not only have a revolution, but it would be absolutely necessary to have a revolution, because the condition of the worker would become intolerable."

On January 31, 1908, Roosevelt sent Congress the most radical presidential message to that time. He charged that businessmen had revived the doctrine of states' rights in order to avoid all meaningful regulation. He observed that there was "no moral difference between gambling at cards . . . and gambling in the stock market." He called for stringent regulation of securities, imprisonment of businessmen who flouted the law, and a comprehensive program of business regula-

tion. He upbraided "decent citizens" for permitting "those rich men whose lives are evil and corrupt" to control the nation's destiny. He lashed the judiciary for "abusing" the writ of injunction in labor disputes. He contemptuously dismissed editors, lawyers, and politicians who had been "purchased by the corporations" as "puppets who move as the strings are pulled." Moreover, he came out for workmen's compensation, compulsory arbitration of labor disputes, and acceptance of big unionism as a countervailing power to big business.

THE DISRUPTION OF THE G.O.P.

Taft's Background. Roosevelt's chosen successor, William Howard Taft, lacked the energy, conviction, and political skill to carry on Roosevelt's policies. He had been an enlightened governor in the Philippines, and he seemed to be sympathetic to Roosevelt's progressive views. But he had marked limitations. He believed implicitly in natural law. He was a good but painfully conventional lawyer. And he had no zest for the give-and-take of politics. He possessed a strain of courage but lacked political boldness and energy.

Big and small business heartily concurred in Taft's nomination in 1908, and he handily defeated William Jennings Bryan by 321 to 162 electoral voltes. But no sooner were the election returns in than Taft's troubles began. He conceived his mission to be to consolidate the Roosevelt reforms (giving them the "sanction of law," as he privately phrased it), not to embark on new ventures. Actually, he was too steeped in legal traditionalism to accept Roosevelt's dynamic conception of the Constitution, and he therefore failed to seize the executive reins. Taft believed that the counsel of lawyers was superior to that of scientists and other experts, and he deplored Roosevelt's reliance on investigatory commissions.

The Tariff Fiasco. By 1908 so many Midwesterners were blaming rising prices on the high schedules of the Dingley Tariff (1897) that Taft implied during the campaign that his administration would revise the tariff downward. Faithfully, he called a special session of Congress for the spring of 1909. But instead of lowering the duties, Old Guardsmen in the Senate raised them. This forced the President to accept a compromise (the Payne-Aldrich Tariff) that left the old schedules more or less intact. Then, to the disgust of progressive Republicans in the Midwest, he defended the measure as "the best bill that the Republican party ever passed." Two years later he negotiated a reciprocity agreement with Canada which the Canadians subsequently rejected because of loose talk that it presaged annexation of their country.

The Rise of Insurgency. Meanwhile, Taft was besieged with troubles on other fronts. In 1910 a group of progressive Republicans in the House, led by George W. Norris of Nebraska, stripped Speaker Joseph G. Cannon of his arbitrary and partisan control over legislation and committee appointments. Taft was secretly pleased, but both the insurgents and the public continued to link the President with the uncouth and reactionary Speaker.

Taft's rather curious stand on conservation led to even worse difficulties. He believed in conservation, but he abhorred the freewheeling methods that Roosevelt had used to achieve his objective. So he replaced Secretary of the Interior James R. Garfield with Richard A. Ballinger, an honest conservative who had earlier resigned from the Land Office because he disagreed with Roosevelt's view that the public's interest in natural resources should be given priority over that of entrepreneurs. Construing the law rigidly when government interests were at stake and loosely when private interests were at issue, Ballinger soon provoked Gifford Pinchot, Chief of the U.S. Forest Service, to charge a "giveaway" of Alaskan mineral lands to the Guggenheims, the great mining industrialists.

Ballinger was eventually exonerated, but the President was fatally stamped as anticonservationist. The characterization was not wholly unfair. Although he withdrew more lands from public entry (closing them to exploitation by private individuals and corporations) than Roosevelt and put millions of acres of forest lands into new reserves, he never did grasp the Roosevelt-Pinchot concepts of controlled development or of multipurpose river valley projects.

Roosevelt Challenges Taft. Roosevelt returned from abroad in 1910 in high indignation over Taft's ineptitude and the implied repudiation of his conservation policies. At Osawatomie, Kansas, on September 1, the former President developed further the social welfare program he had set forth in his memorable messages of 1908, calling it the "New Nationalism" because it put the national need "before sectional or personal advantage." Roosevelt quoted Lincoln's assertion that "Labor is prior to, and independent of, capital." He asserted that the judiciary's primary obligation was to protect "human welfare rather than . . . property." And he called for graduated income and inheritance taxes, workmen's compensation legislation, a federal child labor law, tariff revision, and more stringent regulation of corporations.

The congressional elections in the fall of 1910 produced the most sweeping changes since the great realignment of the mid-nineties. From East to West stand-pat Republicans were turned out of office as the G.O.P. lost fifty-eight seats in the House, ten in the Senate, and a total of seven governorships. Most contemporary observers blamed the tariff and Taft's failure to project a dynamic progressive image. But recent scholarship suggests that resentment among normally Republican Germans of local Republicans'

ELECTION OF 1912: ELECTORAL VOTE

| Wilson: 435 | Roosevelt: 88 | Taft: 8 |

increasingly fervent support of prohibition figured importantly and perhaps decisively.

The "Bull Moose" Party. Early in 1911 Republican progressives began to call for the nomination of La Follette or Roosevelt in 1912. The Wisconsin senator made an early and earnest bid, then refused to bow out gracefully after his most devoted followers concluded that he could not win. Roosevelt's entry into the race in February 1912 precipitated one of the most bitter preconvention campaigns in Republican history. Roosevelt outpolled Taft two to one in the thirteen states that held primaries, but the Old Guard refused to let him have the nomination. "We can't elect Taft," a Kansas regular confessed, "but we are going to hold on to this organization and when we get back four years from now, we will have it and not those d----- insurgents."

Faced with these attitudes, more than three hundred Roosevelt delegates stormed out of the convention hall in Chicago in a dispute over the seating of delegates. Six weeks later they returned to form the Progressive or "Bull Moose" party, nominate their hero, and synthesize their program for a just society.

Roosevelt's following included Social Gospel clergymen and laymen, college presidents and professors, liberal businessmen and editors, Gifford Pinchot and his fellow con-

servationists, and social workers by the hundreds. But when the Democrats nominated a moderate progressive, Governor Woodrow Wilson of New Jersey, Roosevelt and his party were doomed. In the election that autumn Wilson won forty states and 42 percent of the popular vote. Roosevelt ran second and Taft a poor third.

Actually, by the time Taft left office in March 1913 his administration had compiled an impressive legislative record. It included safety regulations for miners, an Employers' Liability Act for work done under government contract, and a measure to establish a Children's Bureau. The Interstate Commerce Commission's authority had been extended to telephone, telegraph, cable, and wireless companies, and a postal savings system had been established to serve farmers and others in remote rural areas. Congress had also adopted two of the progressive movement's most cherished proposals, the Sixteenth Amendment, giving Congress the power to levy an income tax, and the Seventeenth Amendment, providing for direct election of senators. Taft himself had given warm support to some of these measures, perfunctory support to others, and little beyond his signature to one or two. All owed their passage more to a coalition of Democrats and progressive Republicans than to the regular Republican majority.

Ironies of American Socialism. The election of 1912 also drew the largest Socialist vote to that time, though not wholly for reasons of ideology. Probably half the 900,000 voters who cast their ballots for the charismatic Socialist Party candidate, Eugene V. Debs, were simply disaffected by the middle-class character of the Bull Moose leadership and, especially, by the unofficial commitment of the three major parties to prohibition.

The Socialist party itself was hardly more radical in practice than the Progressive party was in theory. Socialist leaders believed firmly in evolution, not revolution, and most of the 1200 party members who held office in railroad, mining, and industrial towns during the era pushed progressive-type programs, including efficiency and economy. Furthermore, the conservative German contingent headed by Victor Berger of Milwaukee was avowedly racist. Not until after the northward trek of blacks made it politically expedient to appeal to them did the party do so, at the end of World War I, though Debs and many others had long been sympathetic.

Conservative Socialists also differed little from organized labor and the major parties on immigration. "Slavonians, Italians, Russians, and Armenians," said Berger before a House committee in 1911, were the "modern white coolies" of the steel industry and had "crowded out the Americans, Germans, Englishmen, and Irishmen." Even Morris Hillquit, leader of the party's strongly Jewish eastern wing, favored selective restriction of immigration. More ironic still, the dirt and tenant farmers of Oklahoma and Texas who constituted the party's largest faction, stood strongly for individual rather than communal ownership of land.

Yet, for all its internal inconsistencies, socialism made a significant impress on American life. As the memoirs of numerous progressives attest, socialist values influenced the social justice wings of the Republican, Democratic, and Progressive parties alike. They also served as a central inspiration to Jane Addams, Florence Kelley, and many of the other great reformers.

THE TRIUMPH OF PROGRESSIVISM

Wilson's Background. Woodrow Wilson was born in a Presbyterian manse in Virginia in 1856 and reared in a South convulsed by Civil War and Reconstruction. As a Ph.D. candidate at Johns Hopkins University, he argued in a brilliant dissertation, *Congressional Government* (1885), that the basic weakness in the

American political system was its separation of executive from legislative leadership. Following a distinguished tenure as president of Princeton University, he became governor of New Jersey in 1910 and changed from a rather academic conservative into a practical progressive. He boldly seized control of the Democratic state machine, pushed a comprehensive reform program through a divided legislature, and gave eloquent voice to high ideals and moderately progressive aspirations.

The New Freedom Program. The program Wilson called the New Freedom was grounded in the theory that no group should receive special privileges. It differed from Roosevelt's New Nationalism in two essentials. First, it advocated regulated competition rather than regulated monopoly. Second, it turned most of the social programs of progressivism back to the states and municipalities. The first goal was to be achieved by downward revision of the tariff, strengthening and relentless enforcement of the antitrust laws, and freeing of banks from dependence on Wall Street.

Tariff and Banking Reform. Wilson began auspiciously by calling a special session of Congress the day of his inauguration and then addressing a joint meeting of the Senate and House in person. He aimed to destroy the Republican system of special privilege for industry and the producers of raw materials by reducing tariff protection and thereby increasing competition. He used patronage to hold wavering Democrats in line, and he marshalled opinion against the G.O.P. Old Guard by charging publicly that Washington had seldom seen "so numerous, so industrious or so insidious a lobby" as had invaded the Capitol. This masterful exertion of leadership resulted in the first substantial reduction of the tariff since before the Civil War.

By the time he signed the Underwood tariff bill (which included a modestly graduated income tax) in October 1913, Wilson was embroiled in conflict over banking legislation. Conservative Republicans wanted a single central bank controlled by private bankers. Conservative Democrats insisted on a decentralized reserve system under private control. Bryan Democrats and progressive Republicans called for a reserve system and currency supply owned and controlled by the government. (The latter were roused especially by sensational revelations of Wall Street's influence over the nation's financial and investment system.) Finally, after consultations with Louis D. Brandeis, his most influential adviser on domestic matters, Wilson worked out a series of constructive compromises that were adopted as the Federal Reserve Act in December 1913.

The measure created twelve Federal Reserve Banks owned and controlled by private bankers but responsible to a seven-member central Federal Reserve Board appointed by the President. The reserve banks were authorized to issue currency and to perform numerous other central banking functions. Provision was also made to meet the seasonal needs of agriculture. The Federal Reserve System was not intended to destroy private ownership and initiative in banking. But it did create new centers of financial power to offset the overweening influence of New York bankers.

Wilson planned to round out his program by revising the antitrust laws. There were to be no special benefits to labor, no aid to agriculture, no such conservation program as Roosevelt had envisaged. Child labor, woman suffrage, workmen's compensation, and all the rest would have to come, if they came at all, by haphazard state action. Indeed, when a bill sponsored by the National Child Labor Committee passed the House in 1914 over the protests of states' rights Southerners, Wilson refused to push it in the Senate.

Politics and Blacks. For the vast majority of blacks, progressivism proved more an illusion than a reality, regardless of who occupied the White House. Violence or the threat of violence continued to be the ultimate means of race control. Although the total number of lynchings decreased because of a sharp decline in the North, the number increased in the South. As often as not, moreover, the burnings and hangings were for imaginary or concocted offenses. In 1906 twelve persons were slaughtered in a race riot in Atlanta. Two years later an antiblack riot occurred a half mile from Lincoln's home in Springfield, Illinois. Meanwhile Southern orators like South Carolina's "Pitchfork Ben" Tillman carried the message of white supremacy to receptive Northern audiences. The production in 1915 of *The Birth of a Nation*, which was based on Thomas Dixon's blatantly racist book, *The Clansman*, brought more violence.

Roosevelt had been moderately sympathetic to blacks. His original objective had been a biracial Southern Republican party led by patrician whites and educated blacks—his immediate end the securing of his own nomination in 1904 through control of the Southern delegations. He had maintained close relations with Booker T. Washington, head of the Tuskeegee Institute, and, unlike McKinley, he had appointed eminently qualified blacks to federal offices in the South. He had also denounced lynching and ordered legal action against peonage, in which a worker, usually black, was forced to pay off a debt through the court-rigged assignment of that debt to a private employer.

By 1904 these actions by Roosevelt had produced a vicious reaction in the South. With the tacit acquiescence of Bryan and Parker, Southern editors and politicians inflamed the region over "Roosevelt Republicanism," and thereby forced enlightened white Southerners on the defensive. Nor was the situation much better in the North, where "scientific" racial theories had penetrated even the universities. Against this background, Roosevelt equivocated. He appointed a few more blacks to

Violence continued to threaten the safety and security of black people during the progressive years. In 1917 in New York 10,000 black Americans marched in silent protest against lynching.

medium-level offices and continued to denounce lynching. But during the race riot in Atlanta in 1906, he gave no moral leadership. Then in the aftermath of an affray at Brownsville, Texas, erroneously thought to involve blacks, he arbitrarily discharged three companies of black soldiers. By the end of his presidency he had concluded that the hope of a viable biracial Republican party in the South was an idle dream. As he sadly reflected, "the North and the South act in just the same way toward the Negro."

His successor had no interest whatever in solving the race problem or helping black

people. "I will not be swerved one iota from my policy to the South . . .," Taft snapped. "I shall not appoint Negroes to office in the South. . . . I shall not relinquish my hope to build up a decent white man's party there."

In 1912 many Northern blacks went over to Woodrow Wilson and the Democratic party. They were soon disillusioned. Blacks were segregated in some federal departments, and virtually no blacks were appointed to any but the lowest-level offices in either the South or the North. Never in his memory, wrote Booker T. Washington, had he seen his people so "discouraged and bitter." During World

War I discrimination became so extreme in the military service that the Federal Council of Churches of Christ established a commission to investigate.

A few small advances—most of them of greater long-range than short-run significance—punctuated this otherwise dreary record. A handful of Northern philanthropists expanded their support of black colleges. A small number of Northern progressives—many the descendants of abolitionists—also formed a common front with blacks. On Lincoln's birthday in 1909, a group of white educators, clergymen, editors, and social workers joined a group of black intellectuals in forming the National Association for the Advancement of Colored People. They dedicated the organization to the abolition of all forced segregation and to the promotion of equal justice and enlarged educational opportunities for blacks. For tactical reasons, only one black, W. E. B. DuBois, served as an official during the NAACP's early years. (See "William E. Burghardt DuBois: Black Intellectual.")

Two years after the founding of the NAACP another group of black intellectuals founded the National Urban League. Neither organization made much headway against the discriminatory conditions that made the average black a person free yet unfree. But they did underline the determination of blacks to survive whether wanted or not.

On the legal front, the Supreme Court struck down peonage in separate decisions during the Taft and Wilson administrations though the system actually continued with modifications into the late 1920s. It also overturned an amendment to the Oklahoma Constitution—the so-called Grandfather Clause—which allowed certain illiterate whites, but not illiterate blacks, to vote. On balance, only the Indians fared worse.

Moving Toward the New Nationalism. By 1914 the progressive movement had gathered too much momentum to be long halted by presidential indifference. While the child labor forces were regrouping for a second assault, new pressures were bearing so heavily on the White House that Wilson had either to accommodate them or risk loss of his office in 1916.

These pressures were first felt when the administration introduced its antitrust program in 1914. Wilson's original measures included legislation to outlaw specific unfair trade practices and to create a federal trade commission with only fact-finding powers. Progressives in both parties thought little of the former and refused to support the latter because it did not grant the commission power to act on its findings.

Finally, Brandeis and others persuaded Wilson that it was impossible to outlaw every conceivable unfair trade practice and that something like Roosevelt's proposal for continuous regulation was the only workable alternative. Wilson signed the Clayton antitrust bill despite its ambiguities and qualifications. But he put his energy and influence into Brandeis' measure to create the Federal Trade Commission empowered, in effect, to define unfair trade practices on its own terms and to suppress them on its own findings, subject to broad court review.

Meanwhile Wilson engaged in a bitter quarrel with organized labor over the Clayton antitrust bill. Samuel Gompers and the AFL hierarchy demanded provisions to exempt labor unions from prosecution for the secondary boycott, the blacklist, and other weapons the Supreme Court had declared in violation of the Sherman Antitrust Act. In effect, labor wanted special privileges to offset management's power.

Wilson held rigidly to the New Freedom line against special privilege for any group. But he did accept an affirmation of rights that labor already possessed in law, if not always in fact, and a few other moderate provisions. His adherence to the New Freedom program on this one point did not signify that he was ordinarily unsympathetic to labor. On the contrary, the AFL lobby spoke with greater effect in Washington during Wilson's administration than did the National Association of Manufacturers.

"We Are Also Progressives." As Wilson's tenure lengthened, it became evident that the New Freedom's opposition to special privilege and commitment to states' rights made it too confining to permit fulfillment of the President's own expanding concept of social justice. It also became clear that the Democrats would have to attract a substantial portion of Roosevelt's disintegrating "Bull Moose" party to retain the presidency in 1916. Against this background, Wilson became more progressive. He began by signing the La Follette Seaman's Act of 1915, which freed sailors from bondage to labor contracts. Then, early in 1916, he nominated Brandeis to the Supreme Court over bitter opposition by Old Guard Republicans and leaders of the legal profession. (Brandeis, a Kentucky-born Jew known as the "people's lawyer," had broken legal tradition in 1908 by presenting a mass of sociological data to the Court in his defense of an Oregon bill establishing maximum working hours for women.)

Next, the President came out in support of a languishing rural-credits bill that he had condemned as class legislation two years before. He successfully urged creation of a tariff commission because he feared that surplus European goods would be dumped in

William E. Burghardt DuBois: Black Intellectual

The most intensely intellectual black spokesman of the first half of the twentieth century was W. E. B. DuBois, whose greatest achievement was to awaken interest in the black past, both African and American. He was born in Great Barrington, Massachusetts, with, as he phrased it, "a flood of Negro blood, a strain of French, a bit of Dutch, but thank God! no Anglo-Saxon." His paternal grandfather, a restless and embittered man, had been the offspring of a wealthy French Huguenot American and a Bahamian mulatto slave. His father, no less restless and embittered, had married Mary Burghardt, whose partly Dutch family were among Great Barrington's earliest settlers; he left her permanently soon after their child was born.

Short and bronze-skinned, with sharp features and an aloof personality that gave him an aristocratic mien, DuBois in his teens was hardly aware that he was "different" until he offered his calling card to a white girl and was rejected "peremptorily, with a glance." Feeling that a "vast veil" had shut him out, he knew "days of secret tears" thereafter. The black man, he wrote in 1903, "feels his two-ness—an American, a Negro, two souls, two thoughts, two unreconciled strivings, two warring ideals in one dark body."

DuBois began to develop an interest in racial matters while still in high school, and

America at the end of World War I. And he threw strong support behind the child labor bill and won its adoption. (Enacted in the summer of 1916, it was declared unconstitutional two years later in *Hammer* v. *Dagenhart*.) He also won approval of a model federal workmen's compensation bill.

The flow of legislation continued until the very eve of the election. A measure to extend federal assistance to the states for highway construction rolled through Congress. The revenue act adopted in the late summer of 1916 increased income taxes sharply and imposed a new estate tax. In September the President personally drove through Congress the Adamson bill to establish the eight-hour day for railroad workers. Finally, during his second administration, Wilson signed both the prohibition and woman suffrage amendments, though his heart was in neither.

Altogether, Wilson's first administration embodied the most imposing and important program of reform legislation in American history to that time. Wilson could truthfully claim, as he did during the presidential campaign of 1916, that he and his party had put a large part of the Progressive party's platform of 1912 onto the federal statute books.

The Progressive Era in Retrospect. Neither the impressive achievements of the Roosevelt, Taft, and Wilson administrations nor the remarkable flow of legislation in the states fulfilled the best hopes of the social justice progressives. In 1920 the distribution of

at the age of fifteen he became the local correspondent of the black New York *Globe*. His princpal, Frank A. Hosmer, recognized his precocity and encouraged him to prepare for college. (DuBois often wondered, he later said, what his fate would have been had Hosmer been "born with no faith in 'darkies.' ") Financed by local white churchpeople, DuBois went to Fisk University, an all-black college in Tennessee in 1885. He completed his degree in three years and entered Harvard with Junior standing as a scholarship student. There, as one of his biographers writes, he came to think of the institution "as a library and a faculty, nothing more." Contemptuous of the lack of purpose of most of Harvard's white students, DuBois took an active part in black affairs in Boston during his first years. His cold and distant personality caused resentment, however, and in time he withdrew into himself. Meanwhile, he was awarded a fellowship to the University of Berlin.

Study in Germany strengthened DuBois' interests in scientific social and historical research, though he had done brilliantly in the natural sciences as an undergraduate. Never—not even after he renounced his American citizenship late in life—did he lose faith that social science would some day triumph over the mythology of racism and the pathology of discrimination. After two years in Germany, DuBois returned to complete a degree in history under Hart in 1895 and to become Harvard's first black Ph.D. Forced to accept a teaching position at Wilberforce College in Ohio, a black institution with a strongly religious orientation, he strutted about the campus with the white gloves and cane of a German student and deplored "the wild screams cries groans & shrieks" of the revival meetings. Only his marriage to Nina Gomer of Cedar Rapids, Iowa, brightened his life. Then, following a temporary appointment in sociology at the University of Pennsylvania, he published his finest work, the pioneering *Philadelphia Negro* (1889). Unmarred by the strong bias of his later books, it marked the founding of black sociology.

wealth was roughly the same as it had been in 1900. The social and economic status of blacks was only marginally better, that of women only modestly so. Basic industry remained unorganized, and thousands of steelworkers labored twelve hours a day, seven days a week. Farm tenancy was continuing to rise, and most farm youths still lacked access to secondary schools. The calls of progressives for social security and unemployment insurance systems were as yet unheeded, and good medical care, like good legal service, remained more a function of the marketplace than a fundamental right.

Civil liberties were no less subject to the whim of the crowd, the local authority, or the business-oriented judge than they had been twenty years earlier. City manager and city council forms of government had altered little more than the face of urban politics, and no perceptible change in the quality of candidates had been wrought by the direct election of United States senators. Neither had the conservation movement halted the abuse of privately owned natural resources or the despoliation of the countryside by individuals and businesses, both big and small.

Despite the highly publicized attacks on trusts, corporations were larger and monopoly or near-monopoly was more widespread at the end of each presidential administration than at its beginning. Many of the regulatory agencies had already become virtual captives of the industries they were supposed to regulate. Close ties had developed in other agencies between the experts who ran them

DuBois differed radically from pragmatic Booker T. Washington, who was tied to Southern roots. Harvard and European educated, living in two worlds yet belonging to neither, DuBois believed fervently in the immediate need to prepare the "Talented Tenth" of blacks for the professions and general leadership. "The Negro race," he wrote, "is going to be saved by its exceptional men." From his new urban base at Atlanta University, he came to deplore Washington's emphasis on vocational and industrial education. In 1903, in a moving and at times poetic book of essays entitled *The Souls of Black Folks*, DuBois criticized Washington as a compromiser whose ideology "practically accepts the alleged inferiority of the Negro." Not only does Washington apologize for injustice, DuBois wrote. "He belittles the emasculating effect of caste distinctions, and opposes the higher training and ambition of our brightest minds." Negroes should realize, he also said, that "Beauty is black."

Two years later DuBois invited a select group of black intellectuals to meet at Fort Erie, Ontario, where they formed the Niagara Movement. Condemning racism as "unreasoning human savagery," they called for federal aid to education, and denounced the discriminatory politics of employers and labor unions alike. They also demanded suffrage for blacks on the same basis as whites. But this program was too advanced for the times, and DuBois himself was too unfitted temperamentally for sustained leadership. The Niagara Movement soon withered.

Subsequently, as editor for twenty-two years of the National Association of Colored People's monthly magazine, *The Crisis*, DuBois vented his often bitter and always intelligent feelings on virtually the entire range of racial issues and personalities, including black editors. "He does do dangerous things" wrote Mary Ovington, his most loyal white supporter on the NAACP board. "He strikes at people with a harshness and directness that appalls me, but the blow is often deserved and it is

and the interests that sought their favors. By any reasonable measure, America in 1920, like all other advanced technological nations, had become a partially formed bureaucratic, corporate society.

Nevertheless, as we have seen, the majority of people led somewhat more comfortable and more interesting lives in 1920 than they had in 1900. Their opportunities for self-fulfillment were also much greater. Technology relieved some of the drudgery of housework, and the increase in leisure time that resulted from the rise in productivity was generating new forms of entertainment and diversion. Government regulations had reduced the industrial accident rate and eased slightly the severity of labor in factories and mines. Modernization of municipal government made cities more manageable, and advances in public health made them more livable.

The growth of urban colleges and evening courses had opened professional careers to thousands of ethnic youths, and the parallel expansion of state colleges and universities was putting higher education within the reach of small town youngsters and the sons and daughters of well-to-do farmers. More important still, the explosion of knowledge sparked by the development of graduate education was creating an almost entirely new professional class and giving both business and government their guiding intelligence.

Philosophically, progressivism raised the level of political discourse far above that of the late nineteenth century and probably to the highest level since the time of the Founding

never below the belt." Meanwhile DuBois became increasingly frustrated by his inability to resolve the paradox of Negro life in the United States: Should blacks regard themselves as Americans or as Afro-Americans? Should they strive for complete integration or for separatism? Incremental reforms or fundamental changes?

In 1912 DuBois had resigned from the Socialist party, partly in disgust over its racism but mainly in the vain hope that the election of Woodrow Wilson would bring modest gains to his people. When the country entered World War I, DuBois suffered the contempt of radical black integrationists for urging creation of a separate Negro Officer Candidate's School. During the 1920s he charged Robert M. La Follette's Progressive presidential campaign with "deliberately dodging" the black question, and he fought with Communist party leaders for the same reason.

DuBois resigned his editorship of *The Crises* in 1932 after a series of policy disputes and returned to Atlanta University. There he edited the *Encyclopedia of the Negro* (1933–1945) and in 1935 published *Black Reconstruction in America*. This brilliant though flawed work did much to wrench white historians from the pro-South bias that marred most histories of Reconstruction till that time.

In 1961, angered by the Cold War and the government's harassment of him for his opposition to it, DuBois joined the Communist party. But by then he had already committed his mind and heart to Africa—"the Spiritual Frontier of humankind," as he called it. He accepted an invitation from the government of Ghana to supervise compilation of the *Encyclopedia Africana* and died in Accra in 1963 at the age of ninety-five. He had become a Ghanian citizen just a few months before his death.

As a white member of the NAACP remarked a half-century earlier, William E. B. DuBois was a classic study of a gifted black damaged emotionally by being "treated as inferior by many men whom he knows to be his inferiors."

Fathers. Educationally, it inculcated the belief that advanced training was both a societal need and a public responsibility. Sociologically, it put into the political realm an environmental and behaviorist interpretation of society that, for all its oversimplifications, was and remains the moral rationale for social reform. Psychologically, it changed the perception of government from a negative to a positive force and more or less fixed the view that the federal government should serve as a countervailing power to the large business corporation. Administratively, progressivism demonstrated both the government's dependence on experts and the apparent impossibility of completely insulating them from the influence of powerful private interests. Constitutionally, it raised important, and partly effective, challenges to the concept of state's rights and to the prerogatives of manufacturers engaged in interstate commerce. Economically, it established a revenue base for the society's current and future needs by winning broad acceptance of the general principle of graduated corporation, income, and inheritance taxes.

Just as important, perhaps, progressivism greatly stimulated the rising expectations and dependence on government for the solutions of social and economic problems that have become the dominant themes of contemporary society.

Chapter 18

The Rise of America as a World Power 1898–1919

THE NEW FRONTIER

Several decades before the historian Frederick Jackson Turner proclaimed in 1893 that the Western frontier had closed, an influential minority of Americans were straining to extend the nation's power and influence to the remote reaches of the globe. Their motives and emphases varied. Some feared that Europe's penetration of South America threatened the United States' security. Others felt that it was the manifest destiny of a "superior" people to extend their influence. Still others believed that expansion would divert the people's attention from slavery or pressing industrial problems. But in almost all cases there was an underlying conviction that assured access to the markets of the world was essential to long-term prosperity and that the possession of outlying territories was one of the hallmarks of greatness.

"Rome expanded and passed away," wrote Theodore Roosevelt, "but all western Europe, both Americas, Australia and large parts of Asia and Africa to this day continue the history of Rome. . . . Spain expanded and fell, but a whole continent to this day speaks Spanish and is covered with commonwealths of the Spanish tongue and culture. . . . England expanded and England will fall. But think of what she will leave behind her. . . ."

The foremost early expansionist was William H. Seward, Secretary of State under Lincoln and Johnson. "Give me . . . fifty, forty, thirty more years of life," he delared in Boston in 1867, "and I will give you possession of the American continent and control of the world." Two months later the United States took over the unoccupied Midway Islands far out in the Pacific. Then, in April 1867, the Senate ratified a treaty with Russia, negotiated by Seward, for the purchase of Alaska for $7,200,000. But most Americans were still too anti-imperialistic to give Seward his rein, and he went out of office in 1869 with his major objectives unfulfilled—annexation by one means or another of Hawaii, Cuba, Puerto Rico, the Danish West Indies (now the Virgin Islands), St. Bartholomew's Island (now St. Barthélemy), Greenland, Iceland, and Canada.

Nevertheless, the expansionist impulse continued to grow. Under President Grant an annexation treaty with Santo Domingo was signed but rejected by the Senate, 24 to 24. And only the consummate diplomacy of Seward's successor, Hamilton Fish, prevented the United States from becoming embroiled in Cuba, where a rebellion against Spain broke out in 1868. Meanwhile the expansionist minority was formulating the intellectual underpinning of its case. As early as 1847 the *New York Sun* had begun to argue that annexation of Cuba would be commercially advantageous. Many Americans subscribed to these sentiments.

More significant in the long run was the growing rapport between naval officers, congressmen, intellectuals, and businessmen. During the 1870s the United States' exports exceeded its imports for the first time, and in the 1880s the aforementioned groups combined forces to promote the revitalization of the navy. Again and again, congressmen justified requests for naval construction in commercial or expansionist terms. "The time has come . . .," Senator John F. Miller of California declared in 1884, "when manufactures are springing up all over the land, when new markets are necessary to be found in order to keep our factories running." Congressmen also deferred to the professional officers' expertise. "We assembled at the Navy Department," the chairman of the House Naval Affairs Committee explained, "and listened to the advice of naval officers, and our bill was changed in obedience to their views." Finally, in 1890, Captain Alfred T. Mahan published *The Influence of Sea Power upon History*. A brilliant synthesis of ideas current in naval circles for ten years or more, it argued that only a large navy could protect the trade that would be the lifeblood of the new American empire.

Many businessmen agreed. The National Association of Manufacturers devoted much of its initial program to promoting expansion of the merchant marine, the navy, and foreign trade. Expansionist intellectuals and politicians continued to trumpet for territorial acquisitions. In 1885 the Reverend Josiah Strong in *Our Country* equated Christianity with those "peculiarly aggressive traits" that would impose Anglo-Saxon civilization "upon Mexico, down upon Central and South America, out upon the islands of the seas, over upon Africa and beyond." That same year John Fiske, the most persuasive of the Social Darwinists, predicted that "every land on the earth's surface that is not already the seat of an old civilization shall become English in its language, in its religion, in its political habits." A decade later Henry Cabot Lodge, a disciple of Captain Mahan, put forth the

Russia and the United States discuss their interests as Uncle Sam tries to straddle the globe. American expansionists wanted to extend the nation's power and influence over much of the world.

commercial rationale for naval expansion in categorical terms:

Commerce follows the flag. The great nations are rapidly absorbing for their future expansion and their present defense all the waste places of the earth. . . . The United States must not fall out of the line of march.

Samoa.   Heard on the completion of the first transcontinental railroad in 1869, American business and naval groups arranged a treaty for a naval station and commercial coaling rights in Samoa in expectation of a quickening of the Asian trade. A decade of jockeying for control of Samoa by Germany, Great Britain, and the United States followed. Open conflict was narrowly avoided in 1889, and the German government proposed that the islands be divided. But at the United States' insistence they agreed instead to establish a tripartite protectorate. Rivalry continued, and in 1899 the fiction of Samoan independence ended. Germany and the United States divided the Samoan Islands, and Great Britain took the Gilbert and Solomon Islands in compensation.

Hawaii.   Another group of naval officers conspired with Hawaiian-American business interests to give the United States control of Hawaii, the crossroads of the central Pacific. Invoking native misgovernment as their rationale, the white leaders who dominated the Hawaiian economy virtually disfranchised the natives in 1887. With the support of the American minister and American marines, they then overthrew Queen Liliuokalani in 1893 and sent a mission to Washington to negotiate a treaty of annexation. They hoped thereby to avoid the sugar tariff and assure orderly government in their own interest.

President Cleveland's refusal to approve the treaty set off a four-year debate. American strategists contended that possession of Hawaii would give naval protection to the Pacific Coast, prevent annexation by Japan, and enable the United States to penetrate the Far East commercially and militarily. Annexation, in their view, was part of a "Large Policy" embracing construction of a Nicaraguan canal and acquisition of Canada. Meanwhile a puppet government ruled Hawaii for white businessmen.

President McKinley announced on taking office that he opposed all acquisition of territory, but he soon changed his mind. Three months after his inauguration he submitted a new treaty of annexation to the Senate. The treaty was rejected. But later, after naval operations in the Pacific during the Spanish-American War dramatized Hawaii's usefulness as a naval base, Congress annexed the islands by joint resolution in July 1898. "As I look back upon the first steps in this miserable business and as I contemplate the outrage," ex-President Cleveland wrote to his former Secretary of State Richard Olney, "I am ashamed of the whole affair."

Venezuela and the Monroe Doctrine.   Yet Cleveland himself had contributed to the jingoism that made the imperialists' triumph possible. Angered by Great Britain's refusal in 1895 to accept American arbitration of a boundary dispute between British Guiana and Venezuela, Secretary of State Olney had bluntly informed the British Foreign Secretary that ". . . the United States is practically sovereign on this continent, and its fiat is law." The British testily replied that the Monroe Doctrine was not recognized in international law and did not apply to boundary disputes in any event. Cleveland then warned that failure to accept the findings of an American investigation would constitute "a willful aggression." Four years later an international commission fixed the boundary largely in accord with Britain's original claims.

Cleveland's rude threat of force had ironic implications. Until then, enforcement of the Monroe Doctrine had actually been dependent on the might of the Royal Navy. Now the Doctrine became an instrument of American initiative. More ironic still, the President's action prompted Great Britain to reappraise its relations with the United States in the context of Germany's rise to world power. This was to lead, in time, to a decision of momentous importance—agreement during the administration of Theodore Roosevelt on a kind of unofficial naval alliance between the United States and Great Britain.

THE GREAT DEPARTURE

Trouble in Cuba.   In spite of the increasingly strong thrust of the imperialists, American foreign policy until 1898 had been generally grounded on a realistic appraisal of the national interest—one which reflected a sharp awareness of both the possibilities and the limitations of American power. The festering crisis in Cuba during the 1890s precipitated the first fateful departure from this policy.

Cubans had always resented Spain's misrule of their island. When their sugar economy collapsed under the weight of European competition, the international depression of 1893, and the restrictive duties of the Wilson-Gorman Tariff of 1894, their smoldering hostilities flamed into a full-scale revolt. Determined to suppress it, Spain sent over its ablest general, Valeriano "Butcher" Weyler, who soon drove much of the civilian population into concentration camps at an estimated cost of 200,000 lives.

An outpouring of propaganda from a revolutionary junta in New York and by the yellow journalism of the New York *World* and New York *Journal* intensified the American people's sympathies for the Cuban people. "You furnish the pictures," *Journal* publisher William Randolph Hearst wired one of his artists who reported that there was no war in Cuba to portray, "and I'll furnish the war." But it was the press as a whole, feeding voraciously on the junta's releases and re-

printing indiscriminately the *World's* and the *Journal's* atrocity stories, that incited the nationwide hysteria.

Genuine sympathy for the Cubans combined with less altruistic attitudes to create a growing demand for a war to liberate the Cubans. Conservative Republicans and Democrats hoped that a war would divert attention from liberal or populist issues such as free silver. Others saw commercial benefits: "Free Cuba would mean a great market to the United States" and "an opportunity for American capital," Senator Lodge asserted. Protestant clergymen felt that American intervention would alleviate suffering and, incidentally, open Cuba to Protestantism. Ultranationalists saw war as a means of testing the nation's military might, uniting the North and South, and even resolving the unemployment problem. As an Atlantan wrote the President, "The South dearly loves a fighter; if you will show yourself strong and courageous in defense of Cuba, you will have a solid South at your call. . . . Strengthen the Army and Navy of this country and in this way give employment to the thousands of idle men who need it."

But Grover Cleveland had a different conception of his duty. Convinced that the Cuban insurrectionists were as barbarous as the Spaniards, he left office in March 1897 without having yielded to the passions of the times.

Escalation of Conflict with Spain.   Cleveland's successor, William McKinley, lacked Cleveland's stubborn courage and iron principle. Neither McKinley nor his industrialist and banker friends wanted war. Under American pressure, Spain recalled General Weyler in the summer of 1897. The Spanish government also promised to abolish the concentration camps and to grant Cuba an autonomy similar to that of Canada. Nevertheless, McKinley gradually locked himself into a policy of full independence for Cuba.

The war fever mounted in early February 1898, when the Hearst press published a stolen letter, written by the Spanish Minister Dupuy de Lome, which called McKinley a "peanut politician" and a "bidder for the admiration of the crowd." Western Republicans introduced three separate resolutions to give the Cuban insurrectionists the status of a warring power, and McKinley dispatched the battleship *Maine* to Havana in a gesture designed to display the American government's resolve to force a settlement.

On February 15 an explosion destroyed the *Maine* in Havana Harbor. The cause was never determined, but the Hearst papers, the New York *Tribune*, and a few other newspapers blamed the disaster on Spain and called for war. Lodge, Senator Albert J. Beveridge of Indiana, and other militant politicians joined them. The *Maine* "was sunk by an act of dirty treachery on the part of the Spaniards," then Assistant Secretary of the Navy Roosevelt charged. But McKinley and most of the financial establishment still hoped for peace.

The cause of the explosion that destroyed the battleship Maine was not determined, but the disaster was blamed on Spain and used to justify increasing cries for war.

The President appointed a commission of inquiry and resumed negotiations with Spain.

As passions mounted, administration circles began to fear that McKinley could not be reelected if he refused to submit. Reluctantly, important business and financial leaders who had little interest in expansion and none whatever in liberating the Cubans or avenging the destruction of the *Maine* now joined the war hawks. Thus presidential adviser Elihu Root warned: "Fruitless attempts to hold back or retard the enormous momentum of the people bent upon war would result in the destruction of the President's power and influence, in depriving the country of its natural leader, in the elevation of the Silver Democracy to power." Under the weight of such counsels McKinley lost the will to resist. "I think . . . possibly the President could have worked out the business without war," one of his intimates later wrote, "but the current was too strong, the demagogues too numerous, the fall elections too near."

On March 27, 1898, the United States sent an ultimatum to Spain demanding an immediate armistice, closing of the concentration camps, and Cuban independence if the United States decided it was advisable. Before Spain could respond, the President began to compose his war message. Then on April 11, two days after Spain had capitulated to his first two demands, he sent the unrevised message to Congress, adding only that Spain had agreed to an armistice. Within two weeks Congress enthusiastically passed, and the President signed, a joint resolution authorizing use of force to compel the Spaniards to evacuate. The Teller Amendment to the resolution pledged the United States to withdraw from Cuba as soon as its independence had been established.

The Spanish-American War. Only the American navy was prepared for hostilities. Modernization and expansion of the fleet had roughly paralleled the rise of interest in the Far East, and by 1898 the United States navy was the fifth largest in the world. The Asiatic squadron was especially strong. Ten days before the destruction of the *Maine*, in accordance with standing plans, Assistant Secretary of the Navy Theodore Roosevelt ordered Commodore George Dewey to attack the Philippines in the event of war with Spain.

On May 1, in less than seven hours, Dewey destroyed an antiquated Spanish fleet in Manila Bay and changed the course of history. Six weeks later 17,000 regular army troops and volunteers, including Theodore Roosevelt's "Rough Riders," landed in Cuba amidst incredible confusion. They were short of every basic supply from arms to medicine. Nevertheless they drove forward, winning a fierce engagement at El Caney and a major battle at San Juan Hill. They then beseiged Santiago. Out of these engagements emerged the usual complement of heroes, but none so dramatic as Colonel Roosevelt. "The instant I received the order I sprang on my horse," he wrote, "and then my 'crowded hour' began."

The end of the war swiftly followed. On July 3 an American squadron commanded by Rear Admiral William T. Sampson destroyed the Spanish fleet after it emerged from Santiago Harbor. Back in the Pacific, American forces took Wake Island the following day. On July 17 the Spanish ground force in Santiago surrounded, and eight days later American troops occupied Puerto Rico with little opposition. An armistice ended further hostilities on August 12. All told, the United States lost 379 men in battle and 5462 from disease and other causes. "It has been a splendid little war," Secretary of State John Hay remarked.

Justification for Imperialism. The self-denying Teller Amendment had reflected the American people's humanitarian strain as distinct from their romantic imperialist impulses. Expansionist sentiment had grown to gale-like proportions during the war. The Hawaiian annexation resolution rolled

American troops won a fierce battle at El Caney and captured the Spanish
fortifications that protected the city of Santiago, shown below the fort.

through Congress three months after hostilities began. Soon afterward the President
decided that Puerto Rico and Guam should be
ceded to the United States. Meanwhile, he
made plans to retain Manila and finally
decided to annex the entire Philippine archipelago.

McKinley later explained his decision to a
delegation of Methodist clergymen:

I went down on my knees and prayed God
Almighty for light and guidance more than one
night. And one night late it came to me this way—I
don't know how it was, but it came: (1) that we
could not give them back to Spain—that would be
cowardly and dishonorable; (2) that we could not

turn them over to France or Germany—our
commercial rivals in the Orient—that would be bad
business and discreditable; (3) that we could not
leave them to themselves—they were unfit for
self-government—and they would soon have anarchy and misrule over there worse than Spain's was;
and (4) that there was nothing left for us to do but to
take them all, and to educate the Filipinos, and
uplift and civilize and Christianize them, and by
God's grace do the very best we could by them, as
our fellow men for whom Christ also died. And
then I went to bed and went to sleep and slept
soundly.

The President's explanation was accurate
and inclusive. Spanish rule had actually been

worse in the Philippines than in Cuba, the Filipinos were unprepared for self-government, and they could not long have remained independent on their own. But McKinley's most fundamental reason was the third: desire for a commercial outpost in the Far East. As Mark Hanna declared, "If it is commercialism to want the possession of a strategic point giving the American people an opportunity to maintain a foothold in the markets of . . . China, for God's sake let us have commercialism."

All through the summer and autumn of 1898 newspapers, religious publications, and civic leaders called for retention of the Phillippines for the same reasons the President gave the Methodist clergymen. McKin-

Filipino insurgents against Spain, like the men shown at this partisan outpost, soon turned against the Americans, their new, would-be masters.

ley sensed the force of this opinion, but he wanted to be certain that the people as a whole would approve such a radical break with tradition. So in October, with a stenographer at his side to time the applause given his various soundings, he toured the Middle West. Convinced finally that national sentiment favored annexation, he cabled his peace commissioners in Paris to demand cession of the entire Philippine archipelago.

The Treaty of Paris. By the terms of the treaty signed on December 10, 1898, Spain ceded the Philippines to the United States for $20 million. Spain also acknowledged Cuban independence and ceded Puerto Rico and Guam outright to the United States. Two months later the Senate ratified the treaty. It would probably have been defeated had not a substantial number of anti-imperialist Republicans put party loyalty above conscience. It would also have been defeated if Bryan had not influenced a handful of Democrats to support it in the hope that imperialism would then become the dominant issue in the presidential campaign of 1900.

The Aftermath of Conquest. By 1900 the United States was tasting the first bitter fruits of imperialism. Filipino partisans had begun a fierce fight for independence from Spain before the Americans arrived. They turned against their new American masters in 1899 and inflicted losses on the American occupation troops heavier than those suffered in the war with Spain. Not until the Americans resorted to methods as ruthless as those used by the Spanish in Cuba were the Filipinos finally defeated formally in 1902. Guerilla warfare continued through 1906.

Partial restitution followed. McKinley, and especially Theodore Roosevelt, took literally the poet's charge to "Take up the White Man's burden—/Send forth the best ye breed." McKinley instituted and Roosevelt greatly strengthened a political system designed to prepare the Filipinos for self-government. Schools were built. Small farmers were installed on lands purchased from the Catholic Church. Numerous other reforms were instituted.

Meanwhile, the United States observed the form of the Teller Amendment by granting nominal independence to Cuba. Many benefits to the people in public health followed. By insisting that Cuba accept an agreement—the Platt Amendment—the United States assured itself control of Cuba's foreign affairs and the right to intervene to protect Cuban national independence and just government. Then, in May 1902, American forces withdrew. But the United States retained a naval base at Guantanamo Bay under what became a permanent lease.

Such minor economic advantages as accrued to the United States from its new island possessions were offset in the long run by vast American expenditures for civic and social improvement. From the outset, moreover, the Philippines were a military liability—"our heel of Achilles," as Roosevelt was calling them by 1907.

Although the United States slowly instituted democratic forms of government on those islands it owned outright, it remains an open question whether on balance native peoples fared better or worse under American rule. Hawaii prospered, but largely as the virtual fief of a half-dozen giant American corporations. Puerto Rico, short of natural resources, suffered from absentee ownership and overpopulation induced by American public health measures. And the Philippines concentrated too much on the production of raw materials for the American market. Everywhere, to be sure, the material standard of living improved considerably. Yet the old social structures and extremes of wealth and poverty persisted, while much of the islanders' cultural integrity disintegrated.

THE FAR EASTERN ABERRATION

The Open Door. The quest for trade, missionary zeal, and illusions of grandeur soon drove the United States into the vortex of Far Eastern affairs. Senator Albert J. Beveridge summed it all up in January 1900:

The Philippines are ours forever. . . . And just beyond . . . are China's illimitable markets. We will not retreat from either . . . will not renounce our part in the mission of our race, trustees under God, of the civilization of the world. . . . The power that rules the Pacific is the power that rules the world.

Yet, in another sense, American policy was grounded more on fear than on the aggressive territorial designs of businessmen and romantics. All the great powers—Japan, Russia, France, Britain, and Germany—and two of the smaller ones, Belgium and Holland, were more stridently imperialistic than the United States during this period. Virtually all Africa had already been taken over by Europeans. Southeast Asia had become the province of the British, the Dutch, and the French. Japan was bursting to take over Korea. And Germany aspired to whatever was available in the Far East, North Africa, or South America. However great the ultimate tragedy of the United States' acquisition of the Philippines, McKinley had correctly assayed French and German designs in making his decision to acquire them.

Alone among the powers, the United States took an enlightened position toward China. The great powers had been carving out spheres of influence in that unhappy land for several years. In 1899 the British began to evade payment of the tariff, the Chinese government's main source of revenue. Such action, if adopted by the French, Germans, Russians, and Japanese (Italy also sought, but failed to get, a sphere of influence), would have forced the collapse of the Peking government and the dismemberment of all

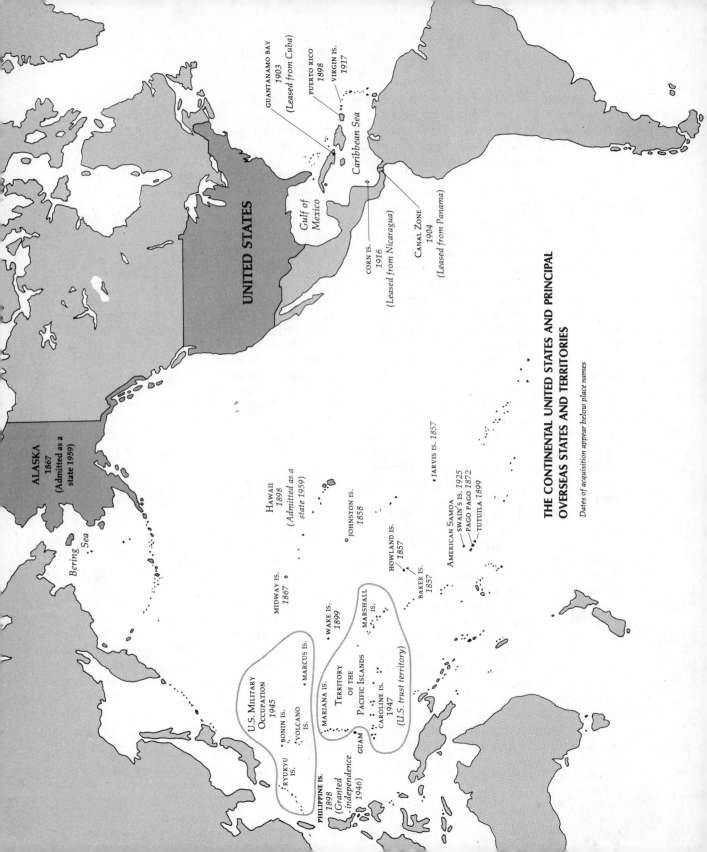

GUANTANAMO BAY
1903
(Leased from Cuba)

PUERTO RICO
1898

VIRGIN IS.
1917

Caribbean Sea

CORN IS.
1916
(Leased from Nicaragua)

CANAL ZONE
1904
(Leased from Panama)

Gulf of
Mexico

UNITED STATES

ALASKA
1867
(Admitted as a
state 1959)

Bering
Sea

HAWAII
1898
(Admitted as a
state 1959)

JOHNSTON IS.
1858

MIDWAY IS.
1867

WAKE IS.
1899

MARSHALL
IS.

HOWLAND IS.
1857

BAKER IS.
1857

• JARVIS IS. 1857

AMERICAN SAMOA
SWAIN'S IS. 1925
PAGO PAGO 1872
TUTUILA 1899

U.S. MILITARY
OCCUPATION
1945

BONIN IS.

VOLCANO
IS.

• MARCUS IS.

MARIANA IS.

TERRITORY
OF THE
PACIFIC ISLANDS
1947
(U.S. trust territory)

CAROLINE IS.

GUAM

RYUKYU
IS.

PHILIPPINE IS.
1898
(Granted
independence
1946)

THE CONTINENTAL UNITED STATES AND PRINCIPAL
OVERSEAS STATES AND TERRITORIES

Dates of acquisition appear below place names

China. Concerned by the implications to American business and persuaded, in any event, that freedom to trade was in the interest of everyone, Secretary of State John Hay sent a round of "Open Door" notes to the powers in 1899 and 1900. The notes proposed, in summary, that Chinese officials continue to collect tariffs and that all nations be guaranteed equal trade rights throughout China. Although most of the powers responded equivocally, Hay baldly announced their acceptance.

The weakness of the Open Door notes was less one of principle than of power. As Admiral Mahan pointed out at this time, the United States lacked the will and the military strength to enforce them. Nevertheless, they marked a heady triumph for the proponents of the "Large Policy," commanding, in the words of one historian, "a measure of interest and support over the years second only to that accorded the Monroe Doctrine." In particular, they led to deep and continuing involvement in the Far East by the United States and, ultimately, to conflict with Japan.

Roosevelt's Policy. More than any other twentieth-century American President, Theodore Roosevelt viewed the Open Door policy with a measure of realism. He felt that the United States could maintain a legitimate interest in the Far East only by recognizing Japan's need for raw materials and markets. He also believed—even more strongly—that Japan was a natural counterpoise to Russia, whose failure to withdraw from southern Manchuria until 1907 he termed an act of "well-nigh incredible mendacity." Thus he approved the Japanese-British naval alliance of 1902, and he privately accepted Japanese suzerainty in Korea in 1905.

By then Roosevelt was mediating the Russo-Japanese War of 1904–1905 at the request of the victorious but nearly insolvent Japanese. Basically, he sought to preserve the balance of power and to protect the Open Door. But he also deemed it his moral duty to end the carnage as soon as possible. He further hoped to cement Japanese-American relations. His mediation fulfilled the first three of these goals but failed in the fourth because the Japanese blamed him for Russia's refusal to pay a war indemnity or to cede to them all of Sakhalin Island.

A decision by the San Francisco board of education to segregate the ninety-three Japanese students in the city's public schools dealt Japanese-American relations a more serious blow in October 1906. Roosevelt labeled the segregation order "a crime against a friendly nation" and threatened to use "all the forces, civil and military," at his command to rectify it. He then called the board members to the White House. They agreed to reverse the order if Japan would curb the emigration of peasants and laborers. A "Gentlemen's Agreement" to that effect was arranged in 1907.

Having thus deferred to Japanese sensibilities, Roosevelt characteristically decided to flaunt American strength by sending the battle fleet on a world cruise in 1907. Before the fleet returned, however, the President made another realistic concession to Japan. By the Root-Takahira Agreement of November 1908 the United States probably, though not certainly, recognized Japan's economic ascendancy in Manchuria in return for a reaffirmation of the status quo in the Pacific and the Open Door in China.

New Far Eastern Policies. Neither Taft nor Wilson shared Roosevelt's view that the United States should accept Japanese preeminence in East Asia. As early as 1910 Roosevelt warned Taft that China was "weak and unreliable" and that the United States should abandon its commercial aspirations in Manchuria. But Taft believed too strongly in the fiction of Chinese independence and was too enamored of trade possibilities to agree. He followed instead a policy of "active intervention to secure for our merchandise and our capitalists opportunity for profitable investment." He permitted his Secretary of State, Philander C. Knox, to demand American participation in an international bankers' consortium to build a network of railways in China. Taft also allowed Knox, who was alarmed by the consolidation of Japanese and Russian influence in Manchuria, to propose internationalization of that province's railways.

President Wilson proved no less determined than Taft to maintain the Open Door. "Our industries have expanded to such a point that they will burst their jackets if they cannot find a free outlet to the markets of the world," he declared in 1912. "Our domestic markets no longer suffice. We need foreign markets." Essentially, however, he conceived of China, which had been penetrated by Christian missionaries, in moralistic terms. He opposed the bankers' consortium because he feared that it would result in European domination, not because he intended to withdraw from the Far East. The United States, he declared at the time, intends "to participate, and participate very generously, in the opening to the Chinese and to the use of the world the almost untouched and perhaps unlimited resources of China." He then urged American bankers to act independently.

Wilson perceived that the outbreak of World War I in 1914 created a power vacuum in China because of the great powers' involvement in Europe. When Japan tried to make China into a satellite by imposing twenty-one far-reaching demands in 1915, the President vigorously defended Chinese integrity and independence. To forestall Japanese economic domination of China, Wilson and Secretary of State Robert Lansing proposed formation of a new four-power consortium to supply China with private capital. With Wilson's approval, Lansing also rejected Tokyo's demand that the United States recognize Japan's paramount interest in

China just as Japan had recognized America's in Mexico. Finally, they arranged a *modus vivendi*—the Lansing-Ishii Agreement of November 1917. By this document the United States recognized Japan's special interests in China while Japan reaffirmed its support of the Open Door and agreed not to use the war situation to seek new privileges in China.

THE CARIBBEAN

Panama. President Roosevelt's Caribbean diplomacy aimed to establish stability, security, and U.S. supremacy in the area. Soon after taking office he arranged negotiation of the second Hay-Pauncefote Treaty (1901), by which Great Britain granted the United States the right to build and defend a canal across Central America. Early American planning envisioned a Nicaraguan route. But in 1902 Roosevelt seized an opportunity to buy for $40 million a French company's rights to a more desirable route through Panama. The President also had Secretary of State Hay draw up a treaty to grant $10 million and $250,000 annual rental for the proposed canal zone to Colombia, which owned Panama.

The Colombian senate's indignant rejection of this arrangement infuriated Roosevelt. Privately castigating the Colombians as "Dagos" and "inefficient bandits," he tacitly encouraged agents of the French company to stimulate a Panamanian revolution against Colombia. When the revolution broke out on November 3, 1903, he sent an American warship to the scene under conditions that assured the revolutionaries' success. Three days later he recognized the new Republic of Panama and approved a treaty, negotiated by Panama's new minister (an agent of the French company), authorizing the United States to build the canal.

Roosevelt later claimed that "our course was straightforward and in absolute accord with the highest standards of international morality." But in 1911 he blurted, "I took the

The Panama Canal, started in 1904, took ten years to build. The workmen and engineers shown in this photo are preparing concrete forms for the Miraflores Locks at the Pacific side of Panama.

canal zone and let Congress debate, and while the debate goes on the canal also does." Ten years after that confession, the United States agreed to pay Colombia $25 million. By then Roosevelt was dead, but the memory of his high-handedness lived on.

Meanwhile, the first great government corporation in American history overcame extraordinary health and engineering problems to complete construction of the Panama Canal. It was opened to the commerce of the world on August 15, 1914, on equal terms to all nations—but only because President Wilson had persuaded Congress to repeal an act of 1912 that exempted American coastwise traffic from payment of tolls.

The Roosevelt Corollary. The need to defend the Panama Canal soon drew the United States deeply into the affairs of the Caribbean. Neither Roosevelt nor his successors wanted this. As the President said of the Dominican Republic, he had "about the same desire to annex it as a gorged boa constrictor might have to swallow a porcupine wrong-end-to." But the poverty, instability, and corruption of the Caribbean countries invited European penetration, and even such an apostle of peace as William Jennings Bryan saw no recourse but to make the Caribbean Sea an American lake.

The first serious incident occurred in December 1902, when the Germans, cooperating with the British in a blockade of Venezuela, bombarded a port town and threatened to take control of Venezuelan customs in order to force payment of debts owed their citizens. Roosevelt and the American people reacted militantly. Kaiser Wilhelm II, reluctant to add the United States to the growing list of nations hostile to Germany, accepted Roosevelt's suggestion for mediation, as did Britain. The dispute was settled by the Hague Tribunal in 1904.

By then the Dominican Republic had been forced by the German, Italian, and Spanish governments to sign protocols for the payment of debts. The Dominicans thereupon requested Roosevelt "to establish some kind of protectorate over the islands," as the President phrased it. In 1905 the United States assumed control of Dominican customs so that funds could be allotted to the European creditors.

To preclude future intervention in the Caribbean by Europeans, Roosevelt also declared that the United States was empowered to serve as an international police force in the event of "chronic wrongdoing, or an impotence which results in a general loosening of the ties of civilized society." This, the so-called Roosevelt Corollary to the Monroe Doctrine, transformed the original doctrine from an external protective device to a justification for internal intervention by the United States. Two years later the President sent American troops into Cuba to avert a revolution.

Dollar Diplomacy. President Taft expanded upon Roosevelt's policies. In 1912 he dispatched marines to Nicaragua to install and maintain a conservative, pro-American government. Meanwhile he and Secretary of State Philander Knox devised a program called "dollar diplomacy"—use of private American capital, often against both the desire and the judgment of the bankers concerned—to displace European bondholders and concessionaires in Latin America. Over the years this drive for stability and protection of the Panama Canal resulted in a clear pattern of American support of ultraconservative and often dictatorial governments in much of Central America and the Caribbean.

Wilson's Mission: Ideal and Reality. President Wilson was not averse to using dollar diplomacy when circumstances seemed to require it. But he and Secretary of State William Jennings Bryan also conceived that they had a mission to democratize the corrupt and revolution-ridden Caribbean republics. "We can have no sympathy with those who seek to seize the power of government to advance their own personal interests or ambition," Wilson warned in a public statement on March 11, 1913. "As friends, therefore, we shall prefer those who act in the interest of peace and honor, who protect private rights and respect the restraints of constitutional provision."

Unparalleled diplomatic and military intervention in the Caribbean and Mexico followed. The Wilson administration regularized the occupation of Nicaragua (which remained occupied by U.S. marines until 1933). It sent marines to Haiti and, by imposing a puppet but nominally democratic regime in 1915, made that state a virtual protectorate of the United States. It dispatched marines to the Dominican Republic in 1916 and governed it directly through military officers. It also fostered road building, school construction, and public health projects.

Triumph and Tragedy in Mexico. Meanwhile, Wilson embarked on a bold new policy toward Mexico, where the classic Latin American alliance of dictator, Church, and foreign investors had provoked a convulsive political upheaval. By 1911 more than half of Mexico's oil, two thirds of its railroads, and three fourths of its mines and smelters were owned by Americans. Much of the remaining oil was British-owned. The Catholic Church was the largest landowner, though William Randolph Hearst and other Americans also had huge holdings. The average Mexican peon or industrial worker lived in abject poverty.

Against this background, a revolution erupted in 1910. The dictator Porfirio Díaz was finally driven out in May 1911 by a group of middle-class intellectuals headed by a constitutionalist named Francisco Madero. Less than a year later Madero himself was overthrown and murdered by counterrevolutionary forces under the army's chief general,

Victoriano Huerta, who became president of Mexico amid revolutionary upheaval.

Wilson's first break with tradition came when he withheld recognition from Huerta on the grounds that the United States should henceforth cooperate only with governments based on the unquestioned consent of the governed. Next he persuaded the British to withdraw their support from Huerta. Then he brought his new policy to fruition by offering to aid Huerta's chief antagonist, the constitutional reformer Venustiano Carranza. Carranza wanted only arms, and on February 3, 1914, Wilson lifted an arms embargo instituted by Taft.

Huerta's strength nevertheless continued to increase, partly as a result of resentment over United States interference. Wilson's sense of frustration became more acute. Seizing finally on a trivial incident at Tampico, he asked Congress for authority to move against the Mexican dictator. Congress had not responded by April 21, 1914, when Wilson ordered the fleet to occupy Vera Cruz to prevent a German ship from unloading ammunition. In the resultant action, 126 Mexicans were killed.

The President's militant action horrified peace-loving Americans and provoked even Carranza to threaten full-scale resistance should American troops march on Mexico City. Abandoned by the liberals of both Mexico and the United States, Wilson resolved his dilemma by agreeing to mediation by the "ABC powers"—Argentina, Brazil, and Chile. Huerta eventually resigned in favor of Carranza, who became *de facto* president of Mexico.

Yet Wilson continued to press Carranza to accept his guidance. He warned against mass executions and made it clear that he would oppose expropriation of the vast holdings of Americans and other foreigners. Then, wrongly concluding that Pancho Villa, an unscrupulous military adventurer tinged with Robin Hoodism, was an honest social reformer, Wilson began to support him. Carranza thereupon broadened his own reform program while his leading general crushed Villa's armies in the field.

Back in Washington, American conservatives put the President under tremendous pressure to mount a full-scale invasion of Mexico. The Catholic hierarchy, the Hearst press, oil and other corporate interests, and ultranationalists like Theodore Roosevelt all urged him to act. But Wilson held firm and in October 1915 extended *de facto* recognition to the Carranza regime.

Reduced to banditry, Villa now strove to regain his power by inciting the United States to war. Early in 1916 he murdered eighteen American engineers in northern Mexico, and Wilson once again braved a nearly overpowering call for war. Then, in a bold sortie into New Mexico, Villa killed seventeen more Americans. The President thereupon ordered Brigadier General John J. Pershing to pursue Villa into Mexico. More incidents followed, and for the third time conservatives and ultranationalists called angrily for an all-out invasion. Wilson responded by mobilizing the National Guard along the Mexican border. But he refused to change the expedition's limited objective. Finally, in late January 1917, he ordered its withdrawal because of the impending conflict with Germany.

WORLD WAR I

Outbreak of Hostilities. On June 28, 1914, an obscure Serbian nationalist shot the heir to the Austro-Hungarian throne, Archduke Francis Ferdinand. The resultant crisis between Austria-Hungary and Serbia might have been localized if Europe had not been organized into a network of alliances which reflected deep divisions of militant nationalism, and if the Russian and Austrian governments had not been spurred to reckless action by dangers of national revolt. After Serbia rejected impossible demands by Austria, the Austrians opened hostilities against the Serbs. Russia then went to the aid of Serbia, and Germany declared war on Russia, prompting France to enter the war on the side of Russia. When German troops pushed through neutral Belgium in a vain effort to knock out France immediately, Great Britain went to war against Germany. Four years and three months later a generation of Europeans—almost 8.5 million—lay dead.

President Wilson believed at first that geography would save the United States from the holocaust. He issued a proclamation of neutrality and then adjured the American people to be "impartial in thought as well as in action." But despite an initial resolve to avoid military involvement, the American public was never disposed to be neutral in thought. The dominant British and French bias was compounded of ethnic, business, and cultural ties and was intensified by a vaguely formed feeling that a German victory would adversely affect American interests by putting an aggressive military regime in control of Europe and possibly of the high seas. Key foreign policy spokesmen, too, believed that the preservation of the European balance of power by Britain had long served American interests and that, as Senator Henry Cabot Lodge phrased it on September 23, if "Germany conquers France, England and Russia she will dominate Europe, and will subsequently extend that domination, if she can, to the rest of the world."

In these circumstances, Germany's violation of Belgian neutrality and later resort to indiscriminate submarine warfare simply solidified standing fears. Similarly, British propaganda served mainly to sharpen perceptions and inflame passions already present. "The principle of Anglo-Saxon liberty seems to have met the irreconcilable conception of the German State," wrote Elihu Root at the time, "and the two ideas are battling for control of the world."

These sentiments were far from unanimous. The great majority of the country's 8 million Germans and German-Americans were strongly attached to the fatherland. The spokesmen of the nation's 4.5 million Irish-Americans were almost universally anti-British. And several million Poles and Jews were almost fanatically anti-Russian. From the outset these groups fed on German propaganda in their foreign-language or diocesan newspapers, and neither the pro-Allied cast of the regular press nor German actions changed their sympathies during the period of 1914–1916. Because most of these groups were lower or lower-middle class, however, they never exercised an influence proportionate to their numbers.

The divisions among the American people were accentuated by the impossibility of genuine neutrality. German might was based on dominance of the land mass of central Europe, Great Britain's on control of the seas. To impose an embargo, as the pro-Germans and many pacifists demanded, would be to deal Britain a paralyzing blow. To supply the Allies, as the United States soon did, was to strengthen them in relation to Germany. Hence the impossiblity of substantive, as distinct from formalistic, neutrality.

President Wilson's decision to accept Britain's control of the seas seems to have been based on two factors: his desire to adhere to traditional rules of neutrality and his fear of a German victory. As he said to his cabinet in 1915, "the Allies are standing with their backs to the wall fighting wild beasts. I will permit nothing to be done by our country to hinder or embarrass them . . . unless admitted rights are grossly violated." Assuredly, he protested Britain's expansion of the contraband list (goods which they could intercept under international law) to include even food. But at no time did Wilson consider military action against Britain to uphold his shifting and, in some cases, historically untenable construction of neutral rights.

As the war progressed, the President authorized positive action to assure the flow of supplies to the Allies. Anticipating a strain on American gold reserves in the summer of 1914, he had permitted Secretary of State Bryan to declare that the administration disapproved of loans to the Allies because they violated the spirit of neutrality. He modified this policy in March 1915 by allowing the Morgan banking house to extend a $50 million credit to the French government. He rejected a German-American proposal to prohibit the export of all war materials. Then, in the summer of 1915, he completely lifted Bryan's ban on loans.

The President's realization that war orders had boosted American prosperity undoubtedly influenced these decisions. By 1916 exports to the Allies exceeded $3 billion in value, four times their 1914 level. "To maintain our prosperity, we must finance it," Secretary of the Treasury McAdoo warned Wilson in August 1915. "Otherwise it may stop and that would be disastrous."

German Submarine Warfare. On February 4, 1915, the German Admiralty marked out a broad war zone around the British Isles in which neutral vessels would run the risk of being sunk without warning by German submarines. Six days later Wilson replied that Germany would be held to "strict accountability" for illegal destruction of American ships and American lives.

The issue was first joined in March when an American was lost on a British liner torpedoed without warning. Arguing passionately that the United States should not indulge the technical right of its citizens to sail through war zones on belligerent ships, Bryan proposed that the government warn them against it. But before a decision was reached, an event of tragic proportions virtually destroyed all hopes of such a solution. On May 7 off the coast of Ireland the British liner *Lusitania* was sunk without warning, with a loss of 1198 lives, 124 of them American.

The immensity of the disaster appalled the nation, but few voices called out for war. From all over the country, in fact, came fervent appeals for peace, and from Democratic leaders in Congress came a warning that Wilson probably could not obtain passage of a war resolution. As a Kansas progressive leader informed Roosevelt, the Midwest's sense of outrage "died down as suddenly as it had risen." When the President soon afterward declared that "There is such a thing as a man being too proud to fight," Roosevelt was almost alone in denouncing him.

Determined to find a peaceful solution, Wilson called on the German government to renew its allegiance to "the rights of humanity" by conforming to the traditional rules of war. The second of his three notes were so stern that Bryan, who feared that it would provoke Germany into hostilities, resigned in protest. The President was prepared at the most to sever relations, but the Germans proved unwilling to gamble on his intent, and on June 6 the Admiralty ordered U-boats to spare large liners.

When a submarine provoked a more severe crisis by sinking the British liner *Arabic* on August 19, 1915, the German government avoided a break with America only by pledging that liners would not be sunk "without warning and without safety of the lives of noncombatants," providing they did not offer resistance or try to escape. Following the torpedoing of the French steamer *Sussex* in March 1916, Wilson sent the Imperial Government an even stronger ultimatum. The Germans again pledged restraint, subject to British observance of international law. Wilson accepted the pledge but not the qualification, and the crisis was temporarily resolved.

Steps Toward U.S. Preparedness. Meanwhile Wilson began to prepare the nation for the hazards of an uncertain future. He was reluctant to do so, but under the hammering

of Roosevelt and a substantial element of the Republican party, he finally faced the implications of his "strict accountability" policy. He took the first tentative steps in the summer of 1915, came out for major increases in the navy and army in December, and then toured the Middle West in January and February 1916 to whip up support for his new preparedness program.

No other issue of the period proved to be so revealing of the configuration of isolationist sentiment. Progressives of all three parties, including the secondary leadership of the disintegrating Bull Moose organization, op-

Wilson's steps toward preparedness meet with Uncle Sam's approval in this cartoon. In reality, however, his actions were strongly opposed by such diverse factions as progressives, farmers, and organized labor.

posed preparedness as a movement of munitions makers in particular and capitalists in general. Farmers in upstate New York, in California, on the Carolina Piedmont, and in the valley of Virginia, no less than on the plains of Kansas and Nebraska, charged that preparedness would lead to war. Organized labor all over the country—in New York and San Francisco as well as in Chicago, Milwaukee, and St. Louis—agreed.

Conversely, conservatives from every section of the nation supported preparedness enthusiastically. The Chamber of Commerce in almost every state endorsed it overwhelmingly. Bankers' and manufacturers' associations in the Midwest and South came out militantly for it.

The main opposition in Congress came from Bryan Democrats and a few Republican progressives. Attributing the movement to conservative Republicans, they resolved to make them bear its cost. "I am persuaded to think that when the income tax will have to pay for the increase in the army and navy," wrote Claude Kitchin of North Carolina to Bryan, "they will not be one-half so frightened over the future invasion by Germany." Not until Wilson agreed to accept their inheritance, munitions-profits, and progressive income tax program did they relax their opposition. Then it was to approve a severely compromised program. The defense legislation of 1916 provided for only moderate increases in the army.

The Election of 1916.   Prewar progressivism had reached full flower by the spring and summer of 1916. In convention at St. Louis in mid-June, the progressive-agrarian Democrats ignored the President's orders to make "Americanism" their keynote and indulged instead in one long and tremendous demand for peace. "He kept us out of war" became their campaign theme, and Wilson had little recourse but to accept it. Compared to the extreme measures advocated by the Roosevelt and Old Guard wings of the reunited Republican party—the so-called jingoes—Wilson's was in fact the policy of moderation. This was widely recognized at the time, and along with the Democrats' remarkable legislative record, it exerted a powerful pull on independents and ex-Bull Moosers.

Divisions within the Republican party also worked to Wilson's advantage. Although the G.O.P. platform criticized the Democratic preparedness program as inadequate and virtually called for war against Mexico, it deferred to the sensibilities of the more than one hundred German-American delegates at the Republican convention by equivocating on neutral rights. As a result, the Republican campaign lacked consistency. The Republican presidential candidate, former Justice Charles Evans Hughes, was forced, on the one hand, to call for a hard policy toward Germany and to contend, on the other hand, that such a policy would assure peace. Graphically, the St. Louis *Post-Dispatch* described his dilemma:

To satisfy the pro-Germans he must quarrel with the pro-British, who demand war with Germany. To satisfy Wall Street, he must quarrel with the western radicals. To satisfy the jingoes and the Munitions Trust, he must quarrel with most of the country. To satisfy privilege and plutocracy, he must quarrel with the people. Even as a candidate Mr. Hughes dare not have a policy, because to have a policy is to antagonize one element or another of his followers.

Wilson squeezed through by a narrow, half-million plurality. The resentment of Irish-, German-, Jewish-, and Polish-American voters possibly cost him much of the East and such Midwestern states as Illinois and Wisconsin, though some recent scholars dispute this. At any rate, he swept most states where isolationism reflected agrarian rather than ethnocentric views and where the progressive impulse was strong. He also carried most of the Western states in which women could vote.

The Failure of Mediation. Hardly were the returns in than the President sought to end the war. For almost two years he had been striving to persuade the belligerents to accept a negotiated peace. His efforts had failed because both the Allies and the Central Powers still aspired to victory in the field. Taking new hope in a German peace overture of December 12, 1916, Wilson six days later called on the belligerents to define their war aims. The British replied privately that they would negotiate on liberal terms (even though the Allies had returned a belligerent public answer), but the Germans answered evasively—and understandably so, for their real terms included control of Belgium and a strip of the French coast.

The President thereupon appealed to world opinion in a speech before the Senate on January 22, 1917. He asserted the right of the United States to share in laying the foundations for a lasting peace, set forth his plan for a League of Nations, and added the noblest of all his perorations: "It must be a peace without victory. Victory would mean peace forced upon the loser, a victor's terms imposed upon the vanquished. . . . Only a peace between equals can last."

People of good will the world over were intoxicated by Wilson's great vision. But realists knew that it was hopeless to expect the German military party to will its own destruction. On January 31 the German government submitted terms that would have assured its hegemony in Europe. It also announced resumption of unrestricted submarine warfare. The President then severed diplomatic relations with Germany.

Although Wilson still hoped to avert war, the onrush of events soon overtook him. From British intelligence on February 25 he received a transcript of the "Zimmermann note," a diplomatic message from German Foreign

Secretary Zimmermann proposing to Mexico that in the event of war between the United States and Germany, Mexico should join Germany against the United States. As a reward, Mexico should recover "the lost territory in Texas, New Mexico, and Arizona."

The next day the President asked Congress for authority to arm American ships for defense and to employ other measures to protect American commerce on the high seas. Bolstered by the public's militant reaction to the Zimmermann note, he castigated progressive senators who prevented adoption of the armed-ship bill as "a little group of willful men representing no opinion but their own." He then ordered ships armed under the authority of earlier statutes.

Events now moved swiftly to a climax. On March 19 three American ships went down with heavy losses. That same week a liberal revolution in Russia overthrew the czar. This softened the pro-German stance of Russian-American Jews and made progressives everywhere more willing to support the Allies. Great throngs of people now called for war in mass meetings in New York and other cities. Meanwhile the White House received reports from London that the Allies were in such desperate straits that only American intervention could save them.

Weighed down by these pressures, the President sorrowfully decided for full-scale war. As his biographer, Arthur S. Link, concludes, he did so mainly for two reasons: First, he believed that the war was already in its final stages and that American participation would bring it to a quick conclusion. Second, and much more important, he believed that Allied war aims posed such a threat to enduring peace that only a decisive American presence at the peace conference could assure a rational reconstruction of the world order. For this reason the United States became an Associate power rather than an Ally.

At eight-thirty in the evening on April 2, 1917, Wilson asked a joint session of Congress to recognize that Germany was at war against the United States and mankind. "The world must be made safe for democracy," he said, ". . . for the right of those who submit to authority to have a voice in their own Governments, for the rights and liberties of small nations, for a universal domination of right by such a concert of free peoples as shall bring peace and safety to all nations and make the world itself at last free."

Four days later, on April 6, 1917, the Senate voted for a war resolution 82 to 6, the House 373 to 50. How much this vote reflected Congress' acceptance of Wilson's concept of a world democratic mission, how much a purely nationalistic reaction against the loss of American shipping, and how much a conviction that British naval supremacy in the Atlantic was in the United States' continuing interest is impossible to say. All that is clear is that many Republican interventionists conceived the war as a power struggle involving American interests and disparaged the proposed League of Nations from the outset. "I am an American," expostulated Congressman Augustus P. Gardner of Massachusetts. "I want no internationalism. I want no conglomerate flag of all nations, with a streak of yellow down the middle."

A PEOPLE AT WAR

The President and his advisers soon learned that disaster loomed on almost every side. On the Western Front a French offensive had been stopped, and ten French divisions had already mutinied. In the Balkans the Allies were being pushed back. In Italy the Austrians, reinforced by the Germans, were soon to win a great victory at Caporetto. In the East the Russian armies were demoralized. On all fronts the Allies were running out of reserves. More ominous still, the Germans were destroying three times as much shipping each month as the Allies were building. Britain faced starvation unless something could be done.

The Washington administration responded boldly. The navy at once began to patrol the Western Hemisphere and to give assistance to the antisubmarine campaign around the British Isles. By July thirty-five American destroyers were based at Queenstown, Ireland. By the end of the war almost four hundred American ships were overseas. Meanwhile, the American navy virtually coerced the British into adopting the convoy system. The results of this critical decision were spectacular. Shipping losses fell from 881,027 tons in April to half that figure in December. By May 1918 they had dropped to 200,000 tons per month, thus destroying the calculations on which the Germans had based their decision to risk hostilities with the United States.

Mobilization for Victory. Three months after American intervention the administration created the War Industries Board to coordinate purchases, allocate raw materials, control production, and supervise labor relations. The WIB made rapid progress in some areas but failed to control military purchases. "The Military Establishment . . . has fallen down," a Democratic senator exclaimed in January 1918. "It has almost stopped functioning . . . because of inefficiency in every bureau and in every department of the Government." Rejecting a Republican demand for a coalition cabinet, Wilson boldly conferred such sweeping authority on the WIB's new head, Bernard Baruch, that the industrial machine was soon hammered into shape.

Meanwhile Herbert Hoover, director of the Food Administration, stimulated dramatic agricultural increases by pegging prices. Food exports to the Allies doubled in 1917–1918 and tripled in 1918–1919. The Fuel Administration was not so spectacularly successful, but it too performed effectively. Conversely, the shipbuilding program proved a failure, less than a half-million new tons being afloat by the end of the war. Only by commandeering 3 million tons already under construction in private yards and by seizing a million tons of German and Dutch shipping did the United States acquire the fleet that saved the Allies.

For a while the railroad situation was even worse. The eastern freight system nearly collapsed in December 1917. But conditions rapidly improved after the President put all railroad transportation under the control of William G. McAdoo, and the demands of the great military effort of 1918 were fully met.

The War on Land. Six weeks after adoption of the war resolution a selective service law that applied to rich and poor alike was enacted, and by the summer of 1917 a great army was being formed. The following winter a small American expeditionary force held a quiet sector of the front and served generally to bolster sagging Allied morale.

Meanwhile the American commander, General John J. Pershing, systematically prepared a major offensive. Appalled by the defense-mindedness of Allied generals, Pershing was determined "to draw the best German divisions to our front and consume them." But before he could do so, he had to throw two divisions into Chateau-Thierry to support the French in May 1918. Two months later 85,000 Americans helped the Allies turn back the last great German drive to break through the Marne pocket and take Paris.

Finally, in mid-September Pershing's army, now greatly reinforced, took the offensive at Saint-Mihiel in its first independent action. It attained its objective after a two-day battle that cost 6000 in dead and wounded. Now more than half a million strong, the Americans turned west and won a fiercely fought battle in the Meuse-Argonne area. Nevertheless, it was British and French successes in the central and northern sectors, not the American offensive, that brought Germany to its knees. Only in the sense that American

involvement convinced the Germans that they would eventually lose did the United States' military contribution prove crucial. An armistice was signed on November 11, 1918.

Progressivism in War Time. The administration's tax and labor policies continued the powerful progressive surge of 1916. Over the bitter protests of conservatives, almost a third of the $38.5 billion total war bill was raised by war profits, income, and luxury taxes.

Moreover, the government threw its power decisively to labor's side. The National War Labor Board promoted harmony between labor and management. The AFL increased its membership from 2,072,702 to 3,260,168. Hours of labor declined from 53.5 per week in 1914 to 50.4 in 1920. And real wages rose sharply—14 percent above the prewar level in 1917 and 20 percent in 1918.

Yet many of the gains proved temporary. The administration failed to devise and implement a viable reconversion plan. Upon the end of hostilities management resumed its old practices. And after a series of long and bitter strikes, labor failed to organize steel and other industries. On the other hand, as we have seen, the progressives won their long struggle for prohibition and woman suffrage with the ratification of the Eighteenth and Nineteenth Amendments in 1919 and 1920.

Propaganda and Civil Liberties. The record on civil liberties proved far less exemplary, partly because of the need to create a solid front. Millions of Americans believed on April 6 that the United States should not have entered the war. In 1917 mayoral candidates of the antiwar Socialist party polled close to half the vote in Dayton, Ohio, more than a third in Chicago, and nearly a quarter in New York and Buffalo—impressive evidence of both the magnitude and the geographic spread of antiwar sentiments.

The administration struck back with a vast propaganda program and legislation to discourage criticism of the war. The Committee on Public Information under George Creel induced the press to accept voluntary censorship and organized some 15,000 writers, scholars, and businessmen into a public-speaking and pamphlet-writing bureau. This helped create a necessary national will to fight. The American people accepted the draft, subscribed liberally to numerous bond drives, and adjusted reasonably well to the dislocations and inconveniences wrought by mobilization. They came also to believe the President's reiterated assertions, echoed again and again by Creel and his speakers and writers, that Americans were fighting to make the world safe for democracy.

At the same time, however, they indulged in an orgy of intolerance and bigotry. State committees of public safety persecuted pacifists, pro-Germans, and radicals almost capriciously. One German-American was lynched. Conservatives read "Bolshevist" and "German socialist" into almost any sign of labor strife. Meanwhile black servicemen were proscribed from full participation in the "crusade for democracy."

American troops helped turn back the last great German drive to take Paris. In June 1918 these American soldiers at the front line in France sought protection in a trench piled high with sandbags.

From the outset the administration was determined to suppress opposition that might cripple the war effort. The Espionage Act of June 1917 forbade interference with the draft or any action calculated to help the enemy. This restrictive program was broadened as the war progressed, partly because the activities of the "Wobblies" (the Industrial Workers of the World) caused production of copper to decline precipitously. The Trading-with-the-Enemy Act of October 1917 and the Sedition Act of 1918 imposed virtual closure on free speech in the United States. By war's end some 1500 people had been convicted for violating the provisions of either these measures or the Espionage Act.

The Lost Peace. As early as the spring of 1916 President Wilson had committed himself both to a liberal peace and to American participation in a postwar league of nations. He had amplified this program in his "Peace without Victory" speech of January 22, 1917, and had spelled out its details in the memorable "Fourteen Points" address a year later.[1] He set out for the peace conference in Paris in the first week of December 1918 determined to impose this program on the Allies in spite of their secret treaties for the division of the German, Austro-Hungarian, and Turkish empires.

The President faced imposing obstacles. A narrow Republican victory in the congression-

The government's propaganda program—like most war propaganda—combined the symbol of a ruthless, horrible enemy with an appeal for positive patriotic action.

---

[1] Wilson's "Fourteen Points," pronounced on January 8, 1918, may be paraphrased as follows:

   I. "Open covenants openly arrived at."
   II. Freedom of the seas in peace and in war alike.
   III. The removal of all economic barriers and the establishment of an equality of trade conditions among all nations.
   IV. Reduction of national armaments.
   V. A readjustment of all colonial claims, giving the interests of the population concerned equal weight with the claims of the ruling government.
   VI. The evacuation of foreign troops from Russian territory and the independent determination by Russia of its own political development and national policy.
   VII. The evacuation of foreign troops and restoration of Belgium.
   VIII. The evacuation of foreign troops and restoration of France and the return of Alsace-Lorraine.
   IX. A readjustment of the frontiers of Italy along national lines.
   X. Self-determination for the peoples of Austria-Hungary.
   XI. Evacuation of foreign troops from Rumania, Serbia, and Montenegro and access to the sea for Serbia.
   XII. Self-determination for the peoples under Turkish rule and freedom of the Dardanelles under international guarantee.
   XIII. The independence of Poland, with free access to the sea guaranteed by international covenant.
   XIV. The formation of a general association of nations (*i.e.* the League of Nations) under specific covenants for the purpose of affording mutual guarantees of political independence and territorial integrity to great and small states alike.

al elections in November 1918 had weakened his moral authority. Many Republicans had already expressed opposition to his program. And Roosevelt and Lodge would soon write Prime Minister David Lloyd George of Great Britain and Premier Georges Clemenceau of France that Wilson did not speak for the American people. Nor did Wilson help matters by failing to select a single prominent Republican as a member of his five-man peace commission.

The President reached France convinced nevertheless that he might well deliver all Europe from the tyranny of history. Triumphal tours of Paris, London, and Rome confirmed his sense of mission. "Wilson heard from his carriage, something different, inhuman or super human," wrote a correspondent who had seen other leaders of the age on parade. Hardly conscious of the fear, lust, and vindictiveness that would shatter his hopes, he sat down with Lloyd George, Clemenceau, and Vittorio Orlando of Italy to forge a lasting peace.

The President first rejected a proposal by the French, who were obsessed with the need for security against Germany, to convert the west bank of the Rhine into buffer states under French control. But he did agree that the west bank should be permanently demilitarized and occupied by the Allies for fifteen years. He also acquiesced in the return of Alsace-Lorraine to France, the reduction of the German army and navy to cadre strength, and the mandating of Germany's colonies to victor nations under the League of Nations. Finally, he won Clemenceau's acceptance of the league idea by agreeing to join Britain and France in a defense treaty against Germany.

At Paris, Wilson also opposed expansion of intervention in Siberia, where the British, Americans, French, and Japanese had sent troops in the summer of 1919. Point VI of the Fourteen Points had called for the evacuation of foreign troops from Russia in order to give that country "an unhampered and unembarrassed opportunity for the independent determination of her own political development and national policy." And though Wilson had reluctantly supported the anti-Bolshevik campaign in Siberia with American troops, he feared that the intervention would backfire by strengthening the Russian people's support of the Bolsheviks.

Actually, he hoped that the Bolshevik government would be supplanted by a liberal-democratic-capitalist regime such as he envisioned for the entire world, including Japan and China. To that end he instituted a policy of nonrecognition of Soviet Russia that persisted until 1933.

More victories and more concessions followed. A new Poland was created without violating unduly the principle of self-determination. Italy gained control of the Brenner Pass for security reasons, but not a long strip of the Dalmation coast, including Fiume, which it had requested. And the Covenant of the League of Nations was firmly embedded in the peace treaty. On the other hand, Germany faced a potentially astronomical reparations bill and was compelled to admit war guilt. More important still, economic barriers within Europe and throughout the world remained intact. Thus Wilson had won considerably more than his critics later conceded and a great deal less than he had hoped.

The President returned to the United States on July 8, 1919, and threw down the gauntlet two days later. "Our isolation was ended twenty years ago," he warned the Senate. "There can be no question of our ceasing to be a world power. The only question is whether we can refuse the moral leadership that is offered, whether we shall accept or reject the confidence of the world."

Wilson's words fell on a divided country. The German-Americans and their powerful journalistic ally, the Hearst press, opposed the treaty's harshness toward Germany.

Italian-Americans sulked over Wilson's refusal to allow Italy to take Fiume. Irish-Americans mounted a virulent opposition because of President Wilson's failure to support the movement for Ireland's independence. Furthermore, a small group of sincere and irreconcilable isolationists in the Senate pledged themselves to the complete defeat of the treaty because of the provision for the League of Nations. Many intellectuals and idealists also revolted. "The European politicians who with American complicity have hatched this inhuman monster," said the *New Republic*," have acted either cynically, hypocritically or vindictively."

Nevertheless, Wilson might still have won the fight for ratification had he not been so uncompromising, and had not Senator Henry Cabot Lodge and a small group of pro-war Republican nationalists feared that the League, by raising false hopes, would compromise the balance-of-power foreign policy which they had always deemed essential to the nation's security. More than two thirds of the Senate approved the League Covenant in broad principle, and the President received a tremendous response as he traveled through the West in September of 1919. It looked as though he must win. "My clients are the children; my clients are the next generation," he exclaimed with tears in his eyes to a cheering throng in Pueblo, Colorado. "I intend to redeem my pledges to the children; they shall not be sent [to France]." Seven days after this memorable peroration, the President suffered a stroke that paralyzed his left side.

The battle now ground slowly to its tragic end. Lodge, as chairman of the foreign relations committee, presented the treaty to the Senate on November 6 for approval, subject to a number of reservations. The most important one had been suggested earlier by Elihu Root. It asserted that the United States assumed no obligations under Article X of the League Covenant to preserve the territorial integrity or political independence of any country, to interfere in controversies between nations, or to use its armed forces to uphold any of the articles of the Treaty for any purpose, *unless Congress by joint resolution so provided.*

The ailing President refused to accept the Lodge reservations on the grounds that they crippled the Covenant. Democrats on November 19 dutifully followed his command and voted against the treaty with reservations. Their vote was sufficient to prevent approval.

Pro-League sentiment throughout the country proved so strong that the Treaty was brought to a second vote on March 19, 1920. By this time Wilson had recovered sufficiently to take an active part in the controversy. "Either we should enter the League fearlessly," he wrote in a public letter, "accepting the responsibility and not fearing the role of leadership which we now enjoy . . . or we should retire as gracefully as possible from the great concert of powers by which the world was saved." If the Senate failed to ratify without crippling reservations, he concluded, the election of 1920 should then be a "great and solemn referendum" on the issue. In spite of—perhaps because of—Wilson's last stand, the Senate again refused to approve ratification of the Versailles Treaty. A change of seven Democratic votes would have won Senate approval.

Most historians doubt that American participation in the League of Nations would have altered more than the tone of postwar foreign affairs. As Part 7 shows, the United States did not become truly isolationist during the 1920s. On the contrary, it pursued about as active (though not invariably constructive) a role in international naval, economic, and diplomatic matters as the American people were willing to countenance.

BIBLIOGRAPHY

The two most influential general interpretations of the Progressive Era during the past decade and a half are Robert H. Wiebe, *The Search for Order 1877–1920* (New York: Hill & Wang, 1968), and Gabriel Kolko, *The Triumph of Conservativism* (New York: The Free Press, 1963). Wiebe's work is a brilliant, but overly schematic, analysis of the rise of the organizational society. Kolko's book is a provocative, one-dimensional analysis of the triumph of corporate progressivism. James Weinstein, *The Corporate Ideal in the Liberal State* (Boston: Beacon Press, 1968), is in the same mold as Kolko's work. Both Richard M. Abrams, *The Burdens of Progress* (Glenview, IL: Scott, Foresman, 1978) and John Whiteclay Chambers II, *The Tyranny of Change* (New York: St. Martin's, 1980), though more in the nature of surveys, come closer to describing historical reality. Two indispensable sources, ideal for term papers on political progressivism, are Elting E. Morison et al., eds., *The Letters of Theodore Roosevelt,* 8 vols. (Cambridge: Harvard University Press, 1951–1954), and Arthur S. Link et al., eds, *The Papers of Woodrow Wilson,* 40 vols. (Princeton, NJ: Princeton University Press, Vols. 1–32 1966–1979). Richard Hofstadter's *The Age of Reform* (New York: Knopf, 1955), now largely obsolete, is still worth reading for its urbanity and specific insights.

The most readable introduction to the social history of the period remains the first three volumes of Mark Sullivan's *Our Times* (New York: Scribner's, 1926–1934). An interesting and comprehensive account of popular culture is Russel B. Nye, *The Unembarrassed Muse: The Popular Arts in America* (New York: Dial Press, 1970). More specialized studies include Rudi Blesh, *Shining Trumpets: A History of Jazz* (New York: Knopf, 1958), Rudi Blesh and Harriet Janis, *They All Played Ragtime* (New York: Knopf, 1950), Edward A. Berlin, *Ragtime: A Musical and Cultural History* (Berkeley: University of California Press, 1980), and Lewis Jacobs, *Rise of the American Film* (New York: Teachers College Press, 1968). Robert Sklar, *Movie-Made America: A Social History of the American Movies* (New York: Random House, 1975), is highly informative, as is Booton Herndon's eminently readable *Mary Pickford and Douglas Fairbanks* (New York: Norton, 1977). Harold Seymour, *Baseball: The Golden Age* (New York: Oxford University Press, 1971), and Foster R. Dulles, *History of Recreation* (Englewood Cliffs, NJ: Prentice-Hall, 1966), are useful sources.

For intellectual and cultural history, in addition to the books by Commager, Goldman, and White listed in the Part 5 bibliography, see Henry F. May, *The End of American Innocence* (New York: Knopf, 1959), and Christopher Lasch, *The New Radicalism in America* (New York: Knopf, 1965). Charles Forcey, *The Crossroads of Liberalism* (New York: Oxford University Press, 1961), analyzes the thought of Croly, Lippmann, and Weyl, while David W. Noble, *The Paradox of Progressive Thought* (Minneapolis: University of Minnesota Press, 1958), treats them and several others.

David M. Chalmers, *The Social and Political Ideas of the Muckrakers* (New York: Citadel, 1964), is suggestive. John E. Burchard and Albert Bush-Brown, *The Architecture of America* (Boston: Little, Brown, 1961), interweaves history and esthetics. Robert C. Twombly, *Frank Lloyd Wright* (New York: Harper & Row, 1973), is a standard biography. Alfred Kazin's classic *On Native Grounds* (New York: Harcourt Brace Jovanovich, 1972) should be supplemented by Charles C. Walcutt, *American Literary Naturalism: A Divided Stream* (Minneapolis: University of Minnesota Press, 1956), and Maxwell Geismer, *Rebels and Ancestors, The American Novel, 1890–1915* (Boston: Houghton Mifflin, 1953).

For the law and the legal profession see Robert G. McCloskey, *The American Supreme Court* (Chicago: University of Chicago Press, 1960), Leon Friedman and Fred L. Israel, eds., *The Justices of the U. S. Supreme Court,* Vol. III (New York: Bowker, 1969), Jerold S. Auerbach, *Unequal Justice: Lawyers and Social Change* (New York: Oxford University Press, 1976), Alpheus T. Mason, *Brandeis: A Free Man's Life* (New York: Viking Press, 1946), William H. Harbaugh, *Lawyer's Lawyer: The Life of John W. Davis* (New York: Oxford University Press, 1973), and Charles Larsen, *The Good Fight: The Life and Times of Ben Linsey* (New York: Times Books, 1972). There are a number of the penetrating essays in G. Edward White, *Patterns of American Legal Thought* (Indianapolis: Bobbs-Merrill, 1978), related to the Progressive Era.

Additional intellectual and social developments are covered in A. Hunter Dupree, ed., *Science and the Emergence of Modern America, 1865–1916* (Chicago: Rand McNally, 1963), Bert N. Adams, *The American Family* (Chicago: Markham, 1971), Dorothy Ross, *G. Stanley Hall: The Psychologist as Prophet* (Chicago: University of Chicago Press, 1972), Daniel M. Fox, *The Discovery of Abundance: Simon Patten and the Transformation of Social Theory* (Ithaca, NY: Cornell University Press, 1967), Julius Weinberg, *Edward Allsworth Ross and the Sociology of Progressivism* (Madison: State Historical Society of Wisconsin, 1972), and Nathan G. Hale, Jr., *Freud and the Americans* (New York: Oxford University Press, 1971). Two other important works are Sidney Fine, *Laissez Faire and the General Welfare State* (Ann Arbor: University of Michigan Press, 1964), and Robert F. Bremner, *From the Depths: The Discovery of Poverty in the United States* (New Haven: Yale University Press, 1956). Roy Lubove, *The Struggle for Social Security 1900-1935* (Cambridge: Harvard University Press, 1968), is also highly informative, as is Lloyd C. Taylor, Jr., *The Medical Profession and Social Reform 1885–1945* (New York: St. Martin's, 1974). Also see William Graebner,

Coal-Mining Safety in the Progressive Period (Lexington: University of Kentucky Press, 1976).

For works on blacks see Gilbert Osofsky, *Harlem* (New York: Harper & Row, 1966); August Meier, *Negro Thought in America 1880–1915* (Ann Arbor: University of Michigan Press, 1963), one of the few works to take a balanced view of Booker T. Washington; and Elliot M. Rudwick, *W.E.B. DuBois: Propagandist of the Negro Protest* (New York: Atheneum, 1968). Other important works include Louis R. Harlan, *Separate and Unequal: Public School Campaigns and Racism in the Southern Seaboard States 1900–1915* (New York: Atheneum, 1968), Rayford W. Logan, *The Betrayal of the Negro* (New York: Collier Books, 1965), Allen H. Spear, *Black Chicago* (Chicago: University of Chicago Press, 1967), Charles Flint Kellogg, *A History of the National Association for the Advancement of Colored People 1909–1920* (Baltimore: Johns Hopkins University Press, 1967), and Louis R. Harlan, *Booker T. Washington* (New York: Oxford University Press, 1972). Also see Richard B. Sherman, *The Republican Party and Black America* (Charlottesville: University Press of Virginia, 1973), and Jack T. Kirby, *Darkness at the Dawning: Race and Reform in the Progressive South* (Philadelphia: Lippincott, 1972).

The literature on immigration and ethnic groups is too voluminous to do more than sample. Among the many works which stand out are Oscar Handlin, *The Uprooted* (Boston: Little, Brown, 1951), John Higham, *Strangers in the Land* (New York: Atheneum, 1963), Donald B. Cole, *Immigrant City: Lawrence, Massachusetts 1845–1921* (Chapel Hill: University of North Carolina Press, 1963), Stephan Thernstrom, *The Other Bostonians* (Cambridge: Harvard University Press, 1973), Moses Rischin, *The Promised City: New York's Jews 1870–1914* (Cambridge: Harvard University Press, 1962), and Josef J. Barton, *Peasants and Strangers* (Cambridge: Harvard University Press, 1975). They should be supplemented by John Higham's collection of essays, *Send These to Me* (New York: Atheneum, 1975), wherein he modifies some of the judgments in *Strangers in the Land,* and Thomas Kessner, *The Golden Door, Italian and Jewish Immigrant Mobility in New York City 1880–1915* (New York: Oxford, 1977), a superb study. Robert Sowell's controversial *Race and Economics* (New York: David McKay, 1975), brings together much of the recent material on rates of mobility of different ethnic groups. A fine general history of immigration is Philip Taylor, *The Distant Magnet* (New York: Harper & Row, 1971).

Various aspects of the history of women, a field in which the literature has also become voluminous in recent years, are covered in the following works: Aileen S. Kraditor, *The Ideas of the Woman Suffrage Movement* (Garden City, NY: Doubleday, 1971), Allen F. Davis, *Spearheads for Reform: The Social Settlements and the Progressive Movement* (New York: Oxford University Press, 1970), and *American Heroine: The Life and Legend of Jane Addams* (New York: Oxford University Press, 1973), Dorothy Rose Blumberg, *Florence Kelley: The Making of a Social Pioneer* (Fairfield, NJ: Augustus M. Kelley, 1966), William L. O'Neill, *Divorce in the Progressive Era* (New Haven: Yale University Press, 1967), David M. Kennedy, *Birth Control in America: The Career of Margaret Sanger* (New Haven: Yale University Press, 1970), Nancy F. Cott, *The Bonds of Womanhood* (New Haven: Yale University Press, 1977), Lois Banner, *Women in Modern America: A Brief History* (New York: Harcourt Brace Jovanovich, 1974), David Morgan, *Suffragists & Democrats: The Politics of Woman Suffrage in America* (East Lansing: Michigan State University Press, 1971), William R. Leach, *True Love and Perfect Union: The Feminist Reform of Sex and Society* (New York: Basic Books, 1980), and Carl Degler, *At Odds: Women and the Family in America* (New York, Oxford University Press, 1980). Also see Mark H. Haller, *Eugenics: Hereditarian Attitudes in American Thought* (New Brunswick, NJ: Rutgers University Press, 1963), and Joseph F. Kett, *Rites of Passage: Adolescence in America* (New York: Basic Books, 1977).

Norman H. Clark, *Deliver Us from Evil: An Interpretation of American Prohibition* (New York: Norton, 1976), is an admirably unbiased and perceptive study which treats prohibition in all its dimensions, including the comparative. Agriculture during the Progressive Era awaits a full-scale study of the quality of Fred Shannon's work on the late nineteenth century. Neither is there a good comprehensive economic study of the era but specialized works include Alfred D. Chandler, Jr., *Strategy and Structure: Chapters in the History of the Industrial Enterprise* (Cambridge: MIT Press, 1962), Allan Nevins and Frank E. Hill, *Ford: The Times, the Man, the Company,* Vol. 1 (New York: Scribner's, 1954) Albert Rees, *Real Wages in Manufacturing 1890–1914* (Princeton: Princeton University Press, 1961), Samuel Haber, *Efficiency and Uplift: Scientific Management in the Progressive Era 1820–1920* (Chicago: University of Chicago Press, 1964), Morton Keller, *The Life Insurance Enterprise 1885–1910* (Cambridge: Harvard University Press, 1963), and Harold Williamson et al., *The American Petroleum Industry,* 2 vols. (Evanston, Ill.: Northwestern University Press, 1963). Albro Martin, *Enterprise Denied: Origins of the Decline of American Railroads* (New York: Columbia University Press, 1971), offers an interesting critique of the regulationist philosophy. For conservation see Samuel P. Hays, *Conservation and the Gospel of Efficiency* (New York: Atheneum, 1959), James Penick, Jr., *Progressive Politics and Conservation* (Chicago: University of Chicago Press, 1968), and Elmo R. Richardson, *The Politics of Conservation* (Berkeley: University of California Press, 1962). In addition to several works cited in the bibliography for Part 5, see the insightful essays on change in Thomas C. Cochran's *Social Change in America: The Twentieth Century* (London: Allen & Unwin, 1971).

A number of works treat progressivism in the cities and states. Among the best are Richard M. Abrams, *Conservatism in a Progressive Era* (Cambridge: Harvard University Press, 1964), Robert S. Maxwell, *La Follette and the Rise of the Progressives in Wisconsin* (Madison: State Historical Society of Wisconsin, 1956), George Wallace Chessman, *Governor Theodore Roosevelt* (Cambridge: Harvard University Press, 1956), William D. Miller, *Memphis During the Progressive Era* (Providence, RI: Brown University Press, 1957), John D. Buenker, *Urban Liberalism and Progressive Reform* (New York: Norton, 1973), Hoyt L. Warner, *Progressivism in Ohio 1897–1917* (Columbus: Ohio State University Press, 1964), Zane L. Miller, *Boss Cox's Cincinnati: Urban Politics in the Progressive Era* (New York: Oxford University Press, 1968), and Robert B. Wesser, *Charles Evans Hughes: Politics and Reform in New York* (Ithaca, NY: Cornell University Press, 1967). Also see the interesting collection of essays in Michael H. Ebner and Eugene M. Tobin, eds., *The Age of Urban Reform: New Perspectives on the Progressive Era* (Port Washington, NY: Kennikat, 1977). David P. Thelen, *The New Citizenship: The Origins of Progressivism in Wisconsin* (Columbia: University of Missouri Press, 1972), is of special importance. Lincoln Steffens' readable and informative articles are reprinted as *The Struggle for Self-Government* (Garden City, NY: Doubleday, 1906), and *The Shame of the Cities* (New York: Hill & Wang, 1957). Many other works could be added, but Martin J. Schiesl, *Municipal Administration and Reform in America: 1880–1920* (Berkeley: University of California Press, 1977), is surely the most balanced and informed treatment of the topic.

George E. Mowry, *The Era of Theodore Roosevelt 1900–1912* (New York: Harper & Row, 1958), is an admirable synthesis of progressivism's early phases. The same author's *Theodore Roosevelt and the Progressive Movement* (New York: Hill & Wang, 1960), is illuminating but dated in its treatment of the trust issue. John Allen Gable, *The Bull Moose Years: Theodore Roosevelt and the Progressive Party* (Port Washington, NY: Kennikat, 1978), both supplements and complements Mowry admirably. Arthur S. Link, *Woodrow Wilson and the Progressive Era 1910–1917* (New York: Harper & Row, 1954), is the best account of Democratic progressivism. A comprehensive regional survey is Russel B. Nye, *Midwestern Progressive Politics 1870–1958*, rev. ed. (East Lansing: Michigan State University Press, 1959). Also see Horace S. Merrill and Marion G. Merrill, *The Republican Command 1897–1913* (Lexington: University of Kentucky Press, 1971). Interesting recent studies are Lewis L. Gould, ed., *The Progressive Era* (Syracuse, NY: Syracuse University Press, 1974), Otis L. Graham, Jr., *The Great Campaigns* (Englewood Cliffs, NJ: Prentice-Hall, 1971), and Arthur A. Ekirch, Jr., *Progressivism in America* (New York: Watts, 1974).

The literature on labor and the left is voluminous. Ira Kipnis, *The American Socialist Movement 1897–1912* (Westport,

CT: Greenwood Press, 1952), should be supplemented by Ray Ginger's brilliant biography *Eugene V. Debs* (New York: Collier Books, 1962), and David A. Shannon, *The Socialist Party of America* (New York: Quadrangle, 1967). Bernard Mandel, *Samuel Gompers* (Kent, Ohio: Kent State University Press, 1963), is the standard work on the AFL leader. Richard Drinnon, *Rebel in Paradise: A Biography of Emma Goldman* (Boston: Beacon Press, 1970), illumines the mind of an anarchist, and David Brody, *Labor in Crisis: The Steel Strike of 1919* (Philadelphia: Lippincott, 1965), puts the abortive effort to organize that industry in historical perspective. Also see James Weinstein, *The Decline of Socialism in America 1912–1925* (New York: Monthly Review Press, 1967). Melvyn Dubofsky, *We Shall Be All: A History of the Industrial Workers of the World* (Chicago: Quadrangle Books, 1969), is a fascinating book. For illumination on why Oklahoma farmers supported the Socialist party so strongly, see Garin Burbank, *When Farmers Voted Red: The Gospel of Socialism in the Oklahoma Countryside* (Westport, CT: Greenwood, 1976).

William H. Harbaugh, *The Life and Times of Theodore Roosevelt* (New York: Oxford University Press, 1975), is a full-length biography. In addition to John M. Blum's *The Republican Roosevelt* (Cambridge: Harvard University Press, 1954), two good short studies are G. Wallace Chessman, *Theodore Roosevelt and the Politics of Power* (Boston: Little, Brown, 1969), and David H. Burton, *Theodore Roosevelt* (New York: Twayne, 1972). For Taft's presidency see Donald F. Anderson, *William Howard Taft* (Ithaca, NY: Cornell University Press, 1973), Paolo E. Colletta, *The Presidency of William Howard Taft* (Lawrence, KS: University of Kansas Press, 1973). For Bryan see Louis W. Koenig, *Bryan: A Political Biography* (New York: Putnam's, 1971); and for Hughes see Merlo J. Pusey, *Charles Evans Hughes*, 2 vols. (New York: Columbia University Press, 1963). Belle C. La Follette and Fola La Follette, *Robert M. La Follette 1855–1925*, 2 vols. (New York: Macmillan, 1953), is a loving but substantial account of the life of Roosevelt's great rival. For a more balanced treatment see David P. Thelen, *Robert M. La Follette and the Insurgent Spirit* (Boston: Little, Brown, 1976). Richard Lowitt, *George W. Norris*, Vol. I (Syracuse, NY: Syracuse University Press, 1963), and Vol. II (Urbana: University of Illinois Press, 1971), carry Norris to 1932. Dewey W. Grantham, Jr., *Hoke Smith and the Politics of the New South* (Baton Rouge: Louisiana State University Press, 1958), is an informative account of one of the Southern progressives. In addition see Hugh C. Bailey, *Liberalism in the New South* (Coral Gables, FL: University of Miami Press, 1969).

Among the many biographies of lesser figures, the following are just a few of those worth examining: John A. Garraty, *Right-Hand Man: The Life of George W. Perkin* (New York: Harper & Row, 1960), Martin L. Fausold, *Gifford Pinchot* (Syracuse, NY: Syracuse University Press, 1961), John

Braeman, *Albert J. Beveridge* (Chicago: University of Chicago Press, 1971), Justin Kaplan, *Lincoln Steffens* (New York: Simon & Schuster, 1974), Michael Wreszin, *Oswald Garrison Villard* (Bloomington: Indiana University Press, 1965), and James B. Lane, *Jacob Riis* (Port Washington, NY: Kennikat Press, 1974).

The most informed and judicious survey of foreign affairs for this period is still Richard W. Leopold, *The Growth of American Foreign Policy* (New York: Knopf, 1962). H. Wayne Morgan, *William McKinley and His America* (Syracuse, NY: Syracuse University Press, 1963), is balanced, though favorable. Ernest R. May, *Imperial Democracy* (New York: Harcourt Brace Jovanovich, 1961), dissects the diplomacy of the decision to go to war in 1898. It is complemented by Walter LaFeber, *The New Empire: An Interpretation of American Expansion* (Ithaca, NY: Cornell University Press, 1963). Both George F. Kennan, *American Diplomacy 1900–1950* (New York: Mentor Books, 1952), and William A. Williams, *The Tragedy of American Diplomacy*, rev. ed. (New York: Dell, 1962), conclude that American intervention in the Far East was deeply unfortunate. Important recent books on the United States and the Far East are Robert L. Beisner, *Twelve Against Empire* (New York: McGraw-Hill, 1968), Jerry Israel, *Progressivism and the Open Door: America and China, 1905–1921* (Pittsburgh: University of Pittsburgh Press, 1971), Thomas J. McCormick, *China Market: America's Quest for Informal Empire 1893–1901* (New York: Quadrangle, 1970), William A. Williams, *Roots of the Modern American Empire* (New York: Random House, 1969), Paul A. Varg, *The Making of a Myth* (East Lansing: Michigan State University Press, 1968), Eugene P. Traini, *The Treaty of Portsmouth* (Lexington: University of Kentucky Press, 1969), Charles Neu, *An Uncertain Friendship: Theodore Roosevelt and Japan 1906–1909* (Cambridge: Harvard University Press, 1967), Raymond A. Esthus, *Theodore Roosevelt and Japan* (Seattle: University of Washington Press, 1966), and Peter Stanley, *A Nation in the Making: The Philippines and the United States* (Cambridge: Harvard University Press, 1974). Walter LaFeber, *The Panama Canal: The Crisis in Historical Perspective* (New York: Oxford University Press, 1978), brings much needed balance to a controversial topic.

For other areas see Bradford Perkins, *The Great Rapprochement: England and the United States 1895–1914* (New York: Atheneum, 1968), Allan R. Millett, *Politics of Intervention: Military Occupation of Cuba 1906–1909* (Columbus: Ohio State University Press, 1968), and Ralph E. Minger, *William Howard Taft and United States Foreign Policy* (Urbana: University of Illinois Press, 1975).

Howard K. Beale, *Theodore Roosevelt and the Rise of America to World Power* (Baltimore: Johns Hopkins University Press, 1956), is a seminal work. But see the new insights in Frederick W. Marks, III, *Velvet on Iron: The Diplomacy of Theodore Roosevelt* (Lincoln: University of Nebraska Press, 1979).

For Wilson, the authoritative work is Arthur S. Link, *Wilson*, Vols. III–V (Princeton: Princeton University Press, 1947–1965). These works should be supplemented by Richard W. Leopold, *Elihu Root and the Conservative Tradition* (Boston: Little, Brown, 1954), Daniel M. Smith, *Robert Lansing and American Neutrality* (Berkeley: University of California Press, 1958), Dana G. Munro, *Intervention and Dollar Diplomacy in the Caribbean 1900–1921* (Princeton: Princeton University Press, 1964), Robert E. Quirk, *An Affair of Honor* (New York: Norton, 1967), John Milton Cooper, Jr., *The Vanity of Power* (Westport, CT: Greenwood Press, 1969), E. Berkeley Tompkins, *Anti-Imperialism in the United States* (Philadelphia: University of Pennsylvania Press, 1970), C. Roland Marchand, *The American Peace Movement and Social Reform 1898–1918* (Princeton: Princeton University Press, 1972), John G. Clifford, *The Citizen Soldiers: The Plattsburg Training Camp Movement* (Lexington: University of Kentucky Press, 1972), and Warren F. Kuehl, *Seeking World Order: The United States and International Organization to 1920* (Nashville, TN: Vanderbilt University Press, 1972). Ernest R. May, *The World War and American Isolation: 1914–1917* (Cambridge, MA: Harvard University Press, 1959), is an original work of high quality. Ross Gregory, *The Origins of American Intervention in the First World War* (New York: Norton, 1971), is a splendid synthesis of the recent literature.

Frederic L. Paxson, *American Democracy and the World War*, 3 vols. (New York: Cooper Square, 1948), is still a useful survey of the nation at war. But see the forthcoming book by David M. Kennedy to be published by Oxford. H. C. Peterson and Gilbert C. Fite, *Opponents of War 1917–1918* (Seattle: University of Washington Press, 1968), is a biting account of the suppression of civil liberties in wartime, as is William Preston, Jr., *Aliens and Dissenters* (New York: Harper & Row, 1963). Robert K. Murray, *Red Scare* (New York: McGraw-Hill, 1954), is a standard work. Stanley Coben, *A. Mitchell Palmer* (New York: Columbia University Press, 1963), offers a rounded evaluation of the man partly responsible for the excesses of the Red Scare. A highly sympathetic account of Wilson and the peacemaking is Arthur Walworth, *Woodrow Wilson*, 2nd ed. (Boston: Houghton Mifflin, 1965). It should be read against John A. Garraty, *Henry Cabot Lodge* (New York: Knopf, 1953). Thomas A. Bailey, *Wilson and the Peacemakers* (New York: Macmillan, 1947), retains much of its original value. Also see N. Gordon Levin, Jr., *Woodrow Wilson and World Politics: America's Response to War and Revolution* (New York: Oxford University Press, 1968). The story of the election of 1920 is ably told in Wesley M. Bagby, *The Road to Normalcy* (Baltimore: Johns Hopkins University Press,

1962). In addition, see Robert D. Cuff, *The War Industries Board* (Baltimore: Johns Hopkins University Press, 1973), Melvin Urofsky, *Big Steel and the Wilson Administration* (Columbus: Ohio State University Press, 1969), and Burl Noggle, *Into the Twenties: The United States from Armistice to Normalcy* (Baltimore: Johns Hopkins University Press, 1972).

Indispensable to understanding the peacemaking are Carl P. Parrini, *Heir to Empire* (Pittsburgh: University of Pittsburgh Press, 1969), Arno J. Mayer, *Politics and the Diplomacy of Peacemaking: Containment and Counterrevolution at Versailles* (New York: Knopf, 1967), and Ralph A. Stone, *The Irreconcilables: The Fight Against the League of Nations* (Lexington: University of Kentucky Press, 1970). A superb new analysis of the Realists, which also includes much on Roosevelt, is William C. Widenor, *Henry Cabot Lodge and the Search for an American Foreign Policy* (Berkeley: University of California Press, 1980). Finally, Arthur S. Link has distilled his mature views on Wilson and the war years in *Woodrow Wilson: Revolution, War, and Peace* (Arlington Heights, IL: AHM Company, 1979).

The student should also consult the bibliography at the end of Chapter 15 for many titles which are also pertinent to this section.

Time Line

1920	League of Nations, Versailles Treaty defeated	**1940**	Hitler conquers France
1921	First immigration quota act		Selective Service (draft) begins in the U.S.
1922	Washington treaties on Far East and naval ratios		Japan joins Axis military alliance
1923	Harding dies, Calvin Coolidge succeeds him	**1941**	Lend-Lease Act to support Allies (March)
1924	Peak of growth of Ku Klux Klan		Germany invades U.S.S.R. (June)
	Dawes Plan cuts reparations		Atlantic Charter announced (August)
	Coolidge wins presidental election		Japan attacks U.S. at Pearl Harbor (December)
1927	Anarchists Sacco and Vanzetti executed	**1942**	War Production Board, War Labor Board set up
1928	Herbert C. Hoover elected President		Declaration of twenty-six United Nations (Jan.)
1929	National Origins Act		Japanese interred in concentration camps (March)
	Stock market boom and panic		U.S. surrenders Philippines (May)
1930	High Smoot-Hawley Tariff Act passed		U.S. gains offensive at Battle of Midway (June)
1931	Beginning of Chinese-Japanese hostilities		U.S. troops land in Africa (November)
1932	Hoover's Reconstruction Finance Corporation Act		Anti-inflation measures for wages, prices, rents
	Franklin D. Roosevelt elected President	**1943**	Germans turned back at Stalingrad (Feb.)
1933	Start of New Deal legislation		Allies invade Italy; Italy surrenders
1934	Wheeler-Howard Indian Reconstruction Act		Smith-Connally Act passed over veto
1935	Basic acts of New Deal declared unconstitutional		Equal pay for equal work ordered for black workers
	National Labor Relations, Social Security Acts		in Virginia
1936	Germany, Italy, Japan sign anti-Communist pact		Teheran summit conference (Nov.–Dec.)
	State minimum wage laws for women upheld	**1944**	Allies land at Normandy, liberate France
1937	Social Security Act upheld	**1945**	Yalta Conference plans UN, postwar arrange-
	Court-packing bill defeated		ments
1938	Last New Deal legislation		Roosevelt dies; Harry S Truman succeeds him
	Start of Nazi anti-Jewish pogroms		Victory in Europe, May 7
	Munich pact for "peace in our time"		Atom bomb dropped on Hiroshima, August 6
1939	Germany, U.S.S.R. sign nonaggression pact		Japan surrenders, August 14
	Germany invades Poland, starting World War II		Potsdam summit conference of victors

7

THE COMING
OF THE
WELFARE STATE

Like all cultural traditions, that in America has combined deep beliefs, acted on but seldom put into words, with admonitions or slogans heard frequently. Franklin's advice on thrift and self-improvement, Samuel Adams' insistence on the equality of all citizens before the law, and Thomas Jefferson's "right to the pursuit of happiness" have long been built into American oratory. On a more basic level, scarcely needing to be put into words, have been the right to private property, to move and think freely, to pursue any legitimate occupation, and to manage one's own life. The precepts of Christianity, even if often disregarded, have formed the moral standards of the culture, while the tradition of women as homemakers has dominated relations between women and men.

Besides these values, Americans—as early as the time of the Revolution—shared two basic beliefs: that individuals were responsible for their own welfare and that success was a reward for effort. To a surprising degree this early heritage has influenced American thought and action throughout the nation's history. But when America's decade of great-est prosperity and economic hope—the 1920s—ended in sudden collapse, giving way to a period of massive unemployment and uncertainty as to any future prosperity, these national beliefs were severely tested and, in part, permanently altered.

Although Americans—and their goals and values—had survived many ups and downs, booms and depressions, before the end of World War I, never had they experienced such severe trials as those that developed between the two World Wars. The twenties, a decade of prosperity, changed ways of living and ways of thinking. In urban areas new, scientific theories of the nature of reality, of human motivation, of child-rearing and of education challenged the guidelines of religion and tradition. Challenged, too, were the old restrictions on women's conduct. Women of the upper middle class saw no reason to give up the new social freedom they had enjoyed during World War I, while the Nineteenth Amendment in 1920 also gave women the right to vote and promised political change. And the automobile alone changed the lives of all but the poorest citizens—mainly those living in central cities or unproductive rural areas.

These changes in family life, education, and conduct were most pronounced among members of the big-city intellectual elite, many of whom were caught up in ideas and values stemming from the pioneer work of Einstein and Freud. The doctrines of both scientists tended to undermine the presumed ability of humans to perceive or rationally understand reality. Freud saw people and society as governed by subconscious urges. Einstein's work implied that reality could be discovered only by mathematical calculations. But though these ideas were popularized in numerous books and magazine articles, surveys suggest that neither thinker ever reached the great majority of the American people, although they may have undermined the moral certainties of social and political leaders.

In contrast, the Great Depression of the 1930s inescapably affected everyone. The sudden changes that struck hardest at the values of the society as a whole were those that forced individuals to recognize that they had lost much of their self-sufficiency, while government was forced to assume new functions. The adjustments that the depression called for went counter to deeply held American beliefs in the self-regulating economy and the virtue of individual initiative and self-help. Thus the thirties too undermined a part of the American heritage and added to inner uncertainties.

The economic problems starkly revealed by the depression had been inherent in the unstable economy of the 1920s. The temporary wartime change in production from consumer goods to military supplies and the creation of a large national debt in private hands generated a strong postwar consumer demand that made the 1920s, in general, a period of prosperity. But in these years slums grew worse, wages were held down, and economic prosperity came to depend not on rising mass consumption but on loans to foreign governments and businesses through the purchase of their bonds, and on speculation in domestic securities and real estate.

Between 1929 and 1931 the unstable system collapsed, ushering in a deep and prolonged depression. Estimated unemployment in the United States rose to well over a quarter of those who had been working in 1929, when there was already an unemployment problem. But the reality was incalculably worse than the statistics. Many who were still employed worked only part-time, and starving staple-crop farmers, particularly numerous in the South, were not included in the statistics at all. Everywhere the unskilled suffered more than the skilled, blacks more than whites, and all wage earners more than managers or professionals. The fact that total man-hours of work declined by 60 percent between 1929 and 1933 provides a clearer notion of the severity of the depression.

The major political issues of the period centered around the partially successful efforts of Franklin D. Roosevelt's administration to solve the economic problems. In general, these took the form of providing greater security for all groups—farmers, workers, investors, householders, the aged, and the unemployed—through the regulatory and financial power of the federal government. Although the measures now seem mildly palliative, they nevertheless contradicted the value America traditionally placed on freedom of action and individual responsibility. They were the subject of bitter contemporary debate, and they have undergone varying interpretations by historians.

To the majority of the people, and to an even larger proportion of the historians who personally experienced these "years of hardship," President Herbert Hoover seemed an obscurantist conservative, while Roosevelt stood forth as a strong, liberal humanitarian, personally responsible for fundamental reforms that combated the depression as effectively as could be done by federal action.

Henry Steele Commager and Allan Nevins serve as outstanding exemplars of this contemporary view. Among the few anti-Roosevelt historians were unfaltering believers in the self-regulating economy, like Edgar E. Robinson; some moderate socialists, like Broadus Mitchell, who thought the President's actions inadequate; and isolationists in foreign policy, led by Charles A. Beard. In the ranks of important professional historians writing on the period, there were no Communists.

Over the next generation the liberal interpretation was eroded by streams of ideas stemming from quite different sources. As economists were gradually won over to the views of the great English theorist, John Maynard Keynes, they learned that there were sound theoretical reasons why the economy was not self-regulating and that had Roosevelt comprehended the importance of government spending, he might have ended the depression by means other than preparation for World War II. His most successful biographer, James MacGregor Burns, writing in the mid-1950s, saw Roosevelt as a man of limited intellectual ability but with a keen grasp of politics—essentially, the charming politican.

As a corollary, the reforms of the period have come to be viewed as the type that any President responsive to congressional and public opinion would have to have made, and Roosevelt as a leader who did no more than was necessary while always trying to conciliate the conservatives. This view gives more credit to the leadership of congressional liberals, like Senator Robert F. Wagner of New York.

By the 1960s, members of a New Left movement among historians saw the period much as had the socialist intellectuals of an earlier time. According to both groups, Roosevelt had saved capitalism without substantially improving it and, as Beard had charged earlier, had cured domestic troubles only by deliberately leading the country into World War II.

These varying interpretations all reveal the preoccupation of earlier generations of historians with politics. In contrast, more recent students of the period, both liberal and conservative, would probably agree that the most important result of the depression was an undermining of the historic American belief that citizens should be responsible for their own welfare, that poverty was the fault of the poor. To holders of this traditional view, such as Herbert Hoover, public assistance undermined character. Reluctantly a majority of the employed upper classes were forced to admit by 1933 that a quarter of their fellow citizens could not all have brought poverty on themselves by moral weakness and that, in a complex industrial state, society had a duty to support those made penniless by forces beyond their personal control. President Roosevelt thought the Social Security Act of 1935 was the most important bill he ever signed, and history is confirming his judgment. In fact, greater security for all groups in society—from jobless widows with children to investors on the stock exchanges—constitutes the major heritage of the New Deal.

TO THINK ABOUT AS YOU READ. . .

1. During the 1920s, social and physical scientists raised a number of questions that seemed to challenge traditional assumptions about the world. What new assumptions were being made, and how did they affect social, intellectual, and political life?
2. The automobile came into its own during the twenties and by 1930 almost every

household owned one. How did the automobile affect American habits, cities, and the economy?

3. The twenties were hailed as the dawning of an era of never-ending prosperity. Yet by the thirties the country and much of the world had been plunged into one of the severest depressions ever known. What forces of instability at work during the twenties do you think were most important?

4. Andrew Carnegie once asserted that for every thousand dollars spent for poor relief, nine hundred fifty would better be thrown into the sea, and most Americans entering the twenties would have been ashamed to accept a public dole. Do you agree? Do you think the legislation of the New Deal was justified? Would other measures have been more effective?

5. Historians have sometimes spoken of World War II as a war for security. Do you agree? Could the United States have remained neutral or was military involvement inevitable? Could the war have been shortened by different military strategies?

Chapter 19

The Culture in Affluence and Deprivation

THE INNER REVOLUTION

A New World of Uncertainty. In the late nineteenth century, middle- and upper-class Americans subscribed to well-defined values of Christian morality and the doctrine of self-improvement through the use of reason and will. They viewed the physical universe as a coherent, understandable system regulated by simple laws. As a result of their certainties, parents and teachers tended to be authoritative, and political and economic leaders tended to be dogmatic.

During the first two decades of the twentieth century, however, this orderly system of beliefs was attacked by several areas of advanced learning. Historical analysis in seminaries and Darwin's theory of evolution cast increasing doubt upon the literal truth of the Bible, while psychology questioned older theories of learning and mental discipline. With the discovery that only mathematics provided a reliable guide to the behavior of matter, understanding the nature of matter seemed lost to all but scientists. Dishearteningly, none of these new ideas were satisfactory substitutes for the old "truths," especially since the new sciences were based on uncertainty and a continual search for answers that could be, at best, only tentative.

The new scientific theories of the twenties, which were difficult for anyone to comprehend, entered the popular culture only partially and imperfectly. Nevertheless, ideas never understood by three quarters of the people may subtly influence all of society. Leaders in America come chiefly from the group with higher education and upper-middle-class family backgrounds. These favored people tend to set the standards, shape the customs, and wield the ultimate power in society. So what is a far-out idea in one generation can become the guide for social action in the next. By the 1920s, the impact of these new scientific ideas were being felt in urban middle-class child-rearing, education, and popular thought.

Psychological Theories. Of great impact were the psychological theories that questioned the human ability to reason objectively and the importance of reason as a basis for action. The founder of behaviorism, John B. Watson, regarded consciousness itself as only a by-product of physical processes, having no role in causing behavior. He insisted that both human and animal learning occurred simply through "conditioned reflexes." The ideas of Sigmund Freud, a Viennese physician and neurologist, also had a lasting social impact.

In his brilliant writings Freud popularized the idea that people were impelled to think and act in certain ways by unconscious pressures rather than by logical reasoning. He further held that these irrational, unconscious urges were of a "sexual" nature, although he used the term *sex* broadly to include many cravings for gratification not normally thought of as sexual. Thus when people thought they were behaving rationally, their behavior might be merely a disguise for a mixture of erotic urges and childhood wants which, though unrecognized by the individuals, influenced their behavior in many ways.

One of the great appeals of Freudianism was that it offered help to people who were emotionally disturbed. By a patient's free association of ideas in the presence of a psychoanalyst, together with the analyst's scientific interpretation of the patient's dreams, it might be possible to bring the disturbing elements to conscious recognition and thus to lessen or end the patient's feelings of conflict or anxiety.

The Freudian emphasis on the *libido*—the instinctive sexual drive in humans—as well as the Freudian denial of the validity of religious feelings had a profound effect upon the thinking of well-educated people all over the Western world. By placing no emphasis on abstinence and little on reason, and by offering salvation through indulgent secular "confession," Freudianism turned older theological doctrine upside down. People who sought Freudian therapy did not necessarily discard their religious faith, and a few clergymen managed to reach a compromise with the new doctrine. But again the scientific approach weakened or contradicted the values of the nineteenth century.

In social life Freudianism provided an excellent weapon for attacking Victorian formalities, rural Protestant virtues, and older educational ideas. Leading intellectuals like Walter Lippmann, Harold Lasswell, and Jerome Frank applied it to politics, public opinion, and the law, with the general effect of further weakening respect for rationality and traditional standards. Magazines and books were full of the new language of psychiatry, and many well-educated people enjoyed being amateur Freudian analysts. Well-informed parents now worried about the danger of suppressing their children's urges, and the child-centered home joined the child-centered school in relaxing discipline.

Changes in Education. The mid-nineteenth-century American view was that education should be directed primarily toward moral or religious rather than intellectual ends. The philosophy of Horace Mann, the most famous American educator of the period, was a "blend of natural law, faith in progress, capitalistic morality, and liberal Protestantism." The teacher's role was to see that the pupils memorized passages that inculcated abstract truths.

A radically progressive approach to education based on the new psychology, already mentioned in Part 5, was now being advanced by John Dewey. In the 1920s his principles became dominant in the major teachers' colleges and spread throughout the urban public school system as theory, if not as practice. Dewey's *Democracy and Education*, written in 1916, was the most influential guide, and the Progressive Education Association, formed in 1919, was the major pressure group. Teachers College of Columbia University was the chief training center for progressive educators. But in estimating the total influence of progressive education on pupils, it should be noted that in 1930 a majority of the nation's students were still in rural schools.

Often allied with progressivism were new movements for efficiency and utility in education. School superintendents applied business methods of "job-analysis" to their schools. Teachers were rated by their efficiency in performing the "housekeeping" necessities of the school, while their intellectual worth was often ignored. The idea of preparing students for daily life, rather than requiring them to master a body of knowledge, led a writer in 1922 to divide school activities into four major categories: health, fundamental processes, civic and social relations, and recreation. Of these, only the second embraced conventional learning.

From the emphasis on utility came more practically oriented curricula on the secondary level. The Smith-Hughes Act of 1917, granting federal aid to vocational education, started a rapid spread of special high schools and manual or trade departments in older schools. More and more a distinction was made between the minority in high school who expected to go to college and the majority who should substitute the development of practical skills for "book learning."

In the 1930s the extreme child-centered philosophy was superseded by a community-centered approach. No doubt the depression put emphasis on social and community duties, but, in addition, child-centeredness had been pushed to such chaotic extremes in a few schools that even Dewey had become critical of the results. The newer view stressed good group relations among students and teachers, plus the responsiveness of schools to the needs and problems of the community. Although it partially restored discipline, this approach did not necessarily place more emphasis on academic learning.

In 1920 the average teacher's salary was $871 a year, and the usual school was a small rural building with one or two teachers. The average teacher did not have a college education, might never have heard of John Dewey, and was not paid enough to support a family. As a result, most teachers were young single women teaching school until they married or found a more promising job. By 1930 the situation had improved somewhat. The average salary had risen to $1400—still inadequate for a middle-class family—and buses were introducing the consolidated school. By 1940 consolidated schools, with their greater degree of specialization among teachers, were becoming the rule in the more

During the 1920s a college degree became increasingly important in securing a good job. These young women are studying physics at Vassar College.

populous areas, and a majority of the children were in urban schools. Because of the fall in prices, teachers' salaries had risen about 25 percent in purchasing power.

During the twenties and thirties, college education followed many of these same trends. There was a decided shift away from the traditional classical program. Schools of education in which physical education could be a major subject multiplied. Women were offered courses in home economics, and most major universities started schools of commerce or business. For students who wanted a mixture of liberal arts and "useful" subjects, junior colleges offered two-year certificates. In 1920 there were only fifty-two such colleges. By 1930 there were ten times that number.

Although many regarded these developments as a lowering of the standards of college education, colleges and universities showed substantial development as centers of learning and research. The 1920s was the first full decade in which general research was supported by massive endowments such as those of the Carnegie and Rockefeller Foundations. Increasing private donations and state grants enabled American universities to rival those of Europe as centers of research. And at the same time more and more Americans were going to college. In 1920, 8 percent of young people aged 18 to 21 were in college. In 1930 it was over 12 percent and in 1940, nearly 16 percent. While some of the 1930–1940 increase was because of lack of employment and government assistance, college degrees were becoming increasingly important in securing jobs and gaining social prestige.

Physical and Social Theory. University departments of science continued an attack on the nineteenth-century belief that human intelligence was on the verge of understanding the nature of things. Over the half century before 1920 a brilliant group of European physicists and mathematicians demonstrated that a human mind could not perceive the nature of physical reality or picture its workings by the ordinary three-dimensional images. Only mathematics had a logic that could handle the four or more dimensions of physical problems. Furthermore, they discovered that matter was not solid substance but a system of particles held together by electrical energy, and that the only guides to this reality were mathematical equations and readings of complicated recording devices. Discoveries in the infinitesimal world inside the atom and the infinite world of outer space made reflective observers uncertain whether reality is precise and orderly or, at least, whether the human imagination is capable of grasping its order if there is one.

Basic philosophical uncertainty, however, did not prevent progress in sub-atomic physics. By the 1930s it was known that tremendous energy in the form of heat could be released by splitting atoms to form new elements. While Germans were in the lead in theory, large investments by the United States government, aided by German émigrés, would produce a bomb from massive atomic fission in 1945. Wartime needs would also speed the development of electronic devices such as radar and digital computers. All these scientific innovations were pragmatic, based on experimentation to find what worked rather than on a complete understanding of electricity or of the inner structure of the atom.

Some popularizers predicted that the scientific uncertainty that was revealed to the reading public in the late 1920s would lead to a new age of faith. But actually such writing had little immediate effect. In fact, the immediate reaction seemed to be a move in the opposite direction. Like the earlier evolutionary theory, the new science undermined theology without offering anything positive to replace it. The highly abstract characterizations of God that seemed consistent with the physical theories were without much appeal to Americans.

The academic world, of course, was required to pay heed, and the changes reported in physics were upsetting to the social sciences and philosophy. Society no longer seemed so simple as it had at the beginning of the century. If general social laws were to be discovered, it would only be by highly complex and sophisticated means. As a result, American social scientists turned to improving their methods and trying them out on limited, carefully defined problems rather than elaborating general systems. Philosophers, also discouraged by the mysterious character of reality, turned to studies of method. "How can any kind of truth be established?" became their major question. The testing of various systems of logic and representation consumed their time. The main body of philosophers lost interest in general systems of thought and, consequently, all contact with the public.

Keynesian Economics. While the social sciences as a whole continued their pursuit of more sophisticated methods, the depression brought the pressure of immediate, practical problems to bear on economic thinking. A few academic social scientists embraced Marxism and gave up hope for the capitalist system, but their number was surprisingly small. The majority turned to solutions of the type that were given a rounded theoretical formulation by the British economist John Maynard Keynes.

Keynes' ideas brought about the first major revision of economic theory in the twentieth century. They offered a more realistic view of the operation of the entire economy than had existed before. His major work, *The General Theory of Employment, Interest and Money,* published in 1936, shifted the main theoretical emphasis from supply and demand to income and investment, or from the mechanics of the market to the distribution of income. Keynes' most important conclusions were: (1) that increasing the income of the poor stimulated demand, while increasing the income of the

rich promoted saving; (2) that increased demand, not increased saving, led to new business investment (his major revision of older theory); (3) that total income could increase only from such investment; (4) that if the functioning of the undisturbed free market did not provide adequate business investment to maintain a sufficient flow of income, government was the only agency with sufficient spending power to see that this result was achieved.

Obviously these doctrines implied the need for higher wages and government investment and were hence resisted by conservatives. But the theory was already partially being applied by the New Deal, although President Roosevelt did not subscribe to Keynesianism or any other economic theory. By the end of World War II the prosperity induced by government spending and massive redistribution of income downward was so obvious that politicans of both major parties implicitly acted on the Keynesian assumptions, and most academic economists gradually made some of Keynes' ideas the starting point for their new theoretical models. These things would have happened without Keynes, but he supplied the rationale for the capitalist revolution that emerged from the disaster of the Great Depression.

Religion. While the pressures of clergymen for sweeping social reform lessened in the prosperous 1920s, religious groups became increasingly concerned with secular matters. Urban churches, in particular, acquired game rooms, gymnasiums, and lecture halls and seemed to be shifting their emphasis from worship to social service and recreation. By the end of the decade the Federal Council of Churches of Christ, the liberal Protestant organization, had commissions for such diverse matters as international justice, social service, race relations, and Christian education. The National Catholic Welfare Conference, formed to help carry out social obligations of the Catholic Church, became a powerful force with a large staff of experts on legislative matters. Missionary activities also were increasingly secularized. By 1920 effectively organized Protestant and Catholic missions in non-Christian areas of the world were emphasizing "civilizing" education, medical care, and other services.

The Great Depression brought liberal Catholic, Jewish, and Protestant organizations closer together. In 1931 the National Catholic Welfare Conference, the General Conference of Rabbis, and the Federal Council of Churches of Christ joined in a conference on "Permanent Preventatives of Unemployment." Such efforts were continued by an interfaith Committee on Religious Welfare Activity. Despite vocal opposition from conservatives, who wanted their churches to refrain from raising political and social questions, liberal religious journals became increasingly secular in content and more concerned with economic problems. But in spite of prodding and articulate social criticism by a small group of religious leaders, parish churches and their ministers tended to remain quite conservative. World War II also shifted religious leaders away from social reform.

The increasingly social orientation of the leading Protestant churches was resisted by fundamentalists—Protestants who believed in the literal interpretation of the Bible as a historical record and prophecy, as well as a guide to faith and morality. The conflict between fundamentalism and current scientific views, either religious or secular, was dramatized by the Scopes trial in 1925. John Scopes, a science teacher in a Tennessee high school, was charged with violating a state law forbidding the teaching in public schools of any theories denying the Biblical account of the creation of man—Darwin's theory of evolution in particular. With his prosecution led by William Jennings Bryan, who championed the literal interpretation of the Bible,

and his defense conducted by the famous liberal lawyer Clarence Darrow, Scopes was convicted of violating the Tennessee law and fined $100, but the penalty later was set aside. The Scopes trial attracted more national and world attention to American fundamentalism than did any other event of the period between the wars.

Equally fundamentalist but with a quite different mission and influence were the ethnic churches in the urban centers. Each immigrant group had quickly established its own congregations, which were centers of neighborhood social life and forces for the preservation of national customs and ceremonies. Wise Catholic bishops usually appointed priests of the same nationality as the parishioners. Second- and third-generation immigrants often supported their churches and church schools more to preserve their national cultures than to show commitment to a particular denominational faith.

As the old-stock white middle class deserted the cities, more and more urban Protestant churches became black. The original Southern Baptist denomination spawned numerous cults and sects whose small churches provided centers where the members, often from the same areas of the South, could rejoice in the promise of a better life to come after death. This emphasis on the hereafter rather than the now made the black churches, as a whole, a conservative influence, tending to reconcile parishioners to their earthly lot.

Except in the South the Protestant church in America had been supported mainly by the urban middle class. Neither farmers in remote areas nor working-class city dwellers generally made the effort to participate in the activities of a Protestant church, but for the increasingly mobile members of the middle class, particularly in suburban areas, the church had a definite social value. It was a place to meet leading citizens and develop friendships through cooperation in religious endeavors. Consequently, the great growth of the urban and suburban middle class and the spread of the automobile to outlying areas led to a steady increase in church membership up to 1929. By 1926, 46 percent of the population were church members.

These reasons for growth go far to explain why the Great Depression reversed the trend in membership. People with only shabby clothes and no money for the collection plate did not want to appear before their more prosperous neighbors. The depression may actually have increased religious feeling, but between 1930 and 1934 the income of Protestant churches declined 50 percent. For the decade as a whole church membership fell about 6 percent. That the decline was caused at least partly by financial hardships is further indicated by the rapid growth in membership in the prosperous years that followed World War II.

Living in Good Times and Bad. If towns with fewer than 2500 people are classed as rural, the nation in 1920 was still less than one-third urban. And except for some suburbs, a community with fewer than 2500 people was not likely to be a center for advanced thought or action. This goes far to

An ingenious contrivance washes clothes on an Iowa farm during World War I. Labor-saving devices rapidly became more sophisticated in the next two decades.

explain the lack of response by the American people to the revolution in ideas, as well as the general passivity with which they bore the deprivations of the depression. If there was such a thing as a "normal" or "ordinary" American family, it lived in or near a small town.

In the twenties people's lives expanded in movement and variety as families acquired an automobile and a radio and towns acquired a movie house. Real incomes advanced somewhat, and manufactured items like vacuum cleaners, washing machines, and ready-made clothes lightened the household chores that wives had been expected to perform throughout recorded history. But this new world of material things probably had little effect on people's ideas. In general, newspapers, radio, and movies were conservative forces, reenforcing the pro-business traditions of American culture. If nothing else, votes cast in the presidential election of 1928 suggested that most people were reasonably contented with things as they were.

The twenties have been called the Jazz Age, characterized by wild parties, assertive females, and heavy drinking. But while the decade had these aspects, they were limited largely to the upper middle class of the largest metropolitan areas. Victorian social decorum could be flagrantly discarded only by those social leaders who had previously imposed it. And while easier, less formal manners spread across the nation and automobiles provided young couples with an opportunity to escape supervision, the change in customs in most parts of the country was gradual and moderate. The real revolution in the manners of youth was still more than a generation away. Deliberate flouting of the liquor laws occurred chiefly in urban industrial communities where public opinion was opposed to prohibition.

The depression had very unequal effects on the world of "mid-America." If the workers of a small town had been employed in manufacturing, they were likely to suffer unemploy-

ment and lack of money during much of the thirties. But in trade, employment kept up, and in many areas local buying and selling of food, even on a barter basis, declined by only a moderate percentage. Conditions were worse in rural regions where crops were grown for export and not for home consumption. Many cotton farmers, for example, had to try their hand at food growing, with mixed results. The middle-class belief that a "dole" would undermine self-reliance delayed a general system of relief payments during Hoover's administration. The worst period was over by 1933, when federal funds lifted the burden of unemployment relief from the bankrupt states and communities. License statistics and gasoline sales indicate that most families living outside of towns kept their automobiles in service, even at the sacrifice of food or clothing. Inadequate diet was more difficult to cope with. In an abstract, theoretical view the American standard of living was high enough in the 1920s for a decline of a quarter to a third to be borne, but unfortunately the burden was not uniformly distributed. Americans did die from malnutrition in the early thirties.

MASS COMMUNICATION

Newspapers. The newspaper continued to be the principal reading matter of adult Americans. Indeed, the transition from prosperity to depression gave most people more time to read and increased the size and circulation of newspapers. Where personal interests were concerned, as in attitudes toward the New Deal, readers were obviously prepared to disagree with their newspapers, most of which were strongly anti-Roosevelt. But publishers and editors, by subtle selection and handling of news and comment, undoubtedly influenced readers to accept many of their ideas.

The major trend in the whole period between the wars was toward papers that were less competitive in opinion and more elaborate in format. While newspaper chains stopped growing in the 1930s, another ultimately more important limitation on competition came from the merger of competing papers within the same city. In 1930 nine tenths of the cities with a population of more than 100,000 had two or more directly competing papers, but of the smaller cities only a fifth had such morning or evening competition.

In the larger cities competition of a sort was often maintained by an all-day tabloid competing against full-sized morning and evening papers. The first American tabloid newspaper was the *New York Daily News*, started by Joseph M. Patterson in 1919. Easy to read on subways and buses, the tabloid also digested news into short, simple stories—illustrated, as never before, by photographs. In 1924 the *News* had the largest circulation in New York City. Other publishers quickly copied Patterson's innovation, and by 1940 there were nearly fifty tabloids.

Another form of potential competition whose effects on the full-sized daily were hard to measure was the radio newscast. To protect themselves, many papers—250 by 1940—bought control of radio stations. In spite of the obvious fact that radio could deliver news more quickly, intimately, and dramatically, the effect of news broadcasts on newspaper circulation was not severe. As people received increasing amounts of news, they appeared to become more interested in local, national, and international events and to spend more time learning about them.

Improvements in technology and press services produced better-quality newspaper illustrations, more detailed last-minute news, and an increase in special departments and columns. The humorous column, by a writer like Will Rogers, successor to "Mr. Dooley," was an old feature, but the column of serious general comment was an innovation in the 1920s. People bought papers just to read some favorite columnist like Heywood Broun or

Walter Lippmann, and writers with such opposing views could appear in the same paper without menacing an "objective" editorial policy. The more popular columns and comics were distributed by press syndicates to newspapers all over the United States.

Magazines. The increasing public appetite for current events was fed by the rise of weekly news magazines. In 1920 only the *Literary Digest*, which took its material on current events largely from the newspapers, was important in this weekly field. In 1923 *Time*, smartly written under the direction of editors Briton Hadden and Henry Luce, made an immediate hit, and in 1936 the Luce organization launched the weekly picture magazine *Life*. Both inspired imitators.

Magazine circulation survived the depression quite well, probably because the readers of most magazines were middle class or above—the groups less affected by depression than the lower half of the income scale. Throughout the 1920s the aged *Saturday Evening Post* was supreme among general weekly magazines. Closely mirroring middle-class interests and attitudes, it mixed good popular fiction with inspirational articles about business leaders and the virtues of the American way of doing things. During the 1930s the *Post*, by turning more liberal, managed to hold much of its circulation, but competition was weakening its position.

Most of the leading "serious" writers of the time, including Faulkner, Fitzgerald, and Hemingway, wrote for magazines. Faulkner, with only a limited audience for his novels, needed the magazine revenue to support his family. Consequently, a magazine reader could sample a wide range of American literature and thought without ever buying a bound book.

For the reader of the early 1920s who felt unable to keep up with all that was being published, Mr. and Mrs. De Witt Wallace started *The Reader's Digest*, a collection of

The radio became an important household fixture during the 1930s and millions of Americans listened regularly.

Radio comedy and variety shows were performed before live audiences. Fred Allen's popular program featured guest stars and a 25-piece orchestra in addition to the regular players.

condensed versions of what they considered the most important magazine articles of the preceding month. As the popularity of their digest grew, they also commissioned articles and condensed books for quick reading. Like the *Post*, the *Digest* appealed to middle-class values and celebrated rugged individualism and business success. Ultimately it became the most widely read magazine in the world.

Radio. In August 1920, Station WWJ of the Detroit *News* initiated commercial broadcasting. The mass development of radio was retarded by many problems, including the control of necessary patents by American Telephone and Telegraph, General Electric, and Westinghouse, and the unwillingness of Associated Press, the largest news service, to have its releases broadcast. But in 1926 AT&T agreed to permit network broadcasting by renting its wires, and the same year AP, pressed by Hearst's International News Service and other competitors, amended its rules to allow broadcast of important news. Between 1926 and 1929 three national radio networks were created. Advertising agencies now brought their big clients to the networks, and radio quickly achieved the form that was to characterize it during the next generation.

The thirties was the first decade of systematic polls of public opinion and hence of the first reasonably reliable estimates of how people spent their time. By 1940 four fifths of American households had radios, and these were turned on nearly five hours a day. Radio listeners heard Hoover, Roosevelt, and other political leaders put forth their views. Franklin Roosevelt, in particular, capitalized on his charming radio personality and on the pseudo-intimacy of home reception in his "fireside chats." These also helped to counterbalance the generally unfavorable newspaper opinion of him.

Since advertisers dictated what was to be performed, programs during the prime evening hours were directed at what were assumed to be the tastes of mass audiences. The leading stars of screen and stage appeared on radio but usually as special attractions in the middle of variety shows that alternated with situation comedy. On less valuable time, however, the networks presented more serious programs. Starting in 1930, CBS broadcast the New York Philharmonic Orchestra on Saturday afternoons. This led NBC to compete the following year with Saturday Opera from New York's Metropolitan and in 1937 to start a series of Sunday performances by Arturo Toscanini conducting his own symphony orchestra. It was estimated that as many as 10 million listeners heard some of these musical programs.

As international tensions mounted in the 1930s, commentators such as H. V. Kaltenborn, Lowell Thomas, and Gabriel Heatter attracted large radio audiences during prime advertising time. In the daytime hours radio listeners were entertained by soap operas, baseball, and college football. Professional football had its successful origin in 1935, and important sporting events like the heavyweight title bouts of Joe Louis were listened to on tens of millions of sets.

Using Unwanted Leisure. During the depression, the unemployed sought ways to occupy their time, and many part-time workers and businessmen with little business to attend to also had leisure problems. Most couldn't afford hardcover books, and really cheap paperbacks appeared only at the end of the decade. So they read more by using the public libraries, perhaps for the first time. The urge to gamble may also have increased with poverty. It took a widespread new form in bingo, which won the approval of many churches as a way of raising money.

The federal government came to the aid of those with unwanted leisure by providing not only subsistence money but also opportunities for recreation. The Civilian Conservation Corps, recruited from unemployed adolescents, built campgrounds, laid out parks with tennis courts and swimming pools, and cleared wilderness trails, erecting hostels at convenient intervals. In the cities after 1935, federal theater and music programs brought serious drama and music to millions who had never before experienced them. Payments were also made to college students for work directed by faculty members.

The Arts. The financial patronage of the arts that had spread during the prosperous twenties halted abruptly with the Great Depression. Rescue came in 1935 from the Federal Arts Project, a branch of the Works Progress Administration (WPA). Forty thousand destitute actors, musicians, writers, and painters were employed at from $60 to $100 a month. This financial support, meager as it was, won many artists back from rebellion to a more balanced judgment of American society.

Painting. A number of major American artists continued to work in one or another of the modes of abstract painting launched earlier in Europe, but during the reaction of the 1920s against prewar enthusiasms, nonrepresentational painting failed to attract young artists, and it diminished in popularity during the depression. A group that included Charles Sheeler and Georgia O'Keefe, whose work was better received by the public, emphasized the abstract esthetic form in machinery, architecture, and nature. Their craftsmanship was exacting, their themes recognizable, and their forms sharply bounded and precise.

The main body of important American painting during the interwar period, however, was of a more conventional type which had close enough contact with reality to permit social commentary. Thomas Hart Benton, Grant Wood, and John Stuart Curry dealt with characters and characteristics of the rural Midwest, both pleasant and unpleasant. Another group of painters also concentrated

on the American scene but explored the problems of urban life. Lois Jones, Ben Shahn, William Gropper, and Philip Evergood were among those stimulated by a strong sense of social justice, engendered primarily by the depression. They sought to use art as a "social weapon," protesting in their paintings against mob violence, political corruption, slums, and strike breaking. Whereas the ashcan school of the early twentieth century had seen poverty as picturesque or pathetic, these angry painters of the 1930s saw it as an inexcusable result of capitalism.

The subsidized painters in the Federal Arts Project had to do many community murals and other public pictures. Perhaps because of this and perhaps because there was a general return in the late thirties to an appreciation of things American, their art tended to embrace the national past and to remain as the last strong surge of popular, realistic painting. It cannot be said with assurance that any great masterpieces were executed by American painters during the interwar period, but the total product of the abler artists was larger and more impressive than in previous generations.

Music. The development of the phonograph and the radio gave composers and performers of serious music a vastly expanded audience. By the 1920s phonographs and records had achieved an accuracy of reproduction that made them acceptable to the best musicians. Undoubtedly many more people than ever before became acquainted with operas, symphonies, and other classical works.

Like other artists in the years before World War I, composers had been attracted by the new scientific attitude of experimentalism and had produced dissonant, multitonal, non-rhythmic compositions. But this group had few representatives in the United States. Instead, an upsurge in musical composition drawing on native materials produced works ranging from popular songs through more sophisticated show tunes and the jazz-based dance music of Duke Ellington to concertos and symphonies. Jazz—which has been called both the major Afro-American contribution to American culture and the only purely American contribution to the arts—was already popular in 1920. Built on these American traditions, the musical comedies of American composers Irving Berlin, Richard Rodgers, George Gershwin, Jerome Kern, and Cole Porter captivated the Western world.

The 1930s was the decade of the dance bands, both "sweet" (Lombardo, Duchin, Whiteman, Wayne King) and "swing" (Goodman, the Dorseys, Lunceford, Basie, Miller). Jazz soloists attracted music enthusiasts as well as dancers. "Jam sessions" given over to improvisation were attended by esthetes as well as "hepcats." Perhaps swing, or perhaps just the quest for novelty by millions of the unemployed young, brought back open dancing in the Big Apple, the Suzie-Q, and other types of "jitterbugging" away from one's partner. George Gershwin made use of jazz motifs and rhythms in *Rhapsody in Blue* (1924), *An American in Paris* (1928), and the opera *Porgy and Bess* (1935), all of which won world acclaim. (See "George Gershwin: Creator of a New American Music.") Aaron Copland, Roy Harris, Charles Ives, William Grant Still, and other Americans also wrote ballet scores and symphonies giving classic form to American rhythms and melodies.

The stage—particularly the musical stage and the bandstand—offered American blacks their best opportunity to escape from poverty and social invisibility. Paul Robeson achieved stardom both as actor and as singer. Robeson and the contralto Marian Anderson won wide acclaim in the concert hall. At a time when practically all sports were still segregated, white jazz musicians looked to the great black jazz artists for both instruction and inspira-

tion, and in the thirties blacks and whites played jazz together publicly as well as privately.

Literature and Drama. Writers of the 1920s experienced a growing dissatisfaction with and alienation from American society and twentieth-century values. In particular, they were disillusioned by the ease with which Woodrow Wilson and other world leaders had converted moral idealism into a zeal for war. They were alienated by the triumph of materialism and business values in the postwar period and exasperated by the smug self-satisfaction of the American upper classes. "The younger generation," wrote Harold Stearns, "*is* in revolt; it *does* dislike almost to the point of hatred and certainly to the point of contempt the type of people dominant in our present civilization."

In *This Side of Paradise* F. Scott Fitzgerald complained that the young writers "had grown up to find all Gods dead, all wars fought, all faiths in men shaken." They deplored American materialism, prosperity, Puritanism, and conformity—in short, much of the national heritage. But unlike confident prewar novelists such as Winston Churchill and Upton Sinclair, the new writers did not preach reform, for they saw no immediate way of correcting the situation. This prevailing nonsocial attitude was sweepingly expressed by the leading drama critic, George Jean Nathan: "What concerns me alone is myself and a few close friends. For all I care the rest of the world can go to hell at today's sunset."

To escape from America writers moved to the relative isolation of Greenwich Village in New York City or to the more complete separation of Paris. Critic H. L. Mencken's pungent but superficial and nihilistic attacks on American values were widely read both in his *American Mercury* magazine and in book form, revealing the desire of many intellectuals to divorce themselves from most traditional American attitudes.

Yet from this alienated generation of writers came as much good drama, poetry, and fiction as the United States had ever seen. Novelists denounced the world in vigorous new prose, used new literary techniques, and wrote with frankness and sincerity. Ernest Hemingway, who gave currency to the phrase "the lost generation," brilliantly pictured its disillusioned, cynical, expatriate society in *The Sun Also Rises* (1925) and traced the causes of that disillusionment and cynicism in his novel of World War I *A Farewell to Arms* (1929). But by 1940 in *For Whom the Bell Tolls* Hemingway had moved gradually to a more positive position of affirming the need for the social solidarity of free peoples against totalitarianism.

Other writers exposed the contradictions and hypocrisies of American culture. *An American Tragedy* (1925), which portrayed a young American hopelessly confused by the false social and religious values of his environment, marked the summit of Theodore Dreiser's career. Sinclair Lewis wrote all of his important attacks on American society during the 1920s. *Main Street* (1920) satirized the small town of the Middle West, where "dullness made God." *Babbitt* (1922) parodied the self-satisfied, conformist, materialistic American businessman so successfully that "Babbitt" and "Babittry" were added to the dictionary. *Arrowsmith* (1925) depicted an America which placed frustrating impediments in the path of a doctor devoted to medical research. *Dodsworth* (1929) satirized

George Gershwin: Creator of a New American Music

After World War I, jazz—a native mixture of Southern folk music filtered through black combos and overlaid with a changeable, free-swinging rhythm—began to replace native American ragtime and the sweet European-inspired melodies of the age of Victor Herbert and Rudolf Friml. The inspired jazz improvisors, from W. C. Handy before World War I to King Oliver, Louis Armstrong, Jelly Roll Morton, and Bessie Smith in the 1920s, played or sang melodies and rhythms that were both new and challenging to the classical traditions of Europe. Although not measurable in dollars, the principal export from the United States to Western Europe during the period between the wars was music. It traveled in sheets, records, and visits by players and was consumed in night clubs, restaurants, and homes. America was having a flowering of native melody comparable to that of Austria two generations earlier.

The formalization of jazz rhythms began in 1922 when George Gershwin incorporated them in a now-forgotten opera, first called *Blue Monday* and later recorded as *135th Street*. Born in 1898 to middle-class Russian-Jewish parents in New York City, Gershwin showed no interest in music until he was thirteen. His talent appeared to be in athletics, particularly in fighting, a great sport on New York's

the upper-middle-class American woman, picturing Fran Dodsworth as a pampered, selfish, superficial, pretentious snob. Sherwood Anderson, in *Winesburg, Ohio* (1919) and in subsequent books, showed from a Freudian viewpoint how small-town morals and customs produced a neurotic society. Perhaps a writer's most brilliant attacks on the lack of proper values in the American upper class, to which he personally aspired, were in F. Scott Fitzgerald's *This Side of Paradise* (1920) and *The Great Gatsby* (1925).

The continuing protest of blacks against the injustices of American life and their growing sense of racial unity were reenforced for a brief period in the twenties by white writers in search of new themes and forms of expression. Urban communities of educated blacks had, from the beginning of the century, produced an increasing volume of prose and poetry. The discovery of this literature, around 1925, by Sherwood Anderson, Carl Van Vechten, and other white novelists and critics called the attention of their readers to what came to be called the Harlem Renaissance. While recognition and attendant pride undoubtedly stimulated black creativity, the sudden flood of publicity produced the false impression that the black literary movement was a new, brief phenomenon. In fact, James Weldon Johnson's novel, *The Autobiography of an Ex-Coloured Man*, was first published in 1912, and Langston Hughes' remarkable output of prose and poetry, fiction and nonfiction, extended into the 1960s. And other writers of the Harlem Renaissance, like

---

lower East Side, unmarred in those days by guns or knives. Learning did not interest him, and he went to a vocational rather than a college-oriented high school.

At the age of twelve he heard eleven-year-old Maxie Rosenberg play Dvořák's *Humoresque* in the auditorium of P.S. 11. By a religious type of conversion Gershwin became a slave to the piano. In a transport of enthusiasm he went to Maxie's house and they became intimate friends. There he learned to play the piano by fingering the notes on a player piano—a process not to be recommended for the less gifted. When the Gershwins bought a piano about a year later with the idea of teaching older brother Ira to play, George unexpectedly demonstrated such proficiency that he won the lessons and Ira was left to his poetry and literature.

At fifteen George left the High School of Commerce and went to work full-time in Tin Pan Alley, 28th Street between Broadway and Fifth Avenue, where musical publishers demonstrated their wares to people from show business. A brilliant performer on the piano, Gershwin won the post of rehearsal pianist for Jerome Kern's and Victor Herbert's *Miss 1917*. But in his spare time he was always composing. Meanwhile brother Ira was turning his poetic talents to the more lucrative art of song writing.

The first show with all-Gershwin music to run on Broadway was *La, La, Lucille* in 1919, but George's rise to fame came from a song "Swanee" that was taken the preceding year by Al Jolson, a famous blackface singer, and interpolated into his show, *Sinbad*. There followed nearly twenty years of popular musical comedies and reviews with words and music by the Gershwins.

George Gershwin's lasting fame came, however, not from songs and dances performed by the Astaires and many other stars in both plays and films, but from introducing the spirit of jazz into formal music. A major effect of jazz is from

Countee Cullen, Alain Locke, Claude McKay, and Jean Toomer, were by no means limited to the last half of the 1920s. As a group, perhaps their greatest achievement was to portray the world of the American black man and woman as they knew it.

In contrast to the preoccupation of writers in the twenties with individual emotional adjustment in the light of new psychological views of personal problems, the Great Depression inevitably brought a return to social issues. Poverty amidst plenty was the writer's lot as well as that of the masses. John Dos Passos, an alienated member of the upper middle class who had begun an attack on American capitalism in *Three Soldiers* (1921), achieved his best work in a trilogy, *U.S.A.*, published between 1930 and 1935.

John Steinbeck's *The Grapes of Wrath* (1939), which chronicles the misery of a family of Oklahoma tenant farmers who migrated to California in search of work, is a graphic description of the contrast between the migratory unemployed and prosperous, propertied Americans, protected by the machinery of government. Accounts of suffering based on experience rather than observation include Henry Roth's *Call It Sleep* (1934), an autobiographical account of childhood in the slums of New York; James T. Farrell's three-volume *Studs Lonigan* (1932–1935), showing the failure of the accepted social institutions to prevent the moral ruin of a young Irish-American in Chicago; and Richard Wright's *Native Son* (1940), picturing the destructive pressures of the same city on a young black.

improvised "blue notes" (flatted notes) and cadenzas, particularly from horns, so that technically the composer writes a suitable basic score and the musicians "jazz" it.

The coming of jazz to New York from Chicago, St. Louis, and New Orleans about 1920 led the famous "big band" leader Paul Whiteman in 1924 to give an "Experiment in Modern Music" at Aeolian Hall, normally devoted to renditions of the standard classics. For this performance Gershwin, working at top speed, composed a single piano script for *Rhapsody in Blue*, leaving the orchestration for another piano and the orchestra to Ferde Grofé, Whiteman's immensely talented assistant. The result has been called the most important single event in American musical history. Coming at the end of a program that was not winning acceptance by the musical elite, it brought a bored audience to its feet, wildly cheering. They had heard something fresher and more alive than had been achieved by any contemporary American or European composer.

From this time on Gershwin led a double life. When musical shows and solo performances gave him time, he composed music to fit the classical molds. Perhaps it should have been the other way around, but Gershwin was hopelessly bound up in the Broadway world of show business, and the great classical piano teachers turned him down as a student who was already beyond their promptings. Since he remained unmarried, sober, and incredibly energetic, he somehow managed while writing shows such as *Lady, Be Good* and *Funny Face* for the Astaires to compose the

The strength of all three writers springs from deep emotional understanding of their subjects. Writing in the same semiautobiographic genre but accepting rather than damning his environment, Thomas Wolfe produced four novels between 1929 and his death in 1938. Characterized by an obsession with his own emotional responses, his long, loose-jointed books were unique in a decade largely given over to novels of social analysis.

The work of one writer, judged by critics in later decades to be the greatest of this period, virtually ignored the passing environments of war, prosperity, and depression. William Faulkner was concerned with the ultimate meaning of human existence, and while he found it in the individual's inescapable relation to nature and the land, his immediate focus was the problem faced by the traditional South in adjusting to the twentieth century. More daring as a writer than his contemporaries, he did not hesitate to depict the world through the eyes of an idiot, to manipulate time, and to imply emotional meanings beyond the range of rational communication. His great period, which ultimately won him a Nobel Prize for Literature, was from *The Sound and the Fury* in 1929 through *Light in August* (1932) and other books in the first half of the 1930s.

American poets of the 1920s, also trying to deal with ultimate, or existential, problems, achieved substantial world acclaim. In 1922 T. S. Eliot, expatriate but still an American citizen, published *The Waste Land*, a poem of despair with modern civilization that exerted

outstanding *Concerto in F for Piano and Orchestra*. On a trip to France in 1928 he wrote *An American in Paris*, which best typifies the serious Gershwin and a decade after his death was made into an opera. When he completed the *Second Rhapsody* in 1931, he thought it was his best work.

For the Western world in general, Gershwin's—and perhaps American music's—greatest success was the opera *Porgy and Bess*. In this case his more popular, but politically serious, musicals such as *Strike Up the Band* and *Of Thee I Sing* delayed production of the opera by several years. Working with poet Du Bose Heyward on a script that had already served for a play depicting the lives of poor blacks on "Catfish Row" in Charleston, South Carolina, George and Ira Gershwin communicated deep levels of human feeling in both the lyrics and the music of *Porgy and Bess*. Produced in 1935, it had a mild success on Broadway. But performed and recorded all over the world after World War II, it became the most universally known and best-loved work by an American composer.

In 1938 Gershwin died of brain cancer. For Americans, at least, his formal compositions mark the last triumph of the great classical traditions of Western music, soon to be silenced by a flood of dissonant and nonrhythmic music, appreciated only by a highly educated musical elite. In a generation that created great music for the general public, Gershwin was the most successful—and may prove to be the most enduring.

Migrant families loaded as many possessions as their vehicles could carry and left their homes in search of work. Here, two families are bound for California in 1936.

tremendous influence. Hart Crane's major work, *The Bridge,* a difficult-to-decipher commentary on time, appeared in 1930. In addition to some of the older poets, Wallace Stevens, William Carlos Williams, Robinson Jeffers, Robert Frost, E. E. Cummings, and Marianne Moore were all writing poetry of the first rank.

In drama the postwar rebellion against the world in general and America in particular also produced important work. The eleven plays of Eugene O'Neill, from *Beyond the Horizon* (1920) to *Mourning Becomes Electra* (1931)—all strongly influenced by Freudian psychology—marked the first major American contribution to serious theater. A number of other dramatists, including Sidney Howard, Maxwell Anderson, Elmer Rice, and

Robert Sherwood, joined in this remarkable upsurge. During the depression a new playwright, Clifford Odets, wrote a strong drama, *Waiting for Lefty* (1935), in praise of collective action and the labor movement. And late in the decade there was a shift from anticapitalist plays to antifascist and antiwar themes. The most talented woman playwright of the times was Lillian Hellman, a severe critic of much in American life. But all in all, neither American drama nor poetry and fiction in the depression period equaled in originality or vigor the work of the twenties.

Motion Pictures. D. W. Griffith's silent movie *Broken Blossoms* (1919), starring Lillian Gish, was widely acclaimed by critics as marking the emergence of a new art form, said by the *Literary Digest* to be as important as music or poetry. Unfortunately, technological success and the work of this one middle-aged pioneer were not followed by a great burst of high-quality motion picture composition, directing, and acting.

The motion picture as an art medium was subordinated to the business interests that marketed the film. The major production studios owned chains of theaters and controlled the circulation of pictures. By 1930, with an investment by the owners of $2 billion to protect, the managers of the companies were unwilling to risk financing films that might not appeal to a major segment of the American public. Consequently, motion pictures of the twenties were massive spectacles of courts and armies directed by Cecil B. De Mille, sentimental melodramas starring Mary Pickford, breathtaking exploits by Douglas Fairbanks, Sr., or romantic seductions by Rudolph Valentino. But comedy remained as one genre that could reconcile profit-oriented producers and talented actors. Most famous of the comedians was Charlie Chaplin who, producing and directing his own pictures, continued in his comedies of the underdog to protest against many of the values of American society.

In the last three years of the 1920s sound and then color began to make the motion picture potentially the equal of the stage. As a result, stock companies and vaudeville practically disappeared, and the professional stage became restricted to a few of the largest cities. From the 1920s to the 1950s the motion picture was the standard form of visual dramatic entertainment for the great majority of Americans.

In the thirties the Hollywood production line turned out a steady stream of highly polished, star-laden escapist films—glittering musicals, gangster stories, Westerns, heroic costume dramas, and comedies, from slapstick to sophisticated. Snubbed by most highbrows, they were embraced by millions of ordinary Americans, for whom the movies—at prices as low as ten cents—provided a warm, dark refuge from reality. The grimmer aspects of depression were treated in a few commercial films and in some excellent documentary films produced by the federal government. Documentary still shots collected by Margaret Bourke-White also created deep impressions of the dire rural poverty of the early thirties.

Architecture. The towering American skyscraper, created in part because of the narrow confines of the Chicago Loop and downtown Manhattan, was regarded as an architectural innovation of worldwide importance. It was a monument to American ideas of marketing. As land values rose in all U.S. cities, it became economical to increase the height of buildings in the most valuable locations, but the altitudes achieved in the 1920s far exceeded this economic need. The advertising value that accrued to the company that built a towering building and the extra amount that tenants were willing to pay for the prestige and convenience of such lofty offices led to a race for height that culminated for that era in the 1200-foot Empire State Building.

The architectural design that was dominant in skyscraper architecture by the late 1920s resulted partly from the New York Zoning Act of 1916, which forced setbacks in buildings rising above certain heights. The plan of the Finnish-born architect Eliel Saarinen, which called for a series of blocks diminishing in size as the building rose, with windows set in vertical panels between continuous strips of stone or concrete, became a general model for skyscraper design.

During both prosperity and depression, older styles of architecture dominated in most public buildings and homes. The Capitol in Washington, D.C., was rebuilt by the Hoover and Roosevelt administrations in the classical Greco-Roman style, the style also chosen for most post offices and state buildings. During

The American skyscraper revolutionized city architecture. This photo of New York's skyline was taken in 1931. The tallest building in the picture is the nearly completed Empire State Building.

the 1920s hundreds of thousands of new homes were built by the well-to-do, but they or their architects and builders generally preferred to adopt or adapt some style from the past rather than experiment with the unfamiliar problems of "modern" design. Needless to say, the builders of small homes, many without architects, avoided experimentation.

SOCIAL CHANGE

Motorization and Urbanization. While the advent of radio and progress in electronics promised great future changes, immediate changes in American society centered around the automobile. Until World War I automobiles had been used chiefly for the recreation of the upper middle class. In 1917 fewer than one farm family in six had an automobile. In the nation as a whole there were fewer than 5 million cars. As forms of transport, trucks and buses were negligible economically and socially.

By 1930 two thirds of America's farms—probably all the prosperous commercial farms—had automobiles, and the nation had about 23 million passenger cars. Since there were only about 26 million households, and many families in big cities did not need private automobiles, the United States was approaching the goal of a car in the garage of every family that wanted one. Even more spectacular than the fivefold increase in passenger cars was a ninefold rise in the number of trucks. Nearly 4 million commercial vehicles, of which 40,000 were buses, signaled the beginning of the change to a society built around motor transport.

In the new geography main highway intersections would replace villages as shopping centers, cities would be within easy reach of farms, factories would move from congested cities to the country, and consolidated grammar and high schools would collect children by bus from miles around. Few places would remain remote from the pressures, advantages, and disadvantages of an urbanized culture.

While the spread of slums had shown the inadequacy of American municipal planning for nearly a century, the automobile, more than the slum, lay back of the rapid rise of city planning commissions and authorities. Although zoning was initiated in New York in 1916 without particular regard to motor transport, that transport, by potentially opening all areas to all types of use, led to the rapid spread of zoning to other cities. The steady migration to major metropolitan areas during the twenties also forced planning on reluctant municipal authorities. By 1930 37 percent of the city population of the United States lived in zoned communities.

Automobiles and trucks required new bridges, tunnels, and thoroughfares into central city business districts. The Port of New York Authority, established by a "treaty" between New York and New Jersey in 1921, initiated interstate agencies to plan transportation. Generally, however, urban efforts to alleviate both traffic problems and slum congestion in the prosperous twenties could be characterized as too little and too late.

The "Automotive Social Ladder." One of the cultural pressures directly connected with the automobile was its rise as a sign of social status. The American automobile, to be sure, depreciated rather rapidly, and for reliable service, replacement was desirable in about five to seven years. But social considerations worked for even briefer ownership. A new car was a symbol of success and prosperity, and the bigger and more expensive the car the higher the presumed status of the owner. For urban and suburban apartment dwellers the automobile took the place of an elaborate house as a mark of social standing. Only farmers and the very rich seem to have been relatively immune to such pressures.

Quickly observing this "automotive social ladder," automobile manufacturers began to differentiate each year's model and to carry on the most intensive advertising of any makers of durable goods. While there were real physical and psychological satisfactions to be gained from a swift, smooth ride in a heavy, powerful car, the lure of social approval was perhaps the strongest force behind the continuous demand for new and bigger machines. Since buyers seldom had saved the money to pay cash, the automobile became the most important item in a rapid growth of installment buying.

The Emancipated Woman. At the time that the Nineteenth Amendment of 1920 gave women the right to vote, upper-middle- and upper-class women in and around the largest urban centers were shaking off the decorum of Victorian customs. They were smoking in public, drinking illegally in speakeasies, talking freely about sex, and in general creating the appearance of demanding equal social rights and privileges. But the publicity accorded the suffrage movement and the "emancipated woman" was hghly misleading. Failing to establish a bloc of voters that could be used to influence legislation, as the Anti-Saloon League had done in the prohibition movement, women soon found that their influence on party politics was minimal.

By the mid-1920s the Women's Joint Congressional Committee was losing power, and the appropriation for the new Women's and Children's Bureau was cut. The mere right to vote in federal elections did not seem to have given substantial new power to the women's movement. In fact, political victory and a decade of general prosperity may have lessened the drive for other forms of equality.

The emancipated upper-class women were too few in number, particularly among the mature and influential, to have an effect beyond journalistic publicity. World War I produced no significant change in the definition or status of "women's work." Although the percentage of women engaged in professional life rose almost 20 percent from 1920 to 1930, women were still substantially excluded from professorships in major universities, from the medical profession, and from the most prestigious law schools.

The proportion of women in the labor force was about the same in 1930 as it was in 1910. In the latter year, 57 percent of working women were blacks or immigrants, which is equivalent to saying they were in low-paying occupations. The percentage of women in clerical jobs remained about the same during the prosperous twenties. Women continued to be paid less than men for doing the same job. There was, in effect, an openly expressed intention by most political, trade union, and business leaders to keep women in their traditional roles, which would avoid difficult adjustments and limit female competition with men. The very fact of lower pay, however, helped many women keep their jobs in the depression, although it lessened their militancy.

For the middle-class women who were homemakers, the trend to smaller houses and apartments and the availability of electrical housekeeping aids such as vacuum cleaners and refrigerators lessened the drudgery of housework. For the few married women who could secure good jobs, there was less social stigma attached to working than in earlier decades. But strong economic and cultural barriers still blocked the road to equality with men.

An Urban Black Society. Since the beginning of the century there had been a steady migration of rural blacks to the cities, but World War I and immigration restriction so increased the movement that the largest Northern cities—New York, Chicago, Philadelphia—became America's major centers of black population. Although frequently able to earn more money than they ever had before, the occupants of these black urban communities soon realized that they had not achieved the Promised Land. Usually they had to move into overcrowded, run-down tenements where they replaced the most recent, poorest immigrants. And though blacks were usually of old American stock, they found themselves looked down on by the foreign-born whites just as they had always been looked down on by the native whites. For a time in the 1920s the singers, dancers, and musicians of black Harlem, and some of its writers and artists as well, were "taken up" by white sophisticates and bohemians. But this fad did not last, nor did it touch the average black person.

There had never been much feeling of labor solidarity in the United States, and black workers in industrial centers were often resented, just as women were, as intruders who threatened white male employment and wage standards. Similar resentment led to attacks on blacks as the ghettos overflowed into white neighborhoods. In 1919 racial violence broke out in a score of cities all over the nation, and blacks learned that they could not rely on either police protection or justice in the courts.

In the early 1920s black activist organizations moved in two, directions. With the support of white middle-class liberals, the

Rural blacks who migrated to the cities in hope of better jobs and living conditions usually found themselves in overcrowded, run-down tenements. This Harlem street scene was photographed for the Federal Art Project in 1939.

National Urban League and the National Association for the Advancement of Colored People (NAACP) sought to establish for blacks the civil and political rights guaranteed by the Constitution. On this front, temporary legal victories were won in the *Sweet* case (1925), which upheld the right of blacks to defend themselves aginst violence, and in the *First Texas Primary* case (1927), which declared exclusion of black voters at the primary election stage in the democratic process to be unconstitutional. But the organization that represented the hopes and dreams of many working-class blacks was the Universal Negro Improvement Association, founded by the charismatic Jamaican, Marcus Garvey. He called on black people to take pride in their race and its history, to turn their backs on white America, and to return to their African homeland. The practical NAACP worked for integration, the romantic Garvey for black unity. The same twin stream has run throughout the Afro-Americans' long history.

Prohibition. Superimposed on this society that was undergoing or resisting confusing changes was America's greatest experiment in more government control over personal habits. Few nations have had a history of more consistent attachment to the consumption of alcohol than the United States. In the decades prior to 1918, however, there had been a trend toward more drinking of beer and wine and less recorded consumption of hard liquor, as well as a trend toward various types of state prohibition. It seems possible that banning the purchase of hard liquor or making it difficult to obtain might have produced a more temperate nation without much public resistance, but this experiment was never tried. Instead, the combination of war hysteria over a shortage of grain, anti-German sentiment against the brewers, and the financing of temperance organizations by important businessmen opposed to beer for workers led to an effort to ban all alcoholic drinks.

The Eighteenth Amendment left interpretation of what was an "intoxicating" beverage to Congress. The Volstead Act of 1919, vetoed by Wilson and repassed by the necessary two-thirds majority, set the limit of alcoholic content at .5 percent. While farmers would continue to make wine and other drinks at home, as they always had, city dwellers were now denied the opportunity of legally buying even the weakest form of beer. As a result, the big urban areas that had opposed the prohibition movement now refused to abide by the law. And as is usual under such circumstances, there was no difficulty in finding entrepreneurs ready to supply illicit demand.

It is an interesting paradox of the triumph of the prohibitionists in Congress that, having passed the amendment and the Volstead Act, they settled back and made no great effort to see that the law was enforced. The number of federal agents began at about 1500 and rose to only a little over 2800 at the peak. With a top salary of around $3000 it was not surprising that these men were often corruptible, but even had they been entirely diligent, they were too few even to check the imports of liquor. Furthermore, the local authorities in "wet" areas gave them little or no help. In 1923 New York state repealed its law for local enforcement, and politicians in other big metropolitan areas connived, almost openly, with those supplying the liquor.

As a result, an illegal traffic in whiskey, wine, and beer, worth hundreds of millions of dollars annually, fell into the hands of underworld leaders. The terms "racket" and "racketeer" came into use, and the newly powerful gangsters quickly branched out into other criminal activities, including bribery, extortion, arson, and murder.

"Where were the police?" one would logically ask. The answer often was: in the pay of racketeers. Al Capone, head of the liquor racket in Chicago, was as powerful politically as anyone in the municipal government of that metropolis, and he was the undisputed ruler of the suburban city of Cicero. In the suburbs of New York and other great cities the liquor interests often controlled county or municipal politics. The sheriffs and police chiefs received a portion of the weekly collections from speakeasies and worked against the occasional federal agent who sought to get evidence of violation of the law.

The national picture was confusing. In dry areas prohibition appeared to work at least as well as it had before the amendment. In wet urban areas, relatively less well represented in Congress, prohibition seemed to be undermining the moral values of both the young elite and honest government. Some manufacturers thought there was less drinking among their employees, while others were sure there was more. The Republican administration continued vaguely to sponsor "the noble experiment." The Wickersham Commission, appointed by Hoover, gave an unfavorable report in January 1931 but illogically concluded that prohibition should be continued.

In the end it was not moral or temperance issues but the depression and need for government revenue in the desperate year of 1932 that apparently tipped the balance in favor of legalizing the liquor business. There was no serious effort to substitute a new law permitting beer and wine for the unworkable Volstead Act. In 1933 the Eighteenth Amendment itself was quickly repealed by the Twenty-first, and the temperance problem was returned to the states.

The Period Between the Wars.   By 1940 the scientific and technological base for the highest level of consumption in the world's history had been achieved, but corresponding institutional adjustments had not taken place. The two decades following World War I were merely an interlude in a much longer period of change from the relatively stable commercial society of Western European nations in the eighteenth century to some new stage that may also have its periods of relative stability. In this transition the 1920s in the United States marked the world's highest peak of material well-being up to that time, and the 1930s the greatest depth of politico-economic failure to make use of existing facilities. It was hardly surprising that each decade produced unusual problems and unique reactions.

Depression inevitably upset most Americans more than any problems caused by prosperity. In 1932 they felt the deep sense of frustration that must come from seeing people starving while crops are being burned for lack of a market, but basic rebellion aginst capitalism or traditional American values was rare. To a remarkable degree people suffered deprivation in silence, comforting themselves with whatever was left. The majority warmly supported Franklin Roosevelt in his programs to provide greater material security, and the protest that feebly sprouted in the dark days from 1931 to 1934 was smothered under a reaffirmation of belief in traditional American values.

But there was a fundamental change. No longer—and probably never again—would it be taken for granted that individual citizens, or at least individual families, were solely responsible for their own welfare. A new tradition of public responsibility for the welfare of private citizens was in the process of creation.

WORLD WAR II

If on balance, dance, fiction, music, painting, and dramatic arts appeared to be more alive and creative in the United States from 1920 to 1940 than ever before, the ongoing artistic vitality of the period was checked by the practical demands of World War II. Wars seen in memory may inspire painters and novelists, but enforced activity while the fighting is in progress precludes contemplative creation. Ten million people of the ages of greatest artistic potential were taken into the armed services, and those at home were occupied with war production. Artists among these who may have had "inspirations" had to put the mood away until after the war. During the war, military and journalistic needs advanced photographic reproduction. But only a few photographers, such as Margaret Bourke-White, made the medium a form of art.

American participation in World War I had been too brief to affect conditions on the home front deeply. The nearly four years of World War II brought more lasting changes. Women did well in manual labor jobs for which they had formerly been thought unfit. Their widespread employment forecast the trend of the postwar decades. People adjusted to the withholding of unprecedentedly high income taxes from paychecks, a burden from which they would never be relieved. In general, the acceptance of government regulation of prices, purchases, and many activities marked first steps toward a more active role for the government.

The mood of most Americans during the Second World War was more liberal than in the First. This time, except for the removal of Japanese from the West Coast, including those who were American citizens, there were no important denials of civil liberties or propaganda of hatred against the people of Germany or Japan. In all, Americans immersed themselves in work, many families having all members above school age either in service or employed. Busy people no longer suffered worries over their ultimate welfare and lack of money. In addition, by mid-1942 there was scarcely anyone not confident that the United States would win the war. Encouraged by the needs of international reconstruction, this wartime optimism continued into the postwar years.

Chapter 20

Prosperity and Depression 1919–1939

THE SWING TOWARD CONSERVATISM

Nineteen-nineteen was a year of disillusionment. During the war progressives, once satisfied with social legislation and national regulation of trusts, had raised their hopes for such fundamental changes as federal control of railroads, shipping, prices, and employment. John Dewey, America's most famous philosopher, had predicted in 1918 that "no matter how many among the special agencies for public control decay with the disappearance of war stress, the movement will never go backward." But during 1919 the movement toward a publicly regulated economy not only receded but was lost altogether in a wave of reaction.

Like all sweeping changes in opinion, the swing to conservatism between early 1919 and 1920 had many causes. The unsatisfactory peace in Europe, publicized in the worst light by opponents of the League of Nations, cooled the popular enthusiasm that President Wilson had temporarily aroused. The result appears to have been an apathy about America's role in world affairs that carried over into domestic issues as well.

Along with this indifference to further reform there was undoubtedly a real fear on the part of middle-class Americans that revolution on the Russian model might spread. Socialism had ceased to be a utopian goal, safe to discuss at social club meetings, and had become a gray, alien world of commissars and secret police. As a result, the unprecedented series of strikes used by labor in 1919 to keep wages abreast of soaring prices was widely regarded as a dangerous indication of revolutionay sentiment, inspired by the subversive activities of a foreign power. In some cases management publicly condemned the strikers as Reds.

The Red Scare. Political demagogues were, of course, ready to ride to power by playing upon such fears. On January 1, 1920, agents of Attorney General A. Mitchell Palmer arrested nearly 3000 allegedly radical aliens and held them without hearings under the Sedition Act of 1918. Friends who subsequently inquired about those arrested were also jailed. Ailing President Wilson protested mildly against Palmer's activities, but the antiradical campaign gained momentum. Of the thousands of aliens rounded up by the Attorney General, 556 were deported, after trial, for radical activity.

Seventeen states passed "criminal syndicalist" laws providing for the arrest of agitators proposing other forms of government. The New York state legislature carried out a lengthy investigation of revolutionary radicalism and refused to seat Socialist representatives from New York City. Meanwhile, Congress refused to admit Victor Berger from Wisconsin until that very moderate Socialist had again been elected by his Milwaukee constituents.

At the height of this "Red scare," the arrest and conviction of two alien anarchists, Nicola Sacco and Bartolomeo Vanzetti, for the murder of a factory paymaster and guard during a robbery in South Braintree, Massachusetts, turned out to be the *cause célèbre* of the 1920s. Because of the alleged bias of the judge and the prejudicial tactics of the prosecuting attorney at the trial, many liberals protested that the men had been convicted for their radicalism rather than for the stated crime. In the six years following their conviction in 1921, protest meetings took place all over the world, and people of international prominence like Albert Einstein and novelist Anatole France gave their support to petitions urging clemency or a retrial. In Massachusetts, however, public opinion remained hostile. A special commission headed by the president of Harvard found that the trial had been fair and that the defendants were guilty. On August 23, 1927, Sacco and Vanzetti were electrocuted in an atmosphere of martyrdom.

The most alarming aspect of the wave of anti-Red hysteria in the 1920s was not the injustices visited upon a few hundred leftists and aliens but the general suppression of free thought that accompanied the unrelenting efforts of the Attorney General and certain "patriotic" societies. Teachers became afraid to impart normal, necessary criticisms of American leaders and American society.

Business employees were afraid to be associated with people or organizations branded by the superpatriots as subversive. Liberal journals were called revolutionary, and people were afraid to be seen reading them. Compared to the Red scare of the 1950s, that of the early twenties was less serious in its impact on government but probably more repressive in its effect on ordinary citizens.

The Klan.   In the back country, especially in the South and a few parts of the Middle West, the anti-foreign and anti-Red hysteria gave a sinister impetus to the Ku Klux Klan, which was revived in 1915 "to unite white male persons, native-born Gentile citizens, who owe no allegiance of any nature to any foreign government, nation, institution, sect, ruler, person or people." The members were united against blacks, Catholics (who were held to owe allegiance to a foreign ruler), Jews, and foreigners. The Klan had shown little tendency to grow until the postwar anti-Red campaign got under way, but in 1920, under Edward Y. Clarke, a professional organizer and fund raiser, it quickly became a powerful force both socially and politically. By 1924 it had several million members. Since the initiation fee was $10, large resources were at the disposal of Klan leaders, who used them to influence—in some cases to control—state politics.

At the level of the local den, however, the Klan was largely an organization for leisure-time enjoyment, community economic pressure, and irresponsible use of force. A congressional investigation revealed that blacks and foreigners were scared into selling property to Klan members at low prices and into avoiding business competition with them. Citizens defending blacks, foreigners, or Catholics might also incur the vengeance of the Klan. The hooded parades, secret meetings, fiery crosses, beatings, and lynchings were signs of the frustration in declining rural areas.

Against the ominous rise of lower-middle-class reaction, the stuff of which fascism was to be made in Germany, must be placed the continuation of liberal and even radical farmer movements in the Northwest. Led by the old Non-Partisan League, a Farmer-Labor party ran second to the victorious Republicans in the election of 1920 in Minnesota, South Dakota, and Washington. Thus, the decentralized character of American politics sustained minority movements while making it difficult for them to win national power.

Immigration Quotas. A major change in American political policy in the early 1920s was the regulation of immigration on a quota basis. While Chinese had been excluded by law in 1882, and Japanese by diplomatic agreements, other Asian and African people had not attempted to immigrate in any large numbers. Meanwhile the door had been held open for most Europeans although organized labor and "old stock" Americans had long tried to restrict the vast flood of newcomers, which in peaceful and prosperous years comprised more than a million annually. Finally, a combination of factors—resumption of heavy immigration from eastern Europe, unemployment at home, and the Red scare—led Congress to establish quotas based on the number of foreign–born residents in the United States in 1910. Opposed vigorously in Congress only by Catholics, the bill met a veto by Wilson. Passed again in the special session of 1921, it was signed by Harding. During the first year of operation the restrictions reduced yearly immigration from around 1 million to 300,000.

To organized labor, nativists, and those who feared communism, the number of "undesirable" or "unassimilable" immigrants from eastern Europe still seemed too large. The National Origins Act of 1924 set up a temporary quota of 2 percent of the foreign-born residents in 1890 (a time when immigrants were still largely of British, German, or Scandinavian origin) and established a commission to work out quotas by a formula based on numbers of foreign-born over the whole range of the United States on the basis of census data. The bill excluded Orientals.

Japan, which had been voluntarily restricting emigration to the United States, regarded this as an affront to its national dignity, but the Japanese protest was brushed aside by Congress. Enacted into law in 1929, the final report of the Commission on National Origins reduced southern and eastern European quotas to negligible size and held the total of restricted immigrants to about 150,000 annually. Citizens of countries in the Western Hemisphere were exempted from restriction. During periods of high employment, like the 1920s, the diminished pool of immigrant labor led to the hiring of more blacks and poor whites in the growing industrial centers.

Triumph of the Conservatives. In the middle of the confusing year 1920 the two national conventions met to nominate candidates for the presidency. The leading Republican contenders—Governor Frank O. Lowden of Illinois and General Leonard Wood—fought each other to a deadlock. The compromise candidate supported by a group of business representatives and conservative congressional leaders was Senator Warren G. Harding of Ohio, a man virtually unknown to the American public but one who had the gracious, commanding look of a President. For Vice-President the convention nominated Calvin Coolidge, the Massachusetts governor famous for his stand against organized labor in the Boston police strike of 1919.

The Democrats had even greater difficulty in choosing a candidate. During thirty-seven indecisive ballots, Attorney General Palmer, the anti-Red champion, fought William G. McAdoo, the liberal ex-Secretary of the Treasury and son-in-law of Woodrow Wilson. Then the convention compromised on a progressive who had been twice elected governor of Ohio, James M. Cox. While Cox was as little known to the general public as Harding, the Democratic ticket was strengthened by the vice-presidential nomination of Assistant Secretary of the Navy Franklin D. Roosevelt.

Partly in deference to President Wilson, Cox and Roosevelt made entry into the League of Nations a major issue of the campaign. The Republicans avoided commitment on the League question and instead advocated higher tariffs and tax reduction. Reading the popular temper correctly, they were extremely confident. During the campaign Harding stayed on his front porch in Marion, Ohio. His speeches, according to McAdoo, were "an army of pompous phrases moving across the landscape in search of an idea." In spite of—or perhaps because of—the assurance of victory, the Republicans were aided by a campaign fund of $8 million.

The Republican landslide was the greatest since the second election of James Monroe. Harding carried every state outside the "solid South," and there he carried Tennessee. He received 61 percent of the popular vote, as much as Franklin D. Roosevelt was to poll in his greatest victory. In Congress the Republican majority was 167 in the House and 22 in the Senate. Although this was the first election following women's suffrage, no significant changes were apparent as a result of women's vote.

The Harding Administration Scandals. Although Harding was probably not far below the average intelligence of the less prominent Presidents of the United States, he was lacking in ideas, vigor, and moral conviction. Easygoing and affable, he delegated too much responsibility. Harding appointed old friends to many important posts, though he offset these weak appointments by naming Charles E. Hughes Secretary of State; Andrew Mellon, Secretary of the Treasury; Henry A. Wallace,

Bribe-taking and misuse of public funds occurred on a huge scale during Harding's administration. The cartoon shows Attorney General Daugherty vainly struggling to keep the skeletons of corruption hidden in the closet.

Secretary of Agriculture; and Herbert Hoover, Secretary of Commerce.

Harding's friends, with whom he often played poker late into the night, soon began taking bribes and misusing funds on a scale that could not be concealed. Late in 1922 Harding learned that Charles R. Forbes had stolen millions from the Veterans' Bureau. By the summer of 1923 there was a rumor that the House, now controlled by Democrats and Progressives, might try to impeach the President. But on August 2, in the midst of the increasing revelations of corruption, Harding died of an apoplectic stroke.

Ultimately investigations and trials revealed the details of other scandals. Attorney General Harry M. Daugherty had profited from the enforcement of prohibition and the handling of alien property. Secretary of the Interior Albert B. Fall had received many thousands of dollars from oil men Harry F. Sinclair and E. L. Doheny for leasing them valuable government oil reserves in Teapot Dome, Wyoming, and in Elk Hills, California. Forbes had cost the taxpayers some $250 million more than necessary for hospitals and other veterans' benefits. And many lesser men had profited from the President's lack of judgment and rigor.

With Vice-President Calvin Coolidge now succeeding to the presidency, the Republican party had a man superbly qualified to make amends for the laxity of the Harding administration. Coolidge, a slight, dry-looking, diffident Vermonter who after graduation from Amherst had won success in Massachusetts law and politics, seemed to personify the traditional virtues of thrift and frugality. He would not be betrayed by his intimate friends, because he had none. At a time when business and most of the middle class seemed satisfied with the status quo, Coolidge could be relied upon not to rock the boat.

Republican National Policy. Led for eight years either by Harding, who had been installed by the right wing of the party, or by Coolidge, whom Hoover called a "real conservative," the Republican administration tried to lessen or remove controls over business activity. In this policy the President was often at odds with Democratic-progressive coalitions in the House and the Senate, but the presidential powers of appointment and veto proved effective weapons in cutting down federal activities.

The Republican Presidents appointed conservative, business-minded members to federal regulatory commissions. This led to such a relaxation in vigilance that, in the words of a famous authority, the Federal Trade Commission "tried to commit *hara-kiri*"—to cease functioning as a regulatory agency. The antitrust division of the Justice Department seldom prosecuted mergers. The Federal Power Commission, established in 1920 to regulate interstate electric power, did little to justify its existence. And the efforts of the Interstate Commerce Commission to bring about railroad consolidation and recapture excess earnings were without significant effect.

Ocean shipping presented special problems. At the end of the war the government owned some 2 million deadweight tons of hastily constructed freighters which were slow and inefficient in comparison with new turbine or diesel electric vessels coming from British and Continental yards. In addition, United States wages and manning requirements made it impossible for American ship owners to compete on an equal basis with foreign operators. To keep some of the ships at sea the Shipping Board for a decade pursued a policy of selling the freighters for $5 to $10 a ton and granting mail subsidies for operation on strategically important routes.

One of the first conflicts between the conservative President and the less conservative Congress was over the soldiers' bonus bill. This proposed legislation provided a twenty-year endowment policy totaling $1 for each day a veteran had served in the United States and $1.25 for each day overseas. President Harding in 1921 and President Coolidge in 1924 vetoed the bill. The Harding veto was sustained, but a more generous Congress overrode that of Coolidge.

Freed from fear of federal regulation, businessmen also were gradually relieved of the higher taxes of the war period. Andrew Mellon, formerly head of the Aluminum Company of America and one of the richest men in the world, believed sincerely that high income taxes retarded economic growth. As Secretary of the Treasury he immediately sponsored a tax bill that repealed the excess profits tax and sharply reduced the surtaxes on personal income. After amendments by the Republican farm bloc and by Democrats in the Senate, the Revenue Act of 1921 repealed the excess profits tax but cut the maximum surtax on personal income only from 65 to 50 percent. Nevertheless, since federal revenues steadily exceeded expenses, there was increasing pressure for tax reduction. By 1929 four subsequent revenue acts had reduced the maximum surtax to 20 percent and the effective initial rate to less than half of 1 percent. The tax on corporate income was slightly reduced, to 11 percent.

These tax reductions, which retarded repayment of the national debt and left it at $16 billion at the beginning of the Great Depression, have been vigorously criticized. Yet Republican administrations faced a real economic dilemma. To have repaid the debt more rapidly would have released to the money markets as much cash as came from the untaxed savings of high incomes, if not more. Only if the government could have found a way to use the money so as to increase lower incomes or to pay it to some of the 2 million unemployed could the surplus have been kept from feeding the inflation in stocks and mortgage bonds. Such a fiscal policy would have been directly contrary to the firmly held beliefs of the conservative majority and, as an explicit policy, probably beyond the imagination of most of the more liberal minority.

One proposed use for federal funds which would not have involved the government in new types of business or competed with private industry was the support of farm incomes. Farmers had been led by the demands of World War I to expand wheat acreage, which in view of long-run trends was already excessive in 1914. After the collapse of the reconstruction boom in 1920, farm prices fell more than those of things the farmer had to buy, and both foreign and domestic markets for such staples as wheat and cotton declined. Farmers were not participating in the general prosperity.

A plan put forward by two farm machinery manufacturers in 1922 did not involve federal subsidy but merely required a federal marketing agency that could maintain a domestic price in excess of the world price. Written into the McNary-Haugen Bill and endorsed by practically all farmer organizations, the proposal was resisted by conservative Republicans as a dangerous extension of federal power. The bill was passed in 1926 and again in 1927 but killed both times by a Coolidge veto.

Although by the late 1930s the Farm Bureau Federation, the chief agricultural pressure group, was to seem conservative, in the 1920s it formed a rallying point for liberals. In spite of the conservative presidential leadership, progressives of both parties maintained their strength in Congress. The greatest obstacle to liberal victories during the decade was probably not the relatively small group of conservatives with substantial incomes but the general political apathy bred by prosperity from 1923 to 1929. Presidential elections drew only a little more than half the voters to the polls. Coolidge was sustained in the 1924 presidential election by a mere 28 percent of the possible electorate.

EXPANSION OF GOVERNMENT

Federal, State, and Local Change. Even within the administration, men like Charles E. Hughes and Herbert Hoover did not share the Coolidge standpat type of conservatism. Hoover, as Secretary of Commerce, tried to bring more efficiency into business operations. To avoid destructive competition he urged small companies to have trade associations administer their mutual concerns, and he invited them to post their prices with the Commerce Department and to refrain from secret rebates. To lower production costs he put his influence behind the movement for standard sizes. The number of shapes of bottles and the various sizes of bricks, for example, were both cut 90 percent. After unsuccessfully preaching self-regulation to the young air transport and radio industries, his department established regulatory agencies in 1926 and 1927 respectively. He and Andrew Mellon also took leading parts in introducing federal budgeting of income and expenses. In these directions Hoover was a planner, but as he saw it, he was using the power of government primarily to suggest better voluntary planning to private industry.

State and local authorities, still the most important forms of government, were led to expand their operations greatly. Increasing high-school education, in particular, demanded new buildings and bigger school budgets. Skyscrapers concentrated so many workers in the centers of the largest cities that new public transportation was required. On the other hand, automobiles moved so many families to the open areas of the cities or suburbs that new streets and sewers were continually needed. New York and some other states increased the scope and size of their expenditures for welfare. New laws or municipal ordinances regulating business practices, sanitation, and housing required new bureaus and squads of inspectors. From all these needs of a growing industrial society the expenses of government soared. Between 1922 and 1927 the annual cost of state and local government rose nearly 40 percent, and the rise had undoubtedly passed 50 percent by 1929. The debts of these governments increased even faster, up nearly 50 percent from 1922 to 1927 and perhaps by two thirds, had figures been collected, by 1929.

It is also worth remembering that in 1929 these governments cost about two and a half times as much to run as the federal government and had about twice as many civilian employees, exclusive of school teachers. Thus what appears on the federal level to have been a period of low government expenditure and reduction of debt was *in toto* one of rapid increase in expenditure and dangerous accumulation of local indebtedness.

Security in the Pacific. While there was a vigorous movement for the League of Nations and world peace, most of the minority of Americans who thought about foreign relations probably wanted to avoid being involved in either European or Far Eastern affairs. The war against Germany was ended by a resolution of Congress on July 2, 1921, and separate treaties were negotiated with the new governments of Germany, Austria, and Hungary, but Far Eastern problems were not settled.

Meanwhile the Navy Department had plans for building the world's largest battle fleet. In spite of congressional refusal to pass the big-navy bills, England and Japan were deeply worried over the possibility of having to compete with the United States in naval construction. Therefore, they readily accepted Secretary of State Hughes' invitation to meet in Washington in 1921 to discuss naval disarmament. Since a naval agreement would have to be linked with treaties establishing and guaranteeing Far Eastern arrangements, France, Italy, Belgium, the Netherlands, and Portugal, nations with Asiatic territories, were invited to the conference together with China.

Early in 1922 Secretary Hughes led the way to a naval agreement whereby the United States, England, and Japan scrapped hundreds of thousands of tons of battleships, afloat or in construction, and agreed to a 5–5–3 ratio for capital ships, with Britain and the United States at equal strength and Japan held to 60 percent of that tonnage. To secure Japan's interests in the western Pacific each party agreed not to fortify new bases or enlarge old ones. World War II was to demonstrate that this arrangement, as planned, gave Japan an initial supremacy in its nearby waters.

After some argument, France and Italy joined in the treaty, each limiting the tonnage of its capital ships to 35 percent of the Anglo-American maximum. A new Four-Power Pact (United States, British Empire, France, Japan) replaced the Anglo-Japanese Alliance and pledged the powers to respect each other's possessions and rights in the Pacific. A Nine-Power Pact, also concluded during the Washington Conference, affirmed the sovereignty, independence, and administrative and territorial integrity of China. The American policy of an "open door" for Chinese trade was reaffirmed. The Washington treaties established a system of security for Asia such as the Treaty of Versailles was presumed to have provided for Europe.

High Tariffs. High tariff continued to be a major Republican policy. Ironically, the protectionist group in Congress in the early 1920s was led by Midwestern farmers who feared Canadian, Irish, and Argentine competition. Their first bill for increased agricultural duties was vetoed by Wilson on the grounds that American farmers also needed foreign markets.

The Harding administration favored higher duties, but the increases in the Fordney-McCumber Tariff of 1922 were generally moderate. Although agricultural products gained protection, the principle of a tariff that would equalize prices of domestic and foreign products was generally maintained. The farm bloc managed to get manufactures like shoes and wagons on the free list, but some industries received very high protection. The Tariff Commission still had the right to recommend changes, and the President had the power to alter the rates by 50 percent.

Neither Harding nor Coolidge made important use of this power.

War Debts. The Treaty of Versailles had a major weakness: an unrealistic structure of reparations and war debts. In 1921 Germany was forced to accept a reparations commission bill for $33 billion, but no such sum could be transferred in a few decades from one European country to the others without severely disrupting the economies involved. Similarly the United States tried to collect war debts of $4.6 billion from England, $4 billion from France, and $2 billion from Italy. The European states advised a cancellation of all international payments that would endanger normal economic growth, but Presidents from Wilson to Roosevelt insisted on the principle of collection.

Since such sums could be paid only in goods and since United States tariffs limited imports, payments were regularly more than balanced by new American lending and investment abroad. Throughout the decade bankers sold annually about $1 billion worth of foreign government, municipal, and corporate bonds to American investors. This was a profitable system for the bankers, and by giving foreigners dollars to spend, it allowed United States manufacturers to maintain large exports. It meant, however, that world financial stability depended on continued prosperity and an easy money market in the United States.

From the start, Germany was unable to pay the reparations assessed by the commission. In 1924 the so-called Dawes Plan, devised by Owen D. Young and Charles G. Dawes of the United States, cut reparations to what seemed like a manageable level, and in 1929 the Young Plan further reduced payments. By now the $33 billion bill had shrunk to about $2 billion. During the 1920s the Allies paid the United States about $2.6 billion in war debts, and the Americans loaned Germany some $2.5 billion,

80 percent of which was paid to the Allies.

Therefore, in fact, there was nearly a mutual balancing. The Allies paid the United States, which loaned to Germany, which paid reparations to Allies, and the cycle continued. But the American investors and banks that had advanced the money were left with foreign bonds that soon defaulted on their interest payments.

Meanwhile, the United States pursued a rather uncertain course of international cooperation. Secretary of State Hughes started the practice of sending "unofficial observers" to League of Nations sessions and to meetings of the principal League committees, but isolationists in the Senate prevented the United States from joining the World Court. This, however, did not prevent Americans, as individuals, from serving as justices. In 1928 Secretary of State Frank B. Kellogg took the lead in negotiating a general agreement to outlaw war as an instrument of national policy. The Pact of Paris, or Kellogg-Briand Pact, was signed ultimately by all the great powers, but Kellogg regarded the pledge as more valuable for appeasing peace sentiment at home than for influencing foreign nations. Providing no means of applying collective sanctions against an aggressor, the pact was an idealistic but empty gesture.

Paradoxically, the idealistic foreign policy of Woodrow Wilson had left the United States deeply involved in the affairs of Caribbean countries. United States troops were in Haiti, Nicaragua, and the Dominican Republic, and diplomatic relations with Mexico had been suspended. On the South American mainland, hostility toward these United States occupations interfered with both trade and investment.

Republican Leadership Reaffirmed. In the depression year of 1922 discontented agrarian and labor elements met in a Conference for Progressive Political Action. Continuing its meetings into 1924, the conference agreed to support the presidential nomination of Senator Robert M. La Follette at the Republican convention and, if defeated there, to organize a third party with La Follette as its candidate.

Obviously the progressive minority had no chance of winning the Republican nomination, but it might have swung over to the Democrats if that party had supported an advanced liberal ticket. The Democratic party, however, was disastrously split over such issues as prohibition, the Ku Klux Klan, Catholicism, and immigration restriction. Hampered additionally by a rule requiring a two-thirds majority for nomination, its convention took 103 ballots to select a relatively unknown New York corporation lawyer, John W. Davis, who failed to inspire enthusiasm in any faction.

When the Republican convention met and nominated Coolidge on the first ballot, the Progressives held their own convention and put forward La Follette. Supported by the American Federation of Labor, many Western farm organizations, and the Socialist party, La Follette ran on a platform advocating the type of action that Europeans called social-democratic. Nationalization was to apply only to railroads and hydroelectric power. Injunctions in labor disputes were to be effectively forbidden. And Congress was to be given power to overrule the Supreme Court.

Coolidge swept the election with 15,718,000 popular votes to 8,385,000 for Davis and 4,831,000 for La Follette. Davis won only the solid South, and La Follette carried only Wisconsin. The Progressive party had failed to develop the strength necessary for survival.

Few American Presidents have enjoyed four such prosperous, peaceful, and generally pleasant years as those from 1924 to 1928. Coolidge could easily have been renominated and reelected had he chosen to run for a second elected term in 1928. But after keeping the bosses in doubt long enough to preserve his influence in the convention, Coolidge gave his support to Herbert Hoover. Quickly nominated, Hoover ran on a platform of continuing the Harding-Coolidge policies. With these, he said, "we shall soon, with the help of God, be in sight of the day when poverty shall be banished from this nation."

The Democratic managers probably had little hope of defeating a strong Republican, but they thought that an unusual candidate might bring new voters to the polls. Such reasoning may explain the swing to Governor Alfred E. Smith of New York, a Catholic of Irish immigrant parentage, who emphasized his origins by wearing a brown derby. The Democratic platform scarcely differed from the Republican, and on economic questions Smith differed little from Hoover. Smith made John J. Raskob, a fellow Catholic and chairman of the Finance Committee of General Motors, manager of the Democratic campaign. Raskob gave the utmost assurance to business that there would be no upsetting changes.

Aside from the immense support given the Republicans by the boom prosperity, the issues came to be Catholicism and prohibition. Smith could do nothing about the former except give assurances of his independence from Rome and his religious tolerance, and these apparently had little effect in the strongly Protestant back country. In the belief that labor and many businessmen were now in favor of repeal of the Eighteenth Amendment, Smith departed from the plank in the party platform that had been inserted to win the support of the dry South and campaigned strongly against prohibition.

While probably no candidate could have defeated Hoover in the year 1928, Smith lost or miscalculated on all fronts save one. His "me-tooism" in support of business probably changed few votes. His Catholicism and antiprohibition sentiments lost seven Southern states and, at the most, gained only two Northern ones. But he did have an appeal for the urban masses. This urban swing, scarcely noticeable in the Hoover landslide, was a portent of the basic change in party strength that was to come from the increase in urban Democrats in the decades ahead.

High Hopes for a Prosperous Nation.   In his inaugural address Hoover said, "I have no fears for the future of our country, it is bright with hope." His *Memoirs* also show the high hopes with which he started his administration: "Mr. Coolidge was reluctant to undertake much that was either new or cost money, and by 1929 many things were already fourteen years overdue." Hoover had a number of plans for bringing more efficiency into government activity, but his first major act, calling a special congressional session to redeem Republican promises to farmers, unfortunately misfired. The President sponsored the Smoot-Hawley Tariff bill to raise the rates on agricultural products, but when the bill finally passed the Senate in June 1930, it carried higher rates on numerous manufactured products and raised the general level of rates on dutiable articles about 25 percent. Although this was not what the President had intended, he signed the bill to give assurance to business. Meanwhile, other nations had been raising their tariffs, some in retaliation for the United States' action, and the outlook for world trade and repayment of international obligations steadily grew darker.

In place of the McNary-Haugen scheme, passed twice by Congress but vetoed both times by Coolidge, the administration planned to help the farmer by the Agricultural Marketing Act of 1929. This originally provided for loans to aid cooperative selling, but progressives added a provision for the use of federal money to stabilize the market price of grain. For these purposes a Federal Farm Board was given a revolving fund of $500 million, the largest single appropriation up to that time for nonmilitary purposes. The plan for buying grain to raise domestic prices and reselling when the market could absorb the surplus might have worked for a time had there been rapid worldwide recovery in 1930. But since the trend toward oversupply in wheat already seemed clear, this cure through manipulating the market was at best a makeshift expedient.

After the onset of the depression in 1929, most of President Hoover's plans for efficiency and mild reform were abandoned in the effort to bring back prosperity. "Instead of being able to devote my four years wholly to these purposes," he lamented, "I was overtaken by the economic hurricane. . . . Then the first need was economic recovery and employment." Fearing that reform would upset business and deepen the depression, the President became as conservative as his predecessors.

POSTWAR ECONOMIC CHANGE

The Decline of Craft Unionism. World War I and the postwar boom brought union membership to a peak of 5 million workers in 1920, about 12 percent of the total labor force. While this was a record for the United States, the level of organization was low in comparison with western Europe. A major reason was that American labor organizations were limited largely to the skilled crafts and older types of industrial activity. The new mass production industries of the twentieth century, such as automobiles, chemicals, and electrical equipment, had successfully resisted efforts at organization.

The union situation of 1920 was essentially unstable. Many union members in war industries and postwar construction soon had to seek other jobs. Employer organizations, held back since 1917 by government policy and competition for workers, were now ready to marshal business-minded people against organized labor. During the Red scare it was easy to convince the middle class that unions had radical intentions.

The American Plan, representing small and medium-sized business, was sponsored by the National Association of Manufacturers and vigorously pursued by various trade and employer organizations. It called for the open shop—a shop in which workers could be hired without joining a union. Some of the organizations associated with the movement insisted that their members should not enter into any union contracts. Advertisements were placed in newspapers, denouncing the closed shop (one restricted to union members) as un-American. Labor spies were hired in larger numbers than before to detect union organizers.

One important "welfare" device for preventing national unions from organizing workers was the employee representation plan or company union. The government demand that contractors in World War I enter into collective bargaining with their employees led 125 of the largest companies to organize their own unions with some 400,000 members. Since these unions and their officers were controlled and supported financially by the companies, they were not generally regarded as true representatives of labor. Yet in the twenties they constituted the one growing area of labor organization. By 1928 it was estimated that company union membership had grown to 1.5 million, half that of the AFL.

In addition to the American Plan and competing company unions, independent unions may also have been weakened by reforms in employee relations. In some big companies, the personnel departments that had been established during the war sought to decrease turnover and increase productivity by improving working conditions and proposing various measures to bolster workers' morale. But it may still be argued that the independent unions declined because of the depression of 1920 to 1922 and because business was growing away from the old skilled crafts. The immediate drop in union membership during those two years of depression was 1.4 million. Another 200,000 members were lost during the prosperous years from 1923 to 1929. By 1930 less than 7 percent of the labor force was organized in independent unions.

Only in coal and textiles were white labor leaders engaged in vigorous campaigns during the mid-twenties. Both industries had the same basic problems: Southern areas were not unionized, and Communists were undermining the existing union leadership. Although John L. Lewis was able to preserve the United Mine Workers' bargaining position in the older areas, he had to agree to wage cuts during the years of high national prosperity. Neither the United Textile Workers nor its Communist-led rival, the National Textile Workers' Union, was able successfully to invade the South and unionize the new mills. With lower wages in that region the industry continued to drift away from New England and the Middle Atlantic states.

As militancy declined in the ranks of labor, there was a trend toward cooperation with employers. Where an employer had a small business and was often poorly informed, as in the garment industry, unions could help to improve shop practices and overall efficiency. Even some of the large railroads found that union-management cooperation increased productivity in their shops. But looking at the labor scene as a whole, the areas of advancing cooperation were small.

Another trend in this period was toward surrender of union leadership to racketeers. In unions where the complacency of the mid-twenties made the members careless about attending meetings, dishonest local officials, supported by so-called gorillas, built up machines that the rank and file dared not oppose. Often these labor racketeers dealt secretly with employers, taking payments from them to prevent the union members from demanding wage increases. The twen-

ties were not a decade of pleasant prosperity for organized labor.

Industrial Distress.   That symbol of modern mass production, the automated assembly line, was increasingly criticized by reformers in the twenties. The speed of the line was set by management, and with no independent unions to protect them, workers who could not maintain the pace were summarily fired. In addition, such plants generally had many workers under a single supervisor or foreman, who consequently had little contact with the workers as individuals. While such big-plant assembly-line jobs involved only a small fraction of the labor force, to many artists and intellectuals they dramatized the plight of the individual in an impersonal, mechanized society.

Blacks who had come to industrial centers during the war and the postwar boom faced problems of a special type. Many companies would not hire them for anything but menial service jobs, and AFL unions would not accept them in the skilled crafts. This discrimination made many blacks quite ready to act as strike breakers against organized white labor. A. Philip Randolph, one of the few influential black labor leaders, organized a union of Pullman Company maids and porters in 1925, but in spite of the all–black personnel on the cars, the Brotherhood of Sleeping Car Porters was unable at that time to displace a company union and force collective bargaining. Other efforts by Randolph to create a national organization of black unions were even less successful.

Agricultural Depression.   The poorer and the less efficient farmers also failed to share in the prosperity of the 1920s. Those who had been encouraged by the government to borrow money in order to bring more land under cultivation to meet the wartime demand now found themselves with heavy debts and a

The automated assembly line was the key to mass production but many people thought it dehumanized the worker. This plant is the Ford Motor Company in 1929.

declining market. The hardest hit were wheat farmers in the Western prairie and plains states and cotton growers in the South. Mortgage foreclosures forced owners to become tenants, and losses on farm loans led to the closing of thousands of small banks in country towns. In the South black sharecroppers, particularly, were forced off the land and had to seek jobs in the growing cities.

During the decade advances in soil biology and chemistry made diversification of crops much safer than formerly. Hybrid seeds were developed which could increase the yield and resistance to unfavorable weather of both corn and wheat. And all-purpose tractors were reduced in cost. But since few farmers had extra capital and the overly competitive situation failed to interest other investors, the

new knowledge and technology were little used until World War II again brought high prices, rural prosperity, and a shortage of labor.

A Slower Rate of Growth. In the long run, economic growth depends upon the making of more and more capital goods such as buildings, factories, roads, and machines. For the decade 1919 to 1928 net capital formation (that is, the creation of new capital goods) in relation to national income was 14 percent less than in the previous decade and nearly 18 percent less than two decades earlier. During the years 1924 to 1929 the annual investment in new capital goods was actually falling. On the other hand, lower taxes were increasing the net income of the wealthiest classes and their savings were rising. These savings of funds for investment were by 1924 beginning to run ahead of the needs of industry and business for capital for physical expansion. In other words, the upper-income groups had more savings each year than there were productive new securities to be bought. As a result, investors were competing for the available securities, and the price of securities went up. A large part of the nation's savings was being used for speculation, while rising interest rates in 1929 were attracting unneeded billions in bank loans from Europe.

Why should the rate of creation of capital goods slow down when there was plenty of saved money to pay for them? Two explanations can be offered. One is that since there was little change in real wages or salaries from 1924 to 1929, consumer demand did not rise rapidly enough to encourage industrial expansion. The other explanation is more speculative. Changes in technology occur in incalculable ways. Some that promise substantial profits require large new investments, as in the case of railroads, while others do not, as in the case of the phonograph. A series of technological innovations requiring large investment absorb savings and labor and produce an expanding economy. But in the 1920s few major capital-absorbing innovations in technology occurred. While some older developments such as electrification, roads for automobiles, and improvements in steel production were still going forward, after 1927 there was a slowing down of the combined rate of growth.

Technological Advance. Although the new technological developments of the 1920s did not actually increase the rate of capital investment, new devices were sought more vigorously than ever before. By 1929 about a thousand large firms were supporting some type of research. Better control of industrial products through careful cost accounting, spot testing, and laboratory analysis (collec-

tively referred to as "quality control") also led to higher efficiency and productivity.

Radio broadcasting and air travel first reached the general public in this decade, and automobiles and electricity came into general use. Until 1919 the federal government forbade private use of radio. Broadcasts by Westinghouse's station KDKA of the results of the presidential election of 1920 demonstrated the great public possibilities of the new medium of communication, and within the next few years the industry assumed the general pattern that was to remain for decades: Competing national networks would subsist on substantial revenue from large advertisers, and high-priced performers would offer variety programs. By 1930 12 million American families, about 40 percent of the total, could tune in stars like Rudy Vallee, Eddie Cantor, and sports announcer Graham McNamee on their radio sets.

The airplaine, invented before World War I, had never attracted much interest in America. During the war the government made an effort to catch up with European development but produced few planes before the Armistice led to cancellation of contracts. The Post Office started an experimental airmail route between New York and Washington in 1918 and after six years extended service to Chicago and San Francisco. Meanwhile, commercial plane production was negligible, and flying was limited to selling rides at airfields and local fairs. In 1925 the government first made an effort to build commercial transport by allowing the Post Office to grant airmail contracts to private firms. The following year Congress gave general regulatory authority to the Commerce Department.

The regular use of air service in Europe and a series of spectacular overseas flights culminating in Charles A. Lindbergh's solo crossing of the Atlantic in 1927 gave some Americans confidence enough to travel by plane. Between 1928 and 1930 passengers increased from 1400 to 32,000, and revenue miles flown multiplied about thirty times to a total of 4.3 million. Although the young industry continued to grow during the depression, the 100 million passenger miles flown in 1940 were almost negligible compared to the 24 billion passenger miles by rail and the incalculable travel by private car.

In the automotive industry, even in the prosperous years of the 1920s, the smaller assemblers of cars had been dropping out. The early years of the depression reduced the number of competitors to fewer than a dozen, all producing similar cars within four or five price ranges. Ford finally had to give up his famous Model T in 1927 and bring out the Model A, a car similar to those of his chief competitors. This episode temporarily convinced American manufacturers that in new cars the public wanted size and luxury rather than cheapness. No one was more easily convinced than Walter P. Chrysler, who had a passion for fine cars. (see "Walter P. Chrysler: Lover of Fine Cars.")

Both homes with electricity and total consumption of electrical energy doubled from 1920 to 1930. In urban and suburban areas five sixths of all residences came to have electricity, but farm electrification was only beginning. In 1920 1.4 percent of farms had electricity and by 1930 only 10 percent.

THE NEW ERA IN BUSINESS

Managerial Enterprise. As usual in times of business prosperity, the number of firms grew faster than the population as a whole. In 1920 there were probably fewer than 2.5 million firms, in 1929 over 3 million. About two thirds of all firms were in trade and service, and very few of these had more than two or three employees. The overall growth figures, however, conceal a great deal of routine change. Every year of the twenties thirty to fifty thousand new firms started, and every year a slightly smaller number left the business scene. While adequately capitalized small companies that were started by people who knew the business they were entering had good chances of success, a large percentage of entrepreneurs lacked both qualifications. At the top, a few medium-sized or large firms disappeared each year through mergers, but these equaled only 1 or 2 percent of the new firms starting up.

The American business structure appeared to have reached a plateau of stability. Big companies continued to dominate highly capitalized manufacturing industries, railroads, and utilities. But the rise of true monopoly had been checked by antitrust laws. In industries dominated by a few companies competition in price was avoided, but competition in quality and marketing was generally vigorous.

By the 1920s the stock of most very large companies was widely held. Neither the officers nor the directors of the company owned any considerable percentage of the shares. The chief officers were chosen from among men who had made successful careers in management and were professional executives rather than either relatives of an owner or large personal investors. The connection of such men with profit was indirect. Profit for the company was a mark of success, a guarantee of security, and a fund from which larger salaries could be drawn, but it did not directly enrich the professional manager. These men were interested in building strong organizations capable of weathering bad times, rather than in reaping quick profits in the market. They favored spending earnings for research, expert advice, and improvement of company morale, rather than using them to pay extra dividends to the stockholders. As a result, the common stock dividends of the biggest companies tended to move toward moderate, stable rates rather than to fluctuate with profits.

While scarcely a thousand companies were big enough to have professional, bureaucratic management remote from control by owners, the thousands of top executives of these big companies were leaders of business opinion. Executives commanded specialized knowledge and expert staff work. They hired the best lawyers, lobbyists, accountants, and engineers. Their assistants wrote speeches and articles for them analyzing business problems. Hence America seemed much more a land of big business than was the case statistically.

Shaping Public Opinion. George Creel's Committee on Public Information, similar to European agencies for propaganda during World War I provided a new emphasis on creating favorable opinion. About 1920 Edward Bernays and Ivy Lee began to call themselves public relations counselors. Soon the major advertising agencies also had public relations departments. The usual techniques were to publicize events that showed the client in a good light and to plant favorable stories in magazines. Much of the content of newspapers in the peaceful years of the twenties originated in public relations offices.

The value of the stockholder as a public relations resource was also exploited. By lowering the price of shares through splitting them two or more ways, and by aggressive selling to small investors, often through agents of the company, it was possible for a big corporation to acquire tens of thousands of new stockholders. American Telephone and Telegraph, which took a leading part in this movement, increased the number of its

Walter P. Chrysler: Lover of Fine Cars

Early in the century Henry Ford had first supplied sturdy, homely, reliable automobiles at moderate prices. By the 1920s Walter P. Chrysler had brought luxury cars within the financial reach of the middle class. In the long view, the high performance of Chryslers from 1924 to after World War II typifies the trend of American automobile design much more than the stark, bare Model Ts. Chrysler's role in setting the pattern for the principal American industry of the twentieth century makes him one of the most important men of his time.

When Chrysler was born in 1875, his father was a locomotive engineer living in Wamego, Kansas. Even such aristocrats of labor, however, couldn't afford to send their children to engineering school. After high school Chrysler went into the railroad shops to learn by doing. His rise was rapid and his devoted wife and young children moved often as he climbed up the ladder of railroad shop positions to a top rung as Superintendent of Motive Power for the Chicago Great Western.

Chrysler was a big, broad-faced, genial man with an emotional power that often controlled his own decisions as well as impressing those around him. Fortunately,

owners from 50,000 in 1920 to 210,000 in 1930. Stockholders were sent attractive annual reports and letters from the president designed to make them feel that they were an important part of the organization. In return many stockholders undoubtedly used their votes and influence for government policies favorable to the company.

Whether as a result of the new public relations, or prosperity, or for other less obvious causes, the American public seemed to have given up much of its traditional hostility to big corporations. Articles in praise of business signed by corporate leaders made popular reading in mass-circulation magazines, and business periodicals boasted of the dominance of the businessman and his values. Advertising executive Bruce Barton

even pictured Christ as a businessman. In this friendly atmosphere business was bold in the use of direct influence in legislatures, in community pressures through business clubs, and in the use of advertising contracts to influence editors. A basic danger, as illustrated in the thirties, was that business developed few new progressive policies to go with its added power.

Stock Market Boom and Bust. Besides lacking a suitable social philosophy, businessmen and their economic advisers lacked understanding of relationships in the economy. Consequently, the stock market boom from 1927 to 1929, though not reflected in any corresponding upswing in real capital formation, was not regarded as dangerous. Confidence that the

his intuitive reactions usually turned out to be right. In 1908 he saw a white Locomobile with red upholstery, four cylinders, and chain drive at the Chicago automobile show. It shared with half a dozen other makes the highest prestige in the luxury part of the market. Chrysler promptly fell in love with fine cars. For a man making $4,200 a year to buy a $5,000 automobile was madness. Yet Chrysler, with the help of a banker friend, managed to do it. He didn't want the car to drive and it was weeks before his family even had a ride. Instead, he wanted to take the car apart. He wanted to learn everything about it, which he proceeded to do during nights and weekends.

Meanwhile, to learn more about the problems of production, still unconsciously driven, no doubt, by his dreams of creating motor cars, he quit his railroad job in 1910 and took one in manufacturing with the American Locomotive Company in Pittsburgh at 20 percent less salary. Within two years the chance came to make automobiles. Although American Locomotive wanted to keep him at $12,000 a year—real wealth in the last year before federal income taxes—he became Works Manager for the Buick division of General Motors at $6,000.

Now he was on the main track of his career in a prodigiously expanding industry. Buick, a medium-priced car, was the most popular of the General Motors lines. An offshoot of William C. Durant's wagon works, Buick construction was still being supervised by men who had originally been craftsmen in wood. Chrysler quickly introduced the techniques of large-scale metalworking he had learned at American Locomotive and actually had part of the works on an assembly line earlier than the Ford Plant.

Chrysler was so successful in both making and marketing cars that in 1915 Durant, the founder of General Motors, who had regained control of the company with help

severe business cycle was a thing of the past pervaded American finance.

The wealthiest class (about 5 percent of the population) received about a third of all income and were taxed at very low rates. Thus, their savings were tremendous. Low corporate taxes allowed big companies to accumulate unprecedented cash surpluses. Both personal savings and corporate surpluses were used for speculation. Moreover, brokers, by means of loans, made it easy for investors of even modest income to purchase securities beyond their means. Investors could buy "on margin"—that is, deposit only a small percentage of the total price of a block of securities, with the broker advancing the rest of the money. The hope was, of course, that the price of the securities would rise and

enable the investor to make a large profit on his small equity. Often brokerage houses and banks would lend three quarters of the cost of new securities, the customer depositing only a 25 percent margin. In practice, margins often were allowed to go down to 10 percent or less. Not only were both domestic and European banks happy to lend on this type of "demand" or "call" loan, but big business companies also employed unused reserves for stock market loans.

Since investors would readily buy the shares of railroad and public utility holding companies, ambitious entrepreneurs like the Van Sweringen brothers in Cleveland, Samuel Insull in Chicago, and S. Z. Mitchell in New York set up pyramids of one holding company on top of another. By selling stock in these

from the du Ponts, made Chrysler President of Buick at a salary of $500,000, payable largely in G.M. stock. By 1919, his division was forging ahead of the others at General Motors, and Chrysler was one of the key men in the industry. He had come to be respected for his great ability at selling and finance as well as in production, and he had enough money in G.M. stock to be independent. Consequently, when he thought Durant was overexpanding early in the inflationary year of 1919, he decided to leave the company and dispose of his stock. Selling out near the peak of the boom, he put the cash in trust for his wife and children and prepared to retire.

General Motors was not the only major automobile company to be caught with too much inventory and too little cash in the rapid market decline of the spring and summer of 1920. Chrysler was soon drawn back into industry affairs, first as a "doctor" for Willys-Overland at an incredible $1 million-a-year salary, and two years later as Chairman of the Reorganization Committee for the ailing Maxwell Motor Company. Meanwhile, in talking with design engineers Fred M. Zeder, Owen Skelton, and Carl Breer, Chrysler succumbed to the overwhelming urge to bring out a new car with his own name and design, using the Maxwell facilities.

Over numerous difficulties, chiefly financial, Chryslers were displayed to large crowds at the Commodore Hotel in New York during the 1924 annual automobile show at nearby Grand Central Palace. Besides being attractive and well made, the

companies to the public, the empire builders got the money to buy dozens of operating companies while keeping personal control of the organization through the top holding company. In theory, economics were being achieved through removal of wasteful competition, but in fact the savings were often consumed by greater managerial costs.

High-pressure selling by the agents of bankers and brokers led investors into buying many other questionable securities. Mortgages on the new urban hotels, apartments, and office buildings that were rising all over the nation were divided into small bonds for sale to investors. Ultimately these buildings would be needed, but in 1929 construction was already outrunning the demand for such space. United States investment firms literally coaxed foreign governments into issuing bonds that could be marketed to the American public. And in spite of all this manufacture of new securities, the demand exceeded the supply and boosted the price of existing stocks higher and higher.

By the summer of 1929 many insiders, convinced that stock prices were too high in relation to earnings, started to sell. But thousands of speculators could only cling to the limb they were on and hope for some miraculous support. Late in October the limb broke. In a series of panic days on the New York Stock Exchange, stocks sank so fast that holders on margin were generally wiped out. Efforts by J. P. Morgan and Company to stabilize the market failed, and European banks began withdrawing $2 billion they had

Chryslers were the first to combine high-compression engines (which meant higher speed), four-wheel hydraulic brakes, and a shorter wheelbase—a majority of the most important engineering innovations that would be made during the next fifteen years. And the cars sold for no more than Buicks of comparable size.

As young people, particularly, swung toward Chryslers, the company quickly took steps to move beyond medium-priced cars sold to hundreds of customers to cheap cars sold to millions. To compete with Ford and Chevrolet, which dominated this market, Chrysler purchased Dodge Brothers in 1927 in one of the largest financial deals in American automotive history. This marked the formation of the still-dominant "big three" in the American automobile market, with Chrysler for many of the early years ahead of Ford in sales.

Chrysler's emphasis on engineering and performance permanently shifted sales efforts toward attractive new models offered at relatively uniform, noncompetitive prices. Chrysler's new ideas created the American automobile market, whose features were to last with little change until the advent of the compact in the late 1950s, and in many respects without much alteration until the gasoline crisis of the 1970s. Few other twentieth-century Americans have been so responsible for shaping the everyday utilities of life.

loaned on call. On October 29, the day of most extreme panic, 16 million shares were traded, and at times stocks could not be sold for want of buyers at any reasonable price. By November stocks had lost 40 percent of their September value.

Stunned by this disaster in what appeared to be stabilized prosperity, business and political leaders insisted that the economy was sound and that the market break would not affect industry. Only about half a million people had margin accounts, and only a million and a half had brokerage accounts of any kind. But since this small group included most of the chief accumulators and users of capital, their importance was not to be measured in numbers. Furthermore, the whole economy had become more closely geared to the stock market than ever before. In the collapse of values, corporations lost their surpluses. Brokerage houses were unable to sell fast enough to cover their loans. Banks in turn were left with demand loans that could be liquidated only at a fraction of their value. And foreign governments were no longer able to borrow on Wall Street.

THE GREAT DEPRESSION

Increasing Force of the Depression. In contrast to the severity of the stock market panic, the Great Depression began gradually. At the end of 1929 and the beginning of 1930 employment declined only slightly more than was seasonally normal. A Wall Street economist thought the collapse of inflated security values "a favorable development from the point of view of general business." Secretary of the Treasury Andrew Mellon saw nothing "in the present situation that is either menacing or warrants pessimism."

Influenced by the prevailing expressions of optimism, President Herbert Hoover sought to end the mild recession by encouraging appropriate business action and by implementing favorable government policies. In conferences with business leaders he urged them to maintain wages, prices, and plans for expansion. In return he promised to continue a normal program of public works, to raise tariffs, and to lower the Federal Reserve System's rediscount rate (the rate of interest at which banks could exchange customers' notes for currency at Federal Reserve Banks) in order to stimulate business activity by making credit more readily available. In addition, the Federal Farm Board, which had been created in 1929, was expected to support agricultural prices by lending funds to marketing cooperatives or to corporations set up by the cooperatives to stabilize the market. The loan funds would be used to purchase basic farm crops and livestock at marketing time so that markets would not be glutted.

The President, however, refused to face realistically the condition of the unemployed and, probably unaware of the weakness of the banks, continued to manipulate figures to encourage a false optimism. In the spring of 1930, just before business unemployment climbed sharply, he assured the nation: "The worst effects of the crash upon unemployment will have passed during the next sixty days."

The chief barrier to effective action in dealing with the advancing depression was that President Hoover, most economists, and practically all businessmen adhered to the traditional laissez-faire view that government should not interfere with business. Thus they considered voluntary private investment the only road to national economic recovery. They did not regard public works projects or other government programs as means of recreating prosperity through increasing demand for workers, goods, and services. Furthermore, allied to the general political failure to appreciate the possibilities of artificially increased employment and demand was the traditional attitude that helping individuals by federal food or relief payments would undermine the initiative of the American people.

A slight upturn in early 1931 supported President Hoover's "wait-and-see" policy. But the business indexes soon started down again, and the international financial structure began to disintegrate. In June 1931, banks on the European continent failed. Reparations and debt payments soon stopped, and by September England went off the gold standard (refused to pay its foreign obligations in gold). In July President Hoover, with the agreement of England, France, and Germany, declared a one-year moratorium on European debt and reparation payments. He hoped that such a temporary lifting of the burden of intergovernmental debts would promote world trade and stimulate economic recovery. However, the European crisis resulted in continued gold withdrawals from banks in the United States, European sale of American securities, and the freezing of most foreign short-term loans owed to banks in this country. These events forced a further contraction of bank loans in the United States and an end to the possibility of a quick return to prosperity. While the collapse of 1929 was initiated in the United States, descent into the

Despite President Hoover's assurances in 1930 that the effects of the crash on unemployment would soon pass, the ranks of the destitute and unemployed continued to grow to unprecedented proportions.

deep trough from 1931 to 1933 was, as President Hoover claimed, precipitated by European events.

Initiation of the Welfare State. Those in "the business world," wrote President Hoover, "threw up their hands and asked for government action." As voluntary action proved inadequate to counteract the deepening depression, Hoover moved step by step toward federal legislation. In December 1931 and January 1932 the President cooperated with leaders of the politically divided Senate and the Democratic House in creating the Reconstruction Finance Corporation (RFC). This conservatively managed agency, with resources of $2 billion, was to make loans to companies such as banks and railroads to prevent bankruptcy and forced liquidation. Aid was given to some 5000 medium-sized to large businesses to help them meet their pressing obligations, such as bond and mortgage interest or short-term debts. The philosophy of aid was to preserve those institutions whose operation was essential to the public and to other businesses. Consequently, banks and railroads received the most aid while small business, in general, was not initially helped.

Until this time the "general welfare" clause of the Constitution had never been interpreted to mean maintenance of the economic system by congressional action. While later Democratic acts continuing the RFC and extending aid to agriculture and individuals were to push the doctrine much further, the nonpartisan RFC Act can be considered the beginning of the federal "welfare state" or "social capitalism." It demonstrated in the sphere of big business that an advanced industrial economy was so complexly interrelated that government could not stand by and see any essential parts break down.

Other recovery measures enacted in the spring of 1932 included the Glass-Steagall Act, which made government bonds and additional types of commercial paper acceptable as collateral for Federal Reserve notes—thus liberalizing the lending powers of banks—and made available to business about $750 million of the government gold supply. In July the Federal Home Loan Bank Act created twelve regional Federal Home Loan Banks to extend federal financial assistance to building and loan associations, savings banks, and insurance companies that were in trouble because of falling prices. But Democratic congressional efforts at direct aid to individuals were defeated by presidential vetoes. Hoover continued to view relief as a function of state and local governments. Consequently relief limped along on the basis of small RFC loans to the states.

Effects of the Depression. By the spring of 1932, conditions in the United States reached what seemed to be an intolerable impasse. Then, after remaining relatively unchanged for some nine months, the situation grew even worse. Yet in all this year of material, social, and moral prostration, there was never

INDEX OF COMMON STOCK PRICES, 1920-1945

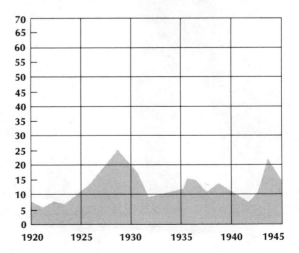

In the early 1930s thousands of people drifted around the country. Most of the homeless men pictured here, trying to keep warm in a Chicago street, had nothing but the sidewalk for a bed and a newspaper for a blanket.

any threat of revolution, or even any important rise of radicalism in American politics. The American cultural traditions of self-help and individual responsibility seemed, for the most part, to make the sufferers feel guilty, and perhaps sullen and resentful, but not ready to fight for a new order.

The overall statement that unemployment rose to between a quarter and a third of the labor force gives too optimistic a picture of the effects of the depression on human beings. To begin with, total man hours worked in mid-1932 were only about 40 percent of those in 1929, and many experienced workers were being paid only five to ten cents an hour. Furthermore, destitute farmers were not considered unemployed, and people who had given up seeking work and students who stayed in school or college solely because they had no hope of finding jobs were not part of the "labor force." In general, the most easily replaceable workers, such as the unskilled, lost their jobs first, and what work remained was apportioned between management and skilled labor. Both managers and women office employees kept their jobs more often than workers in plants.

One-industry towns could be paralyzed by the failure of two or three local companies. By early 1932 the entire county of Williamson in southern Illinois had almost no employment. Some Appalachian mining cities had two or three hundred employed out of many thousands. If a community depended on industries that made goods for other industries, it usually suffered mass unemployment.

Without income or housing to hold them together, many families disintegrated. A father without a job, who washed dishes, made beds, sat around, and failed to provide food, lost status in his family. Sometimes his position became intolerable, and he was driven to suicide. Many more unemployed fathers and older children started drifting around the country, presumably looking for work but perhaps really seeking escape through activity. The drift of a million or more of these "migrants of despair" was aimless but generally toward warm areas, where each city tried to keep the wayfarers moving to somewhere else. In many cities they could get a meal but could not stay.

In the larger cities the major burden of relief fell first on private donors and then on voluntary organizations, like the Red Cross, Salvation Army, Community Chest, and, as these exhausted their resources, on small local and state appropriations. Before the end of 1930, people who administered relief recognized that these resources were inadequate. "Local organizations," said C. A. Dykstra of Cleveland in 1932, "have tried to make $400 million play substitute for $20 or more billion, formerly paid in wages." In small cities conditions were often worse than in the major centers. A survey of fifty-nine cities of upstate New York in the winter of 1930–1931 revealed that most of them had no relief programs. "By the fall of 1931," says Professor Irving Bernstein, "municipal relief—private and public—was bankrupt in virtually every city in the United States," and it is estimated that unemployment rose 50 percent in the next eighteen months.

The farming country presented the most outrageous paradox of all. With no effective means of controlling prices or production, farmers literally ruined each other. To keep his income up when prices were falling, each farmer tried to produce more and more, thus driving prices down still further until the value of some crops and animals was too low to justify taking them to market. And because gifts of food would potentially compete with sales, no permissible way was found to distribute and use agricultural supplies. As a result, a sheep raiser cut the throats of young lambs and threw them into a canyon because he could not afford to feed them, while the families on so-called "bread lines" had watered-down soup. Southern sharecroppers fared worst of all. Owners unable to finance new crops left former tenants without food, and these rural areas generally lacked charitable or other relief organizations.

The Election of 1932. By the summer of 1932 the patience of various groups throughout the nation was becoming exhausted. Organized farmers in Iowa were violently enforcing a "farm holiday" on produce deliveries. An "expeditionary force" of several thousand veterans was encamped in Washington demanding cash payment of the World War i bonus. Numbers of unemployed were killed by police in riots around Detroit, and some

ELECTION OF 1928: ELECTORAL VOTE

	Hoover: 444		Smith: 87

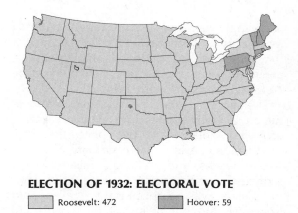

ELECTION OF 1932: ELECTORAL VOTE

	Roosevelt: 472		Hoover: 59

conservative editors were calling for a dictatorship to preserve the state.

Yet a majority of the leaders of both major parties conservatively opposed any substantial change in policy. Of the Democratic leaders only Governor Franklin D. Roosevelt of New York seemed to lean toward a more progressive approach, favoring the use of government power to whatever extent necessary and in whatever ways necessary to reverse the trend of economic events.

Franklin Delano Roosevelt, a fifth cousin of Theodore, had been brought up on a country estate above Poughkeepsie, New York, and educated at Harvard and at Columbia Law School. In 1910 he entered politics and was elected to the New York state assembly, where he stood for progressivism and reform and was an ardent supporter of Woodrow Wilson. President Wilson, aware of the personal charm of the big, strong-jawed, smiling young man, appointed Roosevelt Assistant Secretary of the Navy. The 1920 Democratic convention, needing the magic of the Roosevelt name, nominated him for the vice-presidency.

Shortly after his defeat as Cox's running mate, Roosevelt contracted infantile paralysis, but by 1924 he had recovered sufficiently to appear, supported by crutches, at the Demo

cratic convention and make the nominating speech for Alfred E. Smith. In 1928, at Smith's insistence, Roosevelt ran for governor of New York. Carrying the state by 25,000 votes while Smith lost it for the presidency marked Roosevelt as one of the coming men in the Democratic party. In 1930, after one term as a rather easygoing, liberal governor, he was reelected by a record-breaking 725,000 votes.

These repeated victories made him the party's logical candidate for the presidency in 1932, but Roosevelt, fearful of a strong undercurrent of conservative opposition, left nothing to chance. His able secretary, Louis M. Howe, planned and advised, and New York state Democratic chairman James A. Farley toured the country and talked to politicians. At the Democratic convention Farley skillfully negotiated with William Randolph Hearst and William G. McAdoo for California's support on the fourth ballot in return for the nomination of conservative House Speaker John Nance Garner for Vice-President. This shift swung Garner's state of Texas and other Southern states to the Roosevelt bandwagon, but Al Smith held on to his delegates and left Chicago without congratulating the nominee.

The Republicans had no recourse but to renominate Hoover, and in truth, the prosperous people who financed and ran the national machinery in both parties probably thought that Hoover had done all that could be expected. Yet everyone knew he would not be a strong candidate with the public.

The campaign mirrored the complete confusion in both parties regarding acceptable economic policy. The two platforms were nearly the same, and both candidates talked of public works and relieving misery while reducing spending and balancing the budget. But Garner was no doubt right when he told Roosevelt that to win "all you have to do is to stay alive until election day." Hoover probably gained no votes by his weary and often bitter campaign. On election day he polled 15,759,000 votes to Roosevelt's 22,800,000.

While many middle-class voters supported Socialist party candidate Norman Thomas as the only candidate with a constructive program, Thomas failed utterly to attract the masses. His 881,951 Socialist votes were fewer than in 1920 and relatively less than half the Socialist vote in 1912. Some artists and intellectuals desiring a stronger protest supported William Z. Foster, the Communist, but his meager 102,785 votes indicated that few workers had supported him.

Bottom of the Depression. The depression reached its lowest ebb in the four months between the election and Roosevelt's inauguration. During this critical period there was little constructive leadership. Hoover thought that everything justifiable had been done in the domestic field and was interested in stimulating foreign trade. Roosevelt could not accept Hoover's analysis of the domestic situation and was not prepared to work for return to an international gold standard, the keynote of Hoover's plans. As the nation drifted without leadership, silver shirts, white shirts, khaki shirts, and other fascist organizations strove unsuccessfully for mass support. "Technocracy," a vaguely defined plan for

placing control of the nation's means of production in the hands of technicians in order to realize the full efficiency of industrial equipment, created a midwinter furor, but it died quickly from lack of immediate, practical proposals. In general, the people waited patiently, putting their hopes in the new administration.

The final breakdown of commercial banking was responsible for bringing the economy to its lowest ebb. Of the 16,000 state banks of 1929 that were not members of the Federal Reserve System, nearly half had closed their doors by 1933. These banks had no system to save them, and many of their officers knew little about banking. Of the 7500 members of the Federal Reserve, about 1400 disappeared during the depression, demonstrating that even these banks were too small and poorly connected to stand the strain. Banks that failed drew away deposits kept in the banks of the larger cities. The first major metropolitan area to buckle under the pressure was New Orleans. Early in February 1933 the governor of Louisiana declared a temporary "bank holiday," freezing loans and deposits.

Meanwhile, a Senate committee investigating banking practices had uncovered dishonesty and evasion of responsibility in the highest circles. Major banks had lent money to their officers on no proper security, and bad securities had been sold to banks to save investment subsidiaries or affiliates from disaster. These and other questionable practices had been overlooked by federal examiners. Faced with such uncertainties, depositors began to withdraw their surplus cash from the banks and stuff it into safe deposit boxes.

Closing of the banks in Michigan in mid-February started a chain reaction that ended on March 4, 1933—the day of Roosevelt's inauguration—when Governor Lehman of New York and other governors joined in declaring a "bank holiday" to stop destructive runs as depositors rushed to withdraw savings. The banking crisis had, in turn, hurt business, driving unemployment up to somewhere between 14 and 17 million, perhaps as much as a third of the labor force. The economy was producing at about half the rate of 1929, and the trend was downward.

FDR: THE FIRST TERM

The Honeymoon. Roosevelt's inaugural address on March 4, 1933, struck a note of hope. The nation was strong, he said, and would recover from this crippling depression: "The only thing we have to fear is fear itself—nameless, unreasoning, unjustified terror which paralyzes needed efforts to convert retreat into advance." He closed by affirming, "The people of the United States . . . have asked for discipline and direction under leadership. They have made me the present instrument of their wishes. In the spirit of the gift I take it."

The nation and Congress, which Roosevelt immediately called into emergency session, responded to his appeal, and quickly the pattern of the "New Deal" began to reveal itself. "Our greatest primary task," Roosevelt declared in his inaugural address, "is to put people to work." Preferably the employment should be private firms, but if necessary the federal government should use its resources to provide employment on the most useful work projects that could be quickly devised. Second, the abuses that aggravated the depression must be corrected. Anyone guilty of criminal acts of financial or corporate manipulation must be punished. Banking laws should be made stricter in some respects, controls over the stock exchanges and the commodity markets should be tightened, and abuse of the holding-company device should be corrected by closer control of its use, especially in public utilities. After these emergency corrective measures had been taken, Roosevelt proposed a series of permanent steps to bring about a fuller development of the country and to make the lives of most Americans more secure and prosperous. Roosevelt referred to these three objectives of the New Deal as "Relief, Recovery, and Reform."

On March 6, before Congress met in special session, the President proclaimed a four-day national bank holiday and a four-day embargo on the export of gold, silver, and currency. Congress, convening on March 9, provided for the reopening of banks to relieve the financial emergency. The Emergency Banking Relief Act—enacted that day—confirmed the President's earlier actions and provided for the reopening of sound banks. At the same time Congress prohibited the use of gold except under license for export.

The special session of Congress subsequently was fed a stream of recovery measures drawn up by groups in the administration, often with differing philosophies. But with the force of the President behind them the bills were enacted by sweeping bipartisan majorities. By the time this famous "Hundred Days" or political "honeymoon" ended in June 1933, the basic emergency legislation was complete. The Federal Emergency Relief Administration (FERA) was created with $500 million in funds to be granted to states for direct relief. A Civilian Conservation Corps (CCC) was set up to put unemployed young men into camps to carry out reforestation and erosion-control projects. Beer and light wine with an alcoholic content of 3.2 percent or less by volume were legalized and repeal of the Eighteenth Amendment initiated (passage of the Twenty-first Amendment late in 1933 officially repealed prohibition).

Farm Relief. From the standpoint of loss in money income, farmers were the hardest hit of any occupational group. From 1925 on they were in a vicious circle of increasing overproduction of staple crops and declining prices. Earnings were so low that grain and cotton

These CCC boys are working on a reforestation project in a fire-ravaged national forest in Idaho as part of the government's program to provide work for unemployed young men.

farmers could not afford the investment needed to shift to other produce for which there was a better market. Depression turned hardship into disaster. Total cash income for farmers fell from an average of nearly $11 billion per year in the late twenties to $4.7 billion in 1932. And even these figures fail to suggest the desperate straits of marginal cotton, corn, and wheat growers.

The Agricultural Adjustment Act of June 1933 contained the basic principle of subsequent farm legislation. The government should pay staple crop farmers to plant fewer acres, thus reducing output and raising the prices on farm products. Money to subsidize the farmers was to come from a tax on millers and other processors of staple products. In this way the law would be self-supporting. To get the program going quickly, the Secretary of Agriculture arranged for the plowing up of millions of acres of cotton and the slaughter of six million pigs of less than usual market weights, the pigs to be put to uses other than providing human food. Although many Americans considered the destruction of food and cotton positively sinful when millions were hungry and ill-clothed, farm prices and income did improve in 1934 and 1935.

Mortgage Refinancing. The government had to try not only to revive farm income but also to take care of hundreds of thousands of defaulted mortgages, both farm and nonfarm. In two initial acts creating the Federal Farm Mortgage Corporation and the Home Owners Loan Corporation, the government offered to refinance mortgages on long terms at low interest.

In addition, the Federal Housing Administration Act of 1934 introduced the guaranteed packaged mortgage—one that could be paid, principal and interest, by uniform monthly payments. This government guarantee of loans for a high percentage of the total cost of homes in the low-price range constituted the most important change in the history of American home ownership. Now people with steady jobs could afford to build or buy, where they had had to rent before, and payment was much easier. This new system also marked an important step in the development of less expensive homes and long-term installment buying.

Regional Development. One of the most revolutionary of the acts passed by Congress during the Hundred Days initiated the redevelopment of an entire region—the economically ailing seven-state Tennessee valley area.

The Muscle Shoals–Tennessee Valley Development Act of May 1933 created an independent public corporation, the Tennessee Valley Authority, which was given control of the government property at Muscle Shoals, Alabama, and the power to build and operate other dams and power plants on the Tennessee River and its branches wherever the authority thought advisable. In addition to generation and distribution of electric power, TVA was charged with controlling the flood waters of the Tennessee River and improving its navigation facilities, promoting the conservation of soil in the valley, aiding reforestation, and producing nitrates and other fertilizers for the improvement of the valley's

agriculture. Government-financed improvements in the valley continued over the next generation, leading ultimately to industrial development as well as greatly increasing animal husbandry.

The power dams, plants, and distribution systems of TVA were criticized by private power companies as unfair competition, since the public facilities were not required to pay the same taxes as private companies and received other government subsidies. The constitutionality of the TVA was upheld, however, by the Supreme Court in 1936. The following year President Roosevelt asked Congress to set up six additional regional river valley authorities, but Congress declined. The areas in which they were to be located were not quite such distinct units as the Tennessee valley, nor were the people of these other areas in such a distressed condition as those of the Tennessee valley had been in 1933. The general business outlook was brighter in early 1937, and the business community supported the widespread contention that private capital could develop these valleys as effectively as the federal government.

Partially thwarted in his larger conservation and development plans, the President succeeded in having the Civilian Conservation Corps plant a tree belt across the Great Plains, while the Department of Agriculture checked soil erosion by urging farmers to plow furrows at right angles to the slope of the land, a practice called contour plowing. Thus the New Deal period may be looked upon as the beginning of a heightened federal consciousness of ecological problems.

Industrial Recovery. While banking, currency, mortgages, and agriculture had occupied the President's attention during the first weeks of his administration, he learned in April 1933 that unless he acted quickly Congress would pass a uniform thirty-hour-a-week law governing all industry. Because he regarded such a law as impractical, the

TENNESSEE VALLEY AUTHORITY

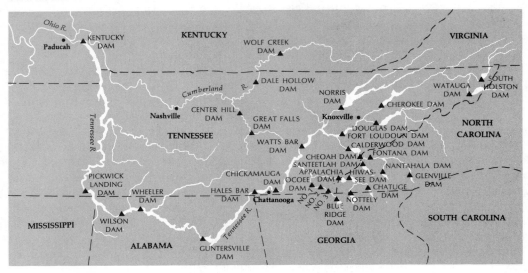

President had his advisers prepare a substitute. The resulting National Industrial Recovery Act (NIRA), though hastily improvised, actually was the outgrowth of much thought by business, labor, and government about how to reconcile "free" private enterprise with effective governmental control of wages and competition.

In many industries excess industrial capacity, unemployed labor, and nearly bankrupt firms had reduced the market to chaos. With women receiving as little as $5 for a full week's work, companies that tried to maintain fair labor standards found themselves undersold. The solution proposed in the act was to have each industry, probably through its trade association, agree to a code of "fair competition" defining wages, hours, and minimum prices. Labor would be represented in the making of such industry agreements by representatives of its own choosing without any pressure from the employer. The public would also be represented so that the interests of consumers would not be lost sight of. When all three parties were represented in the determination of policies for an industry, the government could overlook the fact that a price agreement would appear to be a clear "conspiracy to restrain trade" under the terms of the Sherman Antitrust Act. The National Recovery Administration (NRA) was set up to administer this section of the law.

The second section of NIRA set up the Public Works Administration (PWA) and authorized the expenditure of $3.3 billion for public works projects designed both to provide work for relief and to stimulate recovery.

The bill became law in June 1933, and the President appointed retired General Hugh S. Johnson as administrator of the first section. The negotiation of codes proved difficult and time consuming. In July 1933 President Roosevelt, in an attempt to speed matters, announced a blanket President's Reemployment Agreement (PRA) governing wages and hours for those industries that could not agree upon a code. A blue eagle was adopted as the symbol of the cooperating firms. Those that signed codes or the PRA were allowed to display it on their stores, plants, or merchandise, and the public was strongly urged not to patronize nonsigners. Within months millions of Americans were working under the blue eagle. The original idea of cooperation between the employer, organized labor, and consumer representatives, however, was all but lost in the difficulties of reaching agreements. Furthermore, consumers were unorganized and unable to protect their interests as management and government drew up a flood of codes. As time passed, thousands of cases of noncompliance with codes were reported. Labor was extremely restive because the union organization as authorized by NIRA was often opposed by industry. The country was plagued by strikes. Employers began to fear that they had made a mistake in agreeing to negotiate with labor in drawing up the codes. The public also began to feel that it was being fleeced by prices that were rising faster than income.

Although the NRA contributed to the raising of wages from the low levels of 1932, did away with child labor, and in some industries helped small business stay alive, the NIRA experiment illustrated the difficulty of suddenly regulating a complex economy. More important, it failed to bring back prosperity. The United States Chamber of Commerce and labor leaders as diverse as William Green, John L. Lewis, and Sidney Hillman continued to support the NRA until the Supreme Court ruled the act unconstitutional, but business in general and the rising leaders in the Roosevelt administration lost interest in it or become hostile toward it.

Devaluing the Dollar.   Controllable inflation, the President hoped, would raise farm prices and in general lighten the burden of debts in relation to income. The administration felt that such inflation could be stimulated either by heavy government spending or by altering the value of the dollar. Of the two possibilities, devaluing the dollar had the immediate advantages of not adding to government costs and of stimulating exports.

While the President was supporting the inflationist group in Congress, European nations were meeting in June and July 1933 to attack the worldwide depression by attempting to agree on stabilizing national currencies and restoring the international gold standard. However, contrary to this spirit, an amendment to the Agricultural Adjustment Act of May 1933 gave the President the right to inflate U.S. currency by issuing $3 billion in paper currency, freely coining silver, and devaluing the gold content of the dollar up to 50 percent. For the time being he did none of these things, waiting to see whether the AAA and the NRA would do the inflationary job, but neither would he enter into any international agreement fixing the value of the dollar. As a result, the London Economic Conference was a failure.

Although there was a sharp increase in manufacturing production, employment, and prices between March and July 1933—in part, the result of an effort to produce before the restrictive NRA codes went into effect—by autumn manufacturing and employment were declining, and wholesale prices had again leveled off. At this point the President decided to use his power to devalue the dollar in the expectation that the resulting inflation would lead to higher prices. He reduced the value of the gold content of the dollar to 59.06 cents, a degree of devaluation calculated to restore the price level of 1926. Prices rose slightly, but not nearly so much as the administration had expected. The President's monetary program had no significant effect on the economy.

Rise of Conservative Opposition.   Early criticism of the New Deal had come primarily from advanced liberals and labor leaders. Some members of Congress, for instance, would have nationalized banking and railroads. They and even more moderate liberals regarded the restoration of the banking system in relatively unchanged form as the loss of a great opportunity for progress toward a more stable economy. Organized labor was particularly dissatisfied with its treatment by the NRA, which in labor circles came to be called the "national run-around."

On the other hand, monetary manipulation during the last half of 1933 lost the President the support of many conservative Democratic leaders, who opposed any tinkering with the monetary system. Efforts at permanent reform of financial operations, as distinct from mere recovery, widened the rift between liberals and conservatives.

The reform program really began with the Federal Securities Act of 1933, by which the Federal Trade Commission was given the power to see that underwriters fully disclosed to investors all essential details pertaining to new securities issues. A further reform was effected by the Banking Act of June 1933, which divorced investment banking from commercial banking on the premise that the promoting and selling of new securities by commercial banks gave them an improper amount of power over other businesses and was inconsistent with the policy of caution and prudence which banks should follow. The Banking Act also created the Federal Deposit Insurance Corporation (FDIC) to insure bank deposits up to established limits and prevent losses to depositors. Because it involved more governmental regulation, leading bankers vigorously opposed deposit insurance, and more general business opposition was aroused by the stricter regulation of the securities markets.

The battle between liberals and conservatives was intensified when the Securities Exchange bill was before Congress in the spring of 1934. This bill called for the establishment of a three-member Securities

Uncle Sam is portrayed as getting tangled up by the growing Federal "alphabetocracy." Conservatives thought that Roosevelt's New Deal was creating a vast, irresponsible bureaucracy.

and Exchange Commission to regulate the practices of stock exchanges, including the size of margins; to require full disclosure of details about all securities; and to enforce other parts of the Federal Securities Act of 1933. Stockbrokers and investment bankers complained strongly about the restrictions this legislation would place on them. But despite bitter debate in Congress the bill was passed in June 1934, and the die-hard opponents of all governmental regulation of the financial community were decisively defeated.

Another development in the spring of 1934 that alarmed some businessmen was adoption of the Reciprocal Trade Agreements Act, which gave the President power to make separate agreements with foreign nations to alter U.S. tariff rates by 50 percent in either direction. Even moderate Republicans denounced it as a surrender of power to the President. But the Democrats, with strong Southern support, held firm and enacted this change in American tariff policy.

In the course of debates over the Securities Act and the tariff, business arguments against the New Deal took their permanent shape. The government was condemned for creating a vast and irresponsible bureaucracy, for depriving individuals of their freedom and initiative, and for increasing the national debt. Direct relief, in particular, was condemned as running contrary to the deeply ingrained tradition that self-help was the basis of American greatness.

In August 1934 a group of wealthy Republicans and conservative Democrats formed the Liberty League to defend the rights and liberty of the individual against the New Deal. Backed by DuPont and General Motors executives, the League won the support of previous Democratic presidential candidates John W. Davis and Alfred E. Smith and many other conservative political leaders in both parties. The big city daily newspapers were moving in the same direction. Within a year,

at least two thirds of the metropolitan dailies were strongly in opposition to the New Deal, and their influential columnists were attacking the "third-rate college professors" and other "impractical intellectuals" of the "Brain Trust" that was held to be guiding the policies of the administration.

Reliance upon the Masses. The business attack on the New Deal, though backed by adequate finances and the support of major newspapers, had the fatal weakness of lacking a positive philosophy. Business leaders could only ask the public again to put its faith in the self-regulating economy. That, in fact, the public would not trust self-regulation was shown in the election of 1934. Normally the administration party loses strength in Congress in the nonpresidential elections. Instead the Democrats gained nine seats in the House and nine in the Senate, with nearly 57 percent of the popular vote—an off-year administration victory unmatched since before the Civil War.

What had built the Democratic majority? The answer of a number of presidential advisers was that it was the voters' desire for security—for assurance that when unemployed or old they would be cared for. At this point, therefore, the New Deal became more equalitarian and humanitarian than any of the previous progressive movements.

In the spring of 1935 a new system of relief through useful work was instituted. Jobs ranging from mixing concrete to painting murals were to be created from an appropriation of nearly $5 billion. Pay would be at rates above relief but lower than approved for private employment. The Works Progress Administration lasted until World War II and spent some $11 billion. Although it could employ only from two to three million workers, it kept those with the more valuable skills from deteriorating through idleness. Other minor forms of aid were instituted to help students stay in school and to provide

potential farmers with subsistence homesteads.

In the President's mind, the most important
legislation of this administration was the
Social Security Act of 1935. This act created a
Social Security Board to administer unemployment compensation, old-age security,
and various social services. Payroll taxes were
levied on both employers and employees to
finance old-age pensions of from $10 to $85
per month for retired workers. Pensions
under the new system would not begin until
1942, but meanwhile the federal government
would assist the states in paying small
pensions. In the beginning many groups,
including farm and educational workers, were
not eligible for pensions, but in succeeding
years coverage was broadened and rates
raised to compensate for inflation. The Social
Security Act also extended federal-state unemployment insurance to 28 million workers
and authorized money grants to states to
assist them in relief of the blind, the crippled,
delinquent children, and other dependents.
Now the power of Congress to legislate for the
general welfare had a new meaning.

The Supreme Court: Challenge and Response.

Early in 1935, with the Social Security bill on its way through Congress, the
President regarded his program as virtually
complete. Had the Supreme Court upheld the
legislation of 1933 and 1934, the Roosevelt
administration, like that of Woodrow Wilson,
might have turned its attention to matters
other than domestic reform. But the Supreme
Court had four justices unalterably opposed
to the New Deal, and two others, Owen J.
Roberts and Chief Justice Charles E. Hughes,
who were very doubtful about the constitutionality of delegating congressional power to
administrative agencies and using the commerce power to regulate conditions of production and trade within the states.

The crucial tests came in the spring of 1935,
when the Court declared the NIRA and a

The Social Security Act provided unemployment
compensation and old-age security, but some worried about becoming a number instead of an individual.

number of other basic acts of the New Deal
unconstitutional. There was little hope that
those still to be tested, such as the Agricultural
Adjustment Act, would fare any better. (The
Supreme Court invalidated the first AAA in
January 1936.)

The Court's failure to interpret the Constitution flexibly and to support the type of laws
initially planned in cooperation with business
leaders pushed the President toward further
regulation. The influence of the administration was already behind Senator Robert F.
Wagner's National Labor Relations Act to
replace the labor provisions of the outlawed
NIRA. The Wagner Act created a new
National Labor Relations Board (NLRB) for
administrative purposes and upheld the right
of employees to join labor organizations and
to bargain collectively through representatives of their own choosing.

This support of labor was accompanied by other New Deal measures that antagonized conservatives. A new tax bill introduced in June 1935 had the announced purpose of shifting the tax burden from the poor to the rich. The "Soak the Rich Act" of 1935 actually made few changes in taxes on income under $50,000 a year, and the graduated corporation income tax stopped at 15 percent. But high taxes on big incomes and on inheritance of estates further alarmed the wealthy over the "communistic" trend of the New Deal.

Attack by the rich probably strengthened support for the President. More politically dangerous was the attack on his policies by radical reformers. In his weekly radio broadcasts Father Charles E. Coughlin, a demagogic Catholic priest, first criticized the President for failure to take care of the rural poor and then progressed to a fascist type of attack on Jews and international bankers. In a more constructive vein, Dr. Francis Townsend of California advocated pensions of $200 a month for the elderly. But the most comprehensive political and economic appeal of the day came from Senator Huey P. Long of Louisiana. A mixture of machine politician and shrewd administrator who believed the depression could be cured by government spending, Long advocated a guaranteed minimum income and a capital levy on the rich to provide every family with a home, a car, and a radio. His simple country-boy manner and his slogan, "Every man a king," made him a real threat to Roosevelt's control of the Democratic party until Long was killed by a personal enemy in September 1935. Coughlin and other unorthodox reformers continued to keep the administration under fire, but without Long they lacked a strong political leader.

The Election of 1936.   Many Republicans felt that with Alfred M. Landon, ex-governor of Kansas, they would defeat Roosevelt in 1936. The *Literary Digest*'s poll of telephone sub-

scribers, which indicated a Landon presidential victory, helped sustain this view. (Overlooked was the fact that Roosevelt supporters were not adequately represented among telephone subscribers.) Landon promised to do everything that the New Deal was doing for the common man but to do it in ways more satisfactory to business. The President responded with a more advanced liberalism than in earlier campaigns. In his speech accepting renomination, he denounced the "economic royalists" and said that Americans, in their achievement of economic and social democracy, had a "rendezvous with destiny."

The result was the greatest landslide since 1920. Landon, with 16.7 million votes to the President's 27.8 million, carried only Maine and Vermont. The Coughlin group, supporting a radical farm leader, polled less than a million votes, and the Socialists' and Communists' votes were negligible. No President since Monroe had received such strong second-term support from the people.

LAST PHASE OF THE NEW DEAL

Battle over the Court.   In a surprise move after the election of 1936 Roosevelt boldly attempted to use his great political strength and national popularity to alter the composition of the ultraconservative Supreme Court—and thus to liberalize the Court's attitude toward New Deal legislation.

In February 1937 the President presented Congress with a bill to reorganize the federal judiciary by adding up to fifty judges to the federal court system as a whole. The bill further proposed to increase the membership of the Supreme Court from nine to a maximum of fifteen by permitting the President to appoint one new justice for each justice over seventy who refused to retire. Roosevelt's ostensible argument for the bill was that federal judges were overworked and decisions too long delayed because the judiciary was "handicapped by insufficient personnel." Furthermore, the President contended that the aging judges were antiquated in outlook—"little by little, new facts become blurred through old glasses fitted, as it were, for the needs of another generation." For the lower courts Roosevelt's argument was valid, but the highest tribunal was not far behind in its case work, and the justices over seventy included some of the most vigorous and liberal members of the Court.

The magnitude of the change from nine to fifteen justices when no previous Congress had ever altered the size of the Court so drastically, and the doubtful sincerity of Roosevelt's argument for the major provision of the bill, created unexpected Congressional opposition to the administration. Liberal Democrats and progressive Republicans joined conservatives in opposing the measure. The press was violent in its denunciation, and public opinion polls showed popular distaste for so arbitrary an action by the President.

While Congress debated the President's "Court-packing" bill, the Court itself removed much of Roosevelt's reason for the bill by voluntarily liberalizing its stand on New Deal legislation. Justice Roberts and Chief Justice Hughes abandoned the conservative camp and joined Justices Brandeis, Cardozo, and Stone in reversing the legal doctrines of 1935 and 1936. In March 1937 the Court, by a five-to-four decision, upheld a Washington state minimum wage law for women although the previous year it had declared unconstitutional a similar law of the state of New York. In April the Court declared the National Labor Relations Act constitutional, and the next month it upheld the Social Security Act. Furthermore, Justice Van Devanter's resignation from the Court in May 1937 gave Roosevelt a chance to appoint a justice who would convert the liberal minority of the Court to a majority in future decisions. To succeed Van Devanter, Roosevelt appointed

Senator Hugo L. Black of Alabama, an enthusiastic supporter of the New Deal.

In June 1937 the Senate Judiciary Committee reported the court reform bill unfavorably, and the Senate, after bitter debate, subsequently rejected the proposal by voting 70 to 20 to return it to the Judiciary Committee. Congress did, however, pass a Supreme Court Retirement Act permitting Supreme Court justices to retire, with full pay, at age seventy. It also passed a Judicial Procedure Reform Act which established reforms in the lower courts.

New Dealers found consolation for the defeat of the administration bill in the fact that the few years after defeat of the "Court-packing" plan saw a radical change in the complexion of the Supreme Court. A succession of deaths and resignations enabled

Roosevelt's arbitrary attempt to "pack" the Supreme Court met with strong Congressional opposition and failed to pass.

Roosevelt to make eight new appointments to the Court and gave him the liberal tribunal which Congress had denied him.

A Government-Protected Labor Movement. Early in 1933 the total independent union membership in the United States had fallen to less than 2.7 million, including about 2 million in the AFL. Unemployment had reduced company union membership to less than a million. The morale of union leaders was at a low ebb. In general their proposals for recovery were no more imaginative than Hoover's.

Section 7(a) of NIRA (granting to organized labor the right of collective bargaining through representatives of their own choosing) and the subsequent upswing in employment gave unions a chance to expand. Organizing drives and some help from the National Labor Board of the NRA raised total union membership to 3.6 million in 1935. Meanwhile, faced with the threat of being forced by code authorities to bargain collec-

tively, the larger employers were setting up new company unions. By 1935 this type of membership had passed 2.5 million.

In the same year a group within the AFL, led by John L. Lewis of the United Mine Workers, was urging the organization of all workers in a given industry—skilled or unskilled—into a single union. The AFL as a whole, however, was dominated by craft unions and continued to be officially opposed to all moves toward unionization by industries.

The Wagner Act of 1935 gave industrial organizers new and potentially effective weapons. The powerful National Labor Relations Board created by the Act could hold a plant election at the request of a union but not of an employer. If the union received the vote of a majority of workers, it became the bargaining agent for all. Furthermore, the Board could determine the unit—plants, companies, or industries—for election purposes, and it could prevent employers from interfering in any way with organizers or trying to influence the election. If the winning union was able to negotiate a closed-shop agreement, the employer was required to deduct union dues from the pay of all workers. In view of the decisions of the Supreme Court in 1935 and 1936, however, even labor leaders regarded the law as probably unconstitutional.

Encouraged somewhat by the opportunities the new law might offer and much more by the sweeping reelection of a friendly President, the leaders of eight AFL unions defied the parent body and formed a Committee for Industrial Organization. Led by John L. Lewis, the CIO refused to compromise with the crafts, and the unions involved were expelled by the AFL in 1937. The following year the committee became the Congress of Industrial Organizations with Lewis as president and a membership roughly equal to that of the AFL.

While Lewis in 1936 wanted to use the

**Annual averages (in millions) of
EMPLOYMENT, UNEMPLOYMENT, AND UNION
MEMBERSHIP, 1920–1945**

government-supported power of labor to organize steel workers, the local unions in the automotive industries initiated action on their own front. Late in the year, when General Motors refused to recognize and bargain with the United Automobile Workers, union members in Flint, Michigan, occupied their plants. The sit-down strike left the workers in possession of valuable machinery, while food was brought in by their families. Efforts by local authorities failed to dislodge the workers, and the newly elected Democratic governor, Frank Murphy, refused to enforce court orders to remove them by using the state militia. Meanwhile, orders for cars were mounting as the motor industry enjoyed a return to prosperity, and President Roosevelt kept a steady pressure on General Motors to

bargain with Lewis. As a result of both factors, a settlement was reached that established a pattern of collective bargaining with the UAW. During the prosperous spring of 1937 similar agreements were worked out with the other motor companies except Ford.

In April the Supreme Court, under pressure from the judicial "reform" bill in Congress, reversed its previous attitude and declared the Wagner Act constitutional. Even before this, the two major steel companies, also anxious to avoid a costly and perhaps useless strike, had signed agreements with the CIO. While Ford and the smaller steel companies violently resisted organization for some years more, by World War II they had all been forced into line by government action.

In spite of the sharp downswing of business

These men are engaging in a sit-down strike at the Fisher Body Plant in Michigan. General Motors and the UAW workers reached a peaceful settlement through collective bargaining.

and employment from mid-1937 to 1939, union strength continued to increase. Enthusiastic young organizers, government protection of the processes of organization and election, and compulsory bargaining were building a labor movement of unprecedented strength. In self-defense the AFL was forced to adopt the principle of industrial unionism and compete vigorously with the CIO. In 1940 there were nearly 9 million organized workers: over 4 million in the AFL, 3.5 million in the CIO, and 1 million in independent unions. Although substantially less than the 28 percent organized in Great Britain, the 30 percent in France, and the 50 percent in Australia and Denmark, the total of nonagricultural unionized employees was at a peak for the United States.

Women in the Depression. In most of its unions the AFL would not accept women members, but the new CIO would. Therefore, division in the ranks of labor worked in favor of women's rights. The fact that women worked for lower wages than men also kept a few more of them at their jobs in the worst years of the depression. But with partial recovery the situation returned to about that of 1930. Viewing the record of the 1930s as a whole, William Henry Chafe, a historian of the women's movement in these decades, says: "The advent of Depression provided the final blow to feminist hopes for economic equality."

The inevitable effect of hard times was to move feminist activity from direct efforts to compete more equally with men in the job

But a strike by the CIO against Republic Steel in South Chicago was brutally fought by management and police. Ten people were killed and scores injured in this bloody battle in 1937.

market, which could scarcely succeed in the face of high unemployment, to national legislative reforms. Eleanor Roosevelt took her place as leader in this movement. She encouraged Mary Dewson, head of a Women's Division of the Democratic party, to work hard for FDR and his reform legislation.

In spite of making Frances Perkins Secretary of Labor, it seems doubtful that FDR personally was a strong advocate of women's rights. His pressure on the Supreme Court seems partly responsible for a decision in 1936 upholding state minimum wage laws for women, and one in 1941 validating the equal pay provisions of the Fair Labor Standards Act of 1938. Yet even by 1940, in many states women had not become the legal equals of men. Twenty states still prohibited women from serving on juries, 16 denied a wife the right to make contracts, and 11 forbade a wife to retain earnings without her husband's consent. Thus women entered the war period with few realized gains from the previous decade, but with a potential in both the labor movement and the job market to make some lasting progress.

The Survival of the Indian.   By the mid-twenties it was obvious that government policy concerning the 325,000 Indians scattered across the nation had failed. The Dawes Act of 1887, providing for individual ownership of tribal land, had reduced tribal land acreage by some 60 percent through subsequent white fraud, high-pressure sales, and a variety of illegal schemes to steal more land from the Indians. Indians had been given the land individually, without the equipment to farm it, or schooling on how to use it for grazing, farming, or timber cutting. They were an impoverished people, but psychologically they may have been in still worse shape.

Indian health was a national disgrace. The plains Indians, for example, were forced to cease their nomadic way of life, yet were not taught to handle the sanitation problems of

sedentary living. Indians were made to depend on a government diet which was lacking in vitamin C, proteins, and roughage. Often if they were "unruly," even this food was withheld by local administrators. They were given a very few doctors and nurses when in fact they needed many more than the average white population. And the ones they got were quite often incompetent. Consequently Indians suffered from rampant diseases, high infant mortality, and rates of suicide and alcoholism much higher than those for the rest of the population. Nevertheless they responded to the army volunteer drive of World War I with enthusiasm, and were conspicuous for their bravery in battle. It is believed this war record sparked another reform drive in behalf of the Indians.

Reform was a complex problem. Generally speaking, legislators from states with many Indians fought against giving extra federal funds earmarked for their states to a largely nonvoting minority, who even if they did vote, did not have the numbers to elect anyone. The rest of Congress was generally lacking in knowledge about the variety of problems each of the 250 to 300 tribes faced.

The Bureau of Indian Affairs, run by the Executive branch of the government also had an extremely poor reputation among the Indians, because its policies, usually administered by patronage employees, changed with every new President. These administrators naturally knew and cared very little about Indian cultures. Boarding school education, promoted by the Bureau of Indian Affairs, alienated many children from their hereditary culture, while it equipped them for participation in white society which, in most states, did not want them.

To reformers such as John Collier and the American Indian Defense Association, the best hope for the future appeared to be in strengthening tribal organization and restoring communal land holding. Collier was influential in getting the Wheeler-Howard

Indian Reorganization Act through Congress in 1934. For those tribes who voted to accept it, the Act ended further individual allotments and restored all remaining lands to tribal ownership. More land was to be purchased by the government to resettle landless Indians. Tribes were to be set up as corporations, able to draw on a $10 million revolving fund for new economic enterprises. Each cooperating tribe was also to draw up and ratify a constitution that would restore government by tribal council.

Although education improved, the policies pursued by the Bureau over the next generation were, on the whole, unsuccessful. By congressional mandate, the Act was not applied in Oklahoma, where the "Five Civilized Tribes" lived and enjoyed some unevenly distributed wealth from oil. The Navajo tribe, suspicious of white benevolence—with good historic reasons—numbered about a quarter of all Indians and refused to join. Applying the Act to most of the remaining tribes, who were given over 7 million acres of poor land, led to no considerable gain in their prosperity. But it led to a great deal of trouble between the Indians, the paternalistic local agents, and the remote Bureau. In all, this well-intentioned policy came too late in the history of Indian-government relations to alter the results of decades of neglect and abuse in both policies and administration. By the mid-twentieth century, Indian grazing culture and white industrial society were so far apart that any assimilation could only be slow and difficult. Reconstitution of tribal society, on the other hand, was both artificial and—given the great differences among the Indian peoples—extremely difficult.

Black America. The depression decade was nearly spanned by a particularly well-publicized and flagrant denial of justice to nine young blacks accused early in 1931 of the rape of two white girls on a freight train in Alabama. Tried before an all-white jury in Scottsboro and defended by inadequate counsel, eight of the nine were sentenced to death even after the accusations had been proven false.

In 1932 and 1934 the United States Supreme Court ordered retrials. Even then, only four of the prisoners were released, and in 1938 the Supreme Court refused to order a further trial for three sentenced to life and one to death. (Of these remaining four, two were paroled in 1944 and one in 1951; the fourth escaped in 1948.) During the thirties, the case achieved worldwide notoriety—thanks in part to the action of the legal bureau of the Communist party. Yet the case had pointed out the kind of "justice" blacks often received.

President Roosevelt appointed white race-relations counselors in many government departments, and from 1932 on, as the urban black vote shifted dramatically from Republican to Democratic, Mary M. Bethune became Director of Negro Affairs in the National Youth Administration and Robert C. Weaver adviser to the Department of the Interior—the highest federal posts held by blacks since World War I. In *United States* v. *Classic* (1941) the Supreme Court made the state governments responsible for the conduct of party primaries and hence for the enforcement of constitutional rights in these contests, which were in fact the real elections in the solidly Democratic South. On the whole, however, the President was not prepared to battle Southern congressmen over enforcement of the rights of blacks, and New Deal housing policies actually increased segregation. But the successful struggle of the poor black—and of the impoverished and neglected Indian—to survive was continued as before with growing spiritual strength. As a result, that spirit won allies such as the President's remarkable wife Eleanor.

Toward the middle of the forties some progress was made toward equality of economic opportunity. The NAACP, directing its energy toward winning equal pay for black schoolteachers, had little immediate success. But in 1941 the federal district court for Virginia, at least, ordered equality in pay by 1943. The CIO in principle admitted blacks to all its unions, though in the South they were often put into separate locals and denied true job equality. The growth of the new labor movement brought black workers into the mass production industries and in a few cases to minor administrative positions in big white companies. Although still largely impoverished, blacks were making new efforts to improve their condition.

Return to Depression. Aided by increased federal spending for WPA, more state spending for public works, and payment of the remainder of the World War I soldier's bonus certificates (over the President's veto), 1936 and early 1937 were a period of returning prosperity. But at this point the lack of any clear economic policy by either the administration or most of its critics was disastrously illustrated. To suit the conservatives in Congress, whose votes were needed to pass the Supreme Court bill, the President promised a balanced budget for 1937–1938. His own fear of too strong a boom, even though 6 million were still unemployed, was shown when the Federal Reserve System took steps to tighten the money market.

As a result of this drastic reversal in federal policies, the sharpest business decline in American history began in July 1937 and reached bottom about mid-1938. Not until the beginning of 1940, when the European war and American rearmament had become important economic factors, was there a return to the business volume of 1937. The severity of the depression was about equal to that of late 1931. Unemployment rose above 10 million— a fifth of the labor force. Even with the return toward prosperity in 1940 over 8 million people were still looking for jobs.

New Policies. The renewal of the depression forced the government to institute new policies to promote recovery. Agricultural production had been sharply cut by a severe drought in 1934 which had created a "dust bowl" from Texas to the Dakotas. It had been checked again by a more moderate drought in 1936. In the latter year Congress had passed a soil-conservation act to check planting of soil-depleting crops and encourage planting of soil-restoring crops. As a result of these developments agricultural income, including government payments, stood up during the renewed depression better than did the income of some other sectors. But in 1938 the well-organized farmers won substantial new support in the Agricultural Adjustment Act.

Soil conservation was to be encouraged by payments to staple crop producers who agreed to acreage allotments. Marketing quotas could also be imposed by the vote of two thirds of the growers of a staple crop. And whenever actual prices fell below "parity prices"—government-determined prices intended to keep the farmer's purchasing power in relation to nonfarm commodities at the 1909–1919 level—farmers conforming to these regulations would be given "parity payments" if Congress appropriated the money.

Crop loans were also available to all farmers of crops with marketing quotas, but those who did not accept the quota could borrow only 60 percent as much as could the cooperators. In spite of many loopholes and much subsequent criticism, this law remained the basic plan of agricultural support.

Wage and hour guarantees attempted in the NIRA were now incorporated in a Fair Labor Standards Act. The labor of children under sixteen was prohibited, the minimum wage was set at twenty-five cents an hour, and overtime was to be paid beyond forty-four hours a week. The Housing Act of 1937, now in operation, began the great task of slum clearance. With increases in other parts of the

Severe drought turned the central part of the country into a vast dust bowl. Here a farmer and his two sons walk into the face of a dust storm in Oklahoma in 1936.

federal budget, including public works and defense, federal expenditures in 1939, more than 25 percent above 1938, were the highest of any peacetime year in previous American history.

Failure of the New Deal. While the New Deal had greatly improved stability and security in the national economy, it had not brought satisfactory recovery. For the first time the gross national product per capita had failed to achieve a level higher than in the previous decade. What had been wrong? Several different answers were possible, depending upon different economic theories.

It was possible, first of all, to emphasize the fact that from beginning to end President Roosevelt, either from conviction or for political expediency, held down spending and tried to balance the budget. Prior to the renewed depression of 1938, only 1934 and 1936 showed substantial increases in govern-

ment spending in relation to receipts, and in both cases the level of spending dropped the following year. Put another way, the administration failed to make a clean break with the idea of the self-regulating economy and failed to develop a philosophy of where and how to spend. Yet while failing to spend at the level necessary to promote expansion, the government did not announce policies that encouraged expansion through investment by business.

Another line of reasoning pointed to the failure of NIRA and other legislation to redistribute income enough to create sharply increased consumer demand. Still another was that by chance too few technological innovations had been occurring that would offer profits in return for large capital investment.

Whatever approach one took, the disturbing question remained: How could a healthy economy be assured in time of peace?

Chapter 21

Foreign Policy and World War II

THE ROAD TO WAR

Breakdown of the Security System. Despite prevailing isolationist sentiment, the United States in the 1920s was part of a system of international security which rested on the Washington Treaties of 1922 governing Far Eastern relations; on the structure of international debt and reparations payments worked out in the Dawes and Young Plans; and on the ability of the League of Nations—or its leading members, England and France—to police the settlement of Versailles. Between 1931 and 1935 this entire security structure was demolished, leaving the world perennially on the verge of war.

Partly because Russia had not been invited to take part in the Washington Conference, the treaties of 1922 did not bring peace to China. During the next decade Russia and China first combined to reunify China by defeating local warlords and then fought each other in an undeclared war. When peace was restored with Russia, the Chinese Nationalist leader Chiang Kai-shek tried to assert his power in southern Manchuria, long a Japanese sphere of influence. This gave the strongly imperialist Japanese army the excuse to overthrow the liberal ministry in Tokyo and to wage a war for complete control of Manchuria. The League of Nations, as well as individual countries like Britain and the United States, condemned the Japanese aggression, but Japan ignored the protests, completed its conquest of Manchuria, and in 1933 withdrew from the League. This demonstration that a great power could embark on aggression without meeting effective opposition from the strong members marked the beginning of the disintegration of the League.

International debt and reparation payments depended upon continuing loans from the United States. With the collapse of the Wall Street security market it was only a question of time before payments would end. President Hoover's moratorium in 1931 temporarily eased the debt burden on European nations, but neither the Hoover nor the Roosevelt administration was ready to profit from the inevitable by canceling the war debts. After 1934 only Finland continued to pay. Another part of the World War I settlement had come to an end.

A single man, Adolf Hitler, however, must

bear responsibility for the end of world peace. By 1933 a German democracy weakened by internal conflicts between conservatives, liberals, Socialists, and Communists invited the rise of a man who could impose order and bring back prosperity. Supported by much of labor, by patriots who wanted to undo the hated Versailles Treaty, by the military, and by some businessmen, Hitler won control of the government and became a dictator. Although his aim, set forth in a book, *Mein Kampf,* was to gain control of Europe by war, British and French leaders chose to regard his statements as mere political slogans. Even by 1938, when he had already annexed unresisting neighboring territories and commenced his deadly Jewish pogroms, the conservative leaders of Western Europe valued him as a defense against communism, while President Roosevelt took no decisive action.

Meanwhile, Italy followed Japan's lead in aggressive expansion. In October 1935, the Italian fascist dictator Mussolini launched a wholesale invasion of the African kingdom of Ethiopia. President Roosevelt declared an arms embargo, and the League of Nations, under British pressure, condemned Italy as an aggressor and imposed economic sanctions. But because Britain and France were afraid of driving Germany and Italy into an alliance, the embargo did not include coal and oil. Furthermore, the League had little machinery for enforcing economic sanctions, and nonmembers like Germany and the United States largely ignored the prohibitions. As a result, the conquest of Ethiopia was quickly completed, and the authority of the League was totally undermined.

The conflict over Ethiopia gave Hitler his first big opportunity to use the military force he had been building up in defiance of the Versailles Treaty. In March 1936 Nazi troops marched into the Rhineland, which had been demilitarized by the Versailles Treaty. France mobilized 150,000 troops, but Britain refused to support the use of force to compel German withdrawal. Another World War I agreement had been smashed.

Why had the major military and naval powers of the world failed to enforce the peace? In the first place, Russia, the nation most feared in the long run by Great Britain, was not a party to the Western agreements. (The Soviet Union was not even recognized by the United States until 1933.) The fact that Hitler was a professed enemy of Russia made it difficult for British governments, particularly the Conservative ones, to decide where the ultimate national interest lay. Yet even if the British decided to let Hitler gain strength, they did not want him too strong, and this weakened them in dealing with Italy. Another factor faced by both Britain and the United States was the strength of pacifist and neutralist movements in their own countries. A government embarking on vigorous policies that risked war might find itself lacking in the necessary legislative support. In France many conservatives in the army and the government feared communism much more than they feared Hitler's fascism.

Isolation and Neutrality.   The breakdown of the world order led the United States both to strict isolationist legislation and to an effort to weld the Western Hemisphere into a self-sufficient defense system. The latter presented many difficulties. Aside from Canada, the nations of the Western Hemisphere were further removed from the United States by tradition and national culture than were the nations of northern Europe. The capitals of the three largest South American powers— Argentina, Brazil, and Chile—were also farther removed geographically. Economically as well, the United States had more ties with Europe, and so did each of the major South American nations.

President Roosevelt's inaugural address in

1933 dedicated the United States to "the policy of the good neighbor"—nonaggression, non-intervention, and friendly cooperation to solve mutual problems in the Western Hemisphere. At the seventh Pan-American Conference meeting at Montevideo later the same year, the United States subscribed to a nonintervention pact adopted unanimously by the conference. But the attitude of the United States toward social democratic governments in the Caribbean area remained ambiguous. In the same year that the new pact was adopted, Washington withheld recognition of a liberal government in Cuba which was opposed by the island's landed and business interests, and American warships surrounded the island. These actions, engineered by conservative State Department officials rather than by President Roosevelt, led eventually to the overthrow of the liberal government by the military dictator Fulgencio Batista.

The President's long-range policy was reaffirmed the next year by abrogation of the Platt Amendment authorizing intervention in Cuba and by withdrawal of marines from Haiti. In 1936 the United States ratified a treaty restoring sovereign powers to Panama. Reciprocal trade agreements negotiated with six Latin American nations strengthened economic ties. While the bonds between "good neighbors" five thousand miles apart remained somewhat tenuous, the Roosevelt administration policy marked a great improvement over inter-American relations of the previous thirty years.

Though Americans in the mid-thirties were fully cognizant of the onrush of fascism in Europe, most of them were confident that the United States could remain a neutral bystander in the impending conflict. As Europe's crises deepened, determination mounted in the United States to "sit this one out." The hastily improvised Neutrality Act of 1935, reluctantly signed by Roosevelt, prohibited the export of arms or ammunition to belligerents and required the President to forbid American citizens to travel on the ships of belligerents except at their own risk. A "permanent" Neutrality Act in 1937 retained the earlier restrictions on loans and munitions in time of war and declared travel on belligerent vessels unlawful for American citizens. In addition, it provided that for a period of two years belligerent nations could purchase goods, other than munitions, from the United States only on a "cash-and-carry" basis. During the Spanish Civil War of 1936–1939, in which Germany, Italy, and the Soviet Union all took a hand, the United States remained resolutely neutral.

Rise of the Axis. In 1936 the last safeguards of the World War I diplomatic structure were finally swept away. In October and November Germany, Italy, and Japan entered into an anticommunist pact. These powers, having built new mechanized armies, were now too powerful for England and France to attack. Helped by German military engineers and scientists, Hitler had worked a diplomatic revolution that made defeated and penalized Germany the strongest nation in Europe.

Why had this happened? Causes may be traced far back, but three were abundantly clear in 1936: (1) Mutual distrust between England and France on one side and Russia on the other prevented revival of the old World War I alliance against the central powers; (2) the United States could not be relied upon for active support; and (3) England and France had not kept up with military development. To make their plight worse, England and France guaranteed the independence of Czechoslovakia and, in 1939, of Poland, which they could not possibly defend against Germany. Faced with the choice of arming for possible war or muddling along in the hope that some change would occur in the German situation, the conservative leaders of the Western powers chose the latter course.

Large-scale Japanese inroads in northern

China led President Roosevelt in a speech of October 1937 to test American sentiment by advocating a "quarantine" of aggressor nations. He quickly found that Congress was two to one against cooperation with the League of Nations in bringing effective sanctions against Japan. Underlying much of this isolationist attitude was an implicit confidence that England and France were still capable of controlling the situation. From 1938 on, however, as Germany continued to build up its mechanized army, the European situation was beyond the control of England and France. Hitler was ready to embark on a daring program of expansion, and his territorial demands were to prove limitless.

Hitler's first victim was his neighbor Austria, which Germany invaded and annexed in March 1938. After the Austrian coup, Hitler moved on to his next objective—the annexation of the Sudetenland, a German-speaking portion of Czechoslovakia. Hitler bluntly informed English Prime Minister Neville Chamberlain that he was determined to secure self-determination for the Sudeten Germans. Chamberlain in turn persuaded Édouard Daladier, the French premier, that a sacrifice on the part of Czechoslovakia would save the peace. In September 1938 Hitler, Mussolini, Daladier, and Chamberlain met in Munich and worked out the details of the surrender of the Sudentenland in return for Hitler's promise that he had no further territorial ambitions.

The Sudetenland "becomes German" as Hitler's troops march into northern Czechoslovakia in 1938.

While the Munich Pact gave Britain precious time to build up its air force, British and French hopes that the agreement would appease Hitler's expansionistic cravings were shattered when in March 1939 the German army invaded and seized the remainder of the Czech nation. Mussolini seized Albania the following month, and the two dictators celebrated by signing a military alliance, the "Pact of Steel."

The shock of Hitler's callous violation of the solemn pledge made at Munich ended the appeasement policy of France and Great Britain. Britain launched a tremendous arms program, and in Paris Daladier obtained special emergency powers to push forward national defense.

It was Germany's aggression against Poland, however, that finally precipitated the Second World War. During the summer of 1939 Hitler had made increasingly insistent territorial demands upon Poland while Chamberlain, with the French government concurring, had warned the Nazi government that "in the event of any action which clearly threatened Polish independence" the British would "at once lend the Polish government all support in their power."

As German threats against Poland increased, Britain and France sought an alliance with the Soviet Union but refused to assent to its reannexation of the Baltic states. Meanwhile, the Nazi and Soviet foreign secretaries were secretly working out an agreement of their own. On August 23, 1939, Russia and Germany signed a nonaggression pact. Russia reasoned that a conflict in Western Europe would give the Soviet Union time to build up its armaments. The Soviet Union also secured German recognition of Soviet claims in eastern Poland and the Baltic states.

Now Hitler could attack Poland without fear of intervention by his great rival to the east. Without a declaration of war, Nazi troops crossed the Polish frontier on the morning of September 1, 1939, and the

Luftwaffe began to bomb Polish cities. Hitler hoped that the appeasing governments of France and Great Britain would wring their hands and do nothing, but he had miscalculated. The two Western democracies, knowing that their own time would come sooner or later, declared war on Germany on September 3. The Second World War had begun.

THE AMERICAN QUANDARY

The "Phony" War. War in Europe split American political opinion along new lines. Many liberals opposed defense spending because it would cut down on welfare appropriations. Conservatives who had vigorously opposed domestic spending were, in many cases, willing to support larger military appropriations. Public sentiment, disgusted by Europe's inability to keep the peace, was strongly against anything that would involve the United States in war.

From the start the President favored rearmament and aid to France and England. His political problem was to swing public and congressional opinion behind him. Plans for defense mobilization were drawn up but not acted upon. After the Munich Pact a White House Planning Conference led to a bill in 1939 appropriating a half billion dollars for defense. When polls early in 1940 showed public opinion 60 percent in favor of aid to England and France, the President secured a revised Neutrality Act that lifted the arms embargo for nations paying cash but still prohibited American ships from trading with belligerents and American citizens from traveling on belligerent vessels.

After the rapid conquest of Poland, Germany remained virtually inactive during the winter of 1939–1940. This "Phony War" ended abruptly on April 9, 1940, when Germany simultaneously invaded Denmark and Norway. A month later Nazi armies invaded Belgium, France, and Holland, and in six weeks all had surrendered. After the fall of

In this painting of the evacuation of Dunkirk, France, the artist depicts the enormous scale of the operation. The British suffered many casualties, but managed to rescue 300,000 troops.

France, the British rescued over 300,000 of their troops from the beach at Dunkirk, but they had to abandon practically all their equipment. The army returned to an island without land defense against armored columns. On June 10, when the defeat of France was certain, Italy came into the war on the side of Germany.

A Year of Decision.   What should American policy be now that Hitler with his ally, Italy, controlled western Europe, and military men regarded the conquest of England as likely? The joint planners of the War and Navy Departments thought that the United States should husband its resources at home to prepare for attack. Isolationists, including many leading citizens and scholars, opposed any action that went beyond defense preparations. The President was for as much aid to Britain as he could arrange without being overridden by the antiwar majority in Congress.

The President's decision to take a chance on British survival through all-out U.S. aid was probably the most fateful one of the entire period. He could have pursued a more isolationist policy without alienating his political support. The policy he elected to pursue led almost inevitably to war. In the decisions of both Roosevelt and Wilson the overriding fact appears to have been an unwillingness to permit a Europe in which a militaristic Germany was the dominant power.

In a contest over policy involving military action the President has a great advantage over Congress. He can act and seek support later, whereas Congress, as a nonadministrative body, is always behind a rapid march of events. This is in effect what happened from June 1940 on. The President went ahead administratively to give England as much aid as possible. In so doing, he educated the public toward his point of view, and Congress was usually presented with actions already taken that would be hard to reverse.

In June, for example, Congress thought to restrict the President by passing a law forbidding him to give away military equipment unless the Army Chief of Staff and the Chief of Naval Operations certified it as not essential to the national defense. But on September 2 an executive agreement was signed with England transferring fifty overage American destroyers in return for British bases in Newfoundland, Bermuda, and the Caribbean. Since the bases increased American security, this action was obviously not a violation of the law, yet it tied the United States to the defense of the British Empire and marked the end of any pretext of neutrality. Germany did not declare war at this time because it did not want the United States in the war. But later in the same month Germany, Italy, and Japan formed a military alliance obviously aimed at the United States.

These critical strokes of foreign policy took place during the presidential campaign of 1940. Four days before the Republican convention met in June, the President appointed Republican leaders Henry L. Stimson and Frank Knox to his cabinet as Secretaries of War and of the Navy. Two days before the convention France surrendered. The general confusion favored the internationalists. As none of the leading Republican contenders developed decisive strength, Wendell L. Willkie, a businessman who sympathized with Roosevelt's foreign policy, was skillfully maneuvered to victory. As in 1936, the Republicans had gone far away from the principles of their center and right wing to attract marginal Democratic votes.

The national emergency led the President to seek a third term. Through the manipulations of Harry Hopkins, representing the President, the Democratic bosses were reluctantly forced to accept Henry A. Wallace, the very liberal Secretary of Agriculture, for the vice-presidency.

During the campaign both those favoring all-out aid to Britain and those opposed to risks that might lead to war were nationally organized. The journalist William Allen White of Kansas headed a Committee to Defend America by Aiding the Allies, and business leader Robert E. Wood of Illinois was chairman of the isolationist America First Committee. The effect of the controversy on the campaign was not immediately clear, since both candidates were internationalists.

But by October, as Great Britain withstood Germany's bombing attacks and was not invaded, the argument that aid to Britain was more important than keeping out of war lost its immediate urgency. When public opinion pollsters found that the number of those favoring foreign aid had declined to less than half the voters, Willkie shifted his ground. Having failed to gain support on the issues of the third term and mismanaged defense, Willkie now attacked Roosevelt as a warmonger. Alarmed by the apparent success of the Willkie strategy, the President was pushed further and further away from his true beliefs. Just before election he told his listeners: "I have said this before, but I shall say it again and again and again: Your boys are not going to be sent into any foreign wars." In his mind, conflict resulting from an attack on the United States would not be a "foreign" war.

The Democratic vote was slightly below that of 1936 and the Republican 5.5 million larger, but Willkie won only 82 electoral votes to

Roosevelt's 449. The total minor party vote fell below 200,000. It was hard to call the result a referendum on any policy, since there had been no substantial disagreement. But it could be read as a vote of confidence in Roosevelt personally, or, as Republicans saw it, as proof of the strength of habitual patterns of voting and the Democratic political machine. To the President, it was support for more vigorous foreign aid and military preparation.

Characteristically, the President had put political and foreign problems ahead of domestic ones. By August Congress had appropriated some $16 billion for defense— enough, if it could be used, to move toward a war footing. The following month Congress agreed on a bipartisan basis to a selective service (draft) act. But meanwhile the economic organization essential for defense faltered. Production, the President felt, could be called into existence later when needed.

This was, of course, far from true. Coordination of production was in the hands of a nearly powerless National Defense Advisory Commission. In the words of Donald Nelson, its coordinator for procurement, the commission "began to stagger in the late summer and early autumn of 1940. In November it was punch drunk. It did not fall flat on its face until five days before Christmas." Its successor, the Office of Production Management, had little more success.

The basic difficulty was that private industry did not want to be regimented in time of peace, and, for fear of strengthening the isolationists, the President was reluctant to ask Congress for the necessary power. Fortunately, however, the United States had great capacity for manufacturing the automotive and other steel equipment needed for this war. Incentives such as quick tax write-offs and long-term contracts stimulated big business to undertake much of the new construction that had to precede mass production of military equipment.

Lend-Lease. By December 1940 the opinion polls indicated that around 60 percent of the American people were in favor of helping Great Britain even at the risk of war. Thus, when Churchill told Roosevelt that British credit for the purchase of war supplies was nearing exhaustion, Roosevelt believed he had popular support for extending more liberal, outright aid. A bill was quickly drawn up and introduced in Congress calling for "munitions of war and supplies of many kinds to be turned over to those nations which are now in actual war with aggressor nations," to be paid back in goods and services at the end of the war. Though opposed by Republican leaders, the bill had the compulsion of the situation behind it. On March 11 "Lend-Lease" became law, and the next day the President asked Congress for an initial $7 billion to implement the policy.

The United States had already broken the laws of neutrality beyond repair by aiding only one side and keeping the vessels of the other out of the western Atlantic. Lend-Lease marked the point of no return on the road to war. The bill committed American industrial power, nearly equal to that of all the rest of the world, to the defeat of Germany.

Roosevelt's Dilemma. The Lend-Lease Act of March 1941 was only the first step that President Roosevelt was prepared to take in a broader effort to help Britain resist German aggression. Although he probably overestimated the strength of the vocal isolationist minority, he estimated correctly the great reluctance of most Americans to become directly involved in a war. As a result, in his pursuit of what he thought was the defense of American interests, he was not always open and candid. Sometimes he acted secretly, as he did in late April 1941, when he ordered a naval patrol of the North Atlantic to help the British detect German submarines. Other times he acted as boldly as he thought the majority of the people would permit, as in July 1941, when American troops were ordered to Iceland to relieve the British in protecting it from German invasion.

When Hitler, in a surprise move, invaded the Soviet Union on June 22, 1941, Roosevelt followed Churchill in welcoming a new fighting force in the war against Germany, even though few military advisers believed the Russians could hold out more than three months against the German blitz. Acutely aware of the weakness of British and Russian defenses, Roosevelt, in early July, asked Congress for an extension of the draft law and repeal of the prohibition on overseas service for draftees. Isolationists branded the request as yet another of the President's covert efforts to get the United States into war, but after acrimonious debate the draft extension passed by a single vote in the House of Representatives.

On August 9–12 Roosevelt and Prime Minister Churchill met secretly on the U.S.S. *Augusta* in Placentia Bay, Newfoundland. The result was the Atlantic Charter, setting forth the aims of the war: No territorial changes would be made in favor of the victors, and all nations would be protected in their right to choose their own governments, without fear of aggressive threats. When announced on August 15, this meeting between a technically neutral country and an active belligerent brought loud protests from isolationists in the United States. Nevertheless, upon his return home Roosevelt asked for increased appropriations for aid to Britain and the Soviet Union.

Undeclared War. When in September a German U-boat attacked the American destroyer *Greer*, which, unbeknown to the American public, was sending the British navy information about German submarines, Roosevelt seized the opportunity to issue a "shoot-on-sight" order to the navy and asked Congress for authority to arm American merchant ships. With American naval vessels shooting without even waiting to be attacked, it was only a matter of time before a serious incident would occur. On October 17 the American destroyer *Kearny* was torpedoed and damaged off Iceland, and eleven Americans were killed. Less than three weeks later the *Reuben James* was sunk by a German U-boat with the loss of 115 lives. Yet most Americans seemed to support the President's policy, and in early November Congress authorized Roosevelt to arm merchant vessels and permit their entry into the war zone. Although the fight in Congress had been bitter, the House victory was 212 to 94, far greater than the single-vote margin of the previous summer.

By the end of November 1941 Hitler's armies were deep inside the Soviet Union, seemingly on their way to an early victory, and Japan was obviously readying itself for an offensive against the British and Dutch colonies in Southeast Asia. The President's dilemma was acute. He could not dispel the nagging fear that Russia and Britain, despite American aid, might yet be overwhelmed by the Germans—an event which would leave the United States alone to face Germany. At the same time, he knew that Americans were so divided over the struggle in Europe that he dare not try to lead them immediately into full-scale war against Hitler.

THE END OF HESITATION

Japanese-American Relations, 1940–1941. Ever since the early 1930s, Japanese expansionism on the Asian mainland had met gradual but increasing American opposition. Finally in 1939 the United States began to restrict the flow to Japan of some strategic war materials, like oil and scrap iron. But Roosevelt would not embargo all war materials, as some of his advisers urged. He believed some measures were necessary to warn Japan of American opposition to aggression, but he feared that too strong a stand would push the Japanese into an adventure against the oil-rich and defenseless Dutch East Indies. The Japanese response was to move into northern Indochina in the summer of 1940 and to join the Tripartite Pact with Germany and Italy in September 1940.

By early 1941 the Japanese and American positions in Asia were irreconcilable. Japan's minimum demand was that the United States cease its aid to Chiang Kai-shek, while the United States insisted that Japan end its war against China. During 1941 diplomatic efforts aimed at softening the two positions proved to be in vain. Japanese militarists believed that war was the only answer to America's interference with Japanese ambitions in Asia, and the military's hand was strengthened in April 1941, when the Soviet Union promised to remain neutral in the event of a Japanese-American war. Japan's fear of a two-front war was thus reduced, while Hitler's earlier promise to support Japan in a war against the United States made it clear that the United States would be the one forced to fight on two fronts.

Japanese ambitions became clearer and more alarming in July, when Japanese military units invaded southern Indochina in obvious preparation for an attack upon the Dutch East Indies. In retaliation the United States, Britain, and the Netherlands cut off all vital military supplies to Japan.

On September 6, 1941, Japan's Supreme War Council voted for war if American aid to China did not cease within six weeks. President Roosevelt refused to meet with the liberal Japanese Prime Minister, and before the six weeks elapsed the militant General Hideki Tojo became premier. Though now convinced that war was inevitable, Tojo sent a personal representative, Saburo Kurusu, to Washington in early November for further fruitless talks with the Americans. By the end of the month Americans knew, from their breaking of the Japanese codes, that war was

coming, but they did not know where in the Pacific it would start.

On November 24 American naval authorities sent out warnings of war with Japan to commanders at Pearl Harbor and Manila. On November 27 these bases were warned again, this time that "an aggressive move by Japan is expected within the next few days." On December 1 the emperor gave his consent to war. Already a Japanese task force was steaming across the northern Pacific for a surprise attack on Pearl Harbor. In Washington, the two Japanese envoys, Kurusu and Ambassador Nomura, continued their inconclusive talks with Secretary of State Cordell Hull.

Pearl Harbor. The time was 7:50 on Sunday morning, December 7, 1941. In the sky over Oahu island, Captain Nakaya of the Japanese navy wrote in his log:

Pearl Harbor is still asleep in the morning mist. The orderly groups of barracks, the wriggling white line of the automobile road climbing up to the mountaintop; fine objectives in all directions. . . Inside the harbor were important ships of the Pacific fleet, strung out and anchored two ships side by side in an orderly manner.

Ten minutes later the first wave of Japanese planes struck the great American base. The surprise was complete. Some American sailors thought the first bombs were accidentally dropped from American planes. Although the Americans fought back fiercely, the losses sustained were enormous: All eight battleships, the main object of the attack, were put out of action. Two never saw action again. Except for three aircraft carriers, which happened to be at sea, the whole Pacific fleet was damaged or destroyed. Almost all the aircraft, most of which did not even get off the ground, were knocked out. More than 2400 Americans were killed and 1200 wounded. The Japanese lost twenty-nine airplanes, five midget submarines, and one fleet submarine. Consider-

The USS Arizona sinks in flames after the Japanese attack on Pearl Harbor. Hundreds of men sleeping below decks went down with the ship.

ing the extensive damage, the attack on Pearl Harbor was one of the cheapest victories in the history of warfare.

Despite the devastating success of the raid, the decision to attack Pearl Harbor was a colossal blunder. For some time Roosevelt had feared that if the Japanese attacked British and Dutch possessions in Asia without involving the United States, it would be impossible to unify America behind a war to halt their aggression. After December 7, however, Americans were united in their opposition.

The strike against Pearl Harbor was only one part of an audacious grand plan to destroy British, Dutch, and American power in the western Pacific. Soon after the bombing of Pearl Harbor, Japanese planes attacked the Philippines. Though this time there had been specific warning, the Americans because of bureaucratic tie-ups were again caught unready. On December 8 the Japanese attacked Hong Kong, Borneo, the Malay Peninsula, and the American island outpost of Guam.

The boldness and power of the Japanese advance were brought home on December 10, when Japanese land-based bombers sank the British battleship *Prince of Wales* and the battle cruiser *Repulse* off the coast of Malaya. Never before had air power destroyed a free-moving battleship; the age of the airplane in naval warfare had arrived. Successful amphibious landings in the Philippines and elsewhere also attested to the Japanese' command of the most advanced methods of offensive warfare.

The day after the attack on Pearl Harbor, Congress, at the President's request, voted for war with Japan with only one dissenting vote. On December 11, Hitler fulfilled his promise to the Japanese by declaring war on the United States. Italy followed soon thereafter. The dilemma was resolved. The United States was now in a position to use to the fullest its great power against aggressor nations in both Asia and Europe.

After the initial shock had passed, many Americans grew suspicious that the astonishing success of the Japanese assault must have resulted from traitorous acts, but exhaustive investigations on the part of both the navy and Congress produced no evidence to support such allegations. The fact is that most military experts seriously underestimated Japan's ability to mount the kind of elaborate, multi-pronged assault of which Pearl Harbor was but a part. The commanders at Pearl Harbor were lax in taking precautions after the war warnings of November, but these defects add up to nothing more sinister than inefficiency and carelessness.

WAR IN TWO HEMISPHERES

Creation of the Grand Alliance. Within two weeks after Pearl Harbor Winston Churchill and his chief military advisers arrived in Washington for extended discussions with the President and American military leaders about the long-range strategy of the two-front war in which both countries were now engaged. The basic decision of the conference, as General Marshall later reported, was that "Germany is still the prime enemy and her defeat is the key to victory. Once Germany is defeated the collapse of Italy and the defeat of Japan must follow." Roosevelt, despite pressure to do otherwise, never deviated from this decision, even though Japan appeared to be the greater immediate menace to the United States. The two allies also agreed to pool their resources and military equipment for the duration of the struggle.

Finally, the conference created a Combined Chiefs of Staff in Washington to plan and coordinate global strategy. As a public manifestation of the new association, Churchill, Roosevelt, Maxim Litvinov (representing Stalin), and the representatives of twenty-three other nations at war with one or more Axis powers signed the Declaration of the United Nations on New Year's Day, 1942.

As the arsenal of the alliance, the United States in subsequent months worked out new Lend-Lease agreements with the principal allies. According to these agreements, the costs of the war were to be borne in proportion to ability to pay. By the end of the war in 1945, the United States had contributed over $50 billion in Lend-Lease, the bulk of which went to Great Britain. In return, the Allies provided $8 billion in goods or services to the United States.

Holding the Line. The first months of 1942 were filled with one Japanese success after another. (As a gesture of defiance, the United States dispatched General James Doolittle to lead a small, carrier-borne air strike against Tokyo in April, but its military value was nil.) In a matter of months the Japanese overran all of Southeast Asia. In February they took the great British naval base of Singapore and in March, Java, the main island of the Dutch East Indies. Another Japanese army, meanwhile, had overrun Siam and Burma and now stood poised on the borders of India.

By the end of March the Japanese controlled the western half of the Pacific from the Kuriles in the North to the Solomons in the South as well as the islands and mainland of Southeast Asia from Indochina to India. In the Philippines all American resistance ceased on May 6.

The Japanese had to hold off the United States until they could develop Netherland Indies iron and oil. Not knowing that Americans had broken their naval code the Japanese made the fatal error of trying to expand their defensive perimeter. But in May of 1942 the naval-air Battle of the Coral Sea halted their southward advance, and the following month an American victory over a large Japanese naval task force off Midway Island ended the eastward thrust. Japanese losses at the Battle of Midway were so critical that thereafter the imperial navy was on the defensive. This was thus the decisive victory of the war in the Pacific Ocean.

The third effort to contain the Japanese advance comprised a series of combined land and sea operations on and around the little-known, jungle-covered island of Guadalcanal in the Solomons. The first precarious American landing on Guadalcanal took place on August 7, 1942, but it was not until the fifth major sea and air encounter on November 13–14, 1942, that the southern Solomons rested securely in American hands. Not being able to achieve secure defenses, Japan was bound to lose from lack of supplies.

Unlike the war in the Pacific, the first year of war in Europe brought almost uninterrupted setbacks for the Allies on both land and sea. That spring and summer German submarines sank Allied tankers and merchantmen before the eyes of civilians on the shores of New Jersey and Florida. By the middle of 1942 shipping losses reached a new peak of 4.5 million tons, or more than in all of 1941. Yet in the same six months only twenty-one U-boats were sunk. At the conclusion of eleven months of war and after a furious program of shipbuilding, Allied tonnage was still less than it had been on the day Pearl Harbor was bombed. Although losses were gradually reduced, the submarine menace hung over Allied preparations for counteraction until the middle of 1943. Meanwhile, the Germans had advanced into mid-Russia.

The Turning Point.   Near the end of 1942, Allied forces around the globe assumed the offensive, which they never lost thereafter. November witnessed the victory on Guadalcanal. At about the same time the Russians, after a heroic defense of Stalingrad on the

Volga, seized the offensive against the Germans. On November 8, American forces commanded by General Dwight D. Eisenhower invaded the French colonies of Morocco and Algeria with surprise landings from a giant armada of 500 warships and 350 transports and cargo ships. The German-controlled Vichy French offered only scattered resistance, and total Allied casualties amounted to fewer than 2000. Most important of all, the Germans faltered from lack of supplies at Stalingrad and by 1943 were in retreat.

The Germans, before Eisenhower's landing, had gained control of the North African coast as far east as Egypt. The immediate purpose of the North African landings was to catch the German armies, under General Erwin Rommel, in a giant squeeze. Only a week before, General Bernard L. Montgomery's British Eighth Army had begun an offensive at El Alamein in Egypt. As Rommel's forces retreated westward before Montgomery along the North African coast in December and January, they backed up against the now well-established American forces in Algeria and Tunisia. By the early spring of 1943 Rommel's once invincible Afrika Korps was no more. German losses in Africa reached 350,000.

With all of North Africa in Allied hands, the next target was Sicily, and by the time the Sicilian campaign was concluded at the end of August 1943, Italy was out of the war. A new Italian government joined the Allies in the war against Germany, but the Nazi forces quickly disarmed the Italians, thereby nullifying the diplomatic coup. Despite three amphibious invasions of the Italian peninsula, stubborn German resistance and the Italian mountains kept the Allies fighting in Italy until May 2, 1945.

Setting the Goals of War.   In January 1943, soon after the consolidation of the Allied landings in North Africa, Roosevelt and Churchill met in the Moroccan city of Casablanca to discuss war aims. It was at this meeting that Roosevelt, after consulting with Churchill, announced that only unconditional surrender of Germany and Italy would be acceptable to the Allies. Later critics would argue that such uncompromising terms stiffened German resistance and prolonged the war. Certainly the Nazi propaganda machine played upon the argument that victory for the Allies spelled annihilation for the Germans. But at the time Roosevelt was careful to say that unconditional surrender "does not mean the destruction of the population of Germany, Italy, and Japan, but it does mean the destruction of the philosophies of those countries which are based on conquest and the subjugation of other people." Actually, it appears doubtful that the statement influenced German resistance very much. Certainly it produced exactly the opposite effect upon the Italians, who surrendered with alacrity nine months later.

Late 1943 saw several meetings of the Big Three powers. At the end of October the foreign ministers of the United States, Great Britain, and the Soviet Union met for the first time in Moscow. There it was agreed that the three nations would consult on "all matters relating to the surrender and disarmament" of their common enemies. They also recognized a need for setting "the earliest possible date" for the planning of an international organization of the "peace-loving states." Victory, in short, was already being anticipated.

En route to a meeting with Stalin in Teheran, Iran, Churchill and Roosevelt stopped at Cairo on November 22–26, 1943, to confer with the Nationalist Chinese leader Chiang Kai-shek. The three allies agreed to prosecute the Pacific war until Japan was forced into unconditional surrender. They also agreed that Manchuria, Formosa, and the Pescadore Islands, earlier seized by Japan, should be returned to China after the war.

The Teheran Conference of November 28–December 1, 1943—the first personal en-counter between Stalin, Churchill, and Roosevelt—resulted in no new decisions, although Roosevelt did secure from Stalin, as Hull had from Molotov a month earlier, a promise of Russian help against Japan soon after the end of the war against Germany. Convinced of the need to have Stalin's friendship in the postwar world, Roosevelt did his best to charm the dictator and to dissipate Stalin's obvious suspicion of the two English-speaking allies.

SUPPORT AT HOME

The Battle for Production.   In a very real sense the turning of the tide of war from constant defeat to persistent victory was attributable to the astounding production which flooded from American factories and farms. At Teheran even Stalin acknowledged that without American production the Allies would not be winning the war.

Conversion of the economy to full wartime production did not really begin until after Pearl Harbor. During 1940 and 1941 Roosevelt had created several agencies, headed by businessmen and labor leaders, to speed up and coordinate production. But when the Japanese struck, the level was still far from satisfactory. In January 1942 Roosevelt set up the War Production Board with Donald M. Nelson as chief, and though this more centralized control was the best arrangement yet, the organization of production did not achieve optimum efficiency until the creation of the Office of War Mobilization in May 1943 under James F. Byrnes, former Democratic senator from South Carolina.

While building up an armed force of some 15 million men and women, the United States undertook to expand its productive capacity to feed, clothe, supply, house, and transport this army as well as make sizable support contributions to the British and Russian armies spread around the globe. To meet this gargantuan assignment required not only the expenditure of billions of dollars but also the execution of a host of plans and arrangements. Priorities for materials had to be established, raw materials gathered, labor recruited to replace the men and women serving in the armed services, and civilian industries converted to war work. The automobile industry, for example, was given over entirely to the manufacture of tanks, trucks, and other military vehicles.

The aviation industry expanded its working force from 49,000 in 1939 to a peak of 2.1 million in November 1943, when it employed over 12 percent of the total number of workers in manufacturing. To keep supplies moving, the total tonnage of American shipping increased over five times between 1939 and May 1945. Whole new industries sometimes had to be created. The production of synthetic rubber was inaugurated when the Japanese cut off the major source of natural rubber from Southeast Asia. The volume of industrial production increased so rapidly that by October 1943 some cutbacks were made to prevent surpluses.

Between 1939 and 1946 agricultural production increased some 30 percent, even though the labor force on farms *fell* more than 5 percent. As a result, not only was the United States able to keep the armed forces well supplied with food, but the nation as a whole ate better than ever before, and the Allies were able to draw upon the American larder during the war and after.

The Home Front.   Because the needs of the armed forces came first, many kinds of civilian goods ranging from automobiles to toasters were unobtainable, and necessities in short supply like coffee, sugar, meat, and butter were rationed in order to ensure equitable distribution. Housing, especially in areas where new war plants went up, was hard to obtain, and housing conditions were overcrowded and substandard. Bus and train travel was dirty, uncomfortable, and over-

crowded, if available for a civilian at all. Many commodities still obtainable on the home front declined in quality but not in price as manufacturers tried to get around price controls. However, the average citizen did not suffer unduly. As Director of War Mobilization Byrnes said in January 1945, "It is not as if the civilian economy has been starved. Some items are short. But on the whole the volume of consumption has risen. . . Our level of living is higher than in 1929 or 1940."

As part of the expanding American production effort, women were recruited to work in war plants. A hit song of the day, "Rosie the Riveter," praised the achievements of women like these.

Industrial labor was certainly better off. Unemployment dropped from 9 million in July 1940 to 780,000 in September 1943. And though prices rose by about 30 percent between 1939 and 1945, wage rates rose faster, increasing about 70 percent, thanks to raises and overtime pay. The need for additional labor was so great that at one point the government undertook a house-to-house survey to find workers for war industries. By the middle of 1944 war workers accounted for 45 percent of the nation's labor force, which included millions of women and teenagers (aged 14–17). Because of an acute labor shortage, A. Philip Randolph, leader of the Sleeping Car Porters, was able to score a victory for the Porters by threatening a march on Washington if the President did not enforce equal hiring policies by recipients of government contracts—setting an example for future activists.

Although more workers went on strike during the war years than during the depression years, the number was less than 2.5 million in any one year and only a small proportion of the total labor force of around 55 million. The most notable labor dispute was with John L. Lewis, who twice in 1943 led his United Mine Workers in strikes against government restraints on wage increases. In retaliation, Congress in June 1943 enacted a general anti-labor law, the Smith-Connally Act, which authorized the President to seize any plant where a strike threatened to interfere with the war effort and which imposed criminal penalties on those who called such strikes. Roosevelt vetoed the bill as extreme, but Congress quickly overrode his veto. Only occasionally, however, did the President have to seize plants in order to keep production going.

The job of fitting a free labor force to the needs of war production was formidable. A War Manpower Commission, created in 1942, undertook this task by freezing workers to their jobs unless more important war work required them elsewhere. To handle disputes between labor and management, the President set up the War Labor Board. The board also attempted to hold the line on wages in order to keep prices level, although it had to permit some increases to make up for the rise in the cost of living. In the main, the War Labor Board, which settled thousands of labor disputes amicably during the war years, refused to permit the emergency to be used as an excuse for eroding the gains made by organized labor in the previous decade. As a result, the membership of the unions increased from 9 million in 1940 to almost 15 million in 1945.

Controlling Inflation. Simply because there was so much money and so few consumer goods, the control of prices was a major problem. Essentially, prices were kept under control by two methods—increased taxes and a price freeze. The Office of Price Administration, which was in charge of controlling inflation, failed to put a tight lid on prices until late in 1942 so that some prices, notably those of foods, rose alarmingly through most of that year. Thereafter, however, controls were more effective.

Because Congress would not follow through on legislation, taxation was not so steep as the administration had hoped. Only the Revenue Act of 1942, which increased corporate, private income, and excise taxes, took much of a bite out of civilian purchasing power. In that act, for the first time, the income tax reached into the pockets of the average citizen. About 50 million income-tax payers were recorded in 1943 as compared with 13 million in 1941. Congress refused to heed Roosevelt's demand for a further increase in taxes in 1943. Yet in spite of government spending at a rate as high as $100 million a year, about 40 percent of the ongoing cost of the war was paid for out of taxes, a proportion which had never been achieved in any previous American war.

Civil Liberties.   Fearful of sabotage, the government early in 1942 ordered the rounding up of some 110,000 Japanese living on the West Coast, even though some two thirds of them were American citizens. Although no specific acts of sabotage could be charged against them, these people were held in "relocation centers" in the interior for most of the war. Meanwhile their property was placed in the hands of often incompetent or unfriendly custodians. This action of the government, though generally supported at the time and subsequently upheld by the Supreme Court, was later condemned as an indefensible act of racism, since mere Japanese ancestry was the basis for the internment. Ironically, the Japanese in Hawaii, who made up a much larger proportion of the population, were not affected by the order. No comparable interference with civil liberty was taken against Americans of German or Italian ancestry, nor did the population at large indulge in irrational attacks on Germans like those that had marred the domestic record during the First World War. But *native* minorities did suffer. Large numbers of whites attacked blacks in Detroit in 1943, and whites in other cities resorted to violence against blacks. During the last two years of the war, white servicemen and civilians also harassed young Mexican-Americans in the Los Angeles area in what came to be called the "zoot-suit riots," after the extravagant styles worn by many Mexican-American youths. Later, these incidents were seen to mark the beginning of overt Mexican-American self-consciousness, which by the late 1960s became the Chicano movement.

By and large, however, the position of blacks improved during the war. Thousands moved into Northern cities seeking the new job opportunities. By April 1944 a million more blacks were employed in civilian jobs than in 1940. During the same period the number of blacks in skilled jobs and foreman positions doubled. Under pressure from black leaders the federal government also undertook to make jobs available. The President in June 1941 created a Fair Employment Practices Committee to investigate charges of discrimination against minorities on defense jobs. In 1943 the committee was granted enforcement authority.

The Election of 1944.   In the midst of the Second World War, as in the Civil War, the nation conducted a presidential election. The Republicans, who after Pearl Harbor strongly supported the war effort, now entertained high hopes for victory, since in the congressional elections of 1942 they had gained forty-seven seats in the House and nine in the Senate, dropping the Democratic majority in the House to its lowest level since Roosevelt first took office. Prominently considered for the Republican nomination was Thomas E. Dewey, who had gained national renown as the first Republican since 1920 to be elected governor of New York state. Dewey spoke for the same internationalist wing of the party that had supported Wendell L. Willkie in 1940, but he did not suffer from Willkie's close identification with the administration. Moreover, Dewey, unlike Willkie, enjoyed the support of the professionals in the party.

As a result, the convention nominated Dewey on the first ballot—with only a single dissenting vote. John A. Bricker of Ohio, who as a Midwesterner and an isolationist brought balance to the ticket, received the vice-presidential nomination. The party platform was internationalist in content, but the convention's enthusiasm for Bricker betrayed the persistence of isolationism in Republican ranks.

Roosevelt waited until just a week before the Democratic convention met in July before he indicated his willingness to seek the nomination for a fourth term. The real battle in the convention then raged around the choice

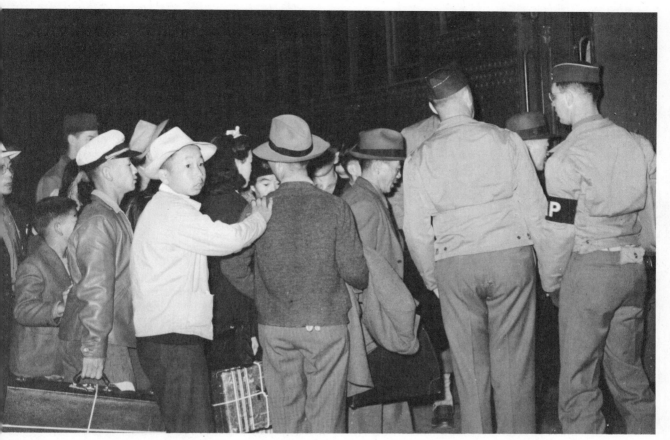

In 1942 a fearful American government rounded up Japanese-Americans who lived on the West Coast. Allowed to take only what they could carry, these families were interned in "relocation centers" for most of the war.

of his running mate. Roosevelt's own choice, though not a strong one, was incumbent Vice-President Henry Wallace, but Wallace was unacceptable to conservatives within the party. The President's second choice was James F. Byrnes, the efficient and capable Director of the Office of War Mobilization. However, labor leaders and liberals in general opposed Byrnes as antiblack and perhaps antilabor. As a consequence, before the convention actually voted, party leaders and the President had decided upon Harry S Truman as a compromise candidate. Truman,

a senator from Missouri, was chairman of a Senate investigating committee that had gained national acclaim for its honest and efficient policing of government war contracts.

His head filled with plans for the postwar settlement, Roosevelt's heart was not in the hustings. Nevertheless, early in the campaign he made one of the most effective political speeches of his career and by the vigor of his few campaign speeches effectively countered Republican charges that he was physically incapable of enduring another term of office.

As usual Roosevelt won, though by a smaller margin in the popular vote than ever before, receiving 25.6 million votes to Dewey's 22 million. The Democrats retained control of both houses, gaining twenty-four new seats in the House of Representatives.

PUSHING TOWARD VICTORY

Island Hopping in the Pacific. When the last Japanese resistance ended on Guadalcanal in February 1943, the United States began the long push northward toward Japan. The task was essentially one for the navy and the marines, since the Japanese were dug in on a multitude of small islands scattered throughout the western Pacific. One by one through 1943, Japanese island fortresses fell to air and amphibious attack, often only after terrible loss of life: the central Solomons in the summer, eastern New Guinea in the fall, and the Gilbert Islands in the late fall. As the great naval task forces of the United States moved northward, other Japanese outposts were bypassed, their garrisons still intact. Cut off from supplies, they would eventually have to surrender without bloodshed. By the end of June 1944 the capture of Saipan in the Marianas placed the air force's giant new B-29 bomber within easy striking distance of Tokyo itself. Systematic bombing of Japan's home islands from Saipan began in November 1944.

The Invasion of Europe. Meanwhile, preparations were well under way for the long-awaited frontal assault upon Hitler's "Fortress Europe." Ever since the middle of 1942 Stalin had been urging the Western allies to open a second front, but aside from the invasion of Italy, which was obviously peripheral, their response had been confined to bombings of the Third Reich. Nevertheless, by the middle of 1943 these air attacks were formidable. In one week in July 1943, for example, the combined British and American air forces dropped 8000 tons of bombs on Hamburg,

devastating three quarters of the city. Later, fifty other large German cities each received a similar pounding. More than 300,000 Germans died in these uninterrupted raids, which by 1944 were deliberately aimed at workers' homes as well as factories in an effort to destroy German morale as well as German industrial capacity. The raids cost the Anglo-American air forces thousands of bombers and their crews.

On December 6, 1943, in appointing Dwight D. Eisenhower Supreme Allied Commander of the West, the Combined Chiefs of Staff told him: "You will enter the continent of Europe and, in conjunction with other Allied Nations, undertake operations aimed at the heart of Germany and the destruction of her armed forces." For months before the actual invasion began and while supplies, shipping, and men were being accumulated in England, Allied planes bombed and strafed German positions along the Channel coast. The Nazis could not help but know in general what was impending, but thanks to superb Allied counterintelligence, they misjudged the exact point of the attack on D-day, June 6, 1944. The main concentration of Allied troops was north of the Cotentin peninsula in Normandy, where the massive invasion force quickly established five connected beachheads. Within two weeks a million troops landed and moved inland. By the end of July both the British and the American armies had broken out of their coastal positions and were striking north and west. On August 15 a new American army invaded southern France, and on August 25 Paris fell to French and American troops.

Concomitantly with the Allied invasion of June 6, the Russians launched a broad offensive on the eastern front, bringing their armies to the Baltic and into Poland and Romania by the end of the summer. By late autumn of 1944 the armies of the Grand Alliance were poised to strike into Germany from both east and west.

Despite the overwhelming land and air

In 1943 American forces began the long push toward Japan. On Leyte Island, GIs build sandbag piers to speed up unloading of two Coast Guard-manned LSTs loaded with supplies and fighting equipment.

power being brought against it, Germany made two desperate attempts to forestall the inevitable. The first was a new secret weapon, a fast-flying rocket bomb, the V-2. (The V-1 or "buzz bomb," used somewhat earlier, was a jet-driven aerial bomb and not a rocket.) The first V-2s landed in England in August. Traveling faster than the speed of sound, the V-2 was impossible to intercept, and it hit without warning. Before the launching bases could be destroyed by Allied bombers, the murderous V-2 attacks killed some 8000 Britons.

The other desperate German effort was a great counteroffensive mounted on December 16, 1944, against the American forces in the Ardennes forest of Belgium. The Battle of the Bulge, as it came to be called, caught the Americans by surprise and forced them to retreat. As a result the whole Allied timetable in the west was set back over six weeks. The first Allied troops did not cross the Rhine until March 7, 1945, when the bridge at Remagen, one of the few remaining Rhine bridges, was unexpectedly taken by soldiers of the American Ninth Armored Division. By that time the Russians stood on the banks of the Oder River, less than forty-five miles from Berlin.

The Big Three at Yalta. As the coils of Allied power tightened around Germany, Roosevelt, Stalin, and Churchill met on February 4–11, 1945, at Yalta, a resort town in the Crimea. Desirous of securing Russian aid

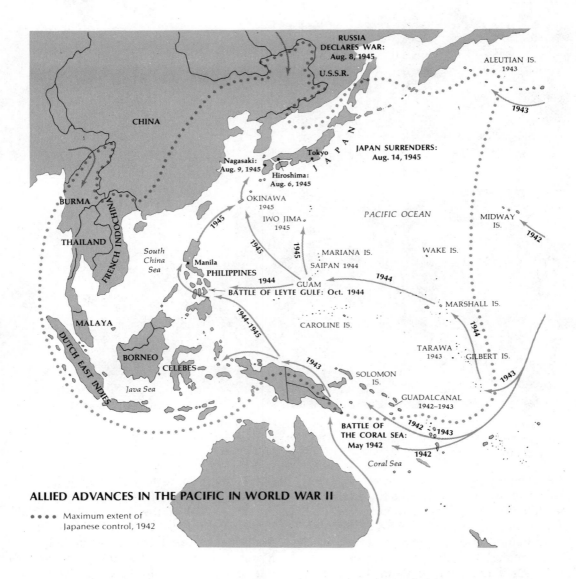

ALLIED ADVANCES IN THE PACIFIC IN WORLD WAR II

● ● ● ● Maximum extent of
Japanese control, 1942

against the Japanese and of bringing the Soviet Union into a new world organization, Roosevelt did his best to assure Stalin that the United States recognized Russia's special interests in Europe. It was agreed that the new government of Poland would be the one established at Lublin by the Russians and not the one in exile in London. But it was also agreed that final recognition of the Lublin government would await "free and unfettered elections." Also, pending the signing of a German peace, Poland would receive German territory to compensate for portions of eastern Poland taken by Russia in 1939.

Russian insistence upon a large figure for German reparations was also favorably received by the Americans, though no final commitment was made. Stalin asked for and received cession of the Kurile Islands from Japan and concessions and bases in China. In

ALLIED ADVANCES IN EUROPE
IN WORLD WAR II

● ● ● ●   Maximum extent of
          Axis control, 1942
░░░░░   Neutral

return, Stalin agreed to participate in the new world organization and to enter the war against Japan within three months after the defeat of Germany.

Despite later criticism, the so-called concessions by Roosevelt do not seem excessive in the context of February 1945. Poland, after all, was in Russian hands, and Russian military assistance against Japan then seemed eminently desirable and worth the granting of

Japanese territory to the Soviet Union. Furthermore, Chiang Kai-shek later consented to the concessions Roosevelt agreed to support in Stalin's behalf.

The End of the Third Reich.   Soon after the Yalta Conference, on April 12, 1945, Franklin D. Roosevelt died of a cerebral hemorrhage at Warm Springs, Georgia. A surprised and shaken Harry S Truman assumed the presidency the same day. Roosevelt's death plunged the nation and the peoples of the Allied world into sorrow, but the military machine he had helped to forge drove on to total victory over Germany and Italy.

With the Russians already fighting in flaming, bombed-out Berlin, Adolf Hitler on April 30 committed suicide in his underground bunker beneath the Reichs chancellery. Faithful guards burned his body. Nazi Germany outlasted its founder by no more than a week. On May 2, Admiral Karl Doenitz, whom Hitler had named as his successor tried to surrender to the British while continuing the war against the Russians, but Field Marshal Bernard L. Montgomery contemptuously rejected this last attempt to divide the Western and Eastern allies. Germany surrendered unconditionally to all the Allied powers on the morning of May 7, 1945.

The United Nations and Potsdam. With Roosevelt's death, President Truman was left to complete the task his predecessor had considered preeminent: the convocation of the representatives of the Allied and other nations at San Francisco to draw up a charter for a new world security organization. The completed Charter of the United Nations was signed by all fifty countries on June 26, 1945. Despite America's long history of isolationism and its rejection of the League of Nations after World War I, the Senate agreed to American membership in the United Nations after only six days of debate and with only two dissenting votes.

President Truman was also called upon to represent the United States at the last conference of the Big Three powers. Since no final decisions on Germany had been made at Yalta and since the United States still wanted Russia's support against Japan, Truman, Stalin, and Churchill (later replaced by Clement Attlee, representing the newly elected Labour government in Britain) met at Potsdam, outside ruined Berlin, on July 17, 1945. Differences between East and West were

more evident than before. Wranglings frequently occurred over details and the meaning of previous agreements. The two Western allies were deeply suspicious of Russian policy in Poland, which Stalin seemed intent upon making a Russian satellite despite agreement on its independence at Yalta. Stalin also insisted that the new border between Germany and Poland was final, though at Yalta the border had been considered only temporary. Furthermore, Stalin now insisted that the tentative agreements on reparations were final.

All three powers agreed that Germany should remain united but that for purposes of temporary military administration each of the three powers (later France was added) would occupy a separate zone. Berlin itself was to be occupied jointly by the victors. Even though Russia had not yet entered the war in the Pacific, the conference issued a demand for Japan's unconditional surrender.

The End of the War with Japan. As the European war reached its climax in the summer and fall of 1944, the American air force and navy moved ever closer to the Japanese home islands. Admiral Chester Nimitz in command of the Pacific fleet wanted to use all available military strength to reach Iwo Jima, an island near enough to mainland Japan so that fighter escorts could protect bombers. He reasoned that with the conquest of the mainland all other Japanese-held areas would have to surrender.

General Douglas MacArthur, the commanding general of the Pacific area, however, wanted to divert planes and ships to reconquer the Phillipines, and he convinced the Joint Chiefs of Staff to divide American forces so as to pursue both policies simultaneously but necessarily more slowly. In February 1945 the reconquest of the Phillipines was completed and the island of Iwo Jima, 500 miles from Japan, was conquered in a bloody assault.

A view of Wall Street on May 7, 1945, as crowds celebrate the end of the war in Europe.

On March 9, B-29s from Saipan dropped a record load of firebombs on Tokyo, igniting the wooden and paper houses of the city. The resulting holocaust was rivaled only by that at Hiroshima five months later.

Even as fierce fighting continued in the Philippines, the Americans invaded Okinawa, close to the home islands. Once again, as at Tarawa in the Gilberts and Iwo Jima in the Bonins, the Japanese dug in and fought virtually to the last man, while Kamikaze (Japanese suicide pilots) hurled their planes at the Americans, sinking thirty-four ships of the invading fleet. By the end of the campaign in June 1945, some 110,000 Japanese had died on Okinawa. Fewer than 8000 had been taken prisoner. The 49,000 American casualties were the heaviest of any engagement in the Pacific theater and a grisly prefiguring of the costs to be expected from the contemplated assault on the Japanese home islands.

That dreaded encounter, however, never came. At 8:15 A.M. on August 6, 1945, a lone B-29 dropped a single atomic bomb on the industrial city of Hiroshima. The tremendous blast waves, fire waves, and radiation leveled 60 percent of the city and killed over 70,000 people outright; 10,000 more were never found. Because the bewildered Japanese did not surrender immediately, a second nuclear bomb was dropped on Nagasaki on August 9 with equally devastating consequences. A day before, on August 8, the Soviet Union had fulfilled its promise by declaring war on Japan and invading Manchuria.

Japan's leaders, recognizing that their country faced certain destruction and heeding the emperor's pleas that no more lives be sacrificed, surrendered unconditionally on August 14. The official surrender took place on September 2 aboard the battleship *Missouri* anchored in Tokyo Bay.

The story of the development of the nuclear bomb began in August 1939, when President Roosevelt received a letter from Albert Einstein informing him that the splitting (fission)

The mushroom-shaped cloud that came to symbolize the atom bomb rises above Nagasaki on August 9, 1945. Japan soon surrendered, and the world entered the age of nuclear power.

of the nucleus of an atom of uranium seemed possible. The consequent release of energy, Einstein wrote, would be enormous. Fearful that Nazi scientists might develop such a bomb, the administration in 1940 began the Manhattan Project to try to beat them to it. Working secretly in a squash court under the stands of the football stadium at the University of Chicago, a team of scientists in December 1942 successfully constructed the first atomic pile. Once it had been shown that a nuclear reaction could be controlled, the engineers took over, constructing plants at Oak Ridge, Tennessee, and Hanford, Washington, for the manufacture of materials needed for assembling a bomb. After more than $2 billion had been invested in the great gamble, the first test of the bomb took place successfully on July 16, 1945, in the desert outside Alamogordo, New Mexico. The secret of the project had been kept so well that Harry Truman did not learn of it until he became President.

The job of building the bomb was so complicated and time-consuming that the two bombs used against Japan were the total world supply. Later it was learned that the Germans had lagged far behind the United States and Great Britain in the development of nuclear fission and probably would not have been able to construct a bomb for months or perhaps years. But no matter who made the first bomb, once its devastating power had been released, the world could not be the same again. Thus, simultaneously with the coming of peace, the world entered the age of nuclear power—an age which would be at once an era of promise and of fear.

BIBLIOGRAPHY

For cultural and intellectual trends between the wars see Merle E. Curti, *The Growth of American Thought,* 3rd ed. (New York: Harper & Row, 1946), Richard H. Pells, *Radical Visions and American Dreams: Culture and Social Thought in the Depression Years* (New York: Harper & Row, 1973), Milton Canter, *The Divided Left: American Radicalism, 1900–1925* (New York: Hill & Wang, 1978), Eric F. Goldman, *Rendezvous with Destiny: A History of Modern American Reform,* abr. rev. ed. (New York: Knopf, 1956), and Charles R. Hearn, *The American Dream and the Great Depression* (Westport: Greenwood, 1977). Morton G. White, ed., *Age of Analysis* (New York: New American Library, 1955), is lively on trends in philosophy. On religion see Robert M. Miller, *American Protestantism and Social Issues 1919–1939* (Chapel Hill: University of North Carolina Press, 1958). Lawrence A. Cremin, *The Transformation of the School* (New York: Knopf, 1961), is an excellent account, with major emphasis on the 1920s and 1930s. Vols. I and II of Erik Barnouw, *A History of Broadcasting in the United States,* 3 vols. (New York: Oxford University Press, 1966–1970), are journalistic in approach but the best source. See also: Paula F. Fass, *The Damned and the Beautiful: American Youth in the 1920's* (New York: Oxford, 1979).

For a general discussion of twentieth-century developments in painting see John H. Bauer, *Revolution and Tradition in Modern American Art* (New York: Praeger, 1951). Oliver W. Larkin, *Art and Life in America,* rev. ed. (New York: Holt, Rinehart and Winston, 1960), contains a provocative survey of the period. Architecture of the period is discussed in James M. Fitch, *American Building: The Historical Forces that Shaped It* (Boston: Houghton Mifflin, 1948). Gilbert Seldes in *The Public Arts* (New York: Simon & Schuster, 1956), gives a highly personal interpretation of moving pictures, radio, and theater. Lewis Jacobs, *Rise of the American Film* (New York: Teachers College Press, 1968), is an excellent scholarly account of social as well as artistic aspects. For modern criticism of cinema in the thirties see James Agee,

Agee on Film, 2 vols. (New York: Grosset & Dunlap, 1969), and Jack C. Ellis, *A History of Film* (Englewood Cliffs, Prentice-Hall, 1979). There are many books on the literature of the period. For an introduction see Alfred Kazin, *On Native Grounds* (New York: Harcourt Brace Jovanovich, 1972), and, for its special emphasis, James O. Young, *Black Writers of the Thirties* (Baton Rouge: Louisiana State University Press, 1973). The federal art projects are well treated in Jerre Mangeoni, *The Dream and the Deal* (Boston: Little, Brown, 1972), Richard D. McKinzie, *The New Deal for Artists* (Princeton: Princeton University Press, 1973), and Malcom Goldstein; *The Political Stage* (New York: Oxford University Press, 1974).

William E. Leuchtenburg, *The Perils of Prosperity 1914–1932* (Chicago: University of Chicago Press, 1959), and Richard S. Kirkendall, *The United States 1929–1945* (New York: McGraw-Hill, 1973), provide more detailed accounts of this period. Otis L. Graham, *Toward a Planned Society: From Roosevelt to Nixon* (New York: Oxford, 1976), stresses the main significance of the New Deal. On political and social thought see Goldman's *Rendezvous with Destiny,* cited previously, and Richard Hofstadter, *The Age of Reform: From Bryan to FDR* (New York: Knopf, 1955). Arthur M. Schlesinger, Jr., *The Crisis of the Old Order,* Vol. I of *The Age of Roosevelt* (Boston: Houghton Mifflin, 1957) is a provocative discussion from a democratic viewpoint, as is Karl Schriftgiesser's more journalistic account, *This Was Normalcy* (Boston: Little, Brown, 1948). William Allen White, *A Puritan in Babylon* (Gloucester, Mass.: Smith reprint of 1938 ed.), is a good picture of Coolidge and his times. On the anti-foreign reaction see Kenneth T. Jackson, *The Ku Klux Klan in the City* (New York: Oxford University Press, 1969). For continuing progressivism see Kenneth MacKay, *The Progressive Movement of 1924* (New York: Octagon Books, 1966), Belle C. La Follette and Fola La Follette, *Robert M. La Follette 1855–1925,* Vol. II (New York: Macmillan, 1953), and Oscar Handlin, *Al Smith and His*

America (Boston: Little, Brown, 1958). For a good treatment of women's activities see William Henry Chafe, *The American Woman: Her Changing Social, Economic and Political Roles, 1920–1970* (New York: Oxford, 1972), and also June Sochen, *Movers and Shakers: American Women Thinkers and Activists 1900–1970* (New York: Quadrangle, 1974). The best general economic account of the period just prior to the Great Depression is George Soule, *Prosperity Decade: From War to Depression 1917–1929* (New York: Harper & Row, 1968). Louis Galambos and Barbara Barrow Spence, *The Public Image of Big Business in America 1880–1940* (Baltimore: Johns Hopkins, 1975), and James R. Flink, *The Car Culture* (Cambridge: MIT Press, 1975), are good on important aspects of the period. An entertaining journalistic, but essentially accurate picture of the period 1919 to 1939 is in two books by Frederick Lewis Allen: *Only Yesterday: An Informal History of the Nineteen Twenties* (New York: Harper & Row, 1931, and later editions), and *Since Yesterday* (New York: Harper & Row, 1972). John K. Galbraith, *The Great Crash 1929*, 3rd ed. (Boston: Houghton Mifflin, 1972) is both lively and authoritative. For labor history see Irving Bernstein, *The Lean Years: A History of the American Worker 1920–1933* (Boston: Houghton Mifflin, 1960), and Bert Cochran, *Labor and Communism: The Conflict that Shaped American Unions* (Princeton: Princeton University Press, 1977).

Black experience from the earliest days is covered in John Hope Franklin, *From Slavery to Freedom,* 4th ed. (New York: Knopf, 1974), August Meier and Elliott M. Rudwick, *From Plantation to Ghetto, enl. ed. (New York: Hill & Wang, 1970),* and Harvard Sitkoff, *A New Deal for Blacks,* Volume 1, *The Depression Decade* (New York: Oxford, 1978). A reprinted classic is Ralph J. Bunche, *The Political Status of the Negro in the Age of FDR,* ed. Dewey W. Grantham (Chicago: University of Chicago Press, 1973). Vishnu V. Oak, *The Negro's Adventure in General Business* (Westport, Conn.: Negro Universities Press, 1949), is short and incomplete, but is the only general account; see also Ivan H. Light, *Ethnic Enterprise in America: Business and Welfare Among Chinese, Japanese and Blacks* (Berkeley: University of California Press, 1972). Elliott M. Rudwick, *W. E. B. Du Bois: Propagandist of the Negro Protest,* 2nd ed. (Philadelphia: University of Pennsylvania Press, 1969), is a good biography. Writing from many periods is collected in *Black Nationalism in America* (Indianapolis: Bobbs-Merrill, 1970), eds. John H. Bracey, Jr., August Meier, and Elliott M. Rudwick. On civil and criminal rights see Bernard H. Nelson, *The Fourteenth Amendment and the Negro Since 1920* (New York: Russell & Russell reprint of 1946 ed.), and Dan T. Carter, *Scottsboro: A Tragedy of the American South* (New York: Oxford University Press, 1971). The Harlem Renaissance is seen in proper perspective by Kenny J. Williams, *They Also Spoke: An Essay on Negro Literature in America 1787–1930* (Nashville, Tenn.: Townsend Press,

1970). On social problems see Domenic Capeci, *The Harlem Riot of 1943* (Philadelphia: Temple, 1977), Raymond Wolters, *Negroes and the Great Depression* (New Haven: Yale, 1970), and Lee Finkle, *Forum for Protest: The Black Press During World War II* (Rutherford, NJ: Fairleigh-Dickinson University Press, 1975). A famous summary of the black position in society at the end of the interwar period is Gunnar Myrdal, *An American Dilemma,* rev. ed. (New York: Harper & Row, 1962)

Harris G. Warren, *Herbert Hoover and the Great Depression* (New York: Norton, 1964), and Albert U. Romasco, *The Poverty of Abundance: Hoover, the Nation, the Depression* (New York: Oxford University Press, 1968), are judicious accounts. Craig Lloyd, *Aggressive Introvert: A Study of Herbert Hoover and Public Relations Management* (Columbus: Ohio State University Press, 1972), is an interesting interpretation. A brief survey of the period 1929–1945 is Thomas C. Cochran, *The Great Depression and World War II* (Glenview, IL.: Scott, Foresman, 1968). More detailed are Basil Rauch, *The History of the New Deal 1933–1938* (New York: Octagon Books reprint of 1963 ed.), and William E. Leuchtenburg, *Franklin D. Roosevelt and the New Deal 1932–1940* (New York: Harper & Row, 1963). Arthur M. Schlesinger, Jr., *The Coming of the New Deal* and *The Politics of Upheaval* (Boston: Houghton Mifflin, 1959 and 1960), take his series on the Age of Roosevelt to 1936. Four volumes by Frank Freidel bring his biography, *Franklin D. Roosevelt* (Boston: Little, Brown, 1952–1974), to 1933. A good, objective biography is James M. Burns, *Roosevelt: The Lion and the Fox* (New York: Harcourt Brace Jovanovich, 1956). A good recent biography is Robert Dallek, *Franklin D. Roosevelt and American Foreign Policy: 1932–1945* (New York: Oxford University Press, 1979).

Legislative opposition is ably discussed in James T. Patterson, *Congressional Conservatism and the New Deal* (Lexington: University of Kentucky Press, 1967), and by the same author, *The New Deal in the States* (Princeton: Princeton University Press, 1969). All types of conservative criticism are included in Edgar E. Robinson, *The Roosevelt Leadership 1933–1945* (New York: Plenum, 1955). Robert Lekachman, *The Age of Keynes* (New York: McGraw-Hill, 1975), is readable and objective about the economics of the New Deal. Roosevelt's strongest opponent on the left is covered well in T. Harry Williams, *Huey Long* (New York: Knopf, 1969). Many of Roosevelt's associates wrote memoirs; of these Frances Perkins, *The Roosevelt I Knew* (New York: Harper & Row, 1964) is favorable, and Raymond Moley, *After Seven Years* (Lincoln, Neb.: Bison Books, 1971), is critical. Robert E. Sherwood, *Roosevelt and Hopkins,* rev. ed. (New York: Harper & Row, 1950), is strong on foreign affairs, while John M. Blum, *From the Diaries of Henry Morgenthau, Jr.,* 3 vols. (Boston: Houghton Mifflin, 1959–1967), is chiefly domestic. A good study of the judiciary is C. Herman Pritchett, *The Roosevelt Court: A Study in Judicial Politics and Values*

1937–1947 (New York: Quadrangle, 1969). For an analysis of important changes in the patterns of voting see Samuel Lubell, *The Future of American Politics*, rev. ed. (New York: Harper & Row, 1966), and Philip J. Fungiello, *The Challenge of Urban Liberalism: Federal-City Relations During World War II* (Knoxville: University of Tennessee Press, 1978).

Broadus Mitchell, *Depression Decade 1929–1939* (New York: Holt, Rinehart and Winston, 1947), is an economic account built around New Deal legislation. J. Douglas Brown, *An American Philosophy of Social Security* (Princeton: Princeton University Press, 1972), is an account by one involved in the New Deal program. John D. Black, *Parity, Parity, Parity* (New York: Da Capo reprint of 1942 ed.), discusses agricultural policies. The effects of NIRA on small business is seen in Louis Galambos, *Competition and Cooperation: The Emergence of a National Trade Association* (Baltimore: John Hopkins University Press, 1966), and on big business in Sidney Fine, *The Automobile Under the Blue Eagle* (Ann Arbor: University of Michigan Press, 1963). Labor history is treated in Walter Galenson, *The CIO Challenge to the AFL* (Cambridge: Harvard University Press, 1960), Irving Bernstein, *The Turbulent Years: A History of the American Worker 1933–1941* (Boston: Houghton Mifflin, 1970), and Sidney Fine, *Sit-Down: The General Motors Strike of 1936–1937* (Ann Arbor: University of Michigan Press, 1969). A comprehensive but uninterpretive social and economic picture of the 1930s is Dixon Wecter, *Age of the Great Depression 1929–1941* (New York: Watts, 1971). Henry F. Bedford, *Trouble Downtown: The Local Context of Twentieth Century America* (New York: Harcourt Brace Jovanovich, 1978), brings up new politico-economic relationships.

There is a considerable literature on Indian history since the 1920s. Good general accounts are Harold E. Fey and D'Arcy McNickle, *Indians and Other Americans* (New York: Harper & Row, 1971), and Hazel W. Hertzberg, *Search for an Indian Identity: Modern Pan-Indian Movements* (Syracuse, N.Y.: Syracuse University Press, 1971). On the immediate effects of New Deal policies see T. H. Haas, *Ten Years of Tribal Government and the Indian Reorganization Act* (Washington, D.C.: Government Printing Office, 1947), and Kenneth R. Philp, *John Collyer's Crusade for Indian Reform, 1920–1954* (Tucson: University of Arizona Press, 1977).

For a history of foreign policy friendly to Roosevelt see Allan Nevins, *The New Deal and World Affairs* (New York: U.S. Publishers Association, 1950); for a critical one see Charles A. Beard, *President Roosevelt: A Study in Appearances and Realities* (Hamden, Conn.: Shoe String Press, 1968). Michael Leigh, *Mobilizing Consent: Public Opinion and American Foreign Policy, 1937–1947* (Westport: Greenwood, 1976), provides important background. See also Ralph B. Levering, *The Public and American Policy* (New York: Morrow, 1978).

The classic account of the coming of the war is William L. Langer and S. Everett Gleason, *The Undeclared War 1940–1941* (New York: Harper & Row, 1953); more readable and as reliable for the Pacific side is Samuel E. Morison, *The Rising Sun in the Pacific* (Boston: Little, Brown, 1948). Full treatment on diplomacy is given in the authoritative Herbert Feis, *The Road to Pearl Harbor* (Princeton: Princeton University Press, 1950). A useful, brief handling of the coming of the war is Robert A. Divine, *Reluctant Belligerent: American Entry into the Second World War* (New York: Wiley, 1965). An intriguing and penetrating study of the causes for the surprise on December 7, 1941, is Roberta Wohlstetter, *Pearl Harbor: Warning and Decision* (Stanford: Stanford University Press, 1962). James M. Burns, *Roosevelt: The Soldier of Freedom* (New York: Harcourt Brace Jovanovich, 1970), completes Burns' readable biography of Roosevelt on a more critical note than most in dealing with foreign policy.

Herbert Feis has devoted himself in several volumes to detailing authoritatively the diplomatic history of the war and immediate postwar years. A central volume in his series is *Churchill-Roosevelt-Stalin* (Princeton: Princeton University Press, 1957). Robert E. Sherwood, *Roosevelt and Hopkins*, rev. ed. (New York: Harper & Row, 1950), is less objective but more readable, and also filled with fascinating selections from the sources. For the transition from neutrality to belligerency, see: Thomas A. Bailey and Paul B. Ryan, *Hitler vs. Roosevelt: The Undeclared Naval War* (Riverside, CA: Free Press, 1979). Robert A. Divine, *Second Chance: The Triumph of Internationalism During World War II* (New York: Atheneum, 1967), traces this great transition. One of the major revisionist works on FDR's handling of foreign affairs is Gabriel Kolki, *The Politics of War* (New York: Random House, 1970). Also critical of FDR and important in relating diplomacy to the atomic bomb is Martin J. Sherwin, *A World Destroyed: The Atomic Bomb and the Grand Alliance* (New York: Knopf, 1975). For an overall view of the war see Gordon Wright, *The Ordeal of Total War 1939–1945* (New York: Harper & Row, 1968), and Christopher Thorne, *Allies of a Kind: The United States, Britain, and the War Against Japan, 1941–1945* (New York: Oxford University Press, 1979). For domestic events see Alan S. Milward, *War, Economy and Society, 1931–1945* (Berkeley: University of California Press, 1977), Chester W. Gregory, *Women in Defense Work During World War II* (Jericho, NY: Exposition, 1974), and Leila J. Rupp, *Mobilizing Women for War: German and American Propaganda, 1939–1945* (Princeton: Princeton University Press, 1978).

Time Line

1945	Death of President Franklin Roosevelt; Harry S Truman becomes President
	Formation of United Nations at San Francisco
1947	Enunciation of Truman Doctrine
1948	European Recovery Program (Marshall Plan) approved by Congress
	Election of Truman for full term
1948–1949	Berlin Blockade
1949	North Atlantic Treaty Organization (NATO) formed
	Triumph of Communists in China; Chiang Kai-shek regime flees to Taiwan
1950–1953	Korean War
1950–1954	Era of Senator Joseph McCarthy
1952	Dwight D. Eisenhower elected President
1954	U.S. Supreme Court in Brown v. Board of Education of Topeka bans racial segregation in public schools
1955	Montgomery bus boycott begins
1957	Federal troops sent to integrate Central High School in Little Rock, Arkansas
	Soviet Union successfully launches first man-made satellite (Sputnik)
1960	Election of John F. Kennedy as President
1961	Bay of Pigs invasion of Cuba
1962	Federal troops sent to integrate University of Mississippi
	Cuban missile crisis with Soviet Union
1963	President John F. Kennedy assassinated; Lyndon B. Johnson becomes President
1963	Publication of Feminine Mystique by Betty Friedan
1964	Comprehensive Civil Rights Act passed
	Tonkin Gulf Resolution passed
	Student riots on Berkeley campus
1967	First large-scale riots by discontented blacks in U.S. cities
1968	President Lyndon Johnson withdraws from upcoming presidential campaign
	Martin Luther King and Robert Kennedy assassinated
	U.S. troops in Vietnam reach peak number of more than 500,000
	Richard M. Nixon elected President
1970	Student protests rock college campuses after U.S. troops invade Cambodia
1972	Nixon visits Communist China
	Democratic National Committee headquarters broken into at Watergate complex in Washington, D.C.
	Richard M. Nixon reelected President
1973	Selective Service (the draft) ends
	Last U.S. troops leave Vietnam
1974	Resignation of President Richard Nixon; Gerald Ford becomes President.
1976	Election of Jimmy Carter to presidency
1978	Senate agrees to Panama Canal Treaty
1979	Formal signing of Israeli-Egyptian accords at White House.
	Iranian Revolution turns against United States.

8

FROM CONFIDENCE TO INDECISION

Historians frequently talk of the need to have perspective on a period in order to understand it. The passage of time, it is pointed out, allows the historically unimportant to fade and partisanship to wane. Sometimes, too, with the passage of time, a recent era pointedly directs people's attention to events of earlier years. Two hundred years after the Revolution, certain developments of the 1970s suddenly made the past sharply relevant to living Americans. The provisions that the Founding Fathers had devised in 1787 for removing a President became front page news in 1974.

Historical perspective often does something else: It may alter the meaning we give to an earlier period. Take, for example, the years immediately after the Second World War. Although Americans had feared that the end of war production would result in a severe depression, the nation entered upon an era of prosperity more extensive and longer lasting than any in its history. For a couple of decades the abundance that poured from farms and factories seemed to justify America's faith in hard work and efficiency. Despite inflation and economic recessions the American worker lived better than any worker in world

history. In the early 1970s, even in the midst of rising food prices, the average American family spent only 18 percent of its income on food, compared with 25 percent by a family in western Europe and almost 50 percent by one in the Sovet Union. Even traditionally disadvantaged black Americans participated more than ever before in the nation's prosperity. Perhaps Thomas Jefferson, with his vision of a predominantly agricultural America, would not have been happy with the highly industrialized and urban United States of the postwar years, but certainly its wealth and power would have warmed the cockles of Alexander Hamilton's mercantilist heart.

Today, however, we look back less positively upon the economic gains since 1945. Industrial growth is no longer the clear-cut benefit it seemed only a decade ago. For example, certain negative consequences must be dealt with if we are to provide enough personal income and produce enough automobiles to allow each family to own a car: City streets become impassable, and the air is filled with fumes, the sky with smog, and the countryside with highways. Furthermore, industrial production throws off wastes that befoul our streams, encumber the land, and cost large amounts of money to remove. Additionally, rising production consumes ever increasing amounts of natural resources, in pursuit of which our forests are denuded, hills scarred, lakes and oceans emptied of fish, and wild and unsettled lands reduced. At the same time, simply to abandon the drive for production promises no solution, for only with wealth can the environment be cleaned up and kept clean.

There were other developments that the 1940s called successes but that a longer perspective reveals as problems. During and after the administration of Franklin Roosevelt, the growth in the power of the presidency was hailed as an effective way of achieving needed reforms, uniting the country, and providing leadership. Harry Truman, John F. Kennedy, Lyndon Johnson, and Richard Nixon all followed Roosevelt's example in their expansion of presidential power. Indeed, one of the principal criticisms of Dwight Eisenhower was that he did not fully use the authority of the presidency that his predecessors had passed on to him. But by the 1970s events provided strong reasons for questioning the wisdom of a continuing expansion of executive powers. The doubts had begun to emerge even before Nixon assumed the office but his abuse of presidential power made the matter a concern for all Americans.

Ironically enough, now that the issue has been confronted, it is not at all clear that in the modern world of nuclear powers there is a real alternative to a strong President. During the Ford administration, for example, when Congress sought to reduce presidential authority, it failed to provide either the political or the personal leadership that even a mediocre President can automatically command simply because of the office. The American presidency was a unique creation of the Founding Fathers. Whatever their intention for the office may have been, by the last half of the twentieth century the United States presidency had become the most powerful as well as

the least responsive office in any democratic government. And so it remained even after the fall of Nixon. And the reason was that no institutions in the American constitutional system functioned to supplement or control it.

The ultimate control that the Founding Fathers provided worked well enough in 1974, when the threat of impeachment forced Nixon out of office. But impeachment is a blunt instrument. What is needed are continuous and flexible controls. The system of checks and balances relies upon a quality of leadership and independence in the other two branches that has not always been present or, perhaps, cannot be expected. Divided by party loyalties, Congress as a body cannot focus its energies and policies as a single executive can. Moreover, Congress will always find it difficult to resist a President in foreign affairs when he speaks for the nation abroad and has access to sources of information that Congress will always lack. And when, as Jimmy Carter's years in office showed, the President does not lead forcefully, the resulting vacuum cannot be filled by Congress. This is especially true when the party system has been weakened and trust in government in general has eroded.

Although many of the promises spawned in the optimism and self-confidence of the 1950s and 1960s have since turned sour, some were at least partly realized. The Black Revolution, the women's movement, and the protest activities of Chicanos and Indians have helped expand the social, political, and economic opportunities that an earlier America had reserved largely for white males of European origin. Moreover, during the 1960s and after, the average American's freedom of expression and access to information were probably greater than at any previous time. Even the revelations of governmental abuse of power during the 1960s and early 1970s testified to the American commitment to an open and socially diverse society. Few other modern societies, for example, permit access to such an array of private governmental sources.

But the very distrust of government that demanded opening of the records reflected a profound lack of self-confidence among Americans. Defeated in Vietnam, divided at home, and ill-served by their government, they were not sure where they wanted to go or why. As President Carter said in his speech on the American spirit in July 1979, Americans were, perhaps for the first time in their history, no longer sure that the future would be better than the present.

The passage of time has also reshaped our interpretation of America's relations with the rest of the world. For some twenty years after the great military victory of World War II, the United States moved swiftly to the center of the world's political and military stage, committing itself to the defense not only of western Europe, but of countries in Asia as well. This dramatic reversal of the foreign policy of the 1930s was praised by many historians and others as proof that Americans had drawn the proper conclusions from the western democracies' failure to stand up to Nazi Germany and Japan during the 1930s. Indeed, it was largely this conclusion that convinced President Harry Truman that United States soldiers must fight in Korea, and President Johnson that large numbers of American troops must also be sent to Vietnam. In 1961 President Kennedy gave eloquent voice to this sense of power and purpose. The United States, he said at his inauguration, would "pay any price, bear any burden, meet any hardship, support any friend, oppose any foe to assure the survival and the success of liberty."

Within ten years, however, another President was disclaiming any such ambitious commitment. In his first State of the World address, Richard Nixon pointed out that "America cannot—and will not—conceive *all* the plans, design *all* the programs, execute *all* of the decisions, and undertake *all* the defenses of the free nations of the world." It had become apparent by then that what was once seen as a world-wide threat to freedom was no longer so. The Communist world was as deeply divided by nationalistic rivalries as the capitalist world. Yet before this lesson could be drawn, the demands of the Cold War had enmeshed the United States in a new and costly war in Southeast Asia.

When that war ended with American defeat and withdrawal from Asia, American dominance in world affairs also came to an end. Thus around 1976 a new era opened in America's relations with the world. Though the United States was still the most productive economy, and one of the world's two military superpowers, Americans no longer viewed international leadership as a necessity or even as an opportunity. The long and internally divisive war in Asia had changed that. Isolationism had not returned, to be sure, nor could it, given the facts of international economics. But military intervention abroad, as in Vietnam or Korea, was no longer an idea Americans could accept. And President Jimmy Carter did not seem disposed to try to change their minds.

Instead, the United States and the industrialized world as a whole found themselves largely on the defensive after 1976. The object of world concern, however, was no longer either European or Asian communism. It was oil—that versatile and crucial source of energy that is the lifeblood of all modern societies. How to keep it flowing and how to obtain alternative sources of energy brought together the domestic and foreign policies of the United States into a novel configuration that promises to endure into the foreseeable future.

TO THINK ABOUT AS YOU READ . . .

1. Economic developments are often seen as shaping other human activities. Can you see ways in which the prosperity of the 1950s and 1960s shaped the developments in education, religion, entertainment, and culture in general? What changes do you think will occur in the 1980s if the economy slowdown is serious and inflation persists?

2. What events and developments in the 1950s at home and abroad do you think might help to explain the strong interest on the part of the government and the American people in improving the economic and social position of blacks? Why do you think that interest has declined in recent years?

3. Diplomatic historians often say that foreign policy is but an extension of domestic policies. What evidence do you see of that being true in the years after 1945? Might a better case be made that it is United States' relations with foreign countries that have shaped domestic policies during these same years?

4. Today the presidency of Harry Truman is held in quite high esteem by historians and by the public. Why do you think this is so, considering how low he stood in the polls when he left office in 1953? Why do you think Dwight Eisenhower's presidency is viewed as less dynamic or inspiring by those who admire Truman's presidency? Which President used presidential power more responsibly, Lyndon Johnson or Richard Nixon?

5. Even though several Republican Presidents have been elected in the past thirty years, the Republican party has been steadily losing popular appeal, as measured in the Congressional elections prior to 1980. Why do you think this happened? Does the decline suggest to you any insights into the cultural and social changes in the United States?

Chapter 22

The Culture of the Postwar Era

THE RISE OF THE CONSUMER SOCIETY

The Prosperous American. The hallmark of life in the United States during most of the thirty-five years after 1945 was the expanding prosperity of the ordinary citizen. The Great Depression had not ended immediately, of course. And even at the conclusion of the period, in the 1970s, millions of Americans, particularly those with dark skins, remained poor and disadvantaged. Yet, measured against any previous period the economic pattern of life for most Americans distinctly improved during the thirty years after World War II. The economic abundance of these years calls for some understanding and explanation, for it was abundance that shaped the life of the ordinary American.

Who was this American? What was his life like? The first point to note is that the average American, in a statistical sense, was not a "he" at all. For the first time in the history of the country, the majority of Americans in the years after 1945 were female. The "average" American was white, married, and probably a mother. Although 80 percent of adult male Americans worked, most women during these years did not. By 1971, however, a majority of married women worked outside the home at least part of the time. That same year over half of married working women were mothers of children under eighteen.

The possessions of the average American and her husband reflected the prosperity of the times. They owned their own home, most likely in an urban area since well over half of all Americans lived in cities. By the end of the period it was likely that the house would be in a suburb rather than a metropolitan city. Regardless of where she lived, the average American would have a car, a telephone, and a television set. In 1974, almost two thirds of American homes contained a color TV, and 45 percent of them had two or more television sets.

So popular was television in the lives of Americans that more owned TV sets than owned washing machines and dishwashers together. Thus 94.4 per cent of families with incomes under $5,000 in 1974 had a TV and a refrigerator, but only 55 per cent of them owned a washing machine. Televisions and refrigerators were the only major appliances the ownership of which did not vary significantly by income.

Neither the average American, if she

worked outside the home, nor her husband worked with their hands at a machine in a factory. Both were likely to be white-collar workers in an office or performing some personal service for others. If she had been born before 1940, it was likely that her children would be attending college, though even in the 1970s when about half the young people continued their education after high school, only about a third of college-age people actually graduated from college.

The recreation of the average American centered around her family, with a heavy dependence upon watching TV. Movies, which had once been a major form of popular entertainment, had become principally an entertainment of young people. Some spectator sports, particularly professional football, had burgeoned into a major popular entertainment. Attendance figures at the National Football League games alone jumped almost 500 per cent between 1950 and 1973. In 1970 some 30 million people attended college football games.

But participatory sports—that is, those that cost money to participate in, such as bowling, golfing, riding, or swimming—also surged. In fact, in 1976 Americans spent more on such sports than on movies or on spectator sports. An equal amount ($3.9 billion) was spent on flowers, plants, and seeds, suggesting that gardening was another significant participatory sport.

Although never avid book readers, Americans had once supported a large number of newspapers. But in the years between 1950 and 1970 the numbers of newspapers declined in the face of rising costs and declining revenues. During the 1970s, however, the number began to rise again. The number of periodicals increased throughout the period, too. They catered increasingly to the specialized interests and hobbies of Americans, like woodworking, sailing, gardening, hunting, sewing, and cooking.

The pursuit of recreation in a period of prosperity can be measured by the fact that 16 million Americans rode horses, 10 million played golf, and 7 million owned motor boats. Between 1950 and 1975 the number of people who took out hunting licenses doubled, while fishing licenses more than doubled, reaching 35 million in 1975.

As the figures on appliances, possessions, and recreation imply, the United States of the 1950s and 1960s was a consumer society of the highest order. The production and acquisition of goods and services became almost an obsession. The very diversity of goods available was at once tantalizing and bewildering. Consumption threatened to outrun production as Americans sought to increase their leisure and reduce their work. Although millions of Americans still lived outside the urban environment, they did not escape city values or materialistic temptations, if only because they had a direct line to the city in their televisions. Few farmhouses were without the thrusting TV aerial to link them to the wider world.

Although more and more Americans traveled outside the United States—the number increased tenfold between 1950 and 1970—the average American spent her vacations with her family inside the United States, usually at the seashore, at lakes, in the mountains, or visiting the national parks in the West. In 1973 there were more visits to the national parks than there were people in the country, reflecting the visits of many people to more than one park or monument. Although the rising price of gasoline began to curtail that kind of vacationing in the late 1970s, the quarter century after the Second World War witnessed an ever growing dependence upon the automobile for pleasure.

One reason Americans could become a nation on wheels in the summer was that vacations had become longer. Before 1940 the average annual vacation was one week. After the war the average doubled, and for increasing numbers of Americans vacation time stretched to three and four weeks.

During the years of prosperity Americans also ate better. The near-full employment that prevailed during these years encouraged people to buy more prepared foods like TV dinners, pastry and other mixes, and frozen vegetables and juices, as well as more costly kinds and cuts of meat. Per capita consumption of frozen foods jumped 300 percent between 1950 and 1973, while per capita purchases of beef went up 150 percent, and those of chicken and turkey more than doubled. The per capita intake of hard liquors rose almost 90 percent after 1950, and of wine, 74 percent. The change in wine drinking over twenty-five years reflected not only an increase in alcoholic intake but a broadening of tastes as well.

Although the federal government and private medical organizations mounted extensive campaigns against cigarette smoking during the 1950s and 1960s because of the clear causal linkage between smoking and cancer, the per capita consumption of cigarettes actually increased from 175 packs a year in 1950 to 210 packs in 1973. It declined then, however, to 203 in 1977.

Despite the increasing richness of the diet and the rise in the consumption of alcohol and tobacco, the life expectancy of the average American significantly improved. In 1940 the average life expectancy at birth was 62.9 years. By 1976 it was up to 72.5. By 1977, it was 73.2. An even more significant measure of improvement was the increase in the life expectancy of black males—from 53 years in 1940 to 68.3 years in 1976. A large part of the improvement stemmed from the lowering of infant mortality rates during those years. A 70 percent drop in infant mortality for whites and 67 percent for blacks reflected not only improvements in medical care, but general prosperity as well.

How was it possible for average Americans to have improved their standard of living so dramatically in the years following World War II? To understand that story let us look at the various segments of the economy and the society.

An Affluent Society. The striking fact about the 1950s and 1960s—in contrast with the 1930s and 1940s—was that unemployment, which as late as 1939 was running at 17 percent of the labor force, did not go above 8 percent at any time in the following thirty years. This was true even though there were at least three rather severe recessions during those years. In the early 1970s economists were puzzled by an increase in prices in the midst of unemployment. In the preceding thirty years, however, they had at least understood the workings of the economy well enough to help prevent a return of the massive unemployment of the Great Depression. The principal single agency responsible for that achievement was the federal government.

After 1940 and down to 1973 high productivity and prosperity were the dominant social facts. Goods spilled from American factories and farms in ever increasing volume and variety. Between 1940 and 1960 the gross national product (GNP), after price changes are discounted, rose 114 percent, though the population grew less than 36 percent. In 1971 the GNP for the first time passed $1 trillion. As recently as 1960 it had been "only" half that. Even when the growth is measured in constant dollars—that is, taking inflation into account—the GNP increased 150 percent between 1950 and 1977. As rates of economic growth go among industrial nations, this was not spectacular. But measured in quantity of goods, American production dwarfed that of any economy in the world. Only Sweden and Switzerland equaled the per capita production of the American economy at the beginning of the 1970s.

The seemingly limitless flood of goods from America's factories and farms in the 1950s did not lack for consumers, as this supermarket scene shows.

Other periods in American history—the 1920s, for example—had been notable for productive capacity and prosperity, but the novelty of the years between 1945 and 1970 was that lower-income groups, as well as upper-income groups, shared in the prosperity. Millions of American families moved up the income ladder. One sign of this rise is that the weekly wage of workers in manufacturing between 1947 and 1957 rose 16 percent—even after the rise in the cost of living is taken into consideration. Another is that since 1950 the average income of the bottom tenth of the population has gone up about 55 percent, after discounting price changes. A third measure is the increase in home ownership. In 1940 fewer than 44 percent of American families, including farmers, lived in homes they had bought. By 1973 the proportion was up to 65 percent. Moreover, the proportion of Americans who lived below the poverty line steadily declined from 22 percent in 1959, when the statistics were first compiled, to 11.4 percent sixteen years later.

Even that decline, however, meant that millions of Americans still lived in want. As a result, federal outlays for welfare rose rapidly, especially in the 1960s as a "war against poverty" was mounted by the Johnson administration. In 1966 federal expenditures on behalf of low-income people amounted to $11.3 billion. By 1971, under the first Nixon administration, the figure had more than doubled to $25.5 billion.

Despite these aids to the poor and the move up the income ladder of millions of lower-class and middle-class Americans, the distribution of income barely changed in these years. In 1950 the top 5 percent of families received 17 percent of aggregate income, while the lowest 20 percent received 4.5 percent. Twenty-five years later the proportion of total aggregate income received by the top 5 percent was down to 15.5 percent, but the proportion received by the lowest 20 percent was up only to 5.4 percent. And the top 20 percent of income receivers got about the same share in 1975 that they had in 1950—that is, about 40 percent. As might be expected in a competitive society, income distribution remained far from equal.

The Corporate Economy. The rapidly expanding economy of the 1950s and 1960s was highly institutionalized. Most people in the labor force worked for someone else, usually a corporation. In 1900, 36 percent of all members of the work force had been self-employed. By 1958 that figure was down to 15 percent. There were still millions of small businesses, but measured by income and production they constituted only a small proportion of the economy. In 1968 less than 3 percent of all corporations received almost

four fifths of the total income of corporations. Corporate enterprises, with their large capital resources and heavy expenditures on research and development, were at once a cause and a consequence of the prosperity of the 1950s and 1960s.

Government, too, with its large outlays of funds, encouraged the corporations and stimulated the economy. Defense expenditures alone reached $50 billion a year in the early 1960s and surged to over $80 billion at the height of the Vietnam War. In fact, after the Second World War the federal government moved far beyond its largely regulatory role under the New Deal. It was now, with its huge budget, a significant participant in the marketplace as well. By 1970 the federal government alone spent a quarter of the nation's money and, with state and local governments, hired almost a fifth of the labor force.

The federal government was also one of the principal forces sustaining the housing boom of the 1950s and 1960s, a major stimulus of the prosperity of those years. Through agencies like the Federal Housing Administration and the Veterans Administration, the government helped finance mortgages for the construction of millions of homes, as well as pouring money into the housing industry in general through its support of low-income public housing. Since residential construction makes up between 20 and 25 percent of all private investment, the significance of government aid to construction can hardly be exaggerated in explaining the economic growth of the postwar years. The extent of the housing boom of the 1950s and 1960s can be measured in the simple fact that in 1971 two fifths of all the houses and apartments occupied in the country had been built in the preceding twenty years.

At the root of economic growth, of course, was the increase in the productivity of the labor force. Generally this gain was achieved through a greater use of machines and power. As machines became more sophisticated and versatile, workers became primarily feeders, supervisors, and operators. The machines did almost all the labor. Even in primary work like digging ditches, machines were used. Heavy lifting by workers, which as recently as the 1930s was common in foundries, mills, and warehouses, was greatly reduced by forklifts, cranes, and other types of lifting equipment. Efficiency was further enhanced by new integration processes whereby interruptions in the manufacture of goods were eliminated. In the so-called continuous-flow processes, a sequence of operations now became a single operation. A result was that whereas in 1947 it took 310.5 hours to make an automobile, by 1962 the time had been cut in half. A single invention like the digital computer and, later,

the microchip made a whole range of clerical and arithmetical activities amazingly rapid, thus releasing money and labor for other tasks.

One consequence of the growth of industry and big business was the expansion of American enterprises abroad in the form of the multinational corporation. Industrial giants like Ford and IBM opened plants in foreign countries in order to tap foreign markets and cheaper labor more easily. Sometimes the products of these American-owned companies in foreign countries competed with American exports, thus arousing the ire of organized labor in the United States. At other times multinational corporations, not all of which were American by any means,

One development that cut the time needed to make an automobile was automatic welding, shown here in a General Motors plant. The large control board indicates any welder malfunction.

encountered opposition from the host countries because they dominated or threatened to stifle local enterprises.

And some of the multinational corporations were enormous. The incomes of the largest dwarfed the national economies of two thirds of the countries of the world. Seen in historical perspective, the multinational corporation imposed a new stability and order on the international economy, not unlike that which the trusts and giant corporations of the nineteenth century had imposed on the national economy of the United States. Like the nineteenth-century trusts, they were great aggregations of economic power—but on an international rather than a national scale and consequently even more difficult to regulate or monitor. The size of the multinational corporations measured, too, how the technological advances of the affluent postwar era had tied together the United States and the rest of the world in a global economy.

Rise of the White-Collar Class.   As the emphasis upon machine production implies, the work performed in the United States in the postwar years was quite different from the industrial labor of previous years. During most of America's history the majority of workers had been farmers, miners, fishermen, and factory workers—that is, blue-collar workers. But ever since the opening of the twentieth century, an increasing proportion of the labor force has comprised white-collar workers—managers, clerks, professionals, government employees, and self-employed proprietors. Beginning in the 1950s more than half of American workers were white-collar and service workers rather than blue-collar workers. In 1970 white-collar workers alone constituted 50.8 percent of the nonagricultural labor force, blue-collars 34.5 percent, and service workers (policemen, bank tellers, domestics, and others) 10.5 percent.

The growth of a white-collar class meant that an increasing number of people were being supplied with goods by an ever smaller proportion of agricultural and manufacturing employees. It also was a measure of the maturity of the economy, since only a highly mechanized and skilled society could achieve such a division of labor. By 1970 less than 5 percent of the work force was in agriculture, compared with 18 percent employed by government—in a society that prided itself on being the antithesis of socialistic! (In officially Communist Yugoslavia in 1972, 20 percent of the work force was employed by the government.)

White-collar predominance also testified to the consumer nature of the economy. Whereas in previous history most paid labor was employed in making new goods, by the end of the 1950s most working people were consuming goods, helping others consume goods, or performing a service.

Traditionally, white-collar workers have resisted joining unions, even though white-collar pay is often inferior to industrial wages. In 1972, for example, only 16.5 percent of all unionized workers were employed in white-collar occupations. The growth in the white-collar class thus seemed to explain, at least partly, the stagnation in labor organizing in the 1950s. Despite its organizing drives and its power, organized labor in the 1960s barely kept pace with the growing size of the labor force. In 1964, for example, about 30 percent of nonagricultural workers were in unions. Eight years later the proportion was down to 26.7 percent.

A large part of the white-collar class was composed of women, who after 1940 entered the labor force in ever increasing numbers. Indeed, between 1950 and 1970 some 13.2 million women joined the labor force, as compared with only 9.5 million men. And among these working women were growing numbers of wives and mothers. By 1970 over two fifths of all married women were employed in paying jobs. Almost a third of women with children under six were working, counting only married women whose husbands were present. In short, women now constituted the largest source of new workers in the economy.

Women entering the labor force, however, were frequently compelled to accept jobs that paid less or were otherwise less rewarding than their education or training warranted. This was espcially true of college-educated women, who, proportionately, returned to work in larger numbers than their noncollege sisters. Furthermore, the needs of the economy apparently did not encourage women to develop their powers. In the 1950s women made up a smaller proportion of all college students than they had in the 1920s, and fewer women, proportionately, were entering graduate schools. By the 1970s, however, there was some reason to believe this pattern was changing.

A Revolution in Agriculture. Like industry, farming experienced a revolution in productivity during the 1950s and 1960s. The increased ability to produce food was an important impetus to the prosperity and the high standard of living of those years. In 1960, for example, an hour of employment in manufacturing bought 2.2 pounds of round steak. In 1929 the same amount of labor had bought only 1.2 pounds. By 1969 an hour's work in a factory bought 2.4 pounds. (Even at the height of inflation in 1974, an hour of factory work bought 2.3 pounds of round steak.) In 1960 about seven minutes of work purchased a quart of milk. In 1969 less than five minutes would buy the same amount.

If, as these figures suggest, American farming was highly productive, it was also in some places backward, inefficient, and a cause of poverty for hundreds of thousands of people who could not afford the costly machines and costly methods that made the agricultural revolution of the postwar years. Even though the number of farmers had been steadily declining ever since the 1920s, as late

as 1961 some 1.6 million farm families, or 44 percent of the total, earned so little from agriculture that they had to engage in other kinds of employment to make ends meet. These people—black and white sharecroppers in the South, farmers on marginal lands in Appalachia and the Middle West—actually were as hard up as the poor of the central cities. Indeed, in 1968 it was estimated that 23 percent of the farm population lived below the poverty line, as compared with 12 percent of the urban population.

It was the highly efficient farms that produced the great bulk of the food, thanks to the encouragement of high government price supports during the 1950s. Capital per farm in 1974 was about 6.6 times in constant dollars what it had been in 1950. Or put another way, in the 1960s the amount of capita per farm work was about $5000 more than the amount of capital per worker in manufacturing. It was this high capitalization that explained the enormous increase in farm productivity. In 1969 over 4.5 million tractors were in use on American farms, and thousands of mechanical cotton pickers had displaced hundreds of thousands of Southern black workers, who left agriculture to seek wider opportunities in Northern cities. New seeds, new machines, and new chemicals of all kinds also gave impetus to the farm revolution of the postwar years. Chemicals were used not only to kill harmful insects but to hasten crop maturity, to kill weeds, to defoliate plants in order to facilitate harvesting, or to inhibit growth in crops like tobacco where only certain kinds of leaves are desired. The chemical industry also developed new feeds for chickens, which speeded up growth and made it possible to raise broilers from egg to maturity in eight to nine weeks. The disastrous effects of some of these chemicals upon wildlife have posed a serious dilemma for a society wanting cheap and abundant food and wildlife at the same time.

The most important consequence of the

changes in agriculture after 1945 is that the family farm as it has been known in the United States since the beginning has almost disappeared. Between 1949 and 1959 some 1.2 million farm families simply left agriculture. By 1960 less than 8 percent of the American population lived on farms, and by 1970 that proportion was down to less than 5 percent. Yet the value of total farm production rose about 20 percent in the same ten-year period. Thus a farmer either was a large-scale operator with a large capital investment or would soon be compelled to withdraw from farming.

Advances in Chemistry.   A large part of the enormous increase in agricultural productivi-ty derived from advances in chemistry. The new chemistry also had a profound effect in areas outside of agriculture. The break-through came just before the Second World War when artificial fibers, such as nylon, which had been created in the laboratory, began to replace cotton, linen, and silk in the manufacture of cloth. Then during the war, when the supply of natural rubber in Asia was cut off by the war with Japan, chemists were able to develop a new synthetic rubber industry. The discovery of how to create giant molecules called polymers allowed chemists to lay the foundation, after the war, of the plastics industry.

Plastics, it was found, could be used in place

Mechanization resulted in enormous increases in farm productivity. But the large capital investment needed for machines like these combines harvesting sorghum in Texas turned farming into big business and threatened the economic viability of the traditional family farm.

of wood, rubber, and metals, and had the decided advantage of being moldable. Thus the shaping of objects made out of plastics did not incur high labor costs. Moreover, plastics were lightweight, resistant to corrosion, and good at insulating. Thus plastics came to be used in a myriad ways, some of which were quite central to the economy. An automobile, for example, now contains about 100 pounds of plastics. All told, about 23 billion pounds of plastics are produced in the United States each year. Since almost all plastics are made from petroleum waste products, the dependence of the American economy on foreign oil derives from more than simply the American love affair with the automobile.

Chemistry also reshaped the field of medicine, for a whole range of new drugs and medicines have been developed for the relief of pain and the treatment of many diseases, including mental illness. Tranquilizers, sleeping aids, birth control pills, fertility pills, and many other kinds of drugs and chemicals not only are new since the Second World War but are now a part of the everyday lives of millions of Americans. It has been estimated that at least half of the current products of the giant chemical industry were unknown before 1950. In the drug branch of the industry no more than 10 percent were known before 1955.

LITERARY AND DRAMATIC EXPRESSION

The Novel. Not surprisingly, the Second World War fostered a number of novels by important American writers. Among them were John Hersey's *A Bell for Adano* (1944), Irwin Shaw's *The Young Lions* (1948), Norman Mailer's *The Naked and the Dead* (1949), James Jones' *From Here to Eternity* (1951), and—ten years later, for another generation—Joseph Heller's *Catch-22*. From a different angle, and still later, was Kurt Vonnegut's macabre *Slaughterhouse Five*, about the bombing of Dresden, which began his popularity among college students. Norman Mailer went on to

write more novels, and then to move over into a highly personal form of journalism that produced, among other works, *Armies in the Night* (1968), his remarkable account of his own participation in an antiwar demonstration at the Pentagon.

By 1960 the final works of a number of novelists of the first and second rank—Faulkner, Hemingway, Dos Passos, Steinbeck, and O'Hara—had appeared. But some of the best of the new writers carried on in the realistic tradition: Saul Bellow (*The Adventures of Augie Mach*, 1953; *Herzog*, 1964; *Humboldt's Gift*, 1975), for example, and Bernard Malamud (*The Assistant*, 1957; *A New Life*, 1961). In 1976 Bellow won the Nobel Prize for Literature. (That Bicentennial Year, in fact, Americans won all five Nobel Prizes.)

Other writers began in the realistic tradition and then moved away from it: Mailer, for one, and for another, Philip Roth, who followed a brilliant short story collection (*Goodbye, Columbus*, 1959) with two traditional novels and then swerved to the wild sexual excess of *Portnoy's Complaint* (1969), and the vitriolic political satire of *Our Gang* (1971), which was about President Nixon. His interest in outrageous fantasy continued with *The Breast* (1972) and *The Professor of Desire* (1977).

John Updike, a virtuoso performer, moved in and out of the realistic tradition with *Rabbit Run* (1960), *The Centaur* (1963), and *Rabbit Redux* (1971). His rising interest in Africa was reflected in his *The Coup* (1978). Of a much more traditional character was the work of Isaac Bashevis Singer, written in Yiddish though Singer now lived in the United States. He recounted in compelling narrative and wry humor the joys and sorrows of Jewish life. His remarkably diverse body of work was recognized internationally in 1978 with the Nobel Prize.

The best known black writers in the opening years of the period were Ralph Ellison, whose *Invisible Man* (1952) became a classic, and James Baldwin (*Go Tell It on the*

Mountain, 1953; *Another Country*, 1962). The most striking black talent in the second half of the century was female: Toni Morrison, whose *The Bluest Eye* (1970) captured attention immediately, and Maya Angelou, whose autobiography, *I Know Why the Caged Bird Sings* (1970), was both popular and significant.

The Movies. The initial impact of television, when it burst upon the entertainment scene in the early 1950s, was to cause a decline in public interest in movies. Hundreds of movie theaters closed down during the 1950s and 1960s, and the Hollywood studios either went unused or were turned over to making movies for TV. In 1948 there were 18,600 movie houses in the country. By 1963 the number was a mere 9200. But then a revival began as independent producers and movie makers came upon the scene. By 1967 there were some 12,000 movie houses and by 1977 the figure was 17,000. Moreover, by 1976 more money was being spent on movie tickets than for all spectator sport events, theater, and opera admissions put together.

By the late 1960s, in sum, it was evident that a sizable segment of the population did not want to stay home nights and stare at the TV set. Reared on television, the young were ready to leave the "tube" to their parents. Many members of the new movie audience were college students or recent graduates, for during the 1960s there was a great increase in college attendance. To reach this expanding potential audience the movies had to grow up. The best of them did. As in the theater and the novel, censorship was virtually dead—a development which conservatives blamed on the "permissive liberalism" of the Supreme Court but which permitted a new realism and a new frankness of both theme and treatment. More significant, perhaps, was the new sophistication the audience demanded. Westerns could still succeed, but movies that laughed at the clichés (*Cat Ballou, True Grit*) or depicted three-dimensional characters in-

stead of cardboard cutouts (*Butch Cassidy and the Sundance Kid*) did best. War, long the subject of romantic or chauvinistic epics, came in for ironic attacks in movies like *Dr. Strangelove, Catch-22*, and *M*A*S*H*. The Vietnam War was treated seriously—and critically—in the poignant *Coming Home*, starring, appropriately enough, the antiwar actress Jane Fonda, and in *The Deerhunter*, which unblinkingly depicted the cost of the war to those who supported it. *The Deerhunter* was also one of several movies dealing realistically with working-class life in America. Another was *Norma Rae*.

Some of the best of the new movies were addressed directly to the young. *The Graduate* came to be considered a classic statement of what young people held against their parents and what they thought of themselves. *Easy Rider* offered a sympathetic view of the drug culture in idyllic settings, and *One Flew Over the Cuckoo's Nest* expressed many a young person's sense of the insanity of the conventional world and its institutions. If some older fans were troubled by the moral ambiguities in the new films, and wondered whether there was, in fact, anything particularly grown up or sophisticated about clinical studies of loveless sex (*Deep Throat*) or celebrations of mindless violence (*Straw Dogs, Clockwork Orange*), by the 1970s the movies were an important emotional and intellectual experience for a great many young Americans. In *Saturday Night Fever* and *Grease* the importance of rock music and dancing in the lives of millions of young people was brought home to all who saw those films.

Older Americans also found certain films in the 1970s attractive, perhaps because they stirred remembrances of things past (*The Great Gatsby, The Sting*) or sentimental ethnicity (*The Godfather*) or the love of being frightened (*Jaws* and *The Exorcist*). Science fiction movies, the ground breaker of which was the highly creative *2001*, proved inordinately attractive to young as well as old. *The Man Who Fell to*

Earth was not a great success in 1976, but in the next two years three science fiction movies each challenged all money-making records: *Star Wars, Close Encounters of the Third Kind,* and *Superman,* the last based upon the old comic strip and TV serial. Was this new interest in science fiction a delayed reaction to the success of the 1960s in putting a man on the moon—or merely escape?

By the 1970s movies made about blacks and for blacks began to appear *(Shaft, Super Fly,* and *Sounder).* Blacks were increasingly a part of the mainstream of America and were recognized as such in the social mirror of the movies. Some blacks as well as whites deplored the separatism and racial chauvinism sometimes depicted in these movies, but others cheered the fact that there were beginning to be some black heroes and heroines with whom black fans could identify. Situation comedies on TV also began to feature blacks, some of the top shows being primarily black in cast and outlook, though generally written by whites.

The most spectacular success in all of television production concerned blacks. It was the series running eight consecutive evenings called *Roots,* which told the story of a black family from its beginnings in Africa, through the darkness of slavery in America, and finally into freedom. Written by black author Alex Haley, *Roots* was seen in January 1977 by almost three quarters of the owners of television sets in the country—in itself a powerful comment on the impact of the black experience on the consciousness of Americans, white as well as black.

THE DARK SIDE AND THE BEGINNINGS OF CHANGE

Sources of Anxiety. The unusual prosperity of these years obscured a number of nagging fears and broad dissatisfactions; these, too, were a part of the postwar social scene. As we shall see in the following chapters, the end of World War II did not mean the end of international suspicions or even of war for the United States. This was the time of the Cold War, when the immense military power and broadened aspirations of the Soviet Union seemed to threaten first Europe and then Asia. Fear of Communist ideology during part of the 1950s so undermined the self-confidence of Americans that a "witch-hunt" was mounted for Communist spies and sympathizers. Hostilities between nations not only threatened, but brought death to, thousands of Americans, first in Korea and then in Vietnam. Fear of nuclear war was sufficiently high in those years to put schoolchildren through bomb drills, and for many citizens to build home bomb shelters.

The very prosperity was a source of anxiety and confusion of values. It encouraged many Americans to buy goods to "keep up with the Joneses," to choose goods over goals. Many adults who had grown up during the Great Depression sacrificed to give their children material advantages they themselves never enjoyed. In doing so, they laid the groundwork for the antimaterialism of the counterculture, which, in turn, alienated many children from their parents. Since even poor people had television, they had first-hand knowledge of the goods they were denied by their poverty. The resentment of many erupted into violence in dozens of cities. For others, the resentment was kept hidden, but it was no less alienating and divisive.

The highly organized corporate economy and its burgeoning bureaucracy, which was in large part responsible for the prosperity, reduced the individual's feelings of significance and effectiveness. The efficient organization of work, on which the prosperity depended, made the work place for millions of Americans monotonous, impersonal, and dispiriting.

New sources of anxiety appeared on a

global scale: rapid population growth; impending world shortages of food and irreplaceable resources like oil and gas; the deadly effects of pollution and toxic wastes; and the growing gap between the rich and poor nations, with the latter increasingly insistent upon a fairer share of the world's production. Behind all these threats stood the most immediate and ominous danger of all: the possibility of a nuclear war that might obliterate half the world. The arms race between the United States and the Soviet Union was still uncontrolled, and nuclear weapons by the 1960s were in the hands of at least four other nations as well.

The bright and dark sides of the years after 1945 were summarized in the achievements and the problems of the nation's cities, then undergoing important changes.

The Transformation of the City. The trend toward urbanization had begun early in the nineteenth century. By 1970 almost three fourths of all Americans lived in urban areas, and the trend appeared irreversible, with each census reporting a further decline in the rural population. But during the fifties and sixties the kinds of urban areas in which Americans chose to live began to change. Central metropolitan districts did not keep up with the general urban growth. Between 1950 and 1960, for example, the aggregate total population of cities over 100,000 increased only 9.3 percent, and four out of five of the giant cities of over a million actually decreased in population.

Increasingly, people moving from the country or small towns were settling in the suburbs of the big cities rather than the cities themselves. Many people were also deserting the central cities for the suburbs. This movement had begun in earnest in the 1920s. By the fifties it was a mass exodus. In 1953 the editors of *Fortune* compared the suburban migration to the great immigration from Europe in the

early years of the twentieth century. About as many people—1.2 million—moved to the suburbs that year as had entered the United States in 1907.

The census of 1970 made it clear that this trend was continuing. Between 1960 and 1970, 61 of the 153 cities of 100,000 or more lost population. For many it was the first loss of population since the beginning of the urbanizing movement. In 1970 less than a third of Americans lived in central cities, while more than two fifths lived in surrounding suburbs, which were now becoming places of work as well as residence. By 1970 the suburbs were providing only slightly fewer jobs than the central cities. They were no longer simply "bedroom communities," though 85 percent of American workers used their cars to get to work.

For the central city, commuters and their automobiles presented a growing problem. The demand for parking facilities alone—not to mention the multiplying demands for new expressways and freeways—ate significantly into the prime real estate of the great cities, thus cutting into the tax base that was needed for increased urban expenditures. Moreover, commuter trains, forced to compete with the automobile, found it more and more difficult to make a profit or even to survive, and many were forced to reduce or discontinue their service. Yet much of the metropolitan labor force still depended on the commuter lines for daily transportation. As a consequence a number of state and local governments faced pressures to subsidize the commuter lines in one way or another.

The Urban Mass Transportation Assistance Act of 1970 brought some federal money for mass transportation to the beleaguered cities, but the need far outran the remedy. The automobile was still a difficult competitor to overcome—as San Francisco's computerized Bay Area Rapid Transportation (BART) discovered soon after it opened in 1972. Seven years later it had not yet fulfilled the promise either to reduce auto traffic significantly or to pay for itself. But the need for mass transit was reflected in the new subways that opened in the late 1970s in New Orleans, Atlanta, and Washington, D.C.—the last pronounced a practical and visual success from the outset—and in the plans for a Texas version of San Francisco's BART in Houston.

The flight to the suburbs was both a symptom and a cause of the decline of the central city as a place of human habitation. As middle-class families fled the overcrowded schools, substandard housing, and polluted air, the city became the home of the poor and metropolitan areas deteriorated still more. High land prices, caused in part by land speculation and by rapid, unplanned growth in the new areas, created a big obstacle to the construction of adequate low- and middle-income housing. Nonexistent or poorly enforced building and housing codes, haphazard zoning laws, and the profits to be made from slum real estate further contributed to the continual rotting of the core cities in America's metropolitan areas.

When the Housing Act of 1968 authorized the building of 1.7 million units—mainly low- and moderate-income—over the next three years, it was estimated that at least 6 million were needed. Added to the problems of housing were those of overcrowded, understaffed urban schools and the fact that large areas of modern cities were generating in-

creasing rates of crime, including juvenile delinquency.

These perplexing urban problems stimulated attempts to restore the nation's cities to economic and social health. Under the generic term "urban renewal," many cities attempted to rehabilitate run-down neighborhoods by land clearance and new construction or by renovating existing structures and bringing such areas into conformity with zoning, housing, health, and safety standards.

But despite the success of urban renewal projects in several of America's metropolitan areas, progress was slow. Land clearance ran into vexing legal delays, the relocation of former tenants was a continuing source of irritation for all concerned. Renewal critics

Builders in the 1950s could hardly build fast enough to meet the demands for housing of people who wanted to move to the suburbs.

attacked everything from spiraling costs to the esthetic and social drawbacks of the new construction. They charged that several billions already spent to rejuvenate America's cities had helped only to destroy their individuality. They called the new middle-income housing "a marvel of dullness and regimentation." And some correctly predicted that new low-income projects would themselves be slums by the 1970s.

One device by which the Johnson administration in 1966 pushed better housing for the poor was to provide rent subsidies permitting people to live in nongovernment housing even if rents were higher than they could afford. Another was to provide federal funds for the renovation of older houses and tenements in established neighborhoods in order to escape the often starkly unattractive housing projects. These efforts, too, often resulted in ownership of still more slums by the federal government when the private owners defaulted.

Since coordination of the many efforts to deal with the problems of the decaying city was a paramount need, Congress in 1965 created a new cabinet post for urban development and, in 1966, another for transportation. The latter was designed to encourage and coordinate efforts in behalf of better intra- and interurban transportation, since the automobile had itself become a problem of urban living.

A New Ethnic and Racial Self-Consciousness. Almost from its inception in 1776, the United States has been a broad mixture of peoples. But for most of those two hundred years the national emphasis has been upon denying or suppressing that diversity in order to create a unified American people. The irony was often recognized in the observation that there were more Irish in Boston than in Dublin or more Germans in Milwaukee than in Heidelberg. And even in the 1970s it was true that there were more blacks in New York City

Herblock's cartoon depicts the plight of the cities beset by tax problems and increasing deterioration.

than in Lagos, Nigeria, and more Jews in Los Angeles than in Tel Aviv. During the years after World War II the ethnic and racial diversity of America began to receive its proper due. Political scientists and historians, as well as movies, TV shows, and novels, began to emphasize the sense of loyalty, community, and identity that people felt toward their national, racial, or religious kin. Jewish humor, Italian families, and Irish political activity became the subjects of studies, novels, and entertainment. Young people took a new pride in their European roots and found no serious conflict, as once their parents had been warned, between their Americanism and their ancestry.

A large part of the reason for the new pride in ethnic and racial identity was the emer-

gence into political and economic prominence of these once-submerged groups. The Irish, it is true, were prominent in urban politics in the late nineteenth century, but the Jews, Poles, and Italians and racial groups like Negroes, Japanese, and Chinese came forward only in the twentieth century and principally after World War II. Part of the new attitude, too, reflected the recognition by the dominant majority that racial and ethnic prejudice had no place in a society that prided itself on equality of opportunity.

Undoubtedly the most conspicuous and immediate impetus to the belated recognition of religious, national, or racial identities in American life was the Black Revolution of the 1960s, which started as a nonviolent civil rights movement and was led by Martin Luther King, Jr., until his assassination in 1968. That movement, simply because of its power and its influence on politics, is treated in subsequent pages, but there can be no question that it was a catalyst, if not a model, for the rise in ethnic self-consciousness of other groups in the 1960s and after. Ironically, the success of the blacks' demands for recognition and a share in the national pie of prosperity caused some ethnic groups to react against black aspirations. In the 1970s, for example, the Irish in Boston and the Poles in Detroit were conspicuous in the demonstrations against busing to integrate public schools.

The new emphasis upon equality and group identity as well as impatience at the slow rate of progress from nonviolent methods, caused new black nationalist or separatist groups to come to the fore during the latter sixties. The Black Muslims, a religious society founded by Elijah Muhammad during the 1930s, attracted national attention in the mid-1950s when the very articulate Malcolm X became head of the Muslims in Harlem. The Muslims preach a form of Islam in religion and black separatism in social policy. After he had turned away from the narrow nationalism of Elijah Muhammad, Malcolm X died at the hands of an assassin in 1965.

The most militant of the nationalist groups was the Black Panther party, which began in the Oakland, California, ghetto in 1966. The best-known spokesman of the party was Eldridge Cleaver, a former convict of some literary talent. His book *Soul on Ice* is one of the classics of the Black Revolution, along with Malcolm X's *Autobiography*. Cleaver fled to Algeria in 1968 after a series of confrontations between police and the Panthers. By 1972 the Panthers were less involved in shoot-outs with the police and more concerned with educational and breakfast programs for black children in the urban ghettos. In 1975 Cleaver returned to the United States, prepared to stand trial on the criminal charges against him.

A third figure of prominence in the new black nationalism of the 1960s was Stokely Carmichael, who in 1966, at twenty-four, became head of the Student Nonviolent Coordinating Committee (SNCC). His slogan "Black Power" aroused a new sense of self-awareness and pride among young blacks and a sense of identification and cohesion among blacks of all ages. As a leader, Carmichael did not last into the 1970s, nor did the idea of Black Power, but both left a sense of positive identity among dark-skinned Americans in regard to their blackness and their African origins. Thenceforth most preferred to call themselves black rather than Negro. (See "Muhammad Ali: Float Like a Butterfly, Sting Like a Bee.")

The Black Revolution by its example spurred into visibility a large minority heretofore almost unknown to most Americans: the Mexican-Americans, who numbered as many as 10 million. Though they were concentrated principally in the Southwest, hundreds of thousands lived in the Detroit-Chicago area, so that their disadvantaged social and economic position was not simply a regional concern. The new Chicano organizations, however, were most active in the Southwest. In Texas, for example, the Raza Unida party was sometimes successful in local politics.

Cesar Chavez was perhaps the best known of the Chicano leaders, principally because of his successful organizing of the California grape pickers, most of whom were Mexican-Americans. Chavez, like King, based his movement on principles of nonviolence, aimed at ultimate reconciliation with the dominant majority rather than victory of one group over another. His grape boycott in the years 1965–1969 compelled the grape growers to recognize the union and to bargain with it. In 1975 Chavez' Farm Workers' Union triumphed over the rival unions in gaining recognition among largely Chicano farm workers in California.

More Mexican-Americans were now entering the universities and politics, particularly in the Southwest, suggesting that soon they would play a role in the life of the region commensurate with their numbers. Both Texas and New Mexico sent Mexican-Americans to Congress, and President Carter appointed a Mexican-American to head the Immigration Service Bureau, an agency now confronting the issue of large numbers of Mexicans entering the United States illegally, in search of jobs and a better life.

Another, but socially quite different Spanish-speaking minority in the United States had already made an impact on its region. That was the Cuban-American community of southern Florida, which grew out of the large number of refugees from Castro's Communist dictatorship in the early 1960s. These largely middle-class refugees soon came to dominate large parts of Dade County (Miami) culturally, economically, and even politically. In 1980, for example, the mayor of Miami was a Cuban-American.

Then, by June 1980, more than 110,000

refugees from Castro's Cuba entered the United States in a flotilla of small boats, the operation being largely financed by the Florida Cuba community. The freedom and economic opportunities available in the United States were still acting as a social magnet—this time for poor Mexicans and for Cubans of all classes.

The newest minority group to assert itself in the late 1960s was also the oldest—the Indians. Books by militant friends of the Indian, like Alvin Josephy's *Red Power* (1971), or by Indians themselves, like Vine Deloria, Jr.'s *Custer Died for Your Sins* (1969) brought the Indians' outlook to a wider public, and the federal government took some steps to recognize the just claims of Indians for fairer treatment. (The occupation of Alcatraz Island in San Francisco Bay by a group of Indians in 1971 and a shoot-out between Indians and federal authorities at Wounded Knee, South Dakota, in 1973 showed that some thought the government was moving too slowly.) Under President Johnson the Bureau of Indian Affairs was headed by an Indian for the first time.

In June 1970 President Nixon proclaimed "that the historic relationship between the Federal Government and the Indian communities cannot be abridged without the consent of the Indians." His announcement ended the policy, begun under the Eisenhower administration, of turning the Indians off the reservations into society. That same year, as a recognition of past injustices to the Indian, the Nixon administration returned to

Muhammad Ali: "Float Like a Butterfly, Sting Like a Bee"

Besides being enormously popular, spectator sports in America have become a big business and a source of cultural idols. And in the turbulent sixties, sports figures became political figures as well. No figure in modern sports has been more successful, more popular, or more controversial than boxer Muhammad Ali.

Ali was born Cassius Marcellus Clay, Jr., in Louisville, Kentucky, on January 17, 1942, the son of a black sign painter. The Clays were proud of their lineage, claiming descent from the South's most famous white opponent of slavery, Cassius Marcellus Clay, a relative of the statesman Henry Clay. At the age of twelve, Clay began amateur boxing when Joe Martin, a local policeman, offered to train him. Later Martin would say Clay had been a model student, never smoking, drinking, or using foul language, always working hard at the gym. After more than a hundred amateur fights, Clay won the competition to represent the United States at the 1960 Olympic games in Rome.

Clay early exhibited a trait that would make him notorious: he talked incessantly, almost always boasting about himself. As a form of psychological warfare, he would

the Taos Pueblo Indians 48,000 acres of land around Blue Lake, New Mexico, which they had long held sacred. Indians were still often caught between two cultures, without much preparation or opportunity to move into the mainstream of American economic life—if that was what they wished to do—but at least more recognition was being given to their situation as a separate culture than at any time since the Indian Reorganization Act under the New Deal.

One of the purposes of the new ethnic and racial consciousness of the 1960s and 1970s had been the expansion of opportunities for minorities in American society. By the opening of the 1980s, however, minority appeals to the remainder of the society were considerably less effective, especially those made by blacks. The white majority was no longer finding Black Power or black nationalism of interest. The consequence was that many of the sources of funds on behalf of black advance were shrinking or drying up.

Even moderate organizations like the NAACP learned that indifference to the cause of racial equality presented serious problems in raising funds and support. Few government programs for minority rights were now being pushed, and since 1968 not a single piece of civil rights legislation had been enacted. Affirmative action on behalf of ethnic and racial minorities and women was also coming under attack. In the Bakke and Weber cases (to be discussed) the Supreme Court compromised on how the affirmative action principle should be carried out.

---

predict the round in which he would defeat his opponent and often he made the prediction come true. Even before he went to the Olympics, fans booed him for his unabashed egotism. After he won an Olympic gold medal for boxing, he ostentatiously wore it around his neck for weeks. His triumphant return to Louisville brought out the whole town, where a group of local wealthy white men agreed to back him as a professional fighter. Clay had just completed high school.

That same year he teamed up with Angelo Dundee, who became both trainer and friend. Clay later summed up their relation with a piece of doggerel: "He's got the connection and the complexion to get me the right protection which leads to good affection."

One of the reasons Clay worked so hard at making himself controversial was that it bettered his chance at a heavyweight championship bout. Fight promoters look for boxers who can attract great numbers of paying spectators. In 1964, when he was just 22, Clay got his chance to fight the champion, Sonny Liston. After six rounds, a battered and stunned Liston could not respond to the bell. Clay was the new champ. In his dressing room a shouting, exuberant Clay taunted the reporters, who had long resented his boasting: "Who is the greatest?" he demanded. "You are," they reluctantly answered.

Soon thereafter he went on a tour of Africa and was received by the Presidents of Ghana and Egypt. Clay used the trip to announce that he was a member of the Black Muslims, a religious sect known for its hostility toward whites and its belief in black separatism. Suddenly Clay was no longer the All-American black but a critic, even an opponent, of the white establishment. He dropped his name, contending it had been given by white slave masters, for one from his new religion—Muhammad Ali. Openly he associated himself with the rising civil rights movement, and the new

By the early eighties gains had certainly been made in the direction of greater equality of opportunity, thanks to the new sense of racial and ethnic identification. But the day when color or race or ethnic origin would not matter in getting a job, making friends, or being accepted into a neighborhood was still far in the future, if it was attainable at all. And many ethnic and racial groups were doubtful whether they wanted to see the day when such distinctions did not count.

Challenges to the Educational System. The Russian launching into orbit around the earth of the first Sputnik, on October 4, 1957, dismayed Americans who liked to think of themselves as first in science and technology. Sputnik not only challenged this comfortable self-image but also seemed to mean that the Soviet Union was doing a better job in training scientists and engineers.

Actually, even before Sputnik began to circle the earth, some educators and others had been calling for more rigorous training and for more emphasis on science and mathematics in the curricula of the nation's schools. These critics now made much of reports on Russian education showing the large amount of time spent on science, mathematics, and languages in the Soviet schools. Soon after Sputnik went up, schools around the country began to revise their curricula to put more emphasis upon these subjects.

The administration and Congress responded to the national concern in September 1958

interest among blacks in Africa. Although his wife divorced him and his parents disapproved, he did not waver. Floyd Patterson's 1965 challenge to Ali's title seemed a defense of the establishment when Patterson proclaimed that he intended to bring "the championship back to America." Ali, however, kept the crown easily.

The most severe test of Ali's convictions came later, over his induction into the Army. When first called up in 1962, Ali failed the achievement test and was deferred. His critics, particularly in the white South, were outraged. Nor did Ali soften their wrath by quipping, "I only said I was the greatest, not the smartest."

The consequence was that in 1966 he was reclassified as eligible. By then over 150,000 Americans were fighting in Vietnam. In that context, Ali's remark, "I ain't got nothing against those Vietcongs," set off a barrage of protests. And when in early 1967 he refused induction on religious grounds, the boxing authorities stripped him of his title. Within another two months he was indicted and convicted of draft evasion by a Texas jury. An indignant judge levied the maximum sentence: five years in prison and a $10,000 fine.

Although he did not go to jail while appealing the conviction, Ali could obtain no matches. Between 1968 and 1970 no promoter could find an opponent and no state would let him fight. By taking away his passport, the federal government prevented him from going abroad to seek matches. He earned what he could by speaking at antiwar rallies and on college campuses, where he was a hero to the opponents of the war. Ultimately, in 1971, the U.S. Supreme Court unanimously upheld Ali's contention that he should have been exempt from the draft because of his religious convictions.

by enacting the National Defense Education Act, which suggested in its title the newly discerned connection between schools and the defense of the country. The law originally provided for financial encouragement to instruction and study in science, mathematics, and modern foreign languages, but that encouragement was soon extended to virtually all fields. In the first ten years of the law more than 1.5 million college students received some $1.3 billion in low-interest loans to continue their education, while some 27,000 fellowships were granted to graduate students for advanced work. The Act was the first major federal effort on behalf of higher education since the College Land Grant Act of 1862. But as would become apparent during the Johnson administration, the interest in

federal support of higher education was only beginning. By the mid-1970s the reevaluation the goals and methods of education sparked by the reaction to Sputnik was to become more urgent and less optimistic.

In any case, the impact of Sputnik on education in America was far-reaching, stirring a new interest in education on all levels. By the 1960s that interest had taken on a life of its own. Of students who entered the fifth grade in 1962, 47 percent went on to college in 1970, as compared with 21 percent of those who had entered the fifth grade in 1942. In 1970, 2.9 million students graduated from high school, and 2 million enrolled in some institution of higher learning, reflecting the fact that many older Americans were also signing up for college courses.

Even before this, the barriers to his fighting had begun to come down. He was still a heavy drawing card, the best-known as well as the most-hated boxer of the century. In 1971 he was matched against Joe Frazier, the official champion. Because Frazier had never fought, much less defeated, Ali, most boxing fans did not consider him the true world's champion. The fight was a sellout, with the contestants each promised $2.5 million. After fifteen rounds of hard slugging, Ali lost by the decision of the judges.

Ali now determined to do what only one other American had done before—to win back the championship. He accomplished this in 1974, against George Foreman, an American, in Kinshasa, Zaire, the first time a heavyweight fight had been set in Africa. Although Foreman was black, too, the 60,000 fans who came to watch rooted for the best-known challenger. "Ali, *bombaye*," they chanted, "Ali, kill him." Ali's victory was not only a spectacular comeback, but an unprecedented one for a fighter over thirty.

Ali said he would soon retire as undefeated champion. But he could not resist the popular acclaim or the money that always came with being on top. The inevitable occurred. In February 1978 he lost his title to Leon Spinks, a man twelve years his junior. Yet the urge to be the best would not die. Later that same year, in a match televised around the world, Ali defeated Spinks, to become the only man to win the world heavyweight championship three times—and at age 36, to boot! In 1979 he announced his "final" retirement while still champion. But it did not last. In 1980 he was again looking for chances to prove that he was the greatest.

In 1971 a group of American Indians took over the former prison island of Alcatraz, declared surplus property by the U.S. Government, in protest against earlier seizures of their tribal lands.

Between 1960 and 1976 the number of full-time students in four-year colleges increased 150 percent to 6.8 million. Never before had a college education seemed so necessary to the average American. In itself this drive to college was at once a sign of the affluence of American society and a measure of the need for highly trained personnel in an advanced economy.

To meet this rising demand, existing facilities were expanded and new institutions were founded across the nation during the 1960s.

New York State, for example, by 1967 had surpassed California with the largest state system of higher education, enrolling 200,000 students in its several branches of a state university system that had started only in 1947. It was reported, moreover, that each week in 1967 saw a new institution of higher learning being founded in the United States. Indeed, the expansion of state systems—with junior colleges, liberal arts colleges, and graduate and professional schools—posed a new and serious threat to even the best of the long-established private institutions as they all competed fiercely for high-quality students and faculty. But if higher education by the middle 1960s was one of the great "growth" industries of the economy, by the early 1970s that growth had slackened considerably, thanks in part at least to some of the unforeseen consequences of the unprecedented expansion.

The state systems, for example, became so large that students began to protest that they were being lost in the rush to "greatness." The first of several spectacular manifestations of student concern was a series of student protests and riots on the Berkeley campus of the University of California in 1964, which brought classes at that huge educational complex to a halt for several days. Though the upheavals at Berkeley and other institutions caused administrators and faculty to think afresh about their enterprise, this did not prevent even more massive disruptions at Columbia University in 1968 and at Harvard in 1969, to mention only two of the more prominent. Indeed, between January and June 1968, the National Student Association counted 221 major demonstrations at 101 colleges and universities, involving some 40,000 students. By this time the protests were against not only the impersonality of the large educational institution and the alleged irrelevance of higher education but also the continuation of the Vietnam War. Suddenly the American student, long known for docility and lack of interest in social protest, was aroused. That the phenomenon was not simply related to the Vietnam War was evident from the riots and disturbances on many campuses in foreign countries in 1968 and 1969. For several days, for example, the whole university system of Paris was brought to a halt by student rebellion.

The student demonstrations in the United States, which had started as nonviolent protests, became more militant and reached a peak in September 1970, with the bombing of a computer center at the University of Wisconsin in which a researcher was killed. Thereafter, the demonstrations as well as the violence subsided sharply. During the academic year 1972 most college campuses were undisturbed by the interruptions of classes and academic routine that had been almost standard at dozens of campuses for half a decade. The reasons for the decline of the demonstrations are not clear, though administrative and curricular changes along the lines demanded by student protesters undoubtedly helped. Certainly the growing violence and the repeated interruptions of classes made many students increasingly intolerant of them. University administrations and faculty also became more adept at defusing or countering demonstrations than had been the case in the beginning. Moreover, the ending of the draft in 1973 removed a good deal of the force behind the student rebellion.

One consequence of the student demonstrations was a more fundamental rethinking of the goals and nature of university education than even Sputnik had spurred. Some educational authorities as well as lay citizens began to question seriously the value of a liberal arts education for all the high-school students who were going on to college each year. Despite the escalating tuition charges and the termination of many of the student amenities, scholarships, and curriculum programs that student activism had initiated, enrollments remained high. But in the face of the rising

Student activism reached its height during the late 1960s. These students are striking Columbia University to force changes in the university structure.

competition for jobs in a weak economy, the less-well-endowed institutions responded more than ever to student demands for practical education.

The Youth Culture. Both the Berkeley protests and the society's apparent indifference to the injustices being dramatized by civil rights leaders in the South led to an increasing self-consciousness among affluent college youth. In increasing numbers they began to challenge the older generation's failure to live up to its professed moral and religious values and, by implication, to examine their own justification for existence.

If any date can be selected for the beginning of this increasing self-consciousness among young people who found American society hypocritical and misdirected, it was the summer of 1964. That was the time when hundreds of white students, predominantly from Northern and Western colleges and universities, descended on Mississippi and other parts of the South to work for the black civil rights movement. Although some were disillusioned by that foray against injustice, many went on to other causes, particularly the movement to end the war in Vietnam. It was this cause that most affected their generation, through the draft, the casualty lists, the emigrations to Canada, the desertions to Sweden; and it was this cause that mobilized their forces. In October 1967 a confrontation at the Pentagon involved some 35,000 people, most of them young. Later, several antiwar demonstrations attracted over 100,000 participants.

It would be a mistake, however, to see the rise of a self-conscious youth movement as simply a consequence of political events or as a political event in itself. At bottom it was a criticism of American society; not infrequently it went beyond criticism to outright rejection of the values of that society and the embracing of a new "counterculture." For a tiny revolutionary minority, rejection came to mean destruction by bombing.

The most visible manifestation of the rejection of society was the revolution in dress and hair style. The dress that many young people assumed—pseudoproletarian blue jeans, denim shirts, and work boots; fringed jackets and Indian headbands; flamboyant colors and designs—set them apart from the "straight" world, even as it created a new uniformity. An even bolder rejection of contemporary mores by young men was the wearing of long hair, a practice that developed

in the mid-sixties. (Fashion designers and the straight society—including in many cases the parental generation—first fought the revolution in dress and hair styling, then adapted it to their own uses. Whether this was victory or a defeat for the young, it undeniably showed their influence and their ability to provide alternatives in life-style.)

Behind the casual dress, however, lay a greater significance: an emphasis upon equality and a denial of deference, rank, and hierarchy. People, many of the young insisted, should be recognized for their individual human dignity and not for what society said they were. The new equality was evident in the impatience of most college-age students with the traditional distinctions of race and sex. Even in many Southern universities young people were much less racially prejudiced than their elders.

The decline in deference was often stigmatized by Establishment spokesmen like President Nixon and Vice-President Agnew as a result of "permissiveness." Yet it was clearly part of a broader world movement toward equal rights and empowerment of the powerless and disadvantaged everywhere. An important facet was the insistence that people have a voice in the making of decisions that would affect them, whether they lived in "third-world" countries emerging from colonialism or in the inner cities of America. This outlook was seen in organizations among welfare recipients as well as in demands on behalf of various other minority groups, including homosexuals seeking respect and freedom from harassment.

Perhaps the most significant difference between the young people of the counterculture and their elders was the emphasis the young now placed upon feeling and emotion. It appeared most obviously in the interest among college students in mysticism, Zen Buddhism, and the works of radical psychologist R. D. Laing. It was also to be seen in the spreading use of hallucinatory drugs, partic-ularly marijuana, which enhances feelings and imagination while dulling reason and rational thought. It is true that the consump-tion of alcohol—the most "successful" drug of all time—continued to exceed by far the use of all other drugs, but the rise in the use of marijuana and later cocaine among both old and young was yet another measure of youth's influence.

The new emphasis upon feeling was also indicated by the enormous popularity during the 1960s—and after—of the loud, rhythmic "rock" music and the vigorous, body-con-torting, often explicitly erotic dancing that accompanied it. These dances were out of a different culture from the ballroom dancing of the previous generation, (as many young people in the early 1980s well recognized when ballroom dancing began to come back onto college campuses.)

The new emphasis on feeling and emotion also helps to explain the new freedom between the sexes that came to be called the *sexual revolution*. Now that pregnancy was reliably controllable by the contraceptive pill, many young people saw no reason to deny their feelings by postponing sexual relations until marriage. The traditional emphasis upon female virginity before marriage was widely abandoned. Living together out of wedlock was accepted in many areas of the country and on levels of society that, only a decade before, had uniformly viewed premarital sexual rela-tions, especially for women, as immoral. Indeed, the whole society in the course of the 1960s and early 1970s came to accept a freedom of expression on sexual matters, on nudity, and in language that was striking considering the great scope of the change and the rapidity with which it had been achieved. Even in small towns in so-called Bible-belt states, pornographic literature and movies were readily available.

A less enduring side of the youth culture

was the attitude toward careers and work. Since personal experience was deemed as of primary importance, many young people in the 1960s saw little reason to put off traveling or experimenting with vocations—or simply enjoying themselves. To many of the young, the good life was not represented by making and saving money or by working hard for a home in the suburbs. It was more likely to be found, they thought, in doing what interested them rather than in choosing what paid well, and in having satisfying relations with people rather than in competing with each other.

To many adults, particularly those with still-sharp memories of the Great Depression, this attitude seemed shockingly impractical. And the onset of the recession in the 1970s made it evident that the prosperity of the 1950s and 1960s had been an important precondition for the youth culture. When faced with the need to confront a competitive world, many young people in the 1970s began to take those courses in high school or college that would prepare them for careers and would promise some economic security in a world no longer running at full employment. Moreover, the cessation of the draft and the ending of the American involvement in Vietnam cooled down the political and social concern of many young people.

The upsurge of the young in the 1960s left enduring marks on the country, however. The essential seriousness and responsibility of young people were acknowledged, for exam-ple, in 1971 when in record time the voting age was lowered to eighteen by the passage of the Twenty-sixth Amendment. Even more signi-ficant was the fact that by 1972 over half the states, including California and New York, had also lowered the age of majority from twenty-one to eighteen in all or almost all legal matters. Young people played a vigorous role in the primary campaigns of Eugene McCarthy and George McGovern, but politi-cal activity by the young in the election of 1972 was less evident than it had been in 1968. Despite the lowering of the voting age, young people did not exercise the franchise in the same proportion as older people in subsequent elections.

Although the youth culture embraced a large number of people in the 1960s and early 1970s, the majority of youth had not participated in the criticism of American society, values, and standards. Most had not demonstrated against the war in Vietnam or campaigned for Eugene McCarthy, Robert Kennedy, or George McGovern. The majority of those who went to college did so in order to get ahead and to do better than their parents. In fact, many young people worked for the reelection of Nixon and Agnew. By 1975 some of the most radical of the young leaders of the 1960s, like Tom Hayden, a founder of Students for a Democratic Society (SDS), were engaging in conventional politics. They were usually found within the Democratic party, though they had derided the conventional parties in the 1960s.

The Women's Movement. Like Chicanos, Indians, and young people, women also responded to the example of the Black Revolution. Although they constituted a majority of the population, women were like the racial and ethnic minorities in that their opportunities for jobs and prestige were arbitrarily limited. They resembled minorities, too, in that they often did not assert themselves. These were among the arguments in Betty Friedan's *Feminine Mystique* (1963), which sparked the new feminist movement of the late 1960s and early 1970s. Beginning as only a weak voice in a society largely complacent about the denial of women's rights and opportunities, the movement by mid-1970s was compelling a new recognition of women's quest for equality. Even older women, observers pointed out, began to call for equal occupational opportunities for persons of their sex, as well as

equal pay. The spreading interest produced a wide range of organizations, some highly militant or politically radical, though the moderate National Organization for Women (NOW), which Betty Friedan founded in 1966, counted the most members. In 1972 the women's movement helped push through Congress a women's equal-rights amendment to the federal Constitution. Ratification by the states, however, did not follow quickly. In fact, the passage of much federal legislation on behalf of women's equality in the preceding eight years convinced many people, a

The 1960s and 1970s saw women move into traditionally male occupations. Here a woman executive talks with the foreman of a natural gas plant.

large number of whom were women, that there was little or no need for a constitutional amendment on behalf of sex equality.

Thanks to the Civil Rights Act of 1964 and executive orders prohibiting discrimination on grounds of sex as well as race or religion, the federal government forced open new jobs for women in private employment while insisting that public institutions increase their proportion of women employees, especially in high-level jobs. The new drive to expand women's opportunities saw traditionally male occupations like those of army general, telephone lineman, jockey, air-tower controller, and FBI agent being filled by women either for the first time or in unprecedented numbers. The new women's organizations also mounted a successful campaign to change state laws to make abortions and birth control information easier to obtain. And they aroused a new popular demand for—and in some instances succeeded in gaining government support for—child-care centers, so that mothers could have a true choice as to whether or not to seek employment.

Although not many more women were actually elected to national political office than in previous years, women participated in politics on a greater scale than ever before. At the Democratic convention in 1972, for example, about 35 percent of the delegates were women—a proportion previously unheard of—and a black woman, Representative Shirley Chisholm of New York, was placed in nomination for President. Even at the Republican convention, which had no minimum quota for women delegates, women made up almost 30 percent of the membership. In 1974 Ella Grasso was elected governor of Connecticut. She was the first woman to reach that level of government unaided by a husband's political prestige or power. Women were also elected to a number of mayoralties, including those of San Jose, California, a city of half a million, and Chicago, the nation's second largest city.

Although women workers were still concentrated in low-paying and low-prestige jobs, the new interest among women and throughout the society in equality of opportunities of all kinds provided broader horizons for women than had previously been the case in the United States. Whether all women wanted to compete with men in the world was still an open question, if antifeminist women's groups were to be believed. But that many women welcomed the widening of their horizons, no one could deny.

A Resurgence of Religion. In the early 1800s the French visitor Alexis de Tocqueville noted the importance of religion in the lives of Americans. Because of the long-standing importance of religion to Americans, their ways of worship have reflected—often quite closely—the social as well as the spiritual changes in their society. Therefore it is not surpising that alterations in religious outlook and practices in the decades after World War II reflected both the prosperity and the anxiety that so strikingly characterized those years.

During the 1950s, for instance, there was a kind of religious revival among Protestants, in which popular preachers like Billy Graham and Norman Vincent Peale extolled traditional Christian morality. It was the time of the Cold War, when contrasts between atheistic communism and religious America served political as well as religious purposes. It was the time when the words "under God" were first added to the Pledge of Allegiance to the Flag.

That turn toward popularizing traditional Christianity, however, proved to be short-lived in the face of the drive for social reform during the 1960s. Most of the established churches became caught up in the great civil rights movement and in the opposition to the war in Vietnam. The heavy involvement of Roman Catholics, both clerical and lay persons, was especially notable inasmuch as the Church had long been recognized as conser-

Some people seeking spiritual meaning looked outside conventional religious groups. These three Hare Krishnas seem oblivious of the curious stares of pedestrians in downtown Chicago.

vative in its outlook on both religion and social change. Efforts to democratize the Church internally were encouraged by liberal Pope John XXIII, whose two Vatican Councils marked a turning point in broadening the Church's outlook on the world. For the American Catholic Church, though, the effect of the changes seemed to be divisive, a sign of which was a drop of one third in the rate of church attendance among Catholics from 75 percent in 1957—among the highest for Americans—to 54 percent in 1975.

This substantial drift away from the traditional Catholic Church was experienced by many traditional Protestant denominations as well. One of the consequences of the churches' emphasis on social issues during the 1960s was that many Americans began to fear that the spiritual message of religion was being forgotten in the process. Moreover, the materialism of the consumer society apparently aroused in many a yearning for a spiritual balance.

As a result, by the 1970s those Christian

churches that emphasized personal salvation and individual fulfillment rather than social action grew rapidly. Sometimes they were old denominations, like the Southern Baptists, which today are the largest Protestant group in the nation. But more often they were new evangelical churches like the Churches of Christ, the Churches of God, or what came to be called the Pentacostals. All of them emphasized forceful, emotional preaching, Christian fellowship, and personal conversion—that is, "being born again." At the same time, they minimized theological doctrines and encouraged a literal interpretation of the Bible. In 1976 a Gallup poll reported that a third of all Americans considered themselves as having been "born again."

The new stress on the search for personal spiritual meaning in an anxious, if affluent society also showed itself outside conventional religious groups. It could be seen in the 6 million people who took up Transcendental Meditation (T.M.) and in the 3 million who practiced yoga. The thirst for personal commitment was noticeable, too, among the young people who joined the studious Jesus Movement, the chanting, begowned Hare Krishnas, or the aggressively proselytizing Unification Church of the Reverend Moon.

Signs that this concern for personal religious commitment was making itself felt in secular politics were President Carter's proud announcement that he was a "born-again" Christian, a similar statement by John Anderson, one of Carter's rivals in the 1980 campaign, and the increasing attractiveness of the conservative politics of Republican candidate Ronald Reagan to the new evangelical churches of the South and Southwest, whose members had usually been Democratic.

In the 1980s religion was still clearly important to many Americans. Surveys showed that, of all the industrial nations of the world, the United States was the most religious. Yet, it should be observed that it was precisely because Americans continued to place a high value on religion that they put pressure on the churches and synagogues to respond to social change. In July 1978, for example, the authoritarian Mormon Church for the first time permitted black men to become full-fledged members of the priesthood, and several Protestant denominations and Jewish synagogues in the late 1970s granted pastoral roles to women in response to demands from their members and the women's movement in general.

The social and economic changes in this country during the last thirty-five years owe much to the altered position of the United States in the world as a result of its total victory over its enemies in World War II. That victory helped to shape not only how Americans thought about their responsibilities in the world, but also what they believed about themselves as a people. In some ways the victory gave Americans a sense of mission and a sense of power that encouraged them to transform their society for the better and to assume a positive role in the preservation of freedom abroad. But that same self-confidence and sense of mission led them to undertake policies and actions that many would later deplore and regret, policies which not only imposed excessive burdens, but also threatened the life of the Republic, repudiated its ideals, and brought destruction upon thousands of people living far beyond the borders of the United States. In the next two chapters we examine those policies and actions at home and abroad that helped to shape the fateful years after 1945.

Chapter 23

The Price of Power 1945–1963

FROM PEACE TO COLD WAR

The surrender of Japan soon after the dropping of the two nuclear bombs in August 1945 caught most Americans, in and out of government, by surprise. Since the Nazi defeat in April, the army and the navy had been readying the great military machine for the final assault upon the Japanese home islands. Yet within weeks after the Japanese surrender, the dismantling of the military establishment, built up over four years of war, had begun. Public clamor to "bring the boys home" was insistent throughout the remainder of 1945. By January 1946 the government was discharging members of the armed forces at the rate of 35,000 a day. By the end of 1946 the military establishment was down to one fifth of wartime strength.

Simultaneously with the discharge of soldiers, the government began the cancellation of war contracts. Within a month after the surrender of Japan $35 billion worth were dropped. The end of war work and the glutting of the labor market with discharged veterans seemed to many to presage a severe depression, but billions of dollars of personal savings and the rapid transition to peacetime production made things turn out otherwise. Instead, inflation became the principal problem in the ensuing years.

The Economic Problems of Reconversion. The ending of overtime work at war plants and the upward movement of prices in 1945 and 1946 provoked organized labor into a wave of strikes. In October 1945, for example, the number of worker days lost through strikes doubled over September. It continued to rise, and all told, about 4.5 million workers went out on strike in 1946. Since the strikes were usually for increased wages, the federal government ran into difficulties trying to hold the line on prices. Demands by Congress and the public for tax reductions also meant increased pressure on prices. In November 1945 Congress cut income taxes by some $9 billion and repealed the wartime excess-profits tax as an inducement to increased production.

The big issues of 1946 were prices and labor unrest. The Truman administration tried to hold the line on prices by continuing wartime price controls, but businessmen, most Republicans, and other large sectors of the population were anxious to remove all wartime restrictions. The results were inadequate price-control legislation and a steadily rising price curve.

With the election of a Republican Congress in November 1946, the Truman administration gave up and abolished virtually all controls over prices. Nevertheless, shortages of all kinds of goods persisted, with the result that prices in 1947 continued to rise to new heights almost every month. Despite the high prices, or perhaps because of them, employment remained high and business activity good. Undoubtedly many workers, especially unorganized labor and white-collar workers, suffered from the steady increase in the cost of living, but the country as a whole enjoyed a boom.

In February 1946, before it was clear that a boom would be the shape of the postwar era, Congress passed the Employment Act, which placed responsibility upon the federal government for the prevention of mass unemployment and economic depression. Although no specific measures were spelled out in the Act (because of the need to win conservative support), it did create a Council of Economic Advisors to the President. In a sense the Act was a reflex from the days of the depression, showing the continuing effect of the New Deal revolution.

Truman versus a Republican Congress. Opposition to price controls, support of labor control bills, and demand for tax reductions marked a rising conservative tide across the country and in the Congress. This conservatism was clearly reflected in the congressional elections of 1946. Brandishing the slogan "Had Enough?" the Republicans elected majorities in both houses for the first time since 1928. First on the agenda of the new Eightieth Congress was legislation to control labor unions, which since the end of the war had been disrupting the economy through nationwide strikes. Earlier in 1946 Truman

had vetoed a severe antilabor law, even though he himself, beset by a national railroad strike in May 1946, had threatened to draft rail workers into the army. In June 1947 the new Republican Congress, under the leadership of conservative Senator Robert A. Taft, passed the Labor-Management Relations, or Taft-Hartley, Act. Truman returned the bill with a stinging veto message, but Congress quickly overrode the veto.

The Taft-Hartley Act attempted to meet two public complaints against labor. In an effort to deal with nationwide strikes that disrupted the economy, the act empowered the President to force a union to accept a sixty-day "cooling-off period" before striking. If at the end of the cooling-off period the dispute was not settled, the employer's last offer would have to be presented to the workers for a secret vote. The act was also intended to reverse the alleged favoritism of New Deal legislation toward labor by listing a number of unfair union practices. It banned the closed shop, permitted employers to sue unions for broken contracts or strike damages, required unions to make their financial statements public, forbade union contributions to political campaigns, limited the "check off" system whereby employers collected union dues, and required union leaders to take oaths that they were not Communists. Despite the opposition of labor organizations and of many liberal Democrats, the Taft-Hartley Act has remained unchanged, a measure of the American people's conviction in the postwar era that national labor unions, like business, need some kind of public control.

Although Truman and the Republican Eightieth Congress rarely agreed on domestic policies, on defense and foreign policy they often did. The army, navy, and air force were merged into the Department of Defense under the National Security Act of July 1947. James V. Forrestal, former Secretary of the Navy, became the first Secretary of Defense.

Russian Expansionism. Even before the Potsdam Conference in July 1945, there had been signs that the Allied unity displayed at Yalta was superficial. Before his death, for example, Roosevelt had warned Stalin that the Yalta agreements concerning Poland must not be ignored. Stalin's initial refusal to send Foreign Minister Molotov to the UN conference in April 1945 also aroused Western suspicions of Russian intentions about the postwar world, while the abrupt stopping of Lend-Lease in early May raised doubts in Russian minds about Western friendship. At Potsdam Stalin insisted on having his way in Poland and with German reparations, which the Russians considered imperative for the rebuilding of their devastated country.

During the last half of 1945 and most of 1946, at the United Nations and at meetings of the Council of Foreign Ministers to draw up peace treaties with the lesser enemy states, the West and Russia clashed repeatedly. Each saw the other as increasingly threatening or uncooperative. Obviously the two sides had different views of the future of Europe—especially of Germany.

Particularly ominous for the peace of the postwar world was the Soviet Union's refusal to withdraw its troops from Iran, which the Russians and the British had jointly occupied during the war. Only vigorous protests by the United States and the United Nations impelled a Russian withdrawal in late May 1946. To the Russians the important point was that they had withdrawn under pressure. To the West, and particularly the Americans, it was the necessity to threaten the Russians that was significant. Two months later, in early August, the Soviets demanded slices of Turkish territory and a share in the control of the Dardanelles. To many Western observers Russian behavior announced a resurgence of historic czarist ambitions.

Actually, Soviet conquests already far exceeded any dreams of the czars. Russian armies stood as far west as Berlin and central Germany, and all of eastern Europe lay under their control. Indeed, throughout the forties and early fifties it was the presence of large Russian armies in central Europe at a time when the West had long since demobilized its wartime forces that sustained the suspicions and aroused the fears of Western leaders. Today the likelihood of a Russian military advance against western Europe seems slight, but to a generation that had seen Russian power move west against Hitler, that likelihood was ever present.

Moreover, although Yugoslavia was not occupied by Russian troops, it was then firmly Communist under the leadership of Marshal Tito. Indeed, in 1946 Tito was more truculent in his dealings with the West than was Stalin himself. The same month that the Soviets served their demands upon Turkey, Tito's planes on two different occasions shot down unarmed American transport planes which had accidentally crossed the Yugoslav frontier. It was Yugoslavia, not Russia, that was supplying Communist-led guerrillas fighting the British-dominated Greek government.

Churchill, now out of office because of a Labour party victory, gave voice to the concern of the Western nations. At Fulton, Missouri, on March 5, 1946, with President Truman sitting conspicuously on the platform, Churchill called attention to the "iron curtain" which "has descended across the continent" from "Stettin in the Baltic to Trieste in the Adriatic." Moreover, he went on, "Nobody knows what Soviet Russia and its Communist international organization intends to do in the immediate future, or what are the limits, if any, to their expansive and proselytising tendencies."

Meanwhile, the Soviets in the UN turned down the American plan for international control of nuclear energy. Since under the plan the United States would have voluntarily surrendered its monopoly of nuclear power,

Americans took the Soviet rejection as another sign that the Soviets were not interested in peace and order in the world. The Russians, apparently, saw the American plan as a way of denying them their own nuclear bomb. On both sides, suspicions grew.

The Problem of Germany.   The major European dispute between East and West concerned the future of Germany. In the view of the Western powers, particularly the United States, the revival of a united Germany had been agreed upon at Yalta and reaffirmed at Potsdam. But Russian insistence upon large German reparations could only mean that Stalin intended to keep Germany weak and without hope of recovery for the foreseeable future. As a result the Russians obtained very little in the way of reparations from the Western occupation zones, though in their own zone they carted eastward everything they could.

By the fall of 1946 Secretary of State James F. Byrnes was convinced that the Russians did not really want a reunited and independent Germany and were using the continued division of Germany as a means of impeding German recovery. He therefore persuaded the British to merge their zone with that of the Americans. (The French, as skeptical of German unification as the Russians, did not join the other Western allies until 1949.) However, in merging the Western zones, Byrnes was helping to divide Germany ever more permanently between East and West. Thus, in Germany as in the United Nations, the Cold War had obviously come into being by the end of 1946. Increasingly in the years ahead, West Germany (which became independent as the German Federal Republic in 1954) would be viewed by the West as the chief bulwark against Russian expansion into western Europe, while the Soviet Union would see it as the chief threat to Russian hegemony in eastern Europe.

The Containment Policy.   For a time after World War II it seemed that the Russians might well be in a position to extend their influence into western as well as eastern Europe. Economically and militarily prostrate from their struggles, the nations of western Europe were in poor position to defend themselves against Soviet military force and subversion. In France and Italy strong Communist parties seemed on the verge of taking power either through the ballot box or by force.

In Greece Communist led guerrillas fought pro-Western government forces for control of the country. Even Great Britain, presumably one of the principal victors of the war, was on the verge of bankruptcy. Economically bled, Britain could no longer sustain its traditional role as guardian of Greek independence. In February 1947 the British announced the imminent withdrawal of aid. In Turkey, too, an unstable government was being pressured by the Soviets for territorial grants and administrative concessions in the Dardanelles.

In Asia and Africa the steady drive for independence had already begun. With their lack of experience in democratic procedures and the difficulties of maintaining stability in the midst of poverty and strife, the new nations were ripe for Communist revolution or subversion, either of which, American leaders anticipated, would make them allies of the Russians.

The American response to this global Communist threat was the establishment and gradual implementation of the policy of "containment." As publicly announced in July 1947 in an article by State Department aide George F. Kennan, "The main element of any U.S. policy toward the Soviet Union must be that of a long-term, patient but firm and vigilant containment of Russian expansive tendencies." While accepting—though not entirely—the accomplished fact of Soviet control over eastern Europe, the policy of containment sought to hold the line against the further extension of Soviet power, military or political.

The Truman Doctrine. Even before the containment policy was officially enunciated, the Truman administration had taken steps to stem the Communist advance. After much soul-searching and consultation with congressional leaders of both parties, President Truman urged the United States to take up the burden of aid to Greece and Turkey. In a historic address to Congress and the nation on March 12, 1947, he called for $400 million in economic and military aid for the two beleaguered countries to save them from "aggressive movements that seek to impose upon them totalitarian regimes." His proposal was opposed by conservatives, who protested the cost, and by liberals and left-wingers, who denounced it as warmongering. All recognized that this "Truman Doctrine," pledging aid to nations resisting aggression or subversion, signaled a sharp departure from the whole previous practice of American foreign policy. For the first time in peace, the United States was being asked to commit its military might (though that part of the proposal was underplayed by the President) and economic power to the defense of countries outside the Western Hemisphere. By a vote of 67 to 23 in the Senate in April and 287 to 107 in the House in May the Republican Congress sanctioned the new turn in foreign policy by voting the funds.

The Marshall Plan. An immediate Soviet military invasion was not the greatest threat to western Europe in the first postwar years. It was the legacy of war—persistent poverty, widespread misery, and mass unemployment—in which communism found its greatest ally, especially in countries like Italy and France, where economic and political instability was an open invitation to subversion. Therefore, to stimulate European recovery,

the Truman administration began plans for extending massive economic assistance. The idea—first suggested in a speech by Under Secretary of State Dean Acheson—was brought to the attention of the world, and Europe in particular, in a Harvard commencement address delivered by Secretary of State George C. Marshall on June 5, 1947.

Marshall's speech offered American economic aid to any European nation seriously interested in restoring the shattered economy of Europe, including those nations closely associated with Soviet Russia. The nations of western Europe accepted the suggestion with enthusiasm, but Russia, after some preliminary exploration, compelled its allies to stay out of the scheme, on the excuse that the Marshall Plan was a cover-up for American imperialistic designs. The proposal also evoked widespread opposition in the United States, from both the right and the left, but leading Republicans, notably Senator Arthur H. Vandenberg, championed it from the outset. Calling the idea a "calculated risk" to "help stop World War III before it starts," Vandenberg countered assertions that it was a gigantic "international WPA" or a "Socialist blueprint." As presented to Congress in December, the measure envisioned the expenditure of $17 billion over a four-year period, with $6.8 billion to be spent in the fifteen months following April 1, 1948.

During the fall and winter of 1947 the continued decline of the European economy and the many stories of starvation and misery in western Europe gave substance to the argument for United States assistance. But equally influential were the continued signs of Soviet pressure. For example, in February 1948 a Communist workers' coup thrust democratic Czechoslovakia behind the Iron Curtain, and in March reports of a Russian advance to the West circulated among government officials. Furthermore, a Communist victory appeared to be a real possibility in the Italian elections coming up in April. Responding to these pressures and to others from an anxious administration, Congress on April 2, 1948, passed the European Recovery Act, or Marshall Plan, granting to the President about 90 percent of the funds he had requested for the first year. Though Congress refused to commit the United States to anything thereafter, subsequent grants were made on an annual basis.

The full four-year plan was never carried out because the Korean War intervened, but the $12.5 billion extended to sixteen western European countries achieved the purpose of reviving the European economy. Between 1948 and 1951 production in all the countries rose about 37 percent. With a more prosperous economy and resultant political stability, the internal threat of communism receded noticeably. Moreover, the international cooperation fostered by the plan afforded the European nations a new insight into the advantages of closer economic union. That insight bore fruit in the 1950s with the formation of the European Coal and Steel Community and, later, the Common Market, or European Economic Community.

NATO.   Soon after the European Recovery Program went into effect, the East-West conflict over Germany reached its most dangerous stage. In July 1948 the Soviets, vexed by the frictions arising from joint administration of Germany and hoping to force Western evacuation of Berlin, ordered a blockade of all ground communication with the city, which lay deep in the Soviet zone. Faced with the prospect of war if they forced their way to Berlin, the Western Allies instead instituted a gigantic airlift to fly in supplies and food. Although the Russians did not molest the airlift, they did not agree to ending the blockade until May 1949. Meanwhile the airlift had proved its ability to sustain the West Berliners and the Western right of access to Berlin.

The Berlin blockade reinforced the Ameri-

can belief in the need for closer military cooperation among the western European nations. The Brussels Pact of March 1948 had already created a defensive alliance among Great Britain, France, Belgium, Luxembourg, and the Netherlands. Toward the end of 1948 the United States encouraged widening the Brussels Pact alliance to include other nations rimming the North Atlantic. In the spring of 1949, twelve countries, including Canada and the United States in the New World, joined the North Atlantic Treaty Organization, which in 1952 expanded to include Turkey and Greece and in 1955 West Germany.

With the signing of the treaty in April 1949, the United States obligated itself to come to the aid of the Europeans—the strongest commitment yet assumed in the course of the diplomatic revolution that had begun only four years earlier with the ratification of the United Nations Charter. The NATO treaty encountered only slight opposition in the Senate, which ratified it on July 21, 1949. In early 1951 General Dwight D. Eisenhower was appointed Supreme Commander of the new integrated defense force to be fashioned out of the national armies of the twelve signatories.

THE ASIAN REVOLUTION

The Overthrow of Colonialism.   If the results of the war in Europe dropped unexpected problems into the laps of Americans, the consequences of the war in Western Asia constituted a revolution. The great colonial powers, though victors in the war, lost virtually all their Asian possessions within five years after the defeat of the Japanese. When the British returned to Malaya and Burma, the Dutch to the East Indies, and the French to Indochina, they were greeted with demands for independence and sometimes by open military rebellion.

One by one the European nations made the only possible response. They got out of Asia. The United States, acting on a prewar

Spectators eagerly watch the arrival of an American supply plane—part of the airlift that broke through the Soviet blockade of Berlin in 1948 and 1949.

promise, led the movement by granting final independence to the Philippines on July 4, 1946. Britain followed next, finally reducing its once vast empire in Asia to a few pin points on the map, like Hong Kong. But not all the European powers recognized the shape of the future as clearly as Britain. The Dutch did not transfer power to the new nationalist government of the United States of Indonesia until 1949, and the French sacrificed the flower of their officer corps and thousands of young men in a futile struggle to suppress the nationalist movement in Indochina until 1954. The liquidation of colonialism was the first part of the Asian revolution.

The Transformation of Japan. The second part of the revolution in Asia was the American occupation of Japan. Although ostensibly representing all the Allied powers, General Douglas MacArthur, the American occupation commander, in reality was the supreme authority in that country, and his policy was dictated by the United States. Aside from stripping Japan of all its colonies, including Formosa and Korea, the United States deliberately undertook to destroy the old Japan. Thoroughgoing land reform, which spread land ownership more widely than ever before, improved the lot of the peasantry. A new democratic constitution, in which the emperor was reduced from a god to a mere symbol of national unity, also removed the army from politics. Women were enfranchised for the first time and given greater freedom in society and within the family. As Edwin O. Reischauer, an authority on Japanese history and ambassador to Japan under the Kennedy administration, once wrote: "During the early postwar years in Japan, MacArthur played the role not only of the most radical American revolutionary of modern times but also of the most successful."

When the Korean War broke out in 1950, the United States and its non-Communist allies in the war against Japan hastened to conclude peace with the Japanese, despite the objections of the Soviet Union. The peace treaty was signed in September 1951, and in a separate agreement the United States was permitted to retain military bases in Japan. As with Germany, the United States also encouraged its former enemy in Asia to rebuild its dismantled military machine.

The Victory of Chinese Communism. The third prong of the Asian revolution was the Communist conquest of China. When World War II ended, China was accorded the status of a great power, receiving, for example, a permanent seat in the Security Council of the United Nations. With the Japanese defeat, most people assumed that Generalissimo Chiang Kai-shek's Nationalists would reinforce their rule over all China. Even Stalin at the close of the war recognized Chiang's Nationalist government, not Communist leader Mao Tse-tung's, as the rightful regime. But the Chinese Communists had a sizable army and a government in northwestern China and were stronger than many observers thought.

At first the United States helped Chiang in his effort to spread his military authority over all of China. When that failed, the United States attempted through most of 1946 and 1947 to find a basis for agreement between

Chiang and Mao Tse-tung. In December 1945 President Truman had dispatched General George C. Marshall to China, where he worked for over a year on such a mission, but without success. By late 1947 the two sides were fighting it out in open civil war, during which Chiang's lack of support from the masses of the Chinese people became increasingly evident.

By the close of 1949 the Nationalists had been forced to flee to the island of Formosa (Taiwan), some one hundred miles off the coast. In October 1949 the Soviet Union extended diplomatic recognition to the new People's Republic of China, and in February 1950 the two Communist powers signed a mutual assistance agreement and pact of alliance. Thus, just as the end of the Berlin blockade and the creation of NATO marked the ebbing of the Communist danger in western Europe, the Cold War came to Asia.

THE DEMOCRATS STAY IN

The Miracle of 1948. . By 1948 Harry Truman had warmed up well to the role of President, which had been thrust upon him so suddenly three years before, and he was eager to try himself before the electorate. Although opposed by many Democrats who thought he lacked popular appeal (according to opinion polls, his presidency was approved by only 36 percent of the people in April 1948), the President controlled the July Democratic convention, which dutifully nominated him on the first ballot, naming Senator Alben W. Barkley of Kentucky as his running mate. When the Republican Congress was called into special session by Truman that summer and refused to enact his liberal program, Truman went into the campaign talking about the "do-nothing" Eightieth Congress.

In the election Truman faced a serious loss of votes from both the right and left wings of his party. Because the Democratic convention adopted a strong civil rights plank, several

Southern states bolted Truman and put forth their own States' Rights party candidate, Governor J. Strom Thurmond of South Carolina. Thurmond, it was expected, would cut deeply into Truman's support in the Deep South. The candidacy of Henry A. Wallace on the newly formed Progressive party ticket promised to draw away left-wing and liberal votes, for Wallace campaigned vigorously against the administration's containment policy, contending that it was anti-Russian and would lead to war instead of peace.

The Republicans, more confident of victory than at any time since the Great Depression, nominated for President their 1944 standard bearer, Governor Thomas E. Dewey of New York, with Governor Earl Warren of California as the vice-presidential nominee. Dewey's campaign was a model of caution. Sure of victory, he preached unity and the need for efficiency. Accepting all of the New Deal reforms, even though they were also Truman's stock in trade, Dewey simply said he would administer them better. Even commentators opposed to Dewey conceded, along with the public opinion polls, that a

President Harry Truman chats with voters in Pittsburgh from the back of the special train that carried him 10,000 miles on the "whistlestop campaign" that helped him to win the election of 1948.

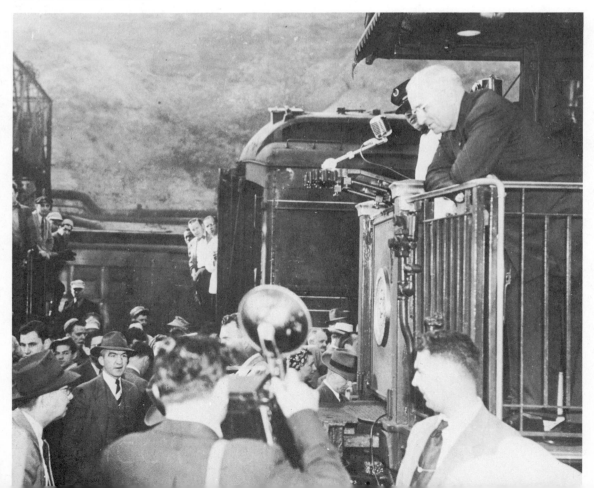

Republican victory was foreordained. Harry Truman, though, was not convinced. He barnstormed around the country, attacking the Republican Congress for being against the people's interests. Republicans, he said, were "old moss backs . . ., gluttons of privilege . . ., all set to do a hatchet job on the New Deal." He traveled some 32,000 miles and made 356 speeches, far exceeding the campign effort of Dewey, his overly confident and much younger opponent.

Election night brought the big surprise: Truman never lost the slight lead he gained in the early returns. By next morning the miracle had occurred. Harry Truman was elected by two million votes. Truman's vigorous appeals to popular memories of the Great Depression and his uncompromising defense of the New Deal had apparently struck fire in millions of voters (though 700,000 who cast votes for state candidates did not even bother to vote for President). Moreover, by emphasizing the decline in farm prices under Republican farm legislation, Truman actually recaptured the farm vote, which Roosevelt had lost in 1940 and 1944. Dewey ran better than Republican congressional candidates, probably because of Truman's vigorous attacks on the Eightieth Congress.

Not surprisingly, the Democrats gained seventy-five new seats in the House and nine in the Senate. Although Truman lost four Southern states (thirty-nine electoral votes) to Thurmond, he had shown that a united South was not necessary for a Democratic victory, especially since his Southern losses were more than made up for in the North by urban black votes. Henry Wallace's candidacy, which at one time had been viewed as a threat to Democratic strength in Northern cities, affected Truman's total hardly at all.

The Fair Deal. In his inaugural speech in January 1949, Truman spoke of his program as the "Fair Deal." In effect, it was a continuation and extension of the New Deal. It called for

civil rights legislation, a national health program, aid for public education, and support for low-income housing. Truman also asked for repeal of the Taft-Hartley Act and enactment of a new farm subsidy program (the Brannan Plan), but the Congress, despite its Democratic complexion, would agree to neither. A coalition of Republicans and conservative Southern Democrats killed off not only civil rights legislation but most of the other measures of the Fair Deal. On the other hand, in 1949 Truman did succeed in obtaining a housing act and a minimum-wage increase to 75 cents an hour. In 1950 Congress also agreed to broadening Social Security coverage, placing some 10 million more persons under the benefits of the system.

After 1949 Truman was increasingly plagued by revelations of corruption in his administration. Although none of the disclosures compared with the Teapot Dome scandals of the twenties, many officials, especially in the Internal Revenue Service, were proved in court to be corrupt. Moreover, some White House officials turned out to have rather casual standards of proper behavior for government officers. In short, the Republican charge that the Democrats had been too long in control of the executive branch of government seemed to have some validity. But an issue of foreign policy was to supersede corruption as a Republican weapon against the administration.

The Outbreak of the Korean War. When in 1945 the United States and the Soviet Union occupied the former Japanese colony of Korea, they arbitrarily divided the country between them along the 38th line of latitude. Originally intended to be temporary, the line, in the suspicious atmosphere of the Cold War, hardened into a border between two Korean regimes—the North under Russian tutelage and the South under American. Because each of the Korean regimes wanted to unite the peninsula under its own rule, border clashes were frequent. When the Americans withdrew their troops from South Korea in 1949, they carefully refrained from leaving behind any offensive weapons like tanks or heavy artillery for fear that the strongly nationalist president of South Korea, Syngman Rhee, would attempt to conquer North Korea by force of arms.

The Russians, withdrawing at about the same time, left a well-trained and heavily equipped North Korean army behind and may even have encouraged the North Koreans to attempt unification by force. In any event, on June 25, 1950, the North Korean army stormed across the 38th parallel, quickly overwhelming the thin South Korean defenses. The next day, before the rapidly advancing invaders, Rhee's government fled the capital of Seoul. Thereupon, the Truman administration, faced with a naked act of military aggression, decided to commit the United States to South Korea's defense, even though the American army then comprised no more than ten and one half infantry divisions and one armored division. On June 30, when it became evident that American air and naval support alone could not save the South Koreans, the first U.S. ground troops landed in Korea.

Prodded by the United States, the United Nations on June 27 branded the North Koreans as aggressors and called upon all member states to "furnish such assistance to the Republic of Korea as may be necessary to repel the armed attack and to restore international peace and security to the area." On July 7 General Douglas MacArthur was designated United Nations commander in chief. Although all during the fighting in Korea, American and South Korean troops made up the great preponderance of UN forces, some twenty nations had sent some kind of support by the end of 1950. Because the Russians had been boycotting the Security Council in protest against the West's refusal to admit Communist China to the UN, their represen-

tative was not present to veto the resolution which propelled the United Nations into the war.

For over two months the American and South Korean forces suffered uninterrupted defeats as the powerful North Korean armies pushed them down the peninsula into a small pocket around the port city of Pusan. Then on September 15, 1950, in a surprise maneuver, General MacArthur led a successful amphibious landing at Inchon on the west coast, far behind the North Korean lines. A simultaneous drive from the Pusan area caught the Communists in a giant pincer movement. By October 1 the United Nations forces were on the verge of crossing the 38th parallel into North Korea. When they did, a new phase of the war in Asia opened.

On November 26, as units of the United Nations forces approached the Yalu River—the border between Korea and Communist China—large contingents of Chinese "volunteers" ambushed them, compelling the UN troops to retreat. Thereafter, increasing numbers of Chinese poured across the Yalu, and the UN troops were once again pushed far south of the 38th parallel. Thus deprived of total victory, General MacArthur asked for permission to bomb the Chinese in what he called their "sanctuary" across the Yalu. The Truman administration turned down his request on the ground that such action might well invoke the Sino-Soviet mutual assistance pact and thus bring on a war with the two chief Communist powers.

But if the nation was spared a world war, a limited war far from American shores produced frustrations that made the Korean struggle immensely unpopular. Public opinion polls indicated that after January 1951 Truman never again received the support of a majority of the American people. Many spoke bitterly of "Truman's War." A draft board in Montana went so far as to refuse to draft any more men until General MacArthur was authorized to bomb as he saw fit in China.

As the leading advocate of striking directly against China, MacArthur inevitably came into fatal clash with the administration. When a letter written to the House Republican minority leader was released to the press—a letter in which MacArthur charged administration "diplomats" with fighting the Asian war "with words" rather than "with arms" and declared that "there is no substitute for victory"—President Truman on April 11, 1951, summarily removed the general from his commands in Korea and Japan. The nation was surprised and shocked. The President was widely attacked and MacArthur accorded a hero's welcome when he returned to the United States.

After an address by the dismissed general before Congress, a Senate investigation exhaustively inquired into the removal. At the end of several weeks of hearings, during which the pitch of emotionalism gradually declined, the Senate committee agreed with General Omar Bradley when he said that MacArthur's policy would have extended the fighting to the mainland of Asia, which would "involve us in the wrong war, at the wrong place, at the wrong time, and with the wrong enemy."

The Effects of the Korean War. By demonstrating that aggression could be halted if the nations of the world were determined to do so, the Korean War stimulated the expansion of America's armed forces and put life into the recently created NATO. Domestically the Korean "police action," as Truman once called the war, forced the administration to institute economic controls, but not to the extent of World War II. Although both income and excise taxes went up in 1950 and a new excess profits tax became law in 1951, there was enough military production by the end of 1952 to permit the easing of many of the economic controls. Indeed, the war had pushed the nation into a new boom, quickly ending the recession of 1948–1949. Thus, conditions of life in the United States were such that many Americans who had no relatives in Korea hardly knew there was a war at all. That such was the case only made the war more unpopular among those who did have sons fighting overseas.

The End of the Korean Fighting. Once the Chinese intervention demonstrated that the whole peninsula could not be united under Syngman Rhee, the Truman administration sought to end the fighting as soon as possible. By the end of 1952, strengthened UN forces had pushed the Chinese northward to the

Heavy snow fails to stop the work of three American combat engineers, members of the UN forces in Korea, as they survey the ground for a shorter supply route to the front lines in 1951.

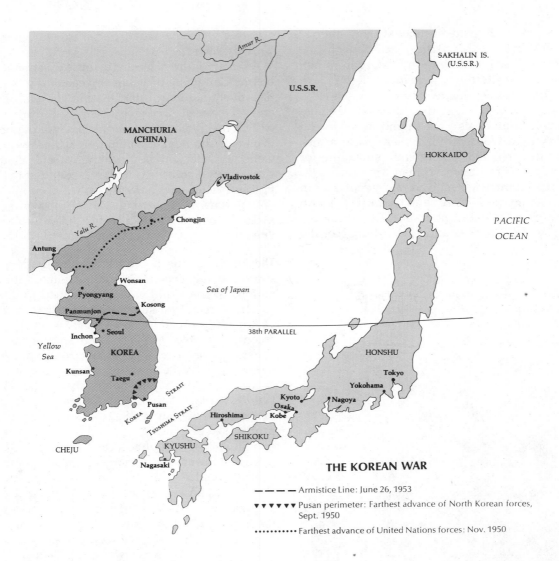

THE KOREAN WAR

— — — Armistice Line: June 26, 1953

▼ ▼ ▼ ▼ ▼ Pusan perimeter: Farthest advance of North Korean forces, Sept. 1950

••••••••• Farthest advance of United Nations forces: Nov. 1950

region of the 38th parallel. Although the United States was prepared to strike a truce at that point, the Communists held off. An armistice was not signed in Korea until the middle of 1953 under the Eisenhower administration.

The Great Fear. Between 1949 and 1954 the nation was gripped by a pervasive fear that communism was about to subvert the Republic. Any program or any idea traceable to Communist ideology became suspect. Even an unproved accusation of having been a Communist was sometimes enough to condemn an individual to lose job or friends. A veritable witch hunt for traitors and disloyal citizens was carried out by government and by private groups. Actually, throughout the whole period the number of disloyal persons discovered in positions of trust was insignificant.

The Great Fear grew out of the deteriorating international situation of 1946 and 1947, when some Communists in the United States, Canada, and Britain showed that regardless of their formal citizenship, they owed first loyalty to the Soviet Union. In 1947 the federal government instituted a program to check on the loyalty of government employees, and many public educational institutions, like the University of California, demanded oaths of loyalty from their faculties. Congressional investigations in 1947 and 1948 revealed evidence of spying in government by Communists during the 1930s. The most notable instance was the case of Alger Hiss, a former high-ranking member of the State Department, who was accused of heading an espionage ring in the 1930s that had passed on classified documents to the Soviets. His two trials in 1949–1950 for perjury (the statute of limitations prevented indictment for espionage) aroused wide public concern over Communist influence in government.

Hiss' trial and conviction, like other revelations about Communists in government, concerned espionage prior to 1945, but in 1950 the FBI revealed that American spies had transmitted secret A-bomb data to the Russians in 1945 and 1946. Several Americans, including Julius and Ethel Rosenberg, were tried and convicted for espionage. The Rosenbergs, whose cause the Communists tried vainly to make into a new Sacco-Vanzetti case, were executed in 1953.

To these and other sensational revelations of Communist activity in the United States, the Congress responded with the Internal Security (or McCarran) Act of 1951, passing it over Truman's veto. The new law required Communist and Communist-front organizations to register with the government and to identify as Communist all their mail and literature. It also forbade employment of Communists in defense work and barred anyone who had belonged to a Communist or fascist organization from entering the country. The most drastic of all provisions and the one which measured the extremity of congressional concern was the authorization for the government to place Communists, citizens and aliens alike, in concentration camps whenever a national emergency occurred. This provision was repealed only in 1970.

The Rise and Fall of McCarthy. The person who more than any other intensified the Great Fear during these years was Joseph McCarthy, a Republican senator from Wisconsin. McCarthy first came into national prominence in February 1950 when he charged in a speech at Wheeling, West Virginia, that fifty-seven or more Communists were then working in the State Department. "In my opinion," he said, "the State Department, which is one of the most important government departments, is thoroughly infested with Communists." And it was all the fault of Secretary of State Dean Acheson, that "pompous diplomat in striped pants, with a phony British accent." A Senate investigating committee later exonerated the department, but McCarthy continued to make similar unsubstantiated charges of Communists in government, in his deep, bass Lone Ranger-type voice, occasionally naming a name but citing numbers by the score. In the context of the Great Fear, his spectacular, headline-making accusations often gained credence. Occasionally he was courageously repudiated and criticized, but most government officials, including his fellow senators, feared to gainsay him. To do so laid his accusers open to charges of being "soft" on communism.

McCarthy's attacks on the State Department and other agencies of the executive branch continued even under Eisenhower's Republican administration. Indeed, during the 1952 campaign Eisenhower hesitated to criticize the senator publicly even though it was widely known that Eisenhower deeply resented the scurrilous attacks that McCarthy had made upon General George C. Marshall, a man Eisenhower greatly admired. As late as January 1954 a Gallup public opinion poll showed that 50 percent of the American people favored McCarthy's activities and only 29 percent opposed him, although by then the senator had driven from the State Department almost all its experts on China on the grounds that they had "lost" China to the Communists. (For the story of another able American sacrificed on the altar of McCarthy's anti-communism, see "J. Robert Oppenheimer: The Destroyer Destroyed.")

McCarthy's power to frighten came to an abrupt end in 1954 when he obliquely attacked President Eisenhower and directly assailed Secretary of the Army Robert Stevens as an "awful dupe" of the Communists. McCarthy's now-apparent demagoguery caused his popularity to plummet. Coming under senatorial investigation himself for his unmannerly conduct, McCarthy was "condemned" for his behavior by sixty-seven senators in December 1954, although a mere twelve months before only one senator had been willing to stand out against an appropriation for McCarthy's Committee on Government Operations. The senator's influence abruptly collapsed. Soon thereafter he went into a physical decline, dying in May 1957.

McCarthy's fall marked the end of the Great Fear. A product of that fear and not a cause of

J. Robert Oppenheimer: The Destroyer Destroyed

To win the Second World War quickly, science and government became linked as they had never been before. The most awesome result was the invention of the nuclear bomb. Its detonation over Hiroshima and Nagasaki in August 1945 made the stakes of the later Cold War the highest imaginable: literally the destruction of the world. At the center of this new relation between science and government stood J. Robert Oppenheimer, often called the father of the atomic bomb. He was also one of the most illustrious victims of the Cold War.

Born in New York City in 1904, Oppenheimer, the son of a well-to-do businessman, was educated at the private Ethical Culture School in New York City and at Harvard. After graduating from college in three years, he spent almost four years more in Europe, earning a Ph.D. at Cambridge in England and studying theoretical physics in Germany, Holland, and Switzerland. Upon his return to the United States in 1929, he accepted posts at the University of California and the California Institute of Technology.

At Berkeley, Oppenheimer at first had only one graduate student, a young man no other professor would accept. Oppenheimer's exciting and lucid teaching, his

it, McCarthyism could last only so long as Americans believed that the internal menace of communism was greater than the external threat. By 1954 they no longer thought so.

A REPUBLICAN INTERLUDE

The Election of 1952. As early as 1950, leading Republicans, especially those of an internationalist persuasion, had been talking of Dwight D. Eisenhower as the ideal candidate for the party in 1952. Still incredibly popular because of his war record, Eisenhower also possessed political appeal because his rise from poor boy in Kansas to international renown seemed to epitomize the American dream. When his name was first suggested for the nomination, Eisenhower announced he was not interested, but in July 1952, after much public and private pressure, he resigned his command of the NATO forces and agreed to try for the nomination.

His most formidable opponent was Senator Robert A. Taft of Ohio, conservative in domestic affairs and neo-isolationist. Twice Taft had been turned down in favor of Dewey. Now the senator's supporters, who were legion, felt Taft's chance had come. But the convention nominated Eisenhower on the first ballot, with Senator Richard M. Nixon of California as his running mate. As a congressman a few years earlier, Nixon had gained national renown as a member of the House Un-American Activities Committee that unmasked Alger Hiss.

After Harry Truman took himself out of the

mastery of the latest in theoretical physics, and his broad cultural interests soon changed that. Within four years the best young brains in physics were seeking him out. At that time Oppenheimer had no interest in public affairs. Outside of physics, his greatest pleasure was studying Hindu scriptures in Sanskrit and reading English Renaissance poetry. He had no telephone or radio. Indeed, it was only in 1930, on a long walk with a fellow physicist, that he first learned of the stock market crash the year before!

This detachment from public affairs began to change in the middle 1930s. Through a love affair, he became caught up, as many idealistic young Americans of the time did, in the cause of the Spanish Republic, which was fighting for its life against a military coup headed by General Francisco Franco and aided by the troops of Hitler and Mussolini. In 1940 Oppenheimer married a young widow whose husband had been a Communist party official, killed in Spain. For a while his new wife was a party member and so were his brother and sister-in-law. These Communist associations, however, did not stand in the way of Oppenheimer's becoming involved in the biggest secret undertaking ever initiated by any government.

The secret was the construction of the first nuclear weapon. Oppenheimer was made the director of the most important—and most secret—part of the Manhattan District Project: the design of the bomb at the isolated mesa in New Mexico called Los Alamos. Without the incentive of a war, the government probably would not have gambled on the project, and without Oppenheimer, there probably would not have been a bomb before the war ended. Oppenheimer brought the necessary scientists together in a totally isolated community of several thousand people and then kept them working amicably and productively to solve the myriad design problems. So intense was the secrecy that even the babies born at Los Alamos were given false birth certificates. During this period, Oppenheimer's weight fell from 130 to 116

race, the Democrats centered their attention upon new prospects, notably Adlai E. Stevenson, governor of Illinois. Although Stevenson was not sure he wanted to run, the July convention "drafted" him on the third ballot. In an effort to heal the wounds from the party split over civil rights in 1948, the convention nominated a Southerner, Senator John J. Sparkman of Alabama, for Vice-President.

From the outset Eisenhower was the favorite. While Stevenson was compelled to defend the Truman administration, the Republicans fiercely attacked it for alleged corruption, for coddling Communists in government, and, above all, for the Korean War. Late in the campaign Stevenson's manager, referring to the Republican barrage of criticism, remarked: "We are suffering from a new kind of KKK—Korea, Communism, and corruption."

Stevenson, however, proved to be an admirable candidate. His speeches were undoubtedly the most sophisticated addresses heard from a presidential candidate since the days of Woodrow Wilson. His ratings on the public opinion polls steadily rose during the campaign, but never to the level of Eisenhower's.

Toward the end of October Eisenhower capitalized on the pervasive discontent over Korea by promising that, if elected, he would personally make a trip to the battlefront in an effort to bring the fighting to an end. Even the prosperous times, which ordinarily would have worked to the advantage of the incumbent party, could not overcome the force of the Korean issue.

pounds. His gangling frame, clothed in an unpressed suit, surmounted by his famous broad-brimmed porkpie hat, seemed never to be still. He was the heart as well as the brain of Los Alamos.

On that July dawn in 1945 when the bomb was tested at Alamagordo, in southern New Mexico, Oppenheimer was so nervous that the military commander had to take him outside for a walk in the desert to calm him. When the bomb exploded with a silent burst of light brighter than the sun itself, illuminating even distant mountains, a line from Hindu scriptures leaped into Oppenheimer's mind: "I am become Death, Destroyer of Worlds." Outwardly though, he smiled with relief; his three-year mission was accomplished. This man who believed in "ahimsa"—the Hindu principle of nonviolence—had built the most devastating weapon the world had ever known.

The success of the Los Alamos enterprise catapulted Oppenheimer into public as well as scientific prominence around the world. He acted as scientific adviser to several government agencies and to the President himself. But his great prestige was not enough to protect him against the fears spawned by the new weapon he had worked so hard to create.

In 1949, years before any American political leader had thought possible, the Soviet Union exploded a nuclear device. With the United States no longer in possession of a nuclear monopoly and the Cold War in full swing, pressure mounted for new military weapons. For some, the answer was the thermonuclear or fusion bomb, many times more powerful than the nuclear bomb, but then little more than a theory. And for a while the practical difficulties seemed to rule it out.

By 1953, though, when Oppenheimer's term in government ended, work on a hydrogen bomb had been moving ahead for some time. Still, the new chairman of the Atomic Energy Commission, Lewis Strauss, was convinced the work was not

Eisenhower scored a sweeping personal victory with 442 electoral votes to Stevenson's 89 and almost 34 million popular votes to Stevenson's 27 million. Eisenhower's popular vote ran 15 percent ahead of his party's vote for Congress, for the Republicans captured both houses by only slim majorities (and, in fact, lost that control to the Democrats in the mid-term elections two years later). Another measure of Eisenhower's victory was that he broke into the Democratic South, capturing not only border states like Maryland and Missouri, and Tennessee and Virginia, but Texas and Florida as well. Even in the traditionally isolationist Middle West Eisenhower won easily despite his record as an internationalist.

Blacks, rural Southerners, and the big city voters in the North remained loyal to the Democrats, but close postelection analyses showed that Eisenhower won support from all classes and income levels. A striking measure of his popularity was that perhaps as much as a quarter of his popular vote came from people who had voted for Truman.

The First Eisenhower Administration. Many Americans, knowing Eisenhower's long record as a military man, anticipated a stern and exacting leader of Congress and the nation. In fact, Eisenhower turned out quite the opposite. Basically he conceived the President's functions to be quite distinct from those of Congress. He generally refused even to comment upon legislation while it was passing through the legislative mill.

proceeding fast enough. He persuaded President Eisenhower that Oppenheimer had delayed progress because of his Communist sympathies. Although by that time Oppenheimer no longer had any connection with the government, and even his advice had not been sought for months, Eisenhower in March 1954 ordered that "a blank wall be placed between Dr. Oppenheimer and any secret data," pending a hearing.

At the hearings all the old information about Oppenheimer's Communist associations in the 1930s was brought forward again. Especially damning, though, was the testimony of his old Los Alamos associate (and strong anti-Communist) Edward Teller, who pronounced Oppenheimer unreliable. No one ever accused Oppenheimer of giving away secrets. Nevertheless the Atomic Energy Commission decided by a four-to-one vote to deny him security clearance. The sole dissenter, significantly, was the single scientist on the Commission.

Only with the moderating of the Cold War in the 1960s did Oppenheimer regain any of the recognition he had earned so laboriously during the war. In 1963 President Lyndon Johnson presented him with the Commission's prestigious Fermi Award for contributions to physics. At the White House ceremony an ill and emaciated Oppenheimer hobbled to the rostrum. In his brief, almost private words to the President, he succinctly described the special new relation between science and politics, which had lain at the root of his own public humiliation. Thomas Jefferson, he recalled, often wrote of " 'the brotherly spirit of science which unites into a family all of its votaries.' " But, Oppenheimer continued, "we have not always given evidence of that brotherly spirit in science. This is . . . because we are engaged in this great enterprise of our time, testing whether men can live without war as the great arbiter of history." Though Oppenheimer died in 1967, that testing continues.

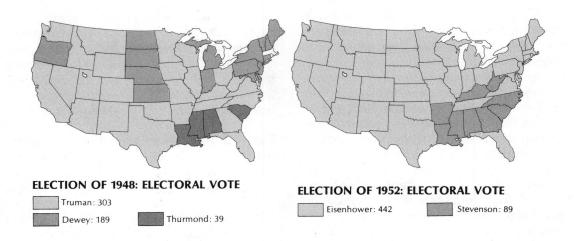

ELECTION OF 1948: ELECTORAL VOTE

Truman: 303

Dewey: 189   Thurmond: 39

ELECTION OF 1952: ELECTORAL VOTE

Eisenhower: 442   Stevenson: 89

The first administration was intended to be a businessman's government in the best sense of the phrase: It would not be subservient to business, but it would do its best to encourage business. Thus all economic controls left over from the Korean War were abolished early in February 1953. Similarly, government enterprises which competed with private business were dropped. A balanced budget became the guiding aim of the administration under the leadership of Secretary of the Treasury George C. Humphrey. When he took office, Eisenhower cut over a billion dollars from Truman's foreign aid budget, but in the main he would not let the drive for economy endanger the national security. When there was any choice, the administration generally gave preference to business over government. Thus it awarded an electric power contract to a private utility instead of to the Tennessee Valley Authority. And in 1956 the Atomic Energy Commission authorized the private development of electric power through nuclear energy.

In at least two respects the Republicans carried on New Deal–Fair Deal policies without question. One was in showing a willingness to use federal authority to counteract the recession of 1954, and the other was in expanding the coverage of the Social Security system in 1953. Eisenhower also tried to overcome the isolationism that still persisted among many Republicans. Indeed, it was to advance the cause of internationalism that he had run in the first place. But it required all of Eisenhower's prestige to prevent the passage in 1954 of the so-called Bricker Amendment, which would have limited the treaty-making power of the government and enlarged congressional control over foreign relations. Although advanced as a means of preventing the treaty-making power from being abused, this proposed amendment to the Constitution would have seriously handicapped the President's handling of foreign affairs.

The Election of 1956. Normally, in view of Eisenhower's immense popularity, his renomination in 1956 would have been unquestioned. But in September 1955 the President suffered a severe heart attack which incapacitated him for two months. Although his steady recovery emboldened the party leaders to call once again for his nomination, the President himself withheld his consent until February 1956. That summer he was renominated along with Richard M. Nixon. The Democrats also renominated Adlai Stevenson, who this time had eagerly sought the nomination.

Eisenhower won again. The Republican campaign capitalized on "peace and prosperity," but the victory is better explained by the character of a man who could inspire millions of voters to display campaign buttons reading "I like Ike." Eisenhower's personal popularity won him 457 electoral votes to Stevenson's 73. That it was a personal victory was attested by the fact that Eisenhower failed to bring a Republican Congress into office with him. The Democrats continued to control the Senate and the House. Ike ran 6.5 million votes ahead of Republican congressional candidates. Not since 1848 had a President failed to carry with him at least one house. For a popular President such a failure was unprecedented.

Working with Democrats. Throughout his second term Eisenhower was confronted with Democratic majorities in both houses. (In the elections of 1958 these majorities reached numbers not seen since the mid-1930s.) Seeing his presidential role as one of resisting a "wasteful" Democratic Congress, Eisenhower regularly vetoed government salary increases and demands for tax cuts during the 1958 recession. Despite the Democratic majorities, all save one of Eisenhower's vetoes of antirecession measures held.

One of the three principal pieces of legislation of Eisenhower's second term was the Labor-Management Reporting and Disclosure Act (1959), growing out of Senate committee hearings on racketeering, corruption, and extortion in labor unions. (The others were the Civil Rights Act of 1957 and the National Defense Education Act of 1958, the latter discussed in the preceding chapter.) The labor act followed the thinking of the Taft-Hartley Act, assuming a divergence of interest between union members and leaders. Senator John L. McClellan, whose committee held the hearings, and Representative Philip M. Landrum, who sponsored the bill in the House, were Southern Democrats, so the bill also symbolized the Republican-Southern Demo-

cratic alliance that usually supported the President on labor and financial measures. The Landrum-Griffin Act, as it was also called, among other things set up a "bill of rights" to protect union members against assessments and coercion by labor leaders; required unions to make public, largely for the benefit of their members, all expenditures and all payments made to officers; and provided that unions must hold regular elections of officers.

THE SECOND RECONSTRUCTION

The 1954 Decision. On May 17, 1954, in handing down a decision in *Brown* v. *Board of Education of Topeka*, the Supreme Court of the United States unanimously concluded "that in the field of public education the doctrine of 'separate but equal' has no place." In the middle of the twentieth century, "separate education facilities are inherently unequal," the Court concluded. In thus overturning the decision in *Plessy* v. *Ferguson* (1896), on which all Southern states rested the validity of their segregated public facilities, the Court opened a new chapter in the history of black people in America.

For over a decade the Supreme Court had been invalidating state laws which discriminated on grounds of race, but the school decision shocked the South. Although a few border-state communities like Baltimore and Washington, D.C., began desegregation of schools in 1954, in most of the South the decision met stiff and determined resistance. By the middle of 1956 only some 350 school districts out of 6300 were desegregated in the South, and none of these desegregated districts was located in the middle or Deep South.

Southern Resistance. In 1957 Southern opposition to school desegregation reached the point of clashes with federal military power. Under a plan of gradual desegregation worked out by the local school board and the

White students look on as heavily armed Federal troops escort black students to classes at the Central High School in Little Rock in 1957.

federal district court, nine black students were scheduled to enter Central High School in Little Rock, Arkansas, in the fall of 1957. But Arkansas' Governor Orville Faubus used state troops to bar their entrance. Faced with state defiance of federal authority, President Eisenhower sent in United States paratroopers to enforce the orders of the federal court. For several weeks soldiers with fixed bayonets escorted the black students to classes. Later, federalized Arkansas troops remained to patrol the school grounds for the entire school year.

If the breakdown of orderly processes of law in Arkansas shocked the nation and the world, the use of federal troops temporarily stiffened resistance in the South. "Massive resistance" statutes, as they were called, were hastily enacted in a number of states, resulting in the closing of schools in Little Rock and in three communities in Virginia. By 1959, though, the more moderate people in Arkansas and Virginia accepted at least token desegregation in preference to no public schools at all. And in 1960 and 1961 token desegregation came to the Deep Southern states of Louisiana and Georgia, particularly in the big cities of New Orleans and Atlanta.

The determined opposition of segregationist leaders and White Citizens Councils in the Deep South was not to be broken so easily, however. In September and October 1962, a transfixed nation watched as the state of Mississippi, through its elected officials, defied a federal court order requiring the University of Mississippi to permit a black man, James Meredith, to enroll as a student. The federal authorities tried their best to avoid the use of armed force by working behind the scenes to secure compliance with the court. But Governor Ross Barnett's public statements of defiance encouraged thousands of segregationists, including many students, to attack physically the federal marshals assigned to protect Meredith upon his arrival at the university.

As a result of the vehemence of the attack, President John F. Kennedy dispatched thousands of federalized Mississippi national guardsmen and regular army troops to the university town of Oxford to restore peace and to ensure the execution of the court's orders. Meredith entered the university as its first known black student.

Prior to the riots, desegregation at the state college and university level had been proceeding almost without incident in the Southern states, excepting Alabama and South Carolina. Thereafter, every state moved to integrate all levels of education, though primary and secondary schools had little more than token integration until 1968. Between then and 1971 the proportion of black children doubled in Southern schools heretofore wholly white, reaching 39 percent. This was a greater increase and a larger proportion than that for the nation as a whole. As early as 1971 only 14 percent of black children in the South were still in schools that were entirely black. In short, the movement toward integration in the South had proceeded further than it had elsewhere in the country.

Even so, resistance continued. The principal evidence was the growing number of private, all-white schools in the South. In 1971 it was estimated that about 4 percent of school-age children attended such schools.

A New Civil Rights Movement.   The decline of segregation in the South during the 1950s and 1960s was hastened by a rising assertiveness among Southern blacks in opposing segregation. One of the most influential efforts, as well as most successful, was the boycott of local buses in Montgomery, Alabama, by the 50,000 black residents. The boycott against segregation on the buses began in December 1955. Although it brought hardship to the blacks who ordinarily depended upon public transportation to get to work, it was sustained for almost a year.

One of the leaders of this boycott was the

Reverend Martin Luther King, Jr., a young Southern black who became nationally known for his remarkably effective oratory and his moral leadership, based upon the principle of nonviolence. His successes at Montgomery and later in other causes on behalf of equality and justice, in the North as well as in the South, brought him worldwide recognition and, in 1964, the Nobel Peace Prize. Segregation of bus passengers was declared unconstitutional by the Supreme Court in November 1956.

The slow pace of desegregation also provoked the federal government to take action against discrimination. In August 1957, Congress, after much debate, passed the first civil rights act since the days of Reconstruction. Its purpose was to protect the voting rights of blacks. Though the provisions were weaker than those originally advocated by the Eisenhower administration, they empowered federal judges to jail for contempt anyone —including state officials—who prevented a qualified person from voting. The law also created a temporary Civil Rights Commission to investigate violations of civil rights and to make recommendations for new legislation. (The Commission was continued into the 1970s.)

A second civil rights act, against which Southerners filibustered unsuccessfully, was passed in 1960 to further protect the voting rights of blacks. It was not until the Johnson administration, however, that a voting rights bill was passed that substantially increased voting by blacks in the South.

From 1960 on, blacks themselves undertook new ways of attacking segregation in the South. There were "sit-ins" at segregated lunch counters and bus depots, "wade-ins" at segregated beaches, and even "pray-ins" at segregated churches—all aimed at nonviolent achievement of integration and equal rights.

Simultaneously with the antisegregation movement in the South, Northern blacks in cities like New York and Chicago campaigned against segregated public schools. Northern segregation resulted from residential patterns rather than from laws, but the effects were often the same. Blacks demanded, with some success, that their children be accepted in white schools outside their local districts, where the schools were often crowded and run-down or underfinanced.

But when in the early 1970s the federal courts used compulsory busing to bring about racial mixture in Northern schools, as it had done in the South, strong white opposition exploded. In some Northern cities, like San Francisco, Pontiac, Michigan, and Brooklyn, New York in the early 1970s parents who opposed busing kept their children out of school for weeks. In Boston during 1974 – 1975, the resistance to busing was as vehement—and violent—as resistance to integration had been at Little Rock in 1957. In 1971, a Gallup poll found that 76 percent of Americans opposed busing as a means of bringing about desegregation. Nevertheless, the courts continued to uphold busing as a constitutional means of breaking segregation. In 1979 the Supreme Court reaffirmed the principle, though by a divided vote.

By the close of the 1970s school segregation was clearly less pronounced in the once completely segregated South than in the North. Only 12 percent of Southern black children were in predominantly black schools as compared to 31 percent of Midwestern and Northeastern children. Yet as recently as 1968 the proportion of black children in segregated schools throughout the nation had been 53 percent.

THE NEW ACTIVIST SUPREME COURT

If in the 1930s the Supreme Court was the center of controversy because of its conservatism, in the 1950s and 1960s it was the object of both criticism and praise because of its willingness to innovate. That willingness, as we shall see, was also the prime source of the strong desire on the part of the first Nixon administration to change its outlook by new, conservative appointments. In at least two different fields the Court exceeded even its customary importance as the final arbiter of American law.

Renewed Interest in Individual Rights. One of these fields was civil rights and individual liberties. The most striking instance was the 1954 decision already mentioned, in which the Court struck down segregated education. But there were other examples, too.

During the 1950s the Court spoke out clearly in defense of individual rights even when the accused were Communists. In the case of *Yates* v. *U.S.* (1957) the Court seriously modified the *Dennis* v. *U.S.* decision of 1951 which had upheld the conviction of eleven Communist leaders for conspiring to overthrow the government by force in violation of the Smith Act. Chief Justice Vinson had stated in his 1951 decision that government could act if "a highly organized conspiracy" to overthrow in the future were established. The *Yates* decision distinguished between "advocacy of forcible overthrow as mere abstract doctrine" (which is within the free speech protection of the First Amendment) and "advocacy which incites to illegal action" (proscribed by the Smith Act). Thus mere advocacy of a theoretical desirability of violence was now not sufficient for conviction. Moreover, "mere membership or the holding of office in the Communist party" was held not to be sufficient proof of specific intent to "incite" persons to overthrow the government.

The Supreme Court's most controversial assertion of individual rights since *Brown* v. *Board of Education* in 1954 was the case of *Roe* v. *Wade*, decided in 1973 by a 7–2 division among the justices. In this decision the Court invalidated all state laws prohibiting abortion on the ground that under the Fourteenth Amendment no state could forbid a woman from terminating a pregnancy during the first six months. Only in the final trimester of pregnancy could a state prohibit a woman from having an abortion, with some procedural regulations being allowed during the middle three months.

The decision was welcomed by the women's movement, but opposed by many conservatives and by some religious groups, notably the Roman Catholic Church. In subsequent years, the question of abortion has become a highly charged political issue. Some anti-abortion organizations have sought to overturn the decision in *Roe* v. *Wade* by constitutional amendment. The necessary public support, however, has so far not been forthcoming. In 1980, though, the Republican party platform called for such an amendment.

During the 1960s the Court also reached out to offer constitutional protection to citizens charged with crimes. In a series of cases beginning with *Gideon* v. *Wainwright* (1962) and culminating in *Miranda* v. *Arizona* (1966), the Court held that the police must not infringe in any way on an individual's right to be presumed innocent until proved guilty. The *Gideon* decision, overturning a twenty-year rule, concluded that paupers had the right to a lawyer even if the court had to pay the lawyer's fee. In the *Miranda* decision the court ruled that an accused person could not be questioned by police unless his or her lawyer was present. Although many police officials contended that these decisions hindered the conviction of known criminals, defenders of civil liberties hailed the decisions as landmarks in the protection of the individual against arbitrary power.

A continuation of this line of reasoning in a case in 1972 was of particular significance because by then four members of the court were appointees of the Nixon administration, which had been among the prominent critics of the Court's liberal view of individual rights in criminal cases. In a 7–2 decision, the Court held that in all cases in which jail sentences resulted, including cases involving minor crimes (misdemeanors), a defendant must be provided with counsel if too poor to pay a lawyer. Only forty years before, anyone convicted of a capital crime could be executed, even though deprived of legal defense because of lack of funds. Now a defendant could not be sent to jail for drunken driving except after a trial with adequate legal representation.

In 1972 the Court extended its protection of individual rights when it ruled in the *Furman* case that capital punishment constituted "cruel and unusual punishment," which the Constitution prohibits. But then in 1976 it modified that position somewhat by deciding that the death penalty was not unconstitutional so long as it was not arbitrarily or unreasonably applied. In *Coker* v. *Georgia,* the next year, however, a divided court held that exacting the death penalty for rape was unconstitutional because it was cruel and unusual punishment.

Despite the Court's concern for individual rights, some other government officials had been less than protective of them. In 1976 the head of the Federal Bureau of Investigation, Clarence Kelley, publicly apologized for the illegalities perpetrated by his agency while under the leadership of the best-known G-man of them all, J. Edgar Hoover. Among the violations were persecution and harassment of citizens and radical groups, and illegal tapping of telephone wires.

The Rights of Urban Dwellers. The Court's decisions in *Baker* v. *Carr,* handed down in March 1962, and in *Reynolds* v. *Sims* two years later, were freighted with almost as much significance for the future as the *Brown* decision on segregation in 1954. The *Baker* case concerned the refusal of Tennessee to reapportion its legislative seats in accordance with changes in the distribution of population. The Court decreed that districts of markedly unequal populations constituted an inequity

'What Do They Think People Are—Innocent Until Proved Guilty?'

Not everyone thought the Supreme Court decisions on individual rights were good ones.

for which the courts could rightly be expected to provide a remedy.

For a number of years, as population flowed from the rural areas to the cities, urban dwellers had smarted under the failure of their growing numbers to be reflected in increased representation in the state legislatures. It was well known that rural-dominated legislatures simply refused, as in the case of Tennessee, to reapportion seats, for to do so might mean loss of rural control. Until the *Baker* decision the courts had always held that such inequity was a "political" question beyond their jurisdiction.

The *Reynolds* decision extended the reasoning of the *Baker* decision to include the upper as well as the lower houses of the state legislatures. These decisions opened up the possibility that with equitable apportionment of representation the cities would be able to get a better hearing in the state legislatures for their many and worsening problems.

The effects of the *Baker* decision were soon apparent. In a number of states where rural dominance in politics had long depended upon underweighting urban populations, the impact of the decisions was almost immediately evident in the new political strength of cities. Atlanta, for example, suddenly gained new strength in the Georgia legislature. In 1967 a reapportioned Tennessee legislature succeeded in repealing the anti-evolution statute passed in 1925, during the heyday of rural domination of the legislature. By 1971 more than half the states had reapportioned their legislatures, though some of the new plans had been thrown out by the courts as inadequate.

SPUTNIK AND THE RACE TO CATCH UP

The Russians' successful launch of the first Sputnik into orbit around the earth on October 4, 1957, shook both the administration and the American people, used to thinking of themselves as second to none in science and technology. The effect of this shock on the educational system was discussed in the preceding chapter. Its effects on our own space capability and on our military hardware was far more dramatic.

America's Space Program. After the launching of Sputnik I, it took four months for the United States to be ready to put a far smaller vehicle into space. By then the Russians had put into orbit a second satellite large enough to carry a dog.

With the prestige of both countries now hinging upon successfully orbiting hardware, satellites were hurled into the skies in profusion during 1958 and in subsequent years. By 1961 the most obvious consequence of the first Sputnik was that the United States had mounted six separate series of rocket probes, each more ambitious and scientifically sophisticated than the preceding one.

In 1961 President John F. Kennedy announced the beginning of the most dramatic of all the rocket series—Project Apollo, which was designed to land a man on the moon by 1970. Despite some cutbacks in funds during the middle 1960s and the death of three astronauts, American successes in orbiting man-carrying satellites around the earth and in landing vehicles on the moon put the United States on a par with, if not ahead of, the U.S.S.R. On July 20, 1969, well ahead of the deadline President Kennedy had set, two American astronauts landed on the moon. Other American visits to the lunar surface followed during the next few years.

The Military Impact of Sputnik. A factor in most Americans' dismay over the initial Russian successes in space rocketry was the fear that the United States was vulnerable to a new kind of military attack. Prior to the orbiting of Sputnik I, the Eisenhower administration had deprecated Russian boasts of being able to shoot off nuclear-tipped missiles that could reach the United States from bases in the Soviet Union. At that time American military missile capability was unable to reach more than five hundred miles. With the orbiting of Sputnik I, the Russians proved their claim, and the immediate American response was a congressional and public clamor for a crash program to catch up with the Russians. In early 1958 Congress and the administration responded with a $1.27 billion program for accelerating missile development. In the budget of 1958–1959 President Eisenhower proposed the largest peacetime military expenditures in American history.

As a result of the new and feverish interest in military rocketry, the United States developed a whole new spectrum of weapons. It included short- and medium-range rockets,

Astronaut Edwin Aldrin looks at the American flag planted on the surface of the moon.

which could be used against planes, troop formations, and ships, and giant intercontinental ballistic missiles (ICBM), which could span oceans at speeds in excess of 15,000 miles per hour and devastate cities with their nuclear warheads. Perhaps the closest to an invulnerable weapon was the 1500-mile-range Polaris missile, which was designed to be fired from a submerged nuclear-powered submarine. Such a submarine could remain submerged for months at a time without refueling and would present an almost impossible target for an enemy to locate and destroy.

One measure of the character of the missile race between the two superpowers was that in

the late sixties even the Polaris missile was being replaced by the more powerful and longer-range Poseidon missile. By the early seventies the Poseidon, in turn, was being replaced by the more sophisticated Trident.

Behind the missile race was the recognition that an all-out attack by nuclear-tipped missiles could devastate the whole country in a matter of an hour or so. The principal defense against nuclear attack became the threat of retaliation from secure bases, as invulnerable to surprise attack as engineers and scientists could make them, for once the first attack had been launched there would be no time for mobilization. So in addition to the submarine missiles, the United States also placed ICBMs in great protective concrete emplacements in the ground in order to have them operational even after a direct enemy strike.

Meanwhile, military authorities on both sides developed an antimissile missile (ABM)—a projectile to knock an enemy missile out of the sky before it could reach its target. By 1970 Moscow was ringed by ABMs and the United States had ABMs around some of its missile sites. Both sides were also beginning to arm their missiles with multiple warheads that could be independently targeted in order to complicate the work of the ABMs.

As weapons of nuclear power became ever more complicated—and more expensive— Congress and a sizable portion of the public began to have doubts that so much power was actually necessary to maintain the balance of terror. It was in the context of astronomical, escalating costs for the new missile systems that the disarmament agreements reached between the United States and the Soviet Union in 1972 and the discussions of further agreements in 1974 under Ford and in 1978 under Carter had such great importance. They will be discussed in the next chapter.

A NEW ERA IN FOREIGN AFFAIRS

The Death of Stalin. In January 1953 a Republican administration took office in Washington. On March 5 Joseph Stalin died in Moscow. In July the Korean War came to a halt. These events, coming so close together, marked a new era in the Cold War. Although no single Soviet leader emerged immediately to inherit Stalin's enormous personal power, the new Russian leaders demonstrated more flexibility and resourcefulness in foreign policy than Stalin had shown.

Notable in this regard was Nikita Khrushchev, who became head of the Communist party in 1953 and premier in 1958. Unlike Stalin, the new Soviet leaders traveled widely outside Russia, selling communism energetically. In 1959 Khrushchev visited the United States.

The Eisenhower administration also sought to alter foreign policy by taking a new approach. Despite his overall commitment to the major policies of the Truman administration, John Foster Dulles, the new Secretary of State, hoped to do more than merely contain communism. Toward the end of 1953, for example, he tried unsuccessfully to badger the European nations into a new defense community which would include a rearmed Germany. A looser grouping, agreed upon in 1954, did provide for a revived German army to be included in NATO.

On the other side of the world in Asia, soon after Communist-led Vietnamese guerrillas drove the French from Indochina in 1954, Secretary Dulles moved to counter further Communist expansion by the formation of the Southeast Asia Treaty Organization (SEATO). It was modeled after NATO but was conspicuously weaker on at least two counts: The signatories were required only to consult, not to take action, in the event of attack, and the organization failed to include the chief powers of the region. Composed of Thailand, Australia, New Zealand, the Philippines, Pakistan, Britain, France, and the United States, SEATO did not include India, Indonesia, Ceylon, and Burma, all of which refused invitations to join.

Dulles also hoped to use the threat of American nuclear capability as a means of countering the superior manpower of the Communist bloc. But his threat of "massive retaliation" in the event of aggression was weakened by the fact that the Soviet Union also possessed the new weapons of war. In 1949 the U.S.S.R. had successfully exploded a nuclear bomb of its own and in 1953 added a thermonuclear (hydrogen) bomb to its arsenal. (The United States had detonated its first thermonuclear device in 1952.) Hence any use of nuclear weapons against the Soviet Union or its allies would presumably set off a war of catastrophic proportions.

The acquisition of nuclear weapons by the Soviet Union spurred arrangements for a meeting of the heads of government of the United States, Great Britain, France, and the Soviet Union. A meeting at the summit, as Winston Churchill called it, took place in the summer of 1955 at Geneva, Switzerland. There was little concrete achievement, but Eisenhower's suggestion that the United States and the U.S.S.R. exchange plans of their military establishments and permit aerial photography of each other's bases seemed, for a while, like a promising idea. Even though the Russians saw little merit in Eisenhower's "open skies" proposal, the suggestion made evident the American President's sincere and anxious search for a way out of the terrible nuclear impasse between the two giant powers.

Crisis in the Middle East; The Hungarian Revolt. The foreign policies of both the United States and Russia were tested more severely in November 1956. Early that month Israeli, French, and British military forces invaded Egypt. All three countries had deep grievances against Colonel Gamal Nasser's nationalistic regime. Nasser had long been a champion of Arab opposition to Israel, refusing to recognize that new country and constantly threatening invasion, and earlier in 1956 he had seized the Suez Canal, contrary to Egypt's treaty obligations. Without informing the United States, their ally, Britain and France, ten days after Israel invaded Egypt, dropped paratroopers on the Suez area, quickly overwhelming the inefficient Egyptian army. At almost the same time, the Soviet Union ruthlessly suppressed a widespread and heroic revolt of the Hungarians against Communist rule.

Both the Suez and Hungarian invasions took the United States by surprise. The administration opposed both, but its power over the Soviets was nil. The opposition of the United States to the Suez adventure was more successful, both because the United States was an ally of Britain and France and because world opinion and the United Nations vehemently condemned it. When the leaders of the Soviet Union threatened to come to Egypt's aid, Britain, France, and Israel, heeding the United Nations resolution for a cease-fire, withdrew their troops.

The immediate consequence of the Suez crisis was that Egypt drew closer to the Soviet Union, and Communist penetration of the Middle East seemed imminent. Reacting to this development and in response to a request from the President, Congress in March 1957 passed a resolution affirming America's intention to aid any country in the Middle East which seemed to be threatened by a Communist coup, internal or external. The first test of what came to be called the Eisenhower Doctrine occurred in July 1958, when American marines landed in Lebanon to forestall a possible invasion from neighboring Syria, then a satellite of Nasser's and judged to be overly friendly toward the Soviet Union. The pro-Western regime in Lebanon was not overthrown, and by the end of October 1958 all American troops had withdrawn.

The Middle East crisis of 1956–1958 brought the Eisenhower administration full circle. Once hopeful of avoiding "brush-fire wars," it found itself dispatching troops to trouble spots much as Truman had done in Korea. It was also evident after 1956 that Moscow was not the only source of instability in the world. Rising nationalism in Asia, Africa, and even the Americas presented new problems and dangers. Khrushchev was adept at winning friends in the new regions, and he consciously identified his country with the fierce opposition of the former colonial peoples to their old rulers. In part to offset Khrushchev's success-

This stockpile of American missiles in West Germany is part of the costly balance of terror—a strategy that has characterized U.S.-Soviet relations since the 1950s.

ful international salesmanship, the President in December 1959 and through the first half of 1960 embarked upon extensive good-will tours of the Middle East and Southeast Asia, Latin America, and eastern Asia. Although the first two tours were eminently successful, the last, to Asia, proved much less so. Anti-American riots in Japan prevented the President from visiting that country at all.

The U-2 Incident. Even before the Tokyo riots of June 1960, other events seriously tarnished the American image abroad and further impaired Soviet-American relations. Early in 1960 the President, still hopeful of being able to arrange some kind of disarmament agreement with Khrushchev, had

agreed to another summit meeting in Paris. But just before the conference opened, the Russians announced the shooting down of a high-flying American espionage plane deep inside the Soviet Union. At first the American officials denied the accusation, but after the Russians triumphantly produced the plane and its pilot, who was still alive, the United States shamefacedly admitted undertaking this and other flights over the Soviet Union. Outraged, Khrushchev called off the summit meeting, deliberately insulting Eisenhower in the process. In their propaganda around the world the Russians made the most of the American admission. The incident of the U-2, as the special plane was called, dealt a heavy blow to American prestige and honor. Not only was the flight contrary to standard usages under international law, but the United States had been caught in an official lie which undermined its credibility before the world.

Troubles with Castro. American relations with Cuba also deteriorated seriously in 1960. On January 1, 1959, a young revolutionary, Fidel Castro, succeeded in overthrowing the corrupt dictatorship of General Fulgencio Batista. At first the new government enjoyed the support of the American people, who welcomed Castro when he visited the United States soon after assuming power. But when it became evident that the social revolution Castro proclaimed also included the confiscation of American property and the wholesale execution of the "enemies of the revolution," the attitude of the American people and their government cooled noticeably.

By early 1960 over a billion dollars worth of American property had been confiscated without compensation, and a steady stream of refugees from Cuba entered Miami. Furthermore, Castro made no secret of his friendship with the Soviet Union, with which he concluded trade agreements. In retaliation, late in May 1960 the United States ended all economic aid to Cuba, and in July, at the recommendation of an angry Congress, the President cut imports of Cuban sugar by 95 percent. Since the United States was Cuba's principal customer and sugar the island's chief export, this action hurt. The Castro regime became increasingly anti-American.

The Election of 1960. Because the recently ratified Twenty-second Amendment limited Presidents to two terms, the Republicans in 1960 did not have to wait to learn whether Eisenhower would run for a third term. Vice-President Richard M. Nixon was the choice of most party leaders, including the President. Nixon was nominated on the first ballot, and Henry Cabot Lodge, the United

States ambassador to the United Nations, was chosen as his running mate.

The front-runner at the Democratic Convention was Massachusetts Senator John F. Kennedy, who had shown strength in a number of state primaries. Thanks to a well-prepared campaign and a highly organized staff, Kennedy was nominated on the first ballot. Astutely, he urged the nomination of his erstwhile opponent, Senator Lyndon Johnson of Texas, for second place on the ticket. The Democrats wrote a deliberately liberal platform, including support of the Supreme Court decision on desegregation.

Since both candidates were in their youthful forties, the campaigning was strenuous, despite extensive use of television and jet travel. Nixon personally visited all fifty states and Kennedy appeared in forty-four. The candidates also inaugurated a series of four joint appearances on television, which helped Kennedy, since he had enjoyed less national recognition than Nixon.

Kennedy also ran under the handicap of being a Roman Catholic. Although the Republicans officially did not allude to his religion or use it against him, a number of private persons and organizations did question the fitness of a Catholic for the presidency. Kennedy met the prejudice head-on, candidly and without rancor. "I am not the Catholic candidate for President," he said at one point in the campaign. "I do not speak for the Catholic Church on issues of public policy, and none in that Church speaks for me. . . . Are we to say that a Jew can be elected Mayor of Dublin, a Protestant be named foreign minister of France . . . but a Catholic cannot be President of the United States?" Subsequent analyses showed that Kennedy's religion was the central issue for most voters.

The election turned out to be one of the closest in American history, with Kennedy winning by fewer than 113,000 votes out of a record 68.6 million votes cast. At least 4.5 million Protestants who had voted for Ste-

John F. Kennedy, an unusually articulate and persuasive speaker, projected a compelling image of youth and vigor during his presidential campaign in 1960.

venson voted for Nixon, it has been estimated, but Kennedy's Catholicism brought out new Catholic voters, and he won support from some Eisenhower Protestants. Few Republican Catholics shifted. Lyndon Johnson was essential in helping to stem the Southern Protestant opposition to a Catholic President. Kennedy's election finally disproved the political platitude that a Catholic could not be elected President.

Although a shift of merely 12,000 votes in five states would have given Nixon an electoral college majority, the congressional elections were one-sidedly Democratic. At that level, at least, it was clear that the country was still strongly Democratic.

THE KENNEDY ADMINISTRATION

Limited Success with Congress. In keeping with the youthful, vigorous image he had projected during the campaign, John Fitzgerald Kennedy called his program "The New Frontier." More eloquent than any President since Woodrow Wilson, more concerned with elevating and educating the people than any President since Theodore Roosevelt, Kennedy entered office surrounded by driving intellectuals and men of high purpose. But he soon found that the conservative Congress was decidedly cool, if not hostile, to his program. Twice during 1961 and 1962 Congress rejected his bills for medical care for the aged and

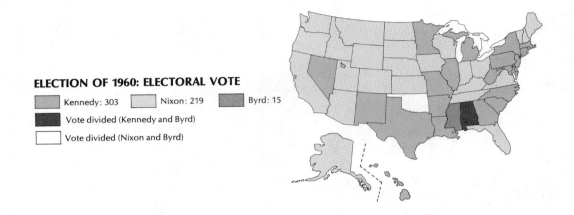

ELECTION OF 1960: ELECTORAL VOTE

Kennedy: 303   Nixon: 219   Byrd: 15

Vote divided (Kennedy and Byrd)

Vote divided (Nixon and Byrd)

federal aid to education. Congress also voted down his recommendation for a new cabinet post of urban affairs. In the first two years of his administration, Congress gave the President only a part of his requests for tax reforms. In 1963 it refused to act on his request for an income tax cut of $11 billion, which Kennedy had strongly urged as a necessary stimulus to the economy.

Like Roosevelt and Truman before him, Kennedy discovered that a heavily Democratic Congress was no guarantee that a Democratic President's program would be enacted. Most of the slowness or hostility of Congress centered in the House of Representatives, which was dominated by conservative Southern Democrats and Republicans, often working in coalition. In the congressional elections of 1962 the President vigorously campaigned for a Democratic Congress, and, contrary to the usual results of mid-term elections, the Democrats lost very few seats in the House and actually gained some in the Senate. Yet the result for the President's program was largely negative. At the time of Kennedy's death by assassination on November 22, 1963, Congress had failed to pass a single major piece of the legislative program he had enunciated the previous January.

The administration's principal legislative success had come in the previous year. The Trade Expansion Act of 1962 was important because it marked an even more significant departure from protectionism than the Reciprocal Trade Act of 1934. It gave the President new and unprecedentedly wide powers to cut tariff rates, although for decades Congress had jealously guarded its prerogatives in this field. The act also provided for federal aid to business firms and workers adversely affected by the resulting increased competition from abroad. Kennedy correctly hailed the act because it provided means for increasing the rate of American economic growth through the expansion of American exports. By permitting the importation of certain foreign goods, especially those from the booming European Common Market (composed of France, Italy, West Germany, and the Benelux countries) and from Japan, the administration hoped to secure important and wider markets for American goods abroad, while increasing, through competition, the efficiency of industry at home.

Several times Kennedy publicly denied that his administration harbored any of that hostility toward business usually associated with the Democratic regimes of Roosevelt and

Truman. But the business community clearly felt uneasy about Kennedy's leadership—particularly after he used threats of government intervention and harassment to force United States Steel to rescind its price increases in the spring of 1962.

Losses and Gains in Foreign Affairs. The Kennedy administration's foreign policy record was mixed. At his death the long-term problems of the Cold War were still unresolved and some new ones had been added. Germany and Berlin were still divided, and the several thousand advisers and support troops that Kennedy had sent to South Vietnam to help its anti-Communist government fight Communist rebels constituted the beginning of a much larger involvement to come.

During the early days of his administration, Kennedy launched the Alliance for Progress in Latin America, a long-range economic aid program designed to combat the conditions of poverty that contributed to the spread of communism and denied a decent living to millions. Through technical advice, loans, and grants, the Alliance endeavored to help Latin Americans help themselves in effecting land reform, improving farming techniques, and accelerating industrial development.

Unfortunately, the Alliance's laudable aim of not permitting United States funds to be used to bolster undemocratic or unpopular regimes was not easily put into practice. Military juntas in Argentina, Brazil, and Peru in 1962 and in the Dominican Republic in 1963 interfered with or actually overthrew constitutional governments, thereby bringing into serious question the political stability and commitment to constitutional and democratic procedures of those nations. It could be said, though, that the Alliance at least ended the long neglect of Latin America, whose leaders and intellectuals had both resented United States indifference and feared its power and its intentions.

In 1965 President Johnson admitted that the program would have to continue for twenty years instead of the original ten before it could be properly evaluated. By 1970 the rate of economic growth among members of the Alliance was higher than it had been in the early years of the program, but the average still fell below the planned-for 2.5 percent growth per year. An enduring problem was the unwillingness of governments in Latin America to encourage birth control, although birth rates in most of these countries were among the highest in the world.

During the Kennedy administration the storm center of Latin American affairs proved to be Cuba. In April 1961, Kennedy ill-advisedly lent token naval support to an invasion of Cuba by a small group of anti-Castro Cuban refugees at a place called Bay of Pigs. But the effort to overthrow Castro's avowedly Communist regime ended in fiasco when the 1500-man invasion force was easily defeated and its members killed or captured. The United States suffered grievously in prestige because it had once again, as in the U-2 incident, contravened the normal procedures of international law and had broken its own agreements under the inter-American security system. The immediate result was the strengthening of the Castro regime and the tightening of Cuba's connection with the Soviet Union.

How close that Russo-Cuban tie actually was became painfully clear in the summer and fall of 1962, when the Soviet Union began supplying the island nation with large amounts of economic and military aid. Then, in early October, American reconnaissance planes photographed Soviet medium-range missile sites under construction on Cuban soil. Alarmed at what he termed the upsetting of the "nuclear status quo" in the world, Kennedy on October 22, 1962, declared a naval quarantine of Cuba, broadcasting to the world and particularly to the Soviet Union the American intention to risk war rather than to permit a buildup of Soviet missile power in Cuba, only ninety miles from the United States.

The carefully considered confrontation brought the world to the very brink of nuclear war. But within three days the Russians agreed to withdraw their missiles in exchange for an American agreement not to support any future invasion of Cuba. Although Soviet technicians and support troops remained on the island, the extension of Soviet missiles to the Western Hemisphere had been stopped.

Then and later Kennedy was criticized for risking a world holocaust in order to show the Russians how determined he was. But most observers in the United States and western Europe praised his coolness and his success in dealing with the crisis. In any event, he did not gloat over the Soviet retreat. Instead he continued to seek ways of breaking the circle of mutual suspicion that perpetuated the Cold War. His success in making some accommodations with the Russians suggests that the ordeal of the missile crisis of 1962 marked a significant shift in Soviet-American relations.

Kennedy's most concrete accommodation was the working out of a limited test-ban treaty with the Soviet Union during the summer of 1963. The treaty, which was ratified overwhelmingly by the Senate in October 1963, prohibited any testing of nuclear weapons in the atmosphere, in outer space, or under water. Although the stockpiles of nuclear weapons on both sides continued to grow, the test-ban treaty promised to reduce the contamination of the atmosphere and showed that careful and limited negotiations with the Russians could bear fruit.

The United States and the Soviet Union also agreed to establish a "hot line," or direct teletype circuit, between the Kremlin and the White House for instant communication between the two superpowers should an international emergency arise that made it crucial for them to know each other's intentions. The hot line proved valuable at the outbreak of the Arab-Israeli war of June 1967 and again in the war of 1973, when the leaders of the U.S.S.R. and the U.S. used it to assure each other of their intentions to refrain from direct intervention.

The Assassination of President Kennedy.   On November 22, 1963, in Dallas, Texas, to the horror of a stunned nation and a shocked world on both sides of the Iron Curtain, an assassin's bullet turned to ashes the shining but unfulfilled promise of John Fitzgerald Kennedy. In the short time that he had been before the world, his youthful vigor, self-deprecating wit, and incisive intellect had won favor among Americans of all political persuasions. Young adults especially were deeply affected by this novel political figure who spoke inimitably to and for their generation. Foreign nations, from leaders to ordinary citizens, responded to his image of the United States as a nation compassionate toward the weak, imaginative in confronting old problems, and firm in leadership. His eloquence and bright intelligence moved people in all walks of life, from affluent suburbanites to the inner-city poor. His death seemed horrifying even to an age hardened to violence and inured to irrationality.

In later years, the reputation of John F. Kennedy would tarnish somewhat as less admirable sides of his personality and administration became known or were so interpreted, but his assassination left unanswered forever the question of what John F. Kennedy might have been and done, given his potentialities and great popular appeal.

Chapter 24

Reform, War,
and a New Era
1963–1980

JOHNSON AND DOMESTIC REFORM

Within ninety minutes of Kennedy's assassination, Vice-President Johnson, who was also in Dallas that day, was sworn in as President. Immediately he flew back to Washington to evade any other possible attacks on high officials. The smell of conspiracy was strong in Dallas that November day.

The new President was quite a different man from the wealthy, Eastern-born Kennedy. Born in Texas in modest circumstances in 1908, Lyndon Johnson had spent almost all his adult years in the swirling politics of Texas and Washington, first as a member of the House of Representatives in the Roosevelt era and then as senator and majority leader during the Eisenhower years.

"The Great Society." In his State of the Union message in January 1964, President Johnson called for "a war against poverty" as the central goal of his administration. The Economic Opportunity Act, passed in August 1964, was only the first of the legislative steps to be taken in that war. The act recognized that

most of the poverty in the nation resulted from lack of education and training among the unemployed rather than from a dearth of jobs. The law appropriated almost $1 billion for agencies and programs designed to train or retrain the workless in order to fit them for the more highly skilled jobs available in an advanced society. The name the President gave to his program was the Great Society, which he defined as "a place where men are more concerned with the quality of their goals than the quantity of their goods."

Johnson's long and distinguished career in the legislative branch gave him an understanding of Congress that enabled him to push through legislation that had been stalled for half a year under Kennedy. Within Johnson's first year in office, Congress passed the first reduction in income taxes in thirty years, the Economic Opportunity Act already mentioned, the long-pending foreign-aid bill, the Higher Education Facilities Act, and the strongest and most far-reaching civil rights act ever put into law. Not all the measures that were asked for the Great Society were enacted that first year. But the record made clear that in his dealings with Congress, Johnson was highly successful, despite the handicap of following a martyred President.

President in His Own Right. Inasmuch as Johnson was advocating the same kind of a liberal program advanced by Democratic Presidents since Franklin Roosevelt, conservatives in the Republican party were convinced that, to win the presidency in 1964, the G.O.P. had to put forward a candidate with a different political philosophy from that of Eisenhower and Dewey—someone who did not represent the Eastern, liberal wing of the party. For too long, conservative Republicans contended, the party had been merely an echo of the Democrats. Victory would come, they believed, only if the voters were presented with a real choice.

The man the conservatives selected as their standard-bearer was Barry Goldwater, a senator from Arizona who, ever since his election to the Senate in 1958, had been publicly opposing the liberal point of view and the liberal programs which had long dominated both parties. In 1963, for example, he said that social security should be voluntary and that the TVA should be sold. As a result of careful organization and arduous preconvention campaigning, the Goldwater forces won the Republican nomination for their candidate. The platform of the party reflected his philosophy: It called for an end to deficit spending, further tax reduction, and a more militant foreign policy, which it characterized as a "dynamic strategy aimed at victory," a reference to the increasingly frustrating war in Vietnam.

There was no doubt, of course, that Lyndon Johnson would be the Democratic candidate, although his selection of Hubert Humphrey as his running mate came as something of a surprise. Humphrey had long been associated with the more liberal wing of the party, toward which Johnson was not thought to be favorably disposed. The platform was as liberal as Humphrey ever was, stressing civil rights for blacks, medical insurance for the aged, full employment, and aid to education. Also, it denounced not only the Communist party but such supernationalistic organizations as the John Birch Society and the Ku Klux Klan. The contest between the Republican and Democratic parties, in short, was unusually ideological for an American presidential campaign, since it was devoid of the usual balancing of philosophies in candidates and platforms.

Johnson proved to be not only the more relaxed and experienced campaigner but also the more popular. His margin of votes was the largest in U.S. history, topping even Franklin Roosevelt's in 1936. He carried 44 states and won 295 seats in the House of Representatives and 68 seats out of 100 in the Senate. Goldwater's record as a believer in military solutions to problems of foreign policy, such as that in Vietnam, and his repudiation of the social gains of the New Deal lost him many votes among moderate Republicans, the poor, the aged, and ethnic minorities. Not surprisingly, Johnson's proportion of the black vote in the big cities of the North and in several Southern states reached as high as 90 and 95 percent.

Farmers, too, voted Democratic, because they feared that Goldwater's laissez-faire views would jeopardize the government support program for agriculture. Four of the six states Goldwater carried were in the Deep South, where it was believed that his position on the rights of black Americans (he had voted against the Civil Rights Act of 1964) was less dangerous to white supremacy than that of Johnson. He also endeared himself to the white South by his emphasis upon states' rights and his steady denunciations of centralization of power in Washington.

The debacle that the Republicans suffered in 1964 was somewhat repaired in the November elections of 1966, when the party was able to win forty-seven new seats in the

House of Representatives and eight new governorships. That almost all the Republican winners had either opposed Goldwater's nomination in 1964 or simply ignored his conservative ideology in 1966 indicated once again how damaging the party's shift to the right two years before had been.

Constructing the Great Society.   Thanks to his overwhelming victory at the polls in 1964, Johnson found that the legislation he wanted was passed quickly by the new Congress. To continue the war against poverty, the legislators appropriated $1.1 billion to alleviate rural poverty in Appalachia and $3.3 billion for the economic development of depressed urban areas. By the end of 1968 some 162,000 new housing units had been constructed through federal aid, as compared with 34,000 five years before. A high of 400,000 units was reached in 1970.

At the President's urging, Congress in 1965 also authorized rent subsidies to the poor living in privately owned housing. The program was designed to help low-income people living outside public housing. Johnson called the Act "the single most important breakthrough" in housing legislation. That same year Johnson secured the passage of the Medicare bill, which provided for medical aid for persons over sixty-five through the social security system—a measure that Kennedy

An important goal of President Johnson's war on poverty was to improve the housing that was available to low-income families like these.

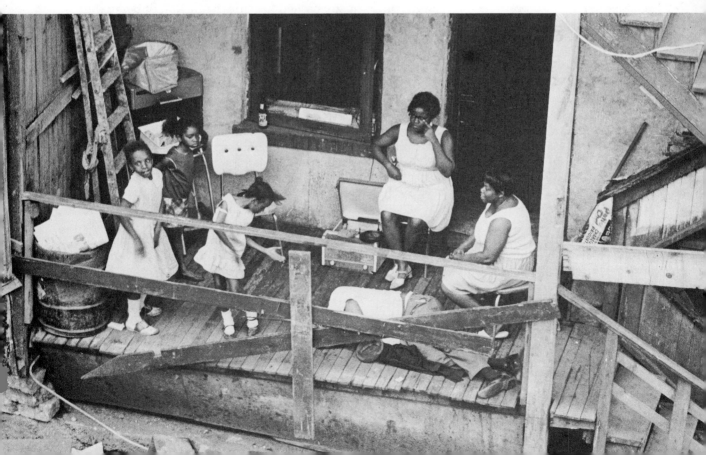

had advocated earlier but had twice failed to get through Congress.

Johnson also redeemed Kennedy's 1960 pledge to revise the immigration laws in order to remove the discrimination against immigrants from eastern and southern Europe that had been a part of national policy since the 1920s. The Immigration Act of 1965 provided for the elimination by 1968 of quotas based on national origin but kept a ceiling on the total number of immigrants admitted each year and introduced the first ceiling on immigrants from the Western Hemisphere.

The Education President. Johnson's most dramatic and path-breaking contribution was in education. For years the role of the federal government in supporting education had been vehemently debated, without either side being able to prevail. Under Johnson the question was settled positively. From now on it would be a question only of how much support the federal government ought to provide. The National Defense Education Act of 1964, for example, offered federal support for the teaching of the humanities as well as the sciences in college. Federal support of education no longer needed to be confined to subjects useful in repelling foreign threats, as it had at the passage of the first NDEA under Eisenhower in 1958.

The Elementary and Secondary Education Act of 1965 was also a landmark measure. It provided for the expenditure of over $1 billion for improving education in schools below the college level and, also for the first time, permitted federal money to be granted to private church-supported schools. For thirty years the major stumbling block in the path of federal aid to education had been the demand of such schools—principally Roman Catholic—for funds and the refusal of many people to countenance such aid on the ground that it would violate the traditional separation of church and state. These obstacles were transcended in the Act by confining the federal

funds to nonreligious expenditures, while justifying such grants as aid to pupils rather than as aid to religious institutions.

In the Higher Education Act of 1965, the federal government for the first time provided scholarships for college students in an effort to realize President Johnson's goal of making it financially possible for any young American to attend college. The Act also constituted a continuation of the long-term trend toward popularization of higher education that had begun in the 1920s and had been continued by measures such as the G. I. Bill, which had offered financial aid to World War II veterans wishing to attend college.

A Southern President and Black America. John F. Kennedy's moving television appeal to all Americans in 1963 to accept the moral challenge of full equality for blacks justly earned him the distinction of being the first President in the twentieth century to attack the question of discrimination against black Americans in clearly moral terms. But to Lyndon Johnson must go the credit for the most sweeping attack on the unequal treatment of black people mounted by any President at any time. The Civil Rights Act of 1964 really originated under the Kennedy administration, but it remained for Johnson to push it through a three-month filibuster in the Senate. The Act prohibited racial discrimination in public places, in employment, and in labor unions. As a sanction of compliance, it provided for the withholding of federal funds from any state that practiced racial discrimination. Since much federal money went to support schools, hospitals, and other state services, this provision gave bite to the law.

The Act also sought to get around the literacy requirements for voting, which were often used in the South as a means of disfranchising blacks. It provided that any adult with a sixth-grade education was presumed to be literate. The immediate effect was to open public accommodations in many cities of the South for the first time in the twentieth century—though not much was changed in the rural and small-town South—and to increase voting by blacks in many communities.

It is also worth noting that the Civil Rights Act of 1964 was the broadest statement of American belief in equality ever enacted. It outlawed not only racial discrimination but discrimination in employment for reasons of sex, nationality, and religion as well. The federal government was now committed to enforcing equality of treatment for two of the most visible groups in the United States— blacks and women.

The Johnson administration also pushed through a new voting bill in 1965. Despite protections for black voters in the acts of 1957, 1960, and 1964, blacks were still being kept from the polls in the South by subterfuge, intimidation, or outright refusal by state officials. The Voting Act of 1965 provided for federal officers to register black voters in any county in which the Justice Department found less than 50 percent of the eligible voters actually participating in presidential elections. A striking measure of how far the country had come on the question of federal power as well as on the rights of blacks was that in 1890 a similar bill by Representative Henry Cabot Lodge had been denounced and killed in the Senate for being a "Force Bill." In 1965 such a bill seemed a mild and necessary measure to most Americans.

As a result of the protection and support provided by the law, registration drives over the subsequent years brought millions of black voters into the political process. By 1970 about two thirds of the eligible black adults in the South were registered, a proportion that had not been achieved since the days of Reconstruction. As a result, in that same year Alabama counted 105 black elected officials— the second highest number in the nation.

The new interest in black voting, in fact, led in the following years to the election of a large number of black elected officials throughout the country. In 1977, over 4300 blacks held elective office, an increase of 150 percent since 1970. And by mid-decade scores of cities, including Los Angeles, New Orleans, Atlanta, Detroit, Gary, and Newark, were headed by black mayors.

Johnson also took pride in appointing the first black to the cabinet (Robert C. Weaver as Secretary of Housing and Urban Development) and the first to the Supreme Court (Thurgood Marshall).

Two Steps Forward, One Backward.   In 1966, Congress failed to pass an open housing bill—the first civil rights bill to fail in almost ten years. Despite the administration's commitment to civil rights and the passage of four civil rights acts since 1954, resistance to acceptance of blacks as equals was persisting. White violence against black demonstrators in Alabama in the spring of 1965 had caused President Johnson to send federal troops into his native South to provide the protection that George C. Wallace, Alabama's segregationist governor, would not. In the elections of 1966, strong segregationists won the governorships in Alabama and Georgia.

In the spring and summer of 1967, riots in varying degrees of severity occurred in more than thirty cities. In Detroit and Newark alone, 68 persons lost their lives, about 1,400 others were injured, and almost 7,000 were arrested. Property damages from looting and burning were estimated in hundreds of millions of dollars.

President Johnson again asked Congress to enact a civil rights bill that would end discrimination in the sale and rental of housing, one of the bases for all-black schools in the North as well as a major handicap to blacks in achieving equal opportunity. Congress was slow to move on the measure until the assassination of Martin Luther King, Jr., on April 4, 1968, impelled it to action. King was undoubtedly the leading black in the

Blacks line up to vote in Alabama. The rural county in which they live had not a single registered black voter before the passage of the Federal voting rights bill in 1965.

nation, uncompromising in the commitment to the achievement of equality through non-violence. He was shot by a white racist in Memphis where he had been participating in a protest movement on behalf of striking black garbage collectors.

There were outbursts of black rage in some 125 cities across the country. This time Washington, D. C., Baltimore, Chicago, and Kansas City were conspicuous for the level of damage and violence. All told, 46 persons were killed, more than 2,600 injured, and some 22,000 arrested. Property losses were put at $45 million. The civil rights bill that

King's death hastened to the President's desk outlawed discrimination on racial grounds in the sale and rental of about 80 percent of the housing in the country.

During the late 1960s and early 1970s, however, there were many signs in various Northern cities that as the movement for racial equality sought to break down housing barriers and to desegregate schools with enrollments based on segregated housing patterns, white resistance would become stronger rather than weaker. The failure of the 1966 open housing bill was one sign. Another was the approval that greeted the Nixon administration's slowdown on implementing school integration in 1969 and after.

But progress had been made. More blacks were voting in the South than in a century. The whole legal basis of segregation in the South was gone, and by 1972 school integration throughout the region had moved far beyond mere tokenism. Although blacks still experienced a higher rate of unemployment than whites, that disparity in 1970, for the first time, was less than 100 percent. Between 1960 and 1970 the proportion of blacks who had purchasing power equivalent to $10,000 in 1969 dollars rose from 9 percent to 24 percent. That increase was considerably greater than the doubling that took place over the same period for whites. Yet it was still true that blacks, constituting only 11 percent of the population, made up 30 percent of those who were below the official government poverty line.

Toward the end of the Johnson administration it was recognized that equality of opportunity would involve more than removing legal barriers. It would require efforts to eliminate a century of accumulated discrimination in housing, education, and jobs and the deep prejudices underlying it. But neither most white Americans nor the Nixon and Ford administrations, as would be shown by subsequent events, were prepared to do what was needed to achieve that goal.

"Let Us Continue." With these words Lyndon Johnson announced his support of John F. Kennedy's policies after the assassination in Dallas. The same words might be used to sum up the deeper springs of Johnson's policies, for the new President was also following in the path of Franklin Roosevelt's New Deal, during which he had first entered national politics. Indeed, Johnson's programs in education and civil rights went beyond anything done under the New Deal. The Housing and Urban Development Act of 1968, providing $5.3 billion over a three-year period for new housing, especially for low-income families, made New Deal housing expenditures seem paltry. Yet Lyndon Johnson's Great Society never went beyond the New Deal in concept—it simply moved forward in the direction the New Deal had pointed.

It was not, however, the limited imagination of the architects of the Great Society that diminished it in the eyes of the American people and brought it to an unexpected close. It was the inability of the President to end the Vietnam War. Dissatisfaction was already evident in the elections of 1966, when the Republicans picked up forty-seven seats in the House and three in the Senate. By the end of November 1967, according to a Gallup poll, only 38 percent of the American people were satisfied with the President's handling of his office, though three years before he had been elected in a historic landslide. To understand what one historian has called "the tragedy of Lyndon Johnson," we have to look at foreign affairs—an area of presidential activity where Johnson was neither expert nor happy.

JOHNSON AND VIETNAM

If Johnson was responsible for the enactment of much of the liberal legislation that Kennedy could not get through, he benefited, in turn, from his predecessor's superior handling of foreign affairs. Indeed, looking back on their administrations, it appears that Kennedy's successes lay principally in foreign affairs while Johnson's enduring monuments are probably found in his domestic programs. One advantage that Johnson inherited from Kennedy was a more relaxed and understanding relationship with the Soviet Union. The Cold War still remained, but it had obviously been moderated as a result of Kennedy's resistance to Russian pressures, as in Cuba, at the same time that he was working out accommodations to lessen tensions, like the test ban treaty, an agreement to sell wheat to Russia, and his conversations with the

Russians to limit the spread of nuclear weapons.

It was in Southeast Asia that Kennedy's policies ill served his successor. When the French withdrew from their former colony of Indochina in 1954, after defeat by Vietnamese nationalists and Communists under the leadership of Ho Chi Minh, the country was divided into two parts. The northern half was frankly Communist, the southern strongly anti-Communist. The Geneva agreement of 1954, which established the division, also called for unification of Vietnam within two years on the basis of free elections. But since it appeared that the elections would result in the triumph of Ho Chi Minh in both sections of the country, the Eisenhower administration encouraged the establishment of an independent republic in South Vietnam, as part of its global strategy to prevent the spread of communism.

In retrospect the American commitment to resist the spread of Communist power everywhere was based upon an overly simple analysis. Events would show that not all Communist governments were under the control or discipline of Moscow, as many United States officials in the 1950s and even into the 1960s insisted they were. Nor was it evident that a world order of peace depended, as Secretary of State Dean Rusk asserted during the Johnson years, upon resistance at any cost to any form of aggression by Communists. Nor was it accurate to see the war in Vietnam as simply a replay of the Korean conflict. The war in Vietnam began as a civil war in the South—directed largely against the tyrannical rule of Ngo Dinh Diem, the first of the South Vietnamese presidents whose governments were supported by the United States.

During the Eisenhower administration the United States, which had heavily subsidized the unsuccessful French war against Ho, sent economic and military aid to the South. As the situation there continued to deteriorate, Presi-dent Kennedy in 1962–1963 rapidly increased the number of military advisers, helicopters, and other forms of military assistance, though the actual fighting was still left in the hands of the South Vietnamese. Johnson, in the campaign of 1964, promised to keep the United States free from a land war in Asia while continuing to support South Vietnam's resistance to the local guerrillas of the National Liberation Front—the "Viet Cong"—and the Communist troops sent from the North.

In early August, however, when two American warships were allegedly attacked by North Vietnamese ships in the Gulf of Tonkin, President Johnson seized the opportunity to broaden his powers. He asked Congress to authorize him to take whatever measures might be necessary to resist aggression. The resolution that Congress passed with only two dissenting votes in the Senate asserted that peace and security in Southeast Asia were vital to the national security of the United States. The Tonkin Gulf Resolution thus became the President's authority for an almost unlimited expansion of the American involvement.

By early 1965, the likelihood of military and therefore political defeat in the South became so great that President Johnson sharply increased the American commitment to contain communism in Asia. In February 1965 he ordered the first bombing of bases and supply dumps in the North. Later that year he not only increased the number of American military personnel in the South but also authorized for the first time the direct engagement of the enemy by American ground troops.

This new turn in American involvement in the war had several consequences. For one thing, by 1966 the military presence of some 400,000 United States troops removed the possibility that the Communist-led guerrillas could take over the South as long as the Americans remained. But it also meant that the war was now being fought largely by

Demonstrators in front of the White House in 1965 protest against the Vietnam War.

Americans, though some 500,000 South Vietnamese troops were also mobilized.

Second, the ever increasing bombing of North Vietnam alarmed many European allies of the United States, who feared that Communist China or the Soviet Union, which supported the Northern regime, would feel compelled to enter the war. Such an act would, of course, involve a direct confrontation between the great powers and perhaps lead to a nuclear war.

Third, within the United States, the Johnson policy of gradually but relentlessly escalating the war divided the American people. Few Americans wanted a full-scale war against China or the Soviet Union, yet it seemed that the policy might lead in that direction. Also many Americans had voted for

Johnson in preference to Goldwater in 1964 on the ground that the war would not be expanded if Johnson were elected, and they now felt that he had misled them. Others found Johnson's policy faulty on moral grounds, contending that the regime the U.S. was keeping in power in South Vietnam was representative of neither its people nor their national aspirations. Still others opposed his policy on the more pragmatic level that the United States was overextended in commitments and power in Vietnam.

Advocates of American abandonment of the long involvement in Vietnam grew in number as the war dragged on. Most Americans, to be sure, supported the general policy of containing communism in Asia, just as they had supported it in Europe. But as the cost of that containment mounted and the connection between the interests and safety of the United States and the interminable war became less and less clear, many Americans began to think that the price was too high. Even those who accepted the administration's claim that the war was primarily a defense against aggression from the North could not help but recognize that, even in 1968, with over a half million American troops in Vietnam, victory was still not in sight. Although President Johnson insisted that American withdrawal could mean national ignominy and national danger, the direct interest of the United States in the war was never spelled out. The administration relied more and more upon the argument that the war involved the prestige of the United States and the "credibility" of its word among its allies.

The effect of the war on American foreign relations elsewhere was evident when Johnson dispatched several thousand marines in 1965 to prevent an alleged Communist coup from overturning the government of the Dominican Republic in the Caribbean. Although the troops were withdrawn within a year, the United States had once again violated its pledge not to intervene in the affairs of Latin American nations.

The consensus was that Johnson had intervened out of fear of another Cuba near American shores. Though the evidence of Communist power in Santo Domingo was slight, the President was not willing to take the chance that the non-Communists could remain in control without help from the United States. In the context of the frustrating war in Vietnam and the continued existence of a Communist regime in Cuba, even the slightest threat of yet another Communist regime in the Western Hemisphere seemed too risky to contemplate.

On the other hand, when war between Egypt and Israel became imminent in May and June of 1967, the United States hesitated to get involved, despite moral and perhaps legal obligations to support Israel against a military threat to its survival. Undoubtedly the heavy involvement in Vietnam played an important part in the hesitation. The United States was unable to prevent the brief war in the Middle East, which began in early June 1967.

At home it was also evident that the rising cost of the war—at least $20 billion a year—was stiffening resistance in Congress and across the country to further expenditures on behalf of the Great Society. In November 1967, Senator Eugene McCarthy, a liberal Democratic senator from Minnesota, announced that he would run in the upcoming primaries against the President in order to provide an alternative on the question of the war. By this time the high cost of the war in both money and personnel, as well as its persistence, had aroused much public hostility, even within the President's own party. Yet few thought McCarthy's challenge would seriously affect the President or the continuance of the war.

On January 29, 1968, at the beginning of Tet, the Vietnamese lunar New Year, the Viet Cong and the North Vietnamese launched a major offensive against thirty provincial capitals held by South Vietnamese forces. The power of the attack took the Americans and their Vietnamese allies by surprise. At one point fighting was going on within the American Embassy in Saigon itself. Although a shaken administration bravely called the Tet offensive a complete failure, few believed it.

That March, Senator McCarthy received almost as many votes in the New Hampshire Democratic primary as the President of the United States. For months the President had been unable to appear in public without insulting harassment and even danger to his person from the opponents of the war, and this new measure of public repudiation put unendurable pressure upon him. He could either abandon the war—a policy he had resolutely refused to consider—or abandon the presidency. In a surprise television announcement at the end of March, Johnson removed himself from consideration for re-nomination, at the same time announcing a partial cessation of the bombing of North Vietnam.

Yet Johnson's withdrawal from political life was only the first of the shocks that preceded the election of 1968. Five days later, Martin Luther King, Jr. was assassinated in Memphis, Tennessee—an event, as we have already noted, which caused violence to erupt in over a hundred cities. Then two months after that, in the midst of the furious primary campaign for the Democratic nomination which Johnson's retirement had begun, Senator Robert Kennedy of New York, brother of the assassinated President, was himself shot and killed by a fanatical anti-Zionist. Kennedy, almost as widely idolized as his brother, had been well on his way to being the Democratic presidential nominee.

THE NIXON YEARS

The Election of 1968. Robert Kennedy's death assured the nomination of Hubert Humphrey, the Vice-President, as Democratic presidential candidate, but not until after the passions stirred up by Vietnam had disrupted the party convention in Chicago. Thousands of disenchanted young people—both moderates who had worked in Senator McCarthy's primary campaign and radicals out to "confront" the Establishment—demonstrated in the streets until they were brutally dispersed by the police in full view of television news cameras. The sight of the bloody clashes shocked the American people. Neither the Democratic platform, which offered no significant alternative to the Johnson war policies, nor the candidate, who was identified with those policies, provided a rallying point for opponents of the war.

Meanwhile, the Republican convention had nominated Richard Nixon, who had survived not only his defeat by John Kennedy in 1960

but the subsequent loss of a race for the governorship of California. Since then he had worked hard at building support within the party and keeping in the public eye through meetings with world leaders. Recognizing that he must win a substantial number of Southern votes, Nixon chose Spiro Agnew, governor of the border state of Maryland, as his running mate.

The campaign was complicated by the candidacy of George Wallace of Alabama, who ran on the American Independent party ticket. No one expected him to win, but he clearly threatened Humphrey in the traditionally Democratic South. And the enthusiasm he stirred in some Northern states reflected the opposition of many blue-collar workers to the Democratic stand on civil rights. There was a possibility that he could prevent either major candidate from winning a majority of the electoral vote and thereby throw the election into the House of Representatives.

The campaign revolved around the war overseas and the social problems at home. Nixon stressed the alarming increase of violence in the cities, which he attributed to the leniency of the Democratic administration toward demonstrators and rioters and of the Supreme Court toward criminals. Playing upon the public's fears, he promised to end the "permissiveness" that, he insisted, fostered lawlessness. Although he had supported the aims of the war against communism in Southeast Asia since his own vice-presidency, he promised to bring the conflict in Vietnam to an end, though he declined to say how. In the television appearances on which he chiefly relied, he shunned the issue of integration, which was unpopular among many whites, and concentrated on "law and order," about which there could be little controversy. Generally, he portrayed himself as a leader dedicated to national unity and peace.

Burdened with the Johnson record on Vietnam, Humphrey finally announced that,

The brutal dispersal of demonstrators by police at the Democratic convention in Chicago shocked the American people in 1968.

if elected, he would stop the bombing of the North. As election day approached, his popular support rose steadily, bolstered by the efforts of his powerful allies in organized labor to win working-class voters back from George Wallace. Just before the election President Johnson announced the cessation of American bombing in North Vietnam.

Given the shambles at the Democratic convention, the election was remarkably close. Nixon won by only a half million votes out of 73 million cast. He carried thirty-two states, however, to Humphrey's fourteen. Nixon won seven Southern states, Wallace five, and Humphrey one—Texas. But while the outcome indicated that the Democrats could no longer count on even a majority of Southern states in a presidential election, the vote for Congress showed that most Americans still voted Democratic. Both House and Senate remained comfortably in Democratic hands.

Nixon and the War. The political destruction of Lyndon Johnson and the mood of the country during the campaign made it clear to the new President that the public would no longer stand for the emotional and financial drain of an endless Asian war. Within six months after taking office, Nixon announced that he would withdraw 25,000 troops from Vietnam over the next ninety days. Thus began the policy of gradual withdrawal that was to continue for the next four years. Meanwhile, the South Vietnamese army was further trained and equipped to carry on the war by itself. This policy President Nixon called Vietnamization.

Nixon's willingness to use American power to ensure the success of his policy marked a new high in brinkmanship. In the spring of 1970 he ordered American forces to support a South Vietnamese invasion of neighboring Cambodia (and eventually of neighboring Laos) in order to destroy enemy supplies and troop buildups. This action, taken at a time when the war was supposedly "winding down," outraged Americans who saw it as expanding the conflict. That same week the killing of four students at Kent State University in Ohio by national guardsmen during an antiwar demonstration, and of two students by police at Jackson State University in Mississippi, triggered student strikes at almost three hundred colleges and universities. Withdrawal of American troops from Cambodia and Laos did not end military action there.

As he continued to remove American ground troops from Vietnam, Nixon also continued the negotiations in Paris that President Johnson had agreed to in 1968. But neither side would accept the other's demands. In the early spring of 1972 North Vietnamese troops launched a powerful assault across the demilitarized zone in the North and the Cambodian border in the West. To support the reeling South Vietnamese forces, President Nixon widened the war once again. He ordered stepped-up bombing raids against North Vietnam, including the capital, Hanoi, and the major port, Haiphong, neither of which had been bombed since 1968, and the rail lines from China. He also ordered the navy, for the first time, to mine Haiphong harbor. His intention was to cut off the military supplies from the Soviet Union and China that made such offensives possible. China and Russia denounced the American "aggression" but took no other action.

The President was gambling for high stakes. In November he would be up for reelection. If the war was still going on then, his Democratic opponent would have an enormous advantage with an electorate that was clearly sick of the war. Yet if he withdrew all American power from Southeast Asia and the Saigon regime collapsed under Communist pressure, he would be held responsible. Thus he needed to continue to withdraw the troops, but he also needed some assurance that Saigon could survive.

To critics of his policy, it seemed that Nixon was following the tactics of the Johnson administration and trying to bomb the North Vietnamese into an acceptable settlement. By 1970 more tons of bombs had been dropped on the small country of Vietnam than had been dropped on Germany and Japan in all of World War II, and the raids of 1972 were setting new records in sheer destructiveness. Yet after all the punishment, the Viet Cong and the North Vietnamese continued to fight and continued to score successes in the South.

Diplomatic Breakthroughs.   In the summer of 1971 the President made the dramatic announcement that he had accepted an invitation to visit the People's Republic of China. The visit had been secretly arranged by Henry Kissinger, a former Harvard professor of political science. Kissinger was the President's trusted adviser on foreign policy, and his influence on the President clearly exceeded that of the Secretary of State. The implications of the trip, which took place in February 1972, were far-reaching. It ended twenty years of frigid enmity between the two powers. Soon after the trip was announced, U.S. opposition to seating Mao's China in the UN ended. Communist China took the place of Chiang Kai-shek's China on the Security Council and in the Assembly in the fall of 1971. Nixon's visit ended China's long isolation. By 1973 Japan too had established commercial and diplomatic relations with the People's Republic of China.

Nixon's visit did not convert China and the United States into instant allies. Diplomatic recognition did not immediately follow, and the United States pledged itself to maintain its treaty obligations to Chiang Kai-shek's regime on Taiwan, even though Communist China claimed the island. Yet a new era in the relations between the United States and the Communist powers seemed to have begun. This was confirmed when the White House announced that, within two months after his

As the war in Vietnam dragged on, antiwar demonstrations continued to errupt. Here, national guardsmen advance on students at Kent State University.

visit to Peking, President Nixon would visit Moscow as well. (He also became the first President to visit Communist Yugoslavia, Romania, and Poland.)

Behind this about-face by the long-time anti-Communist, Richard Nixon, and the leaders of the two largest Communist states was the hostility between the Russians and the Chinese. China, as the weaker of the two Communist giants, wanted a counterweight in the form of better relations with the United States. Russia, on the other hand, feared that the United States and China might combine against it. As a result, President Nixon was welcomed in both capitals, even as his bombers unloaded unprecedented tons of explosives on his hosts' ally, North Vietnam.

The new relationships with both China and the Soviet Union gave Nixon an opportunity to appeal privately to them both to put pressure on North Vietnam to conclude the war on terms the United States could accept. Since American troops were steadily being removed (the last ground combat forces were withdrawn in August 1972), Nixon's desire for an end to hostilities was clear. At the same time, the continued bombing of North Vietnam and the massing of naval power off the Vietnam coast and air power in neighboring Thailand made it equally clear that he intended to keep up the pressure until his minimum conditions were met.

Even after Kissinger had negotiated for months with the North Vietnamese in Paris for a cease-fire, however, the war had not been brought to a close. Just before Christmas 1972, Nixon increased the pressure further by massive bombings of the North, including Hanoi and Haiphong. Later he would contend that it was these B-52 bombings that brought the cease-fire agreement, which was announced in January 1973. Soon thereafter, all remaining U.S. combat troops were withdrawn.

For Americans the fighting was over, but for the Vietnamese it continued until April 30, 1975, when the South surrendered to Northern troops. Earlier that same month rebels friendly to the Communists succeeded in defeating the pro-American government forces in Cambodia, which had gained power as a result of the American and South Vietnamese invasion in May 1970. Later, in 1975, Communist rebels took over Laos. Thus, after more than ten years of active American involvement in Southeast Asia to prevent Communist control, three of the four countries of the Indochinese peninsula were under rule friendly to communism.

On the other hand, for facing up to the changed international realities of the 1970s, the first Nixon administration was likely to go down in history as among the important influences in moderating the Cold War. After the Moscow meetings in the spring of 1972, the Soviet Union and the United States agreed to new limitations on missiles and submarines, as well as on joint explorations of space. By 1972 few Americans continued to look on China as the Great Red Menace a whole generation of Americans had been taught to fear. To have been instrumental in bringing about such an alteration in the world scene was no mean achievement.

President Nixon poses with Mrs. Nixon and Chinese premier Chou En-Lai under a statue of Chairman Mao in Shanghai in 1972.

A Costly War. Although fought far from American shores, the Vietnam struggle had been the longest in American history. Its cost in American lives (56,000) ranked behind only that of the Civil War and the First and Second World Wars. In fifteen years the United States had spent $141 billion on behalf of South Vietnam, or $7000 for each of the 20 million people in that country. Even those astronomical figures were dwarfed by the cost to the

A Vietnamese mother and her children struggle across a river to escape aerial bombardment of their South Vietnam village by the United States.

Vietnamese themselves. Between February 1965 and August 1972 the United States dropped three and one half times as many bombs and shells on Vietnam, both North and South, as all the allies dumped on Germany and Japan during the Second World War. Perhaps as many as 10 million Vietnamese in the South alone became refugees, while civilian deaths there reached almost half a million. Moreover, thirty years of civil war and the corrupting intrusion of American money and power placed severe strains on the social and cultural fabric of the rural, traditional society of Vietnam.

Nixon in Domestic Affairs. Nixon's flexibility in dealing with China and Russia was repeated in some aspects of domestic matters. As in foreign affairs, he surprised friend and foe alike with his ability to abandon or drastically modify attitudes and principles he had stood for during a lifetime in public affairs.

When he took office he proclaimed an end to federal deficits, and for two years he insisted that he would never impose economic controls. In 1969 Congress went along with his recommendations for a tax cut in an effort to stimulate the economy. But in 1970, for the first time in nine years, inflation wiped out the gain in median income for a family of four, and since the economy was sluggish as well as inflationary, government tax receipts fell below expectations. (Unemployment was up from 3 million in 1968 to over 5 million in 1971.) In August 1971 the President ordered a freeze on prices, wages, and rents, and three months later he set up agencies to police observance of federal economic guidelines.

Thus, having for years pronounced himself an opponent of the "New Economics," he ended up embracing Keynesian theory and the familiar Democratic belief that government has a responsibility to regulate the economy. And with the spiraling cost of the Vietnam War, his administration by 1972 had run up not only the largest budgetary deficit since the Second World War but two of the largest in American history.

Nixon also showed his flexibility by recommending that the federal government provide a minimum income of $1600 for every family of four on welfare. Since the idea had been advocated by liberals years earlier, many Democrats could support it in principle, but liberal senators rejected the $1600 figure as inadequate. No agreement was reached and no new welfare program was enacted then or later.

Another Democratic idea that Nixon sought to make a part of what he called his "New American Revolution" was that of sharing federal revenues with the states and cities. A revenue-sharing bill was finally passed in September 1972. Congress also accepted presidential proposals for making the Postal Service an independent agency, and for establishing the National Rail Passenger Corporation (Amtrak) to reorganize and run the nation's passenger rail service.

Congress, however, went far beyond Nixon's lukewarm recommendations on the improvement of the environment. At the end of the 1972 session, it passed a $24.6 billion sewage treatment bill that was vetoed by the President on the ground that such an expenditure was inflationary. Nixon had recommended only $6 billion. Congress, in a rare exhibition of independence, quickly overrode the veto.

In June 1972 the President signed a landmark bill providing for the first time that nearly every college and university would receive some federal money. It also provided that, as a matter of policy, any student needing money to attend college could obtain a loan of up to $1400 a year. Public colleges and graduate schools were prohibited from discriminating against women students on pain of loss of federal funds.

The Act also marked the first interference by Congress in the school desegregation issue: It prohibited any new court-ordered school busing for purposes of racial balance until June 1974. The President angrily denounced the provision for not prohibiting present as well as future court-ordered busing on any grounds and promised to carry the busing issue—merely a new form of the old segregated school issue—into the presidential campaign. In fact busing became an issue in the 1972 campaign even when candidates avoided it.

Especially in some Northern cities, busing continued to be a hotly contested public issue long after Nixon was gone. At the end of the 1970s, despite its continued acceptance of busing, the Supreme Court was taking cognizance of the widely expressed complaint that the defense of minority rights was going too far. In the Bakke case in 1978 the Supreme Court struck down the quota system which a state of California medical school had set up to keep a certain number of places for minority applicants. A white student, Allan Bakke, who had been denied admission, contended that his civil rights had been violated because of the policy.

The opinion of the majority of the court, however, while rejecting the medical school's quota system, did not rule out some kind of preference for minority students in admission to state educational institutions. The intention was to provide some way of compensating minorities for damage done by past discrimination. In *U.S. Steelworkers* v. *Weber* (1979), the Court upheld a private company's policy of affirmative action, which gave some preference to blacks over whites in training programs. In short, the Court was not prepared to countenance rigid quotas for minorities, but was willing to uphold the idea of opening preferential opportunities for minorities through special arrangements.

On balance, despite the liberal character of some of Nixon's policies, both foreign and domestic, his administration frankly repudiated the liberalism of the Kennedy and Johnson years in other areas, particularly civil rights. The conservatism was manifested most ideologically in the speeches of Vice-President Spiro Agnew, who went out of his way to castigate liberals—especially reporters and commentators critical of the administration—as dangerous to America and to condemn youthful protestors and demonstrators for their lack of discipline and lack of respect. The President himself spoke out against laws making abortion easier to obtain, and he vetoed a bill that would have provided federally supported child-care centers for working mothers, arguing that such measures weakened traditional family ties.

Nixon's first Attorney General, John Mitchell (who had been his campaign manager in 1968), considered the Supreme Court decisions protecting the rights of accused persons to be too lenient and sought to slow down school integration in the South. His efforts in this direction were rejected by the federal courts, as was his use of wiretapping without

Students protest busing in Pontiac, Michigan, one of the first northern cities ordered by the courts to integrate its schools by busing.

court orders in the name of national security.

Nixon appointed a new Chief Justice in 1969, but his next two nominees for the Supreme Court—Southern "strict constructionists," to use the President's description—were rejected by the Senate as inadequately qualified. Before his first term was completed, however, he appointed three more justices, all with records that revealed conservative legal philosophies. They soon began to make their views felt. In June 1972, for example, the Court for the first time in eighteen years was unable to render a unanimous decision on school desegregation because two of the new justices voted against the majority.

The Avalanche of 1972. For a long time, Richard Nixon had made clear that he intended to run again for President. Before the Republican convention met in August he had also made evident that he wanted his Vice-President, Spiro Agnew, again as his running mate. The Democrats, however, could not settle as easily upon Nixon's opponent. Hubert Humphrey, who had been only narrowly defeated by Nixon in 1968, was eager to try again. But before the Democratic convention met in July, George McGovern, senator from South Dakota, and long an outspoken opponent of the war in Vietnam, showed that he was a favorite in the various state primaries. Those victories won him the nomination on the first ballot. The Democratic convention itself was unusual that year since its members had been selected by a new process which guaranteed representation to ethnic minorities, women, and young people. This new kind of party convention—more serious and dedicated to the question of political issues than any convention since the Progressives' in 1912—enthusiastically supported McGovern's liberal posture. The platform promised a quick end to the war, a deep reduction in military expenditures, tax revision, and increased expenditures on social services.

The vice-presidential candidate that the convention named, Thomas Eagleton, senator from Missouri, however, was soon compelled to resign because he admitted to having undergone psychological treatment in recent years. Sargent Shriver, a brother-in-law of John F. Kennedy, was named in Eagleton's place. This unexpected change gave a setback to the hitherto highly successful McGovern organization from which it never recovered.

As the weeks of the campaign passed, it became clear that McGovern was really the nominee of only a minority of his party and that his very liberal position on tax reform and welfare and particularly on reductions in military spending were frightening many traditional Democrats into the Nixon camp. Roman Catholics, workingmen, Southerners, and ethnic groups were especially unhappy about McGovern. Rather than putting Nixon on the defensive for failing to end the war after four years in office, McGovern found himself on the defensive for being less than candid in his handling of the resignation of Eagleton and for being less than informed in proposing welfare and tax reform programs that he later had to withdraw. Although McGovern publicized what later became known as the Watergate break-in, the connection to the White House was not known and the country did not seem to think that McGovern's charges were worth taking seriously.

Moreover, when George Wallace was definitively removed from the campaign in May because of permanent paralysis after an attempt upon his life, the Wallace supporters moved to Nixon, not McGovern. The President's stand against busing in school integration, and a "hard line" on urban crime and on welfare won the support of many white Southerners and traditional Democrats in the cities of the North.

The enormous lead that the polls showed for Nixon over McGovern early in the campaign continued to election day. As a result the President left to Vice-President Agnew

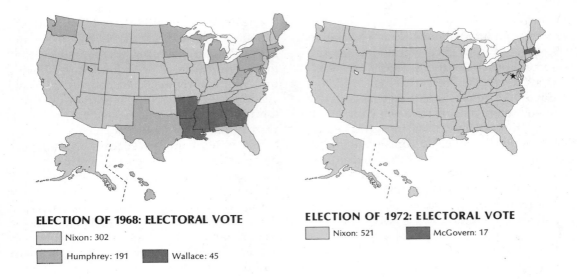

ELECTION OF 1968: ELECTORAL VOTE

☐ Nixon: 302

☐ Humphrey: 191 ■ Wallace: 45

ELECTION OF 1972: ELECTORAL VOTE

☐ Nixon: 521 ■ McGovern: 17

and other subordinates the actual campaigning. Nixon probably made fewer campaign speeches than Franklin Roosevelt did in 1944 in the midst of the Second World War. Although President Nixon and his foreign policy adviser Henry Kissinger worked hard to arrange an agreement with North Vietnam to end the war before the election, the foot-dragging of South Vietnam prevented that feather from being added to the President's cap.

The results of the election made clear that he did not need an end to the war in order to win one of the biggest victories in American history: 49 states and 61 percent of the popular vote. McGovern, by winning only Massachusetts and the District of Columbia, was as badly defeated as Alf Landon in 1936. Those who had contended that McGovern would be the "Democratic Goldwater"—too far out of the mainstream of either party to be able to win—proved to be right. Nixon completed the breakup of the Democratic Solid South, which Harding had begun in 1920. He captured, with large majorities, every one of the former states of the Confederacy, a feat never before achieved by a Republican President. Signifi-

cant for the future politics of the South was the election of three Republican congressmen from Mississippi and Louisiana for the first time since Reconstruction.

Yet it would be a mistake to see Nixon's victory as a Republican resurgence. Indeed, Nixon's campaign had concentrated on "reelecting the President," rather than on winning a Republican majority. In his few campaign speeches the President rarely mentioned his party and in some Southern states Nixon campaigners refused to help Republican candidates who were running against conservative Democrats. The result was that the Democrats continued to control both houses of Congress by substantial majorities, as they had done since 1957. Most Americans, it would seem, were still Democrats, but they apparently did not see George McGovern as their kind of Democratic President.

THE DEPARTURE OF RICHARD NIXON

The intention of the first Nixon administration had been to increase the power and autonomy of the President at the expense of Congress. Its overwhelming victory at the polls in 1972 encouraged the administration to reorganize the government so that the presidential office would be free from Congress on the one hand and from the federal bureaucracy on the other. By enormously increasing the White House staff it would be possible to bypass the permanent staff of the government. Since, as assistants to the President, none of the White House staff would have to be confirmed by the Senate, the office of the President would escape control or even influence from Congress and none of his staff would be a part of the permanent bureaucracy. In effect, the executive would now be accountable only to the voters once every four years.

This move toward plebiscitary government, which was to be put into operation through a reorganization of the executive branch in the first months of the second administration, was stopped in its tracks by the unraveling of the Watergate affair in early 1973. Watergate was a dramatic example of the great danger to constitutional government that could result when a few people whose first loyalty was to a person and not to the office he or she occupied were free to exercise power without accounting to anyone except themselves and the person they served.

Watergate.   On June 17, 1972, as the Democratic convention was approaching, five men were arrested inside the Democratic National Headquarters at the Watergate complex of apartment and office buildings in Washington, D. C. They were caught trying to install secret electronic recording devices. Although the Democrats naturally tried to make political capital out of what the White House immediately dismissed as a "third-rate burglary," the Democrats' effort had no impact on the campaign. But the trial and conviction of the five burglars soon started newspapermen and then Senate investigators along a trail of evidence that quickly led to the White House.

Throughout the spring and early summer of 1973, in the course of several weeks of public,

televised hearings before a Select Committee of the Senate, presided over by Senator Sam Ervin of North Carolina, the public heard some of the evidence linking the illegal act to the President's office. It became clear not only that the men closest to the President, H. R. Haldeman and John D. Ehrlichman, had been instrumental in bringing about the break-in, but that they had conspired with other White House and campaign officials to cover up the involvement of the President's staff in those activities.

The President himself denied knowing anything about the matter, insisting, instead, that he sought only to uncover the extent and nature of the involvement. In seeking to maintain this claim, Nixon was forced eventually to ask for the resignations of Haldeman and Ehrlichman. Soon thereafter the Attorney General, Richard Kleindienst, and Nixon's former Attorney General, John Mitchell, were indicted and later convicted for their involvement in the cover-up and other incidents.

By 1975 some thirty-three former members of the White House staff or cabinet had been indicted or convicted or had pleaded guilty to various criminal acts. Moreover, the FBI, the Internal Revenue Service, and the CIA were all shown to have been used by the administration for purposes that were illegal or unethical. (Still later investigations would show that previous Presidents had also misused these agencies in ways similar to those employed by Nixon, though not in cover-ups of criminal acts.)

Undoubtedly the most sensational revelation that came out of the Senate investigations and hearings was that in 1970 the President had had hidden microphones installed in his own office, thus preserving on tape every conversation in the Oval Office. The news was earthshaking since it promised that the question of the President's involvement in the burglary could be answered, provided that the tape recordings could be obtained. The President, however, refused to permit the tapes to be examined by the Senate Committee or the Watergate trial court on the grounds of the constitutional separation of powers and executive privilege. Even when a Special Prosecutor was named to probe into the scandal, the President continued his adamant refusal. On October 19, 1973, when the Special Prosecutor, Archibald Cox, pressed too hard for the tapes, Nixon fired him.

This effort by the President to blunt the investigation backfired: On the following day the White House was deluged with letters and telegrams expressing the public's outrage over the self-serving dismissal. For the first time Congress seriously considered impeach-

Nixon and his staff are depicted as working hard to cover up Watergate.

'So we're not neat'   © Arkansas Democrat

ment of the President as the sole remedy still open for getting to the bottom of the matter. Nixon then retreated, agreeing to appoint a new prosecutor who would be free from presidential control or interference. The new prosecutor, however, found the President no more cooperative than before.

Meanwhile, Nixon continued to assert his innocence, announcing at one press conference, for example, that "the people have to know whether their President is a crook. Well, I am not a crook. I have earned everything I've got." Up to that point no one had argued that the President had profited financially from the Watergate incident. Indeed, a sinister aspect of the whole affair was that Watergate was not a financial scandal along the lines of those of the Grant and Harding administrations, in which defrauding the government of money was the principal crime. Watergate, rather, was a scandal involving misuse of government power and authority, thus striking at the underlying assumptions of a democratic society. Yet even in his denial of financial gain, the President was not being completely honest. Later investigations would show that he had in fact padded his income-tax deductions while President, thus reducing his personal taxes by almost $450,000.

If the President misgauged what the public would stand for when he fired Cox in October, he repeated his misjudgment in April of 1974. By publishing selected excerpts from the tapes, Nixon sought to quiet the ceaseless public and investigatory clamor for free access to that invaluable evidence. His enemies discounted the usefulness or even the validity of these carefully culled documents, but when the verbatim transcripts were printed they placed the inner councils of the Nixon administration in a devastatingly ugly light. The level of discourse was shockingly low, and was pushed several levels lower by frequent use of the phrase "expletive deleted." Instead of improving the image of the President, this device left entirely to the imagination the degree of obscenity that had actually been used in the Oval Office.

More important was the petty, selfish, and often amoral content of the conversations, though they had been selected for the purpose of putting the best face on the evidence. Even hardened politicians were amazed. Some of the President's staunchest supporters now called for impeachment.

Thereafter, events moved swiftly. In July the Supreme Court ordered the President to turn over all the tapes to the Special Prosecutor, who had been seeking them for half a year. A few weeks later the Judiciary Committee of the House, which for months had been considering in closed session the evidence for impeachment, began to hold public, televised hearings. Not surprisingly, the Democratic majority on the Committee was unanimously in favor of impeachment. More threatening to the President were the seven out of seventeen Republicans who also voted for two of the three charges and the two Republicans who went along with the Democrats on the third. The first charge cited Nixon for obstruction of justice, the second for abuse of power, and the third for contempt of Congress. Unlike the impeachment proceedings against Andrew Johnson over a hundred years before, these were carefully and fairly conducted. Not even Republican partisans could sustain allegations that procedures had been improper or that the President was being "railroaded."

Before the Committee's recommendations could be sent to the full House for a vote, the situation changed dramatically. When the President complied with the Supreme Court's order to deliver up the tapes, those long-sought-for pieces of evidence fully exposed Nixon's involvement in the Watergate cover-up. The tapes revealed that only five days after the break-in, the President was discussing with his aides how the administration's involvement could be hushed up. No longer could there be any doubt that the President

had lied from the beginning about his complicity in crime. Now every one of the Republican members of the House Judiciary Committee turned against him, voting for his impeachment. None of these last-ditch defenders had been taken into the President's confidence.

On August 9, before the House could respond to the recommendation of impeachment, Richard Nixon resigned his office, becoming the first President in history to do so. Characteristically, his emotion-filled farewell statement made no mention of his complicity or guilt. It merely referred to his loss of "a strong enough political base in the Congress" to allow him to remain in office.

The resignation brought into office Gerald R. Ford, the former Republican leader in the House, who had been appointed Vice-President under the Twenty-fifth Amendment only the previous year when Vice-President Spiro Agnew had been compelled to resign because of revelations of financial wrongdoing while governor of Maryland. As Vice-President, Ford had been almost a last-ditch defender of the President's integrity. In assuming the presidency, however, he publicly emphasized the need to recognize that "truth is the glue that holds governments, together." The country was undoubtedly relieved to have a chance to restore some of the faith in government that the Nixon years had severely eroded.

In the White House, Ford proved to be straightforward, relaxed, and low-keyed where Nixon had been devious, tense, and pretentious. Ironically, one of the first acts of the new President was also his least popular. In September, within a month after taking office, Ford pardoned Nixon for any possible crimes he might have committed while President. A pardon implicitly acknowledges guilt, but Nixon, in accepting the pardon, neither alluded to nor admitted any wrongdoing. For some months he remained secluded in his mansion overlooking the Pacific Ocean in southern California, nursing his health, which had deteriorated seriously during the long ordeal of Watergate.

An Abortive Administration. Although Nixon tried to govern during 1973–1974 as if Watergate were not a major public issue, the forced and voluntary resignations of key administration officials because of the scandal weakened and distracted his government. At the same time the federal bureaucracy was increasingly alienated and presidential relations with Congress were blighted by the impeachment proceedings. As a consequence, little effective action could be taken against inflation. By June 1974 prices rose above an annual rate of 10 percent, a level not reached since World War I. The effects of inflation were compounded by a marked slowing down of the economy. This combination of economic burdens aroused more dissatisfaction with the administration and the Republican party than even the revelations about Watergate.

The Nixon administration received further criticism for failing to anticipate the crisis in energy that the Arab-Israeli war of 1973 and then the rise in the price for oil imposed by the Arab oil-producing countries forcefully underlined. The President countered by committing the United States to a policy of self-sufficiency in energy by the end of the 1970s. Although the United States, as an industrialized nation, was second only to the Soviet Union in its ability to meet domestically a large share of its energy needs, the goal of self-sufficiency was unlikely to be achieved by a society as dependent on petroleum as the United States.

If domestically the Nixon administration seemed able only to mark time because of Watergate, in foreign policy there was not much more movement. Although not personally tainted by Watergate, Henry Kissinger, who had become Secretary of State in the fall of 1973, was not able to obtain congressional authorization for the President to revise the

tariff so that the Soviet Union could obtain the trade status of a "most favored nation." Kissinger sought this authority as part of his policy of détente with the Soviet Union. That the Russians, too, had doubts about the survival of the Nixon presidency was suggested by the rapidity with which they concluded agreements on strategic missiles and other military equipment with President Ford in November 1974, after months of dragging their feet during negotiations with the Nixon administration.

The Elections of 1974. The resignation of Nixon did not have the restorative effect upon Republicans in the congressional elections in the fall of 1974 that some members of the party had hoped. Ford's unpopular pardoning of Nixon, however compassionate the intention, probably lost votes for the Republicans. Clearly, the country still held the party responsible for Watergate and the cover-up. Democrats captured three quarters of the seats in the House—enough in theory, if not in fact, to make the body "veto-proof." They also won three fifths of the Senate seats, and almost three quarters of the governors' chairs.

For the first time since the Johnson landslide of 1964, the suburbs voted heavily Democratic. Even Ford's old, sure seat in Michigan went to a Democrat. That Watergate had been an issue in the election was shown by the fact that four of the Republicans who had defended the President until his complicity was fully revealed went down to defeat. On the other hand, only one Republican who had supported impeachment before the final revelations failed to be reelected.

The election appeared to be a repudiation of Nixon's conservatism as well as his criminality. Many of the newly elected members of Congress were not only young but also known for their liberal views on public issues. Another measure of the voters' rejection of conservatism was the widespread success of black candidates, even in the South. Almost one hundred state or national offices were now held by blacks, among them lieutenant-governorships in Colorado and California.

Despite their numbers, however, the liberals did not run the new Congress, as the first year of the Ford administration would show. While Ford may not always have gotten his way, the liberals, despite their numbers, not only failed to get their way but showed themselves unable to agree on what their "way" was.

A further analysis of the election statistics provided a clue as to why the apparent liberal revival was less significant than it seemed. It was probably unrepresentative of the electorate. Only 38 percent of the eligible voters had bothered to go to the polls in 1974, as compared with 45 percent in the previous off-year election. The declining interest in voting undoubtedly stemmed from a disenchantment with government, the cause of which extended back beyond Watergate and Nixon, at least to the Vietnam War.

THE FORD ADMINISTRATION

The New President. Born in Nebraska in 1913 as Leslie King, Jr., but raised in Michigan after his parents were divorced and his mother remarried, Gerald Ford became a star football player in high school and college. Deciding against a promising career in pro football, he went to Yale Law School, then into legal practice, and finally into politics. In 1948 he was elected from Michigan to the House of Representatives, where he served for twenty-five years, eventually becoming Republican leader. Never known for anything but his conservative, rather combative Republicanism, Ford was a natural successor to Vice-President Agnew, who had also been known for his outspokenly conservative views.

As the first appointed Vice-President, and President by the first resignation of a Chief Executive in history, Ford entered the White House with no popular mandate at all. Yet his energetic personality and his willingness to laugh at himself and to recognize his limitations brought him instant appreciation. As he said at the time of his nomination for the vice-presidency, "I am a Ford, not a Lincoln."

In the White House, Ford removed many of the ceremonial, almost monarchical trappings of office that Nixon had insisted upon. Ford's relations with the press were friendly and open, a refreshing change after the secretiveness of Lyndon Johnson and the suspicious hostility of Richard Nixon.

The new First Lady, Betty Ford, was also in striking contrast to Pat Nixon and to most other Presidents' wives. Though a somewhat retiring person, Betty Ford was so open and liberal in her aspirations for women that she quickly became a public personality in her own right. Not since Eleanor Roosevelt had a First Lady cast herself so forthrightly in the role of a champion of policies. Betty Ford made no secret of her efforts to persuade her husband to appoint a woman cabinet officer (which he did in 1975) and a woman Supreme Court justice.

Unlike Nixon, Ford loved meeting people, and in his first two years in office he indulged himself to the fullest. In fact, he was frequently criticized in the press for traveling too much, not only to foreign countries but around the United States as well. Observers wondered how he could find time to think about large national and international issues while on such an incessantly active schedule. When he announced in early 1975 that he would indeed be a candidate to succeed himself, his travels and speechmaking acquired a political as well as a personal explanation. As *The New York Times* sternly noted at the end of 1975, Ford "gives every appearance of having effectively abdicated the presidency today in favor of his candidacy for the nomination next year." Two attempts on his life in California in September 1975 brought the President's propensity for "pressing the flesh" under more serious criticism.

True to his conservative career in the House, Ford as President followed along the Nixon path in minimizing or deploring the government's intervention in the economy. "A government big enough to give you everything you want," he said several times in his first year in the White House, "is big enough to take from you everything you have." Not surprisingly, during his first year in office he kept almost all of the Nixon cabinet officers. Equating large government expenditures with "self-indulgence," the President vetoed several welfare measures on the ground that they were extravagant. In July of 1975, for example, he vetoed a $7.9 billion aid-to-education bill because he thought it inflationary. It was his 35th veto. The Democrats accused him of being niggardly with the poor in the name of cutting back on government costs while permitting increased expenditures for the military and higher prices for petroleum products in the campaign to reduce U.S. dependence on foreign oil. Ford denied that the country needed another Democratic New Deal. More to the point, he insisted, was "a fresh start." It is time, he said, "for us to declare our independence from governmental bureaucracies grown too large, too powerful, too costly, too remote, and yet too deeply involved in our day-to-day lives."

He sought, also, to reduce the regulatory activities of the federal government. Thus in late 1975 the administration submitted a bill removing some governmental controls over the bus and trucking industry in order to stimulate competition. Some of Ford's appointments to vacancies on the regulatory agencies were so favorable to business that in one month alone the Senate turned down four of them almost as soon as the names were submitted. But Ford's conservatism did not cause him to follow Nixon in trying to place a conservative Southerner and strict constructionist on the Supreme Court when liberal Justice William O. Douglas resigned. The new appointee was John Paul Stevens, a moderately conservative federal judge from Chicago.

The administration's assessment of the economic problems of the country also reflected conservative Republican principles. Early in the Ford administration unemployment began to climb until in the spring of 1975 it reached its highest level (over 9 percent of the labor force) since the Great Depression. Simultaneously, inflation spurted to an annual rate of 12 percent. At first the administration concentrated its attention almost entirely on controlling inflation. The President warned Congress against excessive expenditures of any kind, including efforts to put people to work. To back up his warning, Ford vetoed a bill to spend $5.3 billion to create jobs for the unemployed, and another that would have raised farm prices. He also vetoed several environmental bills, notably a stiff anti-strip-mining measure in December 1974, because they would have increased the cost of business operation, thus adding to inflation and reducing the incentive to increase the sources of energy. But as unemployment mounted and the economy remained sluggish, he came to recognize that inflation was not the only menace.

In March 1975 he signed the biggest tax cut in American history as a stimulus to the economy. Even after being pruned by Congress, the cut amounted to $22 billion. Again the President was careful to warn Congress against excessive expenditures that would increase the federal deficit beyond the current (more than $50 billion) figure. As it was, the Ford and Nixon administrations, for all their Republican character and emphasis on fiscal responsibility, had recorded the highest deficits in American history. By the end of 1975 Ford's efforts to deal with economic problems were showing mixed results at best. The rate of unemployment barely declined at all, going from slightly more than 9 percent in early 1975 to about 8 percent in early 1976. Inflation did slow down, from a high of 12 percent a year to a low at the end of 1975 of 6 percent, though the economy as a whole was still not working at capacity.

Despite, or perhaps because of, a political life confined to the House, the President showed himself adept in countering the lopsided Democratic majority in Congress. Although the Democrats promised to come up with energy and economic policies of their own, the administration's policies prevailed, if only because the legislature could not agree on what it wanted. In the contests with the White House, the legislators were no match for someone who had long known the ways of the House. All but seven of Ford's 41 vetoes in his first sixteen months in office were sustained in Congress, even by the allegedly liberal House with its extraordinary majority

of Democrats. Even Ford's veto of the jobs bill to combat unemployment could not be overturned.

At the beginning of his second year, in the fall of 1975, Ford demonstrated his political authority and self-confidence, if not his political shrewdness. He summarily fired James Schlesinger, the Secretary of Defense, and William Colby, the head of the CIA. Colby was dropped because he had been too cooperative with congressional investigations of past undercover operations by the CIA. Schlesinger's removal stemmed from his long conflict with Henry Kissinger over the proper relation between the United States and Russia. Schlesinger thought Kissinger's policy of détente was too trusting of Soviet intentions and aspirations in the world.

A Changing World Scene. Ford, still depending upon Nixon's Secretary of State, Kissinger, tried to implement the breakthrough that his predecessor had made in 1972 in visits of his own to Communist China (the People's Republic of China) and the Soviet Union. Ford met with Leonid Brezhnev in Vladivostok, Soviet Siberia, in November 1974 to discuss missile reduction, and again in Helsinki in August 1975, along with some thirty other heads of government, to recognize formally Soviet and Western boundaries in Europe. Then in December 1975 he traveled to Peking to show the Chinese, who were still fearful of Soviet military intentions, that he continued to be interested in expanding friendly relations with them.

One consequence of the détente with the Communist powers, as well as a measure of it, was a five-year agreement between the Soviet Union and the U.S. on the sale of American grain to Russia. This action assured a ready market for American farmers while avoiding a sudden, inflationary push on domestic American grain prices, as had occurred the year before when the Russians suddenly began to buy grain.

Enthusiastic well-wishers greet Gerald Ford, an open, friendly President who loved meeting people.

An effort to get the Russians to swap grain for oil and thus help the United States reduce its dependence on Arabian oil did not come off. Despite that failure, the Ford administration pressed toward the goal, also inherited from Nixon, that the United States become independent of outside sources of energy by the 1980s. Few observers thought the achievement of the goal was possible, and not many more thought it necessary. No one, however, was optimistic about the future, since oil supplies were entangled in the always smoldering conflict between Israel and the Arab states.

The elusiveness of a firm and enduring settlement in the Middle East threatened to produce a confrontation between the two nuclear superpowers, which were ranged on opposite sides in the controversy over Israel. Alone among the industrial nations of the world, the United States championed Israel. However much the other industrial nations might be mindful of the Nazi horror against the Jews, which had been the justification for the establishment of Israel in 1948, they could not ignore the central importance of Arab oil in their economies. Russia viewed Israel as an outpost of American imperialism and supported the Arab states in their hostility toward Israel.

It was this antagonism that threatened to shatter the peace that the ending of the Vietnam War had finally brought to the United States. For almost the first time since the end of World War II no large-scale war was being waged anywhere. Guerrilla fighters in the Philippines, Thailand, the Middle East, and Africa continued to operate, but no national army actively confronted a national enemy. In fact, the anticolonialism that had lain at the root of most of the wars since 1945, including the Vietnam War, had come to a final close in 1975, when Portugal surrendered its last colony, Angola, to the contending independence forces in that African territory.

The colonial dependencies now left in the world were mostly small islands or bits of territory, which neither desired nor seemed likely to profit from independence.

The Ford administration, then, coincided with the close of an era. The postwar world could now be said to have come to an end. Those social, economic, and political forces that the Second World War had set loose upon the world had run their course. Traditional colonialism had been ended. The relation between the two extra-European victors in the war, the Soviet Union and the United States, was not entirely amicable, but the Cold War as it had been known for a quarter of a century was over. Europe was not united, but it was entirely recovered from the war and once again carrying weight in the world. In Asia Japan was not only the dominant economic power, but the most stable democratic ally of the West. China was no longer hostile to either the West in general or the United States in particular, but was fearful of its Communist neighbor, the U.S.S.R. Economically, too, the world passed over a watershed in the middle seventies when it became clear that the price of energy, thanks to the cartel formed by the oil-producing countries of the Third World, was not only going to rise, but would inevitably diminish that amazing prosperity that had dominated the economies of the industrial countries of the world for the preceding quarter of a century.

Domestically, 1976 was a dividing line because by then the social changes and upheavals associated with the 1960s and the early 1970s were clearly over. The trauma of Watergate, like the nightmare of Vietnam, had been put behind the nation, one way or another, by the Ford Administration. Moreover, as we shall see, the character of the American political party system was in the process of profound change, setting off the years after Ford from those that had gone before. The President elected in 1976 was himself different from not only his immediate predecessors, but from those who had been President earlier.

NEW ERA, NEW PRESIDENT

The Arrival of Jimmy Carter. Just about the time that Gerald Ford assumed office after the resignation of Richard M. Nixon, Governor James Earl Carter, Jr., of Georgia decided to run for the presidency. He was still in his first term as governor, not yet fifty years of age, and virtually unknown outside his own state. In fact, he had never tried for public office before 1962, and had been defeated then. Yet, in January 1977, Jimmy Carter was inaugurated President of the United States, just as he had said all along he would be.

Jimmy Carter, as he insisted upon being known officially as well as unofficially, was unusual in other ways. He was the first candidate from the Deep South since Zachary Taylor in 1848. He was a businessman-farmer rather than a lawyer, and he was the first graduate of the Naval Academy at Annapolis to be President. He actually served in the regular Navy for eight years before returning to his birthplace in the tiny village of Plains, Georgia, where he soon made himself a millionaire by raising peanuts. Carter was unusual for a white Southerner in that as governor he made explicit his belief in equality of opportunity for white and black people.

Thanks to a persistent and energetic campaign of almost two years, in the course of which he traveled around the country, often staying at private homes and talking to no more than handsful of people, Carter captured most of the Democratic primaries in the spring of 1976. He was nominated on the first ballot at the Democratic convention that summer in New York. During his campaign for the nomination he had not always made clear his views, but his choice of Senator Walter Mondale of Minnesota to be his running mate made evident that he intended to be a liberal, activist Democrat in the Roosevelt and Kennedy mold. Indeed, Mondale's professional and effective campaigning helped Carter overcome some of his limitations as a campaigner, especially against the incumbent and more experienced Gerald Ford. On the other hand, Ford's selection of the strongly conservative and acerbic Robert Dole, senator from Kansas, as his candidate for Vice-President, weakened the President's appeal. Even so, the folksy and energetic Ford came from far behind in the public opinion pools in the late summer to almost win in November.

On election day, Carter surpassed Ford by fewer than 2 million votes and the tally in the Electoral College was so close that a shift in 10,000 votes in two states would have given Ford the victory. Both houses of Congress, however, went overwhelmingly Democratic, as they had in 1972 and 1974. To this political inconsistency we will return later in this chapter.

A New Administration. In line with his promise during the campaign, Carter brought two women, one of whom was black, into his Cabinet, and named a black fellow Georgian, Andrew Young, to be the Ambassador to the United Nations. This was not as high a representation of minorities and women as had been anticipated, but it was greater than in any previous administration.

Carter's desire to signal the novelty of his administration was evident immediately after his inauguration when he eschewed the usual ride in a large black Cadillac down Pennsylvania Avenue. Instead he and his wife Rosalyn walked hand-in-hand down the avenue to the White House, waving and smiling broadly to the pleasantly surprised crowds along the way. Another novel act, within a month of taking office, was his pardoning of some 10,000 draft evaders from the days of the

Vietnam War, something none of his immediate predecessors had wanted to do. (Even Carter, however, did not pardon the 69,000 military deserters.)

Carter tried, also early in his administration, to break new ground in foreign policy. He publicly encouraged Soviet dissidents who were seeking greater freedom within the Soviet Union, a gesture Henry Kissinger, the previous Secretary of State, had refused to make on the ground that it would interfere with impending agreements with the Soviet state on larger matters. The Carter administration, however, contended that international agreements were achieved because of self-interest on both sides, not because an American President refrained from criticizing the denials of free speech and press in the Soviet Union. Therefore, early in his administration, Carter dispatched his new Secretary of State, Cyrus Vance, to Moscow with a series of proposals to restrict the number and kinds of missiles that the two superpowers could maintain.

Contrary to his expectations, the Russians coolly turned down the proposals. One interpretation was that Carter had been too quick in his diplomacy. Some feared that Carter's insistence upon denouncing denial of human rights might revive the Cold War.

In subsequent months, as Carter continued to speak out in behalf of human rights, he seemed to be less than consistent in his denouncements. Violations of human rights among our allies were rarely noted. Yet there was no question that Carter's emphasis on human rights was consonant with America's long history of freedom and concern over the denial of freedom in other countries. Some highly placed cynics in some capitals around the world made fun of Carter's addition of human rights concerns to foreign policy, especially when the selectivity of application became evident. But the prominence the issue achieved thereafter at international conferences and at the United Nations suggested that Carter's initiative had made human rights a concern among nations such as it had not been since the 1930s.

Restoring Government to the People. During his campaign Carter had promised to bring government back to the people. Some politicians had complained that he had "campaigned against Washington while trying his best to get there." Early in his administration, Carter emphasized two policies that he thought would give Americans a sense of controlling their future.

One was his promise to balance the federal budget by 1980, though that had not been accomplished under Republican or Democratic Presidents since the beginning of American involvement in the Vietnam War. It could be done only by reducing government expenditures. Although Congress is rarely happy about cutting expenditures, it did stay within the guidelines set by the administration during the first year, though not without the help of some presidential vetoes. A public works appropriation and a plan to build a nuclear carrier were both killed by the President for a saving of some $2 billion. The President demonstrated some willingness to cut down on military spending in his decision not to develop the B-1 superbomber, which many powerful Congressmen were supporting.

Carter's second effort to give Americans a sense of control over their future was his call in March 1977 for a "moral equivalent of war" on the energy shortage, particularly on the dependence of the United States on foreign oil. This was a subject both Ford and Nixon had addressed themselves to, but oil imports had been continuing to rise. Essentially, Carter's program called for a reduction in consumption and provided for a series of incentives to industry and private citizens to use alternative sources of energy, such as coal, which was plentiful in the United States, and solar energy.

Despite the overwhelming majority his party held in both houses of Congress, Carter did not by any means obtain all that he asked for that first year. In fact, the energy program was bogged down for almost eighteen months in Congress, as various groups debated the details of the program. All that the President received that year from Congress in regard to energy was agreement to create a new Cabinet post of Energy. James Schlesinger, the former Secretary of Defense fired by Ford, was named the first Secretary. During the Vietnam War, Congress had been overawed by Johnson and Nixon and had followed their leads without much questioning. When the war was over, revelations about its conduct and about Watergate were evidence that Congress had been negligent. As a result, Congress under Carter became highly independent on both domestic and foreign affairs. Moreover, even Democrats became more conservative in their social outlook. As a result, even though the labor unions had supported Carter and the Democrats in the recent election, the unions' bill to revise the Labor Relations Act in order to control obstructionist employers was killed in the Senate after passing the House. Also, Carter's effort to get a new Department of Education, in order to bring the wide range of federal educational programs under one roof, died in committee.

Congress did agree to an extension of the time allowed for the ratification of the Equal Rights Amendment for women, as Carter recommended. And it approved of his streamlining of the federal bureaucracy through new hiring and firing procedures and salary incentives. But Carter suffered a deep wound officially as well as personally when his trusted friend and adviser, Bert Lance, the Director of the government's Office of Management and Budget was compelled to resign in September 1977 for questionable banking practices in Georgia. Carter's reluctance during several weeks of public hearings to admit his friend's defects spoke well for his sense of personal loyalty but seemed to undercut the high moral claims of his campaign.

Carter entered office with the image of an activist, and during that first year many in Congress were heard to complain of being sent too many proposals from the White House in too short a time. By the second year, however, things had changed if only because so little had been achieved in the first year. The President's first State of the Union message reflected the change. Retrenchment and caution now seemed to be the watchword. "Government cannot solve our problems," he warned. "Government cannot eliminate poverty, or provide a bountiful economy, or reduce inflation, or save our cities, or cure illiteracy, or provide energy, or mandate goodness." Only people cooperating with government can accomplish anything, he asserted.

In his budget message he did present his long-awaited proposal for tax reform and reduction, but it did not stir hearts or bring much that was new. The cuts were designed primarily to relieve the burdens on low- and middle-income Americans, who increasingly were feeling the effects of rising prices.

Although prices had been rising ominously throughout his first eighteen months as President, Carter had hesitated to make a fight against inflation his first priority. He feared that slowing down the economy would produce unemployment. The most he ventured was to set guidelines on prices and wages, but they were only voluntary for business and labor. That half-hearted tactic did not work. By early 1979 the annual rate of inflation was over 10 percent and still rising. That fact probably explained why in early 1979 only 18 percent of Americans thought Carter's handling of the economy was satisfactory.

In the President's mind, a more crucial test

President Carter's tactic of voluntary guidelines on prices and wages proved to be an ineffective weapon against inflation.

of his leadership than the issue of inflation was the question of energy. He had begun his administration by calling for a "moral equivalent of war" on the energy problem, but the measure Congress finally passed was at best a compromise and at worst only an excuse for an energy policy. It cut in half the figure by which importations of oil were to be reduced in the next five years and offered only financial incentives for oil users to shift to coal or solar sources of energy. Obviously the question of energy would have to come before the administration and the nation again, for the problem of American dependence on foreign oil had not been faced up to.

A Promising Start in Foreign Affairs. Just as his personally democratic ways and high intelligence had won the President many admirers domestically, these qualities, at least

at first, won him friends abroad. On an official visit to London in May 1977, to meet with the heads of government of the principal western European nations, Carter was an immediate hit with the British public and the leaders of government. At conferences his command of the issues was quickly evident.

On a two-week tour of Latin America, his wife Rosalyn also impressed governmental officials there with her solid preparation and skillful diplomacy as well as her clear authority to speak for the President. No other American President, including Franklin Roosevelt, had relied so heavily and drawn so much support from his wife as Carter. Rosalyn Carter frequently attended Cabinet meetings as well as accompanying him on virtually every trip abroad.

In fact, trips abroad were so successful for the Carters that in December the President embarked upon another one to Poland, Iran, India, Saudi Arabia, France, and Belgium, covering a distance of 18,500 miles in only nine days. Just when some observers were becoming concerned that travel might turn out to be the only diplomatic achievement of the new President, Carter managed to score two significant gains.

The Canal Treaty. The first was winning the Senate's acceptance of a new treaty with Panama regarding the Panama Canal. Ever since the early years of the Johnson administration, Panamanians had been demanding tha. they be given a more equal role in the management of the canal, but the Vietnam War and then the defeat of the United States in Asia made it difficult to bring the issue before the country. Finally, in August 1977, the American negotiators concluded a treaty that would turn the canal over to Panama by the year 2000.

Although leading foreign policy experts on the Republican side, like Henry Kissinger, supported the treaty, Republican opposition was vocal and adamant. And when it was joined by conservative Democratic opponents, the treaty seemed likely to be defeated in the Senate. After lengthy hearings and sometimes acrimonious public debate, the Senate gave its approval in April 1978, but with only one vote to spare. And to achieve even that narrow victory, certain reservations had to be added. Fortunately, Panama was prepared to accept them so that the treaty could be ratified without renegotiation.

Carter's close victory demonstrated that in foreign policy, as in domestic affairs, the President's influence over Congress was severely limited for a leader with a party majority in both houses. Thanks to the passage of the Canal Treaty, Carter's standing in the opinion polls rose from 37 percent to 42 percent of Americans approving his administration, but, significantly, those who approved were still less than a majority.

Middle East Accord. That minority approval, however, swelled to a majority by the end of the summer. Carter had made the biggest gamble of his career by deliberately undertaking to bring about an agreement between Egypt and Israel in the Middle East.

The opportunity had been created by the surprise visit of President Anwar Sadat of Egypt to Israel in November 1977. This melodramatic break in the long hostility between the two countries seemed pregnant with possibilities for an end to conflict in that war-torn region. Israel and Egypt had been at war with one another four times in the preceding thirty years. Prime Minister Menachem Begin of Israel and Sadat met several times again, their lieutenants met, and Secretary of State Cyrus Vance met with both sides. But it seemed the differences between the two countries could not be ironed out. Suddenly it seemed that Sadat's courageous act of rapprochement would be wasted. The opportunities he had opened up were about to be lost. At that juncture Carter acted.

Undoubtedly worried about his low standing in the polls and his inability to move Congress on energy and other domestic issues, and aware that Congressional elections would be coming up in the fall, Carter invited the two Middle Eastern leaders to come to Camp David, the private presidential retreat in the Maryland mountains, for a confidential conference. Obviously the risk was enormous. If nothing came of the meeting, Carter's prestige would sink still lower and he would be seen as acting impetuously and presumptuously. When before had a President presumed to act as a mediator in a situation so charged with animosity and bad history? Not even Theodore Roosevelt had been intimately involved in the actual negotiations at the Portsmouth Conference that ended the Russo-Japanese War in 1905. And besides, that conference had taken place after a war in which one side had been roundly defeated.

For over ten days the three leaders were secluded at Camp David, a length of time none had expected, but Carter was insistent. The intransigence of Begin almost caused Sadat at one point to leave for Cairo. Then, on the ninth day, Carter convinced Begin to change his mind on one of the major obstacles to agreement. On September 17 a triumphant Carter presented the two leaders to a hastily assembled audience in the East Room of the White House to witness the signing of a framework for peace between the two long-time enemies.

In fact, the delicacy and dangers surrounding the issues of the Mideast animosities were so great that even after the agreement at Camp David, Israel was slow to put into practice the principles that had been agreed upon. Ever fearful for its security after four wars, Israel could not easily give up territory it thought essential to its safety. Nevertheless, after months of further discussion in Cairo and Jerusalem and Washington, a treaty of peace was signed between Israel and Egypt at the White House on March 26, 1979. It not only ended the state of war between the two countries but, among other things, specified the withdrawal of Israel from the Sinai peninsula, which Israel had conquered in the 1967 war and had occupied ever since. The treaty was undoubtedly the most hopeful sign for future peace in the region since the creation of Israel thirty years before. That it should have been brought about by the twentieth-century President least informed or experienced in politics and foreign affairs was at once ironic and a tribute to the intelligence and educability of Jimmy Carter.

Thanks to his successful handling of the Mideast summit, Carter's standing in the polls shot up in September and his ability to convince Congress to go along with foreign policy recommendations improved. He managed, for example, to obtain Congressional approval to sell modern fighter aircraft to Egypt and Saudi Arabia as well as Israel, despite strong objections from pro-Israel members of Congress. Congress also approved his lifting of the arms embargo against Turkey, even though friends of Greece opposed it.

From a certain point of view, there ought not to have been any reason to emphasize his successes with Congress. After all, his own party dominated both houses as well as running all the committees of Congress. Yet it was just that lack of party loyalty to the President and lack of party discipline which was one of the striking aspects of American politics increasingly evident in the middle 1970s. This situation was particularly noticeable in the results of the Congressional elections of 1978.

A NEW POLITICAL SYSTEM?

The Election of 1978. One of the clichés of off-year elections is that the incumbent party usually loses seats in Congress. And the first off-year elections of Carter's presidency were no exception. Republicans gained three seats in the Senate, twelve seats in the House of Representatives, and three gubernatorial chairs in the state capitals. The lack of real significance for these gains, however, was revealed by the tally of state legislatures controlled by Republicans. The number went from four to a mere twelve! Even after adding the off-year gains, the Republicans still remained a decided minority in most of the states and in Congress.

This disparity between Republicans and Democrats was not new in 1978. Between 1960 and 1974 the proportion of seats in the House of Representatives held by Democrats had rarely gone below 60 percent. Though it went over that figure at times, it had never fallen as low as 55 percent. And except for four years (1966–1970) a majority of the governors of the states during that same span of years had also been Democrats. In 1977 only 32 percent of all state legislators were Republicans—as compared with 53 percent in 1948 and 44 percent in 1956.

It was figures like those that caused political commentators in the late 1970s to refer to the American polity as no longer a two-party system, but a "one-and-a-half" party system. When public opinion polls were examined in a similar light, it was evident that the Democrats were the "everyone party." The polls showed that virtually every social group was well represented in the party. Even wealthy people were Democrats, two to one.

At one time in American history it could have been assumed that college graduates would tend to be Republicans, but by the late 1970s, 42 percent of them were listing themselves as Democrats and only 31 percent identified themselves as Republicans. Since the poor, the blacks, and most of the middle class had been captured by the New Deal, if not before, and securely held ever since, no significant social groups were absent from the Democratic coalition.

A Political Paradox. Despite this overwhelming preference of American voters for the Democrats, the party could never be sure of winning the White House. Between 1948 and 1976 the Democrats won only half of the presidential elections and even then the Republicans won 51 percent of the popular vote for the two parties! In short, a two-tier political system seemed to be emerging in the country: presidential and legislative levels. Voters apparently made little connection between their votes for Congress and their votes for President. Part of the explanation for the development of the two-tiered politics were the changes occurring in the South.

One of the consequences of World War II was that the South finally began to catch up with the rest of the nation in industrial and urban development. As a result its politics began to change, too. It was certainly significant that Republican Eisenhower had chalked up much of his unusually strong support for a Republican in the South among city and suburban dwellers. And in the 1960s Southern support for Republican presidents continued to be notable in the cities of the region. Moreover, the Second Reconstruction of the South during the 1960s was associated in the minds of many white Southerners with Democratic Presidents, an association that split off many old-line Southern Democrats from support of their party's presidential candidates.

Only in five elections since the Civil War has the white South failed to give a majority of its votes to a Democratic presidential candidate. Every one of those times was since 1960. The last time was when Jimmy Carter was elected, even though he was himself a son of the South. At the same time, white Southerners continued to support Democratic Congressional candidates, for they were local people, untainted by support for problack programs.

Outside the South the tendency for voters to split their party preferences between Congress and the President has developed more slowly. As late as 1952 only a fifth of voters in the country cast ballots for congressional and presidential candidates from different parties. By 1968 the proportion was up to a third, and by 1972 it was over two fifths. (During the nineteenth century it has been estimated that probably less than 10 percent of voters split their tickets.)

Why voters today so often do not give their presidential candidate the Congressional support he needs is not clear. Perhaps it stems from voter fears about Democratic Presidents being too aggressive or spendthrift while at the same time voters fear that the Republicans cannot be trusted to preserve the social welfare legislation enacted by the Democrats, especially under the New Deal. Whatever the reasons, the two-tiered system of national politics seems now to have seriously modified the old party system, which heretofore had been characterized by a majority and a minority party. As the Republicans are only half a party, so the Democrats are not a true majority party.

Certain other developments of the last two decades suggest that something more profound has been happening to the American political system. Behind the splitting of voters' preferences in national elections lies a deep distrust of parties in general. The most obvious measure of this is the rise in the independent or nonparty vote. At the end of the 1960s pollsters began to find a significant number of voters who said they had no allegiance to any party. By 1974 one third of Americans claimed to be independents; in the 1950s only a fifth had made that self-designation. Among college-educated people in 1973 the proportion who labeled themselves independent (38 percent) outnumbered those who designated themselves as either Republicans or Democrats.

On a superficial level it might be thought that independence of party would constitute a gain for good government. And insofar as party allegiance leads to mindless or blind loyalty, that might be true. But when independence results in the election of a President of a different party from that of the Congress, it can only complicate, if not impede effective relations between legislature and executive.

The tendency of voters to split their votes between the parties has an even more insidious effect. It means that even when Congress and the President are of the *same* party—as has been the case during the Carter administration—the pressure on individual representatives to support the President is correspondingly reduced. Legislators know that voters do not make a connection between their votes for Congress and for President. Hence they can be much more independent of the President even when he is of their own party. It was that situation that confronted Carter in foreign affairs. He simply could not count on support from his own party. In three roll call votes in the Senate, for instance, Republican votes were essential in order for him to carry through his policies. One of those instances was the vote on the crucially important Panama Canal treaty.

A further measure of this decline in Americans' belief in their country's historical political system was underscored by the results of the 1978 elections. That was the tendency of most Americans not to vote at all. The turnout in November 1978 was the lowest in recent history. Only 38 percent of eligible voters bothered to cast their ballots; 96 million people stayed away. As recently as 1962 some 48 percent of voters turned out even for an off-year election. Moreover, in presidential elections, Americans have one of the lowest turnouts of any modern democracy. In short, there is not only a disquieting turning away from political parties, but a disturbing alienation from the whole political process as well.

Part of the explanation is quite properly sought in events of the 1960s and 1970s when government leaders, from the President on down, misused their authority to defend the Vietnam War and to cover up the Watergate crimes. During this period a deep sense of cynicism about authority and its abuse of power spread among many Americans, particularly college-age people. By the end of the 1970s they were a large and influential part of the electorate. The shift can also be seen in a decline in trust of authority generally. In 1966, for example, 72 percent of Americans had said they had a "great deal of confidence" in the leadership of American medicine. By 1977 only 43 percent expressed that degree of confidence. For leaders of higher education the slide was from 61 percent to 37 percent. For the military, as one might expect, the decline was precipitous: from 62 percent in 1966 to 27 percent in 1977.

It was on a promise of restoring confidence in government that Carter campaigned in 1976, and presumably his victory was attributable, at least in part, to the voters' hope that he could do just that. In several ways Carter was in tune with the new mood. He was not authoritarian in his dealings with his family or his subordinates. He probably spent more time as a candidate and as President visiting the homes of ordinary citizens than any President in history. In fact, his thirst for the opinion of the average American was so strong that some observers thought it counterproductive. His effort to maintain an "open presidency" was clearly in response to the popular hostility to the Nixon administration's "bunker mentality," which had produced so many mistakes and abuses of power.

More was involved in the distrust of government, however, than particular evils committed by past Presidents and governments. Also at work were the profound social and cultural changes of the 1960s, among which was a new emphasis upon the dignity of all people—black, brown, and red, poor as well as rich, both female and male. The social order that emerged in America from the turbulent sixties and early seventies was less rigid and less deferential and more democratic than had been true before. As one commentator expressed it, "ordinary people in this country now have a higher estimation of their endowments and broader conceptions of their entitlements than ever before."

The upshot was that the country was probably more difficult to govern than at any time in American history. Americans in the era of Jackson, for example, may have been more turbulent and even harder to discipline or guide, but they also expected less of government. Even with its social diversity, what the nation required for cohesion and growth was less dependence upon the federal government. It was these changes, long germinating, that the Carter administration had to contend with in the closing years of the 1970s. It was soon evident that the encounter and its resolution were not going to be easy. Without a strong sense of party loyalty in Congress and without a strong belief among the people in the virtues of parties, elections, and even the benevolence of government

itself, solutions to the difficult problems of inflation, recession, and energy would be difficult for any President to carry out. That seemed to be the meaning of Carter's many problems as he entered upon the second half of his presidency in January 1979.

Lowering Expectations. In his State of the Union message in January 1979, President Carter stressed good management and efficiency in the federal government, rather than new programs. He talked about laying a "New Foundation," reminiscent of the New Deal and the New Frontier, but he was concerned primarily to steer a path between the continuing inflation and the threat of recession. As a result, established programs received no increases in his new budget and even the military only a 3 percent increase. The national health insurance program he had promised the country at the beginning of his administration was clearly shaped by fears of fueling inflation. It was limited in scope to keep governmental spending down.

Worrisome and potentially dangerous as the long siege of mounting prices was, the sharpest crisis for the President came from a different though not unrelated source. In the spring of 1979 the enduring problem of what to do about American dependence upon foreign oil in the face of growing domestic demand leaped into dramatic prominence. The overthrow of the government of the Shah of Iran by internal revolutionaries abruptly reduced the world's supply of oil, causing new upward pressures on the cost of energy. Then in May and June motorists panicked, first in California and then later on the east coast. Thinking gasoline would be impossible to obtain, they began to buy it in inordinate amounts that so strained the allocation system of the country that suddenly it was hard to find gas, and the price began to shoot up. Long lines of cars appeared outside gasoline stations, depressingly reminiscent of the days of the Arab oil embargo in 1973.

This time, however, when the lines finally disappeared, not only was the price of gasoline considerably higher, but the sense of urgency about the energy shortage remained. For the first time in their history, Americans paid a dollar a gallon for gasoline and the price promised to rise considerably more in short order. (Europeans had been paying a dollar a gallon or more for decades and in June 1979 they were paying twice what Americans were.) The day of cheap gasoline was now definitely over, but American adjustment to the new situation was only beginning.

The gasoline lines, which caught everyone by surprise, showed concretely the weakness of the President's grip on the problem and on the political process. Earlier that spring Carter had asked Congress to give him power to set up a standby gasoline rationing plan for just such an emergency as occurred in June. Congress refused, reflecting the reluctance of most Americans to admit that cheap energy was no longer a given. Once the gas lines materialized, however, the public clamor energized Congress. Within days, several bills setting up machinery for rationing gasoline in an emergency, along the lines advocated by the President only a few weeks before, went into the legislative mill. Congress suddenly became interested in the development of synthetic fuels, too. Meanwhile, the President's stand in the polls plummeted to a level lower than that ever reached by a President, including Nixon at the time of his forced resignation. Only 29 percent of the American people approved of his administration, while a whopping 56 percent said they disapproved.

A feeling that no one in Washington was in charge of the country reached the President himself in early July, soon after he returned from a meeting with European and Japanese heads of government convened to coordinate responses to the world energy shortage. Carter canceled a television address to the people scheduled for July 5 and went instead into seclusion at Camp David. Over the ensuing ten days he invited scores of people from a wide range of professions to discuss the crisis of leadership he, as well as the country, now felt so deeply. In an unprecedented display of presidential self-criticism, Carter pleaded with his visitors and with the ordinary Americans he visited privately at their homes to advise him as to what he might do. At the conclusion of the extraordinary discussions and almost public self-examination, the President appeared on national television. The address he gave was almost devoid of policy statements. It called upon Americans to have faith in themselves and to use the energy crisis as a way of uniting the country and freeing the nation from dependence upon foreign sources of oil. In a second speech the next day he outlined a new program to reduce consumption of oil and to expand the production of energy. The new proposal was monumental in its conception and cost, dwarfing the giant Manhattan District Project during the Second World War that developed the atomic bomb. That had cost $2 billion. Carter's new moral equivalent of war was expected to cost $142 billion over the next ten years. It was to be financed largely by a tax on the so-called windfall profits of oil companies.

The immediate public response was positive. The President's standing in the polls improved considerably, though those who approved his actions constituted still less than half of the voters. For all of the rhetoric of sacrifice in the President's speeches, however, little specific sacrifice was actually demanded. Some of his advisers had hoped that he would take the hard, but necessary road of asking for a sharp increase in the price of gasoline in order to compel Americans to use less. But his plan to reduce consumption relied primarily on exhortations to be patriotic and to conserve.

Some hoped he would abandon reliance upon nuclear energy, which, in the light of a serious and totally unanticipated accident at a nuclear reactor at Three Mile Island, Pennsylvania, shortly before, seemed increasingly dubious, if not dangerous. But the President apparently contemplated no changes in his past policy of including nuclear energy as a substantial part of the national solution to the shortage.

Later in July, presumably in an effort to strengthen his administration internally and to give an impression externally of being in direct control, Carter fired five of his cabinet officers. The replacements, however, did not suggest that there would be much change in policy.

The wholesale firing aroused a furor among many leaders of the Democratic party and in Congress, and puzzled—even alarmed— many observers abroad who were already beginning to view Carter as indecisive or lacking in steadfastness. Nor did the summary dismissals encourage the Senate to act on the second SALT (Strategic Arms Limitation Talks) treaty with the Soviet Union, which Carter had submitted just when the gas lines were capturing the attention of Americans in the spring of 1979. The treaty had been in the works a long time, yet its provisions constituted only a small step in the direction of limiting the largest nuclear weapons of the two superpowers. It placed ceilings on numbers of submarine- and land-based missiles, and on bombers capable of carrying nuclear bombs and limited each side to the development of one new weapon system. Many Republicans and some Democrats thought such acceptance of virtual nuclear equality with the Soviet Union was dangerous and so opposed the treaty. But even those who may have favored it soon were distracted by two significant events in the late fall of 1979.

One was the sudden capturing of the American Embassy in Teheran, Iran, with all its occupants, by a group of armed student supporters of the new religious and secular leader of the Iranian revolution, the Ayatollah Khomeini. They demanded the exchange of the American hostages for the former Shah, who, for a while, was in the United States. When the Administration refused to return the Shah, the militants continued to hold the hostages, threatening to put them on trial as spies.

The second event that virtually killed the SALT discussions in the Senate was the invasion of Afghanistan by Soviet troops in late December 1979, in order to shore up a faltering Communist regime on its southern border. The President reacted strongly—even exaggeratedly—by calling the Soviet intrusion a most serious threat to peace and comity among nations. He sought to arouse other nations to condemn the Soviet action, though not with great success. But at home, the Senate and the country viewed the Soviet measures as inconsistent with SALT, and so the agreement did not even come before the Senate in 1980.

As the 1980 election primaries began, the President was hardly in good political shape. He was burdened with the problem of the American hostages in Teheran and with a rate of inflation that was close to 20 percent on an annual basis. Moreover, all indications were that unemployment, too, would increase as the economy slowed down in response to the high interest rates and other measures aimed at combating inflation. Despite these handicaps, however, the President emerged from most of his primaries as the favored Democratic candidate, easily winning over his once highly favored opponent, Senator Edward Kennedy. Many Democrats, leaders as well as rank and file, were not pleased with Carter, but Kennedy was apparently viewed as even less attractive, despite his vigorous campaign and magical name. Meanwhile, Ronald Reagan, the aging former governor of California, an acknowledged conservative on both domestic and foreign policy issues, easily captured enough delegates in the Republican primaries to win the nomination on the first ballot at the Republican convention.

The Election of 1980. Once the campaign began, it was apparent voters were unhappy about the options. Although Republican Congressman John Anderson offered himself as an alternative, his candidacy soon faded as Americans clung to their historic distrust of third party candidates. Carter and Reagan's campaigning was intensive and vigorous, but neither said much specific about how he would handle inflation—a concern of anxious voters—or any other problem. Neither was able to arouse voter enthusiasm; throughout the fall, polls showed a large proportion of voters stubbornly undecided.

Up until election day, the polls had been predicting a cliffhanger. The disappointing campaign, however, culminated in a stunning surprise when Reagan won by a landslide. Carter won only four states and the District of Columbia for forty-nine electoral votes. Surprising, too, was the Republican capture of the Senate for the first time in twenty-five years. Democrats lost in both the South and the North. The Democratic stronghold in the South crumbled with the victories of four new Republican senators and eleven new Republi-can congressmen. In the North, Republicans defeated three liberal Democratic senators and two congressmen.

These victories seemed to assure Reagan's ability to reshape the judiciary along more conservative lines and to take a harder line in foreign policy. The Republican triumphs also forecast a strong turn to the right in domestic policy, in line with the Republican platform. Among other things, the platform opposed the Equal Rights Amendement and abortion, while favoring higher military spending and a substantial tax cut. Also promised were a greater role for the states in domestic matters and a cutback in Federal spending and social programs.

Yet, some old patterns persisted. Democrats still controlled the House, as they had done since 1930 with only two interruptions. More important, voter turnout continued to decline, as it had been doing for a third of a century. The election seemed more a criticism of the Carter administration's inadequacies in dealing with a weakening economy and declining prestige abroad than a sign of support for Reagan and the Republicans.

BIBLIOGRAPHY

The literature on the cultural life of the period is constantly expanding. J. K. Galbraith, *New Industrial State,* 2nd ed. rev. (Boston: Houghton Mifflin, 1971), notes the limitations on competition in the postwar economy; Herman P. Miller, *Rich Man, Poor Man* (New York: Crowell, 1971), analyzes the distribution of wealth and poverty. Good for appreciating the importance of economic growth is Peter Passell and Leonard Ross, *The Retreat from Riches: Affluence and Its Enemies* (New York: Viking Press, 1973). An excellent analysis of the economy during the Eisenhower years is Harold G. Vatter, *The U.S. Economy in the 1950s* (New York: Norton, 1963). The changing character of agriculture is vigorously and closely examined in Edward C. Higbee, *Farms and Farmers in an Urban Age* (Millwood, NY: Kraus Reprint, 1973). The story has been put into historical perspective and updated in John L. Shover, *First Majority—Last Minority: The Transforming of Rural Life in America* (DeKalb, IL: Northern Illinois University Press, 1976). For some of the social changes of these years a good introduction is William L. O'Neill, *Coming Apart: An Informal History of America in the 1960s* (New York: Quadrangle, 1973). A broader view of the left in short compass is Irwin Unger, *The Movement: A History of the American New Left, 1959–1972* (New York: Harper & Row, 1974). More detailed, but important, is Kirkpatrick Sale, *SDS: Ten Years Toward a Revolution* (New York: Random House, 1973). The book deals with the principal radical youth organization of the 1960s. Morris Dickstein, *Gates of Eden: American Culture in the Sixties* (New York: Basic Books, 1977), looks at the decade from and through literature. At once a description and itself a part of the upheaval in youth's values is Theodore Roszak, *The Making of a Counter-Culture* (Garden City, NY: Doubleday, 1969). A work similarly involved in the movement it describes is the exciting Jane Jacobs, *The Death and Life of Great American Cities* (New York: Random House, 1961). Excellent on religious developments is Johnson Carroll et al., *Religion in America: 1950 to the Present* (New York: Harper & Row, 1979).

Works on minorities and women are numerous. A good introduction to the issues with regard to blacks is Charles E. Silberman, *Crisis in Black and White* (New York: Random House, 1964). Full and highly readable on the Supreme Court decision of 1954 is Richard Kluger, *Simple Justice: The History of Brown v. Board of Education and Black America's Struggle for Equality* (New York: Random House, 1975). For later judicial developments see J. Harris Wilkinson III, *From Brown to Bakke: The Supreme Court and School Integration, 1954–1978* (New York: Oxford University Press, 1979). More scholarly than Kluger is Benjamin Muse, *The American Negro Revolution: From Nonviolence to Black Power, 1963–1967* (Bloomington, IN: Indiana University Press, 1968). Indispensable as well as readable are several books by black leaders: Martin Luther King, Jr., *Stride Toward Freedom: The Montgomery Story* (New York: Harper & Row, 1958), Malcolm X, *Autobiography of Malcolm X* (New York: Grove Press, 1965), and Eldridge Cleaver, *Soul on Ice* (New York: McGraw-Hill, 1968). Important, too, is David L. Lewis, *King: A Critical Biography* (New York: Praeger, 1970).

On the women's movement a good overall view of background and development is William Chafe, *The American Woman: Her Changing Social, Economic, and Political Roles* (New York: Oxford University Press, 1972). Juanita Kreps, *Sex in the Marketplace: American Women at Work* (Baltimore: Johns Hopkins University Press, 1971), is excellent, if brief, on women's economic position. On Muhammad Ali a good introduction is his autobiography, *The Greatest: My Own Story* (New York: Random House, 1975). An excellent analysis of the ideology of the women's movement is Gayle Graham Yates, *What Women Want: The Ideas of the Movement* (Cambridge: Harvard University Press, 1975).

Joan Moore and Alfredo Cuellar, *Mexican American* (Englewood Cliffs, NJ: Prentice-Hall, 1970), is a good introduction to Chicanos. A new and reliable history is Matt S. Meier and Feliciano Rivera, *The Chicanos: A History of Mexican Americans* (New York: Hill & Wang, 1972). For some of the new Indian organizations see Hazel W. Hertzberg, *Search for an American Indian Identity: Modern Pan-Indian Movements* (Syracuse, NY: Syracuse University Press, 1971), and the popular but important writings of Vine De Loria, Jr., who is a Sioux. Most recent is his *God Is Red* (New York: Dell, 1975), which satirically sets forth some of his views. For recent policies see Alan L. Sorkin, *American Indians and Federal Aid* (Washington, D.C.: The Brookings Institution, 1971).

The best overall interpretation of the years since 1945, written with vigor, is by an Englishman familiar with America: Godfrey Hodgson, *America in Our Time* (Garden City, NY: Doubleday, 1976); older but dramatically written is Eric F. Goldman, *The Crucial Decade and After* (New York: Random House, 1960). Although pedestrian in presentation, the *Memoirs of Harry Truman,* 2 vols. (Garden City, NY: Doubleday, 1958), are a must for the immediate postwar years. A most readable memoir on foreign policy for these years is Dean Acheson, *Present at the Creation* (New York: Norton, 1969). The best study of Truman is Robert J. Donovan, *Conflict and Crisis: The Presidency of Harry S Truman, 1945–1948* (New York: Norton, 1977). For critical appraisal of the Truman years see Barton J. Bernstein, ed., *Politics and Policies of the Truman Administration* (New York: Watts, 1970). Less critical and broader in coverage is Alonzo L. Hamby, *Beyond the New Deal: Harry S Truman and American Liberalism* (New York: Columbia University Press, 1973). Susan M. Hartmann, *Truman and the Eightieth Congress* (Columbia: University of Missouri Press, 1971), is one of several good monographs now appearing on special aspects of those years. The Hiss case had been analyzed exhaustively in Allen Weinstein, *Perjury: The Hiss-Chambers Case* (New York: Alfred A. Knopf, 1978), finding Hiss guilty. A scholarly study, critical of both sides in the controversy over Korea, is John W. Spanier, *The Truman–MacArthur Controversy and the Korean War* (Cambridge: Harvard University Press, 1959). Richard Rovere, *Senator Joe McCarthy* (New York: Harcourt Brace Jovanovich, 1959), is the best, albeit hostile study of the Wisconsin Senator. Michael Paul Rogin, *The Intellectuals and McCarthy* (Cambridge: MIT Press, 1967), analyzes the social and political roots of McCarthyism. The whole period is dealt with dramatically in David Caute, *The Great Fear: The Anti–Communist Purge Under Truman and Eisenhower* (New York: Simon & Schuster, 1977). On Oppenheimer's case, read the dramatic Nuel P. Davis, *Lawrence and Oppenheimer* (New York: Simon & Schuster, 1968).

Of a number of general studies of international relations in the postwar years, the following are readable and reliable: Martin J. Sherwin, *A World Destroyed: The Atomic Bomb and the Grand Alliance* (New York: Random House, 1975), Louis J. Halle, *The Cold War as History* (New York: Harper & Row, 1967), John Lewis Gaddis, *The United States and the Origins of the Cold War 1941–1947* (New York: Columbia University Press, 1972), and Raymond Aron, *The Imperial Republic*, tr. Frank Jellinek (Englewood Cliffs, NJ: Prentice-Hall, 1974). Three books that try to look at Russian as well as U.S. policy are Walter LaFeber, *America, Russia, and the Cold War 1945–1966*, 3rd ed. (New York: Wiley, 1976), Adam B. Ulam, *The Rivals: America and Russia Since World War II* (New York: Viking Press, 1972), and Thomas G. Peterson, *Soviet-American Confrontation: Postwar Reconstruction and the Origins of the Cold War* (Baltimore: Johns Hopkins University Press, 1973). The most successful of all in this genre is the balanced Daniel Yergin, *Shattered Peace: The Origins of the Cold War and the National Security State* (Boston: Houghton Mifflin, 1977). Richard M. Freeland, *The Truman Doctrine and the Origins of McCarthyism* (New York: Schocken, 1972), seeks unsuccessfully to link foreign policy goals and the rise of McCarthyism. For a counter and more persuasive view see Richard M. Fried, *Men Against McCarthy* (New York: Columbia University Press, 1976), which unfortunately is misleading in its title since one of McCarthy's courageous opponents was a woman (Sen.) Margeret Chase Smith of Maine.

In addition to the Truman and Acheson memoirs already referred to, indispensable sources for the revolution in American foreign policy in the years after 1945, and interesting in themselves, are *The Forrestal Diaries,* ed. Walter Millis (New York: Viking Press, 1951), and *The Private Papers of Senator Vandenberg,* ed. Arthur H. Vandenberg, Jr. (Boston: Houghton Mifflin, 1952). In somewhat shrill tones Norman A. Graebner, *The New Isolationism* (New York: Ronald Press, 1956), tells the story of the fight for internationalism in the 1950s. Important in that story is the critical *The Devil and John Foster Dulles* (Boston: Little, Brown, 1973), by Townsend Hoopes.

The fullest biography of Eisenhower is the overlong Peter Lyon, *Eisenhower: Portrait of the Hero* (Boston: Little, Brown, 1974); less critical is Herbert S. Parmet, *Eisenhower and the American Crusades* (New York: Macmillan, 1972). See also Robert L. Branyan and Lawrence H. Larsen, eds., *The Eisenhower Administration 1953–1961: A Documentary History,* 2 vols. (New York: Random House, 1971), which covers most issues. Full of accurate and important private information on the administration is Robert J. Donovan's friendly report, *Eisenhower: The Inside Story* (New York: Harper & Row, 1956). Emmett Hughes, *The Ordeal of Power* (New York: Atheneum, 1963), is by someone inside the administration who soon became disenchanted. Reflective of the new appreciation of the Eisenhower presidency is Charles C. Alexander, *The Eisenhower Era 1952–1961* (Bloomington: University of Indiana Press, 1975). The best entry into the various elections of this period or any other is Arthur M. Schlesinger, Jr., and F. L. Israel, *History of American Presidential Elections,* 4 vols. (New York: McGraw-Hill, 1971). The campaigns of 1960 and 1964 have been reported in fluid if purple prose in Theodore White, *The Making of the President 1960* and *The Making of the President 1964* (New York: Atheneum, 1961, 1965). For a similar treatment of the election of 1968, but from the view of English journalists, see Lewis Chester et al., *An American Melodrama* (New York: Viking Press, 1969).

The best biography of Kennedy prior to the presidency is James M. Burns, *John Kennedy: A Political Profile* (New York: Harcourt Brace Jovanovich, 1960). His presidency has been detailed by admiring former associates in Theodore C. Sorenson, *Kennedy* (New York: Harper & Row, 1965), and Arthur Schlesinger, Jr., *A Thousand Days* (Boston: Houghton Mifflin, 1965). The best study of Kennedy's encounter with the U.S.S.R. over Cuba is Herbert S. Dinerstein, *The Making of a Missile Crisis: October, 1962,* (Baltimore: Johns Hopkins University Press, 1978). Critical of Kennedy are Richard J. Walton, *Cold War and Counter-Revolution* (New York: Viking Press, 1972), and Henry Fairlie, *The Kennedy Promise: The Politics of Expectation* (Garden City, NY: Doubleday, 1973). Balanced and thoughtful, but essentially pro–Kennedy, is Carl M. Brauer, *John F. Kennedy and the Second Reconstruction* (New York: Columbia University Press, 1977). More critical is Jim F. Heath, *Decade of Disillusionment: The Kennedy–Johnson Years* (Bloomington: University of Indiana Press, 1975). The best study so far of Johnson's administration is Robert D. Novak and Rowland Evans, Jr., *Lyndon B. Johnson: The Exercise of Power* (New York: New American Library, 1966); it is critical, but fair. More favorable is Sam A. Levitan and Robert Taggart, *The Promise of Greatness* (Cambridge: Harvard University Press, 1976), which defends the effectiveness of the Johnson programs. More from the inside is Eric F. Goldman, *The Tragedy of Lyndon Johnson* (New York: Dell, 1969). The best book on any recent President is Garry Wills, *Nixon Agonistes: The Crisis of the Self-Made Man* (Boston: Houghton Mifflin, 1970), which puts Nixon in a broad ideological framework. Bruce Mazlish, *In Search of Nixon: A Psychohistorical Inquiry* (New York: Basic Books, 1972), is not entirely successful, but it is readable. An engrossing account of the unraveling of the Watergate scandal is Bob Woodward and Carl Bernstein, *All the President's Men* (New York: Simon & Schuster, 1974); the best overall unraveling of the scandal is J. Anthony Lukas, *Nightmare: The Underside of the Nixon Years* (New York: Viking Press, 1976). Theodore White, *Breach of Faith* (New York: Atheneum, 1975), reveals the observer's shock at the scandal; Arthur M. Schlesinger, Jr., *Imperial Presidency* (Boston: Houghton Mifflin, 1973), puts the Nixon presidency in historical context; Rowland Evans, Jr., and Robert D. Novak, *Nixon in the White House* (New York: Random House, 1971), portrays the early years; and William Safire, *Before the Fall* (Garden City, NY: Doubleday, 1975), defends Nixon. A surprisingly strong defense is made in Richard Nixon, *RN: The Memoirs of Richard Nixon* (New York: Grosset and Dunlap, 1978). Jonathan Schell, *The Time of Illusion* (New York: Alfred A. Knopf, 1976), puts the whole episode of Watergate into a broad perspective and with balanced prose. Admiring of Ford is Jerald F. Terhorst, *Gerald Ford and the Future of the Presidency* (New York: The Third Press, 1974), by his press secretary, who resigned over the pardoning of Nixon. More jaundiced is Richard Reeves, *A Ford, Not a Lincoln* (New York: Harcourt Brace Jovanovich, 1975). The best study so far of Carter is James Wooten, *Dasher: The Roots and the Rising of Jimmy Carter* (New York: Summit Books, 1978). Excellent on political developments since the 1960s is Everett C. Ladd, Jr., and Charles D. Hadley, *Transformations of the American Party System: Political Coalitions from the New Deal to the 1970s* (New York: Norton, 1978).

*Denotes availability in paperback.

Appendices

THE DECLARATION OF INDEPENDENCE
In Congress, July 4, 1776

*The Unanimous Declaration
of the thirteen United States of America,*

When in the Course of human events, it becomes necessary for one people to dissolve the political bands which have connected them with another, and to assume among the Powers of the earth, the separate and equal station to which the Laws of Nature and of Nature's God entitle them, a decent respect to the opinions of mankind requires that they should declare the causes which impel them to the separation.

We hold these truths to be self-evident, that all men are created equal, that they are endowed by their Creator with certain unalienable Rights, that among these are Life, Liberty and the pursuit of Happiness. That to secure these rights, Governments are instituted among Men, deriving their just powers from the consent of the governed, That whenever any Form of Government becomes destructive of these ends, it is the Right of the People to alter or to abolish it, and to institute new Government, laying its foundation on such principles and organizing its powers in such form, as to them shall seem most likely to effect their Safety and Happiness. Prudence, indeed, will dictate that Governments long established should not be changed for light and transient causes; and accordingly all experience hath shown, that mankind are more disposed to suffer, while evils are sufferable, than to right themselves by abolishing the forms to which they are accustomed. But when a long train of abuses and usurpations, pursuing invariably the same Object evinces a design to reduce them under absolute Despotism, it is their right, it is their duty, to throw off such Government, and to provide new Guards for their future security.— Such has been the patient sufferance of these Colonies; and such is now the necessity which constrains them to alter their former Systems of Government. The history of the present King of Great Britain is a history of repeated injuries and usurpations, all having in direct object the establishment of an absolute Tyranny over these States. To prove this, let Facts be submitted to a candid world.

He has refused his Assent to Laws, the most wholesome and necessary for the public good.

He has forbidden his Governors to pass Laws of immediate and pressing importance, unless suspended in their operation till his Assent should be obtained; and when so suspended, he has utterly neglected to attend to them.

He has refused to pass other Laws for the accommodation of large districts of people, unless those people would relinquish the right of Representation in the Legislature, a right inestimable to them and formidable to tyrants only.

He has called together legislative bodies at places unusual, uncomfortable, and distant from the depository of their Public Records, for the sole purpose of fatiguing them into compliance with his measures.

He has dissolved Representative Houses repeatedly, for opposing with manly firmness his invasions on the rights of the people.

He has refused for a long time, after such dissolutions, to cause others to be elected; whereby the Legislative Powers, incapable of Annihilation, have returned to the People at large for their exercise; the State remaining in the mean time exposed to all the dangers of invasion from without, and convulsions within.

He has endeavoured to prevent the population of these States; for that purpose obstructing the Laws for Naturalization of Foreigners; refusing to pass others to encourage their migrations hither, and raising the conditions of new Appropriations of Lands.

He has obstructed the Administration of Justice, by refusing his Assent to Laws for establishing Judiciary Powers.

He has made Judges dependent on his Will alone, for the tenure of their offices, and the amount and payment of their salaries.

He has erected a multitude of New Offices, and sent hither swarms of Officers to harass our people, and eat out their substance.

He has kept among us, in times of peace, Standing Armies without the Consent of our legislatures.

He has affected to render the Military independent of and superior to the Civil Power.

He has combined with others to subject us to a jurisdiction foreign to our constitution, and unacknowledged by our laws; giving his Assent to their acts of pretended Legislation:

For quartering large bodies of armed troops among us:

For protecting them, by a mock Trial, from Punishment for any Murders which they should commit on the Inhabitants of these States:

For cutting off our Trade with all parts of the world:

For imposing taxes on us without our Consent:

For depriving us in many cases, of the benefits of Trial by Jury:

For transporting us beyond Seas to be tried for pretended offences:

For abolishing the free System of English Laws in a neighbouring Province, establishing therein an Arbitrary government, and enlarging its Boundaries so as to render it at once an example and fit instrument for introducing the same absolute rule into these Colonies:

For taking away our Charters, abolishing our most valuable Laws, and altering fundamentally the Forms of our Governments:

For suspending our own Legislatures, and declaring themselves invested with Power to legislate for us in all cases whatsoever.

He has abdicated Government here, by declaring us out of his Protection and waging War against us.

He has plundered our seas, ravaged our Coasts, burnt our towns, and destroyed the lives of our people.

He is at this time transporting large armies of foreign mercenaries to compleat the works of death, desolation and tyranny, already begun with circumstances of Cruelty & perfidy scarcely paralleled in the most barbarous ages, and totally unworthy the Head of a civilized nation.

He has constrained our fellow Citizens taken Captive on the high Seas to bear Arms against their Country, to become the executioners of their friends and Brethren, or to fall themselves by their Hands.

He has excited domestic insurrections amongst us, and has endeavoured to bring on the inhabitants of our frontiers, the merciless Indian Savages, whose known rule of warfare, is an undistinguished destruction of all ages, sexes and conditions.

In every stage of these Oppressions We have Petitioned for Redress in the most humble terms: Our repeated Petitions have been answered only by repeated injury. A Prince, whose character is thus marked by every act which may define a Tyrant, is unfit to be the ruler of a free people.

Nor have We been wanting in attentions to our British brethren. We have warned them from time to time of attempts by their legislature to extend an unwarrantable jurisdiction over us. We have reminded them of the circumstances of our emigration and settlement here. We have appealed to their native justice and magnanimity, and we have conjured them by the ties of our common kindred to disavow these usurpations which, would inevitably interrupt our connections and correspondence. They too have been deaf to the voice of justice and of consanguinity. We must, therefore, acquiesce in the necessity, which denounces our Separation, and hold them, as we hold the rest of mankind, Enemies in War, in Peace Friends.

We, therefore, the Representatives of the united States of America, in General Congress, Assembled, appealing to the Supreme Judge of the world for the rectitude of our intentions, do, in the Name, and by authority of the good People of these Colonies, solemnly publish and declare,

That these United Colonies are, and of Right ought to be Free and Independent States; that they are Absolved from all Allegiance to the British Crown, and that all political connection between them and the State of Great Britain, is and ought to be totally dissolved; and that as Free and Independent States, they have full power to levy War, conclude Peace, contract Alliances, establish Commerce, and to do all other Acts and Things which Independent States may of right do. And for the support of this Declaration, with a firm reliance on the Protection of Divine Providence, we mutually pledge to each other our Lives, our Fortunes and our sacred Honor.

JOHN HANCOCK	GEO. TAYLOR
BUTTON GWINNETT	JAMES WILSON
LYMAN HALL	GEO. ROSS
GEO. WALTON	CAESAR RODNEY
WM. HOOPER	GEO. READ
JOSEPH HEWES	THO. M'KEAN
JOHN PENN	WM. FLOYD
EDWARD RUTLEDGE	PHIL. LIVINGSTON
THOS. HEYWARD, Junr.	FRANS. LEWIS
THOMAS LYNCH, Junr.	LEWIS MORRIS
ARTHUR MIDDLETON	RICHD. STOCKTON
SAMUEL CHASE	JNO. WITHERSPOON
WM. PACA	FRAS. HOPKINSON
THOS. STONE	JOHN HART
CHARLES CARROLL	ABRA. CLARK
OF CARROLLTON	JOSIAH BARTLETT
GEORGE WYTHE	WM. WHIPPLE
RICHARD HENRY LEE	SAML. ADAMS
TH. JEFFERSON	JOHN ADAMS
BENJ. HARRISON	ROBT. TREAT PAINE
THOS. NELSON, JR.	ELBRIDGE GERRY
FRANCIS LIGHTFOOT LEE	STEP. HOPKINS
CARTER BRAXTON	WILLIAM ELLERY
ROBT. MORRIS	ROGER SHERMAN
BENJAMIN RUSH	SAM'EL. HUNTINGTON
BENJA. FRANKLIN	WM. WILLIAMS
JOHN MORTON	OLIVER WOLCOTT
GEO. CLYMER	MATTHEW THORNTON
JAS. SMITH	

THE CONSTITUTION OF
THE UNITED STATES OF AMERICA

We the People of the United States, in Order to form a more perfect Union, establish Justice, insure domestic Tranquility, provide for the common defence, promote the general Welfare, and secure the Blessings of Liberty to ourselves and our Posterity, do ordain and establish this Constitution for the United States of America.

ARTICLE I.

Section 1.

All legislative Powers herein granted shall be vested in a Congress of the United States, which shall consist of a Senate and House of Representatives.

Section 2.

The House of Representatives shall be composed of Members chosen every second Year by the People of the several States, and the Electors in each State shall have the Qualifications requisite for Electors of the most numerous Branch of the State Legislature.

No Person shall be a Representative who shall not have attained to the Age of twenty five Years, and been seven Years a Citizen of the United States, and who shall not, when elected, be an Inhabitant of that State in which he shall be chosen.

Representatives and direct Taxes shall be apportioned among the several States which may be included within this Union, according to their respective Numbers, which shall be determined by adding to the whole Number of free Persons, including those bound to Service for a Term of Years, and excluding Indians not taxed, three fifths of all other Persons.[1] The actual Enumeration shall be made within three Years after the first Meeting of the Congress of the United States, and within every subsequent Term of ten Years, in such Manner as they shall by Law direct. The Number of Representatives shall not exceed one for every thirty Thousand, but each State shall have at Least one Representative; and until such enumeration shall be made, the State of New Hampshire shall be entitled to chuse three, Massachusetts eight, Rhode-Island and Providence Plantations one, Connecticut five, New-York six, New Jersey four, Pennsylvania eight, Delaware one, Maryland six, Virginia ten, North Carolina five, South Carolina five, and Georgia three.

When vacancies happen in the Representation from any State, the Executive Authority thereof shall issue Writs of Election to fill such Vacancies.

The House of Representatives shall chuse their Speaker and other Officers; and shall have the sole Power of Impeachment.

Section 3.

The Senate of the United States shall be composed of two Senators from each State, chosen by the Legislature thereof, for six Years; and each Senator shall have one Vote.

Immediately after they shall be assembled in Consequence of the first Election, they shall be divided as equally as may be into three Classes. The Seats of the Senators of the first Class shall be vacated at the Expiration of the second Year, of the second Class at the Expiration of the fourth Year, and of the third Class at the Expiration of the sixth Year, so that one third may be chosen every second Year; and if Vacancies happen by Resignation, or otherwise, during the Recess of the Legislature of any State, the Executive thereof may make temporary Appointments until the next Meeting of the Legislature, which shall then fill such Vacancies.[2]

No Person shall be a Senator who shall not have attained to the Age of thirty Years, and been nine Years a Citizen of the United States, and who shall not, when elected, be an Inhabitant of that State for which he shall be chosen.

The Vice President of the United States shall be President of the Senate, but shall have no Vote, unless they be equally divided.

The Senate shall chuse their other Officers, and also a President pro tempore, in the Absence of the Vice President, or when he shall exercise the Office of President of the United States.

The Senate shall have the sole Power to try all Impeachments. When sitting for that Purpose, they shall be on Oath or Affirmation. When the President of the United States is tried the Chief Justice shall preside: And no Person shall be convicted without the Concurrence of two thirds of the Members present.

Judgment in Cases of Impeachment shall not extend further than to removal from Office, and disqualification to hold and enjoy any Office of honor, Trust or Profit under the United States: but the Party convicted shall nevertheless be liable and subject to Indictment, Trial, Judgment and Punishment, according to Law.

Section 4.

The Times, Places and Manner of holding Elections for Senators and Representatives, shall be prescribed in each State by the Legislature thereof; but the Congress may at

---

[1]"Other Persons" being black slaves. Modified by Amendment XIV, Section 2.

[2]Provisions changed by Amendment XVII.

any time by Law make or alter such Regulations, except as to the Places of chusing Senators.

The Congress shall assemble at least once in every Year, and such Meeting shall be on the first Monday in December, unless they shall by Law appoint a different Day.[3]

Section 5.

Each House shall be the Judge of the Elections, Returns and Qualifications of its own Members, and a Majority of each shall constitute a Quorum to do Business; but a smaller Number may adjourn from day to day, and may be authorized to compel the Attendance of absent Members, in such Manner, and under such Penalties as each House may provide.

Each House may determine the Rules of its Proceedings, punish its Members for disorderly Behaviour, and, with the Concurrence of two thirds, expel a Member.

Each House shall keep a Journal of its Proceedings, and from time to time publish the same, excepting such Parts as may in their Judgment require Secrecy; and the Yeas and Nays of the Members of either House on any question shall, at the Desire of one fifth of those Present, be entered on the Journal.

Neither House, during the Session of Congress, shall, without the Consent of the other, adjourn for more than three days, nor to any other Place than that in which the two Houses shall be sitting.

Section 6.

The Senators and Representatives shall receive a Compensation for their Services, to be ascertained by Law, and paid out of the Treasury of the United States. They shall in all Cases, except Treason, Felony and Breach of the Peace, be privileged from Arrest during their Attendance at the Session of their respective Houses, and in going to and returning from the same; and for any Speech or Debate in either House, they shall not be questioned in any other Place.

No Senator or Representative shall, during the Time for which he was elected, be appointed to any civil Office under the Authority of the United States, which shall have been created, or the Emoluments whereof shall have been encreased during such time; and no Person holding any Office under the United States, shall be a Member of either House during his Continuance in Office.

Section 7.

All Bills for raising Revenue shall originate in the House of Representatives; but the Senate may propose or concur with Amendments as on other Bills.

Every Bill which shall have passed the House of Representatives and the Senate, shall, before it become a Law, be presented to the President of the United States; If he approve he shall sign it, but if not he shall return it, with his Objections to that House in which it shall have originated, who shall enter the Objections at large on their Journal, and proceed to reconsider it. If after such Reconsideration two thirds of that House shall agree to pass the Bill, it shall be sent, together with the Objections, to the other House, by which it shall likewise be reconsidered, and if approved by two thirds of that House, it shall become a Law. But in all such Cases the Votes of both Houses shall be determined by yeas and Nays, and the Names of the Persons voting for and against the Bill shall be entered on the Journal of each House respectively. If any Bill shall not be returned by the President within ten Days (Sundays excepted) after it shall have been presented to him, the Same shall be a Law, in like Manner as if he had signed it, unless the Congress by their Adjournment prevent its Return, in which Case it shall not be a Law.

Every Order, Resolution, or Vote to which the Concurrence of the Senate and House of Representatives may be necessary (except on a question of Adjournment) shall be presented to the President of the United States; and before the Same shall take Effect, shall be approved by him, or being disapproved by him, shall be repassed by two thirds of the Senate and House of Representatives, according to the Rules and Limitations prescribed in the Case of a Bill.

Section 8.

The Congress shall have Power To lay and collect Taxes, Duties, Imposts and Excises, to pay the Debts and provide for the common Defence and general Welfare of the United States; but all Duties, Imposts and Excises shall be uniform throughout the United States;

To borrow Money on the credit of the United States;

To regulate Commerce with foreign Nations, and among the several States, and with the Indian Tribes;

To establish an uniform Rule of Naturalization, and uniform Laws on the subject of Bankruptcies throughout the United States;

To coin Money, regulate the Value thereof, and of foreign Coin, and fix the Standard of Weights and Measures;

To provide for the Punishment of counterfeiting the Securities and current Coin of the United States;

To establish Post Offices and post Roads;

To promote the Progress of Science and useful Arts, by securing for limited Times to Authors and Inventors the exclusive Right to their respective Writings and Discoveries;

To constitute Tribunals inferior to the supreme Court;

To define and punish Piracies and Felonies committed on the high Seas, and Offences against the Law of Nations;

To declare War, grant Letters of Marque and Reprisal, and make Rules concerning Captures on Land and Water;

To raise and support Armies, but no Appropriation of

---

[3]Provision changed by Amendment XX, Section 2.

Money to that Use shall be for a longer Term than two Years;

To provide and maintain a Navy;

To make Rules for the Government and Regulation of the land and naval Forces;

To provide for calling forth the Militia to execute the Laws of the Union, suppress Insurrections and repel Invasions;

To provide for organizing, arming, and disciplining, the Militia, and for governing such Part of them as may be employed in the Service of the United States, reserving to the States respectively, the Appointment of the Officers, and the Authority of training the Militia according to the discipline prescribed by Congress;

To exercise exclusive Legislation in all Cases whatsoever, over such District (not exceeding ten Miles square) as may, by Cession of particular States, and the Acceptance of Congress, become the Seat of the Government of the United States, and to exercise like Authority over all Places purchased by the Consent of the Legislature of the State in which the Same shall be, for the Erection of Forts, Magazines, Arsenals, dock-Yards, and other needful Buildings;—And

To make all Laws which shall be necessary and proper for carrying into Execution the foregoing Powers, and all other Powers vested by this Constitution in the Government of the United States, or in any Department or Officer thereof.

Section 9.

The Migration or Importation of such Persons as any of the States now existing shall think proper to admit, shall not be prohibited by the Congress prior to the Year one thousand eight hundred and eight, but a Tax or duty may be imposed on such Importation, not exceeding ten dollars for each Person.

The Privilege of the Writ of Habeas Corpus shall not be suspended, unless when in Cases of Rebellion or Invasion the public Safety may require it.

No Bill of Attainder or ex post facto Law shall be passed.

No Capitation, or other direct, Tax shall be laid, unless in Proportion to the Census or Enumeration herein before directed to be taken.

No Tax or Duty shall be laid on Articles exported from any State.

No Preference shall be given by any Regulation of Commerce or Revenue to the Ports of one State over those of another: nor shall Vessels bound to, or from, one State, be obliged to enter, clear, or pay Duties in another.

No Money shall be drawn from the Treasury, but in Consequence of Appropriations made by Law; and a regular Statement and Account of the Receipts and Expenditures of all public Money shall be published from time to time.

No Title of Nobility shall be granted by the United States: And no Person holding any Office of Profit or Trust under them, shall, without the Consent of the Congress, accept of any present, Emolument, Office, or Title, of any kind whatever, from any King, Prince, or foreign State.

Section 10.

No State shall enter into any Treaty, Alliance, or Confederation; grant Letters of Marque and Reprisal; coin Money; emit Bills of Credit; make any Thing but gold and silver Coin a Tender in Payment of Debts; pass any Bill of Attainder, ex post facto Law, or Law impairing the Obligation of Contracts, or grant any Title of Nobility.

No State shall, without the Consent of the Congress, lay any Imposts or Duties on Imports or Exports, except what may be absolutely necessary for executing its inspection Laws: and the net Produce of all Duties and Imposts, laid by any State on Imports or Exports, shall be for the Use of the Treasury of the United States; and all such Laws shall be subject to the Revision and Controul of the Congress.

No State shall, without the Consent of Congress, lay any Duty of Tonnage, keep Troops, or Ships of War in time of Peace, enter into any Agreement or Compact with another State, or with a foreign Power, or engage in War, unless actually invaded, or in such imminent Danger as will not admit of delay.

ARTICLE II.

Section 1.

The executive Power shall be vested in a President of the United States of America. He shall hold his Office during the Term of four Years, and, together with the Vice President, chosen for the same Term, be elected, as follows:

Each State shall appoint, in such Manner as the Legislature thereof may direct, a Number of Electors, equal to the whole Number of Senators and Representatives to which the State may be entitled in the Congress: but no Senator or Representative, or Person holding an Office of Trust or Profit under the United States, shall be appointed an Elector.

The Electors shall meet in their respective States, and vote by Ballot for two Persons, of whom one at least shall not be an Inhabitant of the same State with themselves. And they shall make a List of all the Persons voted for, and of the Number of Votes for each; which List they shall sign and certify, and transmit sealed to the Seat of the Government of the United States, directed to the President of the Senate. The President of the Senate shall, in the Presence of the Senate and House of Representatives, open all the Certificates, and the Votes shall then be counted. The Person having the greatest Number of Votes shall be the President, if such Number be a Majority of the whole Number of Electors appointed; and if there be more than one who have such Majority, and have an equal Number of Votes, then the House of

Representatives shall immediately chuse by Ballot one of them for President; and if no Person have a Majority, then from the five highest on the List the said House shall in like Manner chuse the President. But in chusing the President, the Votes shall be taken by States, the Representation from each State having one Vote; A quorum for this Purpose shall consist of a Member or Members from two thirds of the States, and a Majority of all the States shall be necessary to a Choice. In every Case, after the Choice of the President, the Person having the greatest Number of Votes of the Electors shall be the Vice President. But if there should remain two or more who have equal Votes, the Senate shall chuse from them by Ballot the Vice President.[4]

The Congress may determine the Time of chusing the Electors, and the Day on which they shall give their Votes; which Day shall be the same throughout the United States.

No Person except a natural born Citizen, or a Citizen of the United States, at the time of the Adoption of this Constitution, shall be eligible to the Office of President; neither shall any Person be eligible to that Office who shall not have attained to the Age of thirty five Years, and been fourteen Years a Resident within the United States.

In Case of the Removal of the President from Office, or of his Death, Resignation, or Inability to discharge the Powers and Duties of the said Office, the Same shall devolve on the Vice President, and the Congress may by Law provide for the Case of Removal, Death, Resignation or Inability, both of the President and Vice President, declaring what Officer shall then act as President, and such Officer shall act accordingly, until the Disability be removed, or a President shall be elected.

The President shall, at stated Times, receive for his Services, a Compensation, which shall neither be encreased nor diminished during the Period for which he shall have been elected, and he shall not receive within that Period any other Emolument from the United States, or any of them.

Before he enter on the Execution of his Office, he shall take the following Oath or Affirmation:—"I do solemnly swear (or affirm) that I will faithfully execute the Office of President of the United States, and will to the best of my Ability, preserve, protect and defend the Constitution of the United States."

Section 2.

The President shall be Commander in Chief of the Army and Navy of the United States, and of the Militia of the several States, when called into the actual Service of the United States; he may require the Opinion, in writing, of the principal Officer in each of the executive Departments, upon any Subject relating to the Duties of their respective Offices, and he shall have Power to grant

---

[4]Provisions superseded by Amendment XII.

Reprieves and Pardons for Offences against the United States, except in Cases of Impeachment.

He shall have Power, by and with the Advice and Consent of the Senate, to make Treaties, provided two thirds of the Senators present concur; and he shall nominate, and by and with the Advice and Consent of the Senate, shall appoint Ambassadors, other public Ministers and Consuls, Judges of the supreme Court, and all other Officers of the United States, whose Appointments are not herein otherwise provided for, and which shall be established by Law: but the Congress may by Law vest the Appointment of such inferior Officers, as they think proper in the President alone, in the Courts of Law, or in the Heads of Departments.

The President shall have Power to fill up all Vacancies that may happen during the Recess of the Senate, by granting Commissions which shall expire at the End of their next Session.

Section 3.

He shall from time to time give to the Congress Information of the State of the Union, and recommend to their Consideration such Measures as he shall judge necessary and expedient; he may, on extraordinary Occasions, convene both Houses, or either of them, and in Case of Disagreement between them, with Respect to the Time of Adjournment, he may adjourn them to such Time as he shall think proper; he shall receive Ambassadors and other public Ministers; he shall take Care that the Laws be faithfully executed, and shall Commission all the Officers of the United States.

Section 4.

The President, Vice President and all civil Officers of the United States, shall be removed from Office on Impeachment for, and Conviction of, Treason, Bribery, or other high Crimes and Misdemeanors.

ARTICLE III.

Section 1.

The judicial Power of the United States, shall be vested in one supreme Court, and in such inferior Courts as the Congress may from time to time ordain and establish. The Judges, both of the supreme and inferior Courts, shall hold their Offices during good Behaviour, and shall, at stated Times, receive for their Services, a Compensation, which shall not be diminished during their Continuance in Office.

Section 2.

The judicial Power shall extend to all Cases, in Law and Equity, arising under this Constitution, the Laws of the United States, and Treaties made, or which shall be made, under their Authority;—to all Cases affecting

Ambassadors, other public Ministers and Consuls;—to all Cases of admiralty and maritime Jurisdiction;—to Controversies to which the United States shall be a Party;—to Controversies between two or more States;—between a State and Citizens of another State;—between Citizens of different States,—between Citizens of the same State claiming Lands under Grants of different States, and between a State, or the Citizens thereof, and foreign States, Citizens or Subjects.[5]

In all Cases affecting Ambassadors, other public Ministers and Consuls, and those in which a State shall be Party, the supreme Court shall have original Jurisdiction. In all the other Cases before mentioned, the supreme Court shall have appellate Jurisdiction, both as to Law and Fact, with such Exceptions, and under such Regulations as the Congress shall make.

The Trial of all Crimes, except in Cases of Impeachment, shall be by Jury; and such Trial shall be held in the State where the said Crimes shall have been committed, but when not committed within any State, the Trial shall be at such Place or Places as the Congress may by Law have directed.

Section 3.

Treason against the United States, shall consist only in levying War against them, or in adhering to their Enemies, giving them Aid and Comfort. No person shall be convicted of Treason unless on the Testimony of two Witnesses to the same overt Act, or on Confession in open Court.

The Congress shall have Power to declare the Punishment of Treason, but no Attainder of Treason shall work Corruption of Blood, or Forfeiture except during the Life of the Person attainted.

ARTICLE IV.

Section 1.

Full Faith and Credit shall be given in each State to the public Acts, Records, and judicial Proceedings of every other State. And the Congress may by general Laws prescribe the Manner in which such Acts, Records and Proceedings shall be proved, and the Effect thereof.

Section 2.

The Citizens of each State shall be entitled to all Privileges and Immunities of Citizens in the several States.

A Person charged in any State with Treason, Felony, or other Crime, who shall flee from Justice, and be found in another State, shall on Demand of the executive Authority of the State from which he fled, be delivered up, to be removed to the State having Jurisdiction of the Crime.

No Person held to Service or Labour in one State, under the Laws thereof, escaping into another, shall, in Consequence of any Law or Regulation therein, be discharged from such Service or Labour, but shall be delivered up on Claim of the Party to whom such Service or Labour may be due.

Section 3.

New States may be admitted by the Congress into this Union; but no new State shall be formed or erected within the Jurisdiction of any other State; nor any State be formed by the Junction of two or more States, or Parts of States, without the Consent of the Legislatures of the States concerned as well as of the Congress.

The Congress shall have Power to dispose of and make all needful Rules and Regulations respecting the Territory or other Property belonging to the United States; and nothing in this Constitution shall be so construed as to Prejudice any Claims of the United States, or of any particular State.

Section 4.

The United States shall guarantee to every State in this Union a Republican Form of Government, and shall protect each of them against Invasion; and on Application of the Legislature, or of the Executive (when the Legislature cannot be convened) against domestic Violence.

ARTICLE V.

The Congress, whenever two thirds of both Houses shall deem it necessary, shall propose Amendments to this Constitution, or, on the Application of the Legislatures of two thirds of the several States, shall call a Convention for proposing Amendments, which, in either Case, shall be valid to all Intents and Purposes, as Part of this Constitution, when ratified by the Legislatures of three fourths of the several States, or by Conventions in three fourths thereof, as the one or the other Mode of Ratification may be proposed by the Congress; Provided that no Amendment which may be made prior to the Year One thousand eight hundred and eight shall in any Manner affect the first and fourth Clauses in the Ninth Section of the first Article; and that no State, without its Consent, shall be deprived of its equal Suffrage in the Senate.

ARTICLE VI.

All Debts contracted and Engagements entered into, before the Adoption of this Constitution, shall be as valid against the United States under this Constitution, as under the Confederation.

---

[5]Clause changed by Amendment XI.

This Constitution, and the Laws of the United States which shall be made in Pursuance thereof; and all Treaties made, or which shall be made, under the Authority of the United States, shall be the supreme Law of the Land; and the Judges in every State shall be bound thereby, any Thing in the Constitution or Laws of any State to the Contrary notwithstanding.

The Senators and Representatives before mentioned, and the Members of the several State Legislatures, and all executive and judicial Officers, both of the United States and of the several States, shall be bound by Oath or Affirmation, to support this Constitution; but no religious Test shall ever be required as a Qualification to any Office or public Trust under the United States.

[6]The Constitution was submitted on September 17, 1787, by the Constitutional Convention, was ratified by the conventions of several states at various dates up to May 29, 1790, and became effective on March 4, 1789.

ARTICLE VII.

The Ratification of the Conventions of nine States, shall be sufficient for the Establishment of this Constitution between the States so ratifying the Same.

done in Convention by the Unanimous Consent of the States present the Seventeenth Day of September in the Year of our Lord one thousand seven hundred and Eighty seven and of the Independence of the United States of America the Twelfth[6] IN WITNESS whereof We have hereunto subscribed our Names,

GEORGE WASHINGTON,
President and Deputy
from Virginia

New Hampshire
JOHN LANGDON
NICHOLAS GILMAN
Massachusetts
NATHANIEL GORHAM
RUFUS KING
Connecticut
WILLIAM S. JOHNSON
ROGER SHERMAN
New York
ALEXANDER HAMILTON
New Jersey
WILLIAM LIVINGSTON
DAVID BREARLEY
WILLIAM PATERSON
JONATHAN DAYTON
Pennsylvania
BENJAMIN FRANKLIN
THOMAS MIFFLIN
ROBERT MORRIS
GEORGE CLYMER
THOMAS FITZSIMONS
JARED INGERSOLL
JAMES WILSON
GOUVERNEUR MORRIS

Delaware
GEORGE READ
GUNNING BEDFORD, JR.
JOHN DICKINSON
RICHARD BASSETT
JACOB BROOM
Maryland
JAMES McHENRY
DANIEL OF ST. THOMAS JENIFER
DANIEL CARROLL
Virginia
JOHN BLAIR
JAMES MADISON, JR.
North Carolina
WILLIAM BLOUNT
RICHARD DOBBS SPRAIGHT
HU WILLIAMSON
South Carolina
J. RUTLEDGE
CHARLES C. PINCKNEY
PIERCE BUTLER
Georgia
WILLIAM FEW
ABRAHAM BALDWIN

AMENDMENTS TO THE CONSTITUTION

[AMENDMENT I]

Congress shall make no law respecting an establishment of religion, or prohibiting the free exercise thereof; or abridging the freedom of speech, or of the press; or the right of the people peaceably to assemble, and to petition the Government for a redress of grievances.

[AMENDMENT II]

A well regulated Militia being necessary to the security of a free State, the right of the people to keep and bear Arms, shall not be infringed.

[AMENDMENT III]

No Soldier shall, in time of peace be quartered in any house, without the consent of the Owner, nor in time of war, but in a manner to be prescribed by law.

[AMENDMENT IV]

The right of the people to be secure in their persons, houses, papers, and effects, against unreasonable searches and seizures, shall not be violated, and no Warrants shall issue, but upon probable cause, supported by Oath or affirmation, and particularly describing the place to be searched, and the persons or things to be seized.

[AMENDMENT V]

No person shall be held to answer for a capital, or otherwise infamous crime, unless on a presentment or indictment of a Grand Jury, except in cases arising in the land or naval forces, or in the Militia, when in actual service in time of War or public danger; nor shall any person be subject for the same offense to be twice put in jeopardy of life or limb; nor shall be compelled in any criminal case to be a witness against himself, nor be deprived of life, liberty, or property, without due process of law; nor shall private property be taken for public use, without just compensation.

[AMENDMENT VI]

In all criminal prosecutions, the accused shall enjoy the right to a speedy and public trial, by an impartial jury of the State and district wherein the crime shall have been committed, which district shall have been previously ascertained by law, and to be informed of the nature and cause of the accusation; to be confronted with the witnesses against him; to have compulsory process for obtaining witnesses in his favor, and to have the Assistance of Counsel for his defence.

[AMENDMENT VII]

In Suits at common law, where the value in controversy shall exceed twenty dollars, the right of trial by jury shall be preserved, and no fact tried by a jury, shall be otherwise re-examined in any Court of the United States, than according to the rules of the common law.

[AMENDMENT VIII]

Excessive bail shall not be required, nor excessive fines imposed, nor cruel and unusual punishments inflicted.

[AMENDMENT IX]

The enumeration in the Constitution, of certain rights, shall not be construed to deny or disparage others retained by the people.

[AMENDMENT X]

The powers not delegated to the United States by the Constitution, nor prohibited by it to the States, are reserved to the States respectively, or to the people.[7]

[AMENDMENT XI]

The Judicial power of the United States shall not be construed to extend to any suit in law or equity, commenced or prosecuted against one of the United States by Citizens of another State, or by Citizens or Subjects of any Foreign State.[8]

[AMENDMENT XII]

The Electors shall meet in their respective states, and vote by ballot for President and Vice-President, one of

---

[7]The first ten amendments were all proposed by Congress on September 25, 1789, and were ratified and adoption certified on December 15, 1791.

[8]Proposed by Congress on March 4, 1794, and declared ratified on January 8, 1798.

whom, at least, shall not be an inhabitant of the same state with themselves; they shall name in their ballots the person voted for as President, and in distinct ballots the person voted for as Vice-President, and they shall make distinct lists of all persons voted for as President, and of all persons voted for as Vice-President, and of the number of votes for each, which lists they shall sign and certify, and transmit sealed to the seat of the government of the United States, directed to the President of the Senate;— The President of the Senate shall, in the presence of the Senate and House of Representatives, open all the certificates and the votes shall then be counted;—The person having the greatest number of votes for President, shall be the President, if such number be a majority of the whole number of Electors appointed; and if no person have such majority, then from the persons having the highest numbers not exceeding three on the list of those voted for as President, the House of Representatives shall choose immediately, by ballot, the President. But in choosing the President, the votes shall be taken by states, the representation from each state having one vote; a quorum for this purpose shall consist of a member or members from two-thirds of the states, and a majority of all the states shall be necessary to a choice. And if the House of Representatives shall not choose a President whenever the right of choice shall devolve upon them, before the fourth day of March next following, then the Vice-President shall act as President, as in the case of the death or other constitutional disability of the President.—The person having the greatest number of votes as Vice-President, shall be the Vice-President, if such number be a majority of the whole number of Electors appointed, and if no person have a majority, then from the two highest numbers on the list, the Senate shall choose the Vice-President; a quorum for the purpose shall consist of two-thirds of the whole number of Senators, and a majority of the whole number shall be necessary to a choice. But no person constitutionally ineligible to the office of President shall be eligible to that of Vice-President of the United States.[9]

[AMENDMENT XIII]

Section 1.

Neither slavery nor involuntary servitude, except as a punishment for crime whereof the party shall have been duly convicted, shall exist within the United States, or any place subject to their jurisdiction.

Section 2.

Congress shall have power to enforce this article by appropriate legislation.[10]

---

[9]Proposed by Congress on December 9, 1803; declared ratified on September 25, 1804; supplemented by Amendments XX and XXIII.

[10]Proposed by Congress on January 31, 1865; declared ratified on December 18, 1865.

[AMENDMENT XIV]

Section 1.

All persons born or naturalized in the United States, and subject to the jurisdiction thereof, are citizens of the United States and of the State wherein they reside. No State shall make or enforce any law which shall abridge the privileges or immunities of citizens of the United States; nor shall any State deprive any person of life, liberty, or property, without due process of law; nor deny to any person within its jurisdiction the equal protection of the laws.

Section 2.

Representatives shall be apportioned among the several States according to their respective numbers, counting the whole number of persons in each State, excluding Indians not taxed. But when the right to vote at any election for the choice of electors for President and Vice-President of the United States, Representatives in Congress, the Executive and Judicial officers of a State, or the members of the Legislature thereof, is denied to any of the male inhabitants of such State, being twenty-one years of age, and citizens of the United States, or in any way abridged, except for participation in rebellion, or other crime, the basis of representation therein shall be reduced in the proportion which the number of such male citizens shall bear to the whole number of male citizens twenty-one years of age in such State.

Section 3.

No person shall be a Senator or Representative in Congress, or elector of President and Vice President, or hold any office, civil or military, under the United States, or under any State, who, having previously taken an oath, as a member of Congress, or as an officer of the United States, or as a member of any State legislature, or as an executive or judicial officer of any State, to support the Constitution of the United States, shall have engaged in insurrection or rebellion against the same, or given aid or comfort to the enemies thereof. But Congress may by a vote of two-thirds of each House, remove such disability.

Section 4.

The validity of the public debt of the United States, authorized by law, including debts incurred for payment of pensions and bounties for services in suppressing insurrection or rebellion, shall not be questioned. But neither the United States nor any State shall assume or pay any debt or obligation incurred in aid of insurrection or rebellion against the United States, or any claim for the loss or emancipation of any slave; but all such debts, obligations and claims shall be held illegal and void.

736

Section 5.

The Congress shall have power to enforce, by appropriate legislation, the provisions of this article.[11]

[AMENDMENT XV]

Section 1.

The right of citizens of the United States to vote shall not be denied or abridged by the United States or by any State on account of race, color, or previous condition of servitude.

Section.

The Congress shall have power to enforce this article by appropriate legislation.[12]

[AMENDMENT XVI]

The Congress shall have power to lay and collect taxes on incomes, from whatever source derived, without apportionment among the several States, and without regard to any census or enumeration.[13]

[AMENDMENT XVII]

The Senate of the United States shall be composed of two Senators from each State, elected by the people thereof, for six years; and each Senator shall have one vote. The electors in each State shall have the qualifications requisite for electors of the most numerous branch of the State legislatures.

When vacancies happen in the representation of any State in the Senate, the executive authority of such State shall issue writs of election to fill such vacancies: *Provided,* That the legislature of any State may empower the executive thereof to make temporary appointments until the people fill the vacancies by election as the legislature may direct.

This amendment shall not be so construed as to affect the election or term of any Senator chosen before it becomes valid as part of the Constitution.[14]

[11]Proposed by Congress on June 13, 1866; declared ratified on July 28, 1868.

[12]Proposed by Congress on February 26, 1869; declared ratified on March 30, 1870.

[13]Proposed by Congress on July 12, 1909; declared ratified on February 25, 1913.

[14]Proposed by Congress on May 13, 1912; declared ratified on May 31, 1913.

[AMENDMENT XVIII]

Section 1.

After one year from the ratification of this article the manufacture, sale, or transportation of intoxicating liquors within, the importation thereof into, or the exportation thereof from the United States and all territory subject to the jurisdiction thereof for beverage purposes is hereby prohibited.

Section 2.

The Congress and the several States shall have concurrent power to enforce this article by appropriate legislation.

Section 3.

This article shall be inoperative unless it shall have been ratified as an amendment to the Constitution by the legislatures of the several States, as provided in the Constitution, within seven years from the date of the submission hereof to the States by the Congress.[15]

[AMENDMENT XIX]

The right of citizens of the United States to vote shall not be denied or abridged by the United States or by any State on account of sex.

Congress shall have power to enforce this article by appropriate legislation.[16]

[AMENDMENT XX]

Section 1.

The terms of the President and Vice President shall end at noon on the 20th day of January, and the terms of Senators and Representatives at noon on the 3d day of January, of the years in which such terms would have ended if this article had not been ratified; and the terms of their successors shall then begin.

Section 2.

The Congress shall assemble at least once in every year, and such meeting shall begin at noon on the 3d day of January, unless they shall by law appoint a different day.

[15]Proposed by Congress on December 18, 1917; declared ratified on January 29, 1919; repealed by Amendment XXI.

[16]Proposed by Congress on June 4, 1919; declared ratified on August 26, 1920.

Section 3.

If, at the time fixed for the beginning of the term of the President, the President elect shall have died, the Vice President elect shall become President. If a President shall not have been chosen before the time fixed for the beginning of his term, or if the President elect shall have failed to qualify, then the Vice President elect shall act as President until a President shall have qualified; and the Congress may by law provide for the case wherein neither a President elect nor a Vice President elect shall have qualified, declaring who shall then act as President, or the manner in which one who is to act shall be selected, and such person shall act accordingly until a President or Vice President shall have qualified.

Section 4.

The Congress may by law provide for the case of the death of any of the persons from whom the House of Representatives may choose a President whenever the right of choice shall have devolved upon them, and for the case of the death of any of the persons from whom the Senate may choose a Vice President whenever the right of choice shall have devolved upon them.

Section 5.

Sections 1 and 2 shall take effect on the 15th day of October following the ratification of this article.

Section 6.

This article shall be inoperative unless it shall have been ratified as an amendment to the Constitution by the legislatures of three-fourths of the several States within seven years from the date of its submission.[17]

[AMENDMENT XXI]

Section 1.

The eighteenth article of amendment to the Constitution of the United States is hereby repealed.

Section 2.

The transportation or importation into any States, Territory, or possession of the United States for delivery or use therein of intoxicating liquors, in violation of the laws thereof, is hereby prohibited.

Section 3.

This article shall be inoperative unless it shall have been ratified as an amendment to the Constitution by

conventions in the several States, as provided in the Constitution, within seven years from the date of the submission hereof to the States by the Congress.[18]

[AMENDMENT XXII]

Section 1.

No person shall be elected to the office of the President more than twice, and no person who has held the office of President, or acted as President, for more than two years of a term to which some other person was elected President shall be elected to the office of the President more than once. But this Article shall not apply to any person holding the office of President when this Article was proposed by the Congress, and shall not prevent any person who may be holding the office of President, or acting as President, during the term within which this Article becomes operative from holding the office of President or acting as President during the remainder of such term.

Section 2.

This article shall be inoperative unless it shall have been ratified as an amendment to the Constitution by the legislatures of three-fourths of the several States within seven years from the date of its submission to the States by the Congress.[19]

[AMENDMENT XXIII]

Section 1.

The District constituting the seat of Government of the United States shall appoint in such manner as the Congress shall direct:

A number of electors of President and Vice President equal to the whole number of Senators and Representatives in Congress to which the District would be entitled if it were a State, but in no event more than the least populous State; they shall be in addition to those appointed by the States, but they shall be considered, for the purposes of the election of President and Vice President, to be electors appointed by a State; and they shall meet in the District and perform such duties as provided by the twelfth article of amendment.

Section 2.

The Congress shall have power to enforce this article by appropriate legislation.[20]

---

[17]Proposed by Congress on March 2, 1932; declared ratified on February 6, 1933.

[18]Proposed by Congress on February 20, 1933; declared ratified on December 5, 1933.

[19]Proposed by Congress on March 24, 1947; declared ratified on March 1, 1951.

[20]Proposed by Congress on June 16, 1960; declared ratified on April 3, 1961.

[AMENDMENT XXIV]

Section 1.

The right of citizens of the United States to vote in any primary or other election for President or Vice President, for electors for President or Vice President, or for Senator or Representative in Congress, shall not be denied or abridged by the United States or any state by reason of failure to pay any poll tax or other tax.

Section 2.

The Congress shall have the power to enforce this article by appropriate legislation.[21]

[AMENDMENT XXV]

Section 1.

In case of the removal of the President from office or his death or resignation, the Vice President shall become President.

Section 2.

Whenever there is a vacancy in the office of the Vice President, the President shall nominate a Vice President who shall take the office upon confirmation by a majority vote of both houses of Congress.

Section 3.

Whenever the President transmits to the President pro tempore of the Senate and the Speaker of the House of Representatives his written declaration that he is unable to discharge the powers and duties of his office, and until he transmits to them a written declaration to the contrary, such powers and duties shall be discharged by the Vice President as Acting President.

Section 4.

Whenever the Vice President and a majority of either the principal officers of the executive departments or of such other body as Congress may by law provide, trans-

mit to the President pro tempore of the Senate and the Speaker of the House of Representatives their written declaration that the President is unable to discharge the powers and duties of his office, the Vice President shall immediately assume the powers and duties of the office as Acting President.

Thereafter, when the President transmits to the President pro tempore of the Senate and the Speaker of the House of Representatives his written declaration that no inability exists, he shall resume the powers and duties of his office unless the Vice President and a majority of either the principal officers of the executive department or of such other body as Congress may by law provide, transmit within four days to the President pro tempore of the Senate and the Speaker of the House of Representatives their written declaration that the President is unable to discharge the powers and duties of his office. Thereupon Congress shall decide the issue, assembling within 48 hours for that purpose if not in session. If the Congress, within 21 days after receipt of the latter written declaration, or, if Congress is not in session, within 21 days after Congress is required to assemble, determines by two-thirds vote of both houses that the President is unable to discharge the powers and duties of his office, the Vice President shall continue to discharge the same as Acting President; otherwise, the President shall resume the powers and duties of his office.[22]

[AMENDMENT XXVI]

Section 1.

The right of citizens of the United States, who are 18 years of age or older, to vote shall not be denied or abridged by the United States or any state on account of age.

Section 2.

The Congress shall have the power to enforce this article by appropriate legislation.[23]

---

[21]Proposed by Congress on August 27, 1962; declared ratified on January 23, 1963.

[22]Proposed by Congress on July 6, 1965; declared ratified on February 10, 1967.

[23]Proposed by Congress on March 23, 1971; declared ratified on June 30, 1971.

PRESIDENTIAL ELECTIONS*: ELECTORAL AND POPULAR VOTE

Presidential Candidate[1]	Electoral Vote	Popular Vote	Presidential Candidate[1]	Electoral Vote	Popular Vote
1789[2]: 11 States			S. Johnston	2	
GEORGE WASHINGTON	69		*Independent-Federalist*		
John Adams	34		C. C. Pinckney	1	
John Jay	9		*Independent-Federalist*		
R. H. Harrison	6				
John Rutledge	6		**1800[2]: 16 States**		
John Hancock	4		THOMAS JEFFERSON	73	
George Clinton	3		*Republican*		
Samuel Huntington	2		Aaron Burr	73	
John Milton	2		*Republican*		
James Armstrong	1		John Adams	65	
Benjamin Lincoln	1		*Federalist*		
Edward Telfair	1		C. C. Pinckney	64	
(Not voted)	12		*Federalist*		
			John Jay	1	
1792[2]: 15 States			*Federalist*		
GEORGE WASHINGTON	132				
Federalist			**1804: 17 States**		
John Adams	77		THOMAS JEFFERSON	162	
Federalist			*Republican*		
George Clinton	50		C. C. Pinckney	14	
Republican			*Federalist*		
Thomas Jefferson	4				
Aaron Burr	1				
			1808: 17 States		
1796[2]: 16 States			JAMES MADISON	122	
JOHN ADAMS	71		*Republican*		
Federalist			C. C. Pinckney	47	
Thomas Jefferson	68		*Federalist*		
Republican			George Clinton	6	
Thomas Pinckney	59		*Independent-Republican*		
Federalist			(Not voted)	1	
Aaron Burr	30				
Anti-Federalist			**1812: 18 States**		
Samuel Adams	15		JAMES MADISON	128	
Republican			*Republican*		
Oliver Ellsworth	11		DeWitt Clinton	89	
Federalist			*Fusion*		
George Clinton	7		(Not voted)	1	
Republican					
John Jay	5		**1816: 19 States**		
Independent-Federalist			JAMES MONROE	183	
James Iredell	3		*Republican*		
Federalist			Rufus King	34	
George Washington	2		*Federalist*		
Federalist			(Not voted)	4	
John Henry	2				
Independent					

*Source: U.S. Bureau of the Census, *Historical Statistics of the United States, Colonial Times to 1957* (Washington, D.C., 1960).

[1] Excludes unpledged tickets and minor candidates polling under 10,000 votes; various party labels may have been used by a candidate in different states; the more important of these are listed.

[2] Prior to the election of 1804, each elector voted for two candidates for President; the one receiving the highest number of votes, if a majority, was declared elected President, the next highest, Vice-President. This provision was modified by adoption of the Twelfth Amendment which was proposed by the Eighth Congress, December 12, 1803, and declared ratified by the legislatures of three fourths of the states in a proclamation of the Secretary of State, September 25, 1804.

[3] No candidate having a majority in the electoral college, the election was decided in the House of Representatives.

PRESIDENTIAL ELECTIONS: ELECTORAL AND POPULAR VOTE

Presidential Candidate[1]	Electoral Vote	Popular Vote
1820: 24 States		
JAMES MONROE	231	
Republican		
John Quincy Adams	1	
Independent-Republican		
(Not voted)	3	
1824: 24 States		
JOHN QUINCY ADAMS	84[3]	108,740
Andrew Jackson	99[3]	153,544
Henry Clay	37	47,136
W. H. Crawford	41	46,618
1828: 24 States		
ANDREW JACKSON	178	647,286
Democratic		
John Quincy Adams	83	508,064
National Republican		
1832: 24 States		
ANDREW JACKSON	219	687,502
Democratic		
Henry Clay	49	530,189
National Republican		
William Wirt	7	
Anti-Masonic		
John Floyd	11	
Nullifiers		
(Not voted)	2	
1836: 26 States		
MARTIN VAN BUREN	170	765,483
Democratic		
William Henry Harrison	73	
Whig		
Hugh L. White	26	739,795[4]
Whig		
Daniel Webster	14	
Whig		
W. P. Mangum	11	
Anti-Jackson		
1840: 26 States		
WILLIAM HENRY HARRISON	234	1,274,624
Whig		
Martin Van Buren	60	1,127,781
Democratic		
1844: 26 States		
JAMES K. POLK	170	1,338,464
Democratic		
Henry Clay	105	1,300,097
Whig		
James G. Birney		62,300
Liberty		

Presidential Candidate[1]	Electoral Vote	Popular Vote
1848: 30 States		
ZACHARY TAYLOR	163	1,360,967
Whig		
Lewis Cass	127	1,222,342
Democratic		
Martin Van Buren		291,263
Free Soil		
1852: 31 States		
FRANKLIN PIERCE	254	1,601,117
Democratic		
Winfield Scott	42	1,385,453
Whig		
John P. Hale		155,825
Free Soil		
1856: 31 States		
JAMES BUCHANAN	174	1,832,955
Democratic		
John C. Frémont	114	1,339,932
Republican		
Millard Fillmore	8	871,731
American		
1860: 33 States		
ABRAHAM LINCOLN	180	1,865,593
Republican		
John C. Breckinridge	72	848,356
Democratic (South)		
Stephen A. Douglas	12	1,382,713
Democratic		
John Bell	39	592,906
Constitutional Union		
1864: 36 States		
ABRAHAM LINCOLN	212	2,206,938
Republican		
George B. McClellan	21	1,803,787
Democratic		
(Not voted)	81	
1868: 37 States		
ULYSSES S. GRANT	214	3,013,421
Republican		
Horatio Seymour	80	2,706,829
Democratic		
(Not voted)	23	
1872: 37 States		
ULYSSES S. GRANT	286	3,596,745
Republican		
Horace Greeley		2,843,446
Democratic		
Charles O'Conor		29,489
Straight Democratic		
Thomas A. Hendricks	42	
Independent-Democratic		

[4]Whig tickets were pledged to various candidates in various states.

[3]Greeley died shortly after the election and presidential electors supporting him cast their votes as indicated, including three for Greeley, which were not counted.

Presidential Candidate[1]	Electoral Vote	Popular Vote
B. Gratz Brown	18	
Democratic		
Charles J. Jenkins	2	
Democratic		
David Davis	1	
Democratic		
(Not voted)	17	
1876: 38 States		
RUTHERFORD B. HAYES	185	4,036,572
Republican		
Samuel J. Tilden	184	4,284,020
Democratic		
Peter Cooper		81,737
Greenback		
1880: 38 States		
JAMES A. GARFIELD	214	4,453,295
Republican		
Winfield S. Hancock	155	4,414,082
Democratic		
James B. Weaver		308,578
Greenback-Labor		
Neal Dow		10,305
Prohibition		
1884: 38 States		
GROVER CLEVELAND	219	4,879,507
Democratic		
James G. Blaine	182	4,850,293
Republican		
Benjamin F. Butler		175,370
Greenback-Labor		
John P. St. John		150,369
Prohibition		
1888: 38 States		
BENJAMIN HARRISON	233	5,447,129
Republican		
Grover Cleveland	168	5,537,857
Democratic		
Clinton B. Fisk		249,506
Prohibition		
Anson J. Streeter		146,935
Union Labor		
1892: 44 States		
GROVER CLEVELAND	277	5,555,426
Democratic		
Benjamin Harrison	145	5,182,690
Republican		
James B. Weaver	22	1,029,846
People's		
John Bidwell		264,133
Prohibition		
Simon Wing		21,164
Socialist Labor		

Presidential Candidate[1]	Electoral Vote	Popular Vote
1896: 45 States		
WILLIAM McKINLEY	271	7,102,246
Republican		
William Jennings Bryan	176	6,492,559
Democratic[6]		
John M. Palmer		133,148
National Democratic		
Joshua Levering		132,007
Prohibition		
Charles M. Matchett		36,274
Socialist Labor		
Charles E. Bentley		13,969
Nationalist		
1900: 45 States		
WILLIAM McKINLEY	292	7,218,491
Republican		
William Jennings Bryan	155	6,356,734
Democratic[6]		
John C. Wooley		208,914
Prohibition		
Eugene V. Debs		87,814
Socialist		
Wharton Barker		50,373
People's		
Joseph F. Malloney		39,739
Socialist Labor		
1904: 45 States		
THEODORE ROOSEVELT	336	7,628,461
Republican		
Alton B. Parker	140	5,084,223
Democratic		
Eugene V. Debs		402,283
Socialist		
Silas C. Swallow		258,536
Prohibition		
Thomas E. Watson		117,183
People's		
Charles H. Corregan		31,249
Socialist Labor		
1908: 46 States		
WILLIAM HOWARD TAFT	321	7,675,320
Republican		
William Jennings Bryan	162	6,412,294
Democratic		
Eugene V. Debs		420,793
Socialist		
Eugene W. Chafin		253,840
Prohibition		
Thomas L. Hisgen		82,872
Independence		
Thomas E. Watson		29,100
People's		
August Gillhaus		14,021
Socialist Labor		

[6]Includes a variety of joint tickets with People's party electors commited to Bryan.

PRESIDENTIAL ELECTIONS: ELECTORAL AND POPULAR VOTE

Presidential Candidate[1]	Electoral Vote	Popular Vote
1912: 48 States		
WOODROW WILSON	435	6,296,547
Democratic		
Theodore Roosevelt	88	4,118,571
Progressive		
William Howard Taft	8	3,486,720
Republican		
Eugene V. Debs		900,672
Socialist		
Eugene W. Chafin		206,275
Prohibition		
Arthur E. Reimer		28,750
Socialist Labor		
1916: 48 States		
WOODROW WILSON	277	9,127,695
Democratic		
Charles Evans Hughes	254	8,533,507
Republican		
A. L. Benson		585,113
Socialist		
J. Frank Hanly		220,506
Prohibition		
Arthur E. Reimer		13,403
Socialist Labor		
1920: 48 States		
WARREN G. HARDING	404	16,143,407
Republican		
James M. Cox	127	9,130,328
Democratic		
Eugene V. Debs		919,799
Socialist		
P. P. Christensen		265,411
Farmer-Labor		
Aaron S. Watkins		189,408
Prohibition		
James E. Ferguson		48,000
American		
W. W. Cox		31,715
Socialist Labor		
1924: 48 States		
CALVIN COOLIDGE	382	15,718,211
Republican		
John W. Davis	136	8,385,283
Democratic		
Robert M. La Follette	13	4,831,289
Progressive		
Herman P. Faris		57,520
Prohibition		
Frank T. Johns		36,428
Socialist Labor		
William Z. Foster		36,386
Workers		
Gilbert O. Nations		23,967
American		
1928: 48 States		
HERBERT HOOVER	444	21,391,993
Republican		
Alfred E. Smith	87	15,016,196
Democratic		
Norman Thomas		267,835
Socialist		

Presidential Candidate[1]	Electoral Vote	Popular Vote
Verne L. Reynolds		21,603
Socialist Labor		
William Z. Foster		21,181
Workers		
William F. Varney		20,106
Prohibition		
1932: 48 States		
FRANKLIN D. ROOSEVELT	472	22,809,638
Democratic		
Herbert Hoover	59	15,758,901
Republican		
Norman Thomas		881,951
Socialist		
William Z. Foster		102,785
Communist		
William D. Upshaw		81,869
Prohibition		
William H. Harvey		53,425
Liberty		
Verne L. Reynolds		33,276
Socialist Labor		
1936: 48 States		
FRANKLIN D. ROOSEVELT	523	27,752,869
Democratic		
Alfred M. Landon	8	16,674,665
Republican		
William Lemke		882,479
Union		
Norman Thomas		187,720
Socialist		
Earl Browder		80,159
Communist		
D. Leigh Colvin		37,847
Prohibition		
John W. Aiken		12,777
Socialist Labor		
1940: 48 States		
FRANKLIN D. ROOSEVELT	449	27,307,819
Democratic		
Wendell L. Willkie	82	22,321,018
Republican		
Norman Thomas		99,557
Socialist		
Roger Q. Babson		57,812
Prohibition		
Earl Browder		46,251
Communist		
John W. Aiken		14,892
Socialist Labor		
1944: 48 States		
FRANKLIN D. ROOSEVELT	432	25,606,585
Democratic		
Thomas E. Dewey	99	22,014,745
Republican		
Norman Thomas		80,518
Socialist		
Claude A. Watson		74,758
Prohibition		
Edward A. Teichert		45,336
Socialist Labor		

Presidential Candidate[1]	Electoral Vote	Popular Vote	Presidential Candidate	Electoral Vote	Popular Vote
1948: 48 States			**1964: 50 States and D.C.**		
HARRY S. TRUMAN	303	24,105,812	LYNDON B. JOHNSON	486	43,126,506
Democratic			*Democratic*		
Thomas E. Dewey	189	21,970,065	Barry Goldwater	52	27,176,799
Republican			*Republican*		
J. Strom Thurmond	39	1,169,063	Eric Haas		45,186
States' Rights			*Socialist Labor*		
Henry Wallace		1,157,172	Clifton DeBerry		32,705
Progressive			*Socialist Workers*		
Norman Thomas		139,414	Earle H. Munn		23,267
Socialist			*Prohibition*		
Claude A. Watson		103,224	John Kasper		6,953
Prohibition			*States' Rights*		
Edward A. Teichert		29,244	Joseph B. Lightburn		5,060
Socialist Labor			*Constitution*		
Farrell Dobbs		13,613			
Socialist Workers			**1968: 50 States and D.C.**		
			RICHARD NIXON	301	31,770,237
1952: 48 States			*Republican*		
DWIGHT D. EISENHOWER	442	33,936,234	Hubert Humphrey	191	31,270,533
Republican			*Democratic*		
Adlai E. Stevenson	89	27,314,992	George Wallace	46	9,906,141
Democratic			*American Independent*		
Vincent Hallinan		140,023	Hennings Blomen		52,588
Progressive			*Socialist Labor*		
Stuart Hamblen		72,949	Dick Gregory		47,097
Prohibition			*Freedom and Peace*		
Eric Haas		30,267	Fred Halstead		41,300
Socialist Labor			*Socialist Worker*		
Darlington Hoopes		20,203	Eldridge Cleaver		36,385
Socialist			*Peace and Freedom*		
Douglas A. MacArthur		17,205	Eugene McCarthy		25,858
Constitution			*New Party*		
Farrell Dobbs		10,312	Earle H. Munn		14,519
Socialist Workers			*Prohibition*		
			Charlene Mitchell		1,075
1956: 48 States			*Communist*		
DWIGHT D. EISENHOWER	457	35,590,472			
Republican			**1972: 50 States and D.C.**		
Adlai E. Stevenson	73[7]	26,022,752	RICHARD NIXON	520	47,168,963
Democratic			*Republican*		
T. Coleman Andrews		107,929	George McGovern	17	29,169,615
States' Rights			*Democratic*		
Eric Haas		44,300	John G. Schmitz		1,080,541
Socialist Labor			*American*		
Enoch A. Holtwick		41,937	Benjamin Spock		78,801
Prohibition			*People's*		
			John Hospers	1	
1960: 50 States			*Libertarian*		
JOHN F. KENNEDY	303	34,227,096			
Democratic; Liberal			**1976: 50 States and D.C.**		
Richard M. Nixon	219	34,108,546	JAMES EARL CARTER, JR.	297	40,828,605
Republican			*Democratic*		
Harry F. Byrd	15*	116,248	Gerald R. Ford	240	39,147,633
Independent			*Republican*		
Orville Faubus		214,549	Eugene McCarthy		751,842
States' Rights			*Independent*		
Eric Haas		46,560	Roger MacBride		183,187
Socialist Labor			*Libertarian*		
Rutherford B. Decker		46,203	Lester Maddox		170,780
Prohibition			*American Independent*		
Farrell Dobbs		39,541	Thomas Anderson		160,600
Socialist Workers			*American*		
Charles L. Sullivan		19,570	Peter Camejo		91,226
Constitution			*Socialist Workers*		
J. Bracken Lee		12,912	Gus Hall		59,114
Conservative			*Communist*		

[7]One Democratic elector voted for Walter Jones. *Byrd's electoral count includes the votes of fourteen unpledged electors from Mississippi and Alabama, in addition to one vote pledged to Nixon but cast for Byrd by an Oklahoma elector.

PRESIDENTS, VICE-PRESIDENTS, AND CABINET MEMBERS

President and Vice-President	Secretary of State	Secretary of the Treasury	Secretary of War
George Washington (F) .... 1789 J. Adams .... '89	T. Jefferson .... '89 E. Randolph .... '94 T. Pickering.......... '95	A. Hamilton .... '89 O. Wolcott.......... '89	H. Knox .... '89 T. Pickering.......... '95 J. McHenry .... '96
John Adams (F)..................... 1797 T. Jefferson (R^J).................. '97	T. Pickering.......... '97 J. Marshall .... '00	O. Wolcott .... '97 S. Dexter .... '01	J. McHenry .... '97 J. Marshall .... '00 S. Dexter .... '00 R. Griswold.......... '01
Thomas Jefferson (R^J) .... 1801 A. Burr (R^J) .... '01 G. Clinton (R^J)..................... '05	J. Madison.......... '01	S. Dexter .... '01 A. Gallatin........... '01	H. Dearborn .... '01
James Madison (R^J) .... 1809 G. Clinton (R^J).................... '09 E. Gerry (R^J)...................... '13	R. Smith............ '09 J. Monroe........... '11	A. Gallatin .... '09 G. Campbell .... '14 A. Dallas .... '14 W. Crawford......... '16	W. Eustis .... '09 J. Armstrong .... '13 J. Monroe .... '14 W. Crawford......... '15
James Monroe (R^J) .... 1817 D. Tompkins (R^J) .... '17	J. Q. Adams.......... '17	W. Crawford......... '17	I. Shelby............. '17 G. Graham........... '17 J. Calhoun .... '17
John Quincy Adams (NR)............ 1825 J. Calhoun (R^J) .... '25	H. Clay............. '25	R. Rush............. '25	J. Barbour........... '25 P. Porter............. '28
Andrew Jackson (D)................ 1829 J. Calhoun (D)..................... '29 M. Van Buren (D).................. '33	M. Van Buren........ '29 E. Livingston .... '31 L. McLane .... '33 J. Forsyth .... '34	S. Ingham .... '29 L. McLane .... '31 W. Duane........... '33 R. Taney............ '33 L. Woodbury......... '34	J. Eaton............. '29 L. Cass .... '31 B. Butler .... '37
Martin Van Buren (D) .... 1837 R. Johnson (D)..................... '37	J. Forsyth .... '37	L. Woodbury......... '37	J. Poinsett .... '37
William H. Harrison (W)............ 1841 J. Tyler (W)....................... '41	D. Webster .... '41	T. Ewing .... '41	J. Bell............... '41
John Tyler (W and D)................ 1841	D. Webster .... '41 H. Legare............ '43 A. Upshur .... '43 J. Calhoun .... '44	T. Ewing .... '41 W. Forward......... '41 J. Spencer........... '43 G. Bibb............. '44	J. Bell .... '41 J. McLean........... '41 J. Spencer .... '41 J. Porter .... '43 W. Wilkins .... '44
James K. Polk (D) .... 1845 G. Dallas (D)...................... '45	J. Buchanan.......... '45	R. Walker........... '45	W. Marcy .... '45
Zachary Taylor (W)................. 1849 M. Fillmore (W)................... '49	J. Clayton........... '49	W. Meredith .... '49	G. Crawford .... '49
Millard Fillmore (W)................ 1850	D. Webster .... '50 E. Everett............ '52	T. Corwin .... '50	C. Conrad .... '50
Franklin Pierce (D)................. 1853 W. King (D)....................... '53	W. Marcy........... '53	J. Guthrie............ '53	J. Davis............. '53
James Buchanan (D)................ 1857 J. Breckinridge (D) .... '57	L. Cass .... '57 J. Black .... '60	H. Cobb............. '57 P. Thomas .... '60 J. Dix............... '61	J. Floyd............. '57 J. Holt .... '61
Abraham Lincoln (R)................ 1861 H. Hamlin (R)..................... '61 A. Johnson (U)..................... '65	W. Seward........... '61	S. Chase .... '61 W. Fessenden .... '64 H. McCulloch .... '65	S. Cameron .... '61 E. Stanton .... '62
Andrew Johnson (U) 1865	W. Seward........... '65	H. McCulloch .... '65	E. Stanton .... '65 U. Grant............. '67 L. Thomas .... '68 J. Schofield .... '68

Party affiliations: D, Democratic; F, Federalist; NR, National Republican; R, Republican; R^J, Republican (Jeffersonian); U, Unionist; W, Whig.

Secretary of the Navy	Attorney General	Postmaster General	Secretary of the Interior
Established April 30, 1798	E. Randolph.............. '89		
	W. Bradford.............. '94		
	C. Lee.................. '95		
B. Stoddert.............. '98	C. Lee.................. '97		
	T. Parsons.............. '01		
B. Stoddert.............. '01	L. Lincoln.............. '01		
R. Smith................ '01	R. Smith................ '05		
J. Crowninshield .... '05	J. Breckinridge.......... '05		
	C. Rodney.............. '07		
P. Hamilton.............. '09	C. Rodney.............. '09		
W. Jones................ '13	W. Pinkney............. '11		
B. Crowninshield........ '14	R. Rush................. '14		
B. Crowninshield........ '17	R. Rush................. '17		
S. Thompson............. '18	W. Wirt................ '17		
S. Southard .... '23		*Cabinet status since March 9, 1829*	
S. Southard .... '25	W. Wirt................ '25		
J. Branch................ '29	J. Berrien............... '29	W. Barry................ '29	
L. Woodbury............. '31	R. Taney................ '31	A. Kendall .... '35	
M. Dickerson............. '34	B. Butler................ '33		
M. Dickerson............. '37	B. Butler................ '37	A. Kendall .... '37	
J. Paulding.............. '38	F. Grundy............... '38	J. Niles................. '40	
	H. Gilpin............... '40		
G. Badger................ '41	J. Crittenden .... '41	F. Granger .... '41	
G. Badger................ '41	J. Crittenden .... '41	F. Granger .... '41	
A. Upshur............... '41	H. Legare .... '41	C. Wickliffe .... '41	
D. Henshaw.............. '43	J. Nelson................ '43		
T. Gilmer............... '44			
J. Mason................ '44			
G. Bancroft.............. '45	J. Mason .... '45	C. Johnson.............. '45	*Established March 3, 1849*
J. Mason................ '46	N. Clifford .... '46		
	I. Toucey................ '48		
W. Preston.............. '49	R. Johnson .... '49	J. Collamer.............. '49	Thomas Ewing .... '49
W. Graham.............. '50	J. Crittenden .... '50	N. Hall .... '50	A. Stuart................ '50
J. Kennedy.............. '52		S. Hubbard .... '52	
J. Dobbin .... '53	C. Cushing.............. '53	J. Campbell .... '53	R. McClelland .... '53
I. Toucey................ '57	J. Black .... '57	A. Brown .... '57	J. Thompson .... '57
	E. Stanton............... '60	J. Holt................. '59	
G. Welles .... '61	E. Bates................. '61	H. King................. '61	C. Smith................ '61
	T. Coffey................ '63	M. Blair................. '61	J. Usher................ '63
	J. Speed................ '64	W. Dennison............. '64	
G. Welles .... '65	J. Speed................ '65	W. Dennison............. '65	J. Usher................ '65
	H. Stanbery .... '66	A. Randall .... '66	J. Harlan .... '65
	W. Evarts .... '68		O. Browning .... '66

PRESIDENTS, VICE-PRESIDENTS, AND CABINET MEMBERS

President and Vice-President	Secretary of State	Secretary of the Treasury	Secretary of War	Secretary of the Navy
Ulysses S. Grant (R) ..... 1869 S. Colfax (R) .... '69 H. Wilson (R) .... '73	E. Washburne . . '69 H. Fish .... '69	G. Boutwell .... '69 W. Richardson . '73 B. Bristow ..... '74 L. Morrill ...... '76	J. Rawlins..... '69 W. Sherman .. '69 W. Belknap ... '69 A. Taft .... '76 J. Cameron.... '76	A. Borie ...... '69 G. Robeson ... '69
Rutherford B. Hayes (R) .. 1877 W. Wheeler (R) .... '77	W. Evarts...... '77	J. Sherman..... '77	G. McCrary ... '77 A. Ramsey.... '79	R. Thompson . '77 N. Goff .... '81
James A. Garfield (R).... 1881 C. Arthur (R) .... '81	J. Blaine....... '81	W. Windom ... '81	R. Lincoln ..... '81	W. Hunt ...... '81
Chester A. Arthur (R) 1881	F. Freling- huysen...... '81	C. Folger...... '81 W. Gresham ... '84 H. McCulloch.. '84	R. Lincoln ..... '81	W. Chandler... '81
Grover Cleveland (D)...... 1885 T. Hendricks (D)........ '85	T. Bayard...... '85	D. Manning .... '85 C. Fairchild.... '87	W. Endicott.... '85	W. Whitney ... '85
Benjamin Harrison (R)..... 1889 L. Morton (R)........... '89	J. Blaine....... '89 J. Foster....... '92	W. Windom ... '89 C. Foster ...... '91	R. Proctor ..... '89 S. Elkins ...... '91	B. Tracy....... '89
Grover Cleveland (D)..... 1893 A. Stevenson (D)........ '93	W. Gresham ... '93 R. Olney ...... '95	J. Carlisle...... '93	D. Lamont..... '93	H. Herbert .... '93
William McKinley (R) .... 1897 G. Hobart (R)........... '97 T. Roosevelt (R)......... '01	J. Sherman .... '97 W. Day .... '97 J. Hay......... '98	L. Gage .... '97	R. Alger....... '97 E. Root........ '99	J. Long........ '97
Theodore Roosevelt (R).... 1901 C. Fairbanks (R) .... '05	J. Hay......... '01 E. Root........ '05 R. Bacon ...... '09	L. Gage .... '01 L. Shaw....... '02 G. Cortelyou... '07	E. Root........ '01 W. Taft....... '04 L. Wright...... '08	J. Long........ '01 W. Moody..... '02 P. Morton ..... '04 C. Bonaparte... '05 V. Metcalf ..... '07 T. Newberry... '08
William Howard Taft (R) .. 1909 J. Sherman (R).......... '09	P. Knox .... '09	F. MacVeagh .. '09	J. Dickinson ... '09 H. Stimson .... '11	G. Meyer...... '09
Woodrow Wilson (D)...... 1913 T. Marshall (D) .... '13	W. Bryan...... '13 R. Lansing .... '15 B. Colby ...... '20	W. McAdoo ... '13 C. Glass....... '18 D. Houston.... '20	L. Garrison.... '13 N. Baker ...... '16	J. Daniels..... '13
Warren G. Harding (R) .... 1921 C. Coolidge (R) .... '21	C. Hughes..... '21	A. Mellon ..... '21	J. Weeks....... '21	E. Denby...... '21
Calvin Coolidge (R) .... 1923 C. Dawes (R) .... '25	C. Hughes..... '23 F. Kellogg ..... '25	A. Mellon ..... '23	J. Weeks....... '23 D. Davis .... '25	E. Denby...... '23 C. Wilbur ..... '24
Herbert Hoover (R) .... 1929 C. Curtis (R)............ '29	H. Stimson .... '29	A. Mellon ..... '29 O. Mills....... '32	J. Good........ '29 P. Hurley...... '29	C. Adams ..... '29
Franklin D. Roosevelt (D) .. 1933 J. Garner (D)........... '33 H. Wallace (D).......... '41 H. Truman (D).......... '45	C. Hull........ '33 E. Stettinius ... '44	W. Woodin.... '33 H. Morgen- thau .... '34	G. Dern .... '33 H. Woodring .. '36 H. Stimson .... '40	C. Swanson.... '33 C. Edison ..... '40 F. Knox .... '40 J. Forrestal..... '44
Harry S. Truman (D) ...... 1945 A. Barkley (D) .... '49	J. Byrnes ...... '45 G. Marshall.... '47 D. Acheson.... '49	F. Vinson ..... '45 J. Snyder ...... '46	R. Patterson ... '45 K. Royall ...... '47	J. Forrestal..... '45

Party affiliations: D, Democratic; R, Republican.

Attorney General	Postmaster General	Secretary of the Interior	Secretary of Agriculture	Secretary of Commerce and Labor	
E. Hoar .... '69 A. Ackerman ... '70 G. Williams .... '71 E. Pierrepont ... '75 A. Taft .... '76	J. Creswell .... '69 J. Marshall ... '74 M. Jewell ..... '74 J. Tyner .... '76	J. Cox .... '69 C. Delano ..... '70 Z. Chandler ... '75			
C. Devens ...... '77	D. Key .... '77 H. Maynard ... '80	C. Schurz ..... '77			
W. Mac-Veagh ..... '81	T. James .... '81	S. Kirkwood ... '81			
B. Brewster .... '81	T. Howe ...... '81 W. Gresham ... '83 F. Hatton...... '84	H. Teller ...... '81	*Cabinet status since Feb. 9, 1889*		
A. Garland .... '85	W. Vilas .... '85 D. Dickinson .. '88	L. Lamar ...... '85 W. Vilas....... '88	N. Colman .... '89		
W. Miller...... '89	J. Wanamaker.. '89	J. Noble........ '89	J. Rusk .... '89		
R. Olney ...... '93 J. Harmon ..... '95	W. Bissell ..... '93 W. Wilson..... '95	H. Smith ...... '93 D. Francis ..... '96	J. Morton ...... '93		
J. McKenna.... '97 J. Griggs .... '97 P. Knox .... '01	J. Gary .... '97 C. Smith ...... '98	C. Bliss .... '97 E. Hitchcock... '99	J. Wilson ...... '97	*Established Feb. 14, 1903*	
P. Knox .... '01 W. Moody..... '04 C. Bonaparte... '07	C. Smith ...... '01 H. Payne...... '02 R. Wynne ..... '04 G. Cortelyou... '05 G. Meyer...... '07	E. Hitchcock... '01 J. Garfield ..... '07	J. Wilson ...... '01	G. Cortelyou... '03 V. Metcalf ..... '04 O. Straus...... '07	
G. Wickersham........ '09	F. Hitchcock... '09	R. Ballinger.... '09 W. Fisher ..... '11	J. Wilson ...... '09	C. Nagel ...... '09	
J. McReynolds . '13 T. Gregory..... '14 A. Palmer ..... '19	A. Burleson.... '13	F. Lane........ '13 J. Payne....... '20	D. Houston.... '13 E. Meredith.... '20	**Secretary of Commerce** *Established March 4, 1913* W. Redfield.... '13 J. Alexander ... '19	**Secretary of Labor** *Established March 4, 1913* Wm. Wilson ... '13
H. Daugherty.. '21	W. Hays ...... '21 H. Work ...... '22 H. New .... '23	A. Fall .... '21 H. Work ...... '23	H. C. Wallace.. '21	H. Hoover..... '21	J. Davis .... '21
H. Daugherty.. '23 H. Stone ...... '24 J. Sargent...... '25	H. New .... '23	H. Work ...... '23 R. West .... '28	H. C. Wallace.. '23 H. Gore .... '24 W. Jardine..... '25	H. Hoover..... '23 W. Whiting.... '28	J. Davis .... '23
W. Mitchell.... '29	W. Brown ..... '29	R. Wilbur ..... '29	A. Hyde........ '29	R. Lamont..... '29 R. Chapin ..... '32	J. Davis .... '29 W. Doak ...... '30
H. Cummings . '33 F. Murphy..... '39 R. Jackson ..... '40 F. Biddle ...... '41	J. Farley....... '33 F. Walker...... '40	H. Ickes........ '33	H. A. Wallace.. '33 C. Wickard .... '40	D. Roper ...... '33 H. Hopkins.... '39 J. Jones........ '40 H. A. Wallace.. '45	F. Perkins ..... '33
T. Clark .... '45 J. McGrath..... '49 J. McGranery .. '52	R. Hannegan .. '45 J. Donaldson.. '47	H. Ickes........ '45 J. Krug........ '46 O. Chapman... '49	C. Anderson... '45 C. Brannan .... '48	H. A. Wallace.. '45 W. A. Harriman .... '46 C. Sawyer ..... '48	L. Schwellenbach .... '45 M. Tobin...... '48

PRESIDENTS, VICE-PRESIDENTS, AND CABINET MEMBERS

President and Vice-President	Secretary of State	Secretary of the Treasury	Secretary of Defense[1]	Attorney General	Postmaster General	Secretary of the Interior
			Established July 26, 1947 J. Forrestal[2] .... '47 L. Johnson[2] .... '49 G. Marshall[2] ... '50 R. Lovett[2] ..... '51			
Dwight D. Eisenhower (R).................. 1953 R. Nixon (R)............. '53	J. Dulles....... '53 C. Herter...... '59	G. Humphrey.. '53 R. Anderson... '57	C. Wilson ..... '53 N. McElroy.... '57	H. Brownell ... '53 W. Rogers ..... '57	A. Summer- field .... '53	D. McKay......'53 F. Seaton........'56
John F. Kennedy (D) ...... 1961 L. Johnson (D).......... '61	D. Rusk....... '61	D. Dillon...... '61	R. McNamara.. '61	R. Kennedy.... '61	J. Day......... '61 J. Gronouski... '63	S. Udall ...... '61
Lyndon B. Johnson (D) .... 1963 H. Humphrey (D)....... '65	D. Rusk....... '63	D. Dillon...... '63 H. Fowler ..... '65 J. Barr......... '68	R. McNamara.. '63 C. Clifford..... '68	R. Kennedy.... '63 N. Katzenbach. '65 R. Clark .... '67	J. Gronouski... '63 L. O'Brien..... '65 W. Watson .... '68	S. Udall ...... '63
Richard M. Nixon (R) ..... 1969 S. Agnew (R) .... '69 G. Ford (R) .... '73	W. Rogers .... '69 H. Kissinger .. '73	D. Kennedy... '69 J. Connally ... '71 G. Shultz .... '72 W. Simon .... '74	M. Laird ..... '69 E. Richardson . '72 J. Schlesinger . '73	J. Mitchell .... '69 R. Kleindienst . '73 E. Richardson . '73 W. Saxbe ..... '73	W. Blount .... '69 ——————— *Terminated July 1, 1971*	W. Hickel ... '69 R. Morton ... '71
Gerald R. Ford (R) .... 1974 N. Rockefeller (R) ..... '74	H. Kissinger . '74	W. Simon .... '74	J. Schlesinger . '74 D. Rumsfeld .. '75	W. Saxbe ..... '74 E. Levi ...... '75		R. Morton ... '74 S. Hathaway . '75 T. Kleppe ... '75
James E. Carter, Jr. (D) ....1977 W. Mondale (D)........'77	C. Vance .... '77 E. Muskie..... '80	W. Blumenthal '77 G. Miller...... '79	H. Brown .... '77	G. Bell ....'77 B. Civiletti.... '79		C. Andrus .. '77

Party affiliations: D, Democratic; R, Republican.

[1]The Department of Defense, established during the Truman Administration, was a combination of the Departments of War and the Navy.

[2]Appointed during the Truman Administration.

Secretary of Agriculture	Secretary of Commerce	Secretary of Labor	Secretary of Health, Education, and Welfare	Department of Education³	Secretary of Housing and Urban Development	Secretary of Transportation	Secretary of Energy
			Established April 1, 1953				
E. Benson .... '53	S. Weeks ..... '53 L. Strauss .... '58 F. Mueller .... '59	M. Durkin.... '53 J. Mitchell .... '53	O. Hobby .... '53 M. Folsom... '55 A. Flemming . '58				
O. Freeman... '61	L. Hodges.... '61	A. Goldberg .. '61 W. Wirtz ..... '62	A. Ribicoff ... '61 A. Celebrezze. '62				
O. Freeman... '63	L. Hodges .... '63 J. Connor..... '65 A. Trow- bridge ...... '67 C. Smith ..... '68	W. Wirtz ..... '63	A. Celebrezze. '63 J. Gardner .... '65 W. Cohen .... '68		*Established Sept. 9, 1965* R. Weaver .... '66 R. Wood ..... '68	*Established Oct. 15, 1966* A. Boyd ...... '66	
C. Hardin ... '69 E. Butz ..... '71	M. Stans .... '69 P. Peterson .. '72 F. Dent ..... '73	G. Shultz .... '69 J. Hodgson .. '70 P. Brennan .. '73	R. Finch ..... '69 E. Richardson '70 C.Weinberger '73		G. Romney .. '69 J. Lynn ..... '73	J. Volpe ..... '69 C. Brinegar .. '73	
E. Butz ..... '74	F. Dent ..... '74 R. Morton ... '75 E. Richardson '75	P. Brennan .. '74 J. Dunlop .... '75 W. Usery ... '76	C.Weinberger '74 F. Matthews . '75	*Established October 17, 1979*	J. Lynn ..... '74 C. Hills ..... '75	C. Brinegar .. '74 W. Coleman . '75	*Established Aug. 4, 1977*
B. Bergland... '77	J. Kreps ..... '77 P. Klutznick.. '79	R. Marshall ..'77	J. Califano .. '77	S. Hufstedler '80	P. Harris ... '77 M. Landrieu. '79	B. Adams .... '77 N. Goldschmidt .... '79	J. Schlesinger '77 C. Duncan, Jr. '79
			Reorganized into Department of Health and Human Services *Established October 17, 1979* P. Harris...... '79				

³Department of Health, Education, and Welfare split into Department of Health and Human Services and Department of Education under the Carter Administration.

PARTY DISTRIBUTION IN CONGRESS

CONGRESS	YEAR	PRESIDENT		SENATE			HOUSE		
				Majority Party	Minority Party	Others	Majority Party	Minority Party	Others
1	1789–91	F	(Washington)	Ad 17	Op 9	0	Ad 38	Op 26	0
2	1791–93	F	(Washington)	F 16	R' 13	0	F 37	R' 33	0
3	1793–95	F	(Washington)	F 17	R' 13	0	R' 57	F 48	0
4	1795–97	F	(Washington)	F 19	R' 13	0	F 54	R' 52	0
5	1797–99	F	(J. Adams)	F 20	R' 12	0	F 58	R' 48	0
6	1799–01	F	(J. Adams)	F 19	R' 13	0	F 64	R' 42	0
7	1801–03	R'	(Jefferson)	R' 18	F 14	0	R' 69	F 36	0
8	1803–05	R'	(Jefferson)	R' 25	F 9	0	R' 102	F 39	0
9	1805–07	R'	(Jefferson)	R' 27	F 7	0	R' 116	F 25	0
10	1807–09	R'	(Jefferson)	R' 28	F 6	0	R' 118	F 24	0
11	1809–11	R'	(Madison)	R' 28	F 6	0	R' 94	F 48	0
12	1811–13	R'	(Madison)	R' 30	F 6	0	R' 108	F 36	0
13	1813–15	R'	(Madison)	R' 27	F 9	0	R' 112	F 68	0
14	1815–17	R'	(Madison)	R' 25	F 11	0	R' 117	F 65	0
15	1817–19	R'	(Monroe)	R' 34	F 10	0	R' 141	F 42	0
16	1819–21	R'	(Monroe)	R' 35	F 7	0	R' 156	F 27	0
17	1821–23	R'	(Monroe)	R' 44	F 4	0	R' 158	F 25	0
18	1823–25	R'	(Monroe)	R' 44	F 4	0	R' 187	F 26	0
19	1825–27	C	(J. Q. Adams)	Ad 26	J 20	0	Ad 105	J 97	0
20	1827–29	C	(J. Q. Adams)	J 28	Ad 20	0	J 119	Ad 94	0
21	1829–31	D	(Jackson)	D 26	NR 22	0	D 139	NR 74	0
22	1831–33	D	(Jackson)	D 25	NR 21	2	D 141	NR 58	14
23	1833–35	D	(Jackson)	D 20	NR 20	8	D 147	AM 53	60
24	1835–37	D	(Jackson)	D 27	W 25	0	D 145	W 98	0
25	1837–39	D	(Van Buren)	D 30	W 18	4	D 108	W 107	24
26	1839–41	D	(Van Buren)	D 28	W 22	0	D 124	W 118	0
27	1841–43	W	(W. Harrison)						
		W	(Tyler)	W 28	D 22	2	W 133	D 102	6
28	1843–45	W	(Tyler)	W 28	D 25	1	D 142	W 79	1
29	1845–47	D	(Polk)	D 31	W 25	0	D 143	W 77	6
30	1847–49	D	(Polk)	D 36	W 21	1	W 115	D 108	4
31	1849–51	W	(Taylor)						
		W	(Fillmore)	D 35	W 25	2	D 112	W 109	9
32	1851–53	W	(Fillmore)	D 35	W 24	3	D 140	W 88	5
33	1853–55	D	(Pierce)	D 38	W 22	2	D 159	W 71	4
34	1855–57	D	(Pierce)	D 40	R 15	5	R 108	D 83	43
35	1857–59	D	(Buchanan)	D 36	R 20	8	D 118	R 92	26
36	1859–61	D	(Buchanan)	D 36	R 26	4	R 114	D 92	31
37	1861–63	R	(Lincoln)	R 31	D 10	8	R 105	D 43	30
38	1863–65	R	(Lincoln)	R 36	D 9	5	R 102	D 75	9
39	1865–67	R	(Lincoln)						
		R	(Johnson)	U 42	D 10	0	U 149	D 42	0
40	1867–69	R	(Johnson)	R 42	D 11	0	R 143	D 49	0
41	1869–71	R	(Grant)	R 56	D 11	0	R 149	D 63	0
42	1871–73	R	(Grant)	R 52	D 17	5	D 134	R 104	5
43	1873–75	R	(Grant)	R 49	D 19	5	R 194	D 92	14
44	1875–77	R	(Grant)	R 45	D 29	2	D 169	R 109	14
45	1877–79	R	(Hayes)	R 39	D 36	1	D 153	R 140	0
46	1879–81	R	(Hayes)	D 42	R 33	1	D 149	R 130	14
47	1881–83	R	(Garfield)						
		R	(Arthur)	R 37	D 37	1	R 147	D 135	11
48	1883–85	R	(Arthur)	R 38	D 36	2	D 197	R 118	10
49	1885–87	D	(Cleveland)	R 43	D 34	0	D 183	R 140	2
50	1887–89	D	(Cleveland)	R 39	D 37	0	D 169	R 152	4
51	1889–91	R	(B. Harrison)	R 39	D 37	0	R 166	D 159	0
52	1891–93	R	(B. Harrison)	R 47	D 39	2	D 235	R 88	9

CONGRESS	YEAR	PRESIDENT	SENATE			HOUSE		
			Majority Party	Minority Party	Others	Majority Party	Minority Party	Others
53	1893–95	D (Cleveland)	D 44	R 38	3	D 218	R 127	11
54	1895–97	D (Cleveland)	R 43	D 39	6	R 244	D 105	7
55	1897–99	R (McKinley)	R 47	D 34	7	R 204	D 113	40
56	1899–01	R (McKinley)	R 53	D 26	8	R 185	D 163	9
57	1901–03	R (McKinley)						
		R (T. Roosevelt)	R 55	D 31	4	R 197	D 151	9
58	1903–05	R (T. Roosevelt)	R 57	D 33	0	R 208	D 178	0
59	1905–07	R (T. Roosevelt)	R 57	D 33	0	R 250	D 136	0
60	1907–09	R (T. Roosevelt)	R 61	D 31	0	R 222	D 164	0
61	1909–11	R (Taft)	R 61	D 32	0	R 219	D 172	0
62	1911–13	R (Taft)	R 51	D 41	0	D 228	R 161	1
63	1913–15	D (Wilson)	D 51	R 44	1	D 291	R 127	17
64	1915–17	D (Wilson)	D 56	R 40	0	D 230	R 196	9
65	1917–19	D (Wilson)	D 53	R 42	0	D 216	R 210	6
66	1919–21	D (Wilson)	R 49	D 47	0	R 240	D 190	3
67	1921–23	R (Harding)	R 59	D 37	0	R 303	D 131	1
68	1923–25	R (Coolidge)	R 51	D 43	2	R 225	D 205	5
69	1925–27	R (Coolidge)	R 56	D 39	1	R 247	D 183	4
70	1927–29	R (Coolidge)	R 49	D 46	1	R 237	D 195	3
71	1929–31	R (Hoover)	R 56	D 39	1	R 267	D 167	1
72	1931–33	R (Hoover)	R 48	D 47	1	D 220	R 214	1
73	1933–35	D (F. Roosevelt)	D 60	R 35	1	D 310	R 117	5
74	1935–37	D (F. Roosevelt)	D 69	R 25	2	D 319	R 103	10
75	1937–39	D (F. Roosevelt)	D 76	D 16	4	D 331	R 89	13
76	1939–41	D (F. Roosevelt)	D 69	R 23	4	D 261	R 164	4
77	1941–43	D (F. Roosevelt)	D 66	R 28	2	D 268	R 162	5
78	1943–45	D (F. Roosevelt)	D 58	R 37	1	D 218	R 208	4
79	1945–47	D (F. Roosevelt)						
		D (Truman)	D 56	R 38	1	D 242	R 190	2
80	1947–49	D (Truman)	R 51	D 45	0	R 246	D 188	1
81	1949–51	D (Truman)	D 54	R 42	0	D 263	R 171	1
82	1951–53	D (Truman)	D 49	R 47	0	D 235	R 199	1
83	1953–55	R (Eisenhower)	R 48	D 47	1	R 221	D 212	1
84	1955–57	R (Eisenhower)	D 48	R 47	1	D 232	R 203	0
85	1957–59	R (Eisenhower)	D 49	R 47	0	D 232	R 199	0
86	1959–61	R (Eisenhower)	D 62	R 34	0	D 280	R 152	0
87	1961–63	D (Kennedy)	D 65	R 35	0	D 261	R 176	0
88	1963–65	D (Kennedy)						
		D (Johnson)	D 68	R 32	0	D 258	R 177	0
89	1965–67	D (Johnson)	D 68	R 32	0	D 295	R 140	0
90	1967–69	D (Johnson)	D 64	R 36	0	D 248	R 187	0
91	1969–71	R (Nixon)	D 57	R 43	0	D 243	R 192	0
92	1971–72	R (Nixon)	D 54	R 44	2	D 254	R 180	0
93	1973–74	R (Nixon)	D 56	R 42	2	D 240	R 192	0
		R (Ford)						
94	1975–	R (Ford)	D 60	R 37	2	D 291	R 144	0
94	1975–77	R (Ford)	D 62	R 38	0	D 291	R 144	0
95	77–79	D (Carter)	D 61	R 38	1	D 292	R 143	0
96	79–81	D (Carter)	D58	R41	1	D276	R 159	0

Ad: Administration; AM: Anti-Masonic; C: Coalition; D: Democratic; F: Federalist; J: Jacksonian; NR: National Republican; Op: Opposition; R: Republican; R^J: Republican (Jeffersonian); U: Unionist; W: Whig.

JUSTICES OF THE UNITED STATES SUPREME COURT

NAME *Chief Justices in Capital Letters*	Terms of Service[1]	Appointed By	NAME *Chief Justices in Capital Letters*	Terms of Service[1]	Appointed By
JOHN JAY, N.Y.	1789–1795	Washington	Henry B. Brown, Mich.	1891–1906	B. Harrison
James Wilson, Pa.	1789–1798	Washington	George Shiras, Jr., Pa.	1892–1903	B. Harrison
John Rutledge, S.C.	1790–1791	Washington	Howell E. Jackson, Tenn.	1893–1895	B. Harrison
William Cushing, Mass.	1790–1810	Washington	Edward D. White, La.	1894–1910	Cleveland
John Blair, Va.	1790–1796	Washington	Rufus W. Peckham, N.Y.	1896–1909	Cleveland
James Iredell, N.C.	1790–1799	Washington	Joseph McKenna, Cal.	1898–1925	McKinley
Thomas Johnson, Md.	1792–1793	Washington	Oliver W. Holmes, Mass.	1902–1932	T. Roosevelt
William Paterson, N.J.	1793–1806	Washington	William R. Day, Ohio	1903–1922	T. Roosevelt
JOHN RUTLEDGE, S.C.[2]	1795	Washington	William H. Moody, Mass.	1906–1910	T. Roosevelt
Samuel Chase, Md.	1796–1811	Washington	Horace H. Lurton, Tenn.	1910–1914	Taft
OLIVER ELLSWORTH, Conn.	1796–1800	Washington	Charles E. Hughes, N.Y.	1910–1916	Taft
Bushrod Washington, Va.	1799–1829	J. Adams	Willis Van Devanter, Wy.	1911–1937	Taft
Alfred Moore, N.C.	1800–1804	J. Adams	Joseph R. Lamar, Ga.	1911–1916	Taft
JOHN MARSHALL, Va.	1801–1835	J. Adams	EDWARD D. WHITE, La.	1910–1921	Taft
William Johnson, S.C.	1804–1834	Jefferson	Mahlon Pitney, N.J.	1912–1922	Taft
Brockholst Livingston, N.Y.	1807–1823	Jefferson	James C. McReynolds, Tenn.	1914–1941	Wilson
Thomas Todd, Ky.	1807–1826	Jefferson	Louis D. Brandeis, Mass.	1916–1939	Wilson
Gabriel Duvall, Md.	1811–1835	Madison	John H. Clarke, Ohio	1916–1922	Wilson
Joseph Story, Mass.	1812–1845	Madison	WILLIAM H. TAFT, Conn.	1921–1930	Harding
Smith Thompson, N.Y.	1823–1843	Monroe	George Sutherland, Utah	1922–1938	Harding
Robert Trimble, Ky.	1826–1828	J. Q. Adams	Pierce Butler, Minn.	1923–1939	Harding
John McLean, Ohio	1830–1861	Jackson	Edward T. Sanford, Tenn.	1923–1930	Harding
Henry Baldwin, Pa.	1830–1844	Jackson	Harlan F. Stone, N.Y.	1925–1941	Coolidge
James M. Wayne, Ga.	1835–1867	Jackson	CHARLES E. HUGHES, N.Y.	1930–1941	Hoover
ROGER B. TANEY, Md.	1836–1864	Jackson	Owen J. Roberts, Penn.	1930–1945	Hoover
Philip P. Barbour, Va.	1836–1841	Jackson	Benjamin N. Cardozo, N.Y.	1932–1938	Hoover
John Catron, Tenn.	1837–1865	Van Buren	Hugo L. Black, Ala.	1937–1971	F. Roosevelt
John McKinley, Ala.	1838–1852	Van Buren	Stanley F. Reed, Ky.	1938–1957	F. Roosevelt
Peter V. Daniel, Va.	1842–1860	Van Buren	Felix Frankfurter, Mass.	1939–1962	F. Roosevelt
Samuel Nelson, N.Y.	1845–1872	Tyler	William O. Douglas, Conn.	1939–1975	F. Roosevelt
Levi Woodbury, N.H.	1845–1851	Polk	Frank Murphy, Mich.	1940–1949	F. Roosevelt
Robert C. Grier, Pa.	1846–1870	Polk	HARLAN F. STONE, N.Y.	1941–1946	F. Roosevelt
Benjamin R. Curtis, Mass.	1851–1857	Fillmore	James F. Byrnes, S.C.	1941–1942	F. Roosevelt
John A. Campbell, Ala.	1853–1861	Pierce	Robert H. Jackson, N.Y.	1941–1954	F. Roosevelt
Nathan Clifford, Me.	1858–1881	Buchanan	Wiley B. Rutledge, Iowa	1943–1949	F. Roosevelt
Noah H. Swayne, Ohio	1862–1881	Lincoln	Harold H. Burton, Ohio	1945–1958	Truman
Samuel F. Miller, Iowa	1862–1890	Lincoln	FREDERICK M. VINSON, Ky.	1946–1953	Truman
David Davis, Ill.	1862–1877	Lincoln	Tom C. Clark, Texas	1949–1967	Truman
Stephen J. Field, Cal.	1863–1897	Lincoln	Sherman Minton, Ind.	1949–1956	Truman
SALMON P. CHASE, Ohio	1864–1873	Lincoln	EARL WARREN, Cal.	1953–1969	Eisenhower
William Strong, Pa.	1870–1880	Grant	John Marshall Harlan, N.Y.	1955–1971	Eisenhower
Joseph P. Bradley, N.J.	1870–1892	Grant	William J. Brennan, Jr., N.J.	1956–	Eisenhower
Ward Hunt, N.Y.	1873–1882	Grant	Charles E. Whittaker, Mo.	1957–1962	Eisenhower
MORRISON R. WAITE, Ohio	1874–1888	Grant	Potter Stewart, Ohio	1958–	Eisenhower
John M. Harlan, Ky.	1877–1911	Hayes	Byron R. White, Colo.	1962–	Kennedy
William B. Woods, Ga.	1881–1887	Hayes	Arthur J. Goldberg, Ill.	1962–1965	Kennedy
Stanley Matthews, Ohio	1881–1889	Garfield	Abe Fortas, Tenn.	1965–1970	Johnson
Horace Gray, Mass.	1882–1902	Arthur	Thurgood Marshall, Md.	1967–	Johnson
Samuel Blatchford, N.Y.	1882–1893	Arthur	WARREN E. BURGER, Va.	1969–	Nixon
Lucius Q. C. Lamar, Miss.	1888–1893	Cleveland	Harry A. Blackmun, Minn.	1970–	Nixon
MELVILLE W. FULLER, Ill.	1888–1910	Cleveland	Lewis F. Powell, Jr., Va.	1971–	Nixon
David J. Brewer, Kan.	1890–1910	B. Harrison	William H. Rehnquist, Ariz.	1971–	Nixon
			John Paul Stevens, Ill.	1975–	Ford

[1]The date on which the justice took his judicial oath is here used as the date of the beginning of his service, for until that oath is taken he is not vested with the prerogatives of his office. Justices, however, receive their commissions ("letters patent") before taking their oath—in some instances, in the preceding year.

[2]Acting Chief Justice; Senate refused to confirm appointment.

POPULATION OF THE UNITED STATES: 1800-1880

Division and State	1800	1810	1820	1830	1840	1850	1860	1870	1880
UNITED STATES	5,308,483	7,239,881	9,638,453	12,866,020	17,069,453	23,191,876	31,443,321	39,818,449	50,189,209
New England	1,233,011	1,471,973	1,660,071	1,954,717	2,234,822	2,728,116	3,135,283	3,487,924	4,010,529
Maine	151,719	228,705	298,335	399,455	501,793	583,169	628,279	626,915	648,936
New Hampshire	183,858	214,160	244,161	269,328	284,574	317,976	326,073	318,300	346,991
Vermont	154,465	217,895	235,981	280,652	291,948	314,120	315,098	330,551	332,286
Massachusetts	422,845	472,040	523,287	610,408	737,699	994,514	1,231,066	1,457,351	1,783,085
Rhode Island	69,122	76,931	83,059	97,199	108,830	147,545	174,620	217,353	276,531
Connecticut	251,002	261,942	275,248	297,675	309,978	370,792	460,147	537,454	622,700
Middle Atlantic	1,402,565	2,014,702	2,669,845	3,587,664	4,526,260	5,898,735	7,458,985	8,810,806	10,496,878
New York	589,051	959,049	1,372,812	1,918,608	2,428,921	3,097,394	3,880,735	4,382,759	5,082,871
New Jersey	211,149	245,562	277,575	320,823	373,306	489,555	672,035	906,096	1,131,116
Pennsylvania	602,365	810,091	1,049,458	1,348,233	1,724,033	2,311,786	2,906,215	3,521,951	4,282,891
South Atlantic	2,286,494	2,674,891	3,061,063	3,645,752	3,925,299	4,679,090	5,364,703	5,835,610	7,597,197
Delaware	64,273	72,674	72,749	76,748	78,085	91,532	112,216	125,015	146,608
Maryland	341,548	380,546	407,350	447,040	470,019	583,034	687,049	780,894	934,943
Dist. of Columbia	8,144	15,471	23,336	30,261	33,745	51,687	75,080	131,700	177,624
Virginia	886,149	983,152	1,075,069	1,220,978	1,249,764	1,421,661	1,596,318	1,225,163	1,512,565
West Virginia	....	....	....	....	....	....	....	442,014	618,457
North Carolina	478,103	555,500	638,829	737,987	753,419	869,039	992,622	1,071,361	1,399,750
South Carolina	345,591	415,115	502,741	581,185	594,398	668,507	703,708	705,606	995,577
Georgia	162,686	252,433	340,989	516,823	691,392	906,185	1,057,286	1,184,109	1,542,180
Florida	....	....	....	34,730	54,477	87,445	140,424	187,748	269,493
East South Central	335,407	708,590	1,190,489	1,815,969	2,575,445	3,363,271	4,020,991	4,404,445	5,585,151
Kentucky	220,955	406,511	564,317	687,917	779,828	982,405	1,155,684	1,321,011	1,648,690
Tennessee	105,602	261,727	422,823	681,904	829,210	1,002,717	1,109,801	1,258,520	1,542,359
Alabama	1,250	9,046	127,901	309,527	590,756	771,623	964,201	996,992	1,262,505
Mississippi	7,600	31,306	75,448	136,621	375,651	606,526	791,305	827,922	1,131,597
West South Central	....	77,618	167,680	246,127	449,985	940,251	1,747,667	2,029,965	3,334,220
Arkansas	....	1,062	14,273	30,388	97,574	209,897	435,450	484,471	802,525
Louisiana	....	76,556	153,407	215,739	352,411	517,762	708,002	726,915	939,946
Oklahoma	....	....	....	....	....	....	....	....	....
Texas	....	....	....	....	....	212,592	604,215	818,579	1,591,749
East North Central	51,006	272,324	792,719	1,470,018	2,924,728	4,523,260	6,926,884	9,124,517	11,206,668
Ohio	41,365	230,760	581,434	937,903	1,519,467	1,980,329	2,339,511	2,665,260	3,198,062
Indiana	5,641	24,520	147,178	343,031	685,866	988,416	1,350,428	1,680,637	1,978,301
Illinois	....	12,282	55,211	157,445	476,183	851,470	1,711,951	2,539,891	3,077,871
Michigan	....	4,762	8,896	31,639	212,267	397,654	749,113	1,184,059	1,636,937
Wisconsin	....	....	....	....	30,945	305,391	775,881	1,054,670	1,315,497
West North Central	....	19,783	66,586	140,455	426,814	880,335	2,169,832	3,856,594	6,157,443
Minnesota	....	....	....	....	....	6,077	172,023	439,706	780,773
Iowa	....	....	....	....	43,112	192,214	674,913	1,194,020	1,624,615
Missouri	....	19,783	66,586	140,455	383,702	682,044	1,182,012	1,721,295	2,168,380
North Dakota	....	....	....	....	....	....	....	2,405	36,909
South Dakota	....	....	....	....	....	....	....	11,776	98,268
Nebraska	....	....	....	....	....	....	28,841	122,993	452,402
Kansas	....	....	....	....	....	....	107,206	364,399	996,096
Mountain	....	....	....	....	....	72,927	174,923	315,385	653,119
Montana	....	....	....	....	....	....	....	20,595	39,159
Idaho	....	....	....	....	....	....	....	14,999	32,610
Wyoming	....	....	....	....	....	....	....	9,118	20,789
Colorado	....	....	....	....	....	....	34,277	39,864	194,327
New Mexico	....	....	....	....	....	61,547	93,516	91,874	119,565
Arizona	....	....	....	....	....	....	....	9,658	40,440
Utah	....	....	....	....	....	11,380	40,273	76,786	143,963
Nevada	....	....	....	....	....	....	6,857	42,491	62,266
Pacific	....	....	....	....	....	105,871	444,053	675,125	1,148,004
Washington	....	....	....	....	....	1,201	11,594	23,955	75,116
Oregon	....	....	....	....	....	12,093	52,465	90,923	174,768
California	....	....	....	....	....	92,597	379,994	560,247	864,694
Alaska	....	....	....	....	....	....	....	....	33,426
Hawaii	....	....	....	....	....	....	....	....	....

POPULATION OF THE UNITED STATES: 1890–1970

Division and State	1890	1900	1910	1920	1930	1940	1950	1960	1970
UNITED STATES	62,979,766	76,212,168	92,228,622	106,021,568	123,202,660	132,165,129	151,325,798	179,323,175	203,184,772
New England	4,700,749	5,592,017	6,552,681	7,400,909	8,166,341	8,437,290	9,314,453	10,509,367	11,847,186
Maine	661,086	694,466	742,371	768,014	797,423	847,226	913,774	969,265	993,663
New Hampshire	376,530	411,588	430,572	443,083	465,293	491,524	533,242	606,921	737,681
Vermont	332,422	343,641	355,956	352,428	359,611	359,231	377,747	389,881	444,732
Massachusetts	2,238,947	2,805,346	3,366,416	3,852,356	4,249,614	4,316,721	4,690,514	5,148,578	5,689,170
Rhode Island	345,506	428,556	542,610	604,397	687,497	713,346	791,896	859,488	949,723
Connecticut	746,258	908,420	1,114,756	1,380,631	1,606,903	1,709,242	2,007,280	2,535,234	3,032,217
Middle Atlantic	12,706,220	15,454,678	19,315,892	22,261,144	26,260,750	27,539,487	30,163,533	34,168,452	37,152,813
New York	6,003,174	7,268,894	9,113,614	10,385,227	12,588,066	13,479,142	14,830,192	16,782,304	18,190,740
New Jersey	1,444,933	1,883,669	2,537,167	3,155,900	4,041,334	4,160,165	4,835,329	6,066,782	7,168,164
Pennsylvania	5,258,113	6,302,115	7,665,111	8,720,017	9,631,350	9,900,180	10,498,012	11,319,366	11,793,909
South Atlantic	8,857,922	10,443,480	12,194,895	13,990,272	15,793,589	17,823,151	21,182,335	25,971,732	30,671,337
Delaware	168,493	184,735	202,322	223,003	238,380	266,505	318,085	446,292	548,104
Maryland	1,042,390	1,188,044	1,295,346	1,449,661	1,631,526	1,821,244	2,343,001	3,100,689	3,922,399
Dist. of Columbia	230,392	278,718	331,069	437,571	486,869	663,091	802,178	763,956	756,510
Virginia	1,655,980	1,854,184	2,061,612	2,309,187	2,421,851	2,677,773	3,318,680	3,966,949	4,648,494
West Virginia	762,794	958,800	1,221,119	1,463,701	1,729,205	1,901,974	2,005,552	1,860,421	1,744,237
North Carolina	1,617,949	1,893,810	2,206,287	2,559,123	3,170,276	3,571,623	4,061,929	4,556,155	5,082,059
South Carolina	1,151,149	1,340,316	1,515,400	1,683,724	1,738,765	1,899,804	2,117,027	2,382,594	2,590,516
Georgia	1,837,353	2,216,331	2,609,121	2,895,832	2,908,506	3,123,723	3,444,578	3,943,116	4,589,575
Florida	391,422	528,542	752,619	968,470	1,468,211	1,897,414	2,771,305	4,951,560	6,789,443
East South Central	6,429,154	7,547,757	8,409,901	8,893,307	9,887,214	10,778,225	11,477,181	12,050,126	12,804,552
Kentucky	1,858,635	2,147,174	2,289,905	2,416,630	2,614,589	2,845,627	2,944,806	3,038,156	3,219,311
Tennessee	1,767,518	2,020,616	2,184,789	2,337,885	2,616,556	2,915,841	3,291,718	3,567,089	3,924,164
Alabama	1,513,401	1,828,697	2,138,093	2,348,174	2,646,248	2,832,961	3,061,743	3,266,740	3,444,165
Mississippi	1,289,600	1,551,270	1,797,114	1,790,618	2,009,821	2,183,796	2,178,914	2,178,141	2,216,912
West South Central	4,740,983	6,532,290	8,784,534	10,242,224	12,176,830	13,064,525	14,537,572	16,951,255	19,322,458
Arkansas	1,128,211	1,311,564	1,574,449	1,752,204	1,854,482	1,949,387	1,909,511	1,786,272	1,923,295
Louisiana	1,118,588	1,381,625	1,656,388	1,798,509	2,101,593	2,363,880	2,683,516	3,257,022	3,643,180
Oklahoma	258,657	790,391	1,657,155	2,028,283	2,396,040	2,336,434	2,233,351	2,328,284	2,559,253
Texas	2,235,527	3,048,710	3,896,542	4,663,228	5,824,715	6,414,824	7,711,194	9,579,677	11,196,730
East North Central	13,478,305	15,985,581	18,250,621	21,475,543	25,297,185	26,626,342	30,309,368	36,225,024	40,252,678
Ohio	3,672,329	4,157,545	4,767,121	5,759,394	6,646,697	6,907,612	7,946,627	9,706,397	10,652,017
Indiana	2,192,404	2,516,462	2,700,876	2,930,390	3,238,503	3,427,796	3,934,224	4,662,498	5,193,669
Illinois	3,826,352	4,821,550	5,638,591	6,485,280	7,630,654	7,897,241	8,712,176	10,081,158	11,113,976
Michigan	2,093,890	2,420,982	2,810,173	3,668,412	4,842,325	5,256,106	6,371,766	7,823,194	8,875,083
Wisconsin	1,693,330	2,069,042	2,333,860	2,632,067	2,939,006	3,137,587	3,434,575	3,951,777	4,417,933
West North Central	8,932,112	10,347,423	11,637,921	12,544,249	13,296,915	13,516,990	14,061,394	15,394,115	16,324,389
Minnesota	1,310,283	1,751,394	2,075,708	2,387,125	2,563,953	2,792,300	2,982,483	3,413,864	3,805,069
Iowa	1,912,297	2,231,853	2,224,771	2,404,021	2,470,939	2,538,268	2,621,073	2,757,537	2,825,041
Missouri	2,679,185	3,106,665	3,293,335	3,404,055	3,629,367	3,784,664	3,954,653	4,319,813	4,677,399
North Dakota	190,983	319,146	577,056	646,872	680,845	641,935	619,636	632,446	617,761
South Dakota	348,600	401,570	583,888	636,547	692,849	642,961	652,740	680,514	666,257
Nebraska	1,062,656	1,066,300	1,192,214	1,296,372	1,377,963	1,315,834	1,325,510	1,411,330	1,483,791
Kansas	1,428,108	1,470,495	1,690,949	1,769,257	1,880,999	1,801,028	1,905,299	2,178,611	2,249,071
Mountain	1,213,935	1,674,657	2,633,517	3,336,101	3,701,789	4,150,003	5,074,998	6,855,060	8,283,585
Montana	142,924	243,329	376,053	548,889	537,606	559,456	591,024	674,767	694,409
Idaho	88,548	161,772	325,594	431,866	445,032	524,873	588,637	667,191	713,008
Wyoming	62,555	92,531	145,965	194,402	225,565	250,742	290,529	330,066	332,416
Colorado	413,249	539,700	799,024	939,629	1,035,791	1,123,296	1,325,089	1,753,947	2,207,259
New Mexico	160,282	195,310	327,301	360,350	423,317	531,818	681,187	951,023	1,016,000
Arizona	88,243	122,931	204,354	334,162	435,573	499,261	749,587	1,302,161	1,772,482
Utah	210,779	276,749	373,351	449,396	507,847	550,310	688,862	890,627	1,059,273
Nevada	47,355	42,335	81,875	77,407	91,058	110,247	160,083	285,278	488,738
Pacific	1,920,386	2,634,285	4,448,660	5,877,819	8,622,047	10,229,116	15,114,964	21,198,044	26,525,774
Washington	357,232	518,103	1,141,990	1,356,621	1,563,396	1,736,191	2,378,963	2,853,214	3,409,169
Oregon	317,704	413,536	672,765	783,389	953,786	1,089,684	1,521,341	1,768,687	2,091,385
California	1,213,398	1,485,053	2,377,549	3,426,861	5,677,251	6,907,387	10,586,223	15,717,204	19,953,134
Alaska	32,052	63,592	64,356	55,036	59,278	72,524	128,643	226,167	302,173
Hawaii	....	154,001	192,000	255,912	368,336	423,330	499,794	632,772	769,913

ACKNOWLEDGMENTS

Credits for illustrations and photographs not given on the page where they appear are listed below. The New York Public Library is abbreviated N.Y.P.L. To all, the authors and publisher wish to express their appreciation.

11 from Campbell, *Travelling*, 1793
12 Courtesy American Antiquarian Society
14 Rare Book Division, N.Y.P.L., Astor, Lenox and Tilden Foundations
18 John R. Freeman
21 Courtesy The New-York Historical Society, New York City
23 Stokes Collection, N.Y.P.L.
28 Tate Gallery, London, photo by John Webb
31 N.Y.P.L.
33 from Robert Johnson, *Offering Most*, 1609
35 from William Tatham, *An Historical and Practical Essay on the Culture and Commerce of Tobacco*, 1800
39 Courtesy Pennsylvania Academy of the Fine Arts
42 Bettmann Archive
48 The Metropolitan Museum of Art, Gift of Edgar William and Bernice Garbisch, 1963
53 The Franklin Institute, Philadelphia
54 Library of Congress
56 Library of Congress
60 Manuscript Division, N.Y.P.L. (top), *Pennsylvania Journal*, October 31, 1765 (bottom)
64 Library of Congress
66 Library of Congress
87 Missouri Historical Society
88 The Metropolitan Museum of Art, Rogers Fund, 1942
90 Smithsonian Institution
96 National Gallery of Art, Washington, D.C.
98 Prints Division, N.Y.P.L., Astor, Lenox and Tilden Foundations
104 Culver Pictures
108 Library of Congress
109 Courtesy Pennsylvania Academy of the Fine Arts
112 Public Archives of Canada
117 N.Y.P.L., Astor, Lenox and Tilden Foundations
125 Courtesy The New-York Historical Society, New York City
128 Bettmann Archive
130 Culver Pictures
139 Franklin D. Roosevelt Library
143 Henry E. Huntington Library and Art Gallery
144 Montana Historical Society
152 Library of Congress
155 Courtesy Maryland Historical Society
162 Bettmann Archive
171 State Historical Society of Wisconsin
174 Bettmann Archive

178 Library of Congress
180 Courtesy The New-York Historical Society, New York City
181 Harvard University Library
186 Museum of the City of New York
188 Courtesy The New-York Historical Society, New York City
190 Courtesy The Brooklyn Museum
191 Courtesy The New-York Historical Society, New York City
197 Library of Congress
201 Bettmann Archive
203 from Stephan Lorant, *The Glorious Burden: The American Presidency*
208 Franklin D. Roosevelt Library
210 Bettman Archive
217 Harry T. Peters Collection
220 Scotts Bluff National Monument
225 Library of Congress
233 Courtesy The New-York Historical Society, New York City
236 *Frank Leslie's Illustrated Newspaper*, July 1, 1865
238 *Frank Leslie's Illustrated Newspaper*, March 17, 1860
249 Museum of Fine Arts, Boston, M. and M. Karolik Collection
252 The Metropolitan Museum of Art, Harris Brisbane Dick Fund, 1934
254 Courtesy The New-York Historical Society, New York City
256 Library of Congress
260 Bettmann Archive
264 N.Y.P.L., Astor, Lenox and Tilden Foundations
267 *Harper's New Monthly Magazine*, March, 1854
268 Library of Congress
276 *Harper's New Monthly Magazine*, March, 1854
277 *The Outlook*, September, 1898
281 Courtesy The Kansas State Historical Society
282 *Frank Leslie's Illustrated Newspaper*, June 7, 1856
289 Library of Congress
290 from J.S. Buckingham, *Slave States of America*, 1842
297 Library of Congress
303 *Harper's Weekly*, August 2, 1862
305 U.S. Signal Corps
309 Union Pacific Railroad Museum Collection
313 Library of Congress
315 Library of Congress
321 Rutherford B. Hayes Library
334 Kaufman & Fabry Co.

336 Library of Congress
339 Museum of the City of New York, The Byron Collection
340 Courtesy Brandeis University
343 Museum of the City of New York, Harry T. Peters Collection
348 Jones & Laughlin Steel Corporation
350 Culver Pictures
355 Library of Congress
362 Courtesy Southern Pacific Railroad
366 Library of Congress
367 Prints Division, N.Y.P.L., Astor, Lenox and Tilden Foundations
371 *Frank Leslie's Illustrated Newspaper*, 1886
374 *Harper's Weekly*, July 16, 1892
376 Montana Historical Society, Helena
379 Courtesy Whitney Gallery of Western Art, Cody, Wyoming, © Charles J. Belden
380 The Kansas Historical Society, Topeka
384 *Puck*, May 12, 1880
387 Library of Congress
392 Library of Congress
395 Library of Congress
397 American Telephone & Telegraph Company
398 Bettmann Archive
402 *Harper's Weekly*, October 20, 1877
409 Library of Congress
411 Bettmann Archive
430 Library of Congress
438 Historical Pictures Service
442 Wide World
444 from Charles Stelzle, *Why Prohibition*, 1918
449 Library of Congress
454 Photograph by Jacob A. Riis, The Jacob A. Riis Collection, Museum of the City of New York
457 Culver Pictures
460 Photograph by Lewis W. Hine
462 Library of Congress
464 Underwood & Underwood
467 Library of Congress
474 N.Y.P.L.
476 Milton Meltzer
482 Bettmann Archive
485 Library of Congress
487 Library of Congress
488 Library of Congress
493 National Archives
498 *The New York Times*
503 U.S. Signal Corps
504 West Point Museum Collection, U.S. Military Academy
519 Vassar College Library
523 J.C. Allen and Son
526 Library of Congress (top), Courtesy Columbia Broadcasting System (bottom)
530 Culver Pictures

534 Library of Congress
536 Library of Congress
539 Museum of the City of New York
541 Museum of the City of New York
555 Courtesy Ford Motor Co.
558 Brown Brothers
563 *New Masses*, February 11, 1933
565 UPI
570 U.S. Forest Service
574 Brown Brothers
576 Library of Congress
578 Historical Pictures Service
580 Library of Congress
581 Archives of Labor and Urban Affairs, Wayne State University
585 Library of Congress
588 International News Photo
591 The National Maritime Museum, London
596 U.S. Navy
600 Margaret Bourke-White, LIFE Magazine © Time Inc.
603 Library of Congress
605 U.S. Coast Guard
609 UPI
610 U.S. Air Force
622 Rus Arnold
624 Fisher Body Division, General Motors
627 Bob Kral, USDA-SCS
632 State Historical Society of Wisconsin
634 Herblock, *The Washington Post*
636 Wide World
640 Wide World
641 Gerry Adler
644 Ellis Herwig/Stock, Boston
646 Bob Amft
654 Consulate General of Germany
656 UPI
659 U.S. Army
662 UPI
668 UPI
672 Engelhardt, *U.S. Post-Dispatch*
674 NASA
677 Cornell Capa/Magnum
679 UPI
685 Plus 4
688 UPI
691 Wide World
694 Paul Sequeira
696 Jack Davis, Kent State University
697 UPI
698 UPI
700 UPI
704 Jon Kennedy, *Arkansas Democrat*
709 Peter L. Gould/FPG
714 Frank Evers, Copyright 1979 New York News Inc. Reprinted by permission.

INDEX

ABOUT OUR COVER

Our cover shows a small sample of the many flags that have been part of the Democratic Experience. As carefully thought out expressions of symbolism and unity, these flags have inspired pride and recognition.

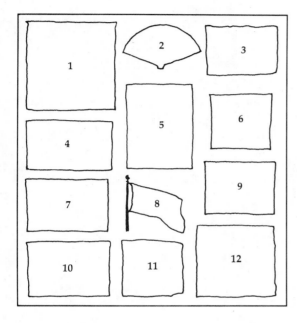

The Bunker Hill Flag of Massachusetts **(7)** combines the symbolism of the pine tree, representing New England, with the cross of Saint George, an ancient symbol of England. The flag was used on land and sea from the 1680s until the Revolution. (Replica courtesy Library of Congress.)

On January 1, 1776, George Washington ordered the Continental Colors or "great Union Flag" **(4)** raised to celebrate the official formation of the Continental Army. Created six months before the colonies declared their independence, the flag combines the symbolism of the Union Jack as a sign of loyalty to Britain and thirteen stripes to symbolize the colonies' unity in seeking redress for their grievances. (Replica courtesy Library of Congress.)

The Gadsden flag of South Carolina. **(10),** dated about 1776, was just one of many flags inspired by Benjamin Franklin's "Join or Die" cartoon depicting the colonies as a dismembered snake. The alertly coiled snake and defiant motto signal the new mood of rebellion. (Replica courtesy Library of Congress.)

The Bedford Flag **(11)**, an English army flag made in the 1600s, was the Company colors of the Three County Troop stationed in Essex, Middlesex, and Suffolk Counties in Massachusetts. It is believed that minuteman Nathaniel Page carried the flag at the Battle of Concord on April 19, 1778. (Courtesy Bedford, Massachusetts, Public Library.)

The Texel flag **(9)** was being flown by John Paul Jones when he captured the *HMS Serapis* off the coast of Scotland on September 23, 1779. Jones transferred his flag to the British ship and sailed to Texel, The Netherlands, with the *Alliance*, another of his ships, which flew a slightly different version of the Stars and Stripes. To establish that Jones was sailing under recognized flags and thus help Jones circumvent British charges of piracy, Dutch authorities commissioned watercolors of the two flags. (Replica courtesy Library of Congress.)

The Star-Spangled Banner **(5)** of fifteen stars and fifteen stripes flew over Fort McHenry, Maryland, during its bombardment by the British on the night of September 13–14, 1814. When he saw the flag still waving the next morning, Francis Scott Key wrote the song that was to be officially adopted as the national anthem in 1931. (Courtesy Smithsonian Institution.)

The Garrison Banner **(1)**, one of many antislavery banners displayed at abolitionist fairs and festivals, carries the slogan first published in William Lloyd Garrison's abolitionist paper, *The Liberator,* founded in 1831. (Courtesy The Massachusetts Historical Society.)

Once Texas won its freedom from Mexico, the Lone Star Flag **(3)** was adopted as the official flag of the Republic of Texas. Today, this is the state flag of Texas. (Courtesy Texas Memorial Museum, Austin.)

The regimental colors of the United States Eighth Infantry Regiment **(12)** may have been the first American banner to fly over Chapultepec after its fall on September 13, 1847. (Courtesy West Point Museum Collection, U.S. Military Academy–American Heritage.)

The Confederate Battle Flag **(6)** combines the symbolism of St. Andrew's Cross with thirteen stars representing the thirteen states of the Confederacy. This flag is believed to have been captured at the battle of Antietam on September 17, 1862, by the 35th New York Regiment. (Courtesy The Museum of the Confederacy, Richmond, Virginia.)

The flag fan **(2)** was one of many items created to commemorate the proclamation of the flag of forty-eight stars on July 4, 1912. (Courtesy Mastai Collection, New York.)

The fifty-star flag **(8),** the official flag of the United States since 1960, is made according to Executive orders specifying its exact configuration and the precise proportions of stars and stripes. (Courtesy Scott, Foresman and Company).